McKINNEY'S®
NEW YORK
RULES OF COURT
2009 EDITION

STATE

Mat #40580501

ISBN: 978–0–314–97435–8

PREFACE

This edition of *McKinney's New York Rules of Court, State, 2009*, replaces the 2008 edition. This volume provides in convenient form court rules governing state practice in New York and is current with amendments received through September 15, 2008.

THE PUBLISHER

October 2008

*

RELATED PRODUCTS
FROM WEST

WEST'S McKINNEY'S FORMS

Civil Practice Law and Rules

Uniform Commercial Code

Business Corporation Law

Matrimonial and Family Law

Real Property Practice

Estates and Surrogate Practice

Criminal Procedure Law

Not–For–Profit Corporation Law

Tax Practice and Procedure

Local Government Forms

Selected Consolidated Law Forms

McKinney's Consolidated Laws of New York Annotated

McKinney's Consolidated Laws of New York, Compact Edition

West's New York Legal Update

New York Digest

New York Law Finder

New York Official Reports, 3d Series

New York Pattern Jury Instructions—Civil

New York Forms, Legal and Business

New York Supplement, 2d Series

New York Practice 4th Edition
David D. Siegel

New York Court of Appeals on Criminal Law 2d Edition
William C. Donnino

Charges to the Jury and Requests to Charge in a Criminal Case in New York
Howard Leventhal

RELATED PRODUCTS

Criminal Law in New York, 4th Edition
Gary Muldoon, Esq.

Hon. Karen Morris

Nicole L. Black, Esq.

Criminal Procedure in New York, 2d Edition
Hon. Robert G. Bogle

Handling a Criminal Case in New York
Gary Muldoon, Esq.

Handling the DWI Case in New York
Peter Gerstenzang

Eric H. Sills

Modern New York Discovery, 2d
Abraham Fuchsberg, et al.

New York Driving While Intoxicated, 2d Edition
Edward Louis Fiandach

New York DWI Defense Forms
Michael S. Taheri, Esq.

James F. Orr

New York Vehicle and Traffic Law, 2d Edition
James M. Rose

Trial Handbook for New York Lawyers, 3d Edition
Aaron J. Broder

RELATED PRODUCTS

Village, Town and District Courts in New York
Hon. James E. Morris
Hon. Robert G. Bogle
Hon. Thomas F. Liotti
Maryita Dobiel, Esq.

WEST'S NEW YORK PRACTICE SERIES

Vol. 1
New York Limited Liability Companies and Partnerships
Walker, et al.

Vols. 2–4B
Commercial Litigation in New York State Courts 2d
Haig, et al.

Vol. 5
Evidence in New York State and Federal Courts
Barker and Alexander

Vol. 6
New York Criminal Law 3d
Greenberg, Marcus, Fahey and Cary

Vol. 7
New York Pretrial Criminal Procedure 2d
Marks, et al.

Vol. 8
New York Civil Appellate Practice 2d
Davies, Stecich and Gold

Vol. 9
Environmental Law and Regulation in New York
Ginsberg, Weinberg, et al.

Vol. 10
New York Family Court Practice
Sobie, et al.

Vols. 11–12
New York Law of Domestic Relations
Scheinkman

Vol. 13
Employment Litigation in New York
Taber, et al.

VII

RELATED PRODUCTS

Vol. 13A
Employment Law in New York
Stiller

Vols. 14–16
New York Law of Torts
Kreindler, Rodriguez, et al.

Vols. 20–25
General Practice in New York
Ostertag, Benson, et al.

Vol. 26
New York Administrative Procedure and Practice
Borchers and Markell

Vol. 27
New York Workers' Compensation
Minkowitz

Vol. 28
New York Contract Law
Banks

Vol. A
Enforcing Judgments and Collecting Debts in New York
Borges, et al.

Vols. B–C
Personal Injury Practice in New York
Bensel, Frank, McKeon, et al.

Vols. D–E
Trusts and Estates Practice in New York
Preminger, et al.

Vols. F–G
Landlord and Tenant Practice in New York
Finkelstein and Ferrara

PAMPHLETS

McKinney's Criminal and Motor Vehicle Law
McKinney's Law and the Family—New York
McKinney's New York Rules of Court—State, Federal and Local Civil
McKinney's New York Civil Practice Law and Rules
McKinney's New York Estate and Surrogate Practice

RELATED PRODUCTS

New York Sentence and Related Law Charts
Simon's New York Code of Professional Responsibility

———————

TEXTS

New York Jurisprudence 2d
Carmody–Wait 2d

———————

Westlaw®
WestCheck.com™
West CD–ROM Libraries™

———————

To order any of these New York practice tools, call
your West Representative or **1–800–328–9352.**

NEED RESEARCH HELP?

You can get quality research results with free help—call the West Reference
Attorneys when you have questions concerning Westlaw or West
Publications at 1–800–REF–ATTY (1–800–733–2889).

INTERNET ACCESS

Contact the West Editorial Department directly with your questions and suggestions by e-
mail at west.editor@thomson.com. Visit West's home page at west.thomson.com.

*

WESTLAW ELECTRONIC RESEARCH GUIDE

Westlaw—Expanding the Reach of Your Library

Westlaw is West's online legal research service. With Westlaw, you experience the same quality and integrity that you have come to expect from West books, plus quick, easy access to West's vast collection of statutes, case law materials, public records, and other legal resources, in addition to current news articles and business information. For the most current and comprehensive legal research, combine the strengths of West books and Westlaw.

When you research with westlaw.com you get the convenience of the Internet combined with comprehensive and accurate Westlaw content, including exclusive editorial enhancements, plus features found only in westlaw.com such as ResultsPlus™ or StatutesPlus.™

Accessing Databases Using the Westlaw Directory

The Westlaw Directory lists all databases on Westlaw and contains links to detailed information relating to the content of each database. Click Directory on the westlaw.com toolbar. There are several ways to access a database even when you don't know the database identifier. Browse a directory view. Scan the directory. Type all or part of a database name in the Search these Databases box. The Find a Database Wizard can help you select relevant databases for your search. You can access up to ten databases at one time for user-defined multibase searching.

Retrieving a Specific Document

To retrieve a specific document by citation or title on westlaw.com click **Find&Print** on the toolbar to display the Find a Document page. If you are unsure of the correct citation format, type the publication abbreviation, e.g., **xx st** (where xx is a state's two-letter postal abbreviation), in the Find this document by citation box and click **Go** to display a fill-in-the-blank template. To retrieve a specific case when you know one or more parties' names, click **Find a Case by Party Name**.

KeyCite®

KeyCite, the citation research service on Westlaw, makes it easy to trace the history of your case, statute, administrative decision or regulation to determine if there are recent updates and to find other documents that cite your document. KeyCite will also find pending legislation relating to federal or state statutes. Access the powerful features of KeyCite from the westlaw.com toolbar, the **Links** tab, or KeyCite flags in a document display. KeyCite's red and yellow warning flags tell you at a glance whether your document has negative history. Depth-of-treatment stars help you focus on the most important citing references. KeyCite Alert allows you to monitor the status of your case, statute or rule, and automatically sends you updates at the frequency you specify.

ResultsPlus™

ResultsPlus is a Westlaw technology that automatically suggests additional information related to your search. The suggested materials are accessible by a set of links that appear to the right of your westlaw.com search results:

- Go directly to relevant ALR® articles and Am Jur® annotations.
- Find on-point resources by key number.
- See information from related treatises and law reviews.

StatutesPlus™

When you access a statutes database in westlaw.com you are brought to a powerful Search Center which collects, on one toolbar, the tools that are most useful for fast, efficient retrieval of statutes documents:

- Have a few key terms? Click **Statutes Index**.
- Know the common name? Click **Popular Name Table**.
- Familiar with the subject matter? Click **Table of Contents**.
- Have a citation or section number? Click **Find by Citation**.
- Interested in topical surveys providing citations across multiple state statutes? Click **50 State Surveys.**
- Or, simply search with **Natural Language** or **Terms and Connectors.**

When you access a statutes section, click on the **Links** tab for all relevant links for the current document that will also include a KeyCite section with a description of the KeyCite status flag. Depending on your document, links may also include administrative, bill text, and other sources that were previously only available by accessing and searching other databases.

Additional Information

Westlaw is available on the Web at westlaw.com.

For search assistance, call the West Reference Attorneys at
1–800–REF–ATTY (1–800–733–2889).

For technical assistance, call West Customer Technical Support at
1–800–WESTLAW (1–800–937–8529).

TABLE OF CONTENTS

STATE COURTS

TABLE OF CONTENTS

TABLE OF CONTENTS

TABLE OF CONTENTS

TABLE OF CONTENTS

TABLE OF CONTENTS

TABLE OF CONTENTS

*

STATE RULES OF COURT
STANDARDS AND ADMINISTRATIVE POLICIES

Including Amendments Received Through September 15, 2008

_____

Westlaw Electronic Research

*These rules may be searched electronically on Westlaw® in the NY–RULES
database; updates to these rules may be found on* Westlaw *in NY–RULESUP-
DATES. For search tips and a summary of database content, consult the* Westlaw
Scope Screens for each database.

_____

Table of Sections

RULES OF THE CHIEF JUDGE

PART 1. STANDARDS AND ADMINISTRATIVE POLICIES: GENERAL

§ 1.0. Preamble

The purpose of these standards and policies is to assign and regulate administrative authority in a complex, multi-tiered court system. The Constitution now vests in a Chief Administrator of the Courts, on behalf of the Chief Judge, responsibility for supervising the administration and operation of our courts. Heretofore this has been the constitutional responsibility of the Appellate Divisions of the Supreme Court and the Administrative Board of the Judicial Conference. These standards and policies reflect the judgment of the Chief Judge and of the Court of Appeals that sound management of our court system requires that the Appellate Divisions, through their presiding justices, have a significant consultative role in management decisions which affect the trial courts in each of the diverse areas of our State. This participation of the Appellate Divisions in court administration is consistent with our judicial tradition and is important to the intelligent and effective exercise of the Chief Administrator's constitutional functions and responsibilities.

Paramount, however, is the constitutional mandate for a unified administration of the courts, within the framework of which the consultative role of the Appellate Divisions may appropriately function. The Chief Administrator should also consult with the trial judges, the bar, and the public, either directly or through deputies, local administrative judges, and advisory committees.

Cross References

Constitution, see McKinney's Book 2.

§ 1.1. Chief Judge and Chief Administrator; Exercise of Administrative Powers and Duties

(a) Establishment of the regular hours, terms and parts of court, other than temporary hours, terms and parts, and assignments of judges and justices to them, other than temporary assignments, shall be done in consultation and agreement with the presiding justices of the appropriate Appellate Divisions on behalf of their respective courts; provided that if the Chief Administrator and a presiding justice are unable to agree, the matter shall be determined by the Chief Judge. Retired judges or justices certificated pursuant to article VI, section 25 of the Constitution shall be subject to assignment by the Appellate Divisions pursuant to that section, in consultation with the Chief Administrator.

(b) Appointments of nonjudicial officers and employees of trial courts shall be made upon nomination of the appropriate administrative judge, supervising judge or judge of the court in which the position is to be filled, or other administrator designated by the Chief Administrator. Judges and justices having personal assistants who serve as law clerks (law secretaries) and secretaries may continue to appoint and remove them, subject to standards and administrative policies established, approved and promulgated pursuant to article VI, section 28(c) of the Constitution, and to the final determination of budgets pursuant to article VI, section 29.

(c) Designation of the places where appellate terms shall be held, pursuant to article VI, section 8(a) of the Constitution, shall be made in consultation with the presiding justices of the appropriate Appellate Divisions.

(d) Adoption of administrative rules for the efficient and orderly transaction of business in the trial courts, including but not limited to calendar practice, shall be done in consultation with the Administrative Board of the Courts or the appropriate Appellate Divisions.

(e) If the Chief Judge designates deputy chief administrators and administrative judges, he shall do so in consultation with the presiding justices of the appropriate Appellate Divisions on behalf of their respective courts. If the Chief Administrator of the Courts designates deputy chief administrators and administrative judges pursuant to delegated authority, the designations shall be made in consultation with the presiding justices of the appropriate Appellate Divisions on behalf of their respective courts, and shall require the approval of the Chief Judge.

(f) Designation of the presiding justice and associate justices of an Appellate Term shall require the approval of the presiding justice of the appropriate Appellate Division.

Cross References

Constitution, see McKinney's Book 2.

§ 1.2. Chief Administrator of the Courts; Compensation

The salary of the Chief Administrator shall be fixed by the Chief Judge within the amount available by appropriation. He shall also be entitled to reimbursement for expenses actually and necessarily incurred by him in the performance of his duties. If a judge is appointed, he shall receive his judicial salary and such additional compensation as may be available by appropriation, and his actual and necessary expenses.

§ 1.3. Existing Rules

Before amending or repealing an administrative rule of an Appellate Division for the efficient and orderly transaction of business in the trial courts, including but not limited to calendar practice, that was in effect on March 31, 1978, the Chief Judge or Chief Administrator shall consult with that Appellate Division.

PART 3. HOURS OF COURT

§ 3.1. Hours of Court

Notwithstanding any provision of law or rule of court to the contrary, throughout the State of New York the sessions of the Supreme Court, Court of Claims, County Court, Surrogate's Court, Family Court, Civil Court of the City of New York, Criminal Court of the City of New York, City Courts and District Courts, for the disposition of business before the court shall commence not later than 9:30 a.m. and conclude not earlier than 5 p.m. Where warranted, the Chief Administrator of the Courts may authorize variances in the opening and closing hours of the courts, but, in such event, daily sessions shall total not less than six hours.

PART 4. REPORTS OF PENDING MATTERS

§ 4.1. Statement of Pending Cases; Report of Pending Transcripts; Requirements

(a) The Chief Administrator of the Courts shall regularly obtain, in such form and at such times as such Chief Administrator may require, (1) a statement from every judge and justice of every court indicating the matters which have been pending undecided before such judge or justice for a period of 60 days after final submission, and the reasons therefor, and (2) a statement from every justice of the Supreme Court indicating any motions for or related to interim maintenance or child support pending undecided before such justice for a period of 30 days after final submission, and the reasons therefor.

(b) The appropriate administrative judge in each judicial district shall obtain, from each court reporter or court stenographer in the district, a report, in such form and at such times as the Chief Administrator may prescribe, detailing the matters in which a transcript has not been furnished within 40 days after an order therefor has been placed, and the reasons for the delay.

PART 5. PERSONAL ASSISTANTS

§ 5.1. Requirements for Appointment of Personal Assistants to Justices and Judges

(a) Each justice of the Supreme Court may appoint and at pleasure remove one law clerk to justice and one secretary to justice. A law clerk to justice appointed pursuant to this section must meet the requirements set forth in subdivision (b) of this section. No justice of the Supreme Court may appoint or continue to employ any other personal assistant to render legal or clerical services unless approved by the Chief Administrator of the Courts.

(b) No person shall be appointed, by a judge or justice of the Court of Appeals, Appellate Division, Supreme Court, Court of Claims, County Court, Surrogate's Court, and Civil Court of the City of New York, as a law clerk who is not a member of the bar of the State of New York or a graduate of an approved law school eligible to take the New York State bar examination. Such appointee, if not a member of the bar, must pass the first such bar examination following his or her appointment, or else the appointment terminates upon publication of the examination results. An application in writing for continuance in service may be made to the Chief Judge of the Court of Appeals on behalf of a person so employed in that

court, or to the presiding justice of a judicial department on behalf of a person employed in an Appellate Division or Appellate Term of that department, or to the Chief Administrator of the Courts by the appointing authority in any other court in the unified court system except a Town or Village Court, on behalf of the appointee, and, if approved, said appointee may continue in service upon condition of taking the next succeeding bar examination. If the appointee fails to pass the second examination, his or her continuance in service automatically terminates upon publication of the results. This rule shall be subject to applicable statutory provisions, if any.

PART 6. GRATUITIES [REPEALED]

PART 7. LAW GUARDIANS

§ 7.1. Standards to Regulate Designation of Lawyers Who May Be Appointed Law Guardians to Represent Minors in Family Court Proceedings

(a) Each of the appellate divisions shall by January 1, 1980 promulgate rules pertaining to the establishment and operation of a panel of lawyers qualified for assignment as law guardians to represent minors in proceedings in Family Court.

(b) The panel plan, which consists of the rules so promulgated, may provide for the creation of a departmental advisory committee, whose membership may be representative of the bar associations, law school faculties and the lay public, among others.

(c) The panel plan shall contain standards and administrative procedures for continuing evaluation of the panel plan and panel lawyers.

(d) The panel plan shall set forth standards for appointment to the panel, which may include litigation experience in matters within the jurisdiction of the Family Court, participation in a panel plan training program, or other qualifying criteria.

(e) The panel plan shall set forth standards for removal from the panel and provide a removal process or mechanism.

(f) The panel plan shall provide for a continuing program of training and education for members of the panel.

(g) Annual reports on the operation of the panels, for each calendar year, shall be filed by the Appellate Divisions with the Chief Administrator of the Courts, no later than July 1st of the next succeeding calendar year.

§ 7.2. Function of the Attorney for the Child

(a) As used in this part, "attorney for the child" means a law guardian appointed by the family court

pursuant to section 249 of the Family Court Act, or by the supreme court or a surrogate's court in a proceeding over which the family court might have exercised jurisdiction had such action or proceeding been commenced in family court or referred thereto.

(b) The attorney for the child is subject to the ethical requirements applicable to all lawyers, including but not limited to constraints on: ex parte communication; disclosure of client confidences and attorney work product; conflicts of interest; and becoming a witness in the litigation.

(c) In juvenile delinquency and person in need of supervision proceedings, where the child is the respondent, the attorney for the child must zealously defend the child.

(d) In other types of proceedings, where the child is the subject, the attorney for the child must zealously advocate the child's position.

(1) In ascertaining the child's position, the attorney for the child must consult with and advise the child to the extent of and in a manner consistent with the child's capacities, and have a thorough knowledge of the child's circumstances.

(2) If the child is capable of knowing, voluntary and considered judgment, the attorney for the child should be directed by the wishes of the child, even if the attorney for the child believes that what the child wants is not in the child's best interests. The attorney should explain fully the options available to the child, and may recommend to the child a course of action that in the attorney's view would best promote the child's interests.

(3) When the attorney for the child is convinced either that the child lacks the capacity for knowing, voluntary and considered judgment, or that following the child's wishes is likely to result in a substantial risk of imminent, serious harm to the child, the attor-

ney for the child would be justified in advocating a position that is contrary to the child's wishes. In these circumstances, the attorney for the child must inform the court of the child's articulated wishes if the child wants the attorney to do so, notwithstanding the attorney's position.

PART 8. APPOINTMENT OF RELATIVES OF JUDGES

§ 8.1. Prohibited Appointments

No person shall be appointed to a position in any state-paid court of the Unified Court System if he or she is a relative within the fourth degree of relationship, or the spouse of such relative, of any judge or the spouse of such judge of the same court within the county in which the appointment is to be made. The Appellate Division and Appellate Terms of the Supreme Court shall not be considered the same court as the Supreme Court for purposes of this Part.

§ 8.2. Application

This Part shall not apply to appointments to positions in the competitive class nor to persons who have held permanent appointments in positions in the Unified Court System prior to the effective date of this Part or prior to the relative becoming a judge.

PART 9. FILING AND PUBLICATION OF RULES AND REGULATIONS

§ 9.1. Filing of Rules and Regulations Required

(a) All rules and regulations hereafter promulgated by any court or agency of the Unified Court System shall be filed with the Chief Administrator of the Courts. This section shall not apply to instructions issued by individual judges governing the hearing of cases pursuant to the Individual Assignment System.

(b) The Chief Administrator shall arrange for the publication of such rules and regulations, including in the *Official Compilation of Codes, Rules and Regulations* and the *State Register*.

(c) The provisions of subdivision (b) of this section shall not be applicable to:

(1) general rules and orders of the Court of Appeals published in the *State Register* pursuant to section 52 of the Judiciary Law;

(2) rules of the Appellate Divisions or Appellate Terms for those courts; or

(3) rules of the Appellate Divisions for court-related agencies administered by the Appellate Divisions.

Cross References

Judiciary Law, see McKinney's Book 29.

PART 11. EXAMINATION OF JURORS [REPEALED]

PART 12. ATTENDANCE OF INMATES AT JUDICIAL HEARINGS

§ 12.1. Attendance of Inmates at Judicial Hearings

Whenever a court directs the temporary removal of an inmate from an institution under the jurisdiction of the State Department of Correctional Services for the purposes of attendance at a judicial hearing, its order shall recite that the hearing therein provided must be held within 30 days of the arrival of the inmate at the temporary place of detention.

PART 13. RELIEF FROM DISABILITIES [REPEALED]
PART 14. CRIMINAL RECORD [REPEALED]
PART 16. COURT APPEARANCES BY FORMER APPELLATE COURT JUDGES AND JUSTICES

§ 16.1. Appearances by Former Appellate Court Judges and Justices Before the Courts in Which They Were Members

No former judge of the New York State Court of Appeals or former justice of the Appellate Divisions or Appellate Terms of the Supreme Court of the State of New York shall appear in person in the Appellate Court on which he or she served, or use or permit the use of his or her name on a brief filed in such court, within two years after having left such court. Nothing in this Part shall prohibit a law firm with which said judge is associated from appearing before a court and using the name of the firm on its papers consistent with that appearance.

PART 17. JUDICIAL EDUCATION AND TRAINING

§ 17.1. Visitation of Facilities and Institutions for Detention, Treatment, Examination and Confinement; Visitation of Residential Facilities for Victims of Domestic Violence

(a) In order to ensure that every judge or justice be familiar with those facilities where the judge or justice is authorized to direct the detention, treatment, examination or confinement of any person in connection with Criminal or Family Court proceedings, the following steps shall be taken:

(1) each judge or justice designated in subdivision (d) of this section, holding office before October 1, 1981, shall visit a facility or institution of each type specified in subdivision (d). To comply with this requirement, visits shall be completed no later than October 1, 1982, or shall have been made no earlier than January 1, 1979;

(2) each judge or justice designated in subdivision (d) of this section, who shall assume office on or after October 1, 1981, shall visit a facility or institution of each type specified in subdivision (d). To comply with this requirement, visits shall be completed no later than one year after the assumption of office, or shall have been made no earlier than three years before the assumption of office;

(3) each judge or justice whose term of office is four years or longer or who is appointed to or elected to consecutive terms of office that, in the aggregate, equal four years or more, and who regularly sits in a criminal term or in a term with criminal as well as civil jurisdiction, each judge of the New York City Criminal Court, and each judge of the Family Court, having complied with the provisions of paragraph (a)(1) or (a)(2) of this section, shall, within every four years thereafter during the term or terms of office of said judge or justice, visit at least one facility or institution of each type specified in subdivision (d);

(4) a judge or justice, for the purposes of this Part, shall be deemed to regularly sit in a criminal term, or in a term with criminal as well as civil jurisdiction, if such judge or justice sits in a part of court exercising criminal jurisdiction for at least one trial term in a year.

(b) The Deputy Chief Administrator of the Courts for the courts outside the city of New York shall be responsible for ensuring compliance with subdivision (a) of this section by the judges and justices of courts outside the city of New York and shall report to the Chief Administrator of the Courts as to the implementation of the provisions thereof at such times and in such form as the Chief Administrator of the Courts shall require.

(c) The Deputy Chief Administrator of the Courts for the courts within the city of New York shall be responsible for ensuring compliance with subdivision (a) of this section by the judges and justices of courts within the city of New York, and shall report to the Chief Administrator of the Courts as to the implementation of the provisions thereof at such times and in such form as the Chief Administrator of the Courts shall require.

(d) The following types of facilities and institutions shall be visited.

(1) Justices of the Supreme Court, judges of the County Court, and judges of the Court of Claims, regularly sitting in a criminal term or in a term with criminal as well as civil jurisdiction, shall visit one facility in each of the following categories:

(i) a facility operated by the New York State Department of Correctional Services for the confinement of persons convicted of a felony;

(ii) a facility operated by (a) the city of New York or (b) a county or municipality outside the city of New York for the confinement of persons convicted of a misdemeanor or violation;

(iii) a facility operated by (a) the city of New York or (b) a county or municipality outside the city of New York for the detention of persons accused of an offense;

(iv) a secure facility maintained by the New York State Office of Children and Family Services for the care and confinement of juvenile offenders; and

(v) a facility certified by the New York State Office of Children and Family Services as a juvenile detention facility for the reception of children.

(2) Judges of the New York City Criminal Court shall visit one facility in each of the following categories:

(i) a facility operated by the New York City Department of Correction for the confinement of persons convicted of a misdemeanor or violation;

(ii) a facility operated by the New York City Department of Correction for the detention of persons accused of an offense; and

(iii) a facility certified by the New York State Office of Children and Family Services as a juvenile detention facility for the reception of children.

(3) Judges of the District Court and judges of the City Court, regularly sitting in a criminal term or in a term with criminal as well as civil jurisdiction, shall visit one facility in each of the following categories. Justices of the Town and Village Courts shall visit one facility in each of the following categories if located in the county where the justice is sitting:

(i) a facility operated by a county or municipality for the confinement of persons convicted of a misdemeanor or violation;

(ii) a facility operated by a county or municipality for the detention of persons accused of an offense; and

(iii) a facility certified by the New York State Office of Children and Family Services as a juvenile detention facility for the reception of children.

(4) Judges of the Family Court shall visit one facility in each of the following categories:

(i) a secure facility certified by the New York State Office of Children and Family Services for the detention of alleged juvenile delinquents held prior to completion of a Family Court proceeding;

(ii) a nonsecure facility certified by the New York State Office of Children and Family Services for the detention of alleged juvenile delinquents and Persons In Need of Supervision held prior to completion of a Family Court proceeding;

(iii) a facility of the New York State Office of Children and Family Services for the care, treat-

ment or confinement of juvenile delinquents or Persons In Need of Supervision;

(iv) a facility operated by a voluntary authorized agency, as defined by section 371, subdivision 10(a) of the Social Services Law, for the care and treatment of children; and

(v) either (a) or (b):

(a) a children's psychiatric center or children's unit of a psychiatric center operated by the New York State Office of Mental Health, or a developmental center or intermediate care facility for the mentally retarded or developmentally disabled operated by the New York State Office of Mental Retardation and Developmental Disabilities for the evaluation and treatment of children; or

(b) a facility of a county or municipality, or a private institution, to which the Family Court refers children for evaluation or in which the Family Court places children for treatment of mental illness or retardation.

Cross References

Social Services Law, see McKinney's Book 52A.

§ 17.2. Training and Education of Town and Village Justices

Training programs, under the auspices of the Chief Administrator of the Courts, shall be conducted for town and village justices at least three times per year at various locations in the State, in the following manner:

(a) The training programs shall consist of a basic and an advanced course. All newly selected justices, who are not members of the Bar of this State, shall attend the first available basic course after their selection. Upon successful completion of such basic course, certification shall be issued which shall be valid until the next available advanced course. The aforesaid justices shall then be required to successfully complete such advanced course and thereupon shall receive a certificate of completion.

(b) Every incumbent nonlawyer justice heretofore certified or certified pursuant to this section, shall be required to successfully complete an advanced course of training once in each calendar year thereafter while holding office in order to maintain certification.

(c) Successful completion of a training program, as herein provided, shall mean attendance at no less than 80 percent of the sessions thereof and a passing grade on a written examination in such course as established by the Chief Administrator.

(d) The Chief Administrator may issue temporary certificates to nonlawyer justices which shall be valid until the time of the next available course.

(e) Each newly elected or appointed justice who is a member of the Bar of this State shall attend the first available advanced course of training after his or her election or appointment. Each such justice shall attend an advanced course of training each calendar year thereafter while holding office. Attendance at an advanced course shall mean attendance at no less than 80 percent of the sessions thereof. The Chief Administrator shall issue appropriate certificates of attendance.

§ 17.3. Training and Education of Judges and Justices Other than Town and Village Justices

The Unified Court System shall provide training and education for its judges and justices, other than town and village justices, which shall include annual seminars, special seminars for new judges, and such other courses, classes and presentations as the Chief Administrator of the Courts deems appropriate. Judges and justices shall attend at least 24 hours of such training and education courses, classes and presentations every two calendar years, which may include, with the approval of the Chief Administrator,

courses, classes and presentations provided outside of the Unified Court System. The Chief Administrator also may grant credit in complying with the requirements of this rule for the teaching of courses and classes, the making of presentations, and the writing of publications, directed to the training and education of judges or to the presentation of a judicial perspective.

§ 17.4. Domestic Violence Program

(a) Each judge or justice in a court that exercises criminal jurisdiction, including town and village justices, each judge of the Family Court, and each justice of the Supreme Court who regularly handles matrimonial matters shall attend, every two years, a program approved by the Chief Administrator of the Courts addressing issues relating to domestic violence.

(b) Attendance at such program shall be counted toward fulfillment of the training and education requirements for justices and judges subject to section 17.3.

PART 18. SHERIFF'S JURORS [REPEALED]

PART 19. JUDICIAL ANNUAL LEAVE—TRIAL COURTS

§ 19.1. Annual Leave for Judges and Justices

A full-time judge or justice of a trial court of the unified court system shall be entitled to four weeks (20 days) of annual leave each year, except that a full-time judge or justice of a trial court who has served full-time as a judge or justice for more than five years shall be entitled to five weeks (25 days) of annual leave each year.

PART 20. NONPUBLIC FACILITIES

§ 20.1. Transaction of Official Business in Nonpublic Facilities

(a) The transaction of official business by judges, justices and nonjudicial personnel of the unified court system, when permitted to be held in a nonpublic facility, shall not knowingly be conducted in a facility which by practice, by law or other regulation restricts

membership or admission thereto on the basis of sex, race, color, ethnic origin, religion, creed or sexual orientation. Reimbursement from State funds shall be denied for knowing violation of this subdivision.

(b) The term "transaction of official business," for purposes of this section only, shall mean and apply to sessions, conferences and seminars conducted by or under the auspices of the unified court system.

PART 23. GRIEVANCE PROCEDURE

§ 23.1. Application and Definitions

(a) **Application of Grievance.** The provisions of this Part shall apply to all nonjudicial employees of the State-paid courts and court-related agencies of the unified court system who are not represented for purposes of collective negotiations pursuant to article 14 of the Civil Service Law. A nonjudicial employee to whom the provisions of this Part applies shall have the right to present his or her grievance in accordance with this Part, free from interference, coercion, restraint, discrimination or reprisal.

(b) **Definitions.** When used in this Part, the term "administrative authority" means:

(1) the clerk of the Court of Appeals with respect to nonjudicial employees of the Court of Appeals;

(2) the presiding justice of each appellate division with respect to nonjudicial employees of the appellate divisions and the courts and agencies which they supervise;

(3) the presiding judge of the Court of Claims with respect to nonjudicial employees of the Court of Claims;

(4) the deputy chief administrator for management support with respect to nonjudicial employees of the Office of Court Administration; or

(5) the deputy chief administrative judge having administrative jurisdiction over the court or agency in which the employee is employed, with respect to all other nonjudicial employees in the unified court system.

Cross References

Civil Service Law, see McKinney's Book 9.

§ 23.2.　Initiating a Grievance

(a) An employee shall initiate a grievance by submitting the grievance, in writing, to the administrative authority not later than 45 calendar days after the date on which the act or omission giving rise to the grievance occurred, or when the employee could reasonably have been expected to become aware of, or to have knowledge, that he or she had a grievance. After receipt of the grievance, the administrative authority or his or her designee shall meet with the employee for a review of the grievance. The employee may be represented by a representative of his or her choosing at this meeting, and the employee may present oral statements and written material. The administrative authority or his or her designee shall issue a written decision, and a copy of such decision shall be sent to the employee and to the Chief Administrator of the Courts.

(b) Nothing in this section shall be construed as discouraging the informal resolution of grievances by the administrative authority or his designee.

§ 23.3.　Appeal to the Reviewing Authority

In the event the employee wishes to appeal the decision of the administrative authority, the appeal must be presented in writing to the Chief Administrator of the Courts within 15 days of the date of the determination by the administrative authority. Such appeal shall contain a short, clear statement of the grievance, the basis of the grievance, the relief sought and a copy of the decision by the administrative authority. A copy of such appeal also shall be sent to the administrative authority who previously passed upon such grievance. The Chief Administrator shall conduct such review as he or she deems necessary, and the Chief Administrator shall determine the grievance in consultation with, and with the approval of, the Chief Judge. The determination of the Chief Administrator shall be final. The Chief Administrator, with the approval of the Chief Judge, also shall have the power to reverse or modify any decision made by an administrative authority that is not appealed by the employee.

§ 23.4.　Areas of Employment Subject to the Grievance Procedure

Grievances subject to this procedure shall be limited to:

(a) claims concerning discriminatory supervisory practices, except insofar as such practices as alleged would constitute violations of law;

(b) claims concerning unreasonable work assignments or conditions; and

(c) claims concerning the application of the time and leave rules contained in Part 24 of this Title.

§ 23.5.　Pending Grievances

This grievance procedure shall apply to grievances filed after the effective date of this Part [January 1, 1987]. Grievances filed before that date shall be processed in accordance with the procedures of this Part that were in effect immediately prior to the effective date of this Part.

§§ 23.6 and 23.7.　[Repealed]

PART 24.　TIME AND LEAVE

§ 24.1.　Application

(a) Except as otherwise provided in this section the provisions of this Part shall apply to all nonjudicial employees of the State-paid courts and court-related agencies of the unified court system who are not represented for purposes of collective negotiations pursuant to article 14 of the Civil Service Law. Only employees who are compensated on a full-time annual salary basis, and employees who are compensated on a part-time, per diem or hourly basis who are employed at least half time and who are expected by the deputy chief administrator for management support to be so employed continuously for nine months without a break in service exceeding one full payroll period, shall be eligible to observe holidays pursuant to section 24.9 of this Part and to accrue annual leave and sick leave pursuant to sections 24.3 and 24.4 of this Part and shall be eligible for leaves with pay or leaves without pay pursuant to sections 24.4, 24.5, 24.6 and 24.7 of this Part. Such part-time, per diem or hourly paid employees shall be eligible to observe holidays and shall accrue annual leave and sick leave on a pro rata basis subject to the same limitations and restrictions as would apply if they were compensated on a full-time annual salary basis.

(b) **Definitions.** When used in this Part, the term "administrative authority" means:

(1) the clerk of the Court of Appeals with respect to nonjudicial employees of the Court of Appeals;

(2) the presiding justice of each appellate division with respect to nonjudicial employees of the appellate

divisions and the courts and agencies which they supervise;

(3) the presiding judge of the Court of Claims with respect to nonjudicial employees of the Court of Claims;

(4) the deputy chief administrator for management support with respect to nonjudicial employees of the Office of Court of Administration; and

(5) the deputy chief administrative judge having administrative jurisdiction over the court or agency in which the employee is employed, with respect to all other nonjudicial employees in the unified court system.

(c) An administrative authority may delegate any responsibilities set forth in this Part.

(d) No provision of this Part shall be construed to require extension of any employment beyond the time at which it would otherwise terminate by operation of law, rule or regulation.

Cross References

Civil Service Law, see McKinney's Book 9.

§ 24.2. Attendance

(a) **Record of Attendance.** All employees in the classified service of the unified court system shall maintain time and attendance records. These records shall be maintained in accordance with procedures established by the deputy chief administrator for management support. No time and leave credits shall be deemed earned for purposes of any provision of this Part unless accurate records of time and attendance have been kept in accordance with the procedures established by the deputy chief administrator.

(b) **Tardiness.** The Chief Administrator or his or her designee may establish rules and schedules of penalties for tardiness. Such penalties shall not preclude disciplinary action in cases of excessive tardiness. In the event of public transportation difficulties, strikes, severe storms or floods, or similar uncontrollable conditions affecting employees, tardiness may be excused by the administrative authority.

(c) The administrative authority shall excuse a reasonable amount of tardiness caused by direct emergency duties of duly authorized volunteer firefighters and volunteer ambulance drivers. The employee may be required to submit satisfactory evidence that lateness was due to such emergency duties.

§ 24.3. Annual Leave

(a) An employee shall be entitled to combined vacation, personal business and religious holiday leave of 20 workdays annually and, unless otherwise provided in this Part, shall be entitled on his or anniversary date to one additional day for each completed year of continuous service in the unified court system up to a maximum of 27 workdays annually. Thereafter, such employees shall earn annual leave for completed bi-

weekly pay periods at a rate equal to 26 days for 26 such pay periods, and also shall earn one additional day of annual leave on his or her anniversary date.

(b) An employee who has completed 25 years of service in the unified court system or the State shall be entitled on his or her anniversary date to one additional annual leave day each year.

(c) An employee who has completed 30 years of service in the unified court system or the State shall be entitled on his or her anniversary date to one additional annual leave day each year, in addition to the one additional annual leave day provided in subdivision (b) of this section.

(d) Employees who were officially entitled prior to April 1, 1977 to receive additional annual leave days and religious holiday leave days, and who have received such additional leave days continuously thereafter, may continue to receive such leave, provided that such leave is limited to a maximum of 30 annual leave days and three religious holiday leave days per year. Religious holiday leave days shall be credited on a calendar-year basis. Such days may be used only in the calendar year in which they are credited and may not be carried over from one calendar year to the next. Religious holiday leave days may be used only for recognized days of religious observance for which the faith requires its members to make religious observance.

(e) Employees entering the service of the unified court system shall be entitled to accrue annual leave from their initial date of hire. An employee shall not earn annual leave credits for any biweekly pay period unless he or she is in full-pay status for at least seven workdays during such biweekly pay period.

(f) A part-time, per diem or hourly paid employee eligible to earn annual leave credits pursuant to this Part shall earn annual leave credits as provided herein, but such employee's total pay when absent on such leave shall be the amount which would have been due if the employee had worked his or her usual number of hours or days during such period.

(g) The time at which annual leave may be drawn by an employee shall be subject to the prior approval of the administrative authority.

(h) Annual leave credits shall be used in units of not less than 15 minutes.

(i) No accumulation of annual leave credits in excess of 54 days may be carried over from one fiscal year to the next. Any such accumulation in excess of 54 days at the end of a fiscal year shall be converted into sick leave. The administrative authority may grant an employee specific permission to exceed the 54-day maximum for a period of no longer than one year where the needs of the court or agency require that the employee postpone his or her vacation.

(j) A leave of absence without pay, or a resignation followed by reemployment in the unified court system within one year following such leave of absence or resignation, shall not constitute an interruption of continuous service for the purposes of this Part; provided, however, that leave without pay for more than six months or the period between resignation and reemployment during which the employee is not in the service of the unified court system, shall not be counted in determining eligibility for additional annual leave credits under this Part.

(k) to the extent practicable, annual leave credits be used prior to appointment, promotion, reassignment or transfer to a different court or agency. The court or agency to which an employee is appointed, promoted, reassigned or transferred shall credit him with all of his accumulated annual leave credits not used prior to such appointment, promotion, reassignment or transfer.

(l) In the event the administrative authority determines that operations in a particular court or courts will be recessed for at least four consecutive workdays, the administrative authority may require employees during such recess to charge up to four days' annual leave in each fiscal year.

§ 24.4. Sick Leave

(a)(1) "Sick leave" is absence with pay necessitated by the illness or disability of the employee, including illness or disability caused by pregnancy or childbirth.

(2) An employee shall be allowed to charge a maximum of 15 days of sick leave in any one calendar year for absences from work to care for a close family member during a time of illness. For purposes of this section, a close family member shall be the employee's spouse; domestic partner; natural, foster or step child; natural, foster or step parent; or any relative residing with the employee or an individual for whom the employee is the primary caregiver.

(b) Employees shall earn sick leave credits at the rate of one-half day per biweekly pay period. No more than 200 days of such credits may be used for retirement service credit unless a greater benefit is provided by law, rule or regulation, and no more than 200 days of such credits may be used to pay for health insurance in retirement.

(c) An employee shall not earn sick leave credit for any biweekly pay period unless he or she is in full-pay status for at least seven workdays during such biweekly pay period.

(d) A part-time, per diem or hourly employee eligible to earn sick leave credits pursuant to this Part shall earn sick leave credits as provided herein, but such employee's total pay when absent on such leave shall be the amount which would have been due if the employee had worked his or her usual number of hours or days during such period.

(e) An employee absent on sick leave shall notify his or her supervisor, or the supervisor's designee, of such absence and the reason therefor on the day of such absence and within 90 minutes after the beginning of his or her workday; provided, however, that where the work is such that a substitute may be required, the administrative authority may require earlier notification, but not earlier than two hours prior to the beginning of the employee's workday.

(f) Sick leave credits may be used in such units as the administrative authority may approve, but shall not be used in units of less than 15 minutes.

(g) Before absence for personal illness may be charged against accumulated sick leave credits, the administrative authority may require such proof of illness as may be satisfactory to the administrative authority, or may require the employee to be examined, at the expense of the unified court system, by a physician designated by the administrative authority. In the event of failure to submit proof of illness upon request, or in the event that, upon such proof as is submitted or upon the report of medical examination, the administrative authority finds that there is not satisfactory evidence of illness sufficient to justify the employee's absence from the performance of his or her duties, such absence may be considered as unauthorized leave and shall not be charged against accumulated sick leave credits. Abuse of sick leave shall be cause for disciplinary action.

(h) The administrative authority may require an employee who has been absent because of personal illness, prior to and as a condition of his or her return to duty, to be examined, at the expense of the unified court system, by a physician designated by the administrative authority, to establish that he or she is not disabled from the performance or his or her normal duties and that his or her return to duty will not jeopardize the health of other employees.

(i) In addition to personal illness of an employee, personal visits by such employee to a doctor, dentist or other medical practitioner, when approved by the administrative authority, may be charged against accumulated sick leave credits. Proof of the need for such visits, satisfactory to the administrative authority, may be required.

(j) When an employee is transferred or reassigned, the court or agency to which the employee is transferred or reassigned shall credit the employee with all of his or her accumulated sick leave credits not used prior to such transfer or reassignment. When an employee is separated from service for other than disciplinary reasons and is subsequently reinstated or reemployed within one year after such separation, or is reinstated by action of the Chief Administrator of the Courts, or is reinstated or reemployed while eligible for reinstatement from a preferred list, his or her sick leave credits accumulated and unused at the time of his or her separation shall be restored; provided, however, that such sick leave credits shall not be restored except where leave records satisfactory to the administrative authority are available.

(k) Sick Leave Bank Program. The Chief Administrator or his or her designee may establish rules and procedures permitting an employee who has exhausted all of his or her sick leave, annual leave and overtime credits to draw sick leave credits from a sick leave bank established through the contribution of leave credits by employees who participate in the program.

§ 24.5. Workers' Compensation Leave

(a)(1) Employees necessarily absent from duty because of an occupational injury, disease or condition as defined in the Workers' Compensation Law, incurred on or after the effective date of this section, shall be eligible for a workers' compensation benefit as provided by law, and the treatment of time and leave benefits shall be as provided in this section.

(2) A workers' compensation injury shall mean any occupational injury, disease or condition found compensable as defined in the Workers' Compensation Law.

(3) The treatment of time and leave benefits for an employee necessarily absent from duty because of an occupational injury, disease or condition incurred through an assault to the employee, suffered by the employee in the pursuit of a criminal, or incurred while coming to the aid of an employee, member of the public or in response to an emergency, shall be as provided to nonjudicial uniformed employees covered by the collective bargaining agreement between the Unified Court System and The Civil Service Employees Association, Inc., Local 1000, AFSCME (AFL–CIO).

(b) An employee who suffers compensable occupational injury shall, upon completion of a ten–workday waiting period, be placed on a leave of absence without pay for all absences necessitated by such injury and shall receive the benefit provided by the Workers' Compensation Law except as modified in this section.

(c) An employee necessarily absent for less than a full day in connection with a workers' compensation injury due to therapy, a doctor's appointment, or other required continuing treatment may charge accrued leave for said absences.

(d) An employee required to serve a waiting period pursuant to subdivision (b) shall have the option of using accrued leave credits or being placed on leave without pay. When an employee has charged credits, upon receipt of documentation from the State Insurance Fund issuing a credit for the time charged, the employee shall be entitled to restoration of credits charged proportional to the net monetary award credited to the Unified Court System by the Workers' Compensation Board.

(e) When annual leave credits are restored pursuant to this section and such restoration causes the total annual leave credits to exceed 54 days, a period of one year from the date of the return of the credits or the date of return to work, whichever is later, shall be allowed to reduce the total accumulation to 54 days.

(f) An employee receiving workers' compensation payments for a period of disability found compensable by the Workers' Compensation Board shall be treated as though the employee is on the payroll for the length of the disability, not to exceed twelve months per injury, for the sole purposes of accruing seniority, credit for continuous service, eligibility for health insurance, accrual of vacation and sick leave credit, and retirement credit and contributions.

(g)(1) Where an employee's workers' compensation claim is controverted by the State Insurance Fund, the employee may utilize leave credits (including sick leave at half pay, if eligible) pending a determination by the Workers' Compensation Board.

(2) If the employee's controverted or contested claim is decided in the employee's favor, any leave credits charged (and sick leave at half pay eligibility) shall be restored proportional to the net monetary award credited to the Unified Court System by the Workers' Compensation Board.

(3) If the employee was in leave without pay status pending determination of a controverted or contested claim, and the claim is decided in the employee's favor, the employee shall receive the benefits in subdivision (f) for the period covered by the award, not to exceed twelve months per injury.

(h) If the date of the disability incident is prior to the effective date of this section, the benefits available shall be provided as set forth in the provisions of section 24.5 in effect immediately prior to the effective date of this section.

Cross References

Workers' Compensation Law, see McKinney's Book 64.

§ 24.6. Other Leaves With Pay

(a) Leave for Subpoenaed Appearance and Jury Attendance. Upon application to the administrative authority, together with proof satisfactory to the administrative authority of the necessity of each day's absence from work, an employee shall be granted a leave of absence with pay for documented absences resulting from jury service or appearance as a witness pursuant to subpoena or other order of a court or body. Provided, however, that this subdivision shall not apply to any absence by an employee occasioned by such an appearance where the employee, or his or her relative as defined in subdivision (f) of this section, has a personal interest in the underlying action or proceeding; nor shall this subdivision apply to any absence by an employee who receives a fee for testifying as an expert witness. Employees entitled to leave under this subdivision shall not be entitled to receive any remuneration for jury service except mileage and transportation expenses. Should an employee receive a jury fee, the unified court system will require reimbursement from the employee.

(b) Leave for Civil Service Examinations. Employees shall be allowed leave with pay to take civil service examinations for positions in the unified court system at the appropriate center, or to appear for an official investigation or appointment interview for positions in the competitive, noncompetitive or exempt classes, provided that due notice is given by the employee to the administrative authority.

(c) Leave for Quarantine. If an employee who is not ill is required to remain absent because of quarantine and presents a written statement of the attending physician or local health officer proving the necessity of such absence, such employee shall be granted leave with pay for the period of his or her required absence, without charge against accumulated sick leave, annual leave or overtime credits. Prior to return to duty, such employee may be required to submit a written statement from the local health officer having jurisdiction that his or her return to duty will not jeopardize the health of other employees.

(d) Leaves Required by Law. An employee shall be allowed such other leaves of absence with pay, including military leave, as are required by law.

(e) Leave for Civil Defense Duties. Upon certification by the State Director of Civil Defense of the necessity for the participation in State or local civil defense drills of an employee enrolled as a civil defense volunteer and required to perform civil defense duties, pursuant to the State Defense Emergency Act, the administrative authority may allow such employee to absent himself or herself from his or her position, without loss of pay or charge against leave credits, for such time as is necessary for participation in such drills, but not exceeding cumulatively five workdays per calendar year.

(f) Death in the Immediate Family. Leave of up to four consecutive workdays (not to exceed a total of 28 work hours) shall be allowed immediately following the death of an employee's spouse; domestic partner; natural, foster or step: parent, child, brother or sister; father-in-law or mother-in-law; grandparent or grandchild; or any relative residing with the employee or an individual for whom the employee has been the primary caregiver. Leave of up to two consecutive workdays (not to exceed a total of 14 work hours) shall be allowed immediately following the death of an employee's son-in-law or daughter-in-law. Prior notice and authorization is not required for leave under this subdivision. When a death in an employee's family occurs while the employee is on annual leave, such time as is excusable for death in the family shall not be charged to annual leave.

Up to four days leave with pay may be granted in the discretion of the Deputy Chief Administrator for Management Support or his or her designee for the death of an individual for whom the employee has been the primary caregiver.

(g) Conferences. Four days' leave per annum without charge to an employee's leave credits may be allowed to attend conferences of recognized professional organizations. Such conferences must be directly related to the employee's profession or professional duties. This leave is subject to the prior approval of the administrative authority and to the staffing needs of the court or agency.

(h) An employee who has reported for duty and, because of extraordinary circumstances beyond his or her control, is directed to leave work, shall not be required to charge such directed absence during such day against leave credits. An employee who does not report for duty because of circumstances beyond his or her control shall not be required to charge such absence during such day against leave credits if the court or other facility where the employee is required to report is closed due to extraordinary circumstances. Any release or excusal of employees due to extraordinary circumstances does not create any right to equivalent time off by employees not adversely affected by the extraordinary circumstances. Only the administrative authority may direct employees to leave work.

(i) Blood Donations. Subject to the reasonable operating needs of the court or court-related agency, an employee shall be allowed up to three and one-half hours leave with pay for blood donations made during the employee's normal working hours. Such leave shall be used only on the day the donation is made and shall include all time spent making the donation, including travel time to and from the collection point. In the event that an employee donates blood during working hours pursuant to a court-sponsored blood drive and is required to return to work immediately following such donation, and the employee is not allowed the full three and one-half hours to make such donation, the employee shall be granted three and one-half hours of compensatory time. This subdivision shall not apply to an employee who receives a fee for such donation.

(j) Internal Discrimination Claims. Subject to the reasonable operating needs of the court or court-related agency, and with the prior written approval of the Equal Employment Opportunity ("EEO") Unit of the Unified Court System, an employee shall be allowed leave with pay (i) to consult with the EEO Unit prior to filing an internal discrimination claim or (ii) to attend meetings or consultations with the EEO Unit in relation to a filed internal discrimination claim. Such leave shall include reasonable travel time.

(k) Leaves for medical screening. An employee shall be entitled to leave with pay for breast cancer screening and bone marrow screening and donation.

(*l*) The Chief Administrator of the Courts or his or her designee may grant leaves with pay for reasons not itemized in this Part.

§ 24.7. Leaves Without Pay

(a) **Leave of Absence; Duration.** A permanent employee may, in the discretion of the administrative authority, be granted a leave of absence, without pay, for a period not exceeding two years. Such leave may be extended beyond two years, for periods aggregating not in excess of an additional two years. In an exceptional case, a further extension may be permitted for good cause shown and where the interests of the unified court system would be served. For the purposes of this Part, time spent in active service in the military forces of the United States or of the State of New York shall not be considered in computing the period of leave.

(b) **Successive Leaves of Absence.** Where a leave of absence without pay has been granted for a period which aggregates two years, or more if extended pursuant to subdivision (a) of this section, a subsequent leave of absence without pay may not be granted until after the employee returns to his or her position and serves continuously therein for six months immediately preceding the subsequent leave of absence.

(c) **Leave for Child Care.** A combined confinement and child-care leave of absence without pay shall be granted to an employee (male or female) who becomes the parent of a child up to four years of age, either by birth or by adoption, for a period of up to 12 months. In one instance per employee only, a period beyond 12 months, but not more than another successive 12–month period, may be granted at the discretion of the administrative authority, subject to the staffing needs of the court or agency.

(d) A grant of leave pursuant to this section shall not be construed to require extension of any employment beyond the time at which it would otherwise terminate by operation of law, rule or regulation.

§ 24.8. Workweek

The workweek shall be 35 hours.

§ 24.9. Holidays

(a) All legal holidays enumerated herein shall be allowed as paid days off, or holiday pay as set forth in subdivision (b) of this section shall be allowed in lieu thereof. The days prescribed by law for the observance of New Year's Day, Martin Luther King, Jr.'s Birthday, Lincoln's Birthday, Washington's Birthday, Memorial Day, Independence Day, Labor Day, Columbus Day, Election Day, Veterans' Day, Thanksgiving Day and Christmas Day shall be observed as holidays. A holiday falling on a Saturday or a Sunday shall be observed on the preceding Friday or following Monday subject to the operational or staffing needs of the court or agency.

(b) **Holiday Pay.** An employee who is entitled to time off with pay on days observed as holidays by the unified court system as an employer will receive, at such employee's option, additional compensation for time worked on such days or compensatory time off. Such additional compensation for each such full day worked will be at the rate of 1/10 of the employee's biweekly rate of compensation. Such additional compensation for less than a full day of such work will be prorated. Such rate of compensation will include geographic, location, inconvenience and shift pay as may be appropriate to the place or hours worked. In no event will an employee be entitled to such additional compensation or compensatory time off unless he or she has been scheduled or directed to work. An employee required to work on Thanksgiving Day (the fourth Thursday in November), Christmas Day (December 25) or New Year's Day (January 1) shall receive a 100% cash premium for all hours worked on such day in addition to any holiday pay or compensatory time off granted pursuant to this subdivision.

§ 24.10. Overtime Meal Allowance

(a) A meal allowance of $6 will be paid to any employee required to work at least three hours beyond his or her regularly scheduled workday unless he or she is receiving cash compensation for such overtime work.

(b) An employee ineligible to receive cash compensation for overtime worked, who is required to work at least seven hours on his or her regularly scheduled day off, shall be entitled to receive one overtime meal allowance. An employee required to work at least 10 hours on his or her regularly scheduled day off shall be entitled to receive a second overtime meal allowance.

§ 24.11. Payment for Accruals Upon Separation

(a) At the time of separation from service in the Unified Court System, an employee or the employee's estate or beneficiary, as the case may be, shall be compensated in cash for overtime credits not in excess of 30 days accrued and unused as of the effective date of separation; and further, except where provision is made for the transfer of leave credits, the employee or the employee's estate or beneficiary shall be compensated in cash for annual leave credits not in excess of 45 days accrued and unused as of the effective date of separation, except, that in the case of resignation, the Chief Administrator of the Courts or his or her designee may require, as a condition for such payment, that written notice of such resignation be given to the Chief Administrator or his or her designee at least two weeks prior to the last day of work. Effective April 1, 1998, the employee or the employee's estate or beneficiary shall be compensated in cash for annual leave credits not in excess of 50 days. No employee who is removed from Unified Court System service as a result of disciplinary action, or who resigns after charges of incompetency or misconduct have been served upon him or her, shall be entitled to compensation for annual leave credits under this subdivision.

(b) An employee on leave from his or her position on account of entry into the Armed Forces of the United States for active duty (other than for training as defined by title 10 of the United States Code), may elect to receive compensation in cash for accrued and unused annual leave and overtime credits not in excess of 30 days in each category accrued and unused as of the last date on which his or her name appeared on the unified court system payroll.

§ 24.12. Written Agreement Required for Transfer of Leave Credits

For the purpose of applying the provisions of this Part, employment in the Executive or Legislative Branch of State service shall be credited as service in the unified court system; provided, however, that, except as otherwise provided by law, leave credits may not be transferred upon movement from such positions to positions subject to this Part except where such credits were earned and accumulated in accordance with attendance and leave regulations which are substantially equivalent to the provisions of this Part and there is a written agreement between the President of the Civil Service Commission and the Chief Administrator of the Courts governing the transfer of leave credits upon such movements. Other public employment may be credited as service in the unified court system for purposes of determining transferabil-ity of leave credits, provided such employment was subject to attendance and leave regulations substantially equivalent to the provisions of this Part, and provided there is a written agreement between the Chief Administrator and the public agency wherein such employment occurred governing the crediting of such employment and the transfer of leave credits upon movement of employees to and from such agency and positions subject to this Part.

§ 24.13. Retroactive Time Credits

(a) Nothing in this Part shall be construed to provide for the granting of annual leave, sick leave or other time or leave credits for service rendered prior to the effective date of this Part [January 1, 1987]; provided, however, that nothing in this Part shall affect time or leave credits lawfully earned prior to the effective date of this Part.

(b) No employee who has been placed on the payroll of the unified court system pursuant to section 39 of the Judiciary Law shall be entitled to compensation under this Part for any time or leave credits lawfully earned before April 1, 1977, except in accordance with section 39.

Cross References

Judiciary Law, see McKinney's Book 29.

§ 24.14. Suspension of Rules

The Chief Administrator of the Courts may suspend these rules, in whole or in part, in an emergency.

PART 25. CAREER SERVICE

§ 25.1. Application

This Part shall apply to employees of the unified court system other than judges and elective officers.

§ 25.2. Intent

The purpose of these rules is to provide for the employees of the unified court system a career and merit system consistent with the Civil Service Law.

Cross References

Civil Service Law, see McKinney's Book 9.

§ 25.3. [Repealed]

§ 25.4. General Provisions

(a) **Delegation.** All powers and duties of the Chief Administrator of the Courts set forth in this Part may be delegated by the Chief Administrator to any deputy, assistant, administrative judge or court.

(b) **Changes in Civil Service Law.** The Chief Administrator of the Courts may implement for employees of the unified court system, for a period of no greater than six months, procedures consistent with any changes in the Civil Service Law pending formal consideration of these changes through amendments to this Part.

(c) Any provision in this Part requiring the return to a previously held position by an employee on any type of leave of absence shall be deemed to permit the assignment of said employee to any position with the same title in the same promotion unit as the former position.

Cross References

Civil Service Law, see McKinney's Book 9.

§ 25.5. Classification and Allocation

(a) The Chief Administrator of the Courts shall have the power to classify and reclassify, and to allocate and reallocate to an appropriate salary grade, all positions in the classified service of the unified court system.

(b) The Chief Administrator of the Courts may, in order to implement a plan for the progressive advancement of employees in an occupational group, based on their acquiring, as prescribed by the Chief Administrator, training or experience or both, reclassify the positions of the incumbents who meet the prescribed qualifications to titles allocated to higher salary grades. The advancement of an incumbent pursuant to this subdivision shall not be deemed a reallocation.

(c) The effective date of any classification, reclassification, allocation or reallocation shall be such date as is determined by the Chief Administrator of the Courts. No employee whose salary would be increased by any classification, reclassification, allocation or reallocation shall have any claim for the difference, if any, between his or her former salary and that which he or she should receive as a result of that classification, reclassification, allocation or reallocation for the period prior to the date the change in title or salary grade becomes effective.

(d) **Review of Classification and Allocation.** Any nonjudicial employee, employee organization or court administrator directly concerned in any classification or allocation of a position in the unified court system may seek review of that classification or allocation by submitting a request, in writing, to the director of personnel of the unified court system setting forth the basis of the change requested, together with any supporting papers. The director of personnel shall conduct such inquiry as is necessary and recommend to the Chief Administrator any required adjustments in the classification or allocation. The Chief Administrator shall determine the request for review and shall notify the employee, employee organization or administrator of that determination.

(e) No classification or reclassification of a position of a permanent employee shall diminish any existing salary compensable on an annual basis so long as such position is held by the then permanent incumbent.

§ 25.6. [Repealed]

§ 25.7. Classified Service

The classified service shall comprise all offices and positions in the unified court system except justices, judges, county clerks and housing judges appointed pursuant to section 110 of the New York City Civil Court Act. The offices and positions in the classified service of the unified court system shall be divided into four classes, to be designated as the exempt class, the noncompetitive class, the labor class and the competitive class. The Chief Administrator of the Courts shall determine the appropriate class for each job title in the unified court system.

Cross References

New York City Civil Court Act, see McKinney's Book 29A, Part 3.

§ 25.8. Exempt Class

The exempt class shall consist of all offices or positions, other than unskilled labor positions, for the filling of which competitive or noncompetitive exami-

nations may be found by the Chief Administrator of the Courts not to be practicable.

§ 25.9. Noncompetitive Class

The noncompetitive class shall include all positions that are not in the exempt class or the labor class and for which it is found by the Chief Administrator of the Courts not to be practicable to ascertain the merit and fitness of applicants by competitive examination. Appointments to positions in the noncompetitive class shall be made after such noncompetitive examination as is prescribed by the Chief Administrator.

§ 25.10. Labor Class

The labor class shall comprise all unskilled laborers in the unified court system. The Chief Administrator of the Courts may, where practicable, require applicants for employment in the labor class to meet minimum qualifications and to qualify by examination.

§ 25.11. Competitive Class

The competitive class shall include all positions for which the Chief Administrator of the Courts finds it is practicable to determine the merit and fitness of applicants by competitive examination.

§ 25.12. Private Institutions or Enterprises Acquired by Unified Court System

(a) Whenever the unified court system shall acquire a private institution or enterprise for the purpose of operating it as a public function, the unified court system may continue the employment of all officers or employees thereof deemed necessary, who shall have been in the employ of such private institution or enterprise for at least one year prior to such acquisition. The positions so held by such employees shall be in the noncompetitive class, pending the jurisdictional classification or reclassification of such positions by the Chief Administrator of the Courts, and such employees shall continue to be employed in similar or corresponding positions and shall have the seniority theretofore held by them as among themselves. The Chief Administrator, however, after notice to any such employee of the reasons therefor, and after according such employee a hearing, may exclude such employee from further employment if found by the Chief Administrator not to be a person of good character.

(b) Not later than one year after the acquisition of such private institution or enterprise, the Chief Administrator of the Courts shall classify or reclassify the various positions. The then incumbents of such positions who are employed therein at the time of the acquisition of the private institution or enterprise and who were so employed for at least one year prior to such acquisition shall continue to hold their positions without further examination and shall have all the rights and privileges of the jurisdictional class to which such positions may be allocated; provided, however, that after such acquisition all new positions thereafter created and vacancies occurring in positions already established shall be filled in accordance with the provisions of this Part.

§ 25.13.   Applications and Examinations

(a) Positions Subject to Competitive Examinations. The merit and fitness of applicants for positions which are classified in the competitive class shall be ascertained by such examinations as may be prescribed by the Chief Administrator of the Courts.

(b) Announcement of Examination. The Chief Administrator of the Courts shall issue an announcement of each competitive examination, setting forth the minimum qualifications required, the subjects of examination, and such other information as he or she may deem necessary, and shall advertise such examination in such manner as the nature of the examination may require. Such announcement and advertisement shall each inform prospective applicants of the availability of special accommodations for taking of examinations as provided in subdivisions (g) and (h) of this section.

(c) Applications. The Chief Administrator of the Courts shall require prospective applicants for any positions to file, during a prescribed time, a formal application in which the applicant shall state such information as may reasonably be required regarding his or her background, experience and qualifications for the position sought, and his or her merit and fitness for the public service. The application shall be subscribed by the applicant and shall contain an affirmation by him or her that the statements therein are true, and shall bear a form notice to the effect that false statements made therein are punishable under section 210.45 of the Penal Law. Blank forms of such applications shall be furnished by the Chief Administrator without charge to all persons requesting the same. The Chief Administrator may require in connection with such application such information as the good of the service may require.

(d) Disqualification of Applicants or Eligibles.

(1) The Chief Administrator of the Courts may refuse to examine an applicant, or after examination to include a candidate on the eligible list, or may remove or restrict from the eligible list, or may refuse to appoint, an applicant or eligible:

(i) who is found to lack any of the established requirements for admission to the examination or for appointment to the position for which he or she applies; or

(ii) who is found to have a physical or mental disability which renders him or her unfit for the performance, with or without reasonable accommodation, of the essential functions of the position in which he or she seeks employment, or which creates a significant risk to the health or safety of the individual or of others that cannot be eliminated with reasonable accommodation; or

(iii) who has been guilty of a crime; or

(iv) who has been dismissed from a permanent position in the public service upon stated written charges of incompetency or misconduct, after an opportunity to answer such charges in writing, or who has resigned from, or whose service has otherwise been terminated in, a permanent or temporary position in the public service, where it is found after appropriate investigation or inquiry that such resignation or termination resulted from his or her incompetency or misconduct; or

(v) who has intentionally made a false statement of any material fact in his or her application; or

(vi) who has practiced, or attempted to practice, any deception or fraud in his or her application, in his or her examination, or in securing eligibility or appointment; or

(vii) who has been dismissed from private employment because of poor performance, incompetency or misconduct; or

(viii) who lacks good moral character; or

(ix) who has a record of disrespect for the requirements and processes of law, including repeated traffic offenses or disregard of summonses for traffic offenses.

(2) No person shall be disqualified pursuant to this subdivision unless he or she has been given a written statement of the reasons therefor and afforded an opportunity to make an explanation and to submit facts in opposition to such disqualification. The applicant shall have the burden of establishing his or her qualifications to the satisfaction of the Chief Administrator of the Courts. Any applicant who refuses to permit the Chief Administrator to investigate matters necessary for the verification of his or her qualifications or who otherwise hampers, impedes or fails to cooperate in such investigation shall be disqualified as set forth in paragraph (1) of this subdivision.

(3) Notwithstanding any other provision of this Part, the Chief Administrator of the Courts may investigate the qualifications and background of an eligible after he or she has been appointed from the list, and upon finding facts which, if known prior to appointment, would have warranted his or her disqualification, or upon a finding of illegality, irregularity or fraud of a substantial nature in his or her application, examination or appointment, may revoke such eligible's certification and appointment and direct that his or her employment be terminated; provided, however, that no such certification shall be revoked or appointment terminated more than three years after it is made, except in the case of fraud.

(e) Application Fees. The Chief Administrator of the Courts may require applicants for any positions to pay application and processing fees in a manner and amount prescribed by the Chief Administrator.

(f) Scope of Examination. Examinations shall relate to those matters which will fairly test the relative capacity and fitness of the persons examined to discharge the duties of that service into which they seek to be appointed. The Chief Administrator of the Courts shall establish an eligible list on the basis of ratings received by the candidates in the competitive portions of the examination, and may thereafter conduct medical, physical ability, psychological and other appropriate noncompetitive qualifying tests as required.

(g) Examination of Candidates Unable to Attend Tests Because of Religious Observance. A person who, because of religious beliefs, is unable to attend and take an examination scheduled to be held on a day which is a religious holiday observed by such person shall be permitted to take such examination on some other day designated by the Chief Administrator of the Courts at a reasonable comparable time and place without any additional fee or penalty.

(h) Examinations of Disabled Persons. Where an applicant is not so physically or mentally disabled as to prevent him or her from satisfactorily performing, with or without reasonable accommodation, the essential functions of the position for which he or she is applying, to insure competitive equality between the disabled person and persons not so disabled in connection with interviews and the taking of examinations, the Chief Administrator, upon request, may furnish appropriate auxiliary aids or services and, when necessary, allow additional time for examinations.

(i) Residence Requirements for Unified Court System Positions. The Chief Administrator of the Courts may prescribe residency requirements for positions in the unified court system.

(j) Rating of Examinations.

(1) The subjects of an examination shall be given such relative weight as the Chief Administrator of the Courts may prescribe; provided, however, that in a promotion examination, credit granted for seniority and for performance rating, may be applied by the addition of points to the scores earned by passed candidates who have passed all other parts of the examination.

(2) After a candidate's rating has been determined, he or she shall be notified of such rating unless he or she has otherwise been disqualified.

(3) In an examination in which the number of candidates is expected to greatly exceed the number of existing and anticipated vacancies, the Chief Administrator of the Courts may prescribe that the passing mark shall be the lowest grade received among a certain fixed number of candidates graded highest in such examination or in any subject of such examination. Whenever the Chief Administrator shall determine upon such a passing mark in any examination or

in any subject of an examination, notice thereof shall be set forth in the announcement of the examination.

(4) The Chief Administrator of the Courts may authorize the use of any professionally recognized examination scoring and conversion methods, taking into consideration the type of examination, the examination difficulty, the size of the applicant population in relation to the number of positions to be filled, labor market conditions, or other factors which can affect the number and quality of eligibles.

(k) Establishment of Eligible Lists. Every candidate who attains a passing mark in an examination as a whole and who meets the standards prescribed, if any, for separate subjects or parts of subjects of the examination shall be eligible for appointment to the position for which he or she was examined, and his or her name shall be entered on the eligible list in the order of his or her final rating; but if two or more eligibles receive the same final rating in the examination, they shall be ranked in accordance with such uniform, impartial procedure as may be prescribed therefor by the Chief Administrator of the Courts.

§ 25.14. Filling Vacancies by Open Competitive Examination

The Chief Administrator of the Courts may conduct an open competitive examination for filling a vacancy or vacancies instead of a promotion examination. Any employee or employee organization may submit to the Chief Administrator a request, in writing, for a promotion examination, rather than an open competitive examination, stating the reasons why it is practicable and in the public interest to fill the vacancy by promotion examination.

§ 25.15. Filling Vacancies by Promotion Examinations

(a) Filling Vacancies by Promotion. Except as provided in section 25.14 of this Part, vacancies in positions in the competitive class shall be filled, as far as practicable, by promotion from among persons holding, at the time of the examination for promotion or at the time of appointment, competitive class positions on a permanent basis in a lower title in the promotion unit in which the vacancy exists, provided that such lower-titled positions are in direct line of promotion, as determined by the Chief Administrator of the Courts; except that where the Chief Administrator determines that it is impracticable or against the public interest to limit eligibility for promotion to persons holding lower-titled positions in direct line of promotion, the Chief Administrator may extend eligibility for promotion to persons holding competitive class positions in lower titles which the Chief Administrator determines to be in related or collateral lines of promotion, or in any comparable positions in the unified court system. The Chief Administrator may prescribe minimum training and experience qualifications for eligibility to take a promotion examination and for promotion.

(b) Factors in Promotion. Promotion shall be based on merit and fitness as determined by examination, due weight being given to seniority. The previous training and experience of the candidates, and performance ratings where available, may be considered and given due weight as factors in determining the relative merit and fitness of candidates for promotion.

(c) Promotion Eligibility of Persons on Preferred Lists and Employees on Leave of Absence. Any employee who has been suspended from his or her position through no fault of his or her own and whose name is on a preferred list, and any employee on leave of absence from his or her position, shall be allowed to compete in a promotion examination for which he or she would otherwise be eligible on the basis of his or her actual service before suspension or leave of absence.

(d) General and Promotion Unit Eligible Lists. Promotion examinations may be held for such subdivisions of the unified court system as the Chief Administrator may determine to be appropriate promotion units. No general promotion eligible list shall be certified for any promotion unit until after the promotion unit eligible list for that promotion unit has been exhausted.

(e) Promotion by Noncompetitive Examination.

(1) Whenever there are no more than three persons eligible for examination for promotion to a vacant competitive class position, or whenever no more than three persons file applications for examination for promotion to such position, one of such persons may be nominated and, upon passing an examination appropriate to the duties and responsibilities of the position, may be promoted. Any person who is nominated for noncompetitive examination for promotion to such position and who fails to pass two examinations for such promotion shall not thereafter be eligible for employment in such position, except by appointment or promotion from an eligible list established following competitive examination.

(2) An examination may be waived for noncompetitive promotion where the nominee has already qualified in an examination appropriate to the duties and responsibilities of the position.

(f) Limitation Upon Promotion. No person shall be promoted to a position or title for which there is required an examination involving essential tests or qualifications different from or higher than those required for the position or title held by such person unless he or she has passed the examination and is eligible for appointment to such higher position or title.

(g) Credit for Provisional Service. No credit in a promotion examination shall be granted to any person

for any time served as a provisional appointee in the position to which promotion is sought or in any similar position; provided, however, such provisional appointee by reason of such provisional appointment shall receive credit in his or her permanent position from which promotion is sought for such time served in such provisional appointment.

(h) Extension of Promotion Examinations. Notwithstanding any other provision in this Part, the Chief Administrator of the Courts may, for designated titles:

(1) extend to employees in the unified court system who are holding or who have held a position in the noncompetitive, exempt or labor class of such service, the same opportunity as employees in the competitive class to take promotion examinations (i) if said employees in the past have held qualifying competitive class positions for that examination on a permanent basis, or (ii) if such examinations are to be held in conjunction with open competitive examinations; and

(2) extend to employees in the unified court system who are holding or who have held a position in the noncompetitive class pursuant to the provisions of section 25.16(b) of this Part, or to disabled veterans of the Vietnam era as defined in section 85 of the Civil Service Law, the same opportunities to take promotion examinations as provided to employees in the competitive class.

(i) Appointment or promotion to noncompetitive or exempt positions from competitive positions. An employee holding a permanent position in the competitive class who accepts an appointment or promotion to a position in the noncompetitive or exempt class, and to any successive positions in either of those classes, shall be eligible to return to his or her former competitive class position, in the manner provided herein, upon termination of employment in the noncompetitive or exempt position for reasons other than misconduct or incompetency. Upon such termination, and upon request, the name of the employee shall be placed on a preferred list for his or her former position pursuant to section 25.31 of this Part, and the employee shall be eligible for reinstatement from such preferred list for a period of four years.

§ 25.16. Equal Employment Opportunity

(a) It is the policy of the New York State Unified Court System to ensure equal employment opportunity for all employees and applicants for employment, without regard to race, color, national origin, religion, creed, sex (including freedom from sexual harassment), sexual orientation, age, marital status, disability, military status, or, in certain circumstances, prior criminal record. No person shall be prevented from qualifying for employment in any position in the unified court system because of any of these factors, unless these factors are bona fide occupational qualifications.

(b) The Chief Administrator of the Courts may determine up to 100 positions in the competitive class with duties such as can be performed by physically or mentally disabled persons who are found otherwise qualified to perform satisfactorily the duties of any such position. Upon such determination, the position shall be classified in the noncompetitive class, and may be filled only by persons who shall have been certified by an appropriate agency as being either physically or mentally disabled but capable of performing the duties of such positions.

§ 25.17. Duration of an Eligible List

The duration of an eligible list shall be fixed at not less than one nor more than four years, provided that:

(a) where vacancies cannot be filled from an eligible list because of restrictions on filling vacancies based upon a financial emergency, the Chief Administrator of the Courts may extend the duration of that eligible list up to a period equal to the length of such restriction against the filling of vacancies; and

(b) in exceptional circumstances and where an examination already has been scheduled for a title, the Chief Administrator may extend the duration of an eligible list for that title up to the date of the certification of the new eligible list resulting from that examination, but in no event for more than one year.

An eligible list that has been in existence for one year or more shall terminate upon establishment of an appropriate new list, unless otherwise prescribed by the Chief Administrator.

§ 25.18. Establishment of a Continuing Eligible List

The Chief Administrator of the Courts may establish a continuing eligible list for any class of positions for which inadequate numbers of qualified persons are found available for recruitment or appointment. Names of eligibles shall be inserted in such list from time to time as applicants are tested and found qualified in examinations held at such intervals as may be prescribed by the Chief Administrator. Such successive examinations shall, so far as practicable, be constructed and rated so as to be equivalent tests of the merit and fitness of candidates. The name of any candidate who passes any such examination and who is otherwise qualified shall be placed on the continuing eligible list in the rank corresponding to his or her final rating on such examination. The period of eligibility of successful candidates for certification and appointment from such continuing eligible list, as a result of any such examination, shall be fixed by the Chief Administrator but, except as a list may reach an announced terminal date, such period shall not be less than one year; nor shall such period of eligibility exceed four years, except as provided in section 25.17 of this Part. Subject to such conditions and limitations as the Chief Administrator may prescribe, a candidate may take more than one such examination; provided, however, that no such candidate shall be certified simultaneously with more than one rank on the continuing eligible list. With respect to any candidate who applies for and is granted additional credit in any such examination as a disabled or nondisabled veteran, and for the limited purpose of granting such additional credit, the eligible list shall be deemed to be established on the date on which his or her name is added thereto.

§ 25.19. Certification of Eligibles

(a) Certification of Eligibles From Prior List. When an eligible list has been in existence for less than one year and contains the names of fewer than three persons willing to accept appointment, and a new list for the same position or group of positions is established, the names of the persons remaining on the old list shall have preference in certification over the new list until such old list is one year old, and during such period such names shall be certified along with enough names from the new list to provide the appointing officer with a sufficient number of eligibles from which selection for appointment may be made. Where an old list which has been in existence for one year or more is continued upon the establishment of a new list which contains fewer than three names, the Chief Administrator of the Courts may certify the names on the old list along with enough names from the new list to provide the appointing officer with a sufficient number of eligibles from which selection for appointment may be made.

(b) Certification on Basis of Sex. The Chief Administrator may limit certification from an eligible list to one sex when the duties of the position involved require sex selection as a bona fide occupational qualification.

(c) Certification of Lists for Court Positions.

(1) Certifications for appointments to positions in the court service, regardless of the location thereof, shall be made from statewide lists of eligibles.

(2) The Chief Administrator of the Courts shall determine the eligible list most nearly appropriate for the position to be filled, and shall certify a sufficient number of eligibles from which selection for appointment may be made. When the name of any eligible is included in a certification for appointment, the names of all other eligibles on the list having the same final rating as such eligible shall likewise be included in such certification.

(3) When an eligible is canvassed for or is offered appointment in writing, and fails to state his or her willingness to accept such appointment within seven business days after the mailing of such canvass or offer, or before the end of the second succeeding business day if such canvass or offer is sent by telegram or express mail, he or she may be considered

as ineligible for purposes of making selection for such particular appointment.

(4) The name of any eligible who fails to reply to an offer of or canvass for appointment, or who declines or indicates unwillingness to accept appointment, or who fails to report for work after accepting an offer of appointment, may be withheld from further certification from the eligible list. The name of such eligible may again be certified upon his or her request, and the submission by such eligible of reasons satisfactory to the Chief Administrator for declination or failure to reply or to accept appointment or to report to work.

§ 25.20. Appointment or Promotion of Eligibles

(a) Appointment or Promotion From Eligible Lists.

(1) Appointment or promotion from an eligible list to a position in the competitive class shall be made by the selection of one of the three persons certified by the Chief Administrator of the Courts as standing highest on such eligible list who are willing to accept such appointment or promotion; provided, however, that where it is necessary to break ties among eligibles having the same final examination ratings in order to determine their respective standings on the eligible list, appointment or promotion may be made by the selection of any eligible whose final examination rating is equal to or higher than the final examination rating of the third highest standing eligible willing to accept such appointment or promotion. Appointments and promotions shall be made from the eligible list most nearly appropriate for the position to be filled. Persons on a certified eligible list who are considered and not selected for appointment or promotion pursuant to this paragraph shall, whenever another candidate is appointed or promoted, be given written notice of such nonselection.

(2) Whenever a vacancy exists in a competitive class position and an open competitive examination does not result in an eligible list containing the names of at least three persons willing to accept appointment, a person may be nominated for noncompetitive examination for such position. If such nominee shall be certified by the Chief Administrator as qualified, he or she may be appointed to fill such vacancy. The Chief Administrator also may designate an eligible list as a continuing eligible list in accordance with section 25.18 of this Part.

(b) Prohibition Against Out-of-Title Work. No person shall be appointed, promoted or employed under any title not appropriate to the duties to be performed and, except upon assignment by proper authority during the continuance of a temporary emergency situation, no person shall be assigned to perform the duties of any position unless he or she has been duly appointed, promoted, transferred, reassigned or reinstated to such position in accordance

with the provisions of this Part. No credit shall be granted in a promotion examination for out-of-title work.

(c) Trainee Appointments. The Chief Administrator may require that permanent appointments or promotions to designated positions shall be conditioned upon the satisfactory completion of a term of service as a trainee in such a position or in an appropriate, lower, training title or the completion of specified training or academic courses, or both. Upon the satisfactory completion of such training term, and of specified courses if required, an appointee shall be entitled to full permanent status in the position for which appointment was made. Any appointment hereunder shall be subject to such probationary period as is prescribed in this Part. The employment of such person may be discontinued at the end of the term of training service if his or her conduct, capacity or fitness is not satisfactory, or at any time if he or she fails to pursue or continue satisfactorily such training or academic courses as may be required.

(d) Seasonal Positions.

(1) Positions in the competitive class where the nature of service is such that it is not continuous throughout the year, but recurs in each successive year, except as herein otherwise provided, shall be designated as seasonal positions and shall be subject to the provisions of this Part applicable generally to positions in such class. Upon the expiration of the employment season, the names of all persons employed in such seasonal positions shall be entered upon a seasonal reemployment list in the order of their first appointment to the title vacated by them at the expiration of such employment season. Such seasonal reemployment list shall be certified at the commencement of or during the next employment season, and the persons whose names appear thereon as still qualified shall be entitled to reemployment in such positions in the order in which their names appear on such list. Any person may be reexamined with respect to physical fitness for the performance of the duties of the position, and may be disqualified for reemployment in the same manner and for any of the reasons applicable to the disqualification of an eligible on an eligible list resulting from open competitive examination.

(2) The name of any person on such list who is not reached for reemployment shall remain on such list and shall be certified, in the order of the date of his or her first appointment to such position, during subsequent employment seasons; provided, however, that the eligibility for reemployment of any such person shall not continue for a period longer than three years from the date of his or her separation from such seasonal employment. A seasonal reemployment list shall not be deemed to be a preferred list.

(3) Where a vacancy occurs in a full-time position having a title and duties similar to those of a seasonal

position and for which no appropriate open competitive eligible list is available, it may be filled by selection from among seasonal employees. For that purpose, the Chief Administrator of the Courts may certify, to fill such vacancy, the names of persons holding comparable seasonal positions in the order of their dates of original appointment in such positions or, if the vacancy occurs at a time other than during the employment season, the appropriate seasonal reemployment list. In such case, appointment shall be made by the selection of a person whose date of original appointment to the seasonal position is the same as or earlier than the date of original appointment of the third highest standing person certified who indicates willingness to accept such appointment.

§ 25.21. Oath of Office

Every person employed by the unified court system, except an employee in the labor class, before he or she shall be entitled to enter upon the discharge of any of his or her duties, shall take and file an oath or affirmation in the form and language prescribed by the Constitution for executive, legislative and judicial officers, which may be administered by any officer authorized to take the acknowledgment of the execution of a deed of real property, or by an officer in whose office the oath is required to be filed. In lieu of such oath administered by an officer, an employee may comply with the requirements of this section by subscribing and filing the following statement: "I do hereby pledge and declare that I will support the Constitution of the United States, and the Constitution of the State of New York, and that I will faithfully discharge the duties of the position of _____ according to the best of my ability." Such oath or statement shall be required only upon original appointment or upon a new appointment following an interruption of continuous service, defined in section 25.30(b) of this Part, and shall not be required upon promotion, demotion, transfer, or other change of title during the continued service of the employee, or upon reinstatement, pursuant to law or rules, of an employee whose services have been terminated and whose last executed oath or statement is on file. The oath of office heretofore taken by any employee as previously required by law, and the oath of office hereafter taken or statement hereafter subscribed by any employee pursuant to this section, shall extend to and encompass any position or title in which such person may serve as an employee during the period of his or her continuous service following the taking of such oath or subscribing of such statement, and his or her acceptance of such new title shall constitute a reaffirmance of such oath or statement. The oath or statement of every employee of the unified court system shall be filed in the administrative office for the courts. The refusal or willful failure of such employee to take and file such oath or subscribe and file such statement shall terminate his or her employment until such oath shall be taken and filed, or statement subscribed and filed, as herein provided.

Cross References

Constitution, see McKinney's Book 2.

§ 25.22. Probation

(a) Probationary Term.

(1) Except as otherwise provided every permanent appointment from an open competitive list and every original appointment to the noncompetitive, exempt or labor class shall be subject to a probationary term of not less than 26 nor more than 52 weeks. This probationary term also shall apply to each appointment to a position in which the appointee is not under the regular supervision of the appointing authority until the completion of prescribed schooling or off-the-job training; provided, however, that such probationary term, in this case, shall commence after the successful completion of such training.

(2) Except as otherwise provided, every promotion to a position shall be subject to a probationary term of not less than 12 weeks nor more than 52 weeks. For the purposes of this subdivision, the term "promotion" shall include the appointment of an employee to a higher-grade position in the noncompetitive, exempt or labor class.

(3) Every transfer and reassignment, as defined in section 25.26 of this Part, to a position shall be subject to a probationary term of not less than 12 weeks nor more than 52 weeks, provided, however, (i) that this paragraph shall apply to a reassignment only where the reassignment is to a court under the supervision of a different Administrative Judge, and (ii) that the appointing authority having jurisdiction over a position to which transfer or reassignment is sought may elect to waive the probationary term required for such position.

(4) The Chief Administrator of the Courts may establish, for specified titles, shorter periods of probation for promotion, transfers and reassignments than those set forth in paragraphs (2) and (3) of this subdivision.

(5)(i) An appointment, promotion, transfer or reassignment shall become permanent upon the retention of the probationer after completion of the maximum period of service of the probationary term or upon earlier written notice, following completion of the minimum period, that the probationary term is successfully completed, or, in the case of a transfer or reassignment, upon written notice that the appointing authority has elected to waive the serving of the probationary term.

(ii) If the conduct or performance of a probationer is not satisfactory, his or her employment from such position may be terminated at any time after eight weeks and before completion of the maximum period of service, provided that the appointing authority may, in his or her discretion, and with notice to the probationer prior to the end of the probationary term, extend the probationary period for an additional term of not less than 12 nor more than 26 weeks in a different assignment, in which case the appointment may be made permanent at any time after completion of 12 weeks of service, or the employment terminated at any time after the completion of eight weeks of service, and on or before the completion of 26 weeks of service.

(iii) The probationer's supervisor shall carefully observe the probationer's conduct and performance and, at least two weeks prior to the end of the probationary term, shall report thereon in writing to the appointing authority or his or her designee. The supervisor shall also, from time to time during the probationary term, advise the probationer of his or her status and progress. A probationer whose services are to be terminated for unsatisfactory service shall receive written notice at least one week prior to such termination and, upon request, shall be granted an interview with the appointing authority or his or her representative.

(b) Trainee Appointment or Promotion. The probationary term for a trainee appointment or trainee promotion shall coincide with the term of training service. If the conduct or performance of the probationer is not satisfactory, his or her employment may be terminated at any time after the completion of a specified minimum period of service and on or before the completion of the term of training service. Such specified minimum period of service, unless otherwise prescribed in the announcement of examination, shall be eight weeks.

(c) Transfers and Reassignments. A probationer shall be eligible for transfer or reassignment, provided, that upon such transfer, or upon a reassignment requiring service of a probationary period, he or she shall serve a complete probationary period in the new position in the same manner and subject to the same conditions as required upon his or her employment in the position from which transfer or reassignment is made.

(d) Leave of Absence. When a permanent employee is promoted, transferred or reassigned to a position in which he or she is required to serve a probationary term, the position thus vacated shall not be filled during such probationary term except on a temporary basis or by an appointment made pursuant to section 25.24 of this Part. The employee so promoted, transferred or reassigned shall be deemed to be on leave of absence from the vacated position. At any time during such probationary term, the employee shall have the right, upon reasonable notice, to return to his or her previous position at his or her own election. If the conduct or performance of the probationer is not satisfactory, the probationer shall be restored to his or her former permanent position.

(e) Reinstatement. An employee who is reinstated to a position in accordance with section 25.28 of this Part shall serve a new probationary period in the same manner and subject to the same requirements as apply upon original appointment to such position, unless otherwise provided by the Chief Administrator of the Courts.

(f) Absence During Probationary Term. Any periods of authorized or unauthorized absence aggregating up to 10 workdays during the probationary term, or aggregating up to 20 workdays if the maximum term exceeds 26 weeks, may, in the discretion of the appointing authority, be considered as time served in the probationary term. Any such periods of absence not so considered by the appointing authority as time served in the probationary term, and any periods of absence in excess of periods considered by the appointing authority as time served in the probationary term pursuant to this subdivision, shall not be counted as time served in the probationary term. The minimum and maximum periods of the probationary term of any employee shall be extended by the number of workdays of absence which, pursuant to this subdivision, are not counted as time served in the probationary term.

(g) Restoration to Eligible List. A probationer whose employment is terminated, or who resigns, before the end of his or her probationary term may request that his or her name be restored to the eligible list from which he or she was appointed, provided such list is still in existence. The probationer's name may be restored to such list if the Chief Administrator, after due inquiry, determines that the probationer's service was such that he or she should be given another opportunity for appointment.

(h) Service in Higher-Level Position. When an employee who has not completed his or her probationary term is appointed to a higher-level position, the period of service rendered by such employee in such higher-level position may, in the discretion of the appointing authority, be considered as satisfactory probationary service in the lower position and may be counted as such in determining the satisfactory completion of such probationary term. At any time after the expiration of the minimum period of the probationary term, or the entire probationary term if it be one of fixed duration, the appointing authority shall, on request of such probationer, furnish a decision in writing as to whether or not service in such higher-level position shall be considered as satisfactory probationary service. In the event of an adverse decision by the appointing authority, such probationer, at his or her request, shall be returned to the lower position for sufficient time to permit the probationer to complete his or her probationary term. The employment of such a probationer in his or her lower position shall not be terminated at the end of the probationary term on account of unsatisfactory service unless he or she shall have actually served in such position, in the aggregate, at least a period of eight weeks.

(i) Removal During Probationary Term. Nothing contained in this section shall be construed to limit or otherwise affect the authority to remove a probationer at any time during the probationary term for job abandonment pursuant to the provisions of section 25.28(e) of this Part, or for incompetency or misconduct.

§ 25.23. Temporary and Emergency Appointments

(a) Temporary Appointments Authorized; Duration. A temporary appointment may be made for a period not exceeding three months when the need for such service is important and urgent. A temporary appointment may be made for a period exceeding three months under the following circumstances only:

(1) When an employee is on leave of absence from his or her position, a temporary appointment to such position may be made for a period not exceeding the authorized duration of such leave of absence as prescribed by statute or rule.

(2) A temporary appointment may be made for a period not exceeding six months when it is found by the appointing authority, upon due inquiry, that the position to which such appointment is proposed will not continue in existence for a longer period; provided, however, that where a temporary appointment is made to a position originally expected to exist for no longer than six months and it subsequently develops that such position will remain in existence beyond such six-month period, such temporary appointment may be extended for a further period not to exceed an additional six months.

(b) Temporary Appointments Upon Abolition of Positions. When a reduction or abolition of positions in the unified court system is planned or imminent and such reduction or abolition of positions will probably result in the suspension or demotion of permanent employees, the appointing authority may make temporary instead of permanent appointments for a period not exceeding one year in positions in the unified court system to which permanent employees to be affected by such abolition or reduction of positions will be eligible for transfer or reassignment. Successive temporary appointments shall not be made to the same position after the expiration of the authorized period of the original temporary appointment to such position.

(c) Temporary Appointments From Eligible Lists.

(1) A temporary appointment for a period not exceeding three months may be made without regard to existing eligible lists.

(2) A temporary appointment for a period exceeding three months, but not exceeding six months may be made by the selection of a person from an appropriate eligible list, without regard to the relative standing of such person on such list.

(3) Any further temporary appointment beyond such six-month period, or any temporary appointment originally made for a period exceeding six months shall be made by the selection of an appointee from among those graded highest on an appropriate eligible list in accordance with section 25.20(a) of this Part.

(d) Temporary Appointments Without Examination in Exceptional Cases. Notwithstanding any other provision of this section, the appointing authority may authorize a temporary appointment, without examination, when the person appointed will render professional, scientific, technical or other expert services on an occasional basis or on a full-time or regular part-time basis in a temporary position established to conduct a special study or project for a period not exceeding 18 months. Such appointment may be authorized only in a case where, because of the nature of the services to be rendered and the temporary or occasional character of such services, it would not be practicable to hold an examination of any kind.

(e) Emergency Appointments. When an emergency requires that a position be filled pending appointment from a list or after noncompetitive examination, the appointing authority may fill the vacancy. Such appointment shall not continue longer than one month without a continuance by the appointing authority.

(f) Effect of Temporary Appointment on Eligibility for Permanent Appointment. The acceptance by an eligible of a temporary appointment shall not affect his or her standing on the eligible list for a permanent appointment, nor shall the period of temporary service be counted as part of the probationary service in that position in the event of subsequent permanent appointment.

(g) Temporary or Provisional Appointment or Promotion of Permanent Employee. When a permanent competitive class employee is given a temporary or provisional appointment or promotion to another competitive class position, he or she shall be deemed to be on leave of absence from his or her permanent position for the period of his or her service under such temporary or provisional appointment or promotion. He or she shall be entitled to return to his or her permanent position upon the termination of such temporary or provisional service. An employee who voluntarily elects to relinquish his or her temporary or provisional status and return to his or her permanent position shall give reasonable notice thereof to the appointing authority.

§ 25.24. Contingent Permanent Appointments

(a) A permanent employee appointed or promoted to a position in a higher title, which is left temporarily vacant by the leave of absence of the permanent incumbent, may, in the discretion of the appointing authority, be appointed or promoted with contingent permanent status in such position, provided that at the time of such appointment or promotion, such employee must have qualified by examination and either be eligible for noncompetitive promotion to such higher-titled position or his or her name must be among the three highest ranking eligibles on an existing list for such higher-titled position who are willing to accept contingent permanent appointment or promotion to such position exclusive of eligibles already appointed or promoted to a similar position on a permanent basis or on a contingent permanent basis.

(b) An employee holding a position on a contingent permanent basis shall have the following rights and be subject to the following conditions:

(1) Unless separated from service, such employee shall be deemed to be on leave of absence from his or her lower-titled position until he or she either returns to such lower-titled position or gains full permanent status in his or her higher-titled position or any higher-titled position.

(2) Such employee may, at his or her election and after reasonable notice, be restored to his or her lower-titled position at any time during such leave of absence, and shall be restored to such position if required in accordance with other provisions of this Part upon the return of the permanent incumbent to his or her or another similar higher-titled position.

(3) His or her contingent permanent status shall not adversely affect or impair eligibility for certification from the eligible list for permanent appointment or promotion to such permanent vacancies as may occur in other similar positions.

(4) He or she shall be deemed to hold such position on a permanent basis for the purposes of section 25.29 of this Part, or under an agreement negotiated pursuant to article 14 of the Civil Service Law, and for purposes of section 25.30(a) of this Part.

(5) For purposes of salary rights and benefits, he or she shall be deemed to hold such position on a permanent basis.

(6) For purposes of subsequent examinations, either open competitive or promotion, service in a position with contingent permanent status shall be counted in the same manner as though it were service on a permanent basis. If such employee received a contingent permanent appointment or promotion as a result of receiving additional credits in an examination as a veteran, he or she shall not be entitled to such credits in any subsequent examination for a higher-titled position for which he or she would not otherwise be eligible without such contingent permanent status.

(7) In the event that return from leave of one or more permanent incumbents or other circumstances necessitates termination of the appointment or promotion of one or more incumbents not having permanent status, such termination shall be made among such incumbents in the unit for suspension or demotion designated pursuant to section 25.30(d) of this Part, wherein such return of permanent incumbents or other circumstances occurs. Incumbents having contingent permanent status shall have preference in retention in their positions or similar positions over temporary incumbents not having such status. If the return of permanent incumbents or other circumstances necessitates termination of the appointment or promotion of incumbents having contingent permanent status, such termination shall be made in the inverse order of date of acquisition of contingent permanent status.

(8) If a permanent vacancy occurs in a position then held by an incumbent having contingent permanent status therein, such vacancy shall be filled by selection by the appointing authority of one of such employees of the promotion unit having such contingent permanent status in such position or a similar position (whether or not he or she is then serving under contingent permanent appointment or promotion in such position); provided, however, that if any such employee has acquired such contingent permanent status by appointment or promotion from an eligible list still in existence, he or she may not be selected for permanent appointment or promotion unless he or she is then reachable for permanent appointment or promotion from such eligible list.

(9) If a permanent vacancy occurs in a position not then held by an incumbent having contingent permanent status therein, such vacancy may be filled without regard to the provisions of this section; or if one or more employees in the promotion unit have contingent permanent status in the same title, the appointing authority may, in his or her discretion, elect to fill such position in the manner provided in paragraph (8) of this subdivision.

(c) Nothing herein shall be construed to limit or adversely affect the right of eligibility for reinstatement of any person from a preferred list as provided in section 25.31 of this Part.

(d) Notwithstanding the provisions of subdivision (a) of this section, an employee may obtain contingent permanent status upon appointment from an open competitive eligible list, in accordance with section 25.20(a) of this Part, to a position which is left temporarily vacant by the leave of absence of the permanent incumbent. An employee obtaining contingent permanent status pursuant to this subdivision shall have the rights and be subject to the conditions set forth in subdivision (b) of this section.

Cross References

Civil Service Law, see McKinney's Book 9.

## § 25.25.	Provisional Appointments

(a) **Provisional Appointments Authorized.** Whenever there is no appropriate eligible list available for filling a vacancy in the competitive class, the appointing authority may appoint provisionally to fill such vacancy a person who qualifies by noncompetitive examination until a selection and appointment can be made after competitive examination. Such noncompetitive examination may consist of a review and evaluation of the training, experience and other qualifications of the nominee, without written, oral or other performance tests.

(b) **Time Limitation on Provisional Appointments.** No provisional appointment shall continue for a period in excess of nine months. The Chief Administrator of the Courts shall order a competitive civil service examination for any position held by provisional appointment for a period of one month. Such an examination shall be conducted, as soon as practicable thereafter, to prevent the provisional appointment from continuing for a period in excess of nine months.

(c) **Termination of Provisional Appointments.** A provisional appointment to any position shall be terminated within two months following the establishment of an appropriate eligible list for filling vacancies in such positions; provided, however, that where there are a large number of provisional appointees to be replaced by permanent appointees from a newly established eligible list, and the appointing authority deems that the termination of the employment of all such provisional appointees within two months following establishment of such list would disrupt or impair essential public services, the appointing authority may terminate the employment of various numbers of such provisional appointees at stated intervals; provided, however, that the employment of any such provisional appointee shall not be continued longer than four months following the establishment of such eligible list.

(d) **Successive Provisional Appointments.** Successive provisional appointments shall not be made to the same position after the expiration of the authorized period of the original provisional appointment to such position; provided, however, that where an examination for a position or group of positions fails to produce a list adequate to fill all positions then held on a provisional basis, or where such list is exhausted immediately following its establishment, a new provisional appointment may be made to any such position remaining unfilled by permanent appointment, and such new provisional appointment may, in the discretion of the appointing authority, be given to a current or former provisional appointee in such position, except that a current or former provisional appointee who becomes eligible for permanent appointment to any such position shall, if he or she is then to be continued in or appointed to any such position, be afforded permanent appointment to such position.

## § 25.26.	Transfer and Reassignments

(a) **Definitions.** Unless otherwise expressly stated or unless the context requires a different meaning, the following terms as used in this section shall be construed as set forth herein:

(1) The term "reassignment" means the change, without further examination, of a permanent employee from his or her present permanent title, position and location to another similar position in the same promotion unit.

(2) The term "transfer" means the change, without further examination, of a permanent employee from his or her present permanent title, position and location within one promotion unit to a similar position within another promotion unit.

(b) **General Provisions.**

(1) Except as provided in subdivision (e) of this section, no employee shall be transferred to a position for which there is required by this Part an examination involving essential tests or qualifications different from or higher than those required for the position held by such employee.

(2) The Chief Administrator of the Courts and the State and municipal civil service commissions may adopt rules governing transfers between positions in their respective jurisdictions and may also adopt reciprocal rules providing for the transfer of employees from one governmental jurisdiction to another.

(3) No employee shall be transferred without his or her consent, except upon the transfer of functions as provided in this section.

(4) A transfer may not be made to a position for which a preferred list exists containing the name of an eligible willing to accept reinstatement to such position, unless the vacancy created by such transfer is in the same geographical area as the position to which transfer is made and such eligible is simultaneously offered reinstatement to such vacancy.

(5) A transfer may be made only if the position to which transfer is sought is at the same or substantially the same or a lower salary level than the position from which transfer is sought.

(6) Every transfer shall require the approval of the Chief Administrator.

(7) A person appointed to a position in the unified court system in any particular court or court agency may not, during the life of the eligible list from which he or she was appointed or for at least one year, whichever is longer, be transferred or reassigned to a similar position in another court or court agency unless he or she is reachable for appointment to such other position from such eligible list, except under a reassignment program approved by the Chief Administrator.

(c) Transfer of Personnel Upon Transfer of Functions. Upon the transfer of a function from a department or agency of the State to the unified court system or vice versa, provision shall be made for the transfer of necessary employees. Employees so transferred shall be transferred without further examination or qualification, and shall retain their respective civil service or court service classifications and status. For the purpose of determining the employees holding permanent appointments in competitive class positions to be transferred, such employees shall be selected within each class of positions in the order of their original appointment, with due regard to the right of preference in retention of disabled and non-durable veterans. All employees so transferred shall, thereafter, be subject to the rules of the Chief Administrator of the Courts or the civil service commission having jurisdiction over the agency to which transfer is made. Employees holding permanent appointments in competitive class positions who are not so transferred shall have their names entered upon an appropriate preferred list for reinstatement to the same or similar positions in the service of the governmental jurisdiction from which transfer is made and in the office or agency to which such function is transferred. Employees transferred to another governmental jurisdiction pursuant to the provisions of this subdivision shall be entitled to full seniority credit for all purposes for service rendered prior to such transfer in the governmental jurisdiction from which transfer is made.

(d) Transfers Between Unified Court System Positions and State or Local Positions.

(1) A transfer may be made between positions in the unified court system and positions in the State service or in the service of a civil division, provided the prospective transferee meets all of the requirements, if any, applicable to the position to which transfer is sought.

(2) A transfer pursuant to this subdivision shall require the approval of the Chief Administrator of the Courts and the State Department of Civil Service or the municipal civil service commission having jurisdiction over the position to or from which transfer is made.

(e) Transfer and Change of Title. Notwithstanding the provisions of subdivision (b) of this section or any other provision of law, any permanent employee in the competitive class who meets all the requirements for a competitive examination, and is otherwise qualified as determined by the Chief Administrator, shall be eligible for participation in a noncompetitive examination in a different classification, provided, however, that such employee is holding a position deemed to be of a comparable level.

§ 25.27. Incapacitated Employees

(a) When there is reason to believe that an employee to whom the disciplinary procedures of section 25.29 of this Part apply is physically or mentally disabled from performing, with or without reasonable accommodation, the essential functions of his or her position, the appropriate administrative authority may require such employee to undergo a physical or psychiatric examination at the expense of the State, to be conducted by a medical officer selected by the Chief Administrator, to establish whether he or she is able to perform, with or without reasonable accommodation, the essential functions of his or her position or whether his or her continued presence on the job creates a significant risk to the health or safety of the individual or of others that cannot be eliminated with reasonable accommodation. For purposes of this section, the appropriate administrative authority shall be the designating authority set forth in section 25.29(b) of this Part. If, upon such medical examination, the medical officer certifies that either condition exists, the employee shall be placed on leave of absence without pay subject to the provisions of subdivision (c) of this section. An employee placed on such leave shall be allowed to draw accumulated and unused sick leave, annual leave, compensatory time, overtime credits and other time allowances standing to his or her credit prior to being placed on such leave. An employee who chooses to draw his or her accumulated leave credits under this section shall cease to earn and accrue sick and annual leave credits during that period.

(b) When an employee who is not permanently incapacitated from performing the duties of his or her position has been absent from and unable to perform the duties of his or her position by reason of sickness or disability either for a consecutive period of one year or more or for a cumulative total of 250 workdays or more within a period of 24 consecutive calendar months, and who reasonably cannot be expected to be able to resume performing, with or without reasonable accommodation, the essential functions of his or her position shortly thereafter, his or her employment may be terminated by the appropriate administrative authority and the position may be filled by a permanent appointment.

(c) Prior to being placed on leave pursuant to subdivision (a) of this section, or terminated pursuant to subdivision (b), an employee shall be provided with written notice thereof, including written notice of the facts relied on therefor and written notice of the employee's right to contest the determination and of the procedures for doing so. Such notice shall be served in person or by first class, registered or certified mail, return receipt requested, upon the employee. If such person elects to contest the determination, he or she shall file a written request for a hearing with the appropriate administrative authority within 10 workdays from service of the notice of the determination to be reviewed. The request for such hearing shall be filed by the employee personally or by first class, certified or registered mail, return receipt requested. Upon receipt of such request, the appropriate administrative authority shall supply to the employee, or his or her personal physician or authorized representative, copies of all diagnoses, test results, observations and other data supporting the determination, and imposition of the leave or termination shall be held in abeyance until a final determination is made by the appropriate administrative authority as provided in subdivision (d) of this section.

(d) A hearing shall be held by a hearing officer designated for that purpose by the appropriate administrative authority. The hearing officer shall be vested with all the powers of the administrative authority and shall make a record of the hearing which shall, with his or her recommendation, be referred to the administrative authority for review and decision and which shall be provided to the employee free of charge. The employee shall, upon request, receive a copy of the transcript of the hearing without charge. The employee may be represented at the hearing by counsel or an authorized representative and may present medical experts and other witnesses or evidence. The burden of proving mental or physical unfitness shall be upon the administrative authority. Compliance with technical rules of evidence shall not be required. The administrative authority shall render a final determination and may either uphold the original notice of leave of absence, withdraw such notice or modify the notice as appropriate. A final determination of an employee's request for review shall contain notice to the employee of his or her right to appeal from such determination and of the procedures for perfecting such appeal.

(e) If the employee elects to appeal, he or she shall make application to the Chief Administrator. The employee shall be afforded an opportunity to present facts and arguments, including medical evidence, in support of his or her position at a time and place and in such manner as may be prescribed by the Chief Administrator. The Chief Administrator shall make a determination on the basis of the medical records and such facts and arguments as are presented.

(f) An employee placed on leave pursuant to this section may, within one year of the commencement of such leave, make application to the appropriate administrative authority for a medical examination to be conducted by a medical officer selected for the purpose by the Chief Administrator. If, upon such medical examination, the medical officer shall certify that the employee is physically and mentally fit to perform, with or without reasonable accommodation, the essential functions of his or her former position, he or she shall be reinstated to the former position, if vacant, or to a vacancy in a similar position or a position in a lower title in the same occupational field in his or her former promotion unit. If no appropriate vacancy shall exist to which such reinstatement may be made, or if the work load does not warrant the filling of such

vacancy, the name of the employee shall be placed on a preferred list for his or her former position in his or her former promotion unit, and the employee shall be eligible for reinstatement in such former promotion unit from such preferred list for a period of four years. In the event that the employee is reinstated in a position in a title lower than that of his or her former position, his or her name shall be placed on the preferred eligible list for the former position or any similar position in such former promotion unit.

(g) An employee placed on leave pursuant to this section who is not reinstated within one year after the date of commencement of such leave, may be terminated by the appropriate administrative authority and his or her position may be filled by permanent appointment.

(h) An employee whose employment status has been terminated pursuant to subdivision (b) or (g) of this section may, within one year after the termination of his or her disability, make application to the appropriate appointing authority for a medical examination and subsequent reinstatement pursuant to the procedures and conditions of subdivision (f) of this section.

(i) Where the continued presence of an employee on the job creates a significant risk to the health or safety of the individual or of others that cannot be eliminated with reasonable accommodation, or would significantly interfere with operations, the appropriate administrative authority may place such employee on an involuntary leave of absence without pay immediately; provided, however, that the employee shall be entitled to draw all accumulated and unused sick leave, annual leave, compensatory time, overtime credits and other time allowances standing to his or her credit. An employee so placed on leave shall thereafter be subject to all of the procedures of this section for placement on leave of absence, except that imposition of such leave shall not be held in abeyance pursuant to subdivision (c) of this section. If it is finally determined pursuant to subdivision (d) of this section, that the employee was physically and mentally fit to perform, with or without reasonable accommodation, the essential functions of his or her position, he or she shall be restored to his or her position and shall have any leave credits or salary that he or she may have lost because of such involuntary leave of absence restored, less any compensation he or she may have earned in other employment or occupation and any unemployment benefits he or she may have received during such period.

(j) Notwithstanding any other provision of this section, when an employee's disability is of such a nature as to permanently incapacitate him or her from the performance, with or without reasonable accommodation, of the essential functions of his or her position, his or her employment status may be terminated once he or she has exhausted any workers' compensation leave to which he or she may be entitled pursuant to section 24.5 of these rules, and his or her position may be filled by a permanent appointment.

(k) This section shall not be construed to require the extension of any employment beyond the time at which it would otherwise terminate by operation of law, rule or regulation, nor shall this section be deemed to modify or supersede any other provisions of law applicable to the reemployment of persons retired from the public service on account of disability.

§ 25.28. Resignations

(a) Resignation in Writing. Except as otherwise provided in this section, every resignation shall be in writing.

(b) Effective Date. If no effective date is specified in a resignation, it shall take effect upon delivery to or filing in the office of the appointing authority. If an effective date is specified in a resignation, it shall take effect on such specified date. However, if a resignation is submitted while the employee is on leave of absence without pay, such resignation, for the purpose of determining eligibility for reinstatement, shall be deemed to be effective as of the date of the commencement of such absence. Notwithstanding the provisions of this section, when charges of incompetency or misconduct have been or are about to be filed against an employee, the appointing authority may elect to disregard a resignation filed by such employee and to prosecute such charges; and, in the event that such employee is found guilty of such charges and dismissed from the service, his or her termination shall be recorded as a dismissal rather than as a resignation.

(c) Withdrawal or Amendment. A resignation may not be withdrawn, cancelled or amended after it is delivered to the appointing authority, without the consent of the appointing authority.

(d) Reinstatement Following Resignation.

(1) A permanent employee who has resigned from his or her position may be reinstated, without examination, within one year from the date of such resignation in the position from which he or she resigned, if then vacant, or in any vacant position to which such employee was eligible for transfer or reassignment. In computing the one-year period within which a person may be reinstated after resignation, the day the resignation takes effect, any time spent in active service in the military or naval forces of the United States or of the State of New York, and any time served in another position in the civil service of the same governmental jurisdiction shall not be counted.

(2) In an exceptional case, the appointing authority may, for good cause shown and where the interests of the government would be served, waive the provisions of this subdivision to permit the reinstatement of a person more than one year after resignation. For the purpose of this subdivision, where an employee on leave of absence resigns, such resignation shall be

deemed effective as of the date of the commencement of such leave.

(e) Job Abandonment. When an employee to whom the procedures of section 25.29 of this Part apply has been absent from work without notice for 15 consecutive workdays, he or she shall be deemed to have resigned from his or her position if he or she (or, if medically unable, a member of his or her family) has not provided a satisfactory written explanation for such absence, to the court or court-related agency to which he or she is assigned, on or before the 15th consecutive workday following the commencement of such unauthorized absence. Prior to the conclusion of the 15–workday period, or at any time thereafter, the court or court-related agency shall send the affected employee notice, to the employee's last known address, by certified mail, return receipt requested, that his or her absence is considered unauthorized and that, as a result of such absence, he or she will be deemed to have resigned from service, effective the 15th workday following the commencement of the unauthorized absence or any specified time thereafter. An employee who has been deemed to have resigned pursuant to this section (or, if medically unable, a member of his or her family) shall have 20 workdays from the date the notice was mailed within which to submit a written explanation concerning his or her absence to the deputy chief administrator for management support. Upon receipt of such explanation, the deputy chief administrator for management support shall reinstate the employee, without examination, to the position from which he or she was deemed to have resigned, if vacant, or to any vacant position to which he or she was eligible for transfer or reassignment, and shall have 20 workdays within which to initiate charges against the employee pursuant to section 25.29 of this Part.

§ 25.29. Removal or Disciplinary Action

(a) An employee described in paragraph (1), (2) or (3) below shall not be removed or otherwise subjected to any disciplinary penalty provided in this section except for incompetency or misconduct shown after a hearing upon stated charges pursuant to this section, unless such employee is granted the option and elects to follow the alternate disciplinary procedure set forth in subdivision (h) of this section.

(1) an employee holding a position by permanent appointment in the competitive class of the classified service;

(2) an employee holding a position by permanent appointment or employment in the classified service, who is an honorably discharged member of the Armed Forces of the United States having served therein as such member in time of war as defined in this Part or who is an exempt volunteer fireman as defined in the General Municipal Law, except when an employee described in this paragraph holds a position designat-

ed by the Chief Administrator of the Courts as confidential or requiring the performance of functions influencing policy; or

(3) an employee holding a position in the noncompetitive class other than a position designated by the Chief Administrator of the Courts as confidential or requiring the performance of functions influencing policy, who since such employee's last entry into the service of the unified court system has completed at least five years of continuous service in the noncompetitive class in a position or positions not designated as confidential or requiring the performance of functions influencing policy.

(b) Procedure.

(1) An employee who at the time of questioning appears to be a potential subject of disciplinary action shall have a right to representation. If representation is requested, a reasonable period of time shall be afforded to obtain such representation. If the employee is unable to obtain representation within a reasonable period of time, the employee may be questioned without representation.

(2) An employee against whom removal or other disciplinary action is proposed shall have written notice thereof and of the reasons therefor, shall be furnished a copy of the charges preferred against him or her by the designating authority as set forth in this subdivision and shall be allowed at least eight days for answering the same in writing. The hearings upon such charges shall be held as follows:

(i) In the instance of an employee of the Court of Appeals, the hearing shall be held by a person designated by the clerk of the Court of Appeals for that purpose.

(ii) In the instance of an employee of an appellate division, the hearing shall be held by a person designated by the presiding justice of that appellate division for that purpose.

(iii) In the instance of an employee of the administrative office for the courts, the hearing shall be held by a person designated by the deputy chief administrator for management support for that purpose.

(iv) In any other instance, the hearing shall be held by a person designated for that purpose by the Deputy Chief Administrator of the Courts having administrative jurisdiction over the court or court-related agency in which the employee is employed.

(3) The person designated shall, for the purpose of such hearing, be vested with all the powers of the designating authority and shall make a record of such hearing which shall, with recommendations, be referred to such designating authority for review and decision. The person or persons holding such hearing shall, upon the request of the employee against whom charges are preferred, permit him or her to be represented by counsel, or by a representative of an em-

ployee organization which represents the employee, and shall allow him or her to summon witnesses in his or her behalf. The burden of proving incompetency or misconduct shall be upon the person alleging the same. Compliance with technical rules of evidence shall not be required. The employee against whom charges are preferred shall, upon request, be entitled to a copy of the recommendations of the person designated to conduct the hearing, and shall be allowed three days to comment upon them, in writing, to the designating authority. The person alleging incompetency or misconduct shall be allowed three days to respond to such comments.

(c) Suspension Pending Determination of Charges. Pending the hearing and determination of charges of incompetency or misconduct, the employee against whom such charges have been preferred may be suspended without pay for a period not exceeding 30 days.

(d) Penalties.

(1) If the employee is found guilty of the charges, the penalty or punishment may consist of a reprimand, a fine not to exceed $200 to be deducted from the salary or wages of such officer of employee, suspension without pay for a period not exceeding three months, a combination of a fine not to exceed $200 and a suspension without pay for a period of up to three months, demotion in salary and title, restitution, probation for up to six months, or dismissal from the service; provided, however, that the time during which an employee is suspended without pay may be considered as part of the penalty. If he or she is acquitted, he or she shall be restored to his or her position with with full pay for the period of suspension less the amount of compensation which he or she may have earned in any other employment or occupation and any unemployment insurance benefits he or she may have received during such period. If the employee is found guilty, a copy of the charges, his or her written answer thereto, a transcript of the hearing, and the determination shall be filed in the office of the Chief Administrator. A copy of the transcript of the hearing shall, upon request of the employee affected, be furnished to him or her without charge.

(2) During a period of suspension without pay pursuant to this section, an employee shall be entitled to continue health insurance, provided the employee pays his or her share of the premium, and shall be eligible to receive welfare fund benefits and have welfare fund payments made on his or her behalf.

(e) Time for Removal or Disciplinary Proceeding. Notwithstanding any other provisions of this Part, and except as provided in section 25.13(d)(3), no removal or disciplinary proceeding shall be commenced more than 18 months after the occurrence of the alleged incompetency or misconduct complained of and described in the charges; provided, however, that such limitation shall not apply where the incompetency or misconduct complained of and described in the charges would, if proved in a court of appropriate jurisdiction, constitute a crime.

(f) Review of Penalty or Punishment. Any employee believing himself aggrieved by a penalty or punishment of demotion in or dismissal from the service, or suspension without pay, or a fine or an official reprimand without the remittance of any pre-hearing suspension without pay, imposed pursuant to the provisions of this section, may appeal from such determination by an application to the Chief Administrator of the Courts or seek relief by an application to the court in accordance with the provisions of article 78 of the Civil Practice Law and Rules.

(1) *Procedure on Appeal.* If such employee elects to appeal to the Chief Administrator, such appeal shall be filed in writing within 20 days after service of written notice of the determination to be reviewed, such written notice to be delivered personally or by registered or certified mail to the last known address of such employee, and when notice is given by registered or certified mail, such employee shall be allowed an additional three days in which to file an appeal. The Chief Administrator shall review the record of the disciplinary proceeding and the transcript of the hearing, and shall determine such appeal on the basis of such record and transcript and such oral or written argument as he or she may determine. The Chief Administrator may designate a representative to hear the appeal who shall report thereon with recommendations to the Chief Administrator. Upon such appeal, the Chief Administrator shall permit the employee to be represented by counsel or by a representative of an employee organization which represents the employee.

(2) *Determination on Appeal.* The determination appealed from may be affirmed, reversed, or modified, and the Chief Administrator may, in his or her discretion, direct the reinstatement of the appellant or permit the transfer or reassignment of such appellant to a vacancy in a similar position in another court or court agency or direct that such employee's name be placed upon a preferred list pursuant to this Part. In the event that a transfer or reassignment is not effected, the Chief Administrator may direct the reinstatement of such employee. An employee reinstated pursuant to this subdivision shall receive the salary or compensation he or she would have been entitled by law to have received in the position for the period of removal including any prior period of suspension without pay, less the amount of any unemployment insurance benefits which may have been received during such period. The decision of the Chief Administrator shall be final and conclusive, and not subject to further review in any court.

(g) Compensation of Employees Reinstated by Court Order. Any employee who is removed from a position in the service of the unified court system in violation of the provisions of this section, and who

thereafter is restored to such position by order of the Supreme Court, shall be entitled to receive and shall receive the salary or compensation which he or she would have been entitled by law to have received in such position but for such unlawful removal, from the date of such unlawful removal to the date of such restoration, less the amount of compensation which may have been earned in any other employment or occupation and any unemployment insurance benefits which may have been received during such period. Such officer or employee shall be entitled to a court order to enforce the payment of such salary or compensation. Such salary or compensation shall be subject to the provisions of sections 474 and 475 of the Judiciary Law for services rendered, but otherwise shall be paid only directly to such employee or his or her legal representatives.

(h) Alternative Disciplinary Procedure. The Chief Administrator or his or her designee may establish rules and procedures implementing an alternative disciplinary procedure permitting an employee to elect, at the option of the designating authority, to accept a penalty to be selected in the sole discretion of the designating authority without the initiation of formal disciplinary charges or the holding of a formal hearing pursuant to subdivision (b) of this section. The penalties under this procedure may be a written reprimand, restitution, probation for up to six months, and the forfeiture of up to ten days of annual leave or compensatory time or the loss of up to ten days pay. The determination of the designating authority shall be final, binding and not renewable in any forum. For purposes of this subdivision only, an eligible employee shall include all employees otherwise not covered by subdivision (a) of this section who are not personal appointees of a judge.

Cross References

CPLR, see McKinney's Book 7B.

General Municipal Law, see McKinney's Book 23.

Judiciary Law, see McKinney's Book 29.

§ 25.30. Abolition or Reduction of Positions

(a) Suspension or Demotion. Where positions in the competitive class or the noncompetitive class are abolished or reduced in rank or salary grade, all suspensions or demotions among incumbent competitive and noncompetitive court personnel holding the same or similar positions shall be made in inverse order of original appointment on a permanent basis in the classified service of the unified court system. The following exceptions shall apply:

(1) Incumbents who have not completed their probationary service shall be suspended or demoted before any permanent incumbents, and among such probationary employees suspension or demotion shall be made in inverse order of original appointment on a

permanent basis in the classified service of the unified court system.

(2) Blind employees shall be granted absolute preference in retention.

(3) The date of original appointment for disabled and nondisabled veterans shall be deemed to be, respectively, 60 months and 30 months earlier than the actual date, determined in accordance with section 30 of the General Construction Law.

(4) The date of original appointment for the spouse of a veteran with 100-percent service-connected disability shall be deemed to be 60 months earlier than the actual date, determined in accordance with section 30 of the General Construction Law, provided the spouse is domiciled with the veteran-spouse and is the head of the household.

(5) The date of original appointment for an incumbent transferred to the unified court system from another governmental jurisdiction upon a transfer of functions shall be the date of original appointment on a permanent basis in the classified service of the governmental jurisdiction from which the transfer was made.

(6) This section shall not apply to noncompetitive employees who do not have tenure protection pursuant to section 25.29(a)(3) of this Part and otherwise do not have tenure protection.

(b) Continuous Service. The original appointment of an incumbent shall mean the date of his or her first appointment on a permanent basis in the classified service followed by continuous service in the classified service on a permanent basis up to the time of the abolition or reduction of his or her position. The following shall not constitute an interruption of continuous service:

(1) a period following an employee's resignation if such employee has been reinstated or reappointed within one year thereafter;

(2) a period of employment on a temporary or provisional basis, or in the unclassified service, immediately preceded and followed by permanent service in the classified service;

(3) a period of leave of absence without pay pursuant to this Part;

(4) any period during which an employee is suspended from his or her position pursuant to this section; or

(5) a period between the termination of an employee because of a disability resulting from occupational injury or disease as defined in the Workers' Compensation Law and his or her reinstatement or reappointment thereafter.

(c) Interrupted Service. An employee who has resigned and who has been reinstated or reappointed in the unified court system more than one year thereafter shall be credited with any previous court service rendered prior to his or her resignation to which he or she would have been entitled for the purposes of this section but for such resignation; provided, however, that any time out of the unified court system exceeding three years shall be subtracted from the employee's previous court service. In such instances, continuous service shall be deemed to have begun on the date which precedes the otherwise applicable date for the commencement of continuous service by the period of actual creditable service provided by this subdivision.

(d) Units for Suspension or Demotion. The Chief Administrator of the Courts may designate as units for suspension or demotion under the provisions of this section any combination of courts or court-related agencies, or any divisions thereof.

(e) Displacement. Permanent employees who are suspended or demoted pursuant to this section shall displace incumbents in other positions in the unified court system in the manner as set forth in subdivisions 6 and 7 of section 80 of the Civil Service Law and subdivision 5 of section 80-a of the Civil Service Law. Probationary employees who are suspended or demoted pursuant to this section shall displace incumbents in other positions in the unified court system in the manner set forth in section 5.5(d) of the rules of the State Department of Civil Service and section 5.6(d) of such rules (4 NYCRR 5.5[d], 5.6[d]). Displacement pursuant to this subdivision shall not be governed by the provisions of section 25.26 of this Part.

(f) Reassignments. Reassignment of court personnel to similar positions in the unified court system necessitated by the abolition or reduction of positions shall be made according to the needs of the unified court system and shall not be governed by the provisions of section 25.26 of this Part. For purposes of implementing this section, all changes of permanent employees from one position to a similar position in the unified court system in the City of New York shall be reassignments, not transfers.

Cross References

Civil Service Law, see McKinney's Book 9.

General Construction Law, see McKinney's Book 21.

Workers' Compensation Law, see McKinney's Book 64.

§ 25.31. Establishment of Preferred Lists

(a) General Provisions.

(1) The Chief Administrator of the Courts shall place on a preferred list the names of all employees suspended or demoted from the same or similar positions in the same jurisdictional class paid by the same fiscal authority, in accordance with the provisions of section 25.30 of this Part. This preferred list shall be used for filling vacancies in the same jurisdictional class paid by the same fiscal authority in the following

order: first, in the same or similar position; second, in any position in a lower title in line of promotion; and third, in any position comparable to the lower title in line of promotion. Such position need not be in the same promotion unit or unit for suspension or demotion as the employee's original position. Except as provided in paragraph (2) of this subdivision, no person shall be appointed from any other list for any such position until such preferred list is exhausted.

(2) Employees reassigned to positions in the unified court system pursuant to section 25.30(f) of this Part, and suspended employees who have accepted appointments from a preferred list to positions other than their original positions pursuant to this section, may be reassigned to their original positions in their original courts or court-related agencies as vacancies occur, in order of seniority. The failure or refusal of an employee after reasonable notice to accept reassignment to such original position shall be deemed a relinquishment of his or her eligibility for reassignment to such position pursuant to this subdivision.

(3) The eligibility to be reinstated or reassigned pursuant to this subdivision shall not continue for more than four years from the date of reassignment, suspension or demotion.

(4) An employee who is eligible to be placed on a preferred list pursuant to this section and who elects, as a member of a public employee retirement system, to retire upon a suspension or demotion, shall be placed on a preferred list and shall be eligible for reinstatement from such list.

(b) Order of Reinstatement From Preferred Lists. Persons on a preferred list who were suspended or demoted from positions in courts or court-related agencies paid by the same fiscal authority shall be reinstated therefrom to vacancies in appropriate positions in the order of their original appointment. The following exceptions shall apply:

(1) Where the vacancy exists in a separate unit for suspension or demotion, persons suspended from or demoted in that unit shall be reinstated first.

(2) No person suspended or demoted before the completion of his or her probationary term shall be reinstated until the reinstatement of all other persons on the preferred list. Upon reinstatement, the probationer shall be required to complete his or her probationary term.

(c) Salary Upon Reinstatement. A person reinstated from a preferred list to his or her former position or a similar position at the same salary grade shall receive at least the same salary received at the time of suspension or demotion.

(d) Notwithstanding any other provision of this Part, any person may voluntarily remove his or her name from a preferred list by application to the Chief Administrator of the Courts.

(e) Effect of Refusal or Failure to Accept Reinstatement From Preferred List.

(1) The failure or refusal of a person on a preferred list after reasonable notice to accept reinstatement therefrom to his or her former position, or any similar position in the same salary grade for which such list is certified, shall be deemed to be a relinquishment of his or her eligibility for reinstatement, and such name shall thereupon be stricken from such preferred list. The name of such person may be restored to such preferred list, and certified to fill such appropriate vacancies as may thereafter occur, only upon the request of such person and such person's submission of reasons satisfactory to the Chief Administrator of the Courts for his or her previous failure or refusal to accept reinstatement.

(2) Notwithstanding the provisions of paragraph (1) of this subdivision, a person on a preferred list shall not be deemed to relinquish eligibility for reinstatement therefrom by reason of a failure or refusal to accept reinstatement to a position in a different city or county from that in which the former position was located, or to a position in a lower salary grade than the position from which he or she was suspended, demoted or displaced. The name of such person may, however, be withheld from further certification for reinstatement to a position in such other city or county or in the same or a lower salary grade than the position to which he or she failed or refused to accept reinstatement.

(3) The restoration of the name of a person to a preferred list, or restoration to eligibility for certification therefrom to positions in any particular city or county or to positions in a lower salary grade than the former position, shall not invalidate or in any manner adversely affect any appointment, promotion, reinstatement, displacement or demotion previously made to any position to which such person would otherwise have been eligible for reinstatement from such preferred list.

(f) Disqualification for Reinstatement. The Chief Administrator of the Courts may disqualify for reinstatement from a preferred list, in the manner set forth in subdivision 7 of section 81 of the Civil Service Law, any person who is physically or mentally disabled from the performance, with or without reasonable accommodation, of the essential functions of the position for which such list is established, or who has been guilty of such misconduct as would warrant his or her dismissal from the public service.

(g) Limitations of Use of Preferred List. A preferred list established pursuant to this section shall have no priority with reference to a new position created by the reclassification of an existing position pursuant to this Part whenever the use of a preferred list for filling such new position would result in the suspension of an employee pursuant to the provisions of section 25.30 of this Part.

(h) The provisions of section 25.26 of this Part shall not apply to the implementation of this section.

Cross References

Civil Service Law, see McKinney's Book 9.

§ 25.32.   Credits and Preferences for Veterans or Disabled Credits

(a) Definitions.

(1) The terms "veteran" and "nondisabled veteran" mean a member of the Armed Forces of the United States who served therein in time of war, who was honorably discharged or released under honorable circumstances from such service, and who is a resident of this State at the time of application for appointment or promotion.

(2) The term "disabled veteran" means a veteran who is certified by the United States Veterans Administration or a military department as entitled to receive disability payments upon the certification of such Veterans Administration or a military department for a disability incurred by him or her in time of war and in existence at the time of application for appointment or promotion or at the time of retention, as the case may be. Such disability shall be deemed to be in existence at the time of application for appointment or promotion or at the time of retention, as the case may be, if the certificate of such Veterans Administration shall state affirmatively that such veteran has been examined by a medical officer of such Veterans Administration on a date within one year of either the date of filing application for competitive examination for original appointment or promotion, or the date of the establishment of the resulting eligible list, or within one year of the time of retention, as the case may be; that at the time of such examination the war-incurred disability described in such certificate was found to exist; and that such disability is rated at 10 per centum or more. Such disability shall also be deemed to be in existence at such time if the certificate of such Veterans Administration shall state affirmatively that a permanent stabilized condition of disability exists to an extent of 10 per centum or more, notwithstanding the fact that such veteran has not been examined by a medical officer of such Veterans Administration within one year of either the time of application for appointment or promotion, or the date of filing application for competitive examination for original appointment or promotion, or within one year of the time of retention, as the case may be. The term "disabled veteran" shall also mean:

(i) a veteran who served in World War I, who continued to serve in the Armed Forces of the United States after November 11, 1918, and who is certified, as hereinbefore provided, by the United States Veterans Administration as receiving disability payments upon the certification of such Veterans Administration for a disability incurred by such veteran in such service on or before July 2, 1921;

(ii) a veteran who served in World War II, who continued to serve in the Armed Forces of the United States after September 2, 1945, or who served aboard merchant vessels as set forth in section 85(1)(b)(2) of the Civil Service Law, and who is certified, as hereinbefore provided, by the United States Veterans Administration as receiving disability payments upon the certification of such Veterans Administration for a disability incurred by such veteran in such service on or before the date that World War II was declared terminated;

(iii) a veteran who served during hostilities participated in by the military forces of the United States subsequent to June 27, 1950, and who continued to serve in the Armed Forces of the United States after January 31, 1955, and who is certified, as hereinbefore provided, by the United States Veterans Administration as receiving disability payments upon the certification of such Veterans Administration for a disability incurred by such veteran in such service;

(3) The term "time of war" shall include the following wars and hostilities for the periods and based upon the evidence herein set forth:

(i) World War I, from April 6, 1917 to and including November 11, 1918;

(ii) World War II, from December 7, 1941 to and including December 31, 1946;

(iii) hostilities participated in by the military forces of the United States from June 27, 1950 to and including January 31, 1955;

(iv) hostilities participated in by the military forces of the United States from December 22, 1961 to May 7, 1975;

(v) hostilities participated in by the military forces of the United States in Lebanon from June 1, 1983 to December 1, 1987, as established by receipt of the armed forces expeditionary medal, the navy expeditionary medal, or the marine corps expeditionary medal;

(vi) hostilities participated in by the military forces of the United States in Grenada, from October 23, 1983 to November 21, 1983, as established by receipt of the armed forces expeditionary medal, the navy expeditionary medal, or the marine corps expeditionary medal;

(vii) hostilities participated in by the military forces of the United States in Panama, from December 20, 1989 to January 31, 1990, as established by receipt of the armed forces expeditionary medal, the navy expeditionary medal, or the marine corps expeditionary medal;

(viii) hostilities participated in by the military forces of the United States in the Persian Gulf, from August 2, 1990 to the end of such hostilities.

(4) The term "time of application for original appointment or promotion" shall mean the date of the establishment of an eligible list resulting from a competitive examination for original appointment or promotion, as the case may be, which date shall be the date on which the term of such eligible list commences.

(5) The term "time of retention" shall mean the time of abolition or elimination of positions.

(b) Additional Credits in Competitive Examinations for Original Appointment or Promotion.

(1) On all eligible lists resulting from competitive examinations, the names of eligibles shall be entered in the order of their respective final earned ratings on examination, with the name of the eligible with the highest final earned rating at the head of such lists; provided, however, that for the purpose of determining final earned ratings:

(i) disabled veterans shall be entitled to receive 10 points additional in a competitive examination for original appointment and five points additional credit in a competitive examination for promotion; and

(ii) nondisabled veterans shall be entitled to receive five points additional credit in a competitive examination for original appointment and 2½ points additional credit in a competitive examination for promotion.

(2) Such additional credits shall be added to the final earned rating of such disabled veteran or nondisabled veteran, as the case may be, after he or she has qualified in the competitive examination, and shall be granted only at the time of establishment of the resulting eligible list.

(c) Application for Additional Credit; Proof of Eligibility; Establishment of Eligible List. Any candidate believing himself or herself to be entitled to additional credit in a competitive examination, as provided herein, may make application for such additional credit at any time between the date of his or her application for examination and the date of the establishment of the resulting eligible list. Such candidate shall be allowed a period of not less than two months from the date of the filing of his or her application for examination in which to establish, by appropriate documentary proof, eligibility to receive additional credit under this section. At any time after two months have elapsed since the final date for filing application for a competitive examination for original appointment or promotion, the eligible list resulting from such examination may be established, notwithstanding the fact that a veteran or disabled veteran who has applied for additional credit has failed to establish eligibility to receive such additional credit. A candidate who fails to establish, by appropriate documentary proof, eligibility to receive additional credit by the time an eligible list is established shall not thereafter be granted additional credit on such eligible list.

(d) Use of Additional Credit.

(1) Except as herein otherwise provided, no person who has received a permanent original appointment or a permanent promotion in the unified court system or in the civil service of the State or of any city or civil division thereof from an eligible list on which he or she was allowed the additional credit granted by this section or by section 85 of the Civil Service Law, either as a veteran or disabled veteran, shall thereafter be entitled to any additional credit under this section either as a veteran or a disabled veteran.

(2) Where, at the time of establishment of an eligible list, the position of a veteran or disabled veteran on such list has not been affected by the addition of credit granted under this section, the appointment or promotion of such veteran or disabled veteran, as the case may be, from such eligible list shall not be deemed to have been made from an eligible list on which he was allowed the additional credit granted by this section.

(3) If, at the time of appointment from an eligible list, a veteran or disabled veteran is in the same relative standing among the eligibles who are willing to accept appointment as if he or she had not been granted the additional credits provided by this section, his or her appointment from among such eligibles shall not be deemed to have been made from an eligible list on which he or she was allowed such additional credits.

(4) Where a veteran or disabled veteran has been originally appointed or promoted from an eligible list on which he or she was allowed additional credit, but such appointment or promotion is thereafter terminated either at the end of the probationary term or by resignation at or before the end of the probationary term, he or she shall not be deemed to have been appointed or promoted, as the case may be, from an eligible list on which he or she was allowed additional credit, and such appointment or promotion shall not affect eligibility for additional credit in other examinations.

(e) Withdrawal of Application; Election to Relinquish Additional Credit. An application for additional credit in a competitive examination under this section may be withdrawn by the applicant at any time prior to the establishment of the resulting eligible list. At any time during the term of existence of an eligible list resulting from a competitive examination in which a veteran or disabled veteran has received the additional credit granted by this section, such veteran or disabled veteran may elect, prior to permanent original appointment or permanent promotion, to relinquish the additional credit theretofore granted and accept the lower position on such eligible list to which he or she would otherwise have been entitled; provided, however, that such election shall thereafter be irrevocable. Such election shall be in writing and signed by the veteran or disabled veteran, and transmitted to the Chief Administrator of the Courts.

(f) Roster. The Chief Administrator of the Courts shall establish and maintain a roster of all veterans and disabled veterans appointed or promoted as a result of additional credits granted by this section. The appointment or promotion of a veteran or disabled veteran as a result of additional credits shall be void if such veteran or disabled veteran, prior to such appointment or promotion, had been appointed or promoted as a result of additional credits granted by this section or by section 85 of the Civil Service Law.

(g) Penalty for Denial of Preference in Retention. A refusal to allow the preference in retention provided for in paragraph (3) of subdivision (a) of section 25.30 of this Part to any veteran or disabled veteran, or a reduction of compensation intended to bring about the resignation of such veteran or disabled veteran, shall be subject to the provisions of subdivision 8 of section 85 of the Civil Service Law.

Cross References

Civil Service Law, see McKinney's Book 9.

§ 25.33. Transfer of Veterans or Exempt Volunteer Firemen Upon Abolition of Positions

If the position in the noncompetitive or in the labor class held by any honorably discharged veteran of the Armed Forces of the United States who served therein in time of war as defined in section 25.32 of this Part, or by an exempt volunteer fireman as defined in the General Municipal Law, shall become unnecessary or be abolished for reasons of economy or otherwise, the honorably discharged veteran or exempt volunteer fireman holding such position shall not be discharged from the public service but shall be transferred to a similar position wherein a vacancy exists, and shall receive the same compensation therein. It is hereby made the duty of all persons clothed with the power of appointment to make such transfer effective. The right to transfer herein conferred shall continue for a period of one year following the date of abolition of the position, and may be exercised only where a vacancy exists in an appropriate position to which transfer may be made at the time of demand for transfer. Where the positions of more than one such veteran or exempt volunteer fireman are abolished and a lesser number of vacancies in similar positions exist to which transfer may be made, the veterans or exempt volunteer firemen whose positions are abolished shall be entitled to transfer to such vacancies in the order of their original appointment in the service. Nothing in this section shall be construed to apply to a person holding a position designated as confidential or requiring the performance of functions influencing policy. This subdivision shall have no application to persons encompassed by subdivision (a) of section 25.30 of this Part.

Cross References

General Municipal Law, see McKinney's Book 23.

§ 25.34. Duties of Public Officers With Respect to This Part

(a) Duties of Public Officers. It shall be the duty of all officers of the unified court system to conform to, comply with and aid in all proper ways in carrying into effect the provisions of this Part. No officer or officers having the power of appointment or employment shall appoint or select any person for appointment, employment, promotion or reinstatement except in accordance with the provisions of this Part. Any person employed or appointed contrary to the provisions of this Part shall be paid by the officer or officers so employing or appointing, or attempting to employ or appoint him or her, the compensation agreed upon for any services performed under such appointment or employment or, in case no compensation is agreed upon, the actual value of such services and any necessary expenses incurred in connection therewith, and shall have such cause of action against such officer or officers as is provided in section 95 of the Civil Service Law.

(b) Waiver of Rights. No public officer nor any employee acting for a public officer shall require a candidate for employment to sign any document whereby such candidate for employment waives any right or rights accruing under this Part.

Cross References

Civil Service Law, see McKinney's Book 9.

§ 25.35. Reports of Appointing Authorities; Official Roster

(a) No person shall be appointed to or be employed in any position in the unified court system until he or she has passed an examination or is exempted from such examination in conformity with the provisions of this Part. Each appointing authority shall report to the Chief Administrator of the Courts forthwith upon such appointment or employment, the name of such appointee or employee, the title and character of his or her office or employment, the date of the commencement of service by virtue thereof and the salary or compensation thereof, and shall report from time to time and upon the date of official action in or knowledge of each case, any separation of a person from the service, or other change therein, and such other information as the Chief Administrator may require in order to keep the roster hereinafter mentioned.

(b) The Chief Administrator shall maintain an official roster of the classified service of the unified court system. Such roster shall contain in detail the employment history of each employee, showing each change of status or compensation from the time he or she enters service until he or she separates from service, except that it shall not be necessary to enter in such roster the compensation or changes in compensation of an employee holding a position classified pursuant to section 25.5 or 25.6 of this Part and listed in a salary grade plan containing titles and specific ranges of salary for each title.

§ 25.36.   Certification of Payrolls

(a) Payroll Certification Required.

(1) The Chief Administrator of the Courts shall certify to the appropriate disbursing or auditing officer that all persons employed in the classified service are employed in their respective positions in accordance with law and rules made pursuant to law. Such certificate may be executed for and on behalf of the Chief Administrator by an employee thereof duly designated in writing for that purpose. Such certificate may, for cause, be withheld from an entire payroll or from any item or items therein. If the Chief Administrator finds that any person has been promoted, transferred, assigned, reinstated or otherwise employed in violation of the Judiciary Law and this part, notification shall be made to the appropriate disbursing and auditing officers.

(2) Any person entitled to be certified as provided herein and refused such certificate, or from whom salary or compensation is otherwise unlawfully withheld, may maintain a proceeding under article 78 of the Civil Practice Law and Rules to compel the issuance of such certificate or the payment of such salary, or both, as the case may be.

(b) Certifications. In order to provide for the payment of salary or compensation to employees on any regular scheduled payday, a duly designated representative of the Chief Administrator of the Courts shall furnish to the Chief Administrator, on prescribed forms, at least five days before the same is required by the appropriate fiscal or disbursing officer, the names of the persons to be paid, the title of the position held or kind of service performed by each, the rate of compensation, and such other information as the Chief Administrator may require. The appointing authority or its duly designated representative shall certify that the persons named are employed in the performance of duties appropriate to their respective positions and employment as indicated. The Chief Administrator shall examine such forms; and if the Chief Administrator finds that the persons named therein are employed in accordance with law, and rules made pursuant to law, the Chief Administrator shall so certify. The Chief Administrator thereafter shall transmit such forms to the appropriate fiscal or disbursing officer for further audit and payment as required by law.

(c) Extended Certifications. The Chief Administrator of the Courts may certify the employment of a person for an extended period without time limitation or, in the case of employment subject to a time limitation, for such limited period as may be applicable. No further certification shall be necessary for the payment of salary or compensation to such person,

so long as his or her title, salary grade and status remain unchanged during the stated limited period, if any, of his or her employment. The Chief Administrator may at any time examine any payroll to determine that any person is employed in accordance with this Part. Nothing herein shall be construed to prevent or preclude the Chief Administrator from terminating or rescinding a certification at any time by giving notice thereof to the appropriate fiscal or disbursing officer.

(d) Temporary Certifications. When the name of any person is first submitted for certification following his or her appointment, reinstatement, promotion, transfer or other change in status, and the Chief Administrator of the Courts requires further information or time to enable a final determination to be made thereon, the Chief Administrator may certify such person temporarily pending such final determination. In such event, the Chief Administrator shall immediately request the necessary additional information. If such information is not furnished promptly, or if the Chief Administrator finds, following receipt of such information, that the employment of such person is not in accordance with the law and rules, the Chief Administrator shall immediately terminate such certification by notice to the appropriate fiscal or disbursing officer.

(e) Effect of Certification. Notwithstanding the provisions of this section, the Chief Administrator of the Courts, in any certificate issued pursuant to this section, shall not be required or deemed to attest that the salary or rate of compensation indicated for such person is that to which he or she is eligible or entitled pursuant to law.

(f) Refusal or Termination of Certification.

(1) Upon satisfactory evidence of intention to evade the provisions of any law or this Part in assigning any employee to perform duties other than those for which he or she was examined and certified or under any title not appropriate to the duties to be performed, the Chief Administrator of the Courts shall refuse certification or shall terminate a certification previously made and then in force.

(2) Any officer who shall willfully pay or authorize the payment of salary or compensation to any person in the classified service of the unified court system with knowledge that the Chief Administrator of the Courts has refused to certify the payroll, estimate or account of such person, or after due notice from the Chief Administrator that such person has been appointed, employed, transferred, assigned to perform duties or reinstated in violation of any of the provisions of this Part, shall be subject to the provisions of section 101 of the Civil Service Law and such court proceedings as are provided by section 102 of the Civil Service Law.

Cross References
CPLR, see McKinney's Book 7B.
Civil Service Law, see McKinney's Book 9.

§§ 25.37 to 25.40. [Repealed]

§ 25.41. Review Procedure for Classification Established by the May 28, 1979 Classification Plan

An employee aggrieved by the classification of his or her position in the classification plan established effective May 28, 1979, including the allocation of his or her position to a salary grade, may seek review as follows:

(a) The employee or the employee's representative shall submit a written notice of an intention to appeal the classification to the Chief Administrator of the Courts within 60 days of his or her receipt of notice of the classification. The Chief Administrator shall notify each employee or representative who files a notice of intention to appeal of the date on which the appeal must be perfected, provided that the employee or the representative shall have at least 30 days to perfect the appeal. An appeal shall be perfected by the submission of a written statement on the basis of the appeal, together with any supporting papers. The Chief Administrator shall review these statements, make any required adjustments, and notify the employee of his or her action.

(b) If the appeal has not been resolved to the satisfaction of the employee, the employee or the employee's representative may then appeal to the Classification Review Board within 60 days of receipt of notice of the action of the Chief Administrator of the Courts. This review board shall consist of three members, one appointed by the President of the State Civil Service Commission, one appointed by the State Comptroller, and a chairman, to be appointed by the Chairman of the Public Employment Relations Board. The Classification Review Board shall determine each appeal. The Classification Review Board shall consider all material submitted by the employee or the employee's representative, and shall send a copy of this material to the Chief Administrator, who shall be given a reasonable opportunity to respond. The Classification Review Board may, in its discretion, hold a hearing with relation to any aspect of any appeal.

(c) Any employee organization may bring an appeal pursuant to this procedure on behalf of any member or group of members.

(d) The Classification Review Board shall have jurisdiction to review appeals only from classifications and allocations determined pursuant to the classification plan established as set forth in subdivision (a) of this section.

(e) A determination of the Classification Review Board shall constitute an administrative order; subject, however, to review in a proceeding brought by either the employee, an employee organization, or the Chief Administrator pursuant to article 78 of the CPLR.

(f) This section shall apply only to appeals pending before the Classification Review Board as of the effective date of this subdivision [January 1, 1987].

§§ 25.42 to 25.45. [Renumbered 25.38 to 25.41]

PART 26. FILING OF STATEMENTS PURSUANT TO JUDICIARY LAW § 35–a

§ 26.1. General

(a) This section applies to any appointments made by a court including but not limited to appraiser, special guardian, guardian ad litem, guardian, referee, counsel, special referee, special examiner, conservator, committee of incompetent, court evaluator or counsel for an incapacitated person appointed pursuant to Article 81 of the Mental Hygiene Law, or receiver, and in connection with which fees of more than $500 for the services performed have been awarded.

(b) This section shall not apply to attorneys appointed to a court to represent indigent persons pursuant to Article 18–B of the County Law, section 35 of the Judiciary Law, or section 407 of the Surrogates' Court Procedure Act, or to law guardians appointed pursuant to the Family Court Act; but in the case of referees or court examiners appointed pursuant to section 78.25 or section 81.32 of the Mental Hygiene Law, a statement shall be filed with the Administrative Office of the Courts, annually, by the judge or special referee who approved compensation for those services.

Cross References
County Law, see McKinney's Book 11.
Judiciary Law, see McKinney's Book 29.
Family Court Act, see McKinney's Book 29A, Part 1.
Mental Hygiene Law, see McKinney's Book 34A.
SCPA, see McKinney's Book 58A.

§ 26.2. Filing of Statements by Judges

Any judge or justice who has approved compensation of more than $500 to a court appointee shall file with the administrative office for the courts, on the first business day of the week following approval, a statement of compensation on a form authorized by the Chief Administrator of the Courts.

§ 26.3. Fixing Amount of Compensation

The judge or justice approving compensation shall certify that the compensation approved is fixed by statute or, if not, is a reasonable award for the services rendered by the appointee. If the fee for services performed is fixed by statute, the judge or justice shall specify the statutory fee and the section of the statute authorizing the payment of the fee.

§ 26.4. Request for Information Regarding Filed Statements

A request for information regarding a filed statement must be made to the Office of Court Administration, Statement of Approval of Compensation, P.O. Box 3171, Church Street Station, New York, N.Y. 10008, in writing, specifying the information desired.

PART 27. COLLECTIVE NEGOTIATIONS WITHIN THE UNIFIED COURT SYSTEM [REPEALED]

PART 28. ALTERNATIVE METHOD OF DISPUTE RESOLUTION BY ARBITRATION

§ 28.1. Definitions

(a) The words "panel of arbitrators" or "panel" in this Part shall mean: (1) a group of three attorneys chosen to serve as arbitrators by the arbitration commissioner pursuant to section 28.4 of this Part; or (2) a single attorney assigned by the arbitration commissioner, as the Chief Administrator of the Courts, (hereinafter denominated the Chief Administrator), shall designate from time to time in a particular county or court; or (3) a single arbitrator in the event the parties, by stipulation, provide for arbitration before a single arbitrator in those cases where a panel of three arbitrators otherwise is required.

(b) The term "chairperson" shall mean the attorney so designated by the arbitration commissioner pursuant to section 28.4 of this Part, or the single arbitrator assigned by the arbitration commissioner.

§ 28.2. Mandatory Submission of Actions to Arbitration

(a) The Chief Administrator may establish in any trial court in any county the arbitration program authorized by this Part.

(b) In each county where an arbitration program is established by order of the Chief Administrator, all civil actions for a sum of money only, except those commenced in small claims parts and not subsequently transferred to a regular part of court, that are noticed for trial or commenced in the Supreme Court, County Court, the Civil Court of the City of New York, a District Court or a City Court, on or after the effective date of the order where recovery sought for each cause of action is $6,000 or less, or $10,000 or less in the Civil Court of the City of New York, or such other sum as may be authorized by law, exclusive of costs and interest, shall be heard and decided by a panel of arbitrators. The Chief Administrator may also, at any time, upon the establishment of the program in any particular court or county or thereafter, provide for the submission to arbitration of actions

seeking recovery of such sums, that are pending for trial in those courts on the effective date of the order.

(c) In addition, upon stipulation filed with the clerk of the court where the action was commenced or, if the case was transferred, the clerk of the court to which it has been transferred, any civil action for a sum of money only, pending or thereafter commenced in such courts, including actions removed to a court of limited jurisdiction from the Supreme Court pursuant to CPLR 325(d), regardless of the amount in controversy, shall be arbitrated, and in any such action the arbitration award shall not be limited to the amounts provided in subdivision (b) of this section, or to the monetary jurisdiction of the court. Any stipulation pursuant to this section may set forth agreed facts, defenses waived or similar terms, and to that extent shall replace the pleadings.

(d) In any action subject to arbitration under these rules or submitted to arbitration by stipulation, the arbitration panel shall have jurisdiction of any counter-claim or crossclaim for a sum of money only that has been interposed, without regard to amount.

(e) All actions subject to arbitration shall be placed on a separate calendar known as the arbitration calendar, in the order of filing of the note of issue, notice of trial or stipulation of submission, except that where a defendant is in default, the plaintiff may seek a default judgment pursuant to the provisions of CPLR 3215.

(f) The appropriate administrative judge, with the approval of the Deputy Chief Administrator, may direct a pretrial calendar hearing by the court of actions pending on the arbitration calendar. If an action is not settled or dismissed, or judgment by default is not directed upon the hearing, it shall be processed thereafter in accordance with the provisions of this Part.

Cross References

CPLR, see McKinney's Book 7B.

§ 28.3. Arbitration Commissioner

(a) The Chief Administrator shall designate, in each county where arbitration is established pursuant to this Part, an arbitration commissioner. The compensation, if any, payable to a commissioner, other than a full time public official or employee who shall receive no compensation as such commissioner, shall be determined by the Chief Administrator within the appropriation made available for that purpose.

(b) The commissioner shall maintain complete and current records of all cases subject to arbitration under this Part and a current list of attorneys consenting to act as arbitrators.

§ 28.4. Selection of Panels of Arbitrators

(a) The members of each panel of arbitrators shall be appointed by the commissioner from the list established by the Chief Administrator of the Courts of attorneys-at-law admitted to practice in the State of New York. The Chief Administrator may establish procedures to evaluate the qualifications of applicants for placement on the list. No attorney shall be appointed unless he or she shall have filed with the commissioner a consent to act and an oath or affirmation equitably and justly to try all actions coming before him or her. An attorney may be removed from the list in the discretion of the commissioner upon approval of the Chief Administrator.

(b) Names of attorneys shall be drawn at random from the list. Where a three-arbitrator panel is utilized, the first name drawn for each three-arbitrator panel shall be the chairperson thereof. The chairperson of each panel shall have been admitted to practice in New York State as an attorney for at least five years; and the second and third members must be admitted to practice but not for any specified period of time, unless the Chief Administrator shall, by order, otherwise determine. Not more than one member or employee of a partnership or firm shall be appointed to any panel.

(c) No attorney who has served as an arbitrator shall be eligible to serve again until all other attorneys on the current list have had an opportunity to serve.

(d) An arbitrator who is related by blood, marriage or professional ties to a party or his counsel shall be disqualified for cause. An arbitrator may disqualify himself upon his own application, or by application of a party made within five days of the receipt of the notice of the hearing as provided by section 28.6 of this Part. Should a party object to the arbitrator's refusal to disqualify himself or herself for cause, the party may apply to the arbitration commissioner for a ruling. The commissioner's ruling shall be binding on all parties. If an arbitrator is disqualified, the commissioner shall select another arbitrator in the manner authorized by this section.

§ 28.5. Assignment of Actions to Panel

(a) The commissioner shall assign to each panel at least the first three, but no more than six, actions pending on the arbitration calendar.

(b) If an action is settled or discontinued before the hearing, the attorney for the plaintiff shall immediately notify the chairperson and the commissioner. If the plaintiff is not represented by an attorney, the chairperson, upon receiving notice of such settlement or discontinuance, shall immediately notify the commissioner. The commissioner, upon receiving such notice, shall assign the next available action to the panel.

§ 28.6. Scheduling of Arbitration Hearings

(a) The hearing shall be held in a place provided by the court, by the commissioner, by the chairperson of the panel or, at the request of the chairperson, by a member of the panel. Unless otherwise agreed by the panel, parties and counsel, such place shall be within the county.

(b) The chairperson shall fix a hearing date and time, not less than 15 nor more than 30 days after the case is assigned, and shall give written notice to the members of the panel and the parties or their counsel at least 10 days before the date set. The commissioner may, on good cause shown, extend for a reasonable period the time within which the hearing shall be commenced. Such date and time shall not be a Saturday, Sunday, legal holiday or during evening hours except by agreement of the panel, parties and counsel. Adjournments may be granted at the discretion of the chairperson only upon good cause shown.

(c) If the chairperson is unable to schedule a hearing within 30 days after the case is assigned, or within such further period as the commissioner may set, he shall notify the commissioner in writing of the reasons for such inability. The commissioner shall mark the action "continued" and place it on the arbitration calendar, and shall assign another action to the panel.

(d) Any action which is continued twice, after assignment to two panels, shall be referred by the commissioner to the court where the action was commenced or, if the action was transferred, to the court to which it was transferred, for a hearing on the cause of the inability to hold an arbitration hearing. The court, upon such hearing, may order a dismissal, or authorize the entry of judgment by default pursuant to CPLR 3215, or refer the action to the commissioner for assignment to another panel.

Cross References

CPLR, see McKinney's Book 7B.

§ 28.7. Defaults

(a) Where a party fails to appear at the hearing, the panel shall nonetheless proceed with the hearing and shall make an award and decision, as may be just and proper under the facts and circumstances of the action, which may be entered as a judgment forthwith pursuant to section 28.11(b) of this Part. The judgment, if any, the default and the award may be vacated and the action may be restored to the arbitration calendar only upon order of the court where the action was commenced or, if the action was transferred, the court to which it was transferred, upon good cause shown. Such order of restoration shall be upon condition that the moving party pay into the court an amount equal to the total fees payable by the administrative office for the courts to the panel.

(b) Should all parties fail to appear at the hearing, the panel must file a report and award dismissing the action. The action may be restored to the arbitration calendar only upon order of the court where the action was commenced or, if the action was transferred, the court to which it was transferred, upon good cause shown. Such order or restoration may provide for the payment by any party into the court of such part of the panel fees payable by the administrative office for the courts to the panel as the court may determine to be just and proper.

§ 28.8. Conduct of Hearings

(a) The panel shall conduct the hearing with due regard to the law and established rules of evidence, which shall be liberally construed to promote justice. In personal injury cases, medical proof may be established by the submission into evidence of medical reports of attending or examining physicians upon stipulation of all parties.

(b) The panel shall have the general powers of a court, including but not limited to:

(1) subpoenaing witnesses to appear;

(2) subpoenaing books, papers, documents and other items of evidence;

(3) administering oaths or affirmations;

(4) determining the admissibility of evidence and the form in which it is to be offered;

(5) deciding questions of law and facts in the actions submitted to them.

§ 28.9. Costs of Hearings; Stenographic Record

(a) Witness fees shall be the same as in the court in which the action was commenced or, if the action was transferred, the court to which the action was transferred and the costs shall be borne by the same parties as in court.

(b) The panel shall not be required to cause a stenographic record to be made, but if any party, at least five days before the hearing, requests such record be kept and deposits $50 or such additional sum as the panel may fix to secure payment therefor, the panel shall provide a stenographer. Any surplus deposited shall be returned to the party depositing it.

The cost of the stenographer shall not be a taxable disbursement.

§ 28.10. Compensation of Arbitrators

(a) [1] The Chief Administrator shall provide for the compensation, including expenses, payable to each arbitrator to the extent of money available to the administrative office for the courts for this purpose. Claims for such compensation shall be made to the commissioner after entry of the award on forms prescribed by the Chief Administrator, except that a claim for compensation of the chairperson of a panel also may be made where the action is settled or withdrawn after a panel hearing date has been scheduled but before the hearing is commenced, and a claim for compensation of an arbitrator other than a chairperson may be made where the action is settled or withdrawn within three days of the date scheduled for the hearing. The commissioner shall forward all claims approved by him to the Chief Administrator. Any arbitrator may apply to the commissioner for reimbursement of extraordinary expenses necessarily incurred by him in the same manner as provided for application for ordinary compensation.

1 So in original. No subd. (b) was promulgated.

§ 28.11. Award

(a) The award shall be signed by the panel of arbitrators or at least a majority of them. The chairperson shall file a report and the award with the commissioner within 20 days after the hearing, and mail or deliver copies thereof to the parties or their counsel. The commissioner shall mark his files accordingly, file the original with the clerk of the court where the action was commenced or, if the action was transferred, the court to which it was transferred, and notify the parties of such filing.

(b) Unless a demand is made for trial de novo, or the award vacated, the award shall be final and judgment shall be entered thereon by the clerk of the court where the action was commenced or, if the action was transferred, the clerk of the court to which it was transferred, with costs and disbursements taxed in accordance with the Civil Practice Law and Rules, the Uniform City Court Act, the New York City Civil Court Act, or the Uniform District Court Act, as the case may be.

Cross References

CPLR, see McKinney's Book 7B.

New York City Civil Court Act, see McKinney's Book 29A, Part 3.

Uniform City Court Act, see McKinney's Book 29A, Part 3.

Uniform District Court Act, see McKinney's Book 29A, Part 3.

Forms

Arbitration award, see West's McKinney's Forms, CPLR, §§ 10:256, 10:257.

§ 28.12. Trial De Novo

(a) Demand may be made by any party not in default for a trial de novo in the court where the action was commenced or, if the action was transferred, the court to which it was transferred, with or without a jury. Any party who is not in default, within 30 days after service upon such party of the notice of filing of the award with the appropriate court clerk, or if service is by mail, within 35 days of such service, may file with the clerk of the court where the award was filed and serve upon all adverse parties a demand for a trial de novo.

(b) If the demandant either serves or files a timely demand for a trial de novo but neglects through mistake or excusable neglect to do one of those two acts within the time limited, the court where the action was commenced or, if the action was transferred, the court to which it was transferred, may grant an extension of time for curing the omission.

(c) The demandant shall also, concurrently with the filing of the demand, pay to the court clerk where the award was filed the amount of the fees payable to the panel by the administrative office for the courts pursuant to section 28.10 of this Part. Where a judicial hearing officer has heard and determined the arbitration, the amount payable shall be the same as would have been payable to a single arbitrator or a panel of three arbitrators, as the case may be, if such judicial hearing officer had not been assigned. Such sum shall not be recoverable by the demandant upon a trial de novo or in any other proceeding.

(d) The arbitrators shall not be called as witnesses nor shall the report or award of the arbitrators be admitted in evidence at the trial de novo.

(e) If the judgment upon the trial de novo is not more favorable than the arbitration award in the amount of damages awarded or the type of relief granted to the demandant, the demandant shall not recover interest or statutory costs and disbursements from the time of the award, but shall pay such statutory costs and disbursements to the other party or parties from the time of the filing of the demand for the trial de novo.

(f) If a judicial hearing officer has heard and determined an arbitration, the trial de novo may not be presided over by a judicial hearing officer, except upon consent of the parties.

§ 28.13. Motion to Vacate Award

(a) Any party, except one who has demanded a trial de novo, within 30 days after the award is filed, may serve upon all other parties who have appeared and file with the appropriate court clerk a motion to vacate the award on only the grounds that the rights of the moving party were prejudiced because:

(1) there was corruption, fraud or misconduct in procuring the award;

(2) the panel making the award exceeded its power or so imperfectly executed it that a final and definite award was not made; or

(3) there was a substantial failure to follow the procedures established by or pursuant to these rules;

unless the party applying to vacate the award continued with the arbitration with notice of the defect and without objection.

(b) Copies of the motion papers shall be served upon the commissioner within two days after filing. If the motion to vacate is granted, the case shall be returned to the top of the arbitration calendar and submitted to a new panel.

Forms

Vacatur of arbitration award, see West's McKinney's Forms, CPLR, § 10:272 et seq.

§ 28.14. General Power of Court

The court where the action was commenced or, if the action was transferred, the court to which it was transferred, shall hear and determine all collateral motions relating to arbitration proceedings.

§ 28.15. Training Courses

The Chief Administrator of the Courts may provide for such orientation courses, training courses and continuing education courses for attorneys applying to be arbitrators and for arbitrators as the Chief Administrator may deem necessary and desirable.

§ 28.16. Judicial Hearing Officers

(a) An arbitration under this part may be heard and determined by a judicial hearing officer instead of a panel of arbitrators, without regard for whether the arbitration otherwise would be triable before a single arbitrator or a panel of three arbitrators. The judicial hearing officer shall be assigned by the commissioner, with the approval of the appropriate administrative judge, to hear and determine such proceedings as shall be assigned by the commissioner. When a judicial hearing officer presides over an arbitration, the procedures followed shall be as set forth in the provisions of this part.

(b) Judicial hearing officers serving as arbitrators pursuant to this part shall receive compensation as provided in section 122.8 of the rules of the Chief Administrator. A location in which a hearing of the arbitration is held shall be deemed a "facility designated for court appearances" within the meaning of that section.

PART 29. ELECTRONIC RECORDING AND AUDIO–VISUAL COVERAGE IN COURT FACILITIES AND OF COURT PROCEEDINGS

§ 29.1. General

(a) Taking photographs, films or videotapes, or audiotaping, broadcasting or telecasting, in a courthouse, including any court room, office or hallway thereof, at any time or on any occasion, whether or not the court is in session, is forbidden, unless permission of the Chief Administrator of the courts or a designee of the Chief Administrator is first obtained; provided, however, that the permission of the Chief Judge of the Court of Appeals or the presiding justice of an Appellate Division shall be obtained with respect to the court over which each presides. Such permission may be granted if:

(1) there will be no detraction from the dignity or decorum of the courtroom or courthouse;

(2) there will be no compromise of the safety of persons having business in the courtroom or courthouse;

(3) there will be no disruption of court activities;

(4) there will be no undue burden upon the resources of the courts; and

(5) granting of permission will be consistent with the constitutional and statutory rights of all affected persons and institutions.

Permission may be conditioned upon compliance with any special requirements that may be necessary to ensure that the above conditions are met.

(b) This section shall not apply to

(1) audio-visual coverage of proceedings in the appellate courts or the trial courts under section 29.2 or 29.3, and

(2) applications made to the appropriate court for photographing, taping or videotaping by or on behalf of the parties to the litigation and not for public dissemination.

§ 29.2. Appellate Courts

In respect to appellate courts, the Chief Judge hereby authorizes electronic photographic recording of proceedings in such courts, subject to the approval of the respective appellate court and subject to the following conditions:

(a) Equipment and Personnel.

(1) Two portable videotape electronic television cameras and two camera operators shall be permitted in any proceeding in any appellate court.

(2) Two photographers to operate two still cameras with not more than two lenses for each camera and related equipment for print purposes shall be permitted in any proceeding in any appellate court.

(3) One audio system for radio broadcast purposes shall be permitted in any proceeding in any appellate court. Audio pickup for all media purposes shall be accomplished from existing audio systems in the court facility. If no technically suitable audio system exists in the court facility, microphones and related wiring essential for media purposes shall be unobtrusive and shall be located in places designated in advance of any proceeding by the presiding judge or justice of the court hearing the appeal.

(4) Notwithstanding the provisions of paragraphs (1) to (3) of this subdivision, the court may increase or decrease within reasonable limits the amount of equipment that will be permitted into the courtroom on finding (i) that there is a need therefor because of special circumstances, and (ii) that it will not impair the dignity of the court or the judicial process.

(5) Notwithstanding the provisions of paragraphs (1) to (3) of this subdivision, the equipment authorized therein shall not be admitted into the courtroom unless interested members of the electronic media and interested print photographers shall have entered into pooling arrangements, for their respective groups, including the establishment of necessary procedures, cost sharing, access to material, and selection of a pool representative. The court may not be called upon to mediate or resolve any dispute as to such arrangements. In making pool arrangements, consideration shall be given to educational users' needs for full coverage of entire proceedings.

(6) The pool operator covering the proceedings shall retain pool material for one year. The pool operator shall make available a copy of pool material at cost to educational users, to the appellate court and to the Court of Appeals at their request.

(b) Sound and Light Criteria.

(1) Only television photographic and audio equipment and still camera equipment which do not produce distracting sound or light shall be employed to cover judicial proceedings. Specifically, television photographic and audio equipment shall produce no greater sound or light than the equipment designated in 22 NYCRR Appendix A–13; and still camera equipment shall produce no greater sound or light than a 33mm Leica "M" Series Rangefinder camera.

(2) It shall be the affirmative duty of media personnel desiring to use equipment other than that authorized in these rules or in 22 NYCRR Appendix A–13, to demonstrate to the court adequately in advance of any proceeding that the equipment sought to be utilized

meets the sound and light criteria enunciated herein. A failure to obtain advance approval for equipment shall preclude its use in any proceeding.

(c) Location of Equipment and Personnel. Television and still camera equipment and camera personnel shall be positioned in such locations as shall be designated by the court. The areas designated shall provide reasonable access to coverage with the least possible interference with court proceedings. Videotape recording equipment which is not a component part of a television camera shall be located in an area outside the court facility.

(d) Movement of Equipment During Proceedings. Electronic still photographic and audio equipment shall not be placed in, moved about or removed from the court facility, and related personnel shall not move about the courtroom except prior to commencement or after adjournment of proceedings each day, or during a recess. Television film magazines and still camera film or lenses shall be changed only during a recess in the proceeding.

(e) Courtroom Light Sources. With the concurrence of the court, modifications and additions may be made in light sources existing in the facility, provided such modification or additions are installed and maintained at media expense and provided they are not distracting or otherwise offensive.

(f) Conferences of Counsel. To protect the attorney-client privilege and effective right to counsel, there shall be no audio pickup or audio broadcast of conferences which occur in a court facility between attorneys and their clients, between co-counsel of a client, or between counsel and the presiding judge held at the bench, without the express consent of all participants in the conference. Nor shall any chambers conference be filmed, recorded or broadcast.

(g) Consent Not Required. Electronic media or print photography coverage of appellate arguments shall not be limited by the objection of counsel or parties, except for good cause shown.

(h) Appellate Review. An order granting or denying the electronic media from access to any proceeding, or affecting other matters arising under these rules and standards, shall not be appealable insofar as it pertains to and arises under these rules and standards except as otherwise provided and authorized by law.

§ 29.3. Trial Courts

Audio-visual coverage of proceedings in the trial courts shall be permitted only in accordance with the provisions of Part 131 of the Rules of the Chief Administrator.

§ 29.4. Videotape Cameras and Recorders

VIDEOTAPE ELECTRONIC CAMERAS

1.	Ikegami	HL–77,	HL–33,
		HL–35,	HL–34,
		HL–51	
2.	RCA	TK–76	
3.	Sony	DXC–1600 Trinicon	
3a.	ASACA	ACC–2006	
4.	Hitachi	SK–80, SK–90	
5.	Hitachi	FP–3030	
6.	Phillips	LDK–25	
7.	Sony BVP–200	ENG Camera	
8.	Fernseh	Video Camera	
9.	JVC–8800 u	ENG Camera	
10.	AKAI	CVC–150, VTS–150	
11.	Panasonic	WV–3085, NV–3085	
12.	JVC	GC–4800 u	

VIDEOTAPE RECORDERS/used
with video cameras

1.	Ikegami	3800
2.	Sony	3800
3.	Sony	BVU–100
4.	Ampex	Video Recorder
5.	Panasonic	1 inch Video Recorder
6.	JVC	4400
7.	Sony	3800H

PART 30. MECHANICAL RECORDING OF PROCEEDINGS IN JUSTICE COURTS

Former Part 30, Uniform Justice Court Rules, was repealed.

§ 30.1. Mechanical Recording of Proceedings in Justice Courts

The chief administrator of the courts may require the mechanical recording of testimony and of other proceedings in cases in a town or village justice court. The mechanical recording of proceedings in accordance with this rule shall not affect the right of the court or any litigant therein to employ a stenographer to take minutes of such proceedings manually.

PART 31. APPOINTMENT OF HEARING EXAMINERS IN FAMILY COURT [REPEALED]

PART 32. VIDEOTAPING OF CONDITIONAL EXAMINATIONS OF WITNESSES IN CRIMINAL CASES

§ 32.1. When Permitted

Conditional examinations authorized pursuant to sections 660.40 and 660.50 of the Criminal Procedure Law may be conducted by means of videotape or photographic recording, provided the recording is made in conformity with this Part.

Cross References

Criminal Procedure Law, see McKinney's Book 11A.

§ 32.2. Application and Notice

An application requesting that a conditional examination be recorded, for audiovisual reproduction and preservation, by videotape or other photographic method, and any order granting that application shall state the name and address of the operator and of his or her employer.

Forms

Application to examine witness conditionally, see West's McKinney's Forms, Criminal Procedure § 660.40, Forms 1 and 2, § 660.50, Form 1.

§ 32.3. Conduct of Examination

(a) The examination shall begin by the operator recording:

(1) his or her name and address;

(2) the name and address of his or her employer;

(3) the date, time and place of the examination;

(4) the caption of the case;

(5) the name of the witness; and

(6) the party on whose behalf the examination is being conducted.

The person being examined shall be sworn as a witness. If the examination requires the use of more than one tape or film, the end of each tape or film and the beginning of each succeeding tape or film shall be announced by the operator.

(b) More than one camera may be used, either in sequence or simultaneously.

(c) At the conclusion of the examination, a statement shall be made on the record that the recording is completed. As soon thereafter as practicable, the videotape or other photographic recording shall be shown to the witness for examination, unless such showing and examination are waived by the witness and the parties. Pursuant to section 660.60 of the Criminal Procedure Law, a transcript and any videotape or photographic recording of the examination must be certified and filed with the court which ordered the examination.

Cross References

Criminal Procedure Law, see McKinney's Book 11A.

§ 32.4. Copies

The parties may make copies of the examination and thereafter may purchase additional copies.

§ 32.5. Custody of Recordings

When the tape or film is filed with the clerk of the court, the clerk shall give an appropriate receipt, shall provide secure and adequate facilities for the storage of such recordings, and thereafter shall keep appropriate records as to the possession and custody of such recordings.

§ 32.6. Use at Trial

The use of recordings of examinations at the trial shall be governed by the provisions of the Criminal Procedure Law, and all other relevant statutes, court rules and decisional law relating to depositions and to the admissibility of evidence. The proponent of the examination shall have the responsibility of providing whatever equipment and personnel may be necessary for presenting the examination.

Cross References

Criminal Procedure Law, see McKinney's Book 11A.

§ 32.7. Cost

The cost of videotaping or photographic recording shall be borne by the applicant.

§ 32.8. Appeal

On appeal, videotaped or photographically recorded examinations shall be transcribed in the same manner as other testimony, and transcripts shall be filed in the appellate court. The transcripts shall remain part of the original record in the case and shall be transmitted therewith.

PART 33.   TEMPORARY ASSIGNMENT OF JUSTICES AND JUDGES

§ 33.0.   General

Temporary assignments of judges and justices of the Unified Court System pursuant to article VI, section 26, of the Constitution shall be made by the Chief Administrator of the Courts, in his or her discretion, subject to the Constitution, article VI, section 28, subdivision b, after determining the need therefor and the advisability thereof consistent with the objectives of the Unified Court System; provided, however, that such temporary assignments shall be made with due regard for the courts from which and to which a temporary assignment is made and with due regard for the official and appropriate interests of the judge being assigned. When made for a period in excess of 20 calendar days, such temporary assignments shall be made by the Chief Administrator in consultation and agreement with the presiding justices of the appropriate appellate divisions on behalf of their respective courts, provided further that if the Chief Administrator and a presiding justice are unable to agree, the matter shall be determined by the Chief Judge.

Cross References

Constitution, see McKinney's Book 2.

§ 33.1.   Temporary Assignment of Judges to the Supreme Court

In addition to the criteria set forth in section 33.0 of this Part, all assignments to the Supreme Court of judges of courts of limited jurisdiction, other than the Court of Claims, shall be made pursuant to rules promulgated by the Chief Administrator which shall provide for:

(a) minimum standards of judicial service as a prerequisite for consideration;

(b) recommendations by administrative judges, bar associations and others who may have knowledge of the capabilities of the judge under consideration; and

(c) limited terms of assignment and a procedure for evaluation of the qualifications of the judge prior to a designation or redesignation for temporary assignment.

PART 34.   GUIDELINES FOR NEW YORK STATE COURT FACILITIES

§ 34.0.   Court Facilities

In the exercise of responsibility for supervision of the administration and operation of the unified court system, the Chief Administrator of the Courts shall encourage, whenever possible and insofar as practicable, compliance with the guidelines for New York State court facilities set forth below.

GUIDELINE I.   SAFETY

I.1: Safety. Court facilities should have structural design, building materials, methods of construction and fire rating as required by local or state building codes that are applicable in the locality.

Court facilities should have fire alarms, fire extinguisher systems, means of egress and emergency exits as required by applicable building and fire codes.

The use of court facilities should conform, to the extent required, to the Occupational Safety and Health Administration Standards of the U.S. Department of Labor for public buildings.

I.2: Emergency Planning and Evacuation Procedures. Court facilities should have established procedures for the evacuation of facilities in case of fire or bomb threats, a system of communication in case of an emergency and the appointment of wardens to conduct fire drills at regular intervals. In addition, there should be safety officers to assure that required safety measures are established and followed at all times. A multi-court facility should have one safety officer with responsibility for the entire facility.

GUIDELINE II.   ACCESS FOR THE HANDICAPPED

Court facilities should be accessible to the physically handicapped as required by Article 15 of the State's Executive Law and accepted architectural standards.

GUIDELINE III.   ENVIRONMENT *

III.1: Overall Appearance. Court facilities should have an overall appearance of dignity and efficiency.

The appearance of court facilities affects the attitude of litigants, attorneys, the public and court employees. Therefore, court facilities should be continuously well maintained.

III.2: Adequate Facilities and Areas. Court facilities should provide the required number of courtrooms, chambers, jury deliberation rooms, attorney/client conference rooms, clerical and other offices of adequate size as set forth below in these guidelines. An inadequate number of facilities delays the administration of justice.

III.3: Heating, Cooling and Humidity. Design should emphasize energy conservation. Court facilities should follow the standards set by the American Society of Heating, Refrigeration and Air-Conditioning Engineers (ASHRAE).

III.4: Ventilation. A fresh, contaminant-free air supply should be provided. ASHRAE standards should be followed.

III.5: Lighting. Court facilities should have adequate lighting levels that comply with the standards set by the Illuminating Engineering Society. Consideration should be given to energy conservation.

III.6: Color Scheme and Contrast. The color scheme should be sober and dignified, the colors easy to maintain. The following level of color contrast is suggested:

- Courtrooms   Low contrast
- Offices, jury rooms, conference rooms, chambers   Medium contrast
- Public lobbies, conference rooms, storage areas   Heavy contrast

III.7: Acoustics. Court facilities should provide a comfortable acoustical environment suitable for public trials, hearings, office work and research.

- There should be no vibration noise due to mechanical systems (heating, air-conditioning, elevators, plumbing, creaky staircases, doors, windows and mechanical equipment).
- Jury deliberation rooms and family court hearing rooms (courtrooms) should be soundproof.
- Courtrooms should be free from outside noise disturbance and should be so constructed as to assure that all the participants in the well area are able to hear the proceedings.
- Sound amplification may be necessary in large courtrooms, jury assembly areas, and large family court waiting rooms.

III.8: Vision and Sightlines. In courtrooms, every participant in the well area should have a clear and adequate view of all other participants.

Prisoner detention areas and prisoner travel path should provide clear and maximum vision for easy supervision of detainees.

III.9: Confidentiality. Functions which require a considerable degree of confidentiality—such as jury deliberation; attorney/client conferences; attorney/defendant interviews; conferences with judges, clerks and probation officers; and adoption proceedings—should be housed in private rooms.

III.10: Cleaning and Maintenance. Court facilities should be clean and hygienic. Floor, wall, ceiling, door and window components should be devoid of deterioration and in working condition. Electrical, plumbing, heating and cooling systems should be maintained in an operating condition.

* Detailed technical criteria may be obtained from the New York State Office of Court Administration.

GUIDELINE IV. SIGNS AND PUBLIC INFORMATION

IV.1: Exterior of the Building. The building should clearly be designated as a courthouse. If there are one or more courtrooms within a building housing other functions, it is particularly important that the existence of these courtrooms is made clear in a place easily seen by the public.

IV.2: Directory. Prominently displayed just within the main doors should be a building directory, bilingual where appropriate. There should be a listing of the location of courtrooms, court-related services, and ancillary agencies. If the courthouse functions are spread among a number of buildings, the courtroom services and the addresses of (and directions to) the other buildings should be posted.

IV.3: Door and Wall Signs. Signs should be posted at the door to each courtroom clearly identifying that part. In addition, directional wall signs, bilingual where appropriate, should be used in buildings where long corridors or confusing layouts indicate they would be useful.

IV.4: Information Service. Where possible, there should be information desks strategically placed in public areas of the courthouse and staffed where necessary by bilingual personnel to direct defendants and their friends and relatives, witnesses, jurors, and spectators to their destinations.

Where personnel are not available to establish such a service, consideration should be given to employing well-trained citizen volunteers.

If such a service is not established, there should be an office, such as that of the Court Clerk, designated as the place for the public to receive information and have their questions answered. Such public information offices should be clearly marked as such, and should be listed in the directory.

IV.5: Posting of Calendars. Copies of all daily part calendars in that courthouse should be posted at a central location, and each courtroom should have that room's calendar posted immediately outside.

GUIDELINE V. DESIGN GUIDELINES FOR PROPOSED COURTHOUSES

V.1: When to Build a New Courthouse. Building a new courthouse should be considered when:

A. The existing structure needs replacement because of structural and other deterioration which would require more financing to remedy than would be needed for a new courthouse.

B. The existing needs for court facilities far exceed those that can be accommodated in the existing structure even with extensive renovation.

C. Expansion of the existing structure to accommodate present and projected future needs cannot be accomplished by building an addition to the existing structure.

D. The space and facility needs of the courts in conjunction with the needs of other governmental agencies would be best met by building a new structure.

E. Where court facilities are substantially located in leased spaces and where it would be more cost-effective to house them in a new publicly-owned structure.

F. Where the historic landmark status or the structure prohibits suitable renovations of the existing courthouse.

V.2: Recycling of Existing Structures. New court facilities may be created by renovating existing structures, such as schools, commercial structures, warehouses or hospitals, as long as the existing structure allows functional layout and design of court facilities with appropriate internal and external symbolism and aesthetic qualities appropriate for a courthouse.

V.3: Long-Term Court Needs. New court facilities should be built to accommodate current and projected needs over the period of the expected life of the new structure. The space and facility needs should be based, wherever possible, on projection of workload, the number of people required to carry out the workload and the space required to house these people.

V.4: Multipurpose Use, Time-Sharing and Flexibility. The translation of projected space and facility needs into a building program should take into account multiple use of facilities, time-sharing of facilities, and inbuilt flexibility of use of spaces.

A. The total number of large courtrooms should be based on the absolute number of full-time, year-round requirements for court parts that have a need for a large public seating capacity (between 100–120).

B. The number of small courtrooms should be based on the total projected needs of all the courts to be housed in the building. No courtroom should be so small that it cannot be converted to properly accommodate a 16-person jury box in its well area.

C. Courtrooms should be so located on the floor as to allow separate prisoner access to all the courtrooms, if so required, in the future.

D. Where judges' chambers are located on the same floor in close proximity to the courtrooms, separate robing and conference rooms adjacent to the courtrooms are not required.

E. The number of jury deliberation rooms to be provided should be based on the current and projected future jury trial rate within the jurisdiction, but that number should not be less than the jury trial rate throughout the State. One jury deliberation room for each courtroom may not be required.

F. The number of attorney/client conference rooms, waiting rooms, and alternate jurors waiting rooms should be based on the principle of shared use of rooms.

G. The prisoner holding facilities adjacent to courtrooms should allow the separation of males and females.

H. Prisoner holding facilities adjacent to courtrooms should provide for at least one secure attorney/defendant interview room.

I. Large multi-courtroom facilities proposed for construction or major renovation should take into account, to the extent feasible, the need for attorneys' waiting rooms, accessible law libraries, public waiting areas, public address systems in public areas, jurors' areas, and designated eating areas for cafeteria facilities.

V.5: Transportation/Accessibility. The courthouse site should be convenient to transportation of the public, attorneys and prisoners.

V.6: Proximity to Court-Related Agencies. The courthouse site should be in close proximity to other related agency locations such as District Attorney's offices, probation offices and County Clerks' offices.

V.7: Separate Building Blocks. Consideration should be given to building two separate blocks—one for courtrooms and ancillary spaces, which require higher ceilings, and the other to accommodate office-type functions with lower ceilings. If appropriately connected to each other, these could lend themselves to the design and installation of cost-effective systems for heating, cooling, security and maintenance, at the same time providing vertical expansion in the future, if required.

V.8: Site Layout, Parking and Landscaping. The site layout should, where feasible, take into account parking needs of court users. Consideration should be given to the security of the parking areas and the separate entrances to the courthouse. The site layout should provide for aesthetically planned, but easy to maintain, grounds and landscape of the surrounding area.

V.9: Character of Building Design and Symbolism. The new courthouse design should project the traditional values of symbolism and retain the character of the area by using appropriate materials and fenestration.

V.10: Placement of Related Functions. Within the building, the functions that require heavy public access, such as clerks' offices and jury assembly area, should be placed on the main and lower floors to minimize the use of elevators, to allow closing off of the upper floors when not in use, and to allow zoning of the heating and cooling systems which can be shut off when the other floors are not in use. By providing clerical space for all courts in the structure on the same or adjacent floors, greater flexibility should be achieved in the allocation of space for clerical functions of different courts. Space can be saved by combining public areas for clerks' offices and photocopying, mail, supplies and general storage areas of all courts. Space can also be saved by allowing flexible use of secondary spaces for record storage by all courts.

V.11: Use of Building Components Offering Flexibility. The design of building components such as non load-bearing partitions, doors, electrical fixtures, ceiling and floor finishes into integrated systems should allow flexibility in rearranging spaces.

V.12: Choice of Building Materials. Building materials should be chosen for cost-effective maintenance, resistance to vandalism, acoustical qualities and safety.

V.13: Separate Circulation Patterns. The layout should provide for a separate pattern of circulation of judges, jurors, prisoners and the public. Spaces and facilities should be appropriately grouped together as secure, private, semi-private and public areas.

The layout should also be readily understandable to users unfamiliar with the facility. This should minimize the need for signs and avoid intrusion of the public into private areas.

GUIDELINE VI. DESIGN GUIDELINES FOR SECURITY

VI.1: Entrances. The entrances to the structure should be kept to a minimum. Separate entrances may be necessary for the public, judges, staff, prisoners and court-related agencies. However, the entrances for judges and staff can be provided with key or card access to minimize security staffing needs.

VI.2: Visibility. The plan and design should provide public corridors and spaces with uninterrupted visibility.

VI.3: Layout and Design. The layout should be devised so that there are three separate patterns of circulation: the first for judges, impanelled jurors and the court staff; the second for prisoners; and the third for the public. Such circulation should limit the crossing of paths of these separate groups in order to minimize conflicts and to provide a degree of privacy for judges and jurors.

The courthouse design and layout should delineate public, semi-private, private and secure areas. Private areas would include such areas as judges' chambers or robing rooms, impanelled or sequestered jurors' areas, jury deliberation rooms and secure areas. The semi-private areas would include the clerical offices. The public areas would include such areas as courtrooms, jury assembly areas, public lobbies, corridors, and public restrooms.

In the Family Court, all areas except the public lobbies, waiting rooms, public restrooms and public areas of the clerk's office should be delineated as private areas to insure confidentiality of proceedings and records.

VI.4: Staircases. Staircases should be so constructed as to prevent unauthorized access to secure areas on other floors.

VI.5: Zoned Areas. The courthouse design and layout should allow for the locking off of entire areas or floors when not in use.

VI.6: Doors and Windows. The design of windows and doors should deter access without compromising aesthetic, natural light and view considerations. The use of better components at somewhat higher initial cost should be considered in order to provide better security than afforded by traditional windows, doors, locks and keys. The use of impact-resistant glass or plastic material should be considered in strategic locations.

VI.7: Lighting and Signs. There should be proper and adequate lighting at strategic locations.

VI.8: Comprehensive Design Approach. When a group of structures is being designed, or a new structure is being added to a group of existing buildings, the layout should consider the security needs of all the structures as a group to eliminate the need for separate security forces and electronic surveillance systems for each structure.

GUIDELINE VII. COURTROOM

VII.1: Courtroom—General. The courtroom is one of the most complex design problems of any courthouse, as well as its focal point. Although there are only four (4) basic types of courtrooms—non-jury, civil, criminal and appellate—a large variety of courtroom layouts are used. Hearing rooms are less formal courtrooms.

All public courtrooms should have two major functional areas:

   i) The well area should provide for the active participants in the judicial proceeding, and

   ii) The public area should provide seating for jurors to be empanelled, attorneys waiting for their cases and the public.

The well area and the public area should be divided by a 3-foot high rail with gates or openings at appropriate places.

The public area should be large enough to accommodate jurors to be empanelled, the attorneys waiting for their cases and the public. In jury trial courtrooms the public seating capacity should not be less than 20.

All courtrooms require a minimum of two and a maximum of four entry/exit points. In a jury courtroom, where possible, an entry/exit point should be provided that allows jurors to avoid mixing with the public. Juries should also be seated at an appropriate distance from the public rail in courtrooms. The judge should have separate direct access to the bench. The public and attorneys should also have an entry/exit point that leads through or by a public seating area. In criminal courtrooms, where possible, a separate entry/exit point should be provided for prisoners away from the bench and the jury box.

Newly constructed or renovated courtrooms in jurisdictions which may wish to hold criminal and civil jury trials in the same courtroom should provide sufficient space in the well area to accommodate a 16-person jury box to handle either criminal or civil cases. (See also guideline V.4 B above.)

Every courtroom should also allow the participants and public to hear all proceedings clearly in normal conversation. Microphones should be used where necessary. (See separate Task Force report on the use of microphones in courtrooms.) The materials used in the courtroom should not produce excessive reverberation or echo. The materials and construction methods used should prevent disruption of court proceedings by outside noise. Where possible, vestibule should be provided at the public entrance to the courtroom or the doors should be soundproof. In existing courtrooms where audibility is poor, microphones should be used. Lighting should be adequate for reading on the work surfaces and for viewing exhibits without producing glare or heat.

The courtroom should have an assigned space for the viewing of exhibits. An exhibit board may be included as an integral part of the courtroom design. If portable stands are to be used, storage space should be provided in an adjacent area, but not necessarily in the courtroom. Coat closets for the public should not be located within the courtroom. Every courtroom should have a working wall clock on the opposite side of the judge's bench.

Where required, adequate electrical outlets and wiring should be provided for the use of audio tapes in evidence, for electronic case processing equipment, for security equipment and for the use of cameras in courtrooms. The basic courtroom design need not be radically changed to accommodate the use of this equipment because the advances in technology are expected to make this equipment unobtrusive.

VII.2: Non-jury, Public Courtroom. (Minimum 600 square feet): The least complicated courtroom type is the non-jury courtroom. Its basic components and requirements are:

—A minimum well area of 24 feet depth and 20 feet width
—A judge's bench
  - separate exit/entrance
  - 8′ × 7′ minimum work area raised 12″ or 18″ above floor level
  - a shielded working desk 8′ × 2′
  - ability to hear and see all court participants
  - ability to be heard and seen in all parts of the courtroom
  - a microphone
  - adequate overhead lighting
  - if local conditions require, an emergency alarm audible in the court security office
—A witness stand
  - raised 6″ or 12″ above floor level
  - visible to the bench, attorneys and court reporter
  - audible throughout the courtroom
  - a rail and shelf
  - a microphone
  - a 3′ × 5′ minimum area, including circulation space
—A court reporter station
  - adjacent to the witness stand
  - ability to observe witness, judge and attorneys
  - ability to hear every word spoken on record
  - lockable drawer for storage, if required
  - lighting similar to judge's
  - a 3′ × 4′ work space
—A clerk's station
  - location next to judge's bench
  - shielded working desk
  - lockable drawers
  - a 5′ × 6′ area
—Litigants' tables
  - two separate 6′ × 3′ tables with at least 3 seats for each table so located as to allow private conversations
  - easy access to the judge's bench and witness stand
  - ability to be heard at bench when speaking conversationally
  - lighting similar to judge's bench
  - clear view of court proceedings
—Spectator seating
  - separated by rail from well area
  - clear view of court proceedings
  - 8–12 square feet per person

VII.3: Civil Jury Trial Courtroom. (Minimum 1200 square feet): Civil courtrooms have components and requirements similar to those in the non-jury courtrooms, with the need for the following spaces as well:

—A minimum well area of 24 feet depth and 30 feet width
—Seven-person jury box, requiring
  - seating for six jurors and one alternate in one or two rows, using comfortable arm swivel chairs in 4′ × 2′ minimum space per juror
  - one step between seat rows
  - ability to clearly see and hear witnesses, judge and attorneys
  - a rail and display shelf with adequate lighting

- location of the rail at least three feet from nearest attorney table and the rail separating the spectator area and the public
- a footrest may be included
- exit/entry outside spectator area

VII.4: Criminal Jury Trial Courtroom. (Minimum 1600 square feet): Criminal courtrooms use these additional components and requirements in addition to those listed above:

—Fourteen (instead of seven) person jury box with capacity to add additional jurors
- seating for twelve jurors and two to four alternates in two or three rows, using comfortable arm swivel chairs in 4' × 2' minimum per juror

VII.5: Hearing Rooms. (Minimum 300 square feet): Hearing rooms are less formal courtrooms. They may have a judge's bench and a witness stand. Large hearing rooms for civil proceedings may range in size from 900 to 1200 square feet, depending upon the need for space for attorneys and public waiting for their cases. They may also be used for sentencing in bail or parole cases if secure access to detention areas is available to transport defendants to custody after sentencing.

VII.5a: Hearing Rooms in Family Court. (600–900 square feet): Family court hearing rooms should have a minimum of 600 square feet in area. The trend towards increased representation and opening of the proceedings to authorized observers may need an area up to 900 square feet. The hearing rooms should be so constructed as to assure the confidentiality of the proceedings both as to sound and vision. The layout and design should satisfy local procedures and degree of formality. Where feasible, separate access and circulation should be provided for persons in custody.

VII.5b: Hearing Rooms for Other Civil Proceedings. (Minimum 300 square feet): These should not be less than 300 square feet in area.

The types of courtrooms used in the New York State court system and their minimum square feet requirements are listed in Table 1 below.

VII.6: Table 1

MINIMUM AREA REQUIREMENTS
COURTROOMS

Facility	Net. Sq. Ft. Minimum Per Unit [1]
Court of Claims Courtroom	1,200
Appellate Term Courtroom	1,200
Special Term Courtroom	1,200
Civil Litigation	
Civil Trial Courtroom (7-person jury box)	1,200

Facility	Net. Sq. Ft. Minimum Per Unit [1]
Small Claims Courtroom [2]	1,200
Hearing Room (Large)	900
Hearing Room (Medium)	600
Hearing Room (Small)	300
Criminal Litigation	
Felony Trial Courtroom (14-person jury box) [3]	1,600
Misdemeanor Trial Courtroom (7-person jury box)	1,200
Arraignment Courtroom and Summons Part Courtroom	1,200
Family Court	
Hearing Room	600–900
Surrogate's Court	
Courtroom (7-person jury box)	1,200
City Court	
Courtroom (7-person jury box)	1,200

[1] These are recommended minimum net areas. Smaller courtrooms with original or unusual design may be satisfactory and adequate for local needs.

[2] Larger courtrooms may be needed where volume of cases and the number of spectators are greater.

[3] For four alternate jurors, two additional chairs could be placed on the side or in front of the jury box.

GUIDELINE VIII. COURTROOM ANCILLARY FACILITIES

VIII.1: Robing Room. (Minimum 200 square feet): If the judge's chambers are located away from the courtrooms, robing rooms should be provided adjacent thereto. Direct access from the robing room to the bench in the courtroom should be provided. The robing rooms should have a table and chairs where the judge can hold conference with attorneys and parties. A robing room should also have a restroom or private access to judges' restroom.

VIII.2: Jury Deliberation Rooms. Six-Person Jury Deliberation Room (Minimum 200 square feet)

Twelve-Person Deliberation Room (Minimum 325 square feet)

The jury deliberation room should be adjacent to courtrooms with access through non-public corridors. It should not be accessible to the public and should be so planned as to allow use of the courtroom for other matters while the jury is deliberating. It should be so constructed as to ensure confidentiality and should include:

- a coat closet
- a minimum of one restroom
- proper ventilation
- a table large enough to accommodate all jurors
- comfortable chairs
- alarm buzzer to call guard
- privacy should be assured both as to vision and sound

VIII.3: Attorney/Client Conference Room, Witness Waiting Room, Alternate Juror Waiting Room. (Minimum 100 square feet—a somewhat larger size is recommended to allow flexibility in use): An adequate number of rooms should be provided on each courtroom floor, adjacent to courtrooms and accessible from public waiting areas or from the courtrooms. The rooms should provide convenient access to a telephone. They should be located and furnished to allow them to be also used in other ways.

Note: In larger, high volume courthouses, it may be desirable or feasible to provide for attorneys' waiting rooms, public address systems in public areas, and additional conveniently located telephones. It is also desirable to take into account, to the extent feasible, the particular needs of defense and prosecution attorneys and court related agencies in busy courthouses handling criminal (or juvenile) matters.

VIII.4: Prisoner Holding Facilities Adjacent to Courtroom. (Minimum 20 square feet per person, 80 square feet per cell):

Courtrooms planned for criminal proceedings should have adjacent prisoner holding facilities planned to allow for separate holding of males and females with adequate privacy. Where feasible, the access to the courtroom should be located away from the bench and the jury box. Access to the central holding area in the courthouse or to the prisoner receiving area of the building should be by secure elevators. Adequate space for the guards should be located so as to allow easy supervision of the prisoners.

Prisoner holding facilities should be provided with a secure alternative means of egress, such as separate staircases, in case of fire. The building materials and methods of construction should comply with appropriate provisions of the New York State Commission of Correction Planning and Design Guidelines for Construction Renovation Programs. Plans for new holding areas are required to be filed with the Commission for approval prior to commencement of construction (Correction Law § 45(10)).

VIII.5: Secure Attorney/Prisoner Interview Room. (Minimum 50 square feet): Prisoner holding facilities next to courtrooms as well as any court supervised central holding facility (if any) in the courthouse should provide secure interview rooms for attorneys to confer with their clients. For busy arraignment courtrooms, large holding areas may be necessary and should provide an adequate number of secure interview rooms. The interview rooms should provide for visual surveillance by security personnel and should be so constructed that the conversation between the attorney and his client is private.

VIII.6: Public Waiting Areas Adjacent to Courtroom. (Minimum 12 square feet per person): Adequate public waiting areas should be provided adjacent to courtrooms with easy access to public restrooms and telephones. These areas should be easy to maintain and should have such ashtrays and refuse receptacles as are necessary. The courtroom number, name of presiding judge, display of case calendars and emergency exit signs should be clearly visible. Where court procedures prevent wearing of hats and coats in the courtroom, coat racks should be provided.

In Family Courts separate waiting rooms for juveniles and adults are mandatory.

VIII.7: Examination Before Trial Room. (Minimum 200 square feet): It is desirable to include an adequate number of Examination Before Trial (EBT) rooms which are accessible from the public area but which can be supervised by the court clerk. These rooms can be used for other purposes when not in use as EBT rooms.

The minimum square foot requirements of courtroom ancillary facilities are listed in Table 2 below.

VIII.8: Children's Center. (Minimum 35 square feet of primary activity space per child exclusive of administrative and ancillary spaces such as staff offices, storage space, bathrooms and hallways, with a minimum total square footage of 150 square feet): A separate, enclosed and safe environment should be provided for children who are in court in connection with matters involving them or their caregivers. The center should be of sufficient size to accommodate a variety of furniture, equipment, toys, books and materials appropriate to the age of the children served, and also should include appropriate storage for such equipment, toys, books and materials, as well as secure storage for children's personal belongings. The center should include toilet facilities and changing tables for children whenever practicable, or such facilities should be otherwise accessible in a nearby restroom.

VIII.9: Table 2.

MINIMUM AREA REQUIREMENTS
COURTROOM ANCILLARY FACILITIES

Facility	Net Sq. Ft. Minimum Per Unit
Robing Room	200
Six–Person Jury Deliberation Room	200
Twelve–Person Jury Deliberation Room	325
Attorney/Client Conference Room, Witness Waiting Room and Alternate Juror Waiting Room	100
Prisoner Holding Facilities Adjacent to Courtrooms	20/Per Person 50/Per Cell
Secure Attorney/Prisoner Interview Room	50
Public Waiting Adjacent to Courtroom	12/Per Person
Examination Before Trial Room	200
Children's Center	35 of primary activity space/ per child

GUIDELINE IX. JUDGE'S FACILITIES

IX.1: Judge's Chambers. The office occupied by the judge (200 square feet minimum) should be located close to the courtrooms or, in large courthouses, on a separate floor. In either case, judge's chambers should be private with as convenient an access to the courtroom as is reasonably possible.

The judge's chambers should have:

- a private office and working area for the judge
- a private restroom or access to a private judges' restroom
- space in the office or in an adjacent conference area
- immediate access to the secretary and any law clerk
- privacy both as to sound and vision

IX.2: Judge's Secretary's Office/Reception. (Minimum 200 square feet): Located at the public access to the chambers, this office should provide waiting space for visitors and work/storage space for the judge's secretary.

IX.3: Law Clerk's Office. (Minimum 150 square feet): The judge's law clerk should have a private office with work area and shelving for a working law library. The law clerk should have easy access to the judge.

IX.4: Central Reception Area. (200–300 square feet): In larger courthouses, if judges' chambers are grouped together on a separate floor or in a separate area, a central reception area should be provided to screen and announce the visitors. Where necessary, security personnel should be present in such an area.

IX.5: Judges' Conference Room. (Minimum 20 square feet per person): In larger courthouses, a room may be provided for the judges for conferences and use as a lunchroom. This room should provide a kitchenette and area for a refrigerator and storage.

IX.6: Law Library. In larger courthouses, a central law library should be conveniently located for use by the judges and the legal staff and, where appropriate, for shared use by such attorneys as are active in the courthouse at the time.

IX.7: Judges' Parking. If car parking provisions are possible, judges' parking should be so planned as to provide adequate security and direct access to the judges' entrance of the courthouse.

The minimum square foot requirements of judges' facilities are listed in Table 3 below.

IX.8: Table 3.

MINIMUM AREA REQUIREMENTS
JUDGE'S FACILITIES

Facility	Net Sq. Ft. Minimum Per Unit
Judge's Office	200
Secretary's Office/Reception	200
Law Clerk's Office	150
Central Reception Area	200–300
Judge's Room	20/Per Person
Law Library	As Required
Judges' Parking	As Required

GUIDELINE X. JUROR FACILITIES

X.1: Jury Assembly. (12–20 square feet per person): Courthouses with three (3) or more jury trial courtrooms should include a juror assembly area adequate in size to accommodate the number of jurors required on an average busy day. The assembly area should be comfortably furnished, with separate restrooms and adequate space designed for appropriate orientation. Separation of smokers and nonsmokers may be advisable.

—The assembly area should:
- be close to the building entrance, but separated from public areas
- have a public counter for identification and processing by court employees
- have adequate means to make announcements in all areas
- be accessible to impanelling rooms
- be accessible to courtrooms without unnecessary exposure to the public

X.2: Jury Impanelling Room—Civil Cases (Minimum 300 square feet for 7-person panel): Jury impanelling rooms should be planned to accommodate up to 20 jurors, attorneys for parties, a table to conduct voir dire, and 7 seats for jurors selected. The impanelling room can double as a waiting room.

X.3: Commissioner of Jurors (Jury Clerk's) Office: Depending upon the size of the jury operation, offices are necessary to provide adequate space and offices for the Commissioner of Jurors (or the Jury Clerk) and his staff. The following may be necessary:

- private offices
- shared clerical offices
- interview booths for juror qualification
- space for juror call-in equipment
- records storage space
- mail, copying and supply storage

These offices should be planned as close to the juror assembly areas as possible to allow better utilization of staff resources.

The minimum square foot requirements of juror facilities are listed in Table 4 below.

X.4: Table 4.

MINIMUM AREA REQUIREMENTS
JUROR FACILITIES

Facility	Net Sq. Ft. Minimum Per Unit
Assembly	12–20/Per Person
Impanelling Room	300
Commissioner of Jurors Office	As Required

GUIDELINE XI. CLERICAL FACILITIES

XI.1: Clerk's Office. The clerk's office is generally the most visible and heavily used part of the court-house. It is responsible for processing all documents, keeping records, and answering questions from the public. The clerks' offices should be located near the main entrance of the building but should, to the extent possible, have private access to judges' chambers and the courtrooms.

The clerk's office should include:

—A public area for waiting/reception (20 square feet per person—minimum 100 square feet)
  • a public counter
  • a cashier's station with adequate security
  • a table for public use
  • seats for waiting
  • copying machine (coin operated) for public use
  • display boards
  • public records access area
—General office area behind counter with no public access
  • working desks—85–95 square feet per employee
  • record files for current work
  • electronic data processing equipment, if necessary
—Private areas
  • offices for chief clerk and assistants
  • conference room (20 square feet/person)
  • microfilm room, if necessary
  • records storage area
  • mail, supply, photocopying and general supplies areas
  • vault or safe for storage of cash, important records or evidence
—Staff facilities as required by law

Table 5 below shows the minimum square foot requirements of clerks' offices by title and type of office.

XI.2: Table 5.

MINIMUM AREA REQUIREMENTS
CLERICAL FACILITIES

Facility	Type of Office	Net Sq. Ft. Minimum Per Unit
Chief Clerk	Private	200
Assistants	As Required	
Public Space and Counter	—	20 sq. ft. per person minimum 100
General Office Area	—	85–95 sq. ft. per person
Records Storage, Vault	—	As Required
Microfilm Room, Storage	—	As Required
Supplies, General Storage	—	As Required
Reproduction and Mail Room		
Staff Facilities:	—	As Required
Male/Female Restrooms	—	As Required by Law
Sick Room for Women	—	As Required by Law
Lounge/Lunch Room	—	As Required

GUIDELINE XII. SUPPORT STAFF FACILITIES

XII.1: General. Office-type space should be provided for law assistants, law stenographers, court reporters, transcribers and interpreters. In large courthouses a number of personnel of the same title performing similar functions may be housed in one area close to other related functions for ease of supervision and assignments and to provide the required degree of privacy or public accessibility to the group as a whole.

XII.2: Law Assistant's Office. (Minimum 150 square feet per office): Private offices should be provided close to the law library and to the judge's chambers. Law assistants perform legal research on pending cases and, therefore, the location of their offices should provide adequate confidentiality.

XII.3: Law Stenographer's Office. (Minimum 80 square feet per person): Law stenographers type legal memoranda prepared by law assistants on pending cases as well as decisions and rulings rendered by judges in cases before them. Location of their offices should not allow public access. A pool of law stenographers should be housed in a shared space with access to photocopy equipment and lockable short-timed storage equipment. A private office for the supervisor may be necessary.

XII.4: Court Reporter's Office. (Minimum 100 square feet per office): Court reporters should have the use of offices in which to transcribe testimony.

In locations where electronic recording equipment is used, secure storage space for equipment, and tapes and space for transcribers should be provided.

XII.5: Transcriber's Office. (Minimum 60 square feet per person): Semi-private offices using sound-absorbent cubicles or shared offices should be provided to transcribers close to the court reporters' offices and tape/equipment storage room. Soundproofing may be necessary.

XII.6: Interpreter's Office. (Minimum 60 square feet per person): Should the court employ full-time interpreters they should be provided with a designated waiting station.

The minimum area requirements for support staff facilities are listed in Table 6 below.

XII.7:   Table 6.

MINIMUM AREA REQUIREMENTS

SUPPORT STAFF FACILITIES

Facility	Type of Office	Net Sq. Ft. Minimum Per Unit
Law Assistant's Office	Private	150
Law Stenographer's Office	Shared	80
Court Reporter's Office	Shared	100
Transcriber's Office	Shared	60
Interpreter's Station	Shared	As Required

GUIDELINE XIII. SECURITY PERSONNEL FACILITIES

XIII.1:   Security Station With First-Aid Facilities. (Minimum 160 square feet): Security stations should be located at strategic locations in the courthouse to complement the courthouse security system composed of electronic equipment, if any, and the security personnel. A security station at the main entrance should allow screening of the persons entering the courthouse. A security control station should also be established as a communication center to act in emergencies. The office of the person in charge of security may act as the control station or the command station.

XIII.2:   Security Chief's Office. (Minimum 120 square feet): The person in charge of security should have a private office which acts as a communications center and a command/control station. Any audio/visual security system should be connected to this station and should be able to be activated from this station in case of emergencies. The security personnel may be required to report here for duty. This office should have a safe for deposit of firearms or confiscated weapons.

XIII.3:   Security Personnel Lockers. (12 square feet per person): Where a courthouse utilizes uniformed security personnel, secure separate locker spaces should be provided. This facility can be located in secondary spaces (basement or windowless spaces) in the building.

The minimum area requirement of security personnel facilities are listed in Table 7 below.

XIII.4:   Table 7.

MINIMUM AREA REQUIREMENTS

SECURITY PERSONNEL FACILITIES

Facility	Type of Office	Net Sq. Ft. Minimum Per Unit
Security Station with first-aid facilities		160
Security Chief's Office	Private	120
Uniformed Security Personnel Lockers	Secondary Space	12/Per Locker

GUIDELINE XIV. FACILITIES FOR THE PUBLIC

XIV.1:   Public Waiting and Information Spaces. The main entrance lobby and areas outside the courtrooms should be adequate for public waiting. These spaces should also prominently display courthouse directory, directional signs, and court calendars. Adequate public pay telephones should be placed in this area. Access doors to private areas should be clearly marked as private. Unmarked doors and panels should be kept locked. Drinking water fountains should be located in these areas.

XIV.2:   Public Restrooms—Male/Female. (As per building code): Restrooms for public use should be located close to public waiting areas and clearly marked.

XIV.3:   Press Room. (120 square feet): A room may be set aside for use by media representatives when assigned to the courthouse. Public pay telephones should be located in or close to this room.

XIV.4:   Table 8.

MINIMUM AREA REQUIREMENTS

FACILITIES FOR THE PUBLIC

Facility	Net Sq. Ft. Minimum Per Unit
Public Waiting	12/Per Person
Information Booth	As Required
Male/Female Restrooms	As Per Building Code
Press Room	120

XIV.5:   Eating Facilities. Where other alternatives are not readily accessible, consideration should be given to providing eating facilities for court employees, attorneys, jury members or the public.

§ 34.1.   Maintenance and Operation Standards for Court Facilities

(a) The Chief Administrator of the Courts shall require from each political subdivision seeking reimbursement of (i) maintenance and operations costs pursuant to § 54–j(2) of the State Finance Law or (ii) workfare administration and supervision expenses pursuant to § 54–j(2–a) of such Law a certification that such political subdivision is in compliance with the Maintenance and Operations Standards set forth below. Failure to comply with such Standards may result in the loss of reimbursement for maintenance and operation costs. The Chief Administrator also shall require from each political subdivision seeking reimbursement of workfare administration and supervision expenses (i) a certification that it has complied with the provisions of § 54–j(2–a)(d) of the State Finance Law and (ii) itemizations of its workfare administration and supervision expenses for the

12–month period concluding September 30, 1994, and for the period for which reimbursement is sought.

(b) A political subdivision may request exemption from one or more of the cleaning frequency schedules or maintenance routines of the Maintenance and Operation Standards. Such request shall be made in writing to the Chief Administrator and may be granted for good cause shown. Exemptions shall be granted for a period of up to two years and may be renewed, upon written request, in the discretion of the Chief Administrator.

(c) **Definitions.** For the purpose of this part, the terms below have the following meanings:

(1) Operation consists of those day-to-day services and activities which are necessary to keep the physical plant open and in a usable condition.

(2) Maintenance includes those services, activities and procedures which are concerned with preserving, protecting and keeping buildings, grounds and equipment in a satisfactory [1] of repair. Included in these activities are some repairs, replacements, renovations and adjustments. Existing court facilities and those which are currently being constructed will require adequate maintenance if they are to function satisfactorily.

(3) Preventive maintenance is a planned schedule for accomplishing required maintenance operations as categorized by the following needs:

(4) Recurring—tasks and jobs which should be performed one or more times each year and should be on a scheduled basis, e.g., floor and furniture care, some types of lawn and grounds maintenance and specialized care of mechanical and heating equipment.

(5) Periodic—tasks and jobs which may need attention less frequently than recurring maintenance. Generally they include repair and renovation items which follow cycles of from 3 to 5 years, such as roof repair; repair of window shades, blinds and drapes; weather proofing windows, doors and walls and repairing heating plants.

(6) Replacement—occurs when circumstances create a need for certain types of maintenance at inopportune times, i.e. plumbing leaks.

(7) Repair—improvement tasks that restore broken items by replacing parts or by mending.

(8) Leased Space—space which is rented in a privately owned building for use by the court or a court agency.

(9) Utilities—services such as water, sewer, gas and electricity which are required to operate a building.

(10) Hard and Resilient Flooring—all hard flooring such as concrete, ceramic, terrazzo, brick and marble requires stripping and sealing. All resilient flooring such as vinyl asbestos tile, linoleum, etc., requires several coats of floor finish.

(11) High Cleaning—space throughout the facility 70 inches or more from the floor. Includes but is not limited to walls, ceiling area adjacent to ventilating and air conditioning outlets, transoms, clocks, moldings around ceilings, tops of partitions, overhead pipes, pictures, plaques, wall or ceiling diffusers, file cases, bookcases, lockers, etc.

(12) Landscape and Grounds Maintenance—includes: mowing lawns, power raking, trimming of and around trees, shrubs, fences, monuments, flag poles, walls, etc., fertilizing, mulching, watering, raking leaves, weed, pest and disease control.

(13) Pest Control—is defined as those measures which are necessary to suppress the population of arachnids, crawling and flying insects, rats, mice and/or any other species which become a pest within or around the facilities covered by this solicitation/contract.

(14) Facilities Management—the total operational responsibility for a facility or group of facilities that includes but is not limited to: maintenance and operations of systems, cleaning, landscape maintenance, trash/debris removal, pest control, and structural and maintenance repairs.

(15) Workfare administration and supervision expenses include (i) the salary and fringe benefit costs to a political subdivision for each person it employs whose duties constitute the supervision of persons who clean and maintain court facilities pursuant to a workfare program provided through the Department of Social Services; and (ii) any other reasonable and necessary administrative costs for the implementation of such a workfare program that may be incurred by a bureau, division or department of a political subdivision that is directly responsible for the maintenance and operation of court facilities.

(d) (See Appendix for Section I–Frequency Cleaning Schedules)

(e) Section II—Maintenance Standards

I SCOPE OF INSPECTION

Facility personnel should perform a complete inspection at least quarterly covering all areas of occupied and unoccupied court space (records storage areas), public areas, grounds, utility systems, equipment and materials storage space.

The primary purpose of the quarterly inspection is to evaluate the physical condition of the facilities and the equipment in order to gain information to establish a progressive maintenance program.

Correction of deficiencies found in the course of the inspection should be limited to emergency and minor items.

[1] So in original.

II SCHEDULING

The inspection should be scheduled to ensure that each facility will be observed at the most appropriate season, e.g., inspection of lawns and plantings during the growing season and the heating plant just before the heating season.

The structure's interior and envelope can be inspected year round, except for roofs when there is snow. Stagger inspection of the structure throughout the year so that correction of found deficiencies will not fall too far behind inspections.

Inspections of the structure's interior should be completed as far as practicable in one visit.

Mechanical areas and related equipment (pumps, refrigerator units, motors, compressors, heating and air conditioning units) should be inspected within reasonable periods of time.

Inspection of items involving health and safety should not be limited to a quarterly basis, but should be made as frequently as necessary to avoid danger to the public and court personnel.

III EXTERIOR

A. Grounds

The entire perimeter of a court facility area should be surveyed systematically paying particular attention to the following: (See Section I—Frequency Cleaning Schedules, Table T–1).

1. Lawns (turf areas)

Establish a formal program of lawn care using the standards of the New York State Department of Parks. Look for density of grass; relative coverage desirable to undesirable growth; bare spots; adequacy of drainage; degree and quality of maintenance, e.g., mowing, watering and fertilizing.

2. Plants (trees, shrubs, hedges and vines)

Look for character of growth; shape and structure; injurious disease and insect infestation; degree and quality of maintenance, e.g. pruning.

3. Paved areas (streets, roads, drives, walks, sitting areas, cut curbs, gutters and traffic markings)

Look for cleanliness; failures in the surface and base; settlement; adequacy of drainage facilities; degree and quality of maintenance and condition of expansion joints.

4. Yard drainage (catch basins, inlets, ditches, pipe lines and swales)

Look for flat undrainable or eroded areas; stoppage by rubbish and silt; adequacy as to capacity to meet peak demand; degree and quality of maintenance.

5. Grounds appurtenances (benches, posts, fences, guard rails, railings, lighting, retaining walls, steps, flag poles, street signs, handicap signage and related equipment)

Look for worn out, damaged, or missing parts, lack of paint or other surface covering; degree and quality of maintenance and services; corrosion at the ground line of metal posts; rotting of wood members; jagged or sharp edges of posts; branches and twigs protruding over walked areas and hanging at eye level or other hazardous conditions.

B. Snow removal

1. Vehicles and related equipment should be in good mechanical condition, winterized and maintained in accordance with manufacturer's specifications.

2. Procedures should be developed and standardized to meet climatic conditions and the court facility's needs.

IV BUILDINGS

A. Structures

Maintain a visual inspection of the buildings for evidence of cracks, joint sealant failure, breaks, deterioration, settling, etc. Any indication of any structural problem should be brought to the attention of the municipality immediately. The exterior appearance of structures must be maintained at levels which are indicative of good building management practices.

For garage buildings and parking areas see Sec. I, Frequency Cleaning Schedules T–18.

B. Roofs

The maintenance program should be implemented by semi-annual inspections of all roofs.

C. Hardware (Exterior Doors)

Hardware, door-checks and other operating mechanisms of exterior doors should be inspected in the spring and fall. Changes in temperature necessitate adjustment of door checks. Lubrication of components should be carried out on a regular basis. Automatic doors require special services which should be handled by the manufacturer's maintenance organization.

D. Interior of Facility

1. Painting and decorating

Examine walls, ceilings, window sashes, trim, doors, closets and other painted surfaces for flaking, peeling, alligatoring, mold markings, wear, discoloration and dirt. Note any cracking, flaking or other damage in plaster or sheetrock covering of walls and ceilings. Inspect windows and door frames for cracking or missing putty and caulking, tightness and drying. Check doors and windows for proper operation.

The right combination of colors can build efficiency in an office as color can complement lighting, thereby relaxing tensions, improving morale and decreasing absenteeism. Colors should not be distracting or disturbing, as this diverts attention from work. Light pastel colors are generally recommended for interior wall surfaces, but it is preferable to use warm colors for rooms which receive little or no sunlight.

2. Floors

Look at floors noting scars, worn areas, broken or loose tile, torn or worn carpet, condition of linoleum; need to vacuum, shampoo, clean and wax; indentation by furniture, evidence of water under floor covering and condition of baseboards or cove molding.

3. Window shades, blinds, draperies

Examine for damaged and worn shades, cords and tapes; defective springs or mechanisms; broken or missing parts; torn, dirty or missing drapes.

4. Space heating equipment

If heating is by means of radiators or convectors, check for cleanliness and freedom from lint and dust; see that valves and traps are operative and do not leak water and that convector covers are properly anchored.

5. Plumbing fixtures & related hardware

Look for any breakage or chipping; easy and complete closing of faucets leakage; proper level of filling in water closet tanks or time flush valves on commodes and urinals; loose, cracked or broken toilet seats.

6. Electrical wiring

Inspect fuses/circuit breakers to see that they have not been tampered with and are not oversize or overloaded. Check all ceiling lights, switches and outlets for broken cover plates, loose connections, missing screws, etc. Inspect occupant-owned appliances and lamps for any frayed cords, broken plugs, or other potentially hazardous elements, i.e., cords running under carpets or across floor surface.

7. Hardware (interior doors)

Loose and missing lock and passage sets, hinges, panic bar hardware, door silencers, stops are the most overlooked items. The improper chocking open of doors, removal of pins, stops, silencers, screws and strike plates can cause safety hazards and failure of hardware. Loose or missing hardware should be reported immediately.

V   ELEVATORS AND ESCALATORS

A. Elevators

Elevator inspection and maintenance requires the services of highly-trained mechanics; control systems of the new automatic elevators require the services of electronic technicians. The condition of floors and sills at landing should be given particular attention, with shafts and pits to be inspected monthly, by the maintenance contractor or a responsible employee. Accumulation of lint on rails, guides or car frame should be removed at once since it constitutes a fire hazard. The same concerns hold for the accumulation of debris in the pits and behind hoistway doors. All elevator cars should be checked periodically to verify that required inspection certificates are posted and up to date.

B. Escalators

Escalators should be checked at the beginning of each day to determine that travel directions are correct and that no hazardous conditions exist. Particular attention should be given to the removable floor panels over the machinery compartments to be sure that no tripping hazards exist.

Escalators should be checked and cleaned each day with particular attention given to handrails, comb-plates, treads and risers.

A record of accidents which occur on escalators should be maintained. These records should contain all available details pertaining to possible cause and brought to the attention of the escalator manufacturer on a regular basis. A review of accident records may reveal a pattern indicating a need for modification in design or operations.

VI   UTILITY SYSTEMS

Air distribution systems must be kept as clean as possible in order to maintain safety and efficiency of operation. Special attention should be given as prescribed below to parts of these systems in order to fulfill that purpose.

A. Inspection and Cleaning of Ducts

Inspection of the ducts should be made in the spring and fall. Cooling and heating coils should be cleaned.

B. Fresh Air Intake

The intakes should be checked at time of duct inspection. Accumulated debris should be removed immediately.

C. Filters

Filters should be inspected, replaced or cleaned in accordance with manufacturers recommendations.

The controls for the HVAC, heating and cooling systems should be inspected to ensure proper operation at the beginning of the heating and cooling seasons.

The controls for the HVAC, heating and cooling systems should be calibrated by a qualified professional yearly.

Repairs and replacement of all controls should be done by qualified technical staff.

D. Fire Doors and Dampers

These should be examined at a minimum of once a year.

E. Maintenance of Machine Rooms

Keep machine and equipment rooms painted, clean and free of foreign objects.

F. Power Distribution–Electrical Systems

All electrical installations must be made in compliance with the National Electrical Code or state and local codes, where applicable.

G. Fans and Fan Motors

Fans and fan motors should be inspected at least quarterly and cleaned and lubricated in accordance with the manufacturer's instructions.

H. Lighting Maintenance

Lamps (fluorescent and incandescent) should be cleaned and replaced on a regular basis.

Regular periodic inspections should be carried out to ascertain if any defective or unsafe conditions exist; including, special attention to exterior illumination of buildings, entrance ways, walks and parking areas.

Particular attention should be given to utilizing energy saving fixtures and relamping products.

I. Emergency Lighting and Power System

The emergency lighting and power system is installed to prevent panic and provide maintenance or security in the event of conventional power failure. Emergency systems must be completely dependable by frequent testing.

J. Fire Protection

Scheduled periodic inspections must be made in order to test fire protection equipment. The frequency of these inspections will generally be regulated by either local fire regulations or codes or the requirements of the National Fire Protection and American Insurance Association, whichever is more stringent.

Visual inspection of standpipes, hoses, smoke detectors, sprinkler systems, fire extinguishers and other equipment should be made to assure that they are being maintained, serviced and properly recorded on a timely basis.

Potential or actual fire hazards should be reported as soon as they are discovered.

VII MAINTENANCE CONTRACTS

A. Government Owned Property

Certain equipment maintenance and building services are furnished to the court by private vendors who have contracts with the municipality. It is the responsibility of the municipality to see that prearranged schedules for performance of these services are properly observed and that all work is satisfactorily completed with as little interruption to court processes as possible.

Special attention should be given to the careful wording of the performance specifications, the areas of responsibility and the required examination frequency schedule. The contractor should specify in the contract the type of staffing to be used for the work as well as the extent and method of their supervision. A

schedule of costs on a unit basis for any additional services which may be required should be furnished by the contractor. The quality of the materials and equipment to be used on the work should be specified. The cost, method of payment and notice of termination of the agreement should be precisely defined.

Localities should have contract compliance and documentation procedures in place to monitor the level of performance, the quality of achievements, safety and other relevant factors.

B. Leased Space—Privately Owned Property

The following should be incorporated into leases providing space to the Unified Court System:

1. The custodial cleaning frequency standards as established by the Unified Court System should appear in their entirety.

2. The method of performing the tasks should be described carefully.

3. The nature of the chemicals and materials to be used or not used should be specified.

4. The nature of the staff should be controlled due to the sensitivity and security factors of the court system, i.e.;

a. The contractor shall submit a master employee roster to the local court administrator. If there are any changes in the roster, the contractor will be responsible to submit an up-dated roster immediately.

b. Each and every employee of the contractor will be required to prominently display an identification badge at all times while on court premises.

c. The local court administrator has the right to reject and bar from the facility any employee hired by the contractor.

d. A full time supervisor will be at the facility during the hours custodial work is being performed.

5. The provider is to schedule the starting time of air conditioning and heating equipment to maintain a proper working and energy efficient environment.

6. In the event any repair is found to be necessary, the building manager is to apprise the court in writing. The work should be progressed in stages and in such manner as to not interfere with the functioning of the courts and with the utmost regard for the safety and convenience of its personnel and the general public.

7. Replacement of all burned out lamps and starters shall be made promptly on call from the court.

8. Repairs should be completed within a specified period of time.

C. Contractor—Failure to Perform

A penalty clause for the contractor's failure to perform the work should be specific as to the court's rights, e.g.

The contractor agrees that in the event any of the services provided for under the terms of this contract, should in any way be omitted or unsatisfactorily performed by the contractor and/or his employees, the court shall so notify the municipality and the contractor in writing of the deficient services for immediate correction. In the event the contractor does not correct the deficient services after receipt of the written notice to correct, the Office of Court Administration (OCA) shall request that the municipality deduct a percentage, based on the work not performed or performed unsatisfactorily as determined by the provider, from the voucher for their services rendered for that contract period. If the contractor continues to omit contracted services and/or performs unsatisfactorily, then the court shall notify the municipality and the contractor to correct the neglected or deficient services within five (5) days from the date of the notice. Should the contractor fail to correct the deficient services, OCA will then arrange with the municipality for the work to be done by another contractor and the cost of such work shall be deducted from any monies due or may become due to the contractor.

VIII UTILITIES STANDARDS

The following standards are based on existing energy conservation regulations established by federal, state and local agencies.

Hot water temperature control devices should be set to achieve results not to exceed the greater of the following: 105 degrees F. or the lowest setting on the control device.

The following general illumination levels should be maintained:

Office	50 foot candles
Corridors	15 foot candles
Storage Areas	10 foot candles
Prolonged or visually difficult tasks	75 foot candles

In specific areas such as court rooms and well areas a higher illumination level is desirable.

A standard air temperature of 78 degrees F. in the summer and 68 degrees F. but not to exceed 75 degrees F. in the winter should be the average room temperatures.

IX OTHER MAINTENANCE CONSIDERATIONS

A. Water

Water should be potable for drinking purposes and pure from chemical or metallic elements that are injurious to human health, equipment and plumbing system.

Where practicable, localities should install separate water meters for court facilities which will allow for cost identification and establishment of programs for conservation of water.

B. Electricity

Lighting fixtures and ceilings should be clean to allow for maximum light reflection.

Consideration should be given to providing separate independent light switches for certain rooms and areas which may result in large electrical savings.

A study should be conducted to evaluate the efficiency of older fixtures.

Maximum use should be made of natural light to help reduce the need for additional electrical illumination. Windows should be regularly cleaned to allow for maximum penetration of natural light to save electrical energy.

Localities should consider using the Power Authority of the State of New York (PASNY) which offers reduced rates to local government.

C. Heating and Air Conditioning—Climate Control

Heating and air conditioning is an important element in the proper operation of a building by providing a reasonable comfort level of environment to users. In addition to electricity, some facilities use gas or oil for heating which also represents a major cost factor in the operation of facilities.

Energy surveys of buildings should be conducted to identify loss of heated or cooled air and to determine corrective actions. Old leaking windows and doors, broken panes, loose caulking, etc. should be repaired.

Municipalities should consider the possibility of installing separate meters or oil tanks to enable identification of costs related only to court facilities.

APPENDIX FOR RULE 34.1—SECTION I—FREQUENCY CLEANING SCHEDULES

Operation Standards—Cleaning tasks and frequency schedules

The abbreviations for the frequency standards are:

D	=	daily
D/2	=	twice daily
W	=	weekly
M/2	=	twice monthly
M	=	monthly
Q	=	quarterly
S/A	=	semi-annually
A	=	annually
A/R	=	as required/requested

1. GROUNDS & BUILDINGS ENTRIES

FREQUENCY SCHEDULE

	D/2	D	W	M/2	M	Q	S/A	A	A/R
Police Area (B)	X								
Clean Lobby Entry Glass			X						
Clean Bright Work Metal						X			
Sweep Outside Entryways	X								
Sweep Steps	X								
Sweep Landings	X								
Empty Litter Containers	X								
Check/Clean Catchbasins & Drains		X							
Check/Replace Burned Out Lights		X							
Check/Replace Missing Signage		X							
Check/Report On Insect/Rodent Control		X							
Check/Report Erosion			X						
Check/Report Quality of Maintenance in Landscaped Areas			X						
Check/Report Deteriorated Surfaces			X						
Maintain Snow Free Walks/Entryways									X
Maintain Clear Passage for Public									X
Maintain Clear Passage for Prisoners									X
Hose & Scrub Down Exterior Entry Areas					X				
Report Any Damage or Hazards (A)		X							
* Painting									X
** Graffiti									X

Turn Off Lights When Appropriate

(A) Clean and Rectify Problem
(B) Free of discarded materials and trash

 * Painting—Touch Up As Required; Cycle Painting ANNUALLY, e.g. Benches, Metal Doors, Frames, Traffic Markings, Etcetera
** Graffiti—To Be Removed Without Delay

2. MAIN/ENTRANCE/LOBBIES

Public Waiting Area(s)
Alcoves—Candy Stand
Telephone Area
Elevator Lobbies

FREQUENCY SCHEDULE

	D/2	D	W	M/2	M	Q	S/A	A	A/R
Unlock and Lock Areas		X							
Check & Close Windows		X							
Check & Replace Missing Signage		X							
Check & Replace Burned Out Lights		X							
Remove Cobwebs			X						
Police Area (B)	X								
Empty & Clean Waste Containers	X								
Empty & Clean Ash Receivers	X								
* Dust High Ceiling & Walls								X	
* Dust Light Fixtures								X	
* Dust Walls & Decorations								X	
* Dust/Clean & Arrange Furniture								X	
* Dust Window Sills, Doors & Frames			X						
* Dust & Adjust Window Blinds/Shades			X						
* Dust Radiators & Covers			X						
* Dust Mop/Sweep Floors		X							
Clean Floors & Remove Stains		X							
Spray Buff Floors (1)			X						
Strip & Refinish Floors								X	
Spot Clean Walls & Partitions			X						
Spot Clean Glass, Doors & Frames			X						
Clean/Polish Metal (Brass, etc.)					X				
Clean/Polish & Arrange Furniture							X		
Clean & Sanitize Drinking Fountains	X								
Clean Door Saddles			X						
Clean Floor Mats/Runners		X							
Repair/Replace Flooring									X
Wash/Clean & Adjust Blinds/Shades							X		
Wash Walls & Partitions							X		
Wash Glass, Doors & Frames							X		
Wash Windows, Exterior/Interior							X		
Disassemble, Clean & Reassemble Light Fixtures								X	
Report Any Damage or Hazards (A)		X							
** Painting									X
*** Graffiti									X

Turn Off Lights When Appropriate

(A)   Clean and Rectify Problem
(B)   Free of Discarded Materials and Trash

(1)   Includes: Sweep, Damp Mop, Spray Buff and Dry Mop
  * Dust—Utilize Treated Cloths/Mops
 ** Painting—Touch Up As Required; Cycle Painting Within THREE YEARS
*** Graffiti—To Be Removed Without Delay

3. CIRCULATION PUBLIC SPACE

Hallways—Passageways
Corridors—Vestibules
Alcove—Lobbies

FREQUENCY SCHEDULE

	D/2	D	W	M/2	M	Q	S/A	A	A/R
Check & Close Windows		X							
Check & Replace Missing Signage		X							
Check & Replace Burned Out Lights		X							
Remove Cobwebs			X						
Police Area(s) (B)		X							
Empty & Clean Waste Containers		X							
Empty & Clean Ash Receivers		X							
* Dust High Ceiling & Walls							X		
* Dust Light Fixtures							X		
* Dust Walls, Decorations & Cabinets							X		
* Dust/Clean & Arrange Furniture							X		
* Dust Window Sills, Doors & Frames			X						
* Dust & Adjust Window Blinds/Shades			X						
* Dust Radiators & Covers			X						
* Dust Mop/Sweep Floors		X							
Clean Floors & Remove Stains		X							
Spray Buff Floors (1)			X						
Strip & Refinish Floors								X	
Spot Clean Walls & Partitions			X						
Spot Clean Glass, Doors & Frames			X						
Clean/Polish (Brass, etc.)		X							
Clean/Polish & Arrange Furniture					X				
Clean/Sanitize Drinking Fountains		X							
Clean Door Saddles			X						
Clean Floor Mats/Runners		X							
Repair/Replace Flooring									X
Wash/Clean & Adjust Blinds/Shades								X	
Wash Walls & Partitions								X	
Wash Glass, Doors & Frames							X		
Wash Windows, Exterior/Interior							X		
Disassemble, Clean & Reassemble Light Fixtures								X	
Report Any Damage or Hazards (A)		X							
** Painting									X
*** Graffiti									X

Turn Off Lights When Appropriate

(A)   Clean and Rectify Problem
(B)   Free of Discarded Materials and Trash

(1)   Includes: Sweep, Damp Mop, Spray Buff and Dry Mop

  * Dust—Utilize Treated Cloths/Mops
 ** Painting—Touch Up As Required, Cycle Painting THREE TO FIVE YEARS
*** Graffiti—To Be Removed Without Delay

4. STAIRS AND LANDINGS

FREQUENCY SCHEDULE

	D/2	D	W	M/2	M	Q	S/A	A	A/R
Check & Close Windows		X							
Check & Report Inoperative Hardware		X							
Check & Replace Burned Out Lights		X							
Check Missing/Broken Fire Apparatus		X							
Check & Report Inoperative Doors		X							
Check & Report Missing Signage		X							
Police Area (B)		X							
* Dust Windows, Frames & Ledges				X					
* Dust Doors, Frames & Handrails				X					
* Dust Fire Apparatus & Vents				X					
* Dust Light Fixtures							X		
Sweep Landings, Steps & Risers			X						
Damp Wipe Surfaces to Door Height					X				
Wash Windows Exterior/Interior							X		
Mop Landings, Steps and Risers				X					
Wash & Dry all Metal Surfaces							X		
Report Missing/Broken Fire Apparatus	X								
Report Any Damage or Hazards (A)	X								
** Painting									X
*** Graffiti									X

(A)   Clean and Rectify Problem
(B)   Free of Discarded Materials and Trash

  * Dust—Utilize Treated Cloths/Mops
 ** Painting—Touch Up As Required; Cycle Painting FIVE TO SEVEN YEARS Except Where Stairways Are Used For General Circulation. ANNUAL Painting May Be Necessary
*** Graffiti—To Be Removed Without Delay

5. ELEVATORS/ESCALATORS (1)

FREQUENCY SCHEDULE

	D/2	D	W	M/2	M	Q	S/A	A	A/R
Check & Replace Missing Signage		X							
Check & Replace Burned Out Lights		X							
Check Current Certificate Operation									X
Check Controls Access Door		X							
Check Indicator Lamps		X							
Check & Report Any Malfunction		X							
Check Emergency Stop & Alarm Operation			X						
Police Elevator Cab & Area (B)					X				
* Dust Light Fixtures					X				
* Dust Ventilation Ducts/Fan Grills					X				
* Dust Elevator Cab & Doors		X							
* Dust Mop Floor		X							
* Spot Clean Elevator Cab & Doors		X							
Clean Floor		X							
Clean, Wax, Polish Panels & Walls					X				
Clean Door Tracks		X							
Wipe, Clean Elevator Hatch Doors									X
Buff Finish Floor			X						
Vacuum/Carpet and Spot Clean		X							
Shampoo Carpet									X
Report Any Damage or Hazards (A)	X								
** Painting									X
*** Graffiti									X

(A) Clean and Rectify Problem
(B) Free of Discarded Materials and Trash

(1) Clean Exposed Surfaces of Treads, Risers and Landings. Polish Bright Metal Surfaces Daily

   * Dust—Utilize Treated Cloths/Mops
  ** Paint—Hatchway Doors As Required; THREE TO FIVE YEARS Cycle
*** Graffiti—To Be Removed Without Delay

6. PUBLIC TOILETS

Jury Assembly Room Toilets
Jurors/Public
Toilets—Washrooms
Lavatories—Powder Rooms

FREQUENCY SCHEDULE

	D/2	D	W	M/2	M	Q	S/A	A	A/R
Lock/Unlock Area		X							
Check & Close Windows		X							
Check & Replace Missing Signage		X							
Check & Replace Burned Out Lights		X							
Remove Cobwebs					X				
Police Area (B)	X								
Empty Waste Containers	X								
* Dust Spot Clean Ceilings					X				
Clean Walls and Disinfect			X						
Clean Floors		X							
Clean Mirrors		X							
Clean Sinks, Urinals & Water Closets		X							
Clean Tile Walls			X						
Clean Toilet Stalls/Partitions			X						
Clean & Shine Chrome		X							
Clean Light Fixtures					X				
Clean Exhaust Vents					X				
Clean Painted Doors & Frames			X						
Resupply Paper, Soap & Hygiene Products	X								
Wash Windows Exterior/Interior							X		
Disassemble, Clean & Reassemble Light Fixtures								X	
Report Any Damage or Hazards (A)	X								
** Painting									X
*** Graffiti									X

REPORT DRIPPING/RUNNING WATER

(A)   Clean and Rectify Problem
(B)   Free of Discarded Materials and Trash

  * Dust—Utilize Treated Cloths/Mops
 ** Paint—Touch Up As Required; Cycle Painting Annually
*** Graffiti—To Be Removed Without Delay

7. EMPLOYEE TOILETS

Toilets—Washrooms
Lavatories—Powder Rooms

FREQUENCY SCHEDULE

	D/2	D	W	M/2	M	Q	S/A	A	A/R
Lock/Unlock Area		X							
Check & Close Windows		X							
Check & Replace Missing Signage		X							
Check & Replace Burned Out Lights		X							
Remove Cobwebs					X				
Police Area (B)		X							
Empty Waste Containers	X								
* Dust & Spot Clean Ceilings					X				
Clean Walls and Disinfect			X						
Clean Floors		X							
Clean Mirrors		X							
Clean Sinks, Urinals & Water Closets		X							
Clean Tile Walls			X						
Clean Toilet Stalls/Partitions			X						
Clean & Shine Chrome		X							
Clean Light Fixtures					X				
Clean Exhaust Vents					X				
Clean Painted Doors & Frames			X						
Resupply Paper, Soap & Hygiene Products	X								
Wash Windows Exterior/Interior							X		
Disassemble, Clean & Reassemble Light Fixtures								X	
Report Any Damage or Hazards (A)	X								
** Painting									X
*** Graffiti									X

REPORT DRIPPING/RUNNING WATER

(A)   Clean and Rectify Problem
(B)   Free of Discarded Materials and Trash

　*Dust—Utilize Treated Cloths/Mops
 ** Paint—Touch Up As Required; Cycle Painting Within THREE YEARS
*** Graffiti—To Be Removed Without Delay

8. PRIVATE TOILETS

Jury Deliberation Room Toilet
Judges—Washrooms
Lavatories—Powder Rooms

FREQUENCY SCHEDULE

	D/2	D	W	M/2	M	Q	S/A	A	A/R
Lock & Unlock Area		X							
Check & Close Windows		X							
Check & Replace Burned Out Lights		X							
Police Area (B)		X							
Empty Waste Containers		X							
* Dust & Spot Clean Ceilings					X				
Clean Walls and Disinfect			X						
Clean Floors		X							
Clean Sink & Fixture		X							
Clean Mirror		X							
Clean Tile Walls			X						
Clean & Shine Chrome		X							
Clean Light Fixtures				X					
Clean Exhaust Vents				X					
Resupply Paper & Soap Products		X							
Wash Window Exterior/Interior						X			
Disassemble, Clean & Reassemble Light Fixtures							X		
Report Any Damage or Hazards (A)		X							
** Painting									X
*** Graffiti									X

REPORT DRIPPING/RUNNING WATER

(A)   Clean and Rectify Problem
(B)   Free of Discarded Materials and Trash

    * Dust—Utilize Treated Cloths/Mops
   ** Painting—Touch Up As Required; Cycle Painting Within THREE YEARS
*** Graffiti—To Be Removed Without Delay

9. OFFICE I

Interpreters,
Clerks, Transcribers,
Court Reporters, Security
Office, File/Storage

FREQUENCY SCHEDULE

	D/2	D	W	M/2	M	Q	S/A	A	A/R
Unlock and Lock Areas		X							
Check & Close Windows		X							
Check & Replace Missing Signage		X							
Check & Replace Burned Out Lights		X							
Remove Cobwebs					X				
Empty & Clean Waste Containers		X							
Empty & Clean Ash Receivers		X							
* Dust High Ceiling & Walls							X		
* Dust Light Fixtures							X		
* Dust Walls, Decorations & Cabinets						X			
* Dust/Clean & Arrange Furniture							X		
* Dust Window Sills, Doors & Frames			X						
* Dust & Adjust Window Blinds/Shades			X						
* Dust Radiators & Covers			X						
* Dust Mop/Sweep Floors		X							
Spray Buff Floors (1)					X				
Strip & Refinish Floors							X		
Spot Clean Walls & Partitions					X				
Spot Clean Glass, Doors & Frames			X						
Clean/Polish & Arrange Furniture							X		
Clean Door Saddles			X						
Repair/Replace Flooring									X
Wash/Clean & Adjust Blinds/Shades								X	
Wash Walls & Partitions								X	
Wash Glass, Doors & Frames							X		
Wash Windows, Exterior/Interior							X		
Disassemble, Clean & Reassemble Light Fixtures								X	
Report Any Damage or Hazards (A)		X							
** Painting									X
*** Graffiti									X

Turn Off Lights When Appropriate

(1) Includes: Sweep, Damp Mop, Spray Buff and Dry Mop
(A) Clean and Rectify Problem
  * Dust—Utilize Treated Cloths/Mops
 ** Painting—Touch Up As Required; Cycle Painting Within THREE/FIVE YEARS
*** Graffiti—To Be Removed Without Delay

10. OFFICE II

Court Clerks,
Examination Before Trial,
Law Assistants, Law Stenographers

FREQUENCY SCHEDULE

	D/2	D	W	M/2	M	Q	S/A	A	A/R
Unlock and Lock Areas		X							
Check & Close Windows		X							
Check & Replace Missing Signage		X							
Check & Replace Burned Out Lights		X							
Remove Cobwebs					X				
Empty & Clean Waste Containers		X							
Empty & Clean Ash Receivers		X							
* Dust High Ceiling & Walls							X		
* Dust Light Fixtures							X		
* Dust Walls, Decorations & Cabinets				X					
* Dust/Clean & Arrange Furniture							X		
* Dust Window Sills, Doors & Frames			X						
* Dust & Adjust Window Blinds/Shades			X						
* Dust Radiators & Covers			X						
* Dust Shelving & Books			X						
* Dust Woodwork & Panels			X						
Spot Clean Walls & Partitions					X				
Spot Clean Glass, Doors & Frames			X						
Spot Clean Upholstered Furniture									X
Spot Clean Rugs/Carpets									X
Clean/Polish & Arrange Furniture							X		
Clean/Polish Woodwork & Panels								X	
Clean Door Saddles			X						
Vacuum Carpet/Rugs			X						
Vacuum Upholstered Furniture							X		
Vacuum Drapes							X		
Shampoo Carpet/Rugs								X	
Restretch Carpet									X
Repair/Replace Carpet									X
Wash/Clean & Adjust Blinds/Shades								X	
Wash Walls & Partitions								X	
Wash Glass, Doors & Frames							X		
Wash Windows, Exterior/Interior							X		
Disassemble, Clean & Reassemble Light Fixtures								X	
Report Any Damage or Hazards (A)		X							
** Painting									X
*** Graffiti									X

Turn Off Lights When Appropriate

(A)   Clean and Rectify Problem

   * Dust—Utilize Treated Cloths/Mops
  ** Painting—Touch Up As Required; Cycle Painting Within THREE/FIVE YEARS
*** Graffiti—To Be Removed Without Delay

11. JUROR FACILITIES

Jury Clerk's Office
Jury Assembly/Waiting Room
Impanelling Rooms
Deliberation Room

FREQUENCY SCHEDULE

	D/2	D	W	M/2	M	Q	S/A	A	A/R
Unlock and Lock Areas		X							
Check & Close Windows		X							
Check & Replace Missing Signage		X							
Check & Replace Burned Out Lights		X							
Remove Cobwebs					X				
Police Area (B)		X							
Empty & Clean Waste Containers		X							
Empty & Clean Ash Receivers		X							
* Dust High Ceiling & Walls						X			
* Dust Light Fixtures						X			
* Dust/Clean & Arrange Furniture		X							
* Dust Window Sills, Doors & Frames		X							
* Dust & Adjust Window Blinds/Shades		X							
* Dust Radiators & Covers		X							
* Dust Mop/Sweep Floors		X							
Spray Buff Floors (1)			X						
Strip & Refinish Floors						X			
Spot Clean Walls & Partitions			X						
Spot Clean Glass, Doors & Frames			X						
Clean/Polish & Arrange Furniture						X			
Clean & Disinfect Drinking Fountains		X							
Clean Door Saddles			X						
Repair/Replace Flooring									X
Wash/Clean & Adjust Blinds/Shades							X		
Wash Walls & Partitions							X		
Wash Glass, Doors & Frames						X			
Wash Windows, Exterior/Interior						X			
Disassemble, Clean & Reassemble Light Fixtures							X		
Report Any Damage or Hazards (A)		X							
** Painting									X
*** Graffiti									X

Turn Off Lights When Appropriate

(A)   Clean and Rectify Problem
(B)   Free of Discarded Materials and Trash
(1)   Includes: Sweep, Damp Mop, Spray Buff and Dry Mop
  * Dust—Utilize Treated Cloths/Mops
 ** Painting—Touch Up As Required; Cycle Painting Within THREE YEARS
*** Graffiti—To Be Removed Without Delay

12. COURT ROOM AREAS

Court Room
Witness Waiting Room
Robing Room
Attorney Conference Room
Conference/Board Room
Lounge/Lunch Room

FREQUENCY SCHEDULE

	D/2	D	W	M/2	M	Q	S/A	A	A/R
Unlock and Lock Areas		X							
Check & Close Windows		X							
Check & Replace Missing Signage		X							
Check & Replace Burned Out Lights		X							
Check Court Room Clock for Accuracy		X							
Remove Cobwebs					X				
Police Area (B)		X							
Empty & Clean Waste Containers		X							
* Dust High Ceiling & Walls						X			
* Dust Light Fixtures						X			
* Dust/Clean & Arrange Furniture		X							
* Dust Window Sills, Doors & Frames			X						
* Dust & Adjust Window Blinds/Shades			X						
* Dust Radiators & Covers			X						
* Dust Mop/Sweep Floors		X							
* Dust Woodwork & Panels			X						
Spray Buff Floors (1)			X						
Strip & Refinish Floors						X			
Spot Clean Walls			X						
Clean/Polish & Arrange Furniture						X			
Clean/Polish Woodwork & Panels							X		
Repair/Replace Flooring									X
Wash/Clean & Adjust Blinds/Shades							X		
Wash Walls							X		
Wash Glass, Doors & Frames						X			
Wash Windows, Exterior/Interiors						X			
Disassemble, Clean & Reassemble Light Fixtures							X		
Report Any Damage or Hazards (A)		X							
** Painting									X
*** Graffiti									X

Turn Off Lights When Appropriate

(A)   Clean and Rectify Problem
(B)   Free of Discarded Materials and Trash

(1)   Includes: Sweep, Damp Mop, Spray Buff and Dry Mop

　* Dust—Utilize Treated Cloths/Mops
　** Painting—Touch Up As Required; Cycle Painting Within THREE YEARS
*** Graffiti—To Be Removed Without Delay

13. JUDGES FACILITIES

Chambers
Secretary's Office
Law Clerk's Office
Reception/Waiting Room

FREQUENCY SCHEDULE

	D/2	D	W	M/2	M	Q	S/A	A	A/R
Unlock and Lock Areas		X							
Check & Close Windows		X							
Check & Replace Missing Signage		X							
Check & Replace Burned Out Lights		X							
Remove Cobwebs					X				
Empty & Clean Waste Containers		X							
Empty & Clean Ash Receivers		X							
* Dust High Ceiling & Walls								X	
* Dust Light Fixtures								X	
* Dust Walls, Decorations & Cabinets						X			
* Dust/Clean & Arrange Furniture						X			
* Dust Window Sills, Doors & Frames			X						
* Dust & Adjust Window Blinds/Shades			X						
* Dust Radiators & Covers			X						
* Dust Shelving & Books			X						
* Dust Woodwork & Panels			X						
Spot Clean Walls & Partitions					X				
Spot Clean Glass, Doors & Frames			X						
Spot Clean Upholstered Furniture									X
Spot Clean Rugs/Carpets									X
Clean/Polish & Arrange Furniture						X			
Clean/Polish Woodwork & Panels								X	
Vacuum Carpet/Rugs			X						
Vacuum Upholstered Furniture						X			
Vacuum Drapes						X			
Shampoo Carpet/Rugs							X		
Restretch Carpet									X
Repair/Replace Carpet									X
Wash/Clean & Adjust Blinds/Shades								X	
Wash Walls & Partitions									X
Wash Glass, Doors & Frames						X			
Wash Windows, Exterior/Interior						X			
Disassemble, Clean & Reassemble Light Fixtures								X	
Report Any Damage or Hazards (A)		X							
**Painting									X
***Graffiti									X

Turn Off Lights When Appropriate

(A)   Clean and Rectify Problem
  * Dust—Utilize Treated Cloths/Mops
 ** Painting—Touch Up As Required; Cycle Painting Within THREE/FIVE YEARS
*** Graffiti—To Be Removed Without Delay

14. LIBRARY FACILITIES

Librarian's Office
Library/Reading Rooms
  Storage

FREQUENCY SCHEDULE

	D/2	D	W	M/2	M	Q	S/A	A	A/R
Unlock and Lock Areas		X							
Check & Close Windows		X							
Check & Replace Missing Signage		X							
Check & Replace Burned Out Lights		X							
Remove Cobwebs					X				
Police Area (B)		X							
Empty & Clean Waste Containers		X							
Empty & Clean Ash Receivers		X							
* Dust High Ceiling & Walls							X		
* Dust Light Fixtures							X		
* Dust Walls, Decorations & Cabinets					X				
* Dust/Clean & Arrange Furniture					X				
* Dust Window Sills, Doors & Frames			X						
* Dust & Adjust Window Blinds/Shades			X						
* Dust Radiators & Covers			X						
* Dust Mop/Sweep Floors		X							
* Dust Shelving & Books			X						
* Dust Woodwork & Panels			X						
Spray Buff Floors (1)		X							
Strip & Refinish Floors								X	
Spot Clean Walls & Partitions					X				
Spot Clean Glass, Doors & Frames			X						
Clean/Polish & Arrange Furniture							X		
Clean/Polish Woodwork & Panels							X		
Repair/Replace Flooring									X
Wash/Clean & Adjust Blinds/Shades							X		
Wash Walls & Partitions							X		
Wash Glass, Doors & Frames							X		
Wash Windows, Exterior/Interior							X		
Disassemble, Clean & Reassemble Light Fixtures								X	
Report Any Damage or Hazards (A)		X							
**Painting									X
***Graffiti									X

Turn Off Lights When Appropriate

(A)   Clean and Rectify Problem
(B)   Free of Discarded Materials and Trash

(1)   Includes: Sweep, Damp Mop, Spray Buff and Dry Mop

  * Dust—Utilize Treated Cloths/Mops
 ** Painting—Touch Up As Required; Cycle Painting Within FIVE YEARS
*** Graffiti—To Be Removed Without Delay

15. SECURITY FACILITIES I

Information Stations
Magnetometer Entries

FREQUENCY SCHEDULE

	D/2	D	W	M/2	M	Q	S/A	A	A/R
Police Area (B)		X							
Empty & Clean Waste Containers	X								
Empty & Clean Ash Receivers	X								
* Dust/Clean & Arrange Furniture		X							
Clean/Polish & Arrange Furniture							X		
Report Any Damage or Hazards (A)		X							
**Painting									X
***Graffiti									X

Turn Off Lights When Appropriate

(A)   Clean and Rectify Problem
(B)   Free of Discarded Materials and Trash

  * Dust—Utilize Treated Cloths/Mops
 ** Painting—Touch Up As Required; Cycle Painting Within THREE YEARS
*** Graffiti—To Be Removed Without Delay

16. SECURITY FACILITIES II

Locker Rooms
Showers & Toilet Areas

FREQUENCY SCHEDULE

	D/2	D	W	M/2	M	Q	S/A	A	A/R
Lock/Unlock Area		X							
Check & Close Windows		X							
Check & Replace Missing Signage		X							
Check & Replace Burned Out Lights		X							
Remove Cobwebs					X				
Police Area (B)		X							
Empty Waste Containers	X								
* Dust & Spot Clean Ceilings					X				
Clean Walls and Disinfect			X						
Clean Floors		X							
Clean Mirrors		X							
Clean Sinks, Urinals & Water Closets		X							
Clean Tile Walls		X							
Clean Toilet Stalls/Partitions		X							
Clean & Shine Chrome		X							
Clean Light Fixtures					X				
Clean Exhaust Vents					X				
Clean Painted Walls			X						
Clean Painted Doors & Frames			X						
Resupply Paper, Soap & Hygiene Products	X								
Wash Windows Exterior/Interior							X		
Disassemble, Clean & Reassemble Light Fixtures								X	
Report Any Damage or Hazards (A)	X								
**Painting									X
***Graffiti									X

REPORT DRIPPING/RUNNING WATER

(A)   Clean and Rectify Problem
(B)   Free of Discarded Materials and Trash

  * Dust—Utilize Treated Cloths/Mops
 ** Painting—Touch Up As Required; Cycle Painting Within FIVE YEARS
*** Graffiti—To Be Removed Without Delay

17. MISCELLANEOUS FACILITIES

Employee Lounge/Lunch Room
Sick Room
Training Rooms & Media
Holding Cells
Children's Center

FREQUENCY SCHEDULE

	D/2	D	W	M/2	M	Q	S/A	A	A/R
Unlock and Lock Areas		X							
Check & Close Windows		X							
Check & Replace Missing Signage		X							
Check & Replace Burned Out Lights		X							
Police Area (B)		X							
Remove Cobwebs					X				
Empty & Clean Waste Containers		X							
Empty & Clean Ash Receivers		X							
* Dust High Ceiling & Walls							X		
* Dust Light Fixtures							X		
* Dust Walls, Decorations & Cabinets						X			
* Dust/Clean & Arrange Furniture						X			
* Dust Window Sills, Doors & Frames			X						
* Dust & Adjust Window Blinds/Shades			X						
* Dust Radiators & Covers			X						
* Dust Mop/Sweep Floors	X								
Spray Buff Floors (1)			X						
Strip & Refinish Floors							X		
Spot Clean Walls & Partitions				X					
Spot Clean Glass, Doors & Frames			X						
Clean Mirror	X								
Clean/Polish & Arrange Furniture							X		
Clean Sink & Shine Chrome	X								
Clean Door Saddles			X						
Clean Exhaust Vents					X				
Repair/Replace Flooring									X
Resupply Paper & Soap Products	X								
Wash/Clean & Adjust Blinds/Shades								X	
Wash Walls & Partitions								X	
Wash Glass, Doors & Frames							X		
Wash Windows, Exterior/Interior							X		
Disassemble, Clean & Reassemble Light Fixtures								X	
Report Any Damage or Hazards (A)	X								
**Painting									X
***Graffiti									X

Turn Off Lights When Appropriate

(A) Clean and Rectify Problem
(B) Free of Discarded Materials and Trash

(1) Includes: Sweep, Damp Mop, Spray Buff and Dry Mop
 * Dust—Utilize Treated Cloths/Mops
 ** Painting—Touch Up As Required; Cycle Painting Within FIVE YEARS
*** Graffiti—To Be Removed Without Delay

18. GARAGE BUILDING PARKING AREAS

FREQUENCY SCHEDULE

	D/2	D	W	M/2	M	Q	S/A	A	A/R
Police Area (B)		X							
Sweep Entryways		X							
Sweep Steps			X						
Sweep Landings			X						
Empty Litter Containers	X								
Check/Clean Catchbasins & Drains			X						
Check/Replace Burned Out Lights		X							
Check/Report Missing Signage		X							
Check/Report on Insect/Rodent Control		X							
Check/Report Erosion				X					
Check/Report Roof Fan Operation		X							
Check/Report Fire Apparatus		X							
Check/Report Missing/Broken Apparatus		X							
Check/Report Any Deterioration of Paved Surfaces		X							
Report Abandoned Equipment/Autos		X							
Maintain Snow Free Walks/Entryways									X
Maintain Clear Passage for Vehicles									X
Hose & Scrub Down Entry Areas						X			
Report Any Damage or Hazards (A)									X
* Painting									X
** Graffiti									X

Turn Off Lights When Appropriate

(A)   Clean and Rectify Problem
(B)   Free of Discarded Materials and Trash

  * Painting—Touch Up As Required; Cycle Painting ANNUALLY, e.g. Benches, Metal Doors, Frames, Traffic Markings, etcetera
** Graffiti—To Be Removed Without Delay

§ 34.2. Reimbursement for Cleaning of Court Facilities

(a) **Purpose.** The purpose of this section is to give effect to the provisions of section 39–b of the Judiciary Law.

(b) **Definitions.** For purposes of this section, the definitions set forth in subdivision (c) of section 34.1 of this Part shall apply. In addition, the following terms shall have the meanings herein provided:

1. The term court facilities shall mean facilities for the transaction of business by the state-paid courts and court-related agencies of the unified court system and the judicial and nonjudicial personnel thereof, including rooms and accommodations for the courts and court-related agencies of the unified court system, the judges, justices and the clerical, administrative and other personnel thereof.

2. The term cleaning of court facilities shall mean those services and activities that are necessary to insure that the interior of each court facility is and remains a clean and healthful environment in which to transact the business of the unified court system.

These services and activities include, but are not limited to: removal of trash and debris; maintenance of appropriate standards of hygiene; painting; pest control; and replacement of consumable items such as light bulbs, soap, toilet paper and paper toweling. They also shall include the making of minor repairs.

3. The term minor repairs shall mean such repairs as are required to replace a part, to put together what is torn or broken, or to restore a surface or finish, where such repairs will preserve and/or restore a court facility to full functionality; and shall include only: (a) painting, carpeting, and other resurfacing of, or finish work related to, or renovation of, the interiors of spaces used by the unified court system and (b) a uniform percentage of other building maintenance costs, said percentage to be established for each state fiscal year by the chief administrator. The chief administrator may set a different percentage for a particular political subdivision upon a showing that minor repairs constitute a greater percentage of other building maintenance costs in that political subdivision than the uniform percentage established by the chief administrator.

4. The term political subdivision shall include each county of the state outside the city of New York and each city of the state.

(c) Contracts with Political Subdivisions.

1. Each political subdivision shall enter into a contract with the unified court system pursuant to which such political subdivision shall provide for the cleaning of court facilities located therein and the state shall reimburse the political subdivision for its actual expenditures therefor.

2. Each contract entered hereunder shall require the political subdivision: (i) to comply with the maintenance and operation standards for court facilities prescribed by section 34.1 of this Part, and (ii) annually, on a form to be prescribed by the chief administrator of the courts and in accordance with such deadline as he or she may fix, to submit to the chief administrator a proposed itemized budget scheduling those expenditures it projects it will incur during the state fiscal year commencing April first next thereafter for the cleaning of its court facilities.

3. The chief administrator shall review each proposed itemized budget submitted pursuant to paragraph two of this subdivision. Following such review, he or she shall notify the political subdivision submitting such budget of the expenditures scheduled therein that have been approved. To the extent practicable, such notification shall be given not later than March first preceding commencement of the state fiscal year in which the expenditures are to be incurred.

4. Notwithstanding the foregoing, the state shall not reimburse a political subdivision for any expenditure during a state fiscal year for the cleaning of its court facilities where:

(i) the need therefor is due to the political subdivisions failure to follow generally accepted preventive maintenance policies and procedures, or

(ii) such expenditure is incurred to pay for cleaning that is undertaken in lieu of replacement of a building system that, in accordance with the political subdivisions normal and usual policies, procedures and practices, should be replaced, or

(iii) such expenditure was not approved for such fiscal year pursuant to paragraph three of this subdivision, unless the need therefor was triggered by a sudden and unexpected failure or by some accident or external force, resulting in a situation that adversely affects the suitability and sufficiency of the court facilities for the dignified transaction of the business of the courts, in which event the state shall reimburse the political subdivision for the amount of the expenditure up to $15,000 (and, notwithstanding any other provision of this section, the political subdivision may include any unreimbursed balance of the expenditure on the proposed itemized budget it submits for the next state fiscal year pursuant to paragraph two of this subdivision), or

(iv) pursuant to the laws, rules and regulations to which the political subdivision is subject, and its own normal and usual policies, procedures and practices, such expenditure is being or could be bonded.

5. Where a political subdivision incurs an expenditure for the cleaning of a court facility that is part of a combined occupancy structure, as that term is defined in section 1676 of the public authorities law, and such cleaning benefits portions of the structure used for purposes not directly or indirectly related to the function of the court facility, the state shall reimburse the political subdivision only for so much of the expenditure as can be attributed to its benefit to the court facility.

PART 35. CHILD WITNESSES

§ 35.1. Development of Methods to Reduce Trauma to Child Witnesses

The Chief Administrator of the Courts shall consult with individuals, agencies and groups concerned with child psychology and child welfare and, based upon that consultation, shall develop and implement methods and techniques designed to reduce significantly the trauma to child witnesses likely to be caused by testifying in court proceedings. The Chief Administrator shall periodically review such methods and techniques to ensure their continuing effectiveness.

Forms

Use of closed-circuit television for vulnerable child witnesses, see West's McKinney's Forms, Criminal Procedure, § 65.20, Forms 1 to 5.

§ 35.2. Training and Education Programs Concerning Treatment of Child Witnesses

The Chief Administrator of the Courts shall include, as appropriate, in education and training programs offered to judges and nonjudicial personnel, programs concerning the social and psychological stages of child development to ensure that, where appropriate, courtroom procedures, including the questioning and treatment of a child witness by the parties, are adopted or modified to protect the child from emotional or psychological harm.

PART 36. APPOINTMENTS BY THE COURT

§ 36.0. Preamble

Public trust in the judicial process demands that appointments by judges be fair, impartial and beyond reproach. Accordingly, these rules are intended to ensure that appointees are selected on the basis of merit, without favoritism, nepotism, politics or other factors unrelated to the qualifications of the appointee or the requirements of the case.

The rules cannot be written in a way that foresees every situation in which they should be applied. Therefore, the appointment of trained and competent persons, and the avoidance of factors unrelated to the merit of the appointments or the value of the work performed are the fundamental objectives that should guide all appointments made, and orders issued, pursuant to this Part.

§ 36.1. Application

(a) Except as set forth in subdivision (b), this Part shall apply to the following appointments made by any judge or justice of the Unified Court System:

(1) guardians;

(2) guardians ad litem, including guardians ad litem appointed to investigate and report to the court on particular issues, and their counsel and assistants;

(3) law guardians who are not paid from public funds, in those judicial departments where their appointments are authorized;

(4) court evaluators;

(5) attorneys for alleged incapacitated persons;

(6) court examiners;

(7) supplemental needs trustees;

(8) receivers;

(9) referees (other than special masters and those otherwise performing judicial functions in a quasi-judicial capacity);

(10) the following persons or entities performing services for guardians or receivers:

    (i) counsel

    (ii) accountants

    (iii) auctioneers

    (iv) appraisers

    (v) property managers

    (vi) real estate brokers

(11) a public administrator within the City of New York and for the counties of Westchester, Onondaga, Erie, Monroe, Suffolk and Nassau and counsel to the public administrator, except that only sections 36.2(c) and 36.4(e) of this Part shall apply, and that section 36.2(c) shall not apply to incumbents in these positions

until one year after the effective date of this paragraph.

(b) Except for sections 36.2(c)(6) and 36.2(c)(7), this Part shall not apply to:

(1) appointments of law guardians pursuant to section 243 of the Family Court Act, guardians ad litem pursuant to section 403–a of the Surrogate's Court Procedure Act, or the Mental Hygiene Legal Service;

(2) the appointment of, or the appointment of any persons or entities performing services for, any of the following:

    (i) a guardian who is a relative of (A) the subject of the guardianship proceeding or (B) the beneficiary of a proceeding to create a supplemental needs trust; a person or entity nominated as guardian by the subject of the proceeding or proposed as guardian by a party to the proceeding; a supplemental needs trustee nominated by the beneficiary of a supplemental needs trust or proposed by a proponent of the trust; or a person or entity having a legally recognized duty or interest with respect to the subject of the proceeding;

    (ii) a guardian ad litem nominated by an infant of 14 years of age or over;

    (iii) a nonprofit institution performing property management or personal needs services, or acting as court evaluator;

    (iv) a bank or trust company as a depository for funds or as a supplemental needs trustee;

    (v) except as set forth in section 36.1(a)(11), a public official vested with the powers of an administrator:

    (vi) a person or institution whose appointment is required by law;

    (vii) a physician whose appointment as a guardian ad litem is necessary where emergency medical or surgical procedures are required.

(3) an appointment other than above without compensation, except that the appointee must file a notice of appointment pursuant to section 36.4(a) of this Part.

§ 36.2. Appointments

(a) **Appointments by the judge.** All appointments of the persons or entities set forth in section 36.1, including those persons or entities set forth in section 36.1(a)(10) who perform services for guardians or receivers, shall be made by the judge authorized by law to make the appointment. In making appointments of persons or entities to perform services for guardians or receivers, the appointing judge may consider the recommendation of the guardian or receiver.

(b) Use of lists.

(1) All appointments pursuant to this Part shall be made by the appointing judge from the appropriate list of applicants established by the Chief Administrator of the Courts pursuant to section 36.3 of this Part.

(2) An appointing judge may appoint a person or entity not on the appropriate list of applicants upon a finding of good cause, which shall be set forth in writing and shall be filed with the fiduciary clerk at the time of the making of the appointment. The appointing judge shall send a copy of such writing to the Chief Administrator. A judge may not appoint a person or entity that has been removed from a list pursuant to section 36.3(e).

(3) Appointments made from outside the lists shall remain subject to all of the requirements and limitations set forth in this Part, except that the appointing judge may waive any education and training requirements where completion of these requirements would be impractical.

(c) Disqualifications from appointment.

(1) No person shall be appointed who is a judge or housing judge of the Unified Court System of the State of New York, or who is a relative of, or related by marriage to, a judge or housing judge of the Unified Court System within the fourth degree of relationship.

(2) No person serving as a judicial hearing officer pursuant to Part 122 of the Rules of the Chief Administrator shall be appointed in actions or proceedings in a court in a county where he or she serves on a judicial hearing officer panel for such court.

(3) No person shall be appointed who is a full-time or part-time employee of the Unified Court System. No person who is the spouse, sibling, parent or child of an employee who holds a position at salary grade JG24 or above, or its equivalent, shall be appointed by a court within the judicial district where the employee is employed or, with respect to an employee with statewide responsibilities, by any court in the state.

(4)(i) No person who is the chair or executive director, or their equivalent, of a state or county political party, or the spouse, sibling, parent or child of that official, shall be appointed while that official serves in that position and for a period of two years after that official no longer holds that position. This prohibition shall apply to the members, associates, counsel and employees of any law firms or entities while the official is associated with that firm or entity.

(ii) No person who has served as a campaign chair, coordinator, manager, treasurer or finance chair for a candidate for judicial office, or the spouse, sibling, parent or child of that person, or anyone associated with the law firm of that person,

shall be appointed by the judge for whom that service was performed for a period of two years following the judicial election. If the candidate is a sitting judge, the disqualifications shall apply as well from the time the person assumes any of the above roles during the campaign for judicial office.

(5) No former judge or housing judge of the Unified Court System, or the spouse, sibling, parent or child of such judge, shall be appointed, within two years from the date the judge left judicial office, by a court within the jurisdiction where the judge served. Jurisdiction is defined as follows:

(i) The jurisdiction of a judge of the Court of Appeals shall be statewide.

(ii) The jurisdiction of a justice of an Appellate Division shall be the judicial department within which the justice served.

(iii) The jurisdiction of a justice of the Supreme Court and a judge of the Court of Claims shall be the principal judicial district within which the justice or judge served.

(iv) With respect to all other judges, the jurisdiction shall be the principal county within which the judge served.

(6) No attorney who has been disbarred or suspended from the practice of law shall be appointed during the period of disbarment or suspension.

(7) No person convicted of a felony, or for five years following the date of sentencing after conviction of a misdemeanor (unless otherwise waived by the Chief Administrator upon application), shall be appointed unless that person receives a certificate of relief from disabilities.

(8) No receiver or guardian shall be appointed as his or her own counsel, and no person associated with a law firm of that receiver or guardian shall be appointed as counsel to that receiver or guardian, unless there is a compelling reason to do so.

(9) No attorney for an alleged incapacitated person shall be appointed as guardian to that person, or as counsel to the guardian of that person.

(10) No person serving as a court evaluator shall be appointed as guardian for the incapacitated person except under extenuating circumstances that are set forth in writing and filed with the fiduciary clerk at the time of the appointment.

(d) Limitations on appointments based upon compensation.

(1) No person or entity shall be eligible to receive more than one appointment within a calendar year for which the compensation anticipated to be awarded to the appointee in any calendar year exceeds the sum of $15,000.

(2) If a person or entity has been awarded more than an aggregate of $75,000 in compensation by all

courts during any calendar year, the person or entity shall not be eligible for compensated appointments by any court during the next calendar year.

(3) For purposes of this Part, the term "compensation" shall mean awards by a court of fees, commissions, allowances or other compensation, excluding costs and disbursements.

(4) These limitations shall not apply where the appointment is necessary to maintain continuity of representation of or service to the same person or entity in further or subsequent proceedings.

§ 36.3. Procedure for Appointment

(a) **Application for appointment.** The Chief Administrator shall provide for the application by persons or entities seeking appointments pursuant to this Part on such forms as shall be promulgated by the Chief Administrator. The forms shall contain such information as is necessary to establish that the applicant meets the qualifications for the appointments covered by this Part and to apprise the appointing judge of the applicant's background.

(b) **Qualifications for appointment.** The Chief Administrator shall establish requirements of education and training for placement on the list of available applicants. These requirements shall consist, as appropriate, of substantive issues pertaining to each category of appointment—including applicable law, procedures, and ethics — as well as explications of the rules and procedures implementing the process established by this Part. Education and training courses and programs shall meet the requirements of these rules only if certified by the Chief Administrator. Attorney participants in these education and training courses and programs may be eligible for continuing legal education credit in accordance with the requirements of the Continuing Legal Education Board.

(c) **Establishment of lists.** The Chief Administrator shall establish separate lists of qualified applicants for each category of appointment, and shall make available such information as will enable the appointing judge to be apprised of the background of each applicant. The Chief Administrator may establish more than one list for the same appointment category where appropriate to apprise the appointing judge of applicants who have substantial experience in that category. Pursuant to section 81.32(b) of the Mental Hygiene Law, the Presiding Justice of the appropriate Appellate Division shall designate the qualified applicants on the lists of court examiners established by the Chief Administrator.

(d) **Reregistration.** The Chief Administrator shall establish a procedure requiring that each person or entity on a list reregister every two years in order to remain on the list.

(e) **Removal from list.** The Chief Administrator may remove any person or entity from any list for unsatisfactory performance or any conduct incompatible with appointment from that list, or if disqualified from appointment pursuant to this Part. A person or entity may not be removed except upon receipt of a written statement of reasons for the removal and an opportunity to provide an explanation and to submit facts in opposition to the removal.

§ 36.4. Procedure After Appointment

(a) **Notice of appointment and certification of compliance.**

(1) Every person or entity appointed pursuant to this Part shall file with the fiduciary clerk of the court from which the appointment is made, within 30 days of the making of the appointment,

(i) a notice of appointment and

(ii) a certification of compliance with this Part, on such form as promulgated by the Chief Administrator. Copies of this form shall be made available at the office of the fiduciary clerk and shall be transmitted by that clerk to the appointee immediately after the making of the appointment by the appointing judge. An appointee who accepts an appointment without compensation need not complete the certification of compliance portion of the form.

(2) The notice of appointment shall contain the date of the appointment and the nature of the appointment.

(3) The certification of compliance shall include:

(i) a statement that the appointment is in compliance with sections 36.2(c) and (d); and

(ii) a list of all appointments received, or for which compensation has been awarded, during the current calendar year and the year immediately preceding the current calendar year, which shall contain

(A) the name of the judge who made each appointment,

(B) the compensation awarded, and

(C) where compensation remains to be awarded,

(i) the compensation anticipated to be awarded and

(ii) separate identification of those appointments for which compensation of $15,000 or more is anticipated to be awarded during any calendar year. The list shall include the appointment for which the filing is made.

(4) A person or entity who is required to complete the certification of compliance, but who is unable to certify that the appointment is in compliance with this Part, shall immediately so inform the appointing judge.

(b) **Approval of compensation.**

(1) Upon seeking approval of compensation of more than $500, an appointee must file with the fiduciary

clerk, on such form as is promulgated by the Chief Administrator, a statement of approval of compensation, which shall contain a confirmation to be signed by the fiduciary clerk that the appointee has filed the notice of appointment and certification of compliance.

(2) A judge shall not approve compensation of more than $500, and no compensation shall be awarded, unless the appointee has filed the notice of appointment and certification of compliance form required by this Part and the fiduciary clerk has confirmed to the appointing judge the filing of that form.

(3) Each approval of compensation of $5,000 or more to appointees pursuant to this section shall be accompanied by a statement, in writing, of the reasons therefor by the judge. The judge shall file a copy of the order approving compensation and the statement with the fiduciary clerk at the time of the signing of the order.

(4) Compensation to appointees shall not exceed the fair value of services rendered. Appointees who serve as counsel to a guardian or receiver shall not be compensated as counsel for services that should have been performed by the guardian or receiver.

(c) Reporting of compensation received by law firms. A law firm whose members, associates and employees have had a total of $50,000 or more in compensation approved in a single calendar year for appointments made pursuant to this Part shall report such amounts on a form promulgated by the Chief Administrator.

(d) Exception. The procedure set forth in this section shall not apply to the appointment of a referee to sell real property and a referee to compute whose compensation for such appointments is not anticipated to exceed $750.

(e) Approval and Reporting of Compensation Received by Counsel to the Public Administrator.

(1) A judge shall not approve compensation to counsel to the public administrator in excess of the fee schedule promulgated by the administrative board of the public administrator under SCPA 1128 unless accompanied by the judge's statement, in writing, of the reasons therefor, and by the appointee's affidavit of legal services under SCPA 1108 setting forth in detail the services rendered, the time spent, and the method or basis by which the requested compensation was determined.

(2) Any approval of compensation in excess of the fee schedule promulgated by the administrative board of the public administrator shall be reported to the Office of Court Administration on a form promulgated by the Chief Administrator and shall be accompanied by a copy of the order approving compensation, the judge's written statement, and the counsel's affidavit of legal services, which records shall be published as determined by the Chief Administrator.

(3) Each approval of compensation of $5,000 or more to counsel shall be reported to the Office of Court Administration on a form promulgated by the Chief Administrator and shall be published as determined by the Chief Administrator.

§ 36.5. Publication of Appointments

(a) All forms filed pursuant to section 36.4 shall be public records.

(b) The Chief Administrator shall arrange for the periodic publication of the names of all persons and entities appointed by each appointing judge, and the compensation approved for each appointee.

PART 37. COSTS AND SANCTIONS

§ 37.1. General

(a) The Chief Administrator of the Courts, with the advice and consent of the Administrative Board of the Courts, shall adopt rules providing for costs and sanctions as follows:

(1) in civil actions and proceedings in any trial or appellate court in the Unified Court System: providing for the award of costs, including reasonable attorney's fees, or the imposition of financial sanctions, or both, for frivolous conduct in litigation by any party or attorney; and

(2) in actions and proceedings in any trial or appellate court in the Unified Court System: providing for the award of costs, including reasonable attorney's fees, or the imposition of financial sanctions, or both, upon an attorney, who, without good cause, fails to appear at a time and date scheduled for an action or proceeding to be heard before a designated court.

(b) The rules shall include:

(1) a definition of frivolous conduct (civil cases);

(2) the factors to be considered in determining whether costs or sanctions should be awarded or imposed;

(3) a provision that the awarding of costs or imposition of financial sanctions by a court may be upon motion or upon the court's own initiative;

(4) a maximum monetary limit on costs or sanctions;

(5) the opportunity to be heard before costs or sanctions are awarded or imposed; and

(6) a requirement that reasons for the award of costs or imposition of sanctions be set forth in writing or on the record.

(c) The rules may provide that, as appropriate, financial sanctions may be made payable to the Lawyers' Fund for Client Protection established pursuant to section 97–t of the State Finance Law or payable to the court.

Cross References

For the text of the rules adopted see Part 130 of the Rules of the Chief Administrator contained in this pamphlet.

PART 38. RETENTION AND DISPOSITION OF THE RECORDS OF THE COURTS OF THE UNIFIED COURT SYSTEM

§ 38.1. Rules of the Chief Administrator of the Courts

(a) The Chief Administrator of the Courts, upon consultation with the Administrative Board of the Courts, shall adopt rules providing for the retention and disposition of the records of the courts of the Unified Court System, including (1) schedules for retention of each category of court record, (2) procedures for disposing of court records, (3) procedures for microphotography of court records, and (4) provisions to ensure the confidentiality of court records sealed or otherwise made confidential by law.

(b) Rules and schedules governing retention and disposition of records of the Court of Appeals and the Appellate Divisions shall be adopted with the approval of the Chief Judge of the Court of Appeals and the presiding Justices of the Appellate Divisions for the records in their respective courts.

PART 39. PROHIBITION OF SMOKING IN THE UNIFIED COURT SYSTEM

§ 39.1. Prohibition of Smoking in the Unified Court System

Smoking is prohibited anywhere in any facility or other indoor area used by courts or agencies of the Unified Court System. This includes courtrooms, offices, cafeterias, lounges, restrooms, elevators, hallways and vehicles.

PART 40. FINANCIAL DISCLOSURE BY JUDGES AND NONJUDICIAL EMPLOYEES; ESTABLISHMENT OF ETHICS COMMISSION

§ 40.1. Ethics Commission

a. There shall be an Ethics Commission for the Unified Court System which shall consist of five members and shall have and exercise the powers and duties set forth herein with respect to all state-paid judges, justices and nonjudicial officers and employees of the courts and court-related agencies of the Unified Court System.

b. The members of the commission shall be appointed by the Chief Judge of the State of New York, upon consultation with the Administrative Board of the Courts. Two members shall be state-paid judges or justices of a court or courts of the Unified Court System, and at least two shall not be public officers or employees.

c. The term of members of the commission shall be five years. Members shall be appointed for no more than one five-year term.

d. The Chief Judge shall designate the chairperson of the commission from among the members thereof, who shall serve as chairperson at the pleasure of the Chief Judge. The chairperson or any three members of the commission may call a meeting.

e. Any vacancy occurring on the commission shall be filled within sixty days of its occurrence by the Chief Judge. A person appointed to fill a vacancy occurring other than by expiration of a term of office shall be appointed for the unexpired term of the member he or she succeeds. Where a member of the commission who is a judge or justice leave judicial office, a vacancy on the commission shall thereby be deemed to have occurred.

f. Three members of the commission shall constitute a quorum, and the commission shall have power to act by majority vote of the total number of members of the commission without vacancy.

g. Members of the commission may be removed by the Chief Judge for substantial neglect of duty, gross misconduct in office, inability to discharge the powers or duties of office or violation of this rule, after written notice and opportunity for a reply.

h. The members of the commission shall not receive compensation but shall be reimbursed for reasonable expenses incurred in the performance of their official duties.

i. The commission shall:

(1) Appoint an executive director who shall act in accordance with the policies of the commission and the provisions of this rule. The commission may delegate authority to the executive director to act in the name of the commission between meetings of the commission provided such delegation is in writing and the specific powers to be delegated are enumerated;

(2) Appoint such other staff, within appropriations made available therefor by the Chief Administrator of the Courts, as are necessary to carry out its duties under this rule;

(3) Adopt, amend and rescind rules and regulations to govern procedures of the commission, which shall be consistent with the provisions of this rule and which shall include, but not be limited to, a procedure for such adjudicatory proceedings as are authorized by this rule and the procedure whereby a person who is required to file an annual financial disclosure statement with the commission may request an additional period of time within which to file such statement, due to justifiable cause or undue hardship; such rules or regulations shall provide for a date beyond which in all cases of justifiable cause or undue hardship no further extension of time will be granted;

(4) Make available forms for annual statements of financial disclosure required to be filed pursuant to law;

(5) Review financial disclosure statements in accordance with the provisions of this rule; provided, however, that the commission may delegate all or part of this review function to the executive director, who shall be responsible for completing staff review of such statements in a manner consistent with the terms of the commission's delegation;

(6) Permit any person required to file a financial disclosure statement to request the commission to delete from the copy thereof made available for public inspection one or more items of information, which may be deleted by the commission upon a finding by a majority of the total number of its members without vacancy that the information which would otherwise be required to be made available for public inspection will have no material bearing on the discharge of the reporting person's official duties;

(7) Permit any person required to file a financial disclosure statement to request an exemption from any requirement to report one or more items of information which pertain to such person's spouse or unemancipated children, which item or items may be exempted by the commission upon a finding by a majority of the total number of its members without vacancy that the reporting individual's spouse, on his or her own behalf or on behalf of an unemancipated child, or the reporting person on behalf of an unemancipated child, objects to providing the information necessary to make such disclosure and that the information which would otherwise be required to be re-

ported will have no material bearing on the discharge of the reporting person's official duties;

(8) Permit any person who is required to file a financial disclosure statement, but who has not been determined pursuant to section 40.2(b) of this Part to hold a policy-making position, to request an exemption from such requirement in accordance with rules and regulations governing such exemptions. Such rules and regulations shall provide for exemptions to be granted either on the application of an individual or on behalf of persons who share the same job title or employment classification which the commission deems to be comparable for purposes of this section. Such rules and regulations may permit the granting of an exemption where, in the discretion of the commission, the public interest does not require disclosure and the applicant's duties do not involve the negotiation, authorization or approval of:

(i) contracts, leases, franchises, revocable consents, concessions, variances, special permits, or licenses as defined in section seventy-three of the Public Officers Law;

(ii) the purchase, sale, rental or lease of real property, goods or services, or a contract therefor;

(iii) the obtaining of grants of money or loans; or

(iv) the adoption or repeal of any rule or regulation having the force and effect of law;

(9) Exemptions granted hereunder shall be for such duration as the commission shall determine;

(10) Prepare an annual report to the Chief Judge and the Administrative Board of the Courts summarizing the activities of the commission; and

(11) In such cases as it shall deem appropriate, the commission may determine a question common to a class or defined category of persons or items of information required to be disclosed, where determination of the question will prevent undue repetition of requests for exemption or deletion or prevent undue complication in complying with the requirements of this rule.

j. The commission, or the executive director and staff of the commission, if responsibility therefor has been delegated, shall inspect all financial disclosure statements filed with the commission to ascertain whether any person required to file a financial disclosure statement has failed to file such a statement or has filed a deficient statement.

k. If a person required to file a financial disclosure statement with the commission has failed to file a disclosure statement or has filed a deficient statement, the commission shall notify the reporting person in writing, state the failure to file or detail the deficiency, provide the person with a fifteen-day period to cure the deficiency, and advise the person of the penalties for failure to comply with the reporting requirements. Such notice shall be confidential. If the person fails to make such filing or fails to cure the deficiency within the specified time period, the commission shall send a notice of delinquency: (1) to the reporting person; (2) in the case of a judge or justice of the Unified Court System, to the State Commission on Judicial Conduct; and (3) in the case of a nonjudicial officer or employee, to the Chief Administrator of the Courts.

l. A reporting individual who knowingly and wilfully fails to file an annual statement of financial disclosure or who knowingly and wilfully with intent to deceive makes a false statement or gives information which such individual knows to be false on such statement of financial disclosure filed pursuant to this section shall be subject to disciplinary action as otherwise permitted by law, rule or collective bargaining agreement. No disciplinary action for false filing may be imposed hereunder in the event a category of "value" or "amount" reported hereunder is incorrect unless such reported information is falsely understated.

m. A copy of any notice of delinquency sent pursuant to subdivision (k) of this section shall be included in the reporting person's file and be available for public inspection.

n. Upon written request from any person who is or may be subject to the requirement of filing a financial disclosure statement, the commission shall render advisory opinions concerning such requirement. Such requests shall be confidential, but the commission may publish such opinions provided that the name of the requesting person and other identifying details shall not be included in the publication.

o. In addition to the other powers and duties specified herein, the commission shall have the power and duty to:

(1) Administer and enforce all the provisions of this section;

(2) Conduct any investigation necessary to carry out the provisions of this section. Pursuant to this power and duty, the commission may administer oaths or affirmations, subpoena witnesses, compel their attendance and require the production of any books or records which it may deem relevant or material; and

(3) Establish an adjudicatory procedure pursuant to which requests for certain deletions or exemptions to be made from a financial disclosure statement as authorized in paragraphs (6), (7) and (8) of subdivision (i) of this section may be heard.

p. (1) Notwithstanding the provision of article six of the Public Officers Law, the only records of the commission which shall be available for public inspection are:

(i) the information set forth in an annual statement of financial disclosure filed pursuant to law except the categories of value or amount and the names of unemancipated children, which shall re-

main confidential, and any other item of information deleted pursuant to paragraph (i) (6) of this section; and

(ii) notices of delinquency sent under subdivision (k) of this section.

(2) Notwithstanding the provisions of article seven of the Public Officers Law, no meeting or proceeding, including any such proceeding contemplated under paragraph (i)(6), (7) or (8) of this section, of the commission shall be open to the public, except if expressly provided otherwise by the commission.

§ 40.2. Financial Disclosure

(a) As herein provided, (1) each state-paid judge or justice, regardless of his or her annual rate of compensation, and (2) each nonjudicial officer and employee of the Unified Court System who, in a calendar year: (i) receives annual compensation at or above the job rate of SG–24 as set forth in paragraph (4) of subdivision (1) of section 130 of the Civil Service Law as of April first of the year in which an annual financial disclosure statement shall be filed and is not otherwise exempted from filing pursuant to this Part, or (ii) holds a policy-making position, as determined in accordance with subdivision (b) of this section, shall file annually with the Ethics Commission of the Unified Court System a financial disclosure statement containing the information and in the form set forth in the Annual Statement of Financial Disclosure adopted by the Chief Judge of the State of New York. Such statement shall be filed on or before the fifteenth day of May following the conclusion of such calendar year, except that:

(A) a person who is subject to the reporting requirements of this section and who timely filed with the Internal Revenue Service an application for automatic extension of time in which to file his or her individual income tax return for the immediately preceding calendar or fiscal year shall be required to file such financial disclosure statement on or before May fifteenth but may, without prejudice on account of a deficient statement, indicate with respect to any item of the disclosure statement that information with respect thereto is lacking but will be supplied in a supplementary statement of financial disclosure, which shall be filed on or before the seventh day after the expiration of the period of such automatic extension of time within which to file such individual income tax return, provided that failure to file or to timely file such supplementary statement of financial disclosure or the filing of an incomplete or deficient supplementary statement of financial disclosure shall be subject to the provisions of section 40.1(k) of this Part as if such supplementary statement were an annual statement; and

(B) a person who is required to file an annual financial disclosure statement with the Ethics Commission of the Unified Court System, and who is granted an additional period of time within which to file such statement due to justifiable cause or undue hardship, in accordance with required rules and regulations on the subject adopted pursuant to section 40.1(i)(3) of this Part, shall file such statement within the additional period of time granted.

(b) During the month of February in each year, the Chief Administrator of the Courts shall file with the Ethics Commission for the Unified Court System a written instrument that shall set forth the names of (1) all state-paid judges and justices, and (2) all state-paid nonjudicial officers and employees of the courts and court-related agencies of the Unified Court System who, during the preceding calendar year, received annual compensation at or above the job rate of SG–24 as set forth in paragraph (a) of subdivision (1) of section 130 of the Civil Service Law as of April first of the year in which an annual financial disclosure statement shall be filed and have not been otherwise exempted from filing pursuant to this rule, and the names of such nonjudicial officers and employees who, during such year, held policy-making positions in the determination of: (i) the Chief Judge of the Court of Appeals, as to personnel of that court; (ii) the Presiding Justice of each Appellate Division, as to personnel of that court; and (iii) the Chief Administrator of the Courts, as to all other State-paid personnel of the Unified Court System.

PART 41. INTEGRATED DOMESTIC VIOLENCE PARTS OF SUPREME COURT

§ 41.1. Integrated Domestic Violence Parts of Supreme Court.

(a) Integrated Domestic Violence Parts of the Supreme Court may be established in one or more counties by order of the Chief Administrator of the Courts following consultation with and agreement of the Presiding Justice of the Judicial Department in which the affected county or counties are located. As provided by rule of the Chief Administrator promulgated pursuant to subdivision (b) of this section, such Parts shall be devoted to the hearing and determination, in a single forum, of cases that are simultaneously pending in the courts if one of them is a domestic violence case in a criminal court and the other is a case in Supreme or Family Court that involves a party or witness in the domestic violence case; or if one is a case in criminal court, Family Court or Supreme Court and the other is a case in any other of these courts having a common party or in which a disposition may affect the interests of a party to the first case. The Chief Administrator also may provide that, where cases are disposed of in an Integrated Domestic Violence Part, subsequent cases that would have been eligible for disposition in such Part were they to have been pending simultaneously with the cases already disposed of shall be eligible for disposition therein. The Chief Administrator may also provide that domestic violence cases pending in a criminal court in the county shall be eligible for disposition in the Integrated Domestic Violence Part if necessary to best utilize available court and community resources for domestic violence cases.

(b) The Chief Administrator shall promulgate rules to regulate operation of Integrated Domestic Violence Parts in Supreme Court. Such rules shall permit a justice of the Supreme Court to transfer to such court, for disposition in an Integrated Domestic Violence Part thereof, any case pending in another court in the same county.

PART 42. CRIMINAL DIVISION OF SUPREME COURT IN BRONX COUNTY

§ 42.1. Criminal Division of the Supreme Court in Bronx County

(a) The purpose of this rule is to promote the administration of justice in the criminal courts in Bronx County by authorizing deployment of the judges of those courts in a manner that assures that all present and future caseload demands in such county will be met as expeditiously and effectively as possible.

(b) The Chief Administrator of the Courts, following consultation with and agreement of the Presiding Justice of the First Judicial Department, may by administrative order establish a Criminal Division of the Supreme Court in Bronx County. As provided by rules of the Chief Administrator promulgated pursuant to subdivision (c) of this section, such Criminal Division, when established, shall be devoted to the hearing and determination of criminal cases commenced in or transferred to the courts sitting in Bronx County.

(c) The Chief Administrator shall promulgate rules to regulate operation of the Criminal Division of Supreme Court in Bronx County. Such rules may authorize the transfer to Supreme Court in such county, for disposition in the Criminal Division thereof, of some or all classes of cases pending in the Criminal Court of the City of New York in Bronx County in which at least one felony or misdemeanor is charged therein.

PART 43. SUPERIOR COURTS FOR DRUG TREATMENT

§ 43.1. Superior Courts for Drug Treatment

(a) A Superior Court for Drug Treatment may be established in Supreme Court or County Court in any county by order of the Chief Administrator of the Courts following consultation with and agreement of the Presiding Justice of the Judicial Department in which such county is located. A Superior Court for Drug Treatment shall have as its purpose the hearing and determination of criminal cases in the courts of the county that are appropriate for disposition by a drug treatment court.

(b) The Chief Administrator, upon consultation with the Administrative Board of the Courts, shall promulgate such rules as are necessary to regulate operation of each Superior Court for Drug Treatment, and to permit transfer to the court, for disposition, of drug cases that are pending in another court in the same county.

PART 44. COURT APPOINTED SPECIAL ADVOCATES PROGRAMS

§ 44.0. General

Recognizing the vital role that a Court Appointed Special Advocates program ("CASA program") can perform in aiding Family Court efforts to further the health, safety and well-being of children, and the need to insure that each such program has adequate resources, this rule is promulgated to standardize use of CASA programs in the courts of this State and to establish a program of State assistance under the direction of the Chief Administrator of the Courts. For purposes of this rule, a CASA program shall mean a not-for-profit corporation affiliated with, and in compliance with, the standards set forth by the National and New York State Court Appointed Special Advocates Associations.

§ 44.1. Use of CASA programs

A CASA program may be appointed by Family Court in its discretion to provide assistance to the Court in cases regarding children in or at risk of out-of-home placement. The CASA program is not a party to the proceeding. To be eligible for such appointment, a program must meet regulations promulgated by the Chief Administrator of the Courts. Such regulations shall insure that each CASA program is capable of regularly providing thorough information about the health, safety, well-being and permanency plans of children and their families to the Court, the parties and law guardian; monitoring Family Court orders; meeting with children in the presence of, or with the consent of, their law guardians or as directed by the Family Court; working with legal and service providers assigned to their cases to facilitate collaborative solutions; and helping to promptly secure safe, stable homes and nurturing families for children so that they may thrive.

§ 44.2. State assistance

The Chief Administrator of the Courts may by rule establish a program for the provision of grants of State assistance to individual CASA programs within appropriations annually made available to the Judiciary.

PART 45. INTEGRATED YOUTH COURT IN WESTCHESTER COUNTY

§ 45.1. Integrated Youth Court in Westchester County

(a) The purpose of this rule is to promote the administration of justice in the courts of Westchester County and for minors who simultaneously are defendants in criminal cases and respondents in Family Court cases in such county.

(b) The Chief Administrator of the Courts, following consultation with and agreement of the Presiding Justice of the Second Judicial Department, may by administrative order establish an Integrated Youth Court in Westchester County to operate as a multi-court part of the County Court and the Family Court in such county. As provided by rules of the Chief Administrator promulgated pursuant to subdivision (c) of this section, such Integrated Youth Court, when established, shall be devoted to the hearing and determination, in a single forum, of cases simultaneously pending in such courts where (1) at least one such case is in a criminal court and at least one such case is in the Family Court; (2) a defendant in each such case in a criminal court also is a respondent in each such case in the Family Court; and (3) such defendant is less than twenty-one years of age at the time of the alleged commission of an offense prosecuted in such case in the criminal court. The Chief Administrator also may provide that a civil action pending in a City Court, Town Court or Village Court in Westchester County, or in the County Court thereof, shall be eligible for disposition in the Integrated Youth Court where such action arises out of substantially the same facts as underlie cases then pending in such Court and a defendant in such action is a party to those pending cases. The Chief Administrator also may provide that, where cases are disposed of in the Integrated Youth Court, subsequent cases that would have been eligible for disposition therein were they to have been

pending simultaneously with the cases already disposed of shall be eligible for disposition therein.

(c) The Chief Administrator shall promulgate rules to regulate the operation of the Integrated Youth Court in Westchester County. Such rules shall permit a judge of the County Court in such county to transfer to such Court, for disposition in the Integrated Youth Court, any case pending in a City Court, Town Court or Village Court in such county upon a finding that such a transfer would promote the administration of justice.

PART 50.   RULES GOVERNING CONDUCT OF NONJUDICIAL COURT EMPLOYEES

§ 50.1. Code of Ethics for Nonjudicial Employees of the Unified Court System

PREAMBLE: A fair and independent court system is essential to the administration of justice. Court employees must observe and maintain high standards of ethical conduct in the performance of their duties in order to inspire public confidence and trust in the fairness and independence of the courts. This code of ethics sets forth basic principles of ethical conduct that court employees must observe, in addition to laws, rules and directives governing specific conducts, so that the court system can fulfill its role as a provider of effective and impartial justice.

I. Court employees shall avoid impropriety and the appearance of impropriety in all their activities.

  A. Court employees shall respect and comply with the law.

  B. Court employees shall not use or attempt to use their positions or the prestige of judicial affiliation to secure privileges or exemptions for themselves or others.

  C. Court employees shall not solicit, accept or agree to accept any gifts or gratuities from attorneys or other persons having or likely to have any official transaction with the court system.

  D. Court employees shall not request or accept any payment in addition to their regular compensation for assistance given as part of their official duties, except as provided by law.

  E. Court employees shall not perform any function in a manner that improperly favors any litigant or attorney.

II. Court employees shall adhere to appropriate standards in performing the duties of their office.

  A. Court employees shall perform their duties properly and with diligence.

  B. Court employees shall be patient and courteous to all persons who come in contact with them.

  C. Court employees shall not discriminate, and shall not manifest by words or conduct bias or prejudice, on the basis of race, color, sex, sexual orientation, religion, creed, national origin, marital status, age or disability.

  D. Court employees shall not disclose any confidential information received in the course of their official duties, except as required in the performance of such duties, nor use such information for personal gain or advantage.

III. Court employees shall conduct their outside activities in a manner that does not conflict with their employment duties.

  A. Court employees shall not engage in outside employment or business activities that interfere with the performance of their official duties or that create an actual or appearance of conflict with those duties.

  B. Court employees shall not engage in political activity during scheduled work hours or at the workplace.

§ 50.2. Rules Governing Conduct for Nonjudicial Court Employees Not Contained in this Part

(a) Appointments by the Court. Court employees may not be appointed as guardians, guardians ad litem, court evaluators, attorneys for alleged incapacitated persons, receivers, referees (to sell real property) or persons designated to perform services for any of these, as provided in section 36.2(c)(3) of the Rules of the Chief Judge.

(b) Financial Disclosure. Court employees who are required to file financial disclosure statements in accordance with section 40.2 of the Rules of the Chief

Judge must comply with the requirements of that section.

(c) Political Activity of Personal Appointees of Judges. Court employees who are personal appointees of judges on the judges' staffs may not engage in political activities as set forth in section 100.5(C) of the Chief Administrator's Rules Governing Judicial Conduct.

§ 50.3. Dual Employment in the Court Service

(a) No employee regularly employed in a position in the classified service in the unified court system shall, while continuing to hold such position, accept appointment or employment in any other position or title, or in any capacity whatsoever, on a full-time or part-time basis, either in the classified or unclassified service, in another department or agency of the State or a political subdivision, or in the Legislature or the Judiciary, for which employment compensation or salary is payable, without the previous consent in writing of his or her appointing authority, except that such consent shall be subject to approval by the Chief Administrator of the Courts for employees of courts other than the appellate courts. Such written consent shall be required, in each case, for each such additional appointment or employment accepted or undertaken by such employee.

(b) A willful violation of the provisions of this section shall be deemed sufficient cause for disciplinary action, including removal.

§ 50.4. Obstruction of Court Service Rights; False Representation; Impersonation in Examination; Misuse or Misappropriation of Examination Material

(a) Any person who shall willfully, by himself or herself, or in cooperation with other persons, defeat, deceive or obstruct any person in respect of his or her right of examination, registration, certification, appointment, promotion or reinstatement, pursuant to the provisions of this Part or who shall willfully and falsely mark, grade, estimate or report upon the examination or proper standing of any person examined, registered or certified pursuant to the provisions of this Part or aid in so doing, or who shall willfully make any false representations concerning the same, or concerning the person examined, or who shall willfully furnish to any person any special or secret information for the purpose of either improving or injuring the prospects or chances of any person so examined, registered or certified, or to be examined, registered or certified, or who shall impersonate any other person, or permit or aid in any manner any other person to impersonate him or her, in connection with any registration or application or request to be registered, shall for each offense be subject to the provisions of section 106 of the Civil Service Law.

(b) A person who shall:

(1) Impersonate, or attempt to or offer to impersonate, another person in taking an examination held pursuant to this Part; or

(2) Take, or attempt to take or offer to take, such an examination in the name of any other person; or

(3) Procure or attempt to procure any other person to falsely impersonate him or her or to take, or attempt to take or offer to take, any such examination in his or her name; or

(4) Have in his or her possession any questions or answers relating to any such examination, or copies of such questions or answers, unless such possession is duly authorized by the appropriate authorities; or

(5) Sell or offer to sell questions or answers prepared for use in any such examination; or

(6) Use in any such examination any questions or answers secured prior to the administration of the examination or secure the questions or secure or prepare the answers to the examination questions prior to the administration of the examination, unless duly authorized to do so by the appropriate authorities; or

(7) Disclose or transmit to any person the questions or answers to such examination prior to its administration, or destroy, falsify or conceal the records or results of such examination from the appropriate authorities to whom such records are required to be transmitted in accordance with this Part, unless duly authorized to do so by the appropriate authorities;

shall be subject to the provisions of section 50(11) of the Civil Service Law. Additionally, a person who is found by the appropriate administrative authority to have violated this section, in addition to any disciplinary penalty that may be imposed, shall be disqualified from appointment to the position for which the examination is being held and may be disqualified from being a candidate for any civil service examination for a period of five years.

§ 50.5. Prohibition Against Certain Political Activities; Improper Influence

(a) Recommendations Based on Political Affiliations. No recommendation or question under the authority of this Part shall relate to the political opinions or affiliations of any person whatever; and no appointment or selection to or removal from an office or employment within the scope of this Part shall be in any manner affected or influenced by such opinions or affiliations. No person in the unified court system is for that reason under any obligation to contribute to any political fund or to render any political service, and no person shall be removed or otherwise prejudiced for refusing so to do. No person in the unified court system shall discharge or promote or reduce, or in any manner change the official rank or compensation of any other person in the unified court system, or promise or threaten so to do, for giving or withholding or neglecting to make any contribution of money or service or any other valuable thing for any political purpose. No person in the unified court system shall use his or her official authority or influence to coerce the political action of any person or body or to interfere with any election.

(b) Inquiry Concerning Political Affiliations.

(1) No person shall directly or indirectly ask, indicate or transmit orally or in writing the political affiliations of any employee in the unified court system or of any person dependent upon or related to such an employee, as a test of fitness for holding office. A violation of this subdivision shall be subject to the provisions of subdivision 2 of section 107 of the Civil Service Law. Nothing herein contained shall be construed to prevent or prohibit inquiry concerning the activities, affiliation or membership of any applicant or employee in any group or organization which advocates that the government of the United States or of any state or of any political subdivision thereof should be overturned by force, violence or any unlawful means.

(2) No question in any examination or application or other proceeding pursuant to this Part shall be so framed as to elicit information concerning, nor shall any other attempt be made to ascertain, the political opinions or affiliations of any applicant, competitor or eligible, and all disclosures thereof shall be disregarded. No discrimination shall be exercised, threatened or promised against or in favor of any applicant, competitor or eligible because of his or her political opinions or affiliations.

(c) Political Assessment. No employee of the unified court system shall, directly or indirectly, use his or her authority or official influence to compel or induce any other employee of the unified court system to pay or promise to pay any political assessment, subscription or contribution. Every employee who may have charge or control in any building, office or room occupied for any governmental purpose is hereby authorized to prohibit the entry of any person, and he or she shall not knowingly permit any person to enter the same for the purpose of making, collecting, receiving or giving notice therein, of any political assessment, subscription or contribution; and no person shall enter or remain in any such office, building or room, or send or direct any letter or other writing thereto, for the purpose of giving notice of, demanding or collecting a political assessment; nor shall any person therein give notice of, demand, collect or receive any such assessment, subscription or contribution. No person shall prepare or take any part in preparing any political assessment, subscription or contribution with the intent that the same shall be sent or presented to or collected from any employee subject to the provisions of this Part, and no person shall knowingly send or present any political assess-

ment, subscription or contribution to or request its payment of any employee. Any person violating any provision of this subdivision shall be subject to the provisions of subdivision 3 of section 107 of the Civil Service Law.

(d) Prohibition Against Promise of Influence. Any person who, while holding any public office, or in nomination for, or while seeking a nomination or appointment for any public office, shall corruptly use or promise to use, whether directly or indirectly, any official authority or influence, whether then possessed or merely anticipated, in the way of conferring upon any person, or in order to secure or aid any person in securing any office or public employment, or any nomination, confirmation, promotion or increase of salary, upon the consideration that the vote or political influence or action of the last-named person, or any other, shall be given or used in behalf of any candidate, officer or party, or upon any other corrupt condition or consideration, shall be subject to the provisions of subdivision 4 of section 107 of the Civil Service Law. Any public officer, or any person having or claiming to have any authority or influence for or affecting the nomination, public employment, confirmation, promotion, removal or increase or decrease of salary of any public officer, who shall corruptly use, or promise, or threaten to use any such authority or influence, directly or indirectly in order to coerce or persuade the vote or political action of any citizen or the removal, discharge or promotion of any officer or public employee, or upon any other corrupt consideration, shall also be subject to the provisions of subdivision 4 of section 107 of the Civil Service Law.

(e) Political Organizations. No employee of the unified court system may hold an elective office in a political party, or a club or organization related to a political party, except that an employee may be a delegate to a judicial nominating convention or a member of a county committee other than the executive committee of a county committee.

§ 50.6. Practice of Law

(a) A lawyer who is employed full-time in any court or agency of the unified court system shall not maintain an office for the private practice of law alone or with others, hold himself or herself out to be in the private practice of law, or engage in the private practice of law except as provided in this section.

(b) Subject to prior written application and approval as to each professional engagement, a person referred to in subdivision (a) of this section may engage in the private practice of law as to matters not pending before a court or a governmental agency, in uncontested matters in the Surrogate's Court, uncontested accountings in the Supreme Court and other ex parte applications not preliminary or incidental to litigated or contested matters. Such approval shall continue only to the completion of the particular engagement for which permission was obtained, except that prior approval for the provision of pro bono services, authorized under subdivision (c) of this section, may be granted on an annual basis with respect to an organization or project that provides such services to persons unable to afford counsel. Prior approval must be obtained from:

(1) the Chief Judge of the Court of Appeals for lawyers employed in that court;

(2) the Presiding Justice of the appropriate Appellate Division for lawyers employed by an Appellate Division; and

(3) the Chief Administrator of the Courts for lawyers employed in every other court or court-related agency in the unified court system.

(c)(1) Persons referred to in subdivision (a) of this section may provide pro bono legal services, which do not interfere with the performance of their jobs, in contested or uncontested matters, except those brought in the courts of their own employment.

(2) Pro bono services in any contested matter shall be performed under such written terms and conditions as may be specified by the approving authority designated in subdivision (b) (1), (2) or (3).

(3) No provision of legal services or related activities authorized pursuant to this section may take place during usual working hours unless appropriate leave is authorized and charged. No public resources may be used in any such connection. Reasonable precautions must be taken in all cases by approving authorities and authorized employees to avoid actual and perceived conflicts of interest and the actual or perceived lending of the prestige or power of the public offices or positions of the employees and conveying the impression that such employees are in special positions to exert influence.

(d) An employee of the Unified Court System who is employed on a part-time basis shall not participate directly or indirectly as a lawyer in any contested action or proceeding in the court in which he or she serves, or in any other practice of law which is incompatible with or which would reflect adversely upon his or her position or the performance of his or her duties. Such employee may participate as a lawyer in uncontested actions or proceedings in the court in which he or she serves only with prior written approval of the Chief Administrator of the Courts.

(e) No partner or associate of a part-time law secretary or law clerk shall practice law before the justice or judge by whom such law secretary or law clerk is employed.

(f) Each approving authority or designee shall report annually to the Chief Administrator of the Courts the number of requests and approvals. With respect to pro bono representation, each authorized employee shall report annually to the Chief Administrator the number of representations and pro bono hours performed.

ADMINISTRATIVE DELEGATIONS OF THE CHIEF JUDGE

PART 80. ADMINISTRATIVE DELEGATION NUMBER 1

§ 80.0. Preamble

Pursuant to article VI, section 28(b) of the State Constitution, the Chief Administrator of the Courts is delegated the following powers and duties.

Cross References

Constitution, see McKinney's Book 2.

§ 80.1. Chief Administrator of the Courts; General Powers and Duties

(a) The Chief Administrator shall supervise on behalf of the Chief Judge the administration and operation of the unified court system, except as otherwise provided in section 80.3 of this Part with respect to the Appellate Divisions and Appellate Terms of the Supreme Court, and section 80.4 with respect to the Court of Appeals.

(b) In the exercise of this delegated responsibility and in accordance with the standards and administrative policies established, approved and promulgated pursuant to article VI, section 28(c) of the Constitution, the Chief Administrator shall:

(1) prepare the itemized estimates of the annual financial needs of the unified court system. These itemized estimates, approved by the Court of Appeals and certified by the Chief Judge, shall be transmitted by the Chief Administrator to the Governor and to the chairmen of the Senate Finance and Judiciary Committees and the Assembly Ways and Means and Judiciary Committees not later than the first day of December;

(2) establish the regular hours, terms and parts of court, and assign judges and justices to them, in consultation and agreement with the Presiding Justices of the appropriate Appellate Divisions on behalf of their respective courts; provided that if the Chief Administrator and the Presiding Justices are unable to agree, the matter shall be determined by the Chief Judge. Consultation and agreement shall not be required for temporary assignments, nor for the establishment of temporary hours, terms and parts of court;

(3) appoint and remove, upon nomination or recommendation of the appropriate administrative judge, supervising judge or judge of the court in which the position is to be filled or the employee works, or other administrator, all nonjudicial officers and employees, except the county clerks, commissioners of jurors, nonjudicial officers and employees of the town and village courts, and personal assistants who serve as law clerks (law secretaries) and secretaries to judges and justices;

(4) designate deputies and administrative judges in accordance with section 80.2 of this Part. The Chief Administrator may delegate to any deputy, administrative judge, assistant or court any administrative power or function delegated to the Chief Administrator;

(5) enforce and supervise the execution of the standards and administrative policies established, approved and promulgated pursuant to article VI, section 28(c) of the Constitution;

(6) adopt administrative rules for the efficient and orderly transaction of business in the trial courts, including but not limited to calendar practice, in consultation with the Administrative Board of the Courts or the appropriate Appellate Divisions;

(7) make rules, in consultation with the Administrative Board of the Courts, to implement article 16 of the Judiciary Law;

(8) establish an administrative office of the courts; appoint and remove deputies, assistants, counsel and employees as may be necessary; fix their salaries within the amounts made available by appropriation; and as may be necessary, establish regional budget and personnel offices for the preparation of budgets of the courts and the conduct of personnel transactions affecting nonjudicial officers and employees of the unified court system located within their regions;

(9) establish programs of education and training for judges and nonjudicial personnel;

(10) appoint advisory committees as he shall require, to advise him in relation to the administration and operation of the unified court system;

(11) supervise the administration and operation of law libraries of the unified court system;

(12) designate law journals for the publication of court calendars, judicial orders, decisions and opinions, and notices of judicial proceedings;

(13) supervise the maintenance and destruction of court records;

(14) accept as agent of the unified court system any grant or gift for the purposes of carrying out any of his powers or duties or the functions of the unified court system, and contract on behalf of the unified court system for goods and services;

(15) exercise all powers and perform all duties on behalf of the unified court system as a public employer, pursuant to article 14 of the Civil Service Law (Taylor Law), as the chief executive officer pursuant to that article;

(16) adopt classifications and allocate positions for nonjudicial officers and employees of the unified court system, and revise them when appropriate; and

(17) have any additional powers and perform any additional duties assigned by the Chief Judge.

Cross References

Constitution, see McKinney's Book 2.

Civil Service Law, see McKinney's Book 9.

Judiciary Law, see McKinney's Book 29.

§ 80.2. Deputy Chief Administrators and Administrative Judges

(a) The Chief Administrator of the Courts, in consultation with the Presiding Justices of the appropriate Appellate Divisions on behalf of their respective courts, and with the approval of the Chief Judge, shall designate the following deputy chief administrators and administrative judges, who shall serve at his pleasure for a period not exceeding one year:

(1) in the City of New York: a deputy chief administrator, who may be a judge, for all the trial courts; one administrative judge each for the Family Court, the Civil Court and the Criminal Court; and one administrative judge each for the Supreme Court in Bronx, New York and Queens Counties and the Second Judicial District;

(2) outside the City of New York: a Deputy Chief Administrator, who may be a judge, for all the trial courts; and an Administrative Judge in each judicial district, except that separate Administrative Judges may be designated for Nassau and Suffolk Counties. The Chief Administrator may designate an Administrative Judge or Administrative Judges for the Family Court outside the City of New York; and

(3) such other deputy chief administrators, administrative judges and supervising judges as may be required.

(b) The Presiding Justice of an appellate term shall be designated by the Chief Administrator with the approval of the Presiding Justice of the appropriate appellate division, and shall be the Administrative Judge of that court.

(c) The Presiding Judge of the Court of Claims shall be the Administrative Judge of that court.

(d) Deputy Chief Administrators and Administrative Judges shall be responsible generally for the orderly administration of the courts within the area of their administrative responsibility, as set forth in their orders of designation.

§ 80.3. Administration of Appellate Divisions and Appellate Terms

(a) The Presiding Justices and the associate justices of the appellate divisions shall administer their respective courts and the appellate terms of the Supreme Court in their respective departments, in accordance with the standards and administrative policies established, approved, and promulgated pursuant to article VI, section 28(c), of the Constitution, and in their respective courts and for their respective appellate terms shall:

(1) establish the hours and terms of court, and assign justices to them;

(2) appoint and remove all nonjudicial officers and employees, except personal assistants who serve as law clerks (law secretaries) and secretaries to justices of those courts;

(3) delegate to the Presiding Justice or to any associate justice or the clerk any administrative power or function enumerated in this section;

(4) enforce and supervise the execution of the standards and administrative policies established, approved, and promulgated pursuant to article VI, section 28(c); and

(5) adopt administrative rules for the efficient and orderly transaction of business.

(b) The Chief Administrator's powers and duties with respect to the appellate divisions and appellate terms shall be limited to the following:

(1) preparation of the itemized estimates of the annual financial needs of the appellate divisions and appellate terms, in consultation with the respective appellate divisions;

(2) enforcement and supervision of the execution of the standards and administrative policies established, approved, and promulgated pursuant to article VI, section 28(c), relating to personnel practices and career service rules;

(3) designation of law journals for the publication of court calendars, judicial orders, decisions and opinions, and notices of proceedings;

(4) acceptance as agent of the appellate divisions and appellate terms of any grant or gift for the purposes of carrying out their functions, and contracting on their behalf for goods and services;

(5) exercise of all powers and performing all duties as a public employer pursuant to article 14 of the Civil Service Law (Taylor Law), and as the chief executive officer pursuant to that article; and

(6) adoption, and revision when appropriate, of classifications and allocations of positions for nonjudicial officers and employees of the appellate divisions and appellate terms.

(c) Supervision of the administration and operation of the following programs shall remain the responsibility of the appellate divisions or Presiding Justices, as now provided by statute: assignments of counsel, law guardians and guardians ad litem; the Mental Health Information Service; appointments of examiners of incompetents' accounts; and admission to the bar, disciplining of lawyers, and regulation of the practice of law.

§ 80.4. Court of Appeals

The Chief Administrator of the Courts shall adopt classifications and allocations of positions for all nonjudicial officers and employees of the Court of Appeals and revise them when necessary and appropriate, and shall have no other and additional powers and duties with respect to the administration of the Court of Appeals except as directed by the Court of Appeals.

PART 81. ADMINISTRATIVE DELEGATION NUMBER 2

§ 81.1. Chief Judge's Administrative Delegation Number 2

(a) Pursuant to article VI, section 28(b), of the State Constitution, and further to the delegation of authority to the Chief Administrator of the Courts effective April 1, 1978, the Chief Administrator of the Courts may designate deputy chief administrators for the courts within and outside the City of New York and a deputy chief administrator for management support. Said deputy chief administrators shall serve at the pleasure of the Chief Judge and the Chief Administrator and shall exercise and perform the following powers and duties, in accordance with and subject to the standards and administrative policies promulgated by the Chief Judge and the policies, rules, orders and directives of the Chief Judge and the Chief Administrator.

(b) The deputy chief administrators for the courts within and outside the City of New York shall:

(1) assist the Chief Judge and the Chief Administrator of the Courts in the supervision of the administration and operation of the unified court system;

(2) enforce and supervise the execution of standards and administrative policies promulgated pursuant to section 28(c) of article VI of the Constitution;

(3) implement within their jurisdictions rules, directives and orders of the Chief Judge and the Chief Administrator of the Courts;

(4) except as provided in paragraphs (c)(4) and (5) of this section, supervise the day-to-day operations of the courts, county clerks' offices and commissioners of jurors, if any, within their jurisdictions and oversee the administrative actions of the Administrative Judges of the courts within their jurisdictions;

(5) temporarily assign judges and justices within and between judicial districts, except certificated judges and justices;

(6) issue directives and orders necessary to implement these powers and duties;

(7) exercise such additional powers and duties as may be expressly delegated by the Chief Administrator of the Courts; and

(8) do all other things appropriate to exercise their aforesaid functions, powers and duties.

(c) The deputy chief administrator for management support shall:

(1) assist the Chief Judge and the Chief Administrator of the Courts in the supervision of the administration and operation of the unified court system;

(2) enforce and supervise the execution of standards and administrative policies promulgated pursuant to section 28(c) of article VI of the Constitution;

(3) with respect to the areas of responsibility set forth in paragraphs (4) and (5) of this subdivision, implement rules, directives and orders of the Chief Judge and the Chief Administrator of the Courts;

(4) supervise the operation of the management support functions of the unified court system, including: budget and finance; personnel; public information; program, systems and facilities management and planning; court information services and statistics; education and training; employee relations; and equal employment opportunity;

(5) appoint all nonjudicial officers and employees of the unified court system except: county clerks; commissioners of jurors; nonjudicial officers and employees of the town and village courts; personal assistants who serve as law clerks or secretaries to judges and justices; nonjudicial officers and employees in the Court of Appeals and appellate divisions and the agencies that they supervise; deputy chief administrators of the unified court system; and counsel to the unified court system. The power to appoint shall include the discretionary extension in service beyond retirement age of a nonjudicial officer or employee;

(6) issue directives and orders necessary to implement these powers and duties;

(7) exercise such additional powers and duties as may be expressly delegated by the Chief Administrator of the Courts; and

(8) do all other things appropriate to exercise the aforesaid functions, powers and duties.

(d) This delegation shall take effect as of January 22, 1981.

PART 82. ADMINISTRATIVE DELEGATION NUMBER 3

§ 82.1. Chief Judge's Administrative Delegation Number 3

(a) Pursuant to article VI, section 28(b), of the State Constitution, and further to the delegation of authority to the Chief Administrator of the Courts in Administrative Delegations Numbers 1 and 2 [22 NYCRR Parts 80 and 81], the Chief Administrator of the Courts, in consultation with the Presiding Justices of the Appellate Divisions, and with the approval of the Chief Judge, may designate a first deputy chief administrator for the courts.

(b) The first deputy chief administrator shall serve at the pleasure of the Chief Judge and Chief Administrator and, at the direction of the Chief Administrator, shall supervise the administration and operation of the trial-level courts and management support functions of the Unified Court System in accordance with and subject to the standards and administrative policies promulgated by the Chief Judge and the policies, rules, orders and directives of the Chief Judge and Chief Administrator.

(c) In exercising this authority, the first deputy chief administrator may exercise and perform any of the powers and duties of the Chief Administrator.

RULES OF THE CHIEF ADMINISTRATOR OF THE COURTS
PART 100. JUDICIAL CONDUCT

Cross References

See the Code of Judicial Conduct set out in McKinney's Bk. 29.

Preamble

The rules governing judicial conduct are rules of reason. They should be applied consistently with constitutional requirements, statutes, other court rules and decisional law and in the context of all relevant circumstances. The rules are to be construed so as not to impinge on the essential independence of judges in making judicial decisions.

The rules are designed to provide guidance to judges and candidates for elective judicial office and to provide a structure for regulating conduct through disciplinary agencies. They are not designed or intended as a basis for civil liability or criminal prosecution.

The text of the rules is intended to govern conduct of judges and candidates for elective judicial office and to be binding upon them. It is not intended, however, that every transgression will result in disciplinary action. Whether disciplinary action is appropriate, and the degree of discipline to be imposed, should be determined through a reasonable and reasoned application of the text and should depend on such factors as the seriousness of the transgression, whether there is a pattern of improper activity and the effect of the improper activity on others or on the judicial system.

The rules are not intended as an exhaustive guide for conduct. Judges and judicial candidates also should be governed in their judicial and personal conduct by general ethical standards. The rules are intended, however, to state basic standards which should govern their conduct and to provide guidance to assist them in establishing and maintaining high standards of judicial and personal conduct.

§ 100.0. Terminology

The following terms used in this Part are defined as follows:

(A) A "candidate" is a person seeking selection for or retention in public office by election. A person becomes a candidate for public office as soon as he or she makes a public announcement of candidacy, or authorizes solicitation or acceptance of contributions.

(B) "Court personnel" does not include the lawyers in a proceeding before a judge.

(C) The "degree of relationship" is calculated according to the civil law system. That is, where the judge and the party are in the same line of descent, degree is ascertained by ascending or descending from the judge to the party, counting a degree for each person, including the party but excluding the judge. Where the judge and the party are in different lines of descent, degree is ascertained by ascending from the judge to the common ancestor, and descending to the party, counting a degree for each person in both lines, including the common ancestor and the party but excluding the judge. The following persons are relatives within the fourth degree of relationship: great-grandparent, grandparent, parent, uncle, aunt, brother, sister, first cousin, child, grandchild, great-grandchild, nephew or niece. The sixth degree of relationship includes second cousins.

(D) "Economic interest" denotes ownership of a more than de minimis legal or equitable interest, or a relationship as officer, director, advisor or other active participant in the affairs of a party, except that

(1) ownership of an interest in a mutual or common investment fund that holds securities is not an economic interest in such securities unless the judge participates in the management of the fund or a proceeding pending or impending before the judge could substantially affect the value of the interest;

(2) service by a judge as an officer, director, advisor or other active participant in an educational, religious, charitable, cultural, fraternal or civic organization, or service by a judge's spouse or child as an officer, director, advisor or other active participant in any organization does not create an economic interest in securities held by that organization;

(3) a deposit in a financial institution, the proprietary interest of a policy holder in a mutual insurance company, of a depositor in a mutual savings association or of a member in a credit union, or a similar proprietary interest, is not an economic interest in the organization, unless a proceeding pending or impending before the judge could substantially affect the value of the interest;

(4) ownership of government securities is not an economic interest in the issuer unless a proceeding pending or impending before the judge could substantially affect the value of the securities.

(5) "De minimis" denotes an insignificant interest that could not raise reasonable questions as to a judge's impartiality.

(E) "Fiduciary" includes such relationships as executor, administrator, trustee, and guardian.

(F) "Knowingly", "knowledge", "known" or "knows" denotes actual knowledge of the fact in question. A person's knowledge may be inferred from circumstances.

(G) "Law" denotes court rules as well as statutes, constitutional provisions and decisional law.

(H) "Member of the candidate's family" denotes a spouse, child, grandchild, parent, grandparent or other relative or person with whom the candidate maintains a close familial relationship.

(I) "Member of the judge's family" denotes a spouse, child, grandchild, parent, grandparent or other relative or person with whom the judge maintains a close familial relationship.

(J) "Member of the judge's family residing in the judge's household" denotes any relative of a judge by blood or marriage, or a person treated by a judge as a member of the judge's family, who resides in the judge's household.

(K) "Nonpublic information" denotes information that, by law, is not available to the public. Nonpublic information may include but is not limited to: information that is sealed by statute or court order, impounded or communicated in camera; and information offered in grand jury proceedings, presentencing reports, dependency cases or psychiatric reports.

(L) A "part-time judge", including an acting part-time judge, is a judge who serves repeatedly on a part-time basis by election or under a continuing appointment.

(M) "Political organization" denotes a political party, political club or other group, the principal purpose of which is to further the election or appointment of candidates to political office.

(N) "Public election" includes primary and general elections; it includes partisan elections, nonpartisan elections and retention elections.

(O) "Require". The rules prescribing that a judge "require" certain conduct of others, like all of the rules in this Part, are rules of reason. The use of the term "require" in that context means a judge is to exercise reasonable direction and control over the conduct of those persons subject to the judge's direction and control.

(P) "Rules"; citation. Unless otherwise made clear by the citation in the text, references to individual components of the rules are cited as follows:

"Part"—refers to Part 100.

"Section"—refers to a provision consisting of 100 followed by a decimal (100.1).

"Subdivision"—refers to a provision designated by a capital letter (A).

"Paragraph"—refers to a provision designated by an arabic numeral (1).

"Subparagraph"—refers to a provision designated by a lower-case letter (a).

(Q) "Window Period" denotes a period beginning nine months before a primary election, judicial nominating convention, party caucus or other party meeting for nominating candidates for the elective judicial office for which a judge or non-judge is an announced candidate, or for which a committee or other organization has publicly solicited or supported the judge's or non-judge's candidacy, and ending, if the judge or non-judge is a candidate in the general election for that office, six months after the general election, or if he or she is not a candidate in the general election, six months after the date of the primary election, convention, caucus or meeting.

(R) "Impartiality" denotes absence of bias or prejudice in favor of, or against, particular parties or classes of parties, as well as maintaining an open mind in considering issues that may come before the judge.

(S) An "independent" judiciary is one free of outside influences or control.

(T) "Integrity" denotes probity, fairness, honesty, uprightness and soundness of character. "Integrity" also includes a firm adherence to this Part or its standard of values.

(U) A "pending proceeding" is one that has begun but not yet reached its final disposition.

(V) An "impending proceeding" is one that is reasonably foreseeable but has not yet been commenced.

§ 100.1. A Judge Shall Uphold the Integrity and Independence of the Judiciary

An independent and honorable judiciary is indispensable to justice in our society. A judge should participate in establishing, maintaining and enforcing high standards of conduct, and shall personally observe those standards so that the integrity and independence of the judiciary will be preserved. The provisions of this Part 100 are to be construed and applied to further that objective.

§ 100.2. A Judge Shall Avoid Impropriety and the Appearance of Impropriety in All of the Judge's Activities

(A) A judge shall respect and comply with the law and shall act at all times in a manner that promotes public confidence in the integrity and impartiality of the judiciary.

(B) A judge shall not allow family, social, political or other relationships to influence the judge's judicial conduct or judgment.

(C) A judge shall not lend the prestige of judicial office to advance the private interests of the judge or others; nor shall a judge convey or permit others to convey the impression that they are in a special position to influence the judge. A judge shall not testify voluntarily as a character witness.

(D) A judge shall not hold membership in any organization that practices invidious discrimination on the basis of age, race, creed, color, sex, sexual orientation, religion, national origin, disability or marital status. This provision does not prohibit a judge from holding membership in an organization that is dedicated to the preservation of religious, ethnic, cultural or other values of legitimate common interest to its members.

§ 100.3. A Judge Shall Perform the Duties of Judicial Office Impartially and Diligently

(A) **Judicial Duties in General.** The judicial duties of a judge take precedence over all the judge's other activities. The judge's judicial duties include all the duties of the judge's office prescribed by law. In the performance of these duties, the following standards apply.

(B) **Adjudicative Responsibilities.**

(1) A judge shall be faithful to the law and maintain professional competence in it. A judge shall not be swayed by partisan interests, public clamor or fear of criticism.

(2) A judge shall require order and decorum in proceedings before the judge.

(3) A judge shall be patient, dignified and courteous to litigants, jurors, witnesses, lawyers and others with whom the judge deals in an official capacity, and shall require similar conduct of lawyers, and of staff, court officials and others subject to the judge's direction and control.

(4) A judge shall perform judicial duties without bias or prejudice against or in favor of any person. A judge in the performance of judicial duties shall not, by words or conduct, manifest bias or prejudice, including but not limited to bias or prejudice based upon age, race, creed, color, sex, sexual orientation, religion, national origin, disability, marital status or socioeconomic status, and shall require staff, court officials and others subject to the judge's direction and control to refrain from such words or conduct.

(5) A judge shall require lawyers in proceedings before the judge to refrain from manifesting, by words or conduct, bias or prejudice based upon age, race, creed, color, sex, sexual orientation, religion, national origin, disability, marital status or socioeconomic status, against parties, witnesses, counsel or others. This paragraph does not preclude legitimate advocacy when age, race, creed, color, sex, sexual orientation, religion, national origin, disability, marital status or socioeconomic status, or other similar factors are issues in the proceeding.

(6) A judge shall accord to every person who has a legal interest in a proceeding, or that person's lawyer, the right to be heard according to law. A judge shall not initiate, permit, or consider ex parte communications, or consider other communications made to the judge outside the presence of the parties or their lawyers concerning a pending or impending proceeding, except:

(a) Ex parte communications that are made for scheduling or administrative purposes and that do not affect a substantial right of any party are authorized, provided the judge reasonably believes that no party will gain a procedural or tactical advantage as a result of the ex parte communication, and the judge, insofar as practical and appropriate, makes provision for prompt notification of other parties or their lawyers of the substance of the ex parte communication and allows an opportunity to respond.

(b) A judge may obtain the advice of a disinterested expert on the law applicable to a proceeding before the judge if the judge gives notice to the parties of the person consulted and a copy of such advice if the advice is given in writing and the substance of the advice if it is given orally, and affords the parties reasonable opportunity to respond.

(c) A judge may consult with court personnel whose function is to aid the judge in carrying out the judge's adjudicative responsibilities or with other judges.

(d) A judge, with the consent of the parties, may confer separately with the parties and their lawyers on agreed-upon matters.

(e) A judge may initiate or consider any ex parte communications when authorized by law to do so.

(7) A judge shall dispose of all judicial matters promptly, efficiently and fairly.

(8) A judge shall not make any public comment about a pending or impending proceeding in any court within the United States or its territories. The judge shall require similar abstention on the part of court personnel subject to the judge's direction and control. This paragraph does not prohibit judges from making public statements in the course of their official duties or from explaining for public information the procedures of the court. This paragraph does not apply to proceedings in which the judge is a litigant in a personal capacity.

(9) A judge shall not:

(a) make pledges or promises of conduct in office that are inconsistent with the impartial performance of the adjudicative duties of the office;

(b) with respect to cases, controversies or issues that are likely to come before the court, make commitments that are inconsistent with the impartial performance of the adjudicative duties of the office.

(10) A judge shall not commend or criticize jurors for their verdict other than in a court order or opinion in a proceeding, but may express appreciation to jurors for their service to the judicial system and the community.

(11) A judge shall not disclose or use, for any purpose unrelated to judicial duties, nonpublic information acquired in a judicial capacity.

(C) Administrative Responsibilities.

(1) A judge shall diligently discharge the judge's administrative responsibilities without bias or prejudice and maintain professional competence in judicial administration, and should cooperate with other judges and court officials in the administration of court business.

(2) A judge shall require staff, court officials and others subject to the judge's direction and control to observe the standards of fidelity and diligence that apply to the judge and to refrain from manifesting bias or prejudice in the performance of their official duties.

(3) A judge shall not make unnecessary appointments. A judge shall exercise the power of appointment impartially and on the basis of merit. A judge shall avoid nepotism and favoritism. A judge shall not approve compensation of appointees beyond the fair value of services rendered. A judge shall not appoint or vote for the appointment of any person as a member of the judge's staff or that of the court of which the judge is a member, or as an appointee in a judicial proceeding, who is a relative within the fourth degree of relationship of either the judge or the judge's spouse or the spouse of such a person. A judge shall refrain from recommending a relative within the fourth degree of relationship of either the judge or the judge's spouse or the spouse of such person for appointment or employment to another judge serving in the same court. A judge also shall comply with the requirements of Part 8 of the Rules of the Chief Judge (22 NYCRR Part 8) relating to the appointment of relatives of judges. Nothing in this paragraph shall prohibit appointment of the spouse of the town or village justice, or other member of such justice's household, as clerk of the town or village court in which such justice sits, provided that the justice obtains the prior approval of the Chief Administrator of the Courts, which may be given upon a showing of good cause.

(D) Disciplinary Responsibilities.

(1) A judge who receives information indicating a substantial likelihood that another judge has committed a substantial violation of this Part shall take appropriate action.

(2) A judge who receives information indicating a substantial likelihood that a lawyer has committed a substantial violation of the Code of Professional Responsibility shall take appropriate action.

(3) Acts of a judge in the discharge of disciplinary responsibilities are part of a judge's judicial duties.

(E) Disqualification.

(1) A judge shall disqualify himself or herself in a proceeding in which the judge's impartiality might reasonably be questioned, including but not limited to instances where:

(a) (i) the judge has a personal bias or prejudice concerning a party or (ii) the judge has personal knowledge of disputed evidentiary facts concerning the proceeding;

(b) the judge knows that (i) the judge served as a lawyer in the matter in controversy, or (ii) a lawyer with whom the judge previously practiced law served during such association as a lawyer concerning the matter, or (iii) the judge has been a material witness concerning it;

(c) the judge knows that he or she, individually or as a fiduciary, or the judge's spouse or minor child residing in the judge's household has an economic interest in the subject matter in controversy or in a party to the proceeding or has any other interest that could be substantially affected by the proceeding;

(d) the judge knows that the judge or the judge's spouse, or a person known by the judge to be within the sixth degree of relationship to either of them, or the spouse of such a person:

(i) is a party to the proceeding;

(ii) is an officer, director or trustee of a party;

(iii) has an interest that could be substantially affected by the proceeding

(e) the judge knows that the judge or the judge's spouse, or a person known by the judge to be within the fourth degree of relationship to either of them, or the spouse of such a person, is acting as a lawyer in the proceeding or is likely to be a material witness in the proceeding.

(f) the judge, while a judge or while a candidate for judicial office, has made a pledge or promise of conduct in office that is inconsistent with the impartial performance of the adjudicative duties of the office or has made a public statement not in the judge's adjudicative capacity that commits the judge with respect to

(i) an issue in the proceeding; or

(ii) the parties or controversy in the proceeding.

(g) notwithstanding the provisions of subparagraphs (c) and (d) above, if a judge would be disqualified because of the appearance or discovery, after the matter was assigned to the judge, that the judge individually or as a fiduciary, the judge's spouse, or a minor child residing in his or her household has an economic interest in a party to the proceeding, disqualification is not required if the judge, spouse or minor child, as the case may be, divests himself or herself of the interest that provides the grounds for the disqualification.

(2) A judge shall keep informed about the judge's personal and fiduciary economic interests, and make a reasonable effort to keep informed about the personal economic interests of the judge's spouse and minor children residing in the judge's household.

(F) Remittal of Disqualification. A judge disqualified by the terms of subdivision (E), except subparagraph (1)(a)(i), subparagraph (1)(b)(i) or (iii) or subparagraph (1)(d)(i) of this section, may disclose on the record the basis of the judge's disqualification. If, following such disclosure of any basis for disqualification, the parties who have appeared and not defaulted and their lawyers, without participation by the judge, all agree that the judge should not be disqualified, and the judge believes that he or she will be impartial and is willing to participate, the judge may participate in the proceeding. The agreement shall be incorporated in the record of the proceeding.

§ 100.4. A Judge Shall so Conduct the Judge's Extra–Judicial Activities as to Minimize the Risk of Conflict With Judicial Obligations

(A) Extra–Judicial Activities in General. A judge shall conduct all of the judge's extra-judicial activities so that they do not:

(1) cast reasonable doubt on the judge's capacity to act impartially as a judge;

(2) detract from the dignity of judicial office; or

(3) interfere with the proper performance of judicial duties and are not incompatible with judicial office.

(B) Avocational Activities. A judge may speak, write, lecture, teach and participate in extra-judicial activities subject to the requirements of this Part.

(C) Governmental, Civic, or Charitable Activities.

(1) A full-time judge shall not appear at a public hearing before an executive or legislative body or official except on matters concerning the law, the legal system or the administration of justice or except when acting pro se in a matter involving the judge or the judge's interests.

(2)(a) A full-time judge shall not accept appointment to a governmental committee or commission or other governmental position that is concerned with issues of fact or policy in matters other than the improvement of the law, the legal system or the administration of justice. A judge may, however, represent a country, state or locality on ceremonial occasions or in connection with historical, educational or cultural activities.

(b) A judge shall not accept appointment or employment as a peace officer or police officer as those terms are defined in section 1.20 of the Criminal Procedure Law.

(3) A judge may be a member or serve as an officer, director, trustee or non-legal advisor of an organization or governmental agency devoted to the improvement of the law, the legal system or the administration of justice or of an educational, religious, charitable, cultural, fraternal or civic organization not conducted for profit, subject to the following limitations and the other requirements of this Part.

(a) A judge shall not serve as an officer, director, trustee or non-legal advisor if it is likely that the organization

(i) will be engaged in proceedings that ordinarily would come before the judge, or

(ii) if the judge is a full-time judge, will be engaged regularly in adversary proceedings in any court.

(b) A judge as an officer, director, trustee or non-legal advisor, or a member or otherwise:

(i) may assist such an organization in planning fund-raising and may participate in the management and investment of the organization's funds, but shall not personally participate in the solicitation of funds or other fund-raising activities;

(ii) may not be a speaker or the guest of honor at an organization's fund-raising events, but the judge may attend such events. Nothing in this subparagraph shall prohibit a judge from being a speaker or guest of honor at a court employee organization, bar association or law school function or from accepting at another organization's fund-raising event an unadvertised award ancillary to such event;

(iii) may make recommendations to public and private fund-granting organizations on projects and programs concerning the law, the legal system or the administration of justice; and

(iv) shall not use or permit the use of the prestige of judicial office for fund-raising or membership solicitation, but may be listed as an officer, director or trustee of such an organization. Use of an organization's regular letterhead for fund-raising or membership solicitation does not violate this provision, provided the letterhead lists only the judge's name and office or other position in the organization, and, if comparable designations are listed for other persons, the judge's judicial designation.

(D) Financial Activities.

(1) A judge shall not engage in financial and business dealings that:

(a) may reasonably be perceived to exploit the judge's judicial position,

(b) involve the judge with any business, organization or activity that ordinarily will come before the judge, or

(c) involve the judge in frequent transactions or continuing business relationships with those lawyers or other persons likely to come before the court on which the judge serves.

(2) A judge, subject to the requirements of this Part, may hold and manage investments of the judge and members of the judge's family, including real estate.

(3) A full-time judge shall not serve as an officer, director, manager, general partner, advisor, employee or other active participant of any business entity, except that:

(a) the foregoing restriction shall not be applicable to a judge who assumed judicial office prior to July 1, 1965, and maintained such position or activity continuously since that date; and

(b) a judge, subject to the requirements of this Part, may manage and participate in a business entity engaged solely in investment of the financial resources of the judge or members of the judge's family; and

(c) any person who may be appointed to fill a full-time judicial vacancy on an interim or temporary basis pending an election to fill such vacancy may apply to the Chief Administrator of the Courts for exemption from this paragraph during the period of such interim or temporary appointment.

(4) A judge shall manage the judge's investments and other financial interests to minimize the number of cases in which the judge is disqualified. As soon as the judge can do so without serious financial detriment, the judge shall divest himself or herself of investments and other financial interests that might require frequent disqualification.

(5) A judge shall not accept, and shall urge members of the judge's family residing in the judge's household not to accept, a gift, bequest, favor or loan from anyone except:

(a) a gift incident to a public testimonial, books, tapes and other resource materials supplied by publishers on a complimentary basis for official use, or an invitation to the judge and the judge's spouse or guest to attend a bar-related function or an activity devoted to the improvement of the law, the legal system or the administration of justice;

(b) a gift, award or benefit incident to the business, profession or other separate activity of a spouse or other family member of a judge residing in the judge's household, including gifts, awards and benefits for the use of both the spouse or other family member and the judge (as spouse or family member), provided the gift, award or benefit could not reasonably be perceived as intended to influence the judge in the performance of judicial duties;

(c) ordinary social hospitality;

(d) a gift from a relative or friend, for a special occasion such as a wedding, anniversary or birthday, if the gift is fairly commensurate with the occasion and the relationship;

(e) a gift, bequest, favor or loan from a relative or close personal friend whose appearance or interest in a case would in any event require disqualification under section 100.3(E);

(f) a loan from a lending institution in its regular course of business on the same terms generally available to persons who are not judges;

(g) a scholarship or fellowship awarded on the same terms and based on the same criteria applied to other applicants; or

(h) any other gift, bequest, favor or loan, only if: the donor is not a party or other person who has come or is likely to come or whose interests have come or are likely to come before the judge; and if its value exceeds $150.00, the judge reports it in the same manner as the judge reports compensation in section 100.4(H).

(E) Fiduciary Activities.

(1) A full-time judge shall not serve as executor, administrator or other personal representative, trustee, guardian, attorney in fact or other fiduciary, designated by an instrument executed after January 1, 1974, except for the estate, trust or person of a member of the judge's family, or, with the approval of the Chief Administrator of the Courts, a person not a member of the judge's family with whom the judge has maintained a longstanding personal relationship of trust and confidence, and then only if such services will not interfere with the proper performance of judicial duties.

(2) The same restrictions on financial activities that apply to a judge personally also apply to the judge while acting in a fiduciary capacity.

(3) Any person who may be appointed to fill a full-time judicial vacancy on an interim or temporary basis pending an election to fill such vacancy may apply to the Chief Administrator of the Courts for exemption from paragraphs (1) and (2) during the period of such interim or temporary appointment.

(F) Service as Arbitrator or Mediator. A full-time judge shall not act as an arbitrator or mediator or otherwise perform judicial functions in a private capacity unless expressly authorized by law.

(G) Practice of Law. A full-time judge shall not practice law. Notwithstanding this prohibition, a judge may act pro se and may, without compensation, give legal advice to a member of the judge's family.

(H) Compensation, Reimbursement and Reporting.

(1) *Compensation and Reimbursement.* A full-time judge may receive compensation and reimbursement of expenses for the extra-judicial activities per-

mitted by this Part, if the source of such payments does not give the appearance of influencing the judge's performance of judicial duties or otherwise give the appearance of impropriety, subject to the following restrictions:

(a) Compensation shall not exceed a reasonable amount nor shall it exceed what a person who is not a judge would receive for the same activity.

(b) Expense reimbursement shall be limited to the actual cost of travel, food and lodging reasonably incurred by the judge and, where appropriate to the occasion, by the judge's spouse or guest. Any payment in excess of such an amount is compensation.

(c) No full-time judge shall solicit or receive compensation for extra-judicial activities performed for or on behalf of: (1) New York State, its political subdivisions or any office or agency thereof; (2) a school, college or university that is financially supported primarily by New York State or any of its political subdivisions, or any officially recognized body of students thereof, except that a judge may receive the ordinary compensation for a lecture or for teaching a regular course of study at any college or university if the teaching does not conflict with the proper performance of judicial duties; or (3) any private legal aid bureau or society designated to represent indigents in accordance with article 18–B of the County Law.

(2) *Public Reports.* A full-time judge shall report the date, place and nature of any activity for which the judge received compensation in excess of $150, and the name of the payor and the amount of compensation so received. Compensation or income of a spouse attributed to the judge by operation of a community property law is not extra-judicial compensation to the judge. The judge's report shall be made at least annually and shall be filed as a public document in the office of the clerk of the court on which the judge serves or other office designated by law.

(I) **Financial Disclosure.** Disclosure of a judge's income, debts, investments or other assets is required only to the extent provided in this section and in section 100.3(F), or as required by Part 40 of the Rules of the Chief Judge (22 NYCRR Part 40), or as otherwise required by law.

Cross References

Criminal Procedure Law, see McKinney's Book 11A.

§ 100.5. A Judge or Candidate for Elective Judicial Office Shall Refrain From Inappropriate Political Activity

(A) Incumbent Judges and Others Running for Public Election to Judicial Office.

(1) Neither a sitting judge nor a candidate for public election to judicial office shall directly or indirectly engage in any political activity except (i) as

otherwise authorized by this section or by law, (ii) to vote and to identify himself or herself as a member of a political party, and (iii) on behalf of measures to improve the law, the legal system or the administration of justice. Prohibited political activity shall include:

(a) acting as a leader or holding an office in a political organization;

(b) except as provided in section 100.5(A)(3), being a member of a political organization other than enrollment and membership in a political party;

(c) engaging in any partisan political activity, provided that nothing in this section shall prohibit a judge or candidate from participating in his or her own campaign for elective judicial office or shall restrict a non-judge holder of public office in the exercise of the functions of that office;

(d) participating in any political campaign for any office or permitting his or her name to be used in connection with any activity of a political organization;

(e) publicly endorsing or publicly opposing (other than by running against) another candidate for public office;

(f) making speeches on behalf of a political organization or another candidate;

(g) attending political gatherings;

(h) soliciting funds for, paying an assessment to, or making a contribution to a political organization or candidate; or

(i) purchasing tickets for politically sponsored dinners or other functions, including any such function for a non-political purpose.

(2) A judge or non-judge who is a candidate for public election to judicial office may participate in his or her own campaign for judicial office as provided in this section and may contribute to his or her own campaign as permitted under the Election Law. During the Window Period as defined in subdivision (Q) of section 100.0 of this Part, a judge or non-judge who is a candidate for public election to judicial office, except as prohibited by law, may:

(i) attend and speak to gatherings on his or her own behalf, provided that the candidate does not personally solicit contributions;

(ii) appear in newspaper, television and other media advertisements supporting his or her candidacy, and distribute pamphlets and other promotional campaign literature supporting his or her candidacy;

(iii) appear at gatherings, and in newspaper, television and other media advertisements with the candidates who make up the slate of which the judge or candidate is a part;

(iv) permit the candidate's name to be listed on election materials along with the names of other candidates for elective public office;

(v) purchase two tickets to, and attend, politically sponsored dinners and other functions, provided that the cost of the ticket to such dinner or other function shall not exceed the proportionate cost of the dinner or function. The cost of the ticket shall be deemed to constitute the proportionate cost of the dinner or function if the cost of the ticket is $250 or less. A candidate may not pay more than $250 for a ticket unless he or she obtains a statement from the sponsor of the dinner or function that the amount paid represents the proportionate cost of the dinner or function.

(3) A non-judge who is a candidate for public election to judicial office may also be a member of a political organization and continue to pay ordinary assessments and ordinary contributions to such organization.

(4) A judge or a non-judge who is a candidate for public election to judicial office:

(a) shall maintain the dignity appropriate to judicial office and act in a manner consistent with the impartiality, integrity and independence of the judiciary, and shall encourage members of the candidate's family to adhere to the same standards of political conduct in support of the candidate as apply to the candidate;

(b) shall prohibit employees and officials who serve at the pleasure of the candidate, and shall discourage other employees and officials subject to the candidate's direction and control, from doing on the candidate's behalf what the candidate is prohibited from doing under this Part;

(c) except to the extent permitted by section 100.5(A)(5), shall not authorize or knowingly permit any person to do for the candidate what the candidate is prohibited from doing under this Part;

(d) shall not:

(i) make pledges or promises of conduct in office that are inconsistent with the impartial performance of the adjudicative duties of the office;

(ii) with respect to cases, controversies or issues that are likely to come before the court, make commitments that are inconsistent with the impartial performance of the adjudicative duties of the office;

(iii) knowingly make any false statement or misrepresent the identity, qualifications, current position or other fact concerning the candidate or an opponent; but

(e) may respond to personal attacks or attacks on the candidate's record as long as the response does not violate subparagraphs 100.5(A)(4)(a) and (d).

(f) shall complete an education program, either in person or by videotape or by internet correspondence course, developed or approved by the Chief Administrator or his or her designee any time after the candidate makes a public announcement of candidacy or authorizes solicitation or acceptance of contributions for a known judicial vacancy, but no later than 30 days after receiving the nomination for judicial office. The date of nomination for candidates running in a primary election shall be the date upon which the candidate files a designating petition with the Board of Elections. This provision shall apply to all candidates for elective judicial office in the Unified Court System except for town and village justices.

(g) shall file with the Ethics Commission for the Unified Court System a financial disclosure statement containing the information and in the form set forth in the Annual Statement of Financial Disclosure adopted by the Chief Judge of the State of New York. Such statement shall be filed within 20 days following the date on which the judge or non-judge becomes such a candidate; provided, however, that the Ethics Commission for the Unified Court System may grant an additional period of time within which to file such statement in accordance with rules promulgated pursuant to section 40.1(i)(3) of the Rules of the Chief Judge of the State of New York (22 NYCRR). Notwithstanding the foregoing, compliance with this subparagraph shall not be necessary where a judge or non-judge already is or was required to file a financial disclosure statement for the preceding calendar year pursuant to Part 40 of the Rules of the Chief Judge.

(5) A judge or candidate for public election to judicial office shall not personally solicit or accept campaign contributions, but may establish committees of responsible persons to conduct campaigns for the candidate through media advertisements, brochures, mailings, candidate forums and other means not prohibited by law. Such committees may solicit and accept reasonable campaign contributions and support from the public, including lawyers, manage the expenditure of funds for the candidate's campaign and obtain public statements of support for his or her candidacy. Such committees may solicit and accept such contributions and support only during the Window Period. A candidate shall not use or permit the use of campaign contributions for the private benefit of the candidate or others.

(6) A judge or a non-judge who is a candidate for public election to judicial office may not permit the use of campaign contributions or personal funds to pay for campaign-related goods or services for which fair value was not received.

(7) Independent Judicial Election Qualifications Commissions, created pursuant to Part 150 of the Rules of the Chief Administrator of the Courts, shall

evaluate candidates for elected judicial office, other than justice of a town or village court.

(B) Judge as Candidate for Nonjudicial Office. A judge shall resign from judicial office upon becoming a candidate for elective nonjudicial office either in a primary or in a general election, except that the judge may continue to hold judicial office while being a candidate for election to or serving as a delegate in a state constitutional convention if the judge is otherwise permitted by law to do so.

(C) Judge's Staff. A judge shall prohibit members of the judge's staff who are the judge's personal appointees from engaging in the following political activity:

(1) holding an elective office in a political organization, except as a delegate to a judicial nominating convention or a member of a county committee other than the executive committee of a county committee;

(2) contributing, directly or indirectly, money or other valuable consideration in amounts exceeding $500 in the aggregate during any calendar year to all political campaigns for political office, and other partisan political activity including, but not limited to, the purchasing of tickets to political functions, except that this $500 limitation shall not apply to an appointee's contributions to his or her own campaign. Where an appointee is a candidate for judicial office, reference also shall be made to appropriate sections of the Election Law;

(3) personally soliciting funds in connection with a partisan political purpose, or personally selling tickets to or promoting a fund-raising activity of a political candidate, political party, or partisan political club; or

(4) political conduct prohibited by section 50.5 of the Rules of the Chief Judge (22 NYCRR 50.5).

Cross References

Election Law, see McKinney's Book 17.

§ 100.6. Application of the Rules of Judicial Conduct

(A) General Application. All judges in the unified court system and all other persons to whom by their terms these rules apply, e.g., candidates for elective judicial office, shall comply with these rules of judicial conduct, except as provided below. All other persons, including judicial hearing officers, who perform judi-cial functions within the judicial system shall comply with such rules in the performance of their judicial functions and otherwise shall so far as practical and appropriate use such rules as guides to their conduct.

(B) Part–Time Judge. A part-time judge:

(1) is not required to comply with sections 100.4(C)(1), 100.4(C)(2)(a), 100.4(C)(3)(a)(ii), 100.4(E)(1), 100.4(F), 100.4(G), and 100.4(H);

(2) shall not practice law in the court on which the judge serves, or in any other court in the county in which his or her court is located, before a judge who is permitted to practice law, and shall not act as a lawyer in a proceeding in which the judge has served as a judge or in any other proceeding related thereto;

(3) shall not permit his or her partners or associates to practice law in the court in which he or she is a judge, and shall not permit the practice of law in his or her court by the law partners or associates of another judge of the same court who is permitted to practice law, but may permit the practice of law in his or her court by the partners or associates of a judge of a court in another town, village or city who is permitted to practice law;

(4) may accept private employment or public employment in a federal, state or municipal department or agency, provided that such employment is not incompatible with judicial office and does not conflict or interfere with the proper performance of the judge's duties.

(C) Administrative Law Judges. The provisions of this Part are not applicable to administrative law judges unless adopted by the rules of the employing agency.

(D) Time for Compliance. A person to whom these rules become applicable shall comply immediately with all provisions of this Part, except that, with respect to sections 100.4(D)(3) and 100.4(E), such person may make application to the Chief Administrator for additional time to comply, in no event to exceed one year, which the Chief Administrator may grant for good cause shown.

(E) Relationship to Code of Judicial Conduct. To the extent that any provision of the Code of Judicial Conduct as adopted by the New York State Bar Association is inconsistent with any of these rules, these rules shall prevail.

PART 101. ADVISORY COMMITTEE ON JUDICIAL ETHICS

§ 101.1. Establishment

There shall be an Advisory Committee on Judicial Ethics to issue advisory opinions to judges and justices of the Unified Court System concerning issues related to ethical conduct, proper execution of judicial duties, and possible conflicts between private interests and official duties.

§ 101.2. Membership

(a) The Chief Administrator of the Courts, in consultation with the Administrative Board of the Courts and with the approval of the Chief Judge of the State of New York, shall appoint members to the Committee in such numbers as deemed necessary to effectively carry out its duties and shall designate the chair.

(b) Each member shall be an active or former judge or justice of the Unified Court System.

(c) The members and the chair shall serve at the pleasure of the Chief Administrator and shall be appointed for terms of up to five years, provided that no member first appointed on or after November 1, 2000, shall serve for more than one five-year term.

§ 101.3. Duties

(a) The Committee shall issue advisory opinions, in writing, to the judge or justice making the request. The Committee may decline to respond to any question it deems inappropriate for the exercise of its jurisdiction.

(b) The Committee may respond to questions concerning judicial ethics posed by persons who exercise quasi-judicial duties in the Unified Court System but who are not judges or justices of the Unified Court System.

§ 101.4. Procedure

(a) Unless the chair provides otherwise, all requests for advisory opinions shall be submitted in writing. Requests shall detail the particular facts and circumstances of the case. The Committee may request such supplemental material as it deems necessary.

(b) The Committee shall adopt procedures for the formulation and transmission of its advisory opinions.

§ 101.5. Compensation

Members of the Committee shall serve without compensation but shall be reimbursed for expenses actually and necessarily incurred in the performance of their official duties for the Committee.

§ 101.6. Confidentiality

Except as set forth in section 101.7, requests for advisory opinions, advisory opinions issued by the Committee, and the facts and circumstances on which they are based shall be confidential and shall not be disclosed by the Committee to any person other than the individual making the request. Deliberations by the Committee shall be confidential.

§ 101.7. Publication

The Committee shall publish its formal advisory opinions, at such times and in such manner as approved by the Chief Administrator, with appropriate deletions of names of persons, places, or things that might tend to identify the judge or justice making the request or any other judge or justice of the Unified Court System.

PART 102. REIMBURSEMENT OF TRAVELING EXPENSES IN CONNECTION WITH PERFORMANCE OF JUDICIAL DUTIES

§ 102.0. General

(a) This Part shall apply to the reimbursement of expenses designated herein incurred by a judge of the Court of Appeals, a justice of the Supreme Court, including a justice of the Appellate Division or Appellate Term, and a judge of the Court of Claims, County Court, Surrogate's Court, Family Court, District Court, and Civil and Criminal Court of the City of New York, and a full-time judge of a City Court outside the City of New York, who is assigned to perform judicial duties outside the county wherein such judge is provided chambers.

(b) Subject to the provisions of this Part, each judge or justice to whom subdivision (a) of this section applies shall receive actual and necessary transportation expenses, and shall also receive such other necessary expenses, including meals, lodging and incidentals, not to exceed the rate determined by the Chief Administrator of the Courts, as such judge or justice shall actually and necessarily incur.

(c) For the purposes of reimbursement of expenses under this Part, the City of New York shall be deemed to be one county. No judge of any court in New York City who is assigned to perform judicial duties in another county in New York City shall be entitled to reimbursement of expenses under this Part.

(d) The reimbursement of expenses provided for in this Part shall be the exclusive method of reimbursing each judge or justice for such expenses.

(e) Each judge or justice shall provide sufficient personal funds to cover all expenses in the first instance.

(f) The Chief Administrator, in consultation with the presiding judge of the Court of Claims, shall designate for Court of Claims judges the county in which chambers are provided or deemed to be provided for the purposes of this Part.

(g) Reimbursement of expenses in connection with the performance of judicial duties outside of New York State shall require the prior approval of the Chief Administrator and shall be allowed only at a daily rate to be fixed by the Chief Administrator.

§ 102.1. Transportation Expenses

Reimbursement for transportation expenses incurred pursuant to this Part shall be allowed in accordance with the following regulations:

(a) Personally Owned Automobile. When transportation is provided by personally owned automobile, a judge or justice shall be reimbursed at a rate determined by the Chief Administrator.[1] In addition, parking charges and bridge and highway tolls shall be reimbursed. Reimbursement for gasoline, insurance, repairs, depreciation, towage and all other operating costs is included in the mileage rate.

(b) Car Rental. Reimbursement of expenses for use of a rental car shall be allowed in exceptional cases, provided that adequate proof of need and of the expenses incurred is provided, and prior approval is obtained from the Chief Administrator. Parking charges and bridge and highway tolls shall be reimbursed.

(c) Publicly Owned Cars. Judges or justices traveling by cars owned by the State or a political subdivision of the State shall so indicate on the expense voucher, giving the license number of the vehicle. Parking charges and bridge and highway tolls shall be reimbursed. Claims for expenses for emergency items and repairs made for cars owned by the State or a political subdivision shall be supported by appropriate receipts. All State vehicles operating in or near Albany shall, when possible, be serviced in the State garage rather than at service stations.

(d) Common Carrier. When transportation is by common carrier, reimbursement of fare shall be allowed. When transportation is by air, or by first class, Pullman or similar rail accommodation, copies of tickets or similar documentation shall be attached to the expense voucher. When air travel is used, less than first class accommodations should be utilized whenever possible. Payments for taxicab, airport limousine, tips or other expenses necessarily incurred in connection with the use of common carrier shall be allowed.

[1] Effective Nunc Pro Tunc Dec. 1, 1988.

§ 102.2. Meals, Lodging and Incidental Expenses

(a) Total allowances for meals, lodging and incidental expenses incurred pursuant to this Part shall not exceed the rate determined by the Chief Administrator. Specific expenses for all or part of a day in travel status shall be reimbursed in accordance with maximum rates established by the Chief Administrator. Miscellaneous expenses for items such as baggage transfer and tips to porters are included under the allowance for lodging and incidentals.

(b) Reimbursement of miscellaneous expenses in connection with travel (such as telephone calls or telegrams) shall be allowed, whether or not an expense for lodging was incurred.

(c) Receipts or other proof of expenses for overnight lodging shall be supplied with the expense voucher. Receipts for meals and incidentals need not be supplied with the expense voucher, but claims for meals and incidental or miscellaneous expenses shall be itemized on the voucher.

(d) A judge or justice traveling to or from the county wherein he or she is provided chambers, in the performance of his or her judicial duties, shall be reimbursed for a meal or meals taken in any place if necessarily purchased in connection with such travel.

(e) A judge or justice traveling on judicial business is exempted from State and local taxes for lodgings. Exemption certificate (form AC 946) shall be used at the hotel or motel to avoid payment of such taxes.

(f) A judge or justice who is continuously assigned to official duties outside the county in which he or she is provided chambers may remain in the county of assignment over weekends and on holidays, or may return home. If he or she elects to remain in the county of assignment, he or she shall be reimbursed pursuant to the rates referred to in subdivision (a) of this section for expenses incurred on Saturdays, Sundays and holidays for meals, lodging and incidentals. If he or she returns home, he or she shall be reimbursed only for transportation expenses, and for a meal or meals in accordance with subdivision (d) of this section.

§ 102.3. Apartment Rental and Long-Term Rental Arrangements

If a judge or justice rents an apartment or hotel or motel room other than at a daily rate, the Chief Administrator may permit reimbursement for lodging expenses at a rate to be determined by the Chief Administrator not to exceed the rate for lodging determined by the Chief Administrator pursuant to section 102.2(a)[1] for each night when the judge or justice stayed overnight in the rented premises, provided that:

(a) the provisions of subdivision (c) of section 102.2 of this Part are satisfied as to each night's lodging expenses for which the judge or justice seeks reimbursement;

(b) prior approval of the rental arrangement is given by the Chief Administrator;

(c) a copy of the rental agreement is filed with the Chief Administrator;

(d) the total reimbursement of expenses for lodging in any period shall not exceed the rent for that period; and

(e) where the amount payable as reimbursement during any one month exceeds the monthly rent, the excess amount payable as reimbursement can be used as an offset against the rent for the same premises for another month during which the amount payable as reimbursement was not sufficient to meet the monthly rent. No judge or justice will be reimbursed for other than actual and necessary expenses for lodging necessitated by the conduct of judicial business.

1 Effective Nunc Pro Tunc July 1, 1979.

§ 102.4. Preparation and Submission of Expense Vouchers

Expense vouchers for reimbursement pursuant to this Part shall be submitted in accordance with the following requirements:

(a) Original copies of evidence of overnight stay, travel by air or by first class, Pullman or similar rail accommodation, car rental, apartment rental and long-term lodging arrangements, if any, shall be attached to the expense voucher (JC 2007).

(b) In cases where extended assignment is authorized, the expense voucher shall be submitted semimonthly, the first voucher covering the 1st to the 15th of each month, inclusive, and the second voucher covering the 16th to the last day of the month. All vouchers shall be submitted for processing no later than 45 days after the trip or completion of the assignment.

(c) Judges of the Court of Appeals and justices of the Appellate Divisions shall submit their expense vouchers to the clerk of their respective court, who shall submit such vouchers to the State Department of Audit and Control for processing. Justices temporarily assigned to a particular Appellate Division shall submit their expense vouchers to the clerk of that Appellate Division.

(d) A judge or justice who is assigned to a court that is under the jurisdiction of the deputy Chief Administrator of the Courts within the City of New York shall submit his or her expense voucher to the office of the Deputy Chief Administrator of the Courts within the City of New York for processing.

(e) A judge of the Court of Claims who is assigned to the Court of Claims shall submit his expense voucher to the clerk of the Court of Claims, who shall submit such voucher to the State Department of Audit and Control for processing.

(f) All other judges and justices shall submit their expense vouchers to the administrative judge of the judicial district to which the judge or justice is assigned, who shall submit them to the State Department of Audit and Control for processing.

§ 102.5. Change of Residence or Chambers

If a judge or justice of any court designated under this Part moves his or her place of residence or chambers outside the county in which he or she resided at the time of election or appointment, such judge or justice is not entitled to receive greater reimbursement for travel than he or she would have received had he or she not moved, unless the Chief Administrator of the Courts specifically approves.

§ 102.6. Reimbursement for Intracounty Travel

Traveling expenses incurred by a judge or justice to whom subdivision (a) of section 102.0 of this Part applies, during the performance of judicial duties within the county in which he or she is provided chambers, will be reimbursed if such travel occurred in accordance with a plan submitted, by an administrative judge on behalf of one or more judges or justices, to the Chief Administrator of the Courts, and approved by the Chief Administrator.

PART 103. ADMINISTRATIVE RULES AND ORDERS EFFECTIVE APRIL 1, 1978

§ 103.1. Administrative Rules and Orders

All administrative regulations, rules, orders and directives for the efficient and orderly transaction of business in the trial courts or the administrative office for the courts in effect on March 31, 1978, adopted pursuant to authority subsequently transferred to the Chief Administrator of the Courts in accordance with article VI, section 28(b) of the Constitution, including but not limited to calendar practice, establishment of hours, terms and parts of court, assignments of judges

and justices to them, and designations of administrative judges, are continued in effect until superseded, repealed or modified. Unless a contrary construction is required, references to the Administrative Board of the Judicial Conference shall be deemed references to the Chief Judge of the Court of Appeals; references to the State Administrator and State Administrative Judge shall be deemed references to the Chief Administrator of the Courts; and references to the Appellate Division or Presiding Justice shall be deemed references to the Chief Administrator of the Courts.

PART 104. RETENTION AND DISPOSITION OF COURT RECORDS

§ 104.1. Application

(a) These rules shall apply to court records of all the courts of the Unified Court System, including records of commissioners of jurors. Any action taken with respect to the records of the Court of Appeals and Appellate Divisions shall be subject to the approval of the Chief Judge of the Court of Appeals and the Presiding Justices of the Appellate Divisions for the records in their respective courts.

(b) The term "court records" shall include all documents and records that are part of the court file of each case and all books, papers, calendars, statistical schedules and reports and other records pertaining to the management of court cases.

(c) The term "alternative format" shall mean a format for the reproduction and maintenance of records, including microphotography and electronic formats, approved by the Deputy Chief Administrator for Management Support.

(d) References to the Deputy Chief Administrator for Management Support shall include a designee of the Deputy Chief Administrator for Management Support.

§ 104.2. Retention Schedules

(a) The Chief Administrator of the Courts shall promulgate schedules for the retention and disposition of court records. These schedules shall include a description of each record and the time period required for its retention. The time periods shall take into account the needs of both the court and the parties appearing before the court, and the historical value of the records for research purposes.

(b) Unless a permanent record in an alternative format first is made and permanently retained, judgment rolls and other records, books and papers that affect the mental illness or the sanity or competency of any person shall be retained for at least 50 years; and that the judgment rolls and other records, books and papers that affect the marital rights or status or the custody or lineage of any person and judgment rolls regardless of their age that affect title to real property shall be retained permanently.

§ 104.3. Procedure for Disposition of Court Records

(a) Any court seeking to dispose of court records shall make a written request for such disposal to the Deputy Chief Administrator for Management Support. The request shall describe in appropriate detail the records sought to be disposed of, including the nature of the records and the range of dates of their filing or creation.

(b) The Deputy Chief Administrator for Management Support shall determine the request based upon the retention schedules created pursuant to section 104.2 of this Part and in accordance with the needs of the courts. The Deputy Chief Administrator may require that a sampling of the records be made, based upon a methodology approved by the Deputy Chief Administrator, and that the sample be retained for research purposes.

(c) Suitability of arrangement for the storage of court records outside of court facilities, including any contracts entered into for such storage, shall be approved by the Deputy Chief Administrator for Management Support.

(d) Nothing in the retention schedules or these rules shall limit the authority of the Deputy Chief Administrator for Management Support to permit the disposition of any court records upon a showing of special circumstances and as permitted by law.

(e) In those actions or proceedings where the retention schedules provide that the period of retention shall commence at the date of disposition of the action or proceeding, where the clerk of any court has opened a case file for such action or proceeding, and where a continuous period of at least five years has elapsed during which such file is totally inactive, there being no additional papers filed therein nor any additional notations made therein or on the file jacket, the required period of retention for such file shall be deemed to have commenced at the end of such five-year period and the file may be disposed of in accordance with these rules and the appropriate retention schedules. This provision shall have no effect upon the action or proceeding or any substantive or procedural rights of any of the parties.

§ 104.4. Reproduction of Court Records in an Alternative Format

(a) All contracts, processes, procedures and apparatus for the reproduction of court records in an alternative format shall be subject to prior approval by the Deputy Chief Administrator for Management Support.

(b) Court records that have been reproduced pursuant to subdivision (a) may be disposed of pursuant to section 104.3, provided that the reproductions are satisfactorily identified and indexed, are in a format that allows for accurate reproduction, and are stored in a facility approved by the Deputy Chief Administrator for Management Support.

§ 104.5. Confidentiality

Court records that are reproduced in an alternative format, retained for research purposes or designated for disposition remain subject to all statutory provisions pertaining to access and confidentiality that are applicable to the original records. Arrangements for the reproduction, retention or disposal of court records that are sealed or otherwise deemed confidential must preserve the level of protection and nonaccess required by law.

PART 105. EXPEDITED CRIMINAL APPEAL OF AN ORDER REDUCING AN INDICTMENT OR DISMISSING AN INDICTMENT AND DIRECTING THE FILING OF A PROSECUTOR'S INFORMATION

§ 105.1. General

This Part shall govern the procedure for an expedited appeal to the Appellate Division, pursuant to CPL 210.20(6)(c), 450.20(1–a) and 450.55, of an order by a superior court reducing a count or counts of an indictment or dismissing an indictment and directing the filing of a prosecutor's information.

§ 105.2. Request to Expedite Appeal

After the People file and serve a notice of appeal pursuant to CPL 460.10(1), either party may request that the Appellate Division to which the appeal has been taken expedite the appeal. If a request is made, the Appellate Division shall hear the appeal on an expedited basis as set forth in this Part.

§ 105.3. Procedure

(a) The Appellate Division shall establish an expedited briefing schedule for the appeal. Briefs may be typewritten or reproduced. The People shall file nine copies of a brief and an appendix, which shall include a copy of the indictment and the trial court's decision and order. The respondent shall file nine copies of a brief and, if necessary, an appendix. One copy of the brief and appendix shall be served on opposing counsel.

(b) The appeal may be taken on one original record, which shall include copies of the indictment, the motion papers, the trial court's decision and order, and the notice of appeal.

(c) The People shall file with the Appellate Division, separately from the record, one copy of the grand jury minutes.

(d) The Appellate Division shall give preference to the hearing of an appeal perfected pursuant to this Part and shall determine the appeal as expeditiously as possible.

§ 105.4. Court-Assigned Counsel to Continue Representation

Unless otherwise ordered by the Appellate Division, if the defendant is represented in the superior court by court-assigned counsel, such counsel shall continue to represent the defendant in any appeal by the People of an order reducing an indictment or dismissing an indictment and directing the filing of a prosecutor's information.

PART 106. ELECTRONIC COURT APPEARANCES

§ 106.1. Authorization

In such counties authorized by law, a court exercising criminal jurisdiction may, except at a hearing or trial, dispense with the personal appearance of the defendant and conduct an electronic appearance in connection with a criminal action.

§ 106.2. Electronic Appearance

(a) An electronic appearance shall consist of an appearance in which some of the participants, including the defendant, are not present in the court, but all of the participants are simultaneously visible and audible to one another by means of an independent audio-visual system.

(b) The independent audio-visual system must be approved by the Commission on Cable Television as technically suitable for the conducting of electronic appearances.

(c) A defendant may participate in an electronic appearance only upon his or her consent on the record after consultation with counsel.

(d) A defendant, on the record, may waive the presence of counsel at the place where the defendant is physically located, but the defendant and counsel must be able to see and hear each other and engage in private conversation.

§ 106.3. Termination

If the court determines on its own or on motion of any party that, for any reason, the conduct of the electronic appearance may impair the legal rights of the defendant, it shall not permit the electronic appearance to proceed. If either party requests at any time, for any articulated reason, that the electronic appearance be terminated, the court shall grant the request and adjourn the proceeding to a date certain. On the adjourned date, the court, if practicable, shall begin the proceeding from the point at which the request to terminate the electronic appearance had been granted.

§ 106.4. Conditions and Limitations

The following conditions and limitations shall apply to all electronic appearances:

(a) The defendant may not enter a plea of guilty to, or be sentenced upon a conviction of, a felony.

(b) The defendant may not enter a plea of not responsible by reason of mental disease or defect.

(c) The defendant may not be committed to the State Department of Mental Hygiene pursuant to article 730 of the Criminal Procedure Law.

(d) The defendant may not enter a plea of guilty to a misdemeanor conditioned upon a promise of incarceration unless such incarceration will be imposed only in the event that the defendant fails to comply with a term or condition imposed under the original sentence.

(e) A defendant who has been convicted of a misdemeanor may not be sentenced to a period of incarceration that exceeds the time the defendant has already served when sentence is imposed.

§ 106.5. Record

(a) An electronic recording may be made of the electronic appearance, but this recording must remain within the custody of the clerk of the court that conducted the proceeding. No electronic recording may be released, duplicated, viewed or inspected without the permission, in writing, of the administrative judge for the court that conducted the proceeding.

(b) Stenographic recording of the electronic appearance shall be made, and shall be made available for inspection or copying, to the same extent and in the same manner as if it were an ordinary appearance rather than an electronic appearance.

PART 107. SALARY SCHEDULE FOR CERTAIN NONJUDICIAL OFFICERS AND EMPLOYEES OF THE UNIFIED COURT SYSTEM

§ 107.0. April 1, 1987 Salary Schedule

Effective April 1, 1987, the salary schedule required by section 2(b) of chapter 477 of the Laws of 1985 shall be as follows:

Grade	Increment	Hiring Rate	1st Year	2nd Year	3rd Year	4th Year	Maximum 5th Year	1st Longevity	2nd Extra Longevity
JG–501	545	11055	11600	12145	12690	13235	13780	14325	14870
JG–502	572	11492	12064	12636	13208	13780	14353	14924	15496
JG–503	599	12078	12677	13276	13875	14474	15073	15672	16271
JG–504	630	12648	13278	13908	14538	15168	15798	16428	17058
JG–505	667	13253	13920	14587	15254	15921	16588	17255	17922
JG–506	693	14018	14711	15404	16097	16790	17483	18176	18869
JG–507	723	14834	15557	16280	17003	17726	18449	19172	19895
JG–508	751	15701	16452	17203	17954	18705	19456	20207	20958
JG–509	789	16594	17383	18172	18961	19750	20539	21328	22117
JG–510	823	17579	18402	19225	20048	20871	21694	22517	23340
JG–511	862	18634	19496	20358	21220	22082	22944	23806	24468
JG–512	896	19725	20621	21517	22413	23309	24205	25101	25997
JG–513	937	20909	21846	22783	23720	24657	25594	26531	27468
JG–514	977	22160	23137	24114	25091	26068	27045	28022	28999
JG–515	1018	23465	24483	25501	26519	27537	28555	29573	30591
JG–516	1068	24804	25872	26940	28008	29076	30144	31212	32280
JG–517	1121	26238	27359	28480	29601	30722	31843	32964	34085
JG–518	1175	27767	28942	30117	31292	32467	33642	34817	35992
JG–519	1230	29303	30533	31763	32993	34223	35453	36683	37913
JG–520	1285	30843	32128	33413	34698	35983	37268	38553	39838
JG–521	1340	32527	33867	35207	36547	37887	39227	40567	41907
JG–522	1399	34313	35712	37111	38510	39909	41308	42707	44106
JG–523	1458	36170	37628	39086	40544	42002	43460	44918	46376
JG–524	1511	38151	39662	41173	42684	44195	45706	47217	48728
JG–525	1577	40305	41882	43459	45036	46613	48190	49767	51344

Grade	Increment	Hiring Rate	1st Year	2nd Year	3rd Year	4th Year	Maximum 5th Year	1st Longevity	2nd Extra Longevity
JG–526	1645	42463	44108	45753	47398	49043	50688	52333	53978
JG–527	1701	44819	46520	48221	49922	51623	53324	55025	56726
JG–528	1764	47235	48999	50763	52527	54291	56055	57819	59583
JG–529	1831	49778	51609	53440	55271	57102	58933	60764	62595
JG–530	1895	52435	54330	56225	58120	60015	61910	63805	65700
JG–531	1957	55303	57260	59217	61174	63131	65088	67045	69002
JG–532	2019	58323	60342	62361	64380	66399	68418	70437	72456
JG–533	2083	61549	63632	65715	67798	69881	71964	74047	76130
JG–534	2145	64913	67058	69203	71348	73493	75638	77783	79928
JG–535	2204	68356	70560	72764	74968	77172	79376	81580	83784
JG–536	2272	71857	74129	76401	78673	80945	83217	85489	87761
JG–537	2332	75714	78046	80378	82710	85042	87374	89706	92038
JG–538		72775+							

§ 107.1. June Twenty-Third, Nineteen Hundred Eighty-Eight Salary Schedule

Effective June 23, 1988, the salary schedule required by Section 2(a)(1) and (2) of Chapter 658 of the Laws of 1988 shall be as follows:

Grade	Increment	Hiring Rate	1st Year	2nd Year	3rd Year	4th Year	5th Year	6th Year	Maximum 7th Year	Longevity
JG–501	572	11,037	11,609	12,181	12,753	13,325	13,897	14,469	15,041	15,613
JG–502	601	11,464	12,065	12,666	13,267	13,868	14,469	15,070	15,671	16,272
JG–503	629	12,053	12,682	13,311	13,940	14,569	15,198	15,827	16,456	17,085
JG–504	661	12,622	13,283	13,944	14,605	15,266	15,927	16,588	17,249	17,910
JG–505	700	13,218	13,918	14,618	15,318	16,018	16,718	17,418	18,118	18,818
JG–506	728	13,990	14,718	15,446	16,174	16,902	17,630	18,358	19,086	19,814
JG–507	759	14,818	15,577	16,336	17,095	17,854	18,613	19,372	20,131	20,890
JG–508	788	15,701	16,489	17,277	18,065	18,853	19,641	20,429	21,217	22,005
JG–509	828	16,598	17,426	18,254	19,082	19,910	20,738	21,566	22,394	23,222
JG–510	864	17,595	18,459	19,323	20,187	21,051	21,915	22,779	23,643	24,507
JG–511	905	18,662	19,567	20,472	21,377	22,282	23,187	24,092	24,997	25,902
JG–512	941	19,770	20,711	21,652	22,593	23,534	24,475	25,416	26,357	27,298
JG–513	984	20,970	21,954	22,938	23,922	24,906	25,890	26,874	27,858	28,842
JG–514	1,026	22,242	23,268	24,294	25,320	26,346	27,372	28,398	29,424	30,450
JG–515	1,069	23,569	24,638	25,707	26,776	27,845	28,914	29,983	31,052	32,121
JG–516	1,121	24,926	26,047	27,168	28,289	29,410	30,531	31,652	32,773	33,894
JG–517	1,177	26,374	27,551	28,728	29,905	31,082	32,259	33,436	34,613	35,790
JG–518	1,234	27,921	29,155	30,389	31,623	32,857	34,091	35,325	36,559	37,793
JG–519	1,291	29,480	30,771	32,062	33,353	34,644	35,935	37,226	38,517	39,808
JG–520	1,349	31,038	32,387	33,736	35,085	36,434	37,783	39,132	40,481	41,830
JG–521	1,407	32,747	34,154	35,561	36,968	38,375	39,782	41,189	42,596	44,003
JG–522	1,469	34,560	36,029	37,498	38,967	40,436	41,905	43,374	44,843	46,312
JG–523	1,531	36,447	37,978	39,509	41,040	42,571	44,102	45,633	47,164	48,695
JG–524	1,587	38,470	40,057	41,644	43,231	44,818	46,405	47,992	49,579	51,166
JG–525	1,656	40,664	42,320	43,976	45,632	47,288	48,944	50,600	52,256	53,912
JG–526	1,727	42,861	44,588	46,315	48,042	49,769	51,496	53,223	54,950	56,677
JG–527	1,786	45,275	47,061	48,847	50,633	52,419	54,205	55,991	57,777	59,563
JG–528	1,852	47,746	49,598	51,450	53,302	55,154	57,006	58,858	60,710	62,562
JG–529	1,923	50,342	52,265	54,188	56,111	58,034	59,957	61,880	63,803	65,726
JG–530	1,990	53,066	55,056	57,046	59,036	61,026	63,016	65,006	66,996	68,986
JG–531	2,055	56,013	58,068	60,123	62,178	64,233	66,288	68,343	70,398	72,453
JG–532	2,120	59,119	61,239	63,359	65,479	67,599	69,719	71,839	73,959	76,079
JG–533	2,187	62,441	64,628	66,815	69,002	71,189	73,376	75,563	77,750	79,937
JG–534	2,252	65,908	68,160	70,412	72,664	74,916	77,168	79,420	81,672	83,924
JG–535	2,314	69,461	71,775	74,089	76,403	78,717	81,031	83,345	85,659	87,973

Grade	Increment	Hiring Rate	1st Year	2nd Year	3rd Year	4th Year	5th Year	6th Year	Maximum 7th Year	Longevity
JG–536	2,386	73,062	75,448	77,834	80,220	82,606	84,992	87,378	89,764	92,150
JG–537	2,449	77,049	79,498	81,947	84,396	86,845	89,294	91,743	94,192	96,641
JG–538	76,414 +									

§ 107.2. April First, Nineteen Hundred Eighty Nine Salary Schedule

Effective April 1, 1989, the salary schedule required by Section 2(b) of Chapter 658 of the Laws of 1988 shall be as follows:

Grade	Increment	Hiring Rate	1st Year	2nd Year	3rd Year	4th Year	5th Year	6th Year	Maximum 7th Year	Longevity
JG–501	601	11,587	12,188	12,789	13,390	13,991	14,592	15,193	15,794	16,395
JG–502	631	12,038	12,669	13,300	13,931	14,562	15,193	15,824	16,455	17,086
JG–503	660	12,659	13,319	13,979	14,639	15,299	15,959	16,619	17,279	17,939
JG–504	694	13,254	13,948	14,642	15,336	16,030	16,724	17,418	18,112	18,806
JG–505	735	13,879	14,614	15,349	16,084	16,819	17,554	18,289	19,024	19,759
JG–506	764	14,693	15,457	16,221	16,985	17,749	18,513	19,277	20,041	20,805
JG–507	797	15,559	16,356	17,153	17,950	18,747	19,544	20,341	21,138	21,935
JG–508	827	16,489	17,316	18,143	18,970	19,797	20,624	21,451	22,278	23,105
JG–509	869	17,431	18,300	19,169	20,038	20,907	21,776	22,645	23,514	24,383
JG–510	907	18,477	19,384	20,291	21,198	22,105	23,012	23,919	24,826	25,733
JG–511	950	19,597	20,547	21,497	22,447	23,397	24,347	25,297	26,247	27,197
JG–512	988	20,759	21,747	22,735	23,723	24,711	25,699	26,687	27,675	28,663
JG–513	1,033	22,020	23,053	24,086	25,119	26,152	27,185	28,218	29,251	30,284
JG–514	1,077	23,357	24,434	25,511	26,588	27,665	28,742	29,819	30,896	31,973
JG–515	1,122	24,751	25,873	26,995	28,117	29,239	30,361	31,483	32,605	33,727
JG–516	1,177	26,173	27,350	28,527	29,704	30,881	32,058	33,235	34,412	35,589
JG–517	1,236	27,692	28,928	30,164	31,400	32,636	33,872	35,108	36,344	37,580
JG–518	1,296	29,315	30,611	31,907	33,203	34,499	35,795	37,091	38,387	39,683
JG–519	1,356	30,951	32,307	33,663	35,019	36,375	37,731	39,087	40,443	41,799
JG–520	1,417	32,587	34,004	35,421	36,838	38,255	39,672	41,089	42,506	43,923
JG–521	1,477	34,387	35,864	37,341	38,818	40,295	41,772	43,249	44,726	46,203
JG–522	1,543	36,285	37,828	39,371	40,914	42,457	44,000	45,543	47,086	48,629
JG–523	1,608	38,267	39,875	41,483	43,091	44,699	46,307	47,915	49,523	51,131
JG–524	1,666	40,396	42,062	43,728	45,394	47,060	48,726	50,392	52,058	53,724
JG–525	1,739	42,696	44,435	46,174	47,913	49,652	51,391	53,130	54,869	56,608
JG–526	1,813	45,007	46,820	48,633	50,446	52,259	54,072	55,885	57,698	59,511
JG–527	1,875	47,541	49,416	51,291	53,166	55,041	56,916	58,791	60,666	62,541
JG–528	1,945	50,131	52,076	54,021	55,966	57,911	59,856	61,801	63,746	65,691
JG–529	2,019	52,861	54,880	56,899	58,918	60,937	62,956	64,975	66,994	69,013
JG–530	2,089	55,723	57,812	59,901	61,990	64,079	66,168	68,257	70,346	72,435
JG–531	2,158	58,812	60,970	63,128	65,286	67,444	69,602	71,760	73,918	76,076
JG–532	2,226	62,075	64,301	66,527	68,753	70,979	73,205	75,431	77,657	79,883
JG–533	2,296	65,566	67,862	70,158	72,454	74,750	77,046	79,342	81,638	83,934
JG–534	2,365	69,201	71,566	73,931	76,296	78,661	81,026	83,391	85,756	88,121
JG–535	2,430	72,932	75,362	77,792	80,222	82,652	85,082	87,512	89,942	92,372
JG–536	2,505	76,718	79,223	81,728	84,233	86,738	89,243	91,748	94,253	96,758
JG–537	2,571	80,905	83,476	86,047	88,618	91,189	93,760	96,331	98,902	101,473
JG–538	80,235									

§ 107.3. April First, Nineteen Hundred Ninety Salary Schedule

Effective April 1, 1990, the salary schedule required by Section 2(c) of Chapter 658 of the Laws of 1988 shall be as follows:

Grade	Increment	Hiring Rate	1st Year	2nd Year	3rd Year	4th Year	5th Year	6th Year	Maximum 7th Year	Longevity
JG–501	634	12,225	12,859	13,493	14,127	14,761	15,395	16,029	16,663	17,297
JG–502	666	12,699	13,365	14,031	14,697	15,363	16,029	16,695	17,361	18,027
JG–503	696	13,358	14,054	14,750	15,446	16,142	16,838	17,534	18,230	18,926
JG–504	732	13,985	14,717	15,449	16,181	16,913	17,645	18,377	19,109	19,841
JG–505	775	14,646	15,421	16,196	16,971	17,746	18,521	19,296	20,071	20,846
JG–506	806	15,502	16,308	17,114	17,920	18,726	19,532	20,338	21,144	21,950
JG–507	841	16,414	17,255	18,096	18,937	19,778	20,619	21,460	22,301	23,142
JG–508	873	17,393	18,266	19,139	20,012	20,885	21,758	22,631	23,504	24,377
JG–509	917	18,389	19,306	20,223	21,140	22,057	22,974	23,891	24,808	25,725
JG–510	957	19,493	20,450	21,407	22,364	23,321	24,278	25,235	26,192	27,149
JG–511	1,002	20,677	21,679	22,681	23,683	24,685	25,687	26,689	27,691	28,693
JG–512	1,042	21,904	22,946	23,988	25,030	26,072	27,114	28,156	29,198	30,240
JG–513	1,090	23,230	24,320	25,410	26,500	27,590	28,680	29,770	30,860	31,950
JG–514	1,136	24,644	25,780	26,916	28,052	29,188	30,324	31,460	32,596	33,732
JG–515	1,184	26,111	27,295	28,479	29,663	30,847	32,031	33,215	34,399	35,583
JG–516	1,242	27,611	28,853	30,095	31,337	32,579	33,821	35,063	36,305	37,547
JG–517	1,304	29,215	30,519	31,823	33,127	34,431	35,735	37,039	38,343	39,647
JG–518	1,367	30,930	32,297	33,664	35,031	36,398	37,765	39,132	40,499	41,866
JG–519	1,431	32,651	34,082	35,513	36,944	38,375	39,806	41,237	42,668	44,099
JG–520	1,495	34,379	35,874	37,369	38,864	40,359	41,854	43,349	44,844	46,339
JG–521	1,558	36,280	37,838	39,396	40,954	42,512	44,070	45,628	47,186	48,744
JG–522	1,628	38,280	39,908	41,536	43,164	44,792	46,420	48,048	49,676	51,304
JG–523	1,696	40,375	42,071	43,767	45,463	47,159	48,855	50,551	52,247	53,943
JG–524	1,758	42,616	44,374	46,132	47,890	49,648	51,406	53,164	54,922	56,680
JG–525	1,835	45,042	46,877	48,712	50,547	52,382	54,217	56,052	57,887	59,722
JG–526	1,913	47,481	49,394	51,307	53,220	55,133	57,046	58,959	60,872	62,785
JG–527	1,978	50,157	52,135	54,113	56,091	58,069	60,047	62,025	64,003	65,981
JG–528	2,052	52,889	54,941	56,993	59,045	61,097	63,149	65,201	67,253	69,305
JG–529	2,130	55,769	57,899	60,029	62,159	64,289	66,419	68,549	70,679	72,809
JG–530	2,204	58,788	60,992	63,196	65,400	67,604	69,808	72,012	74,216	76,420
JG–531	2,277	62,045	64,322	66,599	68,876	71,153	73,430	75,707	77,984	80,261
JG–532	2,348	65,493	67,841	70,189	72,537	74,885	77,233	79,581	81,929	84,277
JG–533	2,422	69,175	71,597	74,019	76,441	78,863	81,285	83,707	86,129	88,551
JG–534	2,495	73,008	75,503	77,998	80,493	82,988	85,483	87,978	90,473	92,968
JG–535	2,564	76,941	79,505	82,069	84,633	87,197	89,761	92,325	94,889	97,453
JG–536	2,643	80,936	83,579	86,222	88,865	91,508	94,151	96,794	99,437	102,080
JG–537	2,712	85,358	88,070	90,782	93,494	96,206	98,918	101,630	104,342	107,054
JG–538	84,648 +									

§ 107.4. April First, Nineteen Hundred Ninety Three Salary Schedule

Effective April 1, 1993, the salary schedule required by Section 2(a) of Chapter 502 of the Laws of 1992 shall be as follows:

Grade	Increment	Hiring Rate	1st Year	2nd Year	3rd Year	4th Year	5th Year	6th Year	7th Year	8th Year	Maximum 9th Year	Longevity
JG–501	577	12137	12714	13291	13868	14445	15022	15599	16176	16753	17330	17907
JG–502	606	12602	13208	13814	14420	15026	15632	16238	16844	17450	18056	18662
JG–503	633	13263	13896	14529	15162	15795	16428	17061	17694	18327	18960	19593
JG–504	666	13880	14546	15212	15878	16544	17210	17876	18542	19208	19874	20540
JG–505	705	14529	15234	15939	16644	17349	18054	18759	19464	20169	20874	21579
JG–506	733	15393	16126	16859	17592	18325	19058	19791	20524	21257	21990	22723
JG–507	765	16309	17074	17839	18604	19369	20134	20899	21664	22429	23194	23959
JG–508	795	17290	18085	18880	19675	20470	21265	22060	22855	23650	24445	25240
JG–509	835	18286	19121	19956	20791	21626	22461	23296	24131	24966	25801	26636
JG–510	871	19401	20272	21143	22014	22885	23756	24627	25498	26369	27240	28111

JG–511	912	20591	21503	22415	23327	24239	25151	26063	26975	27887	28799	29711
JG–512	948	21834	22782	23730	24678	25626	26574	27522	28470	29418	30366	31314
JG–513	992	23167	24159	25151	26143	27135	28127	29119	30111	31103	32095	33087
JG–514	1034	24594	25628	26662	27696	28730	29764	30798	31832	32866	33900	34934
JG–515	1077	26082	27159	28236	29313	30390	31467	32544	33621	34698	35775	36852
JG–516	1130	27588	28718	29848	30978	32108	33238	34368	35498	36628	37758	38888
JG–517	1187	29194	30381	31568	32755	33942	35129	36316	37503	38690	39877	41064
JG–518	1244	30923	32167	33411	34655	35899	37143	38387	39631	40875	42119	43363
JG–519	1302	32657	33959	35261	36563	37865	39167	40469	41771	43073	44375	45677
JG–520	1360	34398	35758	37118	38478	39838	41198	42558	43918	45278	46638	47998
JG–521	1418	36312	37730	39148	40566	41984	43402	44820	46238	47656	49074	50492
JG–522	1482	38326	39808	41290	42772	44254	45736	47218	48700	50182	51664	53146
JG–523	1543	40450	41993	43536	45079	46622	48165	49708	51251	52794	54337	55880
JG–524	1600	42719	44319	45919	47519	49119	50719	52319	53919	55519	57119	58719
JG–525	1670	45173	46843	48513	50183	51853	53523	55193	56863	58533	60203	61873
JG–526	1741	47638	49379	51120	52861	54602	56343	58084	59825	61566	63307	65048
JG–527	1800	50364	52164	53964	55764	57564	59364	61164	62964	64764	66564	68364
JG–528	1867	53141	55008	56875	58742	60609	62476	64343	66210	68077	69944	71811
JG–529	1938	56065	58003	59941	61879	63817	65755	67693	69631	71569	73507	75445
JG–530	2006	59131	61137	63143	65149	67155	69161	71167	73173	75179	77185	79191
JG–531	2072	62456	64528	66600	68672	70744	72816	74888	76960	79032	81104	83176
JG–532	2137	65974	68111	70248	72385	74522	76659	78796	80933	83070	85207	87344
JG–533	2204	69739	71943	74147	76351	78555	80759	82963	85167	87371	89575	91779
JG–534	2270	73662	75932	78202	80472	82742	85012	87282	89552	91822	94092	96362
JG–535	2333	77688	80021	82354	84687	87020	89353	91686	94019	96352	98685	101018
JG–536	2405	81770	84175	86580	88985	91390	93795	96200	98605	101010	103415	105820
JG–537	2468	86304	88772	91240	93708	96176	98644	101112	103580	106048	108516	110984
JG–538	88034 +										

§ 107.5. April First, Nineteen Hundred Ninety Four Salary Schedule

Effective April 1, 1994, the salary schedule required by Section 2(a) of Chapter 502 of the Laws of 1992 shall be as follows:

Grade	Increment	Hiring Rate	1st Year	2nd Year	3rd Year	4th Year	5th Year	6th Year	7th Year	8th Year	Maximum 9th Year	Longevity
JG–501	600	12624	13224	13824	14424	15024	15624	16224	16824	17424	18024	18624
JG–502	630	13109	13739	14369	14999	15629	16259	16889	17519	18149	18779	19409
JG–503	658	13797	14455	15113	15771	16429	17087	17745	18403	19061	19719	20377
JG–504	693	14432	15125	15818	16511	17204	17897	18590	19283	19976	20669	21362
JG–505	733	15112	15845	16578	17311	18044	18777	19510	20243	20976	21709	22442
JG–506	762	16012	16774	17536	18298	19060	19822	20584	21346	22108	22870	23632
JG–507	796	16958	17754	18550	19346	20142	20938	21734	22530	23326	24122	24918
JG–508	827	17980	18807	19634	20461	21288	22115	22942	23769	24596	25423	26250
JG–509	868	19022	19890	20758	21626	22494	23362	24230	25098	25966	26834	27702
JG–510	906	20176	21082	21988	22894	23800	24706	25612	26518	27424	28330	29236
JG–511	948	21419	22367	23315	24263	25211	26159	27107	28055	29003	29951	30899
JG–512	986	22707	23693	24679	25665	26651	27637	28623	29609	30595	31581	32567
JG–513	1032	24091	25123	26155	27187	28219	29251	30283	31315	32347	33379	34411
JG–514	1075	25581	26656	27731	28806	29881	30956	32031	33106	34181	35256	36331
JG–515	1120	27126	28246	29366	30486	31606	32726	33846	34966	36086	37206	38326
JG–516	1175	28694	29869	31044	32219	33394	34569	35744	36919	38094	39269	40444
JG–517	1235	30358	31593	32828	34063	35298	36533	37768	39003	40238	41473	42708
JG–518	1294	32158	33452	34746	36040	37334	38628	39922	41216	42510	43804	45098
JG–519	1354	33964	35318	36672	38026	39380	40734	42088	43442	44796	46150	47504
JG–520	1414	35778	37192	38606	40020	41434	42848	44262	45676	47090	48504	49918
JG–521	1475	37762	39237	40712	42187	43662	45137	46612	48087	49562	51037	52512
JG–522	1541	39862	41403	42944	44485	46026	47567	49108	50649	52190	53731	55272
JG–523	1605	42066	43671	45276	46881	48486	50091	51696	53301	54906	56511	58116
JG–524	1664	44428	46092	47756	49420	51084	52748	54412	56076	57740	59404	61068
JG–525	1737	46979	48716	50453	52190	53927	55664	57401	59138	60875	62612	64349
JG–526	1811	49541	51352	53163	54974	56785	58596	60407	62218	64029	65840	67651
JG–527	1872	52379	54251	56123	57995	59867	61739	63611	65483	67355	69227	71099
JG–528	1942	55264	57206	59148	61090	63032	64974	66916	68858	70800	72742	74684
JG–529	2016	58304	60320	62336	64352	66368	68384	70400	72416	74432	76448	78464
JG–530	2086	61499	63585	65671	67757	69843	71929	74015	76101	78187	80273	82359
JG–531	2155	64954	67109	69264	71419	73574	75729	77884	80039	82194	84349	86504
JG–532	2223	68609	70832	73055	75278	77501	79724	81947	84170	86393	88616	90839
JG–533	2292	72530	74822	77114	79406	81698	83990	86282	88574	90866	93158	95450
JG–534	2361	76607	78968	81329	83690	86051	88412	90773	93134	95495	97856	100217
JG–535	2426	80799	83225	85651	88077	90503	92929	95355	97781	100207	102633	105059

Grade	Increment	Hiring Rate	1st Year	2nd Year	3rd Year	4th Year	5th Year	6th Year	7th Year	8th Year	Maximum 9th Year	Longevity
JG–536	2501	85043	87544	90045	92546	95047	97548	100049	102550	105051	107552	110053
JG–537	2567	89754	92321	94888	97455	100022	102589	105156	107723	110290	112857	115424
JG–538	91556+											

§ 107.6. October First, Nineteen Hundred Ninety Four Salary Schedule

Effective October 1, 1994, the salary schedule required by Section 2(a) of Chapter 502 of the Laws of 1992 shall be as follows:

Grade	Increment	Hiring Rate	1st Year	2nd Year	3rd Year	4th Year	5th Year	6th Year	7th Year	8th Year	Maximum 9th Year	Longevity
JG–501	607	12777	13384	13991	14598	15205	15812	16419	17026	17633	18240	18847
JG–502	638	13262	13900	14538	15176	15814	16452	17090	17728	18366	19004	19642
JG–503	666	13962	14628	15294	15960	16626	17292	17958	18624	19290	19956	20622
JG–504	701	14609	15310	16011	16712	17413	18114	18815	19516	20217	20918	21619
JG–505	742	15292	16034	16776	17518	18260	19002	19744	20486	21228	21970	22712
JG–506	771	16206	16977	17748	18519	19290	20061	20832	21603	22374	23145	23916
JG–507	805	17167	17972	18777	19582	20387	21192	21997	22802	23607	24412	25217
JG–508	837	18196	19033	19870	20707	21544	22381	23218	24055	24892	25729	26566
JG–509	879	19245	20124	21003	21882	22761	23640	24519	25398	26277	27156	28035
JG–510	917	20418	21335	22252	23169	24086	25003	25920	26837	27754	28671	29588
JG–511	960	21671	22631	23591	24551	25511	26471	27431	28391	29351	30311	31271
JG–512	998	22979	23977	24975	25973	26971	27969	28967	29965	30963	31961	32959
JG–513	1044	24384	25428	26472	27516	28560	29604	30648	31692	32736	33780	34824
JG–514	1088	25888	26976	28064	29152	30240	31328	32416	33504	34592	35680	36768
JG–515	1134	27448	28582	29716	30850	31984	33118	34252	35386	36520	37654	38788
JG–516	1189	29040	30229	31418	32607	33796	34985	36174	37363	38552	39741	40930
JG–517	1249	30730	31979	33228	34477	35726	36975	38224	39473	40722	41971	43220
JG–518	1309	32550	33859	35168	36477	37786	39095	40404	41713	43022	44331	45640
JG–519	1370	34375	35745	37115	38485	39855	41225	42595	43965	45335	46705	48075
JG–520	1431	36208	37639	39070	40501	41932	43363	44794	46225	47656	49087	50518
JG–521	1492	38223	39715	41207	42699	44191	45683	47175	48667	50159	51651	53143
JG–522	1560	40337	41897	43457	45017	46577	48137	49697	51257	52817	54377	55937
JG–523	1624	42574	44198	45822	47446	49070	50694	52318	53942	55566	57190	58814
JG–524	1684	44962	46646	48330	50014	51698	53382	55066	56750	58434	60118	61802
JG–525	1758	47542	49300	51058	52816	54574	56332	58090	59848	61606	63364	65122
JG–526	1832	50143	51975	53807	55639	57471	59303	61135	62967	64799	66631	68463
JG–527	1894	53013	54907	56801	58695	60589	62483	64377	66271	68165	70059	71953
JG–528	1965	55932	57897	59862	61827	63792	65757	67722	69687	71652	73617	75582
JG–529	2040	59007	61047	63087	65127	67167	69207	71247	73287	75327	77367	79407
JG–530	2111	62239	64350	66461	68572	70683	72794	74905	77016	79127	81238	83349
JG–531	2181	65733	67914	70095	72276	74457	76638	78819	81000	83181	85362	87543
JG–532	2249	69440	71689	73938	76187	78436	80685	82934	85183	87432	89681	91930
JG–533	2320	73398	75718	78038	80358	82678	84998	87318	89638	91958	94278	96598
JG–534	2389	77531	79920	82309	84698	87087	89476	91865	94254	96643	99032	101421
JG–535	2455	81771	84226	86681	89136	91591	94046	96501	98956	101411	103866	106321
JG–536	2531	86066	88597	91128	93659	96190	98721	101252	103783	106314	108845	111376
JG–537	2598	90832	93430	96028	98626	101224	103822	106420	109018	111616	114214	116812
JG–538	92656+											

§ 107.7. April First, Nineteen Hundred Ninety Six Salary Schedule

Effective April 1, 1996, the salary schedule required by Section 2(a) of Chapter 582 of the Laws of 1996 shall be as follows:

Grade	Increment	Hiring Rate	1st Year	2nd Year	3rd Year	4th Year	5th Year	6th Year	7th Year	8th Year	Maximum 9th Year	Longevity
JG–501	619	13034	13653	14272	14891	15510	16129	16748	17367	17986	18605	19224
JG–502	651	13526	14177	14828	15479	16130	16781	17432	18083	18734	19385	20036
JG–503	679	14245	14924	15603	16282	16961	17640	18319	18998	19677	20356	21035
JG–504	715	14902	15617	16332	17047	17762	18477	19192	19907	20622	21337	22052
JG–505	757	15597	16354	17111	17868	18625	19382	20139	20896	21653	22410	23167
JG–506	786	16534	17320	18106	18892	19678	20464	21250	22036	22822	23608	24394
JG–507	821	17512	18333	19154	19975	20796	21617	22438	23259	24080	24901	25722
JG–508	854	18558	19412	20266	21120	21974	22828	23682	24536	25390	26244	27098
JG–509	897	19627	20524	21421	22318	23215	24112	25009	25906	26803	27700	28597
JG–510	935	20830	21765	22700	23635	24570	25505	26440	27375	28310	29245	30180

JG–511	979	22107	23086	24065	25044	26023	27002	27981	28960	29939	30918	31897
JG–512	1018	23439	24457	25475	26493	27511	28529	29547	30565	31583	32601	33619
JG–513	1065	24871	25936	27001	28066	29131	30196	31261	32326	33391	34456	35521
JG–514	1110	26404	27514	28624	29734	30844	31954	33064	34174	35284	36394	37504
JG–515	1157	27995	29152	30309	31466	32623	33780	34937	36094	37251	38408	39565
JG–516	1213	29619	30832	32045	33258	34471	35684	36897	38110	39323	40536	41749
JG–517	1274	31345	32619	33893	35167	36441	37715	38989	40263	41537	42811	44085
JG–518	1335	33203	34538	35873	37208	38543	39878	41213	42548	43883	45218	46553
JG–519	1397	35067	36464	37861	39258	40655	42052	43449	44846	46243	47640	49037
JG–520	1460	36929	38389	39849	41309	42769	44229	45689	47149	48609	50069	51529
JG–521	1522	38987	40509	42031	43553	45075	46597	48119	49641	51163	52685	54207
JG–522	1591	41146	42737	44328	45919	47510	49101	50692	52283	53874	55465	57056
JG–523	1656	43430	45086	46742	48398	50054	51710	53366	55022	56678	58334	59990
JG–524	1718	45859	47577	49295	51013	52731	54449	56167	57885	59603	61321	63039
JG–525	1793	48495	50288	52081	53874	55667	57460	59253	61046	62839	64632	66425
JG–526	1869	51143	53012	54881	56750	58619	60488	62357	64226	66095	67964	69833
JG–527	1932	54073	56005	57937	59869	61801	63733	65665	67597	69529	71461	73393
JG–528	2004	57054	59058	61062	63066	65070	67074	69078	71082	73086	75090	77094
JG–529	2081	60186	62267	64348	66429	68510	70591	72672	74753	76834	78915	80996
JG–530	2153	63486	65639	67792	69945	72098	74251	76404	78557	80710	82863	85016
JG–531	2225	67045	69270	71495	73720	75945	78170	80395	82620	84845	87070	89295
JG–532	2294	70829	73123	75417	77711	80005	82299	84593	86887	89181	91475	93769
JG–533	2366	74870	77236	79602	81968	84334	86700	89066	91432	93798	96164	98530
JG–534	2437	79080	81517	83954	86391	88828	91265	93702	96139	98576	101013	103450
JG–535	2504	83408	85912	88416	90920	93424	95928	98432	100936	103440	105944	108448
JG–536	2582	87784	90366	92948	95530	98112	100694	103276	105858	108440	111022	113604
JG–537	2650	92649	95299	97949	100599	103249	105899	108549	111199	113849	116499	119149
JG–538	94510+											

§ 107.8. April First, Nineteen Hundred Ninety Seven Salary Schedule

Effective April 1, 1997, the salary schedule required by Section 2(b) of Chapter 582 of the Laws of 1996 shall be as follows:

Grade	Increment	Hiring Rate	1st Year	2nd Year	3rd Year	4th Year	5th Year	6th Year	7th Year	8th Year	Maximum 9th Year	Longevity
JG–501	631	13299	13930	14561	15192	15823	16454	17085	17716	18347	18978	19609
JG–502	664	13797	14461	15125	15789	16453	17117	17781	18445	19109	19773	20437
JG–503	693	14527	15220	15913	16606	17299	17992	18685	19378	20071	20764	21457
JG–504	729	15203	15932	16661	17390	18119	18848	19577	20306	21035	21764	22493
JG–505	772	15911	16683	17455	18227	18999	19771	20543	21315	22087	22859	23631
JG–506	802	16863	17665	18467	19269	20071	20873	21675	22477	23279	24081	24883
JG–507	837	17867	18704	19541	20378	21215	22052	22889	23726	24563	25400	26237
JG–508	871	18930	19801	20672	21543	22414	23285	24156	25027	25898	26769	27640
JG–509	915	20019	20934	21849	22764	23679	24594	25509	26424	27339	28254	29169
JG–510	954	21244	22198	23152	24106	25060	26014	26968	27922	28876	29830	30784
JG–511	999	22546	23545	24544	25543	26542	27541	28540	29539	30538	31537	32536
JG–512	1038	23912	24950	25988	27026	28064	29102	30140	31178	32216	33254	34292
JG–513	1086	25372	26458	27544	28630	29716	30802	31888	32974	34060	35146	36232
JG–514	1132	26934	28066	29198	30330	31462	32594	33726	34858	35990	37122	38254
JG–515	1180	28557	29737	30917	32097	33277	34457	35637	36817	37997	39177	40357
JG–516	1237	30214	31451	32688	33925	35162	36399	37636	38873	40110	41347	42584
JG–517	1300	31968	33268	34568	35868	37168	38468	39768	41068	42368	43668	44968
JG–518	1362	33865	35227	36589	37951	39313	40675	42037	43399	44761	46123	47485
JG–519	1425	35768	37193	38618	40043	41468	42893	44318	45743	47168	48593	50018
JG–520	1489	37670	39159	40648	42137	43626	45115	46604	48093	49582	51071	52560
JG–521	1552	39771	41323	42875	44427	45979	47531	49083	50635	52187	53739	55291
JG–522	1623	41968	43591	45214	46837	48460	50083	51706	53329	54952	56575	58198
JG–523	1689	44300	45989	47678	49367	51056	52745	54434	56123	57812	59501	61190
JG–524	1752	46780	48532	50284	52036	53788	55540	57292	59044	60796	62548	64300
JG–525	1829	49464	51293	53122	54951	56780	58609	60438	62267	64096	65925	67754
JG–526	1906	52170	54076	55982	57888	59794	61700	63606	65512	67418	69324	71230
JG–527	1971	55152	57123	59094	61065	63036	65007	66978	68949	70920	72891	74862
JG–528	2044	58196	60240	62284	64328	66372	68416	70460	72504	74548	76592	78636
JG–529	2123	61387	63510	65633	67756	69879	72002	74125	76248	78371	80494	82617
JG–530	2196	64757	66953	69149	71345	73541	75737	77933	80129	82325	84521	86717
JG–531	2270	68382	70652	72922	75192	77462	79732	82002	84272	86542	88812	91082
JG–532	2340	72245	74585	76925	79265	81605	83945	86285	88625	90965	93305	95645
JG–533	2413	76371	78784	81197	83610	86023	88436	90849	93262	95675	98088	100501
JG–534	2486	80660	83146	85632	88118	90604	93090	95576	98062	100548	103034	105520
JG–535	2554	85077	87631	90185	92739	95293	97847	100401	102955	105509	108063	110617

JG–536	2634	89537	92171	94805	97439	100073	102707	105341	107975	110609	113243	115877
JG–537	2703	94502	97205	99908	102611	105314	108017	110720	113423	116126	118829	121532
JG–538		96401 +										

§ 107.9. October First, Nineteen Hundred Ninety Eight Salary Schedule

Effective October 1, 1998, the salary schedule required by Section 2(c) of Chapter 582 of the Laws of 1996 shall be as follows:

Grade	Increment	Hiring Rate	1st Year	2nd Year	3rd Year	4th Year	5th Year	6th Year	7th Year	8th Year	Maximum 9th Year	Longevity
JG–501	650	13698	14348	14998	15648	16298	16948	17598	18248	18898	19548	20198
JG–502	684	14211	14895	15579	16263	16947	17631	18315	18999	19683	20367	21051
JG–503	714	14961	15675	16389	17103	17817	18531	19245	19959	20673	21387	22101
JG–504	751	15658	16409	17160	17911	18662	19413	20164	20915	21666	22417	23168
JG–505	795	16390	17185	17980	18775	19570	20365	21160	21955	22750	23545	24340
JG–506	826	17370	18196	19022	19848	20674	21500	22326	23152	23978	24804	25630
JG–507	862	18404	19266	20128	20990	21852	22714	23576	24438	25300	26162	27024
JG–508	897	19500	20397	21294	22191	23088	23985	24882	25779	26676	27573	28470
JG–509	942	20624	21566	22508	23450	24392	25334	26276	27218	28160	29102	30044
JG–510	983	21878	22861	23844	24827	25810	26793	27776	28759	29742	30725	31708
JG–511	1029	23223	24252	25281	26310	27339	28368	29397	30426	31455	32484	33513
JG–512	1069	24631	25700	26769	27838	28907	29976	31045	32114	33183	34252	35321
JG–513	1119	26130	27249	28368	29487	30606	31725	32844	33963	35082	36201	37320
JG–514	1166	27742	28908	30074	31240	32406	33572	34738	35904	37070	38236	39402
JG–515	1215	29418	30633	31848	33063	34278	35493	36708	37923	39138	40353	41568
JG–516	1274	31122	32396	33670	34944	36218	37492	38766	40040	41314	42588	43862
JG–517	1339	32928	34267	35606	36945	38284	39623	40962	42301	43640	44979	46318
JG–518	1403	34880	36283	37686	39089	40492	41895	43298	44701	46104	47507	48910
JG–519	1468	36839	38307	39775	41243	42711	44179	45647	47115	48583	50051	51519
JG–520	1534	38798	40332	41866	43400	44934	46468	48002	49536	51070	52604	54138
JG–521	1599	40961	42560	44159	45758	47357	48956	50555	52154	53753	55352	56951
JG–522	1672	43225	44897	46569	48241	49913	51585	53257	54929	56601	58273	59945
JG–523	1740	45627	47367	49107	50847	52587	54327	56067	57807	59547	61287	63027
JG–524	1805	48180	49985	51790	53595	55400	57205	59010	60815	62620	64425	66230
JG–525	1884	50947	52831	54715	56599	58483	60367	62251	64135	66019	67903	69787
JG–526	1963	53737	55700	57663	59626	61589	63552	65515	67478	69441	71404	73367
JG–527	2030	56808	58838	60868	62898	64928	66958	68988	71018	73048	75078	77108
JG–528	2105	59945	62050	64155	66260	68365	70470	72575	74680	76785	78890	80995
JG–529	2187	63226	65413	67600	69787	71974	74161	76348	78535	80722	82909	85096
JG–530	2262	66699	68961	71223	73485	75747	78009	80271	82533	84795	87057	89319
JG–531	2338	70435	72773	75111	77449	79787	82125	84463	86801	89139	91477	93815
JG–532	2410	74415	76825	79235	81645	84055	86465	88875	91285	93695	96105	98515
JG–533	2485	78666	81151	83636	86121	88606	91091	93576	96061	98546	101031	103516
JG–534	2561	83077	85638	88199	90760	93321	95882	98443	101004	103565	106126	108687
JG–535	2631	87626	90257	92888	95519	98150	100781	103412	106043	108674	111305	113936
JG–536	2713	92224	94937	97650	100363	103076	105789	108502	111215	113928	116641	119354
JG–537	2784	97338	100122	102906	105690	108474	111258	114042	116826	119610	122394	125178
JG–538		99294 +										

§ 107.10. March Thirty–First, Nineteen Hundred Ninety–Nine Salary Schedule

Effective March 31, 1999, the salary schedule required by Section 2 of Chapter 69 of the Laws of 2000 shall be as follows:

Grade	Increment	Hiring Rate	1st Year	2nd Year	3rd Year	4th Year	5th Year	6th Year	Maximum	1st Longevity	2nd Extra Longevity
JG–501	836	13,696	14,532	15,368	16,204	17,040	17,876	18,712	19,548	20,384	21,220
JG–502	879	14,214	15,093	15,972	16,851	17,730	18,609	19,488	20,367	21,246	22,125
JG–503	918	14,961	15,879	16,797	17,715	18,633	19,551	20,469	21,387	22,305	23,223
JG–504	966	15,655	16,621	17,587	18,553	19,519	20,485	21,451	22,417	23,383	24,349
JG–505	1,022	16,391	17,413	18,435	19,457	20,479	21,501	22,523	23,545	24,567	25,589
JG–506	1,062	17,370	18,432	19,494	20,556	21,618	22,680	23,742	24,804	25,866	26,928
JG–507	1,108	18,406	19,514	20,622	21,730	22,838	23,946	25,054	26,162	27,270	28,378
JG–508	1,153	19,502	20,655	21,808	22,961	24,114	25,267	26,420	27,573	28,726	29,879
JG–509	1,211	20,625	21,836	23,047	24,258	25,469	26,680	27,891	29,102	30,313	31,524
JG–510	1,264	21,877	23,141	24,405	25,669	26,933	28,197	29,461	30,725	31,989	33,253
JG–511	1,323	23,223	24,546	25,869	27,192	28,515	29,838	31,161	32,484	33,807	35,130

JG–512	1,374	24,634	26,008	27,382	28,756	30,130	31,504	32,878	34,252	35,626	37,000
JG–513	1,439	26,128	27,567	29,006	30,445	31,884	33,323	34,762	36,201	37,640	39,079
JG–514	1,499	27,743	29,242	30,741	32,240	33,739	35,238	36,737	38,236	39,735	41,234
JG–515	1,562	29,419	30,981	32,543	34,105	35,667	37,229	38,791	40,353	41,915	43,477
JG–516	1,638	31,122	32,760	34,398	36,036	37,674	39,312	40,950	42,588	44,226	45,864
JG–517	1,722	32,925	34,647	36,369	38,091	39,813	41,535	43,257	44,979	46,701	48,423
JG–518	1,804	34,879	36,683	38,487	40,291	42,095	43,899	45,703	47,507	49,311	51,115
JG–519	1,887	36,842	38,729	40,616	42,503	44,390	46,277	48,164	50,051	51,938	53,825
JG–520	1,972	38,800	40,772	42,744	44,716	46,688	48,660	50,632	52,604	54,576	56,548
JG–521	2,056	40,960	43,016	45,072	47,128	49,184	51,240	53,296	55,352	57,408	59,464
JG–522	2,150	43,223	45,373	47,523	49,673	51,823	53,973	56,123	58,273	60,423	62,573
JG–523	2,237	45,628	47,865	50,102	52,339	54,576	56,813	59,050	61,287	63,524	65,761
JG–524	2,321	48,178	50,499	52,820	55,141	57,462	59,783	62,104	64,425	66,746	69,067
JG–525	2,422	50,949	53,371	55,793	58,215	60,637	63,059	65,481	67,903	70,325	72,747
JG–526	2,524	53,736	56,260	58,784	61,308	63,832	66,356	68,880	71,404	73,928	76,452
JG–527	2,610	56,808	59,418	62,028	64,638	67,248	69,858	72,468	75,078	77,688	80,298
JG–528	2,706	59,948	62,654	65,360	68,066	70,772	73,478	76,184	78,890	81,596	84,302
JG–529	2,812	63,225	66,037	68,849	71,661	74,473	77,285	80,097	82,909	85,721	88,533
JG–530	2,908	66,701	69,609	72,517	75,425	78,333	81,241	84,149	87,057	89,965	92,873
JG–531	3,006	70,435	73,441	76,447	79,453	82,459	85,465	88,471	91,477	94,483	97,489
JG–532	3,099	74,412	77,511	80,610	83,709	86,808	89,907	93,006	96,105	99,204	102,303
JG–533	3,195	78,666	81,861	85,056	88,251	91,446	94,641	97,836	101,031	104,226	107,421
JG–534	3,293	83,075	86,368	89,661	92,954	96,247	99,540	102,833	106,126	109,419	112,712
JG–535	3,383	87,624	91,007	94,390	97,773	101,156	104,539	107,922	111,305	114,688	118,071
JG–536	3,488	92,225	95,713	99,201	102,689	106,177	109,665	113,153	116,641	120,129	123,617
JG–537	3,579	97,341	100,920	104,499	108,078	111,657	115,236	118,815	122,394	125,973	129,552
JG–538		99,294 +									

§ 107.11. October First, Nineteen Hundred Ninety–Nine Salary Schedule

Effective October 1, 1999, the salary schedule required by Section 2 of Chapter 69 of the Laws of 2000 shall be as follows:

Grade	Increment	Hiring Rate	1st Year	2nd Year	3rd Year	4th Year	5th Year	6th Year	Maximum	1st Longevity	2nd Extra Longevity
JG–501	861	14,108	14,969	15,830	16,691	17,552	18,413	19,274	20,135	20,996	21,857
JG–502	905	14,644	15,549	16,454	17,359	18,264	19,169	20,074	20,979	21,884	22,789
JG–503	946	15,407	16,353	17,299	18,245	19,191	20,137	21,083	22,029	22,975	23,921
JG–504	995	16,125	17,120	18,115	19,110	20,105	21,100	22,095	23,090	24,085	25,080
JG–505	1,053	16,881	17,934	18,987	20,040	21,093	22,146	23,199	24,252	25,305	26,358
JG–506	1,094	17,891	18,985	20,079	21,173	22,267	23,361	24,455	25,549	26,643	27,737
JG–507	1,141	18,960	20,101	21,242	22,383	23,524	24,665	25,806	26,947	28,088	29,229
JG–508	1,188	20,085	21,273	22,461	23,649	24,837	26,025	27,213	28,401	29,589	30,777
JG–509	1,247	21,247	22,494	23,741	24,988	26,235	27,482	28,729	29,976	31,223	32,470
JG–510	1,302	22,533	23,835	25,137	26,439	27,741	29,043	30,345	31,647	32,949	34,251
JG–511	1,363	23,918	25,281	26,644	28,007	29,370	30,733	32,096	33,459	34,822	36,185
JG–512	1,415	25,375	26,790	28,205	29,620	31,035	32,450	33,865	35,280	36,695	38,110
JG–513	1,482	26,914	28,396	29,878	31,360	32,842	34,324	35,806	37,288	38,770	40,252
JG–514	1,544	28,576	30,120	31,664	33,208	34,752	36,296	37,840	39,384	40,928	42,472
JG–515	1,609	30,301	31,910	33,519	35,128	36,737	38,346	39,955	41,564	43,173	44,782
JG–516	1,687	32,057	33,744	35,431	37,118	38,805	40,492	42,179	43,866	45,553	47,240
JG–517	1,774	33,911	35,685	37,459	39,233	41,007	42,781	44,555	46,329	48,103	49,877
JG–518	1,858	35,927	37,785	39,643	41,501	43,359	45,217	47,075	48,933	50,791	52,649
JG–519	1,944	37,945	39,889	41,833	43,777	45,721	47,665	49,609	51,553	53,497	55,441
JG–520	2,031	39,966	41,997	44,028	46,059	48,090	50,121	52,152	54,183	56,214	58,245
JG–521	2,118	42,187	44,305	46,423	48,541	50,659	52,777	54,895	57,013	59,131	61,249
JG–522	2,215	44,517	46,732	48,947	51,162	53,377	55,592	57,807	60,022	62,237	64,452
JG–523	2,304	46,998	49,302	51,606	53,910	56,214	58,518	60,822	63,126	65,430	67,734
JG–524	2,391	49,621	52,012	54,403	56,794	59,185	61,576	63,967	66,358	68,749	71,140
JG–525	2,495	52,476	54,971	57,466	59,961	62,456	64,951	67,446	69,941	72,436	74,931
JG–526	2,600	55,347	57,947	60,547	63,147	65,747	68,347	70,947	73,547	76,147	78,747
JG–527	2,688	58,515	61,203	63,891	66,579	69,267	71,955	74,643	77,331	80,019	82,707
JG–528	2,787	61,748	64,535	67,322	70,109	72,896	75,683	78,470	81,257	84,044	86,831
JG–529	2,896	65,125	68,021	70,917	73,813	76,709	79,605	82,501	85,397	88,293	91,189
JG–530	2,995	68,704	71,699	74,694	77,689	80,684	83,679	86,674	89,669	92,664	95,659
JG–531	3,096	72,550	75,646	78,742	81,838	84,934	88,030	91,126	94,222	97,318	100,414
JG–532	3,192	76,645	79,837	83,029	86,221	89,413	92,605	95,797	98,989	102,181	105,373
JG–533	3,291	81,025	84,316	87,607	90,898	94,189	97,480	100,771	104,062	107,353	110,644
JG–534	3,392	85,566	88,958	92,350	95,742	99,134	102,526	105,918	109,310	112,702	116,094
JG–535	3,485	90,250	93,735	97,220	100,705	104,190	107,675	111,160	114,645	118,130	121,615
JG–536	3,593	94,990	98,583	102,176	105,769	109,362	112,955	116,548	120,141	123,734	127,327
JG–537	3,686	100,264	103,950	107,636	111,322	115,008	118,694	122,380	126,066	129,752	133,438
JG–538		102,273 +									

§ 107.12.   April First, Two Thousand Salary Schedule

Effective April 1, 2000, the salary schedule required by Section 2 of Chapter 69 of the Laws of 2000 shall be as follows:

Grade	Increment	Hiring Rate	1st Year	2nd Year	3rd Year	4th Year	5th Year	6th Year	Maximum	1st Longevity	2nd Extra Longevity
JG–501	887	14,531	15,418	16,305	17,192	18,079	18,966	19,853	20,740	21,627	22,514
JG–502	932	15,085	16,017	16,949	17,881	18,813	19,745	20,677	21,609	22,541	23,473
JG–503	974	15,872	16,846	17,820	18,794	19,768	20,742	21,716	22,690	23,664	24,638
JG–504	1,025	16,608	17,633	18,658	19,683	20,708	21,733	22,758	23,783	24,808	25,833
JG–505	1,085	17,385	18,470	19,555	20,640	21,725	22,810	23,895	24,980	26,065	27,150
JG–506	1,127	18,427	19,554	20,681	21,808	22,935	24,062	25,189	26,316	27,443	28,570
JG–507	1,175	19,531	20,706	21,881	23,056	24,231	25,406	26,581	27,756	28,931	30,106
JG–508	1,224	20,686	21,910	23,134	24,358	25,582	26,806	28,030	29,254	30,478	31,702
JG–509	1,284	21,888	23,172	24,456	25,740	27,024	28,308	29,592	30,876	32,160	33,444
JG–510	1,341	23,210	24,551	25,892	27,233	28,574	29,915	31,256	32,597	33,938	35,279
JG–511	1,404	24,635	26,039	27,443	28,847	30,251	31,655	33,059	34,463	35,867	37,271
JG–512	1,457	26,140	27,597	29,054	30,511	31,968	33,425	34,882	36,339	37,796	39,253
JG–513	1,526	27,725	29,251	30,777	32,303	33,829	35,355	36,881	38,407	39,933	41,459
JG–514	1,590	29,436	31,026	32,616	34,206	35,796	37,386	38,976	40,566	42,156	43,746
JG–515	1,657	31,212	32,869	34,526	36,183	37,840	39,497	41,154	42,811	44,468	46,125
JG–516	1,738	33,016	34,754	36,492	38,230	39,968	41,706	43,444	45,182	46,920	48,658
JG–517	1,827	34,930	36,757	38,584	40,411	42,238	44,065	45,892	47,719	49,546	51,373
JG–518	1,914	37,003	38,917	40,831	42,745	44,659	46,573	48,487	50,401	52,315	54,229
JG–519	2,002	39,086	41,088	43,090	45,092	47,094	49,096	51,098	53,100	55,102	57,104
JG–520	2,092	41,165	43,257	45,349	47,441	49,533	51,625	53,717	55,809	57,901	59,993
JG–521	2,182	43,450	45,632	47,814	49,996	52,178	54,360	56,542	58,724	60,906	63,088
JG–522	2,281	45,856	48,137	50,418	52,699	54,980	57,261	59,542	61,823	64,104	66,385
JG–523	2,373	48,409	50,782	53,155	55,528	57,901	60,274	62,647	65,020	67,393	69,766
JG–524	2,463	51,108	53,571	56,034	58,497	60,960	63,423	65,886	68,349	70,812	73,275
JG–525	2,570	54,050	56,620	59,190	61,760	64,330	66,900	69,470	72,040	74,610	77,180
JG–526	2,678	57,008	59,686	62,364	65,042	67,720	70,398	73,076	75,754	78,432	81,110
JG–527	2,769	60,268	63,037	65,806	68,575	71,344	74,113	76,882	79,651	82,420	85,189
JG–528	2,871	63,598	66,469	69,340	72,211	75,082	77,953	80,824	83,695	86,566	89,437
JG–529	2,983	67,078	70,061	73,044	76,027	79,010	81,993	84,976	87,959	90,942	93,925
JG–530	3,085	70,765	73,850	76,935	80,020	83,105	86,190	89,275	92,360	95,445	98,530
JG–531	3,189	74,726	77,915	81,104	84,293	87,482	90,671	93,860	97,049	100,238	103,427
JG–532	3,288	78,943	82,231	85,519	88,807	92,095	95,383	98,671	101,959	105,247	108,535
JG–533	3,390	83,454	86,844	90,234	93,624	97,014	100,404	103,794	107,184	110,574	113,964
JG–534	3,494	88,132	91,626	95,120	98,614	102,108	105,602	109,096	112,590	116,084	119,578
JG–535	3,590	92,955	96,545	100,135	103,725	107,315	110,905	114,495	118,085	121,675	125,265
JG–536	3,701	97,839	101,540	105,241	108,942	112,643	116,344	120,045	123,746	127,447	131,148
JG–537	3,797	103,269	107,066	110,863	114,660	118,457	122,254	126,051	129,848	133,645	137,442
JG–538		105,342 +									

§ 107.13.   April First, Two Thousand One Salary Schedule

Effective April 1, 2001, the salary schedule required by Section 2 of Chapter 69 of the Laws of 2000 shall be as follows:

Grade	Increment	Hiring Rate	1st Year	2nd Year	3rd Year	4th Year	5th Year	6th Year	Maximum	1st Longevity	2nd Extra Longevity
JG–501	918	15,040	15,958	16,876	17,794	18,712	19,630	20,548	21,466	22,384	23,302
JG–502	965	15,611	16,576	17,541	18,506	19,471	20,436	21,401	22,366	23,331	24,296
JG–503	1,008	16,429	17,437	18,445	19,453	20,461	21,469	22,477	23,485	24,493	25,501
JG–504	1,061	17,189	18,250	19,311	20,372	21,433	22,494	23,555	24,616	25,677	26,738
JG–505	1,123	17,994	19,117	20,240	21,363	22,486	23,609	24,732	25,855	26,978	28,101
JG–506	1,167	19,069	20,236	21,403	22,570	23,737	24,904	26,071	27,238	28,405	29,572
JG–507	1,216	20,216	21,432	22,648	23,864	25,080	26,296	27,512	28,728	29,944	31,160
JG–508	1,267	21,409	22,676	23,943	25,210	26,477	27,744	29,011	30,278	31,545	32,812
JG–509	1,329	22,654	23,983	25,312	26,641	27,970	29,299	30,628	31,957	33,286	34,615
JG–510	1,388	24,022	25,410	26,798	28,186	29,574	30,962	32,350	33,738	35,126	36,514
JG–511	1,453	25,499	26,952	28,405	29,858	31,311	32,764	34,217	35,670	37,123	38,576
JG–512	1,508	27,055	28,563	30,071	31,579	33,087	34,595	36,103	37,611	39,119	40,627
JG–513	1,579	28,699	30,278	31,857	33,436	35,015	36,594	38,173	39,752	41,331	42,910
JG–514	1,646	30,464	32,110	33,756	35,402	37,048	38,694	40,340	41,986	43,632	45,278

JG–515	1,715	32,305	34,020	35,735	37,450	39,165	40,880	42,595	44,310	46,025	47,740
JG–516	1,799	34,171	35,970	37,769	39,568	41,367	43,166	44,965	46,764	48,563	50,362
JG–517	1,891	36,153	38,044	39,935	41,826	43,717	45,608	47,499	49,390	51,281	53,172
JG–518	1,981	38,299	40,280	42,261	44,242	46,223	48,204	50,185	52,166	54,147	56,128
JG–519	2,072	40,455	42,527	44,599	46,671	48,743	50,815	52,887	54,959	57,031	59,103
JG–520	2,165	42,608	44,773	46,938	49,103	51,268	53,433	55,598	57,763	59,928	62,093
JG–521	2,258	44,974	47,232	49,490	51,748	54,006	56,264	58,522	60,780	63,038	65,296
JG–522	2,361	47,460	49,821	52,182	54,543	56,904	59,265	61,626	63,987	66,348	68,709
JG–523	2,456	50,104	52,560	55,016	57,472	59,928	62,384	64,840	67,296	69,752	72,208
JG–524	2,549	52,899	55,448	57,997	60,546	63,095	65,644	68,193	70,742	73,291	75,840
JG–525	2,660	55,942	58,602	61,262	63,922	66,582	69,242	71,902	74,562	77,222	79,882
JG–526	2,772	59,002	61,774	64,546	67,318	70,090	72,862	75,634	78,406	81,178	83,950
JG–527	2,866	62,377	65,243	68,109	70,975	73,841	76,707	79,573	82,439	85,305	88,171
JG–528	2,972	65,821	68,793	71,765	74,737	77,709	80,681	83,653	86,625	89,597	92,569
JG–529	3,087	69,429	72,516	75,603	78,690	81,777	84,864	87,951	91,038	94,125	97,212
JG–530	3,193	73,242	76,435	79,628	82,821	86,014	89,207	92,400	95,593	98,786	101,979
JG–531	3,301	77,339	80,640	83,941	87,242	90,543	93,844	97,145	100,446	103,747	107,048
JG–532	3,403	81,707	85,110	88,513	91,916	95,319	98,722	102,125	105,528	108,931	112,334
JG–533	3,509	86,373	89,882	93,391	96,900	100,409	103,918	107,427	110,936	114,445	117,954
JG–534	3,616	91,219	94,835	98,451	102,067	105,683	109,299	112,915	116,531	120,147	123,763
JG–535	3,716	96,206	99,922	103,638	107,354	111,070	114,786	118,502	122,218	125,934	129,650
JG–536	3,831	101,261	105,092	108,923	112,754	116,585	120,416	124,247	128,078	131,909	135,740
JG–537	3,930	106,883	110,813	114,743	118,673	122,603	126,533	130,463	134,393	138,323	142,253
JG–538		109,029+									

§ 107.14. April First, Two Thousand Two Salary Schedule

Effective April 1, 2002, the salary schedule required by Section 2 of Chapter 69 of the Laws of 2000 shall be as follows:

Grade	Increment	Hiring Rate	1st Year	2nd Year	3rd Year	4th Year	5th Year	6th Year	Maximum	1st Longevity	2nd Extra Longevity
JG–501	950	15,568	16,518	17,468	18,418	19,368	20,318	21,268	22,218	23,168	24,118
JG–502	999	16,156	17,155	18,154	19,153	20,152	21,151	22,150	23,149	24,148	25,147
JG–503	1,043	17,006	18,049	19,092	20,135	21,178	22,221	23,264	24,307	25,350	26,393
JG–504	1,098	17,792	18,890	19,988	21,086	22,184	23,282	24,380	25,478	26,576	27,674
JG–505	1,162	18,626	19,788	20,950	22,112	23,274	24,436	25,598	26,760	27,922	29,084
JG–506	1,208	19,736	20,944	22,152	23,360	24,568	25,776	26,984	28,192	29,400	30,608
JG–507	1,259	20,921	22,180	23,439	24,698	25,957	27,216	28,475	29,734	30,993	32,252
JG–508	1,311	22,161	23,472	24,783	26,094	27,405	28,716	30,027	31,338	32,649	33,960
JG–509	1,376	23,444	24,820	26,196	27,572	28,948	30,324	31,700	33,076	34,452	35,828
JG–510	1,437	24,860	26,297	27,734	29,171	30,608	32,045	33,482	34,919	36,356	37,793
JG–511	1,504	26,391	27,895	29,399	30,903	32,407	33,911	35,415	36,919	38,423	39,927
JG–512	1,561	28,001	29,562	31,123	32,684	34,245	35,806	37,367	38,928	40,489	42,050
JG–513	1,634	29,706	31,340	32,974	34,608	36,242	37,876	39,510	41,144	42,778	44,412
JG–514	1,704	31,528	33,232	34,936	36,640	38,344	40,048	41,752	43,456	45,160	46,864
JG–515	1,775	33,436	35,211	36,986	38,761	40,536	42,311	44,086	45,861	47,636	49,411
JG–516	1,862	35,367	37,229	39,091	40,953	42,815	44,677	46,539	48,401	50,263	52,125
JG–517	1,957	37,420	39,377	41,334	43,291	45,248	47,205	49,162	51,119	53,076	55,033
JG–518	2,050	39,642	41,692	43,742	45,792	47,842	49,892	51,942	53,992	56,042	58,092
JG–519	2,145	41,868	44,013	46,158	48,303	50,448	52,593	54,738	56,883	59,028	61,173
JG–520	2,241	44,098	46,339	48,580	50,821	53,062	55,303	57,544	59,785	62,026	64,267
JG–521	2,337	46,549	48,886	51,223	53,560	55,897	58,234	60,571	62,908	65,245	67,582
JG–522	2,444	49,119	51,563	54,007	56,451	58,895	61,339	63,783	66,227	68,671	71,115
JG–523	2,542	51,858	54,400	56,942	59,484	62,026	64,568	67,110	69,652	72,194	74,736
JG–524	2,638	54,752	57,390	60,028	62,666	65,304	67,942	70,580	73,218	75,856	78,494
JG–525	2,753	57,901	60,654	63,407	66,160	68,913	71,666	74,419	77,172	79,925	82,678
JG–526	2,869	61,068	63,937	66,806	69,675	72,544	75,413	78,282	81,151	84,020	86,889
JG–527	2,966	64,563	67,529	70,495	73,461	76,427	79,393	82,359	85,325	88,291	91,257
JG–528	3,076	68,125	71,201	74,277	77,353	80,429	83,505	86,581	89,657	92,733	95,809
JG–529	3,195	71,860	75,055	78,250	81,445	84,640	87,835	91,030	94,225	97,420	100,615
JG–530	3,305	75,804	79,109	82,414	85,719	89,024	92,329	95,634	98,939	102,244	105,549
JG–531	3,417	80,043	83,460	86,877	90,294	93,711	97,128	100,545	103,962	107,379	110,796
JG–532	3,522	84,568	88,090	91,612	95,134	98,656	102,178	105,700	109,222	112,744	116,266
JG–533	3,632	89,395	93,027	96,659	100,291	103,923	107,555	111,187	114,819	118,451	122,083
JG–534	3,743	94,409	98,152	101,895	105,638	109,381	113,124	116,867	120,610	124,353	128,096
JG–535	3,846	99,574	103,420	107,266	111,112	114,958	118,804	122,650	126,496	130,342	134,188
JG–536	3,965	104,806	108,771	112,736	116,701	120,666	124,631	128,596	132,561	136,526	140,491
JG–537	4,068	110,621	114,689	118,757	122,825	126,893	130,961	135,029	139,097	143,165	147,233
JG–538		112,846+									

PART 108. FORMAT OF COURT TRANSCRIPTS AND RATES OF PAYMENT THEREFOR WHEN THE UNIFIED COURT SYSTEM IS RESPONSIBLE FOR PAYMENT

§ 108.1. General

(a) Unless otherwise provided herein, this Part shall govern the format of each page of a transcript of court proceedings to be furnished by a court reporter who is an employee of the unified court system or who is an independent contractor, the rate of payment to which he or she is entitled therefor, and the requirements for the agreement between court reporter and the requesting party.

(b) For purposes of this Part, the term *"transcript"* shall mean a transcription of the stenographic minutes taken by one or more court reporters, constituting a complete record of all court proceedings in a case.

§ 108.2. Payment for Transcript

(a) [For application of this subsection, see note below. See, also, subsection (a) below.] Unless otherwise provided by law, this section shall apply where the unified court system or persons or parties other than the unified court system are responsible for payment to the court reporter for the transcript, or some portion thereof, that is furnished.

(a) [For application of this subsection, see note below. See, also, subsection (a) above.] This section shall apply where the unified court system is responsible by law for payment to the court reporter for the transcript, or some portion thereof, that is furnished. Where persons or parties other than the unified court system are responsible for payment to the court reporter, this section shall apply to the extent permitted by section 8002 of the CPLR.

(b) [For application of this subsection, see note below. See, also, subsection (b) below.] (1) For furnishing a transcript of court proceedings, or some portion thereof, a court reporter shall be paid at the following rate:

(i) Where the unified court system is responsible by law for payment to the court reporter—$2.50 per page for an original plus $1.00 per page for each copy, except that:

For delivery as required by section 460.70 of the Criminal Procedure Law—$3.50 per page for an original plus no charge for the first copy.

For Regular delivery to a judge pursuant to section 299 of the Judiciary Law—no charge.

(ii) Except as otherwise provided in subparagraph (i) of this paragraph, where payment to the court reporter is to come from public funds:

For Regular delivery—between $2.50 per page and $3.15 per page for an original plus $1.00 per page for each copy.

For Expedited delivery—between $3.15 per page and $4.25 per page for an original plus $1.10 per page for each copy.

For Daily delivery—between $3.75 per page and $5.25 per page for an original plus $1.25 per page for each copy.

(iii) In all instances not covered by subparagraphs (i) and (ii) of this paragraph:

For Regular delivery—between $3.30 per page and $4.30 per page for an original plus $1.00 per page for each copy.

For Expedited delivery—between $4.40 per page and $5.40 per page for an original plus $1.10 per page for each copy.

For Daily delivery—between $5.50 per page and $6.50 per page for an original plus $1.25 per page for each copy.

(2) For purposes of this subdivision and subdivision (e) of this section:

(i) "regular delivery" shall mean production and delivery of a transcript in ordinary circumstances after the conclusion of the proceedings, and including any production and delivery times that exceed those for expedited or daily delivery:

(ii) "expedited delivery" shall mean production and delivery of transcript within five business days for each day's or partial day's proceeding:

(iii) "daily delivery" shall mean production and delivery of a transcript on the morning of the next business day:

(iv) a "copy" of a transcript or a portion thereof must be ordered within 30 days of the date on which the original of such transcript or portion thereof was ordered:

(v) delivery times are measured from the time the court reporter receives the order for the transcript or portion thereof:

(vi) where delivery of a transcript is ordered and this section specifies a range of rates for the category of such delivery (*i.e.*, regular delivery, expedited delivery or daily delivery), the court reporter shall be paid at such rate, within such range, as he or she and the ordering party may agree upon based on consideration of the regional and market cost of transcripts and transcript production, complexity of the subject matter of the proceeding involved, and the court reporter's transcript volume. Where the court reporter and the ordering party cannot agree upon a rate, the court reporter shall not be required to produce and deliver the transcript, except where regular delivery has been ordered, in which event the rate of payment therefor shall be the lowest rate within the range of rates specified in this section for regular delivery.

(vii) a court reporter may, upon agreement with the ordering party, deliver a transcript in the form of a file (in ASCII or other agreed-upon format) on a computer diskette. In such event, such file shall be designated as an original or copy as the court reporter and the ordering party shall agree, and the court reporter shall be entitled to be paid at the otherwise applicable per page rate prescribed hereunder for each page of such transcript included in such file unless the transcript is compressed in which case each quadrant of such transcript (*i.e.*, one of four transcript pages electronically compressed into a single page) shall constitute a separate page for which the court reporter is entitled to be paid at the otherwise applicable per page rate prescribed hereunder.

(b) [For application of this subsection, see note below. See, also, subsection **(b)** above.] (1) For furnishing a transcript of court proceedings, or some portion thereof, a court reporter shall be paid at a rate of $1.375 per page.

(2) Where a court reporter and a private party otherwise enter into an agreement pursuant to section 8002 of the CPLR for the furnishing of a transcript, the following rate maximums should be used as guidelines:

Expedited copy—$4.40 per page

Daily copy—$5.50 per page

Expedited copy means production of the transcript within seven calendar days.

(c)(1) Notwithstanding the provisions of subdivision (b) of this section, no court reporter shall be entitled to receive payment for a transcript, or some portion thereof, at a rate specified in subdivision (b) unless the court reporter or his or her supervisor receives an authorized request therefor on or after the effective date of such rate. For purposes of this subdivision, an authorized request shall mean one that (i) is made in writing by an appellate court or by a judge or nonjudicial court employee acting at the judge's direction, (ii) is dated, and (iii) recites the statutory authority upon which it is made.

(2) The provisions of paragraph (1) of this subdivision shall not apply where preparation of a transcript, or some portion thereof, is not requested by an appellate court, a judge or a nonjudicial employee acting at the judge's direction, but is requested by a party to court proceedings or some other person entitled by law to obtain a copy thereof, or is required by operation of law. In such event, the court reporter who

prepares the transcript, or some portion thereof, shall be entitled to receive payment therefor at the rate specified in subdivision (b) of this section in effect on the date the requirement for its preparation arose.

(d) For purposes of this section, a court reporter shall not be entitled to payment for a page of transcript unless the page complies with the standard transcript specifications set forth in section 108.3 of this Part and has at least 13 lines of material thereon. Where a court reporter is required to furnish only a portion of a transcript, the word transcript as used in this subdivision shall mean that portion.

(e) [For application of this subsection, see note below.] Notwithstanding the provisions of subdivision (b) of this section, a court reporter who has transcribed stenographic minutes of a proceeding prior to the effective date of this subdivision and who, on or after such effective date, receives an order for a transcript of such minutes shall be paid at the following rate if payment to the court reporter is to come from public funds:

(1) Where the unified court system is responsible by law for payment to the court reporter, at the applicable rate specified in subparagraph (i) of paragraph one of subdivision (b) of this section less ten percent thereof.

(2) In all instances in which paragraph (1) of this subdivision does not apply:

For Regular delivery—between $2.25 per page and $2.75 per page for an original plus $1.00 per page for each copy.

For Expedited delivery—between $2.75 per page and $3.85 per page for an original plus $1.10 per page for each copy.

For Daily delivery—between $3.40 per page and $4.75 per page for an original plus $1.25 per page for each copy.

["This order shall take effect on the same day as the chapter of the laws of 2000 (L.2000, c. 279, eff. Aug. 16, 2000) hereinabove cited becomes a law and, except as the amendments otherwise provide, shall apply to all transcripts ordered on or after this date; provided, however, the provisions of Part 108, in effect immediately prior to the effective date of this order shall remain in full force and effect as to nonjudicial officers and employees in a collective negotiating unit not specified in section one of such chapter."]

Cross References

CPLR, see McKinney's Book 7B.

§ 108.3. Standard Transcript Specifications

(a) Transcripts shall be on paper which is 8½ × 11 inches in size.

(b) Each page of a transcript shall conform to the following specifications:

(1) [For application of this subdivision, see note below. See, also, subdivision (1) below.] Each page,

except those listed in subparagraphs (i) through (iii) of this paragraph, shall have 25 numbered lines of material thereon, excluding a line devoted to the title and page number:

(1) [For application of this subdivision, see note below. See, also, subdivision (1) above.] Each page, except those listed in subparagraphs (i) through (iii) of this paragraph, shall have 25 numbered lines of material thereon, including a line devoted to the title and page number:

(i) the page on which the title is included or, if transcription of the title requires more than one page, the last of such pages;

(ii) the page on which the index is included or, if transcription of the index requires more than one page, the last of such pages; and

(iii) for each day on which a court reporter takes minutes of proceedings in a case, the last page of the transcription thereof, or, where more than one court reporter takes minutes of the proceedings in a case, the last such page of each portion of the transcript furnished by each court reporter.

(2) There shall be 10 type characters per inch.

(3) The left-hand margin shall be indented 1¾ inches from the left-hand edge of the page and shall be marked by two lines, 1/16 of an inch apart, extending from the top to the bottom of each page. The right-hand margin shall be indented ⅜ of an inch from the right-hand edge and shall be marked by a single line extending from the top to the bottom of each page. Each line of transcribed material shall extend as closely as possible to the right-hand margin.

(4) The horizontal writing block shall be 6⁵/16 inches. The vertical writing block shall be 9 inches.

(c) The testimony and colloquy portions of a transcript shall be in a format as follows:

(1) In the testimony portion, the first line of each question and each answer shall be indented five spaces from the left-hand margin and shall be commenced by a "Q" or "A," as appropriate. The text of each such line shall then commence 10 spaces from the left-hand margin. Each subsequent line of a question or answer shall commence at the left-hand margin.

(2) [For application of this subdivision, see note below. See, also, subdivision (2) below.] In the colloquy portion, the first line of each speaker's remarks shall be indented 15 spaces from the left-hand margin and shall be commenced with a designation of the speaker's name, followed by a colon, two spaces and the start of his or her remarks. Each subsequent line of such remarks shall be indented 5 spaces from the left-hand margin, except that the first line of each succeeding paragraph of such remarks shall be indented 15 spaces from the left-hand margin.

(2) [For application of this subdivision, see note below. See, also, subdivision (2) above.] In the colloquy portion, the first line of each speaker's remarks shall be indented 15 spaces from the left-hand margin and shall be commenced with a designation of the speaker's name, followed by a colon, two spaces and the start of his or her remarks. Each subsequent line of such remarks shall be indented 10 spaces from the left-hand margin, except that the first line of each succeeding paragraph of such remarks shall be indented 15 spaces from the left-hand margin.

(d) The first page of each transcript shall include a title setting forth only the following:

(1) the court, the county or city of venue, and the part in which the proceedings were held;

(2) the name of the case;

(3) the number of the accusatory instrument(s) or case number(s), the charge and the nature of the proceedings;

(4) the address of the courthouse;

(5) the date(s) of the proceedings;

(6) the presiding authority;

(7) whether the proceedings were before a jury;

(8) the appearances of counsel for the parties; and

(9) the name of each court reporter and each court interpreter, if any.

A transcription of each subsequent day's proceedings shall include an abbreviated title setting forth only the matter specified in paragraphs (1) through (7) of this subdivision. Such abbreviated title shall also include a statement that the appearances of counsel are as previously recited, except that where there are changes in the appearances, such changes shall be set forth.

(e) Each transcript shall include a single index; except that, where more than one court reporter takes minutes of the proceedings in a case, there may be a separate index for each portion of the transcript of the proceedings furnished by each such court reporter. The index shall set forth the following:

(1) the party who called the witness, the name of each witness testifying in the proceedings recorded therein, together with the page or pages on which his or her testimony is given, and whether such testimony was given as part of direct examination, cross-examination or some other form of examination; and

(2) the party who proffered each exhibit, a description of each of the exhibits submitted by each party, together with the page or pages on which it was offered for identification and introduced into evidence.

(f) Sample transcript pages reflecting the specifications required herein are displayed in the Appendix to this Part.[1]

["This order shall take effect on the same day as the chapter of the laws of 2000 (L.2000, c. 279, eff. Aug. 16, 2000) hereinabove cited becomes a law and, except as the amendments otherwise provide, shall apply to all transcripts ordered on or after this date; provided, however, the provisions of Part 108, in effect immediately prior to the effective date of this order shall remain in full force and effect as to nonjudicial officers and employees in a collective negotiating unit not specified in section one of such chapter."]

[1] Such samples are not set out herein. See 22 NYCRR.

§ 108.4. Written Agreement

(a) [For application of this subsection, see note below. See, also, subsection **(a)** below.] Each court reporter who furnishes a transcript of a court proceeding shall, at the time the transcript is requested, enter into a written agreement for its production with the person or party requesting the transcript. The agreement shall be made on the form set forth in the Appendix to this Part.

(a) [For application of this subsection, see note below. See, also, subsection **(a)** above.] Each court reporter who furnishes a transcript of a court proceeding shall, at the time the transcript is requested, enter into a written agreement for its production with the person or party requesting the transcript. The agreement shall be made on a form prescribed by the Chief Administrator of the Courts and shall set forth the rate per page, the estimated number of pages, and the date by which the transcript shall be produced.

(b) Each court reporter who enters into such written agreement shall file a copy of that agreement in the office of the appropriate Administrative Judge, or his or her designee, no later than seven days after entering into the agreement.

(c) [For application of this subsection, see note below. See, also, subsection **(c)** below.] This section shall not apply where payment to the court reporter for the transcript is to come from public funds.

(c) [For application of this subsection, see note below. See, also, subsection **(c)** above.] This section shall not apply where the unified court system is responsible for payment to the court reporter for the transcript.

["This order shall take effect on the same day as the chapter of the laws of 2000 (L.2000, c. 279, eff. Aug. 16, 2000) hereinabove cited becomes a law and, except as the amendments otherwise provide, shall apply to all transcripts ordered on or after this date; provided, however, the provisions of Part 108, in effect immediately prior to the effective date of this order shall remain in full force and effect as to nonjudicial officers and employees in a collective negotiating unit not specified in section one of such chapter."]

§ 108.5. Appendix: Court Reporter Minute Agreement Form

APPENDIX

COURT REPORTER MINUTE AGREEMENT FORM

(As required by section 108.4(a) of the Rules of
the Chief Administrator of the Courts)

Please Type or Print Clearly

1. _____ Court, _____ County.
   Part No. _____ Name of Judge/Justice _____
2. Name of case _____
   _____
3. Court Docket/File/Index Number__ 4. Date minutes requested__
5. Type of proceeding (check one or more):
   Arraignment__ Application__ Hearing__ Plea__ Trial__ Sentence
   Other (specify) _____
6. Pursuant to section 108 of the Rules of the Chief Administrator of the Courts, the rates per page for transcripts of proceedings reported in New York State courts shall be as follows:

      Regular delivery: $3.30 - $4.30 (original)
                      $1.00 (each copy)

      Expedited delivery: $4.40 - $5.40 (original)
                      $1.10 (each copy)

    Daily delivery: $5.50 - $6.50 (original)
            $1.25 (each copy)

7. Rate to be charged per page:
  Regular _____ Expedited _____ Daily _____ Other _____
  No. of copies ordered _____
8. Estimated number of pages: _____ 9. Estimated delivery date _____
10. Agreed to:

_____ _____ _____
 Court Reporter (signature) Attorney/Party (signature) Date of Agreement
 Name of Court Reporter _____ Name of Attorney/Party _____
 Address _____ Firm/Address _____

 Telephone Number _____ Telephone Number _____
 Fax Number _____   Fax Number _____

A copy of this agreement must be filed by the court reporter with his/her supervisor as designated by the Administrative Judge within 7 calendar days following the date of agreement.

INSTRUCTIONS FOR COMPLETING THE COURT REPORTER MINUTE AGREEMENT FORM

A written agreement must be completed whether the initial order is placed by telephone, mail, fax, e-mail or in person. If an order involves minutes to be transcribed for the same case, but from more than one court reporter, each reporter must complete a separate order form.

1. Enter the specific title of the court, *e.g.*, Supreme Court, County Court, etc.; the county in which the court is located; the name or number of the Part in which the matter was heard; and the name of the judge who heard the case.

2. Enter the title of the case.

3. Enter the docket, file or index number, or any other identification assigned by the court to this case. If there is no number assigned, enter "None."

4. Enter the date or dates of the minutes of the proceeding or portion thereof to be transcribed.

5. Indicate one or more types of proceedings to be transcribed.

6. This section is informational and requires no response.

7. Enter the amount of the per page rate to be charged and check the requested time for delivery.

8. The court reporter must estimate the number of pages for which there will be a charge. The actual number of pages cannot be known until the transcript is complete.

9. Enter the estimated date of delivery. Court reporters are expected to adhere to the estimated date of delivery set forth in the agreement. Ordinarily, court reporters are required to transcribe requests for transcripts in the order of receipt. However, where statutory or other provisions set forth in the Court Reporter Manual that require transcripts be produced immediately affect the date of delivery of previously-ordered transcripts, the court reporter will endeavor to use best efforts to notify the person ordering the transcript. Notification must be made in a timely fashion prior to the estimated date of delivery informing the requesting party of the reason for the delay and arranging for a new date of delivery.

10. The court reporter and the attorney or party ordering the transcript each must sign the agreement and provide their addresses and phone and fax numbers. The agreement must be dated.

Definitions:

- "Daily" means produced and delivered the morning of the next UCS workday.
- "Expedited" means produced and delivered within five UCS workdays for each day's or partial day's proceeding.
- "Regular" means produced and delivered in ordinary circumstances after the conclusion of proceedings, and including any production and delivery times that exceed those for daily or expedited copy.
- Delivery times are measured from the time that the reporter receives the order for the transcript or portion thereof.
- To qualify for the "copy" rate, a transcript or portion thereof must be ordered within 30 days from the date that the transcript or that portion thereof was previously ordered.

If you have any questions concerning this form or its contents, please contact the Supervising Court Reporter or Chief Clerk, as appropriate.

PART 109. ATTENDANCE OF PERSONS AT HEARINGS TO DETERMINE THE MENTAL CONDITION OF A PERSON

§ 109.1. Attendance at Civil Proceedings Held Pursuant to Mental Hygiene Law, or Other Law, to Determine the Mental Condition of a Person

In exercising the inherent discretion possessed by the judge who is presiding in the courtroom to exclude any person or the general public from a civil proceeding held pursuant to the provisions of the Mental Hygiene Law, or other law, to determine the mental condition of a person, the judge shall consider whether the orderly and sound administration of justice, including the nature of the proceedings and the privacy of the parties, requires that persons be excluded from the courtroom. Whenever a judge exercises discretion to exclude any person or the general public from such proceeding, the judge shall make findings prior to ordering exclusion.

PART 110. PROCEDURE UNDER CPL 330.20 (JOINTLY ADOPTED BY THE STATE COMMISSIONER OF MENTAL HEALTH AND THE CHIEF ADMINISTRATOR OF THE COURTS)

§ 110.1. Preamble

(a) Section 12 of chapter 548 of the Laws of 1980 requires the State Commissioner of Mental Health and the Chief Administrator of the Courts to implement section 11 of that chapter (which added a new section 330.20 to the Criminal Procedure Law, hereinafter cited as CPL 330.20) by jointly adopting rules respecting the following matters:

(1) the scope of the psychiatric examinations prescribed by CPL 330.20;

(2) the data to be furnished the psychiatric examiners conducting the examinations prescribed in CPL 330.20;

(3) the form and content of the examination reports required to be filed under CPL 330.20;

(4) the form and content of the applications authorized to be filed under CPL 330.20; and

(5) the form and content of the court orders issuable under CPL 330.20.

(b)(1) The rules prescribed in this Part, including the forms appended hereto, have been jointly adopted by the State Commissioner of Mental Health and the Chief Administrator of the Courts. The appended forms shall be the official forms for use in implementing CPL 330.20. Variations in these forms will be permitted if jointly approved by the said commissioner and chief administrator, or if, in the context of a particular case, a variation in a form is required in order to comply with an applicable provision of law.

(2) Since the appended forms do not expressly provide for a defendant who is mentally retarded, the appropriate forms must be modified by the court to conform with the provisions of CPL 330.20 when a defendant, found not responsible by reason of mental disease or defect, is determined by the court to be mentally retarded and not suffering from a dangerous mental disorder. In such case, if the defendant is in need of care and treatment as a resident in the inpatient services of a developmental center or other residential facility for the mentally retarded and de-

velopmentally disabled, jurisdiction is vested by law in the State Office of Mental Retardation and Developmental Disabilities, and not in the State Office of Mental Health.

Cross References

Criminal Procedure Law, see McKinney's Book 11A.

Forms

Procedure following verdict or plea of not responsible by reason of mental disease or defect, see West's McKinney's Forms, Criminal Procedure, § 330.20, Forms 1 to 39.

§ 110.2. Definitions

The definitions set forth in section 1.20, and in subdivision 1 of section 330.20, of the Criminal Procedure Law shall be applicable to this Part and the forms appended hereto.

Cross References

Criminal Procedure Law, see McKinney's Book 11A.

Forms

Procedure following verdict or plea of not responsible by reason of mental disease or defect, see West's McKinney's Forms, Criminal Procedure, § 330.20, Forms 1 to 39.

§ 110.3. Examination Order

(a) Upon entry of a verdict of not responsible by reason of mental disease or defect, or upon the acceptance of a plea of not responsible by reason of mental disease or defect, the court must immediately issue an examination order. The form and contents of this examination order are prescribed in Form A and Form B. Form A directs that the defendant be committed to a secure facility as the place for conducting the psychiatric examination. Form B directs that the examination be conducted on an outpatient basis. Form B may be used in the court's discretion, but only if the defendant was not in custody at the time of the "not responsible" verdict or plea because he was previously released on bail or on his own recognizance.

(b) Form A authorizes confinement in a secure facility for a period not exceeding 30 days. Upon application of the commissioner, the court may authorize confinement for an additional period not exceeding 30 days when a longer period is necessary to complete the examination. Form A–1 prescribes the form and contents of this application and the order authorizing confinement for an additional period.

(c) Form B directs the outpatient psychiatric examination be completed within 30 days after the defendant has first reported to the place designated by the commissioner. Upon application of the commissioner, the court may extend such period for a reasonable time if a longer period is necessary to complete the examination. Form B–1 prescribes the form and contents of this application and the order extending the examination period. If the commissioner informs the court that confinement of the defendant is necessary

for an effective examination, the court must direct that the defendant be confined in a facility designated by the commissioner until the examination is completed. This direction may be made orally, on the record, in open court.

(d) When an examination order is issued, the clerk of the court shall promptly forward or furnish a copy of this order to the persons named in Form A or Form B. In order to assist the psychiatric examiners in their examination of the defendant, the clerk of the court shall also promptly forward to the commissioner, or directly to the designated psychiatric examiners, the following material:

(1) a copy of the indictment and any other accusatory instrument in the court's file;

(2) a copy of any examination report submitted pursuant to CPL article 730;

(3) any psychiatric reports or medical records received in evidence at the trial or other proceedings before the court; and

(4) any other data or material designated by the court or requested by the psychiatric examiners, including any available and transcribed psychiatric testimony given at the trial or other proceedings before the court.

(e) After he has completed his examination of the defendant, each psychiatric examiner must promptly prepare a report of his findings and evaluation concerning the defendant's mental condition. The form of the examination report shall be as prescribed in Form Y. The report shall be submitted to the commissioner. Upon receipt of the examination reports, the commissioner shall submit four copies of each report to the court that issued the examination order. The clerk of the court shall furnish a copy of the reports to the district attorney, counsel for the defendant and the Mental Health Information Service.

(f) After the examination reports are submitted, the court must, within 10 days of receipt of such reports, conduct an initial hearing to determine the defendant's present mental condition. If the defendant is in the custody of the commissioner pursuant to an examination order, the court shall issue the order prescribed in Form C.

Cross References

Criminal Procedure Law, see McKinney's Book 11A.

Forms

Procedure following verdict or plea of not responsible by reason of mental disease or defect, see West's McKinney's Forms, Criminal Procedure, § 330.20, Forms 1 to 39.

§ 110.4. Initial Hearing; Commitment Order; Civil Commitment

(a) At the initial hearing conducted pursuant to subdivision 6 of CPL 330.20, if the court finds that the defendant has a dangerous mental disorder, it must issue a commitment order. The form and contents of this commitment order are prescribed in Form G.

(b) At the initial hearing conducted pursuant to subdivision 6 of CPL 330.20, if the court finds that the defendant is mentally ill but does not have a dangerous mental disorder, the court must issue a civil order committing the defendant to the custody of the commissioner. The form and contents of this civil order are prescribed in Form F. When issuing this civil order, the court must also issue at the same time an order of conditions. The form and contents of the order of conditions are prescribed in Form N.

(c) At the initial hearing conducted pursuant to subdivision 6 of CPL 330.20, if the court finds that the defendant does not have a dangerous mental disorder and is not mentally ill, the court must issue one of the following orders:

(1) an order discharging the defendant unconditionally (Form D); or

(2) an order discharging the defendant subject to an order of conditions (Form E and Form N).

Cross References

Criminal Procedure Law, see McKinney's Book 11A.

Forms

Procedure following verdict or plea of not responsible by reason of mental disease or defect, see West's McKinney's Forms, Criminal Procedure, § 330.20, Forms 1 to 39.

§ 110.5. First Retention Order

(a) When a defendant is in the custody of the commissioner pursuant to a commitment order or a recommitment order, the commissioner must, at least 30 days prior to the expiration of the period prescribed in the order, apply to the court that issued the order, or to a superior court in the county where the secure facility is located, for a first retention order or a release order. Upon receipt of such application, the court may, on its own motion, conduct a hearing to determine whether the defendant has a dangerous mental disorder, and it must conduct such hearing if a demand therefor is made by one of the parties.

(b) Form H prescribes the form and contents of the application for a first retention order and the notice of application. Form Q prescribes the form and contents of the application for a release order and the notice of application. Following the submission of either such application pursuant to subdivision 8 of CPL 330.20, if the court finds that the defendant has a dangerous mental disorder it must issue a first retention order. The form and contents of this first retention order are prescribed in Form I.

(c) Following the submission of an application for a first retention order (Form H) or an application for a release order (Form Q) pursuant to subdivision 8 of CPL 330.20, if the court finds that the defendant is

mentally ill but does not have a dangerous mental disorder, it must issue the following three orders:

(1) a first retention order (Form I);

(2) a transfer order (Form P); and

(3) an order of conditions (Form N).

(d) Following the submission of an application for a first retention order (Form H) or an application for a release order (Form Q) pursuant to subdivision 8 of CPL 330.20, if the court finds that the defendant does not have a dangerous mental disorder and is not mentally ill, it must issue the following two orders:

(1) a release order (Form R); and

(2) an order of conditions (Form N).

Cross References

Criminal Procedure Law, see McKinney's Book 11A.

Forms

Procedure following verdict or plea of not responsible by reason of mental disease or defect, see West's McKinney's Forms, Criminal Procedure, § 330.20, Forms 1 to 39.

§ 110.6. Second Retention Order

(a) When a defendant is in the custody of the commissioner pursuant to a first retention order, the commissioner must, at least 30 days prior to the expiration of the period prescribed in the order, apply to the court that issued the order, or to a superior court in the county where the facility is located, for a second retention order or a release order. Upon receipt of such application, the court may, on its own motion, conduct a hearing to determine whether the defendant has a dangerous mental disorder, and it must conduct such hearing if a demand therefor is made by one of the parties.

(b) Form J prescribes the form and contents of the application for a second retention order and the notice of application. Form Q prescribes the form and contents of the application for a release order and the notice of application. Following the submission of either such application pursuant to subdivision 9 of CPL 330.20, if the court finds that the defendant has a dangerous mental disorder it must issue a second retention order. The form and contents of this second retention order are prescribed in Form K.

(c) Following the submission of an application for a second retention order (Form J) or an application for a release order (Form Q) pursuant to subdivision 9 of CPL 330.20, if the court finds that the defendant is mentally ill but does not have a dangerous mental disorder, it must issue the following three orders:

(1) a second retention order (Form K);

(2) a transfer order (Form P); and

(3) an order of conditions (Form N).

(d) Following the submission of an application for a second retention order (Form J) or an application for a release order (Form Q) pursuant to subdivision 9 of CPL 330.20, if the court finds that the defendant does not have a dangerous mental disorder and is not mentally ill, it must issue the following two orders:

(1) a release order (Form R); and

(2) an order of conditions (Form N).

Cross References

Criminal Procedure Law, see McKinney's Book 11A.

Forms

Procedure following verdict or plea of not responsible by reason of mental disease or defect, see West's McKinney's Forms, Criminal Procedure, § 330.20, Forms 1 to 39.

§ 110.7. Subsequent Retention Order

(a) When a defendant is in the custody of the commissioner pursuant to a second retention order, or a previously issued subsequent retention order, the commissioner must, at least 30 days prior to the expiration of the period prescribed in the order, apply to the court that issued the order, or to a superior court in the county where the facility is located, for a subsequent retention order or a release order. Upon receipt of such application, the court may, on its own motion, conduct a hearing to determine whether the defendant has a dangerous mental disorder, and it must conduct such hearing if a demand therefor is made by one of the parties.

(b) Form L prescribes the form and contents of the application for a subsequent retention order and the notice of application. Form Q prescribes the form and contents of the application for a release order and the notice of application. Following the submission of either such application pursuant to subdivision 9 of CPL 330.20, if the court finds that the defendant has a dangerous mental disorder it must issue a subsequent retention order. The form and contents of this subsequent retention order are prescribed in Form M.

(c) Following the submission of an application for a subsequent retention order (Form L) or an application for a release order (Form Q) pursuant to subdivision 9 of CPL 330.20, if the court finds that the defendant is mentally ill but does not have a dangerous mental disorder, it must issue the following three orders:

(1) a subsequent retention order (Form M);

(2) a transfer order (Form P); and

(3) an order of conditions (Form N).

(d) Following the submission of an application for a subsequent retention order (Form L) or an application for a release order (Form Q) pursuant to subdivision 9 of CPL 330.20, if the court finds that the defendant does not have a dangerous mental disorder and is not mentally ill, it must issue the following two orders:

(1) a release order (Form R); and

(2) an order of conditions (Form N).

Cross References

Criminal Procedure Law, see McKinney's Book 11A.

Forms

Procedure following verdict or plea of not responsible by reason of mental disease or defect, see West's McKinney's Forms, Criminal Procedure, § 330.20, Forms 1 to 39.

§ 110.8. Furlough Order

(a) When a defendant is in the custody of the commissioner in a secure facility pursuant to a commitment order, a recommitment order, or a retention order, the commissioner may apply for a furlough order pursuant to subdivision 10 of CPL 330.20. The application for a furlough order may be made to the court that issued the commitment order or to a superior court in the county where the secure facility is located. Upon receipt of such application the court may, on its own motion, conduct a hearing to determine whether the application should be granted, and must conduct such hearing if a demand therefor is made by the district attorney.

(b) Form U prescribes the form and contents of the application for a furlough order and the notice of application. Following the submission of such application, if the court finds that the issuance of a furlough order is consistent with the public safety and welfare of the community and the defendant, and that the clinical condition of the defendant warrants a granting of the privileges authorized by a furlough order, the court must grant the application and issue a furlough order. The form and contents of this furlough order are prescribed in Form V.

Cross References

Criminal Procedure Law, see McKinney's Book 11A.

Forms

Procedure following verdict or plea of not responsible by reason of mental disease or defect, see West's McKinney's Forms, Criminal Procedure, § 330.20, Forms 1 to 39.

§ 110.9. Transfer Order

(a) When a defendant is in the custody of the commissioner in a secure facility pursuant to a retention order or a recommitment order, the commissioner may apply for a transfer order pursuant to subdivision 11 of CPL 330.20. A transfer order may not be issued when the defendant is in custody of the commissioner pursuant to a commitment order. The application for a transfer order may be made to the court that issued the order under which the defendant is then in custody, or to a superior court in the county where the secure facility is located. Upon receipt of such application, the court may, on its own motion, conduct a hearing to determine whether the application should be granted, and must conduct such hearing if the demand therefor is made by the district attorney.

(b) Form O prescribes the form and contents of the application for a transfer order and the notice of application. Following the submission of such application, the court must grant the application and issue a transfer order if the court finds that the defendant does not have a dangerous mental disorder, or if the court finds that the issuance of a transfer order is consistent with the public safety and welfare of the community and the defendant and that the clinical condition of the defendant warrants his transfer from a secure facility to a nonsecure facility. The form and contents of this transfer order are prescribed in Form P.

(c) A court must also issue a transfer order (Form P) when, in connection with an application for a first retention order (Form H), a second retention order (Form J), or a subsequent retention order (Form L), the court finds that the defendant is mentally ill but does not have a dangerous mental disorder.

(d) Whenever a court issues a transfer order (Form P), it must also issue an order of conditions (Form N).

Cross References

Criminal Procedure Law, see McKinney's Book 11A.

Forms

Procedure following verdict or plea of not responsible by reason of mental disease or defect, see West's McKinney's Forms, Criminal Procedure, § 330.20, Forms 1 to 39.

§ 110.10. Release Order

(a) When a defendant is in the custody of the commissioner pursuant to a retention order or a recommitment order, the commissioner may apply for a release order pursuant to subdivision 12 of CPL 330.20. The application for a release order may be made to the court that issued the order under which the defendant is then in custody, or to a superior court in the county where the facility is located. Upon receipt of such application, the court must promptly conduct a hearing to determine the defendant's present mental condition.

(b) Form Q prescribes the form and contents of the application for a release order and the notice of application. At the conclusion of the hearing conducted pursuant to subdivision 12 of CPL 330.20, if the court finds that the defendant does not have a dangerous mental disorder and is not mentally ill, it must grant the application and issue a release order. The form and contents of this release order are prescribed in Form R.

(c) At the conclusion of the hearing conducted pursuant to subdivision 12 of CPL 330.20, if the court finds that the defendant has a dangerous mental disorder, it must deny the application for a release order.

(d) At the conclusion of the hearing conducted pursuant to subdivision 12 of CPL 330.20, if the court finds that the defendant does not have a dangerous mental disorder but is mentally ill, it must issue a transfer order (Form P) if the defendant is then confined in a secure facility.

(e) A court must also issue a release order (Form R) when, in connection with an application for a first retention order (Form H), a second retention order (Form J), or a subsequent retention order (Form L), the court finds that the defendant does not have a dangerous mental disorder and is not mentally ill.

(f) Whenever a court issues a release order (Form R), it must also issue an order of conditions (Form N).

(g) If the court has previously issued a transfer order (Form P) and an order of conditions (Form N), it must issue a new order of conditions upon issuing a release order (Form R).

Cross References

Criminal Procedure Law, see McKinney's Book 11A.

Forms

Procedure following verdict or plea of not responsible by reason of mental disease or defect, see West's McKinney's Forms, Criminal Procedure, § 330.20, Forms 1 to 39.

§ 110.11. Order of Conditions

(a) An order of conditions is issuable in the following instances:

(1) If the court issues a transfer order, it must also issue an order of conditions.

(2) If the court issues a release order, it must also issue an order of conditions.

(3) If the court at the initial hearing conducted pursuant to CPL 330.20(6) finds that the defendant is mentally ill but does not have a dangerous mental disorder, it must issue an order of conditions and a civil order committing the defendant to the custody of the commissioner pursuant to the applicable provisions of the Mental Hygiene Law.

(4) If the court at the initial hearing conducted pursuant to CPL 330.20(6) finds that the defendant does not have a dangerous mental disorder and is not mentally ill, it must discharge the defendant either unconditionally or subject to an order of conditions.

(b) Form N prescribes the form and contents of an order of conditions.

Cross References

Criminal Procedure Law, see McKinney's Book 11A.

Mental Hygiene Law, see McKinney's Book 34A.

Forms

Procedure following verdict or plea of not responsible by reason of mental disease or defect, see West's McKinney's Forms, Criminal Procedure, § 330.20, Forms 1 to 39.

§ 110.12. Recommitment Order

(a) At any time during the period covered by an order of conditions (Form N), an application may be made by the commissioner or the district attorney for a recommitment order when the applicant is of the view that the defendant has a dangerous mental disorder. The application for a recommitment order may be made to the court that issued the order of conditions, or to a superior court in the county where the defendant is then residing. Form S prescribes the form and contents of an application for a recommitment order.

(b) Upon receipt of an application for a recommitment order (Form S), the court must order the defendant to appear before it for a hearing to determine if the defendant has a dangerous mental disorder. Form S–1 prescribes the form and contents of this order to appear. If the defendant fails to appear in court as directed, the court must issue a warrant. Form S–2 prescribes the form and contents of this warrant. When the defendant is brought before the court on the warrant, the court may direct that the defendant be confined in an appropriate institution. Form S–3 prescribes the form and contents of this temporary confinement order.

(c) When the defendant appears before the court on an application for a recommitment order (Form S), the court must conduct a hearing to determine whether the defendant has a dangerous mental disorder. If the court finds that the defendant has a dangerous mental disorder, it must issue a recommitment order. The form and contents of this recommitment order are prescribed in Form T.

Forms

Procedure following verdict or plea of not responsible by reason of mental disease or defect, see West's McKinney's Forms, Criminal Procedure, § 330.20, Forms 1 to 39.

§ 110.13. Discharge Order

(a) When a defendant has been continuously on an outpatient status for three years or more pursuant to a release order, the commissioner may apply for a discharge order pursuant to subdivision 13 of CPL 330.20. The application for a discharge order may be made to the court that issued the release order, or to a superior court in the county where the defendant is then residing. Upon receipt of such application, the court may, on its own motion, conduct a hearing to determine whether the application should be granted,

and must conduct such hearing if a demand therefor is made by the district attorney.

(b) Form W prescribes the form and contents of the application for a discharge order and the notice of application. Following the submission of such application, the court must grant the application and issue a discharge order if the court finds that the defendant has been continuously on an outpatient status for three years or more, that he does not have a dangerous mental disorder and is not mentally ill, and that the issuance of the discharge order is consistent with the public safety and welfare of the community and the defendant. The form and contents of this discharge order are prescribed in Form X.

Cross References

Criminal Procedure Law, see McKinney's Book 11A.

Forms

Procedure following verdict or plea of not responsible by reason of mental disease or defect, see West's McKinney's Forms, Criminal Procedure, § 330.20, Forms 1 to 39.

§ 110.14. Psychiatric Examination; Scope; Form of Report

(a) The scope of the psychiatric examinations prescribed by CPL 330.20 shall be as follows:

(1) the diagnosis and prognosis made by the psychiatric examiner concerning the defendant's mental condition;

(2) the findings and evaluation made by the psychiatric examiner concerning the defendant's mental condition;

(3) pertinent and significant factors in the defendant's medical and psychiatric history;

(4) the psychiatric signs and symptoms displayed by the defendant; and

(5) the reasons for the opinion stated by the psychiatric examiner (including, when defendant has a dangerous mental disorder, an explanation as to why, because of defendant's mental condition, he currently constitutes a physical danger to himself or others).

(b) Form Y prescribes the form and contents of the psychiatric examination reports required to be filed under CPL 330.20.

Cross References

Criminal Procedure Law, see McKinney's Book 11A.

Forms

Procedure following verdict or plea of not responsible by reason of mental disease or defect, see West's McKinney's Forms, Criminal Procedure, § 330.20, Forms 1 to 39.

PART 111. PROCEDURE UNDER CPL ARTICLE 730

§ 111.1. Definitions

Whenever in this Part or in the forms promulgated or approved hereunder, the following terms appear, they shall have the following meaning:

(a) "Director of community mental health services" means the person responsible for the administration of community mental health and mental retardation services in a county or city, whether known or referred to as director, commissioner, or otherwise.

(b) "Facility director", when used in connection with a hospital, institution or other facility, means the person in charge of the facility, whether known or referred to as director, superintendent, or otherwise.

§ 111.2. Examination of Defendant

(a) An order for the examination of a defendant to determine whether he is an incapacitated person under article 730 of the Criminal Procedure Law shall be addressed to the director of community mental health services of the county where the criminal action is pending, except in the City of New York where the order shall be addressed to the director of community mental health services of such city. If there is no such director of community mental health services, the order shall be addressed to the director of a hospital operated by local government within such county or city that has been certified as having adequate facilities for such purpose by the Commissioner of Mental Health or, in the absence of such local hospital, to the director of the State hospital operated by the Department of Mental Hygiene serving the county where the criminal action is pending.

(b) The hospital in which a defendant may be confined for examination pursuant to subdivision (2) or (3) of section 730.20 of the Criminal Procedure Law shall be a hospital operated by local government that has been certified by the Commissioner of Mental Health as having adequate facilities to examine a defendant to determine if he is an incapacitated person. If there be no such local governmental hospital serving the county where the criminal proceeding is pending, the defendant may be confined in a general hospital having a psychiatric unit approved by the Commissioner of Mental Health or in a State hospital operated by the Department of Mental Hygiene approved for such purpose if the person in charge thereof shall have given his consent to the confinement of such defendant therein.

Cross References

Criminal Procedure Law, see McKinney's Book 11A.

§ 111.3. Examination Report

(a) The examination of the defendant by the psychiatric examiners may be conducted separately or jointly but each examiner shall execute a separate report. Such report shall be made in the form jointly adopted by the Chief Administrator of the Courts and the Commissioner of Mental Health.

(b) The director of community mental health services charged with causing the examination to be made shall furnish six copies of the examination report to the court for filing and necessary distribution. The court shall require that copies be furnished to counsel for the defendant and to the district attorney.

§ 111.4. Commitment to Custody of Commissioner of Mental Health

(a) If the court is satisfied that the defendant is an incapacitated person and the defendant is not in custody, the court shall cause the defendant to appear before it at the time of issuing a final order of observation, temporary order of observation or order of commitment, or other appropriate order, as the case may be.

(b) The court shall forward to the Commissioner of Mental Health the order committing the defendant to his custody together with a copy of the examination reports, a copy of the accusatory instrument and, if available, a copy of the presentence report. Upon receipt thereof, the Commissioner of Mental Health shall designate the institution in which the defendant is to be placed and give notice of such designation to the sheriff or local correction department, as the case may be, who shall deliver the defendant, if in custody, to the person in charge of the designated institution, except that, in the case of final orders of observation, the Department of Mental Hygiene may provide the transportation to the designated institution.

§ 111.5. Order of Retention for Defendant Held Under Orders of Commitment

(a) The application for an order of retention of a defendant held pursuant to an order of commitment or order of retention shall be made within 60 days prior to the expiration of the order pursuant to which the defendant is being held. It shall be prepared by the director of the institution where the defendant is confined and shall have annexed to it a summary of the defendant's history and condition supporting the application, a copy of the indictment and a copy of each prior order of commitment or retention. Such director shall serve notice of the application on the defendant, on the defendant's attorney if known to the director, on the district attorney of the county where the criminal proceeding is pending, and on the Mental Health Information Service. Such director shall then promptly file the application with the court which issued the initial order of commitment of the defendant.

(b) The application shall not be brought on for determination by the court prior to 10 days from the date upon which notice of the application was served upon the defendant. A request by the defendant or anyone on his behalf for a hearing shall be forwarded to the court, with a copy to the district attorney and the Mental Health Information Service. The clerk of the court shall notify the defendant, the defendant's attorney if any, the district attorney, the director of the institution where the defendant is confined, and the Mental Health Information Service of the time and place of the hearing.

(c) Upon issuance of an order of retention, the court shall forward copies thereof to the district attorney, to the director of the institution where the defendant is confined, to the Commissioner of Mental Health and to the Mental Health Information Service. The director of the institution where the defendant is confined shall serve a copy of such order personally upon the defendant.

§ 111.6. Certificate of Custody

When defendant is in the custody of the Commissioner of Mental Health at the expiration of the period prescribed in a temporary order of observation or at the expiration of the authorized period prescribed in the last order of retention, the director of the institution where the defendant is confined may act as the agent of the Commissioner of Mental Health in certifying to the court that the defendant was in the custody of the Commissioner of Mental Health on such expiration date.

§ 111.7. Procedure Following Termination of Custody by Commissioner

When a defendant is in the custody of the commissioner on the expiration date of a final or temporary order of observation or an order of commitment, or on the expiration date of the last order of retention, or on the date an order dismissing an indictment is served upon the commissioner, the director of the institution in which the defendant is confined may, pursuant to section 730.70 of the Criminal Procedure Law, retain him for care and treatment for a period of 30 days from such date. If the director determines that the defendant is so mentally ill or mentally defective as to require continued care and treatment in an institution, he may retain the defendant beyond such period only pursuant to the admission procedures set forth in the Mental Hygiene Law. If the defendant is sought to be retained on an involuntary basis, the certificates of two physicians or, in the case of retention at a school for the mentally retarded, one physician and one psychiatrist, shall be filed and an application to a court for an order authorizing retention shall be made before the expiration of the said 30-day period.

Cross References

Criminal Procedure Law, see McKinney's Book 11A.

Mental Hygiene Law, McKinney's Book 34A.

§ 111.8. Official Forms

Forms promulgated by the Chief Administrator of the Courts and the Commissioner of Mental Health, or either of them, shall be the official forms for uniform use throughout the State in implementation of article 730 of the Criminal Procedure Law. Variations in these forms will be permitted if approved by the official or officials indicated in the following index as having adopted them.

Forms

See West's McKinney's Forms, Criminal Procedure, Article 730.

PART 112. RULES OF THE CHIEF ADMINISTRATOR OF THE COURTS PURSUANT TO CPLR RULES 5529 AND 9703

§ 112.1. Appellate Papers Reproduced by Methods Other Than Printing

Appellate papers reproduced by methods other than printing, pursuant to rule 5529 of the Civil Practice Law and Rules, must be reproduced on a good grade of at least 20-pound, white, opaque, unglazed paper. Any method of reproduction which produces a perma-nent, legible, black-on-white copy on the above paper shall be accepted. Wherever such a paper, presented to a clerk for filing, is not legible or otherwise suitable, the clerk may refuse to accept the same.

Cross References

CPLR, see McKinney's Book 7B.

§ 112.2. [Rescinded]

PART 113. PROCEDURE TO EVALUATE FITNESS OF JUDGES OR JUSTICES WHO BECOME ILL

§ 113.1. Notice to the Chief Administrator

Whenever a judge or justice of the trial courts of the Unified Court System has been unable to fully perform his or her duties for a period of greater than 60 days because of accident or illness, the administrative judge having jurisdiction over the court in which the judge or justice is assigned to sit shall promptly give notice of such inability to perform to the Chief Administrator of the Courts.

§ 113.2. Inquiry and Action by the Chief Administrator

(a) Upon receipt of such notice, the Chief Administrator shall make such inquiry as is necessary to ascertain the reason for the inability to perform, the prognosis for recovery, and the time the judge or justice is expected to be able to return to full performance.

(b) The Chief Administrator, after consultation with the Presiding Justice of the appropriate Appellate Division, may at any time direct a judge or justice who has been unable to fully perform his or her duties for an extended period of time to be examined by a physician selected by the Chief Administrator to ascertain the physical or mental condition of the judge or justice and the prognosis for his or her return to full performance. Except for extraordinary circumstances, any judge who has not fully performed his or her duties for greater than six months because of accident or illness must be examined pursuant to this paragraph.

PART 114. [REPEALED]

PART 115. CASELOAD ACTIVITY REPORTING

§ 115.1. Reports of Caseload Activity Information

The Chief Administrator of the Courts may prescribe forms and systems for the reporting of caseload activity information for each court of the Unified Court System.

§ 115.2. Filing of Caseload Activity Reports

(a) Unless the Chief Administrator shall otherwise direct, the chief clerk of each trial court, other than the Court of Claims, shall report caseload activity information, on a form prescribed pursuant to section 115.1, within ten calendar days following the end of each term of court or calendar month as specified by the Chief Administrator.

(b) Unless the Chief Administrator shall otherwise direct, the chief clerk of each appellate court and the Court of Claims shall report caseload activity information, on a form prescribed pursuant to section 115.1, within 30 calendar days following the end of the last term of the court year.

(c) For the purposes of this section, the County Court shall be deemed a trial court.

(d) This section shall not apply to town and village courts unless the Chief Administrator shall otherwise direct.

§ 115.3. Special Reports

In addition to reports submitted pursuant to section 115.2, all trial and appellate courts shall submit special reports relating to caseload activity as may from time to time be requested by the Chief Administrator.

§ 115.4. Criminal Case Dispositions

In addition to the requirements of section 115.2, each court having jurisdiction over the processing or disposition of criminal actions shall report case activity and disposition information with respect to each criminal action on a form prescribed pursuant to section 115.1 or by electronic media in a manner prescribed by the Chief Administrator. All such information shall be reported within 24 hours following the occurrence of the event, if reported by electronic media, or within 48 hours, if reported by form.

§ 115.5. Signature

All reports submitted to the Chief Administrator pursuant to this Part shall be signed by the chief clerk of the appropriate court or a designee.

PART 116. COMMUNITY DISPUTE RESOLUTION CENTERS PROGRAM

§ 116.1. Definitions

(a) "Center" means a community dispute center which provides conciliation, mediation, arbitration or other forms and techniques of dispute resolution.

(b) "Mediator" means an impartial person who assists in the resolution of a dispute.

(c) "Grant recipient" means any organization that administers a community dispute resolution center receiving funds pursuant to this Part.

(d) "Chief Administrator" means the Chief Administrator of the Courts or his designee.

§ 116.2. Application

(a) The provisions of this Part shall apply to the funding of community centers organized to expeditiously resolve minor disputes, especially those matters that would otherwise be handled by the criminal justice system.

(b) Funds available for disbursement pursuant to this Part shall include those funds appropriated by the

State Legislature for said purposes, and shall also include funds received by the State from any public or private agency or person, including the Federal government, to be used for the purposes of this Part.

§ 116.3.   Eligibility

To be eligible for funding pursuant to this Part, a center must meet the following conditions:

(a) It must be administered by a nonprofit organization organized for the resolution of disputes or for religious, charitable or educational purposes.

(b) It must provide neutral mediators who have received at least 25 hours of training in conflict resolution techniques.

(c) It must provide dispute resolution services without cost to indigents and at nominal or no cost to other participants.

(d) It shall, whenever reasonably possible, make use of public facilities at free or nominal cost.

(e) It must provide, during or at the conclusion of the dispute resolution process, a written agreement or decision, subscribed to by the parties, setting forth the settlement of the issues and future responsibilities of each party, and must make such agreement or decision available to a court which has adjourned a pending action pursuant to section 170.55 of the Criminal Procedure Law.

(f) It may not make monetary awards except upon consent of the parties, and such awards may not exceed $1,500, except that where an action has been adjourned in contemplation of dismissal pursuant to section 215.10 of the Criminal Procedure Law, a monetary award not in excess of $5,000 may be made.

(g) It may not accept for dispute resolution any defendant who is named in a filed felony complaint, superior court information, or indictment, charging:

(1) a class A felony; or

(2) a violent felony offense as defined in section 70.02 of the Penal Law; or

(3) any drug offense as defined in article 220 of the Penal Law; or

(4) a felony upon the conviction of which defendant must be sentenced as a second felony offender, a second violent felony offender, or a persistent violent felony offender pursuant to sections 70.06, 70.04 and 70.08 of the Penal Law, or a felony upon the conviction of which defendant may be sentenced as a persistent felony offender pursuant to section 70.10 of the Penal Law.

(h) It must provide to parties, in advance of the dispute resolution process, a written statement relating:

(1) their rights and obligations;

(2) the nature of the dispute;

(3) their right to call and examine witnesses;

(4) that a written settlement or a written decision with the reasons therefor will be rendered; and

(5) that the dispute resolution process will be final and binding upon the parties.

(i) It must permit all parties to appear with representatives, including counsel, and to present all relevant evidence relating to the dispute, including calling and examining witnesses.

(j) It must keep confidential all memoranda, work products or case files of a mediator, and must not disclose any communications relating to the subject matter of the resolution made during the resolution process by any participant, mediator or any person present at the dispute resolution.

Cross References

Criminal Procedure Law, see McKinney's Book 11A.

Penal Law, see McKinney's Book 39.

§ 116.4.   Application Procedures

Applications for funding pursuant to this Part shall be submitted to the Chief Administrator, and shall include the following information:

(a) a description of the organization administering the center, including a description of any sponsoring organizations;

(b) an itemized description of the annual cost of operating the proposed center, including the compensation of employees;

(c) a description of the geographic area of service, the service population and the number of participants capable of being served on an annual basis;

(d) a description of the facilities available in which the proposed center is to be operated;

(e) a detailed description of the proposed program for dispute resolution, including the types of disputes to be handled and the cost, if any, to the participants;

(f) a statement of the present availability of resources to fund the center;

(g) a description of the applicant's administrative capacity to operate the center, including the educational, training and employment background of every member of the staff of the center;

(h) a list of civic groups, social services agencies and criminal justice agencies available to accept and make referrals, written statements from these groups and agencies indicating an intent to accept and make referrals, and a description of how the program will be publicized to make potential referring agencies, the courts and the public aware of its availability;

(i) a description of the past history of the operation of the center, including specific information for the past two years concerning the program, area of service, staff, source of funding, expenditures, referring agencies, number and types of disputes handled, and number and types of disputes resolved;

(j) a list of all other available dispute resolution services and facilities within the proposed geographical area;

(k) documentation that the center meets the eligibility requirements set forth in section 116.3 of these rules; and

(*l*) such other information as may be required by the Chief Administrator.

§ 116.5. Approval

(a) The Chief Administrator shall select centers for funding pursuant to this Part and shall determine the amount of funds to be disbursed for each center within available appropriations.

(b) No funds provided by the State shall be disbursed for any center in an amount greater than 50 per centum of the estimated annual cost of operating the program as determined by the Chief Administrator.

(c) In determining the centers for which funds may be disbursed, the Chief Administrator shall consider:

(1) the need for the program in that geographical area;

(2) the structure and scope of the proposed program;

(3) the cost of operation;

(4) the availability of sources of funding;

(5) the adequacy and cost of facilities;

(6) the ability of the applicant to administer the program;

(7) the qualifications of the personnel staffing the center;

(8) the effectiveness of the program; and

(9) any other consideration which may affect the provision of dispute resolution services pursuant to this Part.

(d) A center may be rejected if the Chief Administrator determines that it will be unable to comply with any of the conditions set forth in section 116.3 of these rules.

(e) Nothing herein shall require the Chief Administrator to approve funding for any applicant.

§ 116.6. Payment

Payment of funds pursuant to this Part shall be made pursuant to contract entered into between the Unified Court System and the grant recipient.

§ 116.7. Program Evaluation

(a) The Chief Administrator shall monitor and evaluate each program receiving funds pursuant to this Part.

(b) Each grant recipient shall provide to the Chief Administrator on a periodic basis as determined by the Chief Administrator the following information concerning its program:

(1) amount of, and purpose for which, all monies were expended;

(2) number of referrals received by category of cases and the source of each referral;

(3) number of parties serviced;

(4) number of disputes resolved;

(5) nature of the resolution of each dispute, including the type of award and amount of money awarded, if any;

(6) number of cases in which the parties complied with the award, including the nature of the dispute and award in each such case;

(7) number of returnees to the resolution process, including the nature of the dispute and award in each such case;

(8) duration of each hearing;

(9) estimated cost of each hearing; and

(10) any other information as required by the Chief Administrator.

(c) The Chief Administrator shall have the power to inspect at any time the operation of any center receiving funds pursuant to this Part to determine whether the center is complying with the provisions of this Part and the terms of its contract, including the examination and auditing of the fiscal affairs of the program.

(d) The Chief Administrator may halt the disbursement of funds pursuant to this Part at any time he determines that the program is not adequately providing services pursuant to this Part or that any of the provisions of this Part are being violated.

§ 116.8. Records Retention

(a) All financial records of the grant recipient and center pertaining to funding received pursuant to this Part, shall be retained for a minimum of four years after the expiration of the contract entered into with the Unified Court System pursuant to this Part.

(b) A copy of the written agreement or decision subscribed to by the parties, setting forth the settlement of the issues and future responsibilities of each party, referred to in section 116.3(e) of this Part, shall be retained for a period of six years after execution.

(c) A fact sheet or summary of each case from which the center may compile the information required for program evaluation pursuant to section 116.7 of this Part, shall be retained for a period of six years after termination of the case.

(d) No other time requirements for records retention shall apply unless otherwise contracted by the parties.

PART 117. COURT APPOINTED SPECIAL ADVOCATES PROGRAMS

§ 117.0. General

In order to be eligible for appointment by a Family Court to assist the Court, a CASA program must be in compliance with the provisions of section 117.2 of this Part.

§ 117.1. Definitions

(a) "CASA program" means a Court Appointed Special Advocate program structured and administered as provided herein.

(b) "Grant recipient" means any organization receiving funds pursuant to this Part.

(c) "Chief Administrator" means the Chief Administrator of the Courts or his or her designee.

§ 117.2. Program Requirements

(a) Structure. A CASA program shall be a not-for-profit corporation affiliated with, and in compliance with, the standards set forth by the National and New York State CASA Associations. Such a program may be part of a legally incorporated not-for-profit organization or be incorporated (or in the process of being incorporated) as a free-standing not-for-profit organization.

(b) Administration.

(1) Each CASA program shall be governed by a board of directors, which hires and supervises the program's executive director and maintains legal and fiduciary responsibility for the program. The board shall meet a minimum of four times per year. All board members shall receive board training within six months of appointment, be apprised of all duties and responsibilities, sign written conflict of interest statements, and be guided by written bylaws approved by the full board. The board shall develop a written mission statement and shall implement a strategic plan to further its mission.

(2) Each CASA program housed within a multi-program not-for-profit agency shall have an advisory committee with sole responsibility for monitoring such program. A member of the advisory committee shall serve on the not-for-profit agency's board of directors.

(c) Record–keeping. Each CASA program shall have in written form the following:

(1) Goals, objectives, policies, and procedures, including personnel policies, ethics and conflict of interest policies for staff, volunteers and board members;

(2) Staff and volunteer job descriptions, qualification and evaluation forms;

(3) Approved training curricula for a minimum of 30 hours of pre-service and 12 hours of annual in-service training:

(4) A volunteer recruitment plan that encourages diversity of volunteers and that provides for the screening of volunteers;

(5) A plan for the support and supervision of volunteers by qualified and trained supervisory staff;

(6) Guidelines for record-keeping and data collection, including provisions for confidentiality of print and electronic files both at the program's main office and in all off-site locations in conformity with subdivision (d) of this section;

(7) A resource development plan and, with respect to a CASA program housed within a multi-program not-for-profit organization, a fund-raising protocol outlining responsibilities;

(8) Rules for staff and volunteers prohibiting ex parte communications with the Court and with represented parties except with the consent of or in the presence of such parties' attorneys;

(9) A current program budget containing expenditure and income projections and the sources and amounts of income from each source; and

(10) Internal financial control procedures.

(d) Confidentiality of Records. Each CASA program shall safeguard the confidentiality of all information and material in accordance with applicable state and federal laws, rules and regulations, including, but not limited to, court records and social services, health, educational, drug treatment and other records obtained from other agencies. Each CASA program shall ensure that all of its board members, officers, employees and volunteers are trained in, and comply with, these confidentiality requirements.

(e) Reporting. Each CASA program shall report annually and throughout the year on the operation of the program as directed by the Chief Administrator.

(f) Legal consultation. Each CASA program shall ensure that an attorney is available to provide its executive director and members of its board with legal consultation in matters regarding administration of the program.

(g) Liability protection. Each CASA program shall have liability protection for its Board, staff and volunteers and follow standards set by the New York State and National CASA Associations for participation in continual quality improvement.

(h) Screening Procedure for staff and volunteers. Each CASA program shall have a written screening procedure, approved by the local board and the Chief Administrator, for staff and volunteers and appropriate program responses to information obtained from the screening process. The procedure shall address at a minimum the following: written applications for volunteers and staff, screening by the New York State Central Register for child abuse and maltreatment, a criminal history records search, and personal interviews by the program director or other designated staff. Screening shall be accomplished pursuant to prescribed mechanisms established by the Chief Administrator in conjunction with the New York State Office of Children and Family Services.

(i) Eligibility for appointment to assist in Family Court cases. In order to be eligible for appointment by the Family Court to provide assistance in cases, a CASA program shall, in addition to complying with this Part, comply with all statutes, and with all other court rules and standards adopted by the Chief Administrator.

§ 117.3. CASA Assistance Program

(a) Funding. This section establishes a program for the provision of grants of state assistance to individual CASA programs, which shall be known as the CASA Assistance Program. This Program shall be administered by the Chief Administrator in order to disburse funds appropriated by the New York State Legislature, as well as funds received by the Unified Court System from any public or private agency or person, including the Federal government, to be used to assist CASA programs designated by a Family Court to assist the Court. Payment of funds pursuant to this section shall he made pursuant to contract entered into between the Unified Court System and the grant recipient.

(b) Application procedures. No CASA Assistance Program grant funds may be disbursed to any CASA program unless the Chief Administrator first approves an application as provided hereunder.

(1) *Who may apply.* To be eligible for funding pursuant to this section, a CASA program shall comply with the provisions of section 117.2 of this Part and it shall:

(i) provide services without cost to the children and families served; and

(ii) whenever reasonably possible, make use of public facilities at free or nominal cost.

(2) *When and where to apply.* To be eligible for funding pursuant to this section, the CASA program or the not-for-profit corporation of which it is a part must file its application with the Chief Administrator at such time as directed by the Chief Administrator.

(3) *Contents of application.* Each application for grant funding filed with the Chief Administrator pursuant to this section shall be in such form as the Chief Administrator shall prescribe and shall include, at a minimum, the following:

(i) a specification of the amount of funding sought;

(ii) a detailed description of the purpose or purposes to which the funding will be applied and the administrative capacity of the applicant to operate the program;

(iii) a detailed description of the CASA program or programs that will benefit from the funding, including information as to numbers of staff and volunteers; qualifications, professional and employment backgrounds and education level of all staff and volunteers; caseload to be served in each county covered by the application; budget; availability of space and other operational support; facilities needs; information about the county or counties served; and the child protective and foster care populations in each county;

(iv) information concerning financial requirements, current available and anticipated resources, other sources of funding, from both private and government sources, and past applications for funding, if any.

(v) descriptions of: the past history, if any, of the CASA program to benefit from the funding sought, including such information concerning the program as may be specified by the Chief Administrator; the program's area of service; its staff; its sources of funding; its expenditures; and the number and types of Family Court proceedings in which the program has provided assistance and the results of that assistance; and

(vi) such other information as may be required by the Chief Administrator. The Chief Administrator may, at any time following the filing of an application for funding, request that an applicant or applicants furnish additional information or documentation to support the application.

(c) Review of applications and approval of funding. In reviewing an application for funding pursuant to this section, the Chief Administrator shall consider the following factors, among others, in connection with the CASA program on whose behalf the application is made:

(1) the need for the program in the county or counties to be served;

(2) the structure and scope of the program;

(3) the program's caseload and the level of support for a CASA program or programs within the community to be served;

(4) the cost of operation;

(5) the capacity of the applicant to administer the program;

(6) the extent to which the program complies with the provisions of section 117.2 of this Part; and

(7) any other considerations that may affect the provision of CASA services. An applicant for funding may be rejected if the Chief Administrator determines that the CASA program on whose behalf the application is made will be unable to comply with any of the requirements set forth in this Part. Nothing herein shall require the Chief Administrator to approve funding for any applicant.

(d) **Program Review and Evaluation.** The Chief Administrator shall monitor and evaluate each CASA program receiving funds pursuant to this section.

(1) *Program Reports.* Each CASA program receiving funding pursuant to this section shall provide the Chief Administrator with periodic reports summarizing its activities in a manner prescribed by the Chief Administrator. The reports shall include information as to:

(i) the amount of, and purposes for which, all funds received pursuant to this Part were expended;

(ii) the number and type of appointments by the Family Court and the nature of the assistance provided; and

(iii) any other matters as required by the Chief Administrator.

(2) *Access to CASA Program Records.* The State Comptroller and Chief Administrator shall be given complete access to inspect the program operations and financial records of any recipient of funding under this section at any time in order to determine whether the CASA program that benefits from such funding is complying with its contract, all court rules and all applicable Federal, State and local laws and regulations.

(3) *Rescission of Contract.* Where the Chief Administrator determines that a CASA program that benefits from funding hereunder is not adequately meeting its responsibilities, is the subject of a bankruptcy or insolvency filing or is in violation of any provision of this Part or of any other rules, regulations or statutes, the Chief Administrator may rescind the contract for such funding forthwith. In other circumstances, the Chief Administrator may rescind the contract for funding upon 30 days' written notice to the program. A CASA program recipient may rescind the contract for funding upon 60 days' written notice to the Chief Administrator.

(e) **Records Retention.** Each CASA program that receives funding pursuant to this Part shall retain:

(1) all financial records for a minimum of four years after the expiration of the contract entered into with the Unified Court System for such funding pursuant to this Part.

(2) individual case files until the youngest child in the family in the case reaches the age of 18 or, if the child remains in foster care, until the child reaches 21.

(3) a fact sheet or summary of each case from which the program may compile the information required for purposes of program evaluation for a period of six years after termination of such case. No other time requirements for records retention shall apply unless otherwise contracted by the parties, directed by the Family Court or required by statute, rule or regulation.

PART 118. REGISTRATION OF ATTORNEYS

§ 118.1. Filing Requirement

(a) Every attorney admitted to practice in New York State on or before January 1, 1982, whether resident or nonresident, and whether or not in good standing, shall file a registration statement with the Chief Administrator of the Courts no later than March 1, 1982, and during each alternate year thereafter, within 30 days after the attorney's birthday, for as long as the attorney remains duly admitted to the New York bar.

(b) Every attorney admitted to practice in New York State after January 1, 1982, whether resident or nonresident, and whether or not in good standing, shall file a registration statement within 60 days of the date of such admission, and during each alternate year thereafter, within 30 days after the attorney's birthday, for as long as the attorney remains duly admitted to the New York bar.

(c) Every attorney admitted to practice in New York State after January 1, 1986, whether resident or nonresident, and whether or not in good standing, shall file a registration statement prior to taking the constitutional oath of office, and during each alternate year thereafter, within 30 days after the attorney's birthday, for as long as the attorney remains duly admitted to the New York bar.

(d) The registration statement shall be filed in person at the Office of Court Administration, 25 Beaver Street, 8th floor, in the City of New York, or by ordinary mail addressed to:

State of New York
Office of Court Administration
General Post Office
P.O. Box 29327
New York, NY 10087-9327

(e) The registration statement shall be on a form provided by the Chief Administrator and shall include the following information, attested to by affirmation:

(1) name of attorney;

(2) date of birth;

(3) name when admitted to the bar;

(4) law school from which degree granted;

(5) year admitted to the bar;

(6) judicial department of admission to the bar;

(7) office addresses (including department);

(8) home address;

(9) business telephone number; and

(10) social security number.

(f) In the event of a change in any of the information required to be provided pursuant to subdivision (e) of this section, the attorney shall file an amended statement within 30 days of such change.

(g) Each registration statement filed pursuant to this section shall be accompanied by a registration fee of $350. No fee shall be required from an attorney who certifies that he or she has retired from the practice of law. For purposes of this section, the "practice of law" shall mean the giving of legal advice or counsel to, or providing legal representation for, particular body or individual in a particular situation in either the public or private sector in the State of New York or elsewhere, it shall include the appearance as an attorney before any court or administrative agency. An attorney is "retired" from the practice of law when, other than the performance of legal services without compensation, he or she does not practice law in any respect and does not intend ever to engage in acts that constitute the practice of law. For purposes of section 468–a of the Judiciary Law, a full-time judge or justice of the Unified Court System of the State of New York or of a court of any other state or of a federal court, shall be deemed "retired" from the practice of law.

(h) Failure by any attorney to comply with the provisions of this section shall result in referral for disciplinary action by the Appellate Division of the Supreme Court pursuant to section 90 of the Judiciary Law.

Cross References

Judiciary Law, see McKinney's Book 29.

§ 118.2. Public Access to Attorney Registration Information

(a) Except as otherwise provided in this section, the information contained in the registration statement filed pursuant to section 118.1 of this Part shall be made available to the public upon submission of a written request and the payment of a charge for production, pursuant to the following schedule:

(1) Information for individual registered attorney by name:

(i) no charge for single inquiry;

(ii) $2.50 for each additional name.

(2) Names and business addresses of registered attorneys by geographical area:

(i) $25.00 for 100 or fewer names;

(ii) $1.00 for each additional 100 names;

(iii) $100.00 for list of all registered attorneys.

Other requests may entail additional fees as circumstances warrant. Fees may be waived for requests by government agencies. Written requests for information shall be made to the Attorney Registration Unit, Office of Court Administration, 25 Beaver Street, New York, NY 10004.

(b)(1) The home address of an attorney shall be made available to the public only in the following circumstances:

(i) where no office is listed, the home address will be made public;

(ii) where an office address is listed, but a request for information alleges that the attorney cannot be located at that address, the home address will be made public only if the Chief Administrator determines, by independent inquiry, that the attorney cannot be located at the listed office address.

(2) The social security number of the attorney shall not be made available to the public.

(c) All information relating to a particular attorney will be provided to that attorney or, on the attorney's written request, to any person or agency.

(d) All information will be available at all times to the attorney discipline committees of the Appellate Divisions.

PART 120. CALENDAR PRACTICE IN THE CRIMINAL TERMS OF THE SUPREME COURT WITHIN THE CITY OF NEW YORK [REPEALED]

PART 121. TEMPORARY ASSIGNMENT OF JUDGES TO THE SUPREME COURT

§ 121.1. General

All temporary assignments of judges to the Supreme Court from a court of limited jurisdiction, other than the Court of Claims, or designations of eligibility for such assignments, shall be made by the Chief Administrator of the Courts, in his or her discretion, upon consultation with and agreement of the presiding justice of the appropriate Appellate Division, pursuant to Part 33 of the Rules of the Chief Judge and in accordance with the procedure set forth in this Part.

§ 121.2. Procedure for Selection

(a) Selection of judges for temporary assignment pursuant to this Part shall be made by the Chief Administrator upon recommendations from an evaluatory panel consisting of the appropriate Deputy Chief Administrator for the Courts within and without the City of New York, the Deputy Chief Administrator for Management Support, the Administrative Judge for Matrimonial Matters, and the administrative judge of the court where the judge serves. The Chief Administrator may alter the membership of the panel where circumstances require. The panel shall consider the need for judges to be assigned, the availability of judges for assignment and the capability of the judges eligible for assignment.

(b) In determining the capability of judges eligible for assignment, the evaluatory panel shall consult with administrative judges and with bar associations and other persons or groups as may be appropriate, and shall consider the following criteria with respect to each judge:

(1) productivity, including effective docket management and prompt case disposition;

(2) scholarship, including knowledge and understanding of substantive, procedural and evidentiary law of New York State, attentiveness to factual and legal issues before the court, application of judicial precedents and other appropriate sources of authority, and quality and clarity of written opinions;

(3) temperament, including the ability to deal patiently with and be courteous to all parties and participants; and

(4) work ethic, including punctuality, preparation and attentiveness, and meeting commitments on time and according to the rules of the court.

The panel also shall consider any complaints filed with court administrators.

(c) No judge shall be eligible for temporary assignment pursuant to this Part for a period in excess of 20 calendar days unless that judge has served in a court of limited jurisdiction for a period of two years.

(d) The Chief Administrator, upon consultation with and agreement of the Presiding Justice of the appropriate Appellate Division, may except a judge from all or part of the requirements of section 121.2(b) in determining the judge's eligibility for an assignment not in excess of 20 calendar days if the needs of the courts warrant such action.

§ 121.3. Terms of Assignment

Temporary assignments shall be for terms of no greater than one year, provided that the initial assignment shall be for a term of no greater than four months. Where appropriate, the Chief Administrator may designate, pursuant to section 121.2 of this Part, a judge as eligible for being selected for temporary assignments over the course of a term of not more than one year. Judges shall be eligible for redesignation at the conclusion of a term pursuant to the procedure set forth in this section.

§ 121.4. Termination of Assignment

The Chief Administrator, upon consultation with and agreement of the presiding justice of the appropriate appellate division, may terminate at any time any temporary assignment made pursuant to this Part.

§ 121.5. Effect of Discipline by Judicial Conduct Commission

Absent exceptional circumstances, as determined by the Chief Administrator upon consultation with and agreement of the Presiding Justice of the appropriate Appellate Division, no judge shall be eligible to sit as a temporarily assigned justice pursuant to this Part for a period of two years from the date of any order of the State Commission on Judicial Conduct that directs that the judge be publicly admonished or censured.

PART 122. JUDICIAL HEARING OFFICERS

§ 122.1. Application

(a) Any person who has served for at least one year as a judge or justice of a court of the Unified Court System, other than a town or village court, and who no longer is serving in such capacity, except a person who was removed from a judicial position pursuant to section 22 of Article VI of the constitution, may make application to the Chief Administrator of the Courts to be designated as a judicial hearing officer pursuant to article 22 of the Judiciary Law. The Chief Administrator, upon consultation with the Presiding Justice of the appropriate Appellate Division, may waive the one-year service eligibility requirement where the background of the judge, combined with the length and nature of his or her judicial service, permit a finding that the judge meets the qualifications set forth in section 122.2(a) of this Part. The application shall be in such form as may be provided by the Chief Administrator, which shall contain items requesting prior judicial experience, the nature of judicial service sought, and whether any actions against the judge have been taken by, or any claims are pending before, any professional disciplinary body.

Cross References

Constitution, see McKinney's Book 2.

Judiciary Law, see McKinney's Book 29.

§ 122.2. Initial Designation

(a) The Chief Administrator of the Courts, in his or her discretion, may designate as a judicial hearing officer an eligible person who files an application pursuant to section 122.1 of this Part upon determination that the applicant has the physical and mental capacity, competence, work ethic, experience and judicial temperament necessary to perform the duties of a judicial hearing officer, and is well qualified to serve on the panels in the courts to which he or she will be designated.

(b) The applicant shall undergo a comprehensive physical examination by a physician designated by the Chief Administrator, who shall issue a report to the Chief Administrator that the applicant has or has not the physical and mental capacity to perform competently the duties of a judicial hearing officer.

(c) In determining whether to designate an applicant as a judicial hearing officer, the Chief Administrator shall consult with (1) the Presiding Justice of the appropriate Appellate Division, (2) the appropriate Deputy Chief Administrator for the Courts, within or outside the City of New York, (3) the appropriate administrative judge, who shall submit a written evaluation of the applicant, and (4) the appropriate judicial hearing officer selection advisory committee established pursuant to subdivision (e) of this section.

(d) The Chief Administrator also may consult with other appropriate persons and bar associations and conduct whatever investigation the Chief Administrator deems necessary to determine the qualifications of an applicant, including requiring additional medical examinations.

(e)(1) The Chief Administrator, after consultation with the Presiding Justice of the appropriate Appellate Division, shall establish judicial hearing officer selection advisory committees for the First Judicial Department, the Second Judicial Department within the City of New York, the Ninth Judicial District of the Second Judicial Department, the Tenth Judicial District of the Second Judicial Department, the Third Judicial Department and the Fourth Judicial Department, and shall appoint the members thereto. Each committee shall consist of seven members, four nonjudicial members who are practicing attorneys and three members who are either current or former judges or justices of the unified court system. The Chief Administrator shall designate one member of each committee to serve as committee chair. Each member shall serve for a term of two years, which shall be renewable.

(2) Every applicant for initial designation to the office of judicial hearing officer shall be evaluated prior to designation by the committee established for the principal jurisdiction in which the applicant applies to serve, which shall interview the applicant and may require the applicant to submit any appropriate materials. In the event no principal jurisdiction is apparent, the Chief Administrator shall select the committee that shall evaluate the applicant. Where the bulk of the applicant's judicial service was in a jurisdiction other than the principal one in which the applicant is seeking to serve, the committee may consult with the appropriate committee in that other jurisdiction and may refer the applicant to that committee for evaluation. The committee shall set forth whether each applicant is qualified to serve as a judicial hearing officer based upon competence, work ethic, experience and judicial temperament necessary to perform duties of a judicial hearing officer. The Committee also shall specifically advise whether the applicant is qualified to serve as a judicial hearing officer with respect to (a) criminal actions, (b) civil actions other than matrimonial actions, and (c) matrimonial actions.

(f) For purposes of this Part, evaluation of the competence, work ethic, experience and judicial temperament of any applicant pursuant to this Part shall include the following:

(1) Competence: effective case management and prompt case disposition, knowledge of the law, and quality and clarity of written opinions;

(2) Work ethic: punctuality, preparation and attentiveness, and meeting commitments on time and according to the rules of the court.

(3) Experience: the nature, length and proximity in time of judicial service;

(4) Judicial temperament: the ability to deal patiently with and be courteous to all parties and participants.

§ 122.3. Term

A judicial hearing officer shall be designated for a term of one year, which term may be extended without further application for one additional year pursuant to section 122.3–b of this Part. At the end of any term (which shall include any one-year extension thereof), the judicial hearing officer may apply for designation for an additional term, and may be so designated in accordance with the procedures of section 122.3–b. The Chief Administrator may extend the duration of a term for a period not to exceed six months where necessary to complete examination and consultation requirements set forth in this Part.

§ 122.3–a. Performance Evaluation

Each administrative judge shall monitor the performance of every judicial hearing officer who serves in a court within the jurisdiction of the administrative judge, and shall report to the Chief Administrator of the Courts, at such times and in such manner as the Chief Administrator shall require, on the performance of the judicial hearing officer. In evaluating this performance, the administrative judge shall consult with such judges, bar associations, and individual members of the bar as may be appropriate.

§ 122.3–b. Extension of Term; Designation for Additional Term

(a) The Chief Administrator of the Courts, in his or her discretion and in accordance with this section and section 122.3 of this Part, may extend the term of a person serving as a judicial hearing officer or designate a judicial hearing officer to an additional term provided he or she has the physical and mental capacity, and the competence, work ethic, and judicial temperament, necessary to perform the duties of a judicial hearing officer. To be considered for designation to an additional term hereunder, a judicial hearing officer must apply therefor upon such form as may be provided by the Chief Administrator and undergo a comprehensive physical examination as set forth in section 122.2(b) of this Part.

(b) In determining whether to extend the term of a person serving as a judicial hearing officer, or designate a judicial hearing officer to an additional term, the Chief Administrator shall consider recommendations from an evaluatory body consisting of the appropriate Deputy Chief Administrator for the courts within or without the City of New York, the Deputy Chief Administrator for Management Support, the

Administrative Judge for Matrimonial Matters and the administrative judge or judges of the courts where the judicial hearing officer has served. The Chief Administrator, after consultation with the Presiding Justice of the appropriate Appellate Division, may alter the membership of the evaluatory body where circumstances require. In making recommendations whether the judicial hearing officer meets the criteria set forth in the Part, the evaluating body shall examine the performance evaluations prepared pursuant to section 122.3–a of this Part, and any required medical evaluations, and shall consult with administrative judges, bar associations and other persons or groups as may be appropriate.

(c) The Chief Administrator also shall consult with the Presiding Justice of the appropriate Appellate Division and may consult with the appropriate judicial hearing officer selection advisory committee and other persons and conduct whatever investigation the Chief Administrator deems necessary to determine the qualifications of an applicant, including requiring additional medical examinations.

§ 122.4. Oath of Office

(a) Before exercising the functions of judicial hearing officer, a person so designated shall take and file with the Chief Administrator of the Courts a sworn statement that such person will faithfully and fairly do such acts and make such determinations and reports as may be required by the designations as a judicial hearing officer. The statement shall be in the form as set forth in subdivision (b) of this section.

(b) Sworn statement of hearing officer.

I, _____ (give full name), do solemnly swear that I will support the Constitution of the United States, and the Constitution of the State of New York, and I will faithfully and fairly do such acts and make such determinations and reports as may be required by the designation as a judicial hearing officer, according to the best of my ability.

_____
  (Signature)

Sworn to before me this
    day of _____ , 19___ .

_____
Notary Public

§ 122.5. Panels

(a) The Chief Administrator of the Courts, in his or her discretion, shall establish a panel of judicial hearing officers for particular courts in individual counties, where appropriate, to accept assignments in such court in such county, and shall designate judicial hearing officers to each such panel. A judicial hearing officer may serve on more than one panel.

(b) The size and composition of each panel shall be determined by the Chief Administrator, after consultation with the appropriate administrative judge, in accordance with the needs of the courts in each particular county. In determining the need for judicial hearing officers in any court and county, the Chief Administrator shall consider (1) the state of the general calendar in each court in which the use of judicial hearing officers is being considered and (2) the number of proceedings suitable for determination by judicial hearing officers in such court or courts.

(c) The Chief Administrator, in his or her discretion, after consultation with the appropriate presiding justice, may establish a panel of judicial hearing officers in and for an appellate division to perform the functions of the preargument screening program for such appellate division.

(d) A judicial hearing officer who requests that his or her name be removed from any panel of judicial hearing officers during the course of a term of office may not be redesignated to that panel for the duration of that term.

(e) The Chief Administrator, in consultation with the presiding justice of the appropriate appellate division, may remove the name of any judicial hearing officer from any or all panels for unsatisfactory performance or for any conduct incompatible with service as a judicial hearing officer. A judicial hearing officer may not be so removed unless he or she has been given a written statement of the reasons for the removal and afforded an opportunity to make an explanation and to submit facts in opposition to the removal.

§ 122.6. Assignments

(a) A judge or justice of any court for which a panel of judicial hearing officers has been established may recommend to the appropriate administrative judge, designated by the Chief Administrator, particular proceedings for reference to a judicial hearing officer. A judicial hearing officer shall be assigned to a particular proceeding by the administrative judge, in his or her discretion, upon consideration of all relevant factors, including the nature of the matter to be referred, the experience and expertise of the judicial hearing officer with respect to matters of that nature, the expected length and complexity of the matter and the availability of appropriations to pay for the services of the judicial hearing officer.

(b) The administrative judge may assign a judicial hearing officer to preside over a part of court as permitted by law for a specified period. The administrative judge, in making such an assignment, shall take into account the responsibilities of the part and the previous experience and expertise of the judicial hearing officer.

(c) The reference of a matter to a judicial hearing officer and the assignment thereto of the judicial hearing officer shall be in writing. The reference shall indicate the issues referred to such judicial hearing officer and set forth whether the judicial hearing officer is to hear and determine or hear and report or otherwise act in respect to the matter.

(d) The presiding justice of an appropriate appellate division may assign a judicial hearing officer on an appellate division panel to perform the functions of the preargument screening program of such appellate division, within the available appropriations as determined by the Chief Administrator.

§ 122.7. No Vesting of Rights

Nothing herein shall vest any person with any right to be designated as a judicial hearing officer, or to be designated to a panel, or to serve in any particular court or to be assigned to any particular proceeding or type of proceeding.

§ 122.8. Compensation

A judicial hearing officer shall receive $300 per day for each day or part thereof at which such judicial hearing officer actually performs assigned duties in a courtroom or other facility designated for court appearances. There shall be no compensation for out-of-court work performed by such hearing officer. Such hearing officer shall be reimbursed for out-of-pocket expenses reasonably and necessarily incurred in the performance of his or her duties in accordance with the provisions of Part 102 of these rules.

§ 122.9. Reports

A determination required to be made by a judicial hearing officer in respect to any motion or proceeding at which such judicial hearing officer presides, or in respect to any report or decision required to be filed by such judicial hearing officer, shall be rendered and filed within 30 days. All reports and decisions shall be in writing and shall indicate the reasons upon which the decisions or findings and recommendations contained in the report are based.

§ 122.10. Conflicts

(a) A judicial hearing officer shall not preside over any matter in which he or she has represented any party or any witness in connection with that matter, and he or she shall not participate as an attorney in any matter in which he or she has participated as a judge or judicial hearing officer.

(b) A judicial hearing officer shall not preside over a matter in which any party or witness is presented by an attorney who is a partner or associate in a law firm or of counsel to a law firm with which the judicial hearing officer is affiliated in any respect.

(c) A judicial hearing officer shall not participate as an attorney in any contested matter in a court in a county where he or she serves on a judicial hearing officer panel for such court.

(d) A judicial hearing officer shall not appear as an attorney before any other judicial hearing officer in any county in which he or she serves as a judicial hearing officer.

§ 122.11. Disqualification

A judicial hearing officer shall disqualify himself or herself in any proceeding under the same circumstances where a judge or other quasi-judicial officer would be required to disqualify himself or herself under decisional law or pursuant to the provisions of any statute, the Code of Judicial Conduct or Part 100 of these rules.

Cross References

Code of Judicial Conduct, see McKinney's Book 29.

§ 122.12. Continuing Education

The Chief Administrator may require judicial hearing officers to participate in educational courses, seminars and training sessions designed to ensure that they keep current with developments in the law.

PART 123. REQUIREMENTS RELATIVE TO MATERIAL SUBMITTED TO SUPREME COURT LAW LIBRARIES

§ 123.1. Designations

The following Supreme Court Law Libraries are designated to serve as repositories of materials transmitted by State agencies pursuant to section 102(4)(c) of the Executive Law:

(a) Supreme Court Law Library/Civil Branch
60 Centre Street
New York, NY 10007
   (First Judicial District);

(b) Supreme Court Law Library
360 Adams Street
Brooklyn, NY 11201
   (Second Judicial District);

(c) Supreme Court Law Library
Courthouse
Kingston, NY 12401
   (Third Judicial District);

(d) Supreme Court Law Library
72 Clinton Street
Plattsburgh, NY 12901
   (Fourth Judicial District);

(e) Supreme Court Law Library
Onondaga County Courthouse
Syracuse, NY 13202
   (Fifth Judicial District);

(f) Supreme Court Law Library
107 Courthouse
Binghamton, NY 13902
   (Sixth Judicial District);

(g) Supreme Court Law Library
Steuben County Courthouse
Bath, NY 14810
   (Seventh Judicial District);

(h) Supreme Court Law Library
92 Franklin Street
Buffalo, NY 14202
   (Eighth Judicial District);

(i) Supreme Court Law Library
Westchester County Courthouse
White Plains, NY 10601
   (Ninth Judicial District);

(j) Supreme Court Law Library
100 Supreme Court Drive
Mineola, NY 11501
   (Tenth Judicial District);

(k) Supreme Court Law Library
General Courthouse
88–11 Sutphin Boulevard
Jamaica, NY 11435
   (Eleventh Judicial District); and

(l) Supreme Court Law Library/Civil Branch
851 Grand Concourse
Bronx, NY 10451
   (Twelfth Judicial District).

§ 123.2. General Filing Requirements

No material submitted to a Supreme Court Law Library pursuant to section 102(4)(c) of the Executive Law will be accepted for filing therewith unless the following requirements are met:

(a) All material submitted must be (i) in electronic form or (ii) in the form of microfiche or ultrafiche cards, and must comply with the provisions of subdivisions (b–1) and (b–2) of this section, respectively, unless the submitting agency shall certify that such material cannot be obtained commercially in either form, in which event the material shall be in the form prescribed by subdivision (c) of this section.

(b–1) Form for materials submitted in electronic form. Materials submitted in electronic form shall be in such form as approved by the Chief Administrator of the Courts, which may include electronic disks or transmissions between computers or other machines. There also shall be included within each submission the information set forth in subdivision (b–2) of this section.

(b–2) Form for Material Submitted in Microfiche or Ultrafiche.

(1) Material submitted in the form of microfiche or ultrafiche cards shall display the full text of the code, manual, volume or publication of which it is a part.

(2) There shall be included with such cards a separate written index of the material displayed thereon, including the following information for each entry:

(i) the name of the publication, including the volume number and volume title if applicable;

(ii) the name of the publisher or the name of the organization responsible for writing the material, whichever is more useful for identification purposes;

(iii) the date of publication;

(iv) the name of the State agency adopting the publication; and

(v) cross–references to the NYCRR sections which reference the publication pursuant to section 102(1)(c) of the Executive Law.

(c) Form for Material Submitted When Electronic Form, Microfiche and Ultrafiche Are Unavailable.

(1)(i) If the material were published in a permanently bound volume, the bound volume itself must be submitted for filing. Neither photocopies nor pages from bound volumes will be accepted.

(ii) If a soft-bound publication contains fewer than 100 pages, it must be placed in a rigid-cover binder.

(iii) If the publication is self-covering, i.e., the cover and the inside pages are made of the same or similar stock, the publication must be placed in a rigid-cover binder.

(2) Loose–leaf publications must be bound in the loose-leaf binder specially manufactured and imprinted by the publisher for storing the pages.

(3) The following information must appear on an adhesive label placed in the upper left-hand corner of the front cover of each publication or, if the publication is enclosed in a binder, in the upper left-hand corner of the front cover of the binder.

(i) the name of the publication, including the volume number and volume title if applicable;

(ii) the name of the publisher or the name of the organization responsible for writing the material, whichever is more useful for identification purposes;

(iii) the date of the publication;

(iv) the name of the State agency adopting the publication; and

(v) cross-reference to the NYCRR sections which reference the publication pursuant to section 102(1)(c) of the Executive Law.

(4) A rigid-cover binder may not contain more than one publication nor more than one edition of a periodical or series publication.

(d) If for any reason the nature of the material makes it impractical for a State agency to comply with any of the provisions of this section, the agency may request the Chief Administrator of the Courts to grant an exemption therefrom.

(e) No material which is a United States statute or a code, rule or regulation published in the Code of Federal Regulations or in the Federal Register shall be submitted.

PART 124. PUBLIC ACCESS TO RECORDS

§ 124.1. Purpose and Scope

This Part sets forth the procedures governing public access to the administrative records of the Office of Court Administration, pursuant to the Freedom of Information Law (Public Officers Law, article 6).

§ 124.2. Designation of Records Access Officer

(a) The Director of Public Affairs of the Office of Court Administration shall be designated as the records access officer of the Office of Court Administration.

(b) The records access officer shall:

(1) maintain a current list, by subject matter, of all administrative records in the possession of the Office of Court Administration, whether or not available to the public under the Freedom of Information Law;

(2) maintain a list setting forth the name, public office address, title and salary of every officer or employee of the Office of Court Administration; and

(3) respond on behalf of the Office of Court Administration to public requests for access to its records.

(c) The business address of the records access officer is: Records Access Officer, Office of Court Administration, 25 Beaver Street, New York, NY 10004; (212) 428–2116.

(d) The Chief Administrator of the Courts may authorize other officers or employees of the Office of Court Administration to perform any of the duties of records access officer as set forth in this Part.

§ 124.3. Subject Matter List

A reasonably detailed list, by subject matter, of all records in the possession of the Office of Court Administration, whether or not the records are subject to public inspection and copying pursuant to the Freedom of Information Law, shall be available for public inspection and copying at the business office of the records access officer. The subject matter list shall be updated not less than twice per year, and the date of the most recent revision shall be indicated on the first page of the list.

§ 124.4. List of Officers and Employees

A list setting forth the name, public office address, title and salary of every officer or employee of the Office of Court Administration shall be available for public inspection and copying at the business office of the records access officer.

§ 124.5. Requests for Public Access to Records

(a) A person wishing to inspect or copy a record contained within the subject matter list shall file a written application with the records access officer, which shall reasonably describe the record sought. The application shall contain all available data concerning date, title, file designation, department or unit within the Office of Court Administration, and any other information that may help identify the record. If the information supplied by the applicant is not sufficiently detailed to enable the records access officer to determine whether or not the Office of Court Administration maintains the record, the records access officer shall so notify the applicant and may request further identifying information.

(b) A written request shall not be required for materials, such as civil service examination announcements and informational brochures, which customarily have been made available by the Office of Court Administration to the public in the regular course of business, and for any other material which the records access officer deems to be proper to release without a written request.

§ 124.6. Response to Requests

(a) The records access officer shall, within five business days of the receipt of a request for access to a record, provide written notification to the applicant:

(1) approving the request and authorizing inspection and copying of the record;

(2) denying the request in whole or in part, indicating the reason for the denial and advising the applicant of his right to appeal such denial; or

(3) acknowledging receipt of the request and providing the applicant with a statement of the approximate date on which the request will be approved or denied.

(b) Except as provided in paragraph (a)(3) of this section, failure to either approve, deny or acknowledge receipt within 10 business days of receipt of a request

may be construed as a denial of the request and may be appealed.

(c) If the record cannot be located, the records access officer shall certify to the applicant that:

(1) the Office of Court Administration does not maintain the record; or

(2) the Office of Court Administration does maintain the record but, after diligent search, it cannot be found.

§ 124.7. Inspection and Copying of Records

Where a request for inspection or copying of a record is approved, the following provisions shall apply:

(a) **Location.** The record shall be made available for inspection and copying at a location specified by the records access officer, which may include the business office of the records access officer or the office where the record is normally maintained. No record shall be removed, by any person granted access to it, from any office of the Office of Court Administration without the express written consent of the records access officer.

(b) **Hours for Inspection and Copying.** The record shall be made available for inspection and copying at a time specified by the records access officer on any regular business day between the hours of 9:30 a.m. and 5 p.m.

(c) **Photocopies of Records.** Upon request by the applicant, the records access officer shall certify the correctness of any photocopy made from a record of the Office of Court Administration. If, at the request of the applicant, only part of a record is photocopied, a statement to that effect shall be clearly marked on the first page of the photocopy.

(d) **Transcripts of Records.** If a record cannot be photocopied, the applicant may request that a transcript of it be made by the Office of Court Administration. The transcript may, in the discretion of the records access officer, be either typewritten or handwritten.

§ 124.8. Fees

(a) Except as otherwise provided by statute:

(1) the fee for photocopies of records shall be 25 cents per page for photocopies not exceeding 9 inches by 14 inches;

(2) the fee for photocopies of records exceeding 9 inches by 14 inches shall be the actual copying cost, which shall be the average unit cost for photocopying a record, excluding fixed costs such as operator salaries;

(3) if a transcript of a record has been made by the Office of Court Administration at the request of the applicant pursuant to section 124.7 of this Part, the applicant may be charged for the clerical time and

personal expenses involved in producing the transcript.

(b) All fees authorized herein shall be paid in advance by check or money order payable to the Office of Court Administration.

(c) There shall be no fee for:

(1) searching for a record;

(2) inspection of a record;

(3) certification of a photocopy of a record;

(4) certification that a record cannot be located; or

(5) photocopying five or fewer pages of a record, not exceeding 9 inches by 14 inches.

§ 124.9. Appeals

(a) The Chief Administrator of the Courts or his designee shall be the appeals officer. The business address of the appeals officer is: Office of Court Administration, 25 Beaver Street, New York, NY 10004.

(b) An applicant whose request to inspect or copy a record has been denied may, within 30 days of that denial, appeal that determination in writing to the appeals officer at his business address.

(c) The appeal shall set forth:

(1) the name and return address of the applicant;

(2) the date upon which the request for inspection or copying of the record was made;

(3) the record to which the applicant was denied access; and

(4) whether there was a written denial of the request and, if there was, the date upon which the request was denied and the reason for the denial.

(d) Upon receipt of an appeal made in compliance with this section, the appeals officer shall review the denial of the request for inspection or copying of the record. Within 10 business days of receipt of an appeal, the appellant shall be notified in writing of the determination of the appeals officer and the reasons therefor.

(e) A copy of every appeal and the determination thereon shall be transmitted to the Committee on Open Government, Department of State, 162 Washington Avenue, Albany, NY 12231.

PART 125. UNIFORM RULES FOR THE ENGAGEMENT OF COUNSEL

§ 125.1. Engagement of Counsel

(a) Engagement of counsel shall be a ground for adjournment of an action or proceeding in accordance with this rule.

(b) Engagement of counsel shall mean actual engagement on trial or in argument before any state or federal trial or appellate court, or in a proceeding conducted pursuant to rule 3405 of the CPLR and the rules promulgated thereunder.

(c) Subject to the provisions of subdivision (f) of this section, where an attorney has conflicting engagements in the same court or different courts, the affected courts shall determine in which matters adjournments shall be granted and in which matters the parties shall proceed. In making such decisions, they shall, to the extent lawful and practicable, give priority to actions and proceedings in the order in which matters are listed below:

(1) child protective proceedings;

(2) criminal proceedings or juvenile delinquency proceedings wherein the defendant or respondent is incarcerated;

(3) proceedings based on acts which constitute felonies;

(4) proceedings based on acts which constitute misdemeanors; and

(5) matrimonial actions and proceedings; and

(6) civil actions and proceedings, including proceedings conducted pursuant to rule 3405 of the CPLR and the rules promulgated thereunder. Where an attorney's conflicting engagements include two or more engagements within any of these categories of actions and proceedings, as between those engagements the affected courts shall give priority to those involving jury trials.

(d) Subject to the provisions of subdivisions (c) and (f) herein, where an attorney has conflicting engagements, such attorney must proceed in whichever matter is entitled to a statutory preference or, if there is none and none of his or her engagements involves exceptional circumstances, in the particular matter first scheduled for the date on which the conflict arises. Matters involving exceptional circumstances shall be given priority over all others, except those entitled to statutory preference. A court may find exceptional circumstances where: (1) there are four or more attorneys engaged for a trial, hearing or appellate argument therein; (2) a party or material witness will be available for a trial or hearing therein only on the date on which the conflict arises or on any subsequent date during the period such trial or hearing reasonably can be expected to extend; (3) a party or material witness thereto is afflicted with an illness which, because of its nature, requires that the trial of the action or proceeding be held on the date on which the conflict arises; or (4) a trial therein must be conducted within statutory time limits and, if trial of the matter is not held on the date on which the conflict arises, there is a reasonable probability that the time limit applicable thereto will elapse.

(e)(1) Each engagement shall be proved by affidavit or affirmation, filed with the court together with proof of service on all parties, setting forth:

(i) the title of the action or proceeding in which counsel is engaged;

(ii) its general nature;

(iii) the court and part in which it is scheduled or, if it is a proceeding conducted pursuant to rule 3405 of the CPLR, the court in which the underlying action was commenced;

(iv) the name of the judge or panel chairman who will preside over it; and

(v) the date and time the engagement is to commence or did commence and the date and time of its probable conclusion.

(2) In determining an application for adjournment on the ground of engagement elsewhere, the court shall consider the affidavit of engagement and may make such further inquiry as it deems necessary, including:

(i) the dates on which each of the actions or proceedings involved were scheduled for the date on which they conflict;

(ii) whether or not the actions or proceedings involved were marked peremptorily for trial or were the subject of some other special marking;

(iii) the number of times each of the actions or proceedings involved was previously adjourned and upon whose application;

(iv) if any of the attorneys representing a party to one of the actions or proceedings involved is a member or associate of a law firm or office employing more than one attorney, the number of members or associates of his or her firm or office also serving as cocounsel or otherwise involved in such action or proceeding, and their respective engagements elsewhere; and

(v) if applicable, the period of time each of the actions or proceedings involved has been on a calendar from which it has been called.

(f) Where a trial already has commenced, and an attorney for one of the parties has an engagement elsewhere, there shall be no adjournment of the ongoing trial except in the sole discretion of the judge presiding thereat; provided that the judge presiding shall grant a reasonable adjournment where the engagement is in an appellate court.

(g) This subdivision shall apply where a date for trial of an action or proceeding is fixed at least two months in advance thereof upon the consent of all attorneys or by the court. In such event, the attorneys previously designated as trial counsel must appear for trial on that date. If any of such attorneys is actually engaged on trial elsewhere, he or she must produce substitute trial counsel. If neither trial counsel nor substitute trial counsel is ready to try the case on the scheduled date, the court may impose any sanctions permitted by law.

Cross References

CPLR, see McKinney's Book 7B.

PART 126. COMPENSATION AND EXPENSES OF JUDGES AND JUSTICES TEMPORARILY ASSIGNED TO A CITY COURT OR A JUSTICE COURT

§ 126.1. General

Each part-time judge or justice of a city, town or village court who is temporarily assigned to a city court pursuant to section 107 of the Uniform City Court Act shall receive $250 per day, or such lesser amount as his or her order of assignment may specify, for each day or part thereof during which such judge or justice actually performs judicial duties in accordance with such assignment in a courtroom or other facility designated for court appearances, provided that a judge or justice who performs such judicial duties for one half day or less shall receive $125 per day. There shall be no compensation for out-of-court work performed by any such judge or justice while on temporary assignment. Such judge or justice shall be reimbursed for out-of-pocket expenses reasonably or

necessarily incurred in the performance of his or her duties while on temporary assignment in accordance with the provisions of Part 102 of this Title.

Cross References

Uniform City Court Act, see McKinney's Book 29A, Part 3.

§ 126.2. [Temporary Assignment]

Each part-time judge or justice of a city, town or village court who is temporarily assigned to a town or village court pursuant to section 106(2) of the Uniform Justice Court Act shall receive compensation as set forth in section 126.1 of this Part if the temporary assignment is the result of the death, disability or other incapacity of a justice in the receiving court, or any vacancy in that office.

PART 127. ASSIGNMENT AND COMPENSATION OF COUNSEL, PSYCHIATRISTS, PSYCHOLOGISTS AND PHYSICIANS

§ 127.1. Assignment and Compensation of Counsel, Psychiatrists, Psychologists and Physicians

(a) Assignments and appointments of counsel, psychiatrists, psychologists and physicians pursuant to section 35 of the Judiciary Law shall be made by the court in accordance with rules to be adopted by each Appellate Division. Each Appellate Division may compile and maintain such lists of attorneys, psychiatrists, psychologists and physicians as it shall deem appropriate for the implementation of its rules. Such rules may provide that the appointment of psychiatrists, psychologists and physicians shall be made after consultation with the Mental Hygiene Legal Service.

(b) Each claim by assigned counsel, psychiatrist, psychologist or physician payable from State funds for services rendered to indigent persons, pursuant to section 35 of the Judiciary Law, shall be submitted on forms authorized by the Chief Administrator of the Courts for approval within 45 days after completion of service to the court which made the assignment. Upon approval, the court shall thereupon, within 15 days after receipt, forward such claims to the appropriate Appellate Division for certification to the Comptroller for payment.

§ 127.2. Compensation of Counsel and Other Providers in Extraordinary Circumstances

(a) Whenever an attorney, psychiatrist, psychologist or physician, or a person providing investigative, expert or other services, seeks compensation in excess of the statutory limits prescribed by Article 18–B of the County Law or section 35 of the Judiciary Law, because of extraordinary circumstances, he or she shall submit with his or her claim a detailed affidavit stating the nature of the proceeding, the manner in which the time was expended, the necessity therefor, and all other facts that demonstrate extraordinary circumstances. If the claim is by an attorney, the attorney shall state the disposition of the matter.

(b) The order of the trial judge with respect to a claim for compensation in excess of the statutory limits may be reviewed by the appropriate administrative judge, with or without application, who may modify the award if it is found that the award reflects an abuse of discretion by the trial judge. Any order modifying a trial judge's award shall be in writing.

(c) An application for review may be made by any person or governmental body affected by the order.

§ 127.3. Compensation of Counsel and Other Providers in Capital Cases

(a) Each claim for compensation and reimbursement submitted to the court pursuant to section 35–b(9) of the Judiciary Law by an attorney or by a provider of investigative, expert or other services shall be supported by a sworn statement specifying the time expended, services rendered, expenses incurred and reimbursement or compensation applied for or received in the same case from any other source.

(b) Attorneys eligible for awards of compensation by the trial court pursuant to section 35–b(9) may submit vouchers for the court's approval at such times before the case is completed as the court in its discretion may permit.

(c) Requests for reconsideration of any order of the trial court fixing compensation pursuant to section 35–b(9) may be made pursuant to the procedure set forth in section 127.2 of this Part.

Cross References

Judiciary Law, see McKinney's Book 29.

§ 127.4. Compensation of Law Guardians

Claims by law guardians for compensation, expenses and disbursements pursuant to section 245 of the Family Court Act and section 35 of the Judiciary Law shall be determined pursuant to the rules of the appropriate Appellate Division.

§ 127.5. Workload of the Attorney for the Child

(a) Subject to adjustment based on the factors set forth in subdivision (b), the number of children represented at any given time by an attorney appointed pursuant to section 249 of the Family Court Act shall not exceed 150.

(b) For representation provided under an agreement pursuant to section 243(a) and (b) of the Family Court Act, the workload standards set forth in subdivision (a) may be adjusted based on such factors as:

(1) Differences among categories of cases that comprise the workload of the office covered by the agreement;

(2) The level of activity required at different phases of the proceeding;

(3) The weighting of different categories and phases of cases;

(4) Availability and use of support staff;

(5) The representation of multiple children in a case;

(6) Local court practice, including the duration of a case;

(7) Other relevant considerations.

(c) The administrators of offices pursuant to such agreements shall be responsible for managing resources and for allocating cases among staff attorneys to promote the effective representation of children and to ensure that the average workload of the attorneys for children in the office complies with the standards set forth in subdivision (a) as modified by subdivision (b).

(d) For representation provided by a panel of attorneys for children pursuant to section 243 (c) of the Family Court Act, the Appellate Division may adjust the workload standards of subdivision (a) to ensure the effective representation of children.

(e) The Chief Administrator of the Courts, with respect to representation pursuant to section 243(a) of the Family Court Act, and the Appellate Divisions, with respect to representation pursuant to section 243 (b) and (c) of the Family Court Act, shall annually, at the time of the preparation and submission of the judiciary budget, review the workload of such offices and panels, and shall take action to assure compliance with this rule.

PART 128.   UNIFORM RULES FOR THE JURY SYSTEM

§ 128.0.   Applicability and Definitions

(a) This part applies, as the context requires, to the jury system with respect to all courts in the unified court system in which juries are empanelled.

(b) The term "commissioner of jurors" in this part also includes the county clerk of each county within the city of New York and the county clerk or other officer or employee appointed to serve as commissioner of jurors in any county outside the city of New York.

(c) The term "Chief Administrator of the Courts," when used in this part, is deemed to include a designee of the Chief Administrator.

§ 128.1.   Jury Districts

There may be no jury districts from which prospective jurors may be drawn consisting of less than the whole of the governmental subdivision wherein the court convenes.

§ 128.2.   Annual Meeting of County Jury Board

The county jury board shall meet at least annually.

§ 128.3.   Source of Names

The sources of prospective jurors shall be: (a) the names contained on voter registration lists, lists of licensed motor vehicle operators and lists of persons to whom state income tax forms have been mailed; (b) the names of persons who have volunteered to serve in accordance with Section 506 of the Judiciary Law; and (c) the names from such other sources as authorized by the Chief Administrator of the Courts.

Cross References
Judiciary Law, see McKinney's Book 29.

§ 128.4.   Residence

For purposes of article 16 of the Judiciary Law and this Part, a resident of a county or municipality shall mean a person who maintains a fixed permanent and principal home within that county or municipality to which such person, wherever temporarily located, always intends to return. Among the factors that may be considered in determining the principal home is the relative proportion of time in the year that the person customarily resides in the county or municipality.

Cross References
Judiciary Law, see McKinney's Book 29.

§ 128.5.   Qualification of Trial Jurors and Grand Jurors

(a) Prospective jurors shall be selected at random pursuant to a methodology approved by the Chief Administrator of the Courts.

(b) A juror qualification questionnaire shall be sent to prospective jurors by first class mail unless the commissioner of jurors determines that a personal interview is required, in which case the questionnaire shall be completed at the interview. Where a completed questionnaire is returned by mail, the commissioner may require a subsequent personal interview. The qualification questionnaire may be sent with the juror summons during the summoning process as set forth in section 128.6 of this part.

(c) The commissioner of jurors may require prospective grand jurors to appear before the commissioner of jurors to be fingerprinted and interviewed as to their availability to serve as grand jurors.

(d) After the qualification questionnaire has been reviewed and the prospective juror is found otherwise qualified, the juror's name, and fingerprint record in the case of a prospective grand juror, may be forwarded by the commissioner of jurors to an appropriate agency for checking for conviction of a criminal offense.

(e) Upon the basis of the completed questionnaire, the personal interview, if any, and the check for a criminal conviction, where such check was requested, or after at least 30 days without receipt of any report concerning the check for a criminal conviction, the

commissioner of jurors shall note upon each questionnaire whether the person has been found qualified or
not qualified for jury service. If excluded from jury
service, the reasons shall be noted on the questionnaire.

(f) The commissioner of jurors shall maintain a
record of persons who are found not qualified for jury
service, including the reasons therefor.

§ 128.6. Summoning of Trial Jurors and Grand Jurors

(a) Trial jurors and grand jurors shall be selected
for summoning at random from prospective jurors
previously qualified for service. In the alternative,
the Chief Administrator of the Courts may direct that
in any county trial jurors and grand jurors be selected
for summoning at random from the juror source lists
and that their qualifications for service be determined
during the summoning process in accordance with the
procedures set forth in section 128.5 of this part.

(b) The commissioner of jurors shall determine the
number of jurors to be selected for summoning and
shall summon such jurors, unless such number otherwise is specified by the Chief Administrator of the
Courts. At any time during a term of court in a
county, the court may direct an additional specified
number of jurors to be drawn, set the time of the
drawing, and require the commissioner to summon the
additional jurors, giving such notice as the court shall
direct. The drawing shall be conducted in the same
manner as a regular drawing.

(c) Whenever practicable, the summons shall be
served by first class mail at least 14 days before the
day the juror is required to appear, unless a shorter
period is necessary to satisfy court requirements for
sufficient jurors. The commissioner of jurors shall
maintain for one year a record of the date and reason
when the mailing of the summons occurred less than
14 days before the return date of the summons. If
service by first class mail cannot be made or is
impracticable, the summons may be served personally
upon the juror by personal delivery to the juror, or to
a person of suitable age and discretion at the juror's
residence or place of business.

(d) Jurors who appear for the sole purpose of
requesting an excuse, deferment or postponement
from jury service shall not be entitled to any per diem
fee or mileage allowance.

§ 128.6–a. Postponement and Excusal From Jury Service

(a) Postponement.

(1) A prospective juror who has received the initial
jury summons is entitled, upon notifying the commissioner of jurors, to a postponement of jury service to a
specific jury term date that is not more than six
months after the date such service is to commence as
set forth in the summons. The prospective juror may

notify the commissioner by telephone that he or she is
seeking such postponement and shall select an appropriate date to which service is to be postponed. A
request for postponement shall be made at such time
as the commissioner shall require. The commissioner,
in his or her discretion, may grant a postponement of
jury service for greater than six months, but only
upon good cause shown.

(2) The commissioner may grant a prospective juror's subsequent request for a postponement of jury
service, but only upon a written application, containing
documentation acceptable to the commissioner, showing that an inability to obtain a postponement would
result in a hardship that was unanticipated at the time
of the prior postponement. Absent extraordinary circumstances, the commissioner shall not grant a prospective juror more than three postponements of jury
service, nor shall the aggregate period of postponements granted to a prospective juror exceed eighteen
months.

(b) Excusal.

(1) A prospective juror who has received a jury
summons may apply to be excused from jury service
by submitting a written application for excusal to the
commissioner, at such time as the commissioner shall
require. Such application for excusal may be granted
only if the prospective juror has demonstrated satisfactorily that (i) he or she has a mental or physical
condition that renders him or her incapable of performing jury service, or that jury service would cause
undue hardship or extreme inconvenience to the prospective juror, a person under his or her care or
supervision, or the public, and (ii) he or she will be
unable to serve as a juror on a date certain within the
time restrictions applicable to postponements set forth
in subdivision (a) of this section. The application shall
contain documentation, satisfactory to the commissioner, supporting the ground for excusal.

(2) If the application for excusal is granted and the
facts underlying the ground for the excusal are not of
a permanent nature, the excusal shall be for a specific
period of time not to exceed twenty-four months, after
which the prospective juror shall become eligible for
re-qualification as a juror. If the facts underlying the
ground for excusal are of a permanent nature, the
excusal shall be permanent.

(c) Recordkeeping. The commissioner of jurors
shall maintain a list of the names of persons excused
or postponed from service as a trial juror, with an
indication of the reasons therefor insofar as practicable, and which shall include the time periods for which
the persons have been postponed or excused. A judge
hearing an application for postponement or excusal
shall provide notice of his or her determination expeditiously to the commissioner of jurors for inclusion in
such records.

(d) Guidelines. The commissioner of jurors shall conform to such guidelines as may be promulgated by the Chief Administrator of the Courts in determining whether to grant postponements and excusals from jury service.

§ 128.7. Support of Town and Village Courts

(a)[1] The commissioner of jurors shall qualify and maintain source lists or qualified lists of jurors for each town and village court outside the city of New York. The commissioner shall summon jurors to serve in these courts, or if not practicable for the commissioner so to summon jurors, the commissioner shall furnish to each such court a list of qualified jurors who reside within the geographical jurisdiction of such court, or within such geographical area from which the court is authorized by law to summon jurors, to be summoned at random by the court for service in that court. Such lists may be furnished to town courts, which then shall furnish lists to village courts within each town. The notification and summoning of jurors by each such court shall be in the same manner as prescribed for the commissioner in section 516 of the Judiciary Law and this part. Within 30 days of the completion of service by a juror in a town or village court, the court shall notify the commissioner of the identity of a juror who has so served.

[1] No subsec. (b) has been enacted.

Cross References

Judiciary Law, see McKinney's Book 29.

§ 128.8. Duration of Service

(a) Trial Jurors. Unless otherwise specified in the manner provided by subdivision (d) of section 525 of the Judiciary Law, a trial juror shall serve in the court for no more than five consecutive court days, except that service shall continue beyond any time limit fixed pursuant to this section until the conclusion of any trial for which a juror may be empaneled. For the purposes of this section, the duration of a juror's service shall be computed by counting the first day on which the juror is required to appear and each consecutive day thereafter, excluding days in which the court is not in session, until the juror is released from service. The commissioner of jurors may release a trial juror from service at any time, except that a trial juror who has been sworn or selected to sit on a panel in a proceeding may be released before the proceeding is terminated only by a judge or justice unless trial of the proceeding has not been commenced within five court days from the date the juror was sworn, in which case, subject to the discretion of the appropriate administrative judge, the juror shall be released. Service as set forth in this section shall constitute service for purposes of section 128.9(b).

(b) Telephone Standby System. The Chief Administrator may direct the establishment in any county of a telephone standby system for the summoning or service of trial jurors. Service of a trial juror as

provided by subdivision (a) of this section shall include service pursuant to a telephone standby system, and the computation of the duration of a trial juror's service as provided by subdivision (a) shall include any day on which the juror is on telephone standby service.

(c) Grand Jurors. A grand juror shall serve for the duration of the term for which the grand juror has been selected and for any period during which the grand jury panel on which the grand juror has been serving is extended, unless sooner discharged.

§ 128.9. Frequency of Service

(a) When a juror completes service, the juror's name may be restored to the general list of qualified jurors. In the alternative, the Chief Administrator may direct that in any county, when a juror completes service, the commissioner of jurors may summon the juror only if he or she again is selected at random for qualification from the juror source lists and subsequently qualified.

(b) A person who has served on a trial jury or grand jury in any court of record within the state, including service as set forth in section 128.8 of this Part or service in a federal court, is disqualified from further jury service, pursuant to section 524 of the Judiciary Law, for six years following the completion of jury service, and shall not be summoned for such service within that period, except that where, as provided in subdivision (c) of section 524, the commissioner of jurors has determined that compliance with the six-year period would be impracticable, such period of disqualification may be reduced to not less than two years for persons whose service consisted of fewer than three days, and such person shall not be summoned for jury service within such reduced period. Where a person serves on a trial jury or grand jury for more than ten days, that person is disqualified for further jury service for eight years. For purposes of this subdivision, jury service shall include service in the court and telephone standby service.

(c) The commissioner of jurors may extend the period of disqualification for all jurors in excess of the time periods set forth in subdivision (b) where the extension would not interfere with the commissioner's ability to comply with section 508 of the Judiciary Law.

Cross References

Judiciary Law, see McKinney's Book 29.

§ 128.10.   [Repealed]

§ 128.11. Judge to Greet Jurors

Wherever a central juror assembly room is provided for the courts in a county, the administrative judge, where practicable, shall designate a judge in each county in the district to greet newly summoned jurors and generally explain their responsibilities while serving as jurors. In courts not using a central juror assembly room, a judge or justice of the court in which the jurors are serving, where practicable, shall greet newly summoned jurors. A filmed or video-taped greeting from a judge may be used.

§ 128.12. Failure to Respond to Questionnaire or Summons; Procedure for Noncompliance

(a) Inquiry. In exercising the powers set forth in section 502(d) of the Judiciary Law, the commissioner of jurors shall make inquiry of persons who do not respond to the juror qualification questionnaire or jury service summons to determine the reason for nonresponse and shall make reference to the power of a court to cite for contempt or the power of the commissioner of jurors to bring a proceeding for noncompliance, pursuant to section 527 of the Judiciary Law.

(b) Commencement of Noncompliance Proceeding. The commissioner of jurors may bring a non-compliance proceeding against a person who fails to respond to the juror qualification questionnaire or summons to appear for jury service by serving upon such person, either personally or by first-class mail, a notice of noncompliance in a form prescribed by the Chief Administrator of the Courts. The form shall provide that a response to the commissioner of jurors shall be made within 20 days after the date of service of the notice of noncompliance and that the respondent must either admit noncompliance or request a hearing. After 20 days have elapsed from the date of service, the commissioner of jurors shall file with the Supreme Court a copy of the notice of noncompliance with proof of service and any response thereto. The court, or a judicial hearing officer designated pursuant to Part 122, shall review the material submitted and, where the person has failed to respond, or has admitted noncompliance, or has been found not in compliance after a hearing held pursuant to this section, may impose a penalty in accordance with section 527 of the Judiciary Law and shall issue an order fixing a date certain for jury service.

(c)(1) Notwithstanding the provisions of subdivision (b) of this section, where a person has failed to respond and a default judgment is sought, an affidavit shall be submitted that additional notice has been given, at least 20 days before the entry of judgment, to the person who has failed to respond, by mailing a copy of the notice of noncompliance by first class mail to such person at his or her place of residence in an envelope bearing the legend "personal and confidential" and not indicating on the outside of the envelope that the communication is from a court, the commissioner of jurors or any other public officer or official. In the event such mailing is returned as undeliverable by the post office before entry of the default judgment, a copy of the notice of noncompliance then shall be mailed in the same manner to the person who has

failed to respond at his or her place of employment, if known.

(2) The additional notice shall be mailed not less than 20 days after service of the notice of noncompliance pursuant to subdivision (b) of this section. An affidavit of mailing pursuant to this paragraph shall be executed by a person mailing the notice and shall be filed with the judgment.

(d) Hearing. Whenever a respondent served with a notice of noncompliance requests a hearing, the court or judicial hearing officer shall schedule such hearing and shall notify the respondent by mail at least 30 days in advance of the hearing date. The hearing shall be held before the court or the judicial hearing officer assigned to conduct the hearing, and the respondent may be represented by counsel. A finding of noncompliance shall be based upon a preponderance of the credible evidence presented. The charge of noncompliance may not be sustained if there is a finding of undue hardship or extreme inconvenience as set forth in section 517(c) of the Judiciary Law or for any other excuse based upon a good and sufficient cause. Rules of evidence shall not apply except those relating to privileged communications. Oral testimony shall be presented under oath. The court or judicial hearing officer may issue subpoenas to require the attendance at the hearing of persons to give testimony or to produce books, papers or other things relevant to the hearing. The court or judicial hearing officer shall cause a verbatim record of the hearing to be made by stenographic or mechanical means. If the charge is not sustained, the court or judicial hearing officer shall issue an order dismissing the charge, and shall fix a date certain for jury service by the respondent unless the respondent files an affidavit with the commissioner requesting postponement of or excusal from jury service in which case capacity for service then shall be determined by the commissioner pursuant to section 128.6–a of this Part.

(e) Penalty. All penalties imposed pursuant to this section shall be payable to the appropriate commissioner of jurors, who shall transmit such payments to the county clerk for transmittal to the state commissioner of taxation and finance on a monthly basis no later than ten days after the last day of each month.

Cross References

Judiciary Law, see McKinney's Book 29.

§ 128.13. Records to Be Maintained; Retention and Disposition

The commissioner of jurors shall maintain such records as may be necessary for the orderly administration of the county's jury system and as required by the Chief Administrator of the Courts, including, but not limited to, the records required by sections 509 and 514 of the Judiciary Law, qualification questionnaires, notices and summons, records of postponement and excuse, juror attendance records, statistical records of the utilization of jurors, and the minutes of jury empanellings and meetings of the county jury board.

Cross References

Judiciary Law, see McKinney's Book 29.

§ 128.14. Confidentiality and Security of Records

(a) Juror qualification questionnaires and other juror records shall not be disclosed except as permitted by section 509 of the Judiciary Law.

(b) The commissioner of jurors and the Office of Court Administration shall take the necessary precautions to ensure that the records and materials in their respective possession used for the selection, procurement, and utilization of jurors are stored securely and in such a manner as to prevent their unauthorized use, modification or disclosure.

Cross References

Judiciary Law, see McKinney's Book 29.

§ 128.15. Duties of Sheriff

The sheriff of each county may be requested to assist the commissioner of jurors in implementing the provisions of article 16 of the Judiciary Law as provided by law.

Cross References

Judiciary Law, see McKinney's Book 29.

§ 128.16. Selection of Sheriff's Jurors

The commissioner of jurors shall select, at random and in the same manner as regular trial jurors, from the persons qualified to act as regular trial jurors, such number of persons, if any, as may be necessary to constitute the sheriff's jurors.

§ 128.17. Grand Juries; Number; Terms

The Chief Administrator of the Courts, in consultation and agreement with the Presiding Justice of the appropriate Appellate Division, shall designate: (a) the number of grand juries to be drawn and empanelled for each term of the Supreme Court or County Court established within the judicial department and (b) such additional grand juries as may be required.

APPENDIX A.　GUIDELINES FOR POSTPONEMENTS AND EXCUSALS

Judges and Commissioners of Jurors shall utilize the following guidelines in determining whether to grant postponements and excusals from jury service pursuant to section 517 of the Judiciary Law.

I.　Definitions.

1. "Postponement"—A "postponement" of jury service is an adjournment of the date of jury service to a subsequent fixed date. These guidelines shall apply only to postponements of between six and 18 months from the date set forth in the initial juror summons. Postponements of up to six months from the initial summons are not covered by these guidelines, because those postponements must be granted at the request of the person summoned; postponements of greater than 18 months are not permitted by court rules.

2. "Excusal"—An "excusal" from jury service is the cancelling of a juror summons for a period not to exceed 24 months, after which the person so summoned again shall become eligible for requalification as a juror. An excusal may be granted only where jury service cannot be postponed. A person may receive a permanent excusal, and be excluded from selection from any list of prospective jurors, where the judge or Commissioner of Jurors determines that the underlying ground for the excusal is of a permanent nature.

II.　Standards.　Judges and Commissioners of Jurors shall be guided by the following standards in determining whether a person shall receive a postponement of or excusal from jury service. Nothing in these guidelines shall be deemed to limit the documentation that a judge or Commissioner of Jurors may require based upon the facts underlying any individual application for postponement or excusal. A judge or Commissioner of Jurors, in appropriate cases, also may require that any statement submitted be sworn to under oath.

A. *Mental or Physical Capacity.* An application for postponement or excusal may be granted if the applicant has a mental or physical condition that causes him or her to be incapable of performing jury service. The judge or Commissioner of Jurors may require the following documentation in support of the application:

1. A statement signed by an appropriately licensed health care provider, setting forth (i) a diagnosis of the mental or physical condition of the applicant, (ii) a prognosis of the length of time the mental or physical condition is expected to continue to exist, and (iii) a conclusion that the applicant is not capable of performing jury service.

2. A statement from the applicant describing the physical or mental condition and setting forth why the applicant believes the condition prevents his or her service as a juror and when the applicant believes that he or she will become capable to serve as a juror. The applicant may be required to provide documentation concerning his or her employment status. If the applicant describes a condi-

tion associated with advanced age, he or she may be required to provide documentation of his or her age.

B. *Undue Hardship or Extreme Inconvenience.* An application for postponement or excusal may be granted if service as a juror would cause undue hardship or extreme inconvenience to the applicant, a person under his or her care or supervision, or the public. A determination of undue hardship or extreme inconvenience shall be based upon service as a juror for a period of five consecutive court days.

1. Caregivers. An applicant may obtain a postponement or excusal if the applicant (i) has a personal obligation to care for another, including a sick, aged, infirm or disabled dependent or a minor child, who requires the prospective juror's personal care and attention during the time the person will be required to serve as a juror, and (ii) no alternative care is available without severe financial hardship to the applicant or the person requiring care, or because special needs of the person receiving care foreclose the temporary substitution of another caregiver. In determining whether the applicant's personal care and attention are required, the judge or Commissioner of Jurors may require the following documentation in support of the application:

a. A copy of a birth certificate of a minor child;

b. A statement signed by an appropriately licensed health care provider describing the medical condition of an aged, sick, infirm or disabled person;

c. A statement by the applicant that he or she is the primary caregiver and setting forth (i) the circumstances necessitating the caregiving services of the applicant, (ii) the hours that the applicant provides such care and (iii) the reasons why the applicant cannot make arrangements for care to be provided by another during the period of jury service; and

d. Documentation verifying any employment of the applicant, including hours worked and salary earned.

2. Financial Hardship. An applicant may obtain a postponement or excusal if the applicant will suffer a financial hardship that will significantly compromise the applicant's ability to support himself, herself or dependents. In determining whether the applicant's ability to provide such support is significantly compromised, the court or Commissioner of Jurors may require the following documentation:

a. A statement from the applicant setting forth (i) the applicant's sources of income, (ii) the applicant's hours of work, (iii) the amount of money that would be lost as a result of jury service, and (iv) the impact that this loss will have on (A) the applicant's ability to provide support to

the applicant and his or her dependents and (B) where appropriate, the ability of the applicant to maintain his or her business.

b. Forms filed with governmental taxing authorities showing the financial status of the applicant and, where relevant, of his or her business.

3. Needs of the Public. An applicant may obtain a postponement or excusal if his or her absence to serve as a juror would jeopardize to a significant degree the health, welfare or safety of the public. In determining whether the health, welfare or safety of the public would be significantly jeopardized, the judge or Commissioner of Jurors may require a statement by the applicant setting forth (i) the nature and duties of his or her service to the public, (ii) the hours when such service is performed, and (iii) the availability of others to perform such service in his or her absence. The performance of duties that affect the public shall not by itself serve as a ground for postponement or excusal without a showing that the specific individual services performed by the applicant meet the criteria contained in these guidelines.

4. Lack of Transportation. An applicant may obtain a postponement or excusal if (i) the applicant does not have access to a private vehicle, (ii) there is no available public transportation that will permit the applicant to travel to the court in a reasonable time, and (iii) use of other alternate means of transportation to the court would create a severe financial burden. In determining whether an applicant lacks transportation to appear in court to serve as a juror, the judge or Commissioner of Jurors may require a statement by the applicant setting forth (i) the reasons the applicant cannot obtain transportation to the court, (ii) the applicant's current employment status and transportation arrangements to his or her place of employment, and (iii) the anticipated duration of the applicant's inability to obtain the necessary transportation.

C. *Matters of Conscience.* Applications for excusal from jury service based upon matters of conscience should be handled during jury selection or determined by the trial judge.

Members of the clergy who request excusal for matters of conscience shall be excused by the Commissioner of Jurors, unless determined otherwise by the court, and removed from the current list of qualified jurors. In support of each request, the following documentation shall be submitted to the Commissioner of Jurors: (1) a written statement by the applicant identifying the religious beliefs on which the request is based; and (2) a written statement by the head of the religious organization or authorized designee supporting the request.

PART 129. FAIR TREATMENT STANDARDS FOR CRIME VICTIMS

§ 129.1. Purpose

The purpose of these standards is to provide objective guidelines for the fair and uniform treatment of crime victims by the unified court system in order to encourage increased public cooperation and support of the criminal justice process, improve the overall effectiveness of the criminal justice system as it concerns crime victims and the public in general and help ensure that courts in the unified court system treat crime victims and witnesses with dignity and appropriate understanding.

§ 129.2. Definitions

(a) "Criminal justice agency" includes any agency or department of the State or any political subdivision thereof that performs a criminal justice function as defined in 9 NYCRR section 6170.2(c) and a presentment agency as defined in subdivision twelve of section 301.2 of the Family Court Act.

(b) "Criminal justice process" shall mean the process by which a crime charged in an accusatory instrument or in a Family Court petition is processed by the unified court system from the initial appearance of the accused to disposition.

(c) "Crime victim" shall mean a natural person against whom an act defined as a misdemeanor or felony by the Penal Law or section 1192 of the Vehicle and Traffic Law has been committed or attempted, where such act is charged in an accusatory instrument as defined in section 1.20(1) of the Criminal Procedure Law or is alleged in a petition filed in Family Court. Crime victim shall include the immediate family of a homicide victim or the immediate family or guardian of a minor who is a crime victim. Except as otherwise provided in this Part, a victim shall not include a defense witness or an individual reasonably believed to have been involved in the commission of the crime.

(d) "Witness" shall mean a natural person who has evidence or information concerning a crime and who provides such evidence or information to a criminal justice agency. Where the witness is a minor, "witness" shall include an immediate family member or guardian. Except as otherwise provided in this part, a witness shall not include a defense witness or an individual reasonably believed to have been involved in the commission of the crime.

(e) "Court" shall mean any court in the unified court system that has contact with a crime victim or witness.

Cross References

Criminal Procedure Law, see McKinney's Book 11A.

Family Court Act, see McKinney's Book 29A, Part 1.

Penal Law, see McKinney's Book 39.

Vehicle and Traffic Law, see McKinney's Book 62A.

§ 129.3. Standards

(a) When a court has contact with a crime victim or witness, the court shall take steps to ensure:

(1) that the victim had been provided with information concerning:

(i) the victim's role in the criminal justice process, including what the victim can expect from the system as well as what the system expects from the victim;

(ii) the stages of the criminal justice process of significance to the victim and the manner in which information about such stages can be obtained; and

(iii) how the court can address the needs of the victim at sentencing or disposition.

(2) that the victim or witness has been notified as to steps the court can take to protect him or her from intimidation, including the issuance of orders of protection and temporary orders of protection.

(3) that a victim or witness who has provided the appropriate court official or criminal justice agency with a current address and telephone number has been notified, if possible, of judicial proceedings relating to his or her case, including:

(i) the initial appearance of an accused before a judicial officer;

(ii) the release of an accused pending further judicial proceedings;

(iii) proceedings in the prosecution of the accused, including entry of a plea of guilty, trial, sentencing or disposition, and, where a term of imprisonment or confinement is imposed, specific information regarding maximum and minimum terms of such imprisonment or confinement; and

(iv) the reversal or modification of the judgment by an appellate court.

(b) The court shall consider the views of victims of the following felonies regarding disposition of the case by dismissal, plea agreement, trial, or sentence:

(1) a violent felony offense;

(2) a felony involving physical injury to the victim;

(3) a felony involving property loss or damage in excess of $250;

(4) a felony involving attempted or threatened physical injury or property loss or damage in excess of $250; and

(5) a felony involving larceny against the person.

(c) The court shall consider the views of the victim or family of the victim, as appropriate, concerning the release of the defendant in the victim's case pending judicial proceedings upon an indictment or petition, and concerning the availability of sentencing or dispositional alternatives such as community supervision and restitution from the defendant.

(d) The court shall take steps to ensure that, whenever possible, victims and other prosecution witnesses awaiting court appearances have been provided with a secure waiting area separate from all other witnesses.

(e) The court shall assist in and expedite the return of property held for evidentiary purposes, unless there is a compelling law enforcement reason for retaining it relating to proof at trial.

(f) Any judicial or nonjudicial personnel of the unified court system having contact with a crime victim or witness, whether for the prosecution or the defense, shall treat such crime victim or witness with dignity, courtesy and respect.

(g) The court may direct the district attorney or a criminal justice agency to take such steps as may be necessary and appropriate to ensure compliance with these standards.

§ 129.4. Education and Training

Victim assistance education and training shall be given to judicial and nonjudicial personnel of the unified court system so that victims may be promptly, properly and completely assisted.

§ 129.5. Liability

Nothing in this Part shall be construed as creating a cause of action for damages or injunctive relief against the State or any of its political subdivisions or officers or any agency thereof.

PART 130. COSTS AND SANCTIONS

SUBPART 130–1. AWARDS OF COSTS AND IMPOSITION OF FINANCIAL SANCTIONS FOR FRIVOLOUS CONDUCT IN CIVIL LITIGATION

§ 130–1.1. Costs; Sanctions

(a) The court, in its discretion, may award to any party or attorney in any civil action or proceeding before the court, except where prohibited by law, costs in the form of reimbursement for actual expenses reasonably incurred and reasonable attorney's fees, resulting from frivolous conduct as defined in this Part. In addition to or in lieu of awarding costs, the court, in its discretion may impose financial sanctions upon any party or attorney in a civil action or proceeding who engages in frivolous conduct as defined in this Part, which shall be payable as provided in section 130–1.3 of this Part. This Part shall not apply to town or village courts, to proceedings in a small claims part of any court, or to proceedings in the Family Court commenced under Article 3, 7 or 8 of the Family Court Act.

(b) The court, as appropriate, may make such award of costs or impose such financial sanctions against either an attorney or a party to the litigation or against both. Where the award or sanction is against an attorney, it may be against the attorney personally or upon a partnership, firm, corporation, government agency, prosecutor's office, legal aid society or public defender's office with which the attorney is associated and that has appeared as attorney of record. The award or sanctions may be imposed upon any attorney appearing in the action or upon a partnership, firm or corporation with which the attorney is associated.

(c) For purposes of this Part, conduct is frivolous if:

(1) it is completely without merit in law and cannot be supported by a reasonable argument for an extension, modification or reversal of existing law;

(2) it is undertaken primarily to delay or prolong the resolution of the litigation, or to harass or maliciously injure another; or

(3) it asserts material factual statements that are false.

Frivolous conduct shall include the making of a frivolous motion for costs or sanctions under this section. In determining whether the conduct undertaken was frivolous, the court shall consider, among other issues, (1) the circumstances under which the conduct took place, including the time available for investigating the legal or factual basis of the conduct; and (2) whether or not the conduct was continued when its lack of legal or factual basis was apparent, should have been apparent, or was brought to the attention of counsel or the party.

(d) An award of costs or the imposition of sanctions may be made either upon motion in compliance with CPLR 2214 or 2215 or upon the court's own initiative, after a reasonable opportunity to be heard. The form of the hearing shall depend upon the nature of the conduct and the circumstances of the case.

§ 130–1.1–a. Signing of Papers

(a) Signature. Every pleading, written motion, and other paper, served on another party or filed or submitted to the court shall be signed by an attorney, or by a party if the party is not represented by an attorney, with the name of the attorney or party clearly printed or typed directly below the signature. Absent good cause shown, the court shall strike any unsigned paper if the omission of the signature is not corrected promptly after being called to the attention of the attorney or party.

(b) Certification. By signing a paper, an attorney or party certifies that, to the best of that person's knowledge, information and belief, formed after an inquiry reasonable under the circumstances,

(1) the presentation of the paper or the contentions therein are not frivolous as defined in section 130–1.1(c) of this Subpart, and

(2) where the paper is an initiating pleading,

(i) the matter was not obtained through illegal conduct, or that if it was, the attorney or other persons responsible for the illegal conduct are not participating in the matter or sharing in any fee earned therefrom, and

(ii) the matter was not obtained in violation of 22 NYCRR 1200.41–a [DR 7–111].

§ 130–1.2. Order Awarding Costs or Imposing Sanctions

The court may award costs or impose sanctions or both only upon a written decision setting forth the conduct on which the award or imposition is based, the reasons why the court found the conduct to be frivolous, and the reasons why the court found the amount awarded or imposed to be appropriate. An award of costs or the imposition of sanctions or both shall be entered as a judgment of the court. In no event shall the amount of sanctions imposed exceed $10,000 for any single occurrence of frivolous conduct.

§ 130–1.3. Payment of Sanctions

Payments of sanctions by an attorney shall be deposited with the Lawyers' Fund for Client Protection established pursuant to section 97–t of the State Finance Law. Payments of sanctions by a party who is not an attorney shall be deposited with the clerk of the court for transmittal to the Commissioner of Taxation and Finance. The court shall give notice to the Lawyers' Fund of awards of sanctions payable to the Fund by sending a copy of the order awarding sanctions, or by sending other appropriate notice, to the Lawyers' Fund for Client Protection, 119 Washington Avenue, Albany, New York, 12210.

§ 130–1.4. Application to Officers Other Than Judges of the Courts of the Unified Court System

The powers of a court set forth in this subpart shall apply to judges of the Housing Part of the New York City Civil Court and to support magistrates appointed pursuant to section 439 of the Family Court Act, except that the powers of Family Court support magistrates shall be limited to a determination that a party or attorney has engaged in frivolous conduct, which shall be subject to confirmation by a judge of the Family Court who may impose any costs or sanctions authorized by this subpart.

§ 130–1.5. Exception

This rule shall not apply to requests for costs or attorneys' fees subject to the provisions of CPLR 8303–a.

SUBPART 130–2. IMPOSITION OF FINANCIAL SANCTIONS OR COSTS FOR UNJUSTIFIED FAILURE TO ATTEND A SCHEDULED COURT APPEARANCE

§ 130–2.1. Costs; Sanctions

(a) Notwithstanding and in addition to the provisions of subpart 130–1 of this Part, the court, in its discretion, may impose financial sanctions or, in addition to or in lieu of imposing sanctions, may award costs in the form of reimbursement for actual expenses reasonably incurred and reasonable attorney's fees, upon any attorney who, without good cause, fails to appear at a time and place scheduled for an action or proceeding to be heard before a designated court. This Part shall not apply to town or village courts or to proceedings in a small claims part of any court.

(b) In determining whether an attorney's failure to appear at a scheduled court appearance was without good cause and in determining the measure of sanctions or costs to be imposed, the court shall consider all of the attendant circumstances, including but not limited to:

(1) the explanation, if any, offered by the attorney for his or her nonappearance;

(2) the adequacy of the notice to the attorney of the time and date of the scheduled appearance;

(3) whether the attorney notified the court and opposing counsel in advance that he or she would be unable to appear;

(4) whether substitute counsel appeared in court at the time previously scheduled to proffer an explanation of the attorney's nonappearance and whether such substitute counsel was prepared to go forward with the case;

(5) whether an affidavit or affirmation of actual engagement was filed in the manner prescribed in

Part 125 of the Uniform Rules for the Trial Courts of the Unified Court System;

(6) whether the attorney on prior occasions in the same action or proceeding failed to appear at a scheduled court action or proceeding;

(7) whether financial sanctions or costs have been imposed upon the attorney pursuant to this section in some other action or proceeding; and

(8) the extent and nature of the harm caused by the attorney's failure to appear.

(c) The court, as appropriate, may impose any such financial sanctions or award costs upon an attorney personally or upon a partnership, firm, corporation, government agency, prosecutor's office, legal aid society or public defender's office with which the attorney is associated and that has appeared as attorney of record.

(d) The imposition of sanctions or award of costs may be made either upon motion or upon the court's own initiative, after a reasonable opportunity to be heard. The form of the hearing shall depend upon the nature of the attorney's failure to appear and the totality of the circumstances of the case.

§ 130–2.2. Order Imposing Sanctions and Costs

The court may impose sanctions or award costs or both only upon a written memorandum decision or statement on the record setting forth the conduct on which the award or imposition is based and the rea-

sons why the court found the attorney's failure to appear at a scheduled court appearance to be without good cause. The imposition of sanctions or an award of costs or both shall be entered as a judgment of the court. In no event shall the total amount of sanctions imposed and costs awarded exceed $2500 for any single failure to appear at a scheduled court appearance.

§ 130–2.3. Payment of Sanctions

Payments of sanctions shall be deposited with the Lawyers' Fund for Client Protection established pursuant to section 97–t of the State Finance Law.

§ 130–2.4. Application to Officers Other Than Judges of the Courts of the Unified Court System

The power of a court set forth in this subpart shall apply to judges of the housing part of the New York City Civil Court, support magistrates appointed pursuant to section 439 of the Family Court Act, and judicial hearing officers, except that:

(a) the powers of the Family Court support magistrates shall be limited to a determination that an attorney, without good cause, has failed to appear at a time and place scheduled for a Family Court proceeding, which shall be subject to confirmation by a judge of the Family Court who may impose any sanctions authorized by this subpart, and

(b) the powers of judicial hearing officers shall be limited to civil cases.

PART 131. AUDIO–VISUAL COVERAGE OF JUDICIAL PROCEEDINGS

§ 131.1. Purpose; General Provisions

(a) These rules are promulgated to comport with the legislative finding that an enhanced public understanding of the judicial system is important in maintaining a high level of public confidence in the judiciary, and with the legislative concern that cameras in the courts be compatible with the fair administration of justice.

(b) These rules shall be effective for any period when audio-visual coverage in the trial courts is authorized by law and shall apply in all counties in the State.

(c) Nothing in these rules is intended to restrict any pre-existing right of the news media to appear at and to report on judicial proceedings in accordance with law.

(d) Nothing in these rules is intended to restrict the power and discretion of the presiding trial judge to control the conduct of judicial proceedings.

(e) No judicial proceeding shall be scheduled, delayed, reenacted or continued at the request of, or for the convenience of, the news media.

(f) In addition to their specific responsibilities as provided in these rules, all presiding trial judges and all administrative judges shall take whatever steps are necessary to insure that audio-visual coverage is conducted without disruption of court activities, without detracting from or interfering with the dignity or decorum of the court, courtrooms and court facilities, without compromise of the safety of persons having business before the court, and without adversely affecting the administration of justice.

§ 131.2. Definitions

For purposes of this Part:

(a) "Administrative judge" shall mean the administrative judge of each judicial district; the administrative judge of Nassau County or of Suffolk County; the administrative judge of the Civil Court of the City of New York, the Criminal Court of the City of New York or the Family Court of the City of New York; or the presiding judge of the Court of Claims.

(b) "Audio-visual coverage" or "coverage" shall mean the electronic broadcasting or other transmission to the public of radio or television signals from the courtroom, the recording of sound or light in the courtroom for later transmission or reproduction, or the taking of still or motion pictures in the courtroom by the news media.

(c) "News media" shall mean any news reporting or news gathering agency and any employee or agent associated with such agency, including television, radio, radio and television networks, news services, newspapers, magazines, trade papers, in-house publications, professional journals, or any other news reporting or news gathering agency, the function of which is to inform the public or some segment thereof.

(d) "Presiding trial judge" shall mean the justice or judge presiding over judicial proceedings at which audio-visual coverage is authorized pursuant to this Part.

(e) "Covert or undercover capacity" shall mean law enforcement activity involving criminal investigation by peace officers or police officers who usually and customarily wear no uniform, badge, or other official identification in public view.

(f) "Judicial proceedings" shall mean the proceedings of a court or a judge thereof conducted in a courtroom or any other facility being used as a courtroom.

(g) "Child" shall mean a person who has not attained the age of sixteen years.

(h) "Arraignment" shall have the same meaning as such term is defined in subdivision nine of section 1.20 of the Criminal Procedure Law.

(i) "Suppression hearing" shall mean a hearing on a motion made pursuant to the provisions of section 710.20 of the Criminal Procedure Law; a hearing on a motion to determine the admissibility of any prior criminal, vicious or immoral acts of a defendant; and any other hearing held to determine the admissibility of evidence.

(j) "Nonparty witness" shall mean any witness in a criminal trial proceeding who is not a party to such proceeding; except an expert or professional witness, a peace or police officer who acted in the course of his or her duties and was not acting in a covert or undercover capacity in connection with the instant court proceedings, or any government official acting in an official capacity, shall not be deemed to be a "nonparty witness".

(k) "Visually obscured" shall mean that the face of a participant in a criminal trial proceeding shall either not be shown or shall be rendered visually unrecognizable to the viewer of such proceeding by means of special editing by the news media.

§ 131.3. Application for Audio Visual Coverage

(a) Coverage of judicial proceedings shall be permitted only upon order of the presiding trial judge approving an application made by a representative of the news media for permission to conduct such coverage.

(b)(1) Except as provided in paragraph two of this subdivision, an application for permission to conduct coverage of a judicial proceeding shall be made to the presiding trial judge not less than seven days before the scheduled commencement of that proceeding. Where circumstances are such that an applicant cannot reasonably apply more than seven days before commencement of the proceedings, the presiding trial judge may shorten the time period. The application shall be in writing and shall specify such proceeding with sufficient particularity to assist the presiding trial judge in considering the application and shall set forth which of the types of coverage described in subdivision (b) of section 131.2 is sought, including whether live coverage is sought. Upon receipt of any application, the presiding trial judge shall cause all parties to the proceeding to be notified thereof.

(2) An application for permission to conduct coverage of an arraignment in a criminal case or of any other proceeding after it has commenced may be made to the presiding trial judge at any time and shall be otherwise subject to the provisions of paragraph one hereof.

(3) Each application shall relate to one case or proceeding only, unless the presiding trial judge permits otherwise.

(c) Where more than one representative of the news media makes an application for coverage of the same judicial proceeding, such applications shall be consolidated and treated as one.

§ 131.4. Determination of the Application

(a) Upon receipt of an application pursuant to section 131.3, the presiding trial judge shall conduct such review as may be appropriate, including:

(1) consultation with the news media applicant;

(2) consultation with counsel to all parties to the proceeding of which coverage is sought, who shall be responsible for identifying any concerns or objections of the parties, prospective witnesses, and victims, if any, with respect to the proposed coverage, and advising the court thereof;

(3) review of all statements or affidavits presented to the presiding trial judge concerning the proposed coverage.

Where the proceedings of which coverage is sought involve a child, a victim, a prospective witness, or a party, any of whom object to such coverage, and in any other appropriate instance, the presiding trial judge may hold such conferences and conduct any direct inquiry as may be fitting.

(b)(1) Except as otherwise provided in paragraphs two and three hereof or section 131.8 of these rules, consent of the parties, prospective witnesses, victims, or other participants in judicial proceedings of which coverage is sought is not required for approval of an application for such coverage.

(2) An application for audio-visual coverage of a trial proceeding in which a jury is sitting, made after commencement of such proceeding, shall not be approved unless counsel to all parties to such proceeding consent to such coverage; provided, however, this paragraph shall not apply where coverage is sought only of the verdict or sentencing, or both, in such proceeding.

(3) Counsel to each party in a criminal trial proceeding shall advise each nonparty witness that he or she has the right to request that his or her image be visually obscured during said witness' testimony, and upon such request the presiding trial judge shall order the news media to visually obscure the visual image of the witness in any and all audio-visual coverage of the judicial proceeding.

(c) In determining an application for coverage, the presiding trial judge shall consider all relevant factors, including but not limited to:

(1) the type of case involved;

(2) whether the coverage would cause harm to any participant;

(3) whether the coverage would interfere with the fair administration of justice, the advancement of a fair trial, or the rights of the parties;

(4) whether any order directing the exclusion of witnesses from the courtroom prior to their testimony could be rendered substantially ineffective by allowing audio-visual coverage that could be viewed by such witnesses to the detriment of any party;

(5) whether the coverage would interfere with any law enforcement activity;

(6) whether the proceedings would involve lewd or scandalous matters;

(7) the objections of any of the parties, prospective witnesses, victims, or other participants in the proceeding of which coverage is sought;

(8) the physical structure of the courtroom and the likelihood that any equipment required to conduct coverage of proceedings can be installed and operated without disturbance to those proceedings or any other proceedings in the courthouse; and

(9) the extent to which the coverage would be barred by law in the judicial proceeding of which coverage is sought.

The presiding trial judge also shall consider and give great weight to the fact that any party, prospective witness, victim, or other participant in the proceeding is a child.

(d) Following review of an application for coverage of a judicial proceeding, the presiding trial judge, as soon as practicable, shall issue an order, in writing, approving such application, in whole or in part, or denying it. Such order shall contain any restrictions imposed by the judge on the audio-visual coverage and shall contain a statement advising the parties that any violation of the order is punishable by contempt pursuant to article nineteen of the Judiciary Law. Such order shall be included in the record of such proceedings and, unless it wholly approves the application and no party, victim or prospective witness objected to coverage, it shall state the basis for its determination.

(e) Before denying an application for coverage, the presiding trial judge shall consider whether such coverage properly could be approved with the imposition of special limitations, including but not limited to:

(1) delayed broadcast of the proceedings subject to coverage, provided, however, where delayed broadcast is directed, it shall be only for the purpose of assisting the news media to comply with the restrictions on coverage provided by law or by the presiding trial judge;

(2) modification or prohibition of audio-visual coverage of individual parties, witnesses, or other trial participants, or portions of the proceedings; or

(3) modification or prohibition of video coverage of individual parties, witnesses, or other trial participants, or portions of the proceedings.

§ 131.5. Review

(a) Any order determining an application for permission to provide coverage, rendered pursuant to subdivision (d) of section 131.4 of this part, shall be subject to review by the administrative judge in such form, including telephone conference, as he or she may determine, upon the request of a person who is aggrieved thereby and who is either:

(1) a news media applicant; or

(2) a party, victim, or prospective witness who objected to coverage.

(b) Upon review of a presiding trial judge's order determining an application for permission to provide coverage, the administrative judge shall uphold such order unless it is found that the order reflects an abuse of discretion by the presiding trial judge, in which event the administrative judge may direct such modification of the presiding trial judge's order as may be deemed appropriate. Any order directing a modification or overruling a presiding trial judge's order determining an application for coverage shall be in writing.

(c) No judicial proceeding shall be delayed or continued to allow for review by an administrative judge of an order denying coverage in whole or in part.

(d) This section shall authorize review by the administrative judge only of a presiding trial judge's order pursuant to paragraph (b) of subdivision three of section 218 of the Judiciary Law determining an application for permission to provide coverage of judicial proceedings and shall not authorize review of any other orders or decisions of the presiding trial judge relating to such coverage.

§ 131.6. Mandatory Pretrial Conference

(a) Where a presiding trial judge has approved, in whole or in part, an application for coverage of any judicial proceeding, the judge, before any such coverage is to begin, shall conduct a pretrial conference for the purpose of reviewing, with counsel to all parties to the proceeding and with representatives of the news media who will provide such coverage, any objections to coverage that have been raised, the scope of coverage to be permitted, the nature and extent of the technical equipment and personnel to be deployed, and the restrictions on coverage to be observed. The court may include in the conference any other person whom it deems appropriate, including prospective witnesses and their representatives. In an appropriate case, the presiding trial judge may conduct the pretrial conference concurrently with any consultations or conferences authorized by subdivision (a) of section 131.4.

(b) Where two or more representatives of the news media are parties to an approved application for coverage, no such coverage may begin until all such representatives have agreed upon a pooling arrangement for their respective news media prior to the pretrial conference. Such pooling arrangement shall include the designation of pool operators and replacement pool operators for the electronic and motion picture media and for the still photography media, as appropriate. It also shall include procedures for the cost sharing and dissemination of audio-visual material and shall make due provision for educational users' needs for full coverage of entire proceedings. The presiding trial judge shall not be called upon to mediate or resolve any dispute as to such arrangement. Nothing herein shall prohibit a person or organization that was not party to an approved application for coverage from making appropriate arrangements with the pool operator to be given access to the audio-visual material produced by the pool.

(c) In determining the scope of coverage to be permitted, the presiding trial judge shall be guided by a consideration of all relevant factors, including those prescribed in subdivision (c) of section 131.4 of this part. Wherever necessary or appropriate, the presiding trial judge shall, at any time before or during the proceeding, proscribe coverage or modify, expand, impose, or remove special limitations on coverage,

such as those prescribed in subdivision (e) of section 131.4.

§ 131.7. Use and Deployment of Equipment and Personnel by the News Media

(a) Limitations Upon Use of Equipment and Personnel in the Courtroom.

(1) No more than two electronic or motion picture cameras and two camera operators shall be permitted in any proceeding.

(2) No more than one photographer to operate two still cameras, with not more than two lenses for each camera, shall be permitted in any proceeding.

(3) No more than one audio system for broadcast purposes shall be permitted in any proceeding. Audio pickup for all news media purposes shall be effectuated through existing audio systems in the court facility. If no technically suitable audio system is available, microphones and related wiring essential for media purposes shall be supplied by those persons providing coverage. Any microphones and sound wiring shall be unobtrusive and placed where designated by the presiding trial judge.

(4) Notwithstanding the provisions of paragraphs one, two, and three of this subdivision, the presiding trial judge on a finding of special circumstances may modify any restriction on the amount of equipment or number of operating personnel in the courtroom, compatible with the dignity of the court or the judicial process.

(b) Sound and Light Criteria.

(1) Only electronic and motion picture cameras, audio equipment, and still camera equipment that do not produce distracting sound or light may be employed to cover judicial proceedings. The equipment designated in Appendix A to this part shall be deemed acceptable.

(2) Use of equipment other than that authorized in Appendix A may be permitted by the presiding trial judge provided the judge is satisfied that the equipment sought to be utilized meets the sound and light criteria specified in paragraph one of this subdivision. A failure to obtain advance approval shall preclude use of such equipment in the coverage of the judicial proceeding.

(3) No motorized drives, moving lights, flash attachments, or sudden lighting changes shall be permitted during coverage of judicial proceedings.

(4) No light or signal visible or audible to trial participants shall be used on any equipment during coverage to indicate whether it is operating.

(5) With the concurrence of the presiding trial judge and the administrative judge, modifications and additions may be made in light sources existing in the court facility, provided such modifications or additions are installed and maintained at media expense and are not distracting or otherwise offensive.

(c) Location of Equipment and Personnel. Electronic and motion picture cameras, still cameras, and camera personnel shall be positioned in such locations as shall be designated by the presiding trial judge. The areas designated shall provide the news media with reasonable access to the persons they wish to cover while causing the least possible interference with court proceedings. Equipment that is not necessary for audio-visual coverage from inside the courtroom shall be located in an area outside the courtroom.

(d) Movement of Equipment and Media Personnel. During the proceedings, operating personnel shall not move about, nor shall there be placement, movement or removal of equipment, or the changing of film, film magazines or lenses. All such activities shall take place each day before the proceeding begins, after it ends, or during a recess.

(e) Identifying Insignia. Identifying marks, call letters, words, and symbols shall be concealed on all equipment. Persons operating such equipment shall not display any identifying insignia on their clothing.

(f) Other Restrictions. The presiding trial judge may impose any other restrictions on the use and deployment of equipment and personnel as may be appropriate.

§ 131.8. Additional Restrictions on Coverage

(a) No audio pickup or audio broadcast of conferences that occur in a court facility between attorneys and their clients, between co-counsel of a client, or between counsel and the presiding trial judge, shall be permitted without the prior express consent of all participants in the conference.

(b) No conference in chambers shall be subject to coverage.

(c) No coverage of the selection of the prospective jury during voir dire shall be permitted.

(d) No coverage of the jury, or of any juror or alternate juror, while in the jury box, in the courtroom, in the jury deliberation room, or during recess, or while going to or from the deliberation room at any time, shall be permitted provided, however, that, upon consent of the foreperson of a jury, the presiding trial judge may, in his or her discretion, permit audio coverage of such foreperson delivering a verdict.

(e) No coverage shall be permitted of a witness, who as a peace officer or police officer acted in a covert or undercover capacity in connection with the proceedings being covered, without the prior written consent of such witness.

(f) No coverage shall be permitted of a witness, who as a peace officer or police officer is currently engaged in a covert or undercover capacity, without the prior written consent of such witness.

(g) No coverage shall be permitted of the victim in a prosecution for rape, sodomy, sexual abuse, or other sex offense under article one hundred thirty or section 255.25 of the Penal Law; notwithstanding the initial approval of a request for audio-visual coverage of such a proceeding, the presiding trial judge shall have discretion throughout the proceeding to limit any coverage that would identify the victim, except that said victim can request of the presiding trial judge that audio-visual coverage be permitted of his or her testimony, or in the alternative the victim can request that coverage of his or her testimony be permitted but that his or her image shall be visually obscured by the news media, and the presiding trial judge in his or her discretion shall grant the request of the victim for the coverage specified.

(h) No coverage of any participant shall be permitted if the presiding trial judge finds that such coverage is liable to endanger the safety of any person.

(i) No coverage of any judicial proceedings that are by law closed to the public, or that may be closed to the public and that have been closed by the presiding trial judge, shall be permitted.

(j) No coverage of any arraignment or suppression hearing shall be permitted without the prior consent of all parties to the proceeding; provided, however, where a party is not yet represented by counsel, consent may not be given unless the party has been advised of his or her right to the aid of counsel pursuant to subdivision four of section 170.10 or 180.10 of the Criminal Procedure Law and the party has affirmatively elected to proceed without counsel at such proceeding.

(k) No audio-visual coverage shall be permitted which focuses on or features a family member of a victim or a party in the trial of a criminal case, except while such family member is testifying. Audio-visual coverage operators shall make all reasonable efforts to determine the identity of such persons, so that such coverage shall not occur.

The restrictions specified in subdivisions (a) through (k) may not be waived or modified except as provided herein.

§ 131.9. Supervision of Audio-Visual Coverage

(a) Coverage of judicial proceedings shall be subject to the continuing supervision of the presiding trial judge. No coverage shall take place within the courtroom, whether during recesses or at any other time, when the presiding trial judge is not present and presiding.

(b) Notwithstanding the approval of an application for permission to provide coverage of judicial proceedings, the presiding trial judge shall have discretion throughout such proceedings to revoke such approval or to limit the coverage authorized in any way. In the exercise of this discretion, the presiding trial judge shall be especially sensitive and responsive to the needs and concerns of all parties, victims, witnesses, and other participants in such proceedings, particularly where the proceedings unnecessarily threaten the privacy or sensibilities of victims, or where they involve children or sex offenses or other matters that may be lewd or scandalous. The presiding trial judge shall be under a continuing obligation to order the discontinuation or modification of coverage where necessary to shield the identity or otherwise insure the protection of any such person, party, witness, or victim, or in order to preserve the welfare of a child.

(c) Counsel to each party in a trial proceeding that is subject to coverage shall inquire of each witness that he or she intends to call regarding any concerns or objections such witness might have with respect to coverage. Where counsel thereby is advised that a witness objects to coverage, counsel shall so notify the presiding trial judge.

§ 131.10. Cooperation With Committee

All officers and employees of the Unified Court system, and all participants in proceedings where audio-visual coverage was permitted, including judges, attorneys and jurors, shall cooperate with the committee to review audio-visual coverage of court proceedings in connection with the committee's review of the impact of audio-visual coverage on such proceedings.

§ 131.11. Appellate Courts

These rules shall not apply to coverage of proceedings in appellate courts or affect the rules governing such coverage contained in Part 29 of the Rules of the Chief Judge (22 NYCRR Part 29).

§ 131.12. Forms

The Chief Administrator will promulgate and make available forms for applications pursuant to section 131.3 and for judicial orders pursuant to section 131.4.

§ 131.13. Acceptable Equipment

The following equipment shall be deemed acceptable for use in audio-visual coverage of trial court proceedings pursuant to Part 131 of the Rules of the Chief Administrator of the Courts:

(a) Video Cameras.

Sony: BVP–3, BVP–3A, BVP–3U, BVP–5, BVP–30, BVP–33Am, BVP–50J, BVP–110, BVP–150, BVP–250, BVP–300, BVU–300, BVV–1, BVV–5, DXC–3000, M–3

Ikegami: HL–79, HL–79D, HL–79E, HL–83, HL–95, ITC–170, SP–3A, 75–D, 79–E, 95, 730, 730a, 730ap

JVC: KY–1900, KY–2000, KY–2700, BY–110

RCA: TK–76

Thompson: 501, 601

NEC: SP–3A

Sharp: XC–800

Panasonic: X–100 (the recam system in a camera/recorder combination)

Ampex: Betacam

(b) Still Cameras.

Leica: M

Nikon: FE, F–3, FM–2, 2000

Canon: F–1, T–90

(c) Any other audio or video equipment may be used with the permission of the presiding trial judge.

FORMS

APPLICATION FOR PERMISSION TO CONDUCT AUDIO-VISUAL COVERAGE

_____ Court, _____ County
_____x

In the Matter of an Application to
Conduct Audio-Visual Coverage of

Index No. _____
Indictment No. _____
Calendar No. _____
(Complete as applicable, if known)

v.

Judge assigned (if known):

_____

_____x

TO THE COURT:

1. The undersigned hereby applies for permission to conduct audio-visual coverage of the above judicial proceeding as follows (check as appropriate):
   ____ televise live   ____ audio (radio) broadcast live

_____ videotape for later broadcast   _____ audiotape for later broadcast

_____ film   _____ use still photography

_____ tape record   _____ other (specify)

2. The scope of coverage requested is (check as appropriate):
    _____ throughout the above proceeding
    _____ during only the following portion(s) of such proceeding (specify):
    _____

_____
(Signature)
_____
(Name)
_____
(Media organization)
_____
_____
(Address)
Dated: _____   (   )_____
                                     (Telephone number)

ORDER DETERMINING APPLICATION FOR AUDIO–VISUAL COVERAGE

_____ Court, _____ County
_____x
In the Matter of an Application to
Conduct Audio-Visual Coverage of

                                     ORDER DETERMINING APPLI-
                                     CATION FOR AUDIO–VISUAL
                                     COVERAGE

            v.   (Index) (Indictment) (Calendar) No. __

_____x

PRESENT: Hon. _____

    An application having been made to this Court on _____,
19____, pursuant to section 131.3 of the Rules of the Chief Administrative Judge by
_____ (news media applicant), requesting permission to (speci-
fy type of coverage) _____ the above judicial proceeding; and
    The Court having reviewed this application and the attached statements and
affidavits presented to the Court concerning the proposed coverage; and
    The Court having consulted with the news media applicant and counsel to all
parties to the above-named proceeding (and with (specify others—*e.g.*, victims,
witnesses, etc.—as appropriate) _____
_____);
    NOW, upon consideration of all relevant factors, including those specified in
section 131.1(c) of the Rules of the Chief Administrative Judge, it is hereby
    ORDERED that the application is (approved) (denied) (approved with the follow-
ing special limitations: _____
_____) (strike out inapplicable language).

173

The basis for the determination is (to be completed unless the application is approved without special limitations *and* no party, victim or prospective witness objects to coverage):

_____

_____

_____

_____

(Justice)   (Judge)

Dated:

PART 132.   UNIFIED COURT SYSTEM EMPLOYEE SUGGESTION INCENTIVE PROGRAM

§ 132.1.   Program

(a) **Purpose.** The Employee Suggestion Incentive Program (hereinafter "program") is designed to encourage and reward unusual and meritorious suggestions by State employees and retired State employees that promote efficiency and economy in the operation of the unified court system.

(b) **Eligibility.** All State employees, persons who retire from State service, and persons who leave State service for reasons other than retirement shall be eligible to participate in the program, and to receive awards thereunder, subject to the following restrictions:

(1) Except as the Chief Administrator may otherwise provide, no State employee may receive an award for a suggestion:

(i) that relates to his or her duties where such duties involve planning or research;

(ii) where, as part of his or her duties, such employee is assigned a particular problem to solve and the suggestion contributes to the solution of such problem; or

(iii) where such employee serves on a special committee and the suggestion falls within the scope of the committee's assignment.

(2) No justice or judge of the unified court system may receive an award for a suggestion.

(3) No person who has left State service for reasons other than retirement may receive an award for a suggestion except where such suggestion was submitted prior to his or her departure from service.

(4) Where a person dies after submitting a suggestion, and an award is approved for such suggestion, the award, if it consists of a cash payment, will be paid to the deceased person's estate.

(c) **Program Coordinator.** There shall be an Employee Suggestion Incentive Program Coordinator who shall be responsible for operation of the program. The coordinator shall:

(1) ensure that suggestion forms are available to employees;

(2) receive suggestions and screen them to determine whether eligibility requirements are met;

(3) solicit comments from appropriate administrative and supervisory authorities; and

(4) transmit all suggestions to the Employee Suggestion Incentive Program Committee.

(d) **Employee Suggestion Incentive Program Committee; Review of Suggestions.** There shall be an Employee Suggestion Incentive Program Committee, consisting of the Deputy Chief Administrative Judges and the Deputy Chief Administrator for Management Support. At appropriate intervals, the committee shall review suggestions received from the program coordinator and shall recommend to the Chief Administrator those that it believes merit an award under the program, including but not limited to suggestions that would be significantly effective in eliminating safety hazards, reducing operational costs or streamlining procedures. The committee also shall propose an appropriate award for each such suggestion. The Chief Administrator shall then make a final determination thereon.

(e) **Awards.** Each eligible person who submits a suggestion that is approved for an award, as provided herein, shall receive a Certificate of Merit signed by the Chief Judge of the State of New York. Where the Chief Administrator determines that implementation of a suggestion will produce or has produced significant benefits to the Unified Court System, the person submitting such suggestion also shall receive a cash payment. Such cash payment shall be fixed in an amount determined in the discretion of the Chief Administrator and shall be no less than $25 and no more than 10 percent of the actual or projected savings to be derived in the first year following implementation of the suggestion.

PART 133. UNIFIED COURT SYSTEM MERIT PERFORMANCE AWARD PROGRAM

§ 133.1. Program

(a) Purpose. The Merit Performance Award Program (hereinafter "program") is designed to recognize and reward employees of the unified court system for meritorious conduct on the job or in the community.

(b) Eligibility. All employees of the unified court system shall be eligible for nomination for an award under this section. Such nomination may be made by any person.

(c) Program Coordinator. There shall be a Merit Performance Award Program Coordinator who shall be responsible for operation of the program. The coordinator shall:

(1) ensure that nomination forms are made available;

(2) receive nominations;

(3) solicit comments thereon from appropriate authorities; and

(4) transmit to the Merit Performance Award Program Committee each nomination that he or she believes should be subject to consideration for an award.

(d) Merit Performance Award Program Committee; Review of Nominations. There shall be a Merit Performance Award Program Committee, consisting of the Deputy Chief Administrative Judges and the Deputy Chief Administrator for Management Support. At appropriate intervals, the committee shall review nominations received from the program coordinator and shall recommend to the Chief Administrator those that it believes merit an award under the program. The Chief Administrator then shall make a final determination thereon.

(e) Awards. Each nomination that is approved for an award by the Chief Administrator shall receive a certificate of commendation signed by the Chief Judge of the State of New York and a unified court system medallion.

PART 134. REPORTING OF FAMILY OFFENSES BY COURTS EXERCISING CRIMINAL JURISDICTION

§ 134.1. Definition of Family Offense

For purposes of this Part, a family offense shall mean any offense committed by defendant against:

(a) a person related to defendant by consanguinity or affinity, whether or not such person resides with defendant;

(b) a person to whom defendant was or is married, whether or not such person resides with defendant;

(c) a person with whom defendant has a child in common, whether or not such person was or is married to defendant or resides with defendant;

(d) a person with whom defendant resides.

§ 134.2. Family Offenses Designation

(a) An accusatory instrument that charges a defendant in a criminal proceeding with a family offense shall include a designation that an offense charged therein is a family offense and a description of the relationship between defendant and the alleged victim. Such designation and description shall be placed on the upper right hand corner of the accusatory instrument in the following form:

FO

Defendant: _____

(relationship to alleged victim)

Alleged victim: _____

(relationship to defendant)

(b) The designation shall be placed on the accusatory instrument by the criminal justice agency that prepares that instrument, provided that where an accusatory instrument charging a family offense has not been prepared by a criminal justice agency, the court shall place such designation on the accusatory instrument.

(c) Where protection of the identity of an alleged victim of a family offense is required by law or otherwise is deemed appropriate, and where placement of the family offense designation on the accusatory instrument would tend to identify the victim, the criminal justice agency may file instead a separate statement annexed to the accusatory instrument, alerting the court that a family offense is charged therein and describing defendant's relationship to the alleged victim. Such statement shall not be made available to the public.

PART 135.　SICK LEAVE BANK PROGRAM

§ 135.1.　Membership

All employees subject to the provision of Part 24 of this Title shall participate in the sick leave bank program established by this Part unless they decline membership in writing by filing the required waiver form with the Division of Human Resources of the Office of Court Administration.

§ 135.2.　Establishment of sick leave bank

(a) At such date as designated by the Chief Administrator of the Courts, each participating employee shall contribute seven hours of accrued and unused sick leave credits to the bank. Employees with insufficient sick leave time as of that date will have the deduction taken from annual leave, or if none, from compensatory time, or if no accruals, from subsequent accruals of sick leave.

(b) Employees who thereafter are appointed to an unrepresented position shall contribute their first seven hours of sick leave credit to the bank unless they waive membership by filing the notice required in section 135.1.

(c) On each succeeding anniversary of the creation of the bank, the Chief Administrator or his or her designee may require each participant to contribute up to seven additional hours of sick leave time, in the manner as set forth in subdivision (a), upon a finding that the bank requires further accruals of sick leave credits for the program to remain viable.

§ 135.3.　Grants from sick leave bank

(a) **Eligibility.** Bank members are eligible to request a grant of sick leave credits from the bank if they (1) have one year of service with the court system, (2) are necessarily absent from work due to serious injury or illness and (3) have exhausted all leave accruals.

(b) **Procedure.** (1) Application for a grant of bank credits shall be on forms promulgated by the Chief Administrator and must include documentation from a medical practitioner setting forth the nature of the injury or illness, the prescribed treatment and the prognosis for return to work.

(2) The Director of the Division of Human Resources or his or her designee shall review all applications and determine what, if any, grant should be made. In making these determinations, the Director shall take into account the nature of the illness or injury, adequacy of the medical documentation submitted and the applicant's length of service and attendance record.

(3) Employees denied bank credits may resubmit the application with additional documentation or further explanation.

(4) Employees may appeal a denial of bank credits to the Administrative Director based upon the materials submitted to the Director of Human Resources. Appeals shall be taken no later than 30 days after the denial.

(5) The Director of Human Resources or his or her designee may periodically require that an employee receiving bank credits supply medical documentation supporting the need for continued absence and may request that an employee be examined by a physician selected by the court system to determine the need for continued absence.

(6) Employees returning to work at an earlier than anticipated date must return all unused credits to the bank.

(c) All grants of bank credits shall be prospective only.

(d) Employees shall be eligible for ten days of bank credit for each year of court system service up to a maximum of 130 days of bank credit. No grant of credit shall exceed 130 days (at a full-time or part-time rate).

(e) **Accruals of annual leave and sick leave.** Employees who are using bank credits shall continue to accrue annual leave and sick leave. Accruals of annual leave will be charged prior to the charging of bank credits. Accruals of sick leave will not be charged until bank credits are exhausted.

(f) Accumulation of leave credits shall not extend any employment beyond the time at which it would otherwise terminate by operation of law, rule or regulation.

§ 135.4.　Separation from service

Employees who retire from state service and had an unused grant of bank credits prior to retirement may retain any unused grant of bank credits, up to a maximum of 70 hours, for retirement service credit or to pay for health insurance in retirement pursuant to section 24.4(b) of the Rules of the Chief Judge.

PART 136.   FEE ARBITRATION IN DOMESTIC RELATIONS MATTERS [REPEALED]

[Repealed, effective January 1, 2002. "Notwithstanding the above, the provisions of Part 136 shall continue to apply to fee disputes in all domestic relations matters subject to that Part in which representation began prior to January 1, 2002."]

§§ 136.1 to 136.11.   [Repealed]

[Repealed, effective January 1, 2002. See also, Part 137.]

PART 137.   FEE DISPUTE RESOLUTION PROGRAM

§ 137.0.   Scope of Program

This Part establishes the New York State Fee Dispute Resolution Program, which provides for the informal and expeditious resolution of fee disputes between attorneys and clients through arbitration and mediation. In accordance with the procedures for arbitration, arbitrators shall determine the reasonableness of fees for professional services, including costs, taking into account all relevant facts and circumstances. Mediation of fee disputes, where available, is strongly encouraged.

§ 137.1.   Application

(a) This Part shall apply where representation has commenced on or after January 1, 2002, to all attorneys admitted to the bar of the State of New York who undertake to represent a client in any civil matter.

(b) This Part shall not apply to any of the following:

(1) representation in criminal matters;

(2) amounts in dispute involving a sum of less than $1000 or more than $50,000, except that an arbitral body may hear disputes involving other amounts if the parties have consented;

(3) claims involving substantial legal questions, including professional malpractice or misconduct;

(4) claims against an attorney for damages or affirmative relief other than adjustment of fee;

(5) disputes where the fee to be paid by the client has been determined pursuant to statute or rule and allowed as of right by a court; or where the fee has been determined pursuant to a court order;

(6) disputes where no attorney's services have been rendered for more than two years;

(7) disputes where the attorney is admitted to practice in another jurisdiction and maintains no office in the State of New York, or where no material portion of the services was rendered in New York;

(8) disputes where the request for arbitration is made by a person who is not the client of the attorney or the legal representative of the client.

§ 137.2.   General

(a) In the event of a fee dispute between attorney and client, whether or not the attorney already has received some or all of the fee in dispute, the client may seek to resolve the dispute by arbitration under this Part. Arbitration under this Part shall be mandatory for an attorney if requested by a client, and the arbitration award shall be final and binding unless de novo review is sought as provided in section 137.8.

(b) The client may consent in advance to submit fee disputes to arbitration under this Part. Such consent shall be stated in a retainer agreement or other writing that specifies that the client has read the official written instructions and procedures for Part 137, and that the client agrees to resolve fee disputes under this Part.

(c) The attorney and client may consent in advance to arbitration pursuant to this Part that is final and binding upon the parties and not subject to de novo review. Such consent shall be in writing in a form prescribed by the Board of Governors.

(d) The attorney and client may consent in advance to submit fee disputes for final and binding arbitration to an arbitral forum other than an arbitral body created by this Part. Such consent shall be in writing in a form prescribed by the Board of Governors. Arbitration in that arbitral forum shall be governed by the rules and procedures of that forum and shall not be subject to this Part.

§ 137.3.   Board of Governors

(a) There shall be a Board of Governors of the New York State Fee Dispute Resolution Program.

(b) The Board of Governors shall consist of 18 members, to be designated from the following: 12 members of the bar of the State of New York and six members of the public who are not lawyers. Members of the bar may include judges and justices of the New York State Unified Court System.

(1) The members from the bar shall be appointed as follows: four by the Chief Judge from the mem-

bership of statewide bar associations and two each by the Presiding Justices of the Appellate Divisions.

(2) The public members shall be appointed as follows: two by the Chief Judge and one each by the Presiding Justices of the Appellate Divisions.

Appointing officials shall give consideration to appointees who have some background in alternative dispute resolution.

(c) The Chief Judge shall designate the chairperson.

(d) Board members shall serve for terms of three years and shall be eligible for reappointment for one additional term. The initial terms of service shall be designated by the Chief Judge such that six members serve one–year terms, six members serve two–year terms, and six members serve three–year terms. A person appointed to fill a vacancy occurring other than expiration of a term of office shall be appointed for the unexpired term of the member he or she succeeds.

(e) Eleven members of the Board of Governors shall constitute a quorum. Decisions shall be made by a majority of the quorum.

(f) Members of the Board of Governors shall serve without compensation but shall be reimbursed for their reasonable, actual and direct expenses incurred in furtherance of their official duties.

(g) The Board of Governors, with the approval of the four Presiding Justices of the Appellate Divisions, shall adopt such guidelines and standards as may be necessary and appropriate for the operation of programs under this Part, including, but not limited to: accrediting arbitral bodies to provide fee dispute resolution services under this Part; prescribing standards regarding the training and qualifications of arbitrators; monitoring the operation and performance of arbitration programs to insure their conformance with the guidelines and standards established by this Part and by the Board of Governors; and submission by arbitral bodies of annual reports in writing to the Board of Governors.

(h) The Board of Governors shall submit to the Administrative Board of the Courts an annual report in such form as the Administrative Board shall require.

§ 137.4. Arbitral Bodies

(a) A fee dispute resolution program recommended by the Board of Governors, and approved by the Presiding Justice of the Appellate Division in the judicial department where the program is established, shall be established and administered in each county or in a combination of counties. Each program shall be established and administered by a local bar association (the "arbitral body") to the extent practicable. The New York State Bar Association, the Unified Court System through the District Administrative Judges, or such other entity as the Board of Gover-

nors may recommend also may be designated as an arbitral body in a fee dispute resolution program approved pursuant to this Part.

(b) Each arbitral body shall:

(1) establish written instructions and procedures for administering the program, subject to the approval of the board of Governors and consistent with this Part. The procedures shall include a process for selecting and assigning arbitrators to hear and determine the fee disputes covered by this Part. Arbitral bodies are strongly encouraged to include nonlawyer members of the public in any pool of arbitrators that will be used for the designation of multi–member arbitrator panels.

(2) require that arbitrators file a written oath or affirmation to faithfully and fairly arbitrate all disputes that come before them.

(3) be responsible for the daily administration of the arbitration program and maintain all necessary file, records, information and documentation required for purposes of the operation of the program, in accordance with directives and procedures established by the Board of Governors.

(4) prepare an annual report for the Board of Governors containing a statistical synopsis of fee dispute resolution activity and such other data as the Board shall prescribe.

(5) designate one or more persons to administer the program and serve as a liaison to the public, the bar, the Board of Governors and the grievance committees of the Appellate Division.

§ 137.5. Venue

A fee dispute shall be heard by the arbitral body handling disputes in the county in which the majority of the legal services were performed. For good cause shown, a dispute may be transferred from one arbitral body to another. The Board of Governors shall resolve any disputes between arbitral bodies over venue.

§ 137.6. Arbitration Procedure

(a)(1) Except as set forth in paragraph (2), where the attorney and client cannot agree as to the attorney's fee, the attorney shall forward a written notice to the client, entitled "Notice of Client's Right to Arbitrate," by certified mail or by personal service. The notice (i) shall be in a form approved by the Board of Governors; (ii) shall contain a statement of the client's right to arbitrate; (iii) shall advise that the client has 30 days from receipt of the notice in which to elect to resolve the dispute under this Part; (iv) shall be accompanied by the written instructions and procedures for the arbitral body having jurisdiction over the fee dispute, which explain how to commence a fee arbitration proceeding; and (v) shall be accompanied by a copy of the "request for arbitration" form necessary to commence the arbitration proceeding.

(2) Where the client has consented in advance to submit fee disputes to arbitration as set forth in subdivisions (b) and (c) of section 137.2 of this Part, and where the attorney and client cannot agree as to the attorney's fee, the attorney shall forward to the client, by certified mail or by personal service, a copy of the "request for arbitration" form necessary to commence the arbitration proceeding along with such notice and instructions as shall be required by the rules and guidelines of the Board of Governors, and the provisions of subdivision (b) of this section shall not apply.

(b) If the attorney forwards to the client by certified mail or personal service a notice of the clients right to arbitrate, and the client does not file a request for arbitration within 30 days after the notice was received or served, the attorney may commence an action in a court of competent jurisdiction to recover the fee and the client no longer shall have the right to request arbitration pursuant to this Part with respect to the fee dispute at issue. An attorney who institutes an action to recover a fee must allege in the complaint (i) that the client received notice under this Part of the client's right to pursue arbitration or (ii) that the dispute is not otherwise covered by this Part.

(c) In the event the client determines to pursue arbitration on the client's own initiative, the client may directly contact the arbitral body having jurisdiction over the fee dispute. Alternatively, the client may contact the attorney, who shall be under an obligation to refer the client to the arbitral body having jurisdiction over the dispute. The arbitral body then shall forward to the client the appropriate papers set forth in subdivision (a) necessary for commencement to the arbitration.

(d) If the client elects to submit the dispute to arbitration, the client shall file the "request for arbitration form" with the appropriate arbitral body, and the arbitral body shall mail a copy of the "request for arbitration" to the named attorney together with an "attorney fee response" to be completed by the attorney and returned to the arbitral body within 15 days of mailing. The attorney shall include with the "attorney fee response" a certification that a copy of the response was served upon the client.

(e) Upon receipt of the attorney's response, the arbitral body shall designate the arbitrator or arbitrators who will hear the dispute and shall expeditiously schedule a hearing. The parties must receive at least 15 days notice in writing of the time and place of the hearing and of the identity of the arbitrator or arbitrators.

(f) Either party may request the removal of an arbitrator based upon the arbitrator's personal or professional relationship to a party or counsel. A request for removal must be made to the arbitral body no later than five days prior to the scheduled date of the hearing. The arbitral body shall have the final decision concerning the removal of an arbitrator.

(g) The client may not withdraw from the process after the arbitral body has received the "attorney fee response." If the client seeks to withdraw at any time thereafter, the arbitration will proceed as scheduled whether or not the client appears, and a decision will be made on the basis of the evidence presented.

(h) If the attorney without good cause fails to respond to a request for arbitration or otherwise does not participate in the arbitration, the arbitration will proceed as scheduled and a decision will be made on the basis of the evidence presented.

(i) Any party may participate in the arbitration hearing without a personal appearance by submitting to the arbitrator testimony and exhibits by written declaration under penalty of perjury.

§ 137.7. Arbitration Hearing

(a) Arbitrators shall have the power to:

(1) take and hear evidence pertaining to the proceeding;

(2) administer oaths and affirmations; and

(3) compel, by subpoena, the attendance of witnesses and the production of books, papers and documents pertaining to the proceeding.

(b) The rules of evidence need not be observed at the hearing.

(c) Either party, at his or her own expense, may be represented by counsel.

(d) The burden shall be on the attorney to prove the reasonableness of the fee by a preponderance of the evidence and to present documentation of the work performed and the billing history. The client may then present his or her account of the services rendered and the time expended. Witnesses may be called by the parties. The client shall have the right of final reply.

(e) Any party may provide for a stenographic or other record at the party's expense. Any other party to the arbitration shall be entitled to a copy of said record upon written request and payment of the expense thereof.

(f) The arbitration award shall be issued no later than 30 days after the date of the hearing. Arbitration awards shall be in writing and shall specify the bases for the determination. Except as set forth in section 137.8, all arbitration awards shall be final and binding.

(g) Should the arbitrator or arbitral body become aware of evidence of professional misconduct as a result of the fee dispute resolution process, that arbitrator or body shall refer such evidence to the appropriate grievance committee of the Appellate Division for the appropriate action.

(h) In any arbitration conducted under this Part, an arbitrator shall have the same immunity that attaches in judicial proceedings.

§ 137.8.   De Novo Review

(a) A party aggrieved by the arbitration award may commence an action on the merits of the fee dispute in a court of competent jurisdiction within 30 days after the arbitration award has been mailed. If no action is commenced within 30 days of the mailing of the arbitration award, the award shall become final and binding.

(b) Any party who fails to participate in the hearing shall not be entitled to seek de novo review absent good cause for such failure to participate.

(c) Arbitrators shall not be called as witnesses nor shall the arbitration award be admitted in evidence at the trial de novo.

§ 137.9.   Filing Fees

Upon application to the Board of Governors, and approval by the Presiding Justice of the Appellate Division in the judicial department where the arbitral program is established, an arbitral body may require payment by the parties of a filing fee. The filing fee shall be reasonably related to the cost of providing the service and shall not be in such an amount as to discourage use of the program.

§ 137.10.   Confidentiality

All proceedings and hearings commenced and conducted in accordance with this Part, including all papers in the arbitration case file, shall be confidential, except to the extent necessary to take ancillary legal action with respect to a fee matter.

§ 137.11.   Failure to Participate in Arbitration

All attorneys are required to participate in the arbitration program established by this Part upon the filing of a request for arbitration by a client in conformance with these rules. An attorney who without good cause fails to participate in the arbitration process shall be referred to the appropriate grievance committee of the Appellate Division for appropriate action.

§ 137.12.   Mediation

(a) Arbitral bodies are strongly encouraged to offer mediation services as part of a mediation program approved by the Board of Governors. The mediation program shall permit arbitration pursuant to this Part in the event the mediation does not resolve the fee dispute.

(b) All mediation proceedings and all settlement discussions and offers of settlement are confidential and may not be disclosed in any subsequent arbitration.

APPENDIX A.   STANDARDS AND GUIDELINES

Pursuant to Part 137 of the Rules of the Chief Administrator, Title 22 of the Official Compilations of Codes, Rules and Regulations of the State of New York, the following Standards and Guidelines are promulgated by the Board of Governors of the New York State Attorney–Client Fee Dispute Resolution Program ("Board") to implement the Attorney–Client Fee Dispute Resolution Program and Part 137.

Section 1.   Policy

It is the policy of the Appellate Divisions of the Supreme Court and the Board of Governors to encourage out-of-court resolution of fee disputes between attorneys and clients in fair, impartial and efficient programs established and administered by bar associations.

Section 2.   Definitions

A. **"Client"** means a person or entity who receives legal services or advice from a lawyer on a fee basis in the lawyer's professional capacity.

B. **"Board"** means the Board of Governors of the Attorney–Client Fee Dispute Resolution Program established under Part 137 of the Rules of the Chief Administrator.

C. **"Program"** means the Attorney–Client Fee Dispute Resolution Program established under Part 137 and these Standards and Guidelines.

D. **"Local program"** means a bar association-sponsored fee dispute resolution program approved by the Board.

E. **"Neutral"** means a person who serves as an arbitrator or mediator in a local program under Part 137 and these Standards and Guidelines.

F. **"Approval"** by the Board of Governors means, where so required by Part 137, recommendation by the Board of Governors with the approval of the appropriate Presiding Justice of the Appellate Division.

Section 3.   Organizational Framework

A. Arbitration and mediation of fee disputes between attorneys and clients in New York State pursuant to Part 137 shall, to the extent practicable, take place through local programs.

B. Local programs may provide fee dispute resolution services under Part 137 only if they have been duly approved to do so by the Board.

C. A local program may be approved by the Board to provide fee dispute resolution services in more than one county. One or more bar associations may combine to administer a joint local program in one or more counties.

D. In a county where no local program exists, the office of the Administrative Judge of the Judicial District encompassing such county shall administer a program approved by the Board.

Section 4.   Approval Process

A. In order to receive approval from the Board, a prospective local program must complete an approval form adopted by the Board and provide for the Board's review a written statement of rules and procedures for the proposed local program.

B. The local program's written rules and procedures shall comply with Part 137 and these Standards and Guidelines and shall provide for a fair, impartial and efficient process for the resolution of attorney-client fee disputes.

C. The following information must be provided in the approval form and/or in the local program's proposed rules and procedures submitted to the Board:

1. Whether the local program proposes to charge filing fees; the amount, if any, it proposes to charge; and the local program's fee waiver policy, if any;

2. Procedures governing the selection and assignment of neutrals consistent with section 8 of these Standards and Guidelines;

3. A description of the local program's proposal to recruit, train and maintain a sufficient qualified pool of neutrals;

4. A contact person who will have responsibility for the administration of the local program, including the contact person's name, telephone and fax numbers, and business and e-mail addresses;

5. Copies of materials, if any, to be provided to clients and/or attorneys explaining the local program;

6. Copies of manuals or materials, if any, to be used in training neutrals; and

7. The local program's mediation rules and procedures, if applicable.

Section 5.   Responsibilities of Local Programs

A. Local programs shall be responsible for the day-to-day administration of the Program as set forth in section 137.4(b)(3) and these Standards and Guidelines. Each local program shall designate a contact person to serve as liaison to, among others, the disputants, the public, the members of the bar, the Board of Governors and attorney disciplinary authorities.

B. Local programs shall be responsible for determining that the fee dispute falls within the Program's jurisdiction in accordance with screening guidelines or protocols developed by the Board. Any unresolved inquiries shall be referred promptly to the Board for final resolution.

C. Local programs shall prepare a brief annual written report to the Board containing a statistical summary of fee dispute resolution activity and such other data as the Board may request. Local programs shall be responsible for maintaining a log of complaints made by members of the public, clients, attorneys or neutrals regarding the Program, local programs or their personnel, including neutrals. Local programs shall advise the Board of Governors of all complaints in a timely manner, and the complaint log shall be available for review by the Board of Governors upon request.

D. Fee dispute resolution proceedings shall be conducted on neutral sites such as local program premises, Unified Court System facilities and neutrals' offices; they shall not take place in the office of any interested party unless all parties consent in writing.

Section 6.   The Fee Dispute Resolution Process

A. Unless the client has previously consented in writing to submit fee disputes to the fee dispute resolution process established by Part 137, arbitration under this Program shall be voluntary for the client. Mediation under this Program shall be voluntary for the attorney and the client.

B. Prior Written Agreements Between the Attorney and Client Under Section 137.2

1. Under section 137.2(b), the client may consent in advance to submit fee disputes to arbitration under Part 137. To be valid on the part of the client, such consent must be knowing and informed. The client's consent under section 137.2(b) shall be stated in a retainer agreement or other writing specifying that the client has read the official written instructions and procedures for Part 137, and the Board-approved written instructions and procedures for the local program designated to hear fee disputes between the attorney and client, and that the client consents to resolve fee disputes under Part 137.

2. Under section 137.2(c), the attorney and client may consent in advance to submit to arbitration that is final and binding and not subject to a trial de novo. To be valid on the part of the client, such consent must be knowing and informed and obtained in the manner set forth in section 6(B)(1) of these Standards and Guidelines, except that the retainer agreement or other writing shall also state that the client understands that he or she is waiving the right to reject an arbitration award and subsequently commence a trial de novo in court.

3. Where an agreement to arbitrate exists between the attorney and client under either section 137.2(b) or (c), those provisions of section 137.6(a) (1) and (b) relating to the notice of client's right to arbitrate shall not apply and no further notice of the right to arbitrate shall be required. In this circumstance, section 137.6 (a)(2) shall apply and either party may commence the dispute resolution process by filing a "request for arbitration" form with the local program designated to hear fee disputes between the attorney and client, together with a copy of the parties' agreement to arbitrate.

4. Under section 137.2(d), the attorney and client may consent in advance to final and binding fee arbitration in an arbitral forum other than one created under Part 137. To be valid on the part of the client, such consent must be knowing and informed and must be obtained in a retainer agreement or other writing. Arbitration in an arbitral forum outside Part 137 shall be governed by the rules and procedures of that forum. The Board may maintain information concerning other established arbitral programs and shall provide contact information for such programs upon request.

5. Fee disputes may be referred to local programs by means not specifically described in Part 137, including but not limited to, attorney disciplinary authorities, bar associations, and employees, officers or judges of the courts. In those situations, the local program contact person shall provide the client with information about the Program.

Section 7. Board of Governors

A. The Board shall have the power to interpret Part 137 and these Standards and Guidelines.

B. The Board shall monitor the operation and performance of local programs to ensure their conformance with Part 137 and these Standards and Guidelines.

C. The Board shall have the power to deny or revoke approval to local programs for failure to comply with Part 137 and these Standards and Guidelines or where the Board determines that the local program does not provide for a fair, impartial or efficient fee dispute resolution process. The Board shall review and approve the appointment of neutrals for service in local programs under Part 137. The Board shall remove neutrals from such service where they have failed to meet the requirements of Part 137.

D. The Board shall maintain a list of approved local programs under Part 137, including information concerning each local program's rules and procedures.

E. The Board shall submit an annual report to the Administrative Board of the Courts regarding the Program and containing recommendations designed to improve it.

F. The Board shall take appropriate steps to educate and inform the public about the Program.

G. The Board shall have the power to perform acts necessary for the effective operation of the Program and the implementation of Part 137 and these Standards and Guidelines.

Section 8. Selection and Assignment of Neutrals

A. Each local program shall establish procedures governing the selection and assignment of neutrals subject to approval by the Board to ensure that they provide for a fair, impartial and efficient fee dispute resolution process. Each local program shall maintain a list or lists of Board approved neutrals, organized by area of practice, where appropriate. When selecting a neutral, the local program shall select the next available neutral with appropriate experience for the proceeding in question.

B. Unless otherwise approved by the Board:

1. Disputes involving a sum of less than $6,000 shall be submitted to one attorney arbitrator;

2. Disputes involving a sum of $6,000 or more shall be submitted to a panel of three arbitrators, which shall include at least one nonlawyer member of the public.

Section 9. Qualifications and Duties of Arbitrators

A. Both lawyers and nonlawyers may serve as arbitrators.

B. In recruiting arbitrators, local programs should make every effort to ensure that arbitrators represent a wide range of law practices and firm sizes, a diversity of nonlawyer professions within the community and a cross-section of the community.

C. Prospective arbitrators shall submit a summary of credentials to the local program, copies of which the local program shall keep on record. Each local program shall forward to the Board of Governors a list of persons recommended for approval as arbitrators under Part 137 together with a summary of their credentials.

D. Arbitrators shall be appointed by local programs pursuant to their rules and procedures, subject to approval by the Board of Governors to ensure that such arbitrators meet the requirements of Part 137.

E. All arbitrators must sign a written oath or affirmation to faithfully and fairly arbitrate all disputes that come before them, which written oath or affirmation shall be kept on file by the local program.

F. All arbitrators must conduct a conflict of interest check prior to accepting a case. A person who has any personal bias regarding a party or the subject matter of the dispute, a financial interest in the subject matter of the dispute, or a close personal relationship or financial relationship with a party to the dispute shall not serve as an arbitrator. An arbitrator shall disclose any information that he or she has reason to believe may provide a basis for recusal.

G. Arbitrators shall serve as volunteers; provided, however, that local programs may provide for reimbursement of arbitrators' expenses.

H. In making an award, arbitrators shall specify in a concise statement the amount of and basis for the award.

I. Arbitrators have a duty to maintain the confidentiality of all proceedings, hearings and communications conducted in accordance with Part 137, including all papers in the arbitration case file, except to the extent necessary in connection with ancillary legal action with respect to a fee matter. Arbitrators should refer all requests for information concerning a fee dispute to the local program contact person. Arbitrators shall not be competent to testify in a subsequent proceeding or trial de novo.

Section 10.   Training of Arbitrators

Arbitrators shall complete a minimum of six hours of fee dispute arbitration training approved by the Board. The Board may take previous arbitration training and experience under consideration in determining whether the foregoing training requirement has been met; provided, however, that all arbitrators must complete a short orientation program designed to introduce them to Part 137's practices and procedures. Arbitrators may be required to undergo periodic refresher courses.

Section 11.   Mediation

A. Local programs may mediate fee disputes with the written consent of the attorney and client.

B. Participation in mediation does not waive the right to arbitration under Part 137, nor does it waive the right to a trial de novo.

C. Both lawyers and nonlawyers may serve as mediators.

D. In recruiting mediators, local programs should make every effort to ensure that mediators represent a wide range of law practices and firm sizes, a diversity of nonlawyer professions within the community and a cross-section of the community.

E. Mediators shall submit a summary of credentials to the local program, which the local program shall keep on record.

F. Mediators shall complete Board-approved mediation training. The Board may take previous mediation training and experience under consideration in determining whether the foregoing training requirement has been met; provided, however, that all mediators must complete a short orientation program designed to introduce them to Part 137's practices and procedures. Mediators may be required to undergo periodic refresher courses.

G. The local program shall appoint mediators pursuant to its rules of procedure. The attorney or client may challenge a mediator for cause.

H. All mediators must sign a written oath or affirmation to faithfully and fairly mediate all disputes that come before them, which written oath or affirmation shall be kept on file by the local program.

I. All mediators must conduct a conflict of interest check prior to accepting a case. A person who has any personal bias regarding a party or the subject matter of the dispute, a financial interest in the subject matter of the dispute, or a close personal relationship or financial relationship with a party to the dispute shall not serve as a mediator. A mediator shall disclose any information that he or she has reason to believe may provide a basis for recusal.

J. Mediators shall serve as volunteers; provided, however, that local programs may provide for reimbursement of mediators' expenses.

K. A mediator may not serve as an arbitrator in a subsequent arbitration involving the parties to the mediation absent the parties' written consent.

L. Mediators have a duty to maintain the confidentiality of the process, including all communications, documents and negotiations or settlement discussions between the parties and the mediator, except to the extent necessary in connection with ancillary legal action with respect to a fee matter. Mediators should refer all requests for information concerning a fee dispute to the local program contact person. Mediators shall not be competent to testify in any civil or administrative proceeding, including any subsequent fee arbitration or trial de novo, as to any statement, condition, or decision that occurred at or in conjunction with the mediation.

M. During the mediation, upon any agreement of the parties, in whole or in part, the parties shall reduce such agreement to writing. If no agreement is reached by the parties, the mediator shall, in a manner consistent with section 11(L), so inform the local program contact person in writing, and the dispute will be referred for arbitration.

Section 12.   Trial de Novo

A. A party aggrieved by the arbitration award may commence an action on the merits of the fee dispute in a court with jurisdiction over the amount in dispute within 30 days after the arbitration award has been mailed. If no action is commenced within 30 days of the mailing of the arbitration award, the award shall become final and binding.

B. Each local program shall adopt procedures designed to ensure that a party provides notice to the local program when the party commences an action for de novo review.

C. Any party who fails to participate in the arbitration hearing shall not be entitled to a trial de novo absent good cause for such failure to participate.

D. Arbitrators shall not be called as witnesses, nor shall the arbitration award or record of the proceedings be admitted in evidence at the trial de novo.

Section 13. Enforcement

A. In the event that an attorney does not comply with the arbitration award, the local program may appoint an attorney pro bono to assist the client with enforcement of the award. In such an event, the local program contact person shall first write to inform the client's attorney of the obligation to comply with the award and of the local program's policy, if any, of appointing an attorney to assist the client pro bono.

Section 14. Fee Dispute Resolution Forms

A. The following forms are intended to assist in the timely processing of fee arbitration matters. The Board shall develop and disseminate these forms to local programs.

1. Notice of Client's Right to Arbitrate
2. Request for Arbitration
3. Attorney Response
4. Written Instructions and Procedures for Part 137
5. Client Consent to Resolve Fee Disputes Under Part 137.2(b)
6. Consent to Waive Trial De Novo under Part 137.2(c)
7. Consent to Final and Binding Arbitration in an Arbitral Forum Outside Part 137 under Part 137.2(d)
8. Arbitration Award
9. Agreement to Mediate
10. Neutral's Oath

Section 15. Correspondence

All written requests and correspondence to the Board may be sent to:

Board of Governors

Attorney–Client Fee Dispute Resolution Program

c/o UCS State ADR Office

25 Beaver Street, 8th Floor

New York, New York 10004

PART 138. JUSTICE COURT ASSISTANCE PROGRAM.

§ 138.1. General

This Part prescribes rules and regulations governing administration of the Justice Court Assistance Program. This Program was established by the Legislature to provide a means by which towns and villages may obtain limited State funding to improve operation of their Justice Courts.

§ 138.2. Purposes for which Justice Court Assistance Program Funds may be Used

Funding available pursuant to this Part may be used for any purpose having as its end enhancement of the Justice Courts' ability to provide suitable and sufficient services to their respective communities. These purposes may include, but shall not be limited to, automation of court operations; provision of appropriate means for the recording of court proceedings; provision of lawbooks, treatises and related materials; provision of appropriate training for justices and for nonjudicial court staff; and the improvement or expansion of court facilities. Funding shall not be used to compensate justices and nonjudicial court staff, nor shall it be used as a means of reducing funding provided by a town or village to its Justice Court.

§ 138.3. Application procedures

No Justice Court Assistance Program funds may be disbursed unless the Chief Administrator first approves an application therefor as provided hereunder.

(a) **Who May Apply.** Each town and village having a Justice Court may make an individual application for funding, or two or more such towns or villages, or towns and villages, may make a joint application for funding.

(b) **When and where to apply.** For a town or village to be eligible for a disbursement from funds made available by appropriation to the Unified Court System for any State fiscal year, such town or village must file its application with the Chief Administrator on or before the first day of February in such fiscal year.

(c) **Contents of Application.** Each application filed with the Chief Administrator pursuant to this Part must be signed by at least one justice of the court(s) affected thereby other than an acting justice, and by the supervisor of any town, and the mayor of any village, that is party to the application. Each such application shall be in such form as the Chief Administrator shall prescribe and shall include a certified copy of a resolution of the legislative body of each municipality that is a party to the application evidencing its authorization thereof; the information specified in paragraphs (a) through (c) of section 849–i(1) of the Judiciary Law, except to the extent that it already has been made available to the Chief Administrator; and such other information as the Chief Administrator shall require.

The Chief Administrator may, at any time following the filing of an application for funding, request that an applicant or applicants furnish additional information or documentation to support such application.

(d) Special Application by a Magistrates' Association. Notwithstanding any other provision of this section, one or more duly organized county or multi–county magistrates' associations may make an individual or joint application for funding solely for the purpose of enabling the provision of appropriate training for justices and/or for nonjudicial court staff of the courts represented by such association(s). In such event, the other provisions of this section shall not apply except that:

(1) the magistrates' association applicant(s) shall be subject to the same requirements applicable to town and village applicants pursuant to subdivision (b) of this section; and

(2) the application shall be in such form as the Chief Administrator shall prescribe and shall be signed by a duly-authorized officer of the applicant (or by a duly-authorized officer of each of the applicants if it is a joint application).

§ 138.4. Approval

The Chief Administrator shall approve applicants for funding pursuant to this Part. Such approval shall be made as soon as practicable. In determining whether to approve an applicant, the Chief Administrator shall consider:

(a) whether the applicant has complied with these rules and regulations and all pertinent provisions of Article 21–B of the Judiciary Law;

(b) the likely impact of approving its application upon the court or courts to be affected thereby, upon the communities served, and upon the judiciary generally;

(c) the availability of other sources of funding to pay some or all of the costs for which the application seeks funding under the program;

(d) the number and content of all other applications for funding then available under the program, and the amount of such funding; and

(e) the extent of funding already received under the program by the applicant (or joint applicants) pursuant to past applications.

§ 138.5. Payment

(a) General. Once the Chief Administrator approves an application for funding pursuant to this Part, he or she shall authorize a disbursement of funds in any amount up to the amount sought in the application and shall specify the purpose or purposes to which such funds may be applied; provided, however, he or she shall not approve a disbursement of funds exceeding $30,000, unless the application is a joint application in which event he or she shall not approve a disbursement of funds exceeding the product of the number of joint applicants and $30,000. Any disbursement of funds hereunder shall at all times be subject to the availability of appropriations.

(b) How Made. A disbursement of funds pursuant to subdivision (a) of this section may be by advance payment to the applicant (or joint applicants, as appropriate) before it incurs a cost or costs for which funding has been authorized, by reimbursement to the applicant after it incurs and pays such cost or costs in the first instance, or by some combination thereof, as the Chief Administrator may determine to be appropriate. Unless the Chief Administrator shall otherwise provide, funds disbursed hereunder shall be spent within 180 days of the applicant's receipt thereof.

§ 138.6. Program Evaluation

(a) The Chief Administrator may require each town and village for which an application for funding pursuant to this Part has been approved to file such reports as may be necessary to enable him or her to monitor the operation and success of the Justice Court Assistance Program.

(b) The State Comptroller, the Chief Administrator and their authorized representatives shall have the power to inspect, examine and audit the fiscal affairs of each town and village for which an application for funding pursuant to this Part has been approved to the extent necessary to determine whether the funding received has been used for the purpose or purposes specified by the Chief Administrator in approving the application, and whether there has been compliance with these rules and regulations and the provisions of Article 21–B of the Judiciary Law.

(c) The Chief Administrator may halt the disbursement of funds pursuant to this Part or confiscate any property purchased with funds disbursed hereunder at any time he or she determines that the recipient(s) of such funds or the holders of such property are not using them in an authorized manner, or that any of these rules and regulations or the provisions of Article 21–B are being violated.

PART 140.   CIVIL ACTIONS OR PROCEEDINGS BROUGHT BY INMATES

§ 140.1.   General

This Part shall apply where a federal, state or local inmate under sentence for conviction of a crime who is seeking to commence a civil action or proceeding, other than a proceeding brought under CPLR Article 78 that alleges a failure to correctly award or certify jail time credit due an inmate, brings a motion for permission to proceed as a poor person pursuant to Article 11 of the Civil Practice Law and Rules ("CPLR"). For purposes of this Part: (i) "appropriate correctional official" shall mean the superintendent or other public official in charge of the facility where the inmate is confined, and (ii) "inmate's trust fund account" shall mean an inmate's correctional facility trust fund account or the institutional equivalent thereof.

§ 140.2.   Application

(a) As required by subdivision (f) of section 1101 of the CPLR, and in addition to such other papers as may be required by law, such inmate shall complete and file with the court the form affidavit referred to in subdivision (d) of that section along with the summons and complaint or petition or notice of petition or order to show cause. Such affidavit shall be in the form set forth in Appendix A–1 of this Part.

(b) Upon receipt of an inmate's motion, the court may assign an index number to the underlying action or proceeding or, in a court other than Supreme or County Court, such other filing number as is appropriate to the court. The motion shall thereupon be assigned to a judge of the court who, prior to disposition thereof, shall cause to be obtained such information concerning the inmate's trust fund account as is required by paragraph one of subdivision (f) of section 1101 of the CPLR.

§ 140.3.   Disposition of Motion

(a) **Form of Order.** Upon determining an inmate's motion for permission to proceed as a poor person, the court shall issue an order, which shall be in the form set forth in Appendix A–2 of this Part.

(b) **Order Granting Motion.** Where a court grants an inmate's motion for permission to proceed as a poor person, and the court's order requires the inmate to make an initial payment of a portion of the filing fee that is imposed, the inmate may not file a request for judicial intervention in the action or proceeding, nor shall the court report any outstanding fee obligation to the appropriate correctional official, to be collected from the inmate's trust fund account, until such initial payment is fully received by the court. Once such initial payment is fully received by the court, or where the court's order does not require the inmate to make an initial payment, the action or proceeding may go forward as if all fees required therein had been paid and the court shall report such amount of the filing fee as remains unpaid as an outstanding obligation, to be collected from the inmate's trust fund account, to the appropriate correctional official.

(c) **Order Denying Motion.** Where a court denies an inmate's motion for permission to proceed as a poor person, the inmate may not file a request for judicial intervention in the action or proceeding until the inmate pays the proper index number or first paper fee, as appropriate, to the court. In the event no such payment is made within 120 days of the date of the order, the action or proceeding shall be dismissed by the court.

§ 140.4.   Special Procedure Where Fee is Collected From a Source Other Than an Inmate's Trust Fund Account

Where (i) a court issues an order granting an inmate's motion for permission to proceed as a poor person and reports some or all of the filing fee imposed pursuant to such order to the appropriate correctional official as an outstanding obligation to be collected from the inmate's trust fund account, and (ii) thereafter the inmate or a person acting on his or her behalf pays the amount of the outstanding obligation to the clerk of the court, the court shall forthwith issue an order directing the appropriate correctional official to cease collection of the obligation and to restore to the inmate's trust fund account any funds theretofore withheld therefrom to satisfy the obligation. Such order shall be in the form set forth in Appendix A–3 of this Part.

§ 140.5.   Claims in the Court of Claims

This Part shall not apply where an inmate seeks to commence a claim in the court of claims. Such an inmate must comply with the provisions of section 206.5–b of these rules.

APPENDIX A–1

_____COURT

STATE OF NEW YORK

_____COUNTY

-- x

           Plaintiff,   Affidavit in Support of Application
                                        Pursuant to CPLR 1101
                                        (Poor Person Status for an Inmate)

                                        INDEX/FILE#
                                        DIN#
            Defendant.   NYSID#

-- x

State of New York   )
) ss:
County of _____)

_____ being duly sworn, says:

1. I am the Plaintiff/Petitioner in the above-captioned action/proceeding; I am an inmate under sentence for conviction of a crime incarcerated in (include name and mailing address)_____, a federal/state/local correctional facility; and I submit this affidavit in support of my application for poor person status in such action/proceeding.

2. During the past six months:

☐ I was not incarcerated at any other federal/state/local correctional facility.

☐ I was incarcerated in the following federal/state/local correctional facilities) (include name(s) and mailing address(es)) in addition to the facility in which I am now incarcerated:

_____

3. I currently receive income from the following sources, exclusive of correctional facility wages:

_____

_____

4. I own the following property (list all real and personal property, including bank accounts and securities in which you have a beneficial interest, other than miscellaneous personal property of nominal value):

Property: Value:

_____   _____
_____   _____
_____   _____

5. I am responsible for payment of the following debts:

Debt: Amount:

_____   _____
_____   _____
_____   _____

6.   I have no savings, property, assets or income other than as set forth herein.

7.   I am unable to pay the costs, fees and expenses necessary to prosecute the above-captioned action/proceeding.

8.   There is no other person who has a beneficial interest in the recovery I am seeking in the above-captioned action/proceeding who is able to pay the fees, costs and expenses necessary to its prosecution.

9.   The nature of the above-captioned action/proceeding and the facts therein are described in my pleadings and in other papers filed with the court.

10.   I have made no prior request for this relief in the above-captioned action/proceeding.

_____
(signature)

Sworn to before me this_____ day
of _____, _____
_____ Notary Public

AUTHORIZATION

I, _____, inmate number _____ request and authorize the agency holding me in custody to send to the Clerk of the Court certified copies of the correctional facility trust fund account statement (or the institutional equivalent) for the past six months.

In the event my application for poor person status in the above-captioned action/proceeding is granted by the Court, I further request and authorize the agency in which I am incarcerated to deduct the amount of any outstanding obligation reported to such agency by the Court pursuant to CPLR 1101(f)(2) from my correctional facility trust fund account (or institutional equivalent) and to disburse such money as instructed by the Court.

This authorization is furnished in connection with the above-captioned action/proceeding, and shall be valid as to any agency into whose custody I may hereafter be transferred.

I UNDERSTAND THAT THE FULL AMOUNT OF THE OUTSTANDING OBLIGATION REFERRED TO HEREIN WILL BE PAID BY AUTOMATIC DEDUCTION FROM MY CORRECTIONAL FACILITY TRUST FUND ACCOUNT EVEN IF MY CASE IS DISMISSED.

_____
(signature)

APPENDIX A–2

_____COURT
STATE OF NEW YORK
_____COUNTY

-------------------------------------- x

Plaintiff,

ORDER Determining Application for
Poor Person Status for an Inmate
(CPLR 1101)

INDEX/FILE#
DIN#
Defendant.   NYSID#

-------------------------------------- x

Nature of action/proceeding: _____ _____, being a federal/state/local inmate under sentence for conviction of a crime and having made application pursuant to CPLR 1101 poor person status in the above-captioned action/proceeding,

It is hereby ORDERED that this application is:

☐ DENIED, and, as required by section 1101 of the CPLR, all applicable filing fees in the action/proceeding must be paid within 120 days of the date of this order, or else the action/proceeding shall be deemed dismissed without further order of the Court.

☐ GRANTED, and the applicant/inmate is directed to pay a reduced filing fee of $___ dollars and he or she shall be liable for no other fees in the action/proceeding before this Court unless a recovery by judgment or by settlement is had in his or her favor in which event the Court may direct him or her to pay out of the recovery all or part of such fees as are hereby forgiven.

It is further ORDERED:

☐ That, the Court having found that the applicant/inmate can reasonably afford same, the applicant/inmate IS REQUIRED to make an initial payment of $_____ of the reduced filing fee required hereunder; and that, once such initial payment is fully received by the court, the amount of the difference between such initial payment and the reduced filing fee required hereunder, or $_____, shall be assessed as an outstanding obligation of the applicant/inmate and reported to the superintendent or other public official in charge of the facility where the applicant/inmate is confined, who shall collect such amount from the applicant/inmate in the same manner as mandatory surcharges are collected pursuant to section 60.35(5) of the Penal Law.

☐ That, the Court having found that exceptional circumstances render the applicant/inmate unable to pay any filing fee at this time, the applicant/inmate IS NOT REQUIRED to make any initial payment to the Court of a portion of the reduced filing fee required hereunder; and that the full amount of the filing fee required hereunder, or $_____, shall be reported to the superintendent or other public official in charge of the facility where the applicant/inmate is confined, who shall collect such amount from the applicant/inmate in the same manner as mandatory surcharges are collected pursuant to section 60.35(5) of the Penal Law.

☐ _____
_____
_____

_____   _____
    Date   Judge

APPENDIX A–3

_____COURT

STATE OF NEW YORK

_____COUNTY

- x

In the Matter of the Correctional Facility Trust Fund Account of	ORDER to Rescind Order of Collection of a Civil Filing Fee from an Inmate's Trust Account
_____	INDEX/FILE# ORI#

- x

This Court,

Having issued an order dated ___/___/___: (1) granting_____, an inmate at _____ (name of Correctional Facility), poor person status in _____ (name of case); (2) requiring such inmate to pay a filing fee in such case in the amount of $_____; and (3) directing the Superintendent or other public official in charge of the aforesaid Correctional Facility to collect some or all of such filing fee from the inmate's Correctional Facility Trust Fund Account or institutional equivalent, and

Now having received notice that the Clerk of this Court has received payment of the filing fee in full directly from the inmate or a person or persons acting on his/her behalf,

It is hereby ORDERED that so much of the aforesaid order directing the Superintendent or other public official in charge of the aforesaid Correctional Facility to collect some or all of such filing fee from the inmate's Correctional Facility Trust Fund Account or institutional equivalent is rescinded, and that any funds heretofore withheld from such Account pursuant to the aforesaid order shall be restored to such Account.

_____   _____
        Date   Judge

PART 141.   INTEGRATED DOMESTIC VIOLENCE PARTS

§ 141.1.   Definitions

(a) "IDV Part" shall refer to an Integrated Domestic Violence Part established by the Chief Administrator of the Courts pursuant to section 141.2 of this Part.

(b) For purposes of this rule and its application to an IDV Part established in a county, an "IDV–eligible case" shall refer to both of the following when they are simultaneously pending in the county: a domestic violence case commenced in a criminal court and a case commenced in Supreme or Family Court that involves a party or witness in the domestic violence case. If so provided by the administrative order promulgated pursuant to section 141.2 of this Part for such county:

(1) an IDV–eligible case also shall refer to each of the following: any case in criminal court, Family Court or Supreme Court where there is simultaneously pending in the county another case in any other of these courts having a common party or in which a disposition may affect the interests of a party to the first case; and

(2) where cases are IDV–eligible and are disposed of in an IDV Part, subsequent cases that would have been IDV–eligible were they to have been pending simultaneously with the cases already disposed of shall be IDV–eligible; and

(3) in Monroe County, any domestic violence case pending in a criminal court in the county if necessary to best utilize available court and community resources for domestic violence cases.

§ 141.2.   Establishment of IDV Parts

Following consultation with and agreement of the Presiding Justice of the Judicial Department in which a county is located, the Chief Administrator, by administrative order, may establish an IDV Part in Supreme Court in such county and assign one or more justices to preside therein.

§ 141.3.   Identification of IDV–Eligible Cases

Procedures shall be established in each court so as to insure that cases pending before it are identified as IDV–eligible at the earliest possible time.

§ 141.4.   Transfer of IDV–Eligible Cases

Unless the administrative order establishing an IDV Part in a county shall otherwise provide:

(a) Where an IDV–eligible case is pending in a court other than Supreme Court in such county:

(1) Originals or copies of papers and other documents filed in such court in connection with the case shall, directly following its identification as IDV–eligible, be sent by the court to the IDV Part.

(2) Not later than five days following receipt of the original papers and other documents in an IDV–eligible case in an IDV Part, the justice presiding in such Part shall determine whether or not a transfer of the case to the Supreme Court would promote the administration of justice. If the justice determines that it would, he or she may order such transfer, in which event the case shall be referred for disposition to the IDV Part, all original papers, if not already sent, shall be sent from the originating court to the IDV Part, and all further proceedings shall be conducted therein. If the justice determines that such a

transfer would not promote the administration of justice, he or she shall cause all papers and other documents in the case to be returned to the court from which they were received, where all further proceedings in such case shall be conducted in accordance with law.

(3) Notwithstanding the provisions of paragraphs (1) and (2) of this subdivision, where the case is a criminal case and the defendant is held by the local criminal court for the action of a grand jury empaneled by a County Court, only copies of the papers and other documents filed with such court shall be delivered to the IDV Part; and the justice presiding therein may at any time order a transfer of the case to the Supreme Court provided he or she determines that such a transfer would promote the administration of justice. The original papers and other documents filed with the local criminal court shall be delivered to the County Court as required by section 180.30(1) of the Criminal Procedure Law.

(b) Where the IDV–eligible case is a case pending in Supreme Court, it shall be referred for disposition to the IDV Part of such court and all further proceedings shall be conducted therein.

§ 141.5. Procedure in an IDV Part

(a) Unless otherwise authorized or required by law, no case transferred from another court to the Supreme Court and referred for disposition to an IDV Part thereof may be consolidated with any other case pending before such IDV Part.

(b) Each case transferred from another court to the Supreme Court and referred for disposition to an IDV Part thereof shall be subject to the same substantive and procedural law as would have applied to it had it not been transferred, and no party thereto shall be required to pay any fee for the assignment of an index number thereto upon such transfer.

PART 142. CRIMINAL DIVISION OF SUPREME COURT IN BRONX COUNTY

§ 142.1. Establishment of a Criminal Division of Supreme Court in Bronx County

The Chief Administrator of the Courts, following consultation with and agreement of the Presiding Justice of the First Judicial Department, may establish, by administrative order, a Criminal Division of Supreme Court in Bronx County and assign one or more justices to preside therein. Subject to the further limitations prescribed in this part, such Criminal Division shall be devoted to the hearing and determination of all criminal cases commenced in or transferred to the courts sitting in Bronx County provided at least one felony or misdemeanor is charged.

§ 142.2. Transfer of Criminal Cases to the Criminal Division of Supreme Court

Where the Chief Administrator establishes a Criminal Division of Supreme Court in Bronx County pursuant to section 142.1 of this Part:

(a) Each criminal case then pending or thereafter commenced in the Supreme Court in such county, and each criminal case thereafter transferred to Supreme Court in such county from Supreme Court in another county, shall be referred for disposition to such Criminal Division and further proceedings in such case shall be conducted in a part established therein.

(b) All criminal cases then pending or thereafter commenced in the Criminal Court of the City of New York in Bronx County, in which at least one felony or misdemeanor is charged, shall, following arraignment, be transferred therefrom by the Administrative Judge for the Supreme Court in Bronx County to the Supreme Court in such county upon a finding that transfer of these cases would promote the administration of justice, and thereupon such cases shall be referred for disposition to such Criminal Division and further proceedings in such cases shall be conducted in the parts established therein. Provided, however, that no criminal case may be transferred pursuant to this subdivision where such case is returnable in a summons part of the Criminal Court and no felonies or class A misdemeanors are charged therein.

§ 142.3. Procedure Upon Transfer of a Criminal Case Hereunder

Each case transferred from the Criminal Court of the City of New York to the Supreme Court and referred for disposition to the Criminal Division thereof pursuant to section 142.2 of this part shall be subject to the same substantive and procedural law as would have applied to it had it not been transferred. An appeal taken from the trial court in such a case shall be taken to the same intermediate appellate court to which such appeal would have been taken had the case not been transferred hereunder.

PART 143. SUPERIOR COURTS FOR DRUG TREATMENT

§ 143.1. Establishment of Superior Courts for Drug Treatment

Following consultation with and agreement of the Presiding Justice of the Judicial Department in which a county is located, the Chief Administrator of the Courts, by administrative order, may establish a Superior Court for Drug Treatment in Supreme Court or County Court in such county and assign one or more justices or judges to preside therein. Each such Superior Court for Drug Treatment shall have as its purpose the hearing and determination of:

(a) criminal cases that are commenced in the court and that are identified by the court as appropriate for disposition by a drug treatment court; and

(b) criminal cases that are commenced in other courts of the county, and that are identified as appropriate for disposition by a drug treatment court and transferred to the court as provided in section 143.2 of this Part.

§ 143.2. Transfer of cases to Superior Courts for Drug Treatment; How Effectuated

(a) **Transfer of cases pending in local criminal courts.**

1. A local criminal court in a county in which a Superior Court for Drug Treatment has been established in the Supreme or County Court thereof may, upon motion of the defendant and with the consent of the district attorney, cause copies of papers and other documents filed in such local criminal court in connection with a criminal action or proceeding pending therein to be sent to the Superior Court for Drug Treatment:

(i) upon or after arraignment of defendant on a local criminal court accusatory instrument by which such action or proceeding was commenced; or

(ii) upon or after commencement of a proceeding brought against defendant for the violation of a condition of a sentence of probation or a sentence of conditional discharge.

2. Not later than five days following receipt of the papers and other documents, the justice or judge presiding in the Superior Court for Drug Treatment shall determine whether or not a transfer of the action or proceeding to the court would promote the administration of justice. If the justice or judge presiding in the court determines that it would, he or she may order such transfer, in which event the action or proceeding shall be transferred to the Superior Court for Drug Treatment, all originating papers shall then be sent from the originating court to the Superior Court for Drug Treatment, and all further proceedings shall be conducted therein. If the justice or judge determines that a transfer of the action or

proceeding would not promote the administration of justice, he or she shall notify the local criminal court from which the reference was received of such determination, whereupon all further proceedings in such action or proceeding shall be conducted in accordance with law.

(b) **Transfer of cases pending in a superior court.**

1. At any time while a criminal action or proceeding is pending in a superior court in a county in which a Superior Court for Drug Treatment has been established, including a proceeding brought against defendant for the violation of a condition of a sentence of probation or a sentence of conditional discharge, a judge or justice of the court in which the action or proceeding is pending may, upon motion of the defendant and with the consent of the district attorney, cause copies of papers and other documents filed in such court in connection with the action or proceeding to be sent to the judge or justice presiding in the Superior Court for Drug Treatment for review of the appropriateness of the transfer.

2. Not later than five business days following receipt of the papers and other documents, the judge or justice presiding in the Superior Court for Drug Treatment shall determine whether or not a transfer of the action or proceeding to the court would promote the administration of justice. If such judge or justice determines that it would:

(i) he or she, if sitting in Supreme Court, may order such transfer, in which event the action or proceeding shall be referred for disposition to the Superior Court for Drug Treatment, all original papers shall be sent to the Superior Court for Drug Treatment, and all further proceedings in such action or proceeding shall be conducted therein; or

(ii) he or she, if sitting in County Court, shall so notify the justice of the court who caused the papers and other documents to be sent to him or her, and such justice may thereupon order such transfer, in which event the action or proceeding shall be referred for disposition to the Superior Court for Drug Treatment, all original papers shall be sent from the originating court to the Superior Court for Drug Treatment, and all further proceedings in such action or proceeding shall be conducted therein. If the judge or justice presiding in the Superior Court for Drug Treatment determines that a transfer of the action or proceeding would not promote the administration of justice, he or she shall notify the originating court of such determination, whereupon all further proceedings in such action or proceeding shall be conducted in accordance with law.

§ 143.3. Procedure in a Superior Court for Drug Treatment upon Transfer of Case Thereto

Each action or proceeding transferred from a local criminal court to a superior court and referred for disposition to a Superior Court for Drug Treatment thereof shall be subject to the same substantive and procedural law as would have applied to it had it not been transferred.

PART 144. NEW YORK STATE PARENT EDUCATION AND AWARENESS PROGRAM

§ 144.1. Scope of Program

The New York State Parent Education and Awareness Program ("Program") provides information to parents about the impact of parental breakup or conflict on children, how children experience family change, and ways in which parents can help their children manage the family reorganization. The curriculum is child-centered and directed primarily toward promoting children's healthy adjustment and development by educating parents about ways they can minimize the stress of family change and protect their children from the negative effects of ongoing parental conflict. The administration and curriculum of the parent education program is sensitive to domestic violence concerns and must be in compliance with the Guidelines and Procedures for Certification of Parent Education and Awareness Programs.

§ 144.2. Definitions

(a) "Parent education and awareness program": A parent education and awareness program certified by the Office of Court Administration.

(b) "Provider": The entity responsible for applying for certification and for presentation of a parent education and awareness program.

(c) "Program administrator": The individual associated with the parent education provider ultimately responsible for administering all aspects of the parent education and awareness program.

(d) "Court": A justice, judge, judicial hearing officer, matrimonial referee, court attorney-referee, or support magistrate who handles issues of child custody and visitation and child support.

(e) "Guidelines": The Guidelines and Procedures for Certification of Parent Education and Awareness Programs, which contain the minimum standards for parent education programs to be certified and approved by the Office of Court Administration to accept participants referred by the courts of the State of New York.

(f) "Program Director": The individual employed by the Office of Court Administration responsible for administration and oversight of the New York State Parent Education and Awareness Program.

§ 144.3. Application of Program

(a) The New York State Parent Education and Awareness Program may apply in any action or proceeding:

(1) that affects the interests of children under 18 years of age; and

(2) that is brought in Supreme Court or Family Court: (i) to annul a marriage or declare the nullity of a void marriage, (ii) for separation, (iii) for divorce, (iv) to obtain custody of or visitation with minor children, (v) to obtain a modification of a prior order of custody or visitation with minor children, or (vi) where, in the exercise of the court's discretion, a determination is made in a particular matter that attendance by the parents would provide information that would be of benefit to them and their children.

(b) In any action or proceeding to which the Program may apply, the court, in its discretion, may order both parents to attend a parent education and awareness program. The order must direct that both parents attend, not just one parent, but the parents shall not attend the same class session. Such order shall be made as early in the proceeding as practicable.

(c) In determining whether to order parents to attend a parent education and awareness program, a court shall consider all relevant factors bearing upon the parties to the underlying action or proceeding and their children, including, but not limited to, any history, specific allegations or pleadings of domestic violence or other abuse; medical, financial or travel hardship; language barrier; and whether a parent has previously attended parent education. Where there is any history, or there are specific allegations or pleadings, of domestic violence or other abuse involving the parents or their children, the court shall not mandate attendance at the program.

(d) An order to attend a parent education and awareness program shall not delay the expeditious progress of the underlying proceeding.

(e) A parent who is a victim of domestic violence may opt out of attendance by contacting a program administrator.

§ 144.4. Provider Certification

(a) General. Each provider that wishes to accept court-referred participants must be certified by the Office of Court Administration. In order to receive certification, potential providers must submit a certification application and any requested materials to the Program Director and be in compliance prior to being eligible to receive court-referred participants. A provider is under a continuing duty to advise the Program Director of changes in its education and awareness program or administration, including changes in staff, contact information, presenters/facilitators, locations, and class schedules.

(b) Certification Application ("application"). To receive certification, a provider must submit information and documentation that demonstrates that it is in compliance with the Guidelines. Each provider must submit three copies of the application and appended materials for each program, which must address all of the elements. If a provider expects that it will not be able to comply with a requirement, an explanation must be provided. A provider may also be required to submit additional information and materials for continued certification or re-certification, or in the event a complaint or other information is received by the Program Director indicating that the program may not be in compliance with the Guidelines.

(c) Waiver or Modification of Requirements. A waiver or modification of one or more of the requirements for certification or re-certification may be requested by a provider and must be included in the provider's application as well as in the cover letter to the application. Requests must be made by letter to the Program Director sent via first class mail. Such request may be granted in the discretion of the Program Director in consultation with the Chief Administrator of the Courts or his or her designee after review and consideration of the impact of the deviation upon the underlying intent and purpose of the Guidelines.

(d) Review Process. Certification applications shall be reviewed by the Program Director in a timely manner. After a satisfactory initial review of the application, an on-site review of the program shall be conducted by the Program Director or his or her designee. During the on-site review, the Program Director shall observe the presentation of a full program cycle and may interview the program administrator. To promote consistency in the review process, the Program Director shall use a uniform written instrument to evaluate the programs. The determina-

tion of the Program Director shall be communicated to the provider by letter sent via first class mail. The opportunity for a provider to seek a review of any denial of certification or re-certification or suspension or revocation of certification shall be in accordance with the provisions set forth in the Guidelines.

(e) Approved Providers. Approved providers will be compiled in a list that will be updated and distributed regularly to the courts, Supreme and County and Family Court Chief Clerks, and others, as appropriate, and posted on the Program website. A provider is required to keep the Program Director apprised of its current information. Approved providers may indicate in advertisements and other uses that their program is certified by the Office of Court Administration.

§ 144.5. Fees

In accordance with the Guidelines, parent education and awareness programs may require attendees to pay a fee. The fee must be reasonably related to the cost of providing the services, cannot exceed the maximum authorized fee as set forth in the Guidelines, and must be subject to waiver or reduction if requiring a person to pay the full fee would work a hardship on the person or his or her immediate family.

§ 144.6. Confidentiality

(a) Any communication made by a party as part of his or her participation in a parent education and awareness program shall be a confidential communication and shall not be available for evidentiary use in any action or proceeding.

(b) The Court shall obtain information about compliance with its order sending parents to parent education only from the provider pursuant to the provisions in the Guidelines.

(c) Any provider, its program administrator or designee who is provided information from a parent, either in writing or orally, shall not divulge that information to the attorneys representing the parties, the attorney(s) for the children, the other party, or the court, and its chambers or administrative staffs, except that information may be provided, without indication of a parent's name, to the Program Director or his or her designee as part of the certification and evaluation process.

PART 145. INTEGRATED YOUTH COURT IN WESTCHESTER COUNTY

§ 145.1. Definitions

(a) "Integrated Youth Court" shall refer to a multi-court part of the County Court and the Family Court in Westchester County established by the Chief Administrator of the Courts pursuant to section 145.2 of this Part.

(b) "IYC-eligible case" shall refer to both of the following when they are simultaneously pending in Westchester County: a criminal case in a local criminal court or in the County Court and a case in the Family Court in which a respondent therein is a defendant in such criminal case and he or she was under twenty-one years of age at the time of the alleged commission of an offense prosecuted in such criminal case. An IYC-eligible case also shall refer to:

(1) a civil action pending in a City Court, Town Court or Village Court in Westchester County, or in the County Court thereof where such action arises out of substantially the same facts as underlie IYC-eligible cases then pending in the Integrated Youth Court; and

(2) a case that would have been IYC-eligible were it to have been pending simultaneously with other IYC-eligible cases that already have been disposed of in the Integrated Youth Court.

§ 145.2. Establishment of Integrated Youth Court in Westchester County

Following consultation with and agreement of the Presiding Justice of the Second Judicial Department, the Chief Administrator, by administrative order, may establish an Integrated Youth Court in Westchester County and assign one or more judges to preside therein. Such Integrated Youth Court shall be devoted to the hearing and determination, in a single forum, of IYC-eligible cases in accordance with this Part.

§ 145.3. Identification of IYC–Eligible Cases

Procedures shall be established to ensure that IYC-eligible cases are identified at the earliest possible time.

§ 145.4. Assignment and Transfer of Cases

(a) Where an IYC-eligible case is pending in a City Court, Town Court or Village Court in Westchester County:

(1) Originals or copies of papers and other documents filed in such Court in connection with the case shall, directly following its identification as IYC-eligible, be sent by the Court to the Integrated Youth Court.

(2) Not later than five days following receipt of the original papers and documents in an IYC-eligible case in the Integrated Youth Court, the judge presiding therein shall determine whether or not the transfer of such case to the County Court would promote the administration of justice. If the judge determines that it would, he or she may order such transfer, in which event the case shall be referred to the Integrated Youth Court, all original papers, if not already sent, shall be sent from the originating court to the Integrated Youth Court, and further proceedings shall be conducted therein. If the judge determines that such a transfer would not promote the administration of justice, he or she shall cause all papers and other documents in the case to be returned to the court from which they were received, where further proceedings in such case shall be conducted in accordance with law.

(b) Where the IYC-eligible case is a case pending in County Court or Family Court, it shall be referred to the Integrated Youth Court for further proceedings therein.

§ 145.5. Procedure in the Integrated Youth Court

Each case transferred from another court to the County Court and referred to the Integrated Youth Court part thereof shall be subject to the same substantive and procedural law as would have applied to it had it not been transferred.

PART 146. GUIDELINES FOR QUALIFICATIONS AND TRAINING OF ADR NEUTRALS SERVING ON COURT ROSTERS

§ 146.1. Application

These guidelines establish qualifications and training throughout the State for mediators and neutral evaluators serving on court rosters. These guidelines are not intended to cover arbitrators nor to apply to neutrals serving in the UCS Community Dispute Resolution Centers Program.

§ 146.2. Definitions

(a) "Neutral" shall refer to both mediators and neutral evaluators.

(b) "Mediation" shall refer to a confidential dispute resolution process in which a neutral third party (the mediator) helps parties identify issues, clarify perceptions and explore options for a mutually acceptable outcome.

(c) "Neutral evaluation" shall refer to a confidential, non-binding process in which a neutral third party (the neutral evaluator) with expertise in the subject matter relating to the dispute provides an assessment of likely court outcomes of a case or an issue in an effort to help parties reach a settlement.

§ 146.3. Rosters of Neutrals

(a) Each District Administrative Judge may compile rosters in his or her judicial district of neutrals who are qualified to receive referrals from the court. In order to be eligible for appointment to the roster, neutrals must meet the minimum qualifications and training criteria set forth below. Each neutral serves at the pleasure of the District Administrative Judge in his or her district, who may terminate a designation to the roster at any time.

(b) Neutrals shall be redesignated to the roster maintained by the District Administrative Judge in his or her judicial district every two years. In determining whether to redesignate neutrals, District Administrative Judges must determine that each neutral has complied with section 146.5, (Continuing Education for Neutrals) and must consult with the UCS ADR Office regarding any complaints filed against a neutral who is otherwise eligible for redesignation.

§ 146.4. Qualifications and Training of Neutrals

(a) **Neutral Evaluation.** Neutral evaluators who wish to qualify for appointment to a court roster must have successfully completed at least six hours of approved training in procedural and ethical matters related to neutral evaluation and be:

(1) Lawyers admitted to practice law for at least five years who also have at least five years of substantial experience in the specific subject area of the cases that will be referred to them; or

(2) Individuals who have served at least five years as a judge with substantial experience in the specific subject area of the cases that will be referred to them.

(b) **Mediation.** Mediators who wish to qualify for appointment to a court roster must have successfully completed at least 40 hours of approved training as follows:

(1) At least 24 hours of training in basic mediation skills and techniques; and

(2) At least 16 hours of additional training in the specific mediation techniques pertaining to the subject area of the types of cases referred to them.

Mediators must also have recent experience mediating actual cases in the subject area of the types of cases referred to them.

(c) **Mixed Process.** Persons who serve as both mediators and neutral evaluators in the same matter must meet the qualifications and training specified in both subdivisions (a) and (b) of this section.

§ 146.5. Continuing Education for Neutrals

All neutrals must attend at least six hours of additional approved training relevant to their respective practice areas every two years.

§ 146.6. Approval of Training Programs and Qualifications

(a) The UCS ADR Office, with the approval of the Chief Administrative Judge and the four Presiding Justices of the Appellate Divisions, shall adopt such criteria as may be appropriate for the approval of training programs under these guidelines and for defining recent experience mediating actual cases pursuant to section 145.4(b).

(b) The UCS ADR Office, with the approval of the Chief Administrative Judge, may increase the qualifications and training requirements in specific court ADR programs.

PART 150. INDEPENDENT JUDICIAL ELECTION QUALIFICATION COMMISSIONS

§ 150.0. Preamble

It is essential to the effectiveness of an elected judiciary that qualified candidates obtain judicial office. Yet the public frequently is unaware of the qualifications of candidates who run for judicial office, because the candidate-designation process often is not conducted in public view. The public will have greater confidence in the judicial election process if they know that judicial candidates were screened by independent screening panels and found to possess the qualities necessary for effective judicial performance.

§ 150.1. Establishment

There shall be an Independent Judicial Election Qualification Commission established in each judicial district which shall review the qualifications of candidates for public election to the Supreme Court, County Court, Surrogate's Court, Family Court, New York City Civil Court, District Courts and City Courts.

§ 150.2. Membership

(a) Each qualification commission shall have 15 members appointed as follows:

(1) The Chief Judge of the State of New York shall select five members, two of whom shall be non-lawyers;

(2) The Presiding Justice of the Appellate Division encompassing the appropriate district commission shall select five members, two of whom shall be non-lawyers;

(3) The President of the New York State Bar Association shall select one member;

(4) Four local bar associations, located within the appropriate judicial district and designated by the Presiding Justice of the Appellate Division of the appropriate district, shall each select one member.

(b) The Chief Judge of the State of New York shall designate the chair of each commission from the above membership.

(c) Commissioners must be residents of or have a place of business in the judicial district in which they serve.

(d) In making appointments to the commissions, each appointing authority shall give consideration to achieving broad representation of the community, including geographic, racial, ethnic and gender diversity.

(e) Commission members shall act independently and impartially.

§ 150.3. Terms of Office

(a) Except as set forth below, each member shall serve at the pleasure of the appointing authority for a term of three years, and shall be eligible to serve for one additional three-year term.

(b) Initial terms of commissioners shall be staggered so that five commissioners will serve for an initial term of one year, five for an initial term of two years, and five for an initial term of three years.

(c) If a commissioner does not complete the appointed term, the appointing authority shall appoint someone to serve on an interim basis for the remainder of the term.

(d) If a vacancy is not filled by an appointing authority within 30 days after written notification to the appointing authority of its creation, the Chief Judge may fill the vacancy for the remainder of the term.

§ 150.4. Quorum

Two-thirds of the members of the full commission shall constitute a quorum for the purpose of conducting any business.

§ 150.5. Evaluation of Candidates

(a) The qualifications commissions shall evaluate candidates for elected public office for the courts set forth in section 150.1 to determine whether they are qualified for the office to which they seek election.

(b) The criteria for evaluation shall include professional ability; character, independence and integrity; reputation for fairness and lack of bias; and temperament, including courtesy and patience.

(c) Where a quorum exists, a majority vote of the members present shall be required to find a candidate qualified for judicial office.

(d) All votes on whether a candidate is qualified shall be by secret ballot.

(e) Each commission shall publish an alphabetical listing of the names of all candidates that it has found qualified and it has not found qualified for election to judicial office.

§ 150.6. Procedures

(a) The Chief Administrator of the Courts shall establish, with the approval of the Administrative Board of the Courts, uniform procedures for the oper-

ation of the commissions. These procedures shall include:

(1) Wide dissemination by the commission of notice wherever an open judicial position is to be filled by election;

(2) Use of written application forms;

(3) Investigation of the background and qualifications of applicants;

(4) A process for reconsideration upon application of the applicant.

(b) A commission may designate subcommittees to investigate the background and qualifications of applicants and to report to the full committee.

§ 150.7. Compensation

Commission members shall serve without compensation, but shall be entitled to reimbursement for any necessary expenses incurred by them in connection with the performance of their duties.

§ 150.8. Confidentiality

Except as provided in section 150.5(e), all papers filed with or generated by the commission and all proceedings of the commission shall be confidential.

§ 150.9. Conflicts of Interest

(a) No member of a qualifications commission shall be a candidate for judicial office or shall support or act on behalf of any candidate for judicial office.

(b) A member shall recuse himself or herself from participating in a commission proceeding where the member has a relationship with the candidate, or with another candidate competing for the same judicial office, which could reasonably render the member's participation unfair to the public or any candidate, or which might cause others to perceive that such participation is inappropriate or unfair.

(c) The following persons shall not be eligible to serve as a member of a qualification commission:

(1) Any person who presently holds or has held a political party elective office within the past three years, other than a county committee member;

(2) Any person who was a candidate for or who has held elective public office during the three years preceding the year of commission service, or is presently a candidate for public office;

(3) Any person who is an employee of the courts; and

(4) Any person who has been found guilty of professional misconduct or of a class B misdemeanor or more serious crime (or the equivalent under the law of any other jurisdiction).

APPENDIX A. UNIFORM GUIDELINES AND PROCEDURES FOR THE OPERATION OF THE INDEPENDENT JUDICIAL ELECTION QUALIFICATION COMMISSIONS

This Appendix sets forth uniform guidelines and procedures for the operation of the Independent Judicial Election Qualification Commissions established pursuant to Part 150 of the Rules of the Chief Administrator.

Section 1. Notice of Open Judicial Positions

Each commission shall provide to all bar associations, the media and the public, within the judicial district in which the commission is established, notice of current and impending judicial vacancies that are to be filled by election in the courts in that district set forth in section 150.1 of the Chief Administrator's Rules. The notice shall also contain information regarding the commission's role and procedures.

Section 2. Meetings of the Commissions

A. The commissions shall meet at regularly scheduled intervals throughout the calendar year and may meet at such other times as the work of the commission may require.

B. Commission members may attend meetings in person or by video or telephone conference.

Section 3. Scope of the Commissions' Determinations

A. The commissions shall determine whether a candidate is qualified for election to the judicial office (e.g., Supreme Court) in which a vacancy exists.

B. Any candidate found qualified for election to a judicial office shall be deemed qualified for that judicial office for three years in the absence of any new information that may have a negative effect on his or her qualifications and background.

C. Any candidate not found qualified for election to judicial office shall be deemed not to be qualified for that judicial office for one year from the date of submission of the candidate's application to the commission.

Section 4. Use of Subcommittees

A. The commissions may establish subcommittees of no fewer than three commission members to aid the commission in investigating the backgrounds and qualifications of candidates and to report to the full committee.

B. Such subcommittees shall meet to the extent necessary to complete their assigned duties.

Section 5. Investigation of Candidates' Qualifications and Background

A. Each candidate shall submit to the appropriate commission a completed application, on a form promulgated by the Chief Administrator and approved by the Administrative Board, that will provide information for the evaluation of the candidate's qualifications and background.

1. The application shall include items designed to elicit information from the candidates concerning: professional ability, work ethic, character, independence, decisiveness, fairness, integrity, docket management and case disposition skills, temperament, respect for litigants and attorneys, legal experience, education, and scholarship.

2. The application shall also inquire whether the candidate has completed the education program for judicial candidates established by section 100.5(A)(2)(f) of the Rules of the Chief Administrator and, if not, when and how that program is expected to be completed.

3. The application shall be a continuing application and shall require all candidates to immediately submit to the commission any change of circumstances that would substantially change any information previously provided.

B. The commission shall undertake an investigation of the candidates' qualifications and background.

1. If the candidate is or has been a judge, these steps may include, but not be limited to:

a. Ascertaining the view of attorneys who have appeared before the candidate;

b. Ascertaining the views of Administrative or Supervising Judges familiar with the candidate's work performance, professional ability and character;

c. Searching records for activity with the Commission on Judicial Conduct involving the candidate;

d. In the case of a judge who has presided over criminal or Family Court matters, ascertaining the views of the appropriate public defender or Legal Aid Society, District Attorney's office and Family Court agencies;

e. Reviewing professional writings of the candidate, including opinions;

f. Reviewing the disposition of appeals from the candidate's orders and judgments; and

g. Reviewing data regarding docket management and case disposition.

2. If the candidate is currently practicing law, or is a person whose current judicial experience is less than one year, these steps may include, but not be limited to:

   a. Ascertaining the views of judicial or quasi-judicial officers before whom a candidate has appeared;

   b. Ascertaining the views of attorneys who have either appeared opposite the candidate in a litigated matter, or who have otherwise had substantial experience with a candidate;

   c. Searching records for activity with the appropriate Departmental Disciplinary Committees involving the candidate;

   d. Ascertaining the views of colleagues with whom the candidate has served on state or local bar association committees;

   e. Ascertaining the views of representatives of social, civic, cultural or charitable groups to which the candidate belongs;

   f. Ascertaining the views of other attorneys who have been in a position to supervise or otherwise evaluate the candidate's performance and his or her work product; and

   g. Reviewing any professional writings of the candidate that may have a bearing on his or her judicial performance, including briefs and articles.

C. The commission may personally interview the candidate.

   1. Consistent with the restrictions in section 100.5(A)(2)(d) of the Rules of the Chief Administrator, candidates shall not be asked any questions in the personal interview that would require them to pledge or commit to a position on any matter or issue that might come before them as a judge.

   2. Candidates shall not be asked any question inquiring into their political affiliations.

   3. The commission shall not permit an announced candidate for a specific judicial office to withdraw his or her application for evaluation by the commission once a personal interview has commenced.

Section 6.   Results of Evaluation Process

A. Each commission shall notify each candidate, in writing, whether the candidate is qualified for election to the judicial office, not qualified for election to the judicial office, or has not complied with the commission's evaluation process. The commission's written notice informing a candidate that he or she has been found qualified for election to the judicial office shall be accompanied by a statement of ethical guidelines addressing the permitted uses of the commission's rating in any campaign for judicial office.

B. Pursuant to section 150.5(e) of the Rules of the Chief Administrator, each commission shall publish at such times as it may determine, but not less than annually, an alphabetical list of those candidates found qualified and not found qualified for election to judicial offices.

   1. The commission shall make the list available to the public, including but not limited to publishing the list in local newspapers and notifying bar associations and other civic groups.

   2. There shall be no communication to the public regarding those candidates who did not participate in the commission's evaluation process, nor shall the commission provide any additional comment or information regarding any candidate other than the written notice provided for herein.

Section 7.   Requests for Reconsideration

A. Any candidate not found qualified for election to a judicial office may request reconsideration by the commission by making a written request to the commission's chair within seven business days following the date of receipt of notification of the commission's decision.

B. In support of a reconsideration application, the candidate may submit additional material and may request an interview with the commission.

C. The commission shall advise the candidate promptly, in writing, after its determination of the candidate's application upon reconsideration.

D. In the event the candidate, upon reconsideration, is found qualified for the judicial office, the commission shall add his or her name to the publicly available list of candidates found qualified for election to the judicial office. The commission shall also provide the candidate with a statement of ethical guidelines addressing the permitted use of the commission's rating.

Section 8.   Records Retention

All records considered by a commission with respect to a candidate shall be retained by the commission for at least three years from the date of its final determination for that candidate.

Added Appendix A on Feb. 13, 2007.

UNIFORM RULES FOR THE NEW YORK STATE TRIAL COURTS

Effective January 6, 1986

Including Amendments Received Through September 15, 2008

Westlaw Electronic Research

These rules may be searched electronically on Westlaw® in the NY–RULES database; updates to these rules may be found on Westlaw *in NY–RULESUP-DATES. For search tips and a summary of database content, consult the* Westlaw *Scope Screens for each database.*

Table of Sections

201

ADOPTING ORDER

ADMINISTRATIVE ORDER OF THE CHIEF ADMINISTRATIVE JUDGE OF THE COURTS

Pursuant to the authority vested in me, and with the advice and consent of the Administrative Board of the Courts, I hereby adopt, effective January 6, 1986, the following Uniform Rules for the Trial Courts of the Unified Court System:

Uniform Rules for the Engagement of Counsel (Part 125)

Uniform Rules for Courts Exercising Criminal Jurisdiction (Part 200)

Uniform Civil Rules for the Supreme Court and County Court (Part 202)

Uniform Rules for the Family Court (Part 205)

Uniform Rules for the Court of Claims (Part 206)

Uniform Rules for the Surrogate's Court (Part 207)

Uniform Rules for the New York City Civil Court (Part 208)

Uniform Rules for the City Courts Outside of the City of New York (Part 210)

Uniform Civil Rules for the District Courts (Part 212)

Uniform Civil Rules for the Justice Courts (Part 214)

I hereby repeal, also effective January 6, 1986, the following provisions of Title 22 of the Official Compilation of Codes, Rules and Regulations of the State of New York (22 NYCRR), constituting rules for the several trial courts in the State of New York: Part 103 (22 NYCRR Part 103); Part 105 (22 NYCRR Part 105); section 112.2 (22 NYCRR 112.2); Part 113 (22 NYCRR Part 113); Part 114 (22 NYCRR Part 114); Part 117 (22 NYCRR Part 117); Part 120 (22 NYCRR Part 120); Part 150 (22 NYCRR Part 150); Part 151 (22 NYCRR Part 151); Part 340 (22 NYCRR Part 340); Part 360 (22 NYCRR Part 360); Part 420 (22 NYCRR Part 420); Part 421 (22 NYCRR Part 421); Part 422 (22 NYCRR Part 422); Part 440 (22 NYCRR Part 440); Part 580 (22 NYCRR Part 580); Part 605 (22 NYCRR Part 605); Part 630 (22 NYCRR Part 630); all sections of Part 635 (22 NYCRR Part 635), except for section 635.9 (22 NYCRR 635.9) thereof, which is not repealed; sections 636.2, 636.3, 636.4, 636.6, 636.7, 636.8, 636.9 of Part 636 (22 NYCRR 636.2, 636.3, 636.4, 636.6, 636.7, 636.8, 636.9); all sections of Part 660 (22 NYCRR Part 660), except that section 660.24 (22 NYCRR 660.24) thereof is repealed as of April 1, 1986; all sections of Part 661 (22 NYCRR Part 661), except for section 661.7 (22 NYCRR 661.7) thereof, which is not repealed; section 671.8 (22 NYCRR 671.8); Part 672 (22 NYCRR Part 672); Part 673 (22 NYCRR Part 673); Part 674 (22 NYCRR Part 674); Part 675 (22 NYCRR Part 675); Part 676 (22 NYCRR Part 676); Part 677 (22 NYCRR Part 677); Part 678 (22 NYCRR Part 678); Part 680 (22 NYCRR Part 680); Part 681 (22 NYCRR Part 681); Part 682 (22 NYCRR Part 682); Part 683 (22 NYCRR Part 683); Part 685 (22 NYCRR Part 685); section 691.18 (22 NYCRR 691.18); all sections of Part 699 (22 NYCRR Part 699), except for section 699.10 thereof, which is not repealed; Part 704 (22 NYCRR Part 704); sections 711.1 and 711.2 (22 NYCRR 711.1, 711.2); Part 750 (22 NYCRR Part 750); Part 751 (22 NYCRR Part 751); Part 752 (22 NYCRR Part 752); Part 755 (22 NYCRR Part 755); Part 760 (22 NYCRR Part 760); Part 765 (22 NYCRR Part 765); Part 770 (22 NYCRR Part 770); Part 775 (22 NYCRR Part 775); Part 780 (22 NYCRR Part 780); Part 785 (22 NYCRR Part 785); Part 790 (22 NYCRR Part 790); Part 795 (22 NYCRR Part 795); Part 796 (22 NYCRR Part 796); Part 830 (22 NYCRR Part 830); Part 839 (22 NYCRR Part 839); sections 840.1 and 840.3 of Part 840 (22 NYCRR 840.1, 840.3); Part 860 (22 NYCRR Part 860); Part 861 (22 NYCRR Part 861); Part 862 (22 NYCRR Part 862); all sections of Part 863 (22 NYCRR Part 863), except for section 863.5 (22 NYCRR 863.5) thereof, which is not repealed; Part 1024 (22 NYCRR Part 1024); Part 1026 (22 NYCRR Part 1026); Part 1027 (22 NYCRR Part 1027); Part 1030 (22 NYCRR Part 1030); Part 1039 (22 NYCRR Part 1039), except for section 1039.3 thereof (22 NYCRR 1039.3), which is not repealed; Part 1060 (22 NYCRR Part 1060); Part 1085 (22 NYCRR Part 1085); Part 1110 (22 NYCRR Part 1110); Part 1155 (22 NYCRR Part 1155); all the sections of Part 1200 (22 NYCRR Part 1200), except that section 1200.17(b) thereof is repealed as of July 1, 1986; Part 1230 (22 NYCRR Part 1230); Part 1231 (22 NYCRR Part 1231); Part 1280 (22 NYCRR Part 1280); Part 1281 (22 NYCRR Part 1281); Part 1290 (22 NYCRR Part 1290); Part 1291 (22 NYCRR Part 1291); Part 1300 (22 NYCRR Part 1300); Part 1301 (22 NYCRR Part 1301); Part 1302 (22 NYCRR Part 1302); Part 1303 (22 NYCRR Part 1303); Part 1320 (22 NYCRR Part 1320); Part 1420 (22 NYCRR Part 1420); Part 1440 (22 NYCRR Part 1440); Part 1480 (22 NYCRR Part 1480); Part 1500 (22 NYCRR Part 1500); Part 1530 (22 NYCRR Part 1530); Part 1560 (22 NYCRR Part 1560); all sections of Part 1590 (22 NYCRR Part 1590), except for section 1590.11 (22 NYCRR 1590.11), which is not repealed; Part 1600 (22 NYCRR Part 1600); Part 1620 (22 NYCRR Part 1620); Part 1640 (22 NYCRR Part 1640); Part 1660 (22 NYCRR Part 1660); Part 1670 (22 NYCRR Part 1670); Part 1690 (22 NYCRR Part 1690); Part 1700 (22 NYCRR Part 1700); Part 1720 (22 NYCRR Part 1720); Part 1730 (22 NYCRR Part 1730); Part 1740 (22 NYCRR Part 1740); Part 1760 (22 NYCRR Part 1760); Part 1770 (22 NYCRR Part 1770); Part 1780 (22 NYCRR Part 1780); Part 1785 (22 NYCRR Part 1785); Part 1795 (22 NYCRR Part 1795); Part 1810 (22 NYCRR Part 1810); Part 1820 (22 NYCRR Part 1820); Part 1830 (22 NYCRR Part 1830); Part 1940 (22 NYCRR Part 1940); Part 1950 (22 NYCRR Part 1950); Part 1960 (22 NYCRR Part 1960); Part 1980 (22 NYCRR Part 1980); Part 1990 (22 NYCRR Part 1990); Part 2000 (22 NYCRR Part 2000); Part 2050 (22 NYCRR Part 2050); Part 2090 (22 NYCRR Part 2090); Part 2110 (22 NYCRR Part 2110); Part 2120 (22 NYCRR Part 2120); Part 2130 (22 NYCRR Part 2130); Part 2190 (22 NYCRR Part 2190); Part 2200 (22 NYCRR Part 2200); Part 2230 (22 NYCRR Part 2230); Part 2240 (22 NYCRR Part 2240); Part 2250 (22 NYCRR Part 2250); Part 2260 (22 NYCRR Part 2260); Part 2270 (22 NYCRR Part 2270); Part 2280 (22 NYCRR Part

2280); Part 2290 (22 NYCRR Part 2290); Part 2300 (22 NYCRR Part 2300); Part 2310 (22 NYCRR Part 2310); Part 2320 (22 NYCRR Part 2320); Part 2330 (22 NYCRR Part 2330); Part 2340 (22 NYCRR Part 2340); Part 2350 (22 NYCRR Part 2350); Part 2360 (22 NYCRR Part 2360); Part 2370 (22 NYCRR Part 2370); Part 2380 (22 NYCRR Part 2380); Part 2390 (22 NYCRR Part 2390); Part 2400 (22 NYCRR Part 2400); Part 2410 (22 NYCRR Part 2410); Part 2420 (22 NYCRR Part 2420); Part 2430 (22 NYCRR Part 2430); Part 2440 (22 NYCRR Part 2440); Part 2450 (22 NYCRR Part 2450); Part 2501 (22 NYCRR Part 2501); Part 2502 (22 NYCRR Part 2502); Part 2503 (22 NYCRR Part 2503); Part 2504 (22 NYCRR Part 2504); Part 2506 (22 NYCRR Part 2506); Part 2507 (22 NYCRR Part 2507); Part 2508 (22 NYCRR Part 2508); Part 2510 (22 NYCRR Part 2510); Part 2590 (22 NYCRR Part 2590); Part 2655 (22 NYCRR Part 2655); Part 2685 (22 NYCRR Part 2685); Part 2755 (22 NYCRR Part 2755); Part 2770 (22 NYCRR Part 2770); Part 2810 (22 NYCRR Part 2810); Part 2830 (22 NYCRR Part 2830); Part 2900 (22 NYCRR Part 2900); Part 2950 (22 NYCRR Part 2950); Part 3000 (22 NYCRR Part 3000); Part 3020 (22 NYCRR Part 3020); Part 3030 (22 NYCRR Part 3030); Part 3040 (22 NYCRR Part 3040); Part 3050 (22 NYCRR Part 3050); Part 3060 (22 NYCRR Part 3060); Part 3070 (22 NYCRR Part 3070); Part 3080 (22 NYCRR Part 3080); Part 3090 (22 NYCRR Part 3090); Part 3100 (22 NYCRR Part 3100); Part 3110 (22 NYCRR Part 3110); Part 3120 (22 NYCRR Part 3120); Part 3130 (22 NYCRR Part 3130); Part 3200 (22 NYCRR Part 3200); Part 3210 (22 NYCRR Part 3210); Part 3305 (22 NYCRR Part 3305); Part 3400 (22 NYCRR Part 3400); Part 3420 (22 NYCRR Part 3420); Part 3435 (22 NYCRR Part 3435); Part 3445 (22 NYCRR Part 3445); Part 3455 (22 NYCRR Part 3455); Part 3485 (22 NYCRR Part 3485); Part 3495 (22 NYCRR Part 3495); Part 3505 (22 NYCRR Part 3505); Part 3515 (22 NYCRR Part 3515); Part 3525 (22 NYCRR Part 3525); Part 3530 (22 NYCRR Part 3530); Part 3840 (22 NYCRR Part 3840); Part 3935 (22 NYCRR Part 3935); Part 4000 (22 NYCRR Part 4000); Part 4300 (22 NYCRR Part 4300); Part 4301 (22 NYCRR Part 4301); Part 4500 (22 NYCRR Part 4500); Part 5000 (22 NYCRR Part 5000); Part 5300 (22 NYCRR Part 5300); Part 5301 (22 NYCRR Part 5301); and Part 5302 (22 NYCRR Part 5302).

Dated: December 17, 1985

PART 200. UNIFORM RULES FOR COURTS EXERCISING CRIMINAL JURISDICTION

SUBPART A. RULES APPLICABLE TO ALL COURTS

§ 200.1. Application; Definitions

(a) The rules of this Part shall govern procedures in each criminal court of the State.

(b) For purposes of this Part:

(1) "Chief Administrator of the Courts" shall include the designee of the Chief Administrator.

(2) "Clerk," as used in this Part, shall mean the chief clerk or the appropriate clerk of the trial court, unless the context otherwise requires.

(3) Other words or expressions used in this Part shall have the same meanings as they have under provisions of the Criminal Procedure Law.

Cross References

Criminal Procedure Law, see McKinney's Book 11A.

§ 200.2. Terms and Parts of Court

(a) **Terms of Court.** A term of court is a four-week session of court, and there shall be 13 terms of court in a year, unless otherwise provided in the annual schedule of terms established by the Chief Administrator of the Courts, which also shall specify the dates of such terms.

(b) **Parts of Court.** A part of court is a designated unit of the court in which specified business of the court is to be conducted by a judge or quasi-judicial officer. There shall be such parts of court as may be authorized to be established from time to time by the Chief Administrator of the Courts.

§ 200.3. Papers Filed in a Criminal Court; Form

In addition to complying with the applicable provisions of CPLR 2101, every paper filed in court, other than an exhibit or printed form, shall contain writing on one side only, and if typewritten, shall have at least double space between each line, except for quotations and the names and addresses of attorneys appearing in the action, and shall have at least one-inch margins.

Cross References

CPLR, see McKinney's Book 7B.

§ 200.4. Submission of Papers to Judge of a Criminal Court

All papers for signature or consideration of the court shall be presented to the clerk of the trial court in the appropriate courtroom or clerk's office, except that where the clerk is unavailable or the judge so directs, papers may be submitted to the judge and a copy filed with the clerk at the first available opportunity. All papers for any judge that are filed in the clerk's office shall be promptly delivered to the judge by the clerk. The papers shall be clearly addressed to the judge for whom they are intended and prominently show the nature of the papers, the title and the identification number of the accusatory instrument or instruments by which defendant is charged, the name of the assigned judge, if any, the name of the attorney or party submitting them and the return date of any motion to which the papers refer.

§ 200.5. Appearance of Counsel in Criminal Actions

Each attorney appearing in a criminal action is required to file a written notice of appearance on or before the time of the attorney's first appearance in court or not later than 10 days after appointment or retainer, whichever is sooner. The notice shall contain the attorney's name, office address and telephone number, the name of the person on whose behalf he or she is appearing, and the identification number of the accusatory instrument or instruments by which such person is charged.

Forms

Notice of appearance, see West's McKinney's Forms, Criminal Procedure, § 210.10, Form 3.

§ 200.6. Engagement of Counsel

No adjournment shall be granted on the ground of engagement of counsel except in accordance with Part 125 of the Rules of the Chief Administrator of the Courts.

§ 200.7. Authorization to Administer Oaths

(a) All court clerks employed in court parts devoted in whole or in part to the disposition of criminal actions, and such other employees as the judge presiding therein may designate in accordance with section 105 of the Uniform District Court Act, section 105 of the Uniform City Court Act, section 109 of the Uniform Justice Court Act and section 23(1) of the New York City Criminal Court Act, are authorized to administer oaths, take acknowledgments and sign the process of the court under the seal thereof.

(b) Copies of written authorizations to administer oaths required by section fifty-eight of the New York City Criminal Court Act to be filed with the New York City Criminal Court are to be filed with the chief clerk thereof.

Cross References

Uniform Justice Court Act, see McKinney's Book 29A, Part 2.

New York City Criminal Court Act, see McKinney's Book 29A, Part 3.

Uniform City and District Court Acts, see McKinney's Book 29A, Part 3.

§ 200.8. Official Forms

The forms set forth in 22 NYCRR Subtitle D,[1] designated "Forms for use in courts exercising criminal jurisdiction", shall be the official forms of those courts and shall, in substantially the same form as set forth, be uniformly used throughout the State.

[1] Such forms are not set out herein. See Subtitle D of Title 22 of the Codes, Rules and Regulations of the State of New York.

§ 200.9. Certificate of Relief From Disabilities; Notification of Eligibility

(a) In all criminal causes, whenever a pre-sentence probation report is submitted to the court, such report shall contain information bearing upon the eligibility of the defendant to obtain a certificate of relief from forfeitures and disabilities under article 23 of the Correction Law and shall further contain a recommendation as to the appropriateness of granting such discretionary relief at the time sentence is pronounced. Whenever a defendant has been sentenced to a period of probation, and has not received such discretionary relief, and if such defendant is apparently eligible for consideration of such discretionary relief, the probation officer supervising such defendant, prior to the termination of the probation period, shall inform the defendant of his right to make application to the court for a certificate of relief from disabilities, and shall provide such defendant with the required forms in order to enable him or her to make application to the court if he or she should wish to do so.

(b) In all criminal causes, whenever a defendant who is eligible to receive a certificate of relief from disabilities under article 23 of the Correction Law is sentenced, the court, in pronouncing sentence, unless it grants such certificate at that time, shall advise the defendant of his or her eligibility to make application at a later time for such relief.

(c) Failure to comply with the requirements of subdivision (a) or (b) of this section shall not affect the validity of any sentence.

Cross References

Correction Law, see McKinney's Book 10B.

SUBPART B. RULES APPLICABLE TO SUPERIOR COURTS

§ 200.10. Applicability of Sections 200.10 to 200.14

The rules of these sections shall be applicable to each superior court.

§ 200.11. Assignment of Criminal Actions

Criminal actions shall be assigned as follows:

(a) General. Except as the Chief Administrator of the Courts may otherwise provide, all criminal actions in Supreme Court and in County Court shall be heard and disposed of in accordance with an individual assignment system.

(b) Arraignment-Conference Part. The Chief Administrator of the Courts may authorize the establishment of an arraignment-conference part for any superior court. Where an arraignment-conference part has been established, upon commencement of a criminal action in the superior court, the action shall be assigned to such part. The judge presiding therein shall arraign the defendant and hear and determine any bail application. If no plea of guilty is entered within fourteen calendar days of the defendant's arraignment, or if the judge presiding determines that it is unlikely that a plea of guilty will be entered, the action shall be assigned to a judge as provided in subdivision (c) of this section. If a plea of guilty is entered within such time period, the action shall remain in the arraignment-conference part for sentencing and any further proceedings therein.

(c) Assignment of Actions to Individual Assignment Judges. Except as provided in subdivision (b) of this section, upon commencement of a criminal action in the superior court, the action shall be assigned to a judge by the clerk of the court in which it is pending pursuant to a method of random selection authorized by the Chief Administrator. The judge thereby assigned shall be known as the "assigned judge" with respect to such action and, except as otherwise provided in subdivision (d) of this section, shall conduct all further proceedings therein.

(d) Exceptions.

(1) Where the requirements of matters already assigned to a judge are such as to limit the ability of that judge to handle additional cases, the Chief Administrator may authorize that new assignments to that judge be suspended until the judge is able to handle additional cases.

(2) The Chief Administrator may authorize the assignment of one or more special reserve trial judges. Such judges may be assigned matters for trial in exceptional circumstances where the needs of the courts require such assignment.

(3) Matters requiring immediate disposition may be assigned to a judge designated to hear such matters when the assigned judge is not available.

(4) The Chief Administrator may authorize the transfer of any action and any matter relating to an action from one judge to another in accordance with the needs of the court.

§ 200.12. Preliminary Conference

As soon as practicable after the assignment of an action to an individual assignment judge, the assigned judge shall conduct a preliminary conference. The matters to be considered at such conference shall include establishment of a timetable for completion of discovery and filing and hearing of motions, fixing a date for commencement of trial, and consideration of any other matters that the court may deem relevant. At the conclusion of the conference the directions by the court to the parties and any stipulations by counsel shall be placed on the record or incorporated in a written court order. In the discretion of the court, failure of a party to comply with these directions shall result in the imposition of such sanctions as are authorized by law. The court may direct the holding of additional preliminary conferences as may be needed.

§ 200.13. Impaneling of Grand Juries

There shall be a grand jury drawn and impaneled for such terms of a superior court as may be provided on the annual schedule of terms established by the Chief Administrator of the Courts. Whenever the public interest requires, additional grand juries may be drawn and impaneled as authorized by the Chief Administrator.

§ 200.14. Transfer of Indictments Between Superior Courts

Upon authorization by the Chief Administrator:

(a) An indictment pending in the Supreme Court at a term held in a county outside the city of New York may, prior to entry of a plea of guilty thereto or commencement of a trial thereof, be removed to the County Court of such county.

(b) An indictment pending in a County Court may similarly be removed to the Supreme Court at a term held or to be held in the same county.

§ 200.15. Appointment of a Special District Attorney

Any party filing with a superior court an application for appointment of a special district attorney, pursuant to section 701 of the County Law, shall make the application to the Chief Administrator of the Courts. The Chief Administrator, in consultation and agreement with the Presiding Justice of the appropriate Appellate Division, then shall designate a superior court judge to consider the application as provided by law.

Cross References
County Law, see McKinney's Book 11.

§§ 200.16 to 200.19. [Reserved]

SUBPART C. RULES APPLICABLE TO LOCAL CRIMINAL COURTS

§ 200.20. Applicability of Subpart C

The rules of these sections shall be applicable to each local criminal court.

§ 200.21. Procedure in Local Criminal Courts; Local Court Rules

Procedure in each local criminal court shall be as provided by the Criminal Procedure Law and such local court rules as may be adopted in compliance with Part 9 of the Rules of the Chief Judge.

Cross References
Criminal Procedure Law, see McKinney's Book 11A.

§ 200.22. Assignment of Criminal Actions

Criminal actions in a criminal term shall be assigned to judges in a manner authorized by the Chief Administrator of the Courts.

§ 200.23. Recordkeeping Requirements for Town and Village Courts

(a) Each town and village court shall maintain:

(1) case files containing all papers filed, orders issued, any minutes or notes made by the court of proceedings or testimony, and a copy of any original documents or papers forwarded to another court or agency;

(2) an index of cases with a unique number assigned to each case when filed; and

(3) a cashbook which shall chronologically itemize all receipts and disbursements.

(b) In each case, except for parking violations, the court shall assign a unique case number for each defendant. In addition to the papers filed and orders issued, the court shall maintain records which shall include the following information:

(1) the defendant's name, address, and date of birth if under the age of 19;

(2) the State law or local ordinance, including section number, of each offense charged;

(3) a brief description of each offense charged and the date of its alleged commission;

(4) the date of arrest;

(5) the name of the arresting agency or officer;

(6) the date of arraignment;

(7) the name and address of the prosecutor and the defendant's attorney;

(8) a record of the arraignment proceedings, including the following entries: whether the charges were

read to the defendant; the constitutional and statutory rights of which defendant was advised; whether counsel was assigned; the plea entered by defendant; a summary of other actions taken by the court at arraignment, including the form of release and amount of bail set; and the date of the next scheduled appearance;

(9) the defendant's NYSID number and court control number, where available, for fingerprintable offenses;

(10) a summary of all other actions taken and proceedings conducted before trial;

(11) the names and addresses of all witnesses sworn;

(12) whether the defendant waived a jury;

(13) each disposition after trial, and each disposition other than by trial and the reasons therefor;

(14) whether a pre-sentence report was ordered and made available to the defendant or the defendant's attorney;

(15) any sentence imposed by the court; and

(16) a summary of all post-judgment proceedings.

(c) A model recordkeeping system which complies with the requirements of this Part will be prepared and distributed by the Office of Court Administration.

§ 200.24. Recordkeeping in City Courts

Each city court may, consistent with the provisions of section 2019 of the Uniform City Court Act, maintain records of all criminal actions and proceedings in accordance with section 200.23 of this Part.

§ 200.25. Procedure for Accepting Guilty Pleas by Mail in the New York City Criminal Court

(a) **Establishment.** The Administrative Judge of the New York City Criminal Court may establish a procedure for accepting guilty pleas by mail whereby a defendant charged in an information with a designated petty offense defined outside of the Penal Law may enter a plea of guilty to such petty offense, and be sentenced by the Court to pay a fine and any applicable surcharge on the resulting conviction, without making a personal appearance in the action. For purposes of this section, the term "petty offense" shall have the same meaning as in subdivision (39) of section 1.20 of the Criminal Procedure Law

(b) **Applicability.** The procedure established pursuant to subdivision (a) shall apply only where a defendant has been served with an appearance ticket in lieu of an arrest, returnable in the Summons Part of the New York City Criminal Court, for a petty offense defined outside of the Penal Law that has been specifically designated by the Administrative Judge of the New York City Criminal Court as appropriate for disposition under this section.

(c) **Appearance Ticket; Form and Content.**

(1) The appearance ticket shall be in a form prescribed by the Administrative Judge of the New York City Criminal Court, in consultation with appropriate criminal justice agencies, and shall be served upon the defendant by the issuing officer. The appearance ticket shall contain the nature of the charge, the range of applicable penalties if convicted of the charge, a procedure for pleading guilty by mail, and such other information as may be prescribed by the Administrative Judge.

(2) With respect to the procedure for the entry of a plea of guilty by mail, the appearance ticket shall contain the exact amount of the fine and surcharge to be imposed by the Court, and the manner in which and date by which such fine and surcharge must be paid. The appearance ticket also shall include a provision advising the defendant that, by entering a plea of guilty by mail to the charge, he or she:

(i) waives arraignment in open court, the right to receive a copy of the accusatory instrument and the right to the aid of counsel;

(ii) pleads guilty to the offense as charged;

(iii) understands that a plea of guilty to the charge is equivalent to a conviction after trial;

(iv) agrees that the charge be disposed of by payment of the fine and any applicable surcharge in accordance with the amounts designated in the appearance ticket; and

(v) understands that the Court may refuse to accept the plea of guilty, because of the defendant's prior criminal record or other special circumstance, in which case, if ultimately convicted, he or she may be sentenced to the full range of penalties set forth in the appearance ticket.

(d) **Procedure.** A defendant served with an appearance ticket pursuant to this section charging the defendant with a designated petty offense defined outside of the Penal Law may enter a plea of guilty by mail by indicating, in accordance with the instructions in the appearance ticket, that he or she pleads guilty to the charge, and by signing and mailing the completed ticket, by first class, registered or certified mail, to the Court at the address provided on the ticket, together with payment of the amount of the fine and surcharge set forth on the ticket for the offense charged. Provided an information has been filed charging such offense, the Court then may dispose of the case as though the defendant had been convicted upon a plea of guilty in open court, or, because of the defendant's prior criminal record or other special circumstance, may refuse to accept the plea of guilty. If the plea is so refused, the Court shall inform the defendant in writing that he or she is required to appear before the Court at a stated time and place to answer the charge, which shall thereafter be disposed of pursuant to the applicable provisions of law, and shall return to the defendant any fine or surcharge payment that may have accompanied the defendant's proffered plea of guilty. Where an information charging a designated petty offense is dismissed by the court, any plea of guilty to such offense entered pursuant to this section shall be refused, and the court shall inform the defendant of the fact of the dismissal and shall return to the defendant any fine or surcharge payment that may have accompanied the defendant's proffered plea of guilty. A plea of guilty to a designated petty offense that is refused pursuant to this section shall be deemed a nullity.

§ 200.26. Issuance of Certain Securing Orders in Town and Village Courts; Duties of the Court, Assignment Of and Notification to Counsel; Notification to Pretrial Services Agency

(a) Where, following an arrest, a defendant is brought, pursuant to CPL § 120.90, 140.20 or 140.27, before a town or village court for arraignment on an accusatory instrument filed with such court, counsel for the defendant shall be given an opportunity to be heard before the court issues a securing order fixing bail or committing the defendant to the custody of the sheriff.

(b) If the defendant appears at such time without counsel, the court shall:

(i) permit the defendant to communicate free of charge by telephone for the purposes of obtaining counsel and informing a relative or friend that he or she has been charged with an offense.

(ii) prior to issuing a securing order fixing bail or committing the defendant to the custody of the sheriff, make an initial determination as to the defendant's eligibility for assigned counsel, provided, however, that this paragraph, as well as subdivisions (c) and (d) of this section, shall not apply where the court determines that the defendant has sufficient funds available to him or her to immediately post bail with the court in the amount and form to be fixed by the court, and such bail is so posted with the court.

(c) Where it appears, pursuant to paragraph (ii) of subdivision (b) of this section, that the defendant is financially unable to obtain counsel, the court shall, prior to issuing a securing order fixing bail or committing the defendant to the custody of the sheriff, assign counsel. Such assignment shall be in accordance with the plan for representation adopted by the county pursuant to County Law § 722, and shall, in accordance with such plan: (i) direct the administrator of the assigned counsel program to, without delay, select and assign to the defendant, subject to the court's approval, an appropriate attorney from the administrator's list of eligible attorneys: (ii) direct the local public defender office or legal aid society to represent the defendant; or (iii) designate a named attorney to represent the defendant. Where assigned counsel is not present in court at the time of the assignment, the court may issue such securing order in the absence of counsel, and in such case shall provide the defendant, in writing, with the name, business address and telephone number of such assigned counsel, or of the administrator of the assigned counsel program or director of the local public defender office or legal aid society, as appropriate. Upon issuing such securing order in the absence of counsel, or, if not practicable, within 24 hours thereafter, but no later than 48 hours thereafter if extraordinary circumstances so require, the court shall notify such counsel, administrator or director, as well as the director of the local pretrial services agency or head of the pretrial services unit of the county probation department, if any, by telephone, and in writing or by written fax, of the court's assignment, and shall include in such notification the defendant's name, the names of any codefendants, the charge or charges contained in the accusatory instrument, the docket or case number, if available, the adjourn date and time, the terms of the securing order and such other information as the court deems appropriate. The court shall include with such written or faxed notification to such counsel, administrator of the assigned counsel program or director of the local public defender office or legal aid society a copy of the accusatory instrument.

(d) Where it appears, pursuant to paragraph (ii) of subdivision (b) of this section, that the defendant is financially able to retain counsel, the court shall inquire whether the defendant intends to retain counsel, and whether there is a particular attorney the defendant intends to retain. If the defendant identifies a particular attorney he or she intends to retain, the court shall, where such information is readily available, provide the defendant, in writing, with the telephone number of such attorney. Where the defendant does not identify a particular attorney, or where the attorney so identified is not present in court at the time the court intends to issue the securing order fixing bail or committing the defendant to the custody of the sheriff, the court may issue such securing order in the absence of counsel. Upon issuing such securing order in the absence of counsel, or, if not practicable, within 24 hours thereafter, but no later than 48 hours thereafter if extraordinary circumstances so require, the court shall notify the director of the local pretrial services agency or head of the pretrial services unit of the county probation department, if any, and the administrator of the assigned counsel program or director of the local public defender office or legal aid society, as appropriate, by telephone, and in writing or by written fax, of the defendant's appearance before the court and of the court's preliminary determination that the defendant appears to be financially able to retain counsel. Such notification shall also include the defendant's name, the names of any codefendants, the charge or charges contained in the accusatory instrument, the docket or case number, if available, the adjourn date and time, the terms of the securing order and such other information as the court deems appropriate. The court shall include with such written or faxed notification to the administrator of the assigned counsel program or director of the local public defender office or legal aid society a copy of the accusatory instrument.

(e) Each town and village court shall obtain from the administrator of the assigned counsel program, public defender, legal aid society or other provider of indigent criminal defense legal services in that jurisdiction, and from the director of the local pretrial services agency or head of the pretrial services unit of the county probation department, if any, the names, addresses, telephone numbers and fax numbers required to effectuate the notification provisions of subdivisions (c) and (d) of this section.

(f) Nothing contained in this section shall be deemed to preclude the court from:

(i) terminating an assignment of counsel made pursuant to subdivision (c) of this section in accordance with the provisions of County Law § 722–d; or

(ii) issuing a securing order releasing the defendant on his or her own recognizance in accordance with CPL § 170.70, 180.80 or any other relevant provision of the Criminal Procedure Law; or

(iii) issuing a securing order releasing the defendant on bail or on his or her own recognizance in accordance with CPL § 30.30(2); or

(iv) entertaining an application for recognizance or bail made pursuant to CPL § 510.20.

(g) Nothing contained in this section shall be deemed to relieve the court of any obligation imposed pursuant to CPL §§ 170.10 and 180.10.

(h) Each town and village court shall maintain a record in the case file of any communications and correspondence initiated or received by the court pursuant to this section, and shall make such records available to the defendant's counsel and the prosecutor upon request.

(i) The Office of Court Administration shall prepare and distribute to each town and village court such forms as may be necessary to implement the notification provisions of this section.

§§ 200.27 to 200.29. [Reserved]

SUBPART D. CRIMINAL APPEALS TO COUNTY COURTS

§ 200.30. Applicability of Subpart D

The rules of this sub-part shall govern procedures in appeals to county courts in criminal actions.

§ 200.31. Judges Who May Stay Judgment Pending Appeal to County Court

Upon an appeal to county court from a judgment of sentence of a local criminal court, an order pursuant to CPL § 460.50, staying or suspending execution of the judgment pending termination of the appeal and either releasing defendant on his own recognizance or fixing bail, may be issued by a judge of the county court to which the appeal has been taken or a justice of the supreme court in the judicial district in which the local court is located. In the case of an appeal as of right from a judgment or sentence of a city court, such order also may be issued by a judge of such city court.

Cross References

Criminal Procedure Law, see McKinney's Book 11A.

§ 200.32. Duration of Order Staying or Suspending Execution of Judgment

(a) An order issued pursuant to CPL § 460.50 shall contain a statement that if an appeal has not been perfected within 120 days after the issuance of the order, the operation of such order terminates and the defendant must surrender himself to the criminal court in which the judgment was entered in order that execution of the judgment be commenced or resumed.

(b) No extension of the 120–day period specified in CPL § 460.50 shall be granted except by the county court.

Cross References

Criminal Procedure Law, see McKinney's Book 11A.

§ 200.33. Perfection of Criminal Appeals

(a) When a notice of appeal is filed with a local court, a copy shall be filed with the county clerk by the person filing with the local court. After an appeal has been taken pursuant to CPL § 460.10(2), and within 10 days after two transcripts of the stenographic minutes of the proceedings shall have been filed with the local criminal court pursuant to CPL § 460.70(1), the local criminal court shall file with the clerk of the county court the notice of appeal, a transcript of the proceedings, a copy of the accusatory instrument and any decision on pretrial motions, and shall notify the appellant and the respondent. If the local criminal court does not file the notice of appeal and transcript within the prescribed period or if the transcript is defective, the county court, upon application of appellant or respondent, shall order the local criminal court to file them or shall order the parties to settle the transcript before the local court in the manner prescribed by CPLR 5525(c) within a designated time which the county court deems reasonable.

(b) Within 20 days after the affidavit of errors and the return of the lower court have been filed with the county court, where an appeal has been taken pursuant to CPL § 460.10(3), or within 20 days after the notice of appeal and transcript have been filed with the county court, where an appeal has been taken pursuant to CPL § 460.10(2), appellant shall notice the appeal for the next term or special term of county court by filing with the judge of the county court, not less than 14 days prior to the date for which the appeal has been noticed, a brief and notice of argument with proof of service of a copy of each upon respondent. If the defendant is the appellant and the district attorney did not appear in the local criminal court, defendant shall also file proof of service of a copy of the brief and notice of argument upon the district attorney. Respondent's brief, or the district attorney's brief, if any, shall be filed with the judge of the county court within 12 days after service of appellant's brief, with proof of service of a copy upon appellant.

(c) If appellant does not comply herewith, the county court may, upon respondent's motion, or upon its own motion, dismiss the appeal.

(d) Upon motion, the county court judge hearing the appeal may for good cause shown extend the time to a subsequent term or special term, in which case the appellant must notice the appeal for such subsequent term. Unless otherwise ordered by the court, appeals may be submitted without oral argument. Motions for reargument may be made after decision is rendered, and must be made within 30 days after service upon the moving party of a copy of the order entered on the decision, with written notice of its entry.

Cross References

CPLR, see McKinney's Book 7B.

Criminal Procedure Law, see McKinney's Book 11A.

§ 200.40. Obligation of the Court to Advise of Right to Counsel on People's Appeal

(a) When a criminal court issues an order suppressing evidence, dismissing an accusatory instrument, setting aside a verdict or sentence, vacating a judgment or denying a motion made pursuant to CPL § 440.40, where such order may be appealed as of right by the People pursuant to CPL § 450.20, the court promptly shall advise the defendant, on the record or in writing,

(1) that the People have the right to take an appeal;

(2) that the defendant has the right to retain counsel to represent him or her on the appeal or to respond to the appeal pro se;

(3) if the defendant can show no financial ability to pay for the cost of counsel on appeal, the defendant may make application to the appellate court for assignment of counsel to respond to the appeal; and

(4) that the defendant must provide the court and the defendant's trial counsel with an address where he or she can be contacted should the People appeal the order of the criminal court.

(b) In addition to the circumstances set forth in subdivision (a) of this section, where a court imposes a sentence, and where the People have indicated to the sentencing court their belief that the sentence is invalid as a matter of law and may be appealed by them on that ground, the court, upon imposing the sentence, shall advise the defendant of the rights enumerated in subdivision (a).

PART 202. UNIFORM CIVIL RULES FOR THE SUPREME COURT AND THE COUNTY COURT

§ 202.1. Application of Part; Waiver; Additional Rules; Application of CPLR; Definitions

(a) Application. This Part shall be applicable to civil actions and proceedings in the Supreme Court and the County Court.

(b) Waiver. For good cause shown, and in the interests of justice, the court in an action or proceeding may waive compliance with any of these rules other than sections 202.2 and 202.3 unless prohibited from doing so by statute or by a rule of the Chief Judge.

(c) Additional Rules. Local court rules, not inconsistent with law or with these rules, shall comply with Part 9 of the Rules of the Chief Judge (22 NYCRR Part 9).

(d) Application of CPLR. The provisions of this Part shall be construed consistent with the Civil Practice Law and Rules (CPLR), and matters not covered by these provisions shall be governed by the CPLR.

(e) Definitions.

(1) "Chief Administrator of the Courts" in this Part also includes a designee of the Chief Administrator.

(2) The term "clerk" shall mean the chief clerk or other appropriate clerk of the trial court unless the context otherwise requires.

(3) Unless otherwise defined in this Part, or the context otherwise requires, all terms used in this Part shall have the same meaning as they have in the CPLR.

Cross References

CPLR, see McKinney's Book 7B.

§ 202.2. Terms and Parts of Court

(a) Terms of Court. A term of court is a four-week session of court, and there shall be 13 terms of court in a year, unless otherwise provided in the annual schedule of terms established by the Chief Administrator of the Courts, which also shall specify the dates of such terms.

(b) Parts of Court. A part of court is a designated unit of the court in which specified business of the court is to be conducted by a judge or quasi-judicial officer. There shall be such parts of court as may be authorized from time to time by the Chief Administrator of the Courts.

§ 202.3. Individual Assignment System; Structure

(a) General. There shall be established for all civil actions and proceedings heard in the Supreme Court and County Court an individual assignment system which provides for the continuous supervision of each action and proceeding by a single judge. Except as otherwise may be authorized by the Chief Administrator or by these rules, every action and proceeding shall be assigned and heard pursuant to the individual assignment system.

(b) Assignments. Actions and proceedings shall be assigned to the judges of the court upon the filing with the court of a request for judicial intervention pursuant to section 202.6 of this Part. Assignments shall be made by the clerk of the court pursuant to a method of random selection authorized by the Chief Administrator. The judge thereby assigned shall be known as the "assigned judge" with respect to that matter and, except as otherwise provided in subdivision (c), shall conduct all further proceedings therein.

(c) Exceptions.

(1) Where the requirements of matters already assigned to a judge are such as to limit the ability of that judge to handle additional cases, the Chief Administrator may authorize that new assignments to that judge be suspended until the judge is able to handle additional cases.

(2) The Chief Administrator may authorize the establishment in any court of special categories of actions and proceedings, including but not limited to matrimonial actions, medical malpractice actions, tax assessment review proceedings, condemnation actions and actions requiring protracted consideration, for assignment to judges specially assigned to hear such actions or proceedings. Where more than one judge is specially assigned to hear a particular category of action or proceeding, the assignment of such actions or proceedings to the judges so assigned shall be at random.

(3) The Chief Administrator may authorize the assignment of one or more special reserve trial judges. Such judges may be assigned matters for trial in exceptional circumstances where the needs of the courts require such assignment.

(4) Matters requiring immediate disposition may be assigned to a judge designated to hear such matters when the assigned judge is not available.

(5) The Chief Administrator may authorize the transfer of any action or proceeding and any matter relating to an action or proceeding from one judge to another in accordance with the needs of the court.

(6) The Chief Administrator may authorize the establishment in any court or county or judicial district of a dual track system of assignment. Under such system each action and proceeding shall be supervised

continuously by the individually assigned judge until the note of issue and certificate of readiness have been filed and the pretrial conference, if one is ordered, has been held. The action or proceeding then may be assigned to another judge for trial in a manner prescribed by the Chief Administrator.

§ 202.4. County Court Judge; Ex Parte Applications in Supreme Court Actions; Applications for Settlement of Supreme Court Actions

Ex parte applications in actions or proceedings in the Supreme Court, and applications for the settlement of actions or proceedings pending in the Supreme Court, where judicial approval is necessary, may be heard and determined by a judge of the County Court in the county where venue is laid, during periods when no Supreme Court term is in session in the county.

§ 202.5. Papers Filed in Court

(a) Index Number; Form; Label. The party filing the first paper in an action, upon payment of the proper fee, shall obtain from the county clerk an index number, which shall be affixed to the paper. The party causing the first paper to be filed shall communicate in writing the county clerk's index number forthwith to all other parties to the action. Thereafter such number shall appear on the cover and first page to the right of the caption of every paper tendered for filing in the action. Each such cover and first page also shall contain an indication of the county of venue and a brief description of the nature of the paper and, where the case has been assigned to an individual judge, shall contain the name of the assigned judge to the right of the caption. In addition to complying with the provisions of CPLR 2101, every paper filed in court shall have annexed thereto appropriate proof of service on all parties where required, and if typewritten, shall have at least double space between each line, except for quotations and the names and addresses of attorneys appearing in the action, and shall have at least one-inch margins. In addition, every paper filed in court, other than an exhibit or printed form, shall contain writing on one side only, except that papers that are fastened on the side may contain writing on both sides. Papers that are stapled or bound securely shall not be rejected for filing simply because they are not bound with a backer of any kind.

(b) Submission of Papers to Judge. All papers for signature or consideration of the court shall be presented to the clerk of the trial court in the appropriate courtroom or clerk's office, except that where the clerk is unavailable or the judge so directs, papers may be submitted to the judge and a copy filed with the clerk at the first available opportunity. All papers for any judge that are filed in the clerk's office shall be promptly delivered to the judge by the clerk. The papers shall be clearly addressed to the judge for whom they are intended and prominently show the nature of the papers, the title and index number of the action in which they are filed, the judge's name and the name of the attorney or party submitting them.

(c) Papers filed to commence an action or special proceeding. For purposes of CPLR 304, governing the method of commencing actions and special proceedings, the term "clerk of the court" shall mean the county clerk. Each county clerk, and each chief clerk of the Supreme Court, shall post prominently in the public areas of his or her office notice that filing of papers in order to commence an action or special proceeding must be with the county clerk. Should the county clerk, as provided by CPLR 304, designate a person or persons other than himself or herself to accept delivery of the papers required to be filed in order to commence an action or special proceeding, the posted notice shall so specify.

Cross References

CPLR, see McKinney's Book 7B.

§ 202.5–a. Filing by Facsimile Transmission

(a) Application.

(1) There is hereby established a pilot program in which papers may be filed by facsimile transmission with the Supreme Court and, as is provided in section 206.5–a of these rules, with the Court of Claims. In the Supreme Court, the program shall be limited to commercial claims and tax certiorari, conservatorship, and mental hygiene proceedings in Monroe, Westchester, New York and Suffolk Counties.

(2) "Facsimile transmission" for purposes of these rules shall mean any method of transmission of documents to a facsimile machine at a remote location which can automatically produce a tangible copy of such document.

(b) Procedure.

(1) Papers in any civil actions or proceedings designated pursuant to this section, including those commencing an action or proceeding, may be filed with the appropriate court clerk by facsimile transmission at a facsimile telephone number provided by the court for that purpose. The cover page of each facsimile transmission shall be in a form prescribed by the Chief Administrator and shall state the nature of the paper being filed; the name, address and telephone number of the filing party or party's attorney; the facsimile telephone number that may receive a return facsimile transmission, and the number of total pages, including the cover page, being filed. The papers, including exhibits, shall comply with the requirements of CPLR 2101(a) and section 202.5 of these rules and shall be signed as required by law. Whenever a paper is filed that requires the payment of a filing fee, a separate credit card or debit card authorization sheet shall be included and shall contain the credit or

debit card number or other information of the party or attorney permitting such card to be debited by the clerk for payment of the filing fee. The card authorization sheet shall be kept separately by the clerk and shall not be a part of the public record. The clerk shall not be required to accept papers more than 50 pages in length, including exhibits but excluding the cover page and the card authorization sheet.

(2) Papers may be transmitted at any time of the day or night to the appropriate facsimile telephone number and will be deemed filed upon receipt of the facsimile transmission, provided, however, that where payment of a fee is required, the papers will not be deemed filed unless accompanied by a completed credit card or debit card authorization sheet. The clerk shall date-stamp the papers with the date that they were received. Where the papers initiate an action, the clerk also shall mark the papers with the index number. No later than the following business day, the clerk shall transmit a copy of the first page of each paper, containing the date of filing and, where appropriate, the index number, to the filing party or attorney, either by facsimile or first class mail. If any page of the papers filed with the clerk was missing or illegible, a telephonic, facsimile, or postal notification transmitted by the clerk to the party or attorney shall so state, and the party or attorney shall forward the new or corrected page to the clerk for inclusion in the papers.

(c) **Technical Failures.** The appropriate clerk shall deem the UCS fax server to be subject to a technical failure on a given day if the server is unable to accept filings continuously or intermittently over the course of any period of time greater than one hour after 12:00 noon of that day. The clerk shall provide notice of all such technical failures by means of the UCS fax server which persons may telephone in order to learn the current status of the Service which appears to be down. When filing by fax is hindered by a technical failure of the UCS fax server, with the exception of deadlines that by law cannot be extended, the time for filing of any paper that is delayed due to technical failure shall be extended for one day for each day in which such technical failure occurs, unless otherwise ordered by the court.

§ 202.5–b. Electronic Filing in Supreme Court

(a) **Application.**

(1) There is hereby established a pilot program in which documents may be filed and served by electronic means in civil actions in Supreme Court. Documents may be filed or served by such means only to the extent and in the manner authorized in this section and only in the following actions: (i) tax certiorari actions (including small claims actions under Title 1–A of Article 7 of the Real Property Tax Law) and tort and commercial actions in the Supreme Court in Albany, Bronx, Essex, Kings, Livingston, Monroe,

Nassau, New York, Niagara, Onondaga, Queens, Richmond, Suffolk, Sullivan and Westchester Counties; and (ii) actions in Supreme Court in Broome County and Erie County of any type designated by the appropriate Administrative Judge.

(2) For purposes of these rules:

(i) "electronic means" shall mean any method of transmission of information between computers or other machines, other than facsimile machines, designed for the purpose of sending and receiving such transmissions, and which allows the recipient to reproduce the information transmitted in a tangible medium of expression;

(ii) the "e-filing Internet site" shall mean the website located at www.nycourts.gov/efile;

(iii) "e-filing", "electronic filing" and "electronically filing" shall mean the filing and service of documents in a civil action by electronic means through the e-filing Internet site;

(iv) an "authorized e-filing user" shall mean a person who has registered to use e-filing pursuant to subdivision (c) of this section;

(v) an "action" shall include a special proceeding;

(vi) "hard copy" shall mean information set forth in paper form; and

(vii) "party" or "parties" shall mean the party or parties to an action or counsel thereto.

(b) **E–Filing in Actions in Supreme Court.**

(1) *Commencing an action by electronic means.* A party may commence any action specified in paragraph (1) of subdivision (a) of this section by electronically filing the initiating documents with the County Clerk.

(2) *E-filing in an action after commencement.*

(i) Consent of the parties required. After commencement of an action specified in paragraph (1) of subdivision (a) of this section, documents may be electronically filed and served, but only if and when all parties have consented thereto or, if fewer than all parties have so consented, only by and between consenting parties with the permission of the court.

(ii) Consent to e-filing; how obtained. A consent to e-filing in an action shall state that the party providing it agrees to the use of e-filing in the action and to be bound by the filing and service provisions in this section. Consent may be obtained by stipulation or a party who seeks to use e-filing in a pending action may serve upon all other parties to the action a notice regarding use of e-filing in a form approved by the Chief Administrator of the Courts. Service of such a notice shall constitute consent to e-filing in the action by the party causing such service to be made. A party served with such a notice may consent to e-filing in the action not later than ten days after receipt of such service, either by filing with the court and serving on all parties of record a consent to e-filing or if such party or the attorney of record therefor is an authorized e-filing user, by filing the consent electronically in the manner provided at the e-filing Internet site; provided, however, the court, in its discretion, may permit a consent to e-filing at any time thereafter. The filing of a consent to e-filing hereunder shall not constitute an appearance in the action.

(iii) Filing and service after consent to e-filing in an action. Once an action is made subject to e-filing, all documents filed and served by consenting parties shall be served and filed in accordance with this section.

(iv) Documents previously filed with the court; termination or modification of e-filing procedures. When an action becomes subject to e-filing, the court may direct that documents previously filed in the action in hard copy be filed electronically by the parties. The court may at any time order discontinuation of e-filing in such action or modification of e-filing procedures therein in order to prevent prejudice and promote substantial justice. Where a court orders discontinuation of e-filing in an action, the court may direct the clerk to convert into hard copy those documents comprising the case file which had been received electronically.

(c) Authorized E–Filing Users, Passwords and Other Information.

(1) *Registration required.* Documents may be filed or served electronically only by a person who has registered as an authorized e-filing user or as otherwise provided in this subdivision.

(2) *Registering as an authorized e-filing user.*

(i) Who may register. An attorney admitted to practice in the State of New York, or a person seeking to use e-filing as an authorized agent on behalf of attorneys of record in an action or actions (hereinafter "filing agent") may register as an authorized e-filing user of the e-filing Internet site. An attorney admitted *pro hac vice* in an action, a party to an action subject to e-filing who is not represented by an attorney, or a person who has been authorized in writing by an owner or owners of real property to submit a petition as provided in section 730 of the Real Property Tax Law and who has been licensed to engage in such business by the jurisdiction in which the business is operated (hereinafter "small claims assessment review filing agent") may also register as an authorized e-filing user, but solely for purposes of such action or, in the case of a small claims assessment review filing agent, solely for those proceedings under section 730 of the Real Property Tax Law in which he or she has been authorized to submit a petition.

(ii) How to register. Registration shall be on a form prescribed by the Chief Administrator, which shall require such information as he or she shall specify. If so provided by the Chief Administrator, registration shall not be complete until the registering person has been approved as an e-filing user. An authorized e-filing user shall notify the appropriate clerk immediately of any change in the information provided on his or her registration form.

(3) *Identification and password.* Upon registration, an authorized e-filing user shall be issued a confidential User Identification Designation ("User ID") and a password by the Unified Court System ("UCS"). An authorized e-filing user shall maintain his or her User ID and password as confidential, except as provided in paragraph (4) of this subdivision. Upon learning of the compromise of the confidentiality of either the User ID or the password, an authorized e-filing user shall immediately notify the appropriate clerk. At its initiative or upon request, the UCS may at any time issue a new User ID or password to any authorized e-filing user.

(4) An authorized e-filing user may authorize another person to file a document electronically on his or her behalf in a particular action using the User ID and password of the user, but in such event, the authorized e-filing user shall retain full responsibility for any document filed.

(d) Electronic Filing of Documents.

(1) In any action subject to e-filing, all documents required to be filed with the court by a party that has consented to such e-filing shall be filed electronically, except as provided herein. Each document to be filed electronically by a filing agent (other than one employed by a governmental entity) shall be accompanied by a statement of authorization from counsel of record in a form approved by the Chief Administrator.

(2) *Payment of fees.* Whenever documents are filed electronically that require the payment of a filing fee, the person who files the documents shall provide, in payment of the fee: (i) such credit or debit card information as shall be required at the e-filing Internet site to permit a card to be charged or debited by the County Clerk ; or (ii) the form or information required by the County Clerk to permit him or her to debit an account maintained with the County Clerk by an attorney or law firm appearing for a party to the case; or (iii) any other form of payment authorized by the Chief Administrator. Notwithstanding the foregoing, an authorized e-filing user who electronically files documents that require the payment of a filing fee may cause such fee to be paid thereafter in person at the office of the County Clerk.

(3) *Filing and receipt of documents; confirmation; secure information.*

(i) When documents are filed. Documents may be transmitted at any time of the day or night to the e-filing Internet site. Documents are deemed filed on the date on which their electronic transmission is recorded at that site, provided, however, that where payment of a fee is required upon the filing of a document, the document will not be deemed filed until transmission of the information or form or information as required in (i) or (ii), respectively, of paragraph (2) of this subdivision is recorded at the e-filing Internet site; or, if no such transmission is recorded, until payment is physically presented to the County Clerk.

(ii) Confirmation. No later than the close of business on the business day following the electronic filing of a document, a confirmation notice shall be transmitted electronically by the e-filing Internet site to the person filing such document. When documents initiating an action are filed electronically, the County Clerk shall assign an index number or filing number to the action and shall cause that number to be transmitted to the person filing such documents as part of the confirmation notice. If payment is submitted in person after the initiating documents have been transmitted electronically, the County Clerk shall assign the number upon presentation of that payment.

(iii) Secure information. When electronically filing a document, the person filing such document shall indicate whether it contains any of the following: individually identifiable health information, a social security number, a credit card number, a bank account number, an individual's date of birth, an individual's home address, a minor child's name, or trade secrets. If such person indicates that any of this information is contained in the document, access to it on the e-filing Internet site may be restricted to consenting parties to the action, the County Clerk and the court. The document will, however, be available for public inspection at the office of the County Clerk unless sealed by the court.

(4) *Official record; courtesy copies.* When a document has been filed electronically pursuant to this section, the official record shall be the electronic recording of the document stored by the clerk. The court may require the parties to provide courtesy hard copies of documents filed electronically. Unless the court directs otherwise, each such copy shall bear a conspicuous notice on the first page that the document has been electronically filed.

(5) *Orders and judgments.* Unless the court directs otherwise, any document that requires a judge's signature shall be transmitted electronically and in hard copy to the court. Unless the Chief Administrator authorizes use of electronic signatures, orders and judgments signed by a judge shall be signed in hard copy, and shall be converted into electronic form by the appropriate clerk. The County Clerk may sign judgments in hard copy, or may affix a digital image of his or her signature to judgments in electronic form.

(6) *Exhibits in hard copy.* Notwithstanding any other provision of this section, the clerk may permit a party to file in hard copy an exhibit which it is impractical or inconvenient to file electronically.

(e) Signatures.

(1) *Signing of a document.* An electronically filed document shall be considered to have been signed by, and shall be binding upon, the person identified as a signatory, if:

(i) it bears the physical signature of such person and is scanned into an electronic format that reproduces such signature; or

(ii) the signatory has electronically affixed the digital image of his or her signature to the document; or

(iii) it is electronically filed under the User ID and password of that person; or

(iv) in a tax certiorari action in which the parties have stipulated to this procedure, it is an initiating document that is electronically filed without the signature of the signatory in a form provided above in this subparagraph, provided that, prior to filing, the document is signed in hard copy form (which hard copy must be preserved until the conclusion of all proceedings, including appeals, in the case in which it is filed) and the electronic record of the document bears the word "Signed" typed on the signature line; or

(v) it otherwise bears the electronic signature of the signatory in a format conforming to such standards and requirements as may hereafter be established by the Chief Administrator.

(2) *Compliance with Part 130.* A document shall be considered to have been signed by an attorney or party in compliance with section 130–1.1–a of the Rules of the Chief Administrator (22 NYCRR § 130–1.1–a) if it has been signed by such attorney or party as provided in paragraph (1) of this subdivision and it bears the signatory's name, address and telephone number.

(3) *Certification of Signature.* A party or attorney may add his or her signature to a stipulation or other filed document by signing and filing a Certification of Signature for such document in a form prescribed by the Chief Administrator.

(f) Service of Documents.

(1) *Service of initiating documents in an action.* Initiating documents may be served in hard copy pursuant to Article 3 of the CPLR, or in tax certiorari cases, pursuant to the Real Property Tax Law, or by electronic means if the party served agrees to accept such service. A party served by electronic means shall, within 24 hours of service, provide the serving party or attorney with an electronic confirmation that the service has been effected.

(2) *Service of interlocutory documents.* (i) E-mail address for service. Each party in an action subject to electronic filing that has consented thereto shall identify on an appropriate form an e-mail address at which service of interlocutory documents on that party may be made through notification transmitted by the e-filing Internet site (hereinafter the "e-mail service address"). Each attorney of record and each self-represented party shall promptly notify the appropriate clerk in the event he or she changes his or her e-mail service address.

(ii) How service is made. Where parties have consented to e-filing, upon the receipt of an interlocutory document by the e-filing Internet site, the site shall automatically transmit electronic notification to all e-mail service addresses. Such notification shall provide the title of the document received, the date received, and the names of those appearing on the list of e-mail service addresses to whom that notification is being sent. Each party receiving the notification shall be responsible for accessing the e-filing Internet site to obtain a copy of the document received. The electronic transmission of the notification shall constitute service of the document on the e-mail service addresses identified therein, except that such service will not be effective if the filing party learns that it did not reach the address of the person to be served. Proof of such service will be recorded on the e-filing Internet site. A party may, however, utilize other service methods permitted by the CPLR provided that, if one of such other methods is used, proof of service shall be filed electronically.

(g) Addition of Parties or Proposed Intervenors in a Pending E–Filed Action. A party to be added in an action subject to e-filing shall be served with initiating documents in hard copy together with the notice regarding use of e-filing specified in paragraph (2)(ii) of subdivision (b) of this section, to which response shall be made as set forth in that paragraph. A proposed intervenor or other non-party who seeks relief from the court in an action subject to e-filing, if consenting to e-filing, shall promptly file and serve a consent to e-filing. If an added party or intervenor does not so consent, subsequent documents shall be served by and on that party or intervenor in hard copy but the action shall continue as an e-filed one as to all consenting parties.

(h) Entry of Orders and Judgments and Notice of Entry. In an action subject to e-filing, the County Clerk or his or her designee shall file orders and judgments of the court electronically, which shall constitute entry of the order or judgment. The date of entry shall be the date on which transmission of the order or judgment is recorded at the e-filing Internet site. The County Clerk may require that a party seeking entry of judgment electronically serve upon the County Clerk a request for entry of judgment. Upon entry of an order or judgment, the County Clerk, his or her designee, or the e-filing Internet site shall transmit to the e-mail service addresses a notification of such entry, which shall not constitute service of notice of entry by any party. A party shall serve notice of entry of an order or judgment on another party by serving a copy of the notification received from the County Clerk, his or her designee or the e-filing Internet site, a copy of the order or judgment, and an express statement that the transmittal constitutes notice of entry. Service may be made through the e-filing Internet site, or by any other service methods permitted by the CPLR provided that, if one of such other methods is used, proof of service shall be filed electronically.

(i) Technical Failures. The appropriate clerk shall deem the e-filing Internet site to be subject to a technical failure on a given day if the site is unable to accept filings or provide access to filed documents continuously or intermittently over the course of any period of time greater than one hour after 12:00 noon of that day. The clerk shall provide notice of all such technical failures on the site. When filing by electronic means is hindered by a technical failure, a party may file with the appropriate clerk in hard copy. With the exception of deadlines that by law cannot be extended, the time for filing of any paper that is delayed due to technical failure of the site shall be extended for one day for each day on which such failure occurs, unless otherwise ordered by the court.

(j) Electronic Filing of Discovery Materials. In any action subject to e-filing, parties and non-parties producing materials in response to discovery demands may enter into a stipulation authorizing the electronic filing of discovery responses and discovery materials to the degree and upon terms and conditions set forth in the stipulation. In the absence of such a stipulation, no party shall file electronically any such materials except in the form of excerpts, quotations, or selected exhibits from such materials as part of motion papers, pleadings or other filings with the court.

(k) Copyright, Confidentiality, And Other Proprietary Rights.

(1) Submissions pursuant to e-filing procedures shall have the same copyright, confidentiality and proprietary rights as paper documents.

(2) In an action subject to e-filing, any person may apply for an order prohibiting or restricting the electronic filing in the action of specifically identified materials on the grounds that such materials are subject to copyright or other proprietary rights, or trade secret or other privacy interests, and that electronic filing in the action is likely to result in substantial prejudice to those rights or interests. Unless otherwise permitted by the court, a motion for such an order shall be filed not less than ten days before the materials to which the motion pertains are due to be produced or filed with the court.

§ 202.6.   Request for Judicial Intervention

(a) At any time after service of process, a party may file a request for judicial intervention. Except as provided in subdivision (b), in an action not yet assigned to a judge, the court shall not accept for filing a notice of motion, order to show cause, application for ex parte order, notice of Motion, note of issue, notice of medical, dental or podiatric malpractice action, statement of net worth pursuant to section 236 of the Domestic Relations Law or request for a preliminary conference pursuant to section 202.12(a) of this Part, unless such notice or application is accompanied by a request for judicial intervention. Where an application for poor person relief is made, payment of the fee for filing the request for judicial intervention accompanying the application shall be required only upon denial of the application. A request for judicial intervention must be submitted, in duplicate, on a form authorized by the Chief of the Courts, with proof of service on the other parties to the action (but proof of service is not required where the application is ex parte).

(b) The filing of a request for judicial intervention and payment of the fee required by CPLR 8020(a) for said filing shall not be required with respect to an application not filed in an action or proceeding, nor with respect to a petition for the sale of church property, an application for change of name, a habeas corpus proceeding where the movant is institutionalized, an application for default judgment to the clerk pursuant to CPLR 3215(a), an application under CPLR 3102(e) for court assistance in obtaining disclosure in an action pending in another state, a retention proceeding authorized by Article 9 of the Mental Hygiene Law, an appeal to a county court of a civil case brought in a court of limited jurisdiction, an application to vacate a judgment on account of bankruptcy, a motion for an order authorizing emergency surgery, or within the City of New York, an uncontested action for a judgment for annulment, divorce or separation commenced pursuant to Articles 9, 10 or 11 of the Domestic Relations Law.

(c) In the counties within the City of New York, when a request for judicial intervention is filed, the clerk shall require submission of a copy of the receipt of purchase of the index number provided by the county clerk, or a written statement of the county clerk that an index number was purchased in the action. Unless otherwise authorized by the Chief Administrator, the filing of a request for judicial intervention pursuant to this section shall cause the assignment of the action to a judge pursuant to section 202.3 of this Part. The clerk may require that a self-addressed and stamped envelope accompany the request for judicial intervention.

REQUEST FOR JUDICIAL INTERVENTION

_____ COURT, _____ COUNTY

INDEX NO. _____ DATE PURCHASED: _____

PLAINTIFF(S):

DEFENDANT(S):

_____

For Clerk Only

_____

IAS entry date

_____

Judge Assigned

_____

RJI Date

_____

Date issue joined: _____ Bill of particulars served (Y/N): [ ] Yes   [ ] No

NATURE OF JUDICIAL INTERVENTION (check **ONE** box only **AND** enter information)

[ ] Request for preliminary conference

[ ] Note of issue and/or certificate of readiness

[ ] Notice of motion (return date: _____)
Relief sought _____

[ ] Order to show cause
(clerk enter return date: _____)
Relief sought _____

[ ] Other ex parte application (specify: _____)

[ ] Notice of petition (return date: _____)
Relief sought _____

[ ] Notice of medical or dental malpractice action (specify: _____)

[ ] Statement of net worth

[ ] Writ of habeas corpus

[ ] Other (specify: _____)

NATURE OF ACTION OR PROCEEDING (Check **ONE** box only)

MATRIMONIAL
[ ] Contested   -CM
[ ] Uncontested   -UM

COMMERCIAL
[ ] Contract   -CONT
[ ] Corporate   -CORP
[ ] Insurance (where insurer is party, except arbitration)   -INS
[ ] UCC (including sales, negotiable instruments)   -UCC
[ ] *Other Commercial   -OC
_____

REAL PROPERTY
[ ] Tax Certiorari   -TAX
[ ] Foreclosure   -FOR
[ ] Condemnation   -COND
[ ] Landlord/Tenant   -LT
[ ] *Other Real Property   -ORP
_____

OTHER MATTERS
[ ] *_____ -OTH

TORTS
Malpractice
[ ] Medical/Podiatric   -MM
[ ] Dental   -DM
[ ] *Other Professional _____   -OPM
_____

[ ] Motor Vehicle   -MV
[ ] *Products Liability   -PL
[ ] _____
[ ] Environmental   -EN
[ ] Asbestos   -ASB
[ ] Breast Implant   -BI
[ ] *Other Negligence   -OTN
_____

[ ] *Other Tort (including intentional)   -OT
_____

SPECIAL PROCEEDINGS
[ ] Art. 75 (Arbitration)   -ART75
[ ] Art. 77 (Trusts)   -ART77
[ ] Art. 78   -ART78
[ ] Election Law   -ELEC
[ ] Guardianship (MHL Art. 81)   -GUARD81
[ ] *Other Mental Hygiene   -MHYG

* If asterisk used, please specify.   [   ] *Other Special Proceeding   -OSP

Check "YES" or "NO" for each of the following questions:

Is this action/proceeding against a

YES	NO		YES	NO	
[ ]	[ ]	Municipality: (Specify _____)	[ ]	[ ]	Public Authority: (Specify _____)

YES	NO	
[ ]	[ ]	Does this action/proceeding seek equitable relief?
[ ]	[ ]	Does this action/proceeding seek recovery for personal injury?
[ ]	[ ]	Does this action/proceeding seek recovery for property damage?

Pre-Note Time Frames:
(This applies to all cases except contested matrimonial and tax certiorari cases)

Estimated time period for case to be ready for trial (from filing of RJI to filing of Note of Issue):

☐ **Expedited: 0–8 months**   ☐ **Standard: 9–12 months**   ☐ **Complex: 13–15 months**

Contested Matrimonial Cases Only: (Check and give date)

Has summons been served?   ☐ No   ☐ Yes, Date _____

Was a Notice of No Necessity filed?   ☐ No   ☐ Yes, Date _____

ATTORNEY(S) FOR PLAINTIFF(S):

Self Rep.*	Name	Address	Phone #
☐			
☐			

ATTORNEY(S) FOR DEFENDANT(S):

Self Rep.*	Name	Address	Phone #
☐			
☐			

*Self Represented: parties representing themselves, without an attorney, should check the "Self Rep."
box and enter their name, address, and phone # in the space provided above for attorneys.

INSURANCE CARRIERS:

RELATED CASES: (IF NONE, write "NONE" below)

Title	Index #	Court	Nature of Relationship

     I AFFIRM UNDER PENALTY OF PERJURY THAT, TO MY KNOWLEDGE, OTHER THAN AS NOTED ABOVE, THERE ARE AND HAVE BEEN NO RELATED ACTIONS OR PROCEEDINGS, NOR HAS A REQUEST FOR JUDICIAL INTERVENTION PREVIOUSLY BEEN FILED IN THIS ACTION OR PROCEEDING.

Dated: _____

_____
(SIGNATURE)

_____
(PRINT OR TYPE NAME)

_____
ATTORNEY FOR

ATTACH RIDER SHEET IF NECESSARY TO PROVIDE REQUIRED INFORMATION

Cross References

Domestic Relations Law, see McKinney's Book 14.

§ 202.7. Calendaring of Motions; Uniform Notice of Motion Form; Affirmation of Good Faith

(a) There shall be compliance with the procedures prescribed in the CPLR for the bringing of motions. In addition, except as provided in subdivision (d) of this section, no motion shall be filed with the court unless there have been served and filed with the motion papers (1) a notice of motion and (2) with respect to a motion relating to disclosure or to a bill of particulars, an affirmation that counsel has conferred with counsel for the opposing party in a good faith effort to resolve the issues raised by the motion.

(b) The notice of motion shall read substantially as follows:

.... COURT OF THE STATE OF NEW YORK
COUNTY OF ....
....x
A.B.,

                 Plaintiff,

         -against-

C.D.,

                 Defendant.

....x

Notice of Motion
Index No.
....
Name of Assigned Judge
....
Oral argument is requested ☐
(check box if applicable)

    Upon the affidavit of ...., sworn to on ...., 19...., and upon (list supporting papers if any), the .... will move this court (in Room ....) at the .... Courthouse, ..., New York, on the ..... day of ...., 19...., at .... (a.m.) (p.m.) for an order (briefly indicate relief requested).

    The above-entitled action is for (briefly state nature of action, *e.g.*, personal injury, medical malpractice, divorce, etc.).

    This is a motion for or related to interim maintenance or child support ☐.
(check box if applicable)

    An affirmation that a good faith effort has been made to resolve the issues raised in this motion is annexed hereto.
(required only where the motion relates to disclosure or to a bill of particulars)

    Pursuant to CPLR 2214(b), answering affidavits, if any, are required to be served upon the undersigned at least seven days before the return date of this motion. ☐
(check box if applicable)

Dated:

(print name)
....
Attorney [1] (or attorney in charge of
case if law firm) for moving party.
Address:
Telephone number:

                (print name)
TO: ....
          Attorney [1] for (other party)
          Address:
          Telephone number:

                (print name)
....
          Attorney [1] for (other party)
          Address:
          Telephone number:

(c) The affirmation of the good faith effort to re-solve the issues raised by the motion shall indicate the time, place and nature of the consultation and the issues discussed and any resolutions, or shall indicate good cause why no such conferral with counsel for opposing parties was held.

(d) An order to show cause or an application for ex parte relief need not contain the notice of motion set forth in this section, but shall contain the affirmation of good faith set forth in this section if such affirmation otherwise is required by this section.

(e) Ex parte motions submitted to a judge outside of the county where the underlying action is venued or will be venued shall be referred to the appropriate court in the county of venue unless the judge deter-mines that the urgency of the motion requires imme-diate determination.

(f) Any application for temporary injunctive relief, including but not limited to a motion for a stay or a temporary restraining order, shall contain, in addition to the other information required by this section, an affirmation demonstrating there will be significant prejudice to the party seeking the restraining order by giving of notice. In the absence of a showing of significant prejudice, the affirmation must demon-strate that a good faith effort has been made to notify the party against whom the temporary restraining order is sought of the time, date and place that the application will be made in a manner sufficient to permit the party an opportunity to appear in response to the application. This subdivision shall not be appli-cable to orders to show cause or motions in special proceedings brought under Article 7 of the Real Prop-erty Actions and Proceedings Law, nor to orders to show cause or motions requesting an order of protec-tion under section 240 of the Domestic Relations Law, unless otherwise ordered by the court.

[1] If any party is appearing *pro se*, the name, address and telephone number of such party shall be stated.

§ 202.8. Motion Procedure

(a) All motions shall be returnable before the as-signed judge, and all papers shall be filed with the court on or before the return date.

(b) Special Procedure for Unassigned Cases. If a case has not been assigned to a judge, the motion shall be made returnable before the court, and a copy of the moving papers, together with a request for judicial intervention, shall be filed with the court, with proof of service upon all other parties, where required by section 202.6 of this Part, within five days of service upon the other parties. The moving party shall give written notice of the index number to all other parties immediately after filing of the papers. Copies of all responding papers shall be submitted to the court, with proof of service and with the index number set forth in the papers, on or before the return date. The case shall be assigned to a judge as soon as practicable after the filing of the request for judicial intervention pursuant to section 202.6 of this Part, but in no event later than the return date. After assignment to the judge, the court shall provide for appropriate notice to the parties of the name of the assigned judge. Motion papers noticed to be heard in a county other than the county where the venue of the action has been placed by the plaintiff shall be assigned to a judge in accordance with proce-dures established by the Chief Administrator.

(c) The moving party shall serve copies of all affi-davits and briefs upon all other parties at the time of service of the notice of motion. The answering party shall serve copies of all affidavits and briefs as re-quired by CPLR 2214. Affidavits shall be for a statement of the relevant facts, and briefs shall be for a statement of the relevant law.

(d) Motion papers received by the clerk of the court on or before the return date shall be deemed submitted as of the return date. The assigned judge, in his or her discretion or at the request of a party, thereafter may determine that any motion be orally argued and may fix a time for oral argument. A party requesting oral argument shall set forth such request in its notice of motion or in its order to show cause or on the first page of the answering papers, as the case may be. Where all parties to a motion request oral argument, oral argument shall be granted unless the court shall determine it to be unnecessary. Where a motion is brought on by order to show cause, the court may set forth in the order that oral argu-ment is required on the return date of the motion.

(e)(1) Stipulations of adjournment of the return date made by the parties shall be in writing and shall be submitted to the assigned judge. Such stipulation shall be effective unless the court otherwise directs. No more than three stipulated adjournments for an aggregate period of 60 days shall be submitted with-out prior permission of the court. (2) Absent agree-ment by the parties, a request by any party for an adjournment shall be submitted in writing, upon no-tice to the other party, to the assigned judge on or before the return date. The court will notify the requesting party whether the adjournment has been granted.

(f) Where the motion relates to disclosure or to a bill of particulars, and a preliminary conference has not been held, the court shall notify all parties of a scheduled date to appear for a preliminary conference, which shall be not more than 45 days from the return date of the motion unless the court orders otherwise, and a form of a stipulation and order, prescribed by the Chief Administrator of the Courts, shall be made available which the parties may sign, agreeing to a timetable which shall provide for completion of disclo-sure within 12 months, and for a resolution of any other issues raised by the motion. If all parties sign the form and return it to the court before the return date of the motion, such form shall be "so ordered" by the court, and the motion shall be deemed withdrawn. If such stipulation is not returned by all parties, the conference shall be held on the assigned date. Issues raised by the motion and not resolved at the conference shall be determined by the court.

(g) Unless the circumstances require settlement of an order, a judge shall incorporate into the decision an order effecting the relief specified in the decision.

(h) **Reports of Pending Motions in the Supreme Court**

(1) To assist in preparing the quarterly report of pending civil matters required by section 4.1 of the Rules of the Chief Judge, the Chief Administrator of the Court or his or her designee shall provide to a justice of the Supreme Court, upon request, an automated open motion report of all motions pending before the justice which appear undecided 60 days after final submission. This open motion report may be used by the justice to assist in the preparation of his or her official quarterly report.

(2) Since motions are decided on a daily basis and further submissions may be received on a pending motion, the only report that shall be considered current is the official quarterly report submitted by the particular justice.

Cross References

CPLR, see McKinney's Book 7B.

Preliminary Conference Stipulation and Order, see App. D following Uniform Rules.

§ 202.9. Special Proceedings

Special proceedings shall be commenced and heard in the same manner as motions that have not yet been assigned to a judge as set forth in section 202.8, except that they shall be governed by the time requirements of the CPLR relating to special proceedings.

Cross References

CPLR, see McKinney's Book 7B.

§§ 202.10, 202.11. [Reserved]

§ 202.12. Preliminary Conference

(a) A party may request a preliminary conference at any time after service of process. The request shall state the title of the action; index number; names, addresses and telephone numbers of all attorneys appearing in the action; and the nature of the action. If the action has not been assigned to a judge, the party shall file a request for judicial intervention together with the request for a preliminary conference. The request shall be served on all other parties and filed with the clerk for transmittal to the assigned judge. The court shall order a preliminary conference in any action upon compliance with the requirements of this subdivision.

(b) The court shall notify all parties of the scheduled conference date, which shall be not more than 45 days from the date the request for judicial intervention is filed unless the court orders otherwise, and a form of a stipulation and order, prescribed by the Chief Administrator of the Courts, shall be made available which the parties may sign, agreeing to a timetable which shall provide for completion of disclosure within 12 months of the filing of the request for judicial intervention for a standard case, or within 15 months of such filing for a complex case. If all parties sign the form and return it to the court before the scheduled preliminary conference, such form shall be "so ordered" by the court, and, unless the court orders otherwise, the scheduled preliminary conference shall be cancelled. If such stipulation is not returned signed by all parties, the parties shall appear at the conference. Except where a party appears in the action pro se, an attorney thoroughly familiar with the action and authorized to act on behalf of the party shall appear at such conference.

(c) The matters to be considered at the preliminary conference shall include:

(1) simplification and limitation of factual and legal issues, where appropriate;

(2) establishment of a timetable for the completion of all disclosure proceedings, provided that all such procedures must be completed within the timeframes set forth in subdivision (b), unless otherwise shortened or extended by the court depending upon the circumstances of the case;

(3) addition of other necessary parties;

(4) settlement of the action;

(5) removal to a lower court pursuant to CPLR 325, where appropriate; and

(6) any other matters that the court may deem relevant.

(d) At the conclusion of the conference the court shall make a written order including its directions to the parties as well as stipulations of counsel. Alternatively, in the court's discretion, all directions of the court and stipulations of counsel may be recorded by a reporter. Where the latter procedure is followed, the parties shall procure and share equally the cost of a transcript thereof unless the court in its discretion otherwise provides. The transcript, corrected if necessary on motion or by stipulation of the parties approved by the court, shall have the force and effect of an order of the court. The transcript shall be filed by the plaintiff with the clerk of the court.

(e) The granting or continuation of a special preference shall be conditional upon full compliance by the party who has requested any such preference with the foregoing order or transcript. When a note of issue and certificate of readiness are filed pursuant to section 202.21 of this Part, in an action to which this section is applicable, the filing party, in addition to complying with all other applicable rules of the court, shall file with the note of issue and certificate of readiness an affirmation or affidavit, with proof of service on all parties who have appeared, showing specific compliance with the preliminary conference order or transcript.

(f) In the discretion of the court, failure by a party to comply with the order or transcript resulting from the preliminary conference, or with the so-ordered stipulation provided for in subdivision (b) of this section, or the making of unnecessary or frivolous motions by a party, shall result in the imposition upon such party of the costs or such other sanctions as are authorized by law.

(g) A party may move to advance the date of a preliminary conference upon a showing of special circumstances.

(h) Motions in actions to which this section is applicable made after the preliminary conference has been scheduled may be denied unless there is shown good cause why such relief is warranted before the preliminary conference is held.

(i) No action or proceeding to which this section is applicable shall be deemed ready for trial unless there is compliance with the provisions of this section and any order issued pursuant thereto.

(j) The court, in its discretion, at any time may order such conferences as the court may deem helpful or necessary in any matter before the court.

(k) The provisions of this section shall apply to preliminary conferences required in matrimonial actions and actions based upon a separation agreement, in medical malpractice actions, and in real property tax assessment review proceedings within the City of New York, only to the extent that these provisions are not inconsistent with the provisions of sections 202.16, 202.56 and 202.60 of this Part, respectively.

(l) The provisions of this section shall apply where a request is filed for a preliminary conference in an action involving a terminally ill party governed by CPLR 3407 only to the extent that the provisions of this section are not inconsistent with the provisions of CPLR 3407. In an action governed by CPLR 3407 the request for a preliminary conference may be filed at any time after commencement of the action, and shall be accompanied by the physician's affidavit required by that provision, but need not be accompanied by an affirmation of good faith prescribed by subdivision (a) of this section.

Cross References

Preliminary Conference Stipulation and Order, see App. D following Uniform Rules.

§ 202.13. Removal of Actions Without Consent to Courts of Limited Jurisdiction

Actions may be removed to courts of limited jurisdiction without consent pursuant to the provisions of CPLR 325(d) as follows:

(a) from the Supreme Court in counties within the First, Second, Eleventh and Twelfth Judicial Districts to the Civil Court of the City of New York;

(b) from the Supreme Court in counties within the Ninth Judicial District to county and city courts within such counties;

(c) from the Supreme Court in counties within the Tenth Judicial District to county courts within such counties;

(d) from the Supreme Court in counties within the Third Judicial Department to county and city courts within such counties;

(e) from the Supreme Court in counties within the Fourth Judicial Department to county and city courts within such counties;

(f) from the County Court of Broome County to the City Court of Binghamton; and

(g) from the County Court of Albany County to the City Court of Albany.

(h) from the Supreme Court and County Court of Nassau County to the District Court of Nassau County and the city courts within such county; and

(i) from the Supreme Court and County Court of Suffolk County to the District Court of Suffolk County.

Cross References

CPLR, see McKinney's Book 7B.

§ 202.14. Special Masters

The Chief Administrator of the Courts may authorize the creation of a program for the appointment of attorneys as special masters in designated courts to preside over conferences and hear and report on applications to the court. Special masters shall serve without compensation.

§ 202.15. Videotape Recording of Civil Depositions

(a) When Permitted. Depositions authorized under the provisions of the Civil Practice Law and Rules or other law may be taken, as permitted by subdivision (b) of section 3113 of the Civil Practice Law and Rules, by means of simultaneous audio and visual electronic recording, provided such recording is made in conformity with this section.

(b) Other Rules Applicable. Except as otherwise provided in this section, or where the nature of videotaped recording makes compliance impossible or unnecessary, all rules generally applicable to examinations before trial shall apply to videotaped recording of depositions.

(c) Notice of Taking Deposition. Every notice or subpoena for the taking of a videotaped deposition shall state that it is to be videotaped and the name and address of the videotape operator and of the operator's employer, if any. The operator may be an employee of the attorney taking the deposition. Where an application for an order to take a videotaped deposition is made, the application and order shall contain the same information.

(d) Conduct of the Examination.

(1) The deposition shall begin by one of the attorneys or the operator stating on camera:

(i) the operator's name and address;

(ii) the name and address of the operator's employer;

(iii) the date, the time and place of the deposition; and

(iv) the party on whose behalf the deposition is being taken.

The officer before whom the deposition is taken shall be a person authorized by statute and shall identify himself or herself and swear the witness on camera. If the deposition requires the use of more than one tape, the end of each tape and the beginning of each succeeding tape shall be announced by the operator.

(2) Every videotaped deposition shall be timed by means of a time-date generator which shall permanently record hours, minutes, and seconds. Each time the videotape is stopped and resumed, such times shall be orally announced on the tape.

(3) More than one camera may be used, either in sequence or simultaneously.

(4) At the conclusion of the deposition, a statement shall be made on camera that the recording is completed. As soon as practicable thereafter, the videotape shall be shown to the witness for examination, unless such showing and examination are waived by the witness and the parties.

(5) Technical data, such as recording speeds and other information needed to replay or copy the tape, shall be included on copies of the videotaped deposition.

(e) Copies and Transcription. The parties may make audio copies of the deposition and thereafter may purchase additional audio and audio-visual copies. A party may arrange to have a stenographic transcription made of the deposition at his or her own expense.

(f) Certification. The officer before whom the videotape deposition is taken shall cause to be attached to the original videotape recording a certification that the witness was fully sworn or affirmed by the officer and that the videotape recording is a true

record of the testimony given by the witness. If the witness has not waived the right to a showing and examination of the videotape deposition, the witness shall also sign the certification in accordance with the provisions of section 3116 of the Civil Practice Law and Rules.

(g) Filing and Objections.

(1) If no objections have been made by any of the parties during the course of the deposition, the videotape deposition may be filed by the proponent with the clerk of the trial court and shall be filed upon the request of any party.

(2) If objections have been made by any of the parties during the course of the deposition, the videotape deposition, with the certification, shall be submitted to the court upon the request of any of the parties within 10 days after its recording, or within such other period as the parties may stipulate, or as soon thereafter as the objections may be heard by the court, for the purpose of obtaining rulings on the objections. An audio copy of the sound track may be submitted in lieu of the videotape for this purpose, as the court may prefer. The court may view such portions of the videotape recording as it deems pertinent to the objections made, or may listen to an audiotape recording. The court, in its discretion, may also require submission of a stenographic transcript of the portion of the deposition to which objection is made, and may read such transcript in lieu of reviewing the videotape or audio copy.

(3)(i) The court shall rule on the objections prior to the date set for trial and shall return the recording to the proponent of the videotape with notice to the parties of its rulings and of its instructions as to editing. The editing shall reflect the rulings of the court and shall remove all references to the objections. The proponent, after causing the videotape to be edited in accordance with the court's instructions, may cause both the original videotape recording and the deleted version of the recording, clearly identified, to be filed with the clerk of the trial court, and shall do so at the request of any party. Before such filing, the proponent shall permit the other party to view the edited videotape.

(ii) The court may, in respect to objectionable material, instead of ordering its deletion, permit such material to be clearly marked so that the audio recording may be suppressed by the operator during the objectionable portion when the videotape is presented at the trial. In such case the proponent may cause both the original videotape recording and a marked version of that recording, each clearly identified, to be filed with the clerk of the trial court, and shall do so at the request of any party.

(h) Custody of Tape. When the tape is filed with the clerk of the court, the clerk shall give an appropriate receipt for the tape and shall provide secure and adequate facilities for the storage of videotape recordings.

(i) **Use at Trial.** The use of videotape recordings of depositions at the trial shall be governed by the provisions of the Civil Practice Law and Rules and all other relevant statutes, court rules and decisional law relating to depositions and relating to the admissibility of evidence. The proponent of the videotaped deposition shall have the responsibility of providing whatever equipment and personnel may be necessary for presenting such videotape deposition.

(j) **Applicability to Audio Taping of Depositions.** Except where clearly inapplicable because of the lack of a video portion, these rules are equally applicable to the taking of depositions by audio recording alone. However, in the case of the taking of a deposition upon notice by audio recording alone, any party, at least five days before the date noticed for taking the deposition, may apply to the court for an order establishing additional or alternate procedures for the taking of such audio deposition, and upon the making of the application, the deposition may be taken only in accordance with the court order.

(k) **Cost.** The cost of videotaping or audio recording shall be borne by the party who served the notice for the videotaped or audio recording of the deposition, and such cost shall be a taxable disbursement in the action unless the court in its discretion orders otherwise in the interest of justice.

(*l*) **Transcription for Appeal.** On appeal visual and audio depositions shall be transcribed in the same manner as other testimony and transcripts filed in the appellate court. The visual and audio depositions shall remain part of the original record in the case and shall be transmitted therewith. In lieu of the transcribed deposition and, on leave of the appellate court, a party may request a viewing of portions of the visual deposition by the appellate court but, in such case, a transcript of pertinent portions of the deposition shall be filed as required by the court.

Cross References

CPLR, see McKinney's Book 7B.

§ 202.16. Matrimonial Actions; Calendar Control of Financial Disclosure in Actions and Proceedings Involving Alimony, Maintenance, Child Support and Equitable Distribution; Motions for Alimony, Counsel Fees Pendente Lite, and Child Support; Special Rules

(a) **Applicability.** This section shall be applicable to all contested actions and proceedings in the Supreme Court in which statements of net worth are required by section 236 of the Domestic Relations Law to be filed and in which a judicial determination may be made with respect to alimony, counsel fees pendente lite, maintenance, custody and visitation, child support, or the equitable distribution of property, including those referred to Family Court by the Supreme Court pursuant to section 464 of the Family Court Act.

(b) **Form of Statements of Net Worth.** Sworn statements of net worth, except as provided in subdivision (k) of this section, exchanged and filed with the court pursuant to section 236 of the Domestic Relations Law, shall be in substantial compliance with the Statement of Net Worth form contained in appendix A of this Part [see Appendix A, following Part 218].

(c) **Retainer Agreements.**

(1) A signed copy of the attorney's retainer agreement with the client shall accompany the statement of net worth filed with the court, and the court shall examine the agreement to assure that it conforms to Appellate Division attorney conduct and disciplinary rules. Where substitution of counsel occurs after the filing with the court of the net worth statement, a signed copy of the attorney's retainer agreement shall be filed with the court within 10 days of its execution.

(2) An attorney seeking to obtain an interest in any property of his or her client to secure payment of the attorney's fee shall make application to the court for approval of said interest on notice to the client and to his or her adversary. The application may be granted only after the court reviews the finances of the parties and an application for attorney's fees.

(d) **Request for Judicial Intervention.** A request for judicial intervention shall be filed with the court by the plaintiff no later than 45 days from the date of service of the summons and complaint or summons with notice upon the defendant, unless both parties file a notice of no necessity with the court, in which event the request for judicial intervention may be filed no later than 120 days from the date of service of the summons and complaint or summons with notice upon the defendant. Notwithstanding section 202.6(a) of this Part, the court shall accept a request for judicial intervention that is not accompanied by other papers to be filed in court.

(e) **Certification.** Every paper served on another party or filed or submitted to the court in a matrimonial action shall be signed as provided in section 130–1.1–a of the Rules of the Chief Administrator.

(f) **Preliminary Conference.**

(1) In all actions or proceedings to which this section of the rules is applicable, a preliminary conference shall be ordered by the court to be held within 45 days after the action has been assigned. Such order shall set the time and date for the conference and shall specify the papers that shall be exchanged between the parties. These papers must be exchanged no later than 10 days prior to the preliminary conference, unless the court directs otherwise. These papers shall include:

230

(i) statements of net worth, which also shall be filed with the court no later than 10 days prior to the preliminary conference;

(ii) all paycheck stubs for the current calendar year and the last paycheck stub for the immediately preceding calendar year;

(iii) all filed state and federal income tax returns for the previous three years, including both personal returns and returns filed on behalf of any partnership or closely held corporation of which the party is a partner or shareholder;

(iv) all W–2 wage and tax statements, 1099 forms, and K–1 forms for any year in the past three years in which the party did not file state and federal income tax returns;

(v) all statements of accounts received during the past three years from each financial institution in which the party has maintained any account in which cash or securities are held;

(vi) the statements immediately preceding and following the date of commencement of the matrimonial action pertaining to: (A) any policy of life insurance having a cash or dividend surrender value; and (B) any deferred compensation plan of any type or nature in which the party has an interest including, but not limited to, Individual Retirement Accounts, pensions, profit-sharing plans, Keogh plans, 401(k) plans and other retirement plans.

Both parties personally must be present in court at the time of the conference, and the judge personally shall address the parties at some time during the conference.

(2) The matters to be considered at the conference may include, among other things:

(i) applications for pendente lite relief, including interim counsel fees;

(ii) compliance with the requirement of compulsory financial disclosure, including the exchange and filing of a supplemental statement of net worth indicating material changes in any previously exchanged and filed statement of net worth;

(iii) simplification and limitation of the issues;

(iv) the establishment of a timetable for the completion of all disclosure proceedings, provided that all such procedures must be completed and the note of issue filed within six months from the commencement of the conference, unless otherwise shortened or extended by the court depending upon the circumstances of the case; and

(v) any other matters which the court shall deem appropriate.

(3) At the close of the conference, the court shall direct the parties to stipulate, in writing or on the record, as to all resolved issues, which the court then shall "so order," and as to all issues with respect to fault, custody and finance that remain unresolved.

Any issues with respect to fault, custody and finance that are not specifically described in writing or on the record at that time may not be raised in the action unless good cause is shown. The court shall fix a schedule for discovery as to all unresolved issues and, in a noncomplex case, shall schedule a date for trial not later than six months from the date of the conference. The court may appoint a law guardian for the infant children, or may direct the parties to file with the court, within 30 days of the conference, a list of suitable law guardians for selection by the court. The court also may direct that a list of expert witnesses be filed with the court within 30 days of the conference from which the court may select a neutral expert to assist the court. The court shall schedule a compliance conference unless the court dispenses with the conference based upon a stipulation of compliance filed by the parties. Unless the court excuses their presence, the parties personally must be present in court at the time of the compliance conference. If the parties are present in court, the judge personally shall address them at some time during the conference.

(g) Expert Witnesses.

(1) Responses to demands for expert information pursuant to CPLR § 3101(d) shall be served within 20 days following service of such demands.

(2) Each expert witness whom a party expects to call at the trial shall file with the court a written report, which shall be exchanged and filed with the court no later than 60 days before the date set for trial, and reply reports, if any, shall be exchanged and filed no later than 30 days before such date. Failure to file with the court a report in conformance with these requirements may, in the court's discretion, preclude the use of the expert. Except for good cause shown, the reports exchanged between the parties shall be the only reports admissible at trial. Late retention of experts and consequent late submission of reports shall be permitted only upon a showing of good cause as authorized by CPLR 3101(d)(1)(i). In the discretion of the court, written reports may be used to substitute for direct testimony at the trial, but the reports shall be submitted by the expert under oath, and the expert shall be present and available for cross-examination. In the discretion of the court, in a proper case, parties may be bound by the expert's report in their direct case.

(h) Statement of Proposed Disposition.

(1) Each party shall exchange a statement setting forth the following:

(i) the assets claimed to be marital property;

(ii) the assets claimed to be separate property;

(iii) an allocation of debts or liabilities to specific marital or separate assets, where appropriate;

(iv) the amount requested for maintenance, indicating and elaborating upon the statutory factors forming the basis for the maintenance requests;

(v) the proposal for equitable distribution, where appropriate, indicating and elaborating upon the statutory factors forming the basis for the proposed distribution;

(vi) the proposal for a distributive award, if requested, including a showing of the need for a distributive award;

(vii) the proposed plan for child support, indicating and elaborating upon the statutory factors upon which the proposal is based; and

(viii) the proposed plan for custody and visitation of any children involved in the proceeding, setting forth the reasons therefor.

(2) A copy of any written agreement entered into by the parties relating to financial arrangements or custody or visitation shall be annexed to the statement referred to in paragraph (1) of this subdivision.

(3) The statement referred to in paragraph (1) of this subdivision, with proof of service upon the other party, shall, with the note of issue, be filed with the court. The other party, if he or she has not already done so, shall file with the court a statement complying with paragraph (1) of this subdivision within 20 days of such service.

(i) **Filing of Note of Issue.** No action or proceeding to which this section is applicable shall be deemed ready for trial unless there is compliance with this section by the party filing the note of issue and certificate of readiness.

(j) **Referral to Family Court.** In all actions or proceedings to which this section is applicable referred to the Family Court by the Supreme Court pursuant to section 464 of the Family Court Act, all statements, including supplemental statements, exchanged and filed by the parties pursuant to this section shall be transmitted to the Family Court with the order of referral.

(k) **Motions for Alimony, Maintenance, Counsel Fees Pendente Lite and Child Support (Other Than Under Section 237(c) or Section 238 of the Domestic Relations Law).** Unless, on application made to the court, the requirements of this subdivision be waived for good cause shown, or unless otherwise expressly provided by any provision of the CPLR or other statute, the following requirements shall govern motions for alimony, maintenance, counsel fees (other than a motion made pursuant to section 237(c) or section 238 of the Domestic Relations Law for counsel fees for services rendered by an attorney to secure the enforcement of a previously granted order or decree) or child support or any modification of an award thereof:

(1) Such motion shall be made before or at the preliminary conference, if practicable.

(2) No motion shall be heard unless the moving papers include a statement of net worth in the official form prescribed by subdivision (b) of this section.

(3) No motion for counsel fees shall be heard unless the moving papers also include the affidavit of the movant's attorney stating the moneys, if any, received on account of such attorney's fee from the movant or any other person on behalf of the movant, and the moneys such attorney has been promised by, or the agreement made with, the movant or other persons on behalf of the movant, concerning or in payment of the fee.

(4) The party opposing any motion shall be deemed to have admitted, for the purpose of the motion but not otherwise, such facts set forth in the moving party's statement of net worth as are not contravened in:

(i) a statement of net worth, in the official form prescribed by this section, completed and sworn to by the opposing party, and made a part of the answering papers, or

(ii) other sworn statements or affidavits with respect to any fact which is not feasible to controvert in the opposing party's statement of net worth.

(5) The failure to comply with the provisions of this subdivision shall be good cause, in the discretion of the judge presiding, either:

(i) to draw an inference favorable to the adverse party with respect to any disputed fact or issue affected by such failure; or

(ii) to deny the motion without prejudice to renewal upon compliance with the provisions of this section.

(6) The notice of motion submitted with any motion for or related to interim maintenance or child support shall contain a notation indicating the nature of the motion. Any such motion shall be determined within 30 days after the motion is submitted for decision.

(7) Upon any application for an award of counsel fees or appraisal/accounting fees made prior to the conclusion of the trial of the action, the court shall set forth in specific detail, in writing or on the record, the factors it considered and the reasons for its decision.

(*l*) Hearings or trials pertaining to temporary or permanent custody or visitation shall proceed from day to day to conclusion. With respect to other issues before the court, to the extent feasible, trial should proceed from day to day to conclusion.

Cross References

CPLR, see McKinney's Book 7B.

Domestic Relations Law, see McKinney's Book 14.

Family Court Act, see McKinney's Book 29A, Part 1.

§ 202.17. Exchange of Medical Reports in Personal Injury and Wrongful Death Actions

Except where the court otherwise directs, in all actions in which recovery is sought for personal injuries, disability or death, physical examinations and the exchange of medical information shall be governed by the provisions hereinafter set forth:

(a) At any time after joinder of issue and service of a bill of particulars the party to be examined or any other party may serve on all other parties a notice fixing the time and place of examination. Unless otherwise stipulated the examination shall be held not less than 30 nor more than 60 days after service of the notice. If served by any party other than the party to be examined, the notice shall name the examining medical provider or providers. If the notice is served by the party to be examined, the examining parties shall, within five days of receipt thereof, submit to the party to be examined the name of the medical providers who will conduct the examination. Any party may move to modify or vacate the notice fixing the time and place of examination or the notice naming the examining medical providers within ten days of the receipt thereof, on the grounds that the time or place fixed or the medical provider named is objectionable, or that the nature of the action is such that the interests of justice will not be served by an examination, exchange of medical reports or delivery of authorizations.

(b) At least 20 days before the date of such examination, or on such other date as the court may direct, the party to be examined shall serve upon and deliver to all other parties the following, which may be used by the examining medical provider:

(1) copies of the medical reports of those medical providers who have previously treated or examined the party seeking recovery. These shall include a recital of the injuries and conditions as to which testimony will be offered at the trial, referring to and identifying those x-ray and technicians' reports which will be offered at the trial, including a description of the injuries, a diagnosis and a prognosis. Medical reports may consist of completed medical provider, workers' compensation, or insurance forms that provide the information required by this paragraph.

(2) duly executed and acknowledged written authorizations permitting all parties to obtain and make copies of all hospital records and such other records, including x-ray and technicians' reports, as may be referred to and identified in the reports of those medical providers who have treated or examined the party seeking recovery.

(c) Copies of the reports of the medical providers making examinations pursuant to this section shall be served on all other parties within 45 days after completion of the examination. These shall comply with the requirements of paragraph (1) of subdivision (b).

(d) In actions where the cause of death is in issue, each party shall serve upon all other parties copies of the reports of all treating and examining medical providers whose testimony will be offered at the trial, complying with the requirements of paragraph (1) of subdivision (b), and the party seeking to recover shall deliver to all other parties authorizations to examine and obtain copies of all hospital records, autopsy or post-mortem reports, and such other records as provided in paragraph (2) of subdivision (b). Copies of these reports and the required authorizations shall be served and delivered with the bill of particulars by the party seeking to recover. All other parties shall serve copies of the reports of their medical providers within 45 days thereafter. In any case where the interests of justice will not be promoted by service of such reports and delivery of such authorizations, an order dispensing with either or both may be obtained.

(e) Parties relying solely on hospital records may so certify in lieu of serving medical providers' reports.

(f) No case otherwise eligible to be noticed for trial may be noticed unless there has been compliance with this rule, or an order dispensing with compliance or extending the time therefor has been obtained; or, where the party to be examined was served a notice as provided in subdivision (a), and the party so served has not responded thereto.

(g) In the event that the party examined intends at the trial to offer evidence of further or additional injuries or conditions, nonexistent or not known to exist at the time of service of the original medical reports, such party shall, within 30 days after the discovery thereof, and not later than 30 days before trial, serve upon all parties a supplemental medical report complying with the requirements of paragraph (1) of subdivision (b) and shall specify a time not more than 10 days thereafter and a place at which a further examination may be had. Further authorizations to examine and make copies of additional hospital records, other records, x-ray or other technicians' reports as provided in paragraph (2) of subdivision (b) must also be delivered with the medical reports. Copies of the reports of the examining medical providers, complying with the requirements of subdivision (c), shall be served within 10 days after completion of such further examination. If any party desires at the trial to offer the testimony of additional treating or examining medical providers other than whose medical reports have been previously exchanged, the medical reports of such medical providers, complying with the requirements of paragraph (1) of subdivision (b) shall be served upon all parties at least 30 days before trial.

(h) Unless an order to the contrary is made or unless the judge presiding at the trial in the interests of justice and upon a showing of good cause shall hold otherwise, the party seeking to recover damages shall be precluded at the trial from offering in evidence any part of the hospital records and all other records, including autopsy or post-mortem records, x-ray reports or reports of other technicians, not made available pursuant to this rule, and no party shall be permitted to offer any evidence of injuries or conditions not set forth or put in issue in the respective medical reports previously exchanged, nor will the court hear the testimony of any treating or examining medical providers whose medical reports have not been served as provided by this rule.

(i) Orders transferring cases pending in other courts which are subject to the provisions of this section, whether or not such cases are consolidated with cases pending in the court to which transferred, shall contain such provisions as are required to bring the transferred cases into compliance with this rule.

(j) Any party may move to compel compliance or to be relieved from compliance with this rule or any provision thereof, but motions directed to the sufficiency of medical reports must be made within 20 days of receipt of such reports. All motions under this rule may be made on affidavits of attorneys, shall be made on notice, and shall be granted or denied on such terms as to costs, calendar position and dates of compliance with any provision of this rule as the court in its discretion shall direct.

(k) Where an examination is conducted on consent prior to the institution of an action, the party to be examined shall deliver the documents specified in paragraphs (1) and (2) of subdivision (b) hereof, and the report of the examining medical provider shall be delivered as provided in subdivision (c) hereof. In that event, examination after institution of the action may be waived. The waiver, which shall recite that medical reports have been exchanged and that all parties waive further physical examination, shall be filed with the note of issue. This shall not be a bar, however, to proceeding under subdivision (g) in a proper case.

§ 202.18. Testimony of Court–Appointed Expert Witness in Matrimonial Action or Proceeding

In any action or proceeding tried without a jury to which section 237 of the Domestic Relations Law applies, the court may appoint a psychiatrist, psychologist, social worker or other appropriate expert to give testimony with respect to custody or visitation, and may appoint an accountant, appraiser, actuary or other appropriate expert to give testimony with respect to equitable distribution or a distributive award. The cost of such expert witness shall be paid by a party or parties as the court shall direct.

§ 202.19. Differentiated Case Management

(a) Applicability. This section shall apply to such categories of cases designated by the Chief Administrator of the Courts as being subject to differentiated

case management, and shall be implemented in such counties, courts or parts of courts as designated by the Chief Administrator. The provisions of section 202.12 of these rules, relating to the preliminary conference, and section 202.26 of these rules, relating to the pretrial conference, shall apply to the extent not inconsistent with this section.

(b) Preliminary Conference.

(1) In all actions and proceedings to which this section of the rules is applicable, a preliminary conference shall be ordered by the court to be held within 45 days after the request for judicial intervention is filed.

(2) At the preliminary conference, the court shall designate the track to which the case shall be assigned in accordance with the following:

(i) Expedited—discovery to be completed within eight months

(ii) Standard—discovery to be completed within 12 months

(iii) Complex—discovery to be completed within 15 months

The timeframes must be complied with unless otherwise shortened or extended by the court depending upon the circumstances of the case.

(3) No later than 60 days before the date fixed for completion of discovery, a compliance conference shall be held to monitor the progress of discovery, explore potential settlement, and set a deadline for the filing of the Note of Issue.

(c) Pretrial Conference.

(1) A pretrial conference shall be held within 180 days of the filing of the Note of Issue.

(2) At the pretrial conference, the court shall fix a date for the commencement of trial, which shall be no later than eight weeks after the date of the conference.

§ 202.20. [Reserved]

§ 202.21. Note of Issue and Certificate of Readiness

(a) General. No action or special proceeding shall be deemed ready for trial or inquest unless there is first filed a note of issue accompanied by a certificate of readiness, with proof of service on all parties entitled to notice, in the form prescribed by this section. Filing of a note of issue and certificate of readiness is not required for an application for court approval of the settlement of the claim of an infant, incompetent or conservatee. The note of issue shall include the county clerk's index number, the name of the judge to whom the action is assigned, the name, office address and telephone number of each attorney who has appeared, the name, address and telephone number of any party who has appeared pro se, and the name of any insurance carrier acting on behalf of any party. Within ten days after service, the original note of issue, and the certificate of readiness where required, with proof of service where service is required, shall be filed in duplicate with the county clerk together with payment of the calendar fee prescribed by CPLR 8020 or a copy of an order permitting the party filing the note of issue to proceed as a poor person, and a duplicate original with proof of service shall be filed with the clerk of the trial court. The county clerk shall forward one of the duplicate originals of the note of issue to the clerk of the trial court stamped "Fee Paid" or "Poor Person Order."

(b) Forms. The note of issue and certificate of readiness shall read substantially as follows:

NOTE OF ISSUE

Calendar No. (if any) ....   For use of clerk

Index No. ....

.... Court, ... County

Name of assigned judge ....

Notice for trial

Trial by jury demanded ....
... of all issues
... of issues specified below
... or attached hereto
Trial without jury ...
Filed by attorney for ....
Date summons served ....
Date service completed ....
Date issue joined ....

Nature of action or
special proceeding

Tort:
   Motor vehicle negligence   ......
   Medical malpractice   ......
   Other tort   ......
Contract   ......
Contested matrimonial   ......
Uncontested matrimonial   ......

Special preference
claimed under ....
....
on the ground that ....
....

Tax certiorari   ......
   Condemnation   ......
   Other (not itemized above)   ......
      (specify)..............

Attorney(s) for Plaintiff(s)
Office and P.O. Address:
Phone No.

Indicate if this action is   ......
brought as a class action

Attorney(s) for Defendant(s)
Office and P.O. Address:
Phone No.

Amount demanded $ ....
Other relief ....
Insurance carrier(s), if known:

NOTE: The clerk will not accept this note of issue unless accompanied by a certificate of readiness.

CERTIFICATE OF READINESS FOR TRIAL (Items 1–7 must be checked)

	Complete	Waived	Not Required
1. All pleadings served	....	....	....
2. Bill of particulars served	....	....	....
3. Physical examinations completed	....	....	....
4. Medical reports exchanged	....	....	....
5. Appraisal reports exchanged	....	....	....
6. Compliance with section 202.16 of the Rules of the Chief Administrator (22 NYCRR 202.16) in matrimonial actions	....	....	....
7. Discovery proceedings now known to be necessary completed	....	....	....

8. There are no outstanding requests for discovery
9. There has been a reasonable opportunity to complete the foregoing proceedings
10. There has been compliance with any order issued pursuant to section 202.12 of the Rules of the Chief Administrator (22 NYCRR 202.12)
11. If a medical malpractice action, there has been compliance with any order issued pursuant to section 202.56 of the Rules of the Chief Administrator (22 NYCRR 202.56)
12. The case is ready for trial

Dated: _____

(Signature) _____

Attorney(s) for: _____

Office and P.O. address: _____

(c) Jury Trials. A trial by jury may be demanded as provided by CPLR 4102. Where a jury trial has been demanded, the action or special proceeding shall be scheduled for jury trial upon payment of the fee prescribed by CPLR 8020 by the party first filing the demand. If no demand for a jury trial is made, it shall constitute a waiver by all parties and the action or special proceeding shall be scheduled for nonjury trial.

(d) Pretrial Proceedings. Where a party is prevented from filing a note of issue and certificate of readiness because a pretrial proceeding has not been completed for any reason beyond the control of the party, the court, upon motion supported by affidavit, may permit the party to file a note of issue upon such conditions as the court deems appropriate. Where unusual or unanticipated circumstances develop subsequent to the filing of a note of issue and certificate of readiness which require additional pretrial proceedings to prevent substantial prejudice, the court, upon motion supported by affidavit, may grant permission to conduct such necessary proceedings.

(e) Vacating Note of Issue. Within 20 days after service of a note of issue and certificate of readiness, any party to the action or special proceeding may move to vacate the note of issue, upon affidavit showing in what respects the case is not ready for trial, and the court may vacate the note of issue if it appears that a material fact in the certificate of readiness is incorrect, or that the certificate of readiness fails to comply with the requirements of this section in some material respect. However, the 20-day time limitation to make such motion shall not apply to tax assessment review proceedings. After such period, except in a tax assessment review proceeding, no such motion shall be allowed except for good cause shown. At any time, the court on its own motion may vacate a note of issue if it appears that a material fact in the certificate of readiness is incorrect, or that the certificate of readiness fails to comply with the requirements of this section in some material respect. If the motion to vacate a note of issue is granted, a copy of the order vacating the note of issue shall be served upon the clerk of the trial court.

(f) Reinstatement of Note of Issue. Motions to reinstate notes of issue vacated pursuant to this section shall be supported by a proper and sufficient certificate of readiness and by an affidavit by a person having first-hand knowledge showing that there is merit to the action, satisfactorily showing the reasons for the acts or omissions which led to the note of issue being vacated, stating meritorious reasons for its reinstatement and showing that the case is presently ready for trial.

(g) Limited Specification of Damages Demanded in Certain Actions. This subdivision shall apply only in counties where the Chief Administrator of the Courts has established arbitration programs pursuant to Part 28 of the rules of the Chief Judge of the State of New York pertaining to the arbitration of certain actions (22 NYCRR Part 28). In a medical malpractice action or an action against a municipality seeking a sum of money only, where the party filing the note of issue is prohibited by the provisions of CPLR 3017(c) from stating in the pleadings the amount of damages sought in the action, the party shall indicate on the note of issue whether the amount of damages exceeds $6,000, exclusive of costs and interest. If it does not, the party shall also indicate if it exceeds $2,000, exclusive of costs and interest.

(h) Change in Title of Action. In the event of a change in title of an action by reason of a substitution of any party, no new note of issue will be required. Notice of such substitution and change in title shall be given to the assigned judge and to the clerk within ten days of the date of an order or stipulation effecting the party substitution or title change.

(i) Additional Requirements with Respect to Uncontested Matrimonial Actions.

(1) Uncontested matrimonial actions, proceedings for dissolution of marriages and applications of declaratory judgments shall be assigned to judges or special parts of court as the Chief Administrator shall authorize.

(2) There shall be a Unified Court System Uncontested Divorce Packet which shall contain the official forms for use in uncontested matrimonial actions. The Packet shall be available in the Office of the Clerk of the Supreme Court in each county, and the forms shall be filed with the appropriate clerk in accordance with the instructions in the Packet. These forms shall be accepted by the Court for obtaining an uncontested divorce, and no other forms shall be necessary. The Court, in its discretion, may accept other forms that comply with the requirements of law.

(3) The proposed judgments shall be numbered in the order in which they are received and submitted in sequence to the judge or referee.

(4) Unless the court otherwise directs, the proof required by statute must be in writing, by affidavits, which shall include a sufficient factual statement to establish jurisdiction, as well as all elements of the cause of action warranting the relief sought.

(5) If the judge or referee believes that the papers are insufficient, the complaint shall either be dismissed for failure of proof or a hearing shall be directed to determine whether sufficient evidence exists to support the cause of action.

(6) Whether upon written proof or at the conclusion of a hearing, the judge or referee shall render a decision and sign the findings of fact, conclusions of law and the judgment, unless for reasons stated on the record decision is reserved.

(7) Where a hearing has been held, no transcript of testimony shall be required as a condition precedent to the signing of the judgment, unless the judge or referee presiding shall so direct.

Cross References

CPLR, see McKinney's Book 7B.

Domestic Relations Law, see McKinney's Book 14.

§ 202.22. Calendars

(a) A judge to whom cases are assigned under the individual assignment system may establish such calendars of cases as the judge shall deem necessary or desirable for proper case management. These calendars may include:

(1) *Preliminary Conference Calendar.* A preliminary conference calendar is for the calendaring for conference of cases in which a note of issue and certificate of readiness have not yet been filed.

(2) *Motion Calendar.* A motion calendar is for the hearing of motions.

(3) *General Calendar.* A general calendar is for actions in which a note of issue and a certificate of readiness have been filed but which have not as yet been transferred to a pretrial conference calendar or a calendar containing cases that are ready for trial.

(4) *Pretrial Conference Calendar.* A pretrial conference calendar is for actions awaiting conference after the note of issue and certificate of readiness have been filed.

(5) *Reserve Calendar.* A reserve calendar is for actions that have had a pretrial conference or where such conference was dispensed with by the court, but where the actions have not yet been transferred to a ready calendar.

(6) *Ready Calendar.* A ready calendar is for actions in which a trial is imminent.

(7) *Military Calendar.* A military calendar is for cases where a party to an action or a witness necessary upon the trial is in military service and is not presently available for trial, and a deposition cannot be taken, or, if taken, would not provide adequate evidence.

(8) *Continuous Calendars.* In any court not continuously in session, the calendars at the close of one term shall be used to open the following term and actions on the calendars shall retain their positions.

(b) Calendar Progression. With due regard to the requirements of statutory preferences and of section 202.24 of this Part, when actions are advanced from one calendar to another they shall progress from the head of one calendar to the foot of the next calendar and otherwise progress in order insofar as practicable unless otherwise determined by the court.

(c) Call of Calendars. Judges to whom actions and proceedings are assigned pursuant to the individual assignment system may schedule calls of any calendars they have established at such times as they deem appropriate.

(d) Readiness for Trial. When an action has been announced "ready" but a trial is not immediately available, counsel may arrange with the judge to be summoned by telephone, provided they agree to hold themselves available and to appear on one hour's notice, or at such other time as the court may order, at the time assigned for trial.

§ 202.23.   [Reserved]

§ 202.24.   Special Preferences

(a) Applications. Any party claiming a preference under CPLR 3403 may apply to the court in the manner prescribed by that rule.

(b) Special Requirements in Personal Injury and Wrongful Death Action. A party seeking a preference pursuant to CPLR 3403(a)(3) in an action for damages for personal injuries or for causing death shall serve and file in support of the demand or application, whether in the note of issue or subsequent thereto, a copy of:

(1) the summons;

(2) the complaint, answer and bill of particulars, conforming to CPLR 3043 and 3044;

(3) each report required by this Part to be served by the parties relating to medical information;

(4) a statement that the venue of the action was properly laid; and

(5) all other papers material to the application.

(c) Counterclaims and Cross-Claims. A counterclaim or cross-claim which is not entitled to a preference shall not itself defeat the plaintiff's right to a preference under this section.

(d) Result of Preference Being Granted. If a preference is granted, the case shall be placed ahead of all non-preferred cases pending as of that date, unless the court otherwise orders.

Cross References

CPLR, see McKinney's Book 7B.

§ 202.25.   Objections to Applications for Special Preference

(a) Within 20 days of the filing of the note of issue, if the notice of motion for a special preference is filed therewith, or within ten days of the service of a notice of motion to obtain a preference, if served and filed subsequent to service and filing of the note of issue, any other party may serve upon all other parties and file with the court affidavits and other relevant papers, with proof of service, in opposition to granting the preference. In the event opposing papers are filed, the party applying for the preference may, within five days thereafter, serve and file in like manner papers in rebuttal.

(b) In any action which has been accorded a preference in trial upon a motion, the court shall not be precluded, on its own motion at any time thereafter, from ordering that the action is not entitled to a preference under these rules.

(c) Notwithstanding the failure of any party to oppose the application, no preference shall be granted by default unless the court finds that the action is entitled to a preference.

§ 202.26.   Pretrial Conference

(a) After the filing of a note of issue and certificate of readiness in any action, the judge shall order a pretrial conference, unless the judge dispenses with such a conference in any particular case.

(b) To the extent practicable, pretrial conferences shall be held not less than 15 nor more than 45 days before trial is anticipated.

(c) The judge shall consider at the conference with the parties or their counsel the following:

(i) simplification and limitation of the issues;

(ii) obtaining admission of fact and of documents to avoid unnecessary proof;

(iii) disposition of the action including scheduling the action for trial;

(iv) amendment of pleadings or bill of particulars;

(v) limitation of number of expert witnesses; and

(vi) insurance coverage where relevant.

The judge also may consider with the parties any other matters deemed relevant.

(d) In actions brought under the simplified procedure sections of the CPLR, the court shall address those matters referred to in CPLR 3036(5).

(e) Where parties are represented by counsel, only attorneys fully familiar with the action and authorized to make binding stipulations, or accompanied by a person empowered to act on behalf of the party represented, will be permitted to appear at a pretrial conference. Where appropriate, the court may order parties, representatives of parties, representatives of insurance carriers or persons having an interest in any settlement, including those holding liens on any settlement or verdict, to also attend in person or telephonically at the settlement conference. Plaintiff shall submit marked copies of the pleadings. A verified bill of particulars and a doctor's report or hospital record, or both, as to the nature and extent of injuries claimed, if any, shall be submitted by the plaintiff and by any defendant who counterclaims. The judge may require additional data, or may waive any requirement for submission of documents on suitable alternate proof of damages. Failure to comply with this paragraph may be deemed a default under CPLR 3404. Absence of an attorney's file shall not be an acceptable excuse for failing to comply with this paragraph.

(f) If any action is settled or discontinued by stipulation at a pretrial conference, complete minutes of such stipulation shall be made at the direction of the court. Such transcribed stipulation shall be enforceable as though made in open court.

(g)(1) At the pretrial conference, if it appears that the action falls within the monetary jurisdiction of a court of limited jurisdiction, there is nothing to justify its being retained in the court in which it is then pending, and it would be reached for trial more quickly in a lower court, the judge shall order the case transferred to the appropriate lower court, specifying the paragraph of CPLR 325 under which the action is taken.

(2) With respect to transfers to the New York City Civil Court pursuant to CPLR 325, if, at the pretrial conference, the conditions in paragraph (1) are met except that the case will not be reached for trial more quickly in the lower court, the judge, in his or her discretion, may order the case so transferred if it will be reached for trial in the lower court within 30 days of the conference. In determining whether the action will be reached for trial in the lower court within 30 days, the judge shall consult with the administrative judge of his or her court, who shall advise, after due inquiry, whether calendar conditions and clerical considerations will permit the trial of actions in the lower court within the 30-day timeframe. If the action is not transferred to a lower court, it shall be tried in the superior court in its proper calendar progression.

Cross References

CPLR, see McKinney's Book 7B.

§ 202.27. Defaults

At any scheduled call of a calendar or at any conference, if all parties do not appear and proceed or announce their readiness to proceed immediately or subject to the engagement of counsel, the judge may note the default on the record and enter an order as follows:

(a) If the plaintiff appears but the defendant does not, the judge may grant judgment by default or order an inquest;

(b) If the defendant appears but the plaintiff does not, the judge may dismiss the action and may order a severance of counterclaims or cross-claims;

(c) If no party appears, the judge may make such order as appears just.

§ 202.28. Discontinuance of Civil Actions

In any discontinued action, the attorney for the defendant shall file a stipulation or statement of discontinuance with the county clerk within 20 days of such discontinuance. If the action has been noticed for judicial activity within 20 days of such discontinuance, the stipulation or statement shall be filed before the date scheduled for such activity.

Forms

Stipulation of settlement and discontinuance, see West's McKinney's Forms, CPLR, §§ 12:707, 12:708.

§§ 202.29, 202.30. [Reserved]

§ 202.31. Identification of Trial Counsel

Unless the court otherwise provides, where the attorney of record for any party arranges for another attorney to conduct the trial, the trial counsel must be identified in writing to the court and all parties no later than 15 days after the pretrial conference or, if there is no pretrial conference, at least ten days before trial. The notice must be signed by both the attorney of record and the trial counsel.

§ 202.32. Engagement of Counsel

No adjournment shall be granted on the ground of engagement of counsel except in accordance with Part 125 of the Rules of the Chief Administrator of the Courts.

§ 202.33. Conduct of the Voir Dire

a. Trial Judge. All references to the trial judge in this section shall include any judge designated by the administrative judge in those instances where the case processing system or other logistical considerations do not permit the trial judge to perform the acts set forth in this section.

b. Pre-voir Dire Settlement Conference. Where the court has directed that jury selection begin, the trial judge shall meet prior to the actual commencement of jury selection with counsel who will be conducting the voir dire and shall attempt to bring about a disposition of the action.

c. Method of Jury Selection. The trial judge shall direct the method of jury selection that shall be used for the voir dire from among the methods specified in subdivision (f) below.

d. Time Limitations. The trial judge shall establish time limitations for the questioning of prospective jurors during the voir dire. At the discretion of the judge, the limits established may consist of a general period for the completion of the questioning, a period after which attorneys shall report back to the judge on the progress of the voir dire, and/or specific time periods for the questioning of panels of jurors or individual jurors.

e. Presence of Judge at the Voir Dire. In order to ensure an efficient and dignified selection process, the trial judge shall preside at the commencement of the voir dire and open the voir dire proceeding. The trial judge shall determine whether supervision of the voir dire should continue after the voir dire has commenced and, in his or her discretion, preside over part of or all of the remainder of the voir dire.

f. Methods of Jury Selection. Counsel shall select prospective jurors in accordance with the general principles applicable to jury selection set forth in Appendix "E" and using the method designated by the judge pursuant to subdivision (c). The methods that may be selected are:

(1) "White's method," as set forth in Appendix "E" of this Part;

(2) "Struck method," as set forth in Appendix "E" of this Part;

(3) "Strike and replace method," in districts where the specifics of that method have been submitted to the Chief Administrator by the Administrative Judge and approved by the Chief Administrator for that district. The strike and replace method shall be approved only in those districts where the Chief Administrator, in his or her discretion, has determined that experience with the method in the district has resulted in an efficient and orderly selection process; or

(4) Other methods that may be submitted to the Chief Administrator for use on an experimental basis by the appropriate Administrative Judge and approved by the Chief Administrator.

§ 202.34. [Reserved]

§ 202.35. Submission of Papers for Trial

(a) Upon the trial of an action, the following papers, if not yet submitted, shall be submitted to the court by the party who has filed the note of issue:

(1) copies of all pleadings marked as required by CPLR 4012; and

(2) a copy of the bill of particulars, if any.

(b) Upon the trial of an action, a copy of any statutory provision in effect at the time the cause of action arose shall be submitted to the court by the party who intends to rely upon such statute.

(c) If so ordered, the parties shall submit to the court, before the commencement of trial, trial memoranda which shall be exchanged among counsel.

Cross References

CPLR, see McKinney's Book 7B.

§ 202.36. Absence of Attorney During Trial

All trial counsel shall remain in attendance at all stages of the trial until the jury retires to deliberate unless excused by the judge presiding. The court may permit counsel to leave provided that counsel remain in telephone contact with the court. Any counsel not present during the jury deliberation, further requests to charge, or report of the jury verdict shall be deemed to stipulate that the court may proceed in his or her absence and to waive any irregularity in proceedings taken in his or her absence.

§§ 202.37 to 202.39. [Reserved]

§ 202.40. Jury Trial of Less Than All Issues; Procedure

Unless otherwise ordered by the court, whenever a trial by jury is demanded on less than all issues of fact in an action, and such issues as to which a trial by jury is demanded have been specified in the note of issue or in the jury demand, as the case may be, served and filed pursuant to section 202.21 of this Part, the court without a jury first shall try all issues of fact as to which a trial by jury is not demanded. If the determination of these issues by the court does not dispose of the action, a jury shall be empanelled to try the issues as to which a trial by jury is demanded.

§ 202.41. [Reserved]

§ 202.42. Bifurcated Trials

(a) Judges are encouraged to order a bifurcated trial of the issues of liability and damages in any action for personal injury where it appears that bifurcation may assist in a clarification or simplification of issues and a fair and more expeditious resolution of the action.

(b) Where a bifurcated trial is ordered, the issues of liability and damages shall be severed and the issue of liability shall be tried first, unless the court orders otherwise.

(c) During the voir dire conducted prior to the liability phase of the trial, if the damage phase of the trial is to be conducted before the same jury, counsel may question the prospective jurors with respect to the issue of damages in the same manner as if the trial were not bifurcated.

(d) In opening to the jury on the liability phase of the trial, counsel may not discuss the question of damages. However, if the verdict of the jury shall be in favor of the plaintiff on the liability issue or in favor of the defendant on any counterclaim on the liability issue, all parties shall then be afforded an opportunity to address the jury on the question of damages before proof in that regard is presented to the jury.

(e) In the event of a plaintiff's verdict on the issue of liability or a defendant's verdict on the issue of liability on a counterclaim, the damage phase of the trial shall be conducted immediately thereafter before the same judge and jury, unless the judge presiding over the trial, for reasons stated in the record, finds such procedures to be impracticable.

§ 202.43. References of Triable Issues and Proceedings to Judicial Hearing Officers or Referees

(a) No application to refer an action or special proceeding to a judicial hearing officer or referee will be entertained unless a note of issue, where required, has been filed and the index number is set forth in the moving papers and the proposed order.

(b) The proposed order of reference shall be presented in duplicate, and a signed original order shall be delivered to the referee. If such order is not presented for signature within 20 days after the court directs a reference, the application shall be deemed abandoned.

(c) The proposed order of reference, and the actual order of reference shall indicate whether the reference is one to hear and determine or to hear and report.

(d) Every order of reference which does not set forth a date certain for commencement of the trial or hearing shall contain the following provision:

and it is further ORDERED that if trial of the issue or action hereby referred is not begun within 60 days from the date of this order, or before such later date as the referee or judicial hearing officer may fix upon good cause shown, this order shall be cancelled and revoked, shall be remitted by the referee or judicial hearing officer to the court from which it was issued, and the matter hereby referred shall immediately be returned to the court for trial.

(e) The term "referee" in this section shall include but not be limited to commissioners of appraisal, and shall not include receivers or referees in incompetency proceedings or mortgage foreclosure proceedings.

§ 202.44. Motion to Confirm or Reject Judicial Hearing Officer's or Referee's Report

(a) When a judicial hearing officer or a referee appointed to hear and report has duly filed his or her report, together with the transcript of testimony taken and all papers and exhibits before him or her in the proceedings, if any, and has duly given notice to each party of the filing of the report, the plaintiff shall move on notice to confirm or reject all or part of the report within 15 days after notice of such filing was given. If plaintiff fails to make the motion, the defendant shall so move within 30 days after notice of such filing was given.

(b) If no party moves as specified above, the court, on its own motion, shall issue its determination. Costs of such motion, including reasonable attorneys' fees, shall be borne by the parties pro rata, except a party who did not request any relief. However, the Attorney General of New York, or State, Federal or local governmental agencies or officers thereof, shall not be liable for costs. This subdivision shall not apply to a reference to a special referee or a judicial hearing officer or to a reference to a referee in an uncontested matrimonial action.

(c) The term "referee" in this section shall be used as defined in subdivision (e) of section 202.43.

Forms

Motion papers to confirm referee's report, see West's McKinney's Forms, CPLR, §§ 7:623 to 7:631.

Motion papers to reject referee's report, see West's McKinney's Forms, CPLR, §§ 7:631A to 7:631C.

§ 202.45. Rescheduling After Jury Disagreement, Mistrial or Order for New Trial

An action in which there has been an inability by a jury to reach a verdict, a mistrial or a new trial granted by the trial justice or an appellate court shall be rescheduled for trial. Where a new trial is granted by an appellate court, a notice to reschedule shall be filed with the appropriate clerk.

§ 202.46. Damages, Inquest After Default; Proof

(a) In an inquest to ascertain damages upon a default, pursuant to CPLR 3215, if the defaulting party fails to appear in person or by representative, the party entitled to judgment, whether a plaintiff, third-party plaintiff, or a party who has pleaded a cross-claim or counterclaim, may be permitted to submit, in addition to the proof required by CPLR 3215(e), properly executed affidavits as proof of damages.

(b) In any action where it is necessary to take an inquest before the court, the party seeking damages may submit the proof required by oral testimony of witnesses in open court or by written statements of the witnesses, in narrative or question and answer form, signed and sworn to.

Cross References

CPLR, see McKinney's Book 7B.

§ 202.47. Transcript of Judgment; Receipt Stub

Whenever a county clerk issues a transcript of judgment, which shall be in the form prescribed by law, such clerk shall at the same time issue a stub. Such stub shall be 3⅝ × 8½ inches and shall have imprinted thereon the name and address of the issuing county clerk. The stub shall also contain such other information as shall be required to identify it with the transcript with which it was issued, so that it may be readily identified upon its return to the issuing county clerk, with the name of and the date of receipt by the receiving clerk endorsed thereon.

§ 202.48. Submission of Orders, Judgments and Decrees for Signature

(a) Proposed orders or judgments, with proof of service on all parties where the order is directed to be settled or submitted on notice, must be submitted for signature, unless otherwise directed by the court, within 60 days after the signing and filing of the decision directing that the order be settled or submitted.

(b) Failure to submit the order or judgment timely shall be deemed an abandonment of the motion or action, unless for good cause shown.

(c) (1) When settlement of an order or judgment is directed by the court, a copy of the proposed order or judgment with notice of settlement, returnable at the office of the clerk of the court in which the order or judgment was granted, or before the judge if the court has so directed or if the clerk is unavailable, shall be served on all parties either:

(i) by personal service not less than five days before the date of settlement; or

(ii) by mail not less than ten days before the date of settlement.

(2) Proposed counter-orders or judgments shall be made returnable on the same date and at the same place, and shall be served on all parties by personal service, not less than two days, or by mail, not less than seven days, before the date of settlement. Any proposed counter-order or judgment shall be submitted with a copy clearly marked to delineate each proposed change to the order or judgment to which objection is made.

§ 202.49.   [Reserved]

§ 202.50. Proposed Judgments in Matrimonial Actions; Forms

(a) **Form of Judgments.** Findings and conclusions shall be in a separate paper from the judgment, which papers shall be labeled "FINDINGS OF FACT AND CONCLUSIONS OF LAW" and "JUDGMENT," respectively.

(b) **Approved Forms.**

(1) *Contested Actions.* The paragraphs contained in Appendix B of this Part, modified or deleted as may be necessary to conform to the law and facts in a particular action, shall be used in the preparation of "FINDINGS OF FACT AND CONCLUSIONS OF LAW," "JUDGMENT," or "REFEREE'S REPORT OF FINDINGS OF FACT AND CONCLUSIONS OF LAW." Parenthesized portions indicate alternative provisions.

(2) *Uncontested Actions.* Parties in uncontested matrimonial actions shall use the forms in the Unified Court System Uncontested Divorce Packet as set forth in Section 202.21(i)(2) of this Part, unless the court permits otherwise pursuant to that Section.

(c) Judgments submitted to the court shall be accompanied by a completed form UCS 111 (Child Support Summary Form).

§ 202.51.   Proof Required in Dissolution Proceedings

In all actions in which the accounts of a receiver appointed in an action for the dissolution of a corporation are presented for settlement or to be passed upon by the court, a notice or a copy of an advertisement requiring the creditors to present their claims to a referee must be mailed, with the postage thereon prepaid, to each creditor whose name appears on the books of the corporation, at least 20 days before the date specified in such notice or advertisement. Proof of such mailing shall be required on the application for a final decree passing the accounts of the receiver unless proof is furnished that personal service of such notice or copy of advertisement has been made upon the creditors.

Forms

Notice to creditors after dissolution, see West's McKinney's Forms, Business Corporation, § 11:14.

§ 202.52.   Deposit of Funds by Receivers and Assignees

(a) Every receiver or assignee who, as such, receives any funds shall promptly deposit them in a checking account or in an interest-bearing account, as determined by the court, in a bank or trust company designated by the court. Such account shall be in his or her name as receiver or assignee and shall show the name of the case. The depository shall furnish monthly statements to the receiver or assignee and to the attorney for the receiver or the assignee.

(b) No funds shall be withdrawn from a receiver's or assignee's account, and no check thereon shall be honored, unless directed by court order or the check is countersigned by the receiver's or assignee's surety.

(c) The order appointing a receiver or assignee shall incorporate subdivisions (a) and (b) of this section.

(d) All checks by a receiver or assignee for the withdrawal of moneys shall be numbered consecutively. On the stub of each check shall be noted the number, the date, the payee's name and the purpose for which the check is drawn. Checkbooks, stubs, cancelled checks and bank statements of such bank accounts shall be maintained at the office of the receiver or assignee or his or her attorney and shall be available for inspection by creditors or parties during business hours.

(e) Receivers shall file with the court an accounting at least once each year. An application by a receiver for final settlement of his or her account or by an assignee for leave to sell assets shall include a county clerk's certificate stating the date that the bond of the applicant was filed, that it is still on file and that no order has been entered cancelling the bond or discharging the surety thereon.

Forms

Receivership, see West's McKinney's Forms, CPLR, §§ 11:301 to 11:340; West's McKinney's Forms, Business Corporation § 12:01 et seq.

§ 202.53. Trust Accountings; Procedure

(a) Applications by trustees for interlocutory or final judgments or final orders in trust accountings or to terminate trusts shall be by notice of petition or order to show cause after the account has been filed in the county clerk's office.

(b) In all actions involving an accounting of a testamentary trustee or a trustee under a deed, notice must be given to the State Tax Commission before the accounts of such trustees may be approved.

(c) Where all parties file a written consent to the entry of a judgment or order, it may be presented at a motion part for consideration by the court.

§ 202.54. Proceedings Relating to Appointments of Guardians With Respect to Patients in Facilities Defined in the Mental Hygiene Law

Where a patient in a facility defined in the Mental Hygiene Law is the subject of a proceeding for the appointment of a guardian, pursuant to the Mental Hygiene Law or article 17–A of the Surrogate's Court Procedure Act, or for any substitute for or successor to such person:

(a) A copy of the notice of application for the appointment shall be served on the director of the Mental Hygiene Legal Service in the department in which the facility is located. The director shall submit to the court for its consideration such papers as the director may deem appropriate.

(b) Within 10 days after the order determining the application is signed, a copy shall be served on the director.

(c) Within 10 days after qualification of the guardian, proof of qualification shall be served on the director.

(d) A notice of an application for a judicial accounting by the guardian shall be served on the director.

(e) With respect to a patient in a facility located in a judicial department other than the department where the proceeding is initiated, copies of the application, order or proof of qualification shall be served upon the directors in both departments.

(f) Whenever the patient, or a person on behalf of the patient, or the director requests a court hearing, at least five days notice, if notice is given personally or by delivery at the home of the person receiving notice, or eight days notice, if notice is given by mail, excluding Sundays and holidays, of the date and place of the hearing, shall be given to the patient and any person requesting the hearing.

§ 202.55. Procedure for Perfection of Civil Appeals to the County Court

(a) Within 20 days after the papers described in section 1704 of the Uniform Justice Court Act or section 1704 of the Uniform City Court Act have been filed with the county court, appellants shall notice the appeal for the next term or special term of county court by filing with the clerk of the county court, not less than 14 days prior to the date for which the appeal has been noticed, a notice of argument and a brief or statement of contentions with proof of service of a copy of each upon respondent. Respondent's papers shall be filed with the judge of the county court within 12 days after service of appellant's brief or statement of contentions, with proof of service of a copy upon appellant.

(b) If appellant does not comply herewith, the county court may, upon respondent's motion or upon its own motion, dismiss the appeal.

(c) Upon motion, the county court judge hearing the appeal may for good cause shown extend the time to a subsequent term or special term, in which case the appellant must notice the appeal for such subsequent term. Unless otherwise ordered by the court, appeals may be submitted without oral argument. Motions for reargument may be made after decision is rendered, and must be made within 30 days after service upon the moving party of a copy of the order entered on the decision, with written notice of its entry.

Cross References

Uniform Justice Court Act, see McKinney's Book 29A, Part 2.

Uniform City Court Act, see McKinney's Book 29A, Part 3.

§ 202.56. Medical, Dental and Podiatric Malpractice Actions; Special Rules

(a) Notice of Medical, Dental or Podiatric Malpractice Actions.

(1) Within sixty days after joinder of issue by all defendants named in the complaint in an action for medical, dental or podiatric malpractice, or after the time for a defaulting party to appear, answer or move with respect to a pleading has expired, the plaintiff shall obtain an index number and file a notice of such medical, dental or podiatric malpractice action with the appropriate clerk of the county of venue, together with: (i) proof of service of the notice upon all other

parties to the action; (ii) proof that, if demanded, authorizations to obtain medical, dental and hospital records have been served upon the defendants in the action; (iii) copies of the summons, notice of appearance and all pleadings, including the certificate of merit if required by CPLR 3012–a; (iv) a copy of the bill of particulars, if one has been served; (v) a copy of any arbitration demand, election of arbitration or concession of liability served pursuant to CPLR 3045; (vi) if requested and available, all information required by CPLR 3101(d)(1)(i). The notice shall be served simultaneously upon all such parties. If the bill of particulars, papers served pursuant to CPLR 3045, and information required by CPLR 3101(d)(1)(i) are not available, but later become available, they shall be filed with the court simultaneously when served on other parties. The notice shall be in substantially the following form:

NOTICE OF MEDICAL, DENTAL OR
PODIATRIC MALPRACTICE
ACTION

Malpractice
Calendar No.
  (if any) . . . .
           . . . .
             Reserved for Clerk's use

Index No. . . . .

Name of Assigned Judge . . . .

SUPREME COURT
. . . . County
_____

. . . .
     Plaintiff(s)

        vs.

. . . .
     Defendant(s)

_____

    Please take notice that the above action for medical, dental or podiatric malpractice was commenced by service of summons on . . . ., that issue was joined therein on . . . ., and that the action has not been dismissed, settled or otherwise terminated.

1. State full name, address and age of each plaintiff.
2. State full name and address of each defendant.
3. State alleged medical specialty of each individual defendant, if known.
4. Indicate whether claim is for:
    . . . . medical malpractice
    . . . . dental malpractice
    . . . . podiatric malpractice.
5. State date and place claim arose.
6. State substance of claim.
7. (Following items must be checked)

(a) Proof is attached that authorizations to obtain medical, dental, podiatric and hospital records have been served upon the defendants in the action   . . . .
    or
    demand has not been made for such authorizations.   . . . .

(b) Copies of the summons, notice of appearance, all pleadings, certificate of merit, if required, and the bill of particulars, if one has been served, are attached.   . . . .

(c) A copy of any demand for arbitration, election of arbitration or concession of liability is attached   . . . .
    or
    demand has not been made for arbitration.   . . . .

(d) All information required by CPLR 3101(d)(1)(i) is attached   . . . .
    or
    a request for such information has not been made   . . . .
    or
    such information is not available.   . . . .

8. State names, addresses and telephone numbers of counsel for all parties.

         . . . .
            (PRINT NAME)
           Attorney for Plaintiff
           Address
           Telephone number

Dated:

Instructions:

1. Attach additional 8½ × 11 rider sheets if necessary
2. Attach proof of service of this notice upon all other parties to the action
    . . . .

    (2) The filing of the notice of medical, dental or podiatric malpractice action in an action to which a judge has not been assigned shall be accompanied by a request for judicial intervention, pursuant to section 202.6 of this Part, and shall cause the assignment of the action to a judge.

    (3) Such notice shall be filed after the expiration of 60 days only by leave of the court on motion and for good cause shown. The court shall impose such conditions as may be just, including the assessment of costs.

(b) Medical, Dental and Podiatric Malpractice Preliminary Conference.

    (1) The judge, assigned to the medical, dental or podiatric malpractice action, as soon as practicable

after the filing of the notice of medical, dental or podiatric malpractice action, shall order and conduct a preliminary conference and shall take whatever action is warranted to expedite the final disposition of the case, including but not limited to:

(i) directing any party to utilize or comply forthwith with any pretrial disclosure procedure authorized by the Civil Practice Law and Rules;

(ii) fixing the date and time for such procedures provided that all such procedures must be completed within 12 months of the filing of the notice of medical, dental or podiatric malpractice action unless otherwise ordered by the court;

(iii) establishing a timetable for offers and depositions pursuant to CPLR 3101(d)(1)(ii);

(iv) directing the filing of a note of issue and a certificate of readiness when the action otherwise is ready for trial, provided that the filing of the note of issue and certificate of readiness, to the extent feasible, be no later than 18 months after the notice of medical, dental or podiatric malpractice action is filed;

(v) fixing a date for trial;

(vi) signing any order required;

(vii) discussing and encouraging settlement, including use of the arbitration procedures set forth in CPLR 3045;

(viii) limiting issues and recording stipulations of counsel; and

(ix) scheduling and conducting any additional conferences as may be appropriate.

(2) A party failing to comply with a directive of the court authorized by the provisions of this subdivision shall be subject to appropriate sanctions, including costs, imposition of appropriate attorney's fees, dismissal of an action, claim, cross-claim, counterclaim or defense, or rendering a judgment by default. A certificate of readiness and a note of issue may not be filed until a precalendar conference has been held pursuant to this subdivision.

(3) Where parties are represented by counsel, only attorneys fully familiar with the action and authorized to make binding stipulations or commitments, or accompanied by a person empowered to act on behalf of the party represented, shall appear at the conference.

Cross References

CPLR, see McKinney's Book 7B.

Judiciary Law, see McKinney's Book 29.

§ 202.57. Judicial Review of Orders of the State Division of Human Rights; Procedure

(a) Any complainant, respondent or other person aggrieved by any order of the State Commissioner of Human Rights or the State Division of Human Rights may obtain judicial review of such order by commencing a special proceeding, within 60 days after service of the order, in the Supreme Court in the county where the alleged discriminatory practice which is the subject of the order occurred or where any person required by the order to cease and desist from an unlawful discriminatory practice or to take other affirmative action resides or transacts business. Such proceeding shall be commenced by the filing of a notice of petition and petition naming as respondents the State Division of Human Rights and all other parties appearing in the proceeding before the State Division of Human Rights.

(b) Except as set forth in paragraph (c), and unless otherwise ordered by the court, the State Division of Human Rights shall have 20 days after service of the notice of petition and petition to file with the court the written transcript of the record of all prior proceedings upon which its order was made.

(c) Where the petition seeks review of an order issued after a public hearing held pursuant to section 297(4)(a) of the Executive Law:

(1) the petition shall have annexed to it a copy of such order;

(2) the Supreme Court, upon the filing of the petition, shall make an order directing that the proceeding be transferred for disposition to the Appellate Division in the judicial department embracing the county in which the proceeding was commenced; and

(3) the time and manner of the filing of the written transcript of the record of all prior proceedings shall be determined by the Appellate Division to which the proceeding is transferred.

Cross References

Executive Law, see McKinney's Book 18.

Forms

Review of determinations by State Division of Human Rights. See West's McKinney's Forms, Selected Consolidated Laws, Executive Law, § 298, Forms 1 to 6.

§ 202.58. Small Claims Tax Assessment Review Proceedings; Small Claims Sidewalk Assessment Review Proceedings; Special Rules

(a) Establishment.

(1) There is hereby established in the Supreme Court of the State of New York in each county a program to hear special proceedings for small claims tax assessment review pursuant to title 1–A of Article 7 of the Real Property Tax Law; provided, however, that insofar as Hamilton County may lack required personnel and facilities, Fulton and Hamilton Counties shall be deemed one county for the purposes of this rule.

(2) There also is established in the Supreme Court in each county within the City of New York a program

to hear special proceedings for small claims sidewalk assessment review pursuant to section 19–152.3 of the Administrative Code of the City of New York.

(b) Commencement of Small Claims Tax Assessment Review Proceeding.

(1) A special proceeding pursuant to title 1–A of Article 7 of the Real Property Tax Law shall be commenced by a petition in a form in substantial compliance with the forms prescribed by the Chief Administrator of the Courts. Forms shall be available at no cost at each county clerk's office.

(2) Three copies of the petition shall be filed with the county clerk in the county in which the property is located within 30 days after the final completion and filing of the assessment roll containing the assessment at issue, except that in the City of New York, the petition shall be filed before the 25th day of October following the time when the determination sought to be reviewed was made. The petition may be filed with the county clerk by ordinary mail if mailed within the 30-day time period, or in the City of New York, if mailed prior to the 25th day of October, as evidenced by the postmark. A filing fee of $25 shall be paid at the time of filing, which may be in the form of a check payable to the county clerk.

(3) Within ten days of filing the petition with the county clerk, the petitioner shall send, by mail, a copy of the petition to:

    (i) the clerk of the assessing unit named in the petition or, if there is no such clerk, to the officer who performs the customary duties of the clerk, except that in the City of New York the petition shall be mailed to the President of the New York City Tax Commission or to a designee of the President;

    (ii) except in the cities of Buffalo, New York, Rochester, Syracuse and Yonkers, to the clerk of any school district within which any part of the real property on which the assessment to be reviewed is located or, if there is no clerk of the school district or such name and address cannot be obtained, to a trustee of the school district;

    (iii) the treasurer of any county in which any part of the real property is located; and

    (iv) the clerk of a village which has enacted a local law, in accordance with the provisions of subdivision 3 of section 1402 of the Real Property Tax Law, providing that the village shall cease to be an assessing unit and that village taxes shall be levied on a copy of the part of the town or county assessment roll.

(4) The county clerk shall assign a small claims assessment review filing number to each petition, shall retain one copy and shall forward two copies within two days of filing to the clerk designated by the appropriate administrative judge to process assessment review petitions.

(c) Commencement of Small Claims Sidewalk Assessment Review Proceeding.

(1) A special proceeding pursuant to section 19–152.3 of the Administrative Code of the City of New York shall be commenced by a petition in a form prescribed by the Department of Transportation of the City of New York in consultation with the Office of Court Administration. Forms shall be available at no cost at each county clerk's office within the City of New York.

(2) Three copies of the petition shall be filed with the county clerk in the county in which the property is located, provided that at least 30 days have elapsed from the presentation of the notice of claim to the Office of the Comptroller pursuant to section 19–152.2 of the Administrative Code. The petition may be filed with the county clerk by ordinary mail. A filing fee of $25 shall be paid at the time of filing, which may be in the form of a check payable to the county clerk.

(3) Within seven days of filing the petition with the county clerk, the petitioner personally shall deliver or send by certified mail, return receipt requested, a copy of the petition to the Commissioner of Transportation of the City of New York or the Commissioner's designee.

(4) The county clerk shall assign a sidewalk assessment review filing number to each petition, shall retain one copy and shall forward two copies within two days of filing to the clerk designated by the appropriate administrative judge to process sidewalk assessment review petitions.

(d) Selection of Hearing Officer Panels.

(1) The Chief Administrator of the Courts shall establish panels of small claims hearing officers found qualified to hear small claims tax assessment review proceedings pursuant to title 1–A of Article 7 of the Real Property Tax Law and panels of small claims hearing officers found qualified to hear small claims sidewalk assessment review proceedings pursuant to section 19–152.3(d) of the Administrative Code of the City of New York.

(2) The administrative judge of the county in which the panel will serve, or the deputy chief administrative judge for the courts within the City of New York, if the panel is to serve in New York City, shall invite applicants to apply by publishing an announcement in the appropriate law journals, papers of general circulation or trade journals, and by communicating directly with such groups as may produce qualified candidates.

(3) The announcements and communications shall set forth the nature of the position, the qualifications for selection as contained in section 731 of the Real Property Tax Law or section 19–152.3(d) of the Administrative Code of the City of New York, and the compensation.

(4) The administrative judge shall screen each applicant in conformance with the requirements set forth in section 731 of the Real Property Tax Law or section 19–152.3(d) of the Administrative Code of the City of New York, for qualifications, character and ability to handle the hearing officer responsibilities, and shall forward the names of recommended nominees, with a summary of their qualifications, to the Chief Administrator for appointment.

(5) Hearing officers shall serve at the pleasure of the Chief Administrator, and their appointments may be rescinded by the Chief Administrator at any time.

(6) The Chief Administrator may provide for such orientation courses, training courses and continuing education courses for persons applying to be hearing officers and for persons serving on hearing officer panels as the Chief Administrator may deem necessary and desirable.

(e) Assignment of Hearing Officers.

(1) The assessment review clerk of the county in which the panel will serve shall draw names of hearing officers at random from the panel and shall assign to each hearing officer at least the first three, but no more than six, petitions filed with the county clerk pursuant to these rules, provided, however, where necessary to ensure the fair and expeditious administration of justice, the Chief Administrator may authorize the assignment of related petitions and the assignment of more than six petitions to a single hearing officer.

(2) No person who has served as a hearing officer shall be eligible to serve again until all other hearing officers on the panel have had an opportunity to serve.

(3) A hearing officer shall disqualify himself or herself from hearing a matter where a conflict exists as defined by the Public Officers Law or, with respect to small claims tax assessment review hearing officers, by subdivision 2 of section 731 of the Real Property Tax Law. Where a hearing officer disqualifies himself or herself, such hearing officer shall notify the chief administrator or designee and the matter shall be reassigned to another hearing officer.

(4) The hearing officer shall determine, after contacting the parties, the date, time and place for the hearing, which shall be held within 45 days with respect to a small claims tax assessment review proceeding, and within 30 days with respect to a small claims sidewalk assessment review proceeding, after the filing of the petition, or as soon thereafter as is practicable, and which shall be held, where practicable, at a location within the county where the real property is located. The hearing officer shall schedule hearings in the evening at the request of any party, unless special circumstances require otherwise. Written notice of the date, time and place of the hearing shall be sent by mail by the hearing officer to the parties or their attorneys, if represented, at least

10 working days prior to the date of the hearing; provided, however, failure to receive such notice in such period shall not bar the holding of a hearing.

(5) Adjournments shall not be granted by the hearing officer except upon good cause shown.

(6) All parties are required to appear at the hearing. Failure to appear shall result in the petition being dismissed or in the petition being determined upon inquest by the hearing officer based upon the available evidence submitted.

(f) Decision and Order.

(1) The decision and order of the hearing officer shall be rendered expeditiously, and, in a small claims tax assessment review proceeding, the notice required by section 733(4) of the Real Property Tax Law shall be attached to the petition form.

(2) Costs. (i) In a small claims tax assessment review proceeding, if the assessment is reduced by an amount equal to or greater than half the reduction sought, the hearing officer shall award the petitioner costs against the respondent assessing unit in the amount of $25. If the assessment is reduced by an amount less than half of the reduction sought, the hearing officer may award the petitioner costs against the respondent assessing unit in an amount not to exceed $25. (ii) In a small claims sidewalk assessment review proceeding, if the hearing officer grants the petition in full or in part, the hearing officer shall award the petitioner costs against the respondent in the amount of $25. In any other case, the hearing officer, in his or her discretion, may award the petitioner costs in the amount of $25, if he or she deems it appropriate.

(3) The hearing officer in a small claims tax assessment review proceeding shall transmit one copy of the decision and order, by ordinary mail, to the petitioner, the clerk of the assessing unit and the assessment review clerk of the court. The hearing officer in a small claims sidewalk assessment review proceeding shall transmit one copy of the decision and order, by ordinary mail, to the petitioner, the Commissioner of Transportation of the City of New York or the Commissioner's designee, and the assessment review clerk of the court.

(4) The assessment review clerk shall file the petition and the attached decision and order with the county clerk.

(5) The assessment review clerk shall make additional copies of the decision and order, as necessary, and, in the case of a small claims tax assessment review proceeding, shall transmit a copy to the clerk of each tax district relying on the assessment that is named in the petition and to the treasurer of any county in which any part of the real property is located. In the case of a small claims sidewalk assessment review proceeding, where the order grants the petition in full or in part, the assessment review clerk

shall mail a copy of the decision and order to the Collector of the City of New York.

(g) Advertising by Hearing Officers. No person who is appointed a hearing officer shall, in any public advertisement published or distributed to advance such person's business or professional interests, refer to his or her status as a hearing officer. No hearing officer shall use letterhead or business cards bearing the title of hearing officer except in direct connection with such person's official duties as hearing officer.

(h)(1) Proceedings pursuant to Title 1–A of Article 7 of the Real Property Tax Law may be heard and determined by a judicial hearing officer. The judicial hearing officer shall be designated and assigned by the appropriate administrative judge to hear such proceedings as determined by that judge or by the assessment review clerk, and the hearing shall be conducted in accordance with this section.

(2) Judicial hearing officers appointed to hear proceedings pursuant to this section shall receive compensation as provided in section 122.8 of the rules of the Chief Administrator. A location in which a hearing is held pursuant to this section shall be deemed a "facility designated for court appearances" within the meaning of section 122.8.

(i) Collateral Proceedings. All applications for judicial relief shall be made in the supreme court in the county where the real property subject to review is located. If a judicial hearing officer has heard and determined a proceeding under this section, any application for judicial relief may not be heard by a judicial hearing officer, except upon consent of the parties.

Cross References

Public Officers Law, see McKinney's Book 46.

Real Property Tax Law, see McKinney's Book 49A.

§ 202.59. Tax Assessment Review Proceedings in Counties Outside the City of New York; Special Rules

(a) Applicability. This section shall apply to every tax assessment review proceeding brought pursuant to title 1 of article 7 of the Real Property Tax Law in counties outside the City of New York.

(b) Statement of Income and Expenses. Before the note of issue and certificate of readiness may be filed, the petitioner shall have served on the respondent, in triplicate, a statement that the property is not income-producing or a copy of a verified or certified statement of the income and expenses on the property for each tax year under review. For the purposes of this section, a cooperative or condominium apartment building shall be considered income-producing property; an owner-occupied business property shall be considered income-producing as determined by the amount reasonably allocable for rent, but the petitioner is not required to make an estimate of rental income.

(c) Audit. Within 60 days after the service of the statement of income and expenses, the respondent, for the purpose of substantiating petitioner's statement of income and expenses, may request in writing an audit of the petitioner's books and records for the tax years under review. If requested, the audit must be completed within 120 days after the request has been made unless the court, upon good cause shown, extends the time for the audit. Failure of the respondent to request or complete the audit within the time limits shall be deemed a waiver of such privilege. If an audit is requested and the petitioner fails to furnish its books and records within a reasonable time after receipt of the request, or otherwise unreasonably impedes or delays the audit, the court, on motion of the respondent, may dismiss the petition or petitions or make such other order as the interest of justice requires.

(d) Filing Note of Issue and Certificate of Readiness; Additional Requirements.

(1) A note of issue and certificate of readiness shall not be filed unless all disclosure proceedings have been completed and the statement of income and expenses has been served and filed.

(2) A separate note of issue shall be filed for each property for each tax year.

(e) Pretrial Conference.

(1) At any time after filing of the note of issue and certificate of readiness, any party to a tax assessment review proceeding may demand, by application served on all other parties and filed with the court, together with proof of such service, a pretrial conference, or the court on its own motion may direct a pretrial conference at a time and date to be fixed by the court. At the pretrial conference, the judge shall take whatever action is warranted to expedite final disposition of the proceedings, including, but not limited to:

(i) directing the parties to obtain appraisals and sales reports, and to exchange and file appraisal reports and sales reports by dates certain before the trial, provided that if the court dispenses with a pretrial conference, such exchange and filings shall be accomplished at least ten days before trial;

(ii) fixing a date for trial, or by which the parties must be ready for trial;

(iii) signing any order required;

(iv) conducting conferences for the purpose of facilitating settlement; and

(v) limiting issues and recording stipulations of counsel.

(2) Failure to comply with any order or directive of the court authorized by this subdivision shall be subject to the appropriate sanctions.

(f) Consolidation or Joint Trial. Consolidation or joint trial of real property tax assessment review proceedings in the discretion of the court shall be conditioned upon service having been made of the verified or certified income and expense statement, or a statement that the property is not income-producing, for each of the tax years under review.

(g) Exchange and Filing of Appraisal Reports.

(1) The exchange and filing of appraisal reports shall be accomplished by the following procedure:

(i) The respective parties shall file with the clerk of the trial court one copy, or in the event that there are two or more adversaries, a copy for each adversary, of all appraisal reports intended to be used at the trial.

(ii) When the clerk shall have received all such reports, the clerk forthwith shall distribute simultaneously to each of the other parties a copy of the reports filed.

(iii) Where multiple parties or more than one parcel is involved, each appraisal report need be served only upon the taxing authority and the party or parties contesting the value of the property which is the subject of the report. Each party shall provide an appraisal report copy for the court.

(2) The appraisal reports shall contain a statement of the method of appraisal relied on and the conclusions as to value reached by the expert, together with the facts, figures and calculations by which the conclusions were reached. If sales, leases or other transactions involving comparable properties are to be relied on, they shall be set forth with sufficient particularity as to permit the transaction to be readily identified, and the report shall contain a clear and concise statement of every fact that a party will seek to prove in relation to those comparable properties. The appraisal reports also may contain photographs of the property under review and of any comparable property that specifically is relied upon by the appraiser, unless the court otherwise directs.

(3) Where an appraiser appraises more than one parcel in any proceeding, those parts of the separate appraisal reports for each parcel that would be repetitious may be included in one general appraisal report to which reference may be made in the separate appraisal reports. Such general appraisal reports shall be served and filed as provided in paragraph (1) of this subdivision.

(4) Appraisal reports shall comply with any official form for appraisal reports that may be prescribed by the Chief Administrator of the Courts.

(h) Use of Appraisal Reports at Trial. Upon the trial, expert witnesses shall be limited in their proof of appraised value to details set forth in their respective appraisal reports. Any party who fails to serve an appraisal report as required by this section shall be precluded from offering any expert testimony on value, provided, however, upon the application of any party on such notice as the court shall direct, the court may, upon good cause shown, relieve a party of a default in the service of a report, extend the time for exchanging reports, or allow an amended or supplemental report to be served upon such conditions as the court may direct. After the trial of the issues has begun, any such application must be made to the trial judge and shall be entertained only in unusual and extraordinary circumstances.

Cross References

Real Property Tax Law, see McKinney's Book 49A.

§ 202.60. Tax Assessment Review Proceedings in Counties Within the City of New York; Special Rules

(a) Applicability. This section shall apply to every tax assessment review proceeding brought pursuant to title 1 of article 7 of the Real Property Tax Law in a county within the City of New York.

(b) Preliminary Conference.

(1) Any party to a tax assessment review proceeding may demand, by application served on all other parties and filed with the court, together with proof of such service, a preliminary conference, or the court on its own motion may direct a preliminary conference. The court, in its notice to the parties setting the date for the conference, shall direct the petitioner to serve upon the respondent by a date certain before the date of the conference, the completed statement of income and expenses required by this section, together with any ancillary papers or documents that may be necessary. No note of issue may be filed until a preliminary conference has been held.

(2) The judge presiding at the preliminary conference shall take whatever action is warranted to expedite final disposition of the case, including, but not limited to:

(i) directing any party to utilize or comply by a date certain with any pretrial disclosure or bill of particulars procedure authorized by the Civil Practice Law and Rules;

(ii) directing the parties to obtain appraisals and sales reports, and to exchange and file appraisal reports and sales reports by dates certain before the trial;

(iii) directing the filing of a note of issue and certificate of readiness;

(iv) fixing a date for trial, or by which the parties must be ready for trial;

(v) signing any order required;

(vi) conducting conferences for the purpose of facilitating settlement; and

(vii) limiting issues and recording stipulations of counsel.

(3) Failure to comply with any order or directive of the court authorized by this subdivision shall be subject to appropriate sanctions.

(4) Where parties are represented by counsel, only attorneys fully familiar with the action and authorized to make binding stipulations or commitments, or accompanied by a person empowered to act on behalf of the party represented, shall appear at the conference.

(c) **Statement of Income and Expenses.** Before the note of issue and certificate of readiness may be filed, the petitioner shall have served on the respondent, in triplicate, a statement that the property is not income-producing or a copy of a verified or certified statement of the income and expenses of the property for each tax year under review. If the property is income-producing, the petitioner must serve the statement of income and expenses on forms provided by the Tax Certiorari Division of the Office of the Corporation Counsel of the City of New York. The petitioner shall complete all items listed on such form. A copy of such completed form shall also be filed with the note of issue and certificate of readiness. For the purposes of this section, a cooperative or condominium apartment building shall be considered income-producing property; an owner-occupied business property shall be considered income-producing as determined by the amount reasonably allocable for rent, but the petitioner is not required to make an estimate of rental income.

(d) **Audit.** Within 60 days after the first preliminary conference, the respondent, for the purpose of substantiating petitioner's completed statement of income and expenses, as required by subdivision (c), may request in writing an audit of the petitioner's books and records for the tax years under review. If requested, the audit must be completed within 120 days after the request has been made unless the court, upon good cause shown, extends the time for the audit. Failure of the respondent to request or complete the audit within the time limits shall be deemed a waiver of such privilege. If an audit is requested and the petitioner fails to furnish its books and records within a reasonable time after receipt of the request, or otherwise unreasonably impedes or delays the audit, the court, on motion of the respondent, may dismiss the petition or petitions or make such other order as the interest of justice requires.

(e) **Filing Note of Issue and Certificate of Readiness; Additional Requirements.**

(1) A note of issue and certificate of readiness shall not be filed unless all disclosure proceedings have been completed and the statement of income and expenses has been served and filed. A note of issue and certificate of readiness may not be filed in any action where a preliminary conference was requested or was directed by the court until the conference has been held and there has been compliance with any orders or directives of the court or stipulations of counsel made at such conference.

(2) A separate note of issue shall be filed for each property for each tax year.

(f) **Consolidation or Joint Trial.** Consolidation or joint trial of real property tax assessment review proceedings in the discretion of the court shall be conditioned upon service having been made of the verified or certified income and expense statement, or a statement that the property is not income-producing, for each of the tax years under review.

(g) **Exchange and Filing of Appraisal Reports.**

(1) Upon the filing of the note of issue and certificate of readiness, the court, if it has not previously so directed, shall direct that appraisal reports and sales reports be obtained and that appraisal reports and sales reports be exchanged and filed by a date certain a specified time before the date scheduled for trial.

(2) The exchange and filing of appraisal reports shall be accomplished by the following procedure:

(i) The respective parties shall file with the clerk of the trial court one copy, or in the event that there are two or more adversaries, a copy for each adversary, of all appraisal reports intended to be used at the trial.

(ii) When the clerk shall have received all such reports, the clerk forthwith shall distribute simultaneously to each of the other parties a copy of the reports filed.

(iii) Where multiple parties or more than one parcel is involved, each appraisal report need be served only upon the taxing authority and the party or parties contesting the value of the property which is the subject of the report. Each party shall provide an appraisal report copy for the court.

(3) The appraisal reports shall contain a statement of the method of appraisal relied on and the conclusions as to value reached by the expert, together with the facts, figures and calculations by which the conclusions were reached. If sales, leases or other transactions involving comparable properties are to be relied on, they shall be set forth with sufficient particularity as to permit the transaction to be readily identified, and the report shall contain a clear and concise statement of every fact that a party will seek to prove in relation to those comparable properties. The appraisal reports also shall contain photographs of the property under review and of any comparable property that specifically is relied upon by the appraiser, unless the court otherwise directs.

(4) Where an appraiser appraises more than one parcel in any proceeding, those parts of the separate appraisal reports for each parcel that would be repetitious may be included in one general appraisal report to which reference may be made in the separate appraisal reports. Such general appraisal reports

shall be served and filed as provided in paragraph (1) of this subdivision.

(5) Appraisal reports shall comply with any official form for appraisal reports that may be prescribed by the Chief Administrator of the Courts.

(h) Use of Appraisal Reports at Trial. Upon the trial, expert witnesses shall be limited in their proof of appraised value to details set forth in their respective appraisal reports. Any party who fails to serve an appraisal report as required by this section shall be precluded from offering any expert testimony on value, provided, however, upon the application of any party on such notice as the court shall direct, the court may, upon good cause shown, relieve a party of a default in the service of a report, extend the time for exchanging reports, or allow an amended or supplemental report to be served upon such conditions as the court may direct. After the trial of the issues has begun, any such application must be made to the trial judge and shall be entertained only in unusual and extraordinary circumstances.

Cross References

CPLR, see McKinney's Book 7B.

Real Property Tax Law, see McKinney's Book 49A.

§ 202.61. Exchange of Appraisal Reports in Eminent Domain Proceedings

(a)(1) In all proceedings for the determination of the value of property taken pursuant to eminent domain, the exchange of appraisal reports shall be accomplished in the same manner as provided for the exchange of such reports by subdivision (g) of section 202.59 and subdivision (g) of section 202.60 of this Part, except that such reports shall be filed no later than nine months after service of the claim, demand or notice of appearance required by section 503 of the Eminent Domain Procedure Law, unless otherwise extended by the court. A note of issue may not be filed until such reports have been filed.

(2) If a party intends to offer at trial expert evidence in rebuttal to any report, an expert's report shall be filed within 60 days after receipt of the document sought to be rebutted.

(3) Upon application of any party upon such notice as the court in which the proceeding is pending shall direct, the court may, upon good cause shown, relieve a party of a default in filing a report, extend the time for filing reports, or allow an amended or supplemental report to be filed upon such conditions as the court may direct.

(b) In proceedings where more than one parcel is involved, the appraisal reports shall be distributed only to the taking authority and to the claimant or claimants who are owners of parcels which are the subject of the appraisal report. In the event that a party defaults in filing an appraisal report within the time limitation prescribed, the clerk shall return the

filed copies of each party's appraisal report, with notice to the party in default.

(c) The contents and form of each appraisal report, including any rebuttal, amended or supplementary report, shall conform to the requirements of subdivision (g) of section 202.59 and subdivision (g) of section 202.60 of this Part.

(d) All appraisals of fixtures submitted on behalf of the claimants and the condemnor for which claim is made shall be filed and distributed as provided by these rules with respect to appraisal reports and shall set forth the appraisal value of each item in the same numerical order as in the inventory annexed to the claim. (1) Where the condemnor puts in issue the existence of any item in the inventory, the appraisal submitted on its behalf shall so state. (2) Where the condemnor puts in issue the description of any item in the inventory, the appraisal submitted on behalf of the condemnor shall state its appraiser's description of such item and his or her estimate of value. (3) Where the condemnor puts in issue the compensability of any item in the inventory, the appraisal report submitted by the condemnor shall so state and shall state the ground therefor, as well as its appraiser's estimate of the value of such item for consideration in the event that the court should determine that it is compensable.

(e) Upon trial, all parties shall be limited in their affirmative proof of value to matters set forth in their respective appraisal reports. Any party who fails to file an appraisal report as required by this section shall be precluded from offering any appraisal testimony on value.

Cross References

EDPL, see McKinney's Book 16A.

§ 202.62. Payment of Eminent Domain Award to Other Than the Named Awardee

On all applications for payment of awards in eminent domain proceedings by parties other than the party named in the decree, the applicant shall give notice of its motion to all parties with an interest in the award.

§ 202.63. Assignment for Benefit of Creditors

(a) Records and Papers.

(1) In assignments for the benefit of creditors, the clerk shall keep a register and docket. The clerk shall enter in the register in full every final order according to date; the docket shall contain a brief note of each day's proceedings under the respective title.

(2) Every petition, order, decree or other paper shall have endorsed on the outside the nature of such paper, the date of filing, and the name, number and

page of the book in which the proceedings are entered by the clerk.

(3) The papers in each proceeding shall be kept in a separate file, as required by section 18 of the Debtor and Creditor Law. No paper shall be removed from the files of the court except by order of the court.

(4) Except as otherwise provided by law, every notice or citation, subpoena, and all process shall issue out of the court under seal and be attested by the clerk.

(b) Appearances.

(1) Any person interested in an assignment for the benefit of creditors may appear either in person or by attorney. If in person, his or her address and telephone number, and if by attorney, the name, address and telephone number, shall be endorsed on every appearance filed by such attorney. The name of such person or attorney shall be entered in the docket.

(2) The assignee's attorney shall file a written notice of appearance as soon as possible, but not later than ten days after being retained.

(3) When an assignee is removed, voluntarily or involuntarily, and another person has been appointed as assignee, a certified copy of the order shall be filed with the clerk of the county where the original assignment was recorded. The clerk shall make an entry on the record of the original assignment to show the appointment of the substituted assignee, and the copy of the order of substitution shall be attached to the original assignment.

(c) Duties of the Assignor and Assignee.

(1) The assignor shall deliver all books, records and documents to the assignee immediately upon filing the assignment, but the assignee shall make them available to the assignor to prepare the schedules.

(2) The assignee's attorney shall require the person in charge of the assignor's business to submit to examination under oath and shall complete such examinations within 30 days, unless extended by the court for good cause.

(3) The assignee shall promptly require the assignor, if an individual, or its officers and persons in charge of its finances, if a corporation, to pay to the assignee all trust funds withheld for accounting to any governmental authorities together with any preferential payments paid to them or to others by the assignor.

(4) (i) Upon the filing of an assignment, the court, upon application, may stay any prospective sale or transfer to enforce a lien against property in the custody of the court whether by a secured creditor, a judgment creditor, a lienor or otherwise.

(ii) With respect to property not in the custody of the court, possession having been acquired by the secured creditor, judgment creditor or lienor, the assignee may, upon notice to the adverse party,

apply to the court where such assignment proceedings are pending to enjoin any prospective sale and to permit the assignee to conduct the sale, whether private or a public auction, upon such terms and conditions as in its discretion will not prejudice the interest of the secured party and yet preserve the interest of the assigned estate by affording the assignee an opportunity to liquidate the assets under the most favorable terms and conditions.

(5) Every assignee shall keep full, exact and regular books of account of all receipts, payments and expenditures of monies.

(6) In making sales at auction of personal property, the assignee shall give at least ten days' notice of the time and place of sale and of the articles to be sold, by advertisement in one or more newspapers. Such sale shall be held within 15 days after the entry of the order authorizing the same, unless in the meantime an order of the court has been obtained granting an extension of the time for such sale; and he or she shall give notice of the sale at auction of any real estate at least 20 days before such sale. Upon such sale, the assignee shall sell by printed catalogue, in parcels, and shall file a copy of such catalogue with the prices obtained for the goods sold, within 20 days after the date of such sale.

(7) (i) Notwithstanding subdivision (f) of this section, upon receipt of an offer for all or a substantial part of the assets, an assignee may for good cause shown make application to the court for leave to sell at a private sale in lieu of a public auction sale. A hearing thereon shall be scheduled for the purpose of considering that offer or any higher or better offers that may be submitted upon such notice and advertising as the court may deem appropriate.

(ii) Upon application by an assignee or a creditor, setting forth that a part or the whole of the estate is perishable, the nature and location of such perishable property, and that there will be a loss if the same is not sold immediately, the judge presiding, if satisfied of the facts stated and that the sale is required in the interest of the estate, may order the same to be sold with or without notice to creditors.

(8) Upon an application made for a notice of filing of his or her account and for a hearing thereon, the assignee shall file with his or her petition his or her account with the vouchers.

(d) Accounting and Schedules.

(1) The assignee must file and account in all cases.

(2) Failure to file an interim accounting in a pending proceeding within six months after the filing of an assignment may cause a forfeiture of commissions and fees of the assignee and his or her attorney and shall constitute grounds for their removal.

(3) Where more than one sheet of paper is necessary to contain the schedule of liabilities and inventory

of assets required to be filed by the assignor or assignee, each page shall be signed by the person or persons verifying the same. Contingent liabilities shall appear on a separate sheet of paper. The sheets on which such schedule and inventory are written shall be securely fastened before the filing thereof and shall be endorsed with the full name of the assignor and assignee; and when filed by an attorney, the name and address of such attorney shall also be endorsed thereon. Such schedule and inventory shall fully and fairly state the nominal and actual value of the assets and the cause of differences between such values. A separate affidavit will be required explaining such stated cause of difference. If it is deemed necessary, affidavits of disinterested experts as to the claimed values must be furnished; and if such schedule and inventory are filed by the assignee, they must be accompanied by affidavits made by such assignee and by some disinterested expert showing, in detail, the nature and value of the property assigned. The name, residence, occupation and place of business of the assignor, and the name and place of residence of the assignee must be annexed to the schedule and inventory or incorporated in the affidavit verifying the same. There shall be a recapitulation at the end of such schedule and inventory, as follows:

Debts and liabilities amount to............$

Fair value of assets ....$

Assets realized on liquidation ....$

(4) Application to amend the schedule shall be made by verified petition in which the amendment sought to be made shall appear in full, and such amendment shall be verified in the same manner as the original schedule.

(5) The account of the assignee shall be in the nature of a debit and credit statement; he or she shall debit himself or herself with the assets as shown in the schedule, as filed, and credit himself or herself with any decrease and expenses.

(6) The statement of expenditures shall be full and complete and the vouchers for all payments shall be attached to the account.

(7) The affirmative on the accounting shall be with the assignee; the objections to the account may be presented to the court or designated referee in writing or be brought out on a cross-examination. In the latter case, they must be specifically taken and entered in the minutes.

(8) The testimony taken and all exhibits marked in evidence shall be filed with the report of the referee.

(9) It shall be the duty of the assignee to close up the estate as expeditiously as possible; and, unless good cause for greater delay can be shown and authorized by an order of the court obtained prior to the expiration of the permissible time, the assignee's account shall be filed within 15 months from the date of the execution of the assignment deed.

(10) The court may order notice to creditors by publication to present their claims as provided in section 5 of the Debtor and Creditor Law.

(e) Court-Appointed Referee.

(1) The court may appoint a referee to take and state any contested account or to hear and report on any issue of fact raised in an application to the court by any interested party.

(2) Notice of the time and place of the hearing before a referee appointed to take and state an assignee's account or to hear and report on a referred issue of fact shall be given by mail, with the postage thereon prepaid, at least 20 days before the date specified in said notice, to the assignor, the assignee's surety and to each creditor whose name appears on the books of the assignor or on the schedule, or who has presented her or his claim or address to the assignee, and to each attorney who has appeared for any person interested in the assigned estate.

(3) A notice or a copy of an advertisement, requiring the creditors to present their claims, with the vouchers therefor duly verified to the referee, must be mailed to each creditor whose name appears on the books of the assignor or on the schedule, with the postage thereon prepaid, at least ten days before the date specified in such notice or advertisement. Proof of such mailing shall be required on the application for a final decree approving the account of the assignee unless proof is furnished that personal service of such notice or a copy of such advertisement has been made upon the creditor.

(4) The report of the referee shall show all the jurisdictional facts necessary to confer power on the court, such as the proper execution and acknowledgement of the assignment, its recording, the filing of the schedule and bond, the publication and mailing of notice to creditors to present claims, the filing of the assignee's account, the issuance and service of notice of application for settlement of the account, and where any items in the account of the assignee are disallowed, the same shall be fully set out in the report, together with the reason therefor.

(5) The report of the referee after a hearing of a disputed claim under the statute shall be filed with the clerk of the court and a copy served on each party to the proceeding. The court shall, on application of any party, or on its own motion, confirm or disaffirm the referee's report; such report shall then be reviewed only by appeal to the Appellate Division.

(f) Discharge of Assignee.

(1) No discharge shall be granted an assignee who has not advertised for claims pursuant to section 5 of the Debtor and Creditor Law and the applicable provisions of this section.

(2) No discharge shall be granted an assignee and his or her sureties in any case, whether or not the creditors have been paid, or have released, or have entered into composition, except in a regular proceeding for an accounting under the applicable provisions of the Debtor and Creditor Law, commenced by petition, and after due and timely notice thereof to all persons interested in the estate.

(3) *Provisional and Final Bond.* The affidavit upon which application is made for leave to file a provisional bond must show fully and fairly the nature and extent of the property assigned, and good and sufficient reason must be shown why the schedule and inventory cannot be filed. It must appear satisfactorily to the court that a necessity exists for filing of such provisional bond; and the affidavits filed shall be deemed a schedule and inventory of the assigned property until such time as the regular schedule and inventory of the assigned property shall be filed. Upon the filing of the schedule and inventory, the amount of the bond shall be determined finally. Should the provisional bond already filed be deemed sufficient, an order may be granted making such bond, as approved, the final bond.

(4) Upon all applications made to the court by assignees under general assignments for the benefit of creditors for the filing of a provisional bond, or for permission to sell the property of the assignor, the applicant shall present proof by affidavit whether any petition in bankruptcy has been filed by or against the assignor.

(5) The final bond shall be joint and several in form and must be accompanied by the affidavit prescribed by CPLR 2502, and also by the affidavit of each surety, setting forth his business, where it is carried on, and the amount in which he or she is required to justify over and above his debts and liabilities.

(g) Justification of Sureties. The court may in its discretion require any surety to appear and justify. If the penalty of the bond be $20,000 or over, it may be executed by two sureties each justifying in that sum, or by more than two sureties, the amount of whose justification, united, is double the penalty of the bond.

(h) Application to Continue Business of Assignor. An application for authority to continue the business of an assignor must be made upon duly verified petition and upon notice given to, or order to show cause served upon, the assignor, the assignee's surety and all creditors, secured, general or otherwise, of the assigned estate. If more than one application for such authority is subsequently made, the petition must set forth, by a statement of receipts, disbursements and expenses, the result of the continuance of such business for or during the period for which the same was previously authorized.

(i) Involuntary Petition in Bankruptcy of the Assigned Estate. Where an order for relief pursuant to section 503 of Title 11 of the United States Code

has been entered, the assignee shall file with the clerk a certified copy of such petition in bankruptcy, together with proof by affidavit on the part of the assignee showing that he has turned over all assets of the assigned estate to the trustee or receiver in bankruptcy.

(j) Assignee's Commissions and Attorneys Fees. Assignee's allowances and attorney fees are to be fixed by the court upon a motion to settle and approve the assignee's account or upon the confirmation of the referee's report regarding the account. No allowances, fees or commissions shall be paid out until so fixed and directed by the court.

(k) Service of Notice by Mail. When any notice is served by mail on the creditors of the insolvent debtor pursuant to the provisions of the applicable statute or this section, every envelope containing such notice shall have upon it a direction to the postmaster at the place to which it is sent, to return the same to the sender whose name and address shall appear thereon, unless called for or delivered.

Cross References

CPLR, see McKinney's Book 7B.

Debtor and Creditor Law, see McKinney's Book 12.

§ 202.64. Election Law Proceedings

(a) All applications to the Supreme Court, or to a judge thereof, pursuant to the Election Law, shall be made at the special part designated for such proceedings and where there is no special part, before the judge to whom the proceeding is assigned. As far as practicable, the application shall be brought in the county in which it arose.

(b) The judge may hear and determine the proceeding or assign it to a referee for hearing or decision, and such proceedings shall have preference over all other business of the part to which it is assigned or before the judge to whom it is assigned.

(c) The final order in an election proceeding shall state the determination and the facts upon which it was made.

Cross References

Election Law, see McKinney's Book 17.

§ 202.65. Registration of Title to Real Property; Sales of Real Estate Under Court Direction

(a) Petitions for Registration. Petitions for the registration of titles to land made pursuant to article 12 of the Real Property Law shall be made to the Supreme Court in the county where the land or portion thereof affected by the petition is situated. Where a particular part has been designated for this purpose as a title part under the provisions of section 371 of such law, all petitions to register titles to land under the law must be returnable at the said title part. If there is no such part, petitions shall be returnable before the judge assigned. Such title part or assigned judge is hereinafter denominated as the appropriate part or judge in this section.

(b) Application for Final Order and Judgment of Registration. After the time provided in the notice of hearing shall have expired, or within such further time as may have been allowed by the court, if there have been no appearances or answers to the petition, the petitioner may apply to the appropriate part or judge for a final order and judgment of registration, as provided for in the law. In all applications for such final order and judgment of registration, the applicant or petitioner must present to the court proof by affidavit that all the provisions of the law entitling the petitioner to such final order and judgment of registration have been complied with.

(c) Application for Jury Trial. Where an answer is interposed which raises an issue of fact which in an action relating to the title to real property would be triable by a jury, either or any party to the registration proceeding who is entitled to have such issue determined may apply to the appropriate part or judge within 20 days after the issue has been joined to have the issues framed to be tried by a jury, as provided by CPLR 4102(b). The trial of such issues shall be had and the subsequent proceedings in relation thereto shall be such as is prescribed by the CPLR. After such issues are disposed of, either or any party to the registration proceeding may apply to the appropriate part or judge, upon eight days' notice to all who have appeared in the registration proceeding, for a final order and judgment of registration, and on such application the court shall try all other issues in the proceeding not disposed of by the jury, or may refer any such issues undisposed of to be tried by an official examiner of title as referee. Where all issues have been disposed of, any party, upon eight days' notice to all who have appeared in the proceeding, may apply for the final order and judgment of registration at the appropriate part or before the appropriate assigned judge.

(d) Applications; Notice Requirements. All applications to the court after a certificate of registration of title has been issued under the provisions of the law must be made at the appropriate part or before the appropriate assigned judge hereinbefore designated upon 20 days' notice to all persons interested in the said application. All applications to the court under sections 404–a and 422 of the Real Property Law shall be made to the appropriate part or judge upon eight days' notice to all persons in interest, as provided by that section. All applications made to the court under section 428 of the Real Property Law shall also be made to the appropriate part or judge, upon eight days' notice to the city or county treasurer and all other parties who have appeared in the proceeding to recover for loss or damage or deprivation of real

property out of the assurance fund provided for by law.

(e) Sales of Real Estate. All sales of real estate or an interest therein, made pursuant to a judgment, decree or order, or by an officer of the court under its direction, shall be made pursuant to section 231 of the Real Property Actions and Proceedings Law, after notice as prescribed in that section. An auctioneer selected for this purpose must be an attorney, or a licensed real estate broker, or a salesman licensed for at least five years. The auctioneer's fee for conducting the sale shall be as prescribed by law.

Cross References

CPLR, see McKinney's Book 7B.

Real Property Law, see McKinney's Book 49.

RPAPL, see McKinney's Book 49½.

§ 202.66. Workers' Compensation Settlements

(a) Applications for approval of compromises of third-party actions pursuant to subdivision 5 of section 29 of the Workers' Compensation Law must include all papers described therein, and a proposed order providing that the appropriate insuring body file an affidavit within a specified time consenting to or opposing the application. A copy of all such application papers shall be served on the insurance carrier that is liable for the payment of claims under the Workers' Compensation Law.

(b) If prior to the return of the application the court directs that the parties place their stipulation on the record, the transcript shall be filed as part of the papers. In such cases the matter shall be marked settled subject to written consent of the insuring body, or the entry of an order pursuant to subdivision 5 of section 29 of the Workers' Compensation Law.

(c) On the return of the application, the court may hear the matter forthwith or schedule the matter for later hearing if affidavits in opposition to the compromise show that the amount is grossly inadequate in view of the injuries involved, the potential monetary recovery against the third party and the possible exposure of the insuring body to future claims by the plaintiff-petitioner arising out of the same accident.

(d) Nothing in this section shall preclude the insuring body from consenting to a reduction of its lien.

Cross References

Workmen's Compensation Law, see McKinney's Book 64.

Forms

See West's McKinney's Forms, Selected Consolidated Laws, Work Comp § 29, Form 1 et seq., generally.

§ 202.67. Infants' and Incapacitated Persons' Claims and Proceedings

(a) The settlement of an action or claim by an infant or judicially declared incapacitated person (including an incompetent or conservatee) shall comply with CPLR 1207 and 1208 and, in the case of an infant, with section 474 of the Judiciary law. The proposed order in such cases may provide for deduction of the following disbursements from the settlement:

(1) motor vehicle reports;

(2) police reports;

(3) photographs;

(4) deposition stenographic expenses;

(5) service of summons and complaint and of subpoenas;

(6) expert's fees, including analysis of materials;

(7) other items approved by court order. The order shall not provide for attorney's fees in excess of one-third of the amount remaining after deduction of the above disbursements unless otherwise specifically authorized by the court.

(b) The petition or affidavit in support of the application also shall set forth the total amount of the charge incurred for each doctor and hospital in the treatment and care of the infant or incapacitated person and the amount remaining unpaid to each doctor and hospital for such treatment and care. If an order be made approving the application, the order shall provide that all such charges for doctors and hospitals shall be paid from the proceeds, if any, received by the parent, guardian, or other person, in settlement of any action or claim for the loss of the infant's or incapacitated person's services; provided, however, that if there be any bona fide dispute as to such charges, the judge presiding, in the order, may make such provision with respect to them as justice requires. With respect to an incapacitated person, the judge presiding may provide for the posting of a bond as required by the Mental Hygiene Law.

(c) If the net amount obtained for the infant or incapacitated person in any approved settlement does not exceed the amount set forth in CPLR 1206(b), the court may permit it to be paid pursuant to CPLR 1206(b). The court may order in any case that the money be deposited or invested pursuant to CPLR 1206(c) or held for the use and benefit of the infant or incapacitated person as provided in CPLR 1206(d) and CPLR 1210(d).

(d) The affidavit of the attorney for a plaintiff, in addition to complying with CPLR 1208, must show compliance with the requirements for filing a retainer statement and recite the number assigned by the Office of Court Administration, or show that such requirements do not apply.

(e) Applications for approval of an infant's or incapacitated person's compromise shall be made returnable before the judge who presided over the compromise or, where the agreement was reached out-of-court, before the appropriate assigned judge.

(f) A petition for the expenditure of the funds of an infant shall comply with CPLR Article 12, and also shall set forth:

(1) a full explanation of the purpose of the withdrawal;

(2) a sworn statement of the reasonable cost of the proposed expenditure;

(3) the infant's age;

(4) the date and amounts of the infant's and parents' recovery;

(5) the balance from such recovery;

(6) the nature of the infant's injuries and present condition;

(7) a statement that the family of the infant is financially unable to afford the proposed expenditures;

(8) a statement as to previous orders authorizing such expenditures; and

(9) any other facts material to the application.

(g) No authorization will be granted to withdraw such funds, except for unusual circumstances, where the parents are financially able to support the infant and to provide for the infant's necessaries, treatment and education.

(h) Expenditures of the funds of an incapacitated person shall comply with the provisions of the Mental Hygiene Law.

(i) The required notice of the filing of a final account by an incapacitated person's guardian and of a petition for settlement thereof shall show the amounts requested for additional services of the guardian and for legal services. Prior to approving such allowances, the court shall require written proof of the nature and extent of such services. Where notice is given to the attorney for the Veterans Administration, if the Attorney for the Veterans Administration does not appear after notice, the court shall be advised whether the Veteran's Administration attorney has examined the account and whether he objects to it or to any proposed commission or fee.

Cross References

CPLR, see McKinney's Book 7B.

Judiciary Law, see McKinney's Book 29.

Mental Hygiene Law, see McKinney's Book 34A.

Forms

See, generally, West's McKinney's Forms, CPLR, § 3:1301 et seq.

§ 202.68. Proceedings Involving Custody of an Indian Child

In any proceeding in which the custody of a child is to be determined, the court, when it has reason to believe that the child is an Indian child within the meaning of the Indian Child Welfare Act of 1978 (92 St. 3069), shall require the verification of the child's status in accordance with that Act and, proceed further, as appropriate, in accordance with the provisions of that Act.

Cross References

Indian Child Welfare Act of 1978, see 25 U.S.C.A. § 1901 et seq.

§ 202.69. Coordination of Related Actions Pending in More Than One Judicial District

(a) Application. This section shall apply when related actions are pending in the courts of the Unified Court System in more than one judicial district and it may be appropriate for these actions to be coordinated pursuant to the criteria and procedures set forth in this section. Coordination pursuant to this section shall apply to pretrial proceedings, including dispositive motions.

(b) Litigation Coordinating Panel.

(1) Composition. The Chief Administrator of the Courts, in consultation with the Presiding Justice of each Appellate Division, shall create a Litigation Coordinating Panel composed of one justice of the Supreme Court from each judicial department of the state.

(2) Procedure. The Panel shall determine, sua sponte or upon application of a party to an action, a justice before whom such an action is pending, or an administrative judge, whether the related actions should be coordinated before one or more individual justices. The Panel shall provide notice and an opportunity to be heard to all parties to the actions sought to be coordinated and shall inform the justices before whom such actions are pending of the initiation of proceedings before the Panel.

(3) Standards for Coordination. In determining whether to issue an administrative order of coordination, the Panel shall consider, among other things, the complexity of the actions; whether common questions of fact or law exist, and the importance of such questions to the determination of the issues; the risk that coordination may unreasonably delay the progress, increase the expense, or complicate the processing of any action or otherwise prejudice a party; the risk of duplicative or inconsistent rulings, orders or judgments; the convenience of the parties, witnesses and counsel; whether coordinated discovery would be advantageous; efficient utilization of judicial resources and the facilities and personnel of the court; the manageability of a coordinated litigation; whether issues of insurance, limits on assets and potential bankruptcy can be best addressed in coordinated proceedings; and the pendency of related matters in the federal courts and in the courts of other states. The Panel may exclude particular actions from an other-

wise applicable order of coordination when necessary to protect the rights of parties.

(4) Determination.

(i) The Panel shall issue a written decision on each application. If the Panel determines to direct coordination, it shall issue an administrative order identifying the actions that shall be coordinated. The order may address actions subsequently filed or not otherwise then before the Panel.

(ii) The order of the Panel shall specify the number of Coordinating Justices and the county or counties in which the coordinated proceedings shall take place. In making this decision, the Panel shall consider, among other things, the venues of origin of the cases to be coordinated; whether the actions arise out of an accident or events in a particular county; judicial caseloads in prospective venues; fairness to parties; the convenience of the parties and witnesses; the convenience of counsel; and whether the purposes of this section can best be advanced by coordination before more than one Coordinating Justice.

(c) Coordinating Justice.

(1) Designation. The Administrative Judge charged with supervision of the local jurisdiction within which coordinated proceedings are to take place shall select the Coordinating Justice or Justices, in consultation with the appropriate Deputy Chief Administrative Judge. In deciding whom to designate, the Administrative Judge shall consider, among other things, the existing caseload of each prospective appointee and the overall needs of the court in which that justice serves; the familiarity of that justice with the litigation at issue; the justice's managerial ability; and the previous experience of the justice with the field of law involved and with coordinated litigation. The Administrative Judge may designate a justice from another local jurisdiction as a Coordinating Justice with the approval of the Administrative Judge thereof.

(2) Authority. The Coordinating Justice shall have authority to make any order consistent with this section and its purposes, including to remand to the court of origin any portion of a case not properly subject to coordination under the administrative order of the Panel; assign a master caption; create a central case file and docket; establish a service list; periodically issue case management orders after consultation with counsel; appoint and define the roles of steering committees and counsel of parties and liaison counsel, provided that the committees and counsel shall not deprive any party of substantive rights; issue protective orders pursuant to Article 31 of the Civil Practice Law and Rules; establish a document depository; direct the parties to prepare coordinated pleadings and deem service upon liaison counsel or steering committee service upon the respective parties; require service of uniform requests for disclosure and

establish a uniform method for the conduct of physical and mental examinations; rule upon all motions; require the parties to participate in settlement discussions and court–annexed alternative dispute resolution; and try any part of any coordinated case on consent of the parties to that action.

(3) Coordination with Federal or Other States' Actions. If actions related to those pending before a Coordinating Justice are proceeding in federal courts or in the courts of other states, the Coordinating Justice shall consult with the presiding judge(s) in an effort to advance the purposes of this section. Where appropriate, the Coordinating Justice, while respecting the rights of parties under the Civil Practice Law and Rules, may require that discovery in the cases coordinated pursuant to this section proceed jointly or in coordination with discovery in the federal or other states' actions.

(d) Termination of Coordination. The Coordinating Justice, sua sponte or upon motion by any party, may terminate coordination, in whole or in part, if the Justice determines that coordination has been completed or that the purposes of this section can be best advanced by termination of the coordination. Upon termination, the actions shall be remanded to their counties of origin for trial unless the parties to an action consent to trial of that action before the Coordinating Justice.

§ 202.70. Rules of the Commercial Division of the Supreme Court

(a) Monetary thresholds

Except as set forth in subdivision (b), the monetary thresholds of the Commercial Division, exclusive of punitive damages, interests, costs, disbursements and counsel fees claimed, is established as follows:

Albany County	$25,000
Eighth Judicial District	$50,000
Kings County	$75,000
Nassau County	$75,000
New York County	$100,000
Onondaga County	$25,000
Queens County	$50,000
Seventh Judicial District	$25,000
Suffolk County	$50,000
Westchester County	$75,000

(b) Commercial cases

Actions in which the principal claims involve or consist of the following will be heard in the Commercial Division provided that the monetary threshold is met or equitable or declaratory relief is sought:

(1) Breach of contract or fiduciary duty, fraud, misrepresentation, business tort (e.g., unfair competition), or statutory and/or common law violation where the breach or violation is alleged to arise out of business dealings (e.g., sales of assets or securities; corporate restructuring; partnership, shareholder, joint venture, and other business agreements; trade secrets; restrictive covenants; and employment agreements not including claims that principally involve alleged discriminatory practices);

(2) Transactions governed by the Uniform Commercial Code (exclusive of those concerning individual cooperative or condominium units);

(3) Transactions involving commercial property, including Yellowstone injunctions and excluding actions for the payment of rent only;

(4) Shareholder derivative actions — without consideration of the monetary threshold;

(5) Commercial class actions — without consideration of the monetary threshold;

(6) Business transactions involving or arising out of dealings with commercial banks and other financial institutions;

(7) Internal affairs of business organizations;

(8) Malpractice by accountants or actuaries, and legal malpractice arising out of representation in commercial matters;

(9) Environmental insurance coverage;

(10) Commercial insurance coverage (e.g. directors and officers, errors and omissions, and business interruption coverage);

(11) Dissolution of corporations, partnerships, limited liability companies, limited liability partnerships and joint ventures — without consideration of the monetary threshold; and

(12) Applications to stay or compel arbitration and affirm or disaffirm arbitration awards and related injunctive relief pursuant to CPLR Article 75 involving any of the foregoing enumerated commercial issues — without consideration of the monetary threshold.

(c) Non-commercial cases

The following will not be heard in the Commercial Division even if the monetary threshold is met:

(1) Suits to collect professional fees;

(2) Cases seeking a declaratory judgment as to insurance coverage for personal injury or property damage;

(3) Residential real estate disputes, including landlord-tenant matters, and commercial real estate disputes involving the payment of rent only;

(4) Proceedings to enforce a judgment regardless of the nature of the underlying case;

(5) First-party insurance claims and actions by insurers to collect premiums or rescind non-commercial policies; and

(6) Attorney malpractice actions except as otherwise provided in paragraph (b)(8).

(d) Assignment to the Commercial Division

(1) A party seeking assignment of a case to the Commercial Division shall indicate on the Request for Judicial Intervention (RJI) that the case is "commercial." A party seeking a designation of a special proceeding as a commercial case shall check the "other commercial" box on the RJI, not the "special proceedings" box.

(2) The party shall submit with the RJI a brief signed statement justifying the Commercial Division designation, together with a copy of the proceedings.

(e) Transfer into the Commercial Division

If a case is assigned to a non-commercial part because the filing party did not designate the case as "commercial" on the RJI, any other party may apply by letter application (with a copy to all parties) to the Administrative Judge, within ten days after receipt of a copy of the RJI, for a transfer of the case into the Commercial Division. The determination of the Administrative Judge shall be final and subject to no further administrative review or appeal.

(f) Transfer from the Commercial Division

(1) In the discretion of the Commercial Division justice assigned, if a case does not fall within the jurisdiction of the Commercial Division as set forth in this section, it shall be transferred to a non-commercial part of the court.

(2) Any party aggrieved by a transfer of a case to a non-commercial part may seek review by letter application (with a copy to all parties) to the Administrative Judge within ten days of receipt of the designation of the case to a non-commercial part. The determination of the Administrative Judge shall be final and subject to no further administrative review or appeal.

(g) Rules of practice for the Commercial Division

Unless these rules of practice for the Commercial Division provide specifically to the contrary, the rules of Part 202 also shall apply to the Commercial Division, except that Rules 7 through 15 shall supersede section 202.12 (Preliminary Conference) and Rules 16 through 24 shall supersede section 202.8 (Motion Procedure).

Rule 1. Appearance by Counsel with Knowledge and Authority. Counsel who appear in the Commer-

cial Division must be fully familiar with the case in regard to which they appear and fully authorized to enter into agreements, both substantive and procedural, on behalf of their clients. Counsel should also be prepared to discuss any motions that have been submitted and are outstanding. Failure to comply with this rule may be regarded as a default and dealt with appropriately. See Rule 12. It is important that counsel be on time for all scheduled appearances.

Rule 2. Settlements and Discontinuances. If an action is settled, discontinued, or otherwise disposed of, counsel shall immediately inform the court by submission of a copy of the stipulation or a letter directed to the clerk of the part along with notice to chambers via telephone or e-mail. This notification shall be made in addition to the filing of a stipulation with the County Clerk.

Rule 3. Alternative Dispute Resolution (ADR). At any stage of the matter, the court may direct or counsel may seek the appointment of an uncompensated mediator for the purpose of mediating a resolution of all or some of the issues presented in the litigation.

Rule 4. Electronic Submission of Papers.

(a) Papers and correspondence by fax. Papers and correspondence filed by fax should comply with the requirements of section 202.5–a except that papers shall not be submitted to the court by fax without advance approval of the justice assigned. Correspondence sent by fax should not be followed by hard copy unless requested.

(b) Papers submitted in digital format. In cases not pending in the court's Filing by Electronic Means System, the court may permit counsel to communicate with the court and each other by e-mail. In the court's discretion, counsel may be requested to submit memoranda of law by e-mail or on a computer disk along with an original and courtesy copy.

Rule 5. (This rule shall apply only in the First and Second Judicial Departments) Information on Cases. Information on future court appearances can be found at the court system's future appearance site (www.nycourts.gov/ecourts). Decisions can be found on the Commercial Division home page of the Unified Court System's internet website: www.courts.state.ny.us/comdiv or in the New York Law Journal. The clerk of the part can also provide information about scheduling in the part (trials, conferences, and arguments on motions). Where circumstances require exceptional notice, it will be furnished directly by chambers.

Rule 6. Form of Papers. All papers submitted to the Commercial Division shall comply with CPLR 2101 and section 202.5(a). Papers shall be double-spaced and contain print no smaller than twelve-point, or 8½ x 11 inch paper, bearing margins no smaller than one inch. The print size of footnotes shall be no smaller than ten-point. Papers also shall comply with Part 130 of the Rules of the Chief Administrator.

Rule 7. Preliminary Conference; Request. A preliminary conference shall be held within 45 days of assignment of the case to a Commercial Division justice, or as soon thereafter as is practicable. Except for good cause shown, no preliminary conference shall be adjourned more than once or for more than 30 days. If a Request for Judicial Intervention is accompanied by a dispositive motion, the preliminary conference shall take place within 30 days following the decision of such motion (if not rendered moot) or at such earlier date as scheduled by the justice presiding. Notice of the preliminary conference date will be sent by the court at least five days prior thereto.

Rule 8. Consultation prior to Preliminary and Compliance Conferences.

(a) Counsel for all parties shall consult prior to a preliminary or compliance conference about (i) resolution of the case, in whole or in part; (ii) discovery and any other issues to be discussed at the conference; and (iii) the use of alternate dispute resolution to resolve all or some issues in the litigation. Counsel shall make a good faith effort to reach agreement on these matters in advance of the conference.

(b) Prior to the preliminary conference, counsel shall confer with regard to anticipated electronic discovery issues. Such issues shall be addressed with the court at the preliminary conference and shall include but not be limited to (i) implementation of a data preservation plan; (ii) identification of relevant data; (iii) the scope, extent and form of production; (iv) anticipated cost of data recovery and proposed initial allocation of such cost; (v) disclosure of the programs and manner in which the data is maintained; (vi) identification of computer system(s) utilized; (vii) identification of the individual(s) responsible for data preservation; (viii) confidentiality and privilege issues; and (ix) designation of experts.

Rule 9. (Reserved)

Rule 10. Submission of Information. At the preliminary conference, counsel shall be prepared to furnish the court with the following: (i) a complete caption, including the index number; (ii) the name, address, telephone number, e-mail address and fax number of all counsel; (iii) the dates the action was commenced and issue joined; (iv) a statement as to what motions, if any, are anticipated; and (v) copies of any decisions previously rendered in the case.

Rule 11. Discovery

(a) The preliminary conference will result in the issuance by the court of a preliminary conference order. Where appropriate, the order will contain specific provisions for means of early disposition of the case, such as (i) directions for submission to the alternative dispute resolution program; (ii) a schedule of limited-issue discovery in aid of early dispositive mo-

tions or settlement; and/or (iii) a schedule for dispositive motions before disclosure or after limited-issue disclosure.

(b) The order will also contain a comprehensive disclosure schedule, including dates for the service of third-party pleadings, discovery, motion practice, a compliance conference, if needed, a date for filing the note of issue, a date for a pre-trial conference and a trial date.

(c) The preliminary conference order may provide for such limitations of interrogatories and other discovery as may be necessary to the circumstances of the case.

(d) The court will determine, upon application of counsel, whether discovery will be stayed, pursuant to CPLR 3214(b), pending the determination of any dispositive motion.

Rule 12. Non-Appearance at Conference. The failure of counsel to appear for a conference may result in a sanction authorized by section 130.2.1 of the Rules of the Chief Administrator or section 202.27, including dismissal, the striking of an answer, an inquest or direction for judgment, or other appropriate sanction.

Rule 13. Adherence to Discovery Schedule

(a) Parties shall strictly comply with discovery obligations by the dates set forth in all case scheduling orders. Such deadlines, however, may be modified upon the consent of all parties, provided that all discovery shall be completed by the discovery cutoff date set forth in the preliminary conference order. Applications for extension of a discovery deadline shall be made as soon as practicable and prior to the expiration of such deadline. Non-compliance with such an order may result in the imposition of an appropriate sanction against that party pursuant to CPLR 3126.

(b) If a party seeks documents as a condition precedent to a deposition and the documents are not produced by the date fixed, the party seeking disclosure may ask the court to preclude the non-producing party from introducing such demanded documents at trial.

Rule 14. Disclosure Disputes. Counsel must consult with one another in a good faith effort to resolve all disputes about disclosure. See section 202.7. Except as provided in Rule 24 hereof, if counsel are unable to resolve any disclosure dispute in this fashion, the aggrieved party shall contact the court to arrange a conference as soon as practicable to avoid exceeding the discovery cutoff date. Counsel should request a conference by telephone if that would be more convenient and efficient than an appearance in court.

Rule 15. Adjournments of Conferences. Adjournments on consent are permitted with the approval of the court for good cause where notice of the request is given to all parties. Adjournment of a conference will not change any subsequent date in the preliminary conference order, unless otherwise directed by the court.

Rule 16. Motions in General.

(a) Form of Motion Papers. The movant shall specify in the notice of motion, order to show cause, and in a concluding section of a memorandum of law, the exact relief sought. Counsel must attach copies of all pleadings and other documents as required by the CPLR and as necessary for an informed decision on the motion (especially on motions pursuant to CPLR 3211 and 3212). Counsel should use tabs when submitting papers containing exhibits. Copies must be legible. If a document to be annexed to an affidavit or affirmation is voluminous and only discrete portions are relevant to the motion, counsel shall attach excerpts and submit the full exhibit separately. Documents in a foreign language shall be properly translated. CPLR 2101(b). Whenever reliance is placed upon a decision or other authority not readily available to the court, a copy of the case or of pertinent portions of the authority shall be submitted with the motion papers.

(b) Proposed Orders. When appropriate, proposed orders should be submitted with motions, e.g., motions to be relieved, pro hac vice admissions, open commissions, etc. No proposed order should be submitted with motion papers on a dispositive motion.

(c) Adjournment of Motions. Dispositive motions (made pursuant to CPLR 3211, 3212 or 3213) may be adjourned only with the court's consent. Non-dispositive motions may be adjourned on consent no more than three times for a total of no more than 60 days unless otherwise directed by the court.

Rule 17. Length of Papers.
Unless otherwise permitted by the court: (i) briefs or memoranda of law shall be limited to 25 pages each; (ii) reply memoranda shall be no more than 15 pages and shall not contain any arguments that do not respond or relate to those made in the memoranda in chief; (iii) affidavits and affirmations shall be limited to 25 pages each.

Rule 18. Sur–Reply and Post–Submission Papers.
Absent express permission in advance, sur-reply papers, including correspondence, addressing the merits of a motion are not permitted, except that counsel may inform the court by letter of the citation of any post-submission court decision that is relevant to the pending issues, but there shall be no additional argument. Materials submitted in violation hereof will not be read or considered. Opposing counsel who receives a copy of materials submitted in violation of this Rule shall not respond in kind.

Rule 19. Orders to Show Cause.
Motions shall be brought on by order to show cause only when there is genuine urgency (e.g., applications for provisional relief), a stay is required or a statute mandates so proceeding. See Rule 20. Absent advance permission, reply papers shall not be submitted on orders to show cause.

Rule 19–a. Motions for Summary Judgment; Statements of Material Facts.

(a) Upon any motion for summary judgment, other than a motion made pursuant to CPLR 3213, the court may direct that there shall be annexed to the notice of motion a separate, short and concise statement, in numbered paragraphs, of the material facts as to which the moving party contends there is no genuine issue to be tried.

(b) In such a case, the papers opposing a motion for summary judgment shall include a correspondingly numbered paragraph responding to each numbered paragraph in the statement of the moving party and, if necessary, additional paragraphs containing a separate short and concise statement of the material facts as to which it is contended that there exists a genuine issue to be tried.

(c) Each numbered paragraph in the statement of material facts required to be served by the moving party will be deemed to be admitted for purposes of the motion unless specifically controverted by a correspondingly numbered paragraph in the statement required to be served by the opposing party.

(d) Each statement of material fact by the movant or opponent pursuant to subdivision (a) or (b), including each statement controverting any statement of material fact, must be followed by citation to evidence submitted in support of or in opposition to the motion.

Rule 20. Temporary Restraining Orders.
Unless the moving party can demonstrate that there will be significant prejudice by reason of giving notice, a temporary restraining order will not be issued. The applicant must give notice to the opposing parties sufficient to permit them an opportunity to appear and contest the application.

Rule 21. Courtesy Copies.
Courtesy copies should not be submitted unless requested or as herein provided. However, courtesy copies of all motion papers and proposed orders shall be submitted in cases in the court's Filing by Electronic Means System.

Rule 22. Oral Argument.
Any party may request oral argument on the face of its papers or in an accompanying letter. Except in cases before justices who require oral argument on all motions, the court will determine, on a case-by-case basis, whether oral argument will be heard and, if so, when counsel shall appear. Notice of the date selected by the court shall be given, if practicable, at least 14 days before the scheduled oral argument. At that time, counsel shall be prepared to argue the motion, discuss resolution of the issue(s) presented and/or schedule a trial or hearing.

Rule 23. 60-Day Rule. If 60 days have elapsed after a motion has been finally submitted or oral argument held, whichever was later, and no decision has been issued by the court, counsel for the movant shall send the court a letter alerting it to this fact with copies to all parties to the motion.

Rule 24. Advance Notice of Motions

(a) Nothing in this rule shall be construed to prevent or limit counsel from making any motion deemed appropriate to best represent a party's interests. However, in order to permit the court the opportunity to resolve issues before motion practice ensues, and to control its calendar in the context of the discovery and trial schedule, pre-motion conferences in accordance herewith must be held. The failure of counsel to comply with this rule may result in the motion being held in abeyance until the court has an opportunity to conference the matter.

(b) This rule shall not apply to disclosure disputes covered by Rule 14 nor to dispositive motions pursuant to CPLR 3211, 3212 or 3213 made at the time of the filing of the Request for Judicial Intervention or after discovery is complete. Nor shall the rule apply to motions to be relieved as counsel, for pro hac vice admission, for reargument or in limine.

(c) Prior to the making or filing of a motion, counsel for the moving party shall advise the Court in writing (no more than two pages) on notice to opposing counsel outlining the issue(s) in dispute and requesting a telephone conference. If a cross-motion is contemplated, a similar motion notice letter shall be forwarded to the court and counsel. Such correspondence shall not be considered by the court in reaching its decision on the merits of the motion.

(d) Upon review of the motion notice letter, the court will schedule a telephone or in-court conference with counsel. Counsel fully familiar with the matter and with authority to bind their client must be available to participate in the conference. The unavailability of counsel for the scheduled conference, except for good cause shown, may result in granting of the application without opposition and/or the imposition of sanctions.

(e) If the matter can be resolved during the conference, an order consistent with such resolution may be issued or counsel will be directed to forward a letter confirming the resolution to be "so ordered." At the discretion of the court, the conference may be held on the record.

(f) If the matter cannot be resolved, the parties shall set a briefing schedule for the motion which shall be approved by the court. Except for good cause shown, the failure to comply with the briefing schedule may result in the submission of the motion unopposed or the dismissal of the motion, as may be appropriate.

(g) On the face of all notices of motion and orders to show cause, there shall be a statement that there has been compliance with this rule.

(h) Where a motion must be made within a certain time pursuant to the CPLR, the submission of a motion notice letter, as provided in subdivision (a), within the prescribed time shall be deemed the timely making of the motion. This subdivision shall not be construed to extend any jurisdictional limitations period.

Rule 25. Trial Schedule. Counsel are expected to be ready to proceed either to select a jury or to begin presentation of proof on the scheduled trial date. Once a trial date is set, counsel shall immediately determine the availability of witnesses. If, for any reason, counsel are not prepared to proceed on the scheduled date, the court is to be notified within ten days of the date on which counsel are given the trial date or, in extraordinary circumstances, as soon as reasonably practicable. Failure of counsel to provide such notification will be deemed a waiver of any application to adjourn the trial because of the unavailability of a witness. Witnesses are to be scheduled so that trials proceed without interruption. Trials shall commence each court day promptly at such times as the court directs. Failure of counsel to attend the trial at the time scheduled without good cause shall constitute a waiver of the right of that attorney and his or her client to participate in the trial for the period of counsel's absence. There shall be no adjournment of a trial except for good cause shown. With respect to trials scheduled more than 60 days in advance, section 125.1(g) of the Rules of the Chief Administrator shall apply and the actual engagement of trial counsel in another matter will not be recognized as an acceptable basis for an adjournment of the trial.

Rule 26. Estimated Length of Trial. At least ten days prior to trial or such other time as the court may set, the parties, after considering the expected testimony of and, if necessary, consulting with their witnesses, shall furnish the court with a realistic estimate of the length of the trial.

Rule 27. Motions in Limine. The parties shall make all motions in limine no later than ten days prior to the scheduled pre-trial conference date, and the motions shall be returnable on the date of the pre-trial conference, unless otherwise directed by the court.

Rule 28. Pre-Marking of Exhibits. Counsel for the parties shall consult prior to the pre-trial conference and shall in good faith attempt to agree upon the exhibits that will be offered into evidence without objection. At the pre-trial conference date, each side shall then mark its exhibits into evidence as to those to which no objection has been made. All exhibits not consented to shall be marked for identification only. If the trial exhibits are voluminous, counsel shall consult the clerk of the part for guidance. The court will rule upon the objections to the contested exhibits at the earliest possible time. Exhibits not previously demanded which are to be used solely for credibility or rebuttal need not be pre-marked.

Rule 29. Identification of Deposition Testimony. Counsel for the parties shall consult prior to trial and shall in good faith attempt to agree upon the portions of deposition testimony to be offered into evidence without objection. The parties shall delete from the testimony to be read questions and answers that are irrelevant to the point for which the deposition testimony is offered. Each party shall prepare a list of deposition testimony to be offered by it as to which objection has not been made and, identified separately, a list of deposition testimony as to which objection has been made. At least ten days prior to trial or such other time as the court may set, each party shall submit its list to the court and other counsel, together with a copy of the portions of the deposition testimony as to which objection has been made. The court will rule upon the objections at the earliest possible time after consultation with counsel.

Rule 30. Settlement and Pretrial Conferences.

(a) Settlement Conference. At the time of certification of the matter as ready for trial or at any time after the discovery cut-off date, the court may schedule a settlement conference which shall be attended by counsel and the parties, who are expected to be fully prepared to discuss the settlement of the matter.

(b) Pre-trial Conference. Prior to the pretrial conference, counsel shall confer in a good faith effort to identify matters not in contention, resolve disputed questions without need for court intervention and further discuss settlement of the case. At the pre-trial conference, counsel shall be prepared to discuss all matters as to which there is disagreement between the parties, including those identified in Rules 27–29, and settlement of the matter. At or before the pre-trial conference, the court may require the parties to prepare a written stipulation of undisputed facts.

Rule 31. Pre–Trial Memoranda, Exhibit Book and Requests for Jury Instructions

(a) Counsel shall submit pre-trial memoranda at the pre-trial conference, or such other time as the court may set. Counsel shall comply with CPLR 2103(e). A single memorandum no longer than 25 pages shall be submitted by each side. No memoranda in response shall be submitted.

(b) At the pre-trial conference or at such other time as the court may set, counsel shall submit an indexed binder or notebook of trial exhibits for the court's use. A copy for each attorney on trial and the originals in a similar binder or notebook for the witnesses shall be prepared and submitted. Plaintiff's exhibits shall be numerically tabbed and defendant's exhibits shall be tabbed alphabetically.

(c) Where the trial is by jury, counsel shall, on the pre-trial conference date or such other time as the court may set, provide the court with case-specific requests to charge and proposed jury interrogatories. Where the requested charge is from the New York Pattern Jury Instructions—Civil, a reference to the PJI number will suffice. Submissions should be by hard copy and disk or e-mail attachment in WordPerfect 12 format, as directed by the court.

Rule 32. Scheduling of witnesses. At the pretrial conference or at such time as the court may direct, each party shall identify in writing for the court the witnesses it intends to call, the order in which they shall testify and the estimated length of their testimony, and shall provide a copy of such witness list to opposing counsel. Counsel shall separately identify for the court only a list of the witnesses who may be called solely for rebuttal or with regard to credibility.

Rule 33. Preclusion. Failure to comply with Rules 28, 29, 31 and 32 may result in preclusion pursuant to CPLR 3126.

PART 205. UNIFORM RULES FOR THE FAMILY COURT

§ 205.1. Application of Part; Waiver; Additional Rules; Definitions

(a) **Application.** This Part shall be applicable to all proceedings in the Family Court.

(b) **Waiver.** For good cause shown, and in the interests of justice, the court in a proceeding may waive compliance with any of these rules other than sections 205.2 and 205.3 unless prohibited from doing so by statute or by a rule of the Chief Judge.

(c) **Additional Rules.** Local court rules, not inconsistent with law or with these rules, shall comply with Part 9 of the Rules of the Chief Judge (22 NYCRR part 9).

(d) **Statutory Applicability.** The provisions of this part shall be construed consistent with the Family Court Act, the Domestic Relations Law and, where applicable, the Social Services Law. Matters not covered by these rules or the foregoing statutes are governed by the Civil Practice Law and Rules.

(e) **Definitions.**

(1) "Chief Administrator of the Courts" in this part also includes a designee of the Administrator.

(2) Unless otherwise defined in this Part, or the context otherwise requires, all terms used in this part shall have the same meaning as they have in the Family Court Act, the Domestic Relations Law, the Social Services Law and the Civil Practice Law and Rules, as applicable.

Cross References

CPLR, see McKinney's Book 7B.

Domestic Relations Law, see McKinney's Book 14.

Family Court Act, see McKinney's Book 29A, Part 1.

Social Services Law, see McKinney's Book 52A.

§ 205.2. Terms and Parts of Court

(a) **Terms of Court.** A term of court is a four-week session of court, and there shall be 13 terms of court in a year, unless otherwise provided in the annual schedule of terms established by the Chief Administrator of the Courts, which also shall specify the dates of such terms.

(b) **Parts of Court.** A part of court is a designated unit of the court in which specified business of the court is to be conducted by a judge or quasi-judicial officer. There shall be such parts of court, including those mandated by statute, as may be authorized from time to time by the Chief Administrator of the Courts.

§ 205.3. Individual Assignment System; Structure

(a) **General.** There shall be established for all proceedings heard in the Family Court an individual assignment system which provides for the continuous supervision of each proceeding by a single judge or, where appropriate, a single support magistrate. For the purposes of this Part, the word "judge" shall include a support magistrate, where appropriate. Except as otherwise may be authorized by the Chief Administrator or by these rules, every proceeding shall be assigned and heard pursuant to the individual assignment system.

(b) **Assignments.** Proceedings shall be assigned to a judge of the court upon the filing with the court of the first document in the case. Assignments shall be made by the clerk of the court pursuant to a method of random selection authorized by the Chief Administrator. The judge thereby assigned shall be known as the "assigned judge" with respect to that matter and, except as otherwise provided in subdivision (c) or by law, shall conduct all further proceedings therein.

(c) **Exceptions.**

(1) Where the requirements of matters already assigned to a judge are such as to limit the ability of the judge to handle additional cases, the Chief Administrator may authorize that new assignments to the judge be suspended until the judge is able to handle additional cases.

(2) The Chief Administrator may authorize the establishment in any court of special categories of proceedings for assignment to judges specially assigned to hear such proceedings. Where more than one judge is specially assigned to hear a particular category of proceeding, the assignment of such proceedings to the judges so assigned shall be at random.

(3) Matters requiring immediate disposition may be assigned to a judge designated to hear such matters when the assigned judge is not available.

(4) The Chief Administrator may authorize the transfer of any proceeding and any matter relating to a proceeding from one judge to another in accordance with the needs of the court.

(5) Assignment of cases to judges pursuant to this section shall be consistent with section 205.27 of this Part.

(6) Multiple proceedings involving members of the same family shall be assigned to be heard by a single judge to the extent feasible and appropriate, including, but not limited to, child protective, foster care placement, family offense and custody proceedings.

(7) Where a child is under the jurisdiction of the Family Court as a result of a placement in foster care pursuant to Article 10 or 10–A of the Family Court Act or section 358–a of the Social Services Law, a judicial surrender, or a petition for the termination of parental rights, approval of an extra-judicial surren-

der or adoption of the child, shall be assigned, wherever practicable, to the Family Court judge who last presided over the child's proceeding.

§ 205.4. Access to Family Court Proceedings

(a) The Family Court is open to the public. Members of the public, including the news media, shall have access to all courtrooms, lobbies, public waiting areas and other common areas of the Family Court otherwise open to individuals having business before the court.

(b) The general public or any person may be excluded from a courtroom only if the judge presiding in the courtroom determines, on a case-by-case basis based upon supporting evidence, that such exclusion is warranted in that case. In exercising this inherent and statutory discretion, the judge may consider, among other factors, whether:

(1) the person is causing or is likely to cause a disruption in the proceedings;

(2) the presence of the person is objected to by one of the parties, including the law guardian, for a compelling reason;

(3) the orderly and sound administration of justice, including the nature of the proceeding, the privacy interests of individuals before the court, and the need for protection of the litigants, in particular, children, from harm requires that some or all observers be excluded from the courtroom;

(4) less restrictive alternatives to exclusion are unavailable or inappropriate to the circumstances of the particular case.

Whenever the judge exercises discretion to exclude any person or the general public from a proceeding or part of a proceeding in Family Court, the judge shall make findings prior to ordering exclusion.

(c) When necessary to preserve the decorum of the proceedings, the judge shall instruct representatives of the news media and others regarding the permissible use of the courtroom and other facilities of the court, the assignment of seats to representatives of the news media on an equitable basis, and any other matters that may affect the conduct of the proceedings and the well-being and safety of the litigants therein.

(d) Audio-visual coverage of Family Court facilities and proceedings shall be governed by Parts 29 and 131 of this Title.

(e) Nothing in this section shall limit the responsibility and authority of the Chief Administrator of the Courts, or the administrative judges with the approval of the Chief Administrator of the Courts, to formulate and effectuate such reasonable rules and procedures consistent with this section as may be necessary and proper to ensure that the access by the public, including the press, to proceedings in the Family Court shall comport with the security needs of the courthouse, the safety of persons having business before the court and the proper conduct of court business.

§ 205.5. Privacy of Family Court Records

Subject to limitations and procedures set by statute and case law, the following shall be permitted access to the pleadings, legal papers formally filed in a proceeding, findings, decisions and orders and, subject to the provisions of CPLR 8002, transcribed minutes of any hearing held in the proceeding:

(a) the petitioner, presentment agency and adult respondent in the Family Court proceedings and their attorneys;

(b) when a child is either a party to, or the child's custody may be affected by the proceeding:

(1) the parents or persons legally responsible for the care of that child and their attorneys;

(2) the guardian, guardian ad litem and law guardian or attorney for that child;

(3) an authorized representative of the child protective agency involved in the proceeding or the probation service;

(4) an agency to which custody has been granted by an order of the Family Court and its attorney; and

(5) an authorized employee or volunteer of a Court Appointed Special Advocate program appointed by the Family Court to assist in the child's case in accordance with Part 44 of the Rules of the Chief Judge.

(c) a representative of the State Commission on Judicial Conduct, upon application to the appropriate Deputy Chief Administrator, or his or her designee, containing an affirmation that the Commission is inquiring into a complaint under Article 2–A of the Judiciary Law, and that the inquiry is subject to the confidentiality provisions of said Article.

(d) in proceedings under Articles 4, 5, 6 and 8 of the Family Court Act in which temporary or final orders of protection have been issued:

(1) where a related criminal action may, but has not yet been commenced, a prosecutor upon affirmation that such records are necessary to conduct an investigation or prosecution; and

(2) where a related criminal action has been commenced, a prosecutor or defense attorney in accordance with procedures set forth in the criminal procedure law;

Provided, however, that prosecutors may request transcripts of Family Court proceedings in accordance with section 815 of the Family Court Act, and provided further that any records or information disclosed pursuant to this subdivision must be retained as confidential and may not be redisclosed except as necessary for such investigation or use in the criminal action.

(e) another court when necessary for a pending proceeding involving one or more parties or children who are or were the parties in, or subjects of, a proceeding in the Family Court pursuant to Articles 4, 5, 6, 8 or 10 of the Family Court Act. Only certified copies of pleadings and orders in, as well as information regarding the status of, such Family Court proceeding may be transmitted without court order pursuant to this section. Any information or records disclosed pursuant to this paragraph may not be redisclosed except as necessary to the pending proceeding.

Where the Family Court has authorized that the address of a party or child be kept confidential in accordance with Family Court Act § 154–b(2), any record or document disclosed pursuant to this section shall have such address redacted or otherwise safeguarded.

Cross References

CPLR, see McKinney's Book 7B.

§ 205.6. Periodic Reports

Reports on forms to be furnished by the Office of Court Administration shall be filed with that office by the Family Court in each county, as follows:

(a) On or before the 20th day of each term, a report shall be filed in the Office of Court Administration for each of the following instances in which an order of disposition was entered in the preceding month.

(1) Every proceeding instituted under article ten of the Family Court Act.

(2) Every proceeding instituted under article seven of the Family Court Act.

(b) No later than five calendar days thereafter, a separate weekly account for the preceding week ending Sunday shall be filed in the Office of Court Administration concerning:

(1) new cases;

(2) assignment of judges;

(3) appearances of counsel; and

(4) judicial activity;

unless the requirement therefor is otherwise specifically suspended, in whole or in part, by the Office of Court Administration.

(c) On or before the 20th day of the first term of each year, an inventory of the cases pending as of the first day of the first term of that year shall be filed in the Office of Court Administration, and an inventory of pending cases shall also be filed at such other times as may be specified by the Office of Court Administration.

Cross References

Family Court Act, see McKinney's Book 29A, Part 1.

§ 205.7. Papers Filed in Court; Docket Number; Prefix; Forms

(a) The forms set forth in 22 NYCRR Subtitle D [1], designated "Forms of the Family Court of the State of New York" and "Adoption Forms of the Family Court and Surrogate's Court of the State of New York", respectively, shall be the official forms of the court and shall, in substantially the same form as set forth, be uniformly used throughout the State. Examples of these forms shall be available at the clerk's office of any Family Court.

(b) The prefixes for the docket numbers assigned to Family Court proceedings shall be:

A — Adoption
AS — Adoption Surrender
B — Commitment of guardianship and custody (§§ 384, 384–b, Social Services Law)
C — Conciliation
D — Delinquency (including transfers from criminal courts)
E — Designated felony delinquency (including transfers from criminal courts)
F — Support
G — Guardianship (§ 661 FCA)
L — Approval of foster care placement
M — Consent to marry
N — Neglect or child abuse (child protective proceeding)
O — Family offenses
P — Paternity
R — Referred from Supreme Court (except delinquency)
S — Person in need of supervision
U — Uniform Interstate Family Support Law
V — Custody of minors (§ 651 FCA)
W — Material witness
Z — Miscellaneous

(c) Proceedings for extensions of placement in Person in Need of Supervision and juvenile delinquency proceedings and for permanency hearings in child protective and voluntary foster care proceedings pursuant to Article 10–A of the Family Court Act shall bear the prefix and docket number of the original proceeding in which the placement was made. Permanency hearings pursuant to Family Court Act Article 10–A regarding children freed for adoption shall bear the prefix and docket number of the proceeding or proceedings in which the child was freed: the surrender and/or termination of parental rights proceedings. Permanency reports submitted pursuant to Article 10–A shall not be considered new petitions.

(d) The case docket number shall appear on the outside cover and first page to the right of the caption of every paper tendered for filing in the proceeding. Each such cover and first page also shall contain an indication of the county of venue and a brief description of the nature of the paper and, where the case has been assigned to an individual judge, shall contain the name of the assigned judge to the right of the caption. In addition to complying with the provisions of CPLR 2101, every paper filed in court shall have annexed thereto appropriate proof of service on all parties where required, and if typewritten, shall have at least double space between each line, except for quotations and the names and addresses of attorneys appearing in the action, and shall have at least one-inch margins. In addition, every paper filed in court, other than an exhibit or printed official form promulgated in accordance with section 214 of the Family Court Act, shall contain writing on one side only, except that papers that are fastened on the side may contain writing on both sides. Papers that are stapled or bound securely shall not be rejected for filing simply because they are not bound with a backer of any kind.

1 Such forms are not set out herein. See Subtitle D of Title 22 of the Codes, Rules and Regulations of the State of New York.

Cross References

CPLR, see McKinney's Book 7B.

Family Court Act, see McKinney's Book 29A, Part 1.

§ 205.7–a. Electronic Transmission of Orders of Protection.

(a) The Family Courts in Albany, Erie, Kings, Monroe, Nassau, New York, Onondaga, Richmond and Westchester Counties are authorized to implement pilot projects for the electronic transmission of orders of protection and temporary orders of protection through the execution of memoranda of understanding with sheriff's offices, police departments or other law enforcement agencies as set forth in this section.

(b) Unless the party requesting the order of protection or temporary order of protection states on the record that he or she is making alternative arrangements for service or is delivering the order to the law enforcement agency directly, the Family Court may transmit the order of protection or temporary order of protection, together with any associated papers to be served simultaneously, to such agency by facsimile or other electronic means, as defined in subdivision (f) of rule 2103 of the Civil Practice Law and Rules, for expedited service in accordance with subdivision (c) of section one hundred fifty-three-b of the Family Court Act. Proof of service must be provided to the Court pursuant to subdivision (d) of such section and no fees may be charged by the agency for such service.

Such transmission shall constitute the filing required by section one hundred sixty-eight of the Family Court Act.

(c) The Family Court shall keep a record of the numbers of orders of protection and temporary orders of protection transmitted electronically to law enforcement agencies pursuant to the pilot project, the numbers of orders transmitted electronically for service by

such agencies and the length of time between issuance of the orders and service of the orders by the law enforcement agencies, as indicated in the proof of service submitted by such agencies.

§ 205.8. Submission of Papers to Judge

All papers for signature or consideration of the court shall be presented to the clerk of the court in the appropriate courtroom or clerk's office, except that when the clerk is unavailable or the judge so directs, papers may be submitted to the judge and a copy filed with the clerk at the first available opportunity. All papers for any judge which are filed in the clerk's office shall be promptly delivered to the judge by the clerk. The papers shall be clearly addressed to the judge for whom they are intended and prominently show the nature of the papers, the title and docket number of the proceeding in which they are filed, the judge's name and the name of the attorney or party submitting them.

§ 205.9. Miscellaneous Proceedings

All proceedings for which the procedure has not been prescribed by provisions of the Family Court Act, the Domestic Relations Law or the Social Services Law, including but not limited to proceedings involving consent to marry, interstate compact on juveniles and material witnesses, shall be commenced by the filing of a petition and shall require the entry of a written order.

Cross References

Domestic Relations Law, see McKinney's Book 14.

Family Court Act, see McKinney's Book 29A, Part 1.

Social Services Law, see McKinney's Book 52A.

§ 205.10. Notice of Appearance

Each attorney appearing in a proceeding is required to file a written notice of appearance on or before the time of the attorney's first appearance in court or no later than ten days after appointment or retainer, whichever is sooner. The notice shall contain the attorney's name, office address and telephone number, and the name of the person on whose behalf he or she is appearing.

§ 205.11. Service and Filing of Motion Papers

Where motions are required to be on notice:

(a) the motion shall be made returnable at such hour as the assigned judge directs;

(b) at the time of service of the notice of motion, the moving party shall serve copies of all affidavits and briefs upon all of the attorneys for the parties or upon the parties appearing pro se. The answering party shall serve copies of all affidavits and briefs as required by CPLR 2214. Affidavits shall be for a statement of the relevant facts, and briefs shall be for a statement of the relevant law. Unless otherwise directed by the court, answering and reply affidavits and all papers required to be furnished to the court by the Family Court Act or CPLR 2214(c) must be filed no later than the time of argument or submission of the motion;

(c) the assigned judge may determine that any or all motions in that proceeding shall be orally argued and may direct that moving and responding papers shall be filed with the court prior to the time of argument;

(d) unless oral argument has been requested by a party and permitted by the court, or directed by the court, motion papers received by the clerk of the court on or before the return date shall be deemed submitted as of the return date. A party requesting oral argument shall set forth such request in its notice of motion or on the first page of the answering papers, as the case may be. A party requesting oral argument on a motion brought on by an order to show cause shall do so as soon as practicable before the time the motion is to be heard;

(e) hearings on motions shall be held when required by statute or ordered by the assigned judge in the judge's discretion.

Cross References

CPLR, see McKinney's Book 7B.

Family Court Act, see McKinney's Book 29A, Part 1.

§ 205.12.　Conference

(a) In any proceeding, a conference or conferences shall be ordered by the court as required as soon as practicable after the proceeding has been assigned.

(b) The matters which may be considered at such conference may include, among other things:

(1) completion of discovery;

(2) filing of motions;

(3) argument or hearing of motions;

(4) fixing of a date for fact-finding hearing;

(5) simplification and limitation of issues;

(6) amendment of pleadings or bills of particulars;

(7) admissions of fact;

(8) stipulations as to admissibility of documents;

(9) completion or modification of financial disclosure;

(10) possibilities for settlement; and

(11) limitation of number of expert witnesses.

(c) Where parties are represented by counsel, an attorney thoroughly familiar with the action and authorized to act on behalf of the party or accompanied by a person empowered to act on behalf of the party represented shall appear at such conference.

(d) At the conclusion of a conference, the court shall make a written order including its directions to the parties as well as stipulations of counsel. Alternatively, in the court's discretion, all directions of the court and stipulations of counsel shall be formally placed on the record.

§ 205.13.　Engagement of Counsel

No adjournment shall be granted on the ground of engagement of counsel except in accordance with Part 125 of the Rules of the Chief Administrator of the Courts.

§ 205.14.　Time Limitations for Proceedings Involving Custody or Visitation

In any proceeding brought pursuant to sections 467, 651 or 652 of the Family Court Act to determine temporary or permanent custody or visitation, once a hearing or trial is commenced, it shall proceed to conclusion within 90 days.

§ 205.15.　Submission of Orders for Signature

Proposed orders, with proof of service on all parties, must be submitted for signature unless otherwise directed by the court within 30 days after the signing and filing of the decision directing that the order be settled or submitted. Proposed orders in child protective proceedings and permanency hearings pursuant to Articles 10 and 10–A of the Family Court Act, respectively, must be submitted for signature immediately, but in no event later than 14 days of the earlier of the Court's oral announcement of its decision or signing and filing of its decision, unless otherwise directed by the Court, provided, however, that proposed orders pursuant to section 1022 of the Family Court Act must be submitted for signature immediately, but in no event later than the next court date following the removal of the child. Orders in termination of parental rights proceedings pursuant to Article 6 of the Family Court Act or section 384–b of the Social Services Law shall be settled not more than 14 days after the earlier of the Family Court's oral announcement of its decision or signing and filing of its decision.

§ 205.16.　Motion for Judicial Determination that Reasonable Efforts are Not Required for Child in Foster Care

(a) This section shall govern any motion for a judicial determination, pursuant to section 352.2(2)(c), 754(2)(b), 1039–b or 1052(b) of the Family Court Act or section 358–a(3)(b) of the Social Services Law, that reasonable efforts to prevent or eliminate the need for removal of the child from the home or to make it possible to reunify the child with his or her parents are not required.

(b) A motion for such a determination shall be filed in writing on notice to the parties, including the law guardian, on the form officially promulgated by the

Chief Administrator of the Courts and set forth in Chapter IV of Subtitle D of this Title and shall contain all information required therein.

§205.17. Permanency Hearings for Children in Foster Care, Children Directly Placed With Relatives or Other Suitable Persons and Children Freed for Adoption

(a) This section shall govern all permanency hearings conducted pursuant to Article 10–A of the Family Court Act.

(b) Scheduling for dates certain; deadlines for submitting permanency reports.

(1) The first court order remanding a child into foster care or into direct placement with a relative or other suitable person in a proceeding pursuant to article 10 or approving a voluntary placement instrument pursuant to section 358–a of the Social Services Law must contain a date certain for the initial permanency hearing pursuant to article 10–A of the Family Court Act, which must be not later than eight months from the date of removal of the child from his or her home. If the child has a sibling or half-sibling removed from the home, whose permanency hearing is scheduled before this Court, the date certain shall be the same as the date certain for the sibling's or half-sibling's permanency hearing, unless the sibling or half-sibling was removed on a juvenile delinquency or person in need of supervision petition or unless either sibling has been freed for adoption.

(2) A permanency hearing with respect to a child who has been freed for adoption shall be scheduled for a date certain not more than 30 days after the earlier of the Family Court's oral announcement of its decision or the signing and filing of its decision freeing the child for adoption.

(3) In any case in which the court has made a determination, pursuant to section 1039–b or 1052(b) of the Family Court Act or section 358–a(3)(b) of the Social Services Law, that reasonable efforts to reunify the child with his or her parents are not required, a permanency hearing must be scheduled for a date certain within 30 days of the determination and the originally scheduled date shall be cancelled. In such a case, a permanency hearing report shall be transmitted to the parties and counsel, including the law guardian, on an expedited basis as directed by the court.

(4) Each permanency hearing order must contain a date certain for the next permanency hearing, which shall be not more than six months following the completion of the permanency hearing, except as provided in paragraph (3) of this subdivision. Except with respect to a child freed for adoption, if the child has a sibling or half-sibling removed from the home, whose permanency hearing is scheduled before this Court, the date certain shall be the same as the date certain for the sibling's or half-sibling's permanency

hearing, unless the sibling or half-sibling was removed on a juvenile delinquency or person in need of supervision petition or unless either sibling has been freed for adoption.

(5) If the child has been adopted or has been the subject of a final order of discharge or custody or guardianship by the scheduled date certain, the permanency hearing shall be cancelled and the petitioner shall promptly so notify the court, all parties and their attorneys, including the law guardian, as well as all individuals required to be notified of the hearing pursuant to Family Court Act, section 1089.

(c) **Required notice and transmittal of permanency reports.** Except in cases involving children freed for adoption, in addition to sending the permanency hearing report and accompanying papers to the respondent parents' last-known address and to their attorneys not less than 14 days in advance of the hearing date, the petitioner shall make reasonable efforts to provide actual notice of the permanency hearing to the respondent parents through any additional available means, including, but not limited to, case-work, service and visiting contacts. Additionally, not less than 14 days in advance of the hearing date, the petitioner shall send a notice of the permanency hearing and the report and accompanying documents to the non-respondent parent(s) and the foster parent or parents caring for the child, each of whom shall be a party, and to the law guardian. Petitioner shall also send the notice and report to a pre-adoptive parent or relative providing care for the child and shall send a notice, but not the report, to former foster parents who cared for the child in excess of one year unless the court has dispensed with such notice in accordance with paragraph two of subdivision (b) of section 1089 of the Family Court Act. The court shall give such persons an opportunity to be heard, but they shall not be considered parties and their failures to appear shall not constitute cause to delay the hearing. As provided in subdivision (d) of this section, the petitioner shall submit on or before the return date documentation of the notice or notices given to the respondent and non-respondent parents, their attorneys, the law guardian, and any present or former foster parent, pre-adoptive parent or relative.

(d) **Required papers to be submitted.**

(1) A sworn permanency report shall be submitted on the form officially promulgated by the Chief Administrator of the Courts and set forth in Chapter IV of Subtitle D of this Title, and shall contain all information required by section 1089 of the Family Court Act.

(2) The permanency report shall be accompanied by additional reports and documents as directed by the court, which may include, but not be limited to, periodic school report cards, photographs of the child,

clinical evaluations and prior court orders in related proceedings.

(3) The copy of the report submitted to the Family Court must be sworn and must be accompanied by a list of all persons and addresses to whom the report and/or notice of the permanency hearing were sent. Except as otherwise directed by the Family Court, the list containing the addresses shall be kept confidential and shall not be part of the court record that may be subject to disclosure pursuant to Section 205.5 of this title. The copies of the permanency hearing report required to be sent to the parties and their attorneys, including the law guardian, not less than 14 days prior to the scheduled date certain need not be sworn so long as the verification accompanying the Family Court's sworn copy attests to the fact that the copies transmitted were identical in all other respects to the Court's sworn copy.

(e) In any permanency hearing under Article 10–A of the Family Court Act, the child shall be represented by a law guardian and the Family Court shall consider the child's position regarding the child's permanency plan.

§§ 205.18, 205.19. [Reserved]

§ 205.20. Designation of a Facility for the Questioning of Children in Custody (Juvenile Delinquency)

(a) The district administrative judge in each judicial district outside the City of New York and the administrative judge for the Family Court within the City of New York, or a designee, shall arrange for the inspection of any facility within the judicial district proposed for designation as suitable for the questioning of children pursuant to section 305.2 of the Family Court Act, and if found suitable, the district administrative judge or the administrative judge for the Family Court within the City of New York, as appropriate, shall recommend its designation to the Chief Administrator of the Courts.

(b) Every recommendation to the Chief Administrator of the Courts shall include:

(1) the room number or identification, the type of facility in which the room is located, the address and the hours of access;

(2) the name of the police or other law enforcement agency, department of probation, Family Court judge or other interested person or agency which proposed the designation of the particular facility;

(3) a signed and dated copy of the report of inspection of the proposed facility made at the direction of the district administrative judge or the administrative judge for the Family Court within the City of New York; and

(4) the factors upon which the recommendation is based.

(c) Any facility recommended for designation as suitable for the questioning of children shall be separate from areas accessible to the general public and adult detainees.

(d) Insofar as possible, the district administrative judge or the administrative judge for the Family Court within the City of New York, in making a recommendation for designation, shall seek to assure an adequate number and reasonable geographic distribution of designated questioning facilities, and that:

(1) the room is located in a police facility or in a governmental facility not regularly or exclusively used for the education or care of children;

(2) the room presents an office-like, rather than a jail-like, setting;

(3) the room is clean and well-maintained;

(4) the room is well-lit and heated;

(5) there are separate toilet facilities for children, or, in the alternative, procedures insuring the privacy and safety of the children when in use;

(6) there is a separate entrance for children, or, in the alternative, there are procedures which minimize public exposure and avoid mingling with the adult detainees;

(7) a person will be in attendance with the child whenever the room is in use as a questioning facility, such person to be a policewoman or other qualified female person when the child is a female; and

(8) any other factors relevant to suitability for designation are considered.

(e) The appropriate district administrative judge or the administrative judge for the Family Court within the City of New York, or a designee, when notified of any material physical change in a facility designated for the questioning of children, shall arrange for the reinspection of such facility concerning its continued suitability for designation.

(f) A current list of facilities designated for the questioning of children within each judicial district and within the City of New York shall be maintained by the district administrative judge and the administrative judge for the Family Court within the City of New York and shall be kept for easy public inspection in each Family Court in that judicial district and within the City of New York. A current statewide list shall be maintained in the office of the Chief Administrator of the Courts. These lists shall be kept available for public inspection.

Cross References

Family Court Act, see McKinney's Book 29A, Part 1.

§ 205.21. Authorization to Detention Agency for Release of a Child Taken Into Custody Before the Filing of a Petition (Juvenile Delinquency)

(a) When a child is brought to a detention facility prior to the filing of a petition, pursuant to section 305.2 of the Family Court Act, the agency responsible for operating the detention facility is authorized to release the child before the filing of a petition when the events that occasioned the taking into custody do not appear to involve allegations that the child committed a delinquent act.

(b) If the events occasioning the taking into custody do appear to involve allegations that the child committed a delinquent act, the agency is authorized to release the child where practicable and issue an appearance ticket in accordance with section 307.1 of the Family Court Act, unless special circumstances exist which require the detention of the child, including whether:

(1) there is a substantial probability that the child will not appear or be produced at the appropriate probation service at a specified time and place; or

(2) there is a serious risk that before the petition is filed the child may commit an act which, if committed by an adult, would constitute a crime; or

(3) the alleged conduct by the child involved the use or threatened use of violence; or

(4) there is reason to believe that a proceeding to determine whether the child is a juvenile delinquent or juvenile offender is currently pending.

(c) Any child released pursuant to this rule shall be released to the custody of his or her parent or other person legally responsible for his or her care, or if such legally responsible person is unavailable, to a person with whom he or she resides.

Cross References

Family Court Act, see McKinney's Book 29A, Part 1.

§ 205.22. Preliminary Probation Conferences and Procedures (Juvenile Delinquency)

(a) The probation service shall conduct preliminary conferences with any person seeking to have a juvenile delinquency petition filed, the potential respondent and other interested persons, including the complainant or victim, on the same day that such persons appear at a probation service pursuant to sections 305.2(4)(a), 307.1 or 320.6 of the Family Court Act, concerning the advisability of requesting that a juvenile delinquency petition be filed and in order to gather information needed for a determination of the suitability of the case for adjustment. The probation service shall permit any participant who is represented by a lawyer to be accompanied by the lawyer at any preliminary conference.

(b) During the preliminary probation conferences, the probation service shall ascertain from the person seeking to have a juvenile delinquency petition filed a brief statement of the underlying events and, if known to that person, a brief statement of factors that would be of assistance to the court in determining whether the potential respondent should be detained or released in the event that a petition is filed.

(c) In order to determine whether the case is suitable for the adjustment process, the probation service shall consider the following circumstances, among others:

(1) the age of the potential respondent; and

(2) whether the conduct of the potential respondent allegedly involved:

(i) an act or acts causing or threatening to cause death, substantial pain or serious physical injury to another;

(ii) the use or knowing possession of a dangerous instrument or deadly weapon;

(iii) the use or threatened use of violence to compel a person to engage in sexual intercourse, deviant sexual intercourse or sexual contact;

(iv) the use or threatened use of violence to obtain property;

(v) the use or threatened use of deadly physical force with the intent to restrain the liberty of another;

(vi) the intentional starting of a fire or the causing of an explosion which resulted in damage to a building;

(vii) a serious risk to the welfare and safety of the community;

(viii) an act which seriously endangered the safety of the potential respondent or another person;

(3) whether there is a substantial likelihood that a potential respondent will not appear at scheduled conferences with the probation service or with an agency to which he or she may be referred;

(4) whether there is a substantial likelihood that the potential respondent will not participate in or cooperate with the adjustment process;

(5) whether there is a substantial likelihood that in order to adjust the case successfully, the potential respondent would require services that could not be administered effectively in less than four months;

(6) whether there is a substantial likelihood that the potential respondent will, during the adjustment process:

(i) commit an act which if committed by an adult would be a crime; or

(ii) engage in conduct that endangers the physical or emotional health of the potential respondent or a member of the potential respondent's family or household; or

(iii) harass or menace the complainant, victim or person seeking to have a juvenile delinquency petition filed or a member of that person's family or household, where demonstrated by prior conduct or threats;

(7) whether there is pending another proceeding to determine whether the potential respondent is a person in need of supervision, a juvenile delinquent or a juvenile offender;

(8) whether there have been prior adjustments or adjournments in contemplation of dismissal in other juvenile delinquency proceedings;

(9) whether there has been a prior adjudication of the potential respondent as a juvenile delinquent or juvenile offender;

(10) whether there is a substantial likelihood that the adjustment process would not be successful unless the potential respondent is temporarily removed from his or her home and that such removal could not be accomplished without invoking the court process;

(11) whether a proceeding has been or will be instituted against another person for acting jointly with the potential respondent.

(d) At the first appearance at a conference by each of the persons listed in subdivision (a) hereof, the probation service shall inform such person concerning the function and limitations of, and the alternatives to, the adjustment process, and that:

(1) he or she has the right to participate in the adjustment process;

(2) the probation service is not authorized to and cannot compel any person to appear at any conference, produce any papers or visit any place;

(3) the person seeking to have a juvenile delinquency petition filed is entitled to have access to the appropriate presentment agency at any time for the purpose of requesting that a petition be filed under article 3 of the Family Court Act;

(4) the adjustment process may continue for a period of two months and may be extended for an additional two months upon written application to the court and approval thereof;

(5) statements made to the probation service are subject to the confidentiality provisions contained in sections 308.1(6) and 308.1(7) of the Family Court Act; and

(6) if the adjustment process is commenced but is not successfully concluded, the persons participating therein may be notified orally or in writing of that fact and that the case will be referred to the appropriate presentment agency; oral notification will be confirmed in writing.

(e) If the adjustment process is not commenced:

(1) the record of the probation service shall contain a statement of the grounds therefor; and

(2) the probation service shall give written notice to the persons listed in subdivision (a) hereof who have appeared that:

(i) the adjustment process will not be commenced;

(ii) the case will be referred to the appropriate presentment agency; and

(iii) they are entitled to have access to the presentment agency for the purpose of requesting that a petition be filed under article 3 of the Family Court Act.

Cross References

Family Court Act, see McKinney's Book 29A, Part 1.

§ 205.23. Duties of the Probation Service and Procedures Relating to the Adjustment Process (Juvenile Delinquency)

(a) Upon a determination by the probation service that a case is suitable for the adjustment process, it shall include in the process the potential respondent and any other persons listed in subdivision (a) of section 205.22 of these rules who wish to participate therein. The probation service shall permit any participant who is represented by a lawyer to be accompanied by the lawyer at any conference.

(b) If an extension of the period of the adjustment process is sought, the probation service shall apply in writing to the court and shall set forth the services rendered to the potential respondent, the date of commencement of those services, the degree of success achieved, the services proposed to be rendered and a statement by the assigned probation officer that, in the judgment of such person, the matter will not be successfully adjusted unless an extension is granted.

(c) The probation service may discontinue the adjustment process if, at any time:

(1) the potential respondent or the person seeking to have a juvenile delinquency petition filed requests that it do so; or

(2) the potential respondent refuses to cooperate with the probation service or any agency to which the potential respondent or a member of his or her family has been referred.

(d) If the adjustment process is not successfully concluded, the probation service shall notify all the persons who participated therein in writing:

(1) that the adjustment process has not been successfully concluded;

(2) that the appropriate presentment agency will be notified within 48 hours or the next court day, whichever occurs later; and

(3) that access may be had to the presentment agency to request that a petition be filed;

and, in addition to the above, shall notify the potential respondent in writing of the reasons therefor.

(e) The case record of the probation service required to be kept pursuant to section 243 of the Executive Law and the regulations promulgated thereunder shall contain a statement of the grounds upon which:

(1) the adjustment process was commenced but was not successfully concluded; or

(2) the adjustment process was commenced and successfully concluded.

Cross References

Executive Law, see McKinney's Book 18.

§ 205.24. Terms and Conditions of Order Adjourning a Proceeding in Contemplation of Dismissal in Accordance With Section 315.3 of the Family Court Act

(a) An order adjourning a proceeding in contemplation of dismissal pursuant to section 315.3 of the Family Court Act shall be related to the alleged or adjudicated acts or omissions of respondent and shall contain at least one of the following terms and conditions directing the respondent to:

(1) attend school regularly and obey all rules and regulations of the school;

(2) obey all reasonable commands of the parent or other person legally responsible for respondent's care;

(3) avoid injurious or vicious activities;

(4) abstain from associating with named individuals;

(5) abstain from visiting designated places;

(6) abstain from the use of alcoholic beverages, hallucinogenic drugs, habit-forming drugs not lawfully prescribed for the respondent's use, or any other harmful or dangerous substance;

(7) cooperate with a mental health, social services or other appropriate community facility or agency to which the respondent is referred;

(8) restore property taken from the complainant or victim, or replace property taken from the complainant or victim, the cost of said replacement not to exceed $1,500;

(9) repair any damage to, or defacement of, the property of the complainant or victim, the cost of said repair not to exceed $1,500;

(10) cooperate in accepting medical or psychiatric diagnosis and treatment, alcoholism or drug abuse treatment or counseling services and permit an agency delivering that service to furnish the court with information concerning the diagnosis, treatment or counseling;

(11) attend and complete an alcohol awareness program established pursuant to section 19.25 of the mental hygiene law.

(12) abstain from disruptive behavior in the home and in the community;

(13) abstain from any act which if done by an adult would be an offense;

(14) comply with such other reasonable terms and conditions as may be permitted by law and as the court shall determine to be necessary or appropriate to ameliorate the conduct which gave rise to the filing of the petition or to prevent placement with the Commissioner of Social Services or the Office of Children and Family Services.

(b) An order adjourning a proceeding in contemplation of dismissal pursuant to section 315.3 of the Family Court Act may direct that the probation service supervise respondent's compliance with the terms and conditions of said order, and may set a time or times at which the probation service shall report to the court, orally or in writing, concerning compliance with the terms and conditions of said order.

(c) A copy of the order setting forth the terms and conditions imposed and the duration thereof shall be furnished to the respondent and to the parent or other person legally responsible for the respondent.

Cross References

Family Court Act, see McKinney's Book 29A, Part 1.

Forms

Order adjourning juvenile delinquency proceeding in contemplation of dismissal, based on official form, see West's McKinney's Forms, Matrimonial and Family, § 24:22.

§ 205.25. Terms and Conditions of Order Releasing Respondent in Accordance With Section 320.5 of the Family Court Act

(a) An order releasing a respondent at the initial appearance in accordance with section 320.5 of the Family Court Act may contain one or more of the following terms and conditions directing the respondent to:

(1) attend school regularly;

(2) abstain from any act which if done by an adult would be an offense;

(3) observe a specified curfew which must be reasonable in relation to the ends sought to be achieved and narrowly drawn;

(4) participate in a program duly authorized as an alternative to detention;

(5) comply with such other reasonable terms and conditions as the court shall determine to be necessary or appropriate.

(b) A copy of the order setting forth terms and conditions imposed and the duration thereof shall be furnished at the time of issuance to the respondent and, if present, to the parent or other person legally responsible for the respondent.

Cross References

Family Court Act, see McKinney's Book 29A, Part 1.

Forms

Order for conditional release of respondent, based on official form, see West's McKinney's Forms, Matrimonial and Family, § 24:25.

§ 205.26. Procedure When Remanded Child Absconds

(a) When a child absconds from a facility to which he or she was duly remanded, written notice of that fact shall be given within 48 hours by an authorized representative of the facility to the clerk of the court from which the remand was made. The notice shall state the name of the child, the docket number of the pending proceeding in which the child was remanded, the date on which the child absconded and the efforts made to locate and secure the return of the child. Every order of remand shall include a direction embodying the requirements of this subdivision.

(b) Upon receipt of the written notice of absconding, the clerk shall cause the proceeding to be placed on the court calendar no later than the next court day for such action as the court may deem appropriate and shall give notice of such court date to the presentment agency and law guardian or privately-retained counsel of the child.

§ 205.27. Procedure for Assignment in Accordance With Section 340.2(3) of the Family Court Act, of a Proceeding to Another Judge When the Appropriate Judge Cannot Preside

Except for proceedings transferred in accordance with section 302.3(4), when a judge who has presided at the fact-finding hearing or accepted an admission pursuant to section 321.3 in a juvenile delinquency proceeding cannot preside at another subsequent hearing, including the dispositional hearing, for the reasons set forth in section 340.2(3), the assignment of the proceeding to another judge of the court shall be made as authorized by the Chief Administrator of the Courts.

§ 205.28. Procedures for Compliance with the Adoption and Safe Families Act (Juvenile Delinquency Proceeding)

(a) Pre-petition and pretrial detention; required findings. In any case in which detention is ordered by the court pursuant to sections 307.4 or 320.5 of the Family Court Act, the court shall make additional, specific written findings regarding the following issues:

(1) whether the continuation of the respondent in his or her home would be contrary to his or her best interests; and

(2) where appropriate and consistent with the need for protection of the community, whether reasonable efforts were made, prior to the date of the court hearing that resulted in the detention order, to prevent or eliminate the need for removal of the respondent from his or her home, or, if the respondent had been removed from his or her home prior to the initial appearance, where appropriate and consistent with the need for protection of the community, whether reasonable efforts were made to make it possible for the respondent to safely return home.

The court may request the presentment agency and the local probation department to provide information to the court to aid in its determinations and may also consider information provided by the law guardian.

(b) Motion for an order that reasonable efforts are not required. A motion for a judicial determination, pursuant to section 352.2(2)(c) of the Family Court Act, that reasonable efforts to prevent or eliminate the need for removal of the respondent from his or her home or to make it possible to reunify the respondent with his or her parents are not required, shall be governed by section 205.16 of this Part.

(c) Placement; required findings. In any case in which the court is considering ordering placement pursuant to section 353.3 or 353.4 of the Family Court Act, the presentment agency, local probation department, local commissioner of social services and New York State Office of Children and Family Services shall provide information to the court to aid in its required determination of the following issues:

(1) whether continuation in the respondent's home would be contrary to the best interests of the respondent, and, in the case of a respondent for whom the court has determined that continuation in his or her home would not be contrary to the best interests of the respondent, whether continuation in the respondent's home would be contrary to the need for protection of the community;

(2) whether, where appropriate and where consistent with the need for protection of the community, reasonable efforts were made, prior to the date of the dispositional hearing, to prevent or eliminate the need for removal of the respondent from his or her home, and, if the respondent was removed from his or her home prior to the dispositional hearing, where appropriate and where consistent with the need for protection of the community, whether reasonable efforts were made to make it possible for the respondent to return home safely. If the court determines that reasonable efforts to prevent or eliminate the need for removal of the respondent from the home were not made, but that the lack of such efforts was appropriate under the circumstances, or consistent with the

need for protection of the community, or both, the court order shall include such a finding;

(3) in the case of a respondent who has attained the age of 16, the services needed, if any, to assist the respondent to make the transition from foster care to independent living; and

(4) in the case of an order of placement specifying a particular authorized agency or foster care provider, the position of the New York State Office of Children and Family Services or local department of social services, as applicable, regarding such placement.

(d) Permanency hearing; extension of placement.

(1) A petition for a permanency hearing and, if applicable, an extension of placement, pursuant to sections 355.3 and 355.5 of the Family Court Act, shall be filed at least 60 days prior to the expiration of one year following the respondent's entry into foster care; provided, however, that if the Family Court makes a determination, pursuant to section 352.2(2)(c) of the Family Court Act, that reasonable efforts are not required to prevent or eliminate the need for removal of the respondent from his or her home or to make it possible to reunify the respondent with his or her parents, the permanency hearing shall be held within 30 days of such finding and the petition for the permanency hearing shall be filed and served on an expedited basis as directed by the court.

(2) Following the initial permanency hearing in a case in which the respondent remains in placement, a petition for a subsequent permanency hearing and, if applicable, extension of placement, shall be filed at least 60 days prior to the expiration of one year following the date of the preceding permanency hearing.

(3) The permanency petition shall include, but not be limited to, the following: the date by which the permanency hearing must be held; the date by which any subsequent permanency petition must be filed; the proposed permanency goal for the child; the reasonable efforts, if any, undertaken to achieve the child's return to his or her parents or other permanency goal; the visitation plan for the child and his or her sibling or siblings and, if parental rights have not been terminated, for his or her parent or parents; and current information regarding the status of services ordered by the court to be provided, as well as other services that have been provided, to the child and his or her parent or parents.

(4) In all cases, the permanency petition shall be accompanied by the most recent service plan containing, at minimum: the child's permanency goal and projected time-frame for its achievement; the reasonable efforts that have been undertaken and are planned to achieve the goal; impediments, if any, that have been encountered in achieving the goal; and the services required to achieve the goal. Additionally,

the permanency petition shall contain or have annexed to it a plan for the release or conditional release of the child, as required by section 353.3(7) of the Family Court Act.

§ 205.29. [Reserved]

§ 205.30. Preliminary Probation Conferences and Procedures (Support)

(a) Any person except a commissioner of social services, a social services official or a person who is receiving paternity and support services pursuant to Section 111–g of the Social Services Law, seeking to file a petition for support under article 4 of the Family Court Act may first be referred to the probation service concerning the advisability of filing a petition.

(b) The probation service shall be available to meet and confer concerning the advisability of filing a petition with the person seeking to file a petition for support, the potential respondent and any other interested person no later than the next regularly-scheduled court day. The probation service shall permit any participant who is represented by a lawyer to be accompanied at any preliminary conference by the lawyer, who shall be identified by the probation officer to the other party, and shall not discourage any person from seeking to file a petition.

(c) At the first appearance at a conference by each of the persons listed in subdivision (b) hereof, the probation service shall inform such person concerning the function and limitations of, and the alternative to, the adjustment process, and that:

(1) the purpose of the adjustment process is to discover whether it will be possible to arrive at a voluntary agreement for support without filing a petition;

(2) the person seeking to file a petition for support is entitled to request that the probation service confer with him or her, the potential respondent and any other interested person concerning the advisability of filing a petition for support under article 4 of the Family Court Act;

(3) if the assistance of the probation service is not requested or, if requested, is subsequently declined, the person seeking to file a petition for support is entitled to have access to the court at any time for that purpose and may proceed to file a petition for support.

(4) the probation service is not authorized to, and shall not, compel any person, including the person seeking support, to appear at any conference, produce any papers or visit any place;

(5) the adjustment process must commence within 15 days from the date of the request for a conference, may continue for a period of two months from the date of that request and may be extended for an additional 60 days upon written application to the

court containing the consent of the person seeking to file a petition;

(6) if the adjustment process is not successful, the persons participating therein shall be notified in writing of that fact and that the person seeking to file a petition for support is entitled to access to the court for that purpose;

(7) if the adjustment of the matter results in a voluntary agreement for support of the petitioner and any dependents:

(i) it shall be reduced to writing by the probation service, signed by both parties to it, and submitted to the Family Court for approval;

(ii) if the court approves it, the court may, without further hearing, enter an order for support pursuant to section 425 of the Family Court Act in accordance with the agreement;

(iii) the order when entered shall be binding upon the parties and shall in all respects be a valid order, and the Family Court may entertain a proceeding for enforcement of the order should there not be compliance with the order;

(iv) unless the agreement is submitted to the Family Court and an order is issued, the Family Court will not entertain a proceeding for the enforcement of the agreement should the agreement not be complied with.

(d) If the adjustment process is not commenced, the probation service shall give written notice to the persons listed in subdivision (b) that:

(1) the adjustment process will not be commenced and the reasons therefor;

(2) the person seeking to file a petition for support is entitled to access to the court for that purpose; and

(3) if applicable, the adjustment process was not commenced on the ground that the court would not have jurisdiction over the case, and the question of the court's jurisdiction may be tested by filing a petition.

Cross References

Family Court Act, see McKinney's Book 29A, Part 1.

Social Services Law, see McKinney's Book 52A.

§ 205.31. Duties of the Probation Service and Procedures Relating to the Adjustment Process (Support)

(a) If the assistance of the probation service is requested by the person seeking to file a petition for support, and it appears that it may be possible to arrive at a voluntary agreement for support, the adjustment process shall commence within 15 days from the date of request and shall include the person seeking to file a petition for support, the potential respondent and any other person listed in subdivision (b) of section 205.30 of these rules who wishes to participate therein. The probation service shall per-

mit any participant who is represented by a lawyer to be accompanied at any conference by the lawyer, who shall be identified by the probation officer to the other party, and shall not discourage any person from seeking to file a petition.

(b) If an extension of the period of the adjustment process is sought, the probation service shall apply in writing to the court and shall set forth the services rendered, the date of commencement of those services, the degree of success achieved and the services proposed to be rendered. The application shall set forth the reasons why, in the opinion of the assigned probation officer, additional time is needed to adjust the matter, and shall contain the signed consent of the person seeking to file a petition for support.

(c) The probation service shall discontinue its efforts at adjustment if at any time:

(1) the person seeking to file a petition for support or the potential respondent requests that it do so; or

(2) it appears to the probation service that there is no reasonable likelihood that a voluntary agreement for support will result.

(d) If the adjustment process is not successfully concluded, the probation service shall notify all the persons who participated therein in writing:

(1) that the adjustment process has not been successfully concluded and the reasons therefor; and

(2) that the person seeking to file a petition for support is entitled to access to the court for that purpose.

(e) If the adjustment process results in an agreement for the support of the petitioner and any dependents:

(1) it shall be reduced to writing by the probation service, shall be signed by both parties to it, and shall be submitted to the court, together with a petition for approval of the agreement and a proposed order incorporating the agreement;

(2) if the agreement is approved by the court, a copy of the order shall be furnished by the probation service to the person seeking to file a petition for support and the potential respondent, in person if they are present, and by mail if their presence has been dispensed with by the court.

§ 205.32. Support Magistrates

(a) Qualifications. Support magistrates shall be appointed by the Chief Administrator of the Courts to hear and determine support proceedings in Family Court pursuant to section 439 of the Family Court Act. They shall be attorneys admitted to the practice of law in New York for at least five years and shall be knowledgeable with respect to Family Court procedure, family law and federal and state support law and programs.

(b) Term.

(1) Support magistrates shall be appointed as non-judicial employees of the unified court system on a full-time basis for a term of three years and, in the discretion of the Chief Administrator, may be reappointed for subsequent five-year terms, provided that if the Chief Administrator determines that the employment of a full-time support magistrate is not required in a particular court, the services of a full-time support magistrate may be shared by one or more counties or a support magistrate may be appointed to serve within one or more counties on a part-time basis.

(2) In the discretion of the Chief Administrator, an acting support magistrate may be appointed to serve during a support magistrate's authorized leave of absence. In making such appointment, the provisions for selection of support magistrates set forth in subdivision (c) may be modified by the Chief Administrator as appropriate to the particular circumstances.

(3) A support magistrate shall be subject to removal or other disciplinary action pursuant to the procedure set forth in section 25.29(b) of the Rules of the Chief Judge (22 NYCRR 25.29[b]).

(c) Selection of support magistrates.

(1) The district administrative judge for the judicial district in which the county or counties where the support magistrate is authorized to serve is located, or the administrative judge for the courts in Nassau County or the administrative judge for the courts in Suffolk County, if the support magistrate is authorized to serve in either of those counties, or the administrative judge for the Family Court within the City of New York, if the support magistrate is to serve in New York City, shall:

(i) publish an announcement in the law journal serving the affected county or counties inviting applications from the bar or, if there is no law journal serving such area, in a newspaper of general circulation; and

(ii) communicate directly with bar associations in the affected county or counties to invite applicants to apply.

(2) The announcements and communications shall set forth the qualifications for selection as contained in subdivision (a) of this section, the compensation, the term of appointment and requirements concerning restrictions on the private practice of law.

(3) A committee consisting of an administrative judge, a judge of the Family Court and a designee of the Chief Administrator shall screen each applicant for qualifications, character and ability to handle the support magistrate responsibilities, and shall forward the names of recommended nominees, with a summary of their qualifications, to the Chief Administrator, who shall make the appointment. The appointment order shall indicate the court or courts in which the support magistrate shall serve. The Chief Admin-

istrator further may authorize temporary assignments to additional courts.

(d) Training. The Chief Administrator shall authorize such training for support magistrates as appropriate to ensure the effective performance of their duties.

(e) Compensation and Expenses. Compensation for support magistrates shall be fixed by the Chief Administrator. Support magistrates shall be entitled to reimbursement of actual and necessary travel expenses in accordance with the rules governing the reimbursement of the travel expenses of nonjudicial court employees of the State of New York.

Cross References

Family Court Act, see McKinney's Book 29A, Part 1.

§ 205.33. Assignment of Support Magistrates

The supervising judge of the Family Court in the county in which the support magistrate will serve, or the deputy administrative judge for the Family Court within the City of New York, if the support magistrate is to serve in New York City, shall assign support magistrates as required by the needs of the courts, in conformance with law and in conformance with section 205.3 of this part.

§ 205.34. Referrals to Support Magistrates

(a) A summons or warrant in support proceedings shall be made returnable by the clerk of the court before a support magistrate in the first instance, unless otherwise provided by the court. A net worth statement form prescribed by the Chief Administrator shall be appended by the clerk to the summons to be served upon the respondent and shall be given to the petitioner upon the filing of the petition.

(b) Whenever the parties are before a judge of the court when support is an issue, the judge shall make an immediate order, either temporary or permanent, with respect to support. If a temporary order is made, the court shall refer the issues of support to a support magistrate.

(c) The above provisions shall apply to initial determinations of support, subsequent modification or violation proceedings, and support proceedings referred to Family Court by the Supreme Court pursuant to Part 6 of article 4 of the Family Court Act.

Cross References

Family Court Act, see McKinney's Book 29A, Part 1.

Forms

Order upon support agreement, based on official form, see West's McKinney's Forms, Matrimonial and Family, § 25:35.

Temporary support order and referral to hearing examiner, based on official form, see West's McKinney's Forms, Matrimonial and Family, §§ 25:41, 25:42.

Order of support, based on official form, see West's McKinney's Forms, Matrimonial and Family, § 25:43.

Order of support (after referral to hearing examiner and filing of objections), based on official form, see West's McKinney's Forms, Matrimonial and Family, § 25:44.

§ 205.35. Conduct of Hearing

(a) Unless otherwise specified in the order of reference, the support magistrate shall conduct the hearing in the same manner as a court trying an issue without a jury in conformance with the procedures set forth in the Civil Practice Law and Rules and with section 205.3 of these rules.

(b) If a full or partial agreement is reached between the parties during the hearing, it shall be placed on the record and, if approved, shall be incorporated into an order, which shall be duly entered.

(c) The support magistrate shall require the exchange and filing of affidavits of financial disclosure.

Cross References

CPLR, see McKinney's Book 7B.

§ 205.36. Findings of Fact; Transmission of Findings of Fact and Other Information; Quarterly Reports

(a) Findings of fact shall be in writing and shall include, where applicable, the income and expenses of each party, the basis for liability for support and an assessment of the needs of the children. The findings of fact shall be set forth on a form prescribed by the Chief Administrator. A copy of the findings of fact shall accompany the order of support.

(b) At the time of the entry of the order of support, the clerk of the court shall cause a copy of the findings of fact and order of support to be served either in person or by mail upon the parties to the proceeding or their attorneys. When the findings and order are transmitted to a party appearing pro se, they shall be accompanied by information about the objection process, including the requirements for a transcript, the time limitations governing the filing of objections and rebuttals, and the necessity for affidavits of service on the opposing party of all papers filed with the court.

(c) Each support magistrate shall file with the Chief Administrator, in such form as may be required, a quarterly report indicating the matters that have been pending undecided before such hearing examiner for a period of 30 days after final submission, and the reasons therefor.

§ 205.37. Recording of Hearings; Objections

(a) Hearings may be recorded mechanically. Any equipment used for such mechanical recording or for the production of such recording shall have the prior approval of the Chief Administrator of the Courts.

(b) Mechanical recordings shall be appropriately and clearly identified with the name of the case, docket number and date of hearing for storage and retrieval with proper precautions taken for security and preservation of confidentiality. Where hearings are recorded mechanically, the clerk of the court shall provide a means for the making of a duplicate recording or for an alternative method for preparation of a transcript where required by a judge reviewing objections to an order of a support magistrate or when requested by a party.

(c) A transcript of the proceeding before the support magistrate shall be prepared where required by the judge to whom objections have been submitted for review, in which event costs of duplication and of transcript preparation shall be borne by the objecting party. Either party may request a duplicate recording or transcript, in which event costs of duplication of the recording or preparation of the transcript shall be borne by the requesting party. A transcript shall bear the certification of the transcriber that the transcript is a true and accurate transcription of the proceeding. A party who is financially unable to pay the cost of the duplicate recording or the preparation of a transcript may seek leave of the court to proceed as a poor person pursuant to article 11 of the Civil Practice Law and Rules.

(d) Objections to the order of the support magistrate and rebuttals thereto shall be accompanied by an affidavit of service on the opposing party.

Cross References

CPLR, see McKinney's Book 7B

§ 205.38. Record and Report of Unexecuted Warrants Issued Pursuant to Section 428 of the Family Court Act

(a) The clerk of court for the Family Court in each county shall obtain and keep a record of executed warrants issued pursuant to section 428 of the Family Court Act.

(b) At the end of each six-month period, on the first of January and on the first of July in each year, a report concerning all unexecuted warrants issued pursuant to section 428 of the Family Court Act shall be made and filed with the Office of Court Administration on a form to be supplied by the Office of Court Administration.

Cross References

Family Court Act, see McKinney's Book 29A, Part 1.

§ 205.39. Authority of Probation When There Is a Failure to Obey a Lawful Order of the Court (Support)

(a) The probation service, at the request of the petitioner, is authorized to confer with the respondent and the petitioner whenever any respondent fails to obey a lawful order of the court made under article 4 of the Family Court Act or an order of support made under article 5 of the Family Court Act concerning the existence of the violation, the reason for it and the likelihood that there will be compliance in the future. The probation service shall permit any participant who is represented by a lawyer to be accompanied at any conference by the lawyer, who shall be identified by the probation officer to the other party, and shall not discourage any person from seeking to file a petition to enforce compliance.

(b) Before holding any conference pursuant to subdivision (a) of this section:

(1) The probation service shall notify the respondent in writing that:

(i) the probation service is willing to confer with the respondent and must hear from the respondent within seven days if a conference is to be held;

(ii) the petitioner is entitled to petition the court to enforce compliance with the order;

(2) a copy of this notice shall be furnished to the petitioner;

(3) if the respondent does not communicate with the probation service within seven days, the probation service shall advise the petitioner that he or she may petition the court to enforce compliance with the order.

(c) If, at a conference held pursuant to subdivision (a) of this section, it shall appear to the probation service that the failure to comply with the order was not willful and that there is a substantial likelihood that compliance with the order will result, the probation service is authorized to adjust the matter informally. An existing order may not be modified by informal adjustment without the filing of a petition for such modification and the approval of the court thereof. Efforts at adjustment pursuant to this subdivision shall not extend beyond the conference held pursuant to subdivision (a) of this section.

(d) The probation service is not authorized to, and shall not, discuss with the petitioner or the respondent:

(1) the advisability or likely outcome of filing a petition to enforce compliance with the order; or

(2) the amount of arrears that would be awarded or cancelled by the court if a petition to enforce the order were filed.

Cross References

Family Court Act, see McKinney's Book 29A, Part 1.

§ 205.40. Preliminary Probation Conferences and Procedures Upon a Referral From the Supreme Court (Support)

(a) When an application is referred to the Family Court by the Supreme Court pursuant to part 6 of article 4 of the Family Court Act, the parties may first be referred to the probation service, which shall inform them at the first conference concerning the function and limitations of and the alternatives to the adjustment process in accordance with subdivision (c) of section 205.30 of these rules.

(b) The probation service, at the request of either party to the proceeding, shall be available to meet with the parties and other interested persons no later than the next regularly-scheduled court day concerning the willingness of the parties to resolve those issues by voluntary agreement. The probation service shall permit any participant who is represented by a lawyer to be accompanied at any preliminary conference by the lawyer, who shall be identified by the probation officer to the other party, and shall not discourage any person from seeking to file a petition.

Cross References

Family Court Act, see McKinney's Book 29A, Part 1.

§ 205.41. Duties of the Probation Service and Procedures Relating to the Adjustment Process Upon Referral From Supreme Court (Support)

(a) If the assistance of the probation service is requested by either party to the proceeding, efforts at adjustment shall commence within 15 days from the date of the request and may continue for a period of two months from the date of request. The court may extend the adjustment process for an additional 60 days upon written application containing the consent of the person seeking to file a petition.

(b) The probation service shall permit any participant who is represented by a lawyer to be accompanied at any conference by the lawyer, who shall be identified by the probation officer to the other party.

(c) If an extension of the period of the adjustment process is sought, the probation service shall apply in writing to the court and shall set forth the services rendered, the date of commencement of those services, the degree of success achieved and the services proposed to be rendered. The application shall set forth the reasons why, in the opinion of the assigned probation officer, additional time is needed to adjust the matter, and shall contain the signed consent of the parties and a statement by the probation officer that there is a substantial likelihood that a voluntary agreement would be reached if an extension were granted.

(d) The probation service shall discontinue the adjustment process if, at any time:

(1) either party requests that it do so; or

(2) it appears to the probation service that there is no substantial likelihood that a voluntary agreement will result.

(e) If the adjustment process is not successfully concluded, the probation service shall notify the persons who participated therein in writing:

(1) that the adjustment process has not been successfully concluded and the reasons therefor;

(2) that either party is entitled to access to the court to have the issues which have been referred determined at a fact-finding hearing.

(f) If the adjustment process results in a voluntary agreement on the issues referred:

(1) it shall be reduced to writing by the probation service, shall be signed by both parties to it, and shall be submitted to the court, together with a petition for approval of the agreement and a proposed order incorporating the agreement;

(2) if the agreement is approved by the court, a copy of the order made by the court shall be furnished by the probation service to the parties, in person if they are present, and by mail if their presence has been dispensed with by the court.

§ 205.42. Submission by Support Collection Units of Proposed Adjusted Orders of Support

(a) A submission by a support collection unit pursuant to section 413 of the Family Court Act for adjustment of a child support order shall include the following, which shall be submitted on forms promulgated by the Chief Administrator of the Courts:

(1) an affidavit from the support collection unit, with findings in support of adjustment;

(2) a proposed adjusted order of support; and

(3) a notice to the parties of the proposed adjusted order and of the rights of the parties, including the addresses of the court and the support collection unit. The documents set forth in this subdivision shall be filed with the clerk of the court within 10 days of mailing to the parties, together with an affidavit of service of these documents upon the parties.

(b) Where a written objection is received by the clerk of the court within 35 days of mailing to the parties of the documents set forth in subdivision (a), the court shall schedule a hearing upon notice to the support collection unit and the parties.

(c) Where no timely objection is received by the court, the court shall sign the order upon the court's being satisfied that the requirements of sections 111–h of the Social Services Law and 413 of the Family Court Act have been met, and shall transmit copies of the order to the support collection unit for service on the parties. Absent unusual circumstances, the court shall sign the order or dismiss the application within ten business days after the conclusion of the 35–day objection period.

§ 205.43. Hearings to Determine Willful Non-payment of Child Support

(a) A petition that alleges a willful violation or seeks enforcement of an order of support shall be scheduled as soon as possible for a first appearance date in Family Court but in no event more than 30 days of the filing of the violation or enforcement petition.

(b) After service is made, the judge or support magistrate must commence a hearing to determine a willful violation within 30 days of the date noticed in the summons. The hearing must be concluded within 60 days of its commencement.

(c) Neither party shall be permitted more than one adjournment to secure counsel, except for good cause shown.

(d) On the scheduled hearing date on the issue of willfulness, the hearing may not be adjourned except for the following reasons:

(1) actual engagement of counsel pursuant to Part 125 of the Rules of the Chief Administrator;

(2) illness of a party; or

(3) other good cause shown.

No adjournment shall be in excess of 14 days.

(e) If a willfulness hearing has commenced and must be continued, the adjourned date shall be within seven court days.

(f) Upon the conclusion of a willfulness hearing in a case heard by a support magistrate, the support magistrate shall issue written findings of fact within five court days.

(g) In a case heard by a support magistrate, if the support magistrate makes a finding of willfulness, the written findings shall include the following:

(1) the specific facts upon which the finding of willfulness is based;

(2) the specific amount of arrears established and a money judgment for such amount. An award of attorney's fees may be issued with the findings or at a later date after the case is heard by the Family Court judge;

(3) a recommendation regarding the sanctions that should be imposed, including a recommendation whether the sanction of incarceration is recommended;

(4) a recommendation, as appropriate, regarding a specific dollar amount to be paid or a specific plan to repay the arrears.

(h) In a case heard by a support magistrate, if counsel is assigned, the assignment shall continue through the confirmation proceeding before the Family Court judge without further order of the court.

(i) In a case heard by a support magistrate, a Family Court judge may confirm the findings of the support magistrate by adopting his or her findings and recommendations in whole or in part. Alternatively, the Family Court judge may modify or refuse to confirm the findings and recommendations and may refer the matter back to the support magistrate for further proceedings. The court may, if necessary, conduct an evidentiary hearing.

§ 205.44. Testimony by Telephone, Audio-visual or Other Electronic Means in Child Support and Paternity Cases

(a) This section shall govern applications for testimony to be taken by telephone, audio-visual means or other electronic means in accordance with sections 433, 531–a and 580–316 of the Family Court Act.

(b) A party or witness seeking to testify by telephone, audio-visual means or other electronic means must complete an application on the form officially promulgated by the Chief Administrator of the Courts and set forth in Chapter IV of Subtitle D of this Title and, except for good cause shown, must file such application with the court not less than three days in advance of the hearing date. The applicant shall attempt to arrange to provide such testimony at a designated tribunal or the child support enforcement agency, as defined in the federal Social Security Act (42 U.S.C. Title IV–D) in that party's state, or county if within the state. The court may permit the testimony to be taken at any suitable location acceptable to the court, including but not limited to, the party's or witness' counsel's office, personal residence or place of business.

(c) The applicant must provide all financial documentation ordered to be disclosed by the court pursuant to section 424 or 580–316 of the Family Court Act, as applicable, before he or she will be permitted to testify by telephone, audio-visual means or other electronic means. The financial documentation may be provided by personal delivery, mailing, facsimile, telecopier or any other electronic means that is acceptable to the court.

(d) The court shall transmit a copy of its decision by mail, facsimile, telecopier, or electronic means to the applicant and the parties. The court shall state its reasons in writing for denying any request to appear by telephone, audio-visual means or other electronic means.

§§ 205.45 to 205.47. [Reserved]

§ 205.48. Judicial and Extra-judicial Surrenders; Required Papers and Putative Father Determination

(a) In addition to the judicial or extra-judicial surrender instrument and, if applicable, the post-adoption contact agreement and petition for approval of an extra-judicial surrender, the petitioner shall submit a copy of the child's birth certificate.

(b) Where the surrender is by the birth mother:

(1) The petitioner shall also submit:

(i) the response from the putative father registry that is current within 60 days prior to the filing of the surrender proceeding;

(ii) a sworn written statement, if any, by the mother naming the father; and

(iii) a sworn written statement by the caseworker setting forth information regarding any putative father whose consent to adopt is required by section 111 of the Domestic Relations Law or who is entitled to notice of an adoption pursuant to section 111–a of the Domestic Relations Law.

(2) Where a determination has not yet been made by the court regarding any putative father whose consent to adopt is required or who is entitled to notice of an adoption, the proceeding shall be referred to the Family Court judge on the date of filing or the next court date for a determination regarding who must be notified of the surrender proceeding. Except for good cause shown or unless the putative father has previously defaulted in a termination of parental rights proceeding regarding the child, the surrender proceeding shall not be scheduled for execution of a judicial surrender or approval of an extrajudicial surrender, as applicable, until a determination regarding required notices and consents have been made by the Court.

§ 205.49. Termination of Parental Rights; Required Papers; Venue; Putative Father Determination

(a) This section shall apply to petitions filed pursuant to Part 1 of Article Six of the Family Court Act and section 384–b of the Social Services Law.

(b) The petitioner shall submit a copy of the child's birth certificate with the petition.

(c) Where the petition is filed to terminate the birth mother's rights:

(1) The petitioner shall also submit:

(i) the response from the putative father registry that is current within 60 days prior to the filing of the termination of parental rights proceeding;

(ii) a sworn written statement, if any, by the mother naming the father; and

(iii) a sworn written statement by the caseworker setting forth information regarding any putative father who is entitled to notice of the proceeding pursuant to section 384–c of the social services law.

(2) Where a determination has not yet been made by the court regarding any putative father who is entitled to notice of the proceeding pursuant to section 384–c of the social services law, the petition shall be referred to the Family Court judge on the date of filing or the next court date for a determination regarding who must be notified of the proceeding. Except for good cause shown, the petition shall not be scheduled for a fact-finding hearing until a determina-

tion regarding required notices has been made by the court.

(d) Where a child is under the jurisdiction of the Family Court as a result of a placement in foster care pursuant to Article 10 or 10–A of the Family Court Act or section 358–a of the social services law, the petition regarding termination of parental rights to the child shall be assigned, wherever practicable, to the Family Court judge who last presided over the child's child protective, foster care placement or permanency proceeding or over a termination of parental rights proceeding involving the child's other parent. Where the petition has been filed regarding such a child either before a different judge in a different court or before a court in a different county, the petitioner shall so indicate in the petition and the petitioner's attorney shall file an affirmation on a uniform form promulgated by the Chief Administrator of the Courts attesting to the reasons for, and circumstances regarding, such filing. The court in which the petition has been filed shall stay the proceeding for not more than 30 days in order to communicate with the Family Court judge who presided over the child's most recent child protective, foster care placement or permanency hearing or the termination of parental rights or surrender for adoption proceeding involving the child's other parent, and in order to afford the parties and law guardian in the respective proceedings an opportunity to be heard orally, in person or by telephone, or in writing. Pursuant to paragraph (c–1) of subdivision three of section 384–b of the Social Services Law, the Family Court judge who presided over the child's case shall determine whether the termination of parental rights petition should be transferred or should be heard in the court in which it has been filed and shall record that determination on a uniform form promulgated by the Chief Administrator of the Courts. This determination shall be incorporated by the court in which the termination of parental rights petition has been filed into an order on a uniform form promulgated by the Chief Administrator of the Courts either retaining or transferring the petition. If the termination of parental rights petition is to be transferred, the transfer must take place forthwith, but in no event more than 35 days after the filing of the petition.

§ 205.50. Terms and Conditions of Order Suspending Judgment in Accordance With Section 633 of the Family Court Act or Section 384–b(8)(c) of the Social Services Law

(a) An order suspending judgment entered pursuant to section 631 of the Family Court Act or section 384–b(8)(c) of the Social Services Law shall be related to the adjudicated acts or omissions of respondent and shall contain at least one of the following terms and conditions requiring respondent to:

(1) sustain communication of a substantial nature with the child by letter or telephone at stated intervals;

(2) maintain consistent contact with the child, including visits or outings at stated intervals;

(3) participate with the authorized agency in developing and effectuating a plan for the future of the child;

(4) cooperate with the authorized agency's court-approved plan for encouraging and strengthening the parental relationship;

(5) contribute toward the cost of maintaining the child if possessed of sufficient means or able to earn such means;

(6) seek to obtain and provide proper housing for the child;

(7) cooperate in seeking to obtain and in accepting medical or psychiatric diagnosis or treatment, alcoholism or drug abuse treatment, employment or family counseling or child guidance, and permit information to be obtained by the court from any person or agency from whom the respondent is receiving or was directed to receive such services; and

(8) satisfy such other reasonable terms and conditions as the court shall determine to be necessary or appropriate to ameliorate the acts or omissions which gave rise to the filing of the petition.

(b) The order shall set forth the duration, terms and conditions of the suspended judgment and shall contain a date certain for review of respondent's compliance not less than 30 days in advance of the expiration of the suspended judgment. The suspended judgment may last for up to one year and may, if exceptional circumstances warrant, be extended by the Court for one additional period of up to one year. A copy of the order, along with a current service plan, shall be furnished to the respondent. The order shall contain a written statement informing the respondent that a failure to obey the order may lead to its revocation and to the issuance of an order for the commitment of the guardianship and custody of a child. Where the child is in foster care, the order shall set forth the visitation plan for the child and the respondent, as well as for the child and his or her sibling or siblings, if any, and shall require the agency to notify the respondent of case conferences. The order shall further contain a determination in accordance with subdivision 12 of section 384–b of the Social Services Law of the existence of any person or persons to whom notice of an adoption would be required pursuant to section 111–b of the Domestic Relations Law and, if so, whether such person or persons were given notice of the termination of parental rights proceeding and whether such person or persons appeared.

(c) Not later than 60 days in advance of the expiration of the period of suspended judgment, the petitioner shall file a report with the Family Court and all parties, including the respondent and his or her attorney, the law guardian and intervenors, if any, regarding the respondent's compliance with the terms and conditions of the suspended judgment. The court may set additional times at which the respondent or the authorized agency caring for the child shall report to the court regarding compliance with the terms and conditions of the suspended judgment.

(d) If a respondent fails to comply with the terms and conditions of an order suspending judgment made pursuant to section 631 of the Family Court Act or section 384b(8)(c) of the Social Services Law:

(1) a motion or order to show cause seeking the revocation of the order may be filed;

(2) the affidavit accompanying the motion or order to show cause shall contain a concise statement of the acts or omissions alleged to constitute noncompliance with the order;

(3) the motion or order to show cause shall be served upon the respondent by mail at the last known address or as directed by the court and shall be served upon all attorneys, the law guardian and intervenors, if any;

(4) during the pendency of the motion or order to show cause, the period of the suspended judgment is tolled; and

(5) if, after a hearing or upon the respondent's admission, the court is satisfied that the allegations of the motion or order to show cause have been established and upon a determination of the child's best interests, the court may modify, revise or revoke the order of suspended judgment or if exceptional circumstances warrant and the suspended judgment has not already been extended, the court may extend the suspended judgment for an additional period of up to one year.

(e) The court may at any time, upon notice and opportunity to be heard to the parties, their attorneys and the law guardian, revise, modify or enlarge the terms and conditions of a suspended judgment previously imposed.

(f) If the child remains in foster care during the pendency of a suspended judgment or after a suspended judgment has been deemed satisfied or if guardianship and custody have been transferred to the agency as a result of a revocation of the suspended judgment, a permanency hearing must be scheduled for a date certain and must be completed immediately following or not more than 60 days after the earlier of the Family Court's oral announcement of its decision or signing and filing of its written order. Subsequent permanency hearings must be held as required by section 1089 of the Family Court Act at intervals of not more than six months from the date of completion of the prior permanency hearing.

Cross References

Family Court Act, see McKinney's Book 29A, Part 1.

Social Services Law, see McKinney's Book 52A.

§ 205.51. Proceedings Involving Custody of a Native American Child

In any proceeding in which the custody of a child is to be determined, the petition shall set forth whether the child is a Native American child subject to the Indian Child Welfare Act of 1978 (25 U.S.C. §§ 1901–1963) and the Court shall proceed further, as appropriate, in accordance with the provisions of that Act.

§ 205.52. Adoption Rules; Application; Timing and Venue of Filing of Petition

(a) Sections 205.53 through 205.55 hereof shall be applicable to all agency and private-placement adoption proceedings in Family Court.

(b) In any agency adoption, a petition may be filed to adopt a child who is the subject of a termination of parental rights proceeding and whose custody and guardianship has not yet been committed to an authorized agency, provided that

(i) the adoption petition is filed in the same court where the termination of parental rights proceeding is pending; and

(ii) the adoption petition, supporting documents and the fact of their filing shall not be provided to the judge before whom the petition for termination of parental rights is pending until such time as fact-finding is concluded under that petition.

(c) Where a child is under the jurisdiction of the Family Court as a result of a placement in foster care pursuant to Article 10 or 10–A of the Family Court Act or section 358–a of the social services law, the adoption petition regarding the child shall be assigned, wherever practicable, to the Family Court judge who last presided over the child's child protective, foster care placement, permanency, surrender or termination of parental rights proceeding. Where the adoption petition has been filed regarding such a child either before a different judge in a different court or before a court in a different county, the petitioner shall so indicate in the petition and the petitioner's attorney shall file an affirmation by the attorney for the petitioner on a uniform form promulgated by the Chief Administrator of the Courts attesting to the reasons for, and circumstances regarding, such filing. The court in which the adoption petition has been filed shall stay the proceeding for not more than 30 days in order to communicate with the Family Court judge who presided over the child's most recent child protective, foster care placement, permanency, termination of parental rights or surrender proceeding, and afford the agency attorney and law guardian in the respective proceedings an opportunity to be heard orally, in person or by telephone, or in writing. Pursuant to section 113 of the Domestic Relations Law, the Family Court judge who presided over the child's case shall determine whether the adoption petition should be transferred or should be heard in the court in which it has been filed and shall record that determination on a uniform form promulgated by the Chief Administrator of the Courts. This determination shall be incorporated by the court in which the adoption petition has been filed into an order on a uniform form promulgated by the Chief Administrator of the Courts either retaining or transferring the petition. If the adoption petition is to be transferred, the transfer must take place forthwith, but in no event more than 35 days after the filing of the petition.

§ 205.53. Papers Required in an Adoption Proceeding

(a) All papers submitted in an adoption proceeding shall comply with section 205.7 of this Part.

(b) In addition to those papers required by the Domestic Relations Law, the following papers, unless otherwise dispensed with by the court, shall be submitted and filed prior to the placement of any adoption proceeding on the calendar:

(1) a certified copy of the birth certificate of the adoptive child;

(2) an affidavit or affidavits by an attorney admitted to practice in the State of New York or, in the discretion of the court, by a person other than an attorney who is known to the court, identifying each of the parties;

(3) a certified marriage certificate, where the adoptive parents are husband and wife or where an individual adoptive parent is the spouse of the birth parent;

(4) a certified copy of a decree or judgment, where an adoptive parent's marriage has been terminated by decree or judgment;

(5) a certified death certificate, where an adoptive or birth parent's marriage has been terminated by death or where it is alleged that consent or notice is not required because of death;

(6) a proposed order of adoption;

(7) a copy of the attorney's affidavit of financial disclosure filed with the Office of Court Administration pursuant to section 603.23, 691.23, 806.14 or 1022.33 of this Title; and either an attorney's affirmation that the affidavit has been personally delivered or mailed in accordance with such rules or the dated receipt from the Office of Court Administration;

(8) an affidavit of financial disclosure from the adoptive parent or parents, and from any person whose consent to the adoption is required by law, setting forth the following information:

(i) name, address and telephone number of the affiant;

(ii) status of the affiant in the proceeding and relationship, if any, to the adoptive child;

(iii) docket number of the adoption proceeding;

(iv) the date and terms of every agreement, written or otherwise, between the affiant and any attorney pertaining to any fees, compensation or other remuneration paid or to be paid by or on behalf of the adoptive parents or the birth parents, directly or indirectly, including but not limited to retainer fees on account of or incidental to the placement or adoption of the child or assistance in arrangements for such placement or adoption;

(v) the total amount of fees, compensation or other remuneration to be paid to such attorney by the affiant, directly or indirectly, including the date and amounts of each payment already made, if any, on account of or incidental to the placement or adoption of the child or assistance in arrangements for such placement or adoption;

(vi) the name and address of any other person, agency, association, corporation, institution, society or organization who received or will receive any fees, compensation or other remuneration from the affiant, directly or indirectly, on account of or incidental to the birth or care of the adoptive child, the pregnancy or care of the adoptive child's birth mother or the placement or adoption of the child and on account of or incidental to assistance in arrangements for such placement or proposed adoption; the amount of each such fee, compensation or other remuneration; and the reason for or services rendered, if any, in connection with each such fee, compensation or other remuneration; and

(vii) the name and address of any person, agency, association, corporation, society or organization who has or will pay the affiant any fee, compensation or other remuneration, directly or indirectly, on account of or incidental to the birth or care of the adoptive child, the pregnancy or care of the adoptive child's birth mother, or the placement or adoption of the child and on account of or incidental to assistance in arrangements for such placement or adoption; the amount of each such fee, compensation or other remuneration; and the reason for or services rendered, if any, in connection with each such fee, compensation or other remuneration;

(9) in the case of an adoption from an authorized agency in accordance with title 2 of article 7 of the Domestic Relations Law, a copy of the criminal history summary report made by the New York State Office of Children and Family Services to the authorized agency pursuant to section 378–a of the Social Services Law regarding the criminal record or records of the prospective adoptive parent or parents and any adult over the age of 18 currently residing in the home, including fingerprint-based records of the national crime information databases, as defined in section 534(e)(3)(A) of Title 28 of the United States Code,

as well as a report from the New York State Central Registry of Child Abuse and Maltreatment regarding any indicated reports regarding the prospective adoptive parent or parents and any adult over the age of 18 currently residing in the home and from the child abuse and maltreatment registry, if any, of any state in which the prospective adoptive parents and any adult over the age of 18 have resided during the five years immediately prior to the filing of the petition;

(10) in the case of an adoption from an authorized agency, an affidavit by the attorney for the agency attesting to the fact that no appeal from a surrender, surrender revocation or termination of parental rights proceeding is pending in any court and that a notice of entry of the final order of disposition of the surrender, surrender revocation or termination of parental rights proceeding had been served upon the law guardian, the attorneys for the respondent parents or the parents themselves, if they were self-represented, as well as any other parties;

(11) in the case of an adoption from an authorized agency in which a post-adoption contact agreement has been approved by the Family Court in conjunction with a surrender of the child, a copy of the post-adoption contact agreement, as well as the order of the Court that approved the agreement as being in the child's best interests, and

(12) in the case of an adoption petition filed either before a different judge in a different court or a court in a different county regarding a child under the jurisdiction of the Family Court as a result of a placement in foster care pursuant to Article 10 or 10–A of the Family Court Act or section 358–a of the Social Services Law, an affirmation by the attorney for the petitioner on a uniform form promulgated by the Chief Administrator of the Courts attesting to the reasons for, and circumstances regarding, such filing.

(c) Prior to the signing of an order of adoption, the court may in its discretion require the filing of a supplemental affidavit by the adoptive parent or parents, any person whose consent to the adoption is required, the authorized agency and the attorney for any of the aforementioned, setting forth any additional information pertaining to allegations in the petition or in any affidavit filed in the proceeding.

Cross References

Domestic Relations Law, see McKinney's Book 14.

Public Health Law, see McKinney's Book 44.

§ 205.54. Investigation by Disinterested Person; Adoption

(a) The probation service or an authorized agency or disinterested person is authorized to and, at the request of the court, shall interview such persons and obtain such data as will aid the court in determining the truth and accuracy of an adoption petition under article 7 of the Domestic Relations Law, including the

allegations set forth in the schedule annexed to the petition pursuant to section 112(3) of that law and such other facts as are necessary to a determination of the petition;

(b) The adoptive parent or parents and other persons concerned with the proceeding shall be notified of the date, time and place of any interview by a disinterested person or authorized agency designated by the court in accordance with sections 112 and 116 of the Domestic Relations Law.

(c) The written report of the investigation conducted pursuant to subdivision (a) of this section shall be submitted to the court within 30 days from the date on which it was ordered, or earlier as the court may direct, unless, for good cause, the court shall grant an extension for a reasonable period of time not to exceed an additional 30 days.

Cross References

Domestic Relations Law, see McKinney's Book 14.

§ 205.55. Special Applications

All applications, including applications to dispense with statutorily-required personal appearances, the period of residence of a child, or the period of waiting after filing of the adoption petition, shall be made in writing and shall be accompanied by affidavits setting forth the reasons for the application and all facts relevant thereto.

§ 205.56. Investigation by Disinterested Person; Custody; Guardianship

(a) The probation service or an authorized agency or disinterested person is authorized to and, at the request of the court, shall interview such persons and obtain such data as will aid the court in:

(1) determining custody in a proceeding under sections 467 or 651 of the Family Court Act;

(2) exercising its power under section 661 of the Family Court Act to appoint a guardian of the person of a minor under the jurisdiction of the court.

(b) The written report of the investigation conducted pursuant to subdivision (a) of this section shall be submitted to the court within 30 days from the date on which it was ordered, or earlier as the court may direct, unless, for good cause, the court shall grant an extension for a reasonable period of time not to exceed an additional 30 days.

Cross References

Family Court Act, see McKinney's Book 29A, Part 1.

§ 205.57. Petition for Guardianship by Adoptive Parent

(a) When a petition for temporary guardianship has been filed by an adoptive parent or parents pursuant to section 115–c of the Domestic Relations Law, the clerk of the court in which the petition has been filed shall distribute a written notice to the adoptive parents and lawyers who have appeared, and to the commissioner of social services or the director of the probation service, as appropriate, indicating that:

(1) a petition for adoption must be filed in the court in which the application for temporary guardianship has been brought within 45 days from the date of the signing of the consent to the adoption;

(2) any order or decree of temporary guardianship will expire no later than nine months following its issuance or upon the entry of a final order of adoption whichever is sooner, unless, upon application to the court, it is extended for good cause;

(3) any order or decree of temporary guardianship will terminate upon withdrawal or denial of a petition to adopt the child, unless the court orders a continuation of such order or decree;

(b) In addition to and without regard to the date set for the hearing of the petition, the clerk of the court shall calendar the case for the 45th day from the date of the signing of the consent to the adoption. If no petition for adoption has been filed by the 45th day, the court shall schedule a hearing and shall order the appropriate agency to conduct an investigation forthwith, if one had not been ordered previously.

§ 205.58. Proceedings for Certification as a Qualified Adoptive Parent or Parents

(a) Where the petition in a proceeding for certification as a qualified adoptive parent or parents alleges that petitioner or petitioners will cause a pre-placement investigation to be undertaken, the petition shall include the name and address of the disinterested person by whom such investigation will be conducted.

(b) The report of the disinterested person conducting the pre-placement investigation shall be filed by such person directly with the court, with a copy of such report delivered simultaneously to the applicant or applicants.

(c) The court shall order a report (1) from the statewide central register of child abuse and maltreatment setting forth whether the child or the petitioner is, or petitioners are, the subject of or another person named in an indicated report, as such terms are defined in section 412 of the Social Services Law, filed with such register; and (2) from the New York State Division of Criminal Justice Services setting forth any existing criminal record of such petitioner or petitioners, in accordance with section 115–d(3–a) of the Domestic Relations Law; provided, however, that where the petitioner(s) have been fingerprinted pursuant to section 378–a of the Social Services Law, the authorized agency in possession of a current criminal history summary report from the New York State Office of Children and Family Services may be requested to provide such report to the court in lieu of a report from the New York State Division of Criminal Justice Services.

§ 205.59. Calendaring of Proceedings for Adoption From an Authorized Agency

Proceedings for adoption from an authorized agency shall be calendared as follows:

(a) Within 60 days of the filing of the petition and documents specified in section 112–a of the Domestic Relations Law, the court shall schedule a review of said petition and documents to take place to determine if there is adequate basis for approving the adoption.

(b) If such basis is found, the court shall schedule the appearance of the adoptive parent(s) and child before the court, for approval of the adoption, within 30 days of the date of the review.

(c) If, upon the court's review, the court finds that there is not an adequate basis for approval of the adoption, the court shall direct such further hearings, submissions or appearances as may be required, and the proceeding shall be adjourned as required for such purposes.

§ 205.60. Designation of a Facility for the Questioning of Children in Custody (PINS)

Designation of facilities for the questioning of children pursuant to paragraph (ii) of subdivision (b) of section 724 of the Family Court Act shall be in accordance with section 205.20 of this Part.

Cross References

Family Court Act, see McKinney's Book 29A, Part 1.

§ 205.61. Authorization to Release a Child Taken Into Custody Before the Filing of a Petition (PINS)

When a child is brought to a detention facility pursuant to section 724(b)(iii) of the Family Court Act, the administrator responsible for operating the detention facility is authorized, before the filing of a petition, to release the child to the custody of a parent or other relative, guardian or legal custodian when the events that occasioned the taking into custody appear to involve a petition to determine whether the child is a person in need of supervision rather than a petition to determine whether the child is a juvenile delinquent.

Cross References

Family Court Act, see McKinney's Book 29A, Part 1.

§ 205.62. Preliminary Diversion Conferences and Procedures (PINS)

(a) Any person seeking to originate a proceeding under Article 7 of the Family Court Act to determine whether a child is a person in need of supervision shall first be referred to the designated lead diversion agency, which may be either the probation service or the local department of social services. The clerk shall not accept any petition for filing that does not have attached the notification from the lead diversion agency required by section 735 of the Family Court Act and, in the case of a petition filed by a school district or school official, documentation of the efforts made by the school district or official to remediate the child's school problems.

(b) The lead diversion agency shall begin to conduct preliminary conferences with the person seeking to originate the proceeding, the potential respondent and any other interested person, on the same day that such persons are referred to the diversion agency in order to gather information needed to assist in diversion of the case from petition, detention and placement through provision of or referral for services. The diversion agency shall permit any participant who is represented by a lawyer to be accompanied by the lawyer at any preliminary conference.

(c) During the preliminary conferences, the diversion agency shall ascertain, from the person seeking to originate the proceeding, a brief statement of the underlying events, an assessment of whether the child would benefit from diversion services, respite care and other alternatives to detention and, if known to that person, a brief statement of factors that would be of assistance to the court in determining whether the potential respondent should be detained or released in the event that a petition is filed. Such factors include whether there is a substantial probability that the respondent would not be likely to appear in court if released, whether he or she would be likely to benefit from diversion services, whether all available alternatives to detention have been exhausted and, in the case of a child 16 years of age or older, whether special circumstances exist warranting detention. The diversion agency shall also gather information to aid the court in its determination of whether remaining in the home would be contrary to the child's best interests and, where appropriate, whether reasonable efforts were made to prevent or eliminate the need for removal of the child from his or her home.

(d) At the first appearance at a conference by each of the persons listed in subdivision (b) of this section, the diversion agency shall inform such person concerning the function of the diversion process and that:

(1) he or she has the right to participate in the diversion process;

(2) the diversion agency is not authorized to and cannot compel any person to appear at any conference, produce any papers or visit any place, but if the person seeking to originate the proceeding does not cooperate with the diversion agency, he or she will not be able to file a petition. The court may direct the parties to cooperate with the diversion agency even after a petition has been filed;

(3) statements made to the diversion agency are subject to the confidentiality provisions contained in section 735 of the Family Court Act;

(4) if the diversion process is not successfully concluded for reasons other than the noncooperation of the person seeking to originate the proceeding, the diversion agency shall notify the person seeking to originate the proceeding in writing of that fact and that the person seeking to originate the proceeding is entitled to access to the court for the purpose of filing a petition; oral notification shall be confirmed in writing.

(e) If the diversion process is not successfully concluded, the diversion agency shall notify all the persons who participated therein, in writing, of that fact and of the reasons therefor, including a description of the services offered and efforts made to avert the filing of a petition. The notification shall be appended to the petition.

Cross References

Family Court Act, see McKinney's Book 29A, Part 1.

§ 205.63.   [Repealed]

§ 205.64.   Procedure When Remanded Child Absconds (PINS)

(a) When a child absconds from a facility to which he or she was remanded pursuant to section 739 of the Family Court Act, written notice of that fact shall be given within 48 hours by an authorized representative of the facility to the clerk of the court from which the remand was made. The notice shall state the name of the child, the docket number of the pending proceeding in which the child was remanded, the date on which the child absconded, and the efforts made to secure the return of the child. Every order of remand pursuant to section 739 shall include a direction embodying the requirements of this subdivision.

(b) Upon receipt of the written notice of absconding, the clerk shall cause the proceeding to be placed on the court calendar no later than the next court day for such action as the court may deem appropriate and shall give notice of such court date to the petitioner, presentment agency and law guardian or privately-retained counsel of the child.

Cross References

Family Court Act, see McKinney's Book 29A, Part 1.

§ 205.65.   Terms and Conditions of Order Adjourning a Proceeding in Contemplation of Dismissal Entered in Accordance With Section 749(a) of the Family Court Act (PINS)

(a) An order adjourning a proceeding in contemplation of dismissal pursuant to section 749(a) of the Family Court Act shall contain at least one of the following terms and conditions directing the respondent to:

(1) attend school regularly and obey all rules and regulations of the school;

(2) obey all reasonable commands of the parent or other person legally responsible for the respondent's care;

(3) avoid injurious or vicious activities;

(4) abstain from associating with named individuals;

(5) abstain from visiting designated places;

(6) abstain from the use of alcoholic beverages, hallucinogenic drugs, habit-forming drugs not lawfully prescribed for the respondent's use, or any other harmful or dangerous substance;

(7) cooperate with a mental health or other appropriate community facility to which the respondent is referred;

(8) restore property taken from the petitioner, complainant or victim, or replace property taken from the petitioner, complainant or victim, the cost of said replacement not to exceed $1,500;

(9) repair any damage to, or defacement of, the property of the petitioner, complainant or victim, the cost of said repair not to exceed $1,500;

(10) cooperate in accepting medical or psychiatric diagnosis and treatment, alcoholism or drug abuse treatment or counseling services and permit an agency delivering that service to furnish the court with information concerning the diagnosis, treatment or counseling;

(11) attend and complete an alcohol awareness program established pursuant to section 19.25 of the mental hygiene law;

(12) abstain from disruptive behavior in the home and in the community;

(13) comply with such other reasonable terms and conditions as may be permitted by law and as the court shall determine to be necessary or appropriate to ameliorate the conduct which gave rise to the filing of the petition.

(b) An order adjourning a proceeding in contemplation of dismissal pursuant to section 749(b) of the Family Court Act may set a time or times at which the probation service shall report to the court, orally or in writing, concerning compliance with the terms and conditions of said order.

(c) A copy of the order setting forth the terms and conditions imposed and the duration thereof shall be furnished to the respondent and to the parent or other person legally responsible for the respondent.

Cross References

Family Court Act, see McKinney's Book 29A, Part 1.

Forms

Order of adjournment in contemplation of dismissal, based on official form, see West's McKinney's Forms, Matrimonial and Family, § 28:07.

§ 205.66. Terms and Conditions of Order in Accordance With Sections 755 or 757 of the Family Court Act (PINS)

(a) An order suspending judgment entered pursuant to section 755 of the Family Court Act shall be reasonably related to the adjudicated acts or omissions of the respondent and shall contain at least one of the following terms and conditions directing the respondent to:

(1) attend school regularly and obey all rules and regulations of the school;

(2) obey all reasonable commands of the parent or other person legally responsible for the respondent's care;

(3) avoid injurious or vicious activities;

(4) abstain from associating with named individuals;

(5) abstain from visiting designated places;

(6) abstain from the use of alcoholic beverages, hallucinogenic drugs, habit forming drugs not lawfully prescribed for the respondent's use, or any other harmful or dangerous substance;

(7) cooperate with a mental health or other appropriate community facility to which the respondent is referred;

(8) make restitution or perform services for the public good;

(9) restore property taken from the petitioner, complainant or victim, or replace property taken from the petitioner, complainant or victim, the cost of said replacement not to exceed $1000;

(10) repair any damage to, or defacement of, the property of the petitioner, complainant or victim, the cost of said repair not to exceed $1000;

(11) abstain from disruptive behavior in the home and in the community;

(12) cooperate in accepting medical or psychiatric diagnosis and treatment, alcoholism or drug abuse treatment or counseling services, and permit an agency delivering that service to furnish the court with information concerning the diagnosis, treatment or counseling;

(13) attend and complete an alcohol awareness program established pursuant to section 19.25 of the Mental Hygiene Law;

(14) in a case in which respondent has been adjudicated for acts of willful, malicious, or unlawful damage to real or personal property maintained as a cemetery plot, grave, burial place or other place of internment of human remains, provide restitution by performing services for the maintenance and repair of such property; or

(15) comply with such other reasonable terms and conditions as the court shall determine to be neces-

sary or appropriate to ameliorate the conduct which gave rise to the filing of a petition.

(b) An order placing the respondent on probation in accordance with section 757 of the Family Court Act shall contain at least one of the following terms and conditions, in addition to any of the terms and conditions set forth in subdivision (a) of this section, directing the respondent to:

(1) meet with the assigned probation officer when directed to do so by that officer;

(2) permit the assigned probation officer to visit the respondent at home or at school;

(3) permit the assigned probation officer to obtain information from any person or agency from whom the respondent is receiving or was directed to receive diagnosis, treatment or counseling;

(4) permit the assigned probation officer to obtain information from the respondent's school;

(5) cooperate with the assigned probation officer in seeking to obtain and in accepting employment and employment counseling services;

(6) submit records and reports of earnings to the assigned probation officer when requested to do so by that officer;

(7) obtain permission from the assigned probation officer for any absence from the county or residence in excess of two weeks;

(8) attend and complete an alcohol awareness program established pursuant to section 19.25 of the mental hygiene law;

(9) do or refrain from doing any other specified act of omission or commission that, in the opinion of the court, is necessary and appropriate to implement or facilitate the order placing the respondent on probation;

(c) An order entered pursuant to section 754 of the Family Court Act may set a time or times at which the probation service shall report to the court, orally or in writing, concerning compliance with the terms and conditions of said order.

(d) A copy of the order setting forth the terms and conditions imposed and the duration thereof shall be furnished to the respondent and to the parent or other person legally responsible for the respondent.

Cross References

Executive Law, see McKinney's Book 18.

Family Court Act, see McKinney's Book 29A, Part 1.

Forms

Order of fact-finding and disposition based on official form, see West's McKinney's Forms, Matrimonial and Family, § 28:10.

§ 205.67. Procedures for Compliance With Adoption and Safe Families Act (Persons in Need of Supervision Proceeding)

(a) Pretrial detention; required findings. In any case in which detention is ordered by the court pursuant to section 728 or 739 of the Family Court Act, the court shall make additional, specific written findings regarding the following issues:

(1) whether the continuation of the respondent in his or her home would be contrary to his or her best interests; and

(2) whether reasonable efforts, where appropriate, were made, prior to the date of the court hearing that resulted in the detention order, to prevent or eliminate the need for removal of the respondent from his or her home, or, if the respondent had been removed from his or her home prior to such court hearing, whether reasonable efforts, where appropriate, were made to make it possible for the respondent to safely return home.

The court may request the petitioner, presentment agency, if any, and the local probation department to provide information to the court to aid in its determinations and may also consider information provided by the law guardian.

(b) Motion for an order that reasonable efforts are not required. A motion for a judicial determination, pursuant to section 754(2)(b) of the Family Court Act, that reasonable efforts to prevent or eliminate the need for removal of the respondent from his or her home or to make it possible to reunify the respondent with his or her parents are not required shall be governed by section 205.16 of this Part.

(c) Placement; required findings. In any case in which the court is considering ordering placement pursuant to section 756 of the Family Court Act, the petitioner, presentment agency, if any, local probation department and local commissioner of social services shall provide information to the court to aid in its required determination of the following issues:

(1) whether continuation in the respondent's home would be contrary to his or her best interests, and, if the respondent was removed from his or her home prior to the date of such hearing, whether such removal was in his or her best interests;

(2) whether reasonable efforts, where appropriate, were made, prior to the date of the dispositional hearing, to prevent or eliminate the need for removal of the respondent from his or her home, and, if the respondent was removed from his or her home prior to the date of such hearing, whether reasonable efforts, where appropriate, were made to make it possible for the respondent to return safely home. If the court determines that reasonable efforts to prevent or eliminate the need for removal of the respondent from his or her home were not made, but that the lack of

such efforts was appropriate under the circumstances, the court order shall include such a finding;

(3) in the case of a respondent who has attained the age of 16, the services needed, if any, to assist the respondent to make the transition from foster care to independent living; and

(4) in the case of an order of placement specifying a particular authorized agency or foster care provider, the position of the local commissioner of social services regarding such placement.

(d) Permanency hearing; extension of placement.

(1) A petition for a permanency hearing and, if applicable, an extension of placement, pursuant to section 756–a of the Family Court Act, shall be filed at least 60 days prior to the expiration of one year following the respondent's entry into foster care; provided, however, that if the Family Court makes a determination, pursuant to section 754(2)(b) of the Family Court Act, that reasonable efforts are not required to prevent or eliminate the need for removal of the respondent from his or her home or to make it possible to reunify the respondent with his or her parents, the permanency hearing shall be held within 30 days of such finding and the petition for the permanency hearing shall be filed and served on an expedited basis as directed by the court.

(2) Following the initial permanency hearing in a case in which the respondent remains in placement, a petition for a subsequent permanency hearing and, if applicable, extension of placement, shall be filed at least 60 days prior to the expiration of one year following the date of the preceding permanency hearing.

(3) The permanency petition shall include, but not be limited to, the following: the date by which the permanency hearing must be held; the date by which any subsequent permanency petition must be filed; the proposed permanency goal for the child; the reasonable efforts, if any, undertaken to achieve the child's return to his or her parents and other permanency goal; the visitation plan for the child and his or her sibling or siblings and, if parental rights have not been terminated, for his or her parent or parents; and current information regarding the status of services ordered by the court to be provided, as well as other services that have been provided, to the child and his or her parent or parents.

(4) In all cases, the permanency petition shall be accompanied by the most recent service plan containing, at minimum: the child's permanency goal and projected time-frame for its achievement; the reasonable efforts that have been undertaken and are planned to achieve the goal; impediments, if any, that have been encountered in achieving the goal; the services required to achieve the goal; and a plan for the release or conditional release of the child, including information regarding steps to be taken to enroll the child in a school or, as applicable, vocational program.

§§ 205.68, 205.69.   [Reserved]

§ 205.70. Designation of Persons to Inform Complainant of Procedures Available for the Institution of Family Offense Proceedings

Pursuant to section 812 of the Family Court Act, the following persons are hereby designated to inform any petitioner or complainant seeking to bring a proceeding under article 8 of the Family Court Act of the procedures available for the institution of these proceedings, before such proceeding or action is commenced:

(a) Within the City of New York:

(1) the commanding officer of the police precinct wherein the offense is alleged to have occurred; or

(2) any police officer attached to such precinct who is designated by such commanding officer.

(b) Outside the City of New York:

(1) the commanding officer of any law enforcement agency providing police service in the county wherein the offense is alleged to have occurred; or

(2) any police officer attached to such law enforcement agency who is designated by such commanding officer;

(c) the district attorney, corporation counsel or county attorney in the county wherein the offense is alleged to have occurred, or any assistant district attorney, assistant corporation counsel or assistant county attorney who is designated by such district attorney, corporation counsel or county attorney;

(d) any probation officer in the employ of the State of New York, or any political subdivision thereof, providing probation service in the criminal court or in the intake unit of the Family Court in the county in which a proceeding may be instituted;

(e) the Clerk of the Family Court and the Clerk of the criminal court located in the county in which the proceeding may be instituted, or any clerk in that court designated by such Clerk of the Family or criminal court;

(f) judges of all local criminal courts outside the City of New York having jurisdiction over the alleged offense.

Cross References

Family Court Act, see McKinney's Book 29A, Part 1.

§ 205.71. Preliminary Probation Conferences and Procedures (Family Offenses)

(a) Any person seeking to file a family offense petition under article 8 of the Family Court Act may first be referred to the probation service concerning the advisability of filing a petition.

(b) Upon such referral, the probation service shall inform such person:

(1) concerning the procedures available for the institution of family offense proceedings, including the information set forth in subdivision 2 of section 812 of the Family Court Act;

(2) that the person seeking to file a family offense petition is entitled to request that the probation service confer with him or her, the potential respondent and any other interested person concerning the advisability of filing a petition requesting:

   (i) an order of protection;

   (ii) a temporary order of protection;

   (iii) the use of the court's conciliation procedure.

(c) The probation service, at the request of the person seeking to file a family offense petition, shall commence conducting preliminary conferences concerning the advisability of filing a petition with that person, the potential respondent and any other interested person no later than the next regularly-scheduled court day. The probation service shall permit any participant who is represented by a lawyer to be accompanied at any preliminary conference by the lawyer, who shall be identified by the probation officer to the other party, and shall not discourage any person from seeking to file a petition.

(d) At the first appearance at a conference by each of the persons listed in subdivision (c) hereof, the probation service shall inform such person concerning the function and limitations of, and the alternatives to, the adjustment process, and that:

(1) the purpose of the adjustment process is to attempt through conciliation and agreement to arrive at a cessation of the conduct forming the basis of the family offense complaint without filing a petition in court;

(2) the probation service may confer with the persons listed in subdivision (c) of this section if it shall appear to the probation service that:

   (i) there is a reasonable likelihood that the adjustment process will result in a cessation of the conduct forming the basis of the family offense complaint; and

   (ii) there is no reasonable likelihood that the potential respondent will, during the period of the adjustment, inflict or threaten to inflict physical injury on the person seeking to obtain relief or any other member of the same family or household if the filing of a petition is delayed;

(3) the probation service is not authorized to, and shall not, compel any person, including the person seeking to file a family offense; petition, to appear at any conference, produce any papers or visit any place;

(4) the person seeking to file a family offense petition is entitled to request that the probation service confer with him or her, the potential respondent and any other interested person concerning the advisability of filing a family offense petition under article 8 of the Family Court Act;

(5) if the assistance of the probation service is not requested, or if requested, is subsequently declined, the person seeking to file a family offense petition is entitled to have access to the court at any time, even after having consented to an extension of the adjustment period, and may proceed to file a family offense petition;

(6) no statements made during any preliminary conference with the probation service may be admitted into evidence at a fact-finding hearing held in the Family Court or at any proceeding conducted in a criminal court at any time prior to conviction;

(7) the adjustment process must commence within seven days from the date of the request for a conference, may continue for a period of two months from the date of that request and may be twice extended by the court for two periods of up to 60 days each upon written application to the court containing the consent and signature of the person seeking to file a family offense petition;

(8) if a petition is filed, a temporary order of protection may be issued for good cause shown, and unless a petition is filed, the court may not issue any order of protection;

(9) if the adjustment process is not successful, the persons participating therein shall be notified in writing of that fact, and that the person seeking to file a family offense petition is entitled to access to the court for that purpose;

(10) if the matter has been successfully adjusted, the persons participating therein shall be notified in writing of that fact;

(11) if the adjustment of the matter results in a voluntary agreement concerning the cessation of the offensive conduct forming the basis of the family offense complaint:

   (i) it shall be reduced to writing by the probation service, signed by both parties to it and submitted to the Family Court for approval;

   (ii) if the court approves it, the court may, without further hearing, enter an order of protection pursuant to section 823 of the Family Court Act in accordance with the agreement;

   (iii) the order when entered shall be binding on the respondent and shall in all respects be a valid order.

(e) If the adjustment process is not commenced, the probation service shall give written notice to the persons listed in subdivision (c) that:

(1) the adjustment process was not commenced and the reasons therefor;

(2) the person seeking to file a family offense petition is entitled to access to the court for that purpose;

(3) if applicable, the adjustment process was not commenced on the ground that the court would not have jurisdiction over the case, and the person seeking to file a family offense petition may test the question of the court's jurisdiction by filing a petition.

Cross References

Family Court Act, see McKinney's Book 29A, Part 1.

§ 205.72. Duties of the Probation Service and Procedures Relating to the Adjustment Process (Family Offenses)

(a) If the assistance of the probation service is requested by the person seeking to file a family offense petition, the adjustment process shall commence within seven days from the request. The probation service shall permit any participant who is represented by a lawyer to be accompanied at any conference by the lawyer, who shall be identified by the probation officer to the other party, and shall not discourage any person from seeking to file a petition.

(b) If an extension of the period of the adjustment process is sought, the probation service shall, with the written consent of the person seeking to file a family offense petition, apply in writing to the court and shall set forth the services rendered, the date of commencement of those services, the degree of success achieved, the services proposed to be rendered and a statement by the assigned probation officer: that there is no imminent risk that if an extension of the period is granted the potential respondent will, during the extended period of adjustment, endanger the health or safety of the person seeking to file a family offense petition or any other member of the same family or household, and the facts upon which the opinion is based; and that the matter will not be successfully adjusted unless an extension is granted.

(c) The probation service shall discontinue its efforts at adjustment if at any time:

(1) the person seeking to file a family offense petition or the potential respondent requests that it do so;

(2) it appears to the probation service that:

(i) there is no reasonable likelihood that a cessation of the conduct forming the basis of the family offense complaint will result; or

(ii) there is an imminent risk that the potential respondent will inflict or threaten to inflict physical injury upon the person seeking to file a family offense petition or upon any other member of the same family or household; or

(iii) the potential respondent has inflicted or threatened to inflict physical injury on the person seeking to file a family offense petition or any other member of the same family or household since efforts at adjustment began.

(d) If the adjustment process is not successfully concluded, the probation service shall notify in writing all the persons who participated therein:

(1) that the adjustment process has not been successfully concluded and the reasons therefor; and

(2) that the person seeking to file a family offense petition is entitled to access to the court for that purpose.

(e) If the adjustment process results in an agreement for the cessation of the conduct forming the basis of the family offense complaint:

(1) it shall be reduced to writing by the probation service, shall be signed by both parties to it, and shall be submitted to the court, together with a petition for approval of the agreement and a proposed order incorporating the agreement;

(2) if the agreement is approved by the court, a copy of the order shall be furnished by the probation service to the person seeking to file a family offense petition and the potential respondent, in person if they are present, and by mail if their presence has been dispensed with by the court.

§ 205.73. Record and Report of Unexecuted Warrants Issued Pursuant to Section 827 of the Family Court Act (Family Offenses)

(a) The clerk of court for the Family Court in each county shall obtain and keep a record of unexecuted warrants issued pursuant to section 827 of the Family Court Act.

(b) At the end of each six-month period, on the first of January and on the first of July in each year, a report concerning all unexecuted warrants issued pursuant to section 827 of the Family Court Act shall be made and filed with the Office of Court Administration on a form to be supplied by the Office of Court Administration.

Cross References

Family Court Act, see McKinney's Book 29A, Part 1.

§ 205.74. Terms and Conditions of Order in Accordance With Sections 841(b), (c), (d) and (e), 842 and 843 of the Family Court Act (Family Offenses)

(a) An order suspending judgment entered pursuant to section 841(b) of the Family Court Act shall contain at least one of the following terms and conditions directing the respondent to:

(1) stay away from the residence of the person against whom the family offense was committed;

(2) stay away from the place of employment or place of education attended by the person against whom the family offense was committed;

(3) abstain from communicating by any means, including, but not limited to, telephone, letter, e-mail or other electronic means with the person against whom the family offense was committed;

(4) abstain from repeating the conduct adjudicated a family offense at the fact-finding hearing;

(5) cooperate in seeking to obtain and in accepting medical or psychiatric diagnosis and treatment, alcoholism or drug abuse treatment, or employment or counseling or child guidance services, or participate in a batterer's educational program designed to help end violent behavior, and permit information to be obtained by the court from any person or agency from whom the respondent is receiving or was directed to receive such services or participate in such program;

(6) allow medical or psychiatric treatment to be furnished to the person against whom the family offense was committed, or any other named family member or household member who is a dependent of the respondent and whose need for medical or psychiatric treatment was occasioned, in whole or in part, by the conduct adjudicated a family offense;

(7) cooperate with the person against whom the family offense was committed, the head of the household or parent, in maintaining the home or household;

(8) pay restitution in an amount not to exceed ten thousand dollars;

(9) comply with such other reasonable terms and conditions as the court shall deem necessary or appropriate to ameliorate the acts or omissions which gave rise to the filing of the petition.

(b) An order placing the respondent on probation in accordance with section 841(c) of the Family Court Act shall contain at least one of the following terms and conditions, directing the respondent to:

(1) observe one or more of the terms and conditions set forth in subdivision (a) of this section;

(2) meet with the assigned probation officer when directed to do so by that officer;

(3) cooperate with the assigned probation officer in arranging for and allowing visitation in the family residence or household;

(4) cooperate in seeking to obtain and in accepting medical treatment, psychiatric diagnosis and treatment, alcoholism or drug abuse treatment, or employment or counseling services, or participate in a batterer's educational program designed to help end violent behavior, and permit the assigned probation officer to obtain information from any person or agency from whom the respondent is receiving or was directed to receive such services or participate in such program.

(c) An order of protection entered in accordance with section 841(d) of the Family Court Act may, in addition to the terms and conditions enumerated in sections 842 and 842–a of the Family Court Act, require the petitioner, respondent or both, or, if before the court, any other member of the household, to:

(1) abstain from communicating by any means, including, but not limited to, telephone, letter, e-mail or other electronic means with the person against whom the family offense was committed;

(2) stay away from the place of employment or place of education attended by the person against whom the family offense was committed, of a child or a parent, or of another member of the same family or household;

(3) refrain from engaging in any conduct which interferes with the custody of a child as set forth in the order;

(4) cooperate in seeking to obtain and in accepting medical treatment, psychiatric diagnosis and treatment, alcoholism or drug abuse treatment, or employment or counseling services, or participate in a batterer's educational program designated to help end violent behavior, and permit information to be obtained by the court from any person or agency from whom the respondent is receiving or was directed to receive such services or participate in such program;

(5) pay restitution in an amount not to exceed ten thousand dollars;

(6) comply with such other reasonable terms and conditions as the court may deem necessary and appropriate to ameliorate the acts or omissions which gave rise to the filing of the petition.

(d) A copy of the order setting forth its duration and the terms and conditions imposed shall be furnished to the respondent and to the person or persons against whom the family offense was committed.

(e) Each order issued pursuant to section 841(b), (c), or (e) of the Family Court Act shall contain a written statement informing the respondent that a failure to obey the order may result in commitment to jail for a term not to exceed six months. Each order issued pursuant to section 828 or 841(d) shall contain a written statement informing the respondent that a failure to obey the order may result in incarceration up to seven years.

Cross References

Family Court Act, see McKinney's Book 29A, Part 1.

§§ 205.75 to 205.79. [Reserved]

§ 205.80. Procedure When Remanded Child Absconds (Child Protective Proceeding)

(a) When a child absconds from a shelter or holding facility to which the child was remanded pursuant to sections 1027(b) or 1051(d) of the Family Court Act, written notice of that fact, signed by an authorized representative of the facility, shall be sent within 48 hours to the clerk of the court from which the remand was made. The notice shall state the name of the child, the docket number of the pending proceeding in which the child was remanded, the date on which the child absconded, and the efforts made to secure the return of the child. Every order of remand pursuant to sections 1027(b) or 1051(d) shall include a direction embodying the requirement of this subdivision.

(b) Upon receipt of a written notice of absconding, the clerk of the court shall cause the proceeding to be placed on the calendar for the next court day for such action as the court shall deem appropriate and shall give notice of such court date to the petitioner and law guardian or privately-retained counsel of the child.

Cross References

Family Court Act, see McKinney's Book 29A, Part 1.

§ 205.81. Procedures for Compliance with Adoption and Safe Families Act (Child Protective Proceeding)

(a) Temporary removal; required findings. In any case in which removal of the child is ordered by the court pursuant to part 2 of article 10 of the Family Court Act, the court shall set a date certain for a permanency hearing in accordance with section 205.17 of this Part and shall make additional, specific written findings regarding the following issues:

(1) whether the continuation of the child in his or her home would be contrary to his or her best interests; and

(2) whether reasonable efforts, where appropriate, were made, prior to the date of the court hearing that resulted in the removal order, to prevent or eliminate the need for removal of the child from his or her home, and, if the child had been removed from his or her home prior to such court hearing, whether reasonable efforts, where appropriate, were made to make it possible for the child to safely return home. The petitioner shall provide information to the court to aid in its determinations. The court may also consider information provided by respondents, the law guardian, the non-respondent parent or parents, relatives and other suitable persons..

(b) Motion for an order that reasonable efforts are not required. A motion for a judicial determination, pursuant to section 1039–b of the Family Court Act, that reasonable efforts to prevent or eliminate the need for removal of the child from his or her home or to make it possible to reunify the child with his or her parents are not required shall be governed by section 205.16 of this Part.

(c) Placement; required findings. In any case in which the court is considering ordering placement pursuant to section 1055 of the Family Court Act, the petitioner shall provide information to the court to aid in its required determination of the following issues:

(1) whether continuation in the child's home would be contrary to his or her best interests and, if the child was removed from his or her home prior to or at the time of the dispositional hearing and a judicial determination has not yet been made, whether such removal was in his or her best interests;

(2) whether reasonable efforts, where appropriate, were made, prior to the date of the dispositional hearing, to prevent or eliminate the need for removal of the child from his or her home and, if the child was removed from his or her home prior to the date of such hearing, whether reasonable efforts, where appropriate, were made to make it possible for the child to return safely home. If the court determines that reasonable efforts to prevent or eliminate the need for removal of the child from his or her home were not made, but that the lack of such efforts was appropriate under the circumstances, the court order shall include such a finding;

(3) in the case of a child for whom the permanency plan is adoption, guardianship or some other permanent living arrangement other than reunification with the parent or parents of the child, whether reasonable efforts have been made to make and finalize such other permanency plan;

(4) in the case of a respondent who has attained the age of 14, the services needed, if any, to assist the respondent to make the transition from foster care to independent living; and

(5) in the case of an order of placement specifying a particular authorized agency or foster care provider, the position of the local commissioner of social services regarding such placement.

(d) Permanency hearing. If the child or children is or are placed in foster care or directly placed with a relative or other suitable person, the court shall set a date certain for a permanency hearing under Article 10–A of the Family Court Act. All permanency hearings under Article 10–A shall be governed by section 205.17 of this Part.

§ 205.82. Record and Report of Unexecuted Warrants Issued Pursuant to Article Ten of the Family Court Act (Child Protective Proceeding)

(a) The clerk of court for the Family Court in each county shall obtain and keep a record of unexecuted warrants issued pursuant to article ten of the Family Court Act.

(b) At the end of each six-month period, on the first of January and on the first of July in each year, a report concerning all unexecuted warrants issued pursuant to article ten of the Family Court Act shall be made and filed with the Office of Court Administration on a form to be supplied by the Office of Court Administration.

Cross References
Family Court Act, see McKinney's Book 29A, Part 1.

§ 205.83. Terms and Conditions of Order in Accordance With Sections 1053, 1054, and 1057 of the Family Court Act (Child Protective Proceeding)

(a) An order suspending judgment entered pursuant to section 1052 of the Family Court Act shall, where the child is in foster care, set forth the visitation plan between respondent and the child and between the child and his or her sibling or siblings, if any, and shall require the agency to notify the respondent of case conferences. A copy of the order, along with a current service plan, shall be furnished to the respondent. Any order suspending judgment entered pursuant to section 1052 of the Family Court Act shall contain at least one of the following terms and conditions that relate to the adjudicated acts or omissions of the respondent, directing the respondent to:

(1) refrain from or eliminate specified acts or conditions found at the fact-finding hearing to constitute or to have caused neglect or abuse;

(2) provide adequate and proper food, housing, clothing, medical care, and for the other needs of the child;

(3) provide proper care and supervision to the child and cooperate in obtaining, accepting or allowing medical or psychiatric diagnosis or treatment, alcoholism or drug abuse treatment, counseling or child guidance services for the child;

(4) take proper steps to insure the child's regular attendance at school; and

(5) cooperate in obtaining and accepting medical treatment, psychiatric diagnosis and treatment, alcoholism or drug abuse treatment, employment or counseling services, or child guidance, and permit a child protective agency to obtain information from any person or agency from whom the respondent or the child is receiving or was directed to receive treatment or counseling.

(b) An order pursuant to section 1054 of the Family Court Act placing the person to whose custody the child is released under the supervision of a child protective agency, social services officer or duly authorized agency, or an order pursuant to section 1057 placing the respondent under the supervision of a child protective agency, social services official or authorized agency, shall contain at least one of the following terms and conditions requiring the respondent to:

(1) observe any of the terms and conditions set forth in subdivision (a) of this section;

(2) cooperate with the supervising agency in remedying specified acts or omissions found at the fact-finding hearing to constitute or to have caused the neglect or abuse;

(3) meet with the supervising agency alone and with the child when directed to do so by that agency;

(4) report to the supervising agency when directed to do so by that agency;

(5) cooperate with the supervising agency in arranging for and allowing visitation in the home or other place;

(6) notify the supervising agency immediately of any change of residence or employment of the respondent or of the child; or

(7) do or refrain from doing any other specified act of omission or commission that, in the judgment of the court, is necessary to protect the child from injury or mistreatment and to help safeguard the physical, mental and emotional well-being of the child.

(c) When an order is made pursuant to section 1054 or 1057 of the Family Court Act:

(1) the court shall notify the supervising agency in writing of its designation to act and shall furnish to that agency a copy of the order setting forth the terms and conditions imposed;

(2) the order shall be accompanied by a written statement informing the respondent that a willful failure to obey the terms and conditions imposed may result in commitment to jail for a term not to exceed six months; and

(3) the court may, if it concludes that it is necessary for the protection of the child, direct the supervising agency to furnish a written report to the court at stated intervals not to exceed six months, setting forth whether, and to what extent:

(i) there has been any alteration in the respondent's maintenance of the child that is adversely affecting the child's health or well-being;

(ii) there is compliance with the terms and conditions of the order of supervision; and

(iii) the supervising agency has furnished supporting services to the respondent.

(d) A copy of the order, setting forth its duration and the terms and conditions imposed, shall be furnished to the respondent.

(e) If an order of supervision is issued in conjunction with an order of placement pursuant to section 1055 of the Family Court Act, the order shall, unless otherwise ordered by the court, be coextensive in duration with the order of placement and shall extend until the completion of the permanency hearing. The order of supervision shall be reviewed along with the placement at the permanency hearing.

Cross References

Family Court Act, see McKinney's Book 29A, Articles 10 and 10–A.

§ 205.84. [Repealed]

§ 205.85. Procedure When a Child Who Has Been Placed Absconds (Child Protective Proceeding)

(a) When a child placed pursuant to section 1055 of the Family Court Act absconds, written notice of that fact shall be sent within 48 hours to the clerk of the court from which the placement was made. The notice shall be signed by the custodial person or by an authorized representative of the place of placement and shall state the name of the child, the docket number of the proceeding in which the child was placed, the date on which the child absconded, and the efforts made to secure the return of the child. Every order of placement pursuant to section 1055 shall include a direction embodying the requirement of this subdivision.

(b) Upon receipt of the written notice of absconding, the clerk of the court shall cause the proceeding to be placed on the calendar no later than the next court day for such action as the court may deem appropriate.

Cross References

Family Court Act, see McKinney's Book 29A, Part 1.

§ 205.86. Video Recording of Interviews of Children Alleged to Have Been Sexually Abused

(a) In any case in which, pursuant to section 1038(c) of the Family Court Act, a video recording is made of an expert's interview with a child alleged to have been sexually abused, the attorney for the party requesting the video recording, or the party, if unrepresented, shall promptly after the video recording has been completed:

(1) cause to be prepared a duplicate video recording, certified by the preparer as a complete and unaltered copy of the original video recording;

(2) deposit the original video recording, certified by the preparer as the original, with the Clerk of the Family Court; and

(3) submit for signature to the judge before whom the case is pending a proposed order authorizing the retention of the duplicate video recording by the attorney, (or the party, if unrepresented) and directing that retention be in conformance with this section.

Both the original video recording and the duplicate thereof shall be labelled with the name of the case, the Family Court docket number, the name of the child, the name of the interviewer, the name and address of the technician who prepared the video recording, the date of the interview, and the total elapsed time of the video recording.

(b) Up receipt, the clerk shall hold the original video recording in a secure place limited to access only by authorized court personnel.

(c) **(1)** Except as provided in paragraph (2) of this subdivision, the duplicate video recording shall remain in the custody of the attorney for the party who requested it, or the party, if not represented (the "custodian").

(2) The duplicate video recording shall be available for pretrial disclosure pursuant to article 10 of the Family Court Act and any other applicable law. Consistent therewith, the custodian shall permit an attorney for a party, or the party, if not represented by counsel, to borrow the duplicate video recording for a reasonable period of time so that it may be viewed, provided the person to whom it is loaned first certifies, by affidavit filed with the court, that he or she will comply with this subdivision.

(3) A person borrowing the duplicate video recording as provided in paragraph (2) of this subdivision shall not lend it or otherwise surrender custody thereof to any person other than the custodian, and upon returning such video recording to the custodian, such person shall certify, by affidavit filed with the court, that he or she has complied with the provisions of this subdivision.

(4) Subject to court order otherwise, the duplicate video recording may not be viewed by any person other than a party or his or her counsel or prospective expert witnesses. No copy of the duplicate video recording may be made.

(d) Failure to comply with the provisions of this rule shall be punishable by contempt of court.

PART 206. UNIFORM RULES FOR THE COURT OF CLAIMS

§ 206.1. Application of Part; Waiver; Special Rules; Definitions

(a) Application. This Part shall be applicable to all actions and proceedings in the Court of Claims.

(b) Waiver. For good cause shown, and in the interests of justice, the court in an action or proceeding may waive compliance with any of these rules other than section 206.2 and 206.3 unless prohibited from doing so by statute or by rule of the Chief Judge.

(c) Application of the Court of Claims Act and the Civil Practice Law and Rules. The provisions of this Part shall be construed consistent with the Court of Claims Act, and matters not covered by these provisions or the Court of Claims Act shall be governed by the Civil Practice Law and Rules (CPLR).

(d) Definitions.

(1) *"Presiding Judge."* Reference in these rules to the Presiding Judge shall mean the judge of the Court of Claims designated as such by the Governor pursuant to section 2 of the Court of Claims Act.

(2) *"Clerk."* References to the clerk in the Court of Claims Act and in these rules are to the Chief Clerk of the Court in Albany, whose mailing address is:

New York State Court of Claims
P.O. Box 7344—Capitol Station
Albany, New York 12224

and whose filing office is located at:

Justice Building—7th Floor
Governor Nelson A. Rockefeller Empire State Plaza
Albany, New York

(3) "Chief Administrator of the Courts" in this Part also includes a designee of the Chief Administrator.

(4) Unless otherwise defined in this Part, or the context otherwise requires, all terms used in this Part shall have the same meaning as they have in the Court of Claims Act and CPLR.

Cross References

CPLR, see McKinney's Book 7B.

Court of Claims Act, see McKinney's Book 29A, Part 2.

§ 206.2. Terms and Parts of Court

(a) Terms of Court. A term of court is a four-week session of court, and there shall be 13 terms of court in a year, unless otherwise provided in the annual schedule of terms established by the Chief Administrator of the Courts, which also shall specify the dates of such terms.

(b) Parts of Court.

(1) A part of court is a designated unit of the court in which specified business of the court is to be conducted by a judge or quasi-judicial officer.

(2) There shall be such parts of the Court of Claims as may be authorized from time to time by the Chief Administrator of the Courts.

§ 206.3. Individual Assignment System; Structure

(a) General. There shall be established for all actions heard in the Court of Claims an individual assignment system which provides for the continuous supervision of each action by a single judge. Except as otherwise may be authorized by the Chief Administrator or by these rules, every action shall be assigned and heard pursuant to the individual assignment system.

(b) Assignments. Except as otherwise provided by these rules, actions shall be assigned to the judges of the court upon the filing of a claim with the court. Assignments shall be made by the clerk pursuant to a method of random selection authorized by the Chief Administrator. The judge thereby assigned shall be known as the "assigned judge" with respect to that matter and, except as otherwise provided in subdivision (c), shall conduct all further proceedings therein.

(c) Exceptions.

(1) Assignment of public construction contract claims and prisoner pro se claims shall be made at a time and in a manner authorized by the Chief Administrator.

(2) Where the requirements of matters already assigned to a judge are such as to limit the ability of that judge to handle additional cases, the Chief Administrator may authorize that new assignments to that judge be suspended until the judge is able to handle additional cases.

(3) The Chief Administrator may authorize the establishment of special categories of actions, including but not limited to public construction contract actions, prisoner pro se actions, medical malpractice actions, appropriation actions and actions requiring protracted consideration, for assignment to judges specially assigned to hear such actions. Where more than one judge is specially assigned to hear a particular category of action or proceeding, the assignment of such actions or proceedings to the judges so assigned shall be at random.

(4) The Chief Administrator may authorize the assignment of one or more special reserve trial judges. Such judges may be assigned matters for trial in exceptional circumstances where the needs of the court require such assignment.

(5) Matters requiring immediate disposition may be assigned to a judge designated to hear such matters when the assigned judge is not available.

(6) The Chief Administrator may authorize the transfer of any action and any matter relating to an action from one judge to another in accordance with the needs of the court.

§ 206.4. Court Districts; Structure

(a) The court shall be divided into eight districts comprised of the counties listed below. The clerk shall prepare calendars composed of claims arising within the counties constituting said district.

ALBANY DISTRICT

Albany	Essex	Rensselaer	Ulster
Clinton	Franklin	Saratoga	Warren
Columbia	Greene	Schenectady	Washington

BINGHAMTON DISTRICT

Broome	Delaware	Schuyler	Tioga
Chemung	Otsego	Steuben	Yates
Chenango	Schoharie	Sullivan	

BUFFALO DISTRICT

Allegany	Chautauqua	Erie	Niagara
Cattaraugus			

NEW YORK DISTRICT

Bronx	Nassau	Queens	Suffolk
Kings	New York	Richmond	

ROCHESTER DISTRICT

Genesee	Monroe	Orleans	Wyoming
Livingston	Ontario		

SYRACUSE DISTRICT

Cayuga	Jefferson	Oswego	Tompkins
Cortland	Onondaga	Seneca	Wayne

UTICA DISTRICT

Fulton	Herkimer	Madison	Oneida
Hamilton	Lewis	Montgomery	St. Lawrence

WHITE PLAINS DISTRICT

Dutchess	Putnam	Rockland	Westchester
Orange			

(b) No claim shall be transferred for trial from one district to another unless ordered upon motion on notice setting forth the grounds, or upon order of the Presiding Judge.

§ 206.5. Papers Filed With the Court; Numbering Claims

(a) A claim shall be filed by delivering it to the office of the clerk either in person or by facsimile transmission or electronic means pursuant to sections 206.5–a and 206.5–aa of these rules, respectively, or upon the receipt thereof at the clerk's office by mail. Except where filing is made by facsimile transmission or electronic means, at the time of filing of the original claim, the claimant shall file in the clerk's office two copies thereof. Proof of service on the defendant shall be filed in paper form or by facsimile transmission or electronic means with the clerk within ten days of such service. Upon the filing, other than by electronic means, of a claim that is subject to the FBEM ("Filing by Electronic Means") pilot program, the clerk shall provide the claimant with a copy of a Notice Regarding Availability of Electronic Filing in a form approved by the Chief Administrator of the Courts. Regardless of the manner in which a claim is filed, where such claim is subject to the FBEM pilot program and the claimant desires that the action be subject to FBEM, he or she shall serve the defendant with a Notice of Identifying the Claim as Subject to Electronic Filing in a manner authorized by paragraph (1) of subdivision (g) of section 202.5–b of these rules. Such Notice Identifying the Claim as Subject to Electronic Filing shall read substantially as follows:

NOTICE IDENTIFYING THE CLAIM AS SUBJECT TO ELECTRONIC FILING

STATE OF NEW YORK—COURT OF CLAIMS

CLAIM NO. ___

Claimant

- against -

THE STATE OF NEW YORK

Defendant.

Please take notice that, pursuant to chapter 110 of the Laws of 2002, and section 206.5–aa of the Uniform Rules for the Court of Claims (22 NYCRR § 206.5–aa), all papers to be filed or served in this claim shall be filed or served electronically by the parties as provided under section 206.5–aa unless, in accordance with such section: (i) a judge orders otherwise, or (ii) the papers involved are not permitted to be filed or served electronically.

(b) The clerk shall notify the claimant or the claimant's attorney of the date of filing of the claim. The clerk shall number each claim in the order of its filing and advise the claimant or the claimant's attorney of the claim number and of the name of the assigned judge. Thereafter such number and judge's name shall appear on the outside cover and first page to the right of the caption of every paper tendered for filing in the action. A small claim filed pursuant to article 6 of the Eminent Domain Procedure Law shall be numbered in the same manner as other claims except its number shall be followed by the suffix "s." In addition to complying with the provisions of CPLR 2101, unless the court shall otherwise permit in the interest of justice, every paper filed in court shall have annexed thereto appropriate proof of service on all parties where required, and if typewritten, shall have at least double space between each line, except quotations and the names and addresses of attorneys appearing in the action, and shall have at least one-inch margins. In addition, every paper filed in court, other than an exhibit or printed form, shall contain writing on one side only, except that papers that are fastened on the side may contain writing on both sides. Papers that are stapled or bound securely shall not be rejected for filing simply because they are not bound with a backer of any kind.

(c) All other papers required to be served upon a party shall be filed with the clerk either before service or within a reasonable time thereafter, except demands for a verified bill of particulars and bills of particulars, together with proof of service, which shall be filed within ten days after service thereof, and claims, which shall be filed within the times prescribed by the Court of Claims Act. If filing these papers in paper form, a party shall file an original and two copies thereof.

(d) Submission of Papers to Judge. All papers for signature or consideration of the court shall be presented to the clerk. No papers shall be submitted directly to a judge or a member of his or her staff, unless the judge so directs, in which event a copy shall be filed in the clerk's office at the first available opportunity. All papers for any judge that are filed in the clerk's office shall be promptly delivered to the judge by the clerk. The papers shall be clearly addressed to the judge for whom they are intended and prominently show the nature of the papers, the title and claim number of the action in which they are filed, the assigned judge's name, and the name of the attorney or party submitting them.

Cross References

CPLR, see McKinney's Book 7B.

EDPL, see McKinney's Book 16A.

Court of Claims Act, see McKinney's Book 29A, Part 2.

§ 206.5–a. Filing by Facsimile Transmission

(a) Application. This section shall take effect on May 3, 1999, and shall be applicable to the filing of any paper with the court in any action or proceeding commenced on or after such date.

(b) Filing of Papers with the Court.

(1) Except where papers required or permitted to be filed with the court must be filed by electronic means, such papers may be delivered to the clerk of the court by facsimile transmission at a facsimile telephone number provided for such purpose by the clerk. The cover sheet utilized for such facsimile transmission shall be in a form prescribed by the Chief Administrator of the Courts and shall indicate the nature of the paper being filed; any previously

assigned claim number; the name and address of the filing party or the party's attorney; the telephone number of the party or attorney; the facsimile telephone number that may receive a return facsimile transmission; and the number of total pages, including the cover sheet, being filed. All such papers shall comply with the requirements of CPLR 2101(a) and shall be signed and verified as required by law. The clerk shall not be required to accept such filing if it is more than 50 pages in length (including exhibits, but excluding the cover sheet). Documents may be filed by facsimile transmission at any time of the day or night; only documents received before 12 midnight on any day will be considered to have been received as of that day.

(2) Upon receipt of papers filed by facsimile transmission, the clerk shall stamp such papers with the date the papers were received, and no later than the following business day, shall transmit a copy of the first page of each paper received, containing the date of receipt, to the filing party or attorney either by facsimile transmission or by posting by first class mail. If any page of the papers received by the clerk is missing or illegible, the confirmation of receipt transmitted by the clerk shall so state, and the party or attorney forthwith shall transmit a new or corrected page to the clerk for appropriate inclusion in the transmitted papers and notice shall be given by the clerk to said party or attorney that the new or corrected page was received.

§ 206.5–aa. Filing by Electronic Means

(a) There is hereby established a pilot program in which, on or after January 1, 2003, all designated claims in the Court of Claims shall be subject to filing by electronic means (FBEM) in accordance with the provisions of section 202.5–b of these rules.

(b) For purpose of this section:

(1) the term "action," as used in section 202.5–b, shall also include a claim in the Court of Claims;

(2) the term "designated claim" shall mean a claim falling within one or more categories of claims designated pursuant to subdivision (c) of this section; provided, however, the term "designated claim" may not include a claim commenced by a federal, state or local inmate under sentence for conviction of a crime; and

(3) references to the County Clerk, the Chief Clerk of the Supreme Court or the clerk of a court in section 202.5–b shall be deemed to mean the clerk of the Court of Claims.

(c) From time to time, the Presiding Judge of the Court of Claims, at the request of the Attorney General or his or her designee, may designate one or more categories of claims in the Court of Claims, as identified by subject matter, geographic region or otherwise, as claims to be subject to FBEM. The clerk of the Court shall promptly advise the Attorney General of all such designations. Upon designation of a category of claims by the Presiding Judge pursuant to this subdivision, the Attorney General shall be deemed, for all purposes under section 202.5–b, to have agreed to service of all papers upon him or her by electronic means for those claims in which the claimant consents to proceed pursuant to such section.

(d) Notwithstanding the foregoing, the provisions of paragraph (1) of subdivision (b) of section 202.5–b of these rules shall not apply to claims in the Court of Claims.

§ 206.5–b. Filing Fee; Waiver or Reduction

(a) Pursuant to section 11–a of the Court of Claims Act, the claim shall be accompanied by either a filing fee of fifty dollars ($50.00) or a motion, affidavit or certification pursuant to section 1101 of the Civil Practice Law and Rules (CPLR).

(b) No filing fee shall be required for a third party claim filed pursuant to section 9(9–a) of the Court of Claims Act and section 206.6(g) of this Part or for the initiation of a special proceeding.

(c) An application pursuant to CPLR 1101(d) or (f) for waiver or reduction of the filing fee shall be made by completing the affidavit supplied by the clerk's office and filing the affidavit with the claim. The clerk's office will notify the claimant of the court's decision by mail.

§ 206.6. Contents of Claim or Notice of Intention

(a) In addition to the requirements prescribed by section 11 of the Court of Claims Act, the claim or notice of intention shall state the post office address of each claimant therein, and the name, post office address and telephone number of the attorney for each claimant.

(b) To the extent required by Court of Claims Act § 11(b), there shall be included in each claim, or attached thereto, a schedule showing in detail each item of damage claimed and the amount of such item. Where claimant is proceeding upon more than one cause of action, each additional cause of action shall be separately stated and numbered.

(c) In all actions where a notice of intention to file a claim has been served, the claim shall state the date of service on the Attorney General.

(d) Where the claim is for the temporary or permanent appropriation of real property, it shall contain a specific description of the property giving its location and quantity. The original and all filed copies of such claim shall have annexed thereto a duplicate of the official appropriation map or maps filed in the office of the commissioner of the department involved in the taking, covering the property for which the claim is filed.

(e) If the claim is filed under a special statute, such statute shall be pleaded by reference.

(f) Changes in the post office address or telephone number of any attorney or pro se claimant shall be communicated in writing to the clerk within ten days thereof.

(g) **Declaratory Judgment.** Actions for declaratory judgment, pursuant to section 9(9–a) of the Court of Claims Act, shall be commenced by the filing with the clerk and service upon the third-party defendant of a notice of impleader, together with a third-party claim, in the nature of a complaint, and all prior pleadings in the action. Such papers also shall be served upon all other parties. Service upon the third-party defendant shall be made in the same manner as service of a claim under section 11 of the Court of Claims Act. The original third-party claim and two copies thereof shall be filed with the clerk within 10 days of such service. Responsive pleadings shall be served and filed in accordance with Rule 206.7.

Cross References

Court of Claims Act, see McKinney's Book 29A, Part 2.

Forms

Claim for damage arising from acquisition by eminent domain—general form, see West's McKinney's Forms, Selected Consolidated Laws, Em Dom Proc § 504, Forms 1 to 3.

§ 206.7. Responsive and Amended Pleadings

(a) Except in appropriation actions, the defendant shall serve an answer to each claim; the defendant may include a counterclaim in its answer, in which case the claimant shall serve a reply. Except as extended by CPLR 3211 (subd. (f)), service of all responsive pleadings shall be made within 40 days of service of the pleading to which it responds. The original and two copies of each responsive pleading, together with proof of service, shall be filed with the clerk within ten days of such service.

(b) Pleadings may be amended in the manner provided by CPLR 3025, except that a party may amend a pleading once without leave of court within 40 days after its service, or at any time before the period for responding to it expires, or within 40 days after service of a pleading responding to it. Where a response to an amended or supplemental pleading is required, it shall be made within 40 days after service of the amended or supplemental pleading to which it responds.

(c) Stipulations between parties extending the time limits herein shall be executed prior to the expiration of such time limits, and shall be filed with the clerk within ten days thereafter.

Cross References

CPLR, see McKinney's Book 7B.

§ 206.8. Calendaring of Motions; Uniform Notice of Motion Form

(a) There shall be compliance with the procedures prescribed in the CPLR for the bringing of motions. In addition, no motion shall be filed with the court unless a notice of motion is served and filed, with proof of service, with the motion papers.

(b) No motion relating to disclosure shall be placed on the calendar without counsel for the respective parties first conferring with the assigned judge. This subdivision shall not apply to prisoner pro se claims.

(c) No motion by an attorney seeking to be relieved as counsel for a party shall be placed on the calendar unless initiated by order to show cause.

(d) The notice of motion shall read substantially as follows:

STATE OF NEW YORK—COURT OF CLAIMS

A.B.,   Notice of Motion

        Claimant,   Claim No.

—against—

THE STATE OF NEW YORK,   Name of Assigned Judge

        Defendant.

Upon the affidavit of _____, sworn to on _____, 20__, and upon (list supporting papers if any), the _____ will move this court on the ___ day of _____, 20__ for an order (briefly indicate relief requested).

The above-entitled action is for (briefly state nature of action, e.g., personal injury, medical malpractice, etc.).

Dated:

                    (Print Name)
                  Attorney* (or Attorney in charge of case if law firm) for moving party
                  Address:
                  Telephone number:

* If any party is appearing pro se, the name, address and telephone number of such party shall be stated.

(e) The notice of motion set forth in subdivision (d) shall not be required for a motion brought on by order to show cause or an application for ex parte relief.

Cross References

CPLR, see McKinney's Book 7B.

§ 206.9. Motion Procedure

(a) All motions relating to assigned claims shall be returnable before the assigned judge and, unless otherwise directed by the assigned judge, shall be made returnable at 9:30 a.m. on any Wednesday designated by the judge's schedule for the calendaring of motions. Motions relating to applications for permission to file a late claim, and any other motions pertaining to an unassigned claim, shall be made returnable at 9:30

a.m. on any Wednesday at a special part of the court in the district in which the claim arose or is then pending.

(b) Unless brought on by a show cause order, the original and two copies of all motion papers with proof of service annexed shall be filed in the clerk's office at least eight days before the return date thereof. The moving party shall also serve a copy of all affidavits and briefs upon all other parties at the time of service of the notice of motion. The answering party shall serve copies of all affidavits and briefs as required by CPLR 2214(b) and file such copies in accordance with these rules.

(c) Unless oral argument has been requested by a party and permitted by the court, or directed by the court, motions shall be deemed submitted as of the return date. A party requesting oral argument shall set forth such request in its notice of motion or on the first page of the answering papers, as the case may be. A party requesting oral argument on a motion brought on by an order to show cause shall do so as soon as practicable before the time the motion is to be heard.

(d) Ex Parte Applications. Whenever any party shall make an ex parte application to the court for an order, it shall be the duty of the party making the application to present to the assigned judge the proposed original order and to serve on his or her adversary a true conformed copy thereof. The signed original order together with proof of service shall be filed in the clerk's office.

(e) Proposed orders must be submitted for signature, unless otherwise directed, within 60 days of the filing of the decision directing that the order be settled or submitted. Failure to submit the order timely shall be deemed an abandonment of the motion, unless for good cause shown.

Cross References

CPLR, see McKinney's Book 7B.

§ 206.10. Conferences

(a) In all matters, except appropriation claims and prisoner pro se claims, the court shall order a preliminary conference as soon as practicable, but no later than six months, after the claim has been assigned.

(b) The court, in ordering a preliminary conference, shall fix the date and time for the conference and notify the parties. Except where a party appears pro se, an attorney thoroughly familiar with the claim and authorized to act on behalf of the party shall appear at such conference.

(c) The matters to be considered at the preliminary conference shall include:

(1) simplification and limitation of factual and legal issues, where appropriate;

(2) establishment of a timetable for the completion of all disclosure proceedings, provided that all such procedures must be completed within 18 months of the assignment of the claim to the judge, unless otherwise shortened or extended by the court depending upon the circumstances;

(3) settlement of the claim; and

(4) any other matters that the court may deem relevant.

(d) In lieu of a preliminary conference as outlined in this section, and unless the court orders otherwise, the parties may execute a stipulation, to be so ordered by the court, agreeing to a timetable for the completion of disclosure within 18 months of the assignment of the claim to the judge.

(e) The court may direct the holding of additional conferences including, but not limited to, pretrial conferences, as the court may deem helpful or necessary in any matter before the court.

(f) At the conclusion of any conference the court may make a written order including its directions to the parties as well as stipulations of counsel.

(g) If any party fails to appear for a scheduled conference, the court may note the default on the record and enter such order as appears just, including dismissal.

§ 206.11. Videotape Recording of Civil Depositions

(a) **When Permitted.** Depositions authorized under the provisions of the Civil Practice Law and Rules or other law may be taken, as permitted by subdivision (b) of section 3113 of the Civil Practice Law and Rules, by means of simultaneous audio and visual electronic recording, provided such recording is made in conformity with this section.

(b) **Other Rules Applicable.** Except as otherwise provided in this section, or where the nature of videotaped recording makes compliance impossible or unnecessary, all rules generally applicable to examinations before trial shall apply to videotaped recording of depositions.

(c) **Notice of Taking Depositions.** Every notice or subpoena for the taking of a videotaped deposition shall state that it is to be videotaped and the name and address of the videotape operator and of the operator's employer, if any. The operator may be an employee of the attorney taking the deposition or of the Department of Law. Where an application for an order to take a videotaped deposition is made, the application and order shall contain the same information.

(d) **Conduct of the Examination.**

(1) The deposition shall begin by one of the attorneys or the operator stating on camera:

(i) the operator's name and address:

(ii) the name and address of the operator's employer;

(iii) the date, the time and place of the deposition; and

(iv) the party on whose behalf the deposition is being taken.

The officer before whom the deposition is taken shall be a person authorized by statute and shall identify himself or herself and swear the witness on camera. If the deposition requires the use of more than one tape, the end of each tape and the beginning of each succeeding tape shall be announced by the operator.

(2) Every videotaped deposition shall be timed by means of a time-date generator which shall permanently record hours, minutes, and seconds. Each time the videotape is stopped and resumed, such times shall be orally announced on the tape.

(3) More than one camera may be used, either in sequence or simultaneously.

(4) At the conclusion of the deposition, a statement shall be made on camera that the recording is completed. As soon as practicable thereafter, the videotape shall be shown to the witness for examination, unless such showing and examination are waived by the witness and the parties.

(5) Technical data, such as recording speeds and other information needed to replay or copy the tape, shall be included on copies of the videotaped deposition.

(e) **Copies and Transcription.** The parties may make audio copies of the deposition and thereafter may purchase additional audio and audio-visual copies. A party may arrange to have a stenographic transcription made of the deposition at his or her own expense.

(f) **Certification.** The officer before whom the videotape deposition is taken shall cause to be attached to the original videotape recording a certification that the witness was fully sworn or affirmed by the officer and that the videotape recording is a true record of the testimony given by the witness. If the witness has not waived the right to a showing and examination of the videotape deposition, the witness shall also sign the certification in accordance with the provisions of section 3116 of the Civil Practice Law and Rules.

(g) **Filing and Objections.**

(1) If no objections have been made by any of the parties during the course of the deposition, the videotape deposition and one copy may be filed by the proponent with the clerk and shall be filed upon the request of any party.

(2) If objections have been made by any of the parties during the course of the deposition, the video-

tape deposition, with the certification, shall be submitted to the court upon the request of any of the parties within 10 days after its recording, or within such other period as the parties may stipulate, or as soon thereafter as the objections may be heard by the court, for the purpose of obtaining rulings on the objections. An audio copy of the sound track may be submitted in lieu of the videotape for this purpose, as the court may prefer. The court may view such portions of the videotape recording as it deems pertinent to the objections made, or may listen to an audiotape recording. The court, in its discretion, may also require submission of a stenographic transcript of the portion of the deposition to which objection is made, and may read such transcript in lieu of reviewing the videotape or audio copy.

(3)(i) The court shall rule on the objections prior to the date set for trial and shall return the recording to the proponent of the videotape with notice to the parties of its rulings and of its instructions as to editing. The editing shall reflect the rulings of the court and shall remove all references to the objections. The proponent, after causing the videotape to be edited in accordance with the court's instructions, may cause both the original videotape recording and the deleted version of the recording, and a copy of each, clearly identified, to be filed with the clerk, and shall do so at the request of any party. Before such filing, the proponent shall permit the other party to view the edited videotape.

(ii) The court may, in respect to objectionable material, instead of ordering its deletion, permit such material to be clearly marked so that the audio recording may be suppressed by the operator during the objectionable portion when the videotape is presented at the trial. In such case the proponent may cause both the original videotape recording and a marked version of that recording, and a copy of each, clearly identified, to be filed with the clerk of the court, and shall do so at the request of any party.

(h) Custody of Tape. When the tape is filed with the clerk of the court, the clerk shall give an appropriate receipt for the tape and shall provide secure and adequate facilities for the storage of videotape recordings.

(i) Use at Trial. The use of videotape recordings of depositions at the trial shall be governed by the provisions of the Civil Practice Law and Rules and all other relevant statutes, court rules and decisional law relating to depositions and relating to the admissibility of evidence. The proponent of the videotaped deposition shall have the responsibility of providing whatever equipment and personnel may be necessary for presenting such videotape deposition.

(j) Applicability to Audio Taping of Depositions. Except where clearly inapplicable because of the lack of a video portion, these rules are equally applicable to the taking of depositions by audio recording alone. However, in the case of the taking of a deposition upon notice by audio recording alone, any party, at least five days before the date noticed for taking the deposition, may apply to the court for an order establishing additional or alternate procedures for the taking of such audio deposition, and upon the making of the application, the deposition may be taken only in accordance with the court order.

(k) Cost. The cost of videotaping or audio recording shall be borne by the party who served the notice for the videotaped or audio recording of the deposition.

(l) Transcription for Appeal. On appeal visual and audio depositions shall be transcribed in the same manner as other testimony and transcripts filed in the appellate court. The visual and audio depositions shall remain part of the original record in the case and shall be transmitted therewith. In lieu of the transcribed deposition and, on leave of the appellate court, a party may request a viewing of portions of the visual deposition by the appellate court but, in such case, a transcript of pertinent portions of the deposition shall be filed as required by the court.

Cross References

CPLR, see McKinney's Book 7B.

§ 206.12. Note of Issue and Certificate of Readiness

(a) General. No action shall be deemed ready for trial unless there is first filed a note of issue accompanied by a certificate of readiness, with proof of service on all parties entitled to notice, in the form prescribed by this section. Filing of a note of issue and certificate of readiness shall not be required for prisoner pro se claims, for an application for court approval of the settlement of the claim of an infant, incompetent or conservatee, or for an application for court approval of a settlement pursuant to section 20–a of the Court of Claims Act. The note of issue shall include the claim number, the name of the judge to whom the action is assigned, and the name, office address and telephone number of each attorney or individual who has appeared. Within ten days after service, the original note of issue and certificate of readiness, with proof of service, shall be filed with the clerk.

(b) Forms. The note of issue and certificate of readiness shall read substantially as follows:

NOTE OF ISSUE

Calendar No. _____

For use of clerk

Claim No. _____
New York State Court of Claims, _____ District
                        Notice for trial
                            Filed by attorney for _____
                            Date claim filed _____
                            Date claim served _____
                            Date issue joined _____

Nature of action

Tort: Highway or motor vehicle negligence   _____
        Medical malpractice   _____
        Other tort (specify) _____
        Appropriation claim   _____
        Small claim pursuant to
            article 6 EDPL   _____
        Public construction contract claim   _____
        Other contract   _____
        Other type of action (specify)   _____
        _____
        Amount demanded $_____
        Other relief _____

Attorney(s) for Claimant(s)
Office and P.O. Address:
Phone No.
Attorney(s) for Defendant(s)   Insurance carrier(s):
Office and P.O. Address:
Phone No.

NOTE: Clerk will not accept this note of issue unless accompanied
        by a certificate of readiness.

CERTIFICATE OF READINESS FOR TRIAL
(Items 1–6 must be checked)

		Complete	Waived	Not Required
1.	All pleadings served and filed.	....	....	....
2.	Bill of Particulars served and filed.	....	....	....
3.	Physical examinations completed.	....	....	....
4.	Medical reports filed and exchanged.			
5.	Expert reports filed and exchanged.	....	....	....
6.	Discovery proceedings now known to be necessary completed.	....	....	....
7.	There are no outstanding requests for discovery.	....	....	....
8.	There has been a reasonable opportunity to complete the foregoing proceedings.			
9.	There has been compliance with any order issued pursuant to section 206.10 of this part.			
10.	The action is ready for trial.			

Dated: _____

(Signature) _____
Attorney(s) for: _____
Office and P.O. address: _____

(c) Pretrial Proceedings. Where a party is prevented from filing a note of issue and certificate of readiness because a pretrial proceeding has not been completed for any reason beyond the control of the party, the court, upon motion supported by affidavit, may permit the party to file a note of issue upon such conditions as the court deems appropriate. Where unusual or unanticipated circumstances develop subsequent to the filing of a note of issue and certificate of readiness which require additional pretrial proceedings to prevent substantial prejudice, the court, upon motion supported by affidavit, may grant permission to conduct such necessary proceedings.

(d) Striking Note of Issue. Within 20 days after service of a note of issue and certificate of readiness, any party to the action may move to strike the note of issue, upon affidavit showing in what respects the action is not ready for trial, and the court may strike the note of issue if it appears that a material fact in the certificate of readiness is incorrect, or that the certificate of readiness fails to comply with the requirements of this section in some material respect. After such period, no such motion shall be allowed except for good cause shown. At any time, the court on its own motion may strike a note of issue if it appears that a material fact in the certificate of readiness is incorrect, or that the certificate of readiness fails to comply with the requirements of this section in some material respect.

(e) Restoration of Note of Issue. Motions to restore notes of issue struck pursuant to this section shall be supported by a proper and sufficient certificate of readiness and by an affidavit by a person having first-hand knowledge showing that there is merit to the action, satisfactorily showing the reasons for the acts or omissions which led to the note of issue being struck from the calendar, stating meritorious reasons for its restoration and showing that the action is presently ready for trial.

(f) Change in Title of Action. In the event of a change in title of an action by reason of a substitution of any party, no new note of issue will be required. Notice of such substitution and change in title shall be filed with the clerk for transmittal to the assigned judge within ten days of the date of an order or stipulation effecting the party substitution or title change.

(g) Unless for good cause shown, the trial of the action shall commence within 15 months of the filing of the note of issue.

Court of Claims Act, see McKinney's Book 29A, Part 2.

§ 206.13. Calendars

A judge to whom claims are assigned under the individual assignment system may establish such calendars of claims as the judge shall deem necessary or desirable for proper case management.

Judges to whom claims are assigned pursuant to the individual assignment system may schedule calls of any calendars they have established at such times as they may deem appropriate. The Presiding Judge may schedule calls of any claim appearing on a public construction contract calendar or prisoner pro se calendar at such times as he or she may deem appropriate.

Cross References
CPLR, see McKinney's Book 7B.

§ 206.14. Exchange of Medical Reports in Personal Injury and Wrongful Death Actions

Except where the court otherwise directs, in all actions in which recovery is sought for personal injuries, disability or death, physical examinations and the exchange of medical information shall be governed by the provisions hereinafter set forth:

(a) At any time after joinder of issue, and subject to the time limitation set forth in subdivision (b), the defendant may serve on claimant a notice fixing the time and place of examination. The notice shall name the examining medical provider or providers. Claimant may move to modify or vacate the notice within 20 days of the receipt thereof.

(b) At least 30 days before the date of such examination, or on such other date as the court may direct, claimant shall deliver to defendant the following, which may be used by the examining medical provider or providers:

(1) copies of the medical reports of those medical providers who have previously treated or examined the claimant. These shall include a recital of the injuries and conditions as to which testimony will be offered at the trial, referring to and identifying those x-ray and technicians' reports which will be offered at the trial, including a description of the injuries sustained, a diagnosis, and a prognosis. Medical reports may consist of completed medical provider, workers compensation, or insurance forms that provide the information required by this paragraph.

(2) duly executed and acknowledged written authorizations permitting the defendant to obtain and make copies of all hospital records and such other records, including x-ray and technicians' reports, as may be referred to and identified in the reports of those

medical providers who have treated or examined the claimant.

(c) A copy of the report or reports of the medical provider or providers making the examination pursuant to this section shall be furnished to the claimant within 60 days after completion of the examination. Such copy or copies shall comply with the requirements of paragraph (1) of subdivision (b).

(d) In actions where the cause of death is in issue, claimant shall exchange with defendant no later than 45 days after service of the bill of particulars copies of the report or reports of all treating and examining medical providers whose testimony will be offered at the trial, complying with the requirements of paragraph (1) of subdivision (b), and claimant will furnish authorizations to the defendant to examine and obtain copies of all hospital records, autopsy or post-mortem reports, and such other records as provided in paragraph (2) of subdivision (b). In any case where the interests of justice will not be served by exchange of such reports and delivery of such authorizations, an order dispensing with either or both must be obtained upon motion made before the expiration of time set forth in this section.

(e) Unless an order to the contrary is made or unless the judge, at trial, in the interests of justice and upon a showing of good cause shall hold otherwise, claimant shall be precluded at the trial from offering in evidence any part of the hospital records and all other records, including autopsy or post-mortem records, x-ray reports or reports of other technicians, not made available pursuant to this rule, and no party shall be permitted to offer any evidence of injuries or conditions not set forth in the respective medical reports previously exchanged, nor will the court hear the testimony of any treating or examining medical providers whose medical reports have not been exchanged as provided by this rule.

§ 206.15. Default; Restoration; Dismissal

Whenever a note of issue has been filed and the claimant is not ready for trial or fails to appear for a scheduled trial date, or if the assigned judge has directed that the claim be ready for trial by a particular date and the defendant is ready to proceed with the trial but the claimant is not so ready, the assigned judge, upon motion by the defendant or upon his or her own motion, may dismiss the claim unless sufficient reason is shown why such claim should not be tried at that time. An order dismissing a claim pursuant to this section or any section of this Part, or pursuant to the Court of Claims Act or the CPLR, shall not be vacated except upon stipulation of all parties so ordered by the court or by motion on notice to all other parties, supported by affidavit showing sufficient reason why the order should be vacated and the claim restored. Such application shall be made to the judge who granted the order of dismissal unless he or she is no longer a member of the court, in which

event application shall be made to the Presiding Judge.

§ 206.16. Identification of Trial Counsel

(a) Where the attorney of record for any party arranges for another attorney to conduct the trial, the trial counsel must be identified in writing to the clerk and to all parties not less than 15 days before the date assigned for trial. The notice must be signed by both the attorney of record and the trial counsel and filed with the clerk.

(b) After trial counsel is designated as provided above, no substitution shall be permitted unless the substituted counsel is available to try the case when it is reached in regular order. Written notice of such substitution shall be promptly filed with the clerk and given to all parties.

§ 206.17. Engagement of Counsel

No adjournment shall be granted on the ground of engagement of counsel except in accordance with Part 125 of the Rules of the Chief Administrator of the Courts.

§ 206.18. Entry of Judgment

(a) Except as provided in subdivision (b), the clerk shall enter judgment within 20 days of the filing of a decision. Either party may submit a proposed judgment to the clerk within 15 days of said filing on five days' notice to the adverse party.

(b) Where an award is made in a claim for the appropriation of real property or any interest therein, or for any damages to real property, the Attorney General shall have 45 days after filing of the decision to notify the clerk in writing whether any suspension of interest under subdivision 4 of section 19 of the Court of Claims Act is required. After said 45-day period, the clerk shall enter judgment forthwith, unless a motion on notice has been made and filed within said period to stay entry of judgment. Filing such a motion shall temporarily stay entry of judgment pending the court's determination.

Cross References

Court of Claims Act, see McKinney's Book 29A, Part 2.

§ 206.19. Bifurcated Trials

(a) Judges are encouraged to order a bifurcated trial of the issues of liability and damages in any action for personal injury where it appears that bifurcation may assist in a clarification or simplification of issues and a fair and more expeditious resolution of the action.

(b) Where a bifurcated trial is ordered, the issues of liability and damages shall be severed and the issue of liability shall be tried first, unless the court orders otherwise.

(c) In the event of a claimant's judgment on the issue of liability or a defendant's judgment on the issue of liability on a counterclaim, the damage phase of the trial shall be conducted as soon as possible before the same judge, unless the judge presiding over the trial, for reasons stated in the record, finds such procedure to be impracticable.

§ 206.20. Sanctions

The provisions of Part 130 of the Rules of the Chief Administrator of the Courts shall be applicable to the Court of Claims.

§ 206.21. Appropriation Claims; Special Rules

(a) **In an Appropriation Claim the Defendant Is Not Required to Serve or File an Answer.** All allegations in appropriation claims are deemed denied, and issue is joined upon the completion of filing of the claim and proof of service in the clerk's office.

(b) **Appraisal Reports.** Within six months from the date of completion of filing and service of a claim in an appropriation case, the parties shall prepare and file with the clerk of the court an original and three copies of the appraisal of each appraiser whose testimony is intended to be relied upon at trial. Each appraisal shall set forth separately the value of land and improvements, including fixtures, if any, together with the data upon which such evaluations are based, including but not limited to:

(1) the before value and after value,

(2) direct, consequential and total damages,

(3) details of the appropriation,

(4) details of comparable sales, and

(5) other factors which will be relied upon at trial.

If all the details of comparable sales required by section 16 of the Court of Claims Act are included in the appraisals prescribed herein, such shall be deemed compliance with section 16. Parties should confine the use of notices under section 16 to sales or leases of comparable property not reasonably ascertainable at the time of preparation of their respective appraisals.

(c) **Experts' Reports.** Where an expert, other than a valuation expert, is intended to be relied upon at trial, an original and three copies of the expert's report shall be filed within the same time and in the same manner as above set forth.

(d) **Exchange.** When all parties have filed their appraisals and reports as herein provided, the clerk shall send copies of each to all other parties.

(e) **Amendments and Supplements.** If a party intends at trial to offer proof correcting errors in or adding pertinent matter to an appraisal or other expert's report, an original and three copies of an amended or supplemental report shall be filed within two months after the exchange of appraisals and reports. The clerk shall send copies to all other parties.

(f) **Rebuttal Reports.** If a party intends at trial to offer expert evidence in rebuttal to any report or amended or supplemental report, an original and three copies of the expert's report shall be filed within one month after receipt of the document sought to be rebutted. The clerk shall send copies to all other parties.

(g) **Extension of Time.**

(1) A party requiring more time than that prescribed in subdivision (b) of this section may apply for an extension of up to six months by letter to the assigned judge and received not later than six months from the date of the filing and service of the claim. The letter application shall show good cause for the extension, and a copy thereof shall be forwarded by the applicant to each other party. The assigned judge in his or her discretion may, by letter, grant an extension for such period, not to exceed six months, and upon such terms and conditions as may be just. Such extension also shall extend the time of other parties.

(2) An application for any further extension shall be made by motion on notice showing good cause and shall be made to the assigned judge prior to the expiration of any previous extension. The court in its discretion may grant the motion upon such terms and conditions as may be just. Alternatively, a further extension may be set forth in a stipulation which shall be signed by the attorneys and submitted to the assigned judge. The court in its discretion may "so order" said extension.

(3) An application for other or further relief from the requirements or consequences of this section also shall be made to the assigned judge by motion on notice showing unusual and substantial circumstances. However, any application for such relief made after the commencement of trial may be granted only upon a showing of extraordinary circumstances. The court in its discretion may grant the motion upon such terms and conditions as may be just.

(h) **Limitation of Testimony.** At the trial of a claim governed by this section, expert witnesses called by the parties shall be limited in their testimony to matters set forth in their respective appraisals or other reports. A party failing to file appraisals and other reports as provided in this section shall be precluded at trial from offering any expert proof, with the exception of evidence admissible under section 16 of the Court of Claims Act.

(i) **Nonapplicability.** Compliance with this section shall not be required of a party proceeding in this court pursuant to article 6 of the Eminent Domain Procedure Law (special procedure for claims under $25,000) or a party who files, within the time set forth in subdivision (b) of this section, a notice with proof of service, that no expert proof will be offered at trial. When such a notice is received by the clerk, the clerk shall mail to the party filing the notice a copy of any appraisal or report received from any other party.

Cross References

EDPL, see McKinney's Book 16A.

Court of Claims Act, see McKinney's Book 29A, Part 2.

§ 206.22. Small Claims Pursuant to Article 6 of the Eminent Domain Procedure Law (EDPL); Special Rules

(a) The hearing shall be conducted in an informal and simplified manner as to do substantial justice between the parties and to discover expeditiously the facts in order to determine a just result according to the principles and rules of substantive law.

(b) The provisions of the EDPL, the Court of Claims Act, the rules of this court and the CPLR shall apply to small claims so far as the same can be made applicable and are not in conflict with the provisions of article 6 of the EDPL.

(c) An oath or affirmation shall be administered to all witnesses. The court shall liberally construe statutory provisions and rules of practice, procedure and pleading in connection with the conduct of the hearing.

(d) When, at the hearing of a small claim, the defendant has interposed a counterclaim, the court shall hear the entire case, but the trial of the counterclaim shall be conducted as if it were instituted separate and apart from said small claim.

Cross References

CPLR, see McKinney's Book 7B.

EDPL, see McKinney's Book 16A.

§ 206.23. Public Construction Contract Claims; Special Rules

(a)(1) All claims involving public construction contracts shall contain separately captioned and numbered causes of action. When utilized in a claim, detailed schedules of items of damage that pertain to or are allied with a particular cause of action shall be made a part of said cause of action.

(2) Where the claimant has accepted final payment, the claim shall have attached to it a copy of the statement required by section 145 of the State Finance Law.

(b)(1) Within 30 days after the service and filing of its verified answer, the defendant may serve and file an itemized demand for a bill of particulars.

(2) Unless claimant, moves to modify or vacate such demand, said claimant must serve a proper bill of particulars within 60 days of the receipt of the defendant's demand and file the original with proof of service in the office of the clerk or may be precluded under CPLR 3042 for failure to furnish a proper bill unless the time to serve said bill shall be extended as hereinafter provided.

(c)(1) The defendant may serve a notice of an examination before trial of the claimant at any time after the service and filing of its answer, but not later than 60 days after the service of a bill of particulars by the claimant.

(2) The claimant may serve a notice of an examination before trial at any time as provided in the CPLR, but not later than 30 days after the service of a notice by the defendant of an examination before trial of the claimant.

(d) All other motions shall be brought in accordance with the Court of Claims Act, the rules of the Court of Claims and the provisions of the CPLR, and shall be returnable in the district wherein the action is triable.

(e) Subject to the written approval of the court, the parties, within the period of time therein specified, may stipulate to waive or modify any of the requirements of subdivisions (b) or (c) of this section.

(f) A party confronted with unusual and special circumstances requiring more time than prescribed by subdivisions (b) or (c) of this section for compliance with any of the provisions of said subdivisions may move for an extension of time, which the court may grant for such period and under such conditions as the interests of justice require.

Cross References

CPLR, see McKinney's Book 7B.

Court of Claims Act, see McKinney's Book 29A, Part 2.

State Finance Law, see McKinney's Book 55.

§ 206.24. Claims on Submitted Facts

Whenever a claim is submitted to the court on an agreed statement of facts, the claimant, within five days thereafter, shall file in the clerk's office a copy of said statement, which shall be signed at the end thereof by both parties, together with a memorandum stating when and where the claim was submitted and to which judge or judges. Each party, within the same time, shall file in the clerk's office a list of all papers submitted by that party to the court, which list shall sufficiently describe the papers so as to permit their identification.

§ 206.25. Official Forms

The Chief Administrator of the Courts may adopt, amend and rescind official forms for use in the Court of Claims.

PART 207. UNIFORM RULES FOR SURROGATE'S COURT

§ 207.1. Application of Part; Waiver; Special Rules; Definitions

(a) Application. This part shall be applicable to proceedings in all Surrogate's Courts in New York State.

(b) Waiver. For good cause shown, and in the interest of justice, the court in a proceeding may waive compliance with any of these rules, other than section 207.2, unless prohibited from doing so by statute or by rule of the Chief Judge.

(c) Additional Rules. Local court rules, and all court forms not inconsistent with law or with these rules, shall comply with Part 9 of the Rules of the Chief Judge (22 NYCRR Part 9).

(d) Application of SCPA, EPTL and CPLR. The provisions of this part shall be construed consistently with the Surrogate's Court Procedure Act (SCPA) and the Estates Powers and Trusts Law (EPTL). Matters not covered by these provisions, the SCPA and the EPTL shall be governed by the Civil Practice Law and Rules (CPLR).

(e) Definitions.

(1) "Chief Administrator of the Courts" in this Part also includes a designee of the Chief Administrator.

(2) Unless the context requires otherwise, all references to "clerk" shall mean the Chief Clerk of each Surrogate's Court or the designee of the Chief Clerk.

(3) Unless otherwise defined in this Part, or the context otherwise requires, all terms used in this Part shall have the same meaning as they have in the CPLR, EPTL and the SCPA.

Cross References

CPLR, see McKinney's Book 7B.

SCPA, see McKinney's Book 58A.

§ 207.2. Terms of Court

In each Surrogate's Court there shall be held such terms as the Chief Administrator shall designate.

§ 207.3. [Reserved]

§ 207.4. Papers Filed in Court; Clerk's File Number; Official Forms

(a) Unless otherwise specified by the court, attorneys, as well as parties appearing without attorneys, shall prepare and submit all papers, pleadings, orders and decrees to be acted upon by the Surrogate. The party causing the first paper to be filed shall communicate the clerk's file number forthwith to all other parties to the proceeding; service of the citation bearing the file number shall be sufficient. Thereafter such number shall appear on the outside cover and first page to the right of the caption of every paper tendered for filing in the proceeding. The caption also shall contain the title of the proceeding, an indication of the county of venue and a brief description of the nature of the paper. All papers shall comply with the provisions of CPLR 2101 and (other than wills, codicils, exhibits and forms of other governmental agencies) shall be on standard eight and one-half inch by 11–inch paper. The text of all papers must be legible and, other than prompts and instructions, must be in a standard typeface of 10 to 12–point characters and have margins that shall be no less than one-half inch. Papers also shall contain the name of the attorney or party submitting them and, whenever possible, the names, addresses and information regarding parties to the proceeding shall be printed in bold typeface.

(b) The forms set forth in Chapter VII of subtitle D of this title (22 NYCRR), designated "Surrogate Court Forms", and including forms for the Surrogate's Court and adoption forms of the Family Court and Surrogate's Court, shall be the official forms of the court and shall be accepted for filing pursuant to SCPA 106. Forms produced on computers or word processors shall be accepted for filing, provided (1) the text used shall be the same as that contained in the official forms and (2) the attorney or party preparing such form shall certify at the end thereof that the form is the same as the official form and that the substantive text has not been altered. Persons submitting such forms may leave out instructions (contained in brackets) and optional words or phrases that have not been selected or are irrelevant. Submitting a form to be an official form, but upon which the text has been intentionally altered to change the substance or meaning thereof, may be regarded as an attempt to mislead the court.

(c) Examples of the official forms shall be available at the clerks office of any Surrogate's Court.

Cross References

CPLR, see McKinney's Book 7B.

§ 207.4–a. Surrogate's Court E-filing Pilot Program Rules

(a) Application. There is hereby established in designated Surrogate's Courts a pilot program in which documents may be filed or served electronically in Probate or Administration proceedings, miscellaneous proceedings related thereto, or such other types of proceedings as the court may permit. This pilot program shall apply in the Erie County Surrogate's Court.

(b) Definitions. The following definitions shall be used for the purposes of these rules:

(1) "New York State Courts E-filing" ("NYSCEF") shall mean the system, located at the Internet site at www.nycourts.gov/efile, established by the Chief Administrator of the Courts to permit the electronic transmission of documents to courts and parties in authorized cases.

(2) "Consent" shall mean the voluntary agreement by an attorney or party to an estate proceeding to participate in that estate proceeding through NYSCEF pursuant to these rules.

(3) "Document" shall mean any submission to the court for filing.

(4) "Electronic filing" ("e-filing") shall mean the electronic transmission of documents through NYSCEF to the Surrogate's Court.

(5) "Electronic service" ("e-service") shall mean the electronic transmission of documents to a party or that party's attorney or representative in accordance with these rules. E-service shall not include service of process to gain jurisdiction. E-service shall be complete upon transmission of documents to NYSCEF.

(6) "E-filer" shall mean an attorney admitted to practice in New York State and who maintains an office in this state, or admitted *pro hac vice*, or an authorized agent thereof, or a pro se party, any of whom is registered as an e-filer with NYSCEF as set forth below.

(7) "Hard copy" shall mean a document in paper form.

(8) "Party" shall mean an individual or entity who has an interest in the proceeding and without whom the case may not proceed.

(9) "Authorized agent" shall mean a person or filing service company designated by an attorney to file and serve documents on the attorney's behalf in an estate proceeding, pursuant to a form promulgated by the Chief Administrator of the Courts and filed with the court.

(c) Intent.

(1) E-filing is voluntary and nothing herein shall preclude a party from filing and serving documents in hard copy. Except as provided in subdivision (e)(9), a party who initiates a proceeding by e-filing and any other party who chooses to participate as an e-filer must thereafter file, serve, and accept service of all documents electronically unless notice is given to the court and all other parties that the party no longer wishes to participate electronically.

(2) The court may terminate, modify, or suspend the use of e-filing in a proceeding at any time and may in its discretion excuse an e-filer from compliance with any provision of these rules.

(3) A party or that party's attorney or representative who participates as an e-filer consents to be bound by the provisions of these rules, and participates at the discretion of the Court.

(d) E-filers.

(1) In order to file documents electronically pursuant to these rules, an e-filer shall register with the Office of Court Administration of the New York State Unified Court System by filing with that Office a registration form promulgated by the Chief Administrator of the Courts. Upon completion of registration, a user ID and password will be issued to the e-filer by NYSCEF. If, during the course of the proceeding, a pro se party who registered as an e-filer retains an attorney, the attorney shall register, if not already registered as an e-filer, and inform the Chief Clerk of his or her appearance on behalf of the pro se party.

(2) Registration as an e-filer shall not constitute consent to participate in any particular estate proceeding; consent to do so must be provided pursuant to subdivision (b)(2).

(3) Upon learning of the compromise of the confidentiality of either the user ID or the password, the e-filer shall immediately notify NYSCEF, which shall arrange for the issuance of a new user ID or password as appropriate.

(e) Electronic Filing of Documents.

(1) An eligible proceeding may be commenced by filing the initial documents electronically. If the proceeding is commenced electronically, all other parties shall be served with a Notice regarding the use of e-filing and the procedure for participating therein in a form approved by the Chief Administrator of the Courts, which may be obtained through NYSCEF. Such Notice shall be served in person or by regular mail prior to the return date of the citation.

(2) Whenever documents are e-filed that require payment of a court filing fee, the e-filer shall pay such fee through NYSCEF, or by mail, or in person.

(3) Documents may be transmitted at any time to NYSCEF and will be deemed filed when transmission to NYSCEF is complete and payment of any court filing fee due is received by the court. A document due to be filed by a particular date shall be considered to have been timely filed if filed through NYSCEF no later than midnight of that date.

(4) Upon completion of transmission of an e-filed document, an electronic confirmation that includes the date and time of receipt shall be issued through NYSCEF to the e-filer.

(5) Receipt of documents submitted through NYSCEF and issuance of a confirmation shall not be proof of the completeness or technical or legal sufficiency of the documents. If the court identifies any defects as to form, or omissions, in any e-filed documents, the court may direct that the e-filer resubmit them in proper and complete form or amend or supplement them as appropriate.

(6) If an e-filer submits a petition for probate for which the court does not already have in its possession the original purported last will and testament and any codicils thereto being offered for probate, the e-filer shall file directly with the court the paper original purported last will and testament and any codicils thereto and a hard copy of a certified death certificate within two business days of the date of e-filing. Except as otherwise directed by the court, process shall not issue nor shall a fiduciary be appointed before the original purported last will and testament, any codicils thereto and certified death certificate are filed with the court.

(7) If an e-filer submits a petition for administration the e-filer shall file a hard copy of a certified death certificate directly with the court within two business days of the date of e-filing. Except as otherwise directed by the court, process will not issue nor shall a fiduciary be appointed before the certified death certificate is filed with the court.

(8) Whenever a document is e-filed pursuant to this section, the official record of that document shall be the electronic record maintained by the court.

(9) Documents that cannot be e-filed because of size, content, format, or any other reasons satisfactory to the court shall be filed in hard copy directly with the court together with, when required, an affidavit of service upon all parties to the proceeding.

(f) Signatures.

(1) Every document which is e-filed shall be signed as required by Part 130 of the Uniform Rules of the Chief Administrator in accordance with this section. The document shall provide the signatory's name, address, e-mail address of record and telephone number.

(2) A document shall be considered to have been signed by, and shall be binding upon, a person identified therein as a signatory, if it is e-filed bearing the actual signature of such person, or, where the person identified as the signatory is the e-filer and the document is being e-filed under the e-filer's user ID and password, an "/s/" is used in the space where the signature would otherwise appear. An attorney or party who e-files a document that bears an actual signature, or causes such a document to be e-filed, represents that he or she possesses the executed hard copy of such document and that he or she shall make it available at the request of the court or any party.

(g) Service of Parties.

(1) An attorney or party seeking to obtain jurisdiction over a party to a proceeding shall serve that party by any of the methods permitted by the SCPA.

(2) In all other instances where service of documents is required, e-service may be made upon any party who is an e-filer in the proceeding. Upon e-filing of any such document, NYSCEF shall transmit notification of filing of the document to all e-mail service addresses of record. Such notification shall provide the date and time of filing and the names of those appearing on the list of e-mail service addresses of record who are receiving notification. The party receiving the notification shall be responsible for accessing NYSCEF to obtain a copy of the document filed. Proof of transmission to the party or the failure thereof shall be recorded by NYSCEF and displayed in the e-filing case record.

(h) Documents Filed by the Court. Decrees, judgments, orders, and decisions in proceedings governed by these rules shall be electronically filed by the court with the appropriate signature affixed and such e-filing shall constitute filing of the decree, judgment, or order. At the time of the filing of the decree, judgment, order, or decision, NYSCEF shall transmit by e-mail to the e-mail service addresses of record a notification that the decree, judgment, order, or decision has been filed and is accessible through NYSCEF. Such notice shall not constitute service of notice of filing by any party.

(i) Technical Failures.

(1) The Chief Clerk shall deem NYSCEF to be subject to a technical failure on a given date if NYSCEF is unable to accept filings or provide access to filed documents continuously or intermittently over the course of any period of time greater than one hour after 12:00 noon of that day. The court shall provide notice of all such technical failures on the NYSCEF site. When e-filing is hindered by a technical failure, a party may file with the court in hard copy. With the exception of deadlines that by law cannot be extended, the time for filing of any paper that is delayed due to the technical failure as defined herein shall be extended for one day for each day in which such technical failure occurs, unless otherwise ordered by the court.

(2) If the e-filing or e-service does not occur because of any of the following, the court may upon satisfactory proof enter an order permitting the document to be filed *nunc pro tunc* to the date it was first attempted to be sent electronically or extending the date for service of the paper: an error in the transmission of the document to NYSCEF or served party which was unknown to the sending party; the party was erroneously excluded from the service list; or other technical problems experienced by the e-filer.

§ 207.5. Submission of Papers to Surrogate

All papers for signature or consideration of the Surrogate shall be presented in the first instance to the clerk of the court in the appropriate courtroom or clerk's office, except that where the clerk is unavailable or the Surrogate so directs, papers may be filed with the Surrogate and a copy filed with the clerk at the first available opportunity. Where appropriate, orders to show cause may be submitted directly to the Law Department or the Surrogate. The papers shall be clearly addressed to the Surrogate for whom they are intended, and prominently show the nature of the papers, the title and clerk's file number of the proceeding in which they are filed, and the name of the attorney or party submitting them.

§ 207.6. Transfer of Actions From Other Courts

(a) An application under SCPA 501 for the consent of the court to the transfer to the Surrogate's Court of an action pending in the Supreme Court or for the transfer by the Surrogate's Court to itself of any action pending in any other court or for the consolidation of such action with a proceeding pending in the Surrogate's Court shall show whether there is pending a proceeding in the Surrogate's Court and the nature of the proceeding and shall be supported by an affidavit which shall state:

(1) the court in which such action is then pending;

(2) the parties to the action;

(3) the nature of the action;

(4) whether the action is on the trial calendar;

(5) an estimate of the time when the action will be reached for trial in the court in which the same is pending, with the facts upon which such estimate is based;

(6) the reasons why a transfer of the action to this court is desirable;

(7) whether a jury trial has been demanded or whether the same has been waived.

(b) There must be annexed to the moving papers a copy of the pleadings in the action sought to be transferred. Upon compliance with the foregoing requirements, an order will be issued by the court directing the adverse parties to show cause why the application should not be granted.

Cross References

SCPA, see McKinney's Book 58A.

Forms

Procedure for transfer of trial to Surrogate's court, see West's McKinney's Forms, Estates and Surrogate Practice, §§ 3:116 to 3:128.

§ 207.7. Service and Filing of Papers; Motions

(a) Whenever service of a paper or notice is required, copies thereof shall be served upon all parties who have appeared and upon such other persons as the Surrogate may direct. Except as further provided in section 207.9 of this Part, a party has appeared within the meaning of these rules so as to entitle the party to be served with notices or papers (i) if the party has filed a written notice of appearance with a demand for service of all papers at a specified address; or (ii) if the party has filed a pleading upon which is endorsed the name and address of the attor-

ney appearing for the party or the name and address of the party appearing *pro se*.

(b) Proof of service of the paper or notice upon all parties shall be filed with the original paper or notice.

(c) In all proceedings the proof of service of process, notices of motion and orders to show cause shall be filed on or before the second day preceding the return date unless the court otherwise permits. In computing such period of two days, Saturdays, Sundays and legal holidays shall not be taken into account. This provision shall not apply to an order to show cause returnable in such limited time as to make compliance with its provisions impracticable.

(d) All contested motions and proceedings shall be made returnable on any day the court is in session unless otherwise provided in the local rules of the court or by order of the Surrogate.

(e) Unless the court otherwise permits, the moving party shall serve copies of all affidavits and briefs upon all other parties at the time of service of the notice of motion. The answering party shall serve copies of all affidavits and briefs as required by CPLR 2214. Affidavits shall be for a statement of the relevant facts, and briefs shall be for a statement of the relevant law. Unless otherwise directed by the court, answering and reply affidavits and briefs and all papers required to be furnished to the court by CPLR 2214(c) must be filed no later than the time of argument or submission of the motion.

(f) The Surrogate may determine that any or all motions in that court be orally argued and may direct that moving and responding papers be filed with the court prior to the time of argument.

(g)(1) Unless oral argument has been requested by a party and permitted by the court, or directed by the court, motion papers received by the clerk of the court on or before the return date shall be deemed submitted as of the return date. (2) Attendance by counsel at the calendar call shall not be required unless (i) a party intends to make an application to the court that is not on the consent of all parties, (ii) attendance of counsel or oral argument is directed by the court, or (iii) oral argument is requested by a party. (3) Attendance by counsel for a party not requesting oral argument is not required where the hearing of oral argument is based solely upon the request of another party. (4) A party requesting oral argument shall set forth such request in its notice of motion or on the first page of the answering papers, as the case may be. A party requesting oral argument on a motion brought on by order to show cause shall do so as soon as possible prior to the time the motion is to be heard.

Cross References

CPLR, see McKinney's Book 7B.

§ 207.8. Removal of Papers

No record or document filed in the court shall be removed therefrom by any person except on written consent of the Surrogate or the clerk. Suitable facilities shall be designated by the Surrogate for the examination or transcription of records and documents by parties or attorneys.

§ 207.9. Appearances

(a) A person not named in a citation, but who claims to be interested in the proceeding and wishes to intervene therein, shall file a notice of appearance and a petition or affidavit alleging interest.

(b) Unless otherwise directed by the Surrogate, attorneys appearing on behalf of nondomiciliaries or parties not personally served within the state must furnish acknowledged evidence of authority pursuant to SCPA 401.

(c) When directed by the Surrogate, in addition to filing an appearance as required by SCPA 404, a guardian ad litem shall serve a notice of appearance upon all parties.

Cross References

SCPA, see McKinney's Book 58A.

Forms

Notice of appearance by attorney, see West's McKinney's Forms, Estates and Surrogate Practice, §§ 3:03, 3:04.

Authorization of attorney to appear, see West's McKinney's Forms, Estates and Surrogate Practice, §§ 3:05, 3:06.

Notice of appearance by guardian, committee or conservator, see West's McKinney's Forms, Estates and Surrogate Practice, § 3:18.

Notice of appearance by attorney of guardian, committee or conservator, see West's McKinney's Forms, Estates and Surrogate Practice, § 3:19.

§ 207.10. Demand for Pleadings

Unless otherwise ordered by the Surrogate, where a party is entitled under SCPA 302(3) to a copy of a pleading on demand, it shall be served within five days of the demand.

Cross References

SCPA, see McKinney's Book 58A.

§ 207.11. Guardians

(a) Where application is made to appoint a guardian of two or more infants, a separate petition and proposed order must be presented with respect to each infant.

(b) The order appointing a guardian of the property of an infant shall recite the substance of, or contain a reference to, the requirements of SCPA 1719 regarding guardian's annual accounts.

(c) As soon as a ward reaches 18 years of age, the guardian shall forthwith account to the ward and proceed to obtain a discharge upon receipt and re-

lease, by a proceeding for judicial settlement of accounts, or by such other method as directed by the court.

Cross References

SCPA, see McKinney's Book 58A.

§ 207.12. Appointment of Guardian Ad Litem on Nomination

(a) In addition to the requirements of SCPA 403, all applications for the appointment of guardians ad litem upon the petitions of infants over 14 years of age must contain the following information:

(1) the petition of the infant must state whether the infant has been influenced by the proponent or the accounting party or the attorneys for the fiduciaries or anyone connected with them or either of them in the selection of the person the infant nominates as the infant's guardian ad litem, and whether the person nominated by the infant has suggested his or her employment either in person or through others.

(2) the affidavit of the attorney nominated as guardian ad litem must state whether the proponent in a probate proceeding or the petitioner in any other proceeding or the accounting party or the attorney for any of the foregoing persons, or anyone connected with such attorney, has suggested or accelerated the nomination of the attorney as guardian ad litem and, if so, must state the facts.

(b) The papers submitted on an application must satisfy the court that the attorney who is nominated for appointment as guardian ad litem will have no divided loyalty in the performance of his or her duties which might result in failure to protect adequately the infant's rights in the estate.

Cross References

SCPA, see McKinney's Book 58A.

Forms

Petition for appointment of named attorney as guardian ad litem, see West's McKinney's Forms, Estates and Surrogate Practice, § 3:35.

Affidavit of attorney nominated as guardian ad litem, see West's McKinney's Forms, Estates and Surrogate Practice, § 3:36.

§ 207.13. Qualification of Guardians Ad Litem; Filing Report

(a) Each guardian ad litem shall qualify within 10 days of notification of appointment or may be deemed unable to act. He or she shall review the court's guidelines for guardians ad litem, if available, and carefully examine all matters affecting the guardian's client and all processes and papers to ensure that they are regular and have been duly served. No decree shall be made in the proceeding until the guardian shall report these findings. The report shall be made in writing or, with the consent of the Surrogate, orally in open court, except as otherwise provided in SCPA 1754(4), within 10 court days of the guardian's appointment or from the date to which the proceeding was finally adjourned, unless extended by the court.

(b) A guardian ad litem in a proceeding in which a decree has been entered directing payment of money or delivery of property to or for the benefit of the guardian's ward must file a supplemental report within 60 days after a decree settling the account, showing whether the decree has been complied with insofar as it affects the ward. In all such cases the fiduciary shall immediately notify the guardian in writing of the date and details of payment or delivery.

(c) The guardian's allowance may be authorized in the initial decree, but, except as provided in SCPA 2111, no allowance shall be paid until an appropriate report is made.

§ 207.14.　Infants' Funds

(a) No allowances will be made to a guardian or otherwise for the support or maintenance of an infant unless an annual account for the preceding year has been filed or good cause is shown in the petition why it has not been filed. The petition must comply with CPLR 1211.

(b) Where an order is granted authorizing the periodic withdrawal of funds belonging to or held in trust for an infant, it shall specify the number and amounts of such withdrawals and the duration of time in which the funds may be used for the purposes stated.

(c) All guardians, persons acting jointly with a guardian, and depositories designated by the court shall produce for examination, whenever so requested by the court, all securities, evidences of deposit or investment or other records, and shall also furnish an accurate record of receipts and deposits of principal and income and of withdrawals and expenditures.

Cross References

CPLR, see McKinney's Book 7B.

§ 207.15.　Birth and Death Certificates

(a) A birth certificate shall be filed upon an application for letters of guardianship or an order of adoption.

(b) A death certificate shall be filed upon an application for letters testamentary, letters of administration or voluntary administration. Alternate evidence of, death may be accepted in the discretion of the court.

(c) Birth and death certificates may be required to be filed in any other proceeding in the discretion of the court.

§ 207.16.　Petitions for Probate and Administration; Proof of Distributions; Family Tree

(a) All petitions for probate or administration shall:

(1) contain the information required by SCPA 304;

(2) contain an estimate of the gross estate of the decedent passing by will or intestacy, separately showing the values of personal and real property, gross rents for a period of 18 months and information about any cause of action for personal injury or wrongful death; and

(3) indicate whether any distributee is a non-marital child or the issue of a non-marital person under EPTL 4–1.2(a)(1) or (a)(2).

(b) Whenever in a petition for probate or administration a party upon whom the service of process is required is a distributee whose relationship to the decedent is derived through another person who is deceased, the petition must either:

(1) show the relationship of the distributee to the decedent and the name and relationship of each person through whom such distributee claims to be related to the decedent; or

(2) have annexed a family tree table or diagram showing the names, relationships and dates of death of each person through whom such distributee claims to be related to the decedent, which table or diagram shall be supported by an affidavit of a person having knowledge of the contents thereof.

(c) If the petitioner alleges that the decedent was survived by no distributee or only one distributee, or where the relationship of distributees to the decedent is grandparents, aunts, uncles, first cousins or first cousins once removed, proof must be submitted to establish:

(1) how each such distributee is related to the decedent; and

(2) that no other persons of the same or a nearer degree of relationship survived the decedent.

Unless otherwise allowed by the court, the proof submitted pursuant to this subdivision must be by an affidavit or testimony of a disinterested person. Unless otherwise allowed by the court, if only one distributee survived the decedent, proof may not be given by the spouse or children of the distributee. The proof shall include as an exhibit a family tree table or diagram, except no such table or diagram shall be required if the distributee is the spouse or only child of the decedent.

(d) If the petitioner alleges that any of the distributees of the decedent or others required to be cited are unknown or that the names and addresses of some persons who are or may be distributees are unknown, petitioner must submit an affidavit showing that he or she has used due diligence in endeavoring to ascertain the identity, names and addresses of all such persons. Compliance with this due diligence requirement is not intended to burden the estate with costly or overly time-consuming searches. Absent special circumstances, the affidavit will be deemed to satisfy the requirement of due diligence if it indicates the results obtained from among the following:

(1) examination of decedent's personal effects, including address books;

(2) inquiry of decedent's relatives, neighbors, friends, former business associates and employers, the post office and financial institutions;

(3) correspondence to the last known address of any missing distributees;

(4) correspondence or telephone calls to, or internet search for, persons of same or similar name in the area where the person being sought lived;

(5) examination of the records of the motor vehicle bureau and board of elections of the state or county of the last-known address of the person whose whereabouts is unknown.

In probate proceedings, the court may accept, in lieu of the above, an affidavit by decedent setting forth the efforts that he or she made to ascertain relatives.

(e) If a person requesting letters to administer an estate as sole executor or administrator is also an attorney admitted in this State, he or she shall file with the petition requesting letters a statement disclosing:

(1) that the fiduciary is an attorney;

(2) whether the fiduciary or the law firm with which he or she is affiliated will act as counsel; and

(3) if applicable, that the fiduciary was the draftsperson of a will offered for probate with respect to that estate.

Cross References

SCPA, see McKinney's Book 58A.

§ 207.17.   [Repealed]

§ 207.18.   Use of Virtual Representation

(a) In any accounting proceeding where representation is to be utilized pursuant to subdivision 5 of SCPA 315, an affidavit of the petitioner or petitioner's attorney, and of the representor, must be submitted setting forth the following information:

(1) In the affidavit of the petitioner or petitioner's attorney:

(i) the name, address and the interest in the estate of the representor;

(ii) the name, address and the interest in the estate of the representees; and

(iii) the statutory basis for the use of virtual representation; and

(2) In the affidavit of the representor:

(i) that the representor has fully reviewed the proceedings;

(ii) the steps taken by the representor to adequately represent the interest of the representees in order to make a considered judgment whether to appear, default, acquiesce or contest the proceedings; and

(iii) that the representor has no conflict of interest in adequately representing the representees.

(b) If the court in any other proceeding, or in an accounting proceeding in circumstances other than set forth in subdivision (a), questions adequacy of representation by the representor, it may direct the filing of the affidavits set forth in subdivision (a) of this section.

Cross References

SCPA, see McKinney's Book 58A.

§ 207.19.   Probate; Filing of Will; Depositions; Proof by Affidavit

(a) With every petition for probate of a will there must be filed the original will and a copy thereof except in the case of lost or destroyed wills or where the Surrogate dispenses therewith or fixes a later time within which such will must be filed. With such copy there must also be filed an affidavit showing that it is a true copy of the original. If the copy be a reproduction by photographic or similar process, the affidavit shall be by one person; otherwise it shall be by the two persons who have compared the copy with the original. In a proceeding for probate of a will alleged to be lost or destroyed the Surrogate may make such order in respect of the filing of the text thereof as he or she may deem proper.

(b)(1) Unless service is by publication, a copy of the will shall be attached to all citations served and the affidavits of service of citation shall recite the service of a copy of the will.

(2) All waivers and consents filed with the court shall recite in the body of the waiver that a copy of the will was received.

(c) The clerk may require at least two days' notice before taking a deposition or testimony of any attesting witness. When any party is to be represented by a guardian ad litem, proponents should give notice of the time and place of taking a deposition of an attesting witness to such guardian ad litem.

(d) In a probate proceeding where the will purports to exercise a power of appointment, a copy of the instrument creating the power of appointment must be furnished, and the petition for probate shall list those named in said instrument who are adversely affected by the probate of such will. Jurisdiction shall be acquired over such persons in the same manner as over distributees.

Forms

Petition for probate of will—official form, see West's McKinney's Forms, Estates and Surrogate Practice, § 7:434.

§ 207.20. Value of Estate

(a) The fiduciary or the attorney of record shall furnish to the court a list of assets constituting the gross estate for tax purposes, but separately listing:

(1) those assets that either were owned by the decedent individually, including those in which the decedent has a partial interest, or were payable or transferrable to the decedent's estate; and

(2) those assets held in trust, those assets over which the decedent had the power to designate a beneficiary, jointly owned property, and all other non-probate property of the decedent.

This list of assets shall be filed with the court by the later to occur of the following events:

(1) if the estate is required to file a Form 706 Federal Estate Tax Return, the due date for the filing of such return, including any extensions of time received for the filing thereof;

(2) if the estate is not required to file a Form 706, the due date for the filing of the New York Estate Tax Return, including any extensions of time received for the filing thereof;

(3) if the estate is not required to file a New York Estate Tax Return, six months from the issuance of temporary or preliminary letters, limited letters, ancillary letters, full letters of administration or letters testamentary.

At any time after six months from the date of the decedent's death, if any "person interested," as that term is defined by SCPA 103(39), makes a written request for such a list, the fiduciary or attorney of record shall furnish the list, within 21 days of the mailing of such request, in as complete a form as is then possible.

(b) The requirement for filing a list of assets may be satisfied by the filing of a summary schedule together with a copy of either Form 706 Federal Estate Tax Return, Form 706NA Federal Estate Tax Return for Nonresident Aliens, or New York State Estate Tax Return TT–385 or ET–90.

(c) In the event such list of assets is not so filed, the court may refuse to issue certificates, may revoke the letters and may refuse to issue new ones until such list has been filed and the fees paid as provided in SCPA 2402. Failure to voluntarily file such list of assets may also constitute grounds for disallowance of commissions or legal fees.

(d) If any additional filing fees are due, they shall be paid to the court at the time of the submission of any of the documents described in subdivision (a) of this section.

Cross References

SCPA, see McKinney's Book 58A.

§ 207.21. Notification to Foreign Consuls

Where it appears that an intestate who died, or any party interested in the estate of the intestate, is the subject of a foreign power whose consul is entitled by treaty to administration or intervention, notice of the application for the appointment of an administrator shall be given such consul.

§ 207.22. Witnesses Out of County

(a) When, in an uncontested probate proceeding, a witness to a will is outside the jurisdiction of the court, and SCPA section 1406 is not utilized, the court may order that the witness be examined in the Surrogate's Court of another county or in an appropriate court of another state or county or before a commissioner designated by the court pursuant to SCPA 508, specifying the nature and manner of the examination, and shall send such other court or commissioner a copy of such order together with the original will or court-certified reproduction thereof. If the original will is sent, a court-certified copy thereof shall be retained in the office of the court wherein the proceeding is pending.

(b) When the testimony of the witness is obtained, it shall be annexed to the will or to the copy to which it relates, and together they shall be returned to and filed in the court wherein the proceeding is pending, as provided in SCPA 507.

Cross References

SCPA, see McKinney's Book 58A.

Forms

Order directing issuance of commission to take deposition outside state on written questions, see West's McKinney's Forms, Estates and Surrogate Practice, § 3:201.

Order directing issuance of commission to take deposition outside state on oral questions and directing issuance of letters rogatory, see West's McKinney's Forms, Estates and Surrogate Practice, § 3:202.

Commission to take deposition outside state on written questions, see West's McKinney's Forms, Estates and Surrogate Practice, § 3:203.

§ 207.23. Bills of Particulars in Contested Probate Proceedings

(a) In any probate proceeding in which objection to probate is made upon the grounds that the execution of the propounded instrument was procured by fraud or undue influence and the proponent demands or moves for a bill of particulars, the proponent shall be entitled as of course to the following information:

(1) the specific act or acts or course of conduct alleged to have constituted and effected such undue influence; the person or persons charged therewith and the time or times and place or places where it is alleged to have taken place;

(2) the particular false statements, suppressions of fact, misrepresentations, or other fraudulent acts al-

leged to have been practiced upon the decedent, the place or places where these events are claimed to have occurred and the persons who perpetrated them;

(3) whether such acts were accompanied by an act of physical violence or mistreatment of the decedent or threats, and if so, the nature thereof.

(b) If it is claimed by the contestant that the instrument offered for probate is not the last will of the deceased, the proponent shall be entitled to a bill of particulars as of course which shall state:

(1) whether it is claimed that there is an alleged testamentary instrument of later date than the instrument offered for probate;

(2) whether it is claimed that the instrument offered for probate was revoked, and if so, the method by which the alleged revocation was accomplished;

(3) whether it is merely claimed that the instrument offered for probate was not executed in accordance with the prescribed statutory formalities.

(c) In the demand or notice of motion it shall not be necessary for the proponent to set forth at length the foregoing items; he or she may, in lieu thereof, refer to the items specified in this rule. As to any other desired particulars, the proponent shall set them forth at length in the demand or notice of motion.

(d) Nothing contained in the foregoing shall be deemed to limit the court in denying, in a proper case, any one or more of the foregoing particulars, or in a proper case, in granting other, further or different particulars.

§ 207.24. Discontinuance of Proceedings

In any discontinued action or proceeding, the attorney for the plaintiff or petitioner shall file a stipulation or statement of discontinuance with the clerk of the court within 20 days of such discontinuance. If the action or proceeding has been noticed for judicial activity within 20 days of such discontinuance, the stipulation or statement shall be filed before the date scheduled for such activity.

§ 207.25. Kinship Matters

(a) Accounting Proceedings. In all kinship matters, whether the hearing be held by the court or referred to a referee, proof must be completed by the party who seeks to establish kinship in an accounting proceeding within one year from the date fixed for a hearing by the court or the date of referral, or the party's objections shall be dismissed and the monies deposited pursuant to CPLR 2601 for the benefit of unknown distributees.

(b) Administration or Withdrawal Proceedings. In all kinship matters, whether the hearing be held by the court or referred to a referee, proof must be completed by the party who seeks to establish kinship in an administration proceeding or withdrawal proceeding within six months from the date fixed for a

hearing by the court or the date of referral or the petition shall be dismissed, without prejudice.

Cross References

CPLR, see McKinney's Book 7B.

§ 207.26. Contested Probate; Notice of Objections Filed

(a) Objections to probate of a will shall be filed and served with proof of service in conformity with SCPA 1410.

(b) Whenever objections are filed, the proponent shall promptly present a petition for and procure an order directing service of notice of objections filed when required by SCPA 1411. If the proponent fails to present such petition or, having presented it, fails to procure such order or to give the notice prescribed in such section within five days after the return date of the citation or when objections are filed, whichever is later, any other party may present such petition and order and cause such notice to be serviced pursuant thereto.

(c) Since the requirements of SCPA 1411 are jurisdictional, all further pretrial procedures or proceedings shall be stayed until there is compliance with this rule.

Cross References

SCPA, see McKinney's Book 58A.

Forms

Objections to probate, see West's McKinney's Forms, Estates and Surrogate Practice, §§ 7:506, 7:507, 7:508, 7:509, 7:510 and 7:511.

Notice of objections filed, see West's McKinney's Forms, Estates and Surrogate Practice, § 7:532.

Affidavit of service of notice of objections filed, see West's McKinney's Forms, Estates and Surrogate Practice, § 7:533.

Petition for order to serve notice of filing of objections, see West's McKinney's Forms, Estates and Surrogate Practice, § 7:534.

Order directing service of notice of objections filed, see West's McKinney's Forms, Estates and Surrogate Practice, § 7:535.

§ 207.27. Examinations Before Trial in Contested Probate Proceedings

In any contested probate proceeding in which objections to probate are made and the proponent or the objectant seeks an examination before trial, the items upon which the examination will be held shall be determined by the application of Article 31 of CPLR. Except upon the showing of special circumstances, the examination will be confined to a three-year period prior to the date of the propounded instrument and two years thereafter, or to the date of decedent's death, whichever is the shorter period.

§ 207.28. Examination of Attesting Witnesses; Accountants and Adverse Parties or Witnesses

(a) All examinations of attesting witnesses, accountants and adverse parties or witnesses should be conducted on reasonable notice to all attorneys, guardians ad litem and parties entitled under SCPA 302(3). Unless the court otherwise directs, all examinations pursuant to SCPA 1404, 2102, 2103, 2104 and 2211 shall be held at the courthouse.

(b) Unless the court permits, such examinations shall not be conducted until jurisdiction has been obtained over all necessary parties to the proceeding and, where necessary, guardians ad litem have been appointed and qualified.

§ 207.29. Note of Issue; Pretrial Conference

(a) The court may establish such calendars of cases as it deems necessary or desirable for proper case management and may schedule calls of such calendars at such times and in such manner as it deems appropriate.

(b) The court may direct that a trial or hearing date shall not be fixed until after a party shall file in duplicate a note of issue with a certificate of readiness in a form prescribed by the court together with an affidavit of service of said note of issue and certificate of readiness upon all parties who have appeared. The note of issue filed shall contain a statement of the estimated trial time each party will require.

(c) A pretrial conference may be directed by the court, either before or after a trial date is fixed, at which the parties shall attend. At such conference, a schedule of dates for the completion of examinations, disclosure matters, bills of particulars and other pretrial matters may be directed. The court may direct parties to submit for inspection documents and exhibits, may require counsel to stipulate as to facts and issues, and may direct severance or consolidation of issues.

§ 207.30. Statement of Issues

(a) At least ten days prior to the trial of the issues joined in any proceeding except where an order framing issues has theretofore been made, the petitioner shall file with the court a statement, in writing, of the nature of such issues, the party who holds the affirmative as to each issue, and the objections, if any, which the petitioner concedes to be well taken or which may have been withdrawn.

(b) In accounting proceedings, an additional notation shall be included in the statement as to any modifications of the account to which the parties consent.

§ 207.31. Jury Trials; Order Framing Issues

(a) No matter shall be assigned a date for trial by jury until an order framing issues and directing a trial by jury has been made pursuant to SCPA 502.

(b) Whenever a jury trial has been demanded, any party on five days' notice of settlement to the attorneys for all other parties who have appeared may present a proposed order framing the issues and directing such trial by jury. Such order shall state plainly and concisely the controverted questions of fact to be determined by the jury.

(c) In such order, the court may fix a date for trial or on which the matter will be placed on the calendar for assignment of trial date. Such order must be served on all parties who have appeared at least 15 days before date of trial or date of calendar call and proof of service filed at least ten days before such date of trial or calendar call.

§ 207.32. Identification of Trial Counsel

(a) Where the attorney of record for any party arranges for another attorney to conduct the trial, the trial counsel must be identified in writing to the court and all parties within ten days after the filing of the notice of trial. The notice must be signed by both the attorney of record and the trial counsel.

(b) After trial counsel is designated as provided above, no substitution shall be permitted unless the substitute counsel is available to try the case on the day scheduled for trial. Written notice of such substitution shall be given promptly to the court and all parties.

§ 207.33. Engagement of Counsel

No adjournment shall be granted on the ground of engagement of counsel except in accordance with Part 125 of the Rules of the Chief Administrator.

§ 207.34. Exhibits

(a) A party intending to offer an exhibit that can be readily duplicated or reproduced shall prepare extra copies for use at the trial. A party offering in evidence any paper in his or her possession shall submit a copy to opposing counsel for inspection.

(b) If a filed document is to form part of the evidence to be submitted at trial, such document or a certified copy shall be obtained or ordered from the clerk's office or other repository sufficiently in advance of trial to permit its production without delaying the trial.

(c) Whenever practicable, to avoid unnecessary delay during the trial, counsel shall hand exhibits for marking to the court reporter or other designated person prior to the opening statements or during a recess.

§ 207.35. Absence of Attorney During Trial

All trial counsel shall remain in attendance at all stages of the trial until the jury retires to deliberate unless excused by the Surrogate. Any counsel not present during the jury deliberation, further requests to charge, or report of the jury verdict shall be deemed to stipulate that the court may proceed in his or her absence and to waive any irregularity in proceedings taken in his or her absence. The court may permit trial counsel to leave provided that counsel remain in telephone contact with the court.

§ 207.36. Failure to File Timely Objections

Whenever the time to file objections in a proceeding has expired, objections shall not be accepted for filing unless accompanied by a stipulation of all parties to extend the time or unless ordered by the court.

§ 207.37. Submission of Orders, Judgments and Decrees for Signature

(a) Proposed orders or judgments, with proof of service on all parties where the order is directed to be settled or submitted on notice, must be submitted for signature, unless otherwise directed by the court, within 60 days after the signing and filing of the decision directing that the order be settled or submitted.

(b) Failure to submit the order or judgment timely shall be deemed an abandonment of the motion or proceeding unless for good cause shown.

(c)(1) When settlement of an order or judgment is directed by the court, a copy of the proposed order or judgment with notice of settlement, returnable at the office of the clerk of the part in which the order or judgment was granted, or before the judge if the court has so directed or if the clerk is unavailable, shall be served on all parties either:

(i) by personal service not less than five days before the day of settlement; or

(ii) by mail not less than ten days before the date of settlement.

(2) Proposed counter-orders or judgments shall be made returnable on the same date and at the same place, and shall be served on all parties by personal service, not less than two days, or by mail, not less than seven days, before the date of settlement.

§ 207.38. Compromises

(a) Upon any application for leave to compromise a claim for wrongful death or personal injuries or both, the petition and the supporting affidavits shall set forth the time, place and manner in which the decedent sustained the injuries, and a complete statement of all such facts as would justify the granting of the

application. If the cause of action did not arise under the laws of the State of New York, the laws of the jurisdiction under which said cause of action arose must be established to the satisfaction of the court.

(b) The petition also shall show the following:

(1) the age, residence, occupation and earnings of the decedent at time of death;

(2) the names, addresses, dates of birth and ages of all the persons entitled to take or share in the proceeds of the settlement or judgment, as provided by EPTL 5–4.4, or by the applicable law of the jurisdiction under which the claim arose, and a statement whether or not there are any children born out of wedlock.

(3) a complete statement of the nature and extent of the disability other than infancy, of any person set forth in (2);

(4) the gross amount of the proceeds of settlement, the amount to be paid as attorneys' fees, and the net amount to be received by petitioner as a result of the settlement;

(5) any obligations incurred for funeral expenses, or for hospital, medical or nursing services, the name and address of each such creditor, the respective amounts of the obligations so incurred, whether such obligations have been paid in full and/or the amount of the unpaid balance due on each of said claims as evidenced by proper bills filed with the clerk;

(6) whether any hospital notice of lien has been filed under section 189 of the Lien Law, and if so, the particulars relating thereto;

(7) on the basis of the applicable law, a tabulation showing the proposed distribution including the names of the persons entitled to share in the proceeds and the percentage or fraction representing their respective shares, including a reference to the mortality table, if any, employed in the proceeding which resulted in the settlement or judgment, and the mortality table employed in the proposed distribution of the proceeds;

(8) the cost of any annuities in compromises based upon structured settlements in wrongful death actions.

(c) Where the petition also makes application for the compromise of a claim for personal injuries sustained by the decedent, the petition shall set forth the amount allocated to each cause of action, the basis for such allocation, the effect of such allocation on decedent's estate tax liability, and proof of the citation of the New York State Department of Taxation and Finance, or their waiver thereof.

(d) A supporting affidavit by the attorney for petitioner must be filed with each petition for leave to compromise showing:

(1) whether the attorney has become concerned in the application or its subject matter at the instance of

the party with whom the compromise is proposed or at the instance of any representative of such party;

(2) whether the attorney's fee is to be paid by the administrator and whether any payment has been or is to be made to the attorney by any other person or corporation interested in the subject matter of the compromise;

(3) if the attorney's compensation is to be paid by any other person, the name of such person;

(4) the services rendered by the attorney in detail;

(5) the amount to be paid as compensation to the attorney, including an itemization of disbursements on the case, and whether the compensation was fixed by prior agreement or based on reasonable value, and if by agreement, the person with whom such agreement was made and the terms thereof.

(e) In an application for the compromise of a claim solely for personal injuries, the petition shall contain all the facts in relation to such claim and comply with as much of the provisions of this rule as are applicable, and in addition, the petition shall recite the date letters were issued, whether more than seven months have elapsed from such date, the names and post-office addresses of all creditors, or those claiming to be creditors, and the distributees of the decedent, specifying such as are infants or alleged incompetents.

(f) Whenever papers are filed for the compromise of a cause of action in which the original action alleged conscious pain and suffering and wrongful death, and the action is subsequently settled for wrongful death only, the waivers and consents of any adult distributees who will not share in the recovery must recite that they are aware that, by consenting that the entire settlement be considered as a settlement of the cause of action for wrongful death, they are waiving the right to receive any distributive share out of the settlement.

Cross References

EPTL, see McKinney's Book 17B.

Lien Law, see McKinney's Book 32.

Forms

Affidavit of attorney on application to compromise wrongful death action, see West's McKinney's Forms, Estates and Surrogate Practice, § 14:61.

Affidavit of attorney in support of application to compromise wrongful death action, see West's McKinney's Forms, Estates and Surrogate Practice, § 14:65.

Petition to compromise wrongful death action, see West's McKinney's Forms, Estates and Surrogate Practice, §§ 14:59 and 14:60.

§ 207.39. Costs and Allowances

(a) On the settlement of a decree, any party who shall deem himself entitled to costs may present a bill of costs, provided that at least two days' notice of the taxation thereof has been served on all attorneys appearing in the proceeding. Each bill of costs must show the items of costs to which the party deems himself entitled and must contain an itemized list of any disbursements claims, duly verified both as to amount and necessity. The disbursements for referee's and stenographer's fees may be evidenced by affidavit or by such other proof as may be satisfactory to the court.

(b) An application for an allowance may also be made on two days' notice to all attorneys appearing in the proceeding. Such application shall be accompanied by an affidavit setting forth the number of days necessarily occupied in the hearing or trial; the time occupied on each day in the rendition of the services; and a detailed statement of the nature and extent of the services rendered, including services necessarily rendered or to be rendered in the drawing, entering or executing of the decree.

§ 207.40. Accountings

(a) Whenever a petition for a voluntary accounting is presented, the account to which it relates must be filed therewith, if not previously filed, and a citation to settle such account must thereupon be procured and served on the parties required to be cited.

(b) Unless otherwise directed by the court, upon an accounting by an executor, trustee, or administrator c.t.a., a copy of the will or trust instrument must be filed with the petition and account.

(c) Insofar as may be practical, all accounts shall conform with and contain such schedules and information as may be called for in such forms as may from time to time be provided by the Chief Administrator of the Courts or, in the absence thereof, by the court. In the account of a trustee of a common trust fund for a period that begins at the close of the prior intermediate account:

(1) the statements of increases and decreases shall also show gains and losses realized on disposition of assets based upon the fair market values at the beginning of the account of assets held at the beginning of the account and the inventory values of all other assets; and

(2) the statement of assets on hand at the close of the account shall also show that increase or decrease in the fair market value of the assets at the close of the account in relation to the fair market values at the beginning of the account of those assets which were held at the beginning of the account and in relation to the inventory values of the remainder of said assets.

(d) The schedule showing the computation of commissions shall also state in explicit terms whether any personal property listed as an asset of the estate was, at the date of decedent's death, pledged as collateral to any unpaid obligation of the decedent and, if so, shall set forth:

(1) a description of the property so pledged and the value thereof as listed in the account;

(2) the amount due at the date of death on the obligation for which it was pledged;

(3) the equity in such property at the date of death; and

(4) whether the accounting party has included in the claim for commissions any commissions upon the value of the property so pledged and, if so, a statement of the capital value upon which such commissions are claimed with respect to such property.

(e) Unless service is by publication or unless otherwise directed by the court, a copy of the summary statement of account shall be attached to all citations served, and the affidavits of service of citation shall recite the service of a copy of the summary statement of account. Counsel for the accounting party or the accounting party, if not represented by counsel, shall furnish a copy of the full account to all persons cited in the accounting proceeding who request the full account. Failure to furnish such a copy may constitute grounds for disallowance of commissions or legal fees.

(f) Unless otherwise directed by the court, all waivers of citation and consents in accounting proceedings filed with the court shall recite in the body of the waiver that a copy of the summary statement of account was received and shall state that the person waiving understands that he or she may request a copy of the full account from the petitioner or petitioner's attorney.

(g) The cost of producing and delivering a full accounting to persons interested in the estate shall be deemed a proper disbursement and allowed as an expense of administration.

Cross References

Tax Law, see McKinney's Book 59.

§ 207.41. Contested Accountings

On any accounting by an executor, administrator, temporary administrator, guardian or trustee, any creditor or any other party interested may file objections thereto in writing within such time as shall be allowed by the Surrogate. Such objections must be served upon the accounting party or the accounting party's attorney before the filing thereof in the court. A guardian ad litem appointed in an accounting proceeding shall file a report or objections within 20 days after the appointment unless for cause shown the time to file such report or objections is extended by the Surrogate.

§ 207.42. Report of Estates Not Fully Distributed

(a) Whenever the estate of a decedent has not been fully distributed or a final accounting filed with petition for settlement within two years from the date

when the first permanent letters of administration or letters testamentary were issued where the gross taxable estate of such decedent does not require the filing of a federal estate tax return, and within three years if a federal estate tax return is required, the executor or administrator shall, at or before the end of the first complete month following the expiration of such time, file with the clerk of the court a statement in substantially the following form:

SURROGATE'S COURT Report pursuant to 22
NYCRR 207.42

.... COUNTY

Estate of ...., Deceased
File No. ....
Date of issuance of first permanent letters ....
Approximate amount of gross estate ....
Approximate amount that has been distributed to beneficiaries ....
Approximate amount remaining in fiduciary's hands at present ....
This estate has not yet been fully distributed for the following reason: (state briefly)
....
....

Date of this report ....
....
Fiduciary
Address: ....
Phone: ....
....
Attorney for above Fiduciary
Address: ....
Phone: ....

(b) The court shall thereupon take such steps as it deems appropriate to expedite the completion of the administration of the estate and the distribution of all assets.

(c) Failure to file such statement will be considered by the court on any application for commissions or legal fees and may constitute a ground for disallowance of commissions or fees.

(d) The periods set forth in subdivision (a) hereinabove stated are not intended to set a standard time for completion of estate administration but rather to fix a period after which inquiry may be made by the court.

(e) This section shall not limit the power of the court to direct an accounting at any time on its own initiative or on petition pursuant to SCPA 2205.

Cross References

SCPA, see McKinney's Book 58A.

§ 207.43. Filing Estate Tax Return

(a) For all persons who die on or after May 26, 1990, for whom an estate tax return is required to be filed pursuant to section 971 of the Tax Law, if a petition for probate or administration was filed with the Surrogate's Court, the person required to file the tax return shall file a copy of the tax return with such Surrogate's Court, pursuant to section 972(c) of the Tax Law, within ten days of filing the original tax return with the Commissioner of Taxation and Finance; provided, however, this section shall not apply where the decedent died on or after February 1, 2000 and the Surrogate's Court in which the petition for probate or administration was filed has not adopted a rule pursuant to section 972(c) of the Tax Law requiring the filing of a copy of the tax return with such Court.

(b) Failure to file a copy of the estate tax return when required pursuant to this section together with any filing fee required pursuant to law shall authorize the court to compel an accounting pursuant to SCPA 2205 and may constitute grounds for revocation of letters, imposition of a surcharge or disallowance of commissions or legal fees.

§ 207.44. Payment of Estate Tax

(a) No decree of final settlement of an executor's or administrator's account or of the discharge of an executor or administrator shall be signed unless the petition is accompanied or preceded by a copy of the letter from the Estate and Gift Tax Section of the New York Department of Taxation and Finance captioned "New York Estate Tax Discharge from Liability" showing that no final estate tax is due or that the final estate tax plus interest and penalties, if any, have been paid.

(b) Nothing herein shall preclude the discharge of an executor or an administrator who has complied with the requirements of section 1804(3) of the Surrogate's Court Procedure Act where a tax has been fixed but not paid because of insufficient funds in the estate, or the representative seeks a discharge before the estate has been administered, or where no return has been filed, or for other sufficient cause.

§ 207.45. Attorney's Fees; Fixation of Compensation

(a) In any proceeding in which the relief requested includes the determination of compensation of an attorney or the allowance of expenses of counsel, there shall be filed with the petition an affidavit of services which shall state when and by whom the attorney was retained; the terms of the retainer; the amount of compensation requested; whether the client has been consulted as to the fee requested; whether the client consents to the same or, if not, the extent of disagreement or nature of any controversy concerning the same; the period during which services were rendered; the services rendered, in detail; the time spent; and the method or basis by which the requested compensation was determined. The affidavit also shall state whether the fee includes all services rendered and to be rendered up to and including settlement of the decree and distribution, if any, thereunder

and whether the attorney waives a formal hearing as to compensation.

(b) Except when the SCPA otherwise provides or when compelling reasons exist for so doing, the court shall not fix attorneys' compensation or make allowances to parties for counsel expenses unless a proceeding is instituted under SCPA 2110 or unless, in an accounting, the petition and citation state that an application will be made for determination of compensation, the allowance of counsel expenses and the amount thereof.

(c) Reports, affidavits and statements relating to fixation of fees and allowances shall be served upon the petitioner and upon all attorneys, guardians ad litem and parties appearing in person (other than those who have theretofore filed waivers). Proof of such service shall be filed with the court.

(d) In any proceeding for the determination of kinship in which an attorney appears for any party not a resident of the United States, the attorney shall institute a proceeding pursuant to SCPA 2110 for the fixation of his or her compensation and shall comply with the provisions set forth in subdivisions (a) through (c) of this section.

Cross References

SCPA, see McKinney's Book 58A.

§ 207.46. Small Estate Proceedings

In all proceedings for the settlement of small estates without court administration (SCPA Article 13), if additional certificates of voluntary administration are requested, other than updated or replacement certificates for the same asset or assets as the original certificate, such request shall be accompanied by an affidavit from either the voluntary administrator or the attorney of record setting forth the reasons additional certificates are required.

§ 207.47. Recording Assignments of Interest in Estates

(a) No assignment of any right, share or interest in an estate of a decedent shall be filed or recorded unless accompanied by an affidavit in a form satisfactory to the court, which shall state whether any power of attorney or separate agreement exists which relates to such assignment or which fixes presently or prospectively the amount payable by or to the assignor.

(b) A copy of such separate agreement shall be annexed to the affidavit, if such separate agreement be in writing, and a statement of the substance thereof shall be incorporated in the affidavit if such separate agreement be oral. No assignment accompanied by a power of attorney shall be recorded unless such power of attorney be recorded.

§ 207.48. Filing and Recording of Powers of Attorney

(a) No power of attorney affecting any interest in a decedent's estate shall be filed or recorded pursuant to EPTL 13–2.3 unless:

(1) the instrument is satisfactory to the court as to form, content and manner of execution; and

(2) the person offering the instrument for filing or recording shall furnish an affidavit of the attorney-in-fact, stating: the circumstances under which the power of attorney was procured; the post office address of the grantor, the amount of his or her interest and relationship, if any, to the decedent; the financial arrangement and exact terms of compensation of the attorney-in-fact or of any other person concerned with the matter; disbursements to be charged to the grantor; a copy of any agreement concerning compensation; and the name of any attorney representing the attorney-in-fact.

(b) An attorney-in-fact in a proceeding for the determination of kinship shall not accept any payment for acting pursuant to a power of attorney unless there has been filed with the court all the terms of the agreed-upon compensation or the same has been fixed by the court in a proceeding pursuant to SCPA 2112.

§ 207.49. Applications for Appointment of Successor Custodians Under EPTL 7–4.7

(a) A petition for the appointment of a successor custodian under EPTL 7–4.7 shall show:

(1) the relationship between the petitioner and the minor;

(2) the age of the minor;

(3) the facts concerning the original gift;

(4) whether the donor was the original custodian and, if not, whether he or she joins in the application;

(5) the adult members of the minor's family;

(6) whether there is a general or testamentary guardian of the minor and, if so, whether he or she joins in the application;

(7) what was the relationship between the custodian and the petitioner if the donor was the custodian and is now deceased;

(8) if the donor custodian and petitioner were husband and wife, whether they were living together and whether the infant resided with them;

(9) with whom the minor is now living;

(10) the monies and securities to be delivered to the successor custodian and the value of such securities.

(b) If the donor was a relative of the minor and has died leaving a will, a copy of the will should be submitted.

(c) Additional facts and affidavits shall be submitted as will permit the court to determine from the papers, in the absence of a contest, that the best interests of the minor will be served by the appointment of the petitioner as successor custodian, rather than by the appointment of some other eligible person.

(d) Unless otherwise ordered by the court, and unless such person or persons have joined in the application, notice of the application shall be served upon (i) such persons as are required to be served in a proceeding for the appointment of a guardian, (ii) the donor, if he or she is alive, and the guardian, if there is one of the minor.

Cross References

EPTL, see McKinney's Book 17B.

§ 207.50. [Repealed]

§ 207.51. Appearance of a Guardian, Committee or Conservator; Affidavit Required of Attorney

If the affidavit required by SCPA 402 shows that the guardian, committee or conservator is entitled to share in the distribution of the estate or fund in which the infant, incompetent or conservatee is interested or that the guardian, committee or conservator is in any way interested in the estate or fund, such affidavit must state fully the nature of his or her interest. Whenever a guardian, committee or conservator appears by an attorney, the latter shall accompany his or her notice of appearance with an affidavit showing the circumstances which led to his or her employment and whether his or her employment was suggested or accelerated either directly or indirectly by the proponent or accounting party or by the attorney for either of them or by any other person whose interest in the proceeding is adverse to that of the infant, incompetent or conservatee, and showing further that the attorney is free of any restraint, whether professional, personal or otherwise, in his or her complete independence of action on behalf of his or her client or ward.

Cross References

SCPA, see McKinney's Book 58A.

§ 207.52. Accounting of an Attorney-Fiduciary

(a) Within 12 months from the issuance of letters, or 24 months if the estate must file a federal estate tax return, if a sole executor or administrator administering an estate is also an attorney admitted in this state, and he or she or the law firm with which the attorney is affiliated is acting as counsel for the estate, the attorney-fiduciary shall file an affidavit setting forth (1) the total commissions paid or to be paid to him or her and (2) the total attorney's fees paid or to be paid (by court order, if required) to him or her or to the law firm with which he or she is affiliated, for services rendered to the estate.

(b) The court may extend the time for filing the affidavit upon good cause shown to the court in writing.

(c) The court in its discretion may require additional information or documentation from the attorney-fiduciary, including an affidavit of legal services, a cash flow statement and a full accounting pursuant to SCPA 2205.

(d) In the event the affidavit is not so filed, the court may suspend the letters until the affidavit has been filed. Failure to file the affidavit may constitute grounds for disallowance of commissions or legal fees.

(e) Except as otherwise provided by SCPA 2111(1) and (2), or SCPA 2310 or 2311, an attorney-fiduciary as defined in subdivision (a) (or the law firm with which he or she is affiliated) shall not take advances for legal services rendered to the estate, or commissions on account of compensation, until 30 days after filing the affidavit required by subdivision (a).

(f) The provisions of this section also shall apply to each co-fiduciary administering an estate who is an attorney admitted in this state if (1) he or she or the law firm with which the attorney is affiliated is acting as counsel for the estate, and (2) there is no other co-fiduciary who is not an attorney.

Cross References

SCPA, see McKinney's Book 58A.

§ 207.53. [Repealed]

§ 207.54. Adoption Rules; Application

(a) Sections 207.54 through 207.58 hereof shall be applicable to all agency and private-placement adoption proceedings in Surrogate's Court.

(b) In any agency adoption, a petition may be filed to adopt a child who is the subject of a termination of parental rights proceeding and whose custody and guardianship has not yet been committed to an authorized agency, provided that

(i) the adoption petition is filed in the same court where the termination of parental rights proceeding is pending; and

(ii) the adoption petition, supporting documents and the fact of their filing shall not be provided to the judge before whom the petition for termination of parental rights is pending until such time as fact-finding is concluded under that petition.

§ 207.55. Papers Required in an Adoption Proceeding

(a) All papers submitted in an adoption proceeding shall comply with section 207.4 hereof.

(b) In addition to those papers required by the Domestic Relations Law, the following papers, unless otherwise dispensed with by the court, shall be submitted and filed prior to the placement of any adoption proceeding on the calendar:

(1) a certified copy of the birth certificate of the adoptive child;

(2) an affidavit or affidavits by an attorney admitted to practice in the State of New York, or, in the discretion of the court, by a person other than an attorney who is known to the court, identifying each of the parties;

(3) a certified marriage certificate, where the adoptive parents are husband and wife or where an individual adoptive parent is the spouse of the natural parent;

(4) a certified copy of a decree or judgment, where an adoptive parent's marriage has been terminated by decree or judgment;

(5) a certified death certificate, where an adoptive or natural parent's marriage has been terminated by death or where it is alleged that consent or notice is not required because of death;

(6) a proposed order of adoption;

(7) a copy of the attorney's affidavit of financial disclosure filed with the Office of Court Administration pursuant to 22 NYCRR 603.23, 691.23, 806.14 or 1022.33 and either an attorney's affirmation that the affidavit has been personally delivered or mailed in accordance with such rules or the dated receipt from the Office of Court Administration; and

(8) an affidavit of financial disclosure from the adoptive parent or parents, and from any person whose consent to the adoption is required by law, setting forth the following information:

(i) name, address and telephone number of the affiant;

(ii) status of the affiant in the proceeding and relationship, if any, to the adoptive child;

(iii) docket number of adoption proceeding;

(iv) the date and terms of every agreement, written or otherwise between the affiant and any attorney pertaining to any fees, compensation or other remuneration paid or to be paid by or on behalf of the adoptive parents or the natural parents, directly or indirectly, including but not limited to retainer fees on account of or incidental to the placement or adoption of the child or assistance in arrangements for such placement or adoption;

(v) the date and amount of any fees, compensation or other remuneration paid, and the total amount of fees, compensation or other remuneration to be paid to such attorney by the affiant, directly or indirectly, on account of or incidental to the placement or adoption of the child or assistance in arrangements for such placement or adoption;

(vi) the name and address of any other person, agency, association, corporation, institution, society or organization who received or will receive any fees, compensation or other remuneration from the affiant, directly or indirectly, on account of or incidental to the birth or care of the adoptive child, the pregnancy or care of the adoptive child's mother or the placement or adoption of the child and on account of or incidental to assistance in arrangements for such placement or proposed adoption, the amount of each such fee, compensation or other remuneration; and the reason for or services rendered if any, in connection with each such fee, compensation or other remuneration.

(vii) the name and address of any person, agency, association, corporation, society or organization who has or will pay the affiant any fee, compensation or other remuneration, directly or indirectly, on account of or incidental to the birth or care of the adoptive child, the pregnancy or care of the adoptive child's mother, or the placement or adoption of the child and on account of or incidental to assistance in arrangements for such placement or adoption; the amount of each such fee, compensation or other remuneration; and the reason for or services rendered, if any, in connection with each such fee, compensation or other remuneration.

(9) in the case of an adoption from an authorized agency in accordance with Title 2 of Article 7 of the Domestic Relations Law, a copy of the criminal history summary report made by the New York State Office of Children and Family Services to the authorized agency pursuant to section 378–a of the Social Services Law regarding the criminal record or records of the prospective adoptive parent or parents and any adult over the age of 18 currently residing in the home.

(c) Prior to the signing of an order of adoption, the court may in its discretion require the filing of a supplemental affidavit by the adoptive parent or parents, or any person whose consent to the adoption is required, the authorized agency and the attorney for any of the aforementioned, setting forth any additional information pertaining to allegations in the petition or in any affidavit filed in the proceeding.

Cross References

Domestic Relations Law, see McKinney's Book 14.

Public Health Law, see McKinney's Book 44.

§ 207.56. Investigation by Disinterested Person; Adoption

(a) The probation service or an authorized agency or disinterested person is authorized to and, at the request of the court, shall interview such persons and obtain such data as will aid the court in determining the truth and accuracy of an adoption petition under article 7 of the Domestic Relations Law, including the allegations set forth in the schedule annexed to the petition pursuant to section 112(3) of that law and such other facts as are necessary to a determination of the petition;

(b) The adoptive parent or parents and other persons concerned with the proceeding shall be notified of the date, time and place of any interview by a disinterested person or authorized agency designated by the court in accordance with sections 112 and 116 of the Domestic Relations Law.

(c) The written report of the investigation conducted pursuant to subdivision (a) of this section shall be submitted to the court within 30 days from the date on which it was ordered, or earlier as the court may direct, unless, for good cause, the court shall grant an extension for a reasonable period of time not to exceed an additional 30 days.

Cross References

Domestic Relations Law, see McKinney's Book 14.

§ 207.57. Special Applications

All applications, including applications to dispense with statutorily required personal appearances, period of residence of a child, or period of waiting after filing of the adoption petition, shall be made in writing and shall be accompanied by affidavits setting forth the reasons for the application and all facts relevant thereto.

§ 207.58. Petition for Guardianship by Adoptive Parent

(a) When a petition for temporary guardianship has been filed by an adoptive parent or parents pursuant to section 115–c of the Domestic Relations Law, the clerk of the court in which the petition has been filed shall distribute a written notice to the adoptive parents and lawyers who have appeared, and to the commissioner of social services or the director of the probation service, as appropriate, indicating that:

(1) a petition for adoption must be filed in the court in which the application for temporary guardianship has been brought within 45 days from the date of the signing of the consent to the adoption;

(2) any order or decree of temporary guardianship will expire no later than nine months following its issuance or upon the entry of a final order of adoption whichever is sooner, unless, upon application to the court, it is extended for good cause;

(3) any order or decree of temporary guardianship will terminate upon withdrawal or denial of a petition to adopt the child, unless the court orders a continuation of such order or decree;

(b) In addition to and without regard to the date set for the hearing of the petition, the clerk of the court shall calendar the case for the 45th day from the date of the signing of the consent to the adoption. If no petition for adoption has been filed by the 45th day, the court shall schedule a hearing and shall order the appropriate agency to conduct an investigation forthwith, if one had not been ordered previously.

§ 207.59. Proceedings Involving Custody of a Native American Child

In any proceeding in which the custody of a child is to be determined, the petition shall set forth whether the child is a Native American child subject to the Indian Child Welfare Act of 1978 (25 U.S.C. §§ 1901–1963), and the Court shall proceed further, as appropriate, in accordance with the provisions of that Act.

§ 207.60.   [Renumbered § 207.52]

§ 207.61. Proceedings for Certification as a Qualified Adoptive Parent or Parents

(a) Where the petition in a proceeding for certification as a qualified adoptive parent or parents alleges that petitioner or petitioners will cause a pre-placement investigation to be undertaken, the petition shall include the name and address of the disinterested person by whom such investigation will be conducted.

(b) The report of the disinterested person conducting the pre-placement investigation shall be filed by such person directly with the court, with a copy of such report delivered simultaneously to the applicant or applicants.

(c) The court shall order a report (1) from the statewide central register of child abuse and maltreatment setting forth whether the child or the petitioner is, or petitioners are, the subject of or another person named in an indicated report, as such terms are defined in section 412 of the Social Services Law, filed with such register; and (2) from the New York State Division of Criminal Justice Services setting forth any existing criminal record of such petitioner or petitioners in accordance with section 115–d(3–a) of the Domestic Relations Law; provided, however, that where the petitioner(s) have been fingerprinted pursuant to Social Services Law 378–a, the authorized agency in possession of a current criminal history summary report from the New York State Office of Children and Family Services may be requested to provide such report to the court in lieu of a report from the New York State Division of Criminal Justice Services.

§ 207.62. Calendaring of Proceedings for Adoption From an Authorized Agency

Proceedings for adoption from an authorized agency shall be calendared as follows:

(a) Within 60 days of the filing of the petition and documents specified in section 112–a of the Domestic Relations Law, the court shall schedule a review of said petition and documents to take place to determine if there is adequate basis for approving the adoption.

(b) If such basis is found, the court shall schedule the appearance of the adoptive parent(s) and child before the court, for approval of the adoption, within 30 days of the date of the review.

(c) If, upon the court's review, the court finds that there is not an adequate basis for approval of the adoption, the court shall direct such further hearings, submissions or appearances as may be required, and the proceeding shall be adjourned as required for such purposes.

§ 207.63. Annual Report of Public Administrator

(a) Each Surrogate shall request from the public administrator a year-end annual report which, with the participation of the counsel to the public administrator, addresses the following areas: office procedures and record keeping; case management of estates; cash management of estate accounts and financial assets; property management; sale of real and personal property; selection and compensation of outside vendors; and statistical summaries of number of estates under administration, gross value of estates under administration, statutory commissions earned by the public administrator or counsel to the public administrator, legal fees earned by each counsel to the public administrator, and expenditures by the public administrator on vendors, lessors and other service providers other than counsel.

(b) Each Surrogate shall transmit to the Chief Administrator of the Courts the annual report of the public administrator and counsel to the public administrator, together with whatever written commentary thereon the Surrogate deems appropriate and necessary in view of his or her oversight role in connection with the operations and performance of the office of the public administrator and counsel to the public administrator.

PART 208. UNIFORM CIVIL RULES FOR THE NEW YORK CITY CIVIL COURT

§ 208.1. Application of Part; Waiver; Additional Rules; Application of NYCCCA; Definitions

(a) **Application.** This Part shall be applicable to all actions and proceedings in the Civil Court of the City of New York.

(b) **Waiver.** For good cause shown, and in the interests of justice, the court in an action or proceeding may waive compliance with any of these rules other than sections 208.2 and 208.3 unless prohibited from doing so by statute or by a rule of the Chief Judge.

(c) **Additional Rules.** Additional local court rules, not inconsistent with law or with these rules, shall comply with Part 9 of the Rules of the Chief Judge (22 NYCRR Part 9).

(d) **Application of the New York City Civil Court Act.** The provisions of this part shall be construed as consistent with the New York City Civil Court Act (NYCCCA), and matters not covered by these provisions shall be governed by the NYCCCA.

(e) **Definitions.**

(1) "Chief Administrator of the Courts" in this Part includes a designee of the Chief Administrator.

(2) Unless otherwise defined in this Part, or the context otherwise requires, all terms used in this Part shall have the same meaning as they have in the NYCCCA and the CPLR.

Cross References

NYCCCA, see McKinney's Book 29A, Part 3.

§ 208.2. Divisions of Court; Terms and Structure

(a) Divisions of the court shall be designated as follows:

1. The Civil Court of the City of New York, County of Bronx.

2. The Civil Court of the City of New York, County of Kings.

3. The Civil Court of the City of New York, County of New York.

4. The Civil Court of the City of New York, County of Queens.

5. The Civil Court of the City of New York, County of Richmond.

(b) In each division there shall be held such terms as the Chief Administrator of the Courts shall designate. A term of court is a four-week session of court and there shall be 13 terms of court in a year, unless otherwise provided in the annual schedules of terms established by the Chief Administrator, which shall also specify the dates of such terms.

§ 208.3. Parts of Court; Structure

(a) **General.** A part of court is a designated unit of the court in which specified business of the court is to be conducted by a judge or quasijudicial officer.

(b) **Number and Types.** In each division there shall be such number of calendar parts, trial parts, motion parts, conference parts, multi-purpose parts, and other special parts of court, and any combination thereof, as may be established from time to time by the Chief Administrator of the Courts. There shall also be one or more small claims parts in each division for the hearing and disposition of all small claims proceedings, as the Chief Administrator may establish.

(1) *Calendar Part.* A calendar part is a part of court for the maintaining and calling of a calendar of cases, and for the hearing and disposition of all motions and applications, including orders to show cause and applications for adjournments, in civil actions that have been placed on a reserve or ready calendar but not yet assigned to a trial part.

(2) *Trial Part.* A trial part is a part of court for the trial of civil actions and for the hearing and determination of all motions and applications, including orders to show cause, made after an action is assigned to a trial part.

(3) *Motion Part.* A motion part is a part of court for the hearing and determination of motions and applications that are not otherwise required by this Part to be made in a calendar part, trial part or conference part.

(4) *Conference Part.* A conference part is a part of court for the precalendar or pretrial conference of actions as may be provided by this Part or by order of the Chief Administrator.

(5) *Multipurpose Part.* A multipurpose part is a part of court for the performance of the functions of a calendar part, a trial part, a motion part, a conference part, as well as other special parts of court, or any combination thereof.

(6) *Additional Parts.* Additional parts, including parts with special or limited functions, may be established from time to time by order of the Chief Administrator for such purposes as may be assigned by the Chief Administrator.

(7) *Transfer of Actions.* By order of the Chief Administrator, proceedings and matters may be transferred, as the Chief Administrator deems necessary,

from one part of court to another in the same division, regardless of the denomination of the parts.

§ 208.4. Papers Filed in Court; Index Number; Form; Label

The party causing the first paper to be filed shall obtain an index number and communicate it forthwith to all other parties to the action. Thereafter such number shall appear on the outside cover and first page, to the right of the caption, of every paper tendered for filing in the action. Each such cover and first page also shall contain an indication of the county of venue and a brief description of the nature of the paper. In addition to complying with the provisions of CPLR 2101, every paper filed in court shall have annexed thereto appropriate proof of service on all parties where required, and if typewritten, shall have at least a double space between each line, except for quotations and the names and addresses of attorneys appearing in the action, and shall have at least one-inch margins. In addition, every paper filed in court, other than an exhibit or printed form, shall contain writing on one side only, except that papers that are fastened on the side may contain writing on both sides. Papers that are stapled or bound securely shall not be rejected for filing simply because they are not bound with a backer of any kind.

Cross References

CPLR, see McKinney's Book 7B.

§ 208.4–a. Electronic Filing

(a) **Application.** There is hereby established a pilot program in which certain civil actions in the New York City Civil Court ("Civil Court") may be commenced by electronic filing. Documents may be filed by such means only to the extent and in the manner authorized by this section and only in an action brought by a provider of health services specified in section 5102 (a) (1) of the Insurance Law against an insurer for failure to comply with rules and regulations promulgated by the Superintendent of Insurance pursuant to section 5108 (b) of such law.

(b) **Definitions.** For the purposes of these rules:

(1) "Electronic means" shall mean any method of transmission of information between computers or other machines, other than facsimile machines, designed for the purpose of sending and receiving such transmissions and which allows the recipient to receive and to reproduce the information transmitted in a tangible medium of expression.

(2) "Electronic filing address" shall mean the server accessed via the internet protocol address, and any successor thereto, established by the Unified Court System for receipt by the Civil Court of electronic filings as provided in this section.

(3) "Hard copy" shall mean information set forth in paper form.

(4) "Electronic filing" shall mean the filing by electronic means through the electronic filing address.

(5) The "date of receipt" of a document by the electronic filing address shall mean the date on which electronic transmission of such document is recorded at such address.

(c) **Electronic Filing in actions in the Civil Court.**

(1) A party may commence an action specified in subdivision (a) of this section by the electronic filing of such documents as are required to be filed by the CPLR or the Civil Court Act in actions in the Civil Court.

(2)(i) Documents may be transmitted at any time to the electronic filing address.

(ii) Documents that are electronically filed to commence an action in compliance with this section will be deemed filed with the clerk of the Civil Court in the county in which the action is brought for the purposes of section 400 of the Civil Court Act upon the date of receipt of those documents by the electronic filing address, provided, however, no document will be deemed filed unless an index number for the action is endorsed thereon.

(iii) No later than two business days following the date of receipt of documents by the electronic filing address, the clerk of the Civil Court shall make available by electronic means a confirmation of electronic filing. This confirmation will constitute the clerk's return of the copy to the party for the purposes of section 400(1) of the Civil Court Act.

(3) When a document has been filed electronically the official record of that document shall be its electronic recording.

(d) **Service of Documents.**

(1) A person seeking to obtain personal jurisdiction over a person named as a party to an action specified in subdivision (a) of this section may serve the opposing party by electronic means if the opposing party agrees to accept such service in accordance with the CPLR or the Civil Court Act.

(2) Where an action is commenced by electronic filing pursuant to this section, the original proof of service required by section 409 of the Civil Court Act must be electronically filed. Service is deemed complete for the purposes of section 410(b) of the Civil Court Act upon the date of receipt of the electronic proof of service by the electronic filing address.

(e) **Signatures.**

(1) Documents filed electronically shall be signed as required by Part 130 of the Rules of the Chief Administrator ("Part 130") and shall provide the signatory's name, address and telephone number.

(2) A signature on a document filed electronically pursuant to this section, including for the purposes of

Part 130, shall be made (i) by autograph of the signatory on a hard copy that is thereafter scanned into portable document format or (ii) by the signatory electronically affixing the digital image of his or her signature to the document.

§ 208.5. Submission of Papers to Judge

All papers for signature or consideration of the court shall be presented to the clerk of the trial court in the appropriate courtroom or at the clerk's office, except that where the clerk is unavailable or the judge so directs, papers may be submitted to the judge and a copy filed with the clerk at the first available opportunity. All papers for any judge that are filed in the clerk's office shall be promptly delivered to the judge by the clerk. The papers shall be clearly addressed to the judge for whom they are intended and prominently show the nature of the papers, the title and index number of the action in which they are filed, and the name of the attorney or party submitting them.

§ 208.6. Summons

(a) The summons shall state the county division and location of the court in which the action is brought, as well as the names of the parties, and shall comply with all the provisions of the NYCCCA applicable to summonses.

(b) The following form is to be used in all cases:

CIVIL COURT OF   Index No.
THE CITY OF NEW
YORK
COUNTY OF ....

```
_____  )
          Plaintiff, )   SUMMONS
         –against–   )   Plaintiff's Residence
                     )   Address:
          Defendant. )   The basis of the venue
                     )   designated is:
_____  )
```

To the above named defendant:
YOU ARE HEREBY SUMMONED to appear in the Civil Court of the City of New York, County of .... at the office of the Clerk of the said Court at .... in the County of .... City and State of New York, within the time provided by law as noted below and to file your answer to the (endorsed summons) (annexed complaint) * with the Clerk; upon your failure to answer, judgment will be taken against you for the sum of $.......... with interest thereon from the .... day of .... 19..., together with the costs of this action.
Dated, the .... day of .... 19...

```
_____  or  _____
     Clerk               Attorney(s) for Plaintiff
                         Post Office Address
                         Telephone Number
```

NOTE: The law provides that:

(a) If this summons is served by its delivery to you personally within the City of New York, you must appear and answer within TWENTY days after such service; or

(b) if this summons is served by delivery to any person other than you personally, or is served outside the City of New York, or by publication, or by any means other than personal delivery to you within the City of New York, you are allowed THIRTY days after the proof of service thereof is filed with the Clerk of this Court within which to appear and answer.

* If the cause of action is for money only and a formal complaint is not attached to the summons, strike the words "annexed complaint". If a formal complaint is attached to the summons, strike the words "endorsed summons".

(c) Where a defendant appears by an attorney, a copy of his answer shall be served upon the plaintiff's attorney, or upon the plaintiff if the plaintiff appears in person, at or before the time of filing the original answer with proof of service thereof.

(d) In any action arising from a consumer credit transaction, if the form of summons provided for in subdivision (b) of this section is used:

(1) the summons shall have prominently displayed at the top thereof the words "CONSUMER CREDIT TRANSACTION" and the following additional legend or caveat printed in not less than 12-point bold upper case type:

"IMPORTANT!! YOU ARE BEING SUED!!
THIS IS A COURT PAPER—A SUMMONS

DON'T THROW IT AWAY!! TALK TO A LAWYER RIGHT AWAY!! PART OF YOUR PAY CAN BE TAKEN FROM YOU (GARNISHEED). IF YOU DO NOT BRING THIS TO COURT, OR SEE A LAWYER, YOUR PROPERTY CAN BE TAKEN AND YOUR CREDIT RATING CAN BE HURT!! YOU MAY HAVE TO PAY OTHER COSTS TOO!! IF YOU CAN'T PAY FOR YOUR OWN LAWYER BRING THESE PAPERS TO THIS COURT RIGHT AWAY. THE CLERK (PERSONAL APPEARANCE) WILL HELP YOU!!"

(2) where a purchaser, borrower or debtor is a defendant, the summons shall have set forth beneath the designation of the basis of venue the county of residence of a defendant, if one resides within the State, and the county where the consumer credit transaction took place, if it is within the State.

(3) The summons also shall contain a translation in Spanish as follows:

"TRANSACCION DE CREDITO DEL CONSUMIDOR
!IMPORTANTE! UD. HA SIDO DEMANDADO!
ESTE ES UN DOCUMENTO LEGAL—UNA CITACION

!NO LA BOTE! !CONSULTE CON SU ABOGADO ENSEGUIDA! LE PUEDEN QUITAR PARTE DE SU SALARIO (EMBARGARLO). !SI UD. NO SE PRESENTA EN LA CORTE CON ESTA CITACION LE PUEDEN CONFISCAR SUS BIENES (PROPIEDAD) Y PERJUDICAR SU CREDITO! !TAMBIEN ES POSIBLE QUE TENGA QUE PAGAR OTROS GASTOS LEGALES (COSTAS)! SI UD. NO TIENE DINERO PARA UN ABOGADO TRAIGA ESTOS PAPELES A LA CORTE IMMEDIATAMENTE. VENGA EN PERSONA Y EL SECRETARIO DE LA CORTE LE AYUDARA.

Corte Civil de La Ciudad de Neuva York
Condado de ....

No. de Epigrafe .....

	CITACION
	) Residencia de Demand-
	) ante Direccion:
Demandante,	) La Razon de haber de-
	) signado esta Corte es:
–Vs.–	) El Demandado vive
	) en el Condado de
	) ....
Demandado.	) La transaccion de credi-
	) to tuvo lugar en el Con-
	) dado de ....
	)

Al demandado arriba mencionado:

USTED ESTA CITADO a comparecer en la Corte Civil de la Ciudad de Nueva York, Condado de .... a la oficina del Jefe Principal de dicha Corte en .... en el Condado de .... Ciudad y Estado de Nueva York, dentro del tiempo provisto por la ley segun abajo indicado y a presentar su respuesta a la (citacion endorsada) (demanda) * al Jefe de la Corte; si usted no comparece a contestar, se rendira sentencia contra usted en la suma de $......... con intereses en dicha cantidad desde el dia .... de 19..., incluyendo las costas de esta causa.

Fechado, el dia .... de 19...

....
Jefe de la Corte

Abogado(s) del Demandante
Direccion
Telefono

* Si la causa de accion es para dinero solamente y no esta una demanda formal junto a la citacion, tache las palabras "demanda anexada". Si una demanda formal esta junto a la citacion, tache las palabras "citacion endorsada".

NOTA: La Ley provee que:
(a) Si esta citacion es entregada a usted personalmente en la Ciudad de Nueva York, usted debe comparecer y responderia dentro de VIENTE dias despues de la entrega; o
(b) Si esta citacion es entregada a otra persona que no fuera usted personalmente, o si fuera entregada afuera de la Ciudad de Nueva York, o por medio de publicacion, o por otros medios que no fueran entrega personal a usted en la Ciudad de Nueva York, usted tiene TREINTA dias para comparacer y responder la demanda, despues de haberse presentado prueba de entrega de la citacion al Jefe de esta Corte."

(e) In a case in which a notice of motion for summary judgment in lieu of a complaint (pursuant to CPLR 3213 and NYCCCA 1004) is annexed to the summons, the following form of summons is to be used:

Civil Court of the City of New York
County of ....

Index No. ......

	)
Plaintiff,	) SUMMONS
–against–	) Plaintiff's Residence
	) Address:
Defendant.	) The basis of the venue
	) designated is:
	)

To the above named defendant:

YOU ARE HEREBY SUMMONED and required to submit to plaintiff's attorney your answering papers on this motion within the time provided in the notice of motion annexed hereto. In the case of your failure to submit answering papers, summary judgment will be taken against you by default for the relief demanded in the notice of motion.

Dated, the .... day of ...., 19...

....
Attorney(s) for Plaintiff
Post Office Address
Telephone Number

(f) In any action arising from a consumer credit transaction, if the form of summons provided for in subdivision (e) of this section is used:

(1) the summons shall have prominently displayed at the top thereof the words "CONSUMER CREDIT TRANSACTION" and the following additional legend or caveat printed in not less than 12-point bold upper case type:

"IMPORTANT!! YOU ARE BEING SUED!!
THIS IS A COURT PAPER—A SUMMONS

DON'T THROW IT AWAY!! TALK TO A LAW-YER RIGHT AWAY!! PART OF YOUR PAY CAN BE TAKEN FROM YOU (GARNISHEED). IF YOU DO NOT BRING THIS TO COURT, OR SEE A LAWYER, YOUR PROPERTY CAN BE TAKEN AND YOUR CREDIT RATING CAN BE HURT!! YOU MAY HAVE TO PAY OTHER COSTS TOO!! IF YOU CAN'T PAY FOR YOUR OWN LAWYER BRING THESE PAPERS TO THIS COURT RIGHT AWAY. THE CLERK (PERSONAL APPEARANCE) WILL HELP YOU!!"

(2) where a purchaser, borrower or debtor is a defendant, the summons shall have set forth beneath the designation of the basis of venue the county of residence of a defendant, if one resides within the state, and the county where the consumer credit transaction took place, if it is within the State.

(3) the summons also shall contain a translation in Spanish as follows:

"TRANSACCION DE CREDITO DEL
CONSUMIDOR
!IMPORTANTE! !UD. HA SIDO
DEMANDADO!
ESTE ES UN DOCUMENTO
LEGAL—UNA CITACION

!NO LA BOTE! !CONSULTE CON SU ABOGADO ENSEGUIDA! LE PUEDEN QUITAR PARTE DE SU SALARIO (EMBARGARLO). !SI UD. NO SE PRESENTA EN LA CORTE CON ESTA CITA-CION LE PUEDEN CONFISCAR SUS BIENES (PROPIEDAD) Y PERJUDICAR SU CREDI-TO! !TAMBIEN ES POSIBLE QUE TENGA QUE PAGAR OTROS GASTOS LEGALES (COSTAS)! SI UD. NO TIENE DINERO PARA UN ABOGADO TRAIGA ESTOS PAPELES A LA CORTE INME-DIATAMENTE. VENGA EN PERSONA Y EL SECRETARIO DE LA CORTE LE AYUDARA."

Corte Civil de La Ciu-   No. de Epigrafe . . . . . .
dad de Neuva York
Condado de . . . .

_____   CITACION
) Residencia de Demand-
) ante Direccion:
Demandante,) La Razon de haber de-
) signado esta Corte es:
   –Vs.–   ) El Demandado vive en el
) Condado de . . . .
Demandado.) La transaccion de credito
) tuvo lugar en el Condado
) de . . . .
_____)

Al demandado arriba mencionado:

USTED ESTA CITADO y obligado a entregar al abogado del Demandante su contestacion a esta peti-cion dentro del tiempo indicado en el aviso adjunto. En el caso que usted no entregue su contestacion, se dictara sentencia sumaria contra usted por incumpli-miento por la suma demandada en la peticion de demanda.

Fechado, el dia . . . . de 19. . .
. . . .
Abrogado(s) del Demandante
Direccion
Telefono

(g) In any action arising from a consumer credit transaction, a default judgment shall not be entered against the defendant unless the plaintiff first shall have submitted to a judge or to the clerk of the court proof, by affidavit or otherwise, that the summons served upon the defendant had displayed and set forth on its face the words and added legend or caveat required by subdivisions (d) and (f) of this section.

(h) Additional mailing of notice on an action arising from a consumer credit transaction

(1) At the time of filing with the clerk of the proof of service of the summons and complaint in an action arising from a consumer credit transaction, or at any time thereafter, the plaintiff shall submit to the clerk a stamped envelope addressed to the defendant to-gether with a written notice, in both English and Spanish, containing the following language:

CIVIL COURT. CITY OF NEW YORK

TRIBUNAL CIVIL DE LA CIUDAD DE NUEVA YORK

COUNTY OF _____ INDEX (LIBRO) NO. _____

Plaintiff/Demandante _____ Defendant/De-mandado _____

ATTENTION: A SUMMONS AND COMPLAINT HAS BEEN FILED ON A CONSUMER CREDIT TRANSACTION ASKING THE COURT TO REN-DER A JUDGMENT AGAINST YOU. YOU MAY WISH TO CONTACT AN ATTORNEY. YOU MUST ANSWER AT THE LOCATION AND WITH-IN THE TIME SPECIFIED ON THE SUMMONS. IF YOU DO NOT APPEAR IN COURT THE COURT MAY GRANT A JUDGMENT AGAINST YOU. IF A JUDGMENT IS GRANTED AGAINST YOU YOUR PROPERTY CAN BE TAKEN. PART OF YOUR PAY CAN BE TAKEN FROM YOU (GARNISHEED), AND YOUR CREDIT RATING CAN BE AFFECTED. IF YOU HAVE NOT RE-CEIVED THE SUMMONS AND COMPLAINT GO TO THE CIVIL COURT CLERK'S OFFICE SPEC-IFIED ON THE RETURN ADDRESS AND BRING THIS NOTICE WITH YOU.

ATENCIÓN: BASADO EN UNA TRANSAC-CIÓN DE CRÉDITO AL CONSUMIDOR, SE HA

SOMETIDO UNA QUERELLA Y UNA CITACIÓN JUDICIAL ANTE EL TRIBUNAL CIVIL, SOLICITÁNDOLE QUE SE EMITA UN FALLO JUDICIAL EN CONTRA SUYA, POR LO QUE USTED QUERRÁ COMUNICARSE CON UN ABOGADO. USTED TIENE QUE SOMETER UNA RESPUESTA ANTE EL TRIBUNAL, EN EL LUGAR Y EL MOMENTO INDICADO EN LA CITACIÓN. SI NO COMPARECE ANTE EL TRIBUNAL, SE PUEDE EMITIR UN FALLO JUDICIAL EN SU CONTRA. DE SER ASI, SUS PERTENENCIAS PUEDEN SER EMBARGADAS, PARTE DE SU SALARIO PUEDE SER EMBARGADO Y LA CLASIFICACIÓN DE SU CRÉDITO PUEDE SER AFECTADA NEGATIVAMENTE. SI NO HA RECIBIDO LA CITACIÓN Y LA QUERELLA, DIRIJASE AL DESPACHO DEL SECRETARIO JUDICIAL INDICADO EN LA DIRECCIÓN DEL REMITENTE Y TRAIGA ESTA NOTIFICACIÓN CON USTED.

The face of the envelope shall be addressed to the defendant at the address at which process was served in the summons and complaint, and shall contain the defendant's name, address (including apartment number) and zip code. The face of the envelope also shall contain, in the form of a return address, the appropriate address of the clerk's office to which the defendant should be directed. These addresses are:

Bronx: Civil Court of the City of New York

   851 Grand Concourse

   Basement

   Bronx, NY 10451

Kings: Civil Court of the City of New York

   141 Livingston Street

   Room 302

   Brooklyn, New York 11201

New York: Civil Court of the City of New York

   111 Centre Street, Room 118

   New York, New York 10013

Queens: Civil Court of the City of New York

   89–17 Sutphin Boulevard, Room 147

   Jamaica, New York 11435

Richmond: Civil Court of the City of New York

   927 Castleton Avenue, Basement

   Staten Island, New York 10310

(2) The clerk promptly shall mail to the defendant the envelope containing the additional notice set forth in paragraph (1). No default judgment based on defendant's failure to answer shall be entered unless there has been compliance with this subdivision and at least 20 days have elapsed from the date of mailing by the clerk.

Cross References

CPLR, see McKinney's Book 7B.

NYCCCA, see McKinney's Book 29A, Part 3.

§ 208.7. Pleadings

(a) Except as required by statute, a formal pleading may be dispensed with in any case in which the party required to serve the pleading appears in person, and an order to that effect may be entered ex parte by the judge presiding at the appropriate motion part, upon application to the clerk, who shall refer the same to such judge. Any other party may move at the appropriate motion part to modify or vacate such ex parte order.

(b) All formal pleadings in this court and verifications thereof shall be in conformity with CPLR, Article 30.

(c) An order directing the service and filing of a formal pleading, or pleadings, shall specify the time within which the same shall be served and filed.

(d) A defendant's time to move or answer may be extended by ex parte order no more than once, and for no longer than ten days beyond the expiration of the original time to answer, and only if there has been no previous extension by consent. All further applications for extensions shall be made by motion upon notice returnable in the part designated to hear motions on notice.

(e) In any action to recover damages for personal injuries arising out of use or operation of a motor vehicle, plaintiff shall set forth in the complaint, whether in short or long form, the jurisdictional facts that permit plaintiff to maintain the action and avoid the bar of the Comprehensive Automobile Insurance Reparations Act.

Cross References

CPLR, see McKinney's Book 7B.

Comprehensive Motor Vehicle Insurance Reparations Act, see McKinney's Book 27.

§ 208.8. Venue

(a) Motions for a Change of Venue. Motions for a change of venue shall be heard in the county division of the court in which the action was instituted. An order of transfer shall direct the disposition of the papers then on file.

(b) Venue of Transitory Action Laid in Wrong County Division. The clerk shall not accept a summons for filing when it appears upon its face that the proper venue is a county division other than the one where it is offered for filing. The clerk shall stamp upon the summons the date of such rejection and shall enter the date of such rejection in a register maintained by him, together with the county division in which the summons should be filed. Where the wrong county division is stated in the summons, the time of the defendant to appear or answer shall be the later of (i) the original time to answer or (ii) the date ten days after the summons is filed in the proper county division with proof of service upon the defendant by registered or certified mail of notice stating (1) the proper county division, (2) the date of filing of the summons, (3) the date within which the answer or notice of appearance is to be filed and (4) the address at which it is to be filed.

§ 208.9. Preliminary conference.

(a) The Chief Administrator of the Courts may designate a specific class or specific classes of cases in one or more counties to be subject to this section.

(b) The plaintiff in a class of cases designated by the Chief Administrator pursuant to subdivision (a) shall request a preliminary conference within 45 days after joinder of issue. The request shall state the title of the action: index number; date of joinder of issue: name, address, and telephone number of all attorneys appearing in the action; and the nature of the action. The request shall be served on all other parties and filed with the clerk together with stamped postcards addressed to all parties. The court shall order a preliminary conference in the action upon compliance with the requirements of this subdivision.

(c) The clerk shall notify all parties of the scheduled conference date, which shall be not more than 45 days from the date the request for a preliminary conference is filed unless the court orders otherwise. A form of stipulation and order, prescribed by the Administrative Judge, shall be made available which the parties may sign, agreeing to a timetable which shall provide for completion of disclosure. If all parties sign the form and return it to the court before the scheduled preliminary conference, such form shall be "so ordered" by the court, and, unless the court orders otherwise, the scheduled preliminary conference shall be canceled. If such stipulation is not returned signed by all parties, the parties shall appear at the conference. Except where a party appears in the action pro se, an attorney thoroughly familiar with the action and authorized to act on behalf of the party shall appear at such conference.

(d) The matters to be considered at the preliminary conference shall include:

(1) the simplification and limitation of factual and legal issues, where appropriate;

(2) establishment of a timetable for the completion of all disclosure proceedings;

(3) addition of other necessary parties;

(4) settlement of the action;

(5) any other matters that the court may deem relevant.

(e) At the conclusion of the conference the court shall make a written order including its directions to the parties as well as any stipulations of counsel.

(f) When a notice of trial and certificate of readiness is filed pursuant to section 208.17 of this Part in an action to which this section is applicable, the filing party, in addition to complying with all other applicable rules of the court, shall file with the notice of trial and certificate of readiness an affirmation or affidavit, with proof of service on all parties who have appeared, showing specific compliance with the preliminary conference order or with the so-ordered stipulation provided for in subdivision (c) of this section.

(g) In the discretion of the court, failure by a party to comply with the order resulting from the preliminary conference, or with the so-ordered stipulation provided for in subdivision (c) of this section, or the making of unnecessary or frivolous motions by a party, may result in the imposition upon such party of costs or such other sanctions as are authorized by law.

(h) A party may move to advance the date of a preliminary conference upon a showing of special circumstances.

(i) Motions in actions to which this section is applicable made before the preliminary conference is held may be denied or marked off the calendar unless good cause is shown why such relief is warranted before that time.

(j) No action or proceeding to which this section is applicable shall be deemed ready for trial unless there is compliance with the provisions of this section and any order issued pursuant thereto.

(k) The court, in its discretion, may order such further conferences as it may deem helpful or necessary at any time in a matter before the court to which this section is applicable.

(*l*) At the discretion of the Administrative Judge, a judicial hearing officer may preside at a preliminary conference scheduled pursuant to this section.

§ 208.10. Calendaring of Motions; Uniform Notice of Motion Form

(a) There shall be compliance with the procedures prescribed in the NYCCCA and the CPLR for the bringing of motions. In addition, no motion shall be placed on the calendar for hearing in the appropriate part unless a notice of motion is served and filed with the motion papers. The notice of motion shall read substantially as follows:

CIVIL COURT OF THE
CITY OF NEW YORK
COUNTY OF . . . .

_____
)
A.B.,   )   Notice of Motion
      Plaintiff,   )   Index No.
   –against–   )   _____
C.D.,   )   Oral Argument is re-
)   quested ☐
    Defendant.)   (Check box if requested)
_____)

Upon the affidavit of _____, sworn to on _____ 19___, and upon (list supporting papers if any), the _____ will move this court at _____ (specify the Part), at the _____ Courthouse, _____, _____, New York, on the _____ day of _____, 19___, at 9:30 a.m. for an order (briefly indicate relief requested).[1]

The above-entitled action is for (briefly state nature of action, e.g. personal injury, contract, property damage, etc.). This action (is) (is not) on a trial calendar. If on a trial calendar, the calendar number is _____.

Pursuant to CPLR 2214(b), answering affidavits, if any, are required to be served upon the undersigned at least seven days before the return date of the motion.

(check box if applicable) ☐

Dated:

             _____
                   (Print Name)
Attorney[2] (or Attorney in charge of case if law firm) for moving party
Address:
Telephone number:

TO: _____ (Print Name) _____
Attorney[2] for (other party)
Address:
Telephone number:

TO: _____ (Print Name) _____
Attorney[2] for (other party)
Address:
Telephone number:

   [1] If motion is to reargue, vacate or extend, modify or otherwise affect a prior order, state the name of the judge who decided the prior order.

   [2] If any party is appearing pro se, the name, address and telephone number of such party shall be stated.

(b) The notice of motion set forth in subdivision (a) shall not be required for the return of an order to show cause or an application for ex parte relief.

Cross References

CPLR, see McKinney's Book 7B.

NYCCCA, see McKinney's Book 29A, Part 3.

§ 208.11. Motion Parts; Motion Calendars; Motion Procedure

(a) Motion Parts and Calendars. There shall be such motion parts and motion calendars as the Chief Administrator of the Courts shall designate.

(b) Motion Procedure.

(1) All contested motions and proceedings shall be returnable at 9:30 a.m. unless an earlier time is directed by the court. The moving party shall serve copies of all affidavits and briefs upon the adverse parties at the time of service of the notice of motion. The answering party shall serve copies of all affidavits and briefs as required by CPLR 2214. Affidavits shall be for a statement of the relevant facts, and briefs shall be for a statement of the relevant law. Unless otherwise directed by the court, answering and reply affidavits and all other papers required to be furnished to the court by CPLR 2214(c) must be filed no later than the time of argument or submission of the motion.

(2) A judge presiding in any part of court where motions are returnable may determine that any or all motions in that part be orally argued and may direct that moving and responding papers be filed with the court prior to the time of argument.

(3) Unless oral argument has been requested by a party and permitted by the court, or directed by the court, motion papers received by the clerk of the court on or before the return date shall be deemed submitted as of the return date. Attendance by counsel or pro se party at the calendar call shall not be required unless (i) a party intends to make an application to the court that is not on the consent of all parties, (ii) attendance of counsel or oral argument is directed by the court, or (iii) oral argument is requested by a party. Attendance by counsel for a party not requesting oral argument is not required where the hearing of oral argument is based solely upon the request of another party. A party requesting oral argument shall set forth such request in its notice of motion or on the first page of the answering papers, as the case may be. A party requesting oral argument on a motion brought on by an order to show cause shall do so as soon as practicable before the time the motion is to be heard.

(4) Where there is an issue of fact to be tried the court may, in its discretion, order an immediate trial of such issue, in which event the action shall be referred to the administrative judge or a designee for assignment.

Cross References

CPLR, see McKinney's Book 7B.

§ 208.12. Videotape Recording of Depositions

Depositions authorized under the provisions of the CPLR or other law may be taken, as permitted by subdivision (b) of section 3113 of the CPLR, by means of simultaneous audio and visual electronic recording, provided such recording is made in conformity with section 202.15 of the Rules of the Chief Administrator (22 NYCRR Part 202).

Cross References

CPLR, see McKinney's Book 7B.

§ 208.13. Exchange of Medical Reports in Personal Injury and Wrongful Death Actions

Except where the court otherwise directs, in all actions in which recovery is sought for personal injuries, disability or death, physical examinations and the exchange of medical information shall be governed by the provisions hereinafter set forth:

(a) At any time after joinder of issue and service of a bill of particulars the party to be examined or any other party may serve on all other parties a notice fixing the time and place of examination. Unless otherwise stipulated the examination shall be held not less than 30 nor more than 60 days after service of the notice. If served by any party other than the party to be examined, the notice shall name the examining medical provider or providers. If the notice is served by the party to be examined, the examining parties shall, within 10 days of receipt thereof, submit to the party to be examined the name of the medical providers who will conduct the examination. Any party may move to modify or vacate the notice fixing the time and place of examination or the notice naming the examining medical providers within ten days of the receipt thereof, on the grounds that the time or place fixed or the medical provider named is objectionable, or that the nature of the action is such that the interests of justice will not be served by an examination, exchange of medical reports or delivery of authorizations.

(b) At least 20 days before the date of such examination, or on such other date as the court may direct, the party to be examined shall serve upon and deliver to all other parties the following, which may be used by the examining medical provider:

(1) copies of the medical reports of those medical providers who have previously treated or examined the party seeking recovery. These shall include a recital of the injuries and conditions as to which testimony will be offered at the trial, referring to and identifying those x-ray and technicians' reports which will be offered at the trial, including a description of the injuries sustained, a diagnosis, and prognosis. Medical reports may consist of completed medical provider, workers' compensation, or insurance forms that provide the information required by this paragraph.

(2) duly executed and acknowledged written authorizations permitting all parties to obtain and make copies of all hospital records and such other records, including x-ray and technicians' reports, as may be referred to and identified in the reports of those medical providers who have treated or examined the party seeking recovery.

(c) Copies of the reports of the medical providers making examinations pursuant to this section shall be served on all other parties within 45 days after completion of the examination. These shall comply with the requirements of paragraph (1) of subdivision (b).

(d) In actions where the cause of death is in issue, each party shall serve upon all other parties copies of the reports of all treating or examining medical providers whose testimony will be offered at the trial, complying with the requirements of paragraph (1) of subdivision (b), and the party seeking to recover shall deliver to all other parties authorizations to examine and obtain copies of all hospital records, autopsy or post-mortem reports, and such other records as provided in paragraph (2) of subdivision (b). Copies of these reports and the required authorizations shall be served and delivered with the bill of particulars by the party seeking to recover. All other parties shall serve copies of the reports of their medical providers within 45 days thereafter. In any case where the interests of justice will not be promoted by service of such reports and delivery of such authorizations, an order dispensing with either or both may be obtained.

(e) Parties relying solely on hospital records may so certify in lieu of serving medical providers' reports.

(f) No case otherwise eligible to be noticed for trial may be noticed unless there has been compliance with this rule or an order dispensing with compliance or extending the time therefor has been obtained; or, where the party to be examined was served a notice as provided in subdivision (a), and the party so served has not responded thereto.

(g) In the event that the party examined intends at the trial to offer evidence of further or additional injuries or conditions, nonexistent or not known to exist at the time of service of the original medical reports, such party shall, within 30 days after the discovery thereof, and not later than 30 days before trial, serve upon all parties a supplemental medical report complying with the requirements of paragraph (1) of subdivision (b) and shall specify a time not more than 10 days thereafter and a place at which a further examination may be had. Further authorizations to examine and make copies of additional hospital records, other records, x-ray or other technicians' reports as provided in paragraph (2) of subdivision (b) must also be delivered with the medical reports. Copies of the reports of the examining medical providers, complying with the requirements of subdivision (c), shall be served within 10 days after completion of such further examination. If any party desires at the trial to offer the testimony of additional treating or examining medical providers, other than whose medical reports have been previously exchanged, the medical reports of such medical providers complying with the requirements of paragraph (1) of subdivision (b) shall be served upon all parties at least 30 days before trial.

(h) Unless an order to the contrary is made or unless the judge presiding at the trial in the interests of justice and upon a showing of good cause shall hold otherwise, the party seeking to recover damages shall be precluded at the trial from offering in evidence any part of the hospital records and all other records, including autopsy or post-mortem records, x-ray reports or reports of other technicians, not made available pursuant to this rule, and no party shall be permitted to offer any evidence of injuries or conditions not set forth or put in issue in the respective medical reports previously exchanged, nor will the court hear the testimony of any treating or examining medical providers whose medical reports have not been served as provided by this rule.

(i) Orders transferring cases pending in other courts which are subject to the provisions of this section, whether or not such cases are consolidated with cases pending in the court to which transferred, shall contain such provisions as are required to bring the transferred cases into compliance with this rule.

(j) Any party may move to compel compliance or to be relieved from compliance with this rule or any provision thereof, but motions directed to the sufficiency of medical reports must be made within 20 days of receipt of such reports. All motions under this rule may be made on affidavits of attorneys, shall be made on notice, returnable at the appropriate motion part and shall be granted or denied on such terms as to costs, calendar position and dates of compliance with any provision of this rule as the court in its discretion shall direct.

(k) Where an examination is conducted on consent prior to the institution of an action, the party to be examined shall deliver the documents specified in paragraphs (1) and (2) of subdivision (b) hereof, and the report of the examining medical provider shall be delivered as provided in subdivision (c) hereof. In that event examination after institution of the action may be waived. The waiver, which shall recite that medical reports have been exchanged and that all parties waive further physical examination, shall be filed with the note of issue. This shall not be a bar, however, to proceeding under subdivision (g) in a proper case.

§ 208.14. Calendar Default; Restoration; Dismissal

(a) Applicability. This section governs calendar defaults, restorations and dismissals, other than strik-

ing a case from the calendar pursuant to a motion under section 208.17 relating to the notice of trial and certificate of readiness.

(b) At any scheduled call of a calendar or at a pretrial conference, if all parties do not appear and proceed or announce their readiness to proceed immediately or subject to the engagement of counsel, the judge presiding may note the default on the record and enter an order as follows:

(1) if the plaintiff appears but the defendant does not, the judge may grant judgment by default or order an inquest;

(2) if the defendant appears but the plaintiff does not, the judge may dismiss the action and may order a severance of counterclaims or cross-claims;

(3) if no party appears, the judge may strike the action from the calendar or make such other order as appears just.

(c) Actions stricken from the calendar may be restored to the calendar only upon stipulation of all parties so ordered by the court or by motion on notice to all other parties, made within one year after the action is stricken. A motion must be supported by affidavit by a person having firsthand knowledge, satisfactorily explaining the reasons for the action having been stricken and showing that it is presently ready for trial.

(d) If an order of restoration is granted, it shall provide that a new notice of trial be filed forthwith and that the case be placed on the general trial calendar in its regular place as of the date of filing the new notice of trial, unless the court in its discretion orders otherwise. A copy of the order shall be served on the calendar clerk and the case shall receive a new calendar number followed by the letter "R" to designate the case as having been restored. Absent exceptional circumstances, if a restored case is not ready when reached, it shall forthwith be dismissed or an inquest or judgment ordered as provided in paragraph (b).

(e) Applications to restore an action to the ready calendar in the event of a reversal or a direction of a new trial by an appellate court shall be made returnable in the appropriate motion part, except that if all parties do not appear by attorney, the clerk shall, without formal application, restore the action to the ready calendar.

(f) When an action has been tried and the jury has disagreed, or a verdict set aside, or there has been a mistrial for any reason, or if no decision has been made or judgment rendered within the time specified in the CPLR or if the court has ordered a new trial under CPLR 4402, such action must be restored to the appropriate ready calendar for a day certain to be fixed by the court.

CPLR, see McKinney's Book 7B.

§ 208.15. Transfer of Actions

Actions transferred from the Supreme Court to the Civil Court of the City of New York shall be placed in such order and relative position on the appropriate calendars that they will be reached for trial insofar as practicable as if a notice of trial had been filed in the Civil Court of the City of New York for the same date as that for which the note of issue was filed in the Supreme Court.

§ 208.16. Discontinuance of Civil Actions

In any discontinued action, the attorney for the plaintiff shall file a stipulation or statement of discontinuance with the clerk of the court within 20 days of such discontinuance. If the action has been noticed for judicial activity within 20 days of such discontinuance, the stipulation or statement shall be filed before the date scheduled for such activity.

§ 208.17. Notice of Trial Where All Parties Appear by Attorney

(a) The notice of trial filed by any party pursuant to NYCCCA section 1301 shall be accompanied by a certificate of readiness, with proof of service on all parties, in the form prescribed by this section. The notice of trial shall include the index number, name, office address and telephone number of each attorney and pro se party who has appeared, and the name of any insurance carrier acting on behalf of any party.

(b) The clerk shall not place any matter on a trial calendar unless there has been compliance with this rule by the party seeking to place the matter on the calendar.

(c) Within 20 days after service of such notice of trial, any party may move to strike the action from the calendar or to keep it from being placed thereon. The affidavit in support of the application must specify the reason the action is not entitled to be on the calendar.

(d) After any action has been placed on the trial calendar pursuant to this rule, no pretrial examination or other preliminary proceedings may be had, except that if some unusual or unanticipated conditions subsequently develop which make it necessary that further pretrial examination or further preliminary proceedings be had, and if without them the moving party would be unduly prejudiced, the court may make an order granting permission to conduct such examination or proceedings and prescribing the time therefor. Such an order may be made only upon motion on notice showing in detail, by affidavit, the facts claimed to entitle the moving party to relief under this subdivision.

(e) Where a party filing a notice of trial, in a medical malpractice action or an action against a municipality, seeking a sum of money only, is prohibited by the provisions of CPLR 3017(c) from stating in the pleadings the amount of damages sought in the action, the party shall indicate in the notice of trial whether the amount of damages exceeds $6,000, exclusive of costs and interest. If it does not, the party shall also indicate if it exceeds $2,000, exclusive of costs and interest.

(f) The certificate of readiness shall read substantially as follows:

CERTIFICATE OF READINESS FOR TRIAL
(Items 1–5 must be checked)

	Complete	Waived	Not Required
1. All pleadings served	....	....	....
2. Bill of particulars served	....	....	....
3. Physical examinations completed	....	....	....
4. Medical reports exchanged	....	....	....
5. Discovery proceedings now known to be necessary completed	....	....	....
6. There are no outstanding requests for discovery			
7. There has been a reasonable opportunity to complete the foregoing proceedings			
8. The case is ready for trial			

Dated: _____
(Signature) _____
Attorney(s) for: _____
Office and P.O. address: _____

CPLR, see McKinney's Book 7B.

NYCCCA, see McKinney's Book 29A, Part 3.

§ 208.18. Calendars of Triable Actions

There shall be such calendars as may be established, from time to time, in the discretion of the Chief Administrator of the Courts. These calendars may include:

(a)(1) **General Calendar.** A general calendar is for actions in which issue has been joined.

(2) **Preliminary conference calendar.** A preliminary conference calendar is for the calendaring for conference of cases after issue has been joined for specific classes of cases designated by the Chief Administrator of the Courts.

(b) **Pretrial Conference Calendar.** A pretrial conference calendar is for actions awaiting conference in a pretrial conference part. Actions shall be taken in order from the top of the general calendar or preliminary conference calendar and placed at the end of the pretrial conference calendar.

(c) **Reserve Calendars.** A reserve calendar is for actions in which a notice of trial, conforming to § 1301 of the NYCCCA, and a certificate of readiness have been filed. Upon the filing of such notice in any action with the clerk, at least ten days before the day fixed for trial, the action shall be placed at the end of either the reserve jury trial calendar or the reserve nonjury trial calendar, as the case may be. Where an action is placed on a reserve nonjury trial calendar but subsequently a demand for a trial by jury is timely served and filed, the action shall immediately be transferred to the end of the reserve jury trial calendar. Once placed on a calendar, the action shall remain thereon until disposed of, stricken, transferred or otherwise removed. The calendars shall be deemed continuous and no change in the order of original placement shall be made except as provided in this Part, by court order or as may be required by provisions of law.

(d) **Ready Calendars.** A ready calendar is for actions that have been transferred from a reserve calendar because a trial is imminent, for noticed inquests and assessments of damages and for actions in which any party appears in person. There shall be as many ready calendars with such classifications of actions as the Chief Administrator shall direct.

(e) **Continuous Calendars.** In any court not continuously in session, the calendars at the close of one term or session of court shall be used to open the following term or session, and actions on the calendars shall retain their positions.

(f) **Military Calendar.** A military calendar shall be utilized to hold in suspense an action that cannot reasonably be tried because a party or witness is in military service. When it shall appear to the satisfaction of the judge presiding that a party to an action or a witness necessary upon the trial is in military service, and is not presently available for trial, and that a deposition cannot be taken, or, if taken, would not provide adequate evidence, the case shall be designated "military" and transferred to a military calendar. Any case on the military calendar may be removed therefrom by further order of the court or by filing with the calendar clerk, at least five days before such date, a stipulation of the parties who have appeared or a notice to restore, together with proof of service of such notice on all other parties; except that if any party appearing in person seeks such restoration, he may apply to the clerk, who shall refer his application to the judge in the appropriate calendar part for disposition upon such notice to all parties or their attorneys as the judge shall direct.

(g) **Calendar Progression.** With due regard to the requirements of statutory preferences and of section 208.20 of this Part, when actions are advanced from one calendar to another they shall progress from the head of one calendar to the foot of the next calendar and otherwise progress in order insofar as practicable unless otherwise determined by the court.

Cross References

NYCCCA, see McKinney's Book 29A, Part 3.

§ 208.19. Notice of Calendars

A notice shall be published in a law journal designated by the Chief Administrator of the Courts of any and all calls of the reserve calendars at least five court days before such call. The notice shall specify the calendar numbers of the actions to be called. In the event that the call of any reserve calendar is suspended by the Chief Administrator and actions are added to the ready calendar without first being called on the reserve calendar, a notice of actions added to the ready calendar, with their calendar number, shall be published in such law journal at least five court days before the call of the reserve calendar.

§ 208.20. Special Preferences

(a) Any party claiming a preference under CPLR 3403 may apply to the court by making a motion in a motion part, in accordance with CPLR 3403(b), the note of issue therein referred to being deemed a preference to a notice of trial.

(b) **Counterclaims and Cross-Claims.** A counterclaim or cross-claim which is not entitled to a preference shall not itself defeat the plaintiff's right to a preference under this section.

(c) **Result of Preference Being Granted.** If a preference is granted, the action shall be placed on a ready calendar for a day certain ahead of all nonpreferred pending cases, as directed by the court, unless the court otherwise orders.

Cross References

CPLR, see McKinney's Book 7B.

§ 208.21. Objections to Applications for Special Preference

(a) Within 20 days of the filing of the notice of trial, if the notice of motion for a special preference is filed therewith, or within ten days of the service of a notice of motion to obtain a preference, if served and filed subsequent to service and filing of the notice of trial, any other party may serve upon all other parties and file with the clerk affidavits and other relevant papers, with proof of service, in opposition to granting the preference. In the event such opposing papers are filed, the party applying for the preference may, within five days thereafter, serve and file in like manner papers in rebuttal.

(b) In any action which has been accorded a preference in trial upon a motion filed with the clerk, the court shall not be precluded, on its own motion at any time thereafter, from restoring the action to its regular calendar position on the ground that the action is not entitled to a preference under these rules.

(c) Notwithstanding the failure of any party to oppose the application, no preference shall be granted by default unless the court finds that the action is entitled to a preference.

§ 208.22. Pretrial and Prearbitration Conference Calendars

There shall be such pretrial conference parts and calendars and such mandatory pretrial and prearbitration conferences as may be established by the Chief Administrator of the Courts. The attendance of attorneys who are familiar with the case and who are authorized to act shall be required. The court may also require the attendance of parties, and in the event of failure of attendance by attorneys or parties, the court shall have the same powers with respect to dismissals, defaults, or both as it might exercise when a case is reached for trial. Upon the pretrial conference of an action, the judge presiding shall consider with counsel and parties the simplification and limitation of the issues and the obtaining of admissions of facts and of documents to avoid unnecessary proof, as well as the ultimate disposition of the action by settlement or compromise.

§ 208.23. Call of Reserve, Ready and General Calendars

(a) Reserve Calendars. At such times as the Chief Administrator of the Courts shall prescribe, there shall be a call of actions on the reserve calendars in sequence and in sufficient number to insure a steady supply of cases to the ready calendar. When such a call is held, the actions thereon, if marked "ready", shall be passed and subsequently added to the ready calendar, or may be marked "disposed" or stricken from the calendar, as may be appropriate.

(b) Ready Calendars.

(1) The ready calendars shall be called at such time and in such parts as the Chief Administrator shall direct. Actions shall be called in order and shall be announced "ready", "ready subject to engagement", or "disposed". If any party does not so respond, the calendar judge shall treat the action as in default, unless for good cause shown, arising after the action appeared on the ready calendar and not reasonably discoverable or foreseeable, the judge shall direct that the action be held on the ready calendar for a period not to exceed ten days. If the inability to proceed to trial is expected to exceed ten days, the action shall be returned to the reserve calendar or stricken from the calendar as circumstances warrant, unless, for good cause shown, the court on application grants an adjournment.

(2) Actions announced "ready" on the call of the calendar shall be assigned in order to the available trial parts. Jury actions will be sent out for jury selection if a jury trial part is available, or scheduled for jury selection at the opening of court on the next court day or as soon as practicable thereafter. Subject to the provisions of section 208.25 of this Part, no delay will be permitted in selection of a jury, and failure of counsel to proceed as directed or to appear promptly at the directed time on the specified court day will be treated as a calendar default.

(3) The actions on the ready calendar must be answered by or on behalf of the trial counsel each day the calendar is called, unless otherwise ordered by the calendar judge, or unless trial counsel already has demonstrated an engagement during one or more days. The calendar judge may discontinue the call of the ready calendar when sufficient ready cases have been identified to fill all trial parts available on the day of the call and which are expected to become available on the next court day.

(4) When an action has been announced "ready" but no part is immediately available, counsel may arrange with the calendar judge to be summoned by telephone, provided they agree to hold themselves available and to appear on one hour's notice or at such other time as the court may order at the time and part assigned for the trial.

(c) General Calendar. At such time or times and in such manner as the Chief Administrator may direct, a call shall be made of all actions on the general calendar not reached on a ready calendar.

§ 208.24. Day Certain for Trial

(a) Applications for a day certain for trial shall be made to the calendar judge or, if no calendar part has been established, to the trial judge on an affidavit of the attorney of record or a stipulation of the attorneys for all parties, that trial counsel, a party or a material witness resides more than 100 miles from the courthouse or is in the military service or that some other undue hardship exists. Applications to the calendar judge shall be made on notice and must be made before the action is advanced to the ready calendar.

(b) If a day certain is ordered, the action shall be withheld from the ready calendar until that day, at which time it shall appear at the top of the ready calendar. Absent special circumstances, the day designated for trial shall be a date which does not in effect grant a preference to the action. Such day certain actions shall be taken into consideration in determining the number of actions held for counsel under section 208.25 when they appear on the ready calendar.

§ 208.25. Engagement of Counsel

No adjournment shall be granted on the ground of engagement of counsel except in accordance with Part 125 of the Rules of the Chief Administrator of the Courts (22 NYCRR Part 125).

§ 208.26. [Reserved]

§ 208.27. Submission of Papers for Trial

(a) Upon the trial of an action, the following papers, if not yet submitted, shall be submitted to the court by the party who has filed the notice of trial:

(1) copies of all pleadings marked as required by CPLR 4012;

(2) a copy of any statutory provision in effect at the time the cause of action arose upon which either the plaintiff or defendant relies; and

(3) a copy of the bill of particulars, if any.

(b) If so ordered, the parties shall submit to the court, before the commencement of trial, trial memoranda which shall be exchanged among counsel.

Cross References
CPLR, see McKinney's Book 7B.

§ 208.28. Absence of Attorney During Trial

All trial counsel shall remain in attendance at all stages of the trial until the jury retires to deliberate unless excused by the judge presiding. The court may permit counsel to leave, provided counsel remain in telephone contact with the court. Any counsel not present during the jury deliberation, further requests to charge, or report of the jury verdict shall be deemed to stipulate that the court may proceed in his or her absence and to waive any irregularity in proceedings taken in his or her absence.

§ 208.29. Traverse Hearings

Whenever the court has scheduled a hearing to determine whether process was served validly and timely upon a party, and where a process server will testify as to the service, the process server shall be required to bring to the hearing all records in the possession of the process server relating to the matter at issue. Where the process server is licensed, he or she also shall bring the license to the court.

§ 208.30. [Reserved]

§ 208.31. Restoration After Jury Disagreement, Mistrial or Order for New Trial

An action in which there has been an inability by a jury to reach a verdict, a mistrial or a new trial granted by the trial judge or an appellate court shall be restored to the ready calendar by filing a notice thereof with the appropriate clerk.

§ 208.32. Damages, Inquest After Default; Proof

(a) In an inquest to ascertain damages upon a default pursuant to CPLR 3215, if the defaulting party fails to appear in person or by representative, the party entitled to judgment, whether a plaintiff, third-party plaintiff, or a party who has pleaded a cross-claim or counterclaim, shall be permitted to submit, in addition to the proof required by CPLR 3215(e), properly executed affidavits as proof of damages.

(b) In any action where it is necessary to take an inquest before the court, the party seeking damages may submit the proof required by oral testimony of witnesses in open court or by written statements of

the witnesses, in narrative or question and answer form, signed and sworn to.

Cross References
CPLR, see McKinney's Book 7B.

§ 208.33. Submission of Orders, Judgments and Decrees for Signature

(a) Proposed orders or judgments, with proof of service on all parties where the order is directed to be settled or submitted on notice, must be submitted for signature, unless otherwise directed by the court, within 60 days after the signing and filing of the decision directing that the order be settled or submitted.

(b) Failure to submit the order or judgment timely shall be deemed an abandonment of the motion or action, unless for good cause shown.

(c)(1) When settlement of an order or judgment is directed by the court, a copy of the proposed order or judgment with notice of settlement, returnable at the office of the clerk of the part in which the order or judgment was granted, or before the judge if the court has so directed or if the clerk is unavailable, shall be served on all parties either:

(i) by personal service not less than five days before the date of settlement; or

(ii) by mail not less than ten days before the date of settlement.

(2) Proposed counter-orders or judgments shall be made returnable on the same date and at the same place, and shall be served on all parties by personal service, not less than two days, or by mail, not less than seven days, before the date of settlement.

§ 208.34. Absence or Disqualification of Assigned Judge

(a) Whenever a judge is temporarily absent from a multipart court, proceedings in progress or scheduled for appearance in the part presided over by that judge shall be reassigned or otherwise handled by the calendar judge, or the administrative judge if no calendar part has been established. If the judge presiding is unavailable or unable to act for more than two court days in succession, the administrative judge having direct supervisory authority over the court shall make whatever arrangements are necessary to accommodate the proceedings assigned to the judge.

(b) If a proceeding is assigned to a judge who is for any reason disqualified from hearing it, the proceeding shall be reassigned to another judge who is not disqualified, to be heard by the assigned judge as expeditiously as possible.

(c) In an emergency, when neither the calendar judge nor the administrative judge can be contacted, any other judge of or assigned to the court may act in respect to pending proceedings as may be appropriate.

§ 208.35. Bifurcated Trials

(a) Judges are encouraged to order a bifurcated trial of the issues of liability and damages in any action for personal injury where it appears that bifurcation may assist in a clarification or simplification of issues and a fair and more expeditious resolution of the action.

(b) Where a bifurcated trial is ordered, the issues of liability and damages shall be severed and the issue of liability shall be tried first, unless the court orders otherwise.

(c) During the voir dire conducted prior to the liability phase of the trial, if the damage phase of the trial is to be conducted before the same jury, counsel may question the prospective jurors with respect to the issue of damages in the same manner as if the trial were not bifurcated.

(d) In opening to the jury on the liability phase of the trial, counsel may not discuss the question of damages. However, if the verdict of the jury shall be in favor of the plaintiff on the liability issue or in favor of the defendant on any counterclaim on the liability issue, all parties shall then be afforded an opportunity to address the jury on the question of damages before proof in that regard is presented to the jury.

(e) In the event of a plaintiff's verdict on the issue of liability or a defendant's verdict on the issue of liability on a counterclaim, the damage phase of the trial shall be conducted immediately thereafter before the same judge and jury, unless the judge presiding over the trial, for reasons stated in the record, finds such procedures to be impracticable.

§ 208.36. Infants' and Incapacitated Persons' Claims and Proceedings

The settlement of an action by an infant or judicially declared incapacitated person (including an incompetent or conservatee) shall comply with CPLR 1207 and 1208, section 202.67 of the Rules of the Chief Administrator (22 NYCRR 202.67) and, in the case of an infant, with section 474 of the Judiciary Law.

Cross References

CPLR, see McKinney's Book 7B.

Judiciary Law, see McKinney's Book 29.

§ 208.37. Executions

(a) No execution may be issued against any party who has appeared by an attorney in an action or proceeding unless a copy of the judgment has been duly served upon the attorney for such party.

(b) No execution may be issued against any party who has appeared in person in any action and who defaults in answering either the original or an amended or supplemental complaint unless a copy of the judgment has been duly served upon such party personally or mailed to such party by certified mail at the address stated in the notice of appearance or in the last pleading or paper filed by the party with the clerk or at the address last furnished by the party to the clerk in writing.

§ 208.38. Appeals

(a) A notice of appeal shall not be accepted for filing without proof of service upon all parties.

(b) All papers which are to be included in the return on appeal and prepared by the appellant as required by the applicable provisions of the CPLR, shall be furnished by the appellant to the clerk at the time of filing the notice of settlement provided in section 1704 of the NYCCCA.

(c) In the case of the death, disability or prolonged absence from the city of the judge before whom the action was tried, the return on appeal may be settled by any judge presiding in a motion part in the county in which the judgment was entered, with the same force and effect as if he or she had tried the case.

Cross References

CPLR, see McKinney's Book 7B.

NYCCCA, see McKinney's Book 29A, Part 3.

§ 208.39. Procedures for the Enforcement of Money Judgments Under CPLR, Article 52

(a) All subpoenas and processes for the examination of judgment debtors or other persons, including garnishees, in connection with the enforcement of money judgments, as well as adjournments thereof if made returnable in the court, shall be returnable in such motion part of each county division of the court as may be designated by the Chief Administrator of the Courts.

(b) All subpoenas and processes for the examination of judgment debtors or other persons, including garnishees, if made returnable in the court, shall be filed with the clerk of the appropriate motion part, with proper affidavits of service, at least two court days before the return day, except where service was made too late for filing within such time, in which event filing before the hour of the return shall suffice and the clerk shall list all such upon the calendar. Stipulations of adjournments, if attendance in court on the adjourned date is required, shall be similarly filed. Unless so filed, the names of the parties shall not be called; nor shall any such names be called unless they appear on a written or typewritten calendar. The judge presiding may, upon proper proof by affidavit showing good cause for the failure to file in accordance with this rule, add any matter to the calendar.

(c) No adjournment of an examination shall be valid unless reduced to writing and a copy thereof delivered to the judgment debtor or other person, including a garnishee, at the time of such adjournment and his acknowledgement of the receipt thereof is endorsed on the original.

(d) There shall be no more than two adjournments of the examination of a judgment debtor or other person, including a garnishee, unless such additional adjournment is approved and such approval is noted on the papers by the judge presiding at a motion part.

(e) No motion shall be made upon the basis of any testimony taken in examinations unless and until such testimony has been reduced to writing and unless and until there has been compliance with the requirements of CPLR 5224(e).

(f) Every subpoena or other process providing for the examination of a judgment debtor or other person, including a garnishee, in addition to the other requirements of CPLR 5223, shall have endorsed on its face, in bold type, the words: "This subpoena or process (as the case may be) requires your personal appearance at the time and place specified. Failure to appear may subject you to fine and imprisonment for contempt of court."

Cross References

CPLR, see McKinney's Book 7B.

§ 208.40. Arbitration

(a) Alternative method of dispute resolution by arbitration. Where the Chief Administrator of the Courts has established this arbitration program, Part 28 of the Rules of the Chief Judge (22 NYCRR Part 28) shall control the proceedings.

(b) Where the parties agree to arbitrate a claim under NYCCCA § 206, arbitration proceedings shall be conducted in accordance with CPLR, Article 75.

Cross References

CPLR, see McKinney's Book 7B.

§ 208.41. Small Claims Procedure

(a) A small claims action shall be instituted by a plaintiff or someone on his or her behalf paying the filing fee as provided in NYCCCA 1803, and by supplying to the clerk the following information:

(1) plaintiff's name and residence address; (2) defendant's name and place of residence, or place of business or employment; and (3) the nature and amount of the plaintiff's claim, giving dates and other relevant information.

(b) The clerk shall reduce this information to a written statement on a form provided therefor and shall record it in his or her office. The statement shall be in nontechnical, concise and simple language, and shall be signed by the person who shall have supplied the information contained therein.

(c) The clerk shall give to the person who signed the statement a memorandum of the time and place set for the hearing, which shall be as soon as practica-

ble, and shall advise such person to produce at the hearing the supporting witnesses, account books, receipts or other documents required to establish the claim.

(d) Within five days after the action is recorded, the clerk shall send to the defendant by ordinary first class mail and by certified mail, return receipt requested, addressed to one or more of the addresses supplied as shall be deemed necessary, a signed notice bearing the seal of the court, which shall be in substantially the following form:

CIVIL COURT OF THE CITY OF NEW YORK

COUNTY OF _____

SMALL CLAIMS PART

TO: _____

    Take Notice that _____ asks judgment in this Court against you for $_____ together with costs, upon the following claim:

_____

_____

    There will be a hearing before the Court upon this claim on _____, 19__, at ____ o'clock ____M. in the Small Claims Part, held at _____.

    You must appear and present your defense and any counterclaim you may desire to assert at the hearing at the time and place above set forth (a corporation must be represented by an attorney or any authorized officer, director or employee). IF YOU DO NOT APPEAR, JUDGMENT WILL BE ENTERED AGAINST YOU BY DEFAULT EVEN THOUGH YOU MAY HAVE A VALID DEFENSE. If your defense or counterclaim, if any, is supported by witnesses, account books, receipts or other documents, you must produce them at the hearing. The Clerk, if requested, will issue subpoenas for witnesses, without fee thereof.

    If you wish to present a counterclaim against the claimant, you must do so by filing with the Clerk of the Court a statement containing such counterclaim within five days of receiving this notice of claim. At the time of such filing you must pay the Clerk a filing fee of $3.00 plus the cost of postage to send your counterclaim by first class mail to the claimant. If you fail to file a counterclaim within this five-day period, you retain the right to file the counterclaim until the time of the hearing, but the claimant may request and obtain an adjournment of the hearing to a later date.

    If you admit the claim, but desire time to pay, you must appear personally on the day set for the hearing and state to the Court your reasons for desiring time to pay.

Dated: _____, 20____

Clerk

A Guide to Small Claims Court is available at the court listed above.

NOTE: If you desire a jury trial, you must, before the day upon which you have been notified to appear, file with the Clerk of the Court a written demand for a trial by jury. You must also pay to the clerk a jury fee of $55 and file an undertaking in the sum of $50 or deposit such sum in cash to secure the payment of any costs that may be awarded against you. You will also be required to make an affidavit specifying the issues of fact which you desire to have tried by a jury and stating that such trial is desired and demanded in good faith.

Under the law, the Court may award $25 additional costs to the plaintiff if a jury trial is demanded by you and a decision is rendered against you.

(e) The clerk shall note on the statement referred to in subdivision (a) above, the date on which the notice was mailed and the address, the date of delivery shown by the return receipt and the name of the addressee or agent signing the receipt.

(f) Where all parties appear by attorneys, the case may be transferred to the appropriate county division of the Civil Court of the City of New York, and the claimant shall pay any additional filing fees required by law. If the claimant fails or refuses to pay such filing fees, the court shall dismiss the case.

(g) If service of notice cannot be effected upon the defendant within four months following the date on which the action was first instituted, the action shall be dismissed without prejudice.

(h) Unless the court shall otherwise order, a defendant to whom notice was duly given who fails to appear at the hearing on the day and time fixed either in person or by attorney shall be held to be in default, except that no default shall be ordered if the defendant or his attorney appear within one hour after the time fixed.

(i) If at the hearing it shall appear that the defendant has a counterclaim in an amount within the jurisdiction of the part for the hearing of small claims, the judge may either proceed forthwith to hear the entire case or may adjourn the hearing for a period of not more than 20 days or as soon thereafter as may be practicable, at which adjourned time the hearing of the entire case shall be had. An adjournment shall be granted at the request of the claimant if the defendant did not file the counterclaim with the court within five days of receiving the notice of claim.

(j) An oath or affirmation shall be administered to all witnesses. The court shall conduct the hearing in such manner as it deems best suited to discover the facts and to determine the justice of the case. If the plaintiff, or an attorney in his or her behalf, does not appear at the time set for hearing, the court may dismiss the claim for want of prosecution or enter a finding on the merits for the defendant, or make such other disposition as it may deem proper.

(k) Where, after a claim is filed with the clerk, either party to the action desires to implead one or more additional defendants, the clerk shall, upon receipt of the proper fees, issue and mail a notice of claim to each additional defendant under the procedure set forth above.

(l) The undertaking to be filed by a defendant desiring a jury trial shall be in the form prescribed by the relevant provisions of Article 25 of the CPLR.

(m) All motions pertaining to small claims shall be made returnable at a part and session appointed for the hearing of small claims, except that a motion to remove a case from the small claims part shall be made returnable in the appropriate motion part in the county division of the court in which the action is pending and shall be in accord with the rules of the NYCCCA generally applicable to motion practice.

(n) There May Be Arbitration of Any Small Claims Controversy.

(1) The parties to any controversy, except infants and incompetents, may submit the same for arbitration to any attorney, duly appointed as a small claims arbitrator by the administrative judge of this court, so assigned for such duty at that term of the court and upon whom they shall agree.

(2) The parties shall sign a consent which shall contain the name of the arbitrator, a brief recital of the nature of the controversy to be determined, a statement that they will abide by these rules and an affirmation that the decision of the arbitrator is final and that no appeal shall lie from the award. The consent must be filed with the clerk of the small claims part.

(3) The arbitrator shall forthwith proceed to hear the controversy. He or she shall not be bound by the rules regarding the admissibility of evidence, but all testimony shall be given under oath or affirmation. Either party may be represented by counsel, but no record of the proceeding before the arbitrator shall be kept. No expense shall be incurred by the arbitrator except upon the consent in writing of the parties.

(4) After the first hearing, neither party may withdraw from the arbitration unless both parties consent to, or the arbitrator directs, a discontinuance of the proceeding.

(5) The arbitrator shall make an award in writing and file the same forthwith, together with his or her opinion, if any, with the clerk of the small claims part. Unless both parties file a request in writing not to enter judgment, the clerk shall, within two days after the filing of the award, enter judgment in accordance therewith, provided the award has been filed within 30

days from the date of filing the consent. The time within which the clerk shall enter judgment may be extended by a stipulation in writing for a further period not to exceed 30 days.

(6) No fees or disbursements of any kind shall be demanded or received except as hereinabove provided.

Cross References

CPLR, see McKinney's Book 7B.

NYCCCA, see McKinney's Book 29A, Part 3.

§ 208.41–a.   Commercial Claims Procedure

(a) A commercial claims action may be brought by a claimant that is: (1) a corporation, including a municipal or public benefit corporation, partnership, or association, which has its principal office in the State of New York, or (2) an assignee of any commercial claim, subject to the restrictions set forth in NYCCCA § 1809–A. The action shall be instituted by the claimant or someone on its behalf by paying the filing fee and the cost of sending the notice of claim as provided in NYCCCA § 1803–A and by filing and signing a written application containing the following information:

(1) claimant's name and principal office address;

(2) defendant's name and place of residence or place of business or employment;

(3) the nature and amount of the claim, including dates, and other relevant information; where the claim arises out of a consumer transaction (one where the money, property or service which is the subject of the transaction is primarily for personal, family or household purposes), information showing that the transaction is a consumer transaction;

(4) a certification that not more than five claims have been instituted in the courts of this State in the calendar month; and,

(5) in the case of a commercial claim arising out of a consumer transaction, a certification that the claimant has mailed a demand letter, containing the information set forth in NYCCCA § 1803–A, no less than 10 days and no more than 180 days prior to the commencement of the claim.

(b) Unless the clerk shall require the claimant, pursuant to NYCCCA § 1810–A, to apply to the court for leave to prosecute the claim in a commercial claims part, the clerk shall reduce to a concise written form and record in a special docket the information contained in the application, and shall give to the person who signed the statement a memorandum of the time and place set for the hearing, which shall be as soon as practicable and shall advise such person to produce at the hearing supporting witnesses, account books, receipts or other documents required to establish the claim. The clerk shall advise the claimant of the right of the claimant or the defendant to request an evening hearing, which shall not be so scheduled if it would

cause unreasonable hardship to either party, and the clerk shall schedule the hearing so as to minimize the defendant's time away from employment. In the case of a commercial claim arising out of a consumer transaction, the clerk shall mark the claim conspicuously as a consumer transaction and shall record it in the docket marked as a consumer transaction.

(c) Within five days after the action is filed, the clerk shall send to the defendant by ordinary first class mail and by certified mail, return receipt requested, at one of the addresses required by NYCCCA § 1803–A, as shall be deemed necessary, a signed notice bearing the seal of the court, which shall be in substantially the following form:

CIVIL COURT OF THE CITY OF NEW YORK

COUNTY OF _____

COMMERCIAL CLAIMS PART

TO: _____

    Take Notice that _____ asks judgment in this Court against you for $_____ together with costs, upon the following claim:

_____

_____

_____

    There will be a hearing before the Court upon this claim on _____, 19___, at ____ o'clock ___M. in the Commercial Claims Part, held at _____.

    You must appear and present your defense and any counterclaim you may desire to assert at the hearing at the time and place above set forth. You may request that the hearing be scheduled during evening hours if you do so within 14 days of receipt of this notice. IF YOU DO NOT APPEAR, JUDGMENT WILL BE ENTERED AGAINST YOU BY DEFAULT EVEN THOUGH YOU MAY HAVE A VALID DEFENSE. If your defense or counterclaim, if any, is supported by witnesses, account books, receipts or other documents, you must produce them at the hearing. The Clerk, if requested, will issue subpoenas for witnesses, without fee thereof.

    If you wish to present a counterclaim against the claimant, you must do so by filing with the Clerk of the Court a statement containing such counterclaim within five days of receiving this notice of claim. At the time of such filing you must pay the Clerk a filing fee of $3.00 plus the cost of postage to send your counterclaim by first class mail to the claimant. If you fail to file a counterclaim within this five-day period, you retain the right to file the counterclaim until the time of the hearing, but the claimant may request and obtain an adjournment of the hearing to a later date.

    If you admit the claim, but desire time to pay, you must appear personally on the day set for the hearing and state to the Court your reasons for desiring time to pay.

Read the attached sheet for more information.

Dated: _____, 20__

Clerk

A Guide to Commercial Claims Court is available at the court listed above.

NOTE: If you desire a jury trial, you must, before the day upon which you have been notified to appear, file with the Clerk of the Court a written demand for a trial by jury. You must also pay to the clerk a jury fee of $55 and file an undertaking in the sum of $50 or deposit such sum in cash to secure the payment of any costs that may be awarded against you. You will also be required to make an affidavit specifying the issues of fact which you desire to have tried by a jury and stating that such trial is desired and demanded in good faith.

Under the law, the Court may award $25 additional costs to the plaintiff if a jury trial is demanded by you and a decision is rendered against you.

(d) The clerk shall note on the application the date on which the notice was mailed and the address, the date of delivery shown by the return receipt, and the name of the addressee or agent signing the receipt.

(e) If, after the expiration of 21 days (30 days in the case of a commercial claim arising out of a consumer transaction) from the date the notice was mailed, the ordinary first class mailing has not been returned as undeliverable, the defendant shall be presumed to have received notice of the claim.

(f) If service of notice cannot be made upon the defendant within four months following the date on which the action was first instituted, the action shall be dismissed without prejudice.

(g) Where all parties appear by attorney, the case shall be transferred to the appropriate county division of the Civil Court of the City of New York, and the claimant shall pay any additional filing fees required by law. If the claimant fails or refuses to pay such filing fees, the court shall dismiss the case.

(h) Unless the court shall otherwise order, a defendant to whom notice was duly given who fails to appear, either in person or by attorney, at the hearing on the day and time fixed, shall be held to be in default, except that no default shall be ordered if the defendant or his or her attorney appears within one hour after the time fixed. Notice of the default judgment, containing the information set forth in NYCCCA § 1807–A, shall be mailed by first class mail to the claimant and the defendant. The defaulting party may apply to have the default vacated by submitting a written request to the court; proceedings on default shall be governed by, but not limited to, section 5015 of the CPLR.

(i) If at the hearing it shall appear that the defendant has a counterclaim in an amount within the jurisdiction of the part for the hearing of small claims, the judge may either proceed forthwith to hear the entire case or may adjourn the hearing for a period of not more than 20 days or as soon thereafter as may be practicable, at which adjourned time the hearing of the entire case shall be had. An adjournment shall be granted at the request of the claimant if the defendant did not file the counterclaim with the court within five days of receiving the notice of claim.

(j) An oath or affirmation shall be administered to all witnesses. The court shall conduct the hearing in such manner as it deems best suited to discover the facts and to determine the justice of the case. If the claimant, or an attorney in his or her behalf, does not appear at the time set for hearing, the court may dismiss the claim for want of prosecution or enter a finding on the merits for the defendant, or make such other disposition as it may deem proper.

(k) Where, after a claim is filing with the clerk, either party to the action desires to implead one or more additional defendants, the clerk shall, upon receipt of the proper fees, issue and mail a notice of claim to each additional defendant under the procedure set forth above.

(l) The undertaking to be filed by a defendant desiring a jury trial shall be in the form prescribed by the relevant provisions of Article 25 of the CPLR.

(m) All motions pertaining to commercial claims shall be made returnable at a part session appointed for the hearing of commercial claims, except that a motion to remove a case from the commercial claims part shall be made returnable in the appropriate motion part in the county division of the court in which the action is pending, and shall be in accord with the rules of the NYCCCA generally applicable to motion practice.

(n) There may be arbitration of any commercial claims controversy.

(1) The parties to any controversy, except infants and incompetents, may submit the same for arbitration to any attorney, duly appointed as a commercial claims arbitrator by the administrative judge of this court, so assigned for such duty at that term of the court and upon whom they shall agree.

(2) The parties shall sign a consent which shall contain the name of the arbitrator, a brief recital of the nature of the controversy to be determined, a statement that they will abide by these rules, and an affirmation that the decision of the arbitrator is final and that no appeal shall lie from the award. The consent must be filed with the clerk of the commercial claims part.

(3) The arbitrator shall forthwith proceed to hear the controversy. He or she shall not be bound by the rules regarding the admissibility of evidence, but all

testimony shall be given under oath or affirmation. Either party may be represented by counsel, but no record of the proceeding before the arbitrator shall be kept. No expense shall be incurred by the arbitrator except upon the consent in writing of the parties.

(4) After the first hearing, neither party may withdraw from the arbitration unless both parties consent to, or the arbitrator directs, a discontinuance of the proceeding.

(5) The arbitrator shall make his or her award in writing and file the same forthwith, together with an opinion, if any, with the clerk of the commercial claims part. Unless both parties file a request in writing not to enter judgment, the clerk shall, within two days after the filing of the award, enter judgment in accordance therewith, provided the award has been filed within 30 days from the date of filing the consent. The time within which the clerk shall enter judgment may be extended by a stipulation in writing for a further period not to exceed 30 days.

(6) No fees or disbursements of any kind shall be demanded or received except as hereinabove provided.

§ 208.42. Proceedings Under Article 7 of the Real Property Actions and Proceedings Law

(a) Such proceedings involving residential property shall be commenced in the housing part.

(b) Except as provided in subdivision (d) hereof relative to proceedings for nonpayment of rent, the following form is set forth as an example of the notice of petition (the provisions relating to the demand for money judgment should be omitted unless the petition so demands):

CIVIL COURT OF THE
CITY OF NEW YORK,
COUNTY OF . . . .

```
_____ )
                    )
        Petitioner  )
        Address     )
                    )           NOTICE OF
      -against-     )           PETITION
                    )
        Respondent  )
        Address     )
                    )
        Respondent  )
        Address     )
_____ )
```

To the respondents _____ above named and described, in possession of the premises hereinafter described or claiming possession thereof:

PLEASE TAKE NOTICE that a hearing at which you must appear will be held at the Civil Court of the City of New York, _____ Part to be held at

_____, County of _____, on the _____ day of _____, 19___, at _____ am/pm, which prays for a final judgment of eviction awarding to the petitioner the possession of premises designated and described as follows:

the _____ rooms on the _____ floor, Apartment No. ____, _____ Street; City of New York, County of _____, and further granting to the petitioner such other and further relief as is demanded in the petition, which you must answer.

TAKE NOTICE also that demand is made in the petition herein for judgment against you, the respondent, for the sum of $_____, with interest thereon from _____, 19___

TAKE NOTICE that your answer may set forth any defense or counterclaim you may have against the petitioner.

TAKE NOTICE also that if you shall fail at such time to interpose and establish any defense that you may have to the allegations of the petition, you may be precluded from asserting such defense or the claim on which it is based in any other proceeding or action.

TAKE NOTICE that your failure to appear and answer may result in final judgment by default for the petitioner in the amount demanded in the petition.

TAKE NOTICE that under section 745 of the Real Property Actions and Proceedings Law, you may be required by the Court to make a deposit of use and occupancy, or a payment of use and occupancy to the petitioner, upon your second request for an adjournment or if the proceeding is not settled or a final determination has not been made by the Court within 30 days of the first court appearance. Failure to comply with an initial deposit or payment order may result in the entry of a final judgment against you without a trial. Failure to make subsequent required deposits or payments may result in an immediate trial on the issues raised in your answer.

Dated: County of . . . ., the . . . . . . day of . . . . . ., 19. . .

. . . .
Attorney(s) for Petitioner
Office and Post Office Address
Telephone Number

. . . .
Clerk

(c) At the option of the petitioner, on condition that he or she serves the notice of petition at least eight days prior to the return day, the following paragraph may be inserted in the foregoing notice of petition immediately after the paragraph which sets forth the amount of money for which demand is made in the petition:

TAKE NOTICE also that your answer may be made at the time of hearing specified above unless this Notice of Petition is served upon you on or before the . . . . . . day of . . . . . ., 19. . ., in which event you must answer at least three (3) days before the petition is noticed to be heard, either orally before the clerk of the court at his or her office or in writing by serving a copy thereof upon the undersigned attorney for the * petitioner, and by filing the original of such written answer with proof of service thereof in the office of the clerk at least three (3) days before the time the petition is noticed to be heard; in addition thereto, you must appear before the court at the time and place hereinabove set forth for the hearing.

* If the petitioner appears in person, strike out the words "undersigned attorney for the".

(d) Real Property Actions and Proceedings Law, section 732 shall be applicable in this court in a proceeding brought on the ground that the respondent has defaulted in the payment of rent. The following form is set forth as an example of a notice of petition to be used in such proceedings:

CIVIL COURT OF THE
CITY OF NEW YORK
COUNTY OF . . . .

Petitioner (Landlord)	) INDEX NO.
–against–	) L & T . . . . 19. . .
Respondent (Tenant)	) NOTICE OF
	) PETITION
Address	) Petitioner's Residence:
Respondent (Undertenant)	)
	)
Address	) Business Address:
	)

To the respondent[s] above named and described, in possession of the premises hereinafter described or claiming possession thereof:

PLEASE TAKE NOTICE that the annexed petition of _____, verified the ____ day of _____, 19____, prays for a final judgment of eviction, awarding to the petitioner possession of premises described as follows:

Apartment No. ____, on the ____ floor, consisting of ____ rooms, in premises known as and located at _____, County of ____ in the City of New York, as demanded in the petition.

TAKE NOTICE also that demand is made in the petition for judgment against you for the sum of $_____ with interest from _____, 19____

TAKE NOTICE also that within five (5) days after service of this Notice of Petition upon you, you must answer, either orally before the clerk of this Court at _____ County of _____, City and State of New York, or in writing by serving a copy thereof upon the undersigned attorney for the * petitioner, and by filing the original of such answer, with proof of

service thereof, in the Office of the Clerk. Your answer may set forth any defense or counterclaim you may have against the petitioner. On receipt of your answer, the Clerk will fix and give notice of the date for trial or hearing which will be held not less than three (3) nor more than eight (8) days thereafter, at which you must appear. If, after the trial or hearing, judgment is rendered against you, the issuance of a warrant dispossessing you may, in the discretion of the Court, be stayed for five (5) days from the date of such judgment.

TAKE NOTICE also that if you fail to interpose and establish any defense that you may have to the allegations of the petition, you may be precluded from asserting such defense or the claim on which it is based in any other proceeding or action.

In the event you fail to answer and appear, final judgment by default will be entered against you but a warrant dispossessing you will not be issued until the tenth day following the date of the service of this Notice of Petition upon you.

TAKE NOTICE that under Section 745 of the Real Property Actions and Proceedings Law, you may be required by the Court to make a rent deposit, or a rent payment to the petitioner, upon your second request for an adjournment or if the proceeding is not settled or a final determination has not been made by the Court within 30 days of the first court appearance. Failure to comply with an initial rent deposit or payment order may result in the entry of a final judgment against you without a trial. Failure to make subsequent required deposits or payments may result in an immediate trial on the issues raised in your answer.

Dated: City of New York, County of . . . ., the . . . . . . day of . . . ., 19. . . .

. . . .
Clerk of the Civil
Court of the City of
New York

. . . .
Attorney(s) for the Petitioner
. . . .
Address
. . . .
Telephone No.

* If the petitioner appears in person, strike out the words "undersigned attorney for the".

(e)(1) Except as may otherwise be provided by statute, a posttrial application to stay the issuance of a warrant shall be made, or referred, to the judge who directed entry of the judgment.

(2) Applications for an extension of time to comply with orders or judgments to pay moneys, vacate the premises or make repairs, or to correct mathematical errors, may be referred to a judge other than the one who signed the order or judgment.

(f)(1) Commencing May 21, 2001, all summary proceedings for residential premises located in postal zip codes 10035 and 10037, and for the Taft Houses and the Jefferson Houses, except proceedings brought by or at the direction of the New York County District Attorney's office under Real Property Actions and Proceedings Law, sections 711 and 715, shall be noticed and filed in the Harlem courthouse.

(2) Commencing September 1, 2003, all summary proceedings for the following residential premises in which the New York City Housing Authority is a party to the proceeding shall be noticed and filed in the Red Hook Community Justice Center:

Red Hook East Houses

Red Hook West Houses

(g) Allegations required under section 325 of the Multiple Dwelling Law and section 27.2107 of the Administrative Code of the City of New York. In every summary proceeding brought to recover possession of real property pursuant to section 711 of the Real Property Actions and Proceedings Law, the petitioner shall allege either:

(1) that the premises are not multiple dwelling; or

(2) that the premises are a multiple dwelling and, pursuant to the Administrative Code, sections 27–2097 et. seq., there is a currently effective registration statement on file with the office of code enforcement in which the owner has designated a managing agent, a natural person over 21 years of age, to be in control of and responsible for the maintenance and operation of the dwelling.

The petitioner shall also allege the following information: the multiple dwelling registration number, the registered managing agent's name, and either the residence or business address of said managing agent. The petitioner may (optionally) list a telephone number which may be used to call for repair and service.

(h) At the time of the issuance of a notice of petition by a judge or the clerk, or an order to show cause by the judge, in a summary proceeding to recover possession of real property, a copy of such order to show cause or notice of petition shall be filed with the clerk. The original papers with proof of service thereof shall be filed with the clerk within the time specified by statute.

(i)(1) At the time of the filing with the clerk of a notice of petition with proof of service in a summary proceeding under Article 7 of the Real Property Actions and Proceedings Law involving residential property, the petitioner shall submit to the clerk a stamped postcard containing a written notice addressed to the respondent, in both English and Spanish, containing the following language:

CIVIL COURT HOUSING PART
INDEX (LIBRO) NO.
CORTE CIVIL PARTE
DE VIVIENDA

DISPOSSESS OR EVICTION PROCEEDING—
PROCEDIMIENTO DE DESAHUCIO

1. IN NONPAYMENT PROCEEDING:

PAPERS HAVE BEEN SENT TO YOU AND FILED IN COURT ASKING THIS COURT TO EVICT YOU FROM YOUR RESIDENCE. YOU MUST APPEAR IN COURT AND FILE AN ANSWER TO THE LANDLORD'S CLAIM. IF YOU HAVE NOT RECEIVED THE PAPERS, GO TO THE HOUSING PART OF THE CIVIL COURT IMMEDIATELY AND BRING THIS CARD WITH YOU. IF YOU DO NOT APPEAR IN COURT, YOU MAY BE EVICTED. YOU ALSO MAY WISH TO CONTACT AN ATTORNEY.

DOCUMENTOS HAN SIDO ENVIADOS A UD. Y REGISTRADOS EN LA CORTE PARA DESALOJARLO DE SU RESIDENCIA. UD. TIENE QUE COMPARECER EN LA CORTE Y REGISTRAR UNA RESPUESTA A LA RECLAMACION DEL PROPIETARIO. SI NO HA RECIBIDO LOS DOCUMENTOS, VAYA A LA PARTE DE VIVIENDAS DE LA CORTE CIVIL INMEDIATAMENTE Y TRAIGA ESTA TARJETA CON USTED. SI UD. NO COMPARECE EN LA CORTE, PUEDE SER DESALOJADO. SI QUIERE PUEDE PONERSE EN CONTACTO CON UN ABOGADO.

2. IN HOLDOVER PROCEEDING:

PAPERS HAVE BEEN SENT TO YOU AND FILED IN COURT ASKING THIS COURT TO EVICT YOU FROM YOUR RESIDENCE. YOU MUST APPEAR IN COURT ON THE ___ DAY OF _____, 20__, AT ___ A.M./P.M., IN ROOM _____, PART _____. YOU MAY FILE YOUR ANSWER AT THAT TIME. IF YOU HAVE NOT RECEIVED THE PAPERS, YOU STILL MUST APPEAR IN COURT ON THE DATE INDICATED ABOVE AND BRING THIS CARD WITH YOU. IF YOU DO NOT APPEAR IN COURT, YOU MAY BE EVICTED. YOU ALSO MAY WISH TO CONTACT AN ATTORNEY.

DOCUMENTOS HAN SIDO ENVIADOS A UD. Y REGISTRADOS EN LA CORTE PARA DESALOJARLO DE SU RESIDENCIA. UD. TIENE QUE COMPARECER EN LA CORTE EL DIA ___ DE _____, 20__, A LAS ___ A.M./P.M., EN EL SALON _____, PARTE _____. PUEDE REGISTRAR SU RESPUESTA EN ESE MOMENTO. SI UD. NO HA RECIBIDO LOS DOCUMENTOS, DE TODAS MANERAS TIENE QUE COMPARECER EN LA CORTE EN LA FECHA INDICADA ARRIBA, Y TRAER ESTA TARJETA CONSIGO. SI UD. NO COMPARECE EN LA CORTE, PUEDE SER DES-

ALOJADO. SI QUIERE PUEDE PONERSE EN CONTACTO CON UN ABOGADO.

The face of the postcard shall be addressed to the respondent at the premises and at any other address at which process was served in the summary proceeding and shall contain the respondent's name, address (including apartment number) and zip code. The face of the postcard also shall contain, in the form of a return address, the appropriate address of the clerk's office to which the respondent should be directed. These addresses are:

Bronx County — Housing Part of the Civil Court, City of New York, Housing Court Clerk Ground Floor 1118 Grand Concourse Bronx, New York 10456

Kings County — Civil Court of the City of New York Housing Court Clerk Room 203 141 Livingston Street Brooklyn, New York 11201

Red Hook Community Justice Center Civil Court of the City of New York Housing Court Clerk Room 103 88 Visitation Place Brooklyn, New York 11231-1615

New York County — Civil Court of the City of New York Housing Court Clerk Room 225 111 Centre Street New York, New York 10013

Harlem Courthouse Civil Court of the City of New York Housing Court Clerk 170 East 121 Street New York, New York 10035

Queens County — Civil Court of the City of New York Housing Court Clerk 2nd Floor 89–17 Sutphin Boulevard Jamaica, New York 11435

Richmond County — Civil Court of the City of New York Housing Court Clerk

Basement 927 Castleton Avenue Staten Island, New York 10310

(2) The clerk promptly shall mail the postcard to the respondent at the premises and at any other address at which process was served in the summary proceeding. No default judgment for failure to answer shall be entered unless there has been compliance with this rule.

Cross References

Multiple Dwelling Law, see McKinney's Book 35A.

RPAPL, see McKinney's Book 49½.

§ 208.43. Rules of the Housing Part

(a) There shall be a housing part for the hearing of all actions and proceedings in all matters arising under section 110 of the NYCCCA.

(b) All rules of the Civil Court shall apply to the housing part whenever practicable, except when otherwise provided by statute or as otherwise provided in this section.

(c) There shall be paid to the clerk the following sums as a fee in an action or proceeding in the housing part:

(1) upon the request of a tenant for an order directing the owner to correct the violation and to impose a penalty for failure to comply timely with the order—$20;

(2) upon the issuance of a petition by a landlord for the removal of housing violations—$20.

(d) Summons.

(1) The summons shall state the county division and location of the court in which the action is brought, as well as the names of the parties and the address of the premises, and shall comply with all the provisions of the NYCCCA applicable to summonses.

(2) Form of Summons. The summons in a case involving an action in the housing part for the recovery of civil penalties shall be in such form as may be promulgated by the Chief Administrator.

(3) Where a hazardous or nonhazardous violation is alleged and the summons is personally delivered to the landlord or its registered agent within the City of New York, the defendant shall appear and answer within ten days after such service.

(4) Where a summons for a hazardous or nonhazardous violation is delivered by mail or by any other method provided in NYCCCA, § 110(m), the defendant shall appear and answer within 20 days after the proof of service thereof is filed with the clerk of the housing part.

(5) Where the summons for a hazardous or nonhazardous violation is personally delivered to the landlord or its registered agent, the affidavit of service thereof

shall be filed with the clerk of the housing part within five days after personal delivery.

(6) Where the summons for a hazardous or nonhazardous violation is served by any other method provided in NYCCCA, § 110(m), the affidavit of service thereof shall be filed with the clerk of the housing part no later than ten days from the date the summons is posted and mailed (where such mailing is required).

(7) Where the summons for a hazardous or nonhazardous violation is served outside of the City of New York, the affidavit of service thereof shall be filed with the clerk of the housing part within ten days after service.

(8) A penalty action for an immediately hazardous violation shall be commenced by an order to show cause, returnable within five days, or within a lesser time period in the discretion of the court.

(9) Upon the signing of an order to show cause and prior to the service thereof, the clerk of the housing part shall issue an index number.

(10) *Venue.*

(i) In any action or proceeding in the housing part of the Civil Court, the action or proceeding must be brought in the county in which the real property is situated (NYCCCA, § 302).

(ii) An action or proceeding involving premises located in postal zip codes 10035 and 10037, and the Taft Houses and the Jefferson Houses, shall be noticed and filed in the Harlem courthouse.

(iii) An action or proceeding involving the following premises in which the New York City Housing Authority is a party shall be noticed and filed in the Red Hook Community Justice Center:

Red Hook East Houses

Red Hook West Houses

(e) The answer shall be verified and shall include any affirmative defenses or defenses in mitigation of the defendant's liability as set forth in section 27–2116 of the Administrative Code. In cases involving an immediately hazardous violation, the defendant may interpose an oral answer before the court.

(f) Where a defendant defaults by failing to answer the summons or order to show cause, an inquest shall be taken before the court. If the defendant consents to a judgment imposing a civil penalty, no inquest is required to be taken, and judgment shall be entered on consent by direction of the court.

(g) Notice of Trial. Where all parties appear by attorney, any party may serve a notice of trial on the others fixing a date for trial not less than five nor more than eight days after service of such notice, and shall file such notice with proof of service thereof at least four days before the date fixed for trial with the clerk of the housing part of the Civil Court, who shall thereupon place the case on the calendar for trial. Where the defendant appears in person, the clerk of the housing part shall fix a date for trial not less than five nor more than 15 days after joinder of issue, and shall immediately notify all the parties by mail of such date. If any of the parties has appeared by attorney, the clerk shall notify the attorney.

(h) Rules of evidence shall apply in all actions and proceedings in the housing part. The order of proof shall be determined by the court.

(i) The decision of a judge or housing judge shall set forth conclusions of fact. Said judge or housing judge shall render such decision within 30 days after trial of a nonhazardous or hazardous violation, and within 15 days after trial of an immediate hazardous violation or an injunction.

(j) The housing part shall be presided over by a judge of the Civil Court, or, in the discretion of the administrative judge, by a housing judge. The presiding judge shall assign the individual cases to housing judges and Civil Court judges, except actions and proceedings to be tried by jury shall be tried before a judge of the Civil Court.

(k) All applications for impleading shall be made to the judge of the calendar part, or, if the case has been assigned for trial, to the trial judge.

(*l*) No disclosure or bill of particulars shall be allowed without an order of the court in an action or proceeding to impose a civil penalty in the housing part.

(m) The Department of Housing Preservation and Development (HPD) shall not have costs taxed against it and shall be exempt from paying any fees required by this section or the NYCCCA.

Cross References

NYCCCA, see McKinney's Book 29A, Part 3.

PART 210. UNIFORM CIVIL RULES FOR THE CITY COURTS OUTSIDE THE CITY OF NEW YORK

§ 210.1. Application of Part; Waiver; Additional Rules; Application of UCCA; Definitions

(a) Application. This Part shall be applicable to civil actions and proceedings in the City Courts of the State of New York, outside the City of New York.

(b) Waiver. For good cause shown, and in the interests of justice, the court in an action or proceeding may waive compliance with any of these rules other than sections 210.2 and 210.3 unless prohibited from doing so by statute or by a rule of the Chief Judge.

(c) Additional Rules. Additional local court rules, not inconsistent with law or with these rules, shall comply with Part 9 of the Rules of the Chief Judge (22 NYCRR Part 9).

(d) Application of the Uniform City Court Act. The provisions of this part shall be construed as consistent with the Uniform City Court Act (UCCA), and matters not covered by these provisions shall be governed by the UCCA.

(e) Definitions.

(1) "Chief Administrator of the Courts" in this Part also includes a designee of the Chief Administrator.

(2) Unless otherwise defined in this Part, or the context otherwise requires, all terms used in this Part shall have the same meaning as they have in the UCCA and the CPLR.

Cross References

CPLR, see McKinney's Book 7B.

Uniform City Court Act, see McKinney's Book 29A, Part 3.

§ 210.2. Terms and Parts of Court

(a) Terms of Court. In each city court there shall be held such terms as the Chief Administrator of the Courts shall designate. A term of court is a four-week session of court and there shall be 13 terms of court in a year, unless otherwise provided in the annual schedules of terms established by the Chief Administrator which shall also specify the dates of such terms.

(b) Parts of Court. A part of court is a designated unit of the court in which specified business of the court is to be conducted by a judge or a quasi-judicial officer. In each city court there shall be such parts of court including one or more small claims parts, as may be established from time to time by the Chief Administrator of the Courts.

§ 210.3. Individual Assignment System; Structure

(a) General. There shall be established for all civil actions and proceedings heard in city courts an individual assignment system which provides for the continuous supervision of each action and proceeding by a single judge. Except as otherwise may be provided by the Chief Administrator of the Courts or by these rules, every action and proceeding shall be assigned and heard pursuant to the individual assignment system.

(b) Assignments. Actions and proceedings shall be assigned to a judge of the court upon the filing with the court of the first document in the case. Assignments shall be made by the clerk of the court pursuant to a method of selection prescribed by the Chief Administrator. The judge thereby assigned shall be known as the "assigned judge" with respect to that matter and, except as otherwise provided in subdivision (c), shall conduct all further proceedings therein.

(c) Exceptions.

(1) Where the requirements of matters already assigned to a judge are such as to limit the ability of that judge to handle additional cases, the Chief Administrator may authorize that new assignments to that judge be suspended until the judge is able to handle additional cases.

(2) The Chief Administrator may authorize the establishment in any court of special categories of actions and proceedings, for assignment to judges specially assigned to hear such actions or proceedings.

(3) Matters requiring immediate disposition may be assigned to a judge designated to hear such matters when the assigned judge is not available.

(4) The Chief Administrator may transfer any action or proceeding and any matter relating to an action or proceeding from one judge to another in accordance with the needs of the court.

(5) Judges sitting on other than a full-time basis shall be assigned cases in a manner authorized by the Chief Administrator in accordance with the needs of the court.

§ 210.4. Papers Filed in Court; Index Number; Form; Label

The party causing the first paper to be filed shall obtain an index number and communicate it forthwith to all other parties to the action. Thereafter such number shall appear on the outside cover and the first page, to the right of the caption, of every paper tendered for filing in the action. Each such cover and first paper also shall contain an indication of the county of venue and a brief description of the nature of the paper and, where the case has been assigned to an individual judge, shall contain the name of the assigned judge to the right of the caption. In addition to complying with the provisions of CPLR 2101, every paper filed in court shall have annexed thereto appropriate proof of service on all parties where required, and if typewritten, shall have at least a double space between each line, except for quotations and the names and addresses of attorneys appearing in the action, and shall have at least one-inch margins. In addition, every paper filed in court, other than an exhibit or printed form, shall contain writing on one side only, except that papers that are fastened on the side may contain writing on both sides. Papers that are stapled or bound securely shall not be rejected for filing simply because they are not bound with a backer of any kind.

Cross References

CPLR, see McKinney's Book 7B.

§ 210.5. Submission of Papers to Judge

All papers for signature or consideration of the court shall be presented to the clerk of the trial court in the appropriate courtroom or at the clerk's office, except that where the clerk is unavailable or the judge so directs, papers may be submitted to the judge and a copy filed with the clerk at the first available opportunity. All papers for any judge that are filed in the clerk's office shall be promptly delivered to the judge by the clerk. The papers shall be clearly addressed to the judge for whom they are intended and prominently show the nature of the papers, the title and index number of the action in which they are filed, the judge's name and the name of the attorney or party submitting them.

§ 210.6. Summons

(a) The summons shall state the name and location of the court in which the action is brought as well as the names of the parties and shall comply with all provisions of the UCCA applicable to summonses.

(b) The following form shall be used in actions pursuant to UCCA 902(a)(1), where a formal complaint is not served:

.... COURT OF THE CITY OF ....
COUNTY OF ....

```
                            ) Index No. ......
          Plaintiff,        ) SUMMONS
   -against-                ) Plaintiff's Residence
                            )
          Defendant.        ) Address:
                            )
```

To the above named defendant:

YOU ARE HEREBY SUMMONED and required to appear in the .... Court of the City of .... located at ...., in said City, County of ...., State of New York, either (i)

by serving an answer * within 10 days after service of this summons upon you, exclusive of the day of service, upon plaintiff's attorney, at the address stated below, or if there is no attorney, upon the plaintiff at the address stated above or (ii) by appearing at the clerk's office within 10 days after service of this summons upon you, exclusive of the day of service, by having the clerk of the court endorse your answer upon this summons; upon your failure to answer, judgment will be taken against you for the sum of $...... with interest thereon from the .... day of ...., 19... together with the costs of this action.

Dated: the ...... day of ...., 19...

Statement of the nature
and substance of plain-
tiff's cause of action:

             ....
             Attorney(s) for Plaintiff
             Post Office Address
             Telephone Number
             (or, alternatively,

             ....
             Clerk of the ..... Court
             of the City of ....)

* You need not physically go to the court to serve an answer under option (i).

(c) In a case where a formal complaint is annexed to the summons the following form of summons, with all blank spaces appropriately filled in, is to be used:

.... COURT OF THE CITY OF ....
COUNTY OF ....

```
                            ) Index No. ......
          Plaintiff,        ) SUMMONS
   -against-                ) Plaintiff's Residence
                            )
          Defendant.        ) Address:
                            )
```

To the above named defendant:

YOU ARE HEREBY SUMMONED and required to appear in the .... Court of the City of .... located at ...., in said City, County of ...., State of New York, by serving an answer* to the annexed complaint upon plaintiff's attorney at the address stated below, or if there is no attorney, upon the plaintiff at the address stated above, within the time provided by law as noted below; upon your failure to so answer, judgment will be taken against you for the relief demanded in the complaint, together with the costs of this action.

Dated: the ...... day of ...., 19...

....
Attorney(s) for Plaintiff
Post Office Address
Telephone Number

NOTE: The law provides that:

(1) If this summons is served by its delivery to you personally within the County of ...., you must answer within 10 days after such service; or

(2) If this summons is served by delivery to any person other than you personally, or is served outside the County of ...., or by publication, or by any means other than personal delivery to you within the County of ...., you are allowed 30 days after service is complete within which to answer.

* You need not physically go to the court to serve an answer.

Cross References

Uniform City Court Act, see McKinney's Book 29A, Part 3.

§ 210.7. Pleadings

(a) Except as required by statute, a formal pleading may be dispensed with in any case in which the party required to serve the pleading appears in person, and an order to that effect may be entered ex parte by the judge upon application to the clerk, who shall refer the same to such judge. Any other party may move to modify or vacate such ex parte order.

(b) All formal pleadings in this court and verifications thereof shall be in conformity with CPLR, Article 30.

(c) An order directing the service and filing of a formal pleading, or pleadings, shall specify the time within which the same shall be served and filed.

(d) A defendant's time to move or answer may be extended by ex parte order no more than once, and for no longer than ten days beyond the expiration of the original time to answer, and only if there has been no previous extension by consent. All further applications for extensions shall be made by motion upon notice.

(e) In any action to recover damages for personal injuries arising out of use or operation of a motor vehicle, plaintiff shall set forth in the complaint, whether in short or long form, the jurisdictional facts that permit plaintiff to maintain the action and avoid the bar of the Comprehensive Automobile Insurance Reparations Act.

Cross References

CPLR, see McKinney's Book 7B.

Comprehensive Automobile Insurance Reparations Act, see McKinney's Book 27.

§ 210.8. Calendaring of Motions; Uniform Notice of Motion Form

(a) There shall be compliance with the procedures prescribed in the UCCA and CPLR for the bringing of motions. In addition, no motion shall be filed with the court unless a notice of motion is served and filed with the motion papers. The notice of motion shall read substantially as follows:

CITY COURT OF THE
CITY OF/COUNTY OF
_____.

_____
A.B.,   ) Notice of Motion
      Plaintiff,) Index No.
   -against-   ) _____
) Name of Assigned
) Judge
C.D.,   ) Oral argument is re-
) quested ☐
     Defendant.) (Check box if requested)
_____)

Upon the affidavit of _____, sworn to on _____, 19___, and upon (list supporting papers if any), the _____ will move this court at the _____ Courthouse, _____, New York, on the _____ day of _____, 19___, at _____ (a.m.) (p.m.) for an order (briefly indicate relief requested).

The above-entitled action is for (briefly state nature of action, e.g. personal injury, contract, property damage etc.). Pursuant to CPLR 2214(b), answering affidavits, if any, are required to be served upon the undersigned at least seven days before the return date of the motion.

(check box if applicable) ☐

Dated:

_____
(Print Name)
Attorney[1] (or Attorney in charge of case if law firm) for moving party
Address:
Telephone number:

TO: _____
(Print Name)
Attorney[1] for (other party)
Address:
Telephone number:

_____
(Print Name)
Attorney[1] for (other party)
Address:
Telephone number:

[1] If any party is appearing pro se, the name address and telephone number of such party shall be stated.

(b) The notice of motion set forth in subdivision (a) shall not be required for the return of an order to show cause or an application for ex parte relief.

§ 210.9. Motion Procedure

(a) All motions shall be returnable before the assigned judge. The moving party shall serve copies of all affidavits and briefs upon the adverse parties at the time of service of the notice of motion. The answering party shall serve copies of all affidavits and briefs as required by CPLR 2214. Affidavits shall be for a statement of the relevant facts, and briefs shall be for a statement of the relevant law. Unless otherwise directed by the court, answering and reply affidavits and all other papers required to be furnished to the court by CPLR 2214(c) must be filed no later than the time of argument or submission of the motion.

(b) The assigned judge may determine that any or all motions be orally argued and may direct that moving and responding papers be filed with the court prior to the time of argument.

(c) Unless oral argument has been requested by a party and permitted by the court, or directed by the court, motion papers received by the clerk of the court on or before the return date shall be deemed submitted as of the return date. A party requesting oral argument shall set forth such request in the notice of motion or on the first page of the answering papers, as the case may be. A party requesting oral argument on a motion brought on by an order to show cause shall do so as soon as practicable before the time the motion is to be heard.

§ 210.10. Preliminary Conference

In all actions assigned to a judge where disclosure has not been completed the court may order a preliminary conference as soon as practicable after the action has been assigned. The matters to be considered at the preliminary conference may include simplification and limitation of factual and legal issues, establishment of a timetable for the completion of all disclosure proceedings, the addition of other necessary parties and settlement of the action.

§ 210.11. [Reserved]

§ 210.12. Videotape Recording of Depositions

Depositions authorized under the provisions of the CPLR or other law may be taken, as permitted by subdivision (b) of section 3113 of the CPLR, by means of simultaneous audio and visual electronic recording, provided such recording is made in conformity with section 202.15 of the Rules of the Chief Administrator (22 NYCRR Part 202).

§ 210.13. Exchange of Medical Reports in Personal Injury and Wrongful Death Actions

Except where the court otherwise directs, in all actions in which recovery is sought for personal injuries, disability or death, physical examinations and the exchange of medical information shall be governed by the provisions hereinafter set forth:

(a) At any time after joinder of issue and service of a bill of particulars the party to be examined or any other party may serve on all other parties a notice fixing the time and place of examination. Unless otherwise stipulated the examination shall be held not less than 30 nor more than 60 days after service of the notice. If served by any party other than the party to be examined, the notice shall name the examining medical provider or providers. If the notice is served by the party to be examined, the examining parties shall, within 10 days of receipt thereof, submit to the party to be examined the name of the medical providers who will conduct the examination. Any party may move to modify or vacate the notice fixing the time and place of examination or the notice naming the examining medical providers, within 10 days of the receipt thereof, on the grounds that the time or place fixed or the physician named is objectionable, or that the nature of the action is such that the interests of justice will not be served by an examination, exchange of medical reports or delivery or authorizations.

(b) At least 20 days before the date of such examination, or on such other date as the court may direct, the party to be examined shall serve upon and deliver to all other parties the following, which may be used by the examining medical provider:

(1) copies of the medical reports of those medical providers who have previously treated or examined the party seeking recovery. These shall include a recital of the injuries and conditions as to which testimony will be offered at the trial, referring to and identifying those x-ray and technicians' reports which will be offered at the trial, including a description of the injuries sustained, a diagnosis, and a prognosis. Medical reports may consist of completed medical provider, workers' compensation, or insurance forms that provide the information required by this paragraph.

(2) duly executed and acknowledged written authorizations permitting all parties to obtain and make copies of all hospital records and such other records, including x-ray and technicians' reports, as may be referred to and identified in the reports of those

medical providers who have treated or examined the party seeking recovery.

(c) Copies of the reports of the medical providers making examinations pursuant to this section shall be served on all other parties within 45 days after completion of the examination. These shall comply with the requirements of paragraph (1) of subdivision (b).

(d) In actions where the cause of death is in issue, each party shall serve upon all other parties copies of the reports of all treating or examining medical providers whose testimony will be offered at the trial, complying with the requirements of paragraph (1) of subdivision (b), and the party seeking to recover shall deliver to all other parties authorizations to examine and obtain copies of all hospital records, autopsy or post-mortem reports, and such other records as provided in paragraph (2) of subdivision (b). Copies of these reports and the required authorizations shall be served and delivered with the bill of particulars by the party seeking to recover. All other parties shall serve copies of the reports of their medical providers within 45 days thereafter. In any case where the interests of justice will not be promoted by service of such reports and delivery of such authorizations, an order dispensing with either or both may be obtained.

(e) Parties relying solely on hospital records may so certify in lieu of serving medical providers' reports.

(f) No case otherwise eligible to be noticed for trial may be noticed unless there has been compliance with this rule, or an order dispensing with compliance or extending the time therefor has been obtained; or, where the party to be examined was served a notice as provided in subdivision (a), and the party so served has not responded thereto.

(g) In the event that the party examined intends at the trial to offer evidence of further or additional injuries or conditions, nonexistent or not known to exist at the time of service of the original medical reports, such party shall, within 30 days after the discovery thereof, and not later than 30 days before trial, serve upon all parties a supplemental medical report complying with the requirements of paragraph (1) of subdivision (b) and shall specify a time not more than 10 days thereafter and a place at which a further examination may be had. Further authorizations to examine and make copies of additional hospital records, other records, x-ray or other technicians' reports as provided in paragraph (2) of subdivision (b) must also be delivered with the medical reports. Copies of the reports of the examining medical providers, complying with the requirements of subdivision (c), shall be served within 10 days after completion of such further examination. If any party desires at the trial to offer the testimony of additional treating or examining medical providers, other than whose medical reports have been previously exchanged, the medical reports of such medical providers, complying with the

requirements of paragraph (1) of subdivision (b) shall be served upon all parties at least 30 days before trial.

(h) Unless an order to the contrary is made or unless the judge presiding at the trial in the interests of justice and upon a showing of good cause shall hold otherwise, the party seeking to recover damages shall be precluded at the trial from offering in evidence any part of the hospital records and all other records, including autopsy or post-mortem records, x-ray reports or reports of other technicians, not made available pursuant to this rule, and no party shall be permitted to offer any evidence of injuries or conditions not set forth or put in issue in the respective medical reports previously exchanged, nor will the court hear the testimony of any treating or examining medical providers whose medical reports have not been served as provided by this rule.

(i) Orders transferring cases pending in other courts which are subject to the provisions of this section, whether or not such cases are consolidated with cases pending in the court to which transferred, shall contain such provisions as are required to bring the transferred cases into compliance with this rule.

(j) Any party may move to compel compliance or to be relieved from compliance with this rule or any provision thereof, but motions directed to the sufficiency of medical reports must be made within 20 days of receipt of such reports. All motions under this rule may be made on affidavits of attorneys, shall be made on notice, returnable at the appropriate motion part and shall be granted or denied on such terms as to costs, calendar position and dates of compliance with any provision of this rule as the court in its discretion shall direct.

(k) Where an examination is conducted on consent prior to the institution of an action, the party to be examined shall deliver the documents specified in paragraphs (1) and (2) of subdivision (b) hereof, and the report of the examining medical provider shall be delivered as provided in subdivision (c) hereof. In that event examination after institution of the action may be waived. The waiver, which shall recite that medical reports have been exchanged and that all parties waive further physical examination, shall be filed with the note of issue. This shall not be a bar, however, to proceeding under subdivision (g) in a proper case.

§ 210.14. Defaults

At any schedule call of a calendar or at any conference, if all parties do not appear and proceed or announce their readiness to proceed immediately or subject to the engagement of counsel, the judge may note the default on the record and enter an order as follows:

(1) if the plaintiff appears but the defendant does not, the judge may grant judgment by default or order an inquest;

(2) if the defendant appears but the plaintiff does not, the judge may dismiss the action and may order a severance of counterclaims or cross-claims;

(3) if no party appears, the judge may make such order as appears just.

§ 210.15. Transfer of Actions

Actions transferred from the Supreme Court or County Court to a City Court shall be placed in such order and relative position on the appropriate calendars that they will be reached for trial insofar as practicable as if a notice of trial had originally been filed in the City Court for the same date as that for which the note of issue was filed in the Supreme Court or County Court.

§ 210.16. Discontinuance of Civil Actions

In any discontinued action, the attorney for the plaintiff shall file a stipulation or statement of discontinuance with the clerk of the court within 20 days of such discontinuance. If the action has been noticed for judicial activity within 20 days of such discontinuance, the stipulation or statement shall be filed before the date scheduled for such activity.

§ 210.17. Notice of Trial Where All Parties Appear by Attorney

(a) The notice of trial filed by any party pursuant to UCCA section 1301 shall be accompanied by a certificate of readiness, with proof of service on all parties in the form prescribed by this section. The notice of trial shall include the index number, the name of the judge to whom the action is assigned, name, office address and telephone number of each attorney and pro se party who has appeared, and the name of any insurance carrier acting on behalf of any party.

(b) Within 20 days after service of such notice of trial, any party may move to vacate the notice. The affidavit in support of the application must specify the reason for vacating the notice.

(c) After any notice of trial has been filed pursuant to this rule, no pretrial examination or other preliminary proceedings may be had, except that if some unusual or unanticipated conditions subsequently develop which make it necessary that further pretrial examination or further preliminary proceedings be had, and if without them the moving party would be unduly prejudiced, the court may make an order granting permission to conduct such examination or proceedings and prescribing the time therefor. Such an order may be made only upon motion on notice showing in detail, by affidavit, the facts claimed to entitle the moving party to relief under this subdivision.

(d) Where a party filing a notice of trial, in a medical malpractice action or an action against a municipality, seeking a sum of money only, is prohibited by the provisions of CPLR 3017(c) from stating in the pleadings the amount of damages sought in the action, the party shall indicate in the notice of trial whether the amount of damages exceeds $6,000, exclusive of costs and interests. If it does not, the party shall also indicate if it exceeds $2,000, exclusive of costs and interest.

(e) The certificate of readiness shall read substantially as follows:

CERTIFICATE OF READINESS FOR TRIAL
(Items 1–5 must be checked)

	Complete	Waived	Not Required
1. All pleadings served	....	....	....
2. Bill of particulars served	....	....	....
3. Physical examinations completed	....	....	....
4. Medical reports exchanged	....	....	....
5. Discovery proceedings now known to be necessary completed	....	....	....
6. There are no outstanding requests for discovery			
7. There has been a reasonable opportunity to complete the foregoing proceedings			
8. There has been compliance with any order issued pursuant to section 210.11 of the Rules of the Chief Administrator (22 NYCRR Part 210).			
9. The case is ready for trial			

Dated: _____
(Signature) _____
Attorney(s) for: _____
Office and P.O. address: _____

§ 210.18. Calendars

(a) A judge to whom cases are assigned under the individual assignment system may establish such calendar of cases as the judge shall deem necessary or desirable for proper case management.

(b) **Continuous Calendars.** In any court not continuously in session, the calendars at the close of one term or session of court shall be used to open the following term or session, and actions on the calendars shall retain their positions.

(c) **Military Calendar.** A military calendar shall be utilized to hold in suspense an action that cannot reasonably be tried because a party or a witness necessary upon the trial is in military service and is not presently available for trial, and a deposition cannot be taken, or, if taken, would not provide adequate evidence.

(d) **Calendar Progression.** With due regard to the requirements of statutory preferences and of section 210.20 of this Part, when actions are advanced from one calendar to another they shall progress from the head of one calendar to the foot of the next calendar and otherwise progress in order insofar as practicable unless otherwise determined by the court.

(e) Call of Calendars. Judges to whom actions and proceedings are assigned pursuant to the individual assignment system may schedule calls of any calendars they have established at such times as they deem appropriate.

(f) Readiness for Trial. When an action has been announced "ready" but a trial is not immediately available, counsel may arrange with the judge to be summoned by telephone, provided they agree to hold themselves available and to appear on one hour's notice, or at such other time as the court may order, at the time assigned for trial.

§ 210.19.   [Reserved]

§ 210.20.   Special Preferences

(a) Any party claiming a preference under CPLR 3403 may apply to the court in the manner prescribed by that rule, the note of issue therein referred to being deemed a reference to a notice of trial.

(b) Counterclaims and Cross-Claims. A counterclaim or cross-claim which is not entitled to a preference shall not itself defeat the plaintiff's right to a preference under this section.

(c) Result of Preference Being Granted. If a preference is granted, the action shall be placed ahead of all nonpreferred pending cases, as directed by the court, unless the court otherwise orders.

Cross References

CPLR, see McKinney's Book 7B.

§ 210.21.   Objections to Applications for Special Preference

(a) Within 20 days of the filing of the notice of trial, if the notice of motion for a special preference is filed therewith, or within ten days of the service of a notice of motion to obtain a preference if served and filed subsequent to service and filing of the notice of trial, any other party may serve upon all other parties and file with the court affidavits and other relevant papers, with proof of service, in opposition to granting the preference. In the event such opposing papers are filed the party applying for the preference may, within five days thereafter, serve and file in like manner papers in rebuttal.

(b) In any action which has been accorded a preference in trial upon a motion the court shall not be precluded, on its own motion at any time thereafter, from ordering that the action is not entitled to a preference under these rules.

(c) Notwithstanding the failure of any party to oppose the application, no preference shall be granted by default unless the court finds that the action is entitled to a preference.

§ 210.22.   Pretrial and Prearbitration Conference

After the filing of a notice of trial and certificate of readiness in any action, the judge shall order such pretrial and prearbitration conferences as required by the needs of the court. The attendance of attorneys who are familiar with the case and who are authorized to act shall be required. The court may also require the attendance of parties, and in the event of failure of attendance by attorneys or parties, the court shall have the same powers with respect to dismissals, defaults, or both as it might exercise when a case is reached for trial. Upon the pretrial of an action, the judge shall consider with counsel and parties the simplification and limitation of the issues and the obtaining of admissions of facts and of documents to avoid unnecessary proof, as well as the ultimate disposition of the action by settlement or compromise.

§§ 210.23, 210.24.   [Reserved]

§ 210.25.   Engagement of Counsel

No adjournment shall be granted on the ground of engagement of counsel except in accordance with Part 125 of the Rules of the Chief Administrator of the Courts (22 NYCRR Part 125).

§ 210.26.   [Reserved]

§ 210.27.   Submission of Papers for Trial

(a) Upon the trial of an action, the following papers, if not yet submitted, shall be submitted to the court by the party who has filed the notice of trial:

(1) copies of all pleadings marked as required by CPLR 4012;

(2) a copy of any statutory provision in effect at the time the cause of action arose upon which either the plaintiff or the defendant relies; and

(3) a copy of the bill of particulars, if any.

(b) If so ordered, the parties shall submit to the court, before the commencement of trial, trial memoranda which shall be exchanged among counsel.

Cross References

CPLR, see McKinney's Book 7B.

§ 210.28.   Absence of Attorney During Trial

All trial counsel shall remain in attendance at all stages of the trial until the jury retired to deliberate unless excused by the judge presiding. The court may permit counsel to leave, provided counsel remain in telephone contact with the court. Any counsel not present during the jury deliberation, further requests to charge, or report of the jury verdict shall be deemed to stipulate that the court may proceed in his or her absence and to waive any irregularity in proceedings taken in his or her absence.

Reserved

§§ 210.29, 210.30.   [Reserved]

§ 210.31.   Restoration After Jury Disagreement, Mistrial or Order for New Trial

An action in which there has been an inability by a jury to reach a verdict, a mistrial or a new trial granted by the trial judge or an appellate court shall be rescheduled for trial. Where a new trial is granted by an appellate court, a notice to reschedule shall be filed with the appropriate clerk.

§ 210.32.   Damages, Inquest After Default; Proof

(a) In an inquest to ascertain damages upon a default pursuant to CPLR 3215, if the defaulting party fails to appear in person or by representative, the party entitled to judgment, whether a plaintiff, third-party plaintiff, or a party who has pleaded a cross claim or counterclaim, shall be permitted to submit, in addition to the proof required by CPLR 3215(e), properly executed affidavits as proof of damages.

(b) In any action where it is necessary to take an inquest before the court, the party seeking damages may submit the proof required by oral testimony of witnesses in open court or by written statements of the witnesses, in narrative or question and answer form, signed and sworn to.

Cross References

CPLR, see McKinney's Book 7B.

§ 210.33.   Submission of Orders, Judgments and Decrees for Signature

(a) Proposed orders or judgments, with proof of service on all parties where the order is directed to be settled or submitted on notice, must be submitted for signature, unless otherwise directed by the court, within 60 days after the signing and filing of the decision directing that the order be settled or submitted.

(b) Failure to submit the order or judgment timely shall be deemed an abandonment of the motion or action, unless for good cause shown.

(c)(1) When settlement of an order or judgment is directed by the court, a copy of the proposed order or judgment with notice of settlement, returnable at the office of the clerk of the court in which the order or judgment was granted, or before the judges if the court has so directed or if the clerk is unavailable, shall be served on all parties either:

(i) by personal service not less than five days before the date of settlement; or

(ii) by mail not less than ten days before the date of settlement.

(2) Proposed counter-orders or judgments shall be made returnable on the same date and at the same place, and shall be served on all parties by personal service, not less than two days, or by mail, not less than seven days, before the date of settlement.

§§ 210.34, 210.35.   [Reserved]

§ 210.36.   Infants' and Incapacitated Persons' Claims and Proceedings

The settlement of an action by an infant or judicially declared incapacitated person (including an incompetent or conservatee) shall comply with CPLR 1207 and 1208, section 202.67 of the Rules of the Chief Administrator (22 NYCRR 202.67) and, in the case of an infant, with section 474 of the Judiciary law.

Cross References

CPLR, see McKinney's Book 7B.

Judiciary Law, see McKinney's Book 29.

§ 210.37.   Executions

(a) No execution may be issued against any party who has appeared by an attorney in an action or proceeding unless a copy of the judgment has been duly served upon the attorney for such party.

(b) No execution may be issued against any party who has appeared in person in any action and who defaults in answering either the original or an amended or supplemental complaint unless a copy of the judgment has been duly served upon such party personally or mailed to such party by certified mail at the address stated in the notice of appearance or in the last pleading or paper filed by the party with the clerk or at the address last furnished by the party to the clerk in writing.

§ 210.38.   Appeals

(a) A notice of appeal shall not be accepted for filing without proof of service upon all parties.

(b) All papers which are to be included in the return on appeal and prepared by the appellant as required by the applicable provisions of the CPLR, shall be furnished by the appellant to the clerk at the time of filing the notice of settlement provided in section 1704 of the UCCA.

(c) In the case of the death, disability or prolonged absence from the city of the judge before whom the action was tried, the return on appeal may be settled by any judge authorized by the Chief Administrator of the Courts with the same force and effect as if he had tried the case.

Cross References

CPLR, see McKinney's Book 7B.

Uniform City Court Act, see McKinney's Book 29A, Part 3.

§ 210.39. Procedures for the Enforcement of Money Judgments Under CPLR, Article 52

(a) All subpoenas and processes for the examination of judgment debtors or other persons, including garnishees, in connection with the enforcement of money judgments, as well as adjournments thereof if made returnable in the court, shall be returnable in the appropriate motion part of each city court.

(b) All subpoenas and processes for the examination of judgment debtors or other persons, including garnishees, if made returnable in the court, shall be filed with the clerk of the appropriate motion part, with proper affidavits of service, at least two court days before the return day, except where service was made too late for filing within such time, in which event filing before the hour of the return shall suffice and the clerk shall list all such upon the calendar. Stipulations of adjournments, if attendance in court on the adjourned date is required, shall be similarly filed. Unless so filed, the names of the parties shall not be called; nor shall any such names be called unless they appear on a written or typewritten calendar. The judge presiding may, upon proper proof by affidavit showing good cause for the failure to file in accordance with this rule, add any matter to the calendar.

(c) No adjournment of an examination shall be valid unless reduced to writing and a copy thereof delivered to the judgment debtor or other person, including a garnishee, at the time of such adjournment and his acknowledgment of the receipt thereof is endorsed on the original.

(d) There shall be no more than two adjournments of the examination of a judgment debtor or other person, including a garnishee, unless such additional adjournment is approved and such approval is noted on the papers by the judge presiding at a motion part.

(e) No motion shall be made upon the basis of any testimony taken in examinations unless and until such testimony has been reduced to writing and unless and until there has been compliance with the requirements of CPLR 5224(e).

(f) Every subpoena or other process providing for the examination of a judgment debtor or other person, including a garnishee, in addition to the other requirements of CPLR 5223, shall have endorsed on its face, in bold type, the words: "This subpoena or process (as the case may be) requires your personal appearance at the time and place specified. Failure to appear may subject you to fine and imprisonment for contempt of court."

Cross References

CPLR, see McKinney's Book 7B.

§ 210.40. Arbitration

(a) Alternative method of dispute resolution by arbitration. Where the Chief Administrator of the Courts has established this arbitration program, Part 28 of the Rules of the Chief Judge (22 NYCRR Part 28) shall control the proceedings.

(b) Where the parties agree to arbitrate a claim under UCCA 206, arbitration proceedings shall be conducted in accordance with CPLR Article 75.

Cross References

CPLR, see McKinney's Book 7B.

Uniform City Court Act, see McKinney's Book 29A, Part 3.

§ 210.41. Small Claims Procedure

(a) A small claims action shall be instituted by a plaintiff or someone on his or her behalf paying the filing fee as provided in UCCA 1803, and by supplying to the clerk the following information:

(1) plaintiff's name and residence address;

(2) defendant's name and place of residence, or place of business or employment; and

(3) the nature and amount of the plaintiff's claim, giving dates and other relevant information.

(b) The clerk shall reduce this information to a written statement on a form provided therefor and shall record it in his office. The statement shall be in nontechnical, concise and simple language, and shall be signed by the person who shall have supplied the information contained therein.

(c) The clerk shall give to the person who signed the statement a memorandum of the time and place set for the hearing, which shall be as soon as practicable, and shall advise such person to produce at the hearing supporting witnesses, account books, receipts or other documents required to establish the claim.

(d) Within five days after the action is recorded, the clerk shall send to the defendant by ordinary first class mail and by certified mail, return receipt requested, addressed to one or more of the addresses supplied as shall be deemed necessary, a signed notice bearing the seal of the court, which shall be in substantially the following form:

CITY COURT OF THE CITY OF _____

COUNTY OF _____

SMALL CLAIMS PART

TO: _____

Take Notice that _____ asks judgment in this Court against you for $_____ together with costs, upon the following claim:

_____
_____
_____

There will be a hearing before the Court upon this claim on _____, 19__, at ____ o'clock ____M. in the Small Claims Part, held at _____.

You must appear and present your defense and any counterclaim you may desire to assert at the hearing at the time and place above set forth (a corporation must be represented by an attorney or any authorized officer, director or employee). IF YOU DO NOT APPEAR, JUDGMENT WILL BE ENTERED AGAINST YOU BY DEFAULT EVEN THOUGH YOU MAY HAVE A VALID DEFENSE. If your defense or counterclaim, if any, is supported by witnesses, account books, receipts or other documents, you must produce them at the hearing. The Clerk, if requested, will issue subpoenas for witnesses, without fee thereof.

If you wish to present a counterclaim against the claimant, you must do so by filing with the Clerk of the Court a statement containing such counterclaim within five days of receiving this notice of claim. At the time of such filing you must pay the Clerk a filing fee of $3.00 plus the cost of postage to send your counterclaim by first class mail to the claimant. If you fail to file a counterclaim within this five-day period, you retain the right to file the counterclaim until the time of the hearing, but the claimant may request and obtain an adjournment of the hearing to a later date.

If you admit the claim, but desire time to pay, you must appear personally on the day set for the hearing and state to the Court your reasons for desiring time to pay.

Dated: _____, 20__

_____

Clerk

A Guide to Small Claims Court is available at the court listed above.

NOTE: If you desire a jury trial, you must, before the day upon which you have been notified to appear, file with the Clerk of the Court a written demand for a trial by jury. You must also pay to the clerk a jury fee of $55 and file an undertaking in the sum of $50 or deposit such sum in cash to secure the payment of any costs that may be awarded against you. You will also be required to make an affidavit specifying the issues of fact which you desire to have tried by a jury and stating that such trial is desired and demanded in good faith.

Under the law, the Court may award $25 additional costs to the plaintiff if a jury trial is demanded by you and a decision is rendered against you.

(e) The clerk shall note on the statement referred to in subdivision (a) above, the date on which the notice was mailed and the address, the date of delivery shown by the return receipt and the name of the addressee or agent signing the receipt.

(f) If service of notice cannot be effected upon the defendant within four months following the date on which the action was first instituted, the action shall be dismissed without prejudice.

(f-1) Where all parties appear by attorneys, the case may be transferred to a regular part of court, and the claimant shall pay any additional filing fees required by law. If the claimant fails or refuses to pay such filing fees, the court shall dismiss the case.

(g) Unless the court shall otherwise order, a defendant to whom notice was duly given who fails to appear at the hearing on the day and time fixed either in person or by attorney shall be held to be in default, except that no default shall be ordered if the defendant or his attorney appear within one hour after the time fixed.

(h) If at the hearing it shall appear that the defendant has a counterclaim in an amount within the jurisdiction of the part for the hearing of small claims, the judge may either proceed forthwith to hear the entire case or may adjourn the hearing for a period of not more than 20 days or as soon thereafter as may be practicable, at which adjourned time the hearing of the entire case shall be had. An adjournment shall be granted at the request of the claimant if the defendant did not file the counterclaim with the court within five days of receiving the notice of claim.

(i) An oath or affirmation shall be administered to all witnesses. The court shall conduct the hearing in such manner as it deems best suited to discover the facts and to determine the justice of the case. If the plaintiff, or an attorney in his or her behalf, does not appear at the time set for hearing, the court may dismiss the claim for want of prosecution or enter a finding on the merits for the defendant, or make such other disposition as it may deem proper.

(j) Where, after a claim is filed with the clerk, either party to the action desires to implead one or more additional defendants, the clerk shall, upon receipt of the proper fees, issue and mail a notice of claim to each additional defendant under the procedure set forth above.

(k) The undertaking to be filed by a defendant desiring a jury trial shall be in the form prescribed by the relevant provisions of Article 25 of the CPLR.

(l) All motions pertaining to small claims shall be made returnable at a part and session appointed for the hearing of small claims, except that a motion to remove a case from the small claims part shall be assigned to a judge in the manner authorized by the Chief Administrator.

(m) There May Be Arbitration of Any Small Claims Controversy.

(1) The parties to any controversy, except infants and incompetents, may submit the same for arbitration to any attorney, duly appointed as a small claims arbitrator by the administrative judge of the court, so

assigned for such duty at that term of the court and upon whom they shall agree.

(2) The parties shall sign a consent which shall contain the name of the arbitrator, a brief recital of the nature of the controversy to be determined, a statement that they will abide by these rules and an affirmation that the decision of the arbitrator is final and that no appeal shall lie from the award. The consent must be filed with the clerk of the small claims part.

(3) The arbitrator shall forthwith proceed to hear the controversy. He or she shall not be bound by the rules regarding the admissibility of evidence, but all testimony shall be given under oath or affirmation. Either party may be represented by counsel, but no record of the proceeding before the arbitrator shall be kept. No expense shall be incurred by the arbitrator except upon the consent in writing of the parties.

(4) After the first hearing, neither party may withdraw from the arbitration unless both parties consent to, or the arbitrator directs, a discontinuance of the proceeding.

(5) The arbitrator shall make an award in writing and file the same forthwith, together with his or her opinion, if any, with the clerk of the small claims part. Unless both parties file a request in writing not to enter judgment, the clerk shall, within two days after the filing of the award, enter judgment in accordance therewith, provided the award has been filed within 30 days from the date of filing the consent. The time within which the clerk shall enter judgment may be extended by a stipulation in writing for a further period not to exceed 30 days.

(6) No fees or disbursements of any kind shall be demanded or received except as hereinabove provided.

(n) The court or a supervising judge thereof may transfer a small claim to any other part of the court for the purpose of subjecting such claim to arbitration pursuant to Part 28 of the Rules of the Chief Judge (22 NYCRR Part 28) and rule 3405 of the CPLR. In the event a trial de novo is demanded pursuant to Part 28, the transfer shall be deemed rescinded and the claim shall be heard in the small claims part of the court no later than 30 days after the demand is made unless thereafter it is transferred to any other part of court pursuant to law.

Cross References

CPLR, see McKinney's Book 7B.

Uniform City Court Act, see McKinney's Book 29A, Part 3.

§ 210.41–a. Commercial Claims Procedure

(a) A commercial claims action may be brought by a claimant that is (1) a corporation, including a municipal or public benefit corporation, partnership, or association, which has its principal office in the State of New York, or (2) an assignee of any commercial claim, subject to the restrictions set forth in UCCA 1809–A.

The action shall be instituted by the claimant or someone on its behalf by paying the filing fee and the cost of sending the notice of claim as provided in UCCA 1803–A and by filing and signing a written application containing the following information:

(1) claimant's name and principal office address;

(2) defendant's name and place of residence or place of business or employment;

(3) the nature and amount of the claim, including dates, and other relevant information; where the claim arises out of a consumer transaction (one where the money, property or service which is the subject of the transaction is primarily for personal, family or household purposes), information showing that the transaction is a consumer transaction;

(4) a certification that not more than five claims have been instituted in the courts of this State in the calendar month; and,

(5) in the case of a commercial claim arising out of a consumer transaction, a certification that the claimant has mailed a demand letter, containing the information set forth in UCCA § 1803–A, no less than 10 days and no more than 180 days prior to the commencement of the claim.

(b) Unless the clerk shall require the claimant, pursuant to UCCA 1810–A, to apply to the court for leave to prosecute the claim in a commercial claims part, the clerk shall reduce to a concise written form and record in a special docket the information contained in the application, and shall give to the person who signed the statement a memorandum of the time and place set for the hearing, which shall be as soon as practicable and shall advise such person to produce at the hearing supporting witnesses, account books, receipts or other documents required to establish the claim. The clerk shall advise the claimant of the right of the claimant or the defendant to request an evening hearing, which shall not be so scheduled if it would cause unreasonable hardship to either party, and the clerk shall schedule the hearing so as to minimize the defendant's time away from employment. In the case of a commercial claim arising out of a consumer transaction, the clerk shall mark the claim conspicuously as a consumer transaction and shall record it in the docket marked as a consumer transaction.

(c) Within five days after the action is filed, the clerk shall send to the defendant by ordinary first class mail and by certified mail, return receipt requested, at one of the addresses required by UCCA § 1803–A, as shall be deemed necessary, a signed notice bearing the seal of the court, which shall be in substantially the following form:

CITY COURT OF THE CITY OF _____

COUNTY OF _____

COMMERCIAL CLAIMS PART

TO:_____

Take Notice that _____ asks judgment in this Court against you for $_____ together with costs, upon the following claim:

_____

_____

_____

There will be a hearing before the Court upon this claim on _____, 19__, at ____ o'clock ____M. in the Commercial Claims Part, held at _____.

You must appear and present your defense and any counterclaim you may desire to assert at the hearing at the time and place above set forth. (You may request that the hearing be scheduled during evening hours if you do so within 14 days of receipt of this notice.) IF YOU DO NOT APPEAR, JUDGMENT WILL BE ENTERED AGAINST YOU BY DEFAULT EVEN THOUGH YOU MAY HAVE A VALID DEFENSE. If your defense or counterclaim, if any, is supported by witnesses, account books, receipts or other documents, you must produce them at the hearing. The Clerk, if requested, will issue subpoenas for witnesses, without fee thereof.

If you wish to present a counterclaim against the claimant you must do so by filing with the Clerk of the Court a statement containing such counterclaim within five days of receiving this notice of claim. At the time of such filing you must pay the Clerk a filing fee of $3.00 plus the cost of postage to send your counterclaim by first class mail to the claimant. If you fail to file a counterclaim within this five-day period, you retain the right to file the counterclaim until the time of the hearing, but the claimant may request and obtain an adjournment of the hearing to a later date.

If you admit the claim, but desire time to pay, you must appear personally on the day set for the hearing and state to the Court your reasons for desiring time to pay.

Read the attached sheet for more information.

Dated: _____, 20__

_____
Clerk

A Guide for Commercial Claims Court is available at the court listed above.

NOTE: If you desire a jury trial, you must, before the day upon which you have been notified to appear, file with the Clerk of the Court a written demand for a trial by jury. You must also pay to the clerk a jury fee of $55 and file an undertaking in the sum of $50 or deposit such sum in cash to secure the payment of any costs that may be awarded against you. You will also be required to make an affidavit specifying the issues of fact which you desire to have tried by a jury and stating that such trial is desired and demanded in good faith.

Under the law, the Court may award $25 additional costs to the plaintiff if a jury trial is demanded by you and a decision is rendered against you.

(d) The clerk shall note on the application the date on which the notice was mailed and the address, the date of delivery shown by the return receipt, and the name of the addressee or agent signing the receipt.

(e) If, after the expiration of 21 days (30 days in the case of a commercial claim arising out of a consumer transaction) from the date the notice was mailed, the ordinary first class mailing has not been returned as undeliverable, the defendant shall be presumed to have received notice of the claim.

(f) If service of notice cannot be made upon the defendant within four months following the date on which the action was first instituted, the action shall be dismissed without prejudice.

(f-1) Where all parties appear by attorneys, the case may be transferred to a regular part of court, and the claimant shall pay any additional filing fees required by law. If the claimant fails or refuses to pay such filing fees, the court shall dismiss the case.

(g) Unless the court shall otherwise order, a defendant to whom notice was duly given who fails to appear, either in person or by attorney, at the hearing on the day and time fixed, shall be held to be in default, except that no default shall be ordered if the defendant or his or her attorney appears within one hour after the time fixed. Notice of the default judgment, containing the information set forth in UCCA § 1807–A, shall be mailed by first class mail to the claimant and the defendant. The defaulting party may apply to have the default vacated by submitting a written request to the court; proceeding on default shall be governed by, but not limited to, section 5015 of the CPLR.

(h) If at the hearing it shall appear that the defendant has a counterclaim in an amount within the jurisdiction of the part for the hearing of small claims, the judge may either proceed forthwith to hear the entire case or may adjourn the hearing for a period of not more than 20 days or as soon thereafter as may be practicable, at which adjourned time the hearing of the entire case shall be had. An adjournment shall be granted at the request of the claimant if the defendant did not file the counterclaim with the court within five days of receiving the notice of claim.

(i) An oath or affirmation shall be administered to all witnesses. The court shall conduct the hearing in such manner as it deems best suited to discover the facts and to determine the justice of the case. If the claimant, or an attorney in his or her behalf, does not appear at the time set for hearing, the court may dismiss the claim for want of prosecution or enter a finding on the merits for the defendant, or make such other disposition as it may deem proper.

(j) Where, after a claim is filed with the clerk, either party to the action desires to implead one or more additional defendants, the clerk shall, upon receipt of the proper fees, issue and mail a notice of claim to each additional defendant under the procedure set forth above.

(k) The undertaking to be filed by a defendant desiring a jury trial shall be in the form prescribed by the relevant provisions of Article 25 of the CPLR.

(l) All motions pertaining to commercial claims shall be made returnable at a part and session appointed for the hearing of commercial claims, except that a motion to remove a case from the commercial claims part shall be assigned to a judge in the manner authorized by the Chief Administrator.

(m) There may be arbitration of any commercial claims controversy.

(1) The parties to any controversy, except infants and incompetents, may submit the same for arbitration to any attorney, duly appointed as a commercial claims arbitrator by the administrative judge of this court, so assigned for such duty at that term of the court and upon whom they shall agree.

(2) The parties shall sign a consent which shall contain the name of the arbitrator, a brief recital of the nature of the controversy to be determined, a statement that they will abide by these rules, and an affirmation that the decision of the arbitrator is final and that no appeal shall lie from the award. The consent must be filed with the clerk of the commercial claims part.

(3) The arbitrator shall forthwith proceed to hear the controversy. He or she shall not be bound by the rules regarding the admissibility of evidence, but all testimony shall be given under oath or affirmation. Either party may be represented by counsel, but no record of the proceeding before the arbitrator shall be kept. No expense shall be incurred by the arbitrator except upon the consent in writing of the parties.

(4) After the first hearing, neither party may withdraw from the arbitration unless both parties consent to, or the arbitrator directs, a discontinuance of the proceeding.

(5) The arbitrator shall make his or her award in writing and file the same forthwith, together with an opinion, if any, with the clerk of the commercial claims part. Unless both parties file a request in writing not to enter judgment, the clerk shall, within two days after the filing of the award, enter judgment in accordance therewith, provided the award has been filed within 30 days from the date of filing the consent. The time within which the clerk shall enter judgment may be extended by a stipulation in writing for a further period not to exceed 30 days.

(6) No fees or disbursements of any kind shall be demanded or received except as hereinabove provided.

(n) The court or a supervising judge thereof may transfer a commercial claim to any other part of the court for the purpose of subjecting such claim to arbitration pursuant to Part 28 of this Title and rule 3405 of the CPLR. In the event a trial de novo is demanded pursuant to Part 28, the transfer shall be deemed rescinded and the claim shall be heard in the commercial claims part of the court no later than 30 days after the demand is made unless thereafter it is transferred to any other part of court pursuant to law.

§ 210.42. Proceedings Under Article 7 of the Real Property Actions and Proceedings Law

(a) Such proceedings involving residential property shall be commenced in the City Court in which the real property or portion thereof is located. No default shall be noted until at least one hour after the hour when the proceeding is called.

(b) The following form is set forth as an example of the notice of petition (the provisions relating to the demand for a money judgment should be omitted unless the petition so demands):

CITY COURT OF THE CITY OF _____

```
_____  )
                         )
        Petitioner       )
        Address          )
                         )
      -against-          )          NOTICE OF
                         )          PETITION
                         )
        Respondent       )
        Address          )
_____  )
```

To the respondents .... above named and described, in possession of the premises hereinafter described or claiming possession thereof:

PLEASE TAKE NOTICE that a hearing at which you must appear will be held at the City Court of the City of ...., ... District, to be held at ...., City of ...., County of ...., on the .... day of ...., 19..., at .... am/pm, which prays for a final judgment of eviction, awarding to the petitioner the possession of premises designated and described as follows:

the .... rooms on the .... floor, Apartment No. ...., ... Street, City of .... in the County of ...., and further granting to the petitioner such other and further relief as is demanded in the petition, which you must answer.

TAKE NOTICE also that demand is made in the petition herein for judgment against you, the respondent, for the sum of $............, with interest thereon from ...., 19....

TAKE NOTICE that your answer may set forth any defense or counterclaim you may have against the petitioner.

TAKE NOTICE also that if you shall fail at such time to interpose and establish any defense that you may have to the allegations of the petition, you may be precluded from asserting such defense or the claim on which it is based in any other proceeding or action.

TAKE NOTICE that your failure to appear and answer may result in final judgment by default for the petitioner in the amount demanded in the petition.

Dated: County of ...., the ...... day of ...., 19...

....

Attorney(s) for Petitioner
Office and Post Office Address
Telephone Number

....

Clerk

(c) At the option of the petitioner, on condition that he or she serve the notice of petition at least eight days prior to the return day, the following paragraph may be inserted in the foregoing notice of petition immediately after the paragraph which sets forth the amount of money for which demand is made in the petition:

TAKE NOTICE also that your answer may be made at the time of hearing specified above unless this Notice of Petition is served upon you on or before the .... day of ...., 19...., in which event you must answer at least three (3) days before the petition is noticed to be heard, either orally before the clerk of the court at his or her office or in writing by serving a copy thereof upon the undersigned attorney for the * petitioner, and by filing the original of such written answer with proof of service thereof in the office of the clerk at least three (3) days before the time the petition is noticed to be heard; in addition thereto, you must appear before the court at the time and place hereinabove set forth for the hearing.

* If the petitioner appears in person, strike out the words "undersigned attorney for the".

(d) At the time of the issuance of a notice of petition by a judge or the clerk, or an order to show cause by the judge, in a summary proceeding to recover possession of real property, a copy of such order to show cause or notice of petition shall be filed with the clerk. The original papers with proof of service thereof shall be filed with the clerk within the time specified by statute.

(e) Where a part exists to hear proceedings brought pursuant to this section, an action noticed to be heard on a day when a judge is not assigned to the part shall not be accepted for filing. The papers shall be returned to the attorney with a notification as to the days on which a judge is assigned.

Cross References

Real Property Actions and Proceedings Law, see McKinney's Book 49½.

§ 210.43. Powers of Clerks

In accordance with UCCA 105(a), the following shall each have the power to administer oaths, take acknowledgments and sign the process or mandate of the court:

(a) clerks;

(b) deputy clerks;

(c) assistant clerks;

(d) any other nonjudicial person designated by order of the Chief Administrator of the Courts.

Cross References

Uniform City Court Act, see McKinney's Book 29A, Part 3.

PART 212. UNIFORM CIVIL RULES FOR THE DISTRICT COURTS

§ 212.1. Application of Part; Waiver; Additional Rules; Application of UDCA; Definitions

(a) Application. This Part shall be applicable to all actions and proceedings in the District Courts of the State of New York.

(b) Waiver. For good cause shown, and in the interests of justice, the court in an action or proceeding may waive compliance with any of these rules other than sections 212.2 and 212.3 unless prohibited from doing so by statute or by a rule of the Chief Judge.

(c) Additional Rules. Additional local court rules, not inconsistent with law or with these rules, shall comply with Part 9 of the Rules of the Chief Judge (22 NYCRR Part 9).

(d) Application of the Uniform District Court Act. The provisions of this part shall be construed as consistent with the Uniform District Court Act (UDCA), and matters not covered by these provisions shall be governed by the UDCA.

(e) Definitions.

(1) "Chief Administrator of the Courts" in this Part includes a designee of the Chief Administrator.

(2) Unless otherwise defined in this Part, or the context otherwise requires, all terms used in this Part shall have the same meaning as they have in the UDCA and the CPLR.

Cross References

CPLR, see McKinney's Book 7B.

Uniform District Court Act, see McKinney's Book 29A, Part 3.

§ 212.2. Divisions of Court; Terms and Structure

(a) Divisions of the courts shall be designated as follows:

(1) *Suffolk County District Court:*

(i) The District Courts of Suffolk County, first district—Towns of Babylon, Huntington, Smithtown, Islip and Brookhaven;

(ii) The District Court of Suffolk County—second district—Town of Babylon;

(iii) The District Court of Suffolk County, third district—Town of Huntington;

(iv) The District Court of Suffolk County, fourth district—Town of Smithtown;

(v) The District Court of Suffolk County, fifth district—Town of Islip;

(vi) The District Court of Suffolk County, sixth district—Town of Brookhaven.

(2) *Nassau County District Court:*

(i) The District Court of Nassau County, first district—Towns of Hempstead, North Hempstead and Oyster Bay, Cities of Long Beach and Glen Cove;

(ii) The District Court of Nassau County, second district—Town of Hempstead and City of Long Beach;

(iii) The District Court of Nassau County, third district—Town of North Hempstead;

(iv) The District Court of Nassau County, fourth district—Town of Oyster Bay and City of Glen Cove.

(b) In each division there shall be held such terms as the Chief Administrator of the Courts shall designate. A term of court is a four-week session of court, and there shall be 13 terms of court in a year, unless otherwise provided in the annual schedule of terms established by the Chief Administrator, which shall also specify the dates of such terms.

§ 212.3. Parts of Court; Structure

(a) General. A part of court is a designated unit of the court in which specified business of the court is to be conducted by a judge or quasi-judicial officer.

(b) Number and Types. In each division there shall be such number of calendar parts, trial parts, motion parts, conference parts, multipurpose parts, and other special parts of court, and any combination thereof, as may be established from time to time by the Chief Administrator of the Courts. There shall also be one or more small claims parts in each division for the hearing and disposition of all small claims proceedings, as the Chief Administrator may establish.

(1) *Calendar Part.* A calendar part is a part of court for the maintaining and calling of a calendar of cases, and for the hearing and disposition of all motions and applications, including orders to show cause and applications for adjournments, in civil actions that have been placed on a reserve or ready calendar but not yet assigned to a trial part.

(2) *Trial Part.* A trial part is a part of court for the trial of civil actions and for the hearing and determination of all motions and applications, including orders to show cause, made after an action is assigned to a trial part.

(3) *Motion Part.* A motion part is a part of court for the hearing and determination of motions and applications that are not otherwise required by this Part to be made in a calendar part, trial part or conference part.

(4) *Conference Part.* A conference part is a part of court for the precalendar or pretrial conference of actions as may be provided by this Part or by order of the Chief Administrator.

(5) *Multi-Purpose Part.* A multi-purpose part is a part of court for the performance of the functions of a calendar part, a trial part, a motion part, a conference part, as well as other special parts of court, or any combination thereof.

(6) *Additional Parts.* Additional parts, including parts with special or limited functions, may be established from time to time by order of the Chief Administrator for such purposes as may be assigned by the Chief Administrator.

(7) *Transfer of Actions.* By order of the Chief Administrator, proceedings and matters may be transferred, as the Chief Administrator deems necessary, from one part of court to another in the same division, regardless of the denomination of the parts.

§ 212.4. Papers Filed in Court; Index Number; Form; Label

The party causing the first paper to be filed shall obtain an index number and communicate it forthwith to all other parties to the action. Thereafter such number shall appear on the outside cover and first page, to the right of the caption, of every paper tendered for filing in the action. Each such cover and first page also shall contain an indication of the county of venue and a brief description of the nature of the paper. In addition to complying with the provisions of CPLR 2101, every paper filed in court shall have annexed thereto appropriate proof of service on all parties where required, and if typewritten, shall have at least a double space between each line, except for quotations and the names and addresses of attorneys appearing in the action, and shall have at least one-inch margins. In addition, every paper filed in court, other than an exhibit or printed form, shall contain writing on one side only, except that papers that are fastened on the side may contain writing on both sides. Papers that are stapled or bound securely shall not be rejected for filing simply because they are not bound with a backer of any kind.

Cross References

CPLR, see McKinney's Book 7B.

§ 212.5. Submission of Papers to Judge

All papers for signature or consideration of the court shall be presented to the clerk of the trial court in the appropriate courtroom or at the clerk's office, except that where the clerk is unavailable or the judge so directs, papers may be submitted to the judge and a copy filed with the clerk at the first available opportunity. All papers for any judge that are filed in the clerk's office shall be promptly delivered to the judge by the clerk. The papers shall be clearly addressed to the judge for whom they are intended

and prominently show the nature of the papers, the title and index number of the action in which they are filed, and the name of the attorney or party submitting them.

§ 212.6. Summons

(a) The summons shall state the district and location of the court in which the action is brought as well as the names of the parties and shall comply with all the provisions of the UDCA applicable to summonses.

(b) Where an action is brought in any district where there are subdivisions designated as parts for a particular location, there shall also be set forth in the caption of the summons the name of the part, as, for example, "Third District, Great Neck Part."

(c) The following form shall be used in a case in which:

(1) the cause of action is for money only,

(2) the summons is served by personal delivery to the defendant within Nassau or Suffolk County, and

(3) a formal complaint if not served therewith.

DISTRICT COURT OF THE COUNTY OF ......

.............District

_____

                       Index No. ....

)   SUMMONS

        Plaintiff,) Plaintiff's Residence

-against-   ) Address:

     Defendant.) The basis of the venue

_____) designated is:

To the above named defendant:

YOU ARE HEREBY SUMMONED and required to appear in the District Court of the COUNTY OF .... District, at the office of the Clerk of the said court at .... in the County of ...., State of New York, either (i) by serving an answer * within 20 days after service of this summons upon you, exclusive of the day of service, upon plaintiff's attorney, at the address stated below, or if there is no attorney, upon the plaintiff at the address stated above or (ii) by appearing at the clerk's office within 20 days after service of this summons upon you exclusive of the day of service, by having the clerk of the court endorse your answer upon this summons; upon your failure to answer, judgment will be taken against you for the sum of $............ with interest thereon from the .... day of ...., 19..., together with the costs of this action.

Date: the .... day of ...., 19...

Statement of the nature
and substance of plain-
tiff's cause of action:

....

Attorney(s) for Plaintiff
Post Office Address
Telephone Number

* You need not physically go to court to serve an answer under option (i). However, you are required to file a copy of your answer together with proof of service with the clerk of the district in which the action is brought within ten days after service of the answer.

(d) In a case in which a formal complaint is annexed to the summons the following form of summons shall be used:

DISTRICT COURT OF THE COUNTY OF ......

.... District
_____

	Index No. ....
)	SUMMONS
)	Plaintiff's Residence
Plaintiff,)	Address:
-against-)	
Defendant.)	The basis of the venue
)	designated is:
)	

To the above named defendant:

YOU ARE HEREBY SUMMONED and required to appear in the District Court of the COUNTY OF
....
District, at the office of the Clerk of the said court at .... in the County of ...., State of New York, by serving an answer to the annexed complaint upon plaintiff's attorney, at the address stated below, or if there is no attorney, upon the plaintiff, at the address stated above, within the time provided by law as noted below; upon your failure to answer, judgment will be taken against you for the relief demanded in the complaint, together with the costs of this action.

Dated: the .... day of ...., 19...

....

Attorney(s) for Plaintiff

Post Office Address

Telephone Number

NOTE: The law or rules of law provide that:

(a) If the summons is served by its delivery to you, or (for a corporation) an agent authorized to receive service, personally within the County of .... you must answer within 20 days after such service;

(b) If this summons is served otherwise than as designated in subdivision (a) above, you are allowed 30 days to answer after the proof of service is filed with the Clerk of this Court.

(c) You are required to file a copy of your answer together with proof of service with the clerk of the

district in which the action is brought within ten days of the service of the answer.

Cross References

Uniform District Court Act, see McKinney's Book 29A, Part 3.

§ 212.7. Pleadings

(a) Except as required by statute, a formal pleading may be dispensed with in any case in which the party required to serve the pleading appears in person, and an order to that effect may be entered ex parte by the judge presiding at the appropriate motion part, upon application to the clerk, who shall refer the same to such judge. Any other party may move at the appropriate motion part to modify or vacate such ex parte order.

(b) All formal pleadings in this court and verifications thereof shall be in conformity with CPLR, Article 30.

(c) An order directing the service and filing of a formal pleading, or pleadings, shall specify the time within which the same shall be served and filed.

(d) A defendant's time to move or answer may be extended by ex parte order no more than once, and for no longer than ten days beyond the expiration of the original time to answer, and only if there has been no previous extension by consent. All further applications for extensions shall be made by motion upon notice returnable in the part designated to hear motions on notice.

(e) In any action to recover damages for personal injuries arising out of use or operation of a motor vehicle, plaintiff shall set forth in the complaint, whether in short or long form, the jurisdictional facts that permit plaintiff to maintain the action and avoid the bar of the Comprehensive Automobile Insurance Reparations Act.

(f) In addition to those cases in which formal pleadings are required by UDCA 902, the pleadings shall be formal in all of the following actions for money only:

(1) those in which property is held under a levy pursuant to an order of attachment;

(2) upon an agreement of guaranty, surety or indemnification;

(3) upon an insurance policy;

(4) for a penalty of forfeiture;

(5) for a commission;

(6) for fraud and deceit;

(7) for malicious prosecution;

(8) for false imprisonment;

(9) for libel or slander;

(10) for malpractice;

(11) for assault;

(12) for conspiracy; and

on any other cause of action where the amount claimed is more than $1,500.

(g) Unless otherwise directed by the court or by statute, parties shall file a copy of all pleadings together with proof of service with the clerk of the district in which the action is brought within ten days after service.

Cross References

CPLR, see McKinney's Book 7B.

Comprehensive Automobile Insurance Reparations Act, see McKinney's Book 27.

Uniform District Court Act, see McKinney's Book 29A, Part 3.

§ 212.8.　[Reserved]

§ 212.9.　Venue

(a) Motions for a Change of Venue. Motions for a change of venue shall be heard in the division of the court in which the action was instituted. An order of transfer shall direct the disposition of the papers then on file.

§ 212.10.　Calendaring of Motions; Uniform Notice of Motion Form

(a) There shall be compliance with the procedures for the bringing of motions prescribed in the UDCA and CPLR. In addition, no motion shall be placed on the calendar for hearing in the appropriate part unless a notice of motion is served and filed with the motion papers. The notice of motion shall read substantially as follows:

DISTRICT COURT OF
THE COUNTY OF
_____ DISTRICT

_____

A.B.,	)	Notice of Motion
Plaintiff,	)	
	)	Index No.
–against–	)	_____
	)	Oral Argument is Re-
	)	quested
C.D.,	)	(Check box if requested)
Defendant.	)	☐
	)	

_____

Upon the affidavit of _____, sworn to on _____, 19___, and upon (list supporting papers if any), the _____ will move this court at _____ (specify the Part), at the _____ Courthouse, _____, _____, New York, on the _____ day of _____, 19___, at 9:30 a.m. for an order (briefly indicate relief requested).[1]

The above-entitled action is for (briefly state nature of action, e.g. personal injury, contract, property dam-

age etc.). This action (is) (is not) on a trial calendar. If on a trial calendar, the calendar number is _____.

Pursuant to CPLR 2214(b), answering affidavits, if any, are required to be served upon the undersigned at least seven days before the return date of this motion.
(check box if applicable)　☐

Dated:

                    _____
                    (Print Name)
                    Attorney[2] (or Attorney in charge of case if law firm) for moving party
                    Address:
                    Telephone number:

TO:　　　_____
                    (Print Name)
                    Attorney[2] for (other party)
                    Address:
                    Telephone number:

                    _____
                    (Print Name)
                    Attorney[2] for (other party)
                    Address:
                    Telephone number:

[1] If motion is to reargue, vacate or extend, modify or otherwise affect a prior order, state the name of the judge who decided the prior order.

[2] If any party is appearing pro se, the name, address and telephone number of such party shall be stated.

(b) The notice of motion set forth in subdivision (a) shall not be required for the return of an order to show cause or an application for ex parte relief.

Cross References

CPLR, see McKinney's Book 7B.

Uniform District Court Act, see McKinney's Book 29A, Part 3.

§ 212.11.　Motion Parts; Motion Calendars; Motion Procedure

(a) Motion Parts and Calendars. There shall be such motion parts and motion calendars as the Chief Administrator of the Courts may designate.

(b) Motion Procedure.

(1) All contested motions and proceedings shall be returnable at 9:30 a.m., unless an earlier time is directed by the court. The moving party shall serve copies of all affidavits and briefs upon the adverse parties at the time of service of the notice of motion. The answering party shall serve copies of all affidavits and briefs as required by CPLR 2214. Affidavits shall be for a statement of the relevant facts, and briefs shall be for a statement of the relevant law. Unless otherwise directed by the court, answering and reply affidavits and all other papers required to be furnished to the court by CPLR 2214(c) must be filed

no later than the time of argument or submission of the motion.

(2) A judge presiding in any part of court where motions are returnable may determine that any or all motions in that part be orally argued and may direct that moving and responding papers be filed with the court prior to the time of argument.

(3) Unless oral argument has been requested by a party and permitted by the court, or directed by the court, motion papers received by the clerk of the court on or before the return date shall be deemed submitted as of the return date. Attendance by counsel at the calendar call shall not be required unless (i) a party intends to make an application to the court that is not on the consent of all parties, (ii) attendance of counsel or oral argument is directed by the court, or (iii) oral argument is requested by a party. Attendance by counsel for a party not requesting oral argument is not required where the hearing of oral argument is based solely on the request of another party. A party requesting oral argument shall set forth such request in the notice of motion or on the first page of the answering papers, as the case may be. A party requesting oral argument on a motion brought on by an order to show cause shall do so as soon as practicable before the time the motion is to be heard.

(4) Where there is an issue of fact to be tried the court may, in its discretion, order an immediate trial of such issue, in which event the action shall be referred to the administrative judge or a designee for assignment.

Cross References

CPLR, see McKinney's Book 7B.

§ 212.12. Videotape Recording of Depositions

Depositions authorized under the provisions of the CPLR or other law may be taken, as permitted by subdivision (b) of section 3113 of the CPLR, by means of simultaneous audio and visual electronic recording, provided such recording is made in conformity with section 202.15 of the Rules of the Chief Administrator (22 NYCRR Part 202).

Cross References

CPLR, see McKinney's Book 7B.

§ 212.13. Exchange of Medical Reports in Personal Injury and Wrongful Death Actions

Except where the court otherwise directs, in all actions in which recovery is sought for personal injuries, disability or death, physical examinations and the exchange of medical information shall be governed by the provisions hereinafter set forth:

(a) At any time after joinder of issue and service of a bill of particulars the party to be examined or any other party may serve on all other parties a notice fixing the time and place of examination. Unless otherwise stipulated the examination shall be held not less than 30 nor more than 60 days after service of the notice. If served by any party other than the party to be examined, the notice shall name the examining medical provider or providers. If the notice is served by the party to be examined, the examining parties shall, within 10 days of receipt thereof, submit to the party to be examined the name of the medical provider or providers who will conduct the examination. Any party may move to modify or vacate the notice fixing the time and place of examination or the notice naming the examining medical providers, within 10 days of the receipt thereof, on the grounds that the time or place fixed or the medical provider named is objectionable, or that the nature of the action is such that the interests of justice will not be served by an examination, exchange of medical reports or delivery of authorizations.

(b) At least 20 days before the date of such examination, or on such other date as the court may direct, the party to be examined shall serve upon and deliver to all other parties the following, which may be used by the examining medical provider:

(1) copies of the medical reports of the medical providers who have previously treated or examined the party seeking recovery. These shall include a recital of the injuries and conditions as to which testimony will be offered at the trial, referring to and identifying those x-ray and technicians' reports which will be offered at the trial, including a description of the injuries sustained, a diagnosis, and a prognosis. Medical reports may consist of completed medical provider, workers' compensation, or insurance forms that provide the information required by this paragraph.

(2) duly executed and acknowledged written authorizations permitting all parties to obtain and make copies of all hospital records and such other records, including x-ray and technicians' reports, as may be referred to and identified in the reports of those medical providers who have treated or examined the party seeking recovery.

(c) Copies of the reports of the medical providers making examinations pursuant to this section shall be served on all other parties within 45 days after completion of the examination. These shall comply with the requirements of paragraph (1) of subdivision (b).

(d) In actions where the cause of death is in issue, each party shall serve upon all other parties copies of the reports of all treating or examining medical providers whose testimony will be offered at the trial, complying with the requirements of paragraph (1) of subdivision (b), and the party seeking to recover shall deliver to all other parties authorizations to examine and obtain copies of all hospital records, autopsy or post-mortem reports, and such other records as provided in paragraph (2) of subdivision (b). Copies of these reports and the required authorizations shall be served and delivered with the bill of particulars by the party seeking to recover. All other parties shall serve copies of the reports of their medical providers within 45 days thereafter. In any case where the interests of justice will not be promoted by service of such reports and delivery of such authorizations, an order dispensing with either or both may be obtained.

(e) Parties relying solely on hospital records may so certify in lieu of serving medical providers' reports.

(f) No case otherwise eligible to be noticed for trial may be noticed unless there has been compliance with this rule, or an order dispensing with compliance or extending the time therefor has been obtained; or, where the party to be examined was served a notice as provided in subdivision (a), and the party so served has not responded thereto.

(g) In the event that the party examined intends at the trial to offer evidence of further or additional injuries or conditions, nonexistent or not known to exist at the time of service of the original medical reports, such party shall, within 30 days after the discovery thereof, and not later than 30 days before trial, serve upon all parties a supplemental medical report complying with the requirements of paragraph (1) of subdivision (b) and shall specify a time not more than 10 days thereafter and a place at which a further examination may be had. Further authorizations to examine and make copies of additional hospital records, other records, x-ray or other technicians' reports as provided in paragraph (2) of subdivision (b), must also be delivered with the medical reports. Copies of the reports of the examining medical providers, complying with the requirements of subdivision (c), shall be served within 10 days after completion of such further examination. If any party desires at the trial to offer the testimony of additional treating or examining medical providers, other than whose medical reports have been previously exchanged, the medical reports of such medical providers, complying with the requirements of paragraph (1) of subdivision (b) shall be served upon all parties at least 30 days before trial.

(h) Unless an order to the contrary is made or unless the judge presiding at the trial in the interests of justice and upon a showing of good cause shall hold otherwise, the party seeking to recover damages shall be precluded at the trial from offering in evidence any part of the hospital records and all other records, including autopsy or postmortem records, x-ray reports or reports of other technicians, not made available pursuant to this rule, and no party shall be permitted to offer any evidence of injuries or conditions not set forth or put in issue in the respective medical reports previously exchanged, nor will the court hear the testimony of any treating or examining medical providers whose medical reports have not been served as provided by this rule.

(i) Orders transferring cases pending in other courts which are subject to the provisions of this section, whether or not such cases are consolidated with cases pending in the court to which transferred, shall contain such provisions as are required to bring the transferred cases into compliance with this rule.

(j) Any party may move to compel compliance or to be relieved from compliance with this rule or any provision thereof, but motions directed to the sufficiency of medical reports must be made within 20 days of receipt of such reports. All motions under this rule may be made on affidavits of attorneys, shall be made on notice, returnable at the calendar part and shall be granted or denied on such terms as to costs, calendar position and dates of compliance with any provision of this rule as the court in its discretion shall direct.

(k) Where an examination is conducted on consent prior to the institution of an action, the party to be examined shall deliver the documents specified in paragraphs (1) and (2) of subdivision (b) hereof, and the report of the examining medical provider shall be delivered as provided in subdivision (c) hereof. In that event, examination after institution of the action may be waived. The waiver, which shall recite that medical reports have been exchanged and that all parties waive further physical examination, shall be filed with the note of issue. This shall not be a bar, however, to proceeding under subdivision (g) in a proper case.

§ 212.14. Calendar Default; Restoration; Dismissal

(a) **Applicability.** This section governs calendar defaults, restorations and dismissals, other than striking a case from the calendar pursuant to a motion under section 212.17 relating to the notice of trial and statement of readiness.

(b) At any scheduled call of a calendar or at a pretrial conference, if all parties do not appear and proceed or announce their readiness to proceed immediately or subject to the engagement of counsel, the judge presiding may note the default on the record and enter an order as follows:

(1) if the plaintiff appears but the defendant does not, the judge may grant judgment by default or order an inquest;

(2) if the defendant appears but the plaintiff does not, the judge may dismiss the action and may order a severance of counterclaims or cross-claims;

(3) if no party appears, the judge may strike the action from the calendar or make such other order as appears just.

(c) Actions stricken from the calendar may be restored to the calendar only upon stipulation of all parties so ordered by the court or by motion on notice to all other parties, made within one year after the action is stricken. A motion must be supported by affidavit by a person having first-hand knowledge, satisfactorily explaining the reasons for the action having been stricken and showing that it is presently ready for trial.

(d) If an order of restoration is granted, it shall provide that a new notice of trial be filed forthwith and that the case be placed on the general trial calendar in its regular place as of the date of filing the new notice of trial, unless the court in its discretion orders otherwise. A copy of the order shall be served on the calendar clerk and the case shall receive a new calendar number followed by the letter "R" to designate the case as having been restored. If a restored case is not ready when reached, it shall forthwith be dismissed or an inquest or judgment ordered as provided in paragraph (b).

(e) Applications to restore an action to the ready calendar in the event of a reversal or a direction of a new trial by an appellate court shall be made returnable in the appropriate motion part, except that if all parties do not appear by attorney, the clerk shall, without formal application, restore the action to the ready calendar.

(f) When an action has been tried and the jury has disagreed, or a verdict set aside, or there has been a mistrial for any reason, or if no decision has been made or judgment rendered within the time specified in section 1304 of the UDCA or if the court has ordered a new trial under CPLR 4402, such action must be restored to the appropriate ready calendar for a day certain to be fixed by the court.

Cross References

CPLR, see McKinney's Book 7B.

Uniform District Court Act, see McKinney's Book 29A, Part 3.

§ 212.15. Transfer of Actions

Actions transferred from the Supreme Court and County Court to a District Court shall be placed in such order and relative position on the appropriate calendars that they will be reached for trial insofar as practicable as if a notice of trial had originally been filed in the District Court for the same date as that for which the note of issue was filed in the Supreme Court.

§ 212.16. Discontinuance of Civil Actions

In any discontinued action, the attorney for the plaintiff shall file a stipulation or statement of discontinuance with the clerk of the court within 20 days of such discontinuance. If the action has been noticed for judicial activity within 20 days of such discontinuance, the stipulation or statement shall be filed before the date scheduled for such activity.

§ 212.17. Notice of Trial Where All Parties Appear by Attorney

(a) The notice of trial filed by any party pursuant to UDCA section 1301 shall be accompanied by a certificate of readiness, with proof of service on all parties, in the form prescribed by this section. The notice of trial shall include the index number, name, office address and telephone number of each attorney and *pro se* party who has appeared, and the name of any insurance carrier acting on behalf of any party.

(b) The clerk shall not place any matter on a trial calendar unless there has been compliance with this rule by the party seeking to place the matter on the calendar.

(c) Within 20 days after service of such notice of trial, any party may move to strike the action from the calendar or to keep it from being placed thereon. The affidavit in support of the application must specify the reason the action is not entitled to be on the calendar.

(d) After any action has been placed on the trial calendar pursuant to this rule, no pretrial examination or other preliminary proceedings may be had, except that if some unusual or unanticipated conditions subsequently develop which make it necessary that further pretrial examination or further preliminary proceedings be had, and if without them the moving party would be unduly prejudiced, the court may make an order granting permission to conduct such examination or proceedings and prescribing the time therefor. Such an order may be made only upon motion on notice showing in detail, by affidavit, the facts claimed to entitle the moving party to relief under this subdivision.

(e) Where a party filing a notice of trial, in a medical malpractice action or an action against a municipality, seeking a sum of money only, is prohibited by the provisions of CPLR 3017(c) from stating in the pleadings the amount of damages sought in the action, the party shall indicate in the notice of trial whether the amount of damages exceeds $6,000, exclusive of costs and interest. If it does not, the party shall also indicate if it exceeds $2,000, exclusive of costs and interest.

(f) The certificate of readiness shall read substantially as follows:

CERTIFICATE OF READINESS FOR TRIAL
(Items 1–5 must be checked)

	Complete	Waived	Not Required
1. All pleadings served	....	....	....
2. Bills of particulars served	....	....	....
3. Physical examinations completed	....	....	....
4. Medical reports exchanged	....	....	....
5. Discovery proceedings now known to be necessary completed	....	....	....
6. There are no outstanding requests for discovery	....	....	....

7. There has been a reasonable opportunity to com-
plete the foregoing pro-
ceedings
8. The case is ready for trial
Dated: _____
(Signature) _____
Attorney(s) for: _____
Office and P.O. Address: _____
_____

Cross References

CPLR, see McKinney's Book 7B.

Uniform District Court Act, see McKinney's Book 29A, Part 3.

§ 212.18. Calendars of Triable Actions

There shall be such calendars as may be established, from time to time, in the discretion of the Chief Administrator of the Courts. These calendars may include:

(a) General Calendar. A general calendar is for actions in which issue has been joined.

(b) Pretrial Conference Calendar. A pretrial conference calendar is for actions awaiting conference in a pretrial conference part. Actions shall be taken in order from the top of the general calendar and placed at the end of the pretrial conference calendar.

(c) Reserve Calendars. A reserve calendar is for actions in which a notice of trial, conforming to § 1301 of the UDCA, and certificate of readiness have been filed. Upon the filing of such notice in any action with the clerk, at least ten days before the day fixed for trial, the action shall be placed at the end of either the reserve jury trial calendar or the reserve nonjury trial calendar, as the case may be. Where an action is placed on a reserve nonjury trial calendar but subsequently a demand for a trial by jury is timely served and filed, the action shall immediately be transferred to the end of the reserve jury trial calendar. Once placed on a calendar, the action shall remain thereon until disposed of, stricken, transferred or otherwise removed. The calendars shall be deemed continuous and no change in the order of original placement shall be made except as provided in this Part, by court order or as may be required by provisions of law.

(d) Ready Calendars. A ready calendar is for actions that have been transferred from a reserve calendar because a trial is imminent, for noticed inquests and assessments of damages and for actions in which any party appears in person. There shall be as many ready calendars with such classifications of actions as the Chief Administrator shall direct.

(e) Continuous Calendars. In any court not continuously in session, the calendars at the close of one term or session of court shall be used to open the following term or session, and actions on the calendars shall retain their positions.

(f) Military Calendar. A military calendar shall be utilized to hold in suspense any action that cannot reasonably be tried because a party or witness is in military service. When it shall appear to the satisfaction of the judge presiding that a party to an action or a witness necessary upon the trial is in military service, and is not presently available for trial, and that a deposition cannot be taken, or, if taken, would not provide adequate evidence, the case shall be designated "military" and transferred to a military calendar. Any case on the military calendar may be removed therefrom by further order of the court or by filing with the calendar clerk, at least five days before such date, a stipulation of the parties who have appeared or a notice to restore, together with proof of service of such notice on all other parties; except that if any party appearing in person seeks such restoration, he may apply to the clerk, who shall refer his application to the judge in the appropriate calendar part for disposition upon such notice to all parties or their attorneys as the judge shall direct.

(g) Calendar Progression. With due regard to the requirements of statutory preferences and of section 208.20 of this Part, when actions are advanced from one calendar to another they shall progress from the head of one calendar to the foot of the next calendar and otherwise progress in order insofar as practicable unless otherwise determined by the court.

Cross References

Uniform District Court Act, see McKinney's Book 29A, Part 3.

§ 212.19. Notice of Calendars

A notice shall be published in a law journal of any and all calls of the reserve calendars at least five court days before such call if the Chief Administrator of the Courts designates a law journal and directs such publication. The notice shall specify the calendar numbers of the actions to be called. In the event that the call of any reserve calendar is suspended by the Chief Administrator and actions are added to the ready calendar without first being called on the reserve calendar, a notice of actions added to the ready calendar, with their calendar number, shall be published in such law journal at least five court days before the call of the reserve calendar.

§ 212.20. Special Preferences

(a) Any party claiming a preference under CPLR 3403 may apply to the court by making a motion in a motion part, in accordance with CPLR 3403(b), the note of issue therein referred to being deemed a reference to a notice of trial.

(b) Counterclaims and Cross-Claims. A counterclaim or cross-claim which is not entitled to a preference shall not itself defeat the plaintiff's right to a preference under this section.

(c) Result of Preference Being Granted. If a preference is granted, the action shall be placed on a ready calendar for a day certain ahead of all nonpreferred pending cases, as directed by the court, unless the court otherwise orders.

Cross References

CPLR, see McKinney's Book 7B.

§ 212.21. Objections to Applications for Special Preference

(a) Within 20 days of the filing of the notice of trial, if the notice of motion for a special preference is filed therewith, or within ten days of the service of a notice of motion to obtain a preference, if served and filed subsequent to service and filing of the notice of trial, any other party may serve upon all other parties and file with the clerk affidavits and other relevant papers, with proof of service, in opposition to granting the preference. In the event such opposing papers are filed the party applying for the preference, may within five days thereafter, serve and file in like manner papers in rebuttal.

(b) In any action which has been accorded a preference in trial upon a motion filed with the clerk, the court shall not be precluded, on its own motion at any time thereafter, from restoring the action to its regular calendar position on the ground that the action is not entitled to a preference under these rules.

(c) Notwithstanding the failure of any party to oppose the application, no preference shall be granted by default unless the court finds that the action is entitled to a preference.

§ 212.22. Pretrial and Prearbitration Conference Calendars

There shall be such pretrial and prearbitration conference parts and calendars and such mandatory pretrial conferences as may be established by the Chief Administrator of the Courts. The attendance of attorneys who are familiar with the case and who are authorized to act shall be required. The court may also require the attendance of parties, and in the event of failure of attendance by attorneys or parties, the court shall have the same powers with respect to dismissals, defaults, or both as it might exercise when a case is reached for trial. Upon the pretrial conference of an action, the judge presiding shall consider with counsel and parties the simplification and limitation of the issues and the obtaining of admissions of facts and of documents to avoid unnecessary proof, as well as the ultimate disposition of the action by settlement or compromise.

§ 212.23. Call of Reserve, Ready and General Calendars

(a) Reserve Calendars. At such times as the Chief Administrator of the Courts shall prescribe there shall be a call of actions on the reserve calendars in sequence and in sufficient number to insure a steady supply of cases to the ready calendar. When such a call is held, the actions thereon, if marked "ready", shall be passed and subsequently added to the ready calendar, or may be marked "disposed" or stricken from the calendar, as may be appropriate.

(b) Ready Calendars.

(1) The ready calendars shall be called at such time and in such parts as the Chief Administrator shall direct. Actions shall be called in order and shall be announced "ready", "ready subject to engagement", or "disposed". If any party does not so respond, the calendar judge shall treat the action as in default, unless for good cause shown, arising after the action appeared on the ready calendar and not reasonably discoverable or foreseeable, the judge shall direct that the action be held on the ready calendar for a period not to exceed ten days. If the inability to proceed to trial is expected to exceed ten days, the action shall be returned to the reserve calendar or stricken from the calendar as circumstances warrant, unless, for good cause shown, the court on application grants an adjournment.

(2) Actions announced "ready" on the call of the calendar shall be assigned in order to the available trial parts. Jury actions will be sent out for jury selection if a trial part is available, or scheduled for jury selection at the opening of court on the next court day or as soon as practicable thereafter. Subject to the provisions of section 212.25 of this part, no delay will be permitted in selection of a jury, and failure of counsel to proceed as directed or to appear promptly at the directed time on the specified court day will be treated as a calendar default.

(3) The actions on the ready calendar must be answered by or on behalf of the trial counsel each day the calendar is called, unless otherwise ordered by the calendar judge, or unless trial counsel already has demonstrated an engagement during one or more days. The calendar judge may discontinue the call of the ready calendar when sufficient ready cases have been identified to fill all trial parts available on the day of the call and which are expected to become available on the next court day.

(4) When an action has been announced "ready" but no part is immediately available, counsel may arrange with the calendar judge to be summoned by telephone, provided they agree to hold themselves available and to appear on one hour's notice or at such other time as the court may order at the time and part assigned for the trial.

(c) General Calendar. At such time or times and in such manner as the Chief Administrator may direct, a call shall be made of all actions on the general calendar not reached on a ready calendar.

§ 212.24. Day Certain for Trial

(a) Applications for a day certain for trial shall be made to the calendar judge or, if no calendar part has been established, to the trial judge on an affidavit of the attorney of record or a stipulation of the attorneys for all parties, that trial counsel, a party or a material witness resides more than 100 miles from the court-house or is in the military service or that some other undue hardship exists. Applications to the calendar judge shall be made on notice and must be made before the action is advanced to the ready calendar.

(b) If a day certain is ordered, the action shall be withheld from the ready calendar until that day, at which time it shall appear at the top of the ready calendar. Absent special circumstances, the day designated for trial shall be a date which does not in effect grant a preference to the action. Such day certain actions shall be taken into consideration in determining the number of actions held for counsel under section 212.25 when they appear on the ready calendar.

§ 212.25. Engagement of Counsel

No adjournment shall be granted on the ground of engagement of counsel except in accordance with Part 125 of the Rules of the Chief Administrator of the Courts (22 NYCRR Part 125).

§ 212.26. [Reserved]

§ 212.27. Submission of Papers for Trial

(a) Upon the trial of an action, the following papers, if not yet submitted, shall be submitted to the court by the party who has filed the notice of trial:

(1) copies of all pleadings marked as required by CPLR 4012;

(2) a copy of any statutory provision in effect at the time the cause of action arose upon which either the plaintiff or the defendant relies; and

(3) a copy of the bill of particulars, if any.

(b) If so ordered, the parties shall submit to the court, before the commencement of trial, trial memoranda which shall be exchanged among counsel.

Cross References

CPLR, see McKinney's Book 7B.

§ 212.28. Absence of Attorney During Trial

All trial counsel shall remain in attendance at all stages of the trial until the jury retires to deliberate unless excused by the judge presiding. The court may permit counsel to leave, provided counsel remain in telephone contact with the court. Any counsel not present during the jury deliberation, further requests to charge, or report of the jury verdict shall be deemed to stipulate that the court may proceed in his or her absence and to waive any irregularity in proceedings taken in his or her absence.

§§ 212.29, 212.30. [Reserved]

§ 212.31. Restoration After Jury Disagreement, Mistrial or Order for New Trial

An action in which there has been an inability by a jury to reach a verdict, a mistrial or a new trial granted by the trial judge or an appellate court shall be restored to the ready calendar by filing a notice thereof with the appropriate clerk.

§ 212.32. Damages, Inquest After Default; Proof

(a) In an inquest to ascertain damages upon a default pursuant to CPLR 3215, if the defaulting party fails to appear in person or by representative, the party entitled to judgment, whether a plaintiff, third-party plaintiff, or a party who has pleaded a cross-claim or counterclaim, shall be permitted to submit, in addition to the proof required by CPLR 3215(e), properly executed affidavits as proof of damages.

(b) In any action where it is necessary to take an inquest before the court, the party seeking damages may submit the proof required by oral testimony of witnesses in open court or by written statements of the witnesses, in narrative or question and answer form, signed and sworn to.

Cross References

CPLR, see McKinney's Book 7B.

§ 212.33. Submission of Orders, Judgments and Decrees for Signature

(a) Proposed orders or judgments, with proof of service on all parties where the order is directed to be settled or submitted on notice, must be submitted for signature, unless otherwise directed by the court, within 60 days after the signing and filing of the decision directing that the order be settled or submitted.

(b) Failure to submit the order or judgment timely shall be deemed an abandonment of the motion or action, unless for good cause shown.

(c)(1) When settlement of an order or judgment is directed by the court, a copy of the proposed order or judgment with notice of settlement, returnable at the office of the clerk of the part in which the order or judgment was granted, or before the judge if the court has so directed or if the clerk is unavailable, shall be served on all parties either:

(i) by personal service not less than five days before the date of settlement; or

(ii) by mail not less than ten days before the date of settlement.

(2) Proposed counterorders as judgments shall be made returnable on the same date and at the same place, and shall be served on all parties by personal

service, not less than two days, or by mail, not less than seven days, before the date of settlement.

§ 212.34. Absence or Disqualification of Assigned Judge

(a) Whenever a judge is temporarily absent from a multipart court, proceedings in progress or scheduled for appearance in the part presided over by that judge shall be reassigned or otherwise handled by the calendar judge, or the administrative judge if no calendar part has been established. If the judge presiding is unavailable or unable to act for more than two court days in succession, the administrative judge having direct supervisory authority over the court shall make whatever arrangements are necessary to accommodate the proceedings assigned to the judge.

(b) If a proceeding is assigned to a judge who is for any reason disqualified from hearing it, the proceeding shall be reassigned to another judge who is not disqualified, to be heard by the assigned judge as expeditiously as possible.

(c) In an emergency, when neither the calendar judge nor the administrative judge can be contacted, any other judge of, or assigned to, the court may act in respect to pending proceedings as may be appropriate.

§ 212.35. [Reserved]

§ 212.36. Infants' and Incapacitated Persons' Claims and Proceedings

The settlement of an action by an infant or judicially declared incapacitated person (including an incompetent or conservatee) shall comply with CPLR 1207 and 1208, section 202.67 of the Rules of the Chief Administrator (22 NYCRR 202.67) and in the case of an infant, with section 474 of the Judiciary law.

Cross References

CPLR, see McKinney's Book 7B.

Judiciary Law, see McKinney's Book 29.

§ 212.37. Executions

(a) No execution may be issued against any party who has appeared by an attorney in an action or proceeding unless a copy of the judgment has been duly served upon the attorney for such party.

(b) No execution may be issued against any party who has appeared in person in any action and who defaults in answering either the original or an amended or supplemental complaint unless a copy of the judgment has been duly served upon such party personally or mailed to such party by certified mail at the address stated in the notice of appearance or in the last pleading or paper filed by the party with the clerk or at the address last furnished by the party to the clerk in writing.

§ 212.38. Appeals

(a) A notice of appeal shall not be accepted for filing without proof of service upon all parties.

(b) All papers which are to be included in the return on appeal and prepared by the appellant as required by the applicable provisions of the CPLR, shall be furnished by the appellant to the clerk at the time of filing the notice of settlement provided in section 1704 of the UDCA.

(c) In the case of the death, disability or prolonged absence from the city of the judge before whom the action was tried, the return on appeal may be settled by any judge presiding in a motion part in the county in which the judgment was entered, with the same force and effect as if he had tried the case.

Cross References

CPLR, see McKinney's Book 7B.

Uniform District Court Act, see McKinney's Book 29A, Part 3.

§ 212.39. Procedures for the Enforcement of Money Judgments Under CPLR, Article 52

(a) All subpoenas and processes for the examination of judgment debtors or other persons, including garnishees, in connection with the enforcement of money judgments, as well as adjournments thereof if made returnable in the court, shall be returnable in such motion part as may be designated by the Chief Administrator of the Courts.

(b) All subpoenas and processes for the examination of judgment debtors or other persons, including garnishees, if made returnable in the court, shall be filed with the clerk of the appropriate motion part with proper affidavits of service, at least two court days before the return day, except where service was made too late for filing within such time, in which event filing before the hour of the return shall suffice and the clerk shall list all such upon the calendar. Stipulations of adjournments, if attendance in court on the adjourned date is required, shall be similarly filed. Unless so filed, the names of the parties shall not be called; nor shall any such names be called unless they appear on a written or typewritten calendar. The judge presiding may, upon proper proof by affidavit showing good cause for the failure to file in accordance with this rule, add any matter to the calendar.

(c) No adjournment of an examination shall be valid unless reduced to writing and a copy thereof delivered to the judgment debtor or other person, including a garnishee, at the time of such adjournment and his acknowledgement of the receipt thereof is endorsed on the original.

(d) There shall be no more than two adjournments of the examination of a judgment debtor or other person, including a garnishee, unless such additional adjournment is approved and such approval is noted on the papers by the judge presiding at a motion part.

(e) No motion shall be made upon the basis of any testimony taken in examinations unless and until such testimony has been reduced to writing and unless and until there has been compliance with the requirements of CPLR 5224(e).

(f) Every subpoena or other process providing for the examination of a judgment debtor or other person, including a garnishee, in addition to the other requirements of CPLR 5223, shall have endorsed on its face, in bold type, the words: "This subpoena or process (as the case may be) requires your personal appearance at the time and place specified. Failure to appear may subject you to fine and imprisonment for contempt of court."

Cross References

CPLR, see McKinney's Book 7B.

§ 212.40.　Arbitration

(a) Alternative Method of Dispute Resolution by Arbitration. Where the Chief Administrator of the Courts has established this arbitration program, Part 28 of the Rules of the Chief Judge (22 NYCRR Part 28) shall control the proceedings.

(b) Where the parties agree to arbitrate a claim under UDCA 206, arbitration proceedings shall be conducted in accordance with CPLR Article 75.

Cross References

CPLR, see McKinney's Book 7B.

Uniform District Court Act, see McKinney's Book 29A, Part 3.

§ 212.41.　Small Claims Procedure

(a) A small claims action shall be instituted by a plaintiff or someone on his or her behalf paying the filing fee as provided in UDCA 1803, and by supplying to the clerk the following information:

(1) plaintiff's name and residence address; **(2)** defendant's name and place of residence, or place of business or employment; and **(3)** the nature and amount of the plaintiff's claim, giving dates and other relevant information.

(b) The clerk shall reduce this information to a written statement on a form provided therefor and shall record it in his or her office. The statement shall be in nontechnical, concise and simple language, and shall be signed by the person who shall have supplied the information contained therein.

(c) The clerk shall give to the person who signed the statement a memorandum of the time and place set for the hearing, which shall be as soon as practicable, and shall advise such person to produce at the hearing supporting witnesses, account books, receipts or other documents required to establish the claim.

(d) Within five days after the action is recorded, the clerk shall send to the defendant by ordinary first class mail and by certified mail, return receipt requested, addressed to one or more of the addresses supplied as shall be deemed necessary, a signed notice bearing the seal of the court, which shall be in substantially the following form:

DISTRICT COURT OF _____

COUNTY OF _____

SMALL CLAIMS PART

TO:_____

　　Take Notice that _____ asks judgment in this Court against you for $_____ together with costs, upon the following claim:

_____

_____

_____

　　There will be a hearing before the Court upon this claim on _____, 19__, at ____ o'clock ____M. in the Small Claims Part, held at _____.

You must appear and present your defense and any counterclaim you may desire to assert at the hearing at the time and place above set forth (a corporation must be represented by an attorney or any authorized officer, director or employee). IF YOU DO NOT APPEAR, JUDGMENT WILL BE ENTERED AGAINST YOU BY DEFAULT EVEN THOUGH YOU MAY HAVE A VALID DEFENSE. If your defense or counterclaim, if any, is supported by witnesses, account books, receipts or other documents, you must produce them at the hearing. The Clerk, if requested, will issue subpoenas for witnesses, without fee thereof.

If you wish to present a counterclaim against the claimant, you must do so by filing with the Clerk of the Court a statement containing such counterclaim within five days of receiving this notice of claim. At the time of such filing you must pay the Clerk a filing fee of $3.00 plus the cost of postage to send your counterclaim by first class mail to the claimant. If you fail to file a counterclaim within this five-day period, you retain the right to file the counterclaim until the time of the hearing, but the claimant may request and obtain an adjournment of the hearing to a later date.

If you admit the claim, but desire time to pay, you must appear personally on the day set for the hearing and state to the Court your reasons for desiring time to pay.

Dated: _____, 20__

_____

　　　　Clerk

A Guide to Small Claims Court is available at the court listed above.

NOTE: If you desire a jury trial, you must, before the day upon which you have been notified to appear, file with the Clerk of the Court a written demand for a trial by jury. You must also pay to the clerk a jury fee of $55 and file an undertaking in the sum of $50 or deposit such sum in cash to secure the payment of any costs that may be awarded against you. You will also be required to make an affidavit specifying the issues of fact which you desire to have tried by a jury and stating that such trial is desired and demanded in good faith.

Under the law, the Court may award $25 additional costs to the plaintiff if a jury trial is demanded by you and a decision is rendered against you.

(e) The clerk shall note on the statement referred to in subdivision (a) above, the date on which the notice was mailed and the address, the date of delivery shown by the return receipt and the name of the addressee or agent signing the receipt.

(f) If service of notice cannot be effected upon the defendant within four months following the date on which the action was first instituted, the action shall be dismissed without prejudice.

(f–1) Where all parties appear by attorneys, the case may be transferred to a regular part of court, and the claimant shall pay any additional filing fees required by law. If the claimant fails or refuses to pay such filing fees, the court shall dismiss the case.

(g) Unless the court shall otherwise order, a defendant to whom notice was duly given who fails to appear at the hearing on the day and time fixed either in person or by attorney shall be held to be in default, except that no default shall be ordered if the defendant or his attorney appears within one hour after the time fixed.

(h) If at the hearing it shall appear that the defendant has a counterclaim in an amount within the jurisdiction of the part for the hearing of small claims, the judge may either proceed forthwith to hear the entire case or may adjourn the hearing for a period of not more than 20 days or as soon thereafter as may be practicable, at which adjourned time the hearing of the entire case shall be had. An adjournment shall be granted at the request of the claimant if the defendant did not file the counterclaim with the court within five days of receiving the notice of claim.

(i) An oath or affirmation shall be administered to all witnesses. The court shall conduct the hearing in such manner as it deems best suited to discover the facts and to determine the justice of the case. If the plaintiff, or an attorney in his or her behalf, does not appear at the time set for hearing, the court may dismiss the claim for want of prosecution or enter a finding on the merits for the defendant, or make such other disposition as it may deem proper.

(j) Where, after a claim is filed with the clerk, either party to the action desires to implead one or more additional defendants, the clerk shall, upon receipt of the proper fees, issue and mail a notice of claim to each additional defendant under the procedure set forth above.

(k) The undertaking to be filed by a defendant desiring a jury trial shall be in the form prescribed by the relevant provisions of Article 25 of the CPLR.

(l) All motions pertaining to small claims shall be made returnable at a part and session appointed for the hearing of small claims, except that a motion to remove a case from the small claims part shall be made returnable in the appropriate motion part in the county division of the court in which the action is pending and shall be in accord with the rules of the UDCA generally applicable to motion practice.

(m) There may be arbitration of any small claims controversy.

(1) The parties to any controversy, except infants and incompetents, may submit the same for arbitration to any attorney, duly appointed as a small claims arbitrator by the administrative judge of this court, so assigned for such duty at that term of the court and upon whom they shall agree.

(2) The parties shall sign a consent which shall contain the name of the arbitrator, a brief recital of the nature of the controversy to be determined, a statement that they will abide by these rules, and an affirmation that the decision of the arbitrator is final and that no appeal shall lie from the award. The consent must be filed with the clerk of the small claims part.

(3) The arbitrator shall forthwith proceed to hear the controversy. He or she shall not be bound by the rules regarding the admissibility of evidence, but all testimony shall be given under oath or affirmation. Either party may be represented by counsel, but no record of the proceeding before the arbitrator shall be kept. No expense shall be incurred by the arbitrator except upon the consent in writing of the parties.

(4) After the first hearing, neither party may withdraw from the arbitration unless both parties consent to, or the arbitrator directs, a discontinuance of the proceeding.

(5) The arbitrator shall make his or her award in writing and file the same forthwith, together with an opinion, if any, with the clerk of the small claims part. Unless both parties file a request in writing not to enter judgment, the clerk shall, within two days after the filing of the award, enter judgment in accordance therewith, provided the award has been filed within 30 days from the date of filing the consent. The time within which the clerk shall enter judgment may be extended by a stipulation in writing for a further period not to exceed 30 days.

(6) No fees or disbursements of any kind shall be demanded or received except as hereinabove provided.

(n) The court or a supervising judge thereof may transfer a small claim to any other part of the court for the purpose of subjecting such claim to arbitration pursuant to Part 28 of this Title and rule 3405 of the CPLR. In the event a trial de novo is demanded pursuant to Part 28, the transfer shall be deemed rescinded and the claim shall be heard in the small claims part of the court no later than 30 days after the demand is made unless thereafter it is transferred to any other part of court pursuant to law.

Cross References

CPLR, see McKinney's Book 7B.

Uniform District Court Act, see McKinney's Book 29A, Part 3.

§ 212.41–a. Commercial Claims Procedure

(a) A commercial claims action may be brought by a claimant that is (1) a corporation, including a municipal or public benefit corporation, partnership, or association, which has its principal office in the State of New York, or (2) an assignee of any commercial claim, subject to the restrictions set forth in UDCA 1809–A. The action shall be instituted by the claimant or someone on its behalf by paying the filing fee and the cost of sending the notice of claim as provided in UDCA 1803–A and by filing and signing a written application containing the following information:

(1) claimant's name and principal office address;

(2) defendant's name and place of residence or place of business or employment;

(3) the nature and amount of the claim, including dates, and other relevant information; where the claim arises out of a consumer transaction (one where the money, property or service which is the subject of the transaction is primarily for personal, family or household purposes), information showing that the transaction is a consumer transaction;

(4) a certification that not more than five claims have been instituted in the courts of this State in the calendar month; and,

(5) in the case of a commercial claim arising out of a consumer transaction, a certification that the claimant has mailed a demand letter, containing the information set forth in UDCA § 1803–A, no less than 10 days and no more than 180 days prior to the commencement of the claim.

(b) Unless the clerk shall require the claimant, pursuant to UDCA 1810–A, to apply to the court for leave to prosecute the claim in a commercial claims part, the clerk shall reduce to a concise written form and record in a special docket the information contained in the application, and shall give to the person who signed the statement a memorandum of the time and place set for the hearing, which shall be as soon as practicable and shall advise such person to produce at the hearing supporting witnesses, account books, receipts or other documents required to establish the claim. The clerk shall advise the claimant of the right of the claimant or the defendant to request an evening hearing, which shall not be so scheduled if it would cause unreasonable hardship to either party, and the clerk shall schedule the hearing so as to minimize the defendant's time away from employment. In the case of a commercial claim arising out of a consumer transaction, the clerk shall mark the claim conspicuously as a consumer transaction and shall record it in the docket marked as a consumer transaction.

(c) Within five days after the action is filed, the clerk shall send to the defendant by ordinary first class mail and by certified mail, return receipt requested, at one of the addresses required by UDCA § 1803–A, as shall be deemed necessary, a signed notice bearing the seal of the court, which shall be in substantially the following form:

DISTRICT COURT OF _____

COUNTY OF _____

COMMERCIAL CLAIMS PART

TO:_____

    Take Notice that _____ asks judgment in this Court against you for $_____ together with costs, upon the following claim:

_____

_____

_____

    There will be a hearing before the Court upon this claim on _____, 19__, at _____ o'clock _____M. in the Commercial Claims Part, held at _____.

    You must appear and present your defense and any counterclaim you may desire to assert at the hearing at the time and place above set forth. (You may request that the hearing be scheduled during evening hours if you do so within 14 days of receipt of this notice.) IF YOU DO NOT APPEAR, JUDGMENT WILL BE ENTERED AGAINST YOU BY DEFAULT EVEN THOUGH YOU MAY HAVE A VALID DEFENSE. If your defense or counterclaim, if any, is supported by witnesses, account books, receipts or other documents, you must produce them at the hearing. The Clerk, if requested, will issue subpoenas for witnesses, without fee thereof.

    If you wish to present a counterclaim against the claimant, you must do so by filing with the Clerk of the Court a statement containing such counterclaim within five days of receiving this notice of claim. At the time of such filing you must pay the Clerk a filing fee of $3.00 plus the cost of postage to send your counterclaim by first class mail to the claimant. If you fail to file a counterclaim within this five-day period, you retain the right to file the counterclaim until the time of the hearing, but the claimant may request and obtain an adjournment of the hearing to a later date.

If you admit the claim, but desire time to pay, you must appear personally on the day set for the hearing and state to the Court your reasons for desiring time to pay.

Read the attached sheet for more information.

Dated: _____, 20__

_____

Clerk

A Guide to Commercial Claims Court is available at the Court listed above.

NOTE: If you desire a jury trial, you must, before the day upon which you have been notified to appear, file with the Clerk of the Court a written demand for a trial by jury. You must also pay to the clerk a jury fee of $55 and file an undertaking in the sum of $50 or deposit such sum in cash to secure the payment of any costs that may be awarded against you. You will also be required to make an affidavit specifying the issues of fact which you desire to have tried by a jury and stating that such trial is desired and demanded in good faith.

Under the law, the Court may award $25 additional costs to the plaintiff if a jury trial is demanded by you and a decision is rendered against you.

(d) The clerk shall note on the application the date on which the notice was mailed and the address, the date of delivery shown by the return receipt, and the name of the addressee or agent signing the receipt.

(e) If, after the expiration of 21 days (30 days in the case of a commercial claim arising out of a consumer transaction) from the date the notice was mailed, the ordinary first class mailing has not been returned as undeliverable, the defendant shall be presumed to have received notice of the claim.

(f) If service of notice cannot be made upon the defendant within four months following the date on which the action was first instituted, the action shall be dismissed without prejudice.

(f–1) Where all parties appear by attorneys, the case may be transferred to a regular part of court, and the claimant shall pay any additional filing fees required by law. If the claimant fails or refuses to pay such filing fees, the court shall dismiss the case.

(g) Unless the court shall otherwise order, a defendant to whom notice was duly given who fails to appear, either in person or by attorney, at the hearing on the day and time fixed, shall be held to be in default, except that no default shall be ordered if the defendant or his or her attorney appears within one hour after the time fixed. Notice of the default judgment, containing the information set forth in UDCA § 1807–A, shall be mailed by first class mail to the claimant and the defendant. The defaulting party may apply to have the default vacated by submitting a written request to the court; proceeding on default shall be governed by, but not limited to, section 5015 of the CPLR.

(h) If at the hearing it shall appear that the defendant has a counterclaim in an amount within the jurisdiction of the part for the hearing of small claims, the judge may either proceed forthwith to hear the entire case or may adjourn the hearing for a period of not more than 20 days or as soon thereafter as may be practicable, at which adjourned time the hearing of the entire case shall be had. An adjournment shall be granted at the request of the claimant if the defendant did not file the counterclaim with the court within five days of receiving the notice of claim.

(i) An oath or affirmation shall be administered to all witnesses. The court shall conduct the hearing in such manner as it deems best suited to discover the facts and to determine the justice of the case. If the claimant, or an attorney in his or her behalf, does not appear at the time set for hearing, the court may dismiss the claim for want of prosecution or enter a finding on the merits for the defendant, or make such other disposition as it may deem proper.

(j) Where, after a claim is filed with the clerk, either party to the action desires to implead one or more additional defendants, the clerk shall, upon receipt of the proper fees, issue and mail a notice of claim to each additional defendant under the procedure set forth above.

(k) The undertaking to be filed by a defendant desiring a jury trial shall be in the form prescribed by the relevant provisions of Article 25 of the CPLR.

(l) All motions pertaining to commercial claims shall be made returnable at a part and session appointed for the hearing of commercial claims, except that a motion to remove a case from the commercial claims part shall be assigned to a judge in the manner authorized by the Chief Administrator.

(m) There may be arbitration of any commercial claims controversy.

(1) The parties to any controversy, except infants and incompetents, may submit the same for arbitration to any attorney, duly appointed as a commercial claims arbitrator by the administrative judge of this court, so assigned for such duty at that term of the court and upon whom they shall agree.

(2) The parties shall sign a consent which shall contain the name of the arbitrator, a brief recital of the nature of the controversy to be determined, a statement that they will abide by these rules, and an affirmation that the decision of the arbitrator is final and that no appeal shall lie from the award. The consent must be filed with the clerk of the commercial claims part.

(3) The arbitrator shall forthwith proceed to hear the controversy. He or she shall not be bound by the

rules regarding the admissibility of evidence, but all testimony shall be given under oath or affirmation. Either party may be represented by counsel, but no record of the proceeding before the arbitrator shall be kept. No expense shall be incurred by the arbitrator except upon the consent in writing of the parties.

(4) After the first hearing, neither party may withdraw from the arbitration unless both parties consent to, or the arbitrator directs, a discontinuance of the proceeding.

(5) The arbitrator shall make his or her award in writing and file the same forthwith, together with an opinion, if any, with the clerk of the commercial claims part. Unless both parties file a request in writing not to enter judgment, the clerk shall, within two days after the filing of the award, enter judgment in accordance therewith, provided the award has been filed within 30 days from the date of filing the consent. The time within which the clerk shall enter judgment may be extended by a stipulation in writing for a further period not to exceed 30 days.

(6) No fees or disbursements of any kind shall be demanded or received except as hereinabove provided.

(n) The court or a supervising judge thereof may transfer a commercial claim to any other part of the court for the purpose of subjecting such claim to arbitration pursuant to Part 28 of this Title and rule 3405 of the CPLR. In the event a trial de novo is demanded pursuant to Part 28, the transfer shall be deemed rescinded and the claim shall be heard in the commercial claims part of the court no later than 30 days after the demand is made unless thereafter it is transferred to any other part of court pursuant to law.

§ 212.42. Proceedings Under Article 7 of the Real Property Actions and Proceedings Law

(a) Such proceedings involving residential property shall be commenced in the district in which the real property or portion thereof is located. No default shall be noted until at least one hour after the hour when the proceeding is called.

(b) The following form is set forth as an example of the notice of petition (the provisions relating to the demand for a money judgment should be omitted unless the petition so demands):

DISTRICT COURT OF THE COUNTY OF
_____

Petitioner	)	
Address	)	
	)	
–against–	)	NOTICE OF
	)	PETITION
Respondent	)	
Address	)	
Respondent	)	
Address	)	

To the respondents .... above named and described, in possession of the premises hereinafter described or claiming possession thereof:

PLEASE TAKE NOTICE that a hearing at which you must appear will be held at the District Court of the County of ...., ... District, ... Part to be held at ...., Town of ...., County of ...., on the ... day of ...., 19... at .... am/pm, which prays for a final judgment of eviction awarding to the petitioner the possession of premises designated and described as follows:

the .... rooms on the .... floor, Apartment No. ...., ... Street, Town of .... in the County of ...., and further granting to the petitioner such other and further relief as is demanded in the petition, which you must answer.

TAKE NOTICE also that demand is made in the petition herein for judgment against you, the respondent, for the sum of $............, with interest thereon from ...., 19....

TAKE NOTICE that your answer may set forth any defense or counterclaim you may have against the petitioner.

TAKE NOTICE also that if you shall fail at such time to interpose and establish any defense that you may have to the allegations of the petition, you may be precluded from asserting such defense or the claim on which it is based in any other proceeding or action.

TAKE NOTICE that your failure to appear and answer may result in final judgment by default for the petitioner in the amount demanded in the petition.

Dated: County of ...., the ...... day of ......, 19...

....
Attorney(s) for Petitioner
Office and Post Office Address
Telephone Number

....
Clerk   District

(c) At the option of the petitioner, on condition that he serve the notice of petition at least eight days prior to the return day, the following paragraph may be inserted in the foregoing notice of petition immediately after the paragraph which sets forth the amount of money for which demand is made in the petition:

TAKE NOTICE also that your answer may be made at the time of hearing specified above unless this Notice of Petition is served upon you on or before the .... day of ...., 19...., in which event you must answer at least three (3) days before the petition is noticed to be heard, either orally before the clerk of the court at his or her office or in writing by serving a copy thereof upon the undersigned attorney for the* petitioner, and by filing the original of such written answer with proof of service thereof in the office of the clerk at least three (3) days before the time the petition is noticed to be heard; in addition thereto, you must appear before the court at the time and place hereinabove set forth for the hearing.

* If the petitioner appears in person, strike out the words "undersigned attorney for the".

(d) At the time of the issuance of a notice of petition by a judge or the clerk, or an order to show cause by the judge, in a summary proceeding to recover possession of real property, a copy of such order to show cause or notice of petition shall be filed with the clerk. The original papers with proof of service thereof shall be filed with the clerk within the time specified by statute.

(e) An action noticed to be heard on a day when a judge is not assigned to the part shall not be accepted for filing. The papers shall be returned to the attorney with a notification as to the days on which a judge is assigned.

Cross References

Real Property Actions and Proceedings Law, see McKinney's Book 49½.

§ 212.43. Powers of Clerks

The chief clerk, deputy chief clerks and clerks of the court are authorized to administer oaths, take acknowledgments and sign the process and mandates of the court. Other nonjudicial personnel of the court may from time to time likewise be so authorized by order of the Chief Administrator of the Courts.

PART 214. UNIFORM CIVIL RULES FOR THE JUSTICE COURTS

§ 214.1. Application of Part; Waiver; Additional Rules; Definitions

(a) **Application.** This Part shall be applicable to all actions and proceedings in the Town, Village and City Justice Courts of the State of New York, outside the City of New York.

(b) **Waiver.** For good cause shown, and in the interests of justice, the court in an action or proceeding may waive compliance with any of these rules unless prohibited from doing so by statute or by a rule of the Chief Judge.

(c) **Additional Rules.** Additional local court rules, not inconsistent with law or with these rules, shall comply with Part 9 of the Rules of the Chief Judge (22 NYCRR Part 9).

(d) **Application of the Uniform Justice Court Act.** The provisions of this part shall be construed as consistent with the Uniform Justice Court Act (UJCA), and matters not covered by these provisions shall be governed by the UJCA.

(e) **Definitions.**

(1) "Chief Administrator of the Courts" in this Part includes a designee of the Chief Administrator.

(2) Unless otherwise defined in this Part, or the context otherwise requires, all terms used in this Part shall have the same meaning as they have in the UJCA and the CPLR.

Cross References

CPLR, see McKinney's Book 7B.

Uniform Justice Court Act, see McKinney's Book 29A, Part 2.

§ 214.2. Place and Hours of Court

(a) It is the policy that the public is best served by justice courts which function in facilities provided by the municipality, and it is also the policy that each justice of those courts participate equally in the duties of the court. When facilities are provided by the municipality, the sessions of the court shall be held therein.

(b) Each court shall establish the days and times when it shall sit in regular session. Such days and times shall be subject to modification by the Chief Administrator of the Courts. The court's schedule as so established shall be filed with the clerk of the municipality, shall be posted where other official notices are posted and shall be filed with the law enforcement agencies regularly appearing in the court. The clerk's office shall be open at hours established by each court subject to the further order of the Chief Administrator.

(c) Return dates of process shall conform with the above schedule unless otherwise provided by law, rule or order.

§ 214.3. Summons

(a) The summons shall state the name and location of the court in which the action is brought, the names of the parties and a return date to be obtained from the court and shall comply with all provisions of the UJCA applicable to summonses.

(b) The following form is to be used in a case in which the action is for money only and a formal complaint is not served therewith:

JUSTICE COURT OF THE VILLAGE, TOWN OR CITY OF ....
COUNTY OF ....

—————————————————
) Index No. ....
          Plaintiff,)
-against-   )   SUMMONS
)
       Defendant.) Plaintiff's Residence
) Address:
—————————————————
)

To the above named defendant:

YOU ARE HEREBY SUMMONED and required to appear and answer this endorsed summons in the Justice Court of the Village, Town or City of .... located at ...., County of ...., State of New York, on the ...... day of ...., 19... at ...... o'clock in the ......noon; upon your failure to appear and answer, judgment will be taken against you for the sum of $........... with interest thereon from the .... day of ...., 19... together with the costs of this action.

Dated: the ...... day of ...., 19...

                  ....

Statement of the nature   Attorney(s) for Plaintiff
and substance of plain-   Post Office Address
tiff's cause of action: Telephone Number
                      (or, alternatively,

                  ....
                  Clerk of the ....
                  Court)

(c) In an action where a formal complaint is annexed to the summons, the following form of summons shall be used:

JUSTICE COURT OF THE VILLAGE, TOWN OR
CITY OF . . . .
COUNTY OF . . . .

```
———————————————————  )
              Plaintiff, ) Index No. . . . . . . . .
       -against-          )      SUMMONS
                          ) Plaintiff's Residence
              Defendant.  ) Address:
                          )
———————————————————  )
```

To the above named defendant:

YOU ARE HEREBY SUMMONED and required
to appear and answer this complaint in the Justice
Court of the Village, Town or City of . . . .
located at . . . ., County of . . . .,
State of New York, on the . . . . day of
. . . ., 19 . . . at . . . . o'clock in the . . . . noon;
upon your failure to appear and answer, judgment will
be taken against you for the relief demanded in the
complaint, together with the costs of this action.

Dated: the . . . . day of . . . ., 19 . . . .

. . . .
Attorney(s) for Plaintiff
Post Office Address
Telephone Number

Cross References

Uniform Justice Court Act, see McKinney's Book 29A, Part
2.

§ 214.4. Pleadings

(a) Except as required by statute, a formal pleading may be dispensed with in any case in which the
party required to serve the pleading appears in person.

(b) All formal pleadings and verifications thereof
shall be in conformity with CPLR, Article 30.

(c) An order directing the service and filing of a
formal pleading, or pleadings, shall specify the time
within which the same shall be served and filed.

Cross References

CPLR, see McKinney's Book 7B.

§ 214.5. Civil Enforcement Officers

(a) All enforcement officers shall keep accurate and
detailed records, properly indexed, of all functions
performed by them, pursuant to law, rule or order, in
their capacity as law enforcement officers.

(b) In addition to the enforcement officers enumerated in UJCA section 110, the municipal board may
designate other persons to serve as enforcement officers in civil matters.

Cross References

Uniform Justice Court Act, see McKinney's Book 29A, Part
2.

§ 214.6. Power of Clerks to Administer Oaths and Perform Certain Other Duties

The court clerk and one of the deputy or assistant
court clerks designated by the clerk are authorized
and empowered to administer oaths, take acknowl-
edgements, sign the process or mandate of the court
and certify the records of the court.

§ 214.7. Conciliation Conference

(a) Any party who commences an action, proceeding or claim within the court's jurisdiction or against
whom such an action, proceeding or claim is commenced, which, in his or her opinion, may be adjusted
without resort to a trial, may apply to the court for
the issuance, in the discretion of the court, of a notice
of conciliation, or the court on its own motion may
order such conciliation. However, such conciliation
conference may be ordered only upon the prior written consent of the parties that, should the controversy
not be resolved by conciliation, the justice who presides over the conciliation conference may preside
over a subsequent trial of the action, proceeding or
claim.

(b) If the court so orders, the clerk shall immediately fix a date for a conciliation conference and shall
mail notice to all parties to the controversy. At least
ten days' notice shall be given, exclusive of the day of
mailing. The notice shall designate the address of the
court and the time and date where the hearing will be
held.

(c) Conciliation conferences shall be informal, and
the justice presiding shall endeavor to effect an amica-
ble and equitable adjustment between the parties.
The justice shall permit either party to be assisted by
counsel, but no record of the proceeding shall be kept.
At the conference, the justice shall not be bound by
the rules regarding admissibility of evidence.

(d) The justice shall direct the clerk to make an
entry in the docket hereinafter referred to of the
terms of the settlement or that no settlement was
effected. No judgment or order enforceable by law
shall be rendered or made by the justice except upon
the consent or written stipulation of the parties.

(e) A docket shall be kept wherein proper entries
of all proceedings shall be made. Such docket may
not be offered in evidence or referred to upon any
subsequent trial of the controversy.

§ 214.8. Appeals

(a) A notice of appeal shall not be accepted for
filing without proof of service upon all parties.

(b) All papers prepared by the appellant that are
required to be included in the return on appeal as
required by the applicable provisions of the CPLR,
shall be furnished by the appellant to the clerk at the
time of filing the notice of settlement provided in
section 1704 of the UJCA.

(c) In the case of the death, disability or prolonged absence from the municipality of the justice before whom the action was tried, the return on appeal may be settled by any other justice of the court.

Cross References

CPLR, see McKinney's Book 7B.

Uniform Justice Court Act, see McKinney's Book 29A, Part 2.

§ 214.9. Bank Account Requirements for Town Justices and Village Justices

(a) Every town justice and village justice, including acting village justices, shall deposit as soon as practicable all monies received in his or her judicial capacity in a separate bank account in his or her name as such judicial officer, in a bank or trust company in this State, pending disposition as required by law. In no event shall any deposit be made later than 72 hours, exclusive of Sundays and holidays, from the day of receipt.

(b) Withdrawals from such accounts shall be only for purposes permitted by law.

(c) Every justice now having such a bank account or required by subdivision (a) of this section to open such a bank account shall, within 10 days after the effective date of this rule or within 10 days after the opening or transfer of such a bank account, notify the Chief Administrator of the Courts in writing of the name and address of the bank in which the account has been opened or transferred to, the title of the account, the account number and the date that said account was opened or transferred. If, for any reason, the justice, during his or her tenure, shall close or transfer said account to a different bank, within 10 days of such closing or transfer written notification, stating the reasons therefor, shall be given to the Chief Administrator.

(d) With the consent of all the justices of a town or village, a joint account in the names of all the justices may be opened for the deposit of bail monies only. Such an account shall in all other respects comply with the provisions of this section.

(e) The provisions of this section shall not apply to a justice who does not actually receive monies in a judicial capacity, providing he or she files with the Chief Administrator a written statement setting forth the fact that he or she does not receive monies in a judicial capacity and the reasons therefor.

§ 214.10. Small Claims Procedure

(a) Each Town, Village and City Justice Court shall schedule at least one session every other week for the hearing of small claims and may allocate some portion of every session of court specifically for the hearing of such claims as defined in the UJCA. During the times designated for the hearing of small claims, the court shall sit as a small claims part. In those courts having more than one judge, each judge shall participate equally in the handling of small claims.

(b) A small claims action shall be commenced by a plaintiff or someone on his or her behalf paying the filing fee as provided in UJCA 1803, and by supplying to the clerk the following information:

(i) plaintiff's name and residence address;

(ii) defendant's name and place of residence, or place of business or employment; and

(iii) the nature and amount of the plaintiff's claim, giving dates and other relevant information.

(c) The justice or clerk shall reduce this information to a written statement on a form provided therefor and shall record it in his or her office. The statement shall be in nontechnical, concise and simple language, and shall be signed by the person who shall have supplied the information contained therein.

(d) The justice or clerk shall give to the person who signed the statement a memorandum of the time and place set for the hearing, which shall not be less than 22 nor more than 45 days from the date the action is recorded and shall advise such person to produce at the hearing the supporting witnesses, account books, receipts or other documents required to establish the claim.

(e) Within five days after the action is recorded, the clerk shall send to the defendant by ordinary first class mail and by certified mail, return receipt requested, addressed to one or more of the addresses supplied as shall be deemed necessary, a signed notice bearing the seal of the court, which shall be in substantially the following form:

JUSTICE COURT OF THE VILLAGE, TOWN OR CITY OF _____

COUNTY OF _____

SMALL CLAIMS PART

TO: _____

　　Take Notice that _____ asks judgment in this Court against you for $_____ together with costs, upon the following claim:

_____

_____

_____

　　There will be a hearing before the Court upon this claim on _____, 19__, at ____ o'clock ____M. in the Small Claims Part, held at _____.

You must appear and present your defense and any counterclaim you may desire to assert at the hearing at the time and place above set forth (a corporation must be represented by an attorney or any authorized officer, director or employee). IF YOU DO NOT APPEAR, JUDGMENT WILL BE ENTERED AGAINST YOU BY DEFAULT EVEN THOUGH YOU MAY HAVE A VALID DEFENSE. If your defense or counterclaim, if any, is supported by witnesses, account books, receipts or other documents, you must produce them at the hearing. The Clerk, if requested, will issue subpoenas for witnesses, without fee thereof.

If you wish to present a counterclaim against the claimant, you must do so by filing with the Clerk of the Court a statement containing such counterclaim within five days of receiving this notice of claim. At the time of such filing you must pay the Clerk a filing fee of $3.00 plus the cost of postage to send your counterclaim by first class mail to the claimant. If you fail to file a counterclaim within this five-day period, you retain the right to file the counterclaim until the time of the hearing, but the claimant may request and obtain an adjournment of the hearing to a later date.

If you admit the claim, but desire time to pay, you must appear personally on the day set for the hearing and state to the Court your reasons for desiring time to pay.

Dated: _____, 20__

_____

Clerk

A Guide to Small Claims Court is available at the court listed above.

NOTE: If you desire a jury trial, you must, before the day upon which you have been notified to appear, file with the Clerk of the Court a written demand for a trial by jury. You must also pay to the clerk a jury fee of $55 and file an undertaking in the sum of $50 or deposit such sum in cash to secure the payment of any costs that may be awarded against you. You will also be required to make an affidavit specifying the issues of fact which you desire to have tried by a jury and stating that such trial is desired and demanded in good faith.

Under the law, the Court may award $25 additional costs to the plaintiff if a jury trial is demanded by you and a decision is rendered against you.

(f) The justice or clerk shall note on the statement referred to in subdivision (b) above, the date on which the notice was mailed and the address, the date of delivery shown by the return receipt and the name of the addressee or agent signing the receipt.

(g) If service of notice cannot be effected upon the defendant within four months of the date when an action was first instituted, the action shall be dismissed without prejudice.

(h) Unless the court shall otherwise order, a defendant to whom notice was duly given who fails to appear at the hearing on the day and time fixed either in person or by attorney shall be held to be in default, except that no default shall be ordered if the defen-

dant or his attorney appears within one hour after the time fixed.

(i) If at the hearing it shall appear that the defendant has a counterclaim in an amount within the jurisdiction of the part for the hearing of small claims, the judge may either proceed forthwith to hear the entire case or may adjourn the hearing for a period of not more than 20 days or as soon thereafter as may be practicable, at which adjourned time the hearing of the entire case shall be had. An adjournment shall be granted at the request of the claimant if the defendant did not file the counterclaim with the court within five days of receiving the notice of claim.

(j) An oath or affirmation shall be administered to all witnesses. The courts shall conduct the hearing in such manner as it deems best suited to discover the facts and to determine the justice of the case. If the plaintiff, or an attorney in his or her behalf, does not appear at the time set for hearing, the court may dismiss the claim for want of prosecution or enter a finding on the merits for the defendant, or make such other disposition as it may deem proper.

(k) Where, after a claim is filed with the clerk, either party to the action desires to implead one or more additional defendants, the clerk shall, upon receipt of the proper fees, issue and mail a notice of claim to each additional defendant under the procedure set forth above.

(l) The undertaking to be filed by a defendant desiring a jury trial shall be in the form prescribed by the relevant provisions of Article 25 of the CPLR.

Cross References

CPLR, see McKinney's Book 7B.

Uniform Justice Court Act, see McKinney's Book 29A, Part 2.

§ 214.11. Recordkeeping Requirements

(a) Each town and village justice court shall maintain:

(1) case files containing all papers filed, orders issued, any minutes or notes made by the court of proceedings or testimony, and a copy of any original documents or papers forwarded to another court or agency;

(2) an index of cases with a unique number assigned to each case when filed; and

(3) a cashbook which shall chronologically itemize all receipts and disbursements.

(b) In each civil case the following case history shall also be maintained:

(1) the names and addresses of all parties;

(2) the name of the justice presiding;

(3) the name and location of the court;

(4) the dates pleadings were served;

(5) the names and addresses of attorneys;

(6) the date of first appearance, all adjournments and by whom requested;

(7) whether a jury was demanded and by whom;

(8) the names and addresses of all witnesses sworn;

(9) all fees collected by and other funds deposited with the court;

(10) the disposition of the case, including the amount of a money judgment and any costs; and

(11) whether any transcripts of judgment were issued.

(c) A model recordkeeping system which complies with the requirements of this Part will be prepared and distributed by the Office of Court Administration.

PART 215. USE OF RECYCLED PAPER

§ 215.1. Application

The policy set forth in this Part shall apply to all courts of the Unified Court System except those that already have a requirement for the filing of court papers on recycled paper.

§ 215.2. Policy

It is the policy of the Unified Court System that litigants, where practicable, should file or submit to the courts of the Unified Court System of the State of New York papers printed or reproduced on recycled paper. Paper is considered recycled if it contains a minimum content of 30 percent waste paper.

§ 215.3. Statement of Compliance

The signature page of every paper filed or submitted to the court on recycled paper should bear the legend: "Printed [Reproduced] on Recycled Paper."

PART 216. SEALING OF COURT RECORDS IN CIVIL ACTIONS IN THE TRIAL COURTS

§ 216.1. Sealing of Court Records

(a) Except where otherwise provided by statute or rule, a court shall not enter an order in any action or proceeding sealing the court records, whether in whole or in part, except upon a written finding of good cause, which shall specify the grounds thereof. In determining whether good cause has been shown, the court shall consider the interests of the public as well as of the parties. Where it appears necessary or desirable, the court may prescribe appropriate notice and an opportunity to be heard.

(b) For purposes of this rule, "court records" shall include all documents and records of any nature filed with the clerk in connection with the action. Documents obtained through disclosure and not filed with the clerk shall remain subject to protective orders as set forth in CPLR 3103(a).

PART 217. ACCESS TO COURT INTERPRETER SERVICES FOR PERSONS WITH LIMITED ENGLISH PROFICIENCY

§ 217.1. Obligation to Appoint Interpreter in Court Proceedings in the Trial Courts

(a) In all civil and criminal cases, when a court determines that a party or witness, or an interested parent or guardian of a minor party in a Family Court proceeding, is unable to understand and communicate in English to the extent that he or she cannot meaningfully participate in the court proceedings, the court shall appoint an interpreter. The court may permit an interpreter to interpret by telephone or live audiovisual means.

(b) A person with limited English proficiency, other than a person testifying as a witness, may waive a court-appointed interpreter, with the consent of the court, if the person provides his or her own interpreter.

§ 217.2. Provision of Interpreting Services in Clerk's Offices

A court clerk shall provide interpreting services to a person with limited English proficiency seeking assistance at the court clerk's office in accordance with the needs of the person seeking assistance and the availability of court interpreting services. Such services may be provided by telephone or live audiovisual means.

PART 218. UNIFORM RULES FOR THE TRIAL COURTS IN CAPITAL CASES

Preamble

Acting pursuant to the rulemaking authority invested in this Court by New York Constitution, article VI, section 30 and Laws of 1995, chapter 1, the Court of Appeals establishes these Uniform Rules for the Trial Courts in Capital Cases.

§ 218.1. Record Transcription and Reproduction; Settlement

(a) During the course of capital proceedings before the superior court, and at all times thereafter, the clerk of the superior court shall take all necessary steps to insure the accuracy and completeness of the record of the proceedings.

(b) The court reporter shall take, and keep electronically, minutes of all capital proceedings occurring in the superior court. Transcription shall proceed in compliance with any relevant superior court order and the Court of Appeals Capital Appeal Management Order (22 NYCRR 510.4[c][4]; 510.8[a]). Where a copy of the minutes of any proceedings in the superior court was ordered during the course of the superior court proceedings, defense counsel and the prosecutor shall preserve their respective copies of the transcript. Transcripts shall be settled pursuant to CPLR 5525(c) within such time limits and pursuant to such additional procedures as may be set by Court of Appeals order.

(c) Upon the filing of a notice of appeal, the superior court clerk shall expeditiously assemble, reproduce, and transmit to appellant the record of the proceedings. Appellant shall be responsible for the timely preparation and filing of the record on appeal in accordance with the Capital Appeal Management Order issued by the Court of Appeals pursuant to 22 NYCRR 510.4(c)(4) or 510.8(a).

(d) The record on appeal shall comply with 22 NYCRR 510.11(b), and be stipulated to or settled on motion. The parties may stipulate to the correctness of the contents of the record on appeal using the process provided by CPLR 5525(c)(1). Where the parties are unable to agree and stipulate to the contents of the record on appeal, appellant shall move, on notice, to settle the record in the superior court from which the appeal is taken.

§ 218.2. Capital Sentencing Determination and Findings Form

In all criminal actions in which a separate sentencing proceeding is conducted in accordance with the procedures set forth in section 400.27 of the Criminal Procedure Law, the superior court shall provide the jury with a Sentencing Determination and Findings Form, as prescribed by the Court of Appeals, on which the jury must record its determination of sentence and its specification of those mitigating and aggravating factors considered and those mitigating factors established by the defendant. The superior court judge shall instruct the jury on how to complete the form and shall ensure that the form is properly completed.

§ 218.3. Notice to the Capital Defender Office

(a) The clerk of the superior court in whose office a judgment that includes a sentence of death has been entered shall notify the capital defender office by the end of business on the day such determination is handed down.

(b) Notice to the capital defender office required pursuant to subdivision (a) of this section shall consist of telephone, facsimile, electronic mail or other prompt electronic means of communication, which shall be followed by first class mail notification within two business days after rendition of the sentence.

(c) The clerk of the superior court shall retain a written record of the electronic and written notice given pursuant to subdivision (b) of this section.

§ 218.4. Stays of Execution: Automatic or Determined by Superior Court

(a) **Upon appeal from a judgment including a sentence of death (CPL 460.40[1]).** The taking of an appeal by a defendant directly to the Court of Appeals from a superior court judgment including a sentence of death stays the execution of such sentence until determination of the appeal.

(b) **Initial CPL article 440 proceedings (CPL 460.40[3]).** Upon motion to the superior court judge or justice who signed the warrant of execution, a defendant sentenced to death shall be granted a stay of execution of a death warrant issued pursuant to Correction Law article 22–B to allow the defendant an opportunity to prepare and timely file an initial motion in superior court pursuant to CPL 440.10 or 440.20. The order staying execution shall provide that the stay of execution shall continue until (1) the time for taking an appeal to the Court of Appeals from the superior court's denial of such CPL article 440 motion has expired, or (2) if an appeal is taken, until the Court of Appeals determines the appeal.

(c) **Subsequent CPL article 440 proceedings (CPL 460.40[3]).**

(1) In the event a defendant sentenced to death files a motion for post-conviction relief pursuant to CPL 440.10 or 440.20 subsequent to the final determi-

nation of an initial CPL article 440 motion, the superior court may grant a stay of execution of a death warrant issued pursuant to Correction Law article 22–B only for good cause shown.

(2) By the end of business on the date a notice of appeal from a superior court order granting or denying a motion for a stay of execution has been filed, the clerk of the superior court, and appellant or appellant's counsel, shall notify the clerk of the Court of Appeals by telephone of such filing. Telephone notice to the Court of Appeals does not relieve the clerk of the superior court of the duties imposed by section 218.5 of this Part.

§ 218.5. Case History

Within 15 days after the filing of a notice of appeal to the Court of Appeals in a case involving a sentence of death, except in those appeals taken pursuant to CPL 460.40(3) from an order of a superior court granting or denying a motion for a stay of execution, the clerk of the superior court in which the judgment or order being appealed from was rendered shall transmit to the clerk of the Court of Appeals a Case History including:

(1) the duplicate notice of appeal;

(2) a chronological list of all proceedings below giving rise to this particular appeal, noting which transcripts have been, or must be, prepared; and

(3) a list of all exhibits introduced in the proceedings below giving rise to this particular appeal.

The clerk of the superior court shall transmit to counsel for the parties copies of items (2) and (3) above.

§ 218.6. Remittitur

The remittitur of the Court of Appeals containing the court's adjudication, together with the return papers filed with the court, shall be sent to the clerk of the court to which the case is remitted, there to be proceeded upon according to law. Any order to effect the adjudication contained in the Court of Appeals' remittitur shall be sought, entered and enforced in the superior court.

§ 218.7. Capital Case Data Reports

(a) In each criminal action in which the defendant has been indicted for commission of an offense defined in section 125.27 of the Penal Law, except those in which the indictment is dismissed or the defendant is acquitted, the clerk of the superior court, within 45 days after the disposition of the action in such court, shall prepare and send to the Court of Appeals a Capital Case Data Report in the form prescribed by the Court of Appeals. Data reports shall be prepared by the clerk of the superior court by reviewing the record and upon consultation with the prosecutor and counsel for the defendant. Such data reports shall not constitute a part of the record in the underlying criminal action. The clerk of the superior court shall retain, in a confidential file kept separate from the record in the underlying criminal action, a copy of each such data report sent to the Court of Appeals, and may disclose a data report, or any part thereof, only upon order of the Court of Appeals for exceptional cause shown.

(b) All Capital Case Data Reports received by the Court of Appeals shall be compiled into a uniform Capital Case Data Report, which may consist of a computer data base containing the information in each Capital Case Data Report. Upon request, the uniform Capital Case Data Report shall be made available to the parties on appeal to the Court of Appeals in cases where a sentence of death has been imposed.

(c) If the conviction or sentence in such criminal action is subsequently reversed or modified, the Capital Case Data Report shall be notated to reflect the reversal or modification. If an intermediate appellate court reverses or modifies the conviction or sentence, that court shall forward a copy of its remittitur to the Court of Appeals within 10 days after entry. If a new disposition in the action ensues in the superior court, the superior court clerk shall prepare a new Capital Case Data Report. Upon completion, the superior court clerk shall send the new Capital Case Data Report to the clerk of the Court of Appeals with a notice that the new report should be substituted in the data base for the previous report.

PART 220.   UNIFORM RULES FOR JURY SELECTION AND DELIBERATION

SUBPART A.   UNIFORM RULES FOR JURY SELECTION

§ 220.1.   Nondesignated Alternate Jurors

(a) Application. Upon consent of the parties, a court trying a civil case heard by a jury may adopt the procedure provided for in this section concerning the formation of the trial jury.

(b) Number of Jurors. The number of jurors selected shall be as permitted by law.

(c) Designation of Jurors. If more than six jurors are selected, they shall not at that time be designated as trial jurors and alternate jurors. Instead, if at the conclusion of the evidence more than six jurors remain on the jury, at that time the clerk of the court, in the presence of the court and the parties, shall randomly draw the names of six of the remaining jurors, who shall be the jurors who retire to deliberate upon a verdict. Unless otherwise determined by the court, the juror whose name was first drawn shall be designated as the foreperson. After the deliberating jurors have retired to deliberate, the remaining non-deliberating jurors shall be discharged. The court may, in appropriate circumstances, direct the discharged jurors not to discuss the case while the jury deliberates.

(d) Peremptory Challenges. If the court adopts the procedure set forth in this section, the number of peremptory challenges specified in section 4109 of the Civil Practice Law and Rules shall be increased by one for every two jurors selected beyond the first six selected.

SUBPART B.   UNIFORM RULES FOR JUROR DELIBERATION

§ 220.10.   Note-taking by Jurors

(a) Application. This section shall apply to all cases, both civil and criminal, heard by a jury in any court.

(b) After the jury has been sworn and before any opening statements or addresses, the court shall determine if the jurors may take notes at any stage of the proceedings. In making this determination, the court shall consider the probable length of the trial and the nature and complexity of the evidence likely to be admitted.

(c) If the court authorizes note-taking, it shall direct the jurors that they may make written notes if they so desire and that the court will provide materials for that purpose if they so request. The court also shall instruct the jurors in the proper use of any notes taken, and its instructions shall include but not be limited to the following:

(1) Jurors should not permit their note-taking to distract them from the proceedings;

(2) Any notes taken are only an aid to memory and should not take precedence over a juror's independent recollection;

(3) Those jurors who choose not to take notes should rely on their own independent recollection of the evidence and should not be influenced by any notes that another juror may take;

(4) Any notes taken are only for the note-taker's own personal use in refreshing his or her recollection of the evidence;

(5) If there is a discrepancy between a juror's recollection of the evidence and the juror's notes, the jury should request a readback of the record and the court's transcript prevails over a juror's notes; and

(6) Notes are not a substitute for the official record or for the governing principles of law as enunciated by the trial court.

These instructions shall be repeated at the conclusion of the case as part of the court's charge prior to the commencement of jury deliberations.

(d) The court shall require the jurors to print their names or other identifier on the cover of the binder that contains the notes and shall collect each juror's notes at the end of each trial day until the jury retires to deliberate. The jurors may refer to their notes during the proceedings and deliberations.

(e) Any notes taken are confidential and shall not be available for examination or review by any party or other person. After the jury has rendered its verdict, the court shall ensure that the notes are promptly collected and destroyed.

§ 220.11.   Copy of Judge's Charge to Jury

(a) Application. This section shall apply to all civil cases heard by a jury in any court.

(b) Where the court determines that the jury's deliberations may be expedited or assisted by having a copy of the court's instructions available during deliberations, the court, upon its own motion or the motion of a party and after affording the parties an opportunity to be heard, may direct that at least one copy of the instructions be furnished to the jury when it retires to consider its verdict. If the court so directs, it shall state its reasons for doing so on the record. Where the copy thereby furnished is other than a transcript of the minutes of the proceedings, the court shall certify thereon that it is a correct copy of its instructions. Any copy of the instructions provided to the jurors in accordance with this subdivision shall be retrieved from the jury at the close of deliberations, and shall be filed with the clerk of the court.

§ 220.12. Juror Notebooks

(a) **Contents.** At the discretion of the trial court, in cases of appropriate complexity, the court may authorize the distribution to each juror of identical notebooks, which may include copies of:

(1) selected exhibits that have been ruled admissible (or excerpts thereof);

(2) stipulations of the parties;

(3) other material not subject to genuine dispute, which may include:

    (i) curricula vitae of experts;

    (ii) lists or seating charts identifying attorneys and their respective clients;

    (iii) lists or indices of admitted exhibits;

    (iv) glossaries;

    (v) chronologies or timelines; and

    (vi) other material approved by the court for inclusion.

(b) **Procedure to determine contents.**

(1) The court shall require counsel to confer on the contents of the notebooks before trial begins and at any appropriate time thereafter.

(2) If counsel cannot agree on the contents of the notebooks, each party shall be afforded the opportunity to submit its proposal and to comment upon any proposal submitted by another party. The court shall be the final arbiter of the contents of the notebooks.

(c) **Use of notebooks at trial.**

(1) At the time of distribution, the court shall instruct the jurors concerning the purpose and use of the notebooks.

(2) During the course of trial, the court may permit the parties to supplement the materials contained in the notebook with additional documents as these become relevant and after they have been ruled admissible or otherwise approved by the court for inclusion.

(3) The court shall collect the notebooks at the end of each trial day until the jury retires to deliberate. The notebooks shall be available to the jurors during deliberations.

(4) Whenever note-taking is permitted by jurors, the court shall require the jurors to print their names or other identifier on the cover of their notebooks.

PART 221.   UNIFORM RULES FOR THE CONDUCT OF DEPOSITIONS

§ 221.1   Objections at Depositions

(a) Objections in general. No objections shall be made at a deposition except those which, pursuant to subdivision (b), (c) or (d) of Rule 3115 of the Civil Practice Law and Rules, would be waived if not interposed, and except in compliance with subdivision (e) of such rule. All objections made at a deposition shall be noted by the officer before whom the deposition is taken, and the answer shall be given and the deposition shall proceed subject to the objections and to the right of a person to apply for appropriate relief pursuant to Article 31 of the CPLR.

(b) Speaking objections restricted. Every objection raised during a deposition shall be stated succinctly and framed so as not to suggest an answer to the deponent and, at the request of the questioning attorney, shall include a clear statement as to any defect in form or other basis of error or irregularity. Except to the extent permitted by CPLR Rule 3115 or by this rule, during the course of the examination persons in attendance shall not make statements or comments that interfere with the questioning.

Cross References

CPLR, see McKinney's Book 7B, Article 31.

§ 221.2.   Refusal to Answer When Objection Is Made

A deponent shall answer all questions at a deposition, except (i) to preserve a privilege or right of confidentiality, (ii) to enforce a limitation set forth in an order of a court, or (iii) when the question is plainly improper and would, if answered, cause significant prejudice to any person. An attorney shall not direct a deponent not to answer except as provided in CPLR Rule 3115 or this subdivision. Any refusal to answer or direction not to answer shall be accompanied by a succinct and clear statement of the basis therefor. If the deponent does not answer a question, the examining party shall have the right to complete the remainder of the deposition.

Cross References

CPLR, see McKinney's Book 7B, Article 31.

§ 221.3.   Communication With the Deponent

An attorney shall not interrupt the deposition for the purpose of communicating with the deponent unless all parties consent or the communication is made for the purpose of determining whether the question should not be answered on the grounds set forth in section 221.2 of these rules and, in such event, the reason for the communication shall be stated for the record succinctly and clearly.

Cross References

CPLR, see McKinney's Book 7B, Article 31.

APPENDICES

APPENDIX A.   STATEMENT OF NET WORTH
[see Uniform Rules, section 202.16(b)]

COURT
COUNTY OF   Index No.

_____

                          Plaintiff,   STATEMENT OF
     – against –   NET WORTH
                                        (DRL § 236)
                        Defendant.

_____ Date of commencement of action _____

(Complete all items, marking "NONE," "INAPPLICABLE" and "UNKNOWN," if appropriate)

STATE OF   COUNTY OF   SS.:

         , the (Petitioner) (Respondent) (Plaintiff) (Defendant) herein, being duly sworn, deposes and says that the following is an accurate statement as of _____, of my net worth (assets of whatsoever kind and nature and wherever situated minus liabilities), statement of income from all sources and statement of assets transferred of whatsoever kind and nature and wherever situated:

    I.   FAMILY DATA:
        (a)   Husband's age _____
        (b)   Wife's age _____
        (c)   Date married _____
        (d)   Date (separated) (divorced) _____
        (e)   Number of dependent children under 21 years _____
        (f)   Names and ages of children

               _____
               _____
               _____
               _____

        (g)   Custody of Children _____ Husband _____ Wife
        (h)   Minor children of prior marriage: _____ Husband _____ Wife
        (i)   (Husband) (Wife) (paying) (receiving) $_____ as alimony (maintenance) and/or $_____ child support in connection with prior marriage
        (j)   Custody of children of prior marriage:
            Name _____
            Address _____
        (k)   Is marital residence occupied by Husband _____ Wife _____ Both _____
        (l)   Husband's present address

            Wife's present address
            _____

       (m)   Occupation of Husband _____ Occupation of Wife _____
        (n)   Husband's employer

        (o)   Wife's employer

        (p)   Education, training and skills [Include dates of attainment of degrees, etc.]
            Husband _____
            Wife _____

        (q)   Husband's health _____

(r) Wife's health _____
(s) Children's health _____

II. EXPENSES: (You may elect to list all expenses on a weekly basis or all expenses on a monthly basis, however, you must be consistent. If any items are paid on a monthly basis, divide by 4.3 to obtain weekly payments; if any items are paid on a weekly basis, multiply by 4.3 to obtain monthly payment. Attach additional sheet, if needed. Items included under "Other" should be listed separately with separate dollar amounts.)

Expenses listed [ ] weekly   [ ] monthly

(a) Housing
 1. Rent   _____
 2. Mortgage and amortization   _____
 3. Real estate taxes   _____
 4. Condominium charges   _____
 5. Cooperative apartment maintenance   _____

 Total: Housing $_____

(b) Utilities
 1. Fuel oil   _____
 2. Gas   _____
 3. Electricity   _____
 4. Telephone   _____
 5. Water   _____

 Total: Utilities $_____

(c) Food
 1. Groceries   _____
 2. School lunches   _____
 3. Lunches at work   _____
 4. Dining Out   _____
 5. Liquor/alcohol   _____
 6. Home entertainment   _____
 7. Other _____   _____

 Total: Food $_____

(d) Clothing
 1. Husband   _____
 2. Wife   _____
 3. Children   _____
 4. Other _____   _____

 Total: Clothing $_____

(e) Laundry
 1. Laundry at home   _____
 2. Dry cleaning   _____
 3. Other _____   _____

 Total: Laundry $_____

(f) Insurance
 1. Life   _____
 2. Homeowner's/tenant's   _____
 3. Fire, theft and liability   _____
 4. Automotive   _____
 5. Umbrella policy   _____
 6. Medical plan   _____
 7. Dental plan   _____
 8. Optical plan   _____
 9. Disability   _____
 10. Worker's Compensation   _____

11. Other _____ _____

       Total: Insurance $_____

(g) Unreimbursed medical
    1. Medical _____
    2. Dental _____
    3. Optical _____
    4. Pharmaceutical _____
    5. Surgical, nursing, hospital _____
    6. Other _____ _____

       Total: Unreimbursed medical $_____

(h) Household maintenance
    1. Repairs _____
    2. Furniture, furnishings housewares _____
    3. Cleaning supplies _____
    4. Appliances, including maintenance _____
    5. Painting _____
    6. Sanitation/carting _____
    7. Gardening/landscaping _____
    8. Snow removal _____
    9. Extermination _____
   10. Other _____ _____

       Total: Household maintenance $_____

(i) Household help
    1. Babysitter _____
    2. Domestic (housekeeper, maid, etc.) _____
    3. Other _____ _____

       Total: Household help $_____

(j) Automotive
Year: _____ Make: _____ Personal: _____ Business: _____
Year: _____ Make: _____ Personal: _____ Business: _____
Year: _____ Make: _____ Personal: _____ Business: _____
    1. Payments _____
    2. Gas and oil _____
    3. Repairs _____
    4. Car wash _____
    5. Registration and license _____
    6. Parking and tolls _____
    7. Other _____ _____

       Total: Automotive $_____

(k) Educational
    1. Nursery and pre–school _____
    2. Primary and secondary _____
    3. College _____
    4. Post–graduate _____
    5. Religious instruction _____
    6. School transportation _____
    7. School supplies/books _____
    8. Tutoring _____
    9. School events _____
   10. Other _____ _____

       Total: Educational $_____

(l) Recreational
    1. Summer camp _____
    2. Vacations _____
    3. Movies _____

    4.   Theatre, ballet, etc.   _____
    5.   Video rentals   _____
    6.   Tapes, CD's, etc.   _____
    7.   Cable television   _____
    8.   Team sports   _____
    9.   Country club/pool club   _____
   10.   Health club   _____
   11.   Sporting goods   _____
   12.   Hobbies   _____
   13.   Music/dance lessons   _____
   14.   Sports lessons   _____
   15.   Birthday parties   _____
   16.   Other _____   _____

           Total: Recreational $_____

(m)   Income taxes
    1.   Federal   _____
    2.   State   _____
    3.   City   _____
    4.   Social Security and Medicare   _____

           Total: Income taxes $_____

(n)   Miscellaneous
    1.   Beauty parlor/barber   _____
    2.   Beauty aids/cosmetics, drug items   _____
    3.   Cigarettes/tobacco   _____
    4.   Books, magazines, newspapers   _____
    5.   Children's allowances   _____
    6.   Gifts   _____
    7.   Charitable contributions   _____
    8.   Religious organization dues   _____
    9.   Union and organization dues   _____
   10.   Commutation and transportation   _____
   11.   Veterinarian/pet expenses   _____
   12.   Child support payments
         (prior marriage)   _____
   13.   Alimony and maintenance payments
         (prior marriage)   _____
   14.   Loan payments   _____
   15.   Unreimbursed business expenses   _____

           Total: Miscellaneous $_____

(o)   Other
    1.   _____   _____
    2.   _____   _____
    3.   _____   _____
    4.   Other _____   _____

           Total: Other $_____

                   TOTAL EXPENSES: $_____

III.   GROSS INCOME: (State source of income and annual amount. Attach additional sheet, if needed.)
    (a)   Salary or wages: (State whether income has changed during the year preceding date of this affidavit _____. If so, set forth name and address of all employers during preceding year and average weekly wage paid by each. Indicate overtime earnings separately. Attach previous year's W–2 or income tax return.)

    _____   _____

    (b)   Weekly deductions:
        1.   Federal tax ....   _____
        2.   New York State tax ....   _____
        3.   Local tax ....   _____

4. Social Security .... _____
5. Medicare .... _____
6. Other payroll deductions (specify) . _____

(c) Social Security number: _____

(d) Number and names of dependents claimed: _____

(e) Bonus, commissions, fringe benefits (use of auto, memberships, etc.) .... _____

(f) Partnership, royalties, sale of assets (income and installment payments) ...... _____

(g) Dividends and interest (state whether taxable or not) .... _____

(h) Real estate (income only) .... _____

(i) Trust, profit sharing and annuities (principal distribution and income) .... _____

(j) Pension (income only) .... _____

(k) Awards, prizes, grants (state whether taxable) .... _____

(l) Bequests, legacies and gifts .... _____

(m) Income from all other sources .... _____
(including alimony, maintenance or child support from prior marriage)

(n) Tax preference items:
  1. Long term capital gain deduction _____
  2. Depreciation, amortization or depletion .... _____
  3. Stock options—excess of fair market value over amount paid .. _____

(o) If any child or other member of your household is employed, set forth name and that person's annual income ..... _____

(p) Social Security .... _____
(q) Disability benefits .... _____
(r) Public assistance .... _____
(s) Other .... _____

TOTAL INCOME: _____

IV. ASSETS: (If any asset is held jointly with spouse or another, so state, and set forth your respective shares. Attach additional sheets, if needed.)

A. Cash Accounts
Cash
1.1 a. Location _____
    b. Source of funds _____
    c. Amount _____ $_____
                          Total: Cash $_____

Checking Accounts
2.1 a. Financial institution _____
    b. Account number _____
    c. Title holder _____
    d. Date opened _____
    e. Source of funds _____
    f. Balance _____ $_____

2.2 a. Financial institution _____
    b. Account number _____
    c. Title holder _____
    d. Date opened _____
    e. Source of funds _____
    f. Balance _____ $_____
                          Total: Checking $_____

Savings accounts (including individual, joint, totten trust, certificates of deposit, treasury notes)
3.1 a. Financial institution _____
    b. Account number _____

        c.   Title holder _____
        d.   Type of account _____
        e.   Date opened _____
        f.   Source of funds _____
        g.   Balance _____ $_____

   3.2 a.   Financial institution _____
        b.   Account number _____
        c.   Title holder _____
        d.   Type of account _____
        e.   Date opened _____
        f.   Source of funds _____
        g.   Balance _____ $_____
                           Total: Savings $_____

Security deposits, earnest money, etc.
   4.1 a.   Location _____
        b.   Title owner _____
        c.   Type of deposit _____
        e.   Source of funds _____
        f.   Date of deposit _____
        g.   Amount _____ $_____
                         Total: Security
                         Deposits, etc. $_____

Other
   5.1 a.   Location _____
        b.   Title owner _____
        c.   Type of account _____
        d.   Source of funds _____
        e.   Date of deposit _____
        f.   Amount _____ $_____
                         Total: Other $_____

                      Total: Cash Accounts $_____

B. Securities
Bonds, notes, mortgages
   1.1 a.   Description of security _____
        b.   Title holder _____
        c.   Location _____
        d.   Date of acquisition _____
        e.   Original price or value _____
        f.   Source of funds to acquire _____
        g.   Current value _____ $_____
                      Total: Bonds, notes, etc. $_____

Stocks, options and commodity contracts
   2.1 a.   Description of security _____
        b.   Title holder _____
        c.   Location _____
        d.   Date of acquisition _____
        e.   Original price or value _____
        f.   Source of funds to acquire _____
        g.   Current value _____ $_____

   2.2 a.   Description of security _____
        b.   Title holder _____
        c.   Location _____
        d.   Date of acquisition _____
        e.   Original price or value _____
        f.   Source of funds to acquire _____
        g.   Current value _____ $_____

   2.3 a.   Description of security _____
        b.   Title holder _____
        c.   Location _____
        d.   Date of acquisition _____

    e.   Original price or value _____

    f.   Source of funds to acquire _____

    g.   Current value _____ $_____

           Total: Stocks, options, etc. $_____

Broker margin accounts

3.1 a.   Name and address of broker _____

     b.   Title holder _____

     c.   Date account opened _____

     d.   Original value of account _____

     e.   Source of funds _____

     f.   Current value _____ $_____

           Total: Margin accounts $_____

           Total value of securities: $_____

C. Loans to others and accounts receivable

   1.1 a.   Debtor's name and address _____

       b.   Original amount of loan or debt _____

       c.   Source of funds from which loan made

          or origin of debt _____

       d.   Date payment(s) due _____

       e.   Current amount due _____ $_____

   1.2 a.   Debtor's name and address _____

       b.   Original amount of loan or debt _____

       c.   Source of funds from which loan made

          or origin of debt _____

       d.   Date payment(s) due _____

       e.   Current amount due _____ $_____

          Total: Loans and accounts receivable $_____

D. Value of interest in any business

   1.1 a.   Name and address of business _____

       b.   Type of business (corporate, partner-

          ship, sole proprietorship or other) ____

       c.   Your capital contribution _____

       d.   Your percentage of interest _____

       e.   Date of acquisition _____

       f.   Original price or value _____

       g.   Source of funds to acquire _____

       h.   Method of valuation _____

       i.   Other relevant information _____

       j.   Current net worth of business _____ $_____

          Total: Value of business interest $_____

E. Cash surrender value of life insurance

   1.1 a.   Insurer's name and address _____

       b.   Name of insured _____

       c.   Policy number _____

       d.   Face amount of policy _____

       e.   Policy owner _____

       f.   Date of acquisition _____

       g.   Source of funding to acquire _____

       h.   Current cash surrender value _____ $_____

          Total: Value of life insurance $_____

F. Vehicles (automobile, boat, plane, truck, camper, etc.)

   1.1 a.   Description _____

       b.   Title owner _____

       c.   Date of acquisition _____

       d.   Original price _____

       e.   Source of funds to acquire _____

       f.   Amount of current lien unpaid _____

       g.   Current fair market value _____ $_____

   1.2 a.   Description _____

        b.   Title owner _____
        c.   Date of acquisition _____
        d.   Original price _____
        e.   Source of funds to acquire _____
        f.   Amount of current lien unpaid _____
        g.   Current fair market value _____ $_____
                Total: Value of Vehicles $_____

G. Real estate (including real property, leaseholds, life estates, etc. at market value—do not deduct any mortgage)
    1.1 a.   Description _____
          b.   Title owner _____
          c.   Date of acquisition _____
          d.   Original price _____
          e.   Source of funds to acquire _____
          f.   Amount of mortgage or lien unpaid ___
          g.   Estimated current market value _____ $_____

    1.2 a.   Description _____
          b.   Title owner _____
          c.   Date of acquisition _____
          d.   Original price _____
          e.   Source of funds to acquire _____
          f.   Amount of mortgage or lien unpaid ___
          g.   Estimated current market value _____ $_____

    1.3 a.   Description _____
          b.   Title owner _____
          c.   Date of acquisition _____
          d.   Original price _____
          e.   Source of funds to acquire _____
          f.   Amount of mortgage or lien unpaid ___
          g.   Estimated current market value _____ $_____
                Total: Value of real estate $_____

H. Vested interests in trusts (pension, profit sharing, legacies, deferred compensation and others)
    1.1 a.   Description of trust _____
          b.   Location of assets _____
          c.   Title owner _____
          d.   Date of acquisition _____
          e.   Original investment _____
          f.   Source of funds _____
          g.   Amount of unpaid liens _____
          h.   Current value _____ $_____

    1.2 a.   Description of trust _____
          b.   Location of assets _____
          c.   Title owner _____
          d.   Date of acquisition _____
          e.   Original investment _____
          f.   Source of funds _____
          g.   Amount of unpaid liens _____
          h.   Current value _____ $_____
                Total: Vested interest in trusts $_____

I. Contingent interests (stock options, interests subject to life estates, prospective inheritances, etc.)
    1.1 a.   Description _____
          b.   Location _____
          c.   Date of vesting _____
          d.   Title owner _____
          e.   Date of acquisition _____
          f.   Original price or value _____
          g.   Source of funds to acquire _____
          h.   Method of valuation _____
          i.   Current value _____ $_____

Total: Contingent interests $_____

J. Household furnishings
     1.1   a.   Description _____
            b.   Location _____
            c.   Title owner _____
            d.   Original price _____
            e.   Source of funds to acquire _____
            f.   Amount of lien unpaid _____
            g.   Current value _____ $_____
            Total: Household furnishings $_____

K. Jewelry, art, antiques, precious objects, gold and precious metals (only if valued at more than $500)
     1.1   a.   Description _____
            b.   Title owner _____
            c.   Location _____
            d.   Original price or value _____
            e.   Source of funds to acquire _____
            f.   Amount of lien unpaid _____
            g.   Current value _____ $_____

     1.2   a.   Description _____
            b.   Title owner _____
            c.   Location _____
            d.   Original price or value _____
            e.   Source of funds to acquire _____
            f.   Amount of lien unpaid _____
            g.   Current value _____ $_____
            Total: Jewelry, art, etc.: $_____

L. Other (e.g., tax shelter investments, collections, judgments, causes of action, patents, trademarks, copyrights, and any other asset not hereinabove itemized)
     1.1   a.   Description _____
            b.   Title owner _____
            c.   Location _____
            d.   Original price or value _____
            e.   Source of funds to acquire _____
            f.   Amount of lien unpaid _____
            g.   Current value _____ $_____

     1.2   a.   Description _____
            b.   Title owner _____
            c.   Location _____
            d.   Original price or value _____
            e.   Source of funds to acquire _____
            f.   Amount of lien unpaid _____
            g.   Current value _____ $_____
          Total: Other $_____

TOTAL: ASSETS $_____

V. LIABILITIES:

A. Accounts payable
     1.1   a.   Name and address of creditor _____
            b.   Debtor _____
            c.   Amount of original debt _____
            d.   Date of incurring debt _____
            e.   Purpose _____
            f.   Monthly or other periodic payment _____
            g.   Amount of current debt _____ $_____

     1.2   a.   Name and address of creditor _____
            b.   Debtor _____
            c.   Amount of original debt _____
            d.   Date of incurring debt _____
            e.   Purpose _____

    f.   Monthly or other periodic payment ____
    g.   Amount of current debt _____ $_____

1.3 a.   Name and address of creditor _____
     b.   Debtor _____
     c.   Amount of original debt _____
     d.   Date of incurring debt _____
     e.   Purpose _____
     f.   Monthly or other periodic payment ____
     g.   Amount of current debt _____ $_____

1.4 a.   Name and address of creditor _____
     b.   Debtor _____
     c.   Amount of original debt _____
     d.   Date of incurring debt _____
     e.   Purpose _____
     f.   Monthly or other periodic payment ____
     g.   Amount of current debt _____ $_____

1.5 a.   Name and address of creditor _____
     b.   Debtor _____
     c.   Amount of original debt _____
     d.   Date of incurring debt _____
     e.   Purpose _____
     f.   Monthly or other periodic payment ____
     g.   Amount of current debt _____ $_____

                         Total: Accounts payable $_____

B. Notes payable
   1.1 a.   Name and address of note holder ____
      b.   Debtor _____
      c.   Amount of original debt _____
      d.   Date of incurring debt _____
      e.   Purpose _____
      f.   Monthly or other periodic payment ____
      g.   Amount of current debt _____ $_____

   1.2 a.   Name and address of note holder ____
      b.   Debtor _____
      c.   Amount of original debt _____
      d.   Date of incurring debt _____
      e.   Purpose _____
      f.   Monthly or other periodic payment ____
      g.   Amount of current debt _____ $_____
              Total: Notes payable $_____

C. Installment accounts payable (security agreements, chattel mortgages)
   1.1 a.   Name and address of creditor _____
      b.   Debtor _____
      c.   Amount of original debt _____
      d.   Date of incurring debt _____
      e.   Purpose _____
      f.   Monthly or other periodic payment ____
      g.   Amount of current debt _____ $_____

   1.2 a.   Name and address of creditor _____
      b.   Debtor _____
      c.   Amount of original debt _____
      d.   Date of incurring debt _____
      e.   Purpose _____
      f.   Monthly or other periodic payment ____
      g.   Amount of current debt _____ $_____
           Total: Installment accounts $_____

D. Brokers' margin accounts
   1.1 a.   Name and address of broker _____

        b.   Amount of original debt _____
        c.   Date of incurring debt _____
        d.   Purpose _____
        e.   Monthly or other periodic payment ____
        f.   Amount of current debt _____ $_____
                  Total: Brokers' margin accounts $_____

E.   Mortgages payable on real estate
   1.1 a.   Name and address of mortgagee _____
        b.   Address of property mortgaged _____
        c.   Mortgagor(s) _____
        d.   Original debt _____
        e.   Date of incurring debt _____
        f.   Monthly or other periodic payment ____
        g.   Maturity date _____
        h.   Amount of current debt _____ $_____

   1.2 a.   Name and address of mortgagee _____
        b.   Address of property mortgaged _____
        c.   Mortgagor(s) _____
        d.   Original debt _____
        e.   Date of incurring debt _____
        f.   Monthly or other periodic payment ____
        g.   Maturity date _____
        h.   Amount of current debt _____ $_____
                  Total: Mortgages payable $_____

F.   Taxes payable
   1.1 a.   Description of tax _____
        b.   Amount of tax _____
        c.   Date due _____
                  Total: Taxes payable $_____

G.   Loans on life insurance policies
   1.1 a.   Name and address of insurer _____
        b.   Amount of loan _____
        c.   Date incurred _____
        d.   Purpose _____
        e.   Name of borrower _____
        f.   Monthly or other periodic payment ____
        g.   Amount of current debt _____ $_____
                  Total: Life insurance loans $_____

H.   Other liabilities
   1.1 a.   Description _____
        b.   Name and address of creditor _____
        c.   Debtor _____
        d.   Original amount of debt _____
        e.   Date incurred _____
        f.   Purpose _____
        g.   Monthly or other periodic payment ____
        h.   Amount of current debt _____ $_____

   1.2 a.   Description _____
        b.   Name and address of creditor _____
        c.   Debtor _____
        d.   Original amount of debt _____
        e.   Date incurred _____
        f.   Purpose _____
        g.   Monthly or other periodic payment ____
        h.   Amount of current debt _____ $_____
                  Total: Other liabilities $_____

                         TOTAL LIABILITIES: $_____

NET WORTH

TOTAL ASSETS: $_____

TOTAL LIABILITIES: (minus)   ($_____)

NET WORTH: $_____

VI.   ASSETS TRANSFERRED: (List all assets transferred in any manner during the preceding three years, or length of the marriage, whichever is shorter [transfers in the routine course of business which resulted in an exchange of assets of substantially equivalent value need not be specifically disclosed where such assets are otherwise identified in the statement of net worth]).

Description of Property	To Whom Transferred and Relationship to Transferee	Date of Transfer	Value
_____	_____	_____	_____
_____	_____	_____	_____
_____	_____	_____	_____

VII.   SUPPORT REQUIREMENTS:

(a) Deponent is at present (paying) (receiving) $_____ per (week) (month), and prior to separation (paid) (received) $_____ per (week) (month) to cover expenses for _____

These payments are being made (voluntarily) (pursuant to court order or judgment) (pursuant to separation agreement), and there are (no) arrears outstanding (in the sum of $_____ to date).

(b) Deponent requests for support of each child $_____ per (week) (month). Total for children $_____.

(c) Deponent requests for support of self $_____ per (week) (month).

(d) The day of the (week) (month) on which payment should be made is _____.

VIII.   COUNSEL FEE REQUIREMENTS:

(a) Deponent requests for counsel fee and disbursements the sum of $_____.

(b) Deponent has paid counsel the sum of $_____ and has agreed with counsel concerning fees as follows:

_____
_____
_____

(c) There is (not) a retainer agreement or written agreement relating to payment of legal fees. (A copy of any such agreement must be annexed.)

IX.   ACCOUNTANT AND APPRAISAL FEES REQUIREMENTS:

(a) Deponent requests for accountants' fees and disbursements the sum of $_____. (Include basis for fee, e.g., hourly rate, flat rate)

(b) Deponent requests for appraisal fees and disbursements the sum of $_____. (Include basis for fee, e.g., hourly rate, flat rate)

(c) Deponent requires the services of an accountant for the following reasons:

_____
_____

(d) Deponent requires the services of an appraiser for the following reasons:

_____
_____

X.   Other data concerning the financial circumstances of the parties that should be brought to the attention of the Court are:

_____
_____
_____
_____
_____

The foregoing statements and a rider consisting of _____ page(s) annexed hereto and made part hereof, have been carefully read by the undersigned who states that they are true and correct.

_____
(Petitioner)   (Respondent)
(Plaintiff)   (Defendant)

Sworn to before me this
    day of   , 19

_____

SIGNATURE OF ATTORNEY

_____

ATTORNEY'S NAME (PRINT OR TYPE)

_____

_____

_____

ATTORNEY'S ADDRESS AND TELEPHONE NUMBER

APPENDIX B.   FINDINGS OF FACT AND CONCLUSIONS OF LAW; MATRIMONIAL JUDGMENTS; REFEREE'S REPORT ON FINDINGS OF FACT AND CONCLUSIONS OF LAW; MATRIMONIAL JUDGMENT ENTERED UPON REFEREE'S REPORT

[see Uniform Rules, section 202.50(b)]

FINDINGS OF FACT AND CONCLUSIONS OF LAW

Title

The issues of this action having duly come on for hearing before me as one of the Justices of this Court at Part _____ hereof, held in and for the County of _____, on the _____ day(s) of _____, 19__, and having heard the allegations and proofs of the respective parties, and due deliberation having been had thereon

NOW, after hearing _____, Esq., attorney for the plaintiff, and _____, Esq., attorney for the defendant, I do hereby make the following findings of essential facts which I deem established by the evidence and reach the following conclusions of law.

Age of Parties—No Guardian Needed

FIRST: That plaintiff and defendant were both over the age of 18 when this action was commenced.

Age of Parties—Under Age Party

FIRST: That (plaintiff) (defendant) was over the age of 18 years when this action commenced and (defendant) (plaintiff) was then and now is under 18, to wit: _____ years of age and appears herein by _____, (parent and natural guardian) (duly appointed as guardian by order dated _____, 19__).

Residence—One Year

SECOND: That at the time of the commencement of this action and for a continuous period of at least one year immediately preceding such commencement (plaintiff) (defendant) resided in this State and (the parties were married in the State) (the parties have resided in this State as husband and wife) (the cause occurred in this State).

Residence—Two Years

SECOND: That for a continuous period of at least two years immediately preceding commencement of this action (plaintiff) (defendant) resided in this State.

Residence—No Required Time

SECOND: That at the time of the commencement of this action both plaintiff and defendant resided in this State and the cause occurred in this State.

Marriage

THIRD: That plaintiff and defendant were married on _____, 19__ in

No Children

FOURTH: That there is no issue of this marriage.

Children

FOURTH: That there are __ children (born of) (adopted by) the parties to this marriage, whose names and dates of birth are as follows:

Cruelty

FIFTH: That at the following times, none of which is earlier than five years before the date of commencement of this action, defendant committed the following acts which endangered the plaintiff's (physical) (mental) (physical and mental) well-being and rendered it (unsafe) (improper) (unsafe and improper) for plaintiff to continue to reside with defendant.

(Spell out in letter subparagraphs, the acts or omissions to act for which there is proof in the minutes).

Abandonment

FIFTH: That the defendant without cause or justification and without plaintiff's consent on the __ day of _____ 19__ abandoned plaintiff with intent not to return and has been wilfully and continuously absent from the home of the parties since

(in divorce actions add: for a period of one year prior to the commencement of this action).

Confinement to Prison

FIFTH: (a) That after the marriage of plaintiff and defendant, defendant was confined in prison for a period of three or more consecutive years, to wit: that defendant was confined in _____ prison on the __ day of _____ 19__ and remained confined until the __ day of _____ 19__; and

(b) not more than five years elapsed between the date the cause of action arose and the date of commencement of this action.

Adultery

FIFTH: (a) That on the __ day of _____ 19__ at premises _____ the defendant committed adultery with _____; and

(b) not more than five years elapsed between the date of said adultery and the date of commencement of this action.

Neglect to Support

FIFTH: (a) That defendant has (neglected) (refused) to provide for the support of plaintiff since the __ day of _____ 19__; and

(b) not more than five years elapsed between the date the cause of action arose and the date of commencement of this action.

Living Apart Under Separation Decree

FIFTH: (a) That a judgment separating the parties was entered on the __ day of _____ 19__ by the _____ Court of the State of _____; and

(b) that the parties have lived apart pursuant to said judgment for a period of one year after the granting of such judgment; and

(c) that the plaintiff has substantially performed all the terms and conditions of such judgment.

Living Apart Under Separation Agreement

FIFTH: (a) That the plaintiff and defendant entered into a written agreement of separation, which they subscribed and acknowledged on the __ day of _____ 19__ in the form required to entitle a deed to be recorded; and

(b) that the (agreement) (a memorandum of said agreement) was filed in the office of the Clerk of the County of _____, wherein (plaintiff) (defendant) resided on the __ day of _____ 19__; and

(c) that the parties have lived separate and apart for a period of one year after the execution of said agreement; and

(d) that the plaintiff has substantially performed all the terms and conditions of such agreement.

Annulment for Fraud

FIFTH: (a) That prior to the marriage of the parties the defendant represented to plaintiff that

_____

(state representation); and

(b) that said representation was false; and

(c) that said representation was made to induce plaintiff to enter into the marriage; and

(d) that plaintiff believed and relied upon said representation, and would not have entered into the marriage had the representation not been made or had plaintiff known that defendant did not intend to

_____

(refer to representation); and

(e) that defendant after the marriage refused to

_____

(refer to representation); and

(f) that plaintiff has not cohabited with defendant since discovery of the falsity of the representation; and

(g) that three years have not elapsed since discovery of the facts constituting the fraud.

(For other grounds see § 140 DRL).

Declaration of Nullity of Void Marriage

FIFTH: (a) That prior to his marriage to plaintiff and on the __ day of _____ 19__, defendant married _____ (name) in _____ (place); and

(b) that on the date of the marriage of plaintiff and defendant the marriage between defendant and _____ (name) had not been terminated by the judgment of any court; and

(c) on the date of the marriage of plaintiff and defendant, defendant's prior spouse was alive and the prior marriage of defendant was valid and subsisting.

Arrears Due Under Temporary Order

SIXTH: (a) That by order of this court (or by order of the Family Court, _____ County) dated the __ day of _____ 19__, defendant was required to pay to plaintiff as and for maintenance and child support, the sum of $_____ per week and as counsel fee, the sum of $_____; and

(b) that there became due under said order through the week of _____ 19__, the total sum of $_____, no part of which has been paid except $_____; and

(c) that defendant is in arrears under said order in the total sum of $_____ for said period.

Separate and Marital Property

SEVENTH: (a) That the following is separate property owned by plaintiff:

; and

(b) that the following is separate property owned by defendant:

; and _____

(c) that the following is marital property to be disposed of equitably pursuant to DRL § 236B(5):

(List findings required under DRL § 236B(5)(d)(1–10))

Custody

EIGHTH: That the children of the marriage now reside with (plaintiff) (defendant).

Visitation

NINTH: That the (plaintiff) (defendant) is entitled to visitation with the infant child(ren) away from the custodial residence.

Exclusive Occupancy

TENTH: That the parties hereto are the owners of premises known as _____

_____ (*P.O. address*).

Maintenance (pursuant to DRL § 236B(6))

ELEVENTH: (a) That plaintiff is (not) employed and is earning $ (net)_____ per week; and

(b) that defendant is (not) employed and is earning $ (net)_____ per week; and

(c) that (plaintiff) (defendant) now receives $_____ per _____ pursuant to an outstanding _____ Court order;

(d) that (plaintiff) (defendant) requires $_____ per week for maintenance; and

(*List findings required under DRL § 236B(6)(a)(1–10)*); and

(e) that the parties have entered into (a stipulation) (or/and agreement) dated _____ wherein (plaintiff) (defendant) agrees to accept and (plaintiff) (defendant) agrees to pay $_____ per week as maintenance and $_____ per week per child as and for child support. That the terms of the agreement were fair and reasonable at the time of the making of the agreement and are not unconscionable at the time of the entry of judgment herein.

(f) neither of the parties seeks equitable distribution of the marital property.

Child Support

TWELFTH: (a) The award of child support in accordance with DRL § 240(1–b) is based on the following findings:

(i) the children of the marriage entitled to receive parental support are: [state names and dates of birth];

(ii) the income of the plaintiff, who is the (custodial) (non-custodial) parent, is $____ per year;

(iii) the income of the defendant, who is the (custodial) (non-custodial) parent, is $____ per year;

(iv) the applicable child support percentage is ____%;

(v) the basic child support obligation is $____ per (week) (month) [plus, if applicable, expenses for child care, health care not covered by insurance, and educational or other extraordinary expenses]

(vi) the non-custodial parent's pro rata share of the basic child support obligation is calculated as follows:

A. $____ per (week) (month) representing ____% of the combined parental income under $80,000 per year; plus

B. $____ per (week) (month), representing ____% of the combined parental income over $80,000 per year;

C. ____% of future reasonable health care expenses not covered by insurance; [delete if inapplicable]

D. ____% of the reasonable child care expenses; [delete if inapplicable]

E. ____% of educational or other extraordinary expenses; [delete if inapplicable]

[1] (b) The non-custodial parent's pro rata share of the basic child support obligation is neither unjust nor inappropriate.

OR

[2] (b) Upon consideration of the following factors specified in Section 240(1–b)(f) of the Domestic Relations Law:

the non-custodial parent's pro rata share of the basic child support obligation is unjust or inappropriate in that:

OR

[3] (b) The parties have entered into a (stipulation) (agreement) dated _____ wherein (plaintiff) (defendant) agrees to pay $____ per (week) (month) for child support, such (stipulation) (agreement) reciting, in compliance with DRL § 240(1–b)(h), that:

The parties have been advised of the provisions of Section 240(1–b) of the Domestic Relations Law;

The unrepresented party, if any, has received a copy of the child support standards chart promulgated by the commissioner of Social Services pursuant to Social Services Law § 111–i;

The basic child support obligation as defined in DRL Section 240(1–b) presumptively results in the correct amount of child support to be awarded;

The basic child support obligation in this case is $_____ per ___; [plus, if applicable, expenses for child care, health care not covered by insurance, and educational or other extraordinary expenses]; and

[4] (c) The amount of child support agreed to therein conforms to the basic child support obligation.

OR

[5] (c) The amount of child support agreed to therein deviates from the basic child support obligation, and the parties' reasons for not providing that amount are

And the court having found the parties' agreement to deviate from the basic child support obligation is approved for the following reasons: [See DRL § 240(1–b)(f)]

Counsel Fees

THIRTEENTH: That the attorney for the (plaintiff) (defendant) is entitled to counsel fees.

Jurisdiction Obtained

FOURTEENTH: That jurisdiction as required by Section 230 of the Domestic Relations Law has been obtained.

Removal of Barriers to Remarriage

FIFTEENTH: That plaintiff has filed a verified statement that (he) (she) has taken all steps solely within (his) (her) power to remove all barriers to defendant's remarriage following the (annulment) (divorce).

Plaintiff Entitled to Judgment

SIXTEENTH: That plaintiff is entitled to judgment (of divorce) (of separation) (of annulment) (declaring the nullity of the marriage) and granting the incidental relief awarded (herein) (in the JUDGMENT signed this date).

Dated:

_____

Justice Supreme Court

[1] Only one of the three alternative subparagraphs (b) will be appropriate; delete the inapplicable provisions.

[2] Only one of the three alternative subparagraphs (b) will be appropriate; delete the inapplicable provisions.

[3] Only one of the three alternative subparagraphs (b) will be appropriate; delete the inapplicable provisions.

[4] Only one of the three alternative subparagraphs (b) will be appropriate; delete the inapplicable provisions.

[5] Only one of the three alternative subparagraphs (b) will be appropriate; delete the inapplicable provisions.

_____

MATRIMONIAL JUDGMENTS

Title

Nature of Action—Divorce

The plaintiff having brought this action for a judgment of absolute divorce by reason of

(Insert one or more of the following grounds:)

- the cruel and inhuman treatment of the plaintiff by the defendant
- the abandonment of the plaintiff by the defendant for a period of one or more years
- the confinement of defendant in prison for a period of three or more consecutive years after the marriage of plaintiff and defendant
- the commission by the defendant of adultery
- the plaintiff and defendant having lived apart after the granting of a judgment of separation for a period of one or more years
- the plaintiff and defendant having lived separate and apart pursuant to a written agreement for a period of one or more years

Nature of Action—Separation

The plaintiff having brought this action for a judgment of separation by reason of

(Insert one or more of the following grounds:)

- the cruel and inhuman treatment of the plaintiff by the defendant
- the abandonment of the plaintiff by the defendant
- the neglect or refusal of defendant to provide for plaintiff
- the commission by defendant of adultery
- the confinement of defendant in prison for a period of three or more consecutive years after the marriage of plaintiff and defendant

Nature of Action—Annulment

The plaintiff having brought this action for a judgment of annulment by reason of the fraud of the defendant in inducing the marriage

(for other grounds, see § 140 DRL)

Nature of Action—Declaration of the Nullity of a Void Marriage

The plaintiff having brought this action for a judgment declaring the nullity of (his) (her) marriage to the defendant by reason of the prior subsisting marriage of the defendant

Service of Process

and the summons bearing the notation ("Action for a Divorce") ("Action for a Separation") ("Action to Annul a Marriage") ("Action to Declare the Nullity of a Void Marriage") and a statement of any ancillary relief demanded having been duly served upon the defendant (personally within this State) (personally without this State by publication)

Defendant's Non-appearance

and the defendant not having appeared within the time prescribed therefor by statute, and it appearing from (non-military affidavit) (testimony given in open court) that the defendant is not in the military service of the United States

Defendant's Appearance and Non-answer

and the defendant having appeared by _____, Esq. and plaintiff's verified complaint having been duly served upon the attorney for defendant and the defendant not having answered although the time to do so has fully expired

Defendant's Appearance, Answer and Withdrawal of Answer

and the defendant having appeared by _____, Esq. and plaintiff's verified complaint having been duly served upon the attorney for defendant and the defendant having answered the complaint and having thereafter (by written stipulation) (in open court) withdrawn (his) (her) answer

Defendant's Appearance and Answer—Contested Action

and the defendant having appeared by _____, Esq. and plaintiff's verified complaint having been duly served upon the attorney for defendant and defendant having answered the complaint

Inquest Held

and the plaintiff having applied (if defendant has appeared insert: on due notice to defendant's attorney) to the court for judgment for the relief demanded in the complaint and the matter having been set down for trial on the _ day of _____ 19_, and the plaintiff having on that day appeared before me and presented written and oral proof of service and in support of the essential allegations of the complaint, and such proof having been heard and considered by me, I decide and find as stated in the separate FINDINGS OF FACT AND CONCLUSIONS OF LAW of even date herewith

Contested Trial—Non-jury

and the matter having come on for trial before me on the following days _____ and the parties having appeared before me and presented their written and oral proof, and the court having made and filed its memorandum decision dated

Contested Trial—Jury

and the matter having come on before the undersigned and a jury on the following days

_____ and the parties having presented their written and oral proof before the court and jury, and the jury having been instructed to answer each of the following questions "Yes" or "No"

　1.

　2.

and having after due deliberation, made written answers to said questions as follows:

Question 1 _____;　Question 2 _____

NOW, on motion of _____, Esq. attorney for the (plaintiff) (defendant) it is

Adjudged that the marriage between _____, plaintiff, and _____, defendant, is dissolved by reason of (State ground or grounds in the language set forth above); and it is further

Separation

Adjudged that _____, plaintiff be and (s)he hereby is separated from the bed and board of _____, defendant by reason of _____

(State ground or grounds in the language set forth above); and it is further

Annulment

Adjudged that the marriage contract heretofore existing between _____, plaintiff, and _____, defendant, is annulled because of the fraud of the defendant; and it is further

Declaration of Nullity of Void Marriage

Adjudged that the marriage entered into between _____, plaintiff, and _____, defendant, on the _ day of _____ 19_ is declared null and void because of the prior subsisting marriage of the defendant; and it is further

Custody of Children

Adjudged that (plaintiff) (defendant) is awarded custody of the infant issue of the marriage to wit:

　born _____–19_

　born _____–19_

　born _____–19_;

and it is further

Visitation

Ordered and Adjudged that (plaintiff) (defendant) may have visitation with the _____ (number) infant children away from the custodial residence during the following periods:

(a) on Saturday or Sunday of each week between the hours of _ a.m. and _ p.m., provided (defendant) (plaintiff) shall notify (defendant) (plaintiff) not later than Wednesday of each week of the day selected;

(b) on the following holiday days, between the hours of _ a.m. and _ p.m., in odd numbered years (specify holidays);

(c) on the following holiday days between the hours of _ a.m. and _ p.m., in even numbered years (specify holidays); and

(d) for a period of _ consecutive calendar weeks during the summer recess from school beginning on Sunday of the first week selected, provided (defendant) (plaintiff) shall notify (plaintiff) (defendant) not later than June 10th in each year of the particular weeks selected; and it is further

Family Court Order Continued

Ordered and Adjudged that the order made the _____ day of _____ 19_ by the Family Court of the State of New York, County of _____ in the proceeding bearing Docket number _____ is continued, and a copy of this judgment shall be served by plaintiff's attorney upon the Clerk of said Court within 10 days after the date hereof; and it is further

Findings as to Pro Rata Share

and it is further Adjudged that:

(a) The basic child support obligation in this case is $____ per ____; [plus, if applicable, expenses for child care, health care not covered by insurance, and educational or other extraordinary expenses]; and

[3] (b) The non-custodial parent's pro rata share of the basic child support obligation is neither unjust nor inappropriate.

OR

[3] (b) Upon consideration of the following factors specified in § 240(1–b)(f):

;

the non-custodial parent's pro rata share of the basic child support obligation is unjust or inappropriate in that:

;

OR

[3] (b) The parties have voluntarily agreed to child support for the child(ren) [names] ____ payable by ____ to ____ in the amount of $____ per ____, such stipulation reciting, in compliance with DRL § 240(1–b):

The parties have been advised of the provisions of DRL § 240(1–b);

The unrepresented party, if any, has received a copy of the child support standards chart promulgated by the commissioner of Social Services pursuant to Social Services Law § 111–i;

The basic child support obligation as defined in DRL § 240(1–b) presumptively results in the correct amount of child support to be awarded;

The basic child support obligation in this case is $____ per ____ [plus, if applicable, expenses for child care, health care not covered by insurance, and educational or other extraordinary expenses]; and

[4] (c) The amount of child support agreed to therein conforms to the basic child support obligation.

OR

[5] (c) The amount of child support agreed to therein deviates from the basic child support obligation, for the following reasons:

And the Court having found the parties' agreement to deviate from the basic child support obligation is approved for the following reasons: [See DRL § 240(1–b)(f)]

and it is further

Maintenance and Child Support Payable to (Plaintiff) (Defendant) Only

Ordered and Adjudged that the defendant shall pay to the (plaintiff) (third party ____) by check or money order drawn to (his) (her) order and for-

warded on ____ (day) of each week commencing with ____ (date) 19__, the first (date) after the date of this judgment, to the (plaintiff) (third party ____) at (his) (her) residence or at such other place as (he) (she) may designate in writing, the sum of $____ per week as maintenance, plus the sum of $____ per week per child for the support of the children, making a total sum of $____ per week, which total sum is inclusive of all obligations of defendant for the support and maintenance of plaintiff and the children except extraordinary medical or dental expense (*if plaintiff is awarded exclusive possession of marital premises, add:* and extraordinary repairs of marital premises; consider requirement for purchase of insurance policy); and it is further

[1] Only one of the three alternative sub-paragraphs (b) will be appropriate in each case; delete the inapplicable paragraphs.

[2] Only one of the three alternative sub-paragraphs (b) will be appropriate in each case; delete the inapplicable paragraphs.

[3] Only one of the three alternative sub-paragraphs (b) will be appropriate in each case; delete the inapplicable paragraphs.

[4] Only one of the two sub-paragraphs (c) will be appropriate to the agreement or stipulation; delete the inapplicable provisions.

[5] Only one of the two sub-paragraphs (c) will be appropriate to the agreement or stipulation; delete the inapplicable provisions.

Exclusive Possession of Real Property

Ordered and Adjudged that (plaintiff) (defendant) is awarded exclusive possession of the marital premises to wit:

(set forth either street address, or if there is no street number, the metes and bounds description) until the youngest child is 21, or sooner emancipated and (plaintiff) (defendant) shall within ____ days after service upon (him) (her) of a copy of this judgment with notice of entry remove (himself) (herself) therefrom and upon proof by affidavit of (plaintiff) (defendant) and (his) (her) attorney of (defendant's) (plaintiff's) failure to remove from said premises within the time herein provided, a writ of assistance shall issue without further notice to (defendant) (plaintiff); and it is further

Equitable Distribution

Ordered and Adjudged that the marital property shall be distributed as follows: (include disposition of property upon termination of exclusive possession of real property, if any.); and it is further

Counsel Fee

Ordered and Adjudged that the defendant shall pay to the plaintiff, by check or money order, forwarded to (him) (her) at (his) (her) (residence) (the office of (his) (her) attorney) within __ days after service upon him of a copy of this judgment with notice of entry, as and for counsel fee and expenses, the sum of $_____; and it is further

Separation Agreement or Stipulation

Ordered and Adjudged that the (separation agreement) (stipulation) entered into between the parties on the _____ day of _____ 19___, a copy of which is attached to and incorporated in this judgment by reference, shall (not survive and shall be merged) (survive and shall not be merged) in this judgment, and the parties hereby are directed to comply with every legally enforceable term and provision of such (separation agreement) (stipulation) including any provision to submit an appropriate issue to arbitration before a single arbitrator, as if such term or provision were set forth in its entirety herein, and the court retains jurisdiction of the matter concurrently with the Family Court for the purpose of specifically enforcing such of the provisions of that (separation agreement) (stipulation) as are capable of specific enforcement, to the extent permitted by law, and of making such further judgment with respect to maintenance, support, custody or visitation as it finds appropriate under the circumstances existing at the time application for that purpose is made to it, or both; and it is further

Permission to Resume Prior Surname

Ordered and Adjudged that (plaintiff) (defendant) is authorized to resume the use of her maiden name or other former surname, to wit _____; and it is further

Money Judgment for Arrears

Ordered and Adjudged that plaintiff, _____, residing at _____ recover from _____ residing at __ the sum of $_____, as arrears due under the order of this court, (Family Court, _____ County) dated _____ 19__ and that plaintiff have execution therefor.

Signature

ENTER (IN _____ COUNTY)

Justice Supreme Court

REFEREE'S REPORT—FINDINGS OF FACT AND CONCLUSIONS OF LAW

SUPREME COURT OF THE STATE OF NEW YORK

COUNTY OF
TITLE OF ACTION

Cal. No.
Index No.

Nature of Action—Divorce

The plaintiff having brought this action for a judgment of absolute divorce by reason of

(Insert one or more of the following grounds:)

- the cruel and inhuman treatment of the plaintiff by the defendant
- the abandonment of the plaintiff by the defendant for a period of one or more years
- the confinement of defendant in prison for a period of three or more consecutive years after the marriage of plaintiff and defendant
- the commission by the defendant of adultery
- the plaintiff and defendant having lived apart after the granting of a judgment of separation for a period of one or more years
- the plaintiff and defendant having lived separate and apart pursuant to a written agreement for a period of one or more years

Nature of Action—Separation

The plaintiff having brought this action for a judgment of separation by reason of

(Insert one or more of the following grounds:)

- the cruel and inhuman treatment of the plaintiff by the defendant
- the abandonment of the plaintiff by the defendant
- the neglect or refusal of defendant to provide for plaintiff
- the commission by defendant of adultery
- the confinement of defendant in prison for a period of three or more consecutive years after the marriage of plaintiff and defendant

Nature of Action—Annulment

The plaintiff having brought this action for a judgment of annulment by reason of the fraud of the defendant in inducing the marriage *(for other grounds, see § 140 DRL)*

Nature of Action—Declaration of the Nullity of a Void Marriage

The plaintiff having brought this action for a judgment declaring the nullity of (his) (her) marriage to the defendant by reason of the prior subsisting marriage of the defendant

Service of Process

and the summons bearing the notation ("Action for a Divorce") ("Action for a Separation") ("Action to Annul a Marriage") ("Action to Declare the Nullity of a Void Marriage") and a statement of any ancillary relief demanded having been duly served upon the defendant (personally within this State) (personally without this State by publication)

Defendant's Non-appearance

and the defendant not having appeared within the time prescribed therefor by statute, and it appearing from (non-military affidavit) (testimony given in open court) that the defendant is not in the military service of the United States

Defendant's Appearance and Non-answer

and the defendant having appeared by _____, Esq. and plaintiff's verified complaint having been duly served upon the attorney for defendant and the defendant not having answered although the time to do so has fully expired

Defendant's Appearance, Answer and Withdrawal of Answer

and the defendant having appeared by _____, Esq. and plaintiff's verified complaint having been duly served upon the attorney for defendant and the defendant having answered the complaint and having thereafter (by written stipulation) (in open court) withdrawn (his) (her) answer

Defendant's Appearance and Answer—Contested Action

and the defendant having appeared by _____, Esq. and plaintiff's verified complaint having been duly served upon the attorney for defendant and defendant having answered the complaint

Inquest Held

and the plaintiff having applied (*if defendant has appeared insert:* on due notice to defendant's attorney)

to the court for judgment for the relief demanded in the complaint and the matter having been set down for trial on the __ day of _____ 19__, and the plaintiff having on that day appeared before me and presented written and oral proof of service and in support of the essential allegations of the complaint, and such proof having been heard and considered by me, I decide and find as follows:

Contested Trial—Non-jury

and the matter having come on for trial before me on the following days _____ and the parties having appeared before me and presented their written and oral proof, and the court having made and filed its memorandum decision dated

Contested Trial—Jury

and the matter having come on before the undersigned and a jury on the following days _____ and

the parties having presented their written and oral proof before the court and jury, and the jury having been instructed to answer each of the following questions "Yes" or "No"

1.
2.

and having after due deliberation, made written answers to said questions as follows:

Question 1 _____; Question 2 _____

Age of Parties—No Guardian Needed

FIRST: That plaintiff and defendant were both over the age of 18 when this action was commenced.

Age of Parties—Under Age Party

FIRST: That (plaintiff) (defendant) was over the age of 18 years when this action commenced and (defendant) (plaintiff) was then and now is under 18, to wit: __ years of age and appears herein by _____, (parent and natural guardian) (duly appointed as guardian by order dated _____ 19__).

Residence—One Year

SECOND: That at the time of the commencement of this action and for a continuous period of at least one year immediately preceding such commencement (plaintiff) (defendant) resided in this State and (the parties were married in the State) (the parties have resided in this State as husband and wife) (the cause occurred in this State).

Residence—Two Years

SECOND: That for a continuous period of at least two years immediately preceding commencement of this action (plaintiff) (defendant) resided in this State.

Residence—No Required Time

SECOND: That at the time of the commencement of this action both plaintiff and defendant resided in this State and the cause occurred in this State.

Marriage

THIRD: That plaintiff and defendant were married on _____, 19__ in

No Children

FOURTH: That there is no issue of this marriage.

Children

FOURTH: That there are __ children (born of) (adopted by) the parties to this marriage, whose names and dates of birth are as follows:

Cruelty

FIFTH: That at the following times, none of which is earlier than five years before the date of commencement of this action, defendant committed the following acts which endangered the plaintiff's (physical) (mental) (physical and mental) well-being and rendered it (unsafe) (improper) (unsafe and improper) for plaintiff to continue to reside with defendant.

(*Spell out in letter subparagraphs, the acts or omissions to act for which there is proof in the minutes*).

Abandonment

FIFTH: That the defendant without cause or justification and without plaintiff's consent on the __ day of _____ 19__ abandoned plaintiff with intent not to return and has been wilfully and continuously absent from the home of the parties since (*in divorce actions add:* for a period of one year prior to the commencement of this action).

Confinement to Prison

FIFTH: (a) That after the marriage of plaintiff and defendant, defendant was confined in prison for a period of three or more consecutive years, to wit: that defendant was confined in _____ prison on the __ day of _____ 19__ and remained confined until the __ day of _____ 19__; and

(b) not more than five years elapsed between the date the cause of action arose and the date of commencement of this action.

Adultery

FIFTH: (a) That on the __ day of _____ 19__ at premises _____ the defendant committed adultery with _____; and

(b) not more than five years elapsed between the date of said adultery and the date of commencement of this action.

Neglect to Support

FIFTH: (a) That defendant has (neglected) (refused) to provide for the support of plaintiff since the __ day of _____ 19__, and has not done so; and

(b) not more than five years elapsed between the date the cause of action arose and the date of commencement of this action.

Living Apart Under Separation Decree

FIFTH: (a) That a judgment separating the parties was entered on the __ day of _____ 19__ by the _____ Court of the State of _____; and

(b) that the parties have lived apart pursuant to said judgment for a period of one year after the granting of such judgment; and

(c) that the plaintiff has substantially performed all the terms and conditions of such judgment.

Living Apart Under Separation Agreement

FIFTH: (a) That the plaintiff and defendant entered into a written agreement of separation, which they subscribed and acknowledged on the __ day of _____ 19__ in the form required to entitle a deed to be recorded; and

(b) that the (agreement) (a memorandum of said agreement) was filed in the office of the Clerk of the County of _____, wherein (plaintiff) (defendant) resides on the __ day of _____ 19__; and

(c) that the parties have lived separate and apart for a period of one year after the execution of said agreement; and

(d) that the plaintiff has substantially performed all the terms and conditions of such agreement.

Annulment for Fraud

FIFTH: (a) That prior to the marriage of the parties the defendant represented to plaintiff that _____ (*state representation*); and

(b) that said representation was false; and

(c) that said representation was made to induce plaintiff to enter into the marriage; and

(d) that plaintiff believed and relied upon said representation, and would not have entered into the marriage had the representation not been made or had plaintiff known that defendant did not intend to _____ (*refer to representation*); and

(e) that defendant after the marriage refused to (*refer to representation*); and

(f) that plaintiff has not cohabited with defendant since discovery of the falsity of the representation; and

(g) that three years have not elapsed since discovery of the facts constituting the fraud.

(for other grounds see § 140 DRL).

Declaration of Nullity of Void Marriage

FIFTH: (a) That prior to the marriage to plaintiff and on the __ day of _____ 19__, defendant married _____ (name) in _____ (place); and

(b) that on the date of the marriage of plaintiff and defendant the marriage between defendant and _____ (name) had not been terminated by the judgment of any court; and

(c) on the date of the marriage of plaintiff and defendant, defendant's prior spouse was alive and the prior marriage of defendant was valid and subsisting.

Arrears Due Under Temporary Order

SIXTH: (a) That by order of this court (or by order of the Family Court, _____ County) dated the __ day of _____ 19__, defendant was required to pay to plaintiff as and for maintenance and child support, the sum of $_____ per week and as counsel fee, the sum of $_____; and

(b) that there became due under said order through the week of _____ 19__, the total sum of $_____, no part of which has been paid except $_____; and

(c) that defendant is in arrears under said order in the total sum of $_____ for said period.

Separate and Marital Property

SEVENTH: (a) That the following is separate property owned by plaintiff: _____; and

(b) that the following is separate property owned by defendant:

_____

_____; and

(c) that the following is marital property to be disposed of equitably pursuant to DRL § 236B(5):

(*List findings required under DRL § 236(5)(d)(1–10)*)

Custody

EIGHTH: That the children of the marriage now reside with (plaintiff) (defendant).

Visitation

NINTH: That the (plaintiff) (defendant) is entitled to visitation with the infant child(ren) away from the custodial residence.

Exclusive Occupancy

TENTH: That the parties hereto are the owners of premises known as _____

(*P.O. address*).

Maintenance (pursuant to DRL § 236B(6))

ELEVENTH: (a) That plaintiff is (not) employed and is earning $_____ (net) per week; and

(b) that defendant is (not) employed and is earning $_____ (net) per week; and

(c) that (plaintiff) (defendant) now receives $_____ per _____ pursuant to an outstanding Court order; and

(d) that (plaintiff) (defendant) now requires $_____ per week for maintenance; and

(*List findings required under DRL § 236B(6)(a)(1–10)*); and

(e) that the parties have entered into (a stipulation) (or/and agreement) dated _____ wherein (plaintiff) (defendant) agrees to accept and (plaintiff) (defendant) agrees to pay $_____ per week as maintenance and $_____ per week per child as and for child support. That the terms of the agreement were fair and reasonable at the time of the making of the agreement and are not unconscionable at the time of the entry of judgment herein.

(f) Neither of the parties seeks equitable distribution of the marital property.

Child Support

TWELFTH: (a) The award of child support in accordance with DRL § 240(1–b) is based on the following findings:

(i) the children of the marriage entitled to receive parental support are: [state names and dates of birth];

(ii) the income of the plaintiff, who is the (custodial) (non-custodial) parent, is $____ per year;

(iii) the income of the defendant, who is the (custodial) (non-custodial) parent, is $____ per year;

(iv) the applicable child support percentage is ____%;

(v) the basic child support obligation is $____ per (week) (month) [plus, if applicable, expenses for child care, health care not covered by insurance, and educational or other extraordinary expenses]

(vi) the non-custodial parent's pro rata share of the basic child support obligation is calculated as follows:

A. $____ per (week) (month) representing ____% of the combined parental income under $80,000 per year; plus

B. $____ per (week) (month), representing ____% of the combined parental income over $80,000 per year;

C. ____% of future reasonable health care expenses not covered by insurance; [delete if inapplicable]

D. ____% of the reasonable child care expenses; [delete if inapplicable]

E. ____% of educational or other extraordinary expenses; [delete if inapplicable]

[1] (b) The non-custodial parent's pro rata share of the basic child support obligation is neither unjust nor inappropriate.

OR

[2] (b) Upon consideration of the following factors specified in Section 140(1–b)(f) of the Domestic Relations Law:

the non-custodial parent's pro rata share of the basic child support obligation is unjust or inappropriate in that:

                                                        ;

OR

[3] (b) The parties have entered into a (stipulation) (agreement) dated _____ wherein (plaintiff) (defendant) agrees to pay $____ per (week) (month) for child support, such (stipulation) (agreement) reciting, in compliance with DRL § 240(1–b)(h), that:

The parties have been advised of the provisions of Section 240(1–b) of the Domestic Relations Law;

The unrepresented party, if any, has received a copy of the child support standards chart promulgated by the commissioner of Social Services pursuant to Social Services Law § 111–i;

The basic child support obligation as defined in DRL Section 240(1–b) presumptively results in the correct amount of child support to be awarded;

The basic child support obligation in this case is $____ per ____; [plus, if applicable, expenses for child care, health care not covered by insurance, and educational or other extraordinary expenses]; and

[4] (c) The amount of child support agreed to therein conforms to the basic child support obligation.

OR

[5] (c) The amount of child support agreed to therein deviates from the basic child support obligation, and the parties' reasons for not providing that amount are

_____ ;

And the court having found the parties' agreement to deviate from the basic child support obligation is approved for the following reasons: [See DRL § 240(1–b)(f)]

Counsel Fees

THIRTEENTH: That the attorney for the (plaintiff) (defendant) is entitled to counsel fees.

Jurisdiction Obtained

FOURTEENTH: That jurisdiction as required by Section 230 of the Domestic Relations Law has been obtained.

FIFTEENTH: That plaintiff has filed a verified statement that (he) (she) has taken all steps solely within (his) (her) power to remove all barriers to defendant's remarriage following the (annulment) (divorce).

Plaintiff Entitled to Judgment

SIXTEENTH: That plaintiff is entitled to judgment (of divorce) (of separation) (of annulment) (declaring the nullity of the marriage) and granting the incidental relief awarded (herein) (in the JUDGMENT signed this date).

Dated_____: New York, New York

_____ day of _____, 19__.

_____
_____ Referee

[1] Only one of the three alternative subparagraphs (b) will be appropriate; delete the inapplicable provisions.

[2] Only one of the three alternative subparagraphs (b) will be appropriate; delete the inapplicable provisions.

[3] Only one of the three alternative subparagraphs (b) will be appropriate; delete the inapplicable provisions.

[4] Only one of the two alternative subparagraphs (c) will be appropriate; delete the inapplicable provisions.

[5] Only one of the two alternative subparagraphs (c) will be appropriate; delete the inapplicable provisions.

_____

MATRIMONIAL JUDGMENT ENTERED UPON REFEREE'S REPORT

> At the Supreme Court, _____ County, held at the courthouse at _____, New York, on the _____ day of _____, 19__.

PRESENT:

HON. (Justice Supreme Court)

TITLE OF ACTION

The issues in this action having been referred to a referee to hear and report, and the referee having submitted his report,

NOW, on motion of _____, Esq., attorney for the (plaintiff) (defendant), it is

ORDERED, that the Referee's Report is confirmed; and it is further

Adjudged that the marriage between _____, plaintiff, and _____, defendant, is dissolved by reason of _____ (*State ground or grounds in the language set forth above*); and it is further

Separation

Adjudged that _____, plaintiff be and (s)he hereby is separated from the bed and board of _____, defendant by reason of _____ (*State ground or grounds in the language set forth above*); and it is further

Annulment

Adjudged that the marriage contract heretofore existing between _____, plaintiff, and _____, defendant, is annulled because of the fraud of the defendant; and it is further

Declaration of Nullity of Void Marriage

Adjudged that the marriage entered into between _____, plaintiff, and _____, defendant, on the __ day of _____ 19__ is declared null and void because of the prior subsisting marriage of the defendant; and it is further

Custody of Children

Adjudged that (plaintiff) (defendant) is awarded custody of the infant issue of the marriage to wit:

born _____ 19__

born _____ 19__

born _____ 19__

and it is further

Visitation

Ordered and Adjudged that (plaintiff) (defendant) may have visitation with the _____ (number) infant children away from the custodial residence during the following periods:

(a) on Saturday or Sunday of each week between the hours of __ a.m. and __ p.m., provided (defendant) (plaintiff) shall notify (defendant) (plaintiff) not later than Wednesday of each week of the day selected;

(b) on the following holiday days, between the hours of __ a.m. and __ p.m., in odd numbered years (*specify holidays*);

(c) on the following holiday days between the hours of __ a.m. and __ p.m. in even numbered years (*specify holidays*); and

(d) for a period of __ consecutive calendar weeks during the summer recess from school beginning on Sunday of the first week selected, provided (defendant) (plaintiff) (defendant) not later than June 10th in each year of the particular weeks selected; and it is further

Family Court Order Continued

Ordered and Adjudged that the order made the __ day of _____ 19__ by the Family Court of the State of New York, County of _____ in the proceeding bearing Docket number _____ is continued, and a copy of this judgment shall be served by plaintiff's attorney upon the Clerk of said Court within 10 days after the date hereof; and it is further

Findings as to Pro Rata Share

and it is further Adjudged that:

(a) The basic child support obligation in this case is $____ per ____; [plus, if applicable, expenses for child care, health care not covered by insurance, and educational or other extraordinary expenses]; and

[1] (b) The non-custodial parent's pro rata share of the basic child support obligation is neither unjust nor inappropriate.

OR

[2] (b) Upon consideration of the following factors specified in Section 240(1–b)(f):

the non-custodial parent's pro rata share of the basic child support obligation is unjust or inappropriate in that:

;

OR

[3] (b) The parties have voluntarily agreed to child support for the child(ren) [names] _____ payable by _____ to _____ in the amount of $____ per ____, such stipulation reciting, in compliance with DRL § 240(1–b):

The parties have been advised of the provisions of D.R.L. § 240(1–b);

The unrepresented party, if any, has received a copy of the child support standards chart promulgated by the Commissioner of Social Services pursuant to Social Services Law § 111–i;

The basic child support obligation in this case is $____ per ____; and

basic child support obligation as defined in DRL § 240(1–b) presumptively results in the correct amount of child support to be awarded;

The basic child support obligation in this case is $____ per ____ [plus, if applicable, expenses for child care, health care not covered by insurance, and educational or other extraordinary expenses]; and

[4] (c) The amount of child support agreed to therein conforms to the basic child support obligation.

OR

[5] (c) The amount of child support agreed to therein deviates from the basic child support obligation, for the following reasons:

And the Court having found the parties' agreement to deviate from the basic child support obligation is approved for the following reasons: [See DRL § 240(1–b)(f)]

and it is further

Maintenance and Child Support Payable to (Plaintiff) (Defendant) Only

Ordered and Adjudged that the defendant shall pay to the (plaintiff) (third party _____) by check or money order drawn to (his) (her) order and forwarded on _____ (day) of each week commencing with _____ (date) 19__, the first _____ (date) after the date of this judgment, to (the plaintiff) (third _____ party) at (his) (her) residence or at such other place as (he) (she) may designate in writing, the sum of $_____ per week as maintenance, plus the sum of $_____ per week per child for the support of the children, making a total sum of $_____ per week, which sum is inclusive of all obligations of defendant for the support and maintenance of plaintiff and the children except extraordinary medical or dental expense

(*if plaintiff is awarded exclusive possession of marital premises, add*: and extraordinary repairs of marital premises; consider requirement for purchase of insurance policy); and it is further

Exclusive Possession of Real Property

Ordered and Adjudged that (plaintiff) (defendant) is awarded exclusive possession of the marital premises to wit:

(*set forth either street address, or if there is no street number, the metes and bounds description*) until the youngest child is 21, or sooner emancipated and (plaintiff) (defendant) shall within __ days after service upon (him) (her) of a copy of this judgment with notice of entry remove (himself) (herself) therefrom and upon proof by affidavit of (plaintiff) (defendant) and (his) (her) attorney of (defendant's) (plaintiff's) failure to remove from said premises within the time herein provided, a writ of assistance shall issue without further notice to (defendant) (plaintiff); and it is further

Equitable Distribution

Ordered and Adjudged that the marital property shall be distributed as follows:

(*include disposition of property upon termination of exclusive possession of real property, if any*); and it is further

Counsel Fee

Ordered and Adjudged that the defendant shall pay to the plaintiff, by check or money order, forwarded to (him) (her) at (his) (her) (residence) (the office of (his) (her) attorney) within __ days after service upon him of a copy of this judgment with notice of entry, as and for counsel fee and expenses, the sum of $_____; and it is further

Separation Agreement or Stipulation

Ordered and Adjudged that the (separation agreement) (stipulation) entered into between the parties on the _____ day of _____, 19__, a copy of which is attached to and incorporated in this judgment by reference, shall (not survive and shall be merged) (survive and shall not be merged) in this judgment, and the parties hereby are directed to comply with every legally enforceable term and provision of such (separation agreement) (stipulation) including any provision to submit an appropriate issue to arbitration before a single arbitrator, as if such term or provision were set forth in its entirety herein, and the court retains jurisdiction of the matter concurrently with the Family Court for the purpose of specifically enforcing such of the provisions of that (separation agreement) (stipula-

tion) as are capable of specific enforcement, to the extent permitted by law, and of making such further judgment with respect to maintenance, support, custody or visitation as it finds appropriate under the circumstances existing at the time application for that purpose is made to it, or both; and it is further

Permission to Resume Prior Surname

Ordered and Adjudged that (plaintiff) (defendant) is authorized to resume the use of her maiden name or other former surname, to wit _____; and it is further

Money Judgment for Arrears

Ordered and Adjudged that plaintiff, _____, residing at _____ recover from _____ residing at _____, the sum of $_____, as arrears due under the order of this court, (Family Court, _____ County) dated _____ 19__ and that plaintiff have execution therefor.

Signature

ENTER (IN _____ COUNTY)

Justice Supreme Court

[1] Only one of the alternative subparagraphs (b) will be appropriate in each case; delete the inapplicable provisions.

[2] Only one of the alternative subparagraphs (b) will be appropriate in each case; delete the inapplicable provisions.

[3] Only one of the alternative subparagraphs (b) will be appropriate in each case; delete the inapplicable provisions.

[4] Only one of the two subparagraphs (c) will be appropriate to the agreement or stipulation; delete the inapplicable provisions.

[5] Only one of the two sub-paragraphs (c) will be appropriate to the agreement or stipulation; delete the inapplicable provisions.

APPENDIX C. FORMS FOR USE IN COMMERCIAL CLAIMS
PROCEEDINGS IN CITY COURTS AND DISTRICT COURTS
[see Uniform Rules, §§ 210.41–a, 212.41–a]

APPLICATION TO FILE CLAIM   UCS–119 (Rev. 11/90)

FOR CLERK'S USE ONLY

State of New York
_____ Court of _____

Notice was mailed on
_____ day of _____, 19____
to _____
_____
(Address of Defendant)
Date of delivery _____
Home address of person
who signed receipt _____
_____
(from the receipt form)

Application:

Small Claim   _____
Commercial Claim   _____
Commercial Claim   _____
(Consumer Transaction)

Filing Fee:
  Small Claim   – $ 3.00 + postage
  Commercial Claim   – $20.00 + postage
Dated _____
Name of Claimant _____
Address (if commercial claim, give Principal Office Address)
_____
Telephone_____
                —against—
Name of Defendant _____
Address (Home or Bus./Place of Employment) _____
_____

COMPLETE THIS SECTION FOR COMMERCIAL CLAIM
[See next page for commercial claim arising from a consumer transaction]
*CERTIFICATION: (NYCCA 1803–A; UCCA 1803–A; UDCA 1803–A)
 I hereby certify that no more than five (5) actions or proceedings (including the
instant action or proceeding) pursuant to the commercial claims procedure have been
initiated in the courts of this State during the present calendar month.

_____
Signature of Claimant

_____
Signature of Notary/Clerk/Judge

*NOTE: The commercial claims part will dismiss any case where this certification is not
made.

UCS–119 (Rev. 11/90)

—COMPLETE THIS SECTION FOR COMMERCIAL CLAIM— ARISING OUT OF A CONSUMER TRANSACTION

*Certification: (NYCCA 1803–A; UCCA 1803–A; UDCA 1803–A)

I hereby certify that I have mailed a demand letter by ordinary first class mail to the party complained against, no less than ten (10) days and no more than one hundred eighty (180) days before I commenced this claim.

I hereby certify, based upon information and belief, that no more than five (5) actions or proceedings (including the instant action or proceeding) pursuant to the commercial claims procedure have been initiated in the courts of this State during the present calendar month.

_____
Signature of Claimant

_____
Signature of Notary/Clerk/Judge

*NOTE: The commercial claims part will not allow your action to proceed if this certification is not made and properly completed.

UCS–120 (Rev. 11/90)

Notification of Commercial Claims Judgment

_____ Court   of _____ C.C.# _____

Re: Claimant _____

vs.

Defendant _____

DECISION:

After Trial/Inquest, the decision in the above action is as follows:

A.___ Judgment in favor of Claimant.   B.___ Judgment in Favor of Defendant dismissing claim. No monetary award. (Information below and on the reverse side is not applicable.)

Award amount . . . .$_____
Interest . . . .$_____
Costs . . . .$_____
Disbursements . . . .$_____
TOTAL JUDGMENT . . . .$_____
(See information below and on reverse for details).

Date _____ By: _____
                                                              Judge/Arbitrator

INFORMATION FOR THE JUDGMENT CREDITOR
(the party in whose favor a money judgment has been entered)

1. Contact the judgment debtor (either the party you sued or that party's attorney if the party was represented by an attorney) and request payment directly.

2. If the judgment debtor fails to pay within 30 days, then contact (by phone or in person) either a City Marshal or the Sheriff in the County where the judgment debtor (the party who owes you money) may have property. If you do not know where the judgment debtor has property, then you must contact a City Marshal or the Sheriff in the County where the judgment debtor resides.

3. Be prepared to provide the City Marshal or the Sheriff with the following information:
    a) The CC# of your case, which appears above, including the year and the county in which the case was tried.
    b) Your name, address and telephone number.
    c) The name and address of the judgment debtor.
    d) Your knowledge, if any, of the name and address of the judgment debtor's employer.

Fees paid by you (the judgment creditor) to the City Marshal or to the Sheriff in an attempt to collect the judgment will be added to the total judgment.

4. In addition to these rights, a judgment creditor may:

    a) request the issuance by the Commercial Claims Clerk, at nominal cost, of information subpoenas where a judgment remains unsatisfied for 30 days;
    b) bring an action to recover an unpaid judgment through the sale of the judgment debtor's real or personal property;
    c) bring an action to recover an unpaid judgment through suspension of the judgment debtor's motor vehicle license and registration, if the underlying claim is based on the debtor's ownership or operation of a motor vehicle; and
    d) notify the appropriate state or local licensing authority of an unsatisfied judgment as a basis for possible revocation, suspension, or denial or renewal of a business license.

THE JUDGMENT IS VALID FOR A PERIOD OF 20 YEARS, IF THE JUDGMENT IS NOT COLLECTED UPON THE FIRST ATTEMPT, FURTHER ATTEMPTS TO COLLECT MAY BE MADE AT A LATER DATE.

INFORMATION FOR THE JUDGMENT DEBTOR

(the party against whom a money judgment has been entered)

YOU HAVE A LEGAL OBLIGATION TO PAY THIS JUDGMENT.

Your failure to pay the judgment may subject you to any one or a combination of the following:

    a) garnishment of wages;

    b) garnishment of bank accounts;

    c) a lien on real and/or personal property;

    d) seizure and sale of real property;

    e) seizure and sale of personal property, including automobiles;

    f) suspension of motor vehicle license and registration, if claim is based on judgment debtor's ownership or operation of a motor vehicle; and

    g) revocation, suspension, or denial or renewal of any applicable business license or permit.

THE JUDGMENT IS VALID FOR A PERIOD OF 20 YEARS. IF THE JUDGMENT IS NOT COLLECTED UPON THE FIRST ATTEMPT, FURTHER ATTEMPTS TO COLLECT MAY BE MADE AT A LATER DATE.

SPECIAL INFORMATION REGARDING DEFAULT JUDGMENTS

If you did not appear in court on the day the trial was held, you are a defaulting party. A judgment may have been taken against you even though you were not in court. If that is so, you may apply to the court in writing and ask to have the default judgment opened. You must give the judge a reasonable excuse for your failure to appear in court. The judge may open your default judgment and give you another chance to go to court.

UCS–124 (Rev. 11/90)

Commercial Claim Arising Out of a Consumer Transaction

DEMAND LETTER

To: _____   Date:
    Name of Defendant

_____

_____

_____
Address

    You have not paid a debt owed _____,
which you incurred on _____, 199___. The amount
remaining unpaid on the debt is $_____. Demand is hereby made that this
money be paid. Unless payment of this amount is received by the undersigned no later
than _____, 199___, a lawsuit will be brought against you in the Commercial Claims Part of the Court.

    If a lawsuit is brought, you will be notified of the hearing date, and you will be entitled
to appear at the hearing and present any defense you may have to this claim.

    (If applicable) Our records show that you have made the following payment in partial
satisfaction of this debt (fill in dates and amounts paid) _____.

    A copy of the original debt instrument—your agreement to pay—is attached. [The
names and addresses of the parties to that original debt agreement are _____
_____
_____

(to be completed if claimant was not a party to the original transaction)].

_____

_____

_____
Typed or Printed Name and Address
of Claimant

UCS 122 (Rev. 11/90)

Important information for Defendants About the Commercial Claims Court *
Información importante para demandados en la Commercial Claims Court *

The Notice of Claim is the Start of a lawsuit against you. It should not be ignored! The person suing you is the claimant; you are the defendant. Carefully read the Notice of Claim for more information about the lawsuit.

The Commercial Claims Court is an informal court where corporations, partnerships and associations can sue for money only, up to $2,000 without a lawyer. If you have questions about court procedures, contact the clerk of the court or go to the court and pick up a copy of the Commercial Claims Guide. If you are being sued as a result of a consumer transaction, you should have received a letter demanding payment before you received the Notice of Claim. Notify the Court if you did not get the letter.

You MUST go to court on the date specified in the Notice of Claim. If you wish, you may be represented by an attorney at your own expense. If you need an adjournment, call the clerk of the court for information. Note that if you do not have a good excuse, your request will be denied. If the hearing is scheduled in the day, you may request an evening hearing. You also may ask for a jury trial.

If you do not go to the court or do not get an adjournment, a default judgment may be entered against you. If you do not pay it, the claimant may have the Marshal or Sheriff seize certain of your property and sell it to satisfy the judgment, or, if you work, have a portion or your salary turned over to the claimant until the judgment is paid. The claimant also may obtain a restraining order tying up your bank account.

If you have a claim against the claimant, you may bring a "counterclaim" as part of the lawsuit, for money only, up to $2,000. You must inform the court of your counterclaim, and you must be prepared to prove it on the day you go to court.

If you believe a third party is responsible for the claim, you may be able to bring that party into the lawsuit as a defendant. Contact the clerk of the Commercial Claims Court for information about a "third-party action".

When you go to court on the day set for the trial, be prepared for a simple, informal hearing. Bring any evidence necessary to prove your defense, such as photographs, a written agreement, an itemized bill marked "paid", receipts, cancelled checks, etc. If you rely on estimates, two different written estimates of the costs of repairs or services are required. If possible, merchandise that is in dispute should be brought to court. Testimony, including your own, is evidence. Any other witness also may testify. You may have to pay an expert witness for his or her time. If a witness is unwilling to appear voluntarily, you may contact the clerk for information about getting a subpoena.

If you choose arbitration, the hearing will be the same, but it will be held before an arbitrator and no appeal will be allowed.

You may try to end the lawsuit before the court date by offering claimant settlement.

* This information is available in Spanish upon request to the clerk of the court.
* Esta información está disponible en español. Solicítela al secretario de la corte.

UCS 122 (Rev. 11/90)

Información importante para demandados en la Commercial Claims Court (Corte de Reclamaciones Comerciales)

El Aviso de Reclamación es el inicio de un juicio contra usted. Tómelo muy en cuenta! La persona que entabla un juicio contra usted es el demandante; usted es el demandado. Lea el Aviso de Reclamación con cuidado para obtener mayor información acerca del juicio.

La Corte de Reclamaciones Comerciales es un tribunal informal creado para que las sociedades, compañías y asociaciones puedan entablar demandas únicamente por dinero y hasta por la suma de $2000, sin necesidad de contratar a un abogado. Si tiene cualquier duda acerca de los trámites de la corte, comuníquese con el secretario de la corte o vaya personalmente para conseguir un ejemplar de la Guía de Reclamaciones Comerciales. Si le han entablado un juicio como consecuencia de una venta al consumidor, usted debe haber recibido una carta exigiendo el pago antes de haber recibido el Aviso de Reclamación. Si no recibió dicha carta, avise a la corte de ese hecho.

Usted TIENE LA OBLIGACIÓN de presentarse en la corte en la fecha indicada en el Aviso de Reclamación. Si desea, puede hacerse representar por un abogado por su propia cuenta y cargo. Si necesita un aplazamiento, llame al secretario de la corte para que le dé la información correspondiente. Tenga en cuenta que si no tiene una buena disculpa, su solicitud le será denegada. Si la audiencia está programada para horas del día, usted puede solicitar una audiencia nocturna. También tiene derecho de pedir un juicio por jurado.

Si usted no se presenta en la corte o si no consigue aplazamiento, se podría fallar en su contra por negligencia. Si usted no paga, el demandante puede tomar medidas para que el alguacil o márshal confisque ciertos bienes suyos y los venda para satisfacer el fallo, o -si usted está empleado- para que se entregue parte de su sueldo al demandante hasta satisfacer el fallo. El demandante también podrá obtener un juicio de amparo para paralizar su cuenta bancaria.

Si usted tiene alguna reclamación contra el demandante, puede entablar una "contrademanda" como parte del juicio, únicamente por dinero y hasta por una suma de hasta $2000. Es necesario que usted notifique a la corte acerca su contrademanda y que esté preparado a comprobarla en la fecha señalada para presentarse en la corte.

Si usted tiene motivos para creer que hay terceros responsables por la reclamación, puede incluirlos en el juicio como demandante. Comuníquese con el secretario de la Corte de Reclamaciones Comerciales para conseguir información acerca de una "acción de demanda contra terceros".

Cuando se presente en la corte en la fecha señalada para el juicio, venga preparado para una audiencia sencilla y de carácter informal. Traiga cualquier evidencia que sea necesaria para su defensa como, por ejemplo, fotograffas, un acuerdo escrito, una cuenta pormenorizada marcada "pagada", recibos, cheques cancelados, etc. Si usted va a usar como evidencia cálculos estimativos sobre el costo de un servicio, se requieren dos avalúos por escrito en los que conste el costo de los arreglos o servicios prestados. En lo posible, se recomienda que traiga a la corte la mercancía objeto del litigio. Un testimonio, inclusive el suyo propio, constituye una evidencia. También puede prestar testimonio cualquier otro testigo. Es posible que tenga que pagar a un testigo perito por el tiempo que necesite para prestar testimonio. Si algún testigo no está dispuesto a presentarse por su propia voluntad, usted puede comunicarse con el secretario para informarse de cómo emplazarlo.

Si usted prefiere el arbitraje, la audiencia será la misma, pero se realizará en la presencia de un árbitro y no se admitirá recurso de apelación.

Usted puede intentar evitar un juicio antes de la fecha señalada para la audiencia ofreciendo al demandante un arreglo.

UCS–121 (Rev. 11/90)

Transcript of Judgment
Index No. _____

State of New York, _____ Court of _____,
County of _____

Type of proceeding: Civil _____ Summary _____ Small Claim _____
Commercial Claim _____ Commercial Claim (Consumer Transaction) _____

1) _____   1) _____
2) _____   VS   2) _____
3) _____   3) _____
4) _____   4) _____

First paper filed _____ Notice of Trial filed _____
Jury _____ Waived _____ Demanded by _____
Amount sued for _____ Arbitration _____ Non–Arbitration _____
Disposition _____

Date of disposition _____   Date of appeal _____
Attorney for Plaintiff   Attorney for Defendant
Name _____   Name _____
Address _____   Address _____

Phone No. _____   Phone No. _____
Remarks _____

Trade or profession of Judgment Debtor _____
Last known address of Judgment Debtor _____
Address of Judgment Creditor _____
Terms _____

$_____, plus $_____ Court Costs $_____
Judgment rendered _____ (date)
Judgment docketed _____ (date) _____ hr. and min.
Clerk's signature _____ (date) _____
Execution issued on _____ Return satisfied on _____

Remarks (date and manner of change of status of judgment) _____
_____
_____

State of New York
County of _____
(seal)

I, _____ (Clerk, Judge or Justice) of the court named above, hereby
certify that the above is a correct transcript from the docket of judgment in my office.

Satisfaction of judgment on _____. Indicate how and to what extent _____
Clerk's signature _____ (date) _____

APPENDIX D(1).   PRELIMINARY CONFERENCE STIPULATION AND ORDER

SUPREME COURT, COUNTY OF _____ INDIVIDUAL
ASSIGNMENT PART [OR JUSTICE] _____

_____)	INDEX NO. _____
)	
Plaintiff(s),)	PRELIMINARY CONFERENCE
)	STIPULATION AND ORDER
-against-)	(Sections 202.8 and
)	202.12 of the Uniform Rules)
Defendant(s).)	
_____)	

[All items on the form must be completed unless inapplicable.]

It is hereby STIPULATED and ORDERED that disclosure shall proceed as follows:

(1) Insurance Coverage (CPLR 3101(f)): If not already provided, shall be furnished by _____ on or before _____.

(2) Bill of Particulars:

(a) Demand for a bill of particulars shall be served by _____ on or before _____.

(b) Bill of particulars shall be served by _____ on or before _____.

(3) Medical Reports and Authorizations:

Shall be served as follows: _____
                                        _____
                                        _____
                                        _____

(4) Physical Examination:

(a) Examination of _____ shall be held _____
_____

(b) A copy of the physician's report shall be furnished to plaintiff(s) within _____days of the examination.

(5) Depositions: Choose (a) or (b)

(a)

Deponent	Date and Time	Place
_____	_____	_____
_____	_____	_____
_____	_____	_____
_____	_____	_____

[Attach additional sheet if necessary]

(b) The parties shall set a schedule for depositions to be held no later than _____and shall provide the court with the schedule.

Optional:

☐ If one deposition fails to take place as scheduled, the remaining parties' depositions shall nonetheless proceed as scheduled, except that priorities between defendants and plaintiffs shall be preserved.

(6) Other Disclosure:

(a) All parties, on or before _____, shall exchange names and addresses of all eyewitnesses and notice witnesses, statements of opposing parties and photographs, or, if none, provide an affirmation to that effect.

(b) Authorizations for plaintiff(s)' employment records for the period _____ shall be furnished on or before _____.

(c) Demand for discovery and inspection shall be served by _____ on or before _____. The items sought shall be produced to the extent not objected to, and objections, if any, shall be stated on or before _____.

(d) Accident reports prepared in the regular course of business shall be exchanged pursuant to CPLR 3101 (g) by _____.

(e) Other (interrogatories (CPLR 3130), etc.):_____
_____
_____
_____.

All such disclosure, unless otherwise noted herein, shall be completed by _____.

(f) Plaintiff shall provide authorizations for the following collateral source providers (CPLR 4545) within _____ days:
_____
_____
_____
_____.

(7) Impleader Motion(s) to amend the pleadings, or to add parties: Shall be completed on or before _____.

(8) Compliance conference: Shall be held on _____.

(9) End Date for All Disclosure, other than expert disclosure [must be within 12 months, or 15 months for a complex case]: _____.

(10) Expert Disclosure:

Plaintiff(s) shall provide expert disclosure by _____.

Defendant(s) shall provide expert disclosure by _____.

(11) Motions: Any dispositive motion(s) (CPLR 3211 and 3212) shall be made on or before _____.

(12) Note of Issue: _____ shall file a note of issue/certificate of readiness on or before _____. A copy of the stipulation and order, an affirmation stating that the terms of the stipulation and order have been complied with, and an affidavit of service of the affirmation and note of issue shall be served and filed with the note of issue on or before said date.

(13) The parties shall ensure that a stipulation of discontinuance shall be promptly filed if the case settles before the next meeting with the Court.

Failure to comply with any of these directions may result in the imposition of costs or sanctions or other action authorized by law.

_____
Attorney for Plaintiff(s)

_____
Attorney for Defendant(s)

Dated:

SO ORDERED:

_____
J.S.C.

ADDITIONAL DIRECTIVES

In addition to the directives set forth on the annexed pages, it is further ORDERED as follows:

_____

_____

_____

_____

_____

_____

_____

_____

_____

_____

_____

_____

_____

Dated:

SO ORDERED:

_____
      J.S.C.

APPENDIX D(2). PRELIMINARY CONFERENCE STIPULATION AND ORDER FOR COMMERCIAL CASES

SUPREME COURT, COUNTY OF_____ INDIVIDUAL
ASSIGNMENT PART [OR JUSTICE]_____

```
_____)
                                 )
                                 )
                                 )  Index No.
            Plaintiff(s)         )
                                 )  PRELIMINARY CONFERENCE
        -against-                )  STIPULATION AND ORDER
                                 )  FOR COMMERCIAL CASES
                                 )  (Section 202.8 and 202.12 of the
                                 )  the Uniform Rules)
                                 )
            Defendant(s).        )
_____)
```

[All items on the form must be completed unless inapplicable.]

It is hereby STIPULATED and ORDERED that disclosure shall proceed as follows:

(1) <u>Insurance Coverage (CPLR 3101 (f))</u>: If not already provided, shall be furnished by _____ on or before _____.

(2) <u>Depositions</u>: Choose (a) or (b)

  (a)

Deponent	Date and Time	Place
_____	_____	_____
_____	_____	_____
_____	_____	_____
_____	_____	_____
_____	_____	_____

[Attach additional sheet if necessary]

(b) The parties shall set a schedule for depositions to be held no later than _____ and shall provide the court with the schedule.

Optional:

☐ If one deposition fails to take place as scheduled, the remaining parties' depositions shall nonetheless proceed as scheduled, except that priorities between defendants and plaintiffs shall be preserved.

(3) <u>Other Disclosure</u>: (Commissions or letters rogatory (CPLR 3108); identity and location of witnesses; etc.):

_____

_____

_____

All such disclosure, unless otherwise noted herein, shall be completed by _____.

(4) <u>Impleader, Motion(s) to amend the pleadings or to add parties:</u> Shall be completed on or before _____.

(5) <u>Compliance conference:</u> Shall be held on _____.

(6) <u>End Date for All Disclosure</u>, other than expert disclosure [must be within 12 months, or 15 months for a complex case]: _____.

(7) <u>Expert Disclosure:</u>

Plaintiff(s) shall provide expert disclosure by _____.

Defendant(s) shall provide expert disclosure by _____.

(8) <u>Motions:</u> Any dispositive motion(s) (CPLR 3211 and 3212) shall be made on or before _____.

(9) <u>Note of Issue:</u> _____ shall file a note of issue/certificate of readiness on or before _____. A copy of the stipulation and order, an affirmation stating that all of the terms of the stipulation and order have been complied with, and an affidavit of service of the note of issue shall be served and filed with the note of issue on or before said date.

(10) The parties shall ensure that a stipulation of discontinuance shall be promptly filed if the case settles before the next meeting with the Court.

Failure to comply with any of these directions may result in the imposition of costs or sanctions or other action authorized by law.

Dated:

_____
Attorney for Plaintiff(s)

_____
Attorney for Defendant(s)

Dated:

SO ORDERED:

_____
J.S.C.

ADDITIONAL DIRECTIVES

In addition to the directives as set forth on the annexed pages, it is further ORDERED as follows:

_____

_____

_____

_____

_____

_____

_____

_____

_____

_____

_____

Dated:

SO ORDERED:

_____

J.S.C.

APPENDIX E. PROCEDURES FOR QUESTIONING, CHALLENGING AND SELECTING JURORS*

* Suggested title added by Publisher.

Procedures for questioning, challenging and selecting jurors authorized by section 202.33 of the Rules of the Chief Administrator of the Courts.

A. General Principles Applicable to Jury Selection. Selection of jurors pursuant to any of the methods authorized by section 202.33(e) of the Rules of the Chief Administrator shall be governed by the following:

(1) If for any reason jury selection cannot proceed immediately, counsel shall return promptly to the courtroom of the assigned trial judge or the Trial Assignment Part or any other designated location for further instructions.

(2) Generally, a total of eight jurors, including two alternates, shall be selected. The court may permit a greater number of alternates if a lengthy trial is expected or for any appropriate reason. Counsel may consent to the use of "nondesignated" alternate jurors, in which event no distinction shall be made during jury selection between jurors and alternates, but the number of peremptory challenges in such cases shall consist of the sum of the peremptory challenges that would have been available to challenge both jurors and designated alternates.

(3) All prospective jurors shall complete a background questionnaire supplied by the court in a form approved by the Chief Administrator. Prior to the commencement of jury selection, completed questionnaires shall be made available to counsel. Upon completion of jury selection, or upon removal of a prospective juror, the questionnaires shall be either returned to the respective jurors or collected and discarded by court staff in a manner that ensures juror privacy. With Court approval, which shall take into consideration concern for juror privacy, the parties may supplement the questionnaire to address concerns unique to a specific case.

(4) During the voir dire each attorney may state generally the contentions of his or her client, and identify the parties, attorneys and the witnesses likely to be called. However, counsel may not read from any of the pleadings in the action or inform potential jurors of the amount of money at issue.

(5) Counsel shall exercise peremptory challenges outside of the presence of the panel of prospective jurors.

(6) Counsel shall avoid discussing legal concepts such as burden of proof, which are the province of the court.

(7) If an unusual delay or a lengthy trial is anticipated, counsel may so advise prospective jurors.

(8) If counsel objects to anything said or done by any other counsel during the selection process, the objecting counsel shall unobtrusively request that all counsel step outside of the juror's presence, and counsel shall make a determined effort to resolve the problem. Should that effort fail, counsel shall immediately bring the problem to the attention of the assigned trial judge, the Trial Assignment Part judge or any other designated judge.

(9) After jury selection is completed, counsel shall advise the clerk of the assigned Trial Part or of the Trial Assignment Part or other designated part. If counsel anticipates the need during trial of special equipment (if available) or special assistance, such as an interpreter, counsel shall so inform the clerk at that time.

B. "White's Method."

(1) Prior to the identification of the prospective jurors to be seated in the jury box, counsel shall ask questions generally to all of the jurors in the room to determine whether any prospective juror in the room has knowledge of the subject matter, the parties, their attorneys or the prospective witnesses. A response from a juror that requires elaboration may be the subject of further questioning of that juror by counsel on an individual basis. Counsel may exercise challenges for cause at this time.

(2) After general questions have been asked to the group of prospective jurors, jury selection shall continue in rounds, with each round to consist of the following: (1) seating prospective jurors in the jury box; (2) questioning of seated prospective jurors; and (3) removal of seated prospective jurors upon exercise of challenges. Jurors removed for cause shall immediately be replaced during each round. The first round shall begin initially with the seating of six prospective jurors (where undesignated alternates are used, additional prospective jurors equal to the number of alternate jurors shall be seated as well).

(3) In each round, the questioning of the seated prospective jurors shall be conducted first by counsel for the plaintiff, followed by counsel for the remaining parties in the order in which their names appear in the caption. Counsel may be permitted to ask follow-up questions. Within each round, challenges for cause shall be exercised by any party prior to the exercise of peremptory challenges and as soon as the reason therefor becomes apparent. Upon replacement of a prospective juror removed for cause, questioning shall revert to the plaintiff.

(4) Following questioning and the exercise of challenges for cause, peremptory challenges shall be exercised one at a time and alternately as follows: In the first round, in caption order, each attorney shall exercise one peremptory challenge by removing a prospective juror's name from a "board" passed back and forth between or among counsel. An attorney alternatively may waive the making of a peremptory challenge. An attorney may exercise a second, single peremptory challenge within the round only after all other attorneys have either exercised or waived their first peremptory challenges. The board shall continue to circulate among the attorneys until no other peremptory challenges are exercised. An attorney who waives a challenge may not thereafter exercise a peremptory challenge within the round, but may exercise remaining peremptory challenges in subsequent rounds. The counsel last able to exercise a peremptory challenge in a round is not confined to the exercise of a single challenge but may then exercise one or more peremptory challenges.

(5) In subsequent rounds, the first exercise of peremptory challenges shall alternate from side to side. Where a side consists of multiple parties, commencement of the exercise of peremptory challenges in subsequent rounds shall rotate among the parties within the side. In each such round, before the board is to be passed to the other side, the board must be passed to all remaining parties within the side, in caption order, starting from the first party in the rotation for that round.

(6) At the end of each round, those seated jurors who remain unchallenged shall be sworn and removed from the room. The challenged jurors shall be replaced, and a new round shall commence.

(7) The selection of designated alternate jurors shall take place after the selection of the six jurors. Designated alternate jurors shall be selected in the same manner as described above, with the order of exercise of peremptory challenges continuing as the next round following the last completed round of challenges to regular jurors. The total number of peremptory challenges to alternates may be exercised against any alternate, regardless of seat.

C. "Struck Method."

(1) Unless otherwise ordered by the Court, selection of jurors shall be made from an initial panel of 25 prospective jurors, who shall be seated randomly and who shall maintain the order of seating throughout the voir dire. If fewer prospective jurors are needed due to the use of designated alternate jurors or for any other reason, the size of the panel may be decreased.

(2) Counsel first shall ask questions generally to the prospective jurors as a group to determine whether any prospective juror has knowledge of the subject matter, the parties, their attorneys or the prospective witnesses. A response from a juror that requires further elaboration may be the subject of further questioning of that juror by counsel on an individual basis. Counsel may exercise challenges for cause at this time.

(3) After the general questioning has been completed, in an action with one plaintiff and one defendant, counsel for the plaintiff initially shall question the prospective jurors, followed by questioning by defendant's counsel. Counsel may be permitted to ask follow-up questions. In cases with multiple parties, questioning shall be undertaken by counsel in the order in which the parties' names appear in the caption. A challenge for cause may be made by counsel to any party as soon as the reason therefor becomes apparent. At the end of the period, all challenges for cause to any prospective juror on the panel must have been exercised by respective counsel.

(4) After challenges for cause are exercised, the number of prospective jurors remaining shall be counted. If that number is less than the total number of jurors to be selected (including alternates, where non-designated alternates are being used) plus the maximum number of peremptory challenges allowed by the court or by statute that may be exercised by the parties (such sum shall be referred to as the "jury panel number"), additional prospective jurors shall be added until the number of prospective jurors not subject to challenge for cause equals or exceeds the jury panel number. Counsel for each party then shall question each replacement juror pursuant to the procedure set forth in paragraph 3.

(5) After all prospective jurors in the panel have been questioned, and all challenges for cause have been made, counsel for each party, one at a time beginning with counsel for the plaintiff, shall then exercise allowable peremptory challenges by alternately striking a single juror's name from a list or ballot passed back and forth between or among counsel until all challenges are exhausted or waived. In cases with multiple plaintiffs and/or defendants, peremptory challenges shall be exercised by counsel in the order in which the parties' names appear in the caption, unless following that order would, in the opinion of the court, unduly favor a side. In that event, the court, after consulting with the parties, shall specify the order in which the peremptory challenges shall be exercised in a manner that shall balance the interests of the parties.

An attorney who waives a challenge may not thereafter exercise a peremptory challenge. Any *Batson* or other objections shall be resolved by the court before any of the struck jurors are dismissed.

(6) After all peremptory challenges have been made, the trial jurors (including alternates when non-designated alternates are used) then shall be selected in the order in which they have been seated from those prospective jurors remaining on the panel.

(7) The selection of designated alternate jurors shall take place after the selection of the six jurors. Counsel shall select designated alternates in the same manner set forth in these rules, but with an initial panel of not more than 10 prospective alternates unless otherwise directed by the court. The jury panel number for designated alternate jurors shall be equal to the number of alternates plus the maximum number of peremptory challenges allowed by the court or by statute that may be exercised by the parties. The total number of peremptory challenges to alternates may be exercised against any alternate, regardless of seat.

COURT OF APPEALS

Including Amendments Received Through September 15, 2008

Westlaw Electronic Research

These rules may be searched electronically on Westlaw® *in the NY–RULES database; updates to these rules may be found on* Westlaw *in NY–RULESUP-DATES. For search tips and a summary of database content, consult the* Westlaw *Scope Screens for each database.*

Table of Sections

PART 500. RULES OF PRACTICE

GENERAL MATTERS

§ 500.1. General Requirements

(a) All papers shall comply with applicable statutes and rules, particularly the signing requirement of 22 NYCRR 130–1.1–a.

(b) **Method of reproduction.** All briefs, papers submitted pursuant to sections 500.10 and 500.11 of this Part, motion papers and appendices (hereinafter "papers filed") may be reproduced by any method that produces a permanent, legible, black image on white paper. Reproduction on both sides of the paper is encouraged.

(c) **Necessary information.** Where this Part requires the filing of multiple copies of papers, the parties shall identify on its cover the original document filed. All papers filed by or on behalf of a corporation or other business entity shall list all its parents, subsidiaries and affiliates, or state that no such parents, subsidiaries and affiliates exist (hereinafter "disclosure statement"). Where New York authorities are cited in any submissions. New York Official Law Report citations shall be included, if available. Copies of decisions that are not officially published, or are not otherwise readily available, shall

be included in the submission in which such decisions are cited.

(d) **Paper quality, size and binding.** Paper shall be opaque, unglazed, white and eleven by eight and one-half inches. Briefs, appendices, records and motion papers shall be bound on the left side in a manner that keeps all pages securely together, without plastic covers or any metal fasteners or similar hard material that protrudes or presents a bulky surface or sharp edge.

(e) **Computer-generated papers filed.** Papers filed prepared on a computer shall be printed in either a serifed, proportionally spaced typeface, such as Times Roman, or a serifed monospaced typeface, such as Courier. Narrow or condensed typefaces and condensed font spacing shall not be used. Except in headings, words shall not be in bold type or type consisting of all capital letters.

(1) *Papers filed using a proportionally-spaced typeface.* The body of any papers filed using a proportionally-spaced typeface shall be printed in 14-point type. Footnotes shall be printed in type of no less than 12 points.

(2) *Papers filed using a monospaced typeface.* The body of any papers filed using a monospaced typeface

shall be printed in 12-point type containing no more than 10 and one-half characters per inch. Footnotes shall be printed in type of no less than 10 points.

(f) Typewritten papers filed. Typewritten papers filed shall be neatly prepared in clear type no smaller than elite and in a pitch of no more than twelve characters per inch. The original, ribbon typescript of any papers filed shall be signed and filed as the original required by this Part. Carbon copies will not be accepted.

(g) Margins, line spacing and page numbering of computer-generated and typewritten papers filed. Computer-generated and typewritten papers filed shall have margins of one inch on all sides of the page. Text shall be double-spaced, but quotations more than two lines long may be indented and single-spaced. Headings and footnotes may be single-spaced. Pages shall be consecutively numbered in the center of the bottom margin of each page.

(h) Handwritten papers. Self-represented litigants may serve and file handwritten papers. Such papers shall be neatly prepared in cursive script or hand printing in black ink. Pages shall be consecutively numbered in the center of the bottom margin of each page. The filing of handwritten papers is not encouraged. The clerk of the Court may reject illegible papers.

(i) Filing of Papers. All papers filed shall be addressed to the clerk of the Court at 20 Eagle Street, Albany, New York 12207–1095, not to a Judge or Judges of the Court, and shall be served on each other party in accordance with the requirements of this Part. Submissions shall not be filed by facsimile transmission or electronic mail, except when requested by the clerk of the Court.

(j) Acknowledgment of receipt of papers. A request for an acknowledgment of receipt of papers shall be accompanied by the papers filed and a self-addressed, postage pre-paid postcard or envelope. Parties proceeding as poor persons or requesting poor person relief shall comply with this requirement if acknowledgment of receipt of papers is desired.

(k) Nonconforming Papers. The clerk of the Court may reject papers that do not conform to the requirements of this Part.

§ 500.2. Companion Filings on Compact Disk, Read-Only Memory (CD-ROM).

(a) The Court allows the submission of briefs, records or appendices on compact disk, read-only memory (CD-ROM) as companions to the requisite number of printed briefs, records and appendices filed and served in accordance with this Part if all parties have consented to the filing of the companion CD-ROM brief and record or appendix. The Court, by order on motion of any party or on its own motion, may require such filing by a party or amicus.

(b) The companion CD-ROM brief, record or appendix shall comply with the current technical specifications available from the clerk's office.

(c) The companion CD-ROM brief, record or appendix shall be identical in content and format (including page numbering) to the printed version, except that each also shall be word-searchable and shall provide electronic links (hyperlinks) to the complete text of any authorities cited therein, and to all documents or other material constituting the record on appeal. The disk and container shall be labeled to indicate the title of the case and the documents reproduced on the disk.

(d) Unless the Court requires a greater number, 10 disks or sets of disks shall be filed, with (i) proof of service of at least one disk or set on each other party and (ii) a copy of the parties' stipulation permitting, or the Court's order directing, such filing.

(e) Unless the Court requires otherwise, appellant's filing and respondent's filing, or a joint filing by appellant and respondent, are due 10 days after the final due date for filing appellant's reply brief (see section 500.12[d] of this Part).

§ 500.3. Fees

(a) Upon the filing of record material in a civil appeal pursuant to section 500.11, 500.12 or 500.26(a) of this Part, appellant shall provide the clerk of the Court the fee in the amount specified in CPLR 8022 in the form of an attorney's check, certified check, cashier's check or money order payable to "State of New York, Court of Appeals" unless:

(1) appellant demonstrates exemption from the fee requirements by statute or other authority;

(2) other payment arrangements have been made with the clerk of the Court;

(3) the appeal is accompanied by a motion requesting poor person relief or a motion requesting relief from payment of the filing fee; or

(4) appellant in the Court of Appeals provides a copy of an order issued by any court in the action or proceeding to which the appeal relates granting that party poor person relief, together with a sworn affidavit that the same financial circumstances exist at the time of filing in the Court of Appeals as when the order granting poor person relief was issued.

(b) Upon the filing of each motion or cross motion in a civil case pursuant to section 500.21 through 500.24 or 500.26(b) of this Part, movant shall provide the clerk of the Court with the fee in the amount specified in CPLR 8022 in the form of an attorney's check, certified check, cashier's check or money order payable to "State of New York, Court of Appeals" unless:

(1) movant demonstrates exemption from the fee requirements by statute or other authority;

(2) other payment arrangements have been made with the clerk of the Court;

(3) the motion or cross motion is accompanied by a motion requesting poor person relief or a motion requesting relief from payment of the filing fee; or

(4) movant in the Court of Appeals provides a copy of an order issued by any court in the action or proceeding to which the motion relates granting that party poor person relief, together with a sworn affidavit that the same financial circumstances exist at the time of filing in the Court of Appeals as when the order granting poor person relief was issued.

(c) Except as provided in subsections (a) or (b) above or where otherwise specifically required by law or by the Court, no fees shall be charged by the clerk of the Court.

§ 500.4. Pro Hac Vice Admission.

An attorney or the equivalent who is a member of the bar of another state, territory, district or foreign country may apply to appear pro hac vice with respect to a particular matter pending in this Court (see 22 NYCRR 520.11[a] [Rules of the Court of Appeals for the Admission of Attorneys and Counselors at Law—Admission Pro Hac Vice]). The application shall consist of a letter request to the clerk of the Court, with proof of service on each other party, and shall include current certificates of good standing from each jurisdiction in which the applicant is admitted and any orders of the courts below granting such relief in the matter for which pro hac vice status is sought.

§ 500.5. Sealed Documents.

(a) Documents under seal are not available for public viewing.

(b) Any papers sealed by a court below or otherwise required by statute to be sealed shall be sealed in the Court of Appeals.

(c) Any party to an appeal or motion may request that papers not sealed below be sealed in this Court. Such requests shall be by an original and one copy of a motion pursuant to section 500.21 of this Part, with proof of service of one copy on each other party.

(d) Documents and transcripts ordered sealed by the Court of Appeals or a court below shall be reproduced in separate volumes of the record on appeal. Each such volume shall be clearly identified on the cover as containing sealed material.

§ 500.6. Developments Affecting Appeals, Certified Questions, Motions and Criminal Leave Applications.

Counsel shall timely inform the clerk's office and each other party by letter of all developments affect-

ing appeals, section 500.27 certified questions, motions and criminal leave applications pending in this Court, including contemplated and actual settlements, circumstances or facts that could render the matter moot and pertinent developments in applicable case law, statutes and regulations. The writing shall contain proof of service on each other party.

§ 500.7. Post-Briefing, Post-Submission and Post-Argument Communications.

Except for communications providing the information required by section 500.6 of this Part or those specifically requested by the Court, post-briefing, post-submission and post-argument written communications to the Court are not favored, and shall be returned to the sender unless accepted by the clerk of the Court following a written request with a copy of the proposed submission and proof of timely service of one copy on each other party.

§ 500.8. Withdrawal of Appeal, Motion or Criminal Leave Application

(a) Appeals.

(1) Before argument or submission, an appeal shall be marked withdrawn upon receipt by the clerk of the Court of a stipulation of withdrawal signed by counsel for all parties and by all self-represented litigants and, in criminal appeals, additionally by defendant.

(2) After argument or submission, a request to withdraw an appeal shall be supported by a stipulation of withdrawal signed by counsel for all parties and by all self-represented litigants and, in criminal appeals, additionally by defendant. The request shall be submitted to the Court for determination.

(b) Motions.

(1) Before its return date, a motion shall be marked withdrawn upon receipt by the clerk of the Court of a written notice of withdrawal signed by counsel for the moving party, with proof of service of one copy on each other party.

(2) After the return date, a request to withdraw a motion shall be supported by a stipulation of withdrawal signed by counsel for all parties and by all self-represented litigants. The request shall be submitted to the Court for determination.

(c) Criminal Leave Applications. A request to withdraw an application shall be in writing and, if made on behalf of a defendant, shall be signed by defendant. The request shall contain an indication of service of one copy upon all parties and, if the request is made by defendant personally, proof of service upon defense counsel, if defendant is represented. The request shall be submitted to the assigned Judge for determination.

APPEALS

§ 500.9. Preliminary Appeal Statement

(a) Within 10 days after an appeal is taken by (1) filing a notice of appeal in the place and manner required by CPLR 5515, (2) entry of an order granting a motion for leave to appeal in a civil case, or (3) issuance of a certificate granting leave to appeal in a non-capital criminal case, appellant shall file with the clerk of the Court an original and one copy of a preliminary appeal statement on the form prescribed by the Court, with the required attachments and proof of service of one copy on each other party. No fee is required at the time of filing the preliminary appeal statement.

(b) Where a party asserts that a statute is unconstitutional, appellant shall give written notice to the Attorney General before filing the preliminary appeal statement, and a copy of the notification shall be attached to the preliminary appeal statement. The notification and a copy of the preliminary appeal statement shall be sent to the Solicitor General, Department of Law, The Capitol, Albany, New York 12224.

(c) After review of the Preliminary Appeal Statement, the clerk will notify the parties either that review pursuant to section 500.10 or section 500.11 of this Part shall commence or that the appeal shall proceed in the normal course.

APPENDIX TO SECTION 500.9

Preliminary Appeal Statement

Pursuant to section 500.9 of the Rules of the Court of Appeals

1. CAPTION OF CASE (as the parties should be denominated in the Court of Appeals):

STATE OF NEW YORK   COURT OF APPEALS

–against–

2. Name of court or tribunal where case originated, including county, if applicable:

3. Civil index number, criminal indictment number or other number assigned to the matter in the court or tribunal of original instance: _____

4. Docket number assigned to the matter at the Appellate Division or other intermediate appellate court: _____

5. Jurisdictional basis for this appeal:
   _____ Leave to appeal granted by the Court of Appeals or a Judge of the Court of Appeals
   _____ Leave to appeal granted by the Appellate Division or a Justice of the Appellate Division
   _____ CPLR 5601(a): dissents on the law at the Appellate Division
   _____ CPLR 5601(b)(1): constitutional ground (Appellate Division order)
   _____ CPLR 5601(b)(2): constitutional ground (judgment of court of original instance)
   _____ CPLR 5601(c): Appellate Division order granting a new trial or hearing, upon stipulation for judgment absolute
   _____ CPLR 5601(d): from a final judgment, order, determination or award, seeking review of a prior nonfinal Appellate Division order
   _____ Other (specify) _____

6. How this appeal was taken to the Court of Appeals (choose one) (see CPLR 5515[1]):
   NOTICE OF APPEAL   Date filed: _____
                               Clerk's office where filed: _____

ORDER GRANTING LEAVE TO APPEAL (civil case):
                Court that issued order: _____
                Date of order: _____

CERTIFICATE GRANTING LEAVE TO APPEAL (criminal case):
                Justice or Judge who issued order: _____
                Court: _____
                Date of order: _____

7.   Demonstration of timeliness of appeal in civil case (CPLR 5513, 5514):
        Was appellant served by its adversary with a copy of the order, judgment
        or determination appealed from and notice of its entry? ___ yes ___ no
            If yes, date on which appellant was served (if known, or discernable
            from the papers served): _____
            If yes, method by which appellant was served:
                            _____ personal delivery
                            _____ regular mail
                            _____ overnight courier
                            _____ other (describe _____)
        Did the Appellate Division deny a motion for leave to appeal to this
        Court in this case? ___ yes ___ no
        If yes, fill in the following information:
        a.   date appellant served the motion for leave to appeal made at the
              Appellate Division: _____
        b.   date on which appellant was served with the Appellate Division
              order denying such motion with notice of the order's entry:
              _____, and
        c.   method by which appellant was served with the Appellate Divi-
              sion order denying such motion:
                            _____ personal service
                            _____ regular mail
                            _____ overnight courier
                            _____ other (describe _____)

8.   Party Information:
Instructions: Fill in the name of each party to the action or proceeding, one name per line.
Indicate the status of the party in the court of original instance and the party's status in this
Court, if any. Examples of a party's original status include: plaintiff, defendant, petitioner,
respondent, claimant, third-party plaintiff, third-party defendant, intervenor. Examples of a
party's Court of Appeals status include: appellant, respondent, appellant-respondent, respondent-appellant, intervenor-appellant.

No.	Party Name	Original Status	Court of Appeals Status
1			
2			
3			
4			
5			
6			
7			
8			
9			
10			

9.   Attorney information:
Instructions: For each party listed above, fill in the name of the law firm and responsible
attorney, if the party is represented. Where a litigant is self-represented, fill in that party's
data in section 10 below.
For Party No. _____ above:
Law Firm Name: _____
Responsible Attorney: _____
Street Address: _____

City: _____ State: _____ Zip: _____
Telephone No: _____ Ext. _____ Fax: _____
If appearing Pro Hac Vice, has attorney satisfied requirements of section 500.4 of the Rules of the Court of Appeals? _____ yes _____ no

For Party No. _____ above:
Law Firm Name: _____
Responsible Attorney: _____
Street Address: _____
City: _____ State: _____ Zip: _____
Telephone No: _____ Ext. _____ Fax: _____
If appearing Pro Hac Vice, has attorney satisfied requirements of section 500.4 of the Rules of the Court of Appeals? _____ yes _____ no

For Party No. _____ above:
Law Firm Name: _____
Responsible Attorney: _____
Street Address: _____
City: _____ State: _____ Zip: _____
Telephone No: _____ Ext. _____ Fax: _____
If appearing Pro Hac Vice, has attorney satisfied requirements of section 500.4 of the Rules of the Court of Appeals? _____ yes _____ no

For Party No. _____ above:
Law Firm Name: _____
Responsible Attorney: _____
Street Address: _____
City: _____ State: _____ Zip: _____
Telephone No: _____ Ext. _____ Fax: _____
If appearing Pro Hac Vice, has attorney satisfied requirements of section 500.4 of the Rules of the Court of Appeals? _____ yes _____ no

For Party No. _____ above:
Law Firm Name: _____
Responsible Attorney: _____
Street Address: _____
City: _____ State: _____ Zip: _____
Telephone No: _____ Ext. _____ Fax: _____
If appearing Pro Hac Vice, has attorney satisfied requirements of section 500.4 of the Rules of the Court of Appeals? _____ yes _____ no

(Use additional sheets if necessary)

10. Self–Represented Litigant information:
For Party No. _____ above:
Law Firm Name: _____
Responsible Attorney: _____
Street Address: _____
City: _____ State: _____ Zip: _____
Telephone No: _____ Ext. _____ Fax: _____

For Party No. _____ above:
Law Firm Name: _____
Responsible Attorney: _____
Street Address: _____
City: _____ State: _____ Zip: _____
Telephone No: _____ Ext. _____ Fax: _____

11. Related motions and applications:
　　　Does any party to the appeal have any motions or applications related to this appeal pending in the Court of Appeals? _____ yes _____ no
　　　If yes, specify:
　　　a. the party who filed the motion or application: _____
　　　b. the return date of the motion: _____
　　　c. the relief sought: _____

Does any party to the appeal have any motions or applications in this case currently pending in the court from which the appeal is taken? ____ yes ____ no

If yes, specify:

a. the party who filed the motion or application: _____

b. the return date of the motion: _____

c. the relief sought: _____

Are there any other pending motions or ongoing proceedings in this case? If yes, please describe briefly the nature and the status of such motions or proceedings: _____

_____

_____

_____

12. Set forth, in point-heading form, issues proposed to be raised on appeal (this is a nonbinding designation, for preliminary issue identification purposes only):

(use additional sheet, if necessary)

13. Does appellant request that this appeal be considered for resolution pursuant to section 500.11 of the Rules of the Court of Appeals (Alternative Procedure for Selected Appeals)?

_____ yes _____ no

If yes, set forth a concise statement why appellant believes that consideration pursuant to section 500.11 is appropriate (see section 500.11[b]): _____

_____

_____

_____

_____

14. Notice to the Attorney General.

Is any party to the appeal asserting that a statute is unconstitutional? _____ yes _____ no

If yes, has appellant met the requirement of notice to the Attorney General in section 500.9(b) of the Rules of the Court of Appeals? ____ yes ____ no

15. **ITEMS REQUIRED TO BE ATTACHED TO THIS STATEMENT:**

A. **A copy of the filed notice of appeal, a copy of the order granting leave to appeal (civil case), or a copy of the certificate granting leave to appeal (noncapital criminal case), whichever is applicable;**

B. **The order, judgment or determination appealed from to this Court;**

C. **Any order, judgment or determination which is the subject of the order appealed from, or which is otherwise brought up for review;**

D. **All decisions or opinions relating to the orders set forth in subsections B and C above; and**

E. **If required, a copy of the notice sent to the Attorney General pursuant to section 500.9(b) of the Rules of the Court of Appeals.**

Date: _____   Submitted by: _____

(Name of law firm)

_____

_____
(Signature of responsible attorney)

_____
(Typed name of responsible attorney)

Attorneys for appellant _____
(Name of party)

–or–

Date: _____   Submitted by _____, pro se
(Signature of appellant)

_____
(Typed/printed name of self-represented appellant)

§ 500.10. Examination of Subject Matter Jurisdiction

On its own motion, the Court may examine its subject matter jurisdiction over an appeal based on the papers submitted in accordance with section 500.9 of this Part. The clerk of the Court shall notify all parties by letter when an appeal has been selected for examination pursuant to this section, stating the jurisdictional concerns identified in reviewing the preliminary appeal statement and setting a due date for filing and service of comments in letter form from all parties. Such examination shall result in dismissal of the appeal by the Court or in notification to the parties that the appeal shall proceed either under the review process described in section 500.11 of this Part or in the normal course, with or without oral argument. This examination of jurisdiction shall not preclude the Court from addressing any jurisdiction concerns at any time.

§ 500.11. Alternative Procedure for Selected Appeals

(a) On its own motion, the Court may review selected appeals by an alternative procedure. Such appeals shall be determined on the intermediate appellate court record or appendix and briefs, the writings in the courts below and additional letter submissions on the merits. The clerk of the Court shall notify all parties by letter when an appeal has been selected for review pursuant to this section. Appellant may request such review in its preliminary appeal statement. Respondent may request such review by letter to the clerk of the Court, with proof of service of one copy on each other party within five days after the appeal is taken.

(b) Appeals may be selected for alternative review on the basis of:

(1) questions of discretion, mixed questions of law and fact or affirmed findings of fact, which are subject to a limited scope of review:

(2) recent, controlling precedent;

(3) narrow issues of law not of statewide importance;

(4) nonpreserved issues of law;

(5) a party's request for such review; or

(6) other appropriate factors.

(c) **Appellant's filing.** Within 25 days after the date of the clerk of the Court's letter initiating the alternative review procedure, appellant shall:

(1) file three copies of the intermediate appellate court record or appendix and three copies of each brief filed by each party in the intermediate appellate court. Original exhibits to be relied upon which are not in the record or appendix at the intermediate appellate court shall be filed or, if they are on file with the clerk of the trial court, subpoenaed to this Court and the Court so advised by letter. Such exhibits shall be clearly identified and, where appropriate, their authenticity shall be certified or stipulated to;

(2) file an original and two copies of a letter stating its arguments in support of appellant's position on the merits. If appellant objects to review pursuant to this section, the letter shall also explain that position;

(3) file a disclosure statement pursuant to section 500.1(c) of this Part, if necessary;

(4) file proof of service of one copy of its arguments on each other party; and

(5) remit the fee, if any, required by section 500.3(a) of this Part.

(d) **Respondent's filing.** Within 20 days after service of appellant's submission, respondent shall file an original and two copies of a letter stating its arguments in support of its position on the merits. If respondent objects to review pursuant to this section, the letter shall also explain that position. Respondent shall file a disclosure statement pursuant to section 500.1(c) of this Part, if necessary, and proof of service of one copy of its arguments on each other party.

(e) **Abandonment of arguments.** A party shall be deemed to have abandoned any argument made in the intermediate appellate court briefs not addressed or reserved in the written submission to this Court.

(f) **Review of subject matter jurisdiction.** An appeal selected for review pursuant to this section is subject to dismissal on the Court's own motion, should it be determined that the Court is without subject matter jurisdiction.

447

(g) Termination of alternative procedure. If the Court terminates its review of the appeal pursuant to this section before disposition, the clerk of the Court will notify counsel by letter and set a schedule for full briefing of the appeal.

(h) Amicus curiae relief. The Attorney General of the State of New York may file, no later than the filing date set for respondent's submission, an original and two copies of an amicus curiae submission without leave of the Court, with proof of service of one copy on each party. Any other proposed amicus curiae shall request amicus curiae relief pursuant to section 500.23(a)(2) of this Part.

§ 500.12. Filing of Record Material and Briefs in Normal Course Appeals

(a) Scheduling letter. Generally, in an appeal tracked for normal course treatment, the clerk of the Court issues a scheduling letter after the filing of the preliminary appeal statement. A scheduling letter also issues upon the termination of an inquiry pursuant to section 500.10 or 500.11 of this Part. The scheduling letter sets the filing dates for record material and briefs.

(b) Appellant's initial filing. On or before the date specified in the scheduling letter, appellant shall serve and file record material in compliance with section 500.14 of this Part, and shall remit the fee, if any, required by section 500.3(a) of this Part. Appellant also shall file an original and 24 copies of a brief, with proof of service of three copies on each other party. If no scheduling letter is issued, appellant's papers shall be served and filed within 60 days after appellant took the appeal by (1) filing a notice of appeal in the place and manner required by CPLR 5515, (2) entry of an order granting a motion for leave to appeal in a civil case, or (3) issuance of a certificate granting leave to appeal in a non-capital criminal case.

(c) Respondent's filing. On or before the date specified in the scheduling letter, respondent shall serve and file an original and 24 copies of a brief and a supplementary appendix, if any, with proof of service of three copies on each other party. If no scheduling letter is issued, respondent's papers shall be filed within 45 days after service of appellant's brief.

(d) Reply briefs. A reply brief is not required but may be served and filed by appellant on or before the date specified in the scheduling letter. If no scheduling letter is issued, a reply brief may be served and filed within 15 days after service of respondent's brief. Where cross appeals are filed, the cross appellant may serve and file a reply brief to the main appellant's responsive brief. An original and 24 copies of a reply brief shall be served and filed, with proof of service of three copies on each other party.

(e) Amicus curiae briefs. The Attorney General of the State of New York may file, no later than the

filing date set for respondent's brief, an original and 24 copies of an amicus curiae brief without leave of the Court, with proof of service of three copies on each party. Any other proposed amicus curiae shall request amicus curiae relief pursuant to section 500.23(a)(1) of this Part.

(f) Briefs in response to amicus curiae briefs. Briefs in response to an amicus curiae brief are not required but may be served and filed by a party whose position is adverse to that of the amicus curiae. The brief shall be served and filed within 15 days after the date of this Court's order granting a motion for amicus curiae brief within 15 days after the service of an amicus curiae brief by the Attorney General of the State of New York. An original and 24 copies shall be filed, with proof of service of three copies on each other party and one copy on each amicus curiae.

(g) Sur reply briefs. Sur reply briefs are not permitted.

§ 500.13. Content and Form of Briefs in Normal Course Appeals

(a) Content. All briefs shall conform to the requirements of section 500.1 of this Part and contain a table of contents, a table of cases and authorities and a disclosure statement pursuant to section 500.1(c) of this Part, if necessary. Respondent's brief may have a supplementary appendix attached to it. The original of each brief shall be signed and dated, shall have the affidavit of service affixed to the inside of the back cover and shall be identified on the front cover as the original.

(b) Brief covers. Brief covers shall be white and shall contain the caption of the case and name, address, telephone number, and facsimile number of counsel or self-represented litigant and the party on whose behalf the brief is submitted, and the date on which the brief was completed. In the upper right corner, the brief cover shall indicate whether the party proposes to submit the brief without oral argument or, if argument time is requested, the amount of time requested and the name of the person who will present oral argument (see section 500.18 of this Part). If a time request does not appear on the brief, generally no more than 10 minutes will be assigned. The Court will determine the argument time, if any, to be assigned to each party.

§ 500.14. Records, Appendices and Exhibits in Normal Course Appeals

(a) Record material. Appellant shall supply the Court with record material in one of the following ways:

(1) Appellant may subpoena the original file to this Court from the clerk of the court of original instance or other custodian, and submit original exhibits to be relied upon, and supplement these with an original and 24 copies of an appendix conforming to subdivi-

sion (b) below, with proof of service of three copies of the appendix on each other party. If appellant is represented by assigned counsel, or has established indigency, an oral or written request may be made of the clerk of this Court to obtain the original file.

(2) Appellant may file with the clerk of the Court one copy of the reproduced record used at the court below. This record shall be supplemented by an original and 24 copies of an appendix conforming to subdivision (b) below, with proof of service of three copies of the appendix on each other party.

(3) Appellant may file with the clerk of the Court an original and 24 copies of a new and full record which shall include the record used at the court below, the notice of appeal or order granting leave to appeal to this Court, the decision and order appealed from to this Court, and any other decision and order brought up for review, with proof of service of three copies of the new record on each other party.

(b) Appendix. An appendix shall conform to the requirements of CPLR 5528 and 5529, and shall be sufficient by itself to permit the Court to review the issues raised on appeal without resort to the original file (see subsection [a][1] of this section) or reproduced record used at the court below (see subsection [a][2] of this section). The appendix shall include, as relevant to the appeal, the following:

(1) the notice of appeal or order or certificate granting leave to appeal;

(2) the order, judgment or determination appealed from to this Court;

(3) any order, judgment or determination which is the subject of the order appealed from, or which is otherwise brought up for review;

(4) any decision or opinion relating to the orders set forth in subsections (b)(2) and (3) above; and

(5) the testimony, affidavits, and written or photographic exhibits useful to the determination of the questions raised on appeal.

(c) Respondent's appendix. A respondent's brief may include a supplementary appendix.

(d) Inadequate appendix. When appellant has filed an inadequate appendix, respondent may move to strike the appendix (see section 500.21 of this Part) or may submit an original and 24 copies of an appendix containing such additional parts of the record as respondent deems necessary to consider the questions involved, with proof of service of three copies of the appendix on each other party. The Court may direct appellant to supplement the appendix with additional parts of the record it deems necessary to consider the questions involved.

(e) Correctness of the record. The correctness of the reproduced record or the appendix and additional papers shall be authenticated pursuant to CPLR 2105 or stipulated to pursuant to CPLR 5532.

§ 500.15. Extensions of Time

The clerk of the Court is authorized to grant, for good cause shown, a reasonable extension of time for filing papers on an appeal. A request for an extension may be by telephone call to the clerk's office, and shall be made no earlier than 20 days before the filing due date set by the clerk's office or otherwise prescribed by this Part. The party requesting an extension shall advise the clerk of the Court of the position of each other party with regard to the request. A party granted an extension shall file a confirmation letter, with proof of service of one copy on each other party, unless the clerk's office has notified all parties in writing of the determination of the request.

§ 500.16. Failure to Proceed or File Papers

(a) Dismissal of appeal. If appellant has not filed and served the papers required by section 500.11, 500.12 or 500.26(a) of this Part within the time set by the clerk's office or otherwise prescribed by this Part, the clerk of the Court shall enter an order dismissing the appeal.

(b) Preclusion. If respondent has not filed and served the papers required by section 500.11, 500.12 or 500.26(a) of this Part within the time set by the clerk's office or otherwise prescribed by this Part, the clerk of the Court shall enter an order precluding respondent's filing.

(c) Judicial review. The Court may review dismissal and preclusion orders entered pursuant to subsections (a) and (b) above by motion on notice in accordance with section 500.21 of this Part.

§ 500.17. Calendar

(a) Notification of argument time and date. When the calendar has been prepared, the clerk of the Court shall advise counsel by letter of the date and time assigned for oral argument.

(b) Calendar preferences. A party seeking a preference shall address a letter to the clerk of the Court, with proof of service of one copy on each other party. The letter shall state why a preference is needed, why alternative remedies, such as review pursuant to section 500.11 of this Part or submission without argument, are not appropriate, and opposing counsel's position on the request.

(c) Notification of unavailability. Counsel have a continuing obligation to notify the clerk's office of days of known or possible unavailability for oral argument during the Court's scheduled Albany sessions.

(d) Adjournments. Requests for adjournment of a calendared appeal are not favored. A party seeking an adjournment shall address a letter to the clerk of the Court, with proof of service of one copy on each other party. The letter shall state why the adjournment is necessary, why submission on the brief filed and having substitute counsel argue are not viable alternatives, and opposing counsel's position on the request.

§ 500.18. Oral Argument

(a) **Argument time.** Maximum argument time is 30 minutes per party, unless otherwise directed or permitted by the Court upon advance request by letter addressed to the clerk of the Court with proof of service of one copy on each other party. In requesting argument time, counsel shall presume the Court's familiarity with the facts, procedural history and legal issues the appeal presents. The Court may assign time for argument that varies from a party's request and may determine that the appeal be submitted by any party or all parties without oral argument (see section 500.13[b] of this Part).

(b) **Arguing counsel.** Only one counsel is permitted to argue for a party, unless otherwise directed or permitted by the Court upon advance request by letter addressed to the clerk of the Court with proof of service of one copy on each other party.

(c) **Rebuttal.** Prior to beginning argument, appellant may orally request permission from the Chief Judge to reserve a specific number of minutes for rebuttal. The time reserved shall be subtracted from the total time assigned to appellant. Respondent may not request permission to reserve time for sur-rebuttal.

§ 500.19. Remittitur

(a) The remittitur of the Court, containing the Court's adjudication, together with the return papers filed with the Court, shall be sent to the clerk of the court of original instance or to the clerk of the court to which the case is remitted, there to be proceeded upon according to law.

(b) The court of original instance or the court to which the case is remitted issues any order to effect the adjudication in this Court's remittitur, including an award of costs.

CRIMINAL LEAVE APPLICATIONS

§ 500.20. Criminal Leave Applications

(a) **Letter application.** Applications to the Chief Judge for leave to appeal in a criminal case (CPL 460.20) shall be by letter addressed to 20 Eagle Street, Albany, New York 12207-1095, and shall be sent to the clerk of the Court, with proof of service of one copy on the adverse party. The letter shall indicate:

(1) the names of all codefendants in the trial court, if any, and the status of their appeals, if known;

(2) whether an application has been addressed to a justice of the Appellate Division;

(3) whether oral argument in person or by telephone conference call is requested; and

(4) the grounds upon which leave to appeal is sought. Particular written attention shall be given to reviewability and preservation of error, identifying and reproducing the particular portions of the record where the questions sought to be reviewed are raised and preserved. After the application is assigned to a Judge for review, counsel will be given an opportunity to serve and file additional submissions, if any, and opposing counsel will be given an opportunity to respond.

(b) **Material to be provided with application.**

(1) *Orders of intermediate appellate courts determining appeals to those courts.* An application for leave to appeal from an intermediate appellate court order determining an appeal taken to that court shall include:

(i) one copy of each brief submitted by defendant to the intermediate appellate court;

(ii) one copy of each brief submitted by the People to the intermediate appellate court;

(iii) the order and decision of the intermediate appellate court sought to be appealed from; and

(iv) all relevant opinions or memoranda of the courts below, along with any other papers to be relied on in furtherance of the application.

(2) *Orders of intermediate appellate courts determining applications for writs of error coram nobis.* An application for leave to appeal from an intermediate appellate court order determining an application for coram nobis relief shall include:

(i) the order and decision sought to be appealed from;

(ii) the papers in support of and opposing the application filed in the intermediate appellate court; and

(iii) the intermediate appellate court decision and order sought to be vacated, as well as the briefs filed on the underlying appeal, if available.

(c) **Assignment.** The Chief Judge directs the assignment of each application to a Judge of the Court through the clerk of the Court; counsel shall not apply directly to a Judge or request that an application be assigned to a particular Judge. The assigned Judge shall advise the parties if oral argument of the application will be entertained.

(d) **Reargument or reconsideration.** Requests for reargument or reconsideration shall be in letter form addressed to the clerk of the Court, with proof of service on the adverse party, and shall be assigned to the Judge who ruled on the original application. A request for reargument or reconsideration shall not be based on the assertion for the first time of new points, except for extraordinary and compelling reasons. Unless otherwise permitted by the assigned Judge, the reargument or reconsideration request shall be served not later than 30 days after the date of the certificate determining the application of which reargument or reconsideration is sought.

(e) Counsel. This Court does not assign counsel for criminal leave applications. One set of motion papers addressed to this Court under section 500.21 of this Part for assignment of counsel on a criminal appeal may be filed, with proof of service of one copy on the adverse party, only after leave to appeal is granted.

(f) Stay requests. Whether incorporated in an application for leave to appeal or made separately by letter with proof of service of one copy on the adverse party, a request for a stay (CPL 460.60; 530.50) shall state:

(1) whether the relief sought has been previously requested;

(2) whether defendant is presently incarcerated and the incarceration status, if known, of any co-defendants; and,

(3) if the defendant is at liberty,

(i) whether a surrender date has been set; and

(ii) the conditions of release (e.g., on defendant's own recognizance or on a set bail amount).

(g) Applications for extensions of time to seek leave to appeal. An application for an extension of time to seek leave to appeal (CPL 460.30) shall be by one set of motion papers in compliance with section 500.21 of this Part, with proof of service of one copy on the adverse party.

MOTIONS

§ 500.21. Motions—General Procedures

(a) Return date. Regardless whether the Court is in session, motions shall be returnable on a Monday or, if Monday is a legal holiday, the first business day of the week unless otherwise provided by statute, order to show cause or stipulation so ordered by a Judge of the Court. Motions shall be submitted without oral argument, unless the Court directs otherwise. No adjournments shall be permitted other than in those limited instances provided by statute (CPLR 321[c] and 1022).

(b) Notice and service. Movant shall serve a notice of motion and supporting papers on sufficient notice to each other party, as set forth in the CPLR and below. In computing the notice period, the date of service shall not be included.

(1) When movant's papers are personally served, movant shall give at least eight days' notice (CPLR 2214[b]).

(2) When movant's papers are served by regular mail, movant shall give at least 13 days' notice (CPLR 2103[b][2]).

(3) When movant's papers are served by overnight delivery service, movant shall give at least nine days' notice (CPLR 2103[b][6]).

(4) When movant's papers are served by facsimile transmission, movant shall comply with CPLR 2103(b)(5), and give at least eight days' notice.

(c) Filing. Unless otherwise permitted by the Court or clerk of the Court, movant shall file its papers, with proof of service on each other party of the required number of copies, at Court of Appeals Hall no later than noon on the Friday preceding the return date. On or before the return date of the motion, respondent may file papers in opposition to the motion, with proof of service on each other party of the required number of copies. Submissions shall not be filed by facsimile transmission or electronic mail, except when requested by the clerk of the Court. The Court's motion practice does not permit the filing of reply briefs and memoranda. A request for permission to file papers after the return date of the motion is governed by section 500.7 of this Part.

(d) Number of required copies. Except in cases of indigency, where subsection (g) below applies, the number of copies required to be filed is as follows:

(1) *Motions for permission to appeal in civil cases.* Movant shall file an original and six copies of its papers, with proof of service of two copies on each other party. Respondent may file an original and six copies of papers in opposition to the motion, with proof of service of two copies on each other party.

(2) *Motions for reargument of appeals, reargument of motions for permission to appeal and reargument of decisions on certified questions.* Movant shall file an original and six copies of its papers, with proof of service of two copies on each other party. Respondent may file an original and six copies of papers in opposition to the motion, with proof of service of two copies on each other party.

(3) *Other motions.* For motions other than those addressed in subsections (d)(1) and (2) above, movant shall file an original and one copy of its papers, with proof of service of one copy on each other party. Respondent may file an original and one copy of papers in opposition to the motion, with proof of service of one copy on each other party.

(e) Fee required. Movant shall remit the fee, if any, required by section 500.3(b) of this Part with each motion and cross motion filed.

(f) Form of papers. Movant's papers and opposing papers shall comply in form with section 500.1 of this Part. The papers shall include a disclosure statement pursuant to section 500.1(c) of this Part, if required.

(g) Proof of indigency. Any motion may be made on one set of papers, with proof of service of one copy on each other party, where:

(1) the motion requests poor person relief and contains the information required by CPLR 1101(a), or

(2) movant provides a copy of an order, issued by any court in the action or proceeding to which the motion relates, granting that party poor person relief, together with a sworn affidavit that the same financial circumstances exist at the time of filing in the Court of Appeals as when the order granting poor person relief was issued.

§ 500.22. Motions for Permission to Appeal in Civil Cases

(a) Filing and notice. Movant shall file an original and six copies of its papers, with proof of service of two copies on each other party. The motion shall be noticed for a return date in compliance with CPLR 5516 and section 500.21(b) of this Part.

(b) Content. Movant's papers shall be a single document, bound on the left, and shall contain in the order here indicated:

(1) A notice of motion (see CPLR 2214).

(2) A statement of the procedural history of the case, including a showing of the timeliness of the motion.

(i) If no prior motion for leave to appeal to the Court of Appeals was filed at the Appellate Division, movant's papers to this Court shall demonstrate timeliness by stating the date movant was served (see CPLR 2103[b]) with the order or judgment sought to be appealed from, with notice of entry.

(ii) If a prior motion for leave to appeal to the Court of Appeals was filed at the Appellate Division, movant's papers filed in this Court shall demonstrate that the timeliness chain is intact by stating:

(a) the date movant was served with the order or judgment sought to be appealed from, with notice of entry.

(b) the date movant served the notice of motion addressed to the Appellate Division upon each other party, and

(c) the date movant was served with the Appellate Division order denying leave to appeal with notice of entry.

(3) A showing that this Court has jurisdiction of the motion and of the proposed appeal, including that the order or judgment sought to be appealed from is a final determination or comes within the special class of nonfinal orders appealable by permission of the Court of Appeals (see CPLR 5602[a][2]).

(4) A concise statement of the questions presented for review and why the questions presented merit review by this Court, such as that the issues are novel or of public importance, present a conflict with prior decisions of this Court, or involve a conflict among the departments of the Appellate Division. Movant shall identify the particular portions of the record where the questions sought to be reviewed are raised and preserved.

(5) A disclosure statement pursuant to section 500.1(c) of this Part, if required.

(6) Copies of the order or judgment sought to be appealed from with notice of entry, as well as copies of all relevant orders, opinions or memoranda rendered in the courts below. The papers shall state if no opinion was rendered.

(c) Additional documents. Movant shall file with its papers one copy of the record below, or appendix if the appendix method was used in the court below, and one copy of the briefs filed below by each of the parties.

(d) Opposing papers. Respondent may file an original and six copies of papers in opposition to the motion, with proof of service of two copies on each other party. The opposing papers shall state concisely respondent's argument for dismissal or denial of the motion.

§ 500.23. Amicus Curiae Relief

Any non-party other than the Attorney General seeking to file an amicus brief on an appeal, certified question or motion for leave to appeal must obtain permission by motion.

(a) Motions.

(1) *Amicus curiae relief on normal course appeals and normal course certified questions.* Movant shall file an original and one copy of its papers, accompanied by one copy of a proposed brief, with proof of service of one copy on each other party. The motion shall be noticed for a return date no later than the Court session preceding the session in which argument or submission of the appeal or certified question is scheduled. If the motion is granted, an original and 24 copies of the brief shall be filed, with proof of service of three copies on each party, within the time set by the Court's order.

(2) *Amicus curiae relief on appeals selected for review by the alternative procedure.* Movant shall file an original and one copy of its papers, accompanied by an original and two copies of the proposed submission, with proof of service of one copy on each other party. The motion shall be noticed for a return date no later than the filing date set for respondent's submission on the appeal.

(3) *Amicus curiae relief on motions for permission to appeal in civil cases.* Movant shall file an original and one copy of its papers, accompanied by one copy of a proposed brief, with proof of service of one copy on each other party. The motion shall be noticed for a return date as soon as practicable after the return date of the motion for permission to appeal to which it relates. The granting of a motion to appear amicus curiae on a motion for permission to appeal does not authorize the movant to appear amicus on the subsequent appeal. A new motion for amicus curiae relief on the appeal must be brought pursuant to subsection (a) (1) or (2) above.

(4) *Criteria.* Movant shall not present issues not raised before the courts below. A motion for amicus curiae relief shall demonstrate that:

(i) the parties are not capable of a full and adequate presentation and that movants could remedy this deficiency;

(ii) the amicus could identify law or arguments that might otherwise escape the Court's consideration; or

(iii) the proposed amicus curiae brief otherwise would be of assistance to the Court.

(5) *Opposing papers.* Respondent may file an original and one copy of papers in opposition to the motion, with proof of service of one copy on each other party.

(b) Amicus curiae filings by the Attorney General.

(1) *Amicus curiae relief on motions for permission to appeal in civil cases.* The Attorney General shall file an original and one copy of the submission with proof of service of one copy on each other party. The submission shall be filed without leave of the Court on or before the return date of the motion for permission to appeal.

(2) *Amicus curiae relief on normal course appeals and normal course certified questions.* See Rule 500.12(e).

(3) *Amicus curiae relief on appeals selected for review by the alternative procedure.* See Rule 500.11(h).

§ 500.24. Motions for Reargument of Appeals, Motions and Decisions on Certified Questions

(a) Filing and notice. Movant shall file an original and six copies of its papers, with proof of service of two copies on each other party. An original and one copy of a motion for reargument of a motion may be served and filed if filing of an original and one copy of papers was allowed on the underlying motion pursuant to section 500.21(d)(3).

(b) Timeliness. Movant shall serve the notice of motion not later than 30 days after the appeal or motion sought to be reargued has been decided, unless otherwise permitted by the Court.

(c) Content. The motion shall state briefly the ground upon which reargument is sought and the points claimed to have been overlooked or misapprehended by the Court, with proper reference to the particular portions of the record and to the authorities relied upon.

(d) New matters. The motion shall not be based on the assertion for the first time of new arguments or points of law, except for extraordinary and compelling reasons.

(e) Limitation on motions. The Court shall entertain only one motion per party for reargument of a specific appeal, motion or certified question decision.

(f) Opposing papers. Except on those motions described in section 500.21(d)(3), respondent may file an original and six copies of papers in opposition to the motion, with proof of service of two copies on each other party. The opposing papers shall briefly state respondent's argument for dismissal or denial of the motion.

§ 500.25. Emergency Matters; Orders to Show Cause

A request for emergency relief pending the determination of an appeal or a motion for permission to appeal shall be brought on by order to show cause. The applicant shall contact the clerk's office in advance of the filing. The papers shall be filed as directed by the clerk's office. The order to show cause shall include telephone and facsimile numbers for each attorney and self-represented party, and a statement giving reasons for granting the request. If there is no pending appeal or motion for permission to appeal, the order to show cause shall bring on a motion for leave to appeal or be accompanied by a notice of appeal or a motion for permission to appeal complying with section 500.22 of this Part. There is no fee for filing an order to show cause. If a Judge signs an order to show cause bringing on a motion, movant shall pay the fee, if any, required by section 500.3(b) of this Part.

PRIMARY ELECTION SESSION

§ 500.26. Primary Election Session Procedures

(a) Appeals as of right or by permission of the Appellate Division.

(1) Appellant shall immediately contact the clerk's office by telephone upon receipt of the order from which the appeal is taken.

(2) Appellant shall immediately orally notify each respondent of the appeal.

(3) Within the time directed by the clerk of the Court, appellant shall file:

(i) a copy of the notice of appeal or order granting leave and a preliminary appeal statement with proof of service on each other party;

(ii) 25 copies of appellant's Appellate Division brief and, where applicable, the record or appendix;

(iii) the original file, where applicable, which appellant shall obtain;

(iv) the fee, if any, required by section 500.3(a) of this Part;

(v) an original and 24 copies of a letter setting forth appellant's arguments in this Court with proof of service of one copy on each other party; and

(vi) additional papers, if requested.

(4) Within the time directed by the clerk of the Court, respondent shall submit 25 copies of its Appellate Division brief, and may submit an original and 24 copies of a letter in opposition with proof of service of one copy on each other party.

(b) Motions for permission to appeal.

(1) Movant shall immediately contact the clerk's office by telephone upon receipt of the order from which movant seeks leave to appeal.

(2) Movant shall immediately orally notify respondent of the motion.

(3) Within the time directed by the clerk of the Court, movant shall file:

(i) an original and nine copies of a letter requesting permission to appeal with proof of service of one copy on each other party;

(ii) 10 copies of the Appellate Division decision and order;

(iii) 10 copies of the Supreme Court decision and order;

(iv) 10 copies of movant's Appellate Division brief, and, where applicable, the record or appendix;

(v) the original file, where applicable, which movant shall obtain; and

(vi) the fee, if any, required by section 500.3(b) of this Part.

(4) Within the time directed by the clerk of the Court, respondent shall submit 10 copies of its Appellate Division brief, and may submit an original and nine copies of a letter in opposition with proof of service of one copy on each other party.

CERTIFIED QUESTIONS

§ 500.27. Discretionary Proceedings to Review Certified Questions from Federal Courts and Other Courts of Last Resort

(a) Whenever it appears to the Supreme Court of the United States, any United States Court of Appeals, or a court of last resort of any other state that determinative questions of New York law are involved in a case pending before that court for which no controlling precedent of the Court of Appeals exists, the court may certify the dispositive questions of law to the Court of Appeals.

(b) The certifying court shall prepare a certificate which shall contain the caption of the case, a statement of facts setting forth the nature of the case and the circumstances out of which the questions of New York law arise, and the questions of New York law, not controlled by precedent, that may be determinative, together with a statement as to why the issue should be addressed in the Court of Appeals at this time.

(c) The certificate, certified by the clerk of the certifying court under its official seal, together with the original or a copy of all relevant portions of the record and other papers before the certifying court, as it may direct, shall be filed with the clerk of the Court.

(d) The Court, on its own motion, shall examine the merits presented by the certified question, to determine, first, whether to accept the certification, and second, the review procedure to be followed in determining the merits.

(e) If the certification is accepted, the clerk of the Court shall request any additional papers the Court requires for its review. The clerk of the Court shall notify the parties of the time periods for filing of briefs, if any, and calendaring of argument, if any, directed by the Court.

(f) If the constitutionality of an act of the Legislature of this state is involved in a certification to which the State of New York or an agency is not a party, the clerk of the Court shall notify the Attorney General in accordance with the provisions of Executive Law § 71.

(g) When a determination is rendered by the Court with respect to the questions certified, it shall be sent by the clerk of the Court to the certifying court.

PART 510. RULES OF THE COURT OF APPEALS IN CAPITAL CASES

Preamble

Acting pursuant to the rulemaking authority invested in this Court by New York Constitution, article VI, § 30, Judiciary Law § 51 and Laws of 1995, chapter 1, the Court of Appeals establishes these Rules of the Court of Appeals in Capital Cases. Unless otherwise specified, these Rules apply to all appeals taken pursuant to CPL 450.70, 450.80 and 460.40(3).

§ 510.1. Papers

(a) All records, briefs, appendices, motion papers and other required submissions, whether printed, typewritten, or reproduced in other form (no carbon copies), shall conform to CPLR 5529, shall be bound or securely fastened on the left edge, and shall have a fluorescent green sticker on the spine. Pages shall be consecutively numbered and each document filed shall contain an index or table of contents. Records and appendices shall be divided into volumes not to exceed two inches in thickness. Where New York authorities are cited in any paper, New York Official Law Report citations must be included.

(b) Companion filings on interactive compact disk, read-only memory (CD–ROM).

(1)(a) The submission of briefs by parties and amici curiae, and of records or appendices, on interactive compact disk, read-only memory (CD–ROM) as companions to the requisite number of printed briefs, records and appendices filed and served in accordance with the Rules of the Court of Appeals in Capital Cases is allowed and encouraged, provided that all parties have consented to the filing of the companion CD–ROM brief and record or appendix.

(b) The Court may, by order on motion of any party or *sua sponte*, require such filing.

(2) The companion CD–ROM brief, record or appendix must comply with the current technical specifications available from the clerk's office and must be packaged in a box or boxes with a green fluorescent sticker on the spine.

(3) The companion CD–ROM brief, record or appendix must be identical in content and format (including page numbering) to the printed version, except that each also may provide electronic links (hyperlinks) to the complete text of any authorities cited therein, and to any document or other material constituting the record on appeal.

(4) No fewer than 10 disks or sets of disks must be filed, with (a) proof of service of at least one disk or set on each other party and amicus curiae and (b) a

copy of either the parties' stipulation or the Court's order permitting or requesting such filing.

(5) Appellant's filing and respondent's filing, or a joint filing by appellant and respondent, is due 10 days after the final due date for filing appellant's reply brief (see section 510.8[b] of this Part).

(6) Each amicus curiae's filing is due 10 days after the due date for filing the respective amicus brief.

§ 510.2. Duties of Trial-Level Capital Defense Counsel

(a) Where a capital trial results in a judgment including a sentence of death, capital defense counsel shall timely take an appeal. CPL 470.30(2) provides that a defendant sentenced to death may not waive review pursuant to CPL 450.70(1) of the judgment and sentence.

(b) Immediately after being served with an adverse order disposing of a capital matter appealable pursuant to CPL 450.70(2), (3), or (4) or CPL 460.40(3), capital defense counsel shall advise the defendant in writing of the right to appeal. Counsel shall ascertain whether the defendant wishes to appeal and, if so, shall timely take the appeal.

(c) In all instances, capital defense counsel shall advise the defendant in writing of the time limitations for taking an appeal, the manner of taking an appeal and of obtaining a transcript of the testimony, and the right of a defendant unable to pay the cost of an appeal to apply for permission to appeal as a poor person. Capital defense counsel shall also comply with section 510.7(a) of this Part.

§ 510.3. Notice of Appeal

(a) CPL 450.70(1) Mandatory Appeal. A timely appeal must be taken pursuant to CPL 460.10(1). In addition, counsel for defendant must file one copy of the notice of appeal, with proof of service and filing, with the clerk of the Court of Appeals.

(b) Other Capital Appeals. Any other appeal in a case involving a sentence of death shall be taken by the timely service and filing of a notice of appeal pursuant to CPL 460.10(1). In addition, counsel for appellant must file one copy of the notice of appeal, with proof of service and filing, with the clerk of the Court of Appeals.

§ 510.4. Stays of Execution: Automatic or Determined by Superior Court

(a) Upon appeal from a judgment including a sentence of death (CPL 460.40[1]). The taking of an appeal by a defendant directly to the Court of Appeals from a superior court judgment including a sentence of death stays the execution of such sentence until determination of the appeal.

(b) Initial CPL article 440 proceedings (CPL 460.40[3]). Upon motion to the superior court judge or justice who signed the warrant of execution, a defendant sentenced to death shall be granted a stay of execution of a death warrant issued pursuant to Correction Law article 22–B to allow the defendant an opportunity to prepare and timely file an initial motion in superior court pursuant to CPL 440.10 or 440.20. The order staying execution shall provide that the stay of execution shall continue until (1) the time for taking an appeal to the Court of Appeals from the superior court's denial of such CPL article 440 motion has expired, or (2) if an appeal is taken, until the Court of Appeals determines the appeal.

(c) Subsequent CPL article 440 proceedings (CPL 460.40[3]).

(1) In the event a defendant sentenced to death files a motion for post-conviction relief pursuant to CPL 440.10 or 440.20 subsequent to the final determination of an initial CPL article 440 motion, the superior court may grant a stay of execution of a death warrant issued pursuant to Correction Law article 22–B only for good cause shown.

(2) The People and a defendant sentenced to death shall have an appeal as of right directly to the Court of Appeals from a superior court order granting or denying such motion for a stay of execution. On such appeal, the court may affirm, reverse, or modify such order as the court deems appropriate.

(3) By the end of business on the date a notice of appeal from a superior court order granting or denying a motion for a stay of execution has been filed, the clerk of the superior court, and appellant or appellant's counsel, shall notify the clerk of the Court of Appeals by telephone of such filing. Telephone notice to the Court of Appeals does not relieve the clerk of the superior court of the duties imposed by section 510.6 of this Part.

(4) Upon the taking of an appeal from a superior court order granting or denying such a stay, the Court of Appeals shall forthwith issue a Capital Appeal Management Order order establishing a schedule for perfecting the appeal. To the extent other provisions of this Part are inconsistent with a Capital Appeal Management Order so issued, the order shall supersede those provisions for purposes of the subject appeal only.

§ 510.5. Stays of Execution: Requests to the Court of Appeals

(a) Where not otherwise provided, the Court of Appeals may grant a stay on motion brought in accordance with section 510.12 of this Part, provided that the court's jurisdiction has been invoked by the service and filing of a notice of appeal or a motion pursuant to CPL 460.30 for an extension of time to take an appeal.

(b) Emergency motions for interim stay relief shall be brought on by order to show cause filed with the clerk of the Court of Appeals. Any time a party seeks interim stay relief, that party should contact the clerk of the court at (518) 455–7700.

§ 510.6. Case History

Within 15 days after the filing of a notice of appeal to the Court of Appeals in a case involving a sentence of death, except in those appeals taken pursuant to CPL 460.40(3) from an order of a superior court granting or denying a motion for a stay of execution, the clerk of the superior court in which the judgment or order being appealed from was rendered shall transmit to the clerk of the Court of Appeals a Case History including:

(1) the duplicate notice of appeal;

(2) a chronological list of all proceedings below giving rise to this particular appeal, noting which transcripts have been, or must be, prepared; and

(3) a list of all exhibits introduced in the proceedings below giving rise to this particular appeal.

The clerk of the superior court shall transmit to counsel for the parties copies of items (2) and (3) above.

§ 510.7. Poor Person Relief; Assignment of Counsel

The following procedures shall apply in all capital appeals except those appeals taken pursuant to CPL 460.40(3) from an order of a superior court granting or denying a motion for a stay of execution.

(a) Where sought, trial counsel shall move, pursuant to section 510.12 of this Part, for assignment of appellate counsel or other items of poor person relief within 10 days after the filing of the notice of appeal. The motion papers shall include an affidavit setting forth the information required by CPLR 1101(a). On an appeal in a case in which Judiciary Law Section 35–b provides for the assignment of appellate counsel, trial counsel's affidavit shall also state whether counsel is requesting to be considered for assignment as counsel on the appeal.

(b) Where the appeal is taken from a judgment including a sentence of death pursuant to CPL 450.70(1), assigned counsel may move at any time pursuant to section 510.12 of this Part for assignment of Associate Counsel for good cause shown.

(c) Assignment of counsel shall proceed in compliance with any applicable Court of Appeals directives on the matter.

§ 510.8. Capital Appeal Management Orders; Issue Identification by the Parties

The following procedures shall apply in all capital appeals except those appeals taken pursuant to CPL 460.40(3) from an order of a superior court granting or denying a motion for a stay of execution.

(a) After receipt from the superior court of the Case History required by section 510.6 of this Part, the Court of Appeals shall enter and forward to counsel for the parties an Initial Capital Appeal Management Order or Orders:

(1) determining defendant's request, if any, for items of poor person relief,

(2) establishing final dates for transcription and settlement, if necessary, and

(3) establishing a deadline for filing the settled record on appeal in this court, and

(4) for purposes of case management, requiring appellant's counsel to file periodically with the clerk of the Court of Appeals a progress report concerning the capital appeal.

(b) Appellant's counsel shall file, and respondent's counsel may file, a Preliminary Appeal Statement in accordance with section 510.9 of this Part. Following either the filing of respondent's Preliminary Appeal Statement or the expiration of respondent's time to so file, the Court of Appeals shall enter and forward to counsel for the parties a Final Capital Appeal Management Order which shall:

(1) establish a briefing schedule for the appeal;

(2) state whether the appeal will proceed on the full reproduced record or on an appendix, as set forth in section 510.11 of this Part;

(3) for purposes of case management, require counsel to file periodically with the clerk of the Court of Appeals a progress report concerning the capital appeal; and

(4) establish a deadline by which all requests for amicus curiae relief must be noticed to be heard.

Capital appeals shall receive a calendar preference. In the clerk's discretion, a capital appeal management conference may be scheduled prior to, or any time following, issuance of the Initial Capital Appeal Management Order.

(c) For purposes of case management and public notice, appellant must file with the opening brief on appeal a separately bound Issue Identification Statement listing, in point-heading format, all issues raised on the appeal. The Court of Appeals may direct the parties to brief and argue specific issues on the appeal.

§ 510.9. Preliminary Appeal Statements

The following procedures shall apply in all capital appeals except those appeals taken pursuant to CPL 460.40(3) from an order of a superior court granting or denying a motion for a stay of execution.

(a) For issue identification and case management purposes only, within 30 days after the filing of the record on appeal in the Court of Appeals, appellant's counsel shall file with the clerk of the Court of Appeals, with proof of service of one copy on respondent's counsel, two copies of a Preliminary Appeal Statement, which shall include:

(1) the title of the case;

(2) the court from which the appeal is taken;

(3) a copy of the judgment or order of the superior court appealed from;

(4) a copy of any other written order brought up for review;

(5) a copy of all written decisions of the superior court; and

(6) a preliminary, nonbinding statement of issues likely to be raised on appeal.

(b) Within 10 days after service of appellant's Preliminary Appeal Statement, respondent's counsel may file with the clerk of the Court of Appeals, with proof of service of one copy on appellant's counsel, two copies of a Preliminary Appeal Statement which sets forth any additional matters relevant to the appeal or any disagreement with appellant's Preliminary Appeal Statement.

(c) Where appellant's statement of issues pursuant to subdivision (a)(6) of this section includes an assertion that a statute, or a portion of a statute, is unconstitutional, notice must be given to the Attorney General pursuant to section 510.13 of this Part prior to filing the Preliminary Appeal Statement, and a certification of this notification shall be included in the Preliminary Appeal Statement.

§ 510.10. Record Transcription and Reproduction; Settlement

(a) During the course of capital proceedings before the superior court, and at all times thereafter, the clerk of the superior court shall take all necessary steps to insure the accuracy and completeness of the record of the proceedings.

(b) The court reporter shall take, and keep electronically, minutes of all capital proceedings occurring in the superior court. Transcription shall proceed in compliance with any relevant superior court order and the Court of Appeals Capital Appeal Management Orders. Where a copy of the minutes of any proceedings in the superior court was ordered during the course of the superior court proceedings, defense counsel and the prosecutor shall preserve their respective copies of the transcript. Transcripts shall be settled pursuant to CPLR 5525(c) within such time limits and pursuant to such additional procedures as may be set by Court of Appeals order.

(c) Upon the filing of a notice of appeal, the superior court clerk shall expeditiously assemble, reproduce, and transmit to appellant the record of the proceedings. Appellant shall be responsible for the timely preparation and filing of the record on appeal in accordance with the Initial Capital Appeal Management Order issued by the Court of Appeals pursuant to section 510.8(a) of this Part.

(d) The record on appeal shall comply with section 510.11(b) of this Part, and be stipulated to or settled on motion. The parties may stipulate to the correctness of the contents of the record on appeal using the process provided by CPLR 5525(c)(1). Where the parties are unable to agree and stipulate to the contents of the record on appeal, appellant shall move, on notice, to settle the record in the superior court from which the appeal is taken.

(e) Within the time period prescribed in the Initial Capital Appeal Management Order after the superior court clerk's transmission to appellant of the reproduced record of proceedings, appellant shall file with the clerk of the Court of Appeals either the parties' stipulation to the record on appeal or a copy of appellant's notice of motion to settle the record.

(f) The parties' failure to list in the stipulation to the record on appeal any transcript, exhibit, or other document that constituted a part of the underlying prosecution shall not preclude the Court of Appeals from considering such transcript, exhibit, or other document in determining the appeal.

§ 510.11. Record on Appeal; Appendix; Briefs

(a) Record on Appeal. On an appeal in a case involving a sentence of death, appellant shall file with the clerk of the Court of Appeals 15 copies of the settled, reproduced record of the proceedings in the superior court, with proof of service on respondent of three copies of the settled, reproduced record.

(b) The settled, reproduced record shall contain the complete original file, including the transcribed stenographic minutes of all proceedings occurring in the superior court, such as proceedings on pretrial motions and hearings, opening and closing statements, jury voir dire examination, all trial testimony, all legal argument of counsel, including bench and chambers colloquies, the jury instructions, all communications to and from the jury after instructions, proceedings on sentencing, and post-trial motions and hearings. The record shall conform substantially with the requirements of CPLR 5526, except that the subject matter of each page of the record need not be stated at the top. The record shall also conform substantially with the requirements of section 510.1 of this Part, and shall contain in the following order so many of the following items as are relevant to the case:

(1) a cover which shall contain the title of the case on the upper portion and, on the lower portion, the names, addresses, and voice and facsimile telephone numbers of counsel for the parties, and the indictment number;

(2) the statement required by CPLR 5531;

(3) a table of contents which shall list and briefly describe each paper included in the record. The part of the table relating to the transcript of testimony shall separately list each witness and the page at which direct, cross, redirect and recross examinations begin. The part of the table relating to exhibits shall concisely indicate the nature and contents of each exhibit and the page in the record where it is reproduced and where it was admitted into evidence. The table shall also contain references to pages where a motion to dismiss the indictment or to direct or set aside a verdict, or where an oral decision of the court, appears;

(4) the notice of appeal, judgment or order appealed from, judgment roll, corrected transcript, relevant exhibits and any opinions or decisions in the case;

(5) a stipulation, or order settling the transcript; and

(6) a copy of either the stipulation described in section 510.10(d) of this Part or the superior court order settling the record.

(c) Confidential Material

(1) Documents and transcripts ordered sealed by the courts below shall be reproduced in separate volumes of the record on appeal. Each such volume shall be clearly identified on the cover as containing confidential material.

(2) The People shall file, separately from the record on appeal, one copy of all documents and transcripts concerning the nature or substance of any grand jury testimony or evidence, and any decision, result, or other matter attending a grand jury proceeding which is required by CPL 190.25(4)(a) to be kept secret. All such volumes shall be clearly identified on the cover as containing confidential grand jury material.

(d) Appendix. Except on appeals taken pursuant to CPL 450.70(1), the Court of Appeals sua sponte may order appellant, or appellant may seek permission pursuant to section 510.12 of this Part, to prosecute the appeal upon one copy of the settled, reproduced record and 15 copies of an appendix which conforms to the requirements of CPLR 5528 and 5529 and section 510.1 of this Part. The appendix shall be bound separately from the brief and shall include the following items:

(1) the notice of appeal;

(2) the statement required by CPLR 5531;

(3) the order or judgment of the superior court from which the appeal is taken;

(4) any other order sought to be reviewed;

(5) the written and oral decisions of the superior court, as relevant;

(6) findings of fact, as relevant;

(7) the indictment; and

(8) those portions of the testimony, affidavits, legal arguments, and written and photographic exhibits referenced in appellant's brief and reasonably expected to be referenced in respondent's brief, and all other portions that may be useful to the determination of the questions raised on the appeal.

The prior filing of a Preliminary Appeal Statement pursuant to section 510.9 of this Part does not satisfy the requirements of this section. Where appellant has filed an inadequate appendix, respondent may move to strike the appendix pursuant to section 510.12 of this Part or may submit a respondent's appendix containing additional parts of the record deemed necessary for the court to consider the questions involved.

(e) Briefs. Briefs shall conform to the requirements of section 510.1 of this Part. The cover of the brief shall set forth the title of the case. The upper right hand section shall contain a notation stating whether the case shall be argued or submitted. If the case is to be argued, the notation shall state the name of counsel who will argue and the amount of time granted for oral argument. The lower right hand section shall contain the name, address, and voice and facsimile telephone number of counsel filing the brief, and the date the brief was filed, and shall indicate whom counsel represents. Unless authorized by the clerk of the Court of Appeals, briefs shall not contain maps, photographs, or other addenda. Boldface type shall only be used in point headings or subheadings.

(1) Appellant shall file 15 copies of the appellant's brief and the Issue Identification Statement required by section 510.8(c) of this Part, with proof of service of three copies on respondent. The appellant's brief shall contain in the following order:

(i) a table of contents including the titles of the points urged in the brief;

(ii) a list of all authorities cited in the brief;

(iii) a concise statement of the questions involved without names, dates, or particulars. Each question shall be numbered, set forth separately, and followed immediately by the answer, if any, of the court from which the appeal is taken;

(iv) a concise statement of the nature of the case and of the facts which should be known to determine the questions involved, with supporting references to pages in the record or the appendix, including, if such be the case, a statement that proceedings on the judgment or order appealed

from have been stayed pending a determination of the appeal; and

(v) the appellant's argument, which shall be divided into points by appropriate headings distinctively printed.

(2) Respondent shall file 15 copies of the respondent's brief, with proof of service of three copies on appellant. The respondent's brief shall contain, in the following order:

(i) a table of contents including the titles of the points urged in the brief;

(ii) a list of all authorities cited in the brief;

(iii) a counter statement of the questions involved or of the nature and facts of the case, if respondent disagrees with the statement of appellant; and

(iv) the argument for respondent, which shall be divided into points by appropriate headings distinctively printed.

(3) Appellant shall file 15 copies of the appellant's reply brief, with proof of service of three copies on respondent. The appellant's reply brief shall contain, in the following order:

(i) a table of contents;

(ii) a list of all authorities cited in the brief; and

(iii) the reply for appellant, without repetition of the arguments contained in the main brief, which shall be divided into points by appropriate headings distinctively printed.

§ 510.12. Motions

(a) Unless otherwise directed by a judge of the Court of Appeals by order to show cause, the following procedures shall apply to motions concerning capital appeals. A motion addressed to the Court of Appeals may be made on 8 days' notice (personal service), 9 days' notice (overnight delivery service) or 13 days' notice (service by mail) (see CPLR 2103). Motions are returnable at Court of Appeals Hall, 20 Eagle Street, Albany, New York 12207–1095, every Monday, whether or not the court is in session. Whenever a Monday is a State holiday, motions are returnable on the next day of that week that is not a State holiday. All motions shall be submitted without oral argument. Unless otherwise permitted by the court or the clerk, the papers in support of a motion must be filed at Court of Appeals Hall no later than noon on the Friday preceding the return date. All responding papers must be served and filed at Court of Appeals Hall on or before the return date of the motion. Proof of service on each party must be filed with any papers submitted on a motion. Filings by facsimile transmission will not be accepted without prior authorization of the clerk. No adjournments are possible other than in those narrow circumstances provided by CPLR 321(c).

(b) Reply papers are not permitted by the court's motion practice. Requests for permission to file papers after the motion return date are governed by section 510.14 of this Part.

(c) Motion for Amicus Curiae Relief. A brief amicus curiae may be filed only by leave of the Court of Appeals granted on motion, or upon the court's request. Motions for amicus curiae relief must be noticed to be heard no later than the deadline set forth in the Final Capital Appeal Management Order. Movant must file one copy of the motion and 15 copies of the proposed brief, with proof of service of three copies on each party. Motions for amicus curiae relief must demonstrate to the court's satisfaction at least one of the following:

(1) that the parties are not capable of a full and adequate presentation and that movants could remedy this deficiency;

(2) that movants would invite the court's attention to law or arguments which might otherwise escape its consideration; or

(3) that amicus curiae briefs would otherwise be of special assistance to the court.

Proposed briefs amicus curiae shall conform to the requirements set forth in section 510.11(e) of this Part.

(d) Motion for Reargument. A motion for reargument of an appeal shall be made on 10 copies of a brief or memorandum, with proof of service of three copies. A motion to reargue a motion may be made on one copy of a brief or memorandum with proof of service of one copy. A motion to reargue an appeal or motion shall state briefly the grounds upon which reargument is sought and the points claimed to have been overlooked or misapprehended by the court, with proper reference to the particular portions of the record and to the authorities relied upon. A motion to reargue may not be based on the assertion for the first time of new points except for extraordinary and compelling reasons. Unless otherwise permitted by the court, the notice of motion shall be served not later than 30 days after the appeal or motion has been decided.

(e) Other Motions. Motions other than those seeking amicus curiae relief or reargument may be made on a single set of the moving papers, with proof of service of one copy.

(f) Motion papers which do not conform to the requirements of this Part may be rejected by the clerk.

§ 510.13. Notice to the Attorney General

Unless such notice has already been given pursuant to section 510.9(c) of this Part, where a party or an amicus asserts in its brief on appeal that a statute, or a portion of a statute, is unconstitutional, notice shall be given to the Attorney General in writing at the time the party or amicus files its brief, and a certification of the notification shall be included in the brief. The notification and a copy of the brief shall be sent to the Solicitor General, Department of Law, The Capitol, Albany, New York 12224–0341.

§ 510.14. Post-Argument Communications

Post-argument and post-submission communications to the court concerning motions and appeals, in the form of letters, memoranda or briefs, are not permitted and will be returned to the sender, unless specifically requested or authorized by the Court of Appeals or authorized, in writing, by the clerk of the Court of Appeals upon submission to the clerk with a request that they be accepted.

§ 510.15. Withdrawal of Appeal or Motion

With the exception of a defendant's appeal to the Court of Appeals from a judgment including a sentence of death pursuant to CPL 450.70(1), an appeal may be withdrawn and discontinued at any time prior to argument or submission by forwarding to the clerk of the Court of Appeals a duly executed stipulation of withdrawal, which must be signed by all counsel, and by the defendant personally. A motion may be withdrawn at any time prior to its return date by filing with the clerk a written request signed by counsel for the moving party. A request to withdraw a motion after submission must be supported by a stipulation of withdrawal signed by all counsel.

§ 510.16. Notice to the Capital Defender Office

(a) Upon a determination of the Court of Appeals affirming a judgment that includes a sentence of death, the clerk of the Court of appeals shall notify the capital defender office of the determination by the end of business on the day such determination is handed down.

(b) Notice to the capital defender office required pursuant to subdivision (a) of this section shall consist of telephone, facsimile, electronic mail or other prompt electronic means of communication, which shall be followed by first class mail notification within two business days after the affirmance.

(c) The clerk of the Court of Appeals shall retain a written record of the electronic and written notice given pursuant to subdivision (b) of this section.

§ 510.17. Remittitur

The remittitur of the Court of Appeals containing the court's adjudication, together with the return papers filed with the court, shall be sent to the clerk of the court to which the case is remitted, there to be proceeded upon according to law. Any order to effect the adjudication contained in the Court of Appeals' remittitur shall be sought, entered and enforced in the superior court.

§ 510.18. Capital Case Data Reports

[Suspended, until further order, by order of the Court of Appeals, dated January 11, 2008, effective January 30, 2008, or as soon thereafter as section 52 of the Judiciary Law is complied with.]

(a) In each criminal action in which the defendant has been indicted for commission of an offense defined in section 125.27 of the Penal Law, except those in which the indictment is dismissed or the defendant is acquitted, the clerk of the superior court, within 45 days after the disposition of the action in such court, shall prepare and send to the Court of Appeals a Capital Case Data Report in the form prescribed by the Court of Appeals. Data reports shall be prepared by the clerk of the superior court by reviewing the record and upon consultation with the prosecutor and counsel for the defendant. Such data reports shall not constitute a part of the record in the underlying criminal action. The clerk of the superior court shall retain, in a confidential file kept separate from the record in the underlying criminal action, a copy of each such data report sent to the Court of Appeals, and may disclose a data report, or any part thereof, only upon order of the Court of Appeals for exceptional cause shown.

(b) All Capital Case Data Reports received by the Court of Appeals shall be compiled into a uniform Capital Case Data Report, which may consist of a computer data base containing the information in each Capital Case Data Report. Upon request, the uniform Capital Case Data Report shall be made available to the parties on appeal to the Court of Appeals in cases where a sentence of death has been imposed.

(c) If the conviction or sentence in such criminal action is subsequently reversed or modified, the Capital Case Data Report shall be notated to reflect the reversal or modification. If an intermediate appellate court reverses or modifies the conviction or sentence, that court shall forward a copy of its remittitur to the Court of Appeals within 10 days after entry. If a new disposition in the action ensues in the superior court, the superior court clerk shall prepare a new Capital Case Data Report. Upon completion, the superior court clerk shall send the new Capital Case Data Report to the clerk of the Court of Appeals with a notice that the new report should be substituted in the data base for the previous report.

PART 515. STANDARDS FOR APPELLATE COUNSEL AND STATE POST-CONVICTION COUNSEL IN CAPITAL CASES

§ 515.1. Standards for Appellate Counsel in Capital Cases

(1) Appellate Qualifications and Experience.

(a) *Sole Appellate Counsel.* To be eligible to be appointed as sole appellate counsel on direct appeal in a capital case, an attorney must demonstrate that he or she:

(1) has at least five years of criminal trial or criminal appellate or post-conviction experience, or has at least three years of concentrated criminal litigation experience;

(2) is familiar with the practice and procedure of the trial and appellate courts of New York, including the New York Court of Appeals; and

(3) also has had primary responsibility for the appeal of at least five felony convictions in any state or federal court, at least three of which were on behalf of the defendant, and at least three of which were orally argued by the attorney.

(b) *Two Appellate Counsel.* To be eligible to be appointed as one of two appellate counsel on direct appeal in a capital case:

(1) one attorney must demonstrate that he or she has the qualifications set forth in (a) above.

(2) the second attorney must demonstrate that he or she:

(i) has at least three years of criminal litigation or post-conviction experience;

(ii) is familiar with the practice and procedure of the trial and appellate courts of New York, including the New York Court of Appeals; and

(iii) has had primary responsibility for the appeal, in any state or federal court, of at least three felony convictions, at least one of which was on behalf of the defendant.

(c) *Trial Counsel.* If otherwise qualified under these standards, and with the consent of the client, a defendant's capital trial counsel may seek to be appointed capital appellate counsel on the same defendant's appeal.

(d) *Waiver.* If an attorney cannot meet one or more of the requirements set forth above, the Screening Panel, after consideration of the recommendation of the Capital Defender Office, may waive such requirement by demonstration by the attorney that he or she, by reason of extensive civil litigation and/or appellate experience or other exceptional qualifications, is capable of providing effective representation as appellate counsel in a capital case.

(2) Applications to Capital Defender Office.

(a) *Applications.* In support of an application, an attorney shall submit to the Capital Defender Office a form prescribed by the Capital Defender Office and approved by the Administrative Board of the Courts. It shall require the attorney to demonstrate that he or she has fully satisfied the requirements set forth above. The attorney shall also identify any requirements that he or she requests be waived, and shall set forth in detail his or her appellate experience or other exceptional qualifications that justify waiver.

(b) *Required Submissions.* In support of an application, an attorney shall submit to the Capital Defender Office:

(1) at least two appellate briefs, written exclusively or primarily by the applicant, the opposing briefs, and the decisions;

(2) descriptions of any capital or other criminal appellate advocacy or other criminal practice program attended;

(3) the names, addresses and phone numbers of two prosecutors and two defense attorneys, current or former, including at least one appellate adversary, familiar with the applicant's work as an effective advocate;

(4) the applicant may submit the name, address and phone number of one appellate judge, if the judge is familiar with the applicant's work as an effective advocate; and

(5) any other material that may be relevant to fully evaluate the applicant's appellate qualifications and experience.

(3) Creation of Court of Appeals Roster.

(a) *Delivery to Screening Panel.* The Capital Defender Office shall review each application to determine that it is complete. The Capital Defender Office shall deliver all completed applications, within 30 days of their receipt, to the appropriate Screening Panel, together with a statement setting forth the status of the attorney's completion of the training required by Section (5), below, and its recommendations to the Screening Panel with respect to whether the attorney is qualified for appointment as appellate counsel in a capital case. The appropriate Screening Panel shall be the panel in the judicial department in which the attorney has his or her principal office for the practice of law.

(b) *Designation by Screening Panel.* Within 30 days of receipt of the application, each Screening Panel shall designate those attorneys deemed qualified for appointment as appellate counsel in a capital case, and shall report those designations to the Court of Appeals.

(c) *Waiver or Deferral of Required Submissions.* If an attorney cannot provide each of the above items, the Screening Panel, upon demonstration that the attorney is capable of providing effective representation as appellate counsel in a capital case, and after

consideration of the recommendation of the Capital Defender Office, may:

(1) defer submission of any item(s) for a reasonable time, and in the interim designate the attorney as a qualified appellate counsel; or

(2) waive such submission.

(d) *Establishment of the Roster.* The Court of Appeals shall incorporate the names of each attorney found qualified by a Screening Panel into a single roster of attorneys qualified for appointment as appellate counsel in a capital case.

(4) Additions to Court of Appeals Roster.

(a) *Requests for Reconsideration.* Any attorney whose application for designation as qualified appellate counsel is rejected by a Screening Panel may apply to the Court of Appeals for reconsideration of his or her application pursuant to such procedures as may be prescribed by the Court of Appeals.

(b) *Determination by the Court of Appeals.* The Court of Appeals shall review each such application pursuant to the criteria set forth in these standards, including consideration of the recommendations of the Capital Defender Office and of the Screening Panel, and may add that attorney to the roster of qualified appellate counsel if the Court deems the attorney qualified to serve as appellate counsel in a capital case.

(5) Training.

(a) *Certification.* An attorney shall not be eligible to be appointed as appellate counsel in a capital case unless the Capital Defender Office shall certify that the attorney satisfactorily has completed a capital appellate-advocacy course prescribed by the Capital Defender Office and approved by the Administrative Board of the Courts.

(b) *Interim Certification.* The Screening Panel, or the Court of Appeals, in its discretion, may permit an attorney to be eligible for such appointment if the attorney meets all of the other requirements for qualification and experience, and the Capital Defender Office confirms that such attorney is in active pursuit of such training and certification.

(6) Retention of Eligibility.

(a) *On–Going Training.* To remain eligible for appointment as counsel on a capital appeal, an attorney must attend and successfully complete capital training sessions as prescribed by the Capital Defender Office.

(b) *Removal from the Court of Appeals Roster.* The Court of Appeals may remove from its roster of attorneys any attorney who, in the Court's judgment, has not provided competent, thorough representation.

§ 515.2. Standards for State Post–Conviction Counsel in Capital Cases

(1) State Post–Conviction Qualifications and Experience.

(a) *State Post–Conviction Counsel.* To be eligible to be appointed as lead counsel on an initial motion pursuant to section 440.10 or 440.20 of the Criminal Procedure Law and any appeal therefrom in a capital case, an attorney must demonstrate that he or she:

(1) has at least six years criminal trial, criminal appellate or state or federal post-conviction experience, or has at least four years of concentrated criminal or civil litigation experience;

(2) is familiar with:

(i) the practice and procedure of the trial and appellate courts of New York including the New York Court of Appeals; and

(ii) the practice and procedure of the federal courts with regard to federal habeas corpus petitions;

(3) has conducted twelve trials before judges, arbitration panels or juries to verdict, decision, or hung jury, in serious and complex civil or criminal cases;

(4) has had primary responsibility for the appeal of at least five felony convictions in any state or federal court, at least three of which were on behalf of the defendant, and at least three of which were orally argued by the attorney;

(5) has substantial familiarity with, and extensive experience in the use of, expert witnesses and scientific and medical evidence including, but not limited to, mental health and pathology evidence; and

(6) meets two of the following criteria:

(i) has tried five homicides to verdict or hung jury with at least three as defense counsel;

(ii) has, at the trial level, represented to disposition defendants in eight homicide cases;

(iii) has represented capital defendants in three state or federal post-conviction proceedings;

(iv) has brought five motions, pursuant to section 440.10 or 440.20 of the Criminal Procedure Law, where hearings were held and witnesses examined.

(b) *Waiver.* If an attorney cannot meet one or more of the requirements set forth above, the Screening Panel, after consideration of the recommendation of the Capital Defender Office, may waive such requirement upon demonstration by the attorney that he or she, by reason of extensive criminal or civil litigation, 440 motion practice, appellate and/or post-conviction experience or other exceptional qualifications, is capable of providing effective representation as post-conviction counsel in a capital case.

(2) Applications to Capital Defender Office.

(a) *Applications.* In support of an application, an attorney shall submit to the Capital Defender Office a form prescribed by the Capital Defender Office and approved by the Administrative Board of the Courts. It shall require the attorney to demonstrate that he or she has fully satisfied the requirements set forth above. The attorney shall also identify any requirement that he or she requests be waived, and shall set forth in detail his or her criminal or civil litigation, 440 motion practice, appellate and/or post-conviction experience or other exceptional qualification that justify waiver.

(b) *Required Submissions.* In support of an application, an attorney shall submit to the Capital Defender Office:

(1) a description of a trial or post-conviction strategy in a case handled by the attorney and reflective of the attorney's thorough advocacy. This strategy may have, for instance, aimed to achieve a favorable pre-trial disposition or to alter the range of sentencing options;

(2) at least two memoranda of law prepared by the attorney in connection with separate cases;

(3) at least two appellate briefs written exclusively or primarily by the applicant, the opposing briefs, and the decisions;

(4) the names, addresses, and phone numbers of two prosecutors and two defense attorneys, current or former, including at least one adversary, familiar with the applicant's work as an effective advocate;

(5) the applicant may submit the name, address, and phone number of one judge, if the judge is familiar with the applicant's work as an effective advocate;

(6) a description of specialized trial, appellate or post-conviction capital defense training programs regularly attended; and

(7) any other material that may be relevant to fully evaluate the applicant's qualifications and experience.

(3) Creation of Court of Appeals Roster.

(a) *Delivery to Screening Panel.* The Capital Defender Office shall review each application to determine that it is complete. The Capital Defender Office shall deliver all completed applications, within 30 days of their receipt, to the appropriate Screening Panel, together with a statement setting forth the status of the attorney's completion of the training required by Section (5), below, and its recommendations to the Screening Panel with respect to whether the attorney is qualified for appointment as post-conviction counsel in a capital case. The appropriate Screening Panel shall be the panel in the judicial department in which the attorney has his or her principal office for the practice of law.

(b) *Designation by Screening Panel.* Within 30 days of receipt of the application, each Screening Panel shall designate those attorneys deemed qualified for appointment as post-conviction counsel in a capital case, and shall report those designations to the Court of Appeals.

(c) *Waiver or Deferral of Required Submissions.* If an attorney cannot provide each of the above items, the Screening Panel, upon demonstration that the attorney is capable of providing effective representation as post-conviction counsel in a capital case, and after consideration of the recommendation of the Capital Defender Office, may:

(1) defer submission of any item(s) for a reasonable time, and in the interim designate the attorney as a qualified post-conviction counsel; or

(2) waive such submission.

(d) *Establishment of the Roster.* The Court of Appeals shall incorporate the names of each attorney found qualified by a Screening Panel into a single roster of attorneys qualified for appointment as post-conviction counsel in a capital case.

(4) Additions to Court of Appeals Roster.

(a) *Requests for Reconsideration.* Any attorney whose application for designation as qualified post-conviction counsel is rejected by a Screening Panel may apply to the Court of Appeals for reconsideration of his or her application pursuant to such procedures as may be prescribed by the Court of Appeals.

(b) *Determination by the Court of Appeals.* The Court of Appeals shall review each such application pursuant to the criteria set forth in these standards, including consideration of the recommendations of the Capital Defender Office and of the Screening Panel, and may add that attorney to the roster of qualified post-conviction counsel if the Court deems the attorney qualified to serve as post-conviction counsel in a capital case.

(5) Training.

(a) *Certification.* An attorney shall not be eligible to be appointed as post-conviction counsel in a capital case unless the Capital Defender Office shall certify that the attorney satisfactorily has completed a capital post-conviction course prescribed by the Capital Defender Office and approved by the Administrative Board of the Courts.

(b) *Interim Certification.* The Screening Panel, or the Court of Appeals, in its discretion, may permit an attorney to be eligible for such appointment if the attorney meets all of the other requirements for qualification and experience, and the Capital Defender Office confirms that such attorney is in active pursuit of such training and certification.

(6) Retention of Eligibility.

(a) *On–Going Training.* To remain eligible for appointment as counsel on an initial motion pursuant to section 440.10 or 440.20 of the Criminal Procedure Law and an appeal therefrom, an attorney must attend and successfully complete capital training sessions as prescribed by the Capital Defender Office.

(b) *Removal from the Court of Appeals Roster.* The Court of Appeals may remove from its roster of attorneys any attorney who, in the Court's judgment, has not provided competent, thorough representation.

PART 520. RULES OF THE COURT OF APPEALS FOR THE ADMISSION OF ATTORNEYS AND COUNSELORS AT LAW

§ 520.1. General

(a) A person shall be admitted to practice law in the courts of the State of New York only by an order of the Appellate Division of the Supreme Court upon compliance with these rules.

(b) **Saving Clause.** Those provisions of the rules of the Court of Appeals for the admission of attorneys and counselors at law that prescribe the qualifications for admission to the New York State bar examination, which were in effect at the time an applicant for admission commenced the study of law, to the extent that the application thereof was or would have been less restrictive or burdensome, shall determine the applicant's eligibility for admission to such examination.

§ 520.2. Admission Upon Examination

(a) **Proof Required by the New York State Board of Law Examiners.** An applicant for admission to the New York State bar examination shall furnish to the New York State Board of Law Examiners, in accordance with its rules, proof satisfactory to said board:

(1) that applicant is over 21 years of age;

(2) as to the date and place of birth; and

(3) that applicant has complied with section 520.3, 520.4, 520.5 or 520.6 of this Part.

(b) **and (c)** [Rescinded].

§ 520.3. Study of Law in Law School

(a) **General.**

(1) Except as otherwise provided in paragraph (2) of this subdivision, an applicant may qualify to take the New York State bar examination by submitting to the New York State Board of Law Examiners satisfactory proof that applicant attended and was graduated with a first degree in law from a law school or

law schools which at all times during the period of applicant's attendance was or were approved.

(2) An applicant may qualify to take the New York State bar examination by submitting to the New York State Board of Law Examiners satisfactory proof that applicant attended and successfully completed the prescribed course of instruction required for a first degree in law, but the State Board of Law Examiners shall not certify the applicant for admission to the bar pursuant to section 520.7(a) of this Part until the applicant has presented a certificate showing that the applicant has been awarded a first degree in law.

(b) Approved Law School Defined. An approved law school for purposes of these rules is one:

(1) whose program and course of study meet the requirements of this section, as shown by the law school's bulletin or catalogue, which shall be filed annually with the Clerk of the Court of Appeals; and

(2) which is approved by the American Bar Association.

(c) Instructional Requirement.

(1) An approved law school shall require for its first degree in law the successful completion of either a full-time or a part-time program which consists of:

(i) a minimum of 80 semester hours of credit, including at least 60 semester hours in professional law subjects. A maximum of 20 of the required 80 semester hours may be courses related to legal training or clinical courses as provided in sections (2) and (5) of this subdivision; and

(ii) at least 1,120 hours of classroom study, exclusive of examination time.

(2) Other courses related to legal training taught by members of the faculty of said law school or university, or taught by members of the faculty of any university or college with which the law school offers a joint degree program, may, in the discretion of the law school, be substituted for professional law subjects to the extent of no more than 10 of the required 80 semester hours.

(3) No credit shall be allowed for correspondence courses.

(4) All study shall be evaluated by authentic written examination, except where such examination is inappropriate, such as in seminar and practice court courses or courses which are principally concerned with legal writing and research.

(5) Clinical and like courses may, in the discretion of the law school, be substituted for classroom periods to the extent of no more than 20 of the required 80 semester hours, where:

(i) a description of the course has been filed with the Clerk of the Court of Appeals, either separately or in the law school's annual catalogue or bulletin;

(ii) the course is under the direct and immediate supervision of a member or members of the faculty;

(iii) the course includes adequate classroom meetings or seminars during the same semester in which the clinical work is completed in order to insure contemporaneous discussion, review and evaluation of the clinical experience; and

(iv) the law school certificate of attendance filed with the New York State Board of Law Examiners lists separately the credit allowed for clinical courses or other nonclassroom study.

(d) Full–Time Program Defined. A full-time program shall consist of at least 75 and no more than 105 calendar weeks in residence, including reading periods not to exceed one week per semester and examinations, of at least 10 classroom periods per week, scheduled principally between the hours of 8 a.m. and 6 p.m., totaling not less than the equivalent of 1,120 hours of classroom study, exclusive of examination time. A calendar week shall include four days of scheduled classes; however, no more than three three-day weeks per semester may be counted toward the 75–week minimum. A semester which includes successful completion of at least 10 credit hours per week of study shall be counted as 15 full-time weeks in residence toward the residency weeks requirement of this subdivision. As allowed under subdivision (h) of this section, a summer session which includes successful completion of at least 5 credit hours per week of study shall be counted as 7.5 full-time calendar weeks in residence toward the residency weeks requirement of this subdivision.

(e) Part–Time Program Defined. A part-time program shall consist of at least 105 and no more than 135 calendar weeks in residence, including reading periods not to exceed one week per semester and examinations, of at least eight classroom periods per week, irrespective of the hours at which the classroom periods are scheduled, totaling not less the the equivalent of 1,120 hours of classroom study, exclusive of examination time. A calendar week shall include three days of scheduled classes; however, no more than three two-day weeks per semester may be counted toward the 105–week minimum. A semester which includes successful completion of at least 8 credit hours per week of study shall be counted as 15 part-time weeks in residence toward the residency weeks requirement of this subdivision. As allowed under subdivision (h) of this section, a summer session which includes successful completion of at least 4 credit hours per week of study shall be counted as 7.5 part-time calendar weeks in residence toward the residency weeks requirement of this subdivision.

(f) Successful Completion Defined. Complete credit for an academic year, semester, quarter or summer session in an approved law school in which one or more courses have been failed shall not be given until the passing grades in the courses failed have been earned, or substitute courses successfully completed, or unless the failures are compensated for by a sufficiently high average for the same academic year, semester, quarter or summer session under acceptable regulations established by the law school in which the applicant is matriculated.

(g) Transfer from One Law School Program to Another. A student may transfer from a full-time to a part-time program, or from a part-time to a full-time program, at the end of any semester, quarter or other complete academic session. In computing residence credit:

(1) each week of a full-time program shall be deemed equal to one and one-third weeks of a part-time program; and

(2) each week of a part-time program shall be deemed equal to three-fourths of a week of a full-time program.

(h) Summer Session. Credit may be given for successful completion of courses taken in summer session only if such session is approved by the dean of the law school in which the applicant is matriculated.

(i) Credit for Law Study in Foreign Country. An approved law school may, in its discretion, allow such credit as it may determine toward the total credits required for a first degree in law to an applicant who studied law in a law school in a foreign country.

§ 520.4. Study of Law in Law Office

(a) General. An applicant may qualify to take the New York State bar examination by submitting to the New York State Board of Law Examiners satisfactory proof:

(1) that applicant commenced the study of law after applicant's 18th birthday; and

(2) that applicant successfully completed at least one academic year as a matriculated student in a full-time program or the equivalent in a part-time program at an approved law school and at the conclusion thereof was eligible to continue in that school's degree program; and

(3) that applicant thereafter studied law in a law office or offices located within New York State under the supervision of one or more attorneys admitted to practice law in New York State, for such a period of time as, together with the credit allowed pursuant to this section for attendance in an approved law school, shall aggregate four years.

(b) Employment and Instruction Requirements. An applicant studying law in a law office or offices within New York State must be actually and continuously employed during the required period as a regular law clerk and student in a law office, under the direction and subject to the supervision of one or more attorneys admitted to practice law in New York State, and must be actually engaged in the practical work of

such law office during normal business hours. In addition, the applicant must receive instruction from said attorney or attorneys in those subjects which are customarily taught in approved law schools.

(c) Credit for Attendance in Approved Law School. Credit shall be allowed for attendance in an approved law school as follows:

(1) credit of one full year or 52 weeks shall be allowed for any successfully completed year of a full-time law school program;

(2) credit of three quarters of a year or 39 weeks shall be allowed for any successfully completed year of a part-time law school program;

(3) proportionate credit shall be allowed for any successfully completed semester, quarter or summer session in such a full-time or part-time law school program;

(4) for any period of law school study not successfully completed, credit may be allowed for attendance as determined by the New York State Board of Law Examiners based on an evaluation of performance in the individual case.

(d) Vacations. Vacations taken by the applicant in excess of one month in any year of study shall be deducted from the period of law office study for which credit shall be given, but failure by the applicant to take a vacation shall not decrease the period of study required by this section.

(e) Certificate of Commencement of Law Office Study. It shall be the duty of the attorney or attorneys with whom a period of law office study is about to be commenced to obtain from, complete and file with, the Clerk of the Court of Appeals a certificate of commencement of clerkship, Appendix B–2, infra. At the time the certificate of commencement of clerkship is filed, the applicant shall provide the Court of Appeals with a copy of the determination of the New York State Board of Law Examiners of the credit to which the applicant is entitled under subdivision (c) of this section.

(f) Credit for Law Study in Law Office. Credit shall be given only for study in a law office or offices completed subsequent to the filing of the certificate required by subdivision (e) of this section.

(g) Proof Required. Compliance with the requirements of this section shall be proved to the satisfaction of the New York State Board of Law Examiners.

§ 520.5. Study of Law in Law School and Actual Practice

(a) General. An applicant who has studied law in any law school in any other state or territory of the United States or in the District of Columbia, other than a law school which grants credit for correspondence courses, and has received a degree from such law school which qualifies such applicant to practice law in such state, territory or in the District of Columbia, may qualify to take the New York State bar examination by submitting to the New York State Board of Law Examiners satisfactory proof:

(1) that applicant possesses the legal education required by this section:

(2) that applicant's course of study complies with the instructional and program requirements of section 520.3(c) through (i) of this Part, and

(3) that while admitted to the bar in the highest court in any state or territory of the United States or in the District of Columbia, applicant has actually practiced therein for at least five years of the seven years immediately preceding the application to sit for the bar examination.

(b) Proof Required. The applicant shall submit to the New York State Board of Law Examiners such proof of compliance with the provisions of this section as the board may require.

§ 520.6. Study of Law in Foreign Country; Required Legal Education

(a) General. An applicant who has studied in a foreign country may qualify to take the New York State bar examination by submitting to the New York State Board of Law Examiners satisfactory proof of the legal education required by this section.

(b) Legal Education.

(1) The applicant shall show fulfillment of the educational requirements for admission to the practice of law in a country other than the United States by successful completion of a period of law study at least substantially equivalent in duration to that required, under subdivisions (d) and (e) of section 520.3 of this Part, in a law school or schools each of which, throughout the period of applicant's study therein, was recognized by the competent accrediting agency of the government of such other country, or of a political subdivision thereof, as qualified and approved; and

(i) that such other country is one whose jurisprudence is based upon the principles of the English Common Law, and that the program and course of law study successfully completed by the applicant were the substantial equivalent of the legal education provided by an approved law school in the United States; or

(ii) if applicant does not meet the durational equivalency requirements of subdivision (b)(1) of this section but has at least two years of substantively equivalent education, or if the applicant does not meet the substantive equivalency requirements of subdivision (b)(1)(i) of this section, that applicant has successfully completed a full-time or part-time program consisting of a minimum of 20 semester hours of credit, or the equivalent, in professional law subjects, which includes basic courses in American law, in an approved law school in the United States; or

(2) The applicant shall show admission to practice law in a country other than the United States whose jurisprudence is based upon principals of English Common Law, where admission was based upon a program of study in a law school and/or law office recognized by the competent accrediting agency of the government of such other country and which is durationally equivalent yet substantively deficient under subdivision (b)(1)(i) of this section, and that such applicant has successfully completed a full-time or part-time program consisting of a minimum of 20 semester hours of credit, or the equivalent, in professional law subjects, which includes basic courses in American law, in an approved law school in the United States.

(c) Proof Required. The applicant shall submit to the New York State Board of Law Examiners such proof of compliance with the provisions of this section as the board may require.

§ 520.7. Certification by Board of Law Examiners

(a) Except as provided in section 520.10 of this Part, no applicant for admission to practice in this State shall be admitted unless the New York State Board of Law Examiners shall have certified to the Appellate Division of the department in which, as shown by the papers filed by the applicant with the board, the applicant resides, or if not a resident of the State, in which such papers show that applicant is employed full-time, or, if the applicant does not reside and is not employed full-time in the State, to the Appellate Division of the Third Department, that the applicant (1) has passed the written bar examination prescribed in section 520.8 of this Part, and (2) has also passed the Multistate Professional Responsibility Examination described in section 520.9 of this Part.

(b) The requirement of this Part shall first be applicable to those candidates for admission to practice law in New York who qualify for and take the July 1982 regular New York State bar examination and to all those who thereafter qualify for and take such examinations.

§ 520.8. New York State Bar Examination

(a) General. The New York State Board of Law Examiners shall twice each year conduct a written bar examination consisting of legal problems in both adjective and substantive law, and it shall by rule prescribe a list of subjects which will indicate the general scope of the bar examination. The board may use the Multistate Bar Examination as part of the bar examination.

(b) Uniformity of Bar Examinations. The bar examinations shall be as nearly uniform from year to year as is reasonably practicable.

(c) Preservation of Papers. Bar examination papers shall be preserved for a period of four months from the date of the announcement of the results of the bar examination, and may thereafter be destroyed.

(d) Examination Fee. Every applicant for a bar examination shall pay to the New York State Board of Law Examiners the fee prescribed by section 465 of the Judiciary Law.

Cross References

Judiciary Law, see McKinney's Book 29.

§ 520.9. Multistate Professional Responsibility Examination

(a) General. The Multistate Professional Responsibility Examination referred to in section 520.7 of this Part shall be the examination bearing that name which is administered by the National Conference of Bar Examiners.

(b) Requirements and Times and Places for Taking Examination. An applicant may take the Multistate Professional Responsibility Examination prior or subsequent to completion of the requirements for taking the New York State bar examination. An application to take the Multistate Professional Responsibility Examination shall be filed with the National Conference of Bar Examiners and the fee therefor shall be fixed by and paid to that conference, which shall also fix the times and places, within or without the State of New York, for taking the examination.

(c) Passing Score. The New York State Board of Law Examiners may accept the scores attained by individual applicants on the examination as determined and reported to it by the National Conference of Bar Examiners, but such board shall determine the passing score for applicants seeking admission to practice in this State.

(d) Reexamination. There shall be no restriction on the right of a failing applicant to retake the Multistate Professional Responsibility Examination.

§ 520.10. Admission Without Examination

(a) General. In its discretion, the Appellate Division may admit to practice without examination an applicant who:

(1)(i) has been admitted to practice in the highest law court in any other state or territory of the United States or in the District of Columbia; or

(ii) has been admitted to practice as an attorney and counselor-at-law or the equivalent in the highest court in another country whose jurisprudence is based upon the principles of the English Common Law; and

(iii) is currently admitted to the bar in such other jurisdiction or jurisdictions, that at least one such jurisdiction in which the attorney is so admitted would similarly admit an attorney or counselor-at-law admitted to practice in New York State to its bar without examination; and

(2)(i) while admitted to practice as specified in paragraph (1) of this subdivision, has actually practiced therein, for at least five of the seven years immediately preceding the application:

(a) in its highest law court or highest court of original jurisdiction in the state or territory of the United States, in the District of Columbia or in the common law country where admitted; or

(b) in Federal military or civilian legal service in a position which requires admission to the bar for the appointment thereto or for the performance of the duties thereof, even if the government service, civilian or military, was not in a jurisdiction in which the applicant was admitted to practice; or

(c) in legal service as counsel or assistant counsel to a corporation in the state or territory of the United States where admitted, or in the District of Columbia if admitted therein; or in the common law country where admitted; or

(ii) has been employed in any other state or territory of the United States or in the District of Columbia as a judge, magistrate, referee or similar official for the local, state or federal government in a tribunal of record, or as a law clerk to such judicial official, provided that such employment requires admission to the bar for the appointment thereto or for the performance of the duties thereof, for at least five of the seven years immediately preceding the application; or

(iii) has been employed in this State or in any other state or territory of the United States or in the District of Columbia as a full-time member of the law faculty teaching in a law school or schools on the approved list of the American Bar Association and has attained the rank of professor or associate professor for at least five of the seven years immediately preceding the application; or

(iv) has actually practiced as provided in subparagraph (i) of this paragraph, or been employed as a judicial official as provided in subparagraph (ii) of this paragraph, or has been teaching at a law school as provided in subparagraph (iii) of this paragraph, or has actually practiced while admitted pursuant to Rule 520.11(a)(2) of this Part, for a period of up to 18 months, in a combination or cumulation of service among the categories of practice, judicial or legal service or teaching where the Appellate Division determines that such five years of combined or cumulative service is the equivalent of the practice required in clause (a) of subparagraph (i); and

(3) has received a first degree from an approved law school in the United States at the time of applicant's admission to practice in such other state, territory, district or common law country, or at the time of application for admission under this section; and

(4) is over 26 years of age.

(b) Proof Required. An applicant for admission under this section shall file with the Clerk of the Appellate Division of the department in which, as shown by the papers filed by the applicant with the department, the applicant resides or, if not a resident of the state in which such papers show that the applicant is employed full-time or, if such papers do not show that the applicant resides or is employed full-time in the State, the Appellate Division of the Third Department:

(1) a certificate from the clerk of the highest court of the state, territory, district or foreign country in which applicant has been admitted to practice as an attorney and counselor-at-law or the equivalent, certifying to applicant's admission to practice and the date thereof; and

(2) in the case of an applicant seeking admission relying upon teaching, a certificate from the dean of the law school which employs or employed the applicant, certifying to the nature and extent of applicant's employment and the rank attained; and

(3) a certificate from the New York State Board of Law Examiners certifying that the applicant has received a first degree in law from an approved law school as defined in section 520.3(b) of this Part; and

(4) any such other satisfactory evidence of character and qualifications as the Appellate Division may require, which may include a report of the National Conference of Bar Examiners.

(c) Proof to Be Submitted and Fee to Be Paid to New York State Board of Law Examiners. The applicant shall submit to the New York State Board of Law Examiners such proof of compliance with the provisions of paragraph (3) of subdivision (a) of this section as the board may require and shall at the same time pay the board the fee prescribed by section 465 of the Judiciary Law by certified check or money order payable to the order of the board.

(d) Discretion of Appellate Division. The Appellate Division may in its discretion impose as a condition to admission such other tests of character and fitness as it may deem proper.

(e) Admission Pro Hac Vice. [Renumbered § 520.11].

Cross References

Judiciary Law, see McKinney's Book 29.

§ 520.11. Admission Pro Hac Vice

(a) General. An attorney and counselor-at-law or the equivalent who is a member in good standing of the bar of another state, territory, district or foreign country may be admitted pro hac vice:

(1) in the discretion of any court of record, to participate in any matter in which the attorney is employed; or

(2) in the discretion of the Appellate Division, provided applicant is a graduate of an approved law school, to advise and represent clients and participate in any matter during the continuance of the applicant's employment or association with an organization described in subdivision 7 of section 495 of the Judiciary Law or during employment with a District Attorney, Corporation Counsel or the Attorney General, but in no event for longer than 18 months.

(b) New York Law Students. A graduate student or graduate assistant at an approved law school in New York State may be admitted *pro hac vice* in the discretion of the Appellate Division, to advise and represent clients or participate in any matter during the continuance of applicant's enrollment in an approved law school in New York State as a graduate student or graduate assistant, or during applicant's employment as a law school teacher in an approved law school in New York State, if applicant is in good standing as an attorney and counselor-at-law or the equivalent of the bar of another state, territory, district or foreign country and is engaged to advise or represent the client through participation in an organization described in subdivision 7 of section 495 of the Judiciary Law or during employment with a District Attorney, Corporation Counsel or the Attorney General, but in no event for longer than 18 months.

(c) Association of New York Counsel. No attorney may be admitted *pro hac vice* pursuant to paragraph (1) of subdivision (a) to participate in pretrial or trial proceedings unless he or she is associated with an attorney who is a member in good standing of the New York bar, who shall be the attorney of record in the matter.

(d) Professional Responsibility Requirements. An attorney admitted *pro hac vice* pursuant to this section:

(1) shall be familiar with and shall comply with the standards of professional conduct imposed upon members of the New York bar, including the rules of court governing the conduct of attorneys and the Disciplinary Rules of the Code of Professional Responsibility; and

(2) shall be subject to the jurisdiction of the courts of this State with respect to any acts occurring during the course of the attorney's participation in the matter.

§ 520.12. Proof of Moral Character

(a) General. Every applicant for admission to practice must file with a committee on character and fitness appointed by the Appellate Division of the

Supreme Court affidavits of reputable persons that applicant possesses the good moral character and general fitness requisite for an attorney- and counselor-at-law as required by section 90 of the Judiciary Law. The number of such affidavits and the qualifications of persons acceptable as affiants shall be determined by the Appellate Division to which the applicant has been certified.

(b) Affidavits. The affidavits filed shall state that the applicant is, to the knowledge of the affiant, a person of good moral character and possesses the general fitness requisite for an attorney- and counselor-at-law and shall set forth in detail the facts upon which such knowledge is based. Such affidavits shall not be conclusive proof as to character and fitness, and the Appellate Division to which the applicant has been certified may inquire further through its committee on character and fitness or otherwise.

(c) Discretion of Appellate Division. The Appellate Division in each department may adopt for its department such additional procedures for ascertaining the moral character and general fitness of applicants as it may deem proper, which may include submission of a report of the National Conference of Bar Examiners.

(d) Time to File Affidavits.

(1) Except as provided in paragraph (2) of this subdivision, every applicant for admission to practice, other than applicants for admission without examination pursuant to section 520.10 of this Part, shall file the affidavits required under subdivision (a) and any additional material required under subdivision (c) of this section within three years from the date of the letter sent by the New York State Board of Law Examiners notifying the applicant that the applicant has passed the bar examination prescribed in section 520.8 of this Part. The requirements of this subdivision shall first be applicable to those applicants for admission who pass the July 1994 bar examination.

(2) Any applicant for admission to practice who has passed the bar examination prescribed in section 520.8 of this Part, administered prior to July 1994, and who has not filed the affidavits required under subdivision (a) and additional material required under subdivision (c) of this section, must file such affidavits (i) within three years from the date of the letter sent by the New York State Board of Law Examiners notifying the applicant that the applicant has passed the bar examination, or (ii) by November 9, 1995, whichever date is later.

Cross References

Judiciary Law, see McKinney's Book 29.

§ 520.13. Designation of Agent for Service of Process

(a) Every applicant for admission to practice who does not reside and is not employed full-time in the State shall be required, as a condition of admission, to execute and file, with the Appellate Division of the department in which the applicant is being admitted, a duly acknowledged instrument in writing setting forth the applicant's residence or mailing address and designating the clerk of such Appellate Division as the applicant's agent upon whom process may be served, with like effect as if served personally upon the applicant, in any action or proceeding thereafter brought against the applicant and arising out of or based upon any legal services rendered or offered to be rendered by the applicant within the State.

(b) Any such applicant may, at any time after being admitted to practice, revoke a designation filed with the Appellate Division pursuant to subdivision (a) of this section by executing and filing with such Appellate Division an affidavit revoking such designation and showing that, as of the date of such affidavit, the applicant resides or is employed full-time in the State or has an office therein for the practice of law; except such revocation shall be effective only with respect to causes of action accruing after the filing thereof.

(c) Service of process on the clerk of the Appellate Division, pursuant to a designation filed pursuant to subdivision (a) of this section, shall be made by personally delivering to and leaving with such clerk, or with a deputy or assistant authorized to receive such service at the clerk's office, duplicate copies of the process together with a fee of $25. Service of process shall be complete when such clerk has been so served. Such clerk shall promptly send one copy of the process to the person to whom it is directed, by certified mail, return receipt requested, addressed to such person at the address specified in the designation or at such other address as such person shall have specified in a duly acknowledged supplemental instrument in writing which such person shall have filed in the office of such clerk.

§ 520.14. Application for Waiver of Rules

The Court of Appeals, upon application, may in its discretion vary the application of or waive any provision of these rules where strict compliance will cause undue hardship to the applicant. Such application shall be in the form of a verified petition setting forth the applicant's name, age and residence address, the facts relied upon and a prayer for relief.

§ 520.15. Rules of the New York State Board of Law Examiners

The New York State Board of Law Examiners may from time to time adopt, amend or rescind rules, not inconsistent with these Rules, as it shall deem necessary and proper to enable it to discharge its duties as such duties are established by Law and by these Rules. The Rules so established by the Board shall not be adopted, amended or rescinded except by a majority vote of the Members thereof.

A copy of each rule, adopted, amended or rescinded must, within thirty (30) days of such action, be filed in the office of the Secretary of State.

PART 521. RULES OF THE COURT OF APPEALS FOR THE LICENSING OF LEGAL CONSULTANTS

§ 521.1. General Regulation as to Licensing

(a) In its discretion the Appellate Division of the Supreme Court, pursuant to subdivision 6 of section 53 of the Judiciary Law, may license to practice as a legal consultant, without examination, an applicant who:

(1) is a member in good standing of a recognized legal profession in a foreign country, the members of which are admitted to practice as attorneys or counselors at law or the equivalent and are subject to effective regulation and discipline by a duly constituted professional body or a public authority;

(2) for at least three of the five years immediately preceding his or her application, has been a member in good standing of such legal profession and has actually been engaged in the practice of law in such foreign country or elsewhere substantially involving or relating to the rendering of advice or the provision of legal services concerning the law of such foreign country;

(3) possesses the good moral character and general fitness requisite for a member of the bar of this State;

(4) is over 26 years of age; and

(5) intends to practice as a legal consultant in this State and to maintain an office in this State for that purpose.

(b) In considering whether to license an applicant to practice as a legal consultant, the Appellate Division may in its discretion take into account whether a member of the bar of this State would have a reasonable and practical opportunity to establish an office for the giving of legal advice to clients in the applicant's country of admission. Any member of the bar who is seeking or has sought to establish an office in that country may request the court to consider the matter, or the Appellate Division may do so sua sponte.

Cross References

Judiciary Law, see McKinney's Book 29.

§ 521.2. Proof Required

An applicant under this Part shall file with the clerk of the Appellate Division in the department in which he or she resides or intends to practice:

(a) a certificate from the professional body or public authority in such foreign country having final jurisdiction over professional discipline, certifying as to the applicant's admission to practice and the date thereof, and as to his or her good standing as such attorney or counselor at law or the equivalent;

(b) a letter of recommendation from one of the members of the executive body of such professional body or public authority or from one of the judges of the highest law court or court of original jurisdiction of such foreign country;

(c) a duly authenticated English translation of such certificate and such letter if, in either case, it is not in English; and

(d) such other evidence as to the nature and extent of the applicant's educational and professional qualifications, good moral character and general fitness, and compliance with the requirements of section 521.1 of this Part as such Appellate Division may require.

(e) upon a showing that strict compliance with the provisions of paragraph (a) or (b) of this section would cause the applicant unnecessary hardship, such Appellate Division may in its discretion waive or vary the application of such provisions and permit the applicant to furnish other evidence in lieu thereof.

§ 521.3. Scope of Practice

A person licensed to practice as a legal consultant under this Part may render legal services in this State; subject, however, to the limitations that he or she shall not:

(a) appear for a person other than himself or herself as attorney in any court, or before any magistrate or other judicial officer, in this State (other than upon admission pro hac vice pursuant to section 520.11 of this Title);

(b) prepare any instrument effecting the transfer or registration of title to real estate located in the United States of America;

(c) prepare:

(1) any will or trust instrument effecting the disposition on death of any property located in the United States of America and owned by a resident thereof; or

(2) any instrument relating to the administration of a decedent's estate in the United States of America;

(d) prepare any instrument in respect of the marital or parental relations, rights or duties of a resident of the United States of America, or the custody or care of the children of such a resident;

(e) render professional legal advice on the law of this State or of the United States of America (whether rendered incident to the preparation of legal instruments or otherwise), except on the basis of advice from a person duly qualified and entitled (other than by virtue of having been licensed under this Part) to render professional legal advice in this State on such law;

(f) in any way hold himself or herself out as a member of the bar of this State; or

(g) carry on his or her practice under, or utilize in connection with such practice, any name, title or designation other than one or more of the following:

(i) his or her own name;

(ii) the name of the law firm with which he or she is affiliated;

(iii) his or her authorized title in the foreign country of his or her admission to practice, which may be used in conjunction with the name of such country; and

(iv) the title "legal consultant," which may be used in conjunction with the words "admitted to the practice of law in (name of the foreign country of his or her admission to practice)."

§ 521.4.　Rights and Obligations

Subject to the limitations set forth in section 521.3 of this Part, a person licensed as a legal consultant under this Rule shall be considered a lawyer affiliated with the bar of this State and shall be entitled and subject to:

(a) the rights and obligations set forth in the applicable Lawyer's Code of Professional Responsibility or arising from the other conditions and requirements that apply to a member of the bar of this State under the rules of court governing members of the bar; and

(b) the rights and obligations of a member of the bar of this State with respect to:

(1) affiliation in the same law firm with one or more members of the bar of this State, including by:

(i) employing one or more members of the bar of this State;

(ii) being employed by one or more members of the bar of this State or by any partnership or professional corporation which includes members of the bar of this State or which maintains an office in this State; and

(iii) being a partner in any partnership or shareholder in any professional corporation which includes members of the bar of this State or which maintains an office in this State; and

(2) attorney-client privilege, work-product privilege and similar professional privileges.

Cross References

Judiciary Law, see McKinney's Book 29.

Code of Professional Responsibility, see Appendix to McKinney's Judiciary Law, Book 29.

§ 521.5.　Disciplinary Provisions

A person licensed to practice as a legal consultant under this Rule shall be subject to professional discipline in the same manner and to the same extent as members of the bar of this State and to this end:

(a) Every person licensed to practice as a legal consultant under this Part:

(1) shall be subject to control by the Supreme Court and to censure, suspension, removal or revocation of his or her license to practice by the Appellate Division and shall otherwise be governed by subdivisions 2 through 10 of section 90 of the Judiciary Law; and

(2) shall execute and file with the Appellate Division, in the department in which he or she is licensed, in such form and manner as such Appellate Division may prescribe:

(i) his or her commitment to observe the applicable Lawyer's Code of Professional Responsibility and the rules of court governing members of the bar to the extent applicable to the legal services authorized under section 521.3 of this Part;

(ii) an undertaking or appropriate evidence of professional liability insurance, in such amount as such Appellate Division may prescribe, to assure his or her proper professional conduct and responsibility;

(iii) a written undertaking to notify the court of any change in such person's good standing as a member of the foreign legal profession referred to in section 521.1(a)(1) of this Part and of any final action of the professional body or public authority referred to in section 521.2(a) of this Part imposing any disciplinary censure, suspension, or other sanction upon such person; and

(iv) a duly acknowledged instrument, in writing, setting forth his or her address in this State and designating the clerk of such Appellate Division as his or her agent upon whom process may be served, with like effect as if served personally upon him or her, in any action or proceeding thereafter brought against him or her and arising out of or based upon any legal services rendered or offered to be rendered by him or her within or to residents of this State, whenever after due diligence service cannot be made upon him or her at such address or at such new address in this State as he or she shall have filed in the office of such clerk by means of a duly acknowledged supplemental instrument in writing.

(b) Service of process on such clerk, pursuant to the designation filed as aforesaid, shall be made by personally delivering to and leaving with such clerk, or with a deputy or assistant authorized by him or her to receive such service, at his or her office, duplicate copies of such process together with a fee of $10. Service of process shall be complete when such clerk has been so served. Such clerk shall promptly send one of such copies to the legal consultant to whom the process is directed, by certified mail, return receipt requested, addressed to such legal consultant at the address specified by him or her as aforesaid.

§ 521.6. Separate Authority

Nothing in this Part shall be deemed to limit or otherwise affect the provisions of section 520.6 of this Title.

§ 521.7. Application for Waiver of Rules

The Court of Appeals, upon application, may in its discretion vary the application or waive any provision of these rules where strict compliance will cause undue hardship to the applicant. Such application shall be in the form of a verified petition setting forth the applicant's name, age and residence address, the facts relied upon and a prayer for relief.

§ 521.8. Revocation of License

In the event that the Appellate Division determines that a person licensed as a legal consultant under this Part no longer meets the requirements for licensing set forth in section 521.1(a)(1) or section 521.1(a)(3) of this Part, it shall revoke the license granted to such person hereunder.

PART 530. REVIEW OF DETERMINATIONS OF THE STATE COMMISSION ON JUDICIAL CONDUCT

Except as expressly prescribed to the contrary in this Part, the regular practice rules of the Court of Appeals, Part 500 of these rules, are applicable to judicial proceedings in the Court of Appeals to review determinations of the Commission on Judicial Conduct.

§ 530.1. Request for Review

(a) The Commission shall transmit to Court of Appeals Hall in Albany, New York, three copies of its written determination, together with its findings of fact and conclusions of law, and the record of the proceedings upon which the determination is based, including all record and documentary evidence or materials. Two copies shall be addressed to the Chief Judge; the third copy shall be addressed to the Clerk of the Court of Appeals for filing and, upon completion of service, upon the respondent, judge or justice, of the copy required to be served by the Chief Judge, shall also be available for public inspection at the Office of the Clerk in Court of Appeals Hall at Albany.

(b) A written request to the Chief Judge for review by the Court of Appeals, timely made in accordance with Judiciary Law, section 44, subdivision 7, shall commence the proceeding for review of the determination of the State Commission on Judicial Conduct. The respondent in a Commission proceeding shall be denominated the petitioner in the Court of Appeals, and the Commission shall be denominated the respondent in the Court of Appeals. The written request of the Chief Judge by a petitioner shall be transmitted, by personal delivery or certified mail, to the chambers of the Chief Judge at Court of Appeals Hall, Albany, New York, 12207, with copies addressed to the Clerk of the Court of Appeals for filing, and to the Commission.

Cross References

Judiciary Law, see McKinney's Book 29.

§ 530.2. Petitioner's Papers: Content and Time for Filing

No preliminary jurisdictional statement (Rules of Practice section 500.2) shall be required to be filed. A petitioner shall file the papers for review within thirty days of the date of the written request for review by the Court of Appeals. Three copies shall be served on the Commission which may waive receipt of a copy of the record for review. Papers for review to be filed with the court shall consist of ten copies of the petitioner's brief and ten copies of the record for review consisting of, at least: all complaints, whether formal or informal or merely initiatory, except that petitioner or the Commission may apply to the court for good cause shown to exclude irrelevant initiatory material; any answer or other pleading or an agreed statement of facts; and the written determination, findings and conclusions and record of proceedings upon which the determination is based, including all record and documentary evidence or material before the Commission in the making of its determination. The record may be stipulated to by respective counsel in accordance with the procedure set forth in CPLR 5532, or may be certified in accordance with CPLR 2105. Original exhibits may be submitted to the Court of Appeals, upon appropriate stipulation of the respective counsel, without duplication. A reply brief may be served and filed within ten days after receipt of respondent Commission's brief.

Cross References

CPLR, see McKinney's Book 7B.

§ 530.3. Appendix Method

No appendix method, in lieu of the record for review, shall be authorized except by express permission of the court on appropriate motion in accordance with section 530.7(a) of this Part.

§ 530.4. Service and Filing of Respondent's Brief and Appendix

Within 30 days of the service of the petitioner's papers, respondent shall file with the clerk ten copies and shall serve on petitioner three copies of respondent's brief.

§ 530.5. Calendar

A review by the Court of Appeals of a determination of the Commission shall be scheduled for oral argument at the earliest calendar session next after the filing of the respondent Commission's brief, unless otherwise directed by the court.

§ 530.6. Demands, Dismissals and Extensions

(a) If the petitioner shall not have filed and served the papers required by section 530.2 of this Part within the time prescribed, and unless an extension of time has been sought and granted, the court will issue to petitioner, by regular mail to counsel of record, a notice that such service and filing be made within 20 days after the date of the notice. Prior to the expiration of that 20-day period, petitioner may, on good cause shown, request of the clerk of the court an extension of the 20-day period to a day certain. On failure to comply with the terms of the original notice or the terms as extended by the clerk, an order shall be entered by the clerk dismissing the requested review.

(b) If the respondent shall not have filed and served the papers required by section 530.4 of this Part within the time prescribed, and unless an extension of time has been sought and granted, the court will issue to respondent, by regular mail to counsel of record, a notice that such service and filing be made within 20 days after the date of the notice. Prior to the expiration of the 20-day period, respondent may, on good cause shown, request of the clerk of the court an extension of the 20-day period to a day certain. On failure to comply with the terms of the original notice or the terms as extended by the clerk, an order shall be entered by the clerk precluding the right of respondent to submit a brief unless an order is obtained from the court on such conditions as it may impose.

(c) Where, within the time requirements of this section and sections 530.2 and 530.4 of this Part, petitioner or respondent shall establish reasonable ground why there may not be compliance with this Part, the clerk of the court is authorized to grant reasonable extensions of the time for filing papers. When an extension of the time requirements of subdivision (a) or (b) of this section is granted, the case must be ready for argument or submission by the petitioner within the further directed time, or the clerk shall enter an order for the appropriate sanction

of dismissal or preclusion. All determinations made by the clerk may be reviewed by motion to the court on notice in accordance with section 530.7 of this Part.

(d) In all events, under this section, the Court of Appeals may, for cause either sua sponte or on motion, dispense with or modify the requirements of its rules of practice concerning brief filing dates, calendar dates, dismissals for untimeliness and preclusions of brief filing or oral argument.

§ 530.7. Motions

(a) A motion addressed to the court may be made on 8 days' notice (personal service) or 13 days' notice (service by mail). Motions are returnable, at Court of Appeals Hall in Albany, every Monday whether or not the court is in session, unless otherwise directed by order to show cause or by stipulation so ordered by a judge of the court. Motions to dispense with rule requirements or to review determinations of the clerk may be made on a single set of the moving papers with proof of service of one copy. Motions for suspension in accordance with New York State Constitution, article 6, section 22, subdivisions (e), (f) or (g), shall be made on 10 copies of a brief or moving papers, unless the court acts sua sponte on such notice to counsel and with such directions for filing briefs as it may deem appropriate. Oral argument will not be heard unless the court expressly grants permission upon a written request showing need.

(b) Reargument. A motion for reargument shall be made, without oral argument, on 10 copies of a brief, reproduced in conformity with section 500.1 of this Part, which shall state briefly the ground upon which reargument is asked and the points claimed to have been overlooked or misapprehended by the court, with proper reference to the particular portions of the record and to the authorities relied upon. It may not be based on the assertion for the first time of new points except for extraordinary and compelling reasons. Unless otherwise permitted by the court, the notice of motion shall be served not later than 30 days after the court has rendered its judgment or order. One copy of the brief shall be served on the adverse party with the notice of motion.

(c) Amicus Curiae Relief. Motions for permission to file a brief or argue as amicus curiae, when appropriately made sufficiently in advance of the calendaring of the requested review to allow adequate court consideration, must show to the satisfaction of the court at least one of the following criteria:

(1) that a party or parties are not capable of a full and adequate presentation and that movants could remedy this deficiency; or

(2) that movants would invite the court's attention to law or arguments which might otherwise escape the court's consideration; or

(3) that amicus curiae participation would otherwise be of special assistance to the court.

(d) With respect to all motions provided for under subdivisions (a), (b) and (c) of this section, answering papers or briefs shall be served and filed on or before the return day of the motion unless otherwise directed by the court.

Cross References
Constitution, see McKinney's Book 2.

§ 530.8. Order
The order of the court, together with the record filed with the court, shall be entered and filed in the Office of the Clerk at Court of Appeals Hall in Albany.

§ 530.9. Withdrawal of a Request for Review
A request for review may be withdrawn and the proceeding discontinued, upon an order approved by the court, at any time prior to argument or submission, by forwarding to the clerk of the court a duly executed stipulation of withdrawal which must be signed by all counsel and by the petitioner judge or justice personally.

PART 540. UNIFORM PROCEDURES FOR APPEALS FROM PRETRIAL FINDINGS OF MENTAL RETARDATION IN CAPITAL CASES

§ 540.0. Preamble
Acting pursuant to the rulemaking authority invested in this Court by New York Constitution, article VI, section 30 and Laws of 1995, chapter 1, section 20, the Court of Appeals establishes these Uniform Procedures for Appeals from Pretrial Findings of Mental Retardation in Capital Cases.

§ 540.1. Delegation to the Presiding Justices of the Appellate Division
The Presiding Justices of the Appellate Division shall adopt uniform rules to ensure that appeals from pretrial findings of mental retardation in capital cases pursuant to Laws of 1995, chapter 1, section 20 are expeditiously perfected, reviewed and determined.

SUPREME COURT, APPELLATE DIVISION, FIRST DEPARTMENT

Including Amendments Received Through September 15, 2008

Westlaw Electronic Research

These rules may be searched electronically on Westlaw® *in the NY–RULES database; updates to these rules may be found on* Westlaw *in NY–RULESUP-DATES. For search tips and a summary of database content, consult the* Westlaw *Scope Screens for each database.*

Table of Sections

APPENDIX A. CENTRAL SCREENING COMMITTEE
INDIGENT DEFENDANTS ASSIGNED COUNSEL
PLAN

**PART 613. RULES TO IMPLEMENT AN INDIGENT
DEFENSE ORGANIZATION OVERSIGHT
COMMITTEE**

PART 614. COMMITTEE TO CERTIFY LAW GUARDIANS FOR APPOINTMENT IN DOMESTIC RELATIONS MATTERS [RESCINDED]

PART 620. RULES OF THE JURY SYSTEM IN THE CITY OF NEW YORK [REPEALED]

PART 622. MENTAL HYGIENE LEGAL SERVICE

PART 630. MISCELLANEOUS RULES [RESCINDED]

PART 635. JOINT ADMINISTRATIVE ORDERS

PART 636. MISCELLANEOUS ORDERS

Parts 1100 to 1510 (§ 1100.1 et seq.) have been promulgated as joint rules of the Appellate Divisions and are set out following Appellate Division, Fourth Department, Part 1040, post.

PART 600. APPEALS

§ 600.1. Sessions of the Court; Four Justices Present

(a) The court will convene at 2 o'clock in the afternoon during the appointed terms of the court for the hearing of appeals except on Fridays when the court will convene at 10 o'clock in the forenoon.

(b) Special sessions of the court may be scheduled for such time or such purposes as the court may direct.

(c) When a cause is argued or submitted to the court with four justices present, it shall, whenever necessary, be deemed submitted also to any other duly qualified justice of the court, unless objection is noted at the time of argument or submission.

§ 600.2. Motions Generally; Special Proceedings; Calendars; Submission

(a) Motions Generally.

(1) Any application, brought on by notice of motion, may be made returnable on any regular business day of the court during the period September 1 through June 30 and on Mondays during July and August, at 10 o'clock in the forenoon unless otherwise ordered by a justice of the court.

(2) Cross-motions shall be made returnable the same day as the original motion and shall be served not less than three days before the return date.

(3) The moving papers shall state the nature of the application or relief sought; the return day; and the names, addresses and telephone numbers of the attorneys for all parties in support, and who are entitled to notice, of the application. Applications made before the appeal is heard must contain a copy of the notice of appeal or other paper which first invoked the jurisdiction of the court, and the order, judgment or determination sought to be reviewed. Applications made for modification, resettlement, etc. of an order of this court shall contain a copy of the order and opinion, if any.

(4) By noon of the business day preceding the day on which a motion is returnable the moving party must file with the clerk the original moving papers with proof of service thereof within the time:

(i) prescribed by CPLR 2214(b) and 5516; or

(ii) directed by a justice of the court.

(5) Answering and replying papers, if any, must be served within the time:

    (i) prescribed by CPLR 2214(b); or

    (ii) directed by a justice of the court;

and the originals thereof with proof of service must be filed by 4 o'clock in the afternoon of the business day preceding the day on which the application is returnable, unless for good cause shown they are permitted to be filed at a later time.

(6) All papers may be filed either by personal delivery or by ordinary mail. If filed by mail, they shall be considered filed only upon receipt; and the envelope must be marked "Motion Papers". If an acknowledgment of receipt of the papers is desired, there must be enclosed with the papers being filed by mail a self-addressed postage-prepaid postal card bearing the title of the cause, the nature of the motion, the date on which it is returnable and a statement of the papers filed. Such postal card, when stamped and returned by mail, shall serve as a receipt for the papers listed thereon.

(7) When an application is presented for an interim stay or other relief pending the determination of a motion, the party seeking such relief must inform the clerk at the time of submission whether the opposing party has been notified of the application and whether such party opposes or consents to the granting of the relief sought. Time and manner of service of motion papers shall be directed by a justice. The relief granted to the moving party will be by brief order appended to the notice of motion. The justice's signature will apply to the stay or provisional remedy only; there will be no direction to a party "to show cause" why an order should not be entered.

(8) All parties filing papers pertaining to a motion or special proceeding shall include therewith a stamped self-addressed envelope.

(b) Special Proceedings. Unless a justice of the court otherwise directs, all special proceedings originating in the court, except those commenced pursuant to CPLR 506(b)(4), shall be returnable at 10 o'clock in the forenoon of any regular business day of the court during the period August 1 through June 20, and all papers shall be filed in the manner and within the time prescribed in paragraphs (a)(3) and (a)(4) of this section, except that the moving and opposing parties shall submit to the clerk seven conformed copies in addition to the original moving or opposing papers with proof of service of a copy thereof.

(c) No Calendars. No calendar of motions and special proceedings shall be published or called.

(d) Submission of Motions and Special Proceedings.

(1) All motions and special proceedings, except those commenced pursuant to CPLR 506(b)(4), unless adjourned or withdrawn, shall be deemed submitted on the return date thereof. Attendance of attorneys shall not be required and oral argument will not be heard.

(2) Applications brought on by notice of motion or order may be adjourned once by consent of the parties. Except in extraordinary circumstances, in the absence of such consent or approval of the court the application will be deemed submitted on the adjourned return date. Notices or stipulations of adjournment shall be submitted in writing.

Cross References

CPLR, see McKinney's Book 7B.

§ 600.3. Applications for Leave to Appeal to Appellate Division

(a) When Addressed to a Justice. An application to a justice of the court for leave to appeal pursuant to CPLR 5701(c) shall be made within the time prescribed by CPLR 5513(c). The papers upon which such an application is made must state whether any previous application has been made and, if so, to whom and the reason given, if any, for the denial of leave or refusal to entertain the application if that be the case.

(b) When Addressed to the Court.

(1) Where leave of this court is required for an appeal to be taken to it, the application for such leave must be made in the manner and within the time prescribed by CPLR 5513 and 5516. Applications pursuant to CPLR 5703 for leave to appeal from a determination of the Appellate Term shall be made only after denial of a motion for leave to appeal made at the Appellate Term as provided by 640.9 of the Appellate Term rules.

(2) The papers upon which an application for leave to appeal is made must contain a copy of the order or judgment and opinion, if any, of the court below, a copy of the record in the court below, a concise statement of the grounds of alleged error and a copy of the order of the lower court denying leave to appeal, if any. If the application is to review an order of the Appellate Term granting or affirming the granting of a new trial or hearing, the papers must also contain a stipulation by the appellant consenting to the entry of judgment absolute against appellant in the event of an affirmance by the court.

(3) All applications for leave to appeal addressed to the court shall be submitted without oral argument and shall be made returnable at 10 o'clock in the forenoon of a regular business day of the court during the period September 1 through June 20.

Cross References

CPLR, see McKinney's Book 7B.

Forms

Permission to appeal to Appellate Division, see West's McKinney's Forms, CPLR, §§ 9:121 to 9:124.

§ 600.4. Calendars

Appeals shall be noticed as enumerated or nonenumerated.

(a) The following appeals are to be noticed as enumerated:

(1) Appeals from final orders and judgments of the Supreme Court, other than those dismissing a cause for failure to prosecute, for failure to serve a complaint or for failure to obey an order of disclosure or to stay or compel arbitration.

(2) Appeals from decrees or orders of the Surrogate's Court finally determining a special proceeding.

(3) Appeals from orders granting or denying motions for a new trial.

(4) Appeals from orders granting or denying motions for summary judgment.

(5) Appeals from orders granting or denying motions to dismiss a complaint, a cause of action, a counterclaim or an answer in point of law.

(6) Appeals from orders of the Appellate Term.

(7) Appeals from judgments or orders in criminal proceedings.

(8) Special proceedings transferred to this court for disposition.

(9) Controversies on agreed statement of facts.

(10) Appeals from orders of the Family Court finally determining a special proceeding.

(11) Appeals from orders granting or denying custody of minors after a hearing.

(12) Special proceedings challenging determination of the New York City tax appeals tribunal.

(13) Such other appeals as the court or a justice thereof may designate as enumerated.

(b) All other types of appeals not set forth in subdivision (a) of this section shall be noticed as nonenumerated.

§ 600.5. Alternative Methods of Prosecuting Appeal; Time to File Record, Appendix or Agreed Statement

At appellant's option, an appeal may be prosecuted upon a record or statement authorized by CPLR 5526, 5527 or 5528.

(a) The Appendix System.

(1) If the appeal is prosecuted by the appendix system pursuant to CPLR 5528(a)(5), appellant shall subpoena, from the clerk of the court from which the appeal is taken, the papers constituting the record on appeal as set forth in CPLR 5526 and cause them to be filed with the clerk of this court within 30 days after settlement of the transcript of proceedings or statement in lieu of a transcript. At the time the

subpoena is served, the appellant shall deliver to the clerk two copies of the statement required by CPLR 5531.

(2) The clerk from whom the papers are subpoenaed shall prefix one copy of the statement required by CPLR 5531 to the papers and firmly fasten such papers across the top, exclusive of the transcript or statement in lieu thereof, if any, and transmit them to the clerk of this court, together with the additional copy of the statement required by CPLR 5531 and a certificate listing the papers constituting the record on appeal and stating whether all such papers are included in the papers transmitted.

(3) If a transcript of proceedings or statement in lieu of a stenographic transcript as settled is not included in the papers so subpoenaed, appellant shall file the ribbon copy of the transcript or the statement at the time of filing the appellant's brief. Where feasible, the parties shall stipulate, pursuant to CPLR 5525, subdivision (b), that only a portion of the transcript of proceedings need be filed.

(4) Where a full or partial transcript of proceedings is made part of the record on appeal, appellant shall serve upon, or make available to, respondent a conformed copy thereof in the manner and at the time prescribed by subdivision (e) of this section.

(b) Agreed Statement in Lieu of Record.

(1) If the appeal is prosecuted pursuant to CPLR 5527, appellant shall reproduce the statement in lieu of a record on appeal as a joint appendix by printing or such other method of reproduction authorized by CPLR 5529. There shall be prefixed to these papers the statement required by CPLR 5531.

(2) Appellant shall file the original and nine copies of the statement, with proof of service of two copies, within 30 days after approval of the statement by the court from which the appeal is taken, as required by CPLR 5527.

(c) Optional Full Record. If appellant elects to proceed on a completely reproduced record on appeal as authorized by the provisions of paragraph 5, subdivision (a), of CPLR 5528, the record shall be printed or otherwise reproduced as provided in section 600.10 of this Part, and in such case an appendix shall not be required. A copy of the record, duly certified, as provided in section 600.10(b)(1)(viii) of this Part, and nine copies of such certified reproduced record, with proof of service of two copies, shall be filed within 30 days after settlement of the transcript of proceedings. Where feasible, the parties shall stipulate, pursuant to CPLR 5525, subdivision (b), that only a portion of the proceedings need be filed.

(d) When Record Does Not Involve Settlement or Approval. If the appeal is prosecuted upon a record which does not involve a transcript or statement requiring settlement or approval by the court from which the appeal is taken, the record on appeal must be filed or caused to be filed within 30 days after filing of the notice of appeal.

(e) Settlement of Transcript.

(1) Within 15 days after receiving the transcript from the court reporter or any other source, the appellant shall make any proposed amendments and serve them and a copy of the transcript upon the respondent. Appellant may serve on respondent, together with the copy of the transcript and the proposed amendments, a notice of settlement containing a specific reference to this subdivision, and stating that if respondent fails to propose amendments or objections within 15 days, the provisions of paragraph (2) of this subdivision shall apply. Within 15 days after such service, the respondent shall make any proposed amendments or objections to the proposed amendments of the appellant and serve them upon the appellant. At any time thereafter and on at least four days' notice to the adverse party, the transcript and the proposed amendments and objections thereto shall be submitted for settlement to the judge or referee before whom the proceedings were had if the parties cannot agree on the amendments to the transcript. The original of the transcript shall be corrected by the appellant in accordance with the agreement of the parties or the direction of the court, and its correctness shall be certified to thereon by the parties or the judge or referee before whom the proceedings were had. When he serves his brief upon the respondent, the appellant shall also serve a conformed copy of the transcript or deposit it in the office of the clerk of the court of original instance, who shall make it available to respondent.

(2) If the appellant has timely proposed amendments and served them and the transcript and the notice provided by paragraph (1) of this subdivision, and no amendments or objections are proposed by the respondent within the time limited by this rule, the transcript, certified as correct by the court reporter, together with appellant's proposed amendments, shall be deemed correct without the necessity of a stipulation by the parties certifying to its correctness or the settlement of the transcript by the judge or referee. The appellant shall affix to such transcript an affirmation, certifying to his compliance with the time limitation and the respondent's failure to propose amendments or objections within the time prescribed.

(f) Transcript—Number to Be Prepared by Court Reporter. Pursuant to CPLR 5525(a), in all appeals taken from judgments or orders entered in this department, the appellant may request that only the ribbon copy of the typewritten transcript be prepared by the reporter. If such request be made, only the ribbon copy shall be required to be prepared by the reporter and furnished to the appellant. If the appeal is by the appendix method, such ribbon copy shall be included in the record on appeal for use by the parties and the court.

Cross References

CPLR, see McKinney's Book 7B.

Forms

Matters relating to transcript, record, and briefs. See West's McKinney's Forms, CPLR §§ 9:216 to 9:241.

§ 600.6. Appeals From Family Court

An appeal from the Family Court may be prosecuted in accordance with any of the procedures specified in section 600.5 of these rules. Any party to such an appeal may elect to file eight reproduced copies of the brief and appendix, if any, with proof of service of one copy, in lieu of a printed or otherwise reproduced brief and appendix as required by section 600.10 of these rules. The appeal may also be perfected upon the original record (transcript of hearing, if any, to be ordered by appellant and filed with the clerk of the Family Court) and eight reproduced copies of the brief. There shall be prefixed to the record the statement required by CPLR 5531; an additional copy of the statement shall be filed with the clerk of this court.

Cross References

CPLR, see McKinney's Book 7B.

Forms

Statement pursuant to CPLR 5531, see West's McKinney's Forms, CPLR, § 9:226.

§ 600.7. Action on Submitted Facts; Transferred Causes

(a) Submission of a Controversy. Unless the court otherwise directs, the agreed statement of facts in an action submitted to this court pursuant to CPLR 3222 shall be printed or reproduced by any other authorized method. A copy of the statement required by CPLR 5531 shall be prefixed to the papers constituting the submission. The original and 19 copies thereof with proof of service of three copies are to be filed at the time of filing plaintiff's brief and two copies of the note of issue. All such causes shall be noticed as enumerated in accordance with the provisions of section 600.11 of this Part.

(b) Transferred Causes. Article 78 proceedings transferred to this court pursuant to the provisions of CPLR 7804(g) and appeals transferred to this court by an Appellate Division of another department pursuant to CPLR 5711 may be prosecuted in accordance with any of the procedures specified in section 600.5 of this Part, except that the petitioner or appellant, whichever the case may be, shall file the record or cause the same to be filed with the clerk of this court within 30 days after entry of the order of transference.

(c) State Division of Human Rights Proceedings. State Division of Human Rights proceedings, transferred to this court pursuant to Executive Law § 298, shall be deemed enumerated and prosecuted in accordance with sections 600.5 and 600.11 of this Part. No oral argument shall be permitted. The Division, upon receipt by it of petitioner's brief, shall promptly file the original record with this court.

Cross References

CPLR, see McKinney's Book 7B.

Executive Law, see McKinney's Book 18.

Forms

Action on submitted facts, see West's McKinney's Forms, CPLR, §§ 4:409 to 4:417.

§ 600.8. Appeals in Criminal Cases

(a) Record and Briefs.

(1) In appeals in criminal cases, other than those in which permission to proceed on the original record is granted, the appellant may elect to proceed by any of the methods specified in section 600.5 of this Part, and the content and form of the record on appeal or appendix shall be as prescribed by section 600.10 of this Part.

(2) The content and form of briefs shall be as prescribed in section 600.10 of these rules and in addition thereto, there shall be included at the beginning of the main brief submitted by appellant a statement setting forth the decision and judgment appealed from; the sentence imposed, if any, and whether an application for an order of stay of judgment pending determination of the appeal was made and, if so, the date of such application, the court to which it was made, and the decision and opinion of the court.

(b) When to Be Heard. Appeals in criminal cases shall be placed on the calendar in the manner described in section 600.11(b), (c), (d), (e) and (f) of this Part, but must be brought on for argument within 120 days after the last day in which a notice of appeal was required to be filed, unless the time to perfect the appeal is enlarged by the court or a justice thereof.

(c) Enlargements of Time. Every application for an enlargement of time within which to perfect an appeal for argument or submission, or for an extension of time to serve and file the record and brief shall be accompanied by an affidavit satisfactorily explaining the delay and stating whether there is an order of stay of judgment pending determination of the appeal outstanding and, if so, the date such order was granted and whether the appellant is free on bail or his own recognizance.

(d) Application for Certificate Granting Leave to Appeal.

(1) Application for a certificate granting leave to appeal to this court shall be made, in writing, within 30 days after service of the order upon the applicant, shall give 15 days' notice to the district attorney, shall be filed with proof of service and shall be submitted without oral argument.

(2) The moving papers for a certificate granting leave to appeal shall be addressed to the court for assignment to a justice, and shall state:

(i) the return day;

(ii) the name and address of the party seeking leave to appeal and the name of the district attorney;

(iii) the indictment number;

(iv) the questions of law or fact which ought to be reviewed; and

(v) that no prior application for such certificate has been made.

(3) The moving papers must include:

(i) a copy of the order sought to be reviewed; and

(ii) a copy of the memorandum or opinion of the court below or a statement that there was none.

(4) Answering papers or a statement that there is no opposition to the application shall be served and filed not later than noon of the third day before the return date stated in the application. Answering papers shall discuss the merits of the application, or shall state:

(i) that the file has been reviewed and includes a response by the district attorney covering the matters raised in the papers submitted by the applicant in the court below and an opinion or memorandum of the justice of that court; and

(ii) that the application for a certificate granting leave to appeal does not contain any new allegations.

(e) Expedited Appeal of an Order Reducing an Indictment or Dismissing an Indictment and Directing the Filing of a Prosecutor's Information.

(1) This subdivision shall govern the procedure for an expedited appeal to the Appellate Division, pursuant to CPL 210.20(6)(c), 450.20(1–a) and 450.55, of an order by a superior court reducing a count or counts of an indictment or dismissing an indictment and directing the filing of a prosecutor's information.

(2) After the People file and serve a notice of appeal pursuant to CPL 460.10(1), either party may request that the Court expedite the appeal. If a request is made, the Court shall hear the appeal on an expedited basis as set forth in this subdivision.

(3)(i) The Appellate Division shall establish an expedited briefing schedule for the appeal. Briefs may be typewritten or reproduced. The People shall file nine copies of a brief and an appendix, which shall include a copy of the indictment and the trial court's decision and order. The respondent shall file nine copies of a brief and, if necessary, an appendix. One copy of the brief and appendix shall be served on opposing counsel.

(ii) The appeal may be taken on one original record, which shall include copies of the indictment, the motion papers, the trial court's decision and order, and the notice of appeal.

(iii) The People shall file with the Appellate Division, separately from the record, one copy of the grand jury minutes.

(iv) The Court shall give preference to the hearing of an appeal perfected pursuant to this subdivision and shall determine the appeal as expeditiously as possible.

(f) Appeals Taken by the People. An appeal taken by the People must be perfected by serving a copy of the appellant's brief upon respondent's appellate attorney, or in the event that no appellate attorney has appeared for respondent, upon the attorney who last appeared for him in the trial court, within nine months of the filing of the notice of appeal.

(g) Assignment of Appellate Counsel. An attorney who represents a defendant in the superior court and is a member of the Assigned Counsel Plan appellate panel, with defendant's written consent, may apply to the Appellate Division for appointment as appellate counsel.

(h) Appeals to the Court of Appeals. Service of a copy of an order on an appellant as required by CPLR 460.10(5)(a) shall be made pursuant to CPLR 2103.

Forms

Appeals in criminal cases. See West's McKinney's Forms, Criminal Procedure, Articles 450, 460, and 470.

§ 600.9.   Appeals in Election Cases

Appeals from judgment and orders entered in proceedings brought pursuant to any of the provisions of the Election Law may be prosecuted in accordance with any of the methods specified in section 600.5 of this Part or, without printing, upon a record consisting of the original papers, the typewritten transcript of the stenographer's minutes, if any, of the trial or hearing, the statement, in duplicate, required by CPLR 5531, and upon typewritten or reproduced briefs. The typewritten transcript shall be either stipulated as correct by the parties or their attorneys, or settled and certified by the trial judge, as provided in CPLR 5525 and 5532. Such appeals may be brought on for hearing in such manner and on such terms and conditions as the court or a justice thereof may direct by an order granted on the application of any party to the proceeding.

Cross References

CPLR, see McKinney's Book 7B.

Election Law, see McKinney's Book 17.

Forms

Statement pursuant to CPLR 5531, see West's McKinney's Forms, CPLR, § 9:226.

§ 600.10.   Format and Content of Records, Appendices and Briefs

(a) Form and Size.

(1) *Generally—Paper and Page Size.* Records, appendices and briefs shall be reproduced by any method that produces a permanent, legible, black on white copy and shall be on a good grade of white, opaque, unglazed recycled paper that satisfies the requirements of paragraph (e) of this section. Paper shall measure vertically 11 inches on the bound edge and horizontally 8½ inches. The clerk may refuse to accept for filing a paper which is not legible or otherwise does not comply with the provisions of this Part.

(2) *Binding.* Every record, appendix or brief shall be securely bound on the left side; when such binding is done by means of a metal fastener or other hard material which protrudes or presents sharp edges, such binding shall be covered by linen or plastic masking tape or similar material. The use of Acco, spiral or other bulky binding edge binders is discouraged.

(3) *Typeface and Type Size.* Records, appendices and briefs shall be in clear serifed, proportionally spaced typeface, such as times new roman, or serifed monospaced typeface, such as courier. Proportionally spaced typeface shall be no less than 14 point size, with the exception that footnotes shall be in type of no less than 12 point size and headings, shall be in type no greater than 15 point size. Monospaced typeface shall be no less than 12 point size, with the exception that footnotes shall be in type no less than 10 point size and headings shall be in type no greater than 14 point size. Typewritten text shall be no less than elite size.

(4) *Page Format.* Records, appendices and briefs shall be double spaced, with the exception that footnotes, headings, indented quotations, and a full size facsimile reproduction of the opinion of the trial court taken from the official state reports may be single spaced. The margin on each side of each page shall be at least one inch; the text on each page shall not exceed 9 inches by 6½ inches.

(5) *Captions.* The parties to all appeals shall be designated in the record and briefs by adding the word "Appellant", "Respondent", etc., as the case may be, following the party's name, e.g. "Plaintiff-Respondent", "Defendant-Appellant", "Petitioner-Appellant", "Respondent-Respondent", etc. Parties who have not appealed and against whom the appeal has not been taken shall be listed separately and designated as they were in the court below, e.g. "Plaintiff", "Defendant", "Petitioner", "Respondent". In appeals from the Surrogate's Courts or from judgments on trust accountings the caption shall contain the title used in the court below, including the name of the decedent or grantor, followed by a listing of all parties to the appeal, properly designated. In proceedings and ac-

tions originating in this court, the parties shall be designated "Petitioner" and "Respondent" or "Plaintiff" and "Defendant".

(6) *Numbering.* Pages of records and briefs shall be numbered consecutively. Pages of appendices shall be separately numbered consecutively, each number preceded by the letter "A"; a respondent's appendix, if any, shall be numbered consecutively and may be preceded by the letters "RA".

(7) *Page Headings.* The subject matter of each page of the record or appendix shall be stated at the top thereof, except that in the case of papers other than testimony, the subject matter of the paper may be stated at the top of the first page of each paper together with the page numbers of the first and last pages thereof. In the case of testimony, the name of the witness, by whom he was called and whether the testimony is direct, cross, redirect or re-cross examination, shall be stated at the top of each page.

(8) *Motion Papers.* Each affidavit or other paper contained in a record on an appeal from an order shall be preceded by a description thereof that must specify on whose behalf it was read. The name of the affiant shall be stated at the top of each page containing an affidavit.

(9) *Questions and Answers.* The answer to a question in the appendix shall not begin a new paragraph.

(10) *Quotations.* Asterisks or other appropriate means shall be used to indicate omissions in quoted excerpts. Reference shall be made to the source of the excerpts quoted. Quotations in briefs may be single spaced, indented. Where an excerpt in the appendix is testimony of a witness quoted from the record the beginning of each page of the transcript shall be indicated by parenthetical insertion of the transcript page number.

(11) *Citation of Decisions.* New York decisions shall be cited from the official reports, if any. All other decisions shall be cited from the official reports, if any, and also from the National Reporter System if they are there reported. Decisions not reported officially or in the National Reporter System shall be cited from the most available source.

(b) Record, What to Contain.

(1) If appellant elects to proceed on an optional full record as authorized by subdivision (c) of section 600.5 of this Part, the record shall contain, in the following order:

(i) An index of the record's contents, listing and describing each paper separately. That part of the index relating to exhibits shall concisely indicate the contents or nature and date, if given of each exhibit and the pages in the record where it is reproduced and where it is admitted to evidence. The part of the index relating to the transcript of testimony shall separately list each witness and shall state as to each witness the page at which direct, cross, re-

direct and re-cross examination begins. Such index shall also contain a reference to the pages where a motion for the dismissal of a complaint or for the direction of a verdict or an oral decision of the court, appealed from, appears.

(ii) A statement pursuant to CPLR 5531.

(iii) If the appeal be from a final judgment, the notice of appeal, the judgment roll, the corrected transcript of the proceedings or a statement pursuant to subdivision (d) of CPLR 5525 if a trial or hearing was held, any relevant exhibits, or copies of them, in the court of original instance, any other reviewable order, and any opinions in the case.

(iv) If the appeal be from an interlocutory judgment or any order, the notice of appeal, the judgment or order appealed from, the transcript, if any; the papers and other exhibits upon which the judgment or order was founded, and any opinions in the case.

(v) A stipulation or order settling the transcript pursuant to subdivision (c) of CPLR 5525.

(vi) The opinion in the case or a statement that there was none.

(vii) A stipulation, if any, dispensing with the printing or filing of exhibits.

(a) Exhibits may be omitted upon stipulation of the attorneys for the parties, approved by a justice of the court, which shall contain a list of the exhibits to be omitted and a brief description of each exhibit. Exhibits thus omitted unless of a bulky nature as defined in this subparagraph shall be filed with the clerk of the court not later than the Wednesday preceding the first day of the term for which the appeal was noticed. Exhibits of a bulky nature (cartons, file drawers, voluminous folders, ledgers, machinery, weapons, etc.) thus omitted need not be filed with the court but shall be kept in readiness by the parties and delivered to the court on telephone notice; a letter, showing that copy has been sent to the adversary, listing such exhibits and stating that they will be available on telephone notice shall be filed with the clerk of the court not later than the Wednesday preceding the first day of the term for which the appeal was noticed.

(b) Exhibits which are not relevant to an appeal may be omitted upon stipulation of the attorneys for the parties which shall contain a list of the exhibits to be omitted, a brief description of each exhibit and a statement that said exhibits will not be relied upon or cited in the briefs of the parties to the appeal.

(viii) A certificate of the proper clerk, or a stipulation waiving certification of the papers pursuant to CPLR 5532, or a certificate subscribed by the attorney certifying to the correctness of the papers pursuant to CPLR 2105.

(2) On an appeal by permission under CPLR 5701 from an order granting or denying a motion for a more definite statement of a vague or ambiguous pleading or for striking any irrelevant, redundant, scandalous or prejudicial matter unnecessarily inserted in a pleading, the portion of the pleading to which the motion is directed must be italicized if the record is printed or underscored if otherwise reproduced.

(3) On the outside front cover of the record shall appear the title of the case, the names, addresses and telephone numbers of the attorneys for the parties, and the index number in the court of original instance. (See paragraph (a)(5), of this section.)

(c) Appendix, What to Contain.

(1) In accordance with CPLR 5528, the appendix of appellant or the joint appendix shall contain those parts of the record necessary to consider the questions involved. A failure to comply with the requirements may result in rejection of the appendix or may affect the imposition of costs.

(2) The appendix should include at least, if in the record, the following:

(i) Notice of appeal; judgment appealed from; decree appealed from; order appealed from or sought to be enforced; notice of motion; order to show cause; opinion (or a statement that there was none); findings of fact and conclusions of law; report of referee or hearing examiner; charge to the jury; verdict; and pleadings if their sufficiency, content, or form is in issue or material.

(ii) Relevant excerpts from transcripts of testimony or papers in connection with a motion. These must contain all the testimony or averments upon which appellant relies or upon which appellant has reason to believe respondent will rely. Such excerpts must not be misleading because of incompleteness or lack of surrounding context.

(iii) Copies of critical exhibits, including significant photographs, to the extent practicable. Critical exhibits may be omitted upon stipulation of the attorneys for the parties, approved by a justice of the court, which shall contain a list of the exhibits to be omitted and a brief description of each exhibit. A copy of this stipulation shall be included in the appendix.

(iv) Exhibits unless of a bulky nature as defined in clause (a) of this subparagraph shall be filed with the clerk of the court not later than the Wednesday preceding the first day of the term for which the appeal was noticed.

(a) Exhibits of a bulky nature (cartons, file drawers, voluminous folders, ledgers, machinery, weapons, etc.) omitted upon stipulation pursuant to subparagraph (2)(iii) of this subdivision need not be filed with the court but shall be kept in readiness by the parties and delivered to the court on telephone notice; a letter, showing that copy has been sent to the adversary, listing such exhibits and stating that they will be available on telephone notice shall be filed with the clerk of the court not later than the Wednesday preceding the first day of the term for which the appeal was noticed.

(b) Exhibits which are not relevant to an appeal may be omitted upon stipulation of the attorneys for the parties which shall contain a list of the exhibits to be omitted, a brief description of each exhibit and a statement that said exhibits will not be relied upon or cited in the briefs of the parties to the appeal.

(3) On the outside front cover of the appendix, whether bound separately or together with the brief, shall appear the title of the case and the names, addresses and telephone numbers of the attorneys for the parties and the index number in the court of original instance. (See paragraph (a)(5) of this section.)

(4) Each appendix shall contain an index of its contents conforming to the extent feasible to the form of index prescribed by subparagraph (b)(1)(i) of this section.

(d) Briefs, What to Contain.

(1) *Generally.*

(i) Except by permission of the court, principal briefs shall not exceed 70 pages or 14,000 words. The calculation of the length of a brief shall not include pages containing the table of contents, tables of citations and any authorized addendum containing statutes, rules, regulations, etc. A word count calculation shall include all printed text on each page of the body of the brief. Except by permission of the court, reply briefs shall not exceed 35 pages or 7,000 words. An application for permission to file an oversize brief shall be by letter that demonstrates with specificity good cause for the oversize submission and asserts that the brief has been edited for conciseness and to eliminate repetition. A copy of the proposed brief shall be submitted with the letter.

(ii) The name of counsel who is to argue or submit the appeal must appear at the upper right hand corner of the cover of all briefs regardless by whom filed. Only one counsel shall be listed except when the court shall otherwise order (see section 600.11(f)(2) of this Part).

(iii) Unless authorized by the court, briefs to which are added or appended any matter, other than specifically authorized by this rule, shall not be accepted for filing. Boldface type shall not be used except in point headings or subheadings.

(iv) The opinion and findings, if any, of a hearing officer and the determination and decision of an administrative department, board or agency shall be appended to the main brief filed by such department, board or agency in any proceeding in which a printed, reproduced or typewritten record or appendix is dispensed with by statute or court order and the proceeding is permitted to be heard on the original papers.

(v) A brief prepared on a computer shall include at the end of the brief a "Printing Specifications Statement" that specifies the processing system, typeface, point size and word count as calculated by the processing system used to prepare the brief.

(2) *Appellant's Brief.* Each respondent shall file the same number of copies of respondent's brief as appellant is required to file, with proof of service on each appellant of the same number of copies as appellant has served. The brief of the appellant shall contain, in the following order:

(i) an index or table of contents including the titles of the points urged in the brief and a table of cases (alphabetically arranged), statutes and other authorities, indicating the pages of the brief where they are cited;

(ii) a concise statement, not exceeding two pages, of the questions involved without names, dates, amounts or particulars. Each question shall be numbered, set forth separately and followed immediately by the answer, if any, of the court from which the appeal is taken;

(iii) a concise statement of the nature of the case and of the facts which should be known to determine the questions involved, with supporting references to pages in the record or the appendix, including, if such be the case, a statement that proceedings on the judgment or order appealed from have been stayed pending a determination of the appeal. Such statement shall include, if such be the case, a statement that proceedings on the judgment or order appealed from have been stayed in whole or in part, by statute or order, pending a determination of the appeal, or that an application for a stay has been denied, giving the date of any order and the court in which the order granting or denying the stay was made;

(iv) the argument for the appellant, which shall be divided into points by appropriate headings distinctively printed;

(v) the statement required by CPLR 5531, as an addendum at the end of the brief;

(vi) the opinion upon which the judgment or order appealed from was based shall also be appended to the appellant's brief in any case in which the court has dispensed with a printed, reproduced or typewritten record or appendix and has permitted the appeal to be heard on the original papers; and

(vii) if the appeal is from an order involving alimony and counsel fees, the brief shall state the date of joinder of issue, if issue was joined, and whether the case has been noticed for trial.

(3) *Respondent's Brief.* The brief of the respondent shall contain, in the following order:

(i) an index or a table of contents including the titles of points urged in the brief and a table of cases (alphabetically arranged), statutes and other authorities, indicating the pages of the brief where they are cited;

(ii) a counterstatement of the questions involved or of the nature and facts of the case, if the respondent disagrees with the statement of the appellant; and

(iii) the argument for the respondent, which shall be divided into points by appropriate headings distinctively printed.

(4) *Appellant's Reply Brief.* The reply brief of the appellant shall contain, in the following order:

(i) a table of contents and a table of cases (alphabetically arranged), statutes and other authorities, indicating the pages of the brief where they are cited; and

(ii) the reply for the appellant, without repetition of the arguments contained in the main brief, which shall be divided into points by appropriate headings distinctively printed.

(e) Recycled Paper. Every brief and every appendix shall be printed or reproduced on recycled paper. For purposes of this rule, paper is recycled if it contains a minimum content of 50 percent waste paper. Cover and oversized exhibits need not be printed or reproduced on recycled paper. Every brief and every appendix shall bear the legend on the bottom of the cover: "Printed [Reproduced] on Recycled Paper." Submission of briefs or appendices not in conformance with this rule shall not constitute a default, but the clerk may accept nonconforming papers on the condition that they be resubmitted in conformance with the requirements of this rule. This rule shall not apply to parties appearing in forma pauperis or pro se.

Cross References

CPLR, see McKinney's Book 7B.

Forms

Matters relating to transcript, record, briefs, etc. See West's McKinney's Forms, CPLR, §§ 9:216 to 9:241.

§ 600.11. Perfecting and Hearing of Appeals; Calendars; Adjournments

(a) When to Be Noticed.

(1) Unless otherwise ordered by the court, all appeals or causes shall be placed on the calendar within 20 days after filing the record on appeal, statement in lieu of a record, the record in a proceeding commenced pursuant to CPLR 506(b)(4), or the papers in a transferred Article 78 proceeding, except that in the

case of a submission of a controversy it shall be placed on the calendar at the time of filing the agreed statement of facts.

(2) The clerk will place no appeal or cause on the calendar where the necessary papers and brief are not offered for filing within the 20 day period prescribed by this section, unless the time for filing has been enlarged by a justice of the court.

(3) The clerk will place no civil appeal or cause on the calendar where the necessary papers and briefs are not offered for filing within nine months of the date of the notice of appeal from the judgment or order appealed from, in proceedings commenced pursuant to CPLR 506(b)(4) within nine months from the date the petition is filed, in article 78 proceedings within nine months from the date of the order transferring the proceeding to the Appellate Division and in appeals to the Appellate Division by permission within nine months from the date of the order granting leave to appeal, unless the time for filing has been enlarged by order of the court. This nine-month limitation applies to all appeals including cross-appeals and may not be extended by agreement or stipulation of the parties. This paragraph does not extend the time of any party to take any step in connection with any appeal or cause. Such times are fixed by other rules and statutes and the time periods fixed by such other rules and statutes must be complied with.

(b) How Placed on Calendar.

(1)(i) Enumerated Appeals. An appeal or cause required by section 600.4 of this Part to be noticed as enumerated shall be placed on the calendar, by the appellant or moving party filing with the clerk, at least 57 days before the first day of the term for which the matter shall have been noticed, two copies of a note of issue with proof of service stating the date the notice of appeal was served, the date the record on appeal or statement in lieu thereof was filed, the nature of the appeal or cause, the court and county in which the action was commenced, the index or indictment number, the date judgment or order was entered, the name of the justice who made the decision, the term for which noticed, and the names, addresses and telephone numbers of the attorneys for all of the parties.

(ii) Nonenumerated Appeals. All other appeals shall be noticed as nonenumerated and shall be placed on the calendar in a manner identical to that for enumerated appeals.

(2) At the time of filing the note of issue, appellant or the moving party shall also file ten copies of the brief, or brief and appendix conforming to the requirements of section 600.10 of this Part, with proof of service of two copies thereof, except that where a typewritten brief is authorized or the appeal is from the Family Court, eight reproduced copies of the brief with proof of service of one copy may be filed.

(c) Answering and Reply Briefs. At least 27 days before the first day of the term for which the appeal or cause shall have been noticed, the respondent or opposing party shall file ten copies of the answering brief, or brief and appendix conforming to the requirements of section 600.10 of this Part, with proof of service of two copies, except that where a typewritten brief is authorized or the appeal is from the Family Court, eight reproduced copies of the brief with proof of service of one copy may be filed. Within nine days after such service the appellant or moving party may file a like number of copies of a reply as were filed of the main brief, conforming to the requirements of section 600.10 of this Part, with proof of service of the same number of copies as were served of the main brief.

(d) Cross Appeals.

(1) The parties shall consult and thereafter file a joint record or joint appendix which shall include therein a copy of the cross-notice of appeal. The cost of the joint record or joint appendix and the transcript, if any, shall be borne equally among the parties.

(2) It shall be the duty of the first filer of a notice of appeal to perfect the appeal. Respondent-cross-appellant shall file its answering brief pursuant to the scheduled date for a respondent for that specific term and shall include therein the points and arguments on its cross-appeal. Appellant shall have nine days thereafter to file its reply brief and, thereafter, respondent-cross-appellant shall have nine days to file its reply brief.

(e) Service by Mail. Whenever service of a record, appendix, note of issue, appellant's or respondent's briefs, is made through the post office, such service must comply with CPLR 2103(b)(2), *viz.,* be made 5 days prior to the last day designated herein.

(f) Time Permitted for Argument.

(1) Counsel for the parties shall consult and determine whether they wish to argue or submit. If they wish to argue, the clerk shall be notified by the parties in one writing of the time desired for argument by each party. The writing shall be in the possession of the clerk on or before the court's scheduled date therefor in that particular term. In the absence of such notification, the appeal shall be marked submitted with respect to all parties.

(2) On the argument of an enumerated appeal, not more than 15 minutes shall be permitted on either side and only one counsel on each side shall be heard except when the court shall otherwise order. Any party may for good cause request additional time by a writing delivered to the clerk before the day of argument.

(3) Oral argument shall not be allowed in nonenumerated appeals, except by permission of the Court.

(4) No briefs, letters, or other communications in connection with an appeal or a cause will be accepted after the argument or submission of an appeal or cause unless permission is granted by the Court.

(g) Adjournments. Enumerated appeals or causes which have been placed on the calendar may be adjourned once upon the written stipulation of counsel, provided such stipulation is filed with the clerk not later than 26 days before the first day of the term for which the appeal has been noticed and the matter is not being adjourned to the June Term. Any further adjournment by stipulation must be approved by the justice of the court. If the appeal or cause is not argued or submitted during the term to which it has been adjourned, it shall be marked off the calendar.

Cross References

CPLR, see McKinney's Book 7B.

Forms

Notice of time requested for argument or intention to submit appeal without argument, see West's McKinney's Forms, CPLR, § 9:246.

§ 600.12. Preference; Dismissal of Appeal or Cause; Dismissal Calendar Calls

(a) Preference.

(1) Any party to an appeal entitled by law to a preference in the hearing of the appeal may serve and file a demand for a preference which shall set forth the provision of law relied upon for such preference. If the demand is sustained by the court, the appeal shall be preferred.

(2) A preference under CPLR 5521 may be obtained upon good cause shown in an application made to the court on notice to the other parties to the appeal.

(b) Dismissal of Appeal or Cause. In the event the appellant or moving party fails to prosecute the appeal or cause within the time prescribed by this Part, or fails to restore an appeal or cause to the calendar within 60 days after it has been marked off the calendar, any other party to the appeal may move to dismiss the appeal for lack of prosecution on eight days' notice. The moving papers on such an application must include a copy of the notice of appeal.

(c) Dismissal Calendar Calls.

(1) In May of each year the clerk shall make up a calendar of all civil appeals or causes not brought on for hearing within nine months from the filing of the record or papers upon which the matter was to be heard, exclusive of such appeals or causes which are then on the calendar or were marked off the calendar less than 60 days prior to May first.

(2) In May and October of each year the clerk shall make up a calendar of all criminal appeals or causes and all appeals involving writs of habeas corpus in criminal causes not brought on for hearing within eighteen months of the awarding of poor person relief, exclusive of such criminal appeals or causes which are then on the calendar or were marked off the calendar less than 60 days prior to the calendar call. Fifteen days' notice of the time and date of such dismissal calendar call, and of the opportunity to submit an affidavit thereupon pursuant to paragraph (4) of this subdivision, shall be given to the appellants by ordinary mail; if the appellant is a defendant such notice shall be at his last known place of residence, or if imprisoned, at the institution at which confined, and similarly to his attorney if any upon the appeal or who last appeared for him.

(3) The calendars so prepared shall be published in the *New York Law Journal* for five consecutive days and called by the clerk on the fifth day of publication. The clerk shall cause a notice to be published in the *New York Law Journal* during the same period calling attention to the publication of the calendars and stating the date and time the calendars will be called.

(4) In the event the appellant or moving party fails to submit an affidavit with proof of service of a copy thereof prior to or on the call of any of the calendars referred to in paragraphs (1) and (2) of this subdivision satisfactorily explaining the delay and containing the following information:

(i) the nature of the order or judgment appealed from;

(ii) the date the judgment or order appealed from was entered or, if the matter was transferred to this court pursuant to CPLR 7804, the date of the order of transferral;

(iii) the date the notice of appeal was served;

(iv) whether any enlargement of time to perfect the appeal has been granted; and

(v) in the case of criminal appeals, the sentence imposed and whether the defendant is on probation or parole, or free on an order of stay of judgment pending determination of the appeal;

an order will be entered dismissing the appeal or cause.

Cross References

CPLR, see McKinney's Book 7B.

Forms

Order to show cause why a preference in hearing of an appeal should not be granted, see West's McKinney's Forms, CPLR, § 9:244.

Affidavit in support of motion for preference in hearing of appeal, see West's McKinney's Forms, CPLR, § 9:245.

Dismissal of appeal to Appellate Division for failure to prosecute, see West's McKinney's Forms, CPLR, §§ 9:257 to 9:259.

§ 600.13. Costs

Costs upon an appeal under CPLR 8107 shall be allowed only as directed by the court in each case.

Cross References

CPLR, see McKinney's Book 7B.

§ 600.14. Motions for Reargument or Leave to Appeal to the Court of Appeals

(a) **Reargument.** Motions for reargument shall be made within 30 days after the appeal has been decided and shall be submitted without oral argument. The papers in support of the motion shall include a copy of the order entered upon the decision of this court, and shall concisely state the points claimed to have been overlooked or misapprehended by the court, with proper reference to the particular portions of the record and the authorities relied upon.

(b) **Leave to Appeal.** Applications for permission to appeal to the Court of Appeals shall be made in the manner and within the time prescribed by CPLR 5513(b) and 5516 and must be submitted without oral argument. The moving papers shall include a copy of the order of this court from which leave to appeal is requested, and shall set forth the questions of law to be reviewed by the Court of Appeals.

Cross References

CPLR, see McKinney's Book 7B.

Forms

See West's McKinney's Forms, CPLR, §§ 9:126 to 9:134.

§ 600.15. Fees of the Clerk of the Court

(a) On behalf of the State of New York, the clerk of the court is entitled to receive the following fees:

(1) For an embossed and engraved certificate of admission as an attorney and counselor at law, twenty-five dollars;

(2) For a certificate of good standing, five dollars;

(3) For furnishing a copy, certified or uncertified, of an opinion, decision, order, record, or other paper in his custody, one dollar for the first page and 50 cents for each additional page; and

(4) For comparing and certifying a prepared copy of an opinion, decision, order, record, or other paper in his custody, 50 cents for the first page and 25 cents for each additional page, with a minimum fee of one dollar.

(5) for and upon the filing of the record, or the statement in lieu of the record, on a civil appeal, or upon the filing of a notice of petition commencing a special proceeding, $315 by check or money order payable to "Appellate Division, First Department," except in the case of a party who by statute or order of the court has been authorized to prosecute a cause as a poor person pursuant to CPLR 1101 or is exempted from the fee requirement by CPLR 8017.

(6) for and upon the filing of each motion or cross-motion with respect to such appeal, $45 by check or money order payable to "Appellate Division, First Department," except in the case of a motion that seeks leave to appeal as a poor person pursuant to CPLR 1101(a).

(b) None of the fees prescribed in subdivision (a), subsections (1) through (4), of this section shall be charged any department or agency of the Federal, City or State governments or any duly organized bar association. No charge shall be made for furnishing a copy of the order, opinion or decision of the court to any party to an appeal or proceeding pending in the court.

(c) The clerk shall keep proper books of account and records showing the income from fees which books and records shall be subject to examination and audit by the State Comptroller. On or before the 15th day of April and October in each year the clerk shall render an account under oath to the State Comptroller of all the income from fees since the rendition of the last account, and shall pay such income to the State Comptroller. The clerk shall furnish a copy of the account to each justice of the court.

§ 600.16. Appeal From an Order Concerning a Grand Jury Report; Appeal From a Judgment Predicated Upon the Entry of a Plea of Guilty

(a) **Appeal From an Order Concerning a Grand Jury Report.** The mode, time and manner for perfecting an appeal from an order accepting a report of a grand jury pursuant to CPL 190.85(1)(a), or from an order sealing a report of a grand jury pursuant to CPL 190.85(5) shall be in accordance with the sections hereof governing appeals in criminal cases. An appeal from such an order shall be a preferred cause and may be added to the term calendar by stipulation approved by the court or upon motion made in the manner provided by section 600.2 of this Part. The record, briefs and other papers on such an appeal shall be sealed and not be available for public inspection except as permitted by CPL 190.85(3). Unless otherwise directed by the court, oral argument will not be allowed.

(b) **Appeal from a Judgment Predicated Upon the Entry of a Plea of Guilty.** On an appeal from a judgment rendered in a criminal proceeding following entry of a guilty plea pursuant to CPL Article 220, respondent may elect to file a brief that urges an affirmance of the judgment solely upon a claim that there is no reviewable issue because appellant made a valid waiver of the right to appeal. Upon the submission or argument of the appeal, the court in its discretion may direct the respondent to submit a supplemental brief addressing additional issues to which the appellant may reply.

Criminal Procedure Law, see McKinney's Book 11A.

§ 600.17. Pre-argument Conference

(a) In every civil case (except one originating in Family Court) in which a notice of appeal is filed or an order granting leave to appeal to the Appellate Division entered, or an order transferring an Article 78 proceeding to the Appellate Division is entered, counsel for the appellant or petitioner shall file, together with the above, a pre-argument statement, proof of service and, where applicable, a copy of the opinion or short form order which contains a memorandum.

(b) The preargument statement must set forth:

(1) Title of the action;

(2) Full names of original parties and any change in the parties;

(3) Name, address and telephone number of counsel for appellant or petitioner;

(4) Name, address and telephone number of counsel for respondent;

(5) Court and county, or administrative body from which the appeal is taken;

(6) Nature and object of the cause of action or special proceeding (e.g., contract-personal services, sale of goods; tort—personal injury, automobile accident, malpractice, equity—specific performance, injunction, etc.);

(7) Result reached in the court or administrative body below; and

(8) Grounds for seeking reversal, annulment or modification.

Where appropriate, the statement must indicate whether there is any related action or proceeding now pending in any court of this or any jurisdiction, and if so, the status of the case. If an additional appeal is pending in the same action, indicate the date of entry of the order or judgment and attach a copy of the notice of appeal and the preargument statement.

(c) The notice of appeal, or the order granting leave to appeal, or the order transferring the case to the Appellate Division shall be filed by the appellant in duplicate in the office where the judgment or order of the court of original instance is entered.

(d) The clerk of the court from which the appeal is taken shall promptly transmit to the Appellate Division the preargument statement and a copy of the notice of appeal or order granting leave or transferral.

(e) By order of the Court, counsel and the parties to the actions may be directed to attend a preargument conference before a judicial administrative officer or such other person as may be designated by the Appellate Division.

(f) Should a preargument conference not be scheduled within 20 days after the filing of a notice of appeal, any party to the appeal or Article 78 proceeding may apply to the Court to have such a conference.

(g) Within 10 days after an order directing a preargument conference has been entered, counsel for respondent must file with the court a counter preargument statement together with proof of service. The counter statement must set forth the extent to which respondent challenges the assertions made by appellant in the preargument statement. The statement also must include an explanation of grounds for granting the relief sought by respondent.

(h) Any attorney who, without good cause shown, fails to file the materials listed in subdivisions (a) or (g), fails to timely appear for a scheduled conference, fails to abide by the terms of a stipulation or order entered following a preargument conference or fails to demonstrate good faith during the preargument process shall be subject to such sanctions as justice of the court may direct.

(i) Upon the conclusion of the conference, if the parties have entered into a stipulation the Court shall file an order of approval.

CPLR, see McKinney's Book 7B.

§ 600.18. Habeas Corpus Appeals

Appeals from judgments or orders entered in any proceeding or action alleging that a person is illegally imprisoned or otherwise unlawfully restrained in his liberty within the State may be prosecuted in accordance with any of the methods specified in section 600.5 of this Part. Such appeals may also be brought on for hearing in such mode, time and manner and on such terms and conditions as this court or a justice thereof may direct by an order granted on the application of any party to the appeal.

§ 600.19. Appeals From Award of Compensation as to Judicial Appointees

If, subsequent to the filing of a notice of appeal, the sole issue sought to be reviewed is the amount of compensation awarded to a judicial appointee (i.e., referee, arbitrator, guardian, guardian ad litem, conservator, committee of the person or a committee of the property of an incompetent or patient, receiver, person designated to perform services for a receiver, such as but not limited to an agent, accountant, attorney, auctioneer or appraiser, person designated to accept service), the appeal may be prosecuted in accordance with any of the methods specified in section 600.5 of this Part; or in lieu thereof may be prosecuted by motion in accordance with the procedure applicable to special proceedings, subdivision 600.2(b) of this Part. In such event, the review may be had on the original record, and briefs may be filed at the option of the parties.

§ 600.20.   [Rescinded]

PART 601.   NEWSPAPERS

§ 601.1.   Publication of Legal Notices in First Department; Designation of Newspapers

(a) Whenever a notice, summons, citation, order or other paper shall be required by the Civil Practice Law and Rules or other provision of law, or by the order of any court or a judge or justice thereof, or of a surrogate or of the clerk of a court or any other official or individual, to be published in a newspaper in the First Department, or public notice of any application to a court or judge or other officer shall be required to be given by publication thereof in a newspaper in the First Department, or where any court or a judge thereof or a surrogate or other judicial officer or public officer is authorized or required to designate a newspaper in the First Department for the publication of any such notice, summons, citation, order or other paper, the newspaper designated by any court or judge thereof, or surrogate or other judicial officer or public officer, shall be a newspaper designated by the Appellate Division of the Supreme Court in the First Department as hereinafter provided, and no such publication shall be deemed to give the notice required to be given if the same is published in any newspaper in the First Department which has not been designated by an order of the Appellate Division of the Supreme Court in the First Department; and the publication of such notice, summons, citation, order or other paper in any undesignated newspaper in the First Department shall not be deemed a compliance with any provision of the Civil Practice Law and Rules or other provision of law or of the order of any court or judge.

(b) The Appellate Division of the Supreme Court in the First Department shall from time to time designate such newspapers in such Department as in its opinion have such a circulation as is calculated to give public notice of a legal publication, and from time to time revoke such designation. To entitle a newspaper to such a designation, it must file with the clerk a statement, duly verified, showing that it has been established at least one year and has been entered in the United States Post Office as second class matter, the amount of its average net paid circulation, the time and place of its regular publication, a statement of its charges for legal publications which shall not exceed its regularly established classified advertising rate, that it is familiar with the requirements for the publication of legal notices and the proper form of affidavit of publication, and that it will maintain records containing sufficient information to enable it to determine whether a legal notice has been published in any of its issues and to execute an affidavit of publication thereof.

(c) All newspapers designated under this rule for the publication of legal notices must file by January 31 of each year with the Clerk of the Court the following:

(i) a copy of the statement of Ownership, Management and Circulation as filed with the United States Service for the prior years; and

(ii) an affidavit duly acknowledged by an editor, publisher, business manager or owner, affirming the accuracy of the information contained in the statement of Ownership, Management and Circulation.

Failure to file the documents required by this subdivision (c) may result in revocation of the newspaper's designation by order of this Court without further notice.

Cross References

CPLR, see McKinney's Book 7B.

PART 602.   ADMISSION TO PRACTICE

§ 602.1.   Admission of Attorneys

(a) **Filing of Application Papers.** Every applicant for admission to practice as an attorney and counselor at law pursuant to subdivision 1(a) or 1(b) of section 90 of the Judiciary Law, may obtain the standard forms and instructions for that purpose from the secretary of the Committee on Character and Fitness. Every applicant for admission to practice pursuant to subdivision 1(a) of section 90 of the Judiciary Law may obtain such forms and instructions immediately after taking the bar examination, and may file a completed application, consisting of the standard form of questionnaire and the other required papers as directed by the instructions, at any time thereafter, regardless of whether the results of the bar examination have yet been issued. As soon as the applicant shall receive a letter from the State Board of Law Examiners stating that the applicant has passed the bar examination, the applicant shall file that letter with the secretary of the Committee on Character and Fitness, and if the applicant's questionnaire was verified more than 45 days prior to such filing, the applicant shall also file a supplemental affidavit stating whether there have been any changes in the facts stated therein and setting forth any such changes.

(b) Referral to Committee on Character and Fitness. Every completed application shall be referred for investigation of the applicant's character and fitness to a committee on character and fitness designated by the Appellate Division of the department to which the applicant is eligible for certification by the State Board of Law Examiners after passing the bar examination, or to which the applicant is applying for admission without examination in accordance with the rules of the Court of Appeals for the admission of attorneys and counselors at law.

(c) Quorum for Committee Action. A majority of the entire committee shall constitute a quorum for the transaction of business by a committee on character and fitness if it consists of less than ten members, and one-fifth of the entire committee, but not less than five members, shall constitute a quorum if it consists of ten or more members.

(d) Investigation and Interview. The committee may itself conduct the required investigation, including an interview of the applicant, or it may authorize its chairman or acting chairman to designate one or more of its members to do so and to make a recommendation to the committee. The committee or the member or members thereof conducting the investigation may require the applicant to furnish such additional information or proofs of good character as the committee or such member or members may consider pertinent. The committee may commence the required investigation at any time after the applicant's completed application has been filed, except that the personal interview of an applicant for admission pursuant to subdivision 1(a) of section 90 of the Judiciary Law shall not be held until after the applicant has been notified by the State Board of Law Examiners that the applicant has passed the bar examination and has been certified to apply for admission.

(e) Procedure Upon Recommendation of Approval. If the committee shall approve the application following its own investigation, or if it shall accept a recommendation of approval submitted by the member or members conducting an investigation pursuant to designation, the chairman or acting chairman shall certify to the Appellate Division on behalf of the committee that the applicant possesses the requisite character and fitness.

(f) Procedure Upon Recommendation of Disapproval, Deferral or Committee Consideration. If the committee shall fail to approve the application following its own investigation, or following a recommendation submitted by the member or members conducting an investigation pursuant to designation that the application be disapproved or that action thereon be deferred, a hearing on the application shall be held expeditiously before the committee or a subcommittee of at least two members designated by the chairman or acting chairman. Such a hearing shall also be held if the member or members conducting an investigation pursuant to designation shall recommend

consideration of the application by the committee and the committee shall fail to approve the application following such consideration.

(g) Notice of Hearing; Waiver. Unless waived in writing by the applicant, a written notice of hearing of not less than 20 days, specifying the time and place of a hearing, shall be served on the applicant. In addition, the notice of hearing shall inform the applicant of the matters to be inquired into and of the applicant's right to be represented by an attorney, and such information shall also be given to the applicant prior to the hearing if the applicant has waived notice of hearing.

(h) Procedure at Hearing. At the hearing, hearsay evidence may be received and considered and adherence to strict rules of evidence shall not be required. The applicant shall be given an opportunity to call and cross-examine witnesses and to challenge, examine and controvert any adverse evidence. Upon timely request, subpoenas for the attendance of witnesses or the production of papers shall be issued to the applicant by the clerk of the Appellate Division, the subpoena fees and mileage to be paid by the applicant.

(i) Stenographic Record or Tape Recording. A stenographic record or tape recording shall be made of the hearing, and the applicant may obtain a transcript or copy of the recording at the applicant's expense.

(j) Decision or Report Following Hearing. Where the hearing has been conducted by the committee, the committee shall render a decision, and where the hearing has been conducted by a subcommittee, the subcommittee shall render a report, within 60 days after the matter is finally submitted, unless the time is extended by consent of the applicant or order of the Appellate Division. The decision of the committee or the report of the subcommittee, as the case may be, may recommend approval or disapproval of the applicant or deferral of action on the application for a period not to exceed six months.

(k) Transmittal of Decision to Appellate Division Following Hearing Conducted by Committee. Where the hearing has been conducted by the committee, the committee shall transmit its decision to the Appellate Division, together with the appropriate certificate if it recommends approval of the applicant. If the decision recommends disapproval of the applicant or deferral of action on the application, it shall include a statement of the grounds on which it is based and a copy thereof shall be served on the applicant or the applicant's attorney.

(*l*) Review by Committee Following Hearing Conducted by Subcommittee. Where the hearing has been conducted by a subcommittee, the subcommittee's report and the stenographic record or tape recording of the hearing shall be referred for consideration and review to the committee, which shall render a decision thereon expeditiously. The committee's decision may confirm, reverse or modify the subcommittee's report, or direct that a further hearing be held before the same or another subcommittee. If the committee's decision recommends disapproval of the applicant or deferral of action on the application, it shall include a statement of the grounds on which it is based and a copy thereof shall be served on the applicant or the applicant's attorney. The decision shall be transmitted to the Appellate Division, together with the appropriate certificate, if it recommends approval of the applicant. The deliberations of the committee shall be confidential and the applicant shall not be entitled to compel disclosure thereof.

(m) Petition to Appellate Division Following Adverse Decision. If the committee's decision is adverse to the applicant, the applicant may, within 60 days after service of a copy thereof, petition the Appellate Division, in accordance with CPLR 9404, on notice of not less than eight days served on the committee together with any supporting papers, for an order granting the application for admission to practice notwithstanding the committee's decision.

(n) Petition to Appellate Division in Case of Unreasonable Delay. In any case in which it is claimed that the committee has unreasonably delayed action on an application for admission to practice, the applicant may petition the Appellate Division, in accordance with CPLR 9404, on notice of not less than eight days served on the committee together with any supporting papers, for an order granting the application notwithstanding the committee's failure to complete action thereon, or for other appropriate relief.

(*o*) Petition for Advance Ruling With Respect to Past Conduct.

(1) Any person who is a matriculated student in an approved law school, as an approved law school is defined in the rules of the Court of Appeals for the admission of attorneys and counselors at law, or who has applied for admission to such a law school, and who has previously been convicted of a felony or misdemeanor, or suspended, removed, or dismissed from public office or employment, or dishonorably discharged from the armed services of the United States, may petition the Appellate Division of the department in which such person resides or is employed full-time, or if such person does not reside and is not employed full-time in the State, the Appellate Division of the Third Department, for an advance ruling, in accordance with this section, as to whether such conviction, suspension, removal or dismissal from public office or employment, or dishonorable discharge, as the case may be, would operate to disqualify the petitioner, on character grounds, from being admitted to practice as an attorney and counselor at law in this State.

(2) The petition shall include a detailed statement of the facts with respect to the petitioner's conviction, suspension, dismissal or removal from public office or employment, or dishonorable discharge, as the case may be, and of the petitioner's activities subsequent thereto which the petitioner believes bear on character and fitness to practice law.

(3) The petitioner shall also submit a completed and verified questionnaire on the standard form furnished by the committee on character and fitness and affidavits of good moral character from two reputable persons who have known the petitioner for at least one year. In addition, the petitioner shall submit a letter from a person in authority at the approved law school in which the petitioner is a matriculated student or to which the petitioner has applied for admission, stating that such law school would retain or accept the petitioner as a student therein, as the case may be, if the petitioner's conviction, suspension, dismissal or removal from public office or employment or dishonorable discharge, as the case may be, would not operate to disqualify the petitioner from being admitted to practice as an attorney and counselor at law in this State.

(4) The petition and other papers submitted by the petitioner shall be referred to the appropriate committee on character and fitness, which shall process and investigate the petition in accordance with the procedures set forth in the preceding subdivisions of this section. The committee may recommend that a ruling be made either in favor of or against the petitioner, or that no ruling be made, and its recommendation shall be transmitted to the Appellate Division.

(5) A ruling made by the Appellate Division in favor of the petitioner shall determine that the petitioner's prior conviction, suspension, removal or dismissal from public office or employment, or dishonorable discharge, as the case may be, and the acts committed by the petitioner which resulted therein, would not operate to disqualify the petitioner, on character grounds, from being admitted to practice as an attorney and counselor at law in this State. Such a ruling shall have binding force throughout the State with respect to the determination thus made by it. In the event that the Appellate Division should rule against the petitioner or should refuse to make a ruling, its determination shall be without prejudice to the petitioner's right, after passing the bar examination, to apply for a favorable ruling with respect to character and fitness.

(p) Manner of Service. Service of any notice or other papers required under any of these rules may be made by mail or in the manner provided for service of a summons.

Cross References

CPLR, see McKinney's Book 7B.

Judiciary Law, see McKinney's Book 29.

§ 602.2. Admission Pro Hac Vice of Foreign Attorneys and Counselors at Law

(a) **For a Particular Cause.** An attorney and counselor at law, or the equivalent from another state, territory, district or foreign country, may be admitted pro hac vice to participate in the trial or argument of a particular cause in which the attorney may be employed, upon application to and in the discretion of the court in which the cause is pending.

(b) **Graduate Students, Graduate Assistants and Law School Teachers.** An attorney and counselor at law, or the equivalent from another state, territory, district or foreign country, who is a graduate student or graduate assistant enrolled in an approved law school in this department, or a teacher employed in such a law school, may apply to this court, by duly verified petition, for admission pro hac vice to advise and represent clients or participate in the trial or argument of any case during the continuance of such enrollment or employment, if engaged to advise or represent such clients through participation in an organization described in subdivision 7 of section 495 of the Judiciary Law, or during employment with a district attorney, corporation counsel or the Attorney General.

(c) **Law School Graduates.** An attorney and counselor at law, or the equivalent from another state, territory, district or foreign country, who is a graduate of an approved law school, may apply to this court, by duly verified petition, for admission pro hac vice to advise and represent clients and participate in the trial or argument of any case while employed or associated with an organization, described in subdivision 7 of section 495 of the Judiciary Law, whose principal office is located in this department, or during employment with a district attorney, corporation counsel or the Attorney General; but such admission pro hac vice shall be for no longer than 18 months.

(d) **Term for Rendering Legal Services.** Upon granting of the applicant's petition pursuant to either subdivision (b) or (c) of this section, the applicant may render the specified legal services for the organization with which applicant is associated or employed in any court of this State for the period specified in this court's order granting said applicant's petition.

(e) **Filing of Annual Report by the Organization.** An organization described in subdivision 7 of section 495 of the Judiciary Law shall file an annual report with this court in conformance with Part 608 of this court's rules. In addition to the statement required to be filed in the annual report, the organization shall supply the names and addresses of the graduate students, graduate assistants, law school teachers and graduates of approved law schools, and the type of legal services in which they are engaged in the courts of this State, pursuant to their admission pro hac vice.

Cross References

Judiciary Law, see McKinney's Book 29.

§ 602.3. Orientation to the Profession Program

(a) **Orientation Program.** The Chairman of the Committee shall conduct at least quarterly an orientation to professional ethics and professionalism for applicants seeking admission to practice as attorneys and counsellors at law.

(b) **Required Attendance.** Every attorney admitted to the practice of law after September 1, 1999 shall attend an orientation program prior to admission.

(c) **Exemptions.** The following persons shall be exempt from this requirement:

(1) Subject to the requirements in §1500.12(f) of this Part, attorneys who do not practice law in New York. Attorneys practice law pursuant to this section, if during the first two years after admission they give legal advice or counsel to, or provide legal representation for, a particular body or individual in a particular situation in either the public or private sector;

(2) Attorneys who have been engaged in the practice of law in another state, the District of Columbia, any territory of the United States of any foreign jurisdiction, for the five years preceding admission to the New York Bar; and,

(3) Full-time active members of the United States Armed Forces.

(d) **Waivers.** The Chairman of the Committee may, in individual cases involving undue hardship or extenuating circumstances, upon written request, grant waivers and modifications of this requirement.

§ 602.4. Members of Committee on Character and Fitness as Volunteers

The members of the Committee on Character and Fitness, as volunteers, are expressly authorized to participate in a State-sponsored volunteer program within the meaning of subdivision 1 of section 17 of the Public Officers Law.

Cross References

Public Officers Law, see McKinney's Book 46.

PART 603. CONDUCT OF ATTORNEYS

§ 603.1. Application

(a) This Part shall apply to all attorneys who are admitted to practice, reside in, commit acts in or who have offices in this judicial department, or who are admitted to practice by a court of another jurisdiction and who practice within this department as counsel for governmental agencies or as house counsel to corporations or other entities, or otherwise, and to all legal consultants licensed to practice pursuant to the provisions of subdivision 6 of section 53 of the Judiciary Law. In addition, any attorney from another State, territory, district or foreign country admitted pro hac vice to participate in the trial or argument of a particular cause in any court in this judicial department, or who in any way participates in any action or proceeding in this judicial department shall be subject to this Part.

(b) This Part shall apply to any law firm, as that term is used in the Disciplinary Rules of the Code of Professional Responsibility, section 1200.1(b) of this Title, that has as a member, employs, or otherwise retains an attorney or legal consultant described in subdivision (a) of this section.

(c) Neither the conduct of proceedings nor the imposition of discipline pursuant to this Part shall preclude the imposition of any further or additional sanctions prescribed or authorized by law, and nothing herein contained shall be construed to deny to any other court or agency such powers as are necessary for that court or agency to maintain control over proceedings conducted before it, such as the power of contempt, or to prohibit bar associations from censuring, suspending or expelling their members from membership in the association; provided, however, that such action by a bar association shall be reported to the Departmental Disciplinary Committee appointed pursuant to section 603.4(a) of this Part, and provided further that such action by a bar association shall not be a bar to the taking of other and different disciplinary action by the court or such Departmental Disciplinary Committee.

Cross References

Judiciary Law, see McKinney's Book 29.

§ 603.2. Professional Misconduct Defined

(a) Any attorney who fails to conduct himself both professionally and personally, in conformity with the standards of conduct imposed upon members of the bar as conditions for the privilege to practice law and any attorney who violates any provision of the rules of this court governing the conduct of attorneys, or with respect to conduct on or after January 1, 1970, any disciplinary rules of the Code of Professional Responsibility, as adopted by the New York State Bar Association, effective January 1, 1970, as amended, or with respect to conduct on or before December 31, 1969,

any canon of the Canons of Professional Responsibility, as adopted by such bar association and effective until December 31, 1969 or with respect to conduct on or after September 1, 1990, any disciplinary rule of the Code of Professional Responsibility, as jointly adopted by the Appellate Divisions of the Supreme Court, effective September 1, 1990, or any of the special rules concerning court decorum, shall be guilty of professional misconduct within the meaning of subdivision 2 of section 90 of the Judiciary Law.

(b) Any law firm that fails to conduct itself in conformity with the provisions of the Disciplinary Rules of the Code of Professional Responsibility pertaining to law firms shall be guilty of professional misconduct within the meaning of subdivision 2 of section 90 of the Judiciary Law.

Cross References

Judiciary Law, see McKinney's Book 29.

Code of Professional Responsibility, see Appendix to McKinney's Judiciary Law, Book 29.

§ 603.3. Discipline of Attorneys for Professional Misconduct in Foreign Jurisdiction

(a) Any attorney to whom this Part shall apply, pursuant to section 603.1 of this Part who has been disciplined in a foreign jurisdiction, may be disciplined by this court because of the conduct which gave rise to the discipline imposed in the foreign jurisdiction. For purposes of this Part, foreign jurisdiction means another state, territory or district.

(b) Upon receipt of a certified or exemplified copy of the order imposing such discipline in a foreign jurisdiction, and of the record of the proceeding upon which such order was based, this court, directly or by the Departmental Disciplinary Committee, shall give written notice to such attorney pursuant to subdivision 6 of section 90 of the Judiciary Law, according him the opportunity, within 20 days of the giving of such notice, to file a verified statement setting forth evidentiary facts for any defense to discipline enumerated under subdivision (c) of this section, and a written demand for a hearing at which consideration shall be given to any and all such defenses. Such notice shall further advise the attorney that in default of such filing such discipline or such disciplinary action as may be appropriate will be imposed or taken. When a verified statement setting forth evidentiary facts for any defense to discipline and a demand for hearing have been duly filed, no discipline shall be imposed without affording the attorney an opportunity for hearing. The Court may conduct the hearing or it may appoint a Referee to conduct the hearing and further refer the matter to the Departmental Disciplinary Committee. In the event the committee or the attorney desires further action by this court, a petition may be filed in this court together with the record of the proceedings before the committee.

(c) Only the following defenses may be raised:

(1) that the procedure in the foreign jurisdiction was so lacking in notice or opportunity to be heard as to constitute a deprivation of due process; or

(2) that there was such an infirmity of proof establishing the misconduct as to give rise to the clear conviction that this court could not, consistent with its duties, accept as final the finding in the foreign jurisdiction as to the attorney's misconduct; or

(3) that the misconduct for which the attorney was disciplined in the foreign jurisdiction does not constitute misconduct in this jurisdiction.

(d) Any attorney to whom these rules shall apply pursuant to section 603.1 of this Part who has been disciplined in a foreign jurisdiction shall promptly advise this court of such discipline.

(e) Whenever the Departmental Disciplinary Committee learns that an attorney to whom these rules shall apply, pursuant to section 603.1 of this Part, has been disciplined in a foreign jurisdiction, it shall ascertain whether a certified or exemplified copy of the order imposing such discipline has been filed with this court, and if it has not been filed, such committee shall cause such order to be filed.

Cross References

Judiciary Law, see McKinney's Book 29.

§ 603.4. Appointment of Disciplinary Agencies; Commencement of Investigation of Misconduct; Complaints; Procedure in Certain Cases

(a)(1) This court shall appoint a Departmental Disciplinary Committee for the Judicial Department, which shall be charged with the duty and empowered to investigate and prosecute matters involving alleged misconduct by attorneys who, and law firms that, are subject to this Part, and to impose discipline to the extent permitted by section 603.9 of this Part. This court shall, in consultation with the Departmental Disciplinary Committee, appoint a chief counsel to such committee and such assistant counsel, special counsel and supporting staff as it deems necessary.

(2) This court shall appoint as members of the Departmental Disciplinary Committee attorneys in good standing with the Bar of the State of New York and persons who are not attorneys but reside or have a principal place of business in the City of New York. Special counsel may be appointed as members of the committee. At least two-thirds of the committee shall be attorneys. Appointment to the committee shall be for a three-year term. Except for special counsel, a member who has served for two consecutive terms is not eligible for reappointment for at least one year following the expiration of the second term. (The membership of the Departmental Disciplinary Committee shall be appointed by this court for a term of three years, except members who have been appointed to complete unexpired terms, in which case such members may be reappointed for three-year or shorter terms. At least two-thirds of the members of the Departmental Disciplinary Committee shall be members of the Bar of the State of New York in good standing, each of whom shall reside or have an office in the City of New York, and up to one-third of such members shall be persons who are not members of the Bar, each of whom shall reside or have a principal place of business in the City of New York. The court may appoint special counsel who shall be full members of the committee. Appointments to the Departmental Disciplinary Committee may be made from lists of nominees submitted by the Association of the Bar of the City of New York, the New York County Lawyers' Association, and the Bronx County Bar Association, and by such other means which the court deems in the public interest. With the exception of Special Counsel appointed by the Court, a member of the Bar who has served two consecutive terms shall not be eligible for reappointment until one year after the expiration of the second term. The appropriate committees of the Association of the Bar of the City of New York, the New York County Lawyers' Association, and the Bronx County Bar Association may be designated to investigate and prosecute matters involving alleged misconduct of attorneys. Upon such designation, references in sections 603.3, 603.4(a)(3), (b), (c) and (d), 603.5, 603.6, 603.9, 603.11, 603.12(a) and (e), 603.15 and 603.16 of this Part to the Departmental Disciplinary Committee with respect to the matter or matters to which such designation applies shall mean the Committee of the Association of the Bar of the City of New York, the New York County Lawyers' Association or the Bronx County Bar Association so designated.)

(3) The members of the Departmental Disciplinary Committee for the First Judicial Department, as volunteers, are expressly authorized to participate in a State-sponsored volunteer program within the meaning of subdivision 1 of section 17 of the Public Officers Law.

(b) The rules for the conduct of the proceedings and business of the Departmental Disciplinary Committee, set forth in Part 605 of this Title, apply to matters involving alleged misconduct by attorneys and law firms. The Departmental Disciplinary Committee may act through its chairperson, acting chairperson, subcommittees or hearing panels.

(c) Investigation of professional misconduct may be commenced upon receipt of a specific complaint by this court, or by the Departmental Disciplinary Committee or such investigation may be commenced sua

497

sponte by this court or by the Departmental Disciplinary Committee. Complaints must be in writing and subscribed by the complainant but need not be verified. Whenever the Departmental Disciplinary Committee concludes that the issue involved upon the complaint is a fee dispute and, accordingly, dismisses the complaint, the chief counsel to the committee or his assistant shall advise the complainant and the respondent that the dispute might be satisfactorily resolved by referring it for conciliation to the Joint Committee on Fee Disputes organized and administered by the Association of the Bar of the City of New York, the New York County Lawyers' Association and the Bronx County Bar Association and with permission of both the complainant and respondent, will forward the file to said committee headquartered at the New York County Lawyers' Association, 14 Vesey Street, New York, N. Y.

(d) When the Departmental Disciplinary Committee, after investigation, determines that it is appropriate to file a petition against an attorney in this court, the committee shall institute disciplinary proceedings in this court and the court may discipline an attorney on the basis of the record of hearings before such committee, or may appoint a referee, justice or judge to hold hearings.

(e)(1) An attorney who is the subject of an investigation, or of charges by the Departmental Disciplinary Committee of professional misconduct, or who is the subject of a disciplinary proceeding pending in this court against whom a petition has been filed pursuant to this section, or upon whom a notice has been served pursuant to section 603.3(b) of this Part, may be suspended from the practice of law, pending consideration of the charges against the attorney, upon a finding that the attorney is guilty of professional misconduct immediately threatening the public interest. Such a finding shall be based upon:

(i) the attorney's default in responding to the petition or notice, or the attorney's failure to submit a written answer to pending charges of professional misconduct or to comply with any lawful demand of this court or the Departmental Disciplinary Committee made in connection with any investigation, hearing, or disciplinary proceeding, or

(ii) a substantial admission under oath that the attorney has committed an act or acts of professional misconduct, or

(iii) other uncontested evidence of professional misconduct, or,

(iv) the attorney's willful failure or refusal to pay money owed to a client, which debt is demonstrated by an admission, a judgment, or other clear and convincing evidence.

(2) The suspension shall be made upon the application of the Departmental Disciplinary Committee to this court, after notice of such application has been given to the attorney pursuant to subdivision six of

section 90 of the Judiciary Law. The court shall briefly state its reasons for its order of suspension which shall be effective immediately and until such time as the disciplinary matters before the Committee have been concluded, and until further order of the court. Following a temporary suspension under this rule, the Departmental Disciplinary Committee shall schedule a post-suspension hearing within 60 days of the entry of the court's order.

(f) Disciplinary proceedings shall be granted a preference by this court.

(g) An application for suspension pursuant to section 603.4(e)(1) may state that an attorney who is suspended and who has not appeared or applied in writing to the Committee or the Court for a hearing or reinstatement for six months from the date of an order of suspension may be disbarred. If an application does state the foregoing, and the respondent does not appear or apply in writing to the Committee or the Court for a hearing or reinstatement within six months of the suspension date, the respondent may be disbarred without further notice.

Cross References

Judiciary Law, see McKinney's Book 29.

Public Officers Law, see McKinney's Book 46.

§ 603.5. Investigation of Professional Misconduct on the Part of an Attorney; Subpoenas and Examination of Witnesses Under Oath

(a) Upon application by the Departmental Disciplinary Committee, or upon application by counsel to such committee, disclosing that such committee is conducting an investigation of professional misconduct on the part of an attorney, or has commenced proceedings against an attorney, or upon application by an attorney under such investigation, or who is a party to such proceedings, the clerk of this court shall issue subpoenas in the name of the presiding justice for the attendance of any person and the production of books and papers before such committee or such counsel or any subcommittee or hearing panel thereof designated in such application at a time and place therein specified.

(b) The Departmental Disciplinary Committee, or a subcommittee or hearing panel thereof, or its counsel, is empowered to take and cause to be transcribed the evidence of witnesses who may be sworn by any person authorized by law to administer oaths.

§ 603.6. Investigation of Persons, Firms or Corporations Unlawfully Practicing or Assuming to Practice Law

(a) Upon application by the Departmental Disciplinary Committee, or of a committee of a recognized bar association authorized to inquire into possible cases of the unlawful practice of the law, disclosing that there is reason to believe that a person, firm or corporation is unlawfully practicing or assuming to practice law, and that such committee is conducting an investigation into such matter, or upon application by any such person, firm or corporation under such investigation, the clerk of this court shall issue subpoenas in the name of the presiding justice for the attendance of any person and production of books and papers before such committee, or any subcommittee or hearing panel thereof designated in such application, at the time and place therein specified.

(b) Each committee referred to in subdivision (a) of this section or a subcommittee or hearing panel of any of the foregoing, or its counsel, is empowered to take and cause to be transcribed the evidence of witness who may be sworn by any person authorized by law to administer oaths.

§ 603.7. Claims or Actions for Personal Injuries, Property Damage, Wrongful Death, Loss of Services Resulting From Personal Injuries and Claims in Connection With Condemnation or Change of Grade Proceedings

(a) Statements as to Retainers; Blank Retainers.

(1) Every attorney who, in connection with any action or claim for damages for personal injuries or for property damages or for death or loss of services resulting from personal injuries, or in connection with any claim in condemnation or change of grade proceedings, accepts a retainer or enters into an agreement, express or implied, for compensation for services rendered or to be rendered in such action, claim or proceeding, whereby his compensation is to be dependent or contingent in whole or in part upon the successful prosecution or settlement thereof, shall, within 30 days from the date of any such retainer or agreement of compensation, sign personally and file with the Office of Court Administration of the State of New York a written statement of such retainer or agreement of compensation, containing the information hereinafter set forth. Such statement may be filed personally by the attorney or his representative at the main office of the Office of Court Administration in the City of New York, and upon such filing he shall receive a date stamped receipt containing the code number assigned to the original so filed. Such statement may also be filed by ordinary mail addressed to:

Office of Court Administration—Statements
Post Office Box No. 2016
New York, New York 10008

Statements filed by mail must be accompanied by a self-addressed stamped postal card, containing the words "Retainer Statement", the date of the retainer and the name of the client. The Office of Court Administration will date stamp the postal card, make notation thereon of the code number assigned to the retainer statement and return such card to the attorney as a receipt for the filing of such statement. It shall be the duty of the attorney to make due inquiry if such receipt is not returned to him within 10 days after his mailing of the retainer statement to the Office of Court Administration.

(2) A statement of retainer must be filed in connection with each action, claim or proceeding for which the attorney has been retained. Such statement shall be on one side of paper 8½ inches by 11 inches and be in the following form and contain the following information:

Retainer Statement   For office use:

TO THE OFFICE OF COURT ADMINISTRATION OF THE STATE OF NEW YORK

1.   Date of agreement as to retainer ....

2.   Terms of compensation ....

3.   Name and home address of client ....

4.   If engaged by an attorney, name and office address of retaining attorney ....
....

5.   If claim for personal injuries, wrongful death or property damage, date and place of occurrence ....
....

6.   If a condemnation or change of grade proceeding:

   (a) Title and description ....

   (b) Date proceeding was commenced ....

   (c) Number or other designation of the parcels affected ....

7.   Name, address, occupation and relationship of person referring the client ....

Dated: ...., N.Y., ... day of ...., 20...

          Yours, etc.

          ....
                 Signature of Attorney

          ....
                 Attorney's Name

          ....
                 Office and P.O. Address

          ... Dist. ... Dept. ... County

NOTE: CPLR 2104 AND 3217 REQUIRE THAT THE ATTORNEY FOR THE DEFENDANT FILE A STIPULATION OR STATEMENT OF DISCONTINUANCE WITH THE COURT UPON DISCONTINUANCE OF AN ACTION

(3) An attorney retained by another attorney, on a contingent fee basis, as trial or appeal counsel or to assist in the preparation, investigation, adjustment or settlement of any such action, claim or proceeding shall, within 15 days from the date of such retainer, sign personally and file with the Office of Court Administration a written statement of such retainer in the manner and form as above set forth, which statement shall also contain particulars as to the fee arrangement, the type of services to be rendered in the matter, the code number assigned to the statement of retainer filed by the retaining attorney and the date when said statement of retainer was filed.

(4) No attorney shall accept or act under any written retainer or agreement of compensation in which the name of the attorney was left blank at the time of its execution by the client.

(b) Closing Statement; Statement Where No Recovery.

(1) A closing statement shall be filed in connection with every claim, action or proceeding in which a retainer statement is required, as follows: every attorney upon receiving, retaining or sharing any sum in connection with a claim, action or proceeding subject to this section shall, within 15 days after such receipt, retention or sharing, sign personally and file with the Office of Court Administration and serve upon the client a closing statement as hereinafter provided. Where there has been a disposition of any claim, action or proceeding, or a retainer agreement is terminated, without recovery, a closing statement showing such fact shall be signed personally by the attorney and filed with the Office of Court Administration within 30 days after such disposition or termination. Such statement may be filed personally by the attorney or his representative at the main office of the Office of Court Administration in the City of New York and upon such filing he shall receive a date stamped receipt. Such statement may also be filed by ordinary mail addressed to:

The Office of Court Administration—
Statements
Post Office Box No. 2016
New York, New York 10008

Statements filed by mail must be accompanied by a self-addressed stamped postal card containing the words "Closing Statement", the date the matter was completed, and the name of the client. The Office of Court Administration will date stamp the postal card, make notation thereon of the code number assigned to the closing statement and return such card to the attorney as a receipt for the filing of such statement. It shall be the duty of the attorney to make due inquiry if such receipt is not returned to him within 10 days after his mailing of the closing statement to the Office of Court Administration.

(2) Each closing statement shall be on one side of paper 8½ inches by 11 inches and be in the following form and contain the following information:

Closing Statement   For office use:

TO THE OFFICE OF COURT ADMINISTRATION OF THE STATE OF NEW YORK

1. Code number appearing on Attorney's receipt for filing of retainer statement.
. . . .

2. Name and present address of client . . . .

3. Plaintiff(s) . . . .

4. Defendant(s) . . . .

5. (a) If an action was commenced, state the date:
. . . . , 20. . , ... Court, ... County.

(b) Was the action disposed of in open court? . .

If not, and a request for judicial intervention was filed, state the date the stipulation or statement of discontinuance was filed with the clerk of the part to which the action was assigned . . . .

If not, and an index number was assigned but no request for judicial intervention was filed, state the date the stipulation or statement of discontinuance was filed with the County Clerk . . . .

6. Check items applicable: Settled ( ); Claim abandoned by client ( ); Judgment ( ).

Date of payment by carrier or defendant . . . day of . . . , 20 . . .

Date of payment to client . . . day of . . . 20 . . .

7. Gross amount of recovery (if judgment entered, include any interest, costs and disbursements allowed) $ . . . . . . (of which $ . . . . . . was taxable costs and disbursements).

8. Name and address of insurance carrier or person paying judgment or claim and carrier's file number, if any . . . .

9. Net amounts: to client $ . . . . ; compensation to undersigned $ . . . . ; names and addresses and amounts paid to attorneys participating in the contingent compensation.

10. Compensation fixed by: retainer agreement ( ); under schedule ( ); or by court ( ).

11. If compensation fixed by court: Name of Judge . . . . Court . . . . Index No. . . . Date of order . . . .

12. Itemized statement of payments made for hospital, medical care or treatment, liens, assignments, claims and expenses on behalf of the client which have been charged against the client's share of the recovery, together with the name, address, amount and reason for each payment . . . .

13. Itemized statement of the amounts of expenses and disbursements paid or agreed to be paid to others

for expert testimony, investigative or other services properly chargeable to the recovery of damages together with the name, address and reason for each payment . . . .

14. Date on which a copy of this closing statement has been forwarded to the client . . . . . . , 20. . . .

NOTE: CPLR 2104 AND 3217 REQUIRE THAT THE ATTORNEY FOR THE DEFENDANT FILE A STIPULATION OR STATEMENT OF DISCONTINUANCE WITH THE COURT UPON DISCONTINUANCE OF AN ACTION

Dated: . . . . . . , N.Y., ... day of . . . . . . , 20. . .

      Yours, etc.

. . . .
        Signature of Attorney

. . . .
        Attorney's Name

. . . .
      Office and P.O. Address

. . . . Dist. . . . . . . Dept. . . . .
County

(If space provided is insufficient, riders on sheets 8½″ by 11″ and signed by the attorney may be attached).

(3) A joint closing statement may be served and filed in the event that more than one attorney receives, retains or shares in the contingent compensation in any claim, action or proceeding, in which event the statement shall be signed by each such attorney.

(c) Confidential Nature of Statements.

(1) All statements of retainer or closing statements filed shall be deemed to be confidential and the information therein contained shall not be divulged or made available for inspection or examination to any person other than the client of the attorney filing said statements except upon written order of the presiding justice of the Appellate Division.

(2) The Office of Court Administration of the State of New York shall reproduce in an alternative format, as that term is defined in § 104.1(c) of this Title, all statements filed pursuant to this section by a means that shall accurately reproduce the original statements in all details thereof, and shall thereafter destroy the originals so reproduced. Such a reproduction in an alternative format shall be deemed to be an original record for all purposes, and an enlargement or facsimile thereof may be introduced in evidence in all courts and administrative agencies and in any action, hearing or proceeding in place and stead of the original statement so reproduced, with the same force and effect as though the original document were presented.

(d) Deposit of Collections; Notice.

(1) Whenever an attorney, who has accepted a retainer or entered into an agreement as above referred to, shall collect any sum of money upon any such action, claim or proceeding, either by way of settlement or after a trial or hearing, he shall forthwith deposit the same in a special account in accordance with the provisions of section 603.15 of this Part. Within 15 days after the receipt of any such sum he shall cause to be delivered personally to such client or sent by registered or certified mail, addressed to such client at the client's last known address, a copy of the closing statement required by this section. At the same time the attorney shall pay or remit to the client the amount shown by such statement to be due the client, and he may then withdraw for himself the amount so claimed to be due him for compensation and disbursements. For the purpose of calculating the 15 day period, the attorney shall be deemed to have collected or received or been paid a sum of money on the date that he receives the draft endorsed by the client, or if the client's endorsement is not required, on the date the attorney receives the sum. The acceptance by a client of such amount shall be without prejudice to the latter's right in an appropriate action or proceeding, to petition the court to have the question of the attorney's compensation or reimbursement for expenses investigated and determined by it.

(2) Whenever any sum of money is payable upon any such claim, action or proceeding, either by way of settlement or after trial or hearing, and the attorney is unable to locate a client, the attorney shall apply, pursuant to subdivision f–1 of 1200.46 of the Disciplinary Rules of the Code of Professional Responsibility, to the court in which such action or proceeding was pending, or if no action had been commenced, then to the Supreme Court in the county in which the attorney maintains an office, for an order directing payment to be made to the attorney of the fees and reimbursable disbursements determined by the court to be due said attorney and to the Lawyers' Fund for Client Protection of the balance due to the client, for the account of the client, subject to the charge of any lien found by the court to be payable therefrom.

(e) Contingent Fees in Claims and Actions for Personal Injury and Wrongful Death.

(1) In any claim or action for personal injury or wrongful death, other than one alleging medical, dental or podiatric malpractice, whether determined by judgment or settlement, in which the compensation of claimant's or plaintiff's attorney is contingent, that is, dependent in whole or in part upon the amount of recovery, the receipt, retention or sharing by such attorney pursuant to agreement or otherwise, of compensation which is equal to or less than that contained in any schedule of fees adopted by this department is deemed to be fair and reasonable. The receipt, retention or sharing of compensation which is in excess of such scheduled fees shall constitute the exaction of

unreasonable and unconscionable compensation in violation of any provision of the Code of Professional Responsibility, as adopted by the New York State Bar Association, effective Jan. 1, 1970, as amended, or of any canon of the Canons of Ethics, as adopted by such Bar Association effective until Dec. 31, 1969, unless authorized by a written order of the court as hereinafter provided.

(2) The following is the schedule of reasonable fees referred to in paragraph (1) of this subdivision: either,

Schedule A

(i) 50 percent on the first $1,000 of the sum recovered,

(ii) 40 percent on the next $2,000 of the sum recovered,

(iii) 35 percent on the next $22,000 of the sum recovered,

(iv) 25 percent on any amount over $25,000 of the sum recovered; or,

Schedule B

A percentage not exceeding 33⅓ percent of the sum recovered, if the initial contractual arrangement between the client and the attorney so provides, in which event the procedure hereinafter provided for making application for additional compensation because of extraordinary circumstances shall not apply.

(3) Such percentage shall be computed on the net sum recovered after deducting from the amount recovered expenses and disbursements for expert testimony and investigative or other services properly chargeable to the enforcement of the claim or prosecution of the action. In computing the fee, the costs as taxed, including interest upon a judgment, shall be deemed part of the amount recovered. For the following or similar items there shall be no deduction in computing such percentages: liens, assignments or claims in favor of hospitals, for medical care and treatment by doctors and nurses, or of self-insurers or insurance carriers.

(4) In the event that claimant's or plaintiff's attorney believes in good faith that Schedule A, above, because of extraordinary circumstances, will not give him adequate compensation, application for greater compensation may be made upon affidavit with written notice and an opportunity to be heard to the client and other persons holding liens or assignments on the recovery. Such application shall be made to the justice of the trial part to which the action had been sent for trial; or, if it had not been sent to a part for trial, then to the justice presiding at the trial term calendar part of the court in which the action had been instituted; or, if no action had been instituted, then to the justice presiding at the trial term calendar part of the Supreme Court for the county in the judicial department in which the attorney who filed the statement of retainer, pursuant to this section, has an office. Upon such application, the justice, in his discretion, if extraordinary circumstances are found to be present, and without regard to the claimant's or plaintiff's consent, may fix as reasonable compensation for legal services rendered an amount greater than that specified in Schedule A, above, provided, however, that such greater amount shall not exceed the fee fixed pursuant to the contractual arrangement, if any, between the client and the attorney. If the application be granted, the justice shall make a written order accordingly, briefly stating the reasons for granting the greater compensation; and a copy of such order shall be served on all persons entitled to receive notice of the application.

(5) The provisions of subdivision (e) of this section shall not apply to an attorney retained as counsel in a claim or action for personal injury or wrongful death by another attorney, if such other attorney is not subject to the provisions of this section in such claim or action, but all other subdivisions of this section shall apply.

(6) Nothing contained in subdivision (e) of this section shall be deemed applicable to the fixing of compensation for attorneys representing infants or other persons, where the statutes or rules provide for the fixation of such compensation by the court.

(7) Nothing contained in this subdivision shall be deemed applicable to the fixing of compensation for attorneys for services rendered in connection with the collection of first-party benefits as defined by section 5102 of the Insurance Law.

(8) The provisions of paragraph (2) of this subdivision shall not apply to claims alleging medical, dental, or podiatric malpractice. Compensation of claimant's or plaintiff's attorney for services rendered in claims or action for personal injury alleging medical, dental, or podiatric malpractice shall be computed pursuant to the fee schedule in Judiciary Law, § 474–a.

(f) Preservation of Records of Claims and Actions. Attorneys for both plaintiff and defendant in the case of any such claim or cause of action shall preserve, for a period of seven years after any settlement or satisfaction of the claim or cause of action or any judgment thereon or after the dismissal or discontinuance of any action, the pleadings and other papers pertaining to such claim or cause of action, including, but not limited to, letters or other data relating to the claim of loss of time from employment or loss of income; medical reports, medical bills, X-ray reports, X-ray bills; repair bills, estimates of repairs; all correspondence concerning the claim or cause of action; and memoranda of the disposition thereof as well as cancelled vouchers, receipts and memoranda evidencing the amounts disbursed by the attorney to the client and others in connection with the aforesaid claim or cause of action and such other records as are required to be maintained under section 603.15 of this Part.

(g) Omnibus Filings in Property Damage Claims or Actions. Attorneys prosecuting claims or actions for property damages are permitted to make semi-annual omnibus filings of retainer statements and closing statements.

Cross References

Insurance Law, see McKinney's Book 27.

Code of Professional Responsibility, see Appendix to McKinney's Book 29.

§ 603.8. Compromise of Claims or Actions Belonging to Infants

(a) An application for the approval by the court of a settlement of a claim or cause of action belonging to an infant must be made as provided in CPLR 1207 and 1208.

(b) In the case of a claim or demand belonging to an infant, any sum collected by an attorney shall be deposited in a special account apart from his personal account, in accordance with the provisions of section 603.15 of this Part, and a statement of the amount received shall be delivered personally to the duly qualified guardian of the infant or mailed to such guardian by registered or certified mail addressed to said guardian's last known address. But no payment or withdrawal shall be made from such deposit in the said account to the credit of the infant's claim except pursuant to an order of the court after application as provided in section 474 of the Judiciary Law, upon at least two days' notice to the guardian.

Cross References

CPLR, see McKinney's Book 7B.

Judiciary Law, see McKinney's Book 29.

Forms

Settlement of action or claim by infant, incapacitated person, incompetent, or conservatee, see West's McKinney's Forms, CPLR, §§ 3:1321 to 3:1326.

§ 603.9. Discipline by Departmental Disciplinary Committee

(a)[1] The Departmental Disciplinary Committee may issue an admonition or a reprimand in those cases in which professional misconduct, not warranting proceedings before this court, is found. An admonition is discipline imposed without a hearing. A reprimand is discipline imposed after a hearing.

[1] Par. (b) was repealed eff. May 16, 1994.

§ 603.10. Effect of Restitution on Disciplinary Proceedings

Restitution made by an attorney or on his behalf for funds converted or to reimburse a person for losses suffered as a result of the attorney's wrongdoing shall not be a bar to the commencement or continuance of disciplinary proceedings.

§ 603.11. Resignation of Attorneys Under Investigation or the Subject of Disciplinary Proceedings

(a) An attorney who is the subject of an investigation into allegations of misconduct or who is the subject of a disciplinary proceeding pending in the court may submit his resignation by submitting to the Departmental Disciplinary Committee an affidavit stating that he intends to resign and that:

(1) his resignation is freely and voluntarily rendered; he is not being subjected to coercion or duress; and he is fully aware of the implications of submitting his resignation;

(2) he is aware that there is pending an investigation or disciplinary proceeding into allegations that he has been guilty of misconduct, the nature of which shall be specifically set forth; and

(3) he acknowledges that if charges were predicated upon the misconduct under investigation, he could not successfully defend himself on the merits against such charges, or that he cannot successfully defend himself against the charges in the proceedings pending in the court.

(b) On receipt of the required affidavit, such committee shall file it with this court, together with either its recommendation that the resignation be accepted and the terms and conditions, if any, to be imposed upon the acceptance, or its recommendation that the resignation not be accepted.

(c) This court, in its discretion, may accept such resignation, upon such terms and conditions as it deems appropriate or it may direct that proceedings before the Departmental Disciplinary Committee or before this court go forward.

(d) This court, if it accepts such resignation, shall enter an order removing the attorney on consent and may order that the affidavit referred to in subdivision (a) of this section be deemed private and confidential under subdivision 10 of section 90 of the Judiciary Law.

Cross References

Judiciary Law, see McKinney's Book 29.

§ 603.12. Attorneys Convicted of Crimes; Record of Conviction Conclusive Evidence

(a) Upon receipt by the Departmental Disciplinary Committee of a certificate demonstrating that an attorney has been convicted of a crime in this State, or in any foreign jurisdiction, whether the conviction resulted from a plea of guilty or nolo contendere or from a verdict after trial or otherwise, the committee shall determine whether the crime is a serious crime as defined in subdivision (b) of this section. Upon a determination that a crime is a serious crime, the committee shall forthwith file the certificate of conviction with the court. This court shall thereupon enter an order directing the Chairperson of the Departmental Disciplinary Committee to designate a Hearing Panel or appointing a referee, justice or judge, to conduct forthwith disciplinary proceedings. If the committee determines that the crime is not a serious crime as defined in subdivision (b) of this section, it may hear such evidence as is admissible under subdivision (c) of this section and take such other steps as are provided for in Part 605 of this Title.

(b) The term "serious crime" shall include any felony, not resulting in automatic disbarment under the provisions of subdivision 4 of section 90 of the Judiciary Law, and any crime, other than a felony, a necessary element of which, as determined by the statutory or common law definition of such crime, involves interference with the administration of justice, criminal contempt of court, false swearing, misrepresentation, fraud, willful failure to file income tax returns, deceit, bribery, extortion, misappropriation, theft, or an attempt or a conspiracy or solicitation of another to commit a "serious crime".

(c) A certificate of the conviction of an attorney for any crime shall be conclusive evidence of his guilt of that crime in any disciplinary proceeding instituted against him and based on the conviction, and the attorney may not offer evidence inconsistent with the essential elements of the crime for which he was convicted as determined by the statute defining the crime except such evidence as was not available either at the time of the conviction or in any proceeding challenging the conviction.

(d) The clerk of any court within this judicial department in which an attorney is convicted of a crime shall within 10 days of said conviction forward a certificate thereof to the Departmental Disciplinary Committee.

(e) The pendency of an appeal shall not be grounds for delaying any action under this section unless the conviction is from a court which is not a court of record or this court or the Departmental Disciplinary Committee finds there are compelling reasons justifying a delay.

(f) Any attorney to whom these rules shall apply pursuant to section 603.1 of this Part who has been convicted of a crime shall promptly advise the Departmental Disciplinary Committee of that fact.

Cross References

Judiciary Law, see McKinney's Book 29.

§ 603.13. Conduct of Disbarred, Suspended and Resigned Attorneys

(a) Compliance With Judiciary Law. Disbarred, suspended and resigned attorneys at law shall comply fully and completely with the letter and spirit of sections 478, 479, 484 and 486 of the Judiciary Law relating to practicing as attorneys at law without being admitted and registered, and soliciting of business on behalf of an attorney at law and the practice of law by an attorney who has been disbarred, suspended or convicted of a felony.

(b) Compensation. A disbarred, suspended or resigned attorney may not share in any fee for legal services performed by another attorney during the period of his removal from the bar. A disbarred, suspended or resigned attorney may be compensated on a quantum meruit basis for legal services rendered and disbursements incurred by him prior to the effective date of the disbarment or suspension order or of his resignation. The amount and manner of payment of such compensation and recoverable disbursements shall be fixed by the court on the application of either the disbarred, suspended or resigned attorney or the new attorney, on notice to the other as well as on notice to the client. Such applications shall be made at special term in the court wherein the action is pending or at special term of the Supreme Court in the county wherein the moving attorney maintains his office if an action has not been commenced. In no event shall the combined legal fees exceed the amount the client would have been required to pay had no substitution of attorneys been required.

(c) Notice to Clients Not Involved in Litigation. A disbarred, suspended or resigned attorney shall promptly notify by registered or certified mail, return receipt requested, all clients being represented in pending matters, other than litigated or administrative matters or proceedings pending in any court or agency, of his disbarment or suspension or resignation and his consequent inability to act as an attorney after the effective date of his disbarment or suspension or resignation and shall advise said clients to seek legal advice elsewhere.

(d) Notice to Clients Involved in Litigation.

(1) A disbarred or suspended or resigned attorney shall promptly notify, by registered or certified mail, return receipt requested, each of his clients whom he is representing in litigated matters or administrative proceedings, and the attorney or attorneys for every other party in such matter or proceeding, of his disbarment or suspension or resignation and consequent inability to act as an attorney after the effective date of his disbarment or suspension or resignation. The notice to be given to the client shall advise the prompt substitution of another attorney or attorneys in his place.

(2) In the event the client does not obtain substitute counsel before the effective date of the disbarment or suspension or resignation, it shall be the responsibility of the disbarred or suspended or resigned attorney to move in the court in which the action is pending, or before the body in which an administrative proceeding

is pending, for leave to withdraw from the action or proceeding.

(3) The notice to be given to the attorney or attorneys for each other party shall state the place or residence of the client of the disbarred or suspended or resigned attorney. In addition, notice shall be given in like manner to the Office of Court Administration of the State of New York in each matter in which a retainer statement has been filed.

(e) Conduct After Entry of Order. The disbarred or suspended or resigned attorney, after entry of the disbarment or suspension order, or after entry of the order accepting the resignation, shall not accept any new retainer or engage as attorney for another in any new case or legal matter of any nature. However, during the period between the entry date of the order and its effective date he may wind up and complete, on behalf of any client, all matters which were pending on the entry date.

(f) Filing Proof of Compliance and Attorney's Address. Within 10 days after the effective date of the disbarment or suspension order or the order accepting the resignation, the disbarred or suspended or resigned attorney shall file with the clerk of this court, together with proof of service upon the Departmental Disciplinary Committee, an affidavit showing that he has fully complied with the provisions of the order and with these rules. Such affidavit shall also set forth the residence or other address of the disbarred or suspended or resigned attorney where communications may be directed to him.

(g) Appointment of Attorney to Protect Clients' Interests and Interests of Disbarred, Suspended or Resigned Attorney. Whenever it shall be brought to the court's attention that a disbarred or suspended or resigned attorney shall have failed or may fail to comply with the provisions of subdivisions (c), (d) or (f) of this section, this court, upon such notice to such attorney as this court may direct, may appoint an attorney or attorneys to inventory the files of the disbarred or suspended or resigned attorney and to take such action as seems indicated to protect the interests of his clients and for the protection of the interests of the suspended or disbarred or resigned attorney.

(h) [Disclosure of Information.] Any attorney so appointed by this court shall not be permitted to disclose any information contained in any file so inventoried without the consent of the client to whom such file relates except as necessary to carry out the order of this court.

(i) [Attorney Fees.] This court may fix the compensation to be paid to any attorney appointed by this court under this section. This compensation may be directed by this court to be paid as an incident to the costs of the proceeding in which the charges are incurred and shall be charged in accordance with law.

(j) Required Records. A disbarred or suspended or resigned attorney shall keep and maintain records of the various steps taken by him under this Part so that, upon any subsequent proceeding instituted by or against him, proof of compliance with this Part and with the disbarment or suspension order or with the order accepting the resignation will be available.

Cross References

Judiciary Law, see McKinney's Book 29.

§ 603.14. Reinstatement

(a)(1) Unless the Court directs otherwise, any attorney who has been suspended for six months or less pursuant to disciplinary proceedings shall be reinstated at the end of the period of suspension upon an order of the Court. No more than thirty days prior to the expiration of the term of suspension the attorney must file with the Court and serve upon the chief counsel an affidavit stating that the attorney has fully complied with the requirements of the suspension order and has paid any required fees and costs. Upon receipt of the affidavit, the chief counsel shall serve a copy of it upon each complainant in the disciplinary proceeding that led to the suspension and give notice to the complainant(s) that they may submit a response opposing or supporting the lawyer's affidavit. Such response must be filed with the chief counsel within twenty days of the date of the notice. Within thirty days of the date on which the affidavit was served upon the chief counsel, or within such longer time as the Court may allow, the chief counsel may file an affidavit in opposition.

(2) Any attorney who has been disbarred after a hearing, or whose name has been stricken from the roll of attorneys pursuant to section 90(4) of the Judiciary Law or section 603.11 of this part, may not petition for reinstatement until the expiration of seven years from the effective date of the disbarment or removal.

(3) Any attorney suspended under the provisions of this part for more than six months shall be entitled to petition the Court for reinstatement upon the expiration of the period of suspension.

(b) A Petition for reinstatement may be granted only if the petitioner establishes by clear and convincing evidence that:

(1) the petitioner has fully complied with the provisions of the order of disbarment, removal or suspension;

(2) the petitioner possesses the requisite character and general fitness to practice law;

(3) not more than six (6) months prior to the filing of the petition for reinstatement, the petitioner has taken and attained a passing score on the Multistate Professional Responsibility Examination described in section 520.8(a) of the Rules of the Court of Appeals for the Admission of Attorneys and Counselors at

Law, the passing score being that determined by the New York State Board of Law Examiners pursuant to section 520.8(c) of such rules.

(c) In reviewing an application for reinstatement, the court may consider the misconduct for which petitioner was originally disbarred, removed or suspended and any other relevant conduct or information which may come to the attention of the court.

(d) A petition for reinstatement shall be verified and shall be accompanied by a completed questionaire as outlined in subdivision (m) of this section.

(e) A petitioner shall serve a copy of the petition for reinstatement upon the Departmental Disciplinary Committee and upon the Lawyers' Fund for Client Protection. The Court may refer the matter to the Departmental Disciplinary Committee and either direct the Chairperson of the Committee to designate a Hearing Panel or appoint a Referee, or the Court may refer the matter to the Committee on Character and Fitness, to inquire into the facts submitted in support of the petition and all other relevant facts. In its discretion, the Court may require the petitioner to (i) submit additional sworn proof, (ii) submit to a sworn examination, (iii) produce records and other papers in connection with the application, (iv) provide proof of compliance with all disciplinary orders, and (v) submit to medical or psychiatric examinations by qualified experts. The designated committee shall report to the Court in writing.

(f) The Disciplinary Committee may be heard in opposition to the petition for reinstatement.

(g) If the court determines that the petition for reinstatement satisfies the provisions of subsection (b) of this rule, the court may grant the petition, or may refer the petition to the Departmental Disciplinary Committee and direct the Chairperson of the Committee to designate a Hearing Panel or appoint a Referee, or the Court may refer the matter to the Committee on Character and Fitness to conduct a hearing. At such hearing, both petitioner and counsel for the Disciplinary Committee may present evidence bearing upon all relevant issues raised by the petition.

(h) At the conclusion of the hearing, the Committee that conducted it shall submit a written report and recommendation to the court; the report may include a recommendation that the court condition reinstatement upon compliance with such additional orders as are deemed appropriate, including but not limited to the payment of restitution to any person harmed by petitioner's misconduct.

(i) In the event that the court approves the application for reinstatement of an attorney who has resigned, been disbarred, or been suspended and whose petition for reinstatement is made seven or more years after the effective date of his suspension, the petition may thereupon be held in abeyance for a period of not more than two years. It may be a

condition of the granting of the petition that petitioner take and attain a passing score on the New York State Bar Examination described in Section 520.7 of the Rules of the Court of Appeals within the said two year period. Upon proof of successful completion of the said Bar Examination, and in the absence of further misconduct by petitioner, the petition for reinstatement shall be granted.

(j) A petition for reinstatement shall not be accepted for filing within two years following entry of this court's order denying a previous petition for reinstatement filed by or on behalf of the petitioner, unless the order denying the previous petition provides otherwise.

(k) The court may direct the notice of any reinstatement petition be published in one or more newspapers in the First Department pursuant to Section 601.1 of these rules.

(l) Petitions for reinstatement under these rules shall be accompanied by payment of a fee of $315, unless waived or modified by the court upon a showing of hardship.

(m) Petition for reinstatement.

(Applicant's Last Name)_____
(Date)_____

TO: THE APPELLATE DIVISION OF THE SUPREME COURT, FIRST JUDICIAL DEPARTMENT.

STATE OF NEW YORK)
)
COUNTY OF   )

I, _____, hereby apply, pursuant to Judiciary Law, Section 90, and 22 N.Y.C.R.R. Section 603.14, for reinstatement as an attorney and counselor-at-law licensed to practice in all the courts of the State of New York. In support of my application I submit this petition, the form of which has been prescribed by this Court. Inapplicable provisions have been stricken and initialed by me.

1. My full name is _____. I have also been known by the following names _____. (If change of name was made by court order, including marriage, a certified copy of that order is attached.)

2. I was born on __(date)__ at __(city-state-country)__ .

3. I reside at _____ (If you reside in more than one place, state all places in which you reside.)

My home telephone number is _____.

My office telephone number is _____.

4. On _____ I was admitted as an attorney and counselor-at-law by the Appellate Division of the Supreme Court of the State of New York, _____ Judicial Department.

5. By order of this Court, dated _____, I was disciplined to the following extent: _____. A certified copy of this Court's order is attached; this Court's opinion was published in the _____ volume, page _____, of the official reports (2d series) for the Appellate Divisions. My use of the term "discipline" hereafter refers to the action of this Court by the order here referred to.

6. Since the effective date of my discipline, I have resided at the following addresses _____.

7. The discipline imposed upon me was predicated upon, or arose out of, my misappropriation or misuse of the real or personal property of others. Attached to this application is a full listing of each property, its dollar value, the name of the true owner, and the extent to which I have yet to make full restitution. Where I still owe a party under this section, I have also attached a copy of a restitution agreement, signed by that owner and myself, setting forth the terms of my repayment obligations.

8. On the date of my discipline, the following matters, which were not the basis of that order, were pending against me before the Departmental Disciplinary Committee: _____.

9. On the effective date of discipline, I was also admitted to practice in the following Courts/jurisdictions: _____.

10. Based upon this Court's discipline of me, I also have been disciplined in the following way(s): _____.

11. In addition, dating back to my original admission to the bar up until the present, I have also been disciplined for other actions or activities, in the following ways: _____, _____.

12. Prior to my discipline, my law practice involved the following areas of law: _____.

13. Since the effective date of my discipline, I have engaged in the practice of law in other jurisdiction(s), on the date(s) and in the manner specified: _____.

14. Since the effective date of my discipline, I have been engaged in the following legal-type or law-related activities: _____.

15. Since the effective date of my discipline I have had the following employment or been engaged in the following business (set forth names, dates, addresses) _____.

16. I am attaching copies of all federal, state and local tax returns filed by me for the past two years.

17. At the time of my discipline, I took the following affirmative steps to notify my clients of my inability to continue representing them: _____.

18. Pursuant to 22 N.Y.C.R.R. Section 603.13(f), I filed an affidavit of compliance on (date) .

—or—

I did not file an affidavit of compliance, as required by this Court's rules, because _____.

19. Since the date of my discipline, I have maintained the following bank accounts and brokerage accounts _____.

20. There presently exist the following unpaid judgments against me or a partnership, corporation or other business entity of which I am an employee or in which I have an ownership interest _____.

21. Since my discipline, I, or a partnership, corporation or other business entity in which I have an ownership interest, have/has been involved in the following lawsuits, to the extent indicated _____.

22. I, or a partnership, corporation or other business entity in which I have an ownership interest, petitioned to be adjudicated a bankrupt on (date) to (court) .

23. (a) Since my discipline, I applied for the following license(s) which required proof of good character: _____.

(b) These applications resulted in the following action(s): _____.

24. Since my admission to the bar, I have had the following licenses suspended or revoked for the stated reason(s), unrelated to this Court's order of discipline: _____.

25. Since my discipline, on the date(s) specified I have been arrested, charged with, indicted, convicted, tried, and/or have pleaded guilty to the following violation(s), misdemeanor(s) and/or felony(ies): _____.

26. Since my discipline, I have been the subject of the following governmental investigation(s) on the specified date(s), which resulted in the charge or complaint indicated being brought against me: _____.

27. Other than the passage of time and the absence of additional misconduct, the following facts establish that I possess the requisite character and general fitness to be reinstated as an attorney in New York: _____.

28. I have made the following efforts to maintain or renew my general fitness to practice law, including continuing legal education and otherwise, during the period following my disbarment, removal, or suspension: _____.

29. I was treated for alcoholism and/or drug abuse on the date(s) and under the circumstances here set forth: _____.

30. The following fact(s), not heretofore disclosed to this Court, are relevant to this application and might tend by some degree to induce the Court to look less favorably upon this application: _____.

I UNDERSTAND THAT THE DEPARTMENTAL DISCIPLINARY COMMITTEE, THE COMMITTEE ON CHARACTER AND FITNESS, OR OTHER ATTORNEY AUTHORIZED BY THE COURT, MAY TAKE ADDITIONAL INVESTIGATIVE STEPS DEEMED APPROPRIATE IN ACTING UPON THIS APPLICATION FOR REINSTATEMENT. I WILL FULLY COOPERATE WITH ANY REQUEST FOR INFORMATION AND MAKE MYSELF AVAILABLE FOR SWORN INTERVIEWS OR HEARINGS, AS REQUIRED.

————————————————— (Signature of Applicant)

Sworn to before me this ___ day of _____, 19__.

STATE OF NEW YORK　）
　　　　　　　　　　　）
COUNTY OF　　　　　 ）

I, _____ being duly sworn, say: I am the petitioner in the within action; I have read the foregoing petition and know the contents thereof; the same is true to my own knowledge, except as to the matters therein stated to be alleged on information and belief, and as to those matters I believe it to be true.

Sworn to before me this ___ day of _____, 19__.

§ 603.15. Random Review and Audit

(a) Availability of Bookkeeping Records; Random Review and Audit. The financial records required to be maintained pursuant to Rule DR 9–102 of the Code of Professional Responsibility, as jointly adopted by the Appellate Divisions of the Supreme Court, or by any other rule of this Court, shall be made available for inspection, copying and determination of compliance with court rules, to a duly authorized representative of the court pursuant to the issuance, on a randomly selected basis, of a notice or subpoena by the Departmental Disciplinary Committee.

(b) Confidentiality. All matters, records and proceedings relating to compliance with Rule DR 9–102 of the Code of Professional Responsibility and this section, including the selection of an attorney for review hereunder, shall be kept confidential in accordance with applicable law, as and to the extent required of matters relating to professional discipline.

(c) Regulations and Procedures for Random Review and Audit. Prior to the issuance of any notice or subpoena in connection with the random review and audit program established by this section, the Departmental Disciplinary Committee shall propose regulations and procedures for the proper administration of the program. The court shall approve such of the regulations and procedures of the Departmental Disciplinary Committee as it may deem appropriate, and only such regulations and procedures as have been approved by the court shall become effective.

(d) Biennial Affirmation of Compliance. Any attorney subject to this court's jurisdiction shall execute that portion of the biennial registration statement provided by the Office of Court Administration, affirming that the attorney has read and is in compliance with DR 9–102 of the Code of Professional Responsibility, as jointly adopted by the Appellate Divisions of the Supreme Court, and with this section. The affirmation shall be available at all times to the Departmental Disciplinary Committee.

No affirmation of compliance shall be required from a full-time judge or justice of the Unified Court System of the State of New York, or of a court of any other state, or of a federal court.

§ 603.16. Proceedings Where Attorney Is Declared Incompetent or Alleged to Be Incapacitated

(a) Suspension Upon Judicial Determination of Incompetency or on Involuntary Commitment. Where an attorney subject to this Part pursuant to the first sentence of section 603.1 of this Part has been judicially declared incompetent or incapable of caring for his property or has been involuntarily committed to a mental hospital, this court, upon proper proof of the fact, shall enter an order suspending such attorney from the practice of the law, effective immediately and for an indefinite period and until the further order of this court. A copy of such order shall be served upon such attorney, his committee or conservator and/or director of mental hospital in such manner as this court may direct.

(b) Proceeding to Determine Alleged Incapacity and Suspension Upon Such Determination.

(1) Whenever the Departmental Disciplinary Committee shall petition this court to determine whether an attorney is incapacitated from continuing to practice law by reason of physical or mental infirmity or illness or because of addiction to drugs or intoxicants, this court may take or direct such action as it deems necessary or proper to determine whether the attorney is so incapacitated, including examination of the attorney by such qualified experts as this court shall designate. If, upon due consideration of the matter, this court is satisfied and concludes that the attorney is incapacitated from continuing to practice law, it shall enter an order suspending him on the ground of such disability for an indefinite period and until the further order of this court and any pending disciplinary proceedings against the attorney shall be held in abeyance.

(2) This court may provide for such notice to the respondent-attorney of proceedings in the matter as is deemed proper and advisable and may appoint an attorney to represent the respondent, if he is without adequate representation.

(c) Procedure When Respondent Claims Disability During Course of Proceeding.

(1) If, during the course of a disciplinary proceeding, the respondent contends that he is suffering from a disability by reason of physical or mental infirmity or illness, or because of addiction to drugs or intoxicants, which makes it impossible for the respondent adequately to defend himself, this court thereupon shall enter an order suspending the respondent from continuing to practice law until a determination of the respondent's capacity to continue the practice of law is made in a proceeding instituted in accordance with the provisions of subdivision (b) of this section.

(2) If, in the course of a proceeding under this section or in a disciplinary proceeding, this court shall determine that the respondent is not incapacitated from practicing law, it shall take such action as it deems proper and advisable, including a direction for the resumption of the disciplinary proceeding against the respondent.

(d) Appointment of Attorney to Protect Clients' and Suspended Attorney's Interests.

(1) Whenever an attorney is suspended for incapacity or disability, this court, upon such notice to him as this court may direct, may appoint an attorney or attorneys to inventory the files of the suspended attorney and to take such action as seems indicated to protect the interests of his clients and for the protection of the interests of the suspended attorney.

(2) Any attorney so appointed by this court shall not be permitted to disclose any information contained in any file so inventoried without the consent of the client to whom such file relates except as necessary to carry out the order of this court.

(e) Reinstatement Upon Termination of Disability.

(1) Any attorney suspended under the provisions of this section shall be entitled to apply for reinstatement at such intervals as this court may direct in the order of suspension or any modification thereof. Such application shall be granted by this court upon showing by clear and convincing evidence that the attorney's disability has been removed and he is fit to resume the practice of law. Upon such application, this court may take or direct such action as it deems necessary or proper for a determination as to whether the attorney's disability has been removed, including a direction of an examination of the attorney by such qualified experts as this court shall designate. In its discretion, this court may direct that the expense of such an examination shall be paid by the attorney.

(2) Where an attorney has been suspended by an order in accordance with the provisions of paragraph (a) of this section and thereafter, in proceedings duly taken, he has been judicially declared to be competent, this court may dispense with further evidence that his disability has been removed and may direct his reinstatement upon such terms as are deemed proper and advisable.

(f) Burden of Proof. In a proceeding seeking an order of suspension under this section, the burden of proof shall rest with the petitioner. In a proceeding seeking an order terminating a suspension under this section, the burden of proof shall rest with the suspended attorney.

(g) Waiver of Doctor-Patient Privilege Upon Application for Reinstatement. The filing of an application for reinstatement by an attorney suspended for disability shall be deemed to constitute a waiver of any doctor-patient privilege existing between the attorney and any psychiatrist, psychologist, physician or hospital who or which has examined or treated the attorney during the period of his disability. The attorney shall be required to disclose the name of every psychiatrist, psychologist, physician and hospital by whom or at which the attorney has been examined or treated since his suspension and he shall furnish to this court written consent to each to divulge such information and records as requested by court-appointed experts or by the clerk of this court.

(h) Payment of Expenses of Proceedings.

(1) The necessary costs and disbursements of an agency, committee or appointed attorney in conducting a proceeding under this section shall be paid in accordance with subdivision 6 of section 90 of the Judiciary Law.

(2) This court may fix the compensation to be paid to any attorney or expert appointed by this court under this section. This compensation may be directed by this court to be paid as an incident to the costs of the proceeding in which the charges are incurred and shall be charged in accordance with law.

Cross References

Judiciary Law, see McKinney's Book 29.

§ 603.17.   Combining or Grouping of Claims

No attorney for a claimant or plaintiff shall for the purpose of settlement or payment combine or group two or more claims or causes of action or judgments therefor on behalf of separate clients, and each such demand or action shall be settled or compromised independently upon its own merits and with regard to the individual interest of the client. No attorney for a defendant shall participate in the settlement of any such claims or actions on the basis directly or indirectly of combining or grouping claims or actions belonging to different persons.

§ 603.18.   Champerty and Maintenance

No attorney shall by himself, or by or in the name of another person, either before or after action brought, promise, give, or procure, or permit to be promised or given any valuable consideration to any person as an inducement to placing in his hands, or in the hands of another person, any claim for the purpose of making a claim or bringing an action or special proceeding thereon, or defending the same; nor shall any attorney, directly or indirectly, as a consideration for such retainer, pay any expenses attending the prosecution or defense of any such claim or action.

§ 603.19. Attorneys Assigned by the Court as Counsel for a Defendant in a Criminal Case

No attorney assigned by a court as counsel for a defendant in any criminal case shall in any manner demand, accept, receive or agree to accept or receive any payment, compensation, emolument, gratuity or reward, or any promise of payment, compensation, emolument, gratuity or reward or any money, property or thing of value or of personal advantage from such defendant or from any other person, except as expressly authorized by statute or by written order of the court duly entered upon its minutes.

§ 603.20. Prohibition Against Gratuities

No attorney shall give any gift, bequest, favor or loan to any judge or any employee of any court or any member of his family residing in his household or to any member, officer, or employee of any governmental agency or any member of his family residing in his household, where such attorney has had or is likely to have any professional or official transaction with such court or governmental agency.

§ 603.21. Practice of Law by Non-judicial Personnel

(a) An attorney who is employed as a public officer or employee in any court in this judicial department shall not maintain an office for the private practice of law, alone or with others, hold himself out to be in the private practice of law, or engage in the private practice of law; such attorney shall not participate, directly or indirectly, as attorney or counsel in any action or proceeding, pending before any court or any administrative board, agency, committee or commission of any government, or in the preparation or subscription of briefs, papers, or documents pertaining thereto.

(b) By special permission secured from the presiding justice of this judicial department as to each professional engagement, a person referred to in subdivision (a) of this section may engage in the private practice of law as to matters not pending before a court or governmental agency, in uncontested matters in the Surrogate's Court, uncontested accountings in the Supreme Court, and other ex parte applications not preliminary or incidental to litigated or contested matters. Such approval, which shall continue only to the completion of the particular engagement for which permission was obtained, shall be sought by application in writing to the presiding justice of this judicial department (processed through the immediate supervisor and the administrative judge or other head of the court or agency in which applicant is employed for

his comment and recommendation including restrictions, if any), which shall state the position occupied, all pertinent information as to the matter to be handled (including the name of the client engaging such attorney and the prior relationship, if any, between such client and said attorney) and that in the event of litigation the applicant will immediately withdraw as attorney and notify his administrative judge or other head of the court or agency thereof.

(c) A person referred to in subdivision (a) of this section shall not engage in any other practice of law which is incompatible with or would reflect adversely upon the performance of his duties.

§ 603.22. [Rescinded]

Former § 603.22. Section, relating to advertising by attorneys was rescinded effective Sept. 1, 1990. See, now DR 2–101 set out following § 1040, post.

§ 603.23. Attorney's Affidavit in Agency and Private Placement Adoptions

(a) Every attorney appearing for an adoptive parent, a natural parent or an adoption agency in an adoption proceeding in the courts within this judicial department shall, prior to the entry of an adoption decree, file with the Office of Court Administration of the State of New York, and with the court in which the adoption proceeding has been initiated, a signed statement under oath setting forth the following information:

(1) Name of attorney;

(2) Association with firm (if any);

(3) Business address;

(4) Telephone number;

(5) Docket number of adoption proceeding;

(6) Court where adoption has been filed;

(7) The date and terms of every agreement, written or otherwise, between the attorney and the adoptive parents, the natural parents or anyone else on their behalf, pertaining to any compensation or thing of value paid or given or to be paid or given by or on behalf of the adoptive parents or the natural parents, including but not limited to retainer fees;

(8) The date and amount of any compensation paid or thing of value given, and the amount of total compensation to be paid or thing of value to be given to the attorney by the adoptive parents, the natural parents or by anyone else on account of or incidental to any assistance or service in connection with the proposed adoption;

(9) A brief statement of the nature of the services rendered;

(10) The name and address of any other attorney or attorneys who shared in the fees received in connection with the services, or to whom any compensation

or thing of value was paid or is to be paid, directly or indirectly, by the attorney. The amount of such compensation or thing of value;

(11) The name and address of any other attorney or attorneys, if known, who received or will receive any compensation or thing of value, directly or indirectly, from the adoptive parents, natural parents, agency or other source, on account of or incidental to any assistance or service in connection with the proposed adoption. The amount of such compensation or thing of value, if known;

(12) The name and address of any other person, agency, association, corporation, institution, society or organization who received or will receive any compensation or thing of value from the attorney, directly or indirectly, on account of or incidental to any assistance or service in connection with the proposed adoption. The amount of such compensation or thing of value;

(13) The name and address, if known, of any person, agency, association, corporation, institution, society or organization to whom compensation or thing of value has been paid or given or is to be paid or given by any source for the placing out of, or on account of or incidental to assistance in arrangements for the placement or adoption of the adoptive child. The amount of such compensation or thing of value and the services performed or the purposes for which the payment was made; and

(14) A brief statement as to the date and manner in which the initial contact occurred between the attorney and the adoptive parents or natural parents with respect to the proposed adoption.

(b) Names or other information likely to identify the natural or adoptive parents or the adoptive child are to be omitted from the information to be supplied in the attorney's statement.

(c) Such statement may be filed personally by the attorney or his representative at the main office of the Office of Court Administration in the City of New York, and upon such filing he shall receive a date-stamped receipt containing the code number assigned to the original so filed. Such statement may also be filed by ordinary mail addressed to:

Office of Court Administration—
Adoption Affidavits
Post Office Box No. 2016
New York, New York 10008

(d) All statements filed by attorneys shall be deemed to be confidential, and the information therein contained shall not be divulged or made available for inspection or examination to any person other than the client of the attorney in the adoption proceeding, except upon written order of the presiding justice of the Appellate Division.

§ 603.24. Compensation of Attorneys Representing Claimants Against Lawyers' Fund for Client Protection

No attorney shall charge a fee for or accept compensation for representation of claimants against the Lawyers Fund for Client Protection of the state of New York, except as approved by the trustees of the fund.

PART 604. SPECIAL RULES CONCERNING COURT DECORUM

§ 604.1. Obligation of Attorneys and Judges

(a) **Application of Rules.** This Part shall apply to all actions and proceedings, civil and criminal, in courts subject to the jurisdiction of the Appellate Division of the Supreme Court in this Judicial Department. It is intended to supplement but not to supersede, the Code of Professional Responsibility as adopted by the New York State Bar Association and the Rules Governing Judicial Conduct as promulgated by the Administrative Board of the Judicial Conference. In the event of any conflict between the provisions of this Part and the Code of Professional Responsibility or the Rules Governing Judicial Conduct, the Code of Professional Responsibility and the Rules Governing Judicial Conduct shall prevail.

(b) **Importance of Decorum in Court.** The courtroom, as the place where justice is dispensed, must at all times satisfy the appearance as well as the reality of fairness and equal treatment. Dignity, order and decorum are indispensable to the proper administration of justice. Disruptive conduct by any person while the court is in session is forbidden.

(c) **Disruptive Conduct Defined.** Disruptive conduct is any intentional conduct by any person in the courtroom that substantially interferes with the dignity, order and decorum of judicial proceedings.

(d) **Obligation of the Attorney.**

(1) The attorney is both an officer of the court and an advocate. It is his professional obligation to conduct his case courageously, vigorously, and with all the skill and knowledge he possesses. It is also his obligation to uphold the honor and maintain the dignity of the profession. He must avoid disorder or disruption in the courtroom, and he must maintain a respectful attitude toward the court. In all respects the attorney is bound, in court and out, by the provisions of the Code of Professional Responsibility.

(2) The attorney shall use his best efforts to dissuade his client and witnesses from causing disorder or disruption in the courtroom.

(3) The attorney shall not engage in any examination which is intended merely to harass, annoy or humiliate the witness.

(4)(i) No attorney shall argue in support of or against an objection without permission from the court; nor shall any attorney argue with respect to a ruling of the court on an objection without such permission.

(ii) However, an attorney may make a concise statement of the particular grounds for an objection or exception, not otherwise apparent, where it is necessary to do so in order to call the court's attention thereto, or to preserve an issue for appellate review. If an attorney believes in good faith that the court has wrongly made an adverse ruling, he may respectfully request reconsideration thereof.

(5) The attorney has neither the right nor duty to execute any directive of a client which is not consistent with professional standards of conduct. Nor may he advise another to do any act or to engage in any conduct which is in any manner contrary to this Part.

(6) Once a client has employed an attorney who has entered an appearance, the attorney shall not withdraw or abandon the case without (i) justifiable cause, (ii) reasonable notice to the client, and (iii) permission of the court.

(7) The attorney is not relieved of these obligations by what he may regard as a deficiency in the conduct or ruling of a judge or in the system of justice; nor is he relieved of these obligations by what he believes to be the moral, political, social, or ideological merits of the cause of any client.

(e) Obligations of the Judge.

(1) In the administration of justice, the judge shall safeguard the rights of the parties and the interests of the public. The judge at all times shall be dignified, courteous, and considerate of the parties, attorneys, jurors, and witnesses. In the performance of his duties and in the maintenance of proper court decorum the judge is in all respects bound by the Rules Governing Judicial Conduct.

(2) The judge shall use his judicial power to prevent disruptions of the trial.

(3) A judge before whom a case is moved for trial shall preside at such trial unless he is satisfied, upon challenge, or sua sponte, that he is unable to serve with complete impartiality, in fact or appearance, with regard to the matter, or parties in question.

(4) Where the judge deems it appropriate in order to preserve or enhance the dignity, order and decorum of the proceedings, he shall prescribe and make known the rules relating to conduct which the parties, attorneys, witnesses and others will be expected to follow in the courtroom.

(5) The judge should be the exemplar of dignity and impartiality. He shall suppress his personal predilections, control his temper and emotions, and otherwise avoid conduct on his part which tends to demean the proceedings or to undermine his authority in the courtroom. When it becomes necessary during trial for him to comment upon the conduct of witnesses, spectators, counsel, or others, or upon the testimony, he shall do so in a firm and polite manner, limiting his comments and rulings to what is reasonably required for the orderly progress of the trial, and refraining from unnecessary disparagement of persons or issues.

(6) The judge is not relieved of these obligations by what he may regard as a deficiency in the conduct of any attorney who appears before him; nor is he relieved of these obligations by what he believes to be the moral, political, social, or ideological deficiencies of the cause of any party.

Cross References

Code of Judicial Conduct, see Appendix to McKinney's Judiciary Law, Book 29.

Code of Professional Responsibility, see Appendix to McKinney's Judiciary Law, Book 29.

§ 604.2. Judicial Exercise of Contempt Power

(a) Exercise of the Summary Contempt Power.

(1) The power of the court to punish summarily contempt committed in its immediate view and presence shall be exercised only in exceptional and necessitous circumstances, as follows:

(i) Where the offending conduct either

(a) disrupts or threatens to disrupt proceedings actually in progress; or

(b) destroys or undermines or tends seriously to destroy or undermine the dignity and authority of the court in a manner and to the extent that it appears unlikely that the court will be able to continue to conduct its normal business in an appropriate way; and

(ii) The court reasonably believes that a prompt summary adjudication of contempt may aid in maintaining or restoring and maintaining proper order and decorum.

(2) Wherever practical punishment should be determined and imposed at the time of the adjudication of contempt. However, where the court deems it advisable the determination and imposition of punishment may be deferred following a prompt summary adjudication of contempt which satisfies the necessity for immediate judicial corrective or disciplinary action.

(3) Before summary adjudication of contempt the accused shall be given a reasonable opportunity to make a statement in his defense or in extenuation of his conduct.

(b) Exercise of the Contempt Power After Hearing. In all other cases, notwithstanding the occurrence of the contumacious conduct in the view and presence of the sitting court, the contempt shall be adjudicated at a plenary hearing with due process of law including notice, written charges, assistance of counsel, compulsory process for production of evidence and an opportunity of the accused to confront witnesses against him.

(c) Judicial Warning of Possible Contempts. Except in the case of the most flagrant and offensive misbehavior in which the court's discretion requires an immediate adjudication of contempt to preserve order and decorum, the court should warn and admonish the person engaged in alleged contumacious conduct that his conduct is deemed contumacious and give the person an opportunity to desist before adjudicating him in contempt. Where a person so warned desists from further offensive conduct, there is ordinarily no occasion for an adjudication of contempt. Where a person is summarily adjudicated in contempt and punishment deferred and such person desists from further offensive conduct, the court should consider carefully whether there is any need for punishment for the adjudicated contempt.

(d) Disqualification of Judge. The judge before whom the alleged contumacious conduct occurred is disqualified from presiding at the plenary hearing or trial (as distinguished from summary action) except with the defendant's consent:

(1) If the allegedly contumacious conduct consists primarily of personal disrespect to or vituperative criticism of the judge; or

(2) If the judge's recollection of, or testimony concerning the conduct allegedly constituting contempt is necessary for an adjudication; or

(3) If the judge concludes that in view of his recollection of the events he would be unable to make his decision solely on the basis of the evidence at the hearing.

(e) Preference for Appeals From Criminal Court Contempt Convictions. Any appeal by an attorney of his conviction for the misdemeanor of criminal contempt which is pending in any court in this judicial department, shall be granted a preference by the court.

§ 604.3. Conduct of Criminal Trial Threatened by Disruptive Conduct

(a) Removal of Disruptive Defendant.

(1) If a defendant engages in disruptive conduct by word or action in the courtroom in the course of his trial, the trial judge may order the defendant to be removed from the courtroom and placed in custody, and the trial judge may proceed with the trial in the absence of the defendant.

(2) The trial judge may not exclude the defendant except after warning that further disruptive conduct will lead to removal of the defendant from the courtroom.

(3) The defendant shall be returned to the courtroom immediately upon a determination by the court that the defendant is not likely to engage in further disruptive conduct.

(b) Communication Between Defendant and Courtroom. If the defendant is removed from the courtroom under the provisions of paragraph (1) of subdivision (a) of this section, the trial judge shall make reasonable efforts to establish methods of communication linking the defendant with the courtroom while his trial is in progress. For such defendant the judge may provide methods of communication in any way suitable to the physical facilities of the courthouse and consonant with the goal of providing adequate communication to the courtroom and to defense counsel.

(c) Restraint of Defendant.

(1) If a defendant engages in disruptive conduct in the course of the trial, and the trial judge determines not to take action under subdivision (a) of this section, the trial judge may order the defendant to be physically restrained in the courtroom while his trial continues.

(2) The trial judge shall not apply the restraints authorized in the preceding subdivision unless he has warned the defendant, following disruptive conduct by the defendant, that further misconduct will lead to the physical restraint of the defendant in the courtroom.

(3) The physical restraint of the defendant shall be terminated immediately upon a determination by the court that the defendant is not likely to engage in further disruptive conduct.

PART 605.   RULES AND PROCEDURES OF THE DEPARTMENTAL DISCIPLINARY COMMITTEE

§ 605.1. Title, Citation and Construction of Rules

(a) These Rules shall be known, and may be cited, as the "Rules and Procedures of the Departmental Disciplinary Committee of the Appellate Division of the Supreme Court of the State of New York, First Judicial Department" (hereinafter called the Committee).

(b) These Rules are promulgated for the purpose of assisting the Office of Chief Counsel, the Respondent and the Committee to develop the facts relating to, and to reach a just and proper determination of, matters brought to the attention of the Office of Chief Counsel or the Committee. The Committee will not hold action of a Referee or a Hearing Panel invalid by reason of any nonprejudicial irregularity. Any error, defect, irregularity or variance which does not affect substantial rights shall be disregarded.

(c) The use of the term *attorney* in this Part shall apply to a law firm where a firm is the object of an investigation or prosecution of alleged violation of the Code of Professional Responsibility.

§ 605.2.   Definitions

(a) Subject to additional definitions contained in subsequent provisions of these Rules which are applicable to specific sections, subsections or other provisions of these Rules, the following words and phrases, when used in these Rules, shall have, unless the context clearly indicates otherwise, the meanings given to them in this section:

(1) *Admonition.* Discipline administered without hearing, by letter issued by the Committee Chairperson, in those cases in which misconduct in violation of a Disciplinary Rule is found, but is determined to be of insufficient gravity to warrant prosecution of formal charges.

(2) *Answer.* A formal pleading filed by the Respondent in answer to a Notice of Charges.

(3) *Chief Counsel.* The Chief Counsel appointed by the Court or, in the absence of such Chief Counsel, the Deputy Chief Counsel in the case of vacancy in office, or disability of such Chief Counsel, the Deputy Chief Counsel as designated by the Court.

(4) *Code of Professional Responsibility.* The Code of Professional Responsibility as adopted by the New York State Bar Association effective January 1, 1970, as the same may from time to time be amended.

(5) *Committee Chairperson.* The Chairperson of the Committee.

(6) *Complainant.* A person communicating a Grievance to the Committee or to the Office of Chief Counsel, whether or not set forth in a complaint.

(7) *Complaint.* A written statement of the nature described in section 605.6 of this Part with respect to a Grievance concerning an attorney communicated to the Committee or to the Office of Chief Counsel.

(8) *Court.* The Appellate Division of the Supreme Court of the State of New York, First Judicial Department.

(9) *Deputy Chief Counsel.* The Deputy Chief Counsel appointed by the Court, or in the absence of such Deputy Chief Counsel, the Principal Attorney designated by the Chief Counsel to serve as Deputy Chief Counsel; in the case of vacancy in office, or disability of such Deputy Chief Counsel, the Principal Attorney as designated by the Court.

(10) *Disciplinary Rule.* Any provision of the rules of the Court governing the conduct of attorneys, any Disciplinary Rule of the Code of Professional Responsibility, and any Canon of the Canons of Professional

Ethics as adopted by the New York State Bar Association.

(11) *First Department.* The First Judicial Department of the State of New York.

(12) *Formal Proceedings.* Proceedings subject to sections 605.11 through 605.14 of this Part.

(13) *Grievance.* An allegation of misconduct.

(14) *Hearing Panel.* A Hearing Panel established under section 605.18 of this Part.

(15) *Hearing Panel Chairperson.* The member of the Committee designated as chairperson of a Hearing Panel under section 605.18 of this Part.

(16) *Investigation.* Fact gathering under the direction of the Office of Chief Counsel with respect to alleged misconduct.

(17) *Investigator.* Any person designated by the Office of Chief Counsel to assist it in the investigation of alleged misconduct.

(18) *Notice of Charges.* A formal pleading served under § 605.12 of this Part by the Office of Chief Counsel requesting action by the Committee.

(19) *Office of Chief Counsel.* The Office of Chief Counsel provided for by § 605.20 of this Part.

(20) *Parties.* The Office of Chief Counsel and the Respondent.

(21) *Policy Committee.* The Policy Committee established under § 605.21 of this Part.

(22) *Reprimand.* Discipline administered after a hearing, by the Committee through the Hearing Panel Chairperson, in those cases in which misconduct in violation of a Disciplinary Rule is found.

(23) *Respondent.* An attorney or legal consultant described in Section 603.1 of this Title who, or a law firm that, has been named in a complaint or notice of charges.

(24) *Reviewing Member.* The member or members of the Committee designated under Section 605.6(f) of this Part to review the disposition of a Complaint recommended by the Office of the Chief Counsel.

(25) *Rules.* The provisions of these Rules and Procedures.

(26) *Staff Counsel.* The attorneys (including the Chief Counsel) constituting the Office of Chief Counsel, and where appropriate the attorney or attorneys of the Office of Chief Counsel, or such special counsel as may be appointed by the Committee Chairperson with the approval of the Policy Committee, assigned to a particular investigation or proceeding.

§ 605.3.   Location of Office of Chief Counsel

The location of the Office of Chief Counsel and the office of the Chief Counsel is:

Departmental Disciplinary Committee
Appellate Division, First Department
61 Broadway
New York, NY 10006

§ 605.4. Grounds for Discipline

Section 90 of the Judiciary Law of the State of New York, the Disciplinary Rules and decisional law indicate what shall constitute misconduct and shall be grounds for discipline.

§ 605.5. Types of Discipline; Subsequent Consideration of Disciplinary Action

(a) Misconduct under Section 90 of the Judiciary Law of the State of New York, the Disciplinary Rules or decisional law shall be grounds for any of the following:

(1) Disbarment—by the Court.

(2) Suspension—by the Court.

(3) Censure—by the Court.

(4) Reprimand—by the Committee after hearing, with or without referral to the Court for further action.

(5) Admonition—by the Committee without hearing.

(b) The fact that an attorney has been issued an Admonition (which has not yet been vacated), or that an attorney has been the subject of a Reprimand (with or without referral to the Court), or that an attorney has been the subject of disciplinary action by the Court, may (together with the basis thereof) be considered in determining whether to impose discipline, and the extent of discipline to be imposed, in the event other charges of misconduct are brought against the attorney subsequently.

Cross References

Judiciary Law, see McKinney's Book 29.

§ 605.6. Investigations and Informal Proceedings

(a) **Initiation of Investigations.** The Office of Chief Counsel shall, except as otherwise provided by subdivision (g) of this section, undertake and complete an investigation of all matters involving alleged misconduct of attorneys within the jurisdiction of the Committee called to its attention by a Complaint filed pursuant to subdivision (b) of this section, by the Court, or by the Committee by written order, and may, on its own initiative, undertake and complete an investigation of any other matter within the jurisdiction of the Committee otherwise coming to the attention of such Office. The Office of Chief Counsel shall use such Investigators as are deemed appropriate by the Chief Counsel.

(b) **Contents of Complaint.**

(1) *General Rule.* Each Complaint relating to alleged misconduct of an attorney shall be in writing and subscribed by the Complainant and shall contain a concise statement of the facts upon which the Complaint is based. Verification of the Complaint shall not be required. If necessary the Office of Chief Counsel will assist the Complainant in reducing the Grievance to writing. The Complaint shall be deemed filed when received by the Office of Chief Counsel.

(2) *Other Situations.* In the case of an allegation of misconduct originating in the Court or the Committee, or upon the initiative of the Office of Chief Counsel, the writing reflecting the allegation shall be treated as a Complaint.

(c) **Investigation.** The staff of the Office of Chief Counsel shall make such investigation of each Complaint as may be appropriate.

(d) **Notification to Respondent of Complaint.**

(1) *General Rule.* No discipline shall be recommended by the Office of the Chief Counsel until the Respondent shall have been afforded the opportunity to state the Respondent's position with respect to the allegations.

(2) *Transmission of Notice.* Except where it appears that there is no basis for proceeding further, the Office of Chief Counsel shall promptly prepare and forward to the Respondent a request for a statement in response to the Complaint, advising the Respondent of:

(i) the nature of the Grievance and the facts alleged in connection therewith; and

(ii) the Respondent's right to state the Respondent's position with respect to the allegations.

Unless a shorter time is fixed by the Committee Chairperson and specified in such notice, the Respondent shall have 20 days from the date of such notice within which to file such a response in the Office of Chief Counsel.

(e) **Recommendation of the Office of Chief Counsel.** Following completion of any Investigation of the Complaint (including consideration of any statement filed by the Respondent pursuant to section 605.6(d) of this Part), the Office of Chief Counsel shall recommend one of the following dispositions:

(1) referral to another body on account of lack of territorial jurisdiction;

(2) dismissal for any reason (with an indication of the reason therefor), and referral to another body if appropriate;

(3) admonition; or

(4) formal proceedings before a hearing panel.

(f) **Action Following Recommendation.**

(1) *No Jurisdiction.* If the Office of Chief Counsel determines that the Complaint should be referred

under paragraph (e)(1) of this section, it shall notify the Complainant and the Respondent (if previously notified of the Complaint) of such disposition in writing and close the file on the matter. Whenever possible in cases of lack of jurisdiction, the Office of Chief Counsel shall bring the matter to the attention of the authorities of the appropriate jurisdiction, or to any other duly constituted body which may be able to provide a forum for the consideration of the Grievances, and shall advise the Complainant of such referral.

(2) *Other Cases.* In the case of recommendations under paragraph (e)(2) of this section, the Committee chairperson shall designate a lawyer member of the Committee to review the recommendations. In the case of recommendations under paragraph (e)(3) of this section, the Committee chairperson (or a member of the Committee designated by the Committee chairperson) and at least one other member of the Committee shall review the recommendations. In the case of recommendations under paragraph (e)(4) of this section, or under Section 605.15(e)(2) of this part, the Committee chairperson shall designate at least two members of the policy committee, at least one of whom is a lawyer, to review the recommendations.

(g) **Preliminary Screening of Complaints.** Any complaint received by the Office of Chief Counsel against a member of the Committee or Staff counsel involving alleged misconduct shall be transmitted forthwith to the Committee Chairperson, who shall assign it either to the Office of Chief Counsel or to special counsel who shall (1) conduct or direct the appropriate investigation, and (2) give a written recommendation as to the disposition of the Complaint to the Committee Chairperson, who shall determine the appropriate disposition of the Complaint. Any such Complaint which relates to the Committee Chairperson shall, in the first instance, be transmitted to a Hearing Panel Chairperson, who shall conduct the appropriate investigation and determine the appropriate disposition of the Complaint.

§ 605.7. Review of Recommended Disposition of Complaint

(a) **Transmission to Reviewing Member.** In the case of recommendations under § 605.6(e)(3) of this part, the chief counsel shall forward the file (including the proposed disposition letter) to the reviewing member designated under § 605.6(f)(2) of this part for action. In the case of recommendations under § 605.6(e)(4) of this part, the chief counsel shall forward the file, the proposed charges, and a memo summarizing the evidence adduced in support of the charges to the reviewing policy member designated under § 605.6(f)(2) of this part for action. In the case of recommendations to file a motion to disaffirm under § 605.15(e)(2) of this part, the chief counsel shall forward the hearing panel's report, the proposed motion, and memo of law or other memo summarizing

the reasons for the motion, to the reviewing member designated under § 605.6(f)(2) of this part for action.

(b) **Action by Reviewing Member.**

(1) *General Rule.* The Reviewing Member may approve or modify the recommendation of the Office of Chief Counsel concerning the disposition of a Complaint.

(2) *Modification.* If the Reviewing Member determines to modify the recommendation of the Office of Chief Counsel, the Reviewing Member shall set forth such determination in writing together with a brief statement of the reason therefor. Such determination shall be one of the following:

    (i) dismissal of the complaint;

    (ii) further investigation;

    (iii) admonition; or

    (iv) formal proceedings before a hearing panel.

(3) *Return of File.* Upon making such determination, the Reviewing Member shall return the file to the Office of Chief Counsel.

(c) **Reconsideration.** Upon notification of the dismissal of a complaint pursuant to Section 605.6, the complainant may submit a written application for reconsideration that shall be filed with the Office of the Chief Counsel within 30 days of the date of the notification. The Committee chairperson shall designate to examine a request for reconsideration a member of the Committee other than the member who originally reviewed the recommendation of the Office of the Chief Counsel.

§ 605.8. Final Disposition Without Formal Proceedings

(a) **Notification to Respondent of Disposition of Complaint.** Upon the approval of the recommendation of the Office of Chief Counsel by the Reviewing Member, the acceptance of the Reviewing Member's modification by the Office of Chief Counsel, or the determination of the appropriate disposition by the Committee Chairperson, then, unless the disposition involves the institution of Formal Proceedings, as appropriate:

(1) the Office of Chief Counsel by means of written notice shall notify the Respondent of the dismissal of the Complaint; or

(2) the Committee Chairperson shall transmit to the Respondent an Admonition (which shall bear the designation "ADMONITION").

(b) **Admonitions.**

(1) *General Rule.* A written record shall be made of the fact of and basis for Admonitions.

(2) *Notice of Right to Formal Proceedings.* In the Admonition, the Respondent shall be advised of:

(i) the Respondent's right under § 605.8(c) of this Part; and

(ii) the availability of such records for consideration in determining whether to impose discipline, and the extent of discipline to be imposed, in the event other charges of misconduct are brought against the Respondent subsequently.

(c) Action Available to Respondent.

(1) *General Rule.* A Respondent shall not be entitled to appeal an Admonition, but the Respondent may submit a written application for reconsideration which shall be disposed of in accordance with paragraph (3) of this subdivision; or, in the alternative, Respondent may demand as of right that Formal Proceedings be instituted before a Referee, in accordance with subsection (2) of this subdivision.

(2) *Formal Proceedings.* A demand under paragraph (1) of this subdivision that Formal Proceedings be instituted shall be in writing and shall be filed in the Office of Chief Counsel within 30 days after the date on which the Admonition is sent to the Respondent. In the event of such demand, the Admonition shall be vacated and the Referee shall not be bound by its terms, but may take any appropriate action authorized by the Rules of the Committee or the Rules of the Appellate Division, First Department, including a Reprimand or referral to the Court.

(3) *Application for Reconsideration.* An application under paragraph (1) of this subdivision for reconsideration shall be in writing and shall be filed in the Office of Chief Counsel within 30 days after the date on which the Admonition is sent to the Respondent. As soon as practicable after the receipt of an application, the Office of Chief Counsel shall transmit the application and the file relating to the matter to a member of the Departmental Disciplinary Committee (who shall not be a Reviewing Member designated with respect to such matter under § 605.6(f)(2) of the Part) designated to review the matter by the Committee Chairperson (or, upon general or limited written direction of the Committee Chairperson, by the Chief Counsel). The member so designated shall either confirm or vacate the Admonition or otherwise determine to modify the Admonition under § 605.7(b)(2) of this Part.

(d) Notification to Complainant of Disposition of Complaint. The Office of the Chief Counsel, by means of written notice, shall notify the Complainant of the dismissal of a Complaint, or of the issuance of an Admonition. If the complaint has been dismissed pursuant to Section 605.6(e)(2), the notice shall state that the Complainant may seek reconsideration of the dismissal by submitting to the Office of the Chief Counsel a written request within 30 days of the date of the notice.

§ 605.9. Abatement of Investigation

(a) Refusal of Complainant or Respondent to Proceed, etc. Neither unwillingness or neglect of the Complainant to prosecute a charge, nor settlement, compromise or restitution, nor the failure of the Respondent to cooperate, shall, in itself, justify abatement of an Investigation into the conduct of an attorney or the deferral or termination of proceedings under these Rules.

(b) Matters Involving Related Pending Civil Litigation or Criminal Matters.

(1) *General Rule.* The processing of complaints involving material allegations which are substantially similar to the material allegations of pending criminal or civil litigation need not be deferred pending determination of such litigation.

(2) *Effect of Determination.* The acquittal of a Respondent on criminal charges or a verdict or judgment in the Respondent's favor in a civil litigation involving substantially similar material allegations shall not, in itself, justify termination of a disciplinary investigation predicated upon the same material allegations.

§ 605.10. Resignations, Reinstatements, Convictions of Crimes

(a) Resignations by Attorneys Under Disciplinary Investigations.

(1) *Recommendation to the Court.* Upon receipt by the Committee of an affidavit from an attorney who intends to resign pursuant to the rules of the Court, the chief counsel shall review the affidavit and such other matters as the chief counsel deems appropriate and determine either (i) to recommend to the Court that the resignation be accepted and to recommend any terms and conditions of acceptance the chief counsel deems appropriate, or (ii) to recommend to the Court that the resignation not be accepted with the reasons therefor. The chief counsel shall submit the affidavit and the recommendation to the Court, and the proceedings, if any, before the Court shall be conducted by staff counsel.

(2) *Notification of Complainant.* In the event the Court accepts the resignation of a Respondent and removes the Respondent on consent, the Office of Chief Counsel by means of written notice shall notify the Complainant of such action.

(b) Applications for Reinstatement. Upon receipt by the Committee of an application of an attorney who has been disbarred or who has been suspended for more than six months, or whose name has been stricken from the roll of attorneys on consent by order of the Court, applying for reinstatement pursuant to the rules of the Court, the chief counsel shall serve a copy of the petition upon each complainant in the disciplinary proceeding that led to the suspension or disbarment, and shall notify the complainant(s) that they have sixty days to raise objections to or to support the lawyer's petition. Upon the expiration of the sixty-day period, the chief counsel shall either (1) advise the lawyer and the Court that the chief counsel will stipulate to the reinstatement or (2) advise the lawyer and the Court that the chief counsel opposes the reinstatement. If the chief counsel opposes the reinstatement, he shall present the reasons for the opposition and shall request that the Court deny the application or appoint a Referee and refer the matter to the Committee.

(c) Determination of Serious Crimes. Upon receipt by the Committee of a certificate demonstrating that an attorney has been convicted of a crime in the state of New York or in any other state, territory or district, the chief counsel shall determine whether the crime is a "serious crime" as defined in the rules of the court governing the conduct of attorneys. Upon a determination by the chief counsel that the crime is a serious crime, the office of the chief counsel shall file the certificate of conviction with the Court.

§ 605.11. Formal Proceedings; Preliminary Provisions

(a) Representation of Respondent.

(1) *Appearance Pro Se.* When a Respondent appears pro se in a Formal Proceeding, the Respondent shall file with the Office of Chief Counsel an address to which any notice or other written communication required to be served upon the Respondent may be sent.

(2) *Representation of Respondent by Counsel.* When a Respondent is represented by counsel in a Formal Proceeding, counsel shall file with the Office of Chief Counsel, a written notice of such appearance, which shall state such counsel's name, address and telephone number, the name and address of the Respondent on whose behalf counsel appears, and the caption of the subject proceeding. Any additional notice or other written communication required to be served on or furnished to a Respondent may be sent to the counsel of record for such Respondent at the stated address of the counsel in lieu of transmission to the Respondent. In any proceeding where counsel has filed a notice of appearance pursuant to this subsection, any notice or other written communication required to be served on or furnished to the Respondent shall also be served upon or furnished to the Respondent's counsel (or one of such counsel if the Respondent is represented by more than one counsel) in the same manner as prescribed for the Respondent, notwithstanding the fact that such communication may be furnished directly to the Respondent.

(b) Format of Pleadings and Documents. Pleadings or other documents filed in Formal Proceedings shall comply with and conform to the rules from time to time in effect for comparable documents in the Supreme Court in the First Department.

(c) Expeditious Proceedings; Extensions. Formal Proceedings shall be expeditiously conducted. Extension of the time periods specified in this Part regarding proceedings before the Referee or Hearing Panel shall be made in writing to the Court and determined by a Justice of the Court upon good cause shown.

(d) Service by the Departmental Disciplinary Committee.

(1) Orders, notices and other documents originating with the Committee, including all forms of Referee, Hearing Panel or Committee action, petitions and similar process, and other documents designated by the Committee for this purpose, shall be served by the Office of Chief Counsel either personally or by mailing a copy thereof, to the person to be served, addressed to that person at the person's last known address. Whenever any document is to be served by mail upon the Respondent individually, it shall be by both certified mail, return receipt requested, and by first class mail. In all other instances, service by mail shall be by first class mail.

(2) Service by mail shall be complete upon mailing. When service is not accomplished by mail, personal service may be effected by anyone duly authorized by the Office of Chief Counsel in the manner provided in the laws of the State of New York relating to service of process in civil actions.

(e) Number of Copies. The following number of copies of documents shall be served by each Party in a proceeding:

(1) documents being served by the Office of Chief Counsel: one copy of each document to the Respondent, and one copy of each document to the Referee and to each member of the Hearing Panel, as may be appropriate.

(2) documents being served by the Respondent: one copy of each document (plus 10 copies of the Answer) to the Office of Chief Counsel, one copy to the Referee and to each member of the Hearing Panel, as may be appropriate, and one copy of each document to each other Respondent, if any; in each case, to be served personally or by mailing a copy thereof (by certified mail, return receipt requested) to the person to be served.

(3) copies of exhibits to be offered during the hearing shall be provided as specified in section 605.12(d) of this Part.

(f) Amendment and Supplementation of Pleadings. No amendment or supplementation of any Notice of Charges or of any Answer shall be made unless specified in the Pre-Hearing Stipulation or otherwise granted by the Referee. Any objection to a proposed amendment shall be determined by the Referee upon conditions deemed appropriate.

Whenever, in the course of any hearing under these Rules, evidence shall be presented upon which another charge or charges against the Respondent might be made, it shall not be necessary to prepare or serve an additional Notice of Charges with respect thereto, but the Referee may, after reasonable notice to the Respondent and an opportunity to answer and be heard, proceed to the consideration of such additional charge or charges as if they had been made and served at the time of service of the Notice of Charges, and may render its decision upon all such charges as may be justified by the evidence in the case.

§ 605.12. Formal Proceedings

(a) Commencement of Formal Proceedings. The Office of Chief Counsel shall institute formal disciplinary proceedings by serving on the Respondent a Notice of Charges under subdivision (b) of this section in either of the following cases:

(1) pursuant to a determination to institute formal proceedings made under section 605.6 or section 605.7 of this Part; or

(2) pursuant to a referral under the rules of the Court.

(b) Notice of Charges.

(1) *Caption.* A Notice of Charges will be captioned as follows:

Before the Departmental Disciplinary
Committee of the Appellate Division
of the Supreme Court of the State of New York,
First Judicial Department

Notice of Charges   Docket No.
                   Before Referee
In the Matter of
                         _____

_____,
Respondent.

(2) *Contents.* The notice of charges shall set forth the charges of misconduct against the respondent, the disciplinary rules alleged to have been violated, and, in appropriate cases, the fact that the Committee will seek restitution or reimbursement pursuant to section 90 6–a(a) of the Judiciary Law, and costs pursuant to section 605.13(p)(4)(v) of this Part. The notice of charges shall also indicate the Referee appointed to hear the matter, the date, time and place of the hearing, which shall be determined by the Referee and shall advise the respondent that the respondent is entitled to be represented by counsel, to cross-examine witnesses, and to present evidence.

(c) Answer.

(1) *General Rule.* The Respondent shall answer the Notice of Charges by serving and filing an Answer (and 10 copies thereof) in the Office of Chief Counsel within 20 days after service of the Notice of Charges, unless a shorter time is fixed by the Committee Chairperson and specified in the Notice of Charges.

(2) *Contents of Answer.* The Answer shall be in writing and shall respond specifically (by admissions, denials or otherwise) to each allegation of the Notice of Charges and shall assert all affirmative defenses.

(3) *Request to Be Heard in Mitigation.* The Respondent may include in the Answer matters in mitigation.

(4) *Effect of Failure to Answer.* In the event the Respondent fails either to serve and file an Answer or respond specifically to any allegation or charge, such allegation or charge shall be deemed admitted.

(d) Pre-hearing Stipulation. A form of a Pre-Hearing Stipulation specifying the following shall be served on the Respondent together with the Notice of Charges:

(1) amendments;

(2) claims or defenses abandoned; or

(3) undisputed facts:

(i) facts not in dispute as to Staff's Counsel's case;

(ii) facts not in dispute as to the Respondent's case;

(4) facts in dispute:

(i) the Staff Counsel's contentions;

(ii) the Respondent's contentions;

(5) documents to be offered in evidence during the hearing: [1]

(i) the staff will offer the following numbered exhibits;

(ii) the Respondent will offer the following lettered exhibits;

(6) witnesses to be called: [2]

(i) by Staff Counsel;

(ii) by the Respondent;

(7) statement of legal contentions and authorities; [3]

(8) length of trial.

(e) No Other Pleadings. Pleadings shall be limited to a Notice of Charges and any Answer thereto, as amended or supplemented in accordance with section 605.11 of this Part.

(f) Assignment for Hearing.

(1) *Appointment of Referee.* Prior to service of the notice of charges, the Chief Counsel shall request that the Court appoint a Referee to conduct a hearing pursuant to the Rules of this Part.

(2) *Objection to Referee.* Within 7 days of the service of charges the Office of the Chief Counsel or the Respondent may object to the Referee appointed.

The objection shall be made to the Court in writing on notice to the Referee and the adversary.

[1] All documents (including schedules, summaries, charts and diagrams) to be offered (other than those to be used for impeachment or rebuttal) are to be listed in the stipulation with a description of each sufficient for identification. The documents are to be premarked by counsel, and, to the extent practicable, such markings are to be in the sequence of which the documents will be offered. If illegible or handwritten documents are to be offered, counsel shall include a typed version of the document.

Objections as to authenticity must be made in this stipulation or else they shall be deemed waived. Counsel are directed to exchange copies of their exhibits within two business days prior to the scheduled hearing.

Counsel offering an exhibit shall provide a copy for the Referee at that time. Witnesses to be called in rebuttal or for impeachment purposes need not be identified in this stipulation.

[2] Witness identification should include the witness' name (and address) and a brief statement of the overall scope of the witness' testimony. For example, if specific witnesses are to be called to substantiate particular claims or defenses on portions thereof, that should be noted. In addition, any witness being called as a character witness should be so designated.

[3] Only a brief statement of each contention is required, together with the principal authority relied upon; string cites are not necessary.

§ 605.13.　Conduct of Referee Proceedings

(a) Expediting Proceedings.

(1) *Conferences.* In order to provide opportunity for the submission and consideration of facts or arguments, or consideration of means by which the conduct of the hearing may be facilitated and the disposition of the proceeding expedited (including preparation of agreed stipulations of fact) Staff Counsel and Respondent or his attorneys shall meet five (5) days after the Answer is served to complete and sign a Pre–Hearing Stipulation in conformance with the form set forth in section 605.12(d) of this Part. Staff Counsel shall forward the signed stipulation immediately to the Referee.

(2) *Commencement of Hearing.* The hearing before the Referee shall commence within 60 days after service of the Notice of Charges and shall be conducted on consecutive days.

(b) Appearances. The Referee shall cause to be entered upon the record all appearances, with a notation in whose behalf each appearance is made.

(c) Order of Procedure. In proceedings upon a Notice of Charges, the Office of Chief Counsel shall have the burden of proof, shall initiate the presentation of evidence, and may present rebuttal evidence. Opening statements, when permitted in the discretion of the Referee, shall be made first by Staff Counsel. Closing statements shall be made first by the Respondent.

(d) Presentation by the Parties. Respondent and Staff Counsel shall have the right of presentation of evidence, cross-examination, objection, motion and argument. The Referee may examine all witnesses.

(e) Limiting Number of Witnesses. The Referee may limit the number of witnesses who may be heard upon any issue before it to eliminate unduly repetitious or cumulative evidence.

(f) Additional Evidence. At the hearing the Referee may authorize any Party to file specific documentary evidence as a part of the record.

(g) Oral Examination. Witnesses shall be examined orally unless the testimony is taken by deposition as provided in Section 605.17(b) of this Part, or the facts are stipulated in the manner provided in section 605.12(d) or 605.13(i) of this Part. Witnesses whose testimony is to be taken shall be sworn, or shall affirm, before their testimony shall be deemed evidence in the proceeding or any questions are put to them.

(h) Fees of Witnesses. Witnesses subpoenaed by the Office of Chief Counsel or the Respondent shall be paid, by the subpoenaing party, the same fees and mileage as are paid for like service in the Supreme Court in the first Department.

(i) Presentation and Effect of Stipulation. The Parties may stipulate as to any relevant matters of fact or the authenticity of any relevant documents. Such stipulations may be received in evidence at a hearing, and when so received shall be binding on such Parties with respect to the matters therein stipulated.

(j) Admissibility of Evidence.

(1) *General Rule.* All evidence which the Referee deems relevant, competent and not privileged shall be admissible in accordance with the principles set out in section 605.1 of this Part.

(2) *Pleadings.* The Notice of Charges and Answer thereto shall, without further action, be considered as parts of the record.

(3) *Convictions.* A certificate of the conviction of a Respondent for any crime shall be conclusive evidence of the Respondent's guilt of that crime in any disciplinary proceeding instituted against the Respondent and based on the conviction, and the Respondent may not offer evidence inconsistent with the essential elements of the crime for which the Respondent was convicted as determined by the statute defining the crime except such evidence as was not available either at the time of the conviction or in any proceeding challenging the conviction.

(k) Reception and Ruling on Evidence. When objections to the admission or exclusion of evidence are made, the grounds relied upon shall be stated. Formal exceptions are unnecessary. The Referee shall rule on the admissibility of all evidence.

(l) Copies of Exhibits. When exhibits of a documentary character are received in evidence, copies shall, unless impracticable, be furnished to the Parties and to the Referee.

(m) Recording of Proceeding. Hearings shall be recorded by reporters authorized to take oaths, or by mechanical recording devices and a transcript of the hearing so recorded, if such transcription is made, shall be a part of the record and sole official transcript of the proceeding. Such transcript shall consist of a verbatim report of the hearing, an exhibit list and the reporter's certificate, and nothing shall be omitted from the record except as the Referee may direct. After the closing of the record, there shall not be received in evidence or considered as part of the record any document submitted after the close of testimony, except as provided in subdivision (f) of this section or changes in the transcript, except as provided in subdivision (n) of this section.

(n) Transcript Corrections. Corrections in the official transcript may be made only to make it conform to what actually transpired at the hearing. No corrections or physical changes shall be made in or upon the official transcript of the hearing except as provided in this section. Transcript corrections agreed to by all Parties may be incorporated into the record, if the Referee approves, at any time during the hearing or after the close of the hearing, but in no event more than 10 days after the receipt of the transcript. Any dispute among the Parties as to correction of the official transcript shall be resolved by the Referee, whose decision shall be final.

(*o*) Copies of Transcripts. A Respondent desiring copies of an official transcript may obtain such copies at the Respondent's own expense from the official reporter. Any witness may obtain from the official reporter at the witness' own expense a copy of that portion of the transcript relating to the witness' own testimony, or any part thereof. The Office of Chief Counsel shall in either case, bear the expense of one such copy if the Referee so directs upon good cause shown.

(p) Determinations.

(1) *Post-Testimony Procedure.* At the conclusion of the testimony and following the presentation of oral arguments, the Referee shall determine whether an inquiry as to sanction is required and shall, before the commencement of the inquiry, set forth on the record or in writing, the charges that are to be sustained. The inquiry may commence immediately upon the conclusion of the oral arguments, but in no event later than 7 days from the conclusion of the oral arguments whether any charges against the Respondent are to be sustained.

(2) *No Charge Sustained.* If none of the charges against the respondent are sustained, the Referee shall so advise the parties in writing or on the record.

(3) *Any Charge Sustained.* If any charge against the Respondent is sustained, the Referee shall so advise the parties in writing or on the record, and shall thereupon ascertain from Staff Counsel, whether the Respondent has previously been subject to disciplinary action by the Court, the Departmental Disciplinary Committee, any grievance committee established or authorized by any other Appellate Division of the Supreme Court of the State of New York, or by any other court.

(4) *Sanctions.* Following the Referee's determination to sustain one or more charges against the Respondent the Referee shall recommend which of the following disciplinary sanctions should be imposed:

(i) reprimand;

(ii) referral to the Court, with a recommendation as to censure, suspension or disbarment;

(iii) reprimand, with referral to the Court, with a recommendation as to censure, suspension or disbarment;

(iv) referral to the Court under (ii) or (iii) above, with a recommendation as to restitution or reimbursement pursuant to section 90 6–a of the Judiciary Law; and

(v) referral to the Court under (ii) or (iii) above, authorizing a request to the Court that costs be imposed on the respondent.

Upon such recommendation having been made, the Referee shall so advise the parties on the record or reserve decision until the issuance of the Report and Recommendation.

(q) Referee's Report and Recommendation.

(1) *Report and Recommendation.* In all cases the Referee shall prepare a written report and recommendation as to sanction which shall state the Referee's findings of fact and conclusions of law.

(2) *Submissions of the Parties.* In the Referee's discretion staff counsel or respondent may request, or the Referee may require, the submission of briefs or proposed findings of fact and conclusions of law in accordance with such schedule as the Referee may set at the conclusion of the hearing. Any submission by one party shall be served upon the other.

(3) *Service of Report.* The Referee shall file a Report and Recommendation within 60 days of the conclusion of the hearing at the Office of Chief Counsel, which shall serve copies thereof upon the respondent.

§ 605.13–a. Conduct of Hearing Panel Proceedings Directed by the Court

(a) Designation of Hearing Panel. Within 10 days of the date of an order of the court directing the Committee Chairperson to designate a Hearing Panel to conduct disciplinary proceedings pursuant to section 603.12 or 603.14 of this Title, the Chairperson shall assign such Hearing Panel. The Hearing Panel shall not include any Reviewing Member designated pursuant to section 605.6(f)(2) of this Part to review the complaint underlying the Petition, any member of the Committee designated pursuant to section 605.8(c)(3) of this Part to review such matter, or the complainant if a member of the Committee.

(b) Objection to Hearing Panel Member. Within 7 days of the assignment of a Hearing Panel, the Office of the Chief Counsel or Respondent may object to participation of any member of the Hearing Panel. The objection shall be made in writing to the Hearing Panel Chairperson. The Hearing Panel shall consider the objection and determine whether to sustain or deny the objection. The Hearing Panel member who is the subject of an objection shall not participate in the determination of the objection. In his or her discretion, the Committee Chairperson may substitute another member of the Committee for a panel member who is subject of an objection that has been sustained. The Committee Chairperson shall substitute to the extent possible an attorney for an attorney and a non-attorney for a non-attorney.

(c) Conduct of the Proceedings. Proceedings before a Hearing Panel held pursuant to this section shall be conducted in accordance with section 605.13 of this Part.

(d) Procedure Following the Filing of the Hearing Panel Report and Recommendation. Upon the filing of the Hearing Panel Report and Recommendation, the Departmental Disciplinary Committee shall take action in accordance with section 605.15 of this Part.

§ 605.14. Conduct of Hearing Panel Proceedings Following the Filing of the Referee's Report and Recommendation

(a) Designation of Hearing Panel. Within 10 days of the filing of the Referee's Report and Recommendation, the Committee Chairperson shall assign a Hearing Panel to review the Report and Recommendation. The Hearing Panel shall not include any Reviewing Member designated pursuant to section 605.6(f)(2) of this Part to review the complaint underlying in the Report and Recommendation, any member of the Committee designated pursuant to section 605.8(c)(3) of this Part to review such matter, or the complainant if a member of the Committee.

(b) Objection to Hearing Panel Member. Within 7 days of the assignment of a Hearing Panel, the Office of the Chief Counsel or Respondent may object to participation of any member of the Hearing Panel. The objection shall be made in writing to the Hearing Panel Chairperson. The Hearing Panel shall consider the objection and determine whether to sustain or deny the objection. The Hearing Panel member who is the subject of an objection shall not participate in the determination of the objection. In his or her discretion, the Committee Chairperson may substitute another member of the Committee for a panel member who is the subject of an objection that has been sustained. The Committee Chairperson shall substi-

tute to the extent possible an attorney for an attorney and a non-attorney for a non-attorney.

(c) Transmittal of Transcript and Memoranda. Within 10 days of the assignment of a Hearing Panel, the Office of the Chief Counsel shall transmit to the Hearing Panel, one copy of the transcript; and to each Panel Member a copy of the Referee's Report and Recommendation and any other memoranda or briefs submitted to the Referee.

(d) Schedule for Proceedings. Within 30 days of the Hearing Panel's assignment the parties shall present oral argument and submit briefs on the Referee's Report and Recommendation pursuant to a schedule set by the Hearing Panel Chairperson.

(e) Order of Procedure. Oral argument shall be made first by Staff Counsel. The time limits for oral argument shall be set by the Hearing Panel Chairperson.

(f) Transcript. No transcript shall be made of the oral argument.

(g) Determination.

(1) At the conclusion of the oral argument, the Hearing Panel, in executive session, shall determine whether to confirm, disaffirm or modify the findings of fact and conclusions of law set forth in the Referee's Report and Recommendation. Upon making that determination, the Hearing Panel Chairperson shall advise the parties and if the Referee recommends and the Hearing Panel confirms that a reprimand is to be delivered the Hearing Panel Chairperson shall thereupon deliver the reprimand and advise the Respondent of his or her rights under section 605.15(e).

(2) Within ten days of the presentation of the oral argument or the submission of briefs, whichever is later, the Hearing Panel shall file at the Office of the Chief Counsel a written Determination confirming, disaffirming or modifying the Referee's Report and Recommendation. The Hearing Panel Chairperson shall assign a Panel Member to prepare the Determination. Separate dissents or concurrences may be filed.

§ 605.15. Action by the Departmental Disciplinary Committee

(a) Dismissal of All Charges. In the event that the Referee and the Hearing Panel determine that all charges considered at both proceedings should be dismissed, the Office of Chief Counsel shall give written notice of such determination to the respondent and the complainant. This decision shall be final and the matter closed, unless within sixty days of the date on which the Hearing Panel files its determination the Chief Counsel files a motion to disaffirm under § 605.15(e)(2) of this Part.

(b) Reprimand.

(1) *Notice.* In the event that the Referee and Hearing Panel determine that the proceeding should be concluded by Reprimand (with or without referral of the matter to the Court), the Committee Chairperson shall give written confirmation thereof (which shall bear the designation "REPRIMAND") to the Respondent and Staff Counsel, which notice shall also advise the Respondent of:

(i) the charges which were sustained;

(ii) any charges which were dismissed;

(iii) the respondent's right under subdivision (c) of this section to petition the Court; and

(iv) the determination, if made, to refer the matter to the Court.

(2) *Record.* The confirmation shall constitute a written record of the Reprimand, and shall be permanently retained.

(c) Petition by Respondent to Vacate Reprimand. A Respondent shall not be entitled to appeal a Reprimand recommended by a Referee and confirmed by a Hearing Panel, but in the case of a Reprimand without referral of the matter to the Court the Respondent may petition the Court to vacate the Reprimand pursuant to the Rules of the Court. In the event of such petition, if so determined by the Hearing Panel Chairperson, the disciplinary sanction shall become a Reprimand with referral to the Court under section 605.13(p)(4)(iii) of this Part, and shall be treated as such under section 605.13(q) of this Part.

(d) Notification of Complainant. The Office of Chief Counsel by means of written notice shall notify the Complainant of any Reprimand which has become final and is not subject to further review, and the notice shall inform the Complainant of the requirement of confidentiality.

(e) Referral to the Court.

(1) *General Rule.* In the event the Referee and Hearing Panel shall determine that the matter should be concluded by referral to the Court (with or without Reprimand), by Reprimand without referral to the Court in cases where the Respondent is unwilling to have the matter concluded by such Reprimand, or in the event that the Hearing Panel modifies or disaffirms the Referee's Report and Recommendation the Committee shall submit the Referee's Report and Recommendation and the Hearing Panel's Determination together with the entire record as reflected in the docket maintained by the Office of Chief Counsel, to the Court, and the proceedings, if any, before the Court shall be conducted by Staff Counsel.

(2) *Procedure.* The Committee (or, upon the general or limited written direction of the Committee chairperson, the chief counsel) shall transmit the report and the record to the Court with an appropriate petition or motion to disaffirm. If the chief counsel's office accepts the Hearing Panel's report, it shall file a petition. If the chief counsel's office objects to any finding or conclusion contained in the Hearing Panel Determination it may file a motion to disaffirm the Determination in whole or in part, and ask the Court to enter such other and further relief as may be appropriate under the circumstances including, but not limited to, reversal or modification of any finding in the Determination and change in sanction. Copies of such petition or motion to disaffirm shall be served by the office of chief counsel upon the respondent.

(3) *Notification of Complainant.* The Office of Chief Counsel by means of written notice shall notify the Complainant of any referral to the Court (which notice shall inform the Complainant of the requirement of confidentiality), and of any final action by the Court.

§ 605.16. Reopening of Record

(a) Reopening on Application of Respondent.

(1) *Application to Reopen.* No application to reopen a proceeding shall be granted except upon the application of the Respondent prior to the filing by the Referee of the Report and Recommendation or Hearing Panel of its Determination and only upon good cause shown. Such application shall set forth clearly the facts claimed to constitute grounds requiring reopening of the proceedings, and shall be filed with the Office of Chief Counsel. A copy of such application shall be served by the Respondent upon all other parties.

(2) *Responses.* Within five days following the receipt of such application, any other Party may file with the Office of Chief Counsel an answer thereto, and in default thereof shall be deemed to have waived any objection to the granting of such application.

(3) *Action on Application.* As soon as practicable after the filing of an answer to such application or default thereof, as the case may be, the Office of Chief Counsel shall transmit such documents to the Referee or to the Hearing Panel Chairperson, as may be appropriate, who shall grant or deny such petition.

§ 605.17. Subpoenas, Depositions and Motions

(a) Subpoenas. Both Staff Counsel and the Respondent shall have the right to summon witnesses and require production of books and papers by issuance of subpoenas in accordance with the rules of the Court.

(b) Depositions. When there is good cause to believe that the testimony of a potential witness will be unavailable at the time of hearing, testimony may be taken by deposition. Such deposition shall be initiated and conducted in the manner provided for the taking of depositions in the New York Civil Practice Law and Rules, and the use of such depositions at hearings shall be in accordance with the use of depositions at trials under the Civil Practice Law and Rules.

(c) **Motions.** The Referee or the Hearing Panel to which a matter has been assigned, as may be appropriate, will entertain, from time to time, such motions as justice may require, in accordance with the principles set out in section 605.1(b) of this Part.

§ 605.18. Membership, Committees, Officers and Office of Chief Counsel

(a) **Membership.**

(1) *General.* The Committee consists of volunteers appointed by the Court.

(2) *Disqualification.* No person shall, while serving on the Committee, appear before the Committee or any Hearing Panel on behalf of any other person.

(b) **Policy Committee and Hearing Panels; Subcommittees.** The Committee chairperson shall from time to time appoint, subject to the approval of a majority of the total membership of the Departmental Disciplinary Committee, from among the members of the Committee (1) a policy committee consisting of the Committee chairperson and six or more other members, and (2) nine hearing panels each consisting of four members three of whom shall be assigned to a matter. The Committee chairperson shall assign at least two attorneys to each matter. No person shall serve concurrently either on the policy committee and hearing panel, or on more than one hearing panel (except by virtue of substitution in accordance with section 605.14(b) of this part, or when requested by a hearing panel in order to assure the presence of a quorum, and in any such event such person shall also be deemed a member of such other hearing panel with respect to and for the remainder of the proceeding). The Committee Chairperson may from time to time establish one or more subcommittees of the Committee, consisting of one or more members of the Committee for such purposes as the Committee Chairperson shall direct.

(c) **Officers.** The Committee Chairperson shall serve as the chairperson of the Policy Committee. The Committee Chairperson shall appoint a Hearing Panel Chairperson for each of the Hearing Panels from among the members thereof who are attorneys. The Committee Chairperson shall also appoint a Secretary of the Committee. Each Hearing Panel Chairperson and the Secretary shall be appointed for a one year term, and may be appointed for additional terms while serving on the Committee. The Committee Chairperson may from time to time appoint, from among the members of the Policy Committee, an Acting Committee Chairperson who shall, in the absence of the Committee Chairperson, have all the powers of the Committee Chairperson.

(d) **Duties of Officers.** The Committee Chairperson, each Hearing Panel Chairperson and the Secretary shall have such duties as are provided in this Part.

§ 605.19. Meetings of the Departmental Disciplinary Committee

(a) **Meetings, Notice of Time and Place.** The Committee shall meet not less frequently than every other month, and such meetings shall be held upon notice from the Secretary given at the direction of the Committee Chairperson or five members of the Committee. The notice shall be in writing and shall set forth the date and time of the meeting, which shall take place at such place as may be designated by resolution of the Departmental Disciplinary Committee or, in the absence of such resolution, by the Committee Chairperson. In lieu of such written notice, meetings may be called on notice given to each member of the Committee not less than 24 hours prior to the time fixed for the meeting, in person or by telephone or telegraph. All notices shall be given to members of the Committee at the addresses furnished for such purposes by the members to the Secretary.

(b) **Organization.** The Committee Chairperson shall preside at all meetings of the Committee. In the absence of the Committee Chairperson and the Acting Committee Chairperson, any member of the Committee selected for the purpose by the members present at the meeting may preside at the meeting. The Secretary shall keep the minutes of all meetings of the Committee, and in the absence of the Secretary the person presiding at the meeting shall appoint a member present to keep the minutes.

(c) **Agenda.** To the extent possible, an agenda for each meeting of the Committee shall be prepared by or with the approval of the Committee Chairperson, or the members calling the meeting, and distributed by the Secretary to all members of the Committee together with the notice of meeting or subsequent thereto but prior to the meeting.

(d) **Quorum and Manner of Acting.** A majority of the members of the Committee shall constitute a quorum for the transaction of business, and all action shall require an affirmative vote of a majority of the members present at the meeting.

§ 605.20. Office of Chief Counsel

(a) **General.** There shall be an Office of Chief Counsel which shall consist of the Chief Counsel, Deputy Chief Counsel and other Staff Counsel.

(b) **Supervision by Chief Counsel.** The Office of Chief Counsel shall be supervised by the Chief Counsel who shall, either personally or by other Staff Counsel, exercise the powers and perform the duties of the Office of Chief Counsel set forth in these Rules. The Chief Counsel may from time to time designate the Deputy Chief Counsel or in the absence of such Deputy Chief Counsel, an Associate Counsel, to serve as Acting Chief Counsel in the Chief Counsel's absence.

(c) Powers and Duties of the Office of Chief Counsel. The Office of Chief Counsel shall:

(1) have the powers and duties set forth in this Part;

(2) maintain permanent records of all matters processed by it, including the disposition thereof, and maintain dockets and assign such docket numbers as may be appropriate for the clear designation of each matter, which shall include the calendar year in which the matter is originally docketed;

(3) represent the Committee in all proceedings before the Court;

(4) supervise and manage the Bar Mediation Project and Pro Bono Special Counsel Project according to the provisions of this part and as may be from time to time modified by the Court, the Committee Chairperson, the Policy Committee or the entire Disciplinary Committee; and

(5) have such other duties as may be assigned to it from time to time by the Committee Chairperson, the Policy Committee or the Committee.

(d) Bar Mediation Project.

(1) *General.* Bar Mediators shall consist of volunteers appointed by the Court for the purposes described in section 605.22(d)(2) of this part. The Committee Chair may, with the approval of the Policy Committee, recommend lawyers to the Court for such appointments. The Chief Counsel shall forward these recommendations to the Court together with a proposed order requesting the appointment of the volunteers as Bar Mediators.

(2) *Referrals.* The Chief Counsel's Office may refer minor complaints involving lawyers with no significant disciplinary history to Bar Mediators, who shall attempt to mediate and resolve the matters raised by the complaint. If the Bar Mediator is unable to resolve the matter, or if it appears that the matter should be further considered by the Committee, the Bar Mediator shall refer the complaint back to the Chief Counsel's Office for investigation under these rules.

(e) Pro Bono Special Counsel Program.

(1) *General.* Pro Bono Special Counsel shall be volunteer lawyers appointed by the Court for the purpose of expediting cases.

(2) *Procedure for Appointment.* Upon initial determination by the Chief Counsel that a potential volunteer is qualified, the Chief Counsel shall submit the volunteer's resume to the Policy Committee. Upon approval by the Policy Committee, the Chief Counsel shall forward the volunteer's name and descriptive information to the Court, together with a proposed order, requesting the appointment of the volunteer attorney as special counsel.

(f) Other Provisions Governing the Bar Mediation Project and the Pro Bono Special Counsel Program.

(1) *Recruitment.* From time to time, the Chief Counsel's Office shall send notices to the principal bar associations and bar committees on professional discipline or ethics in the First Department, describing the Bar Mediation Project and the Pro Bono Special Counsel Program and soliciting the resumes of interested volunteers. Potential volunteers may also be recruited informally by members of the Court or by members of the Committee. Recommendations for appointment shall be on a non-discriminatory basis.

(2) *Conflicts.* Before accepting the assignment of a case, Pro Bono Special Counsel shall determine whether accepting the assignment would create a conflict under the Lawyer's Code of Professional Responsibility, and shall agree to inform the Chief Counsel's Office of any conflict or potential conflict which arises in the course of handling the case.

(3) *Confidentiality.* Bar Mediators and Pro Bono Special Counsel shall be bound by the confidentiality rules contained in Judiciary Law § 90(10) and all other applicable confidentiality provisions.

(4) *Supervision and Reporting.* The Chief Counsel (or other staff counsel designated by the Chief Counsel) shall assume direct responsibility for supervising a case assigned to Pro Bono Special Counsel. The Chief Counsel shall report to the Policy Committee on an ongoing basis as to the progress of cases assigned to Special Counsel.

(5) *Bar Mediators and Pro Bono Special Counsel as Volunteers.* The members of the Departmental Advisory Committee, as volunteers, are expressly authorized to participate in a State-sponsored volunteer program within the meaning of subdivision 1 of section 17 of the Public Officers Law.

§ 605.21. Policy Committee

(a) General. The Policy Committee shall:

(1) have the powers and duties set forth in this Part;

(2) consult with and report regularly to the full Committee;

(3) consider and recommend to the Committee the establishment of policy for the Committee including, without limitation, the establishment of priorities for type of misconduct to be investigated and prosecuted, standards to insure uniform treatment of cases and, subject to these Rules, the establishment of procedures for the conduct of investigations by the Office of Chief Counsel and hearings by the Hearing Panel;

(4) oversee and evaluate on a continuing basis the effectiveness of the operation of the Committee to assure the integrity of the attorney disciplinary system;

(5) develop and implement a program to make the public aware of the importance and effectiveness of the disciplinary procedures and activities of the Committee; and

(6) engage in such activities as may be assigned to it by the Committee or the Committee Chairperson.

(b) Meetings, Notice of Time and Place, Agenda. The Policy Committee shall meet not less frequently than monthly, and such meetings shall be held upon notice from the Committee Chairperson or three members of the Policy Committee. The notice shall be in writing and shall set forth the date and time of the meeting, which shall take place at such place as may be designated by resolution of the Policy Committee or, in the absence of such resolution, by the Committee Chairperson. In lieu of such written notice, meetings may be called on notice given to each member of the Policy Committee not less than 24 hours prior to the time fixed for the meeting, in person or by telephone or telegraph. All notices shall be given to members of the Policy Committee at the addresses furnished for such purpose by the members to the Secretary. To the extent possible, an agenda for each meeting of the Policy Committee shall be prepared with the approval of the Committee Chairperson, or the members calling the meeting, and distributed by the Secretary to all members of the Policy Committee together with the notice of meeting or subsequent thereto but prior to the meeting.

(c) Organization. The Committee Chairperson shall preside at all meetings of the Policy Committee and shall appoint a secretary who shall keep the minutes of the meetings. In the absence of the Committee Chairperson and the Acting Committee Chairperson, any member of the Policy Committee selected for the purpose by the members of the Policy Committee present at the meeting may preside at the meeting. The Committee Chairperson may from time to time establish subcommittees of the Policy Committee, consisting of one or more members of the Policy Committee, for such purposes as the Committee Chairperson shall direct.

(d) Quorum and Manner of Acting. A majority of the members of the Policy Committee shall constitute a quorum for the transaction of business, and all action shall require an affirmative vote of a majority of the total membership of the Policy Committee.

§ 605.22. Referees; Hearing Panels

(a) A Referee shall:

(1) have the powers and duties set forth in these Rules, including, without limitation, the power and duty to conduct hearings into formal charges of misconduct, and to make such findings of fact and conclusions of law and to recommend such disciplinary sanctions as the Referee may deem appropriate, in accordance with this Part and Part 603 of the Rules of the Court; and

(2) perform such other duties as may be imposed by or pursuant to this Part and Part 603 of the Rules of the Court.

(b) Hearing Panels.

(1) *General.* Each Hearing Panel shall:

(i) have the powers and duties set forth in these Rules, including without limitation, the power and duty to review the Referee's Report and Recommendation and to make such Determination as it may deem appropriate in accordance with this Part; and Part 603 of the Rules of the Court and

(ii) perform such other duties as may be imposed pursuant to this Part and Part 603 of the Rules of the Court.

(c) Officers. Each Hearing Panel shall be presided over by a Hearing Panel Chairperson designated under section 605.18(1) of this Part or by an Acting Hearing Panel Chairperson, who shall be appointed by the Committee Chairperson from among the members of the Hearing Panel who are attorneys to serve in the absence of the Hearing Panel Chairperson shall such powers and duties as are set forth in this Part.

(d) Quorum and Manner of Acting. All matters presented to a Hearing Panel shall be determined by three members of the Panel. Two Panel members assigned to a matter shall constitute a quorum for the transaction of business. All action shall require the concurrence of at least two members. At least two members of a Hearing Panel assigned to a matter shall have heard the entire proceeding. The third assigned member either shall have heard the entire proceeding before the Hearing Panel or shall have read the transcript of proceedings before Referee and briefs submitted to the Referee. In the event that one of the three members assigned to a matter dies, becomes incapacitated, or is otherwise unable to determine a matter, the fourth member shall take his or her place. If the fourth member dies, becomes incapacitated, or is otherwise unable to serve, the Chairperson may designate another member of the Committee to serve in his or her place.

§ 605.23. Committee Chairperson and Secretary

In addition to such other duties as are set forth in this Part, the Committee Chairperson shall perform such duties as may be assigned by the Committee, and the Secretary shall perform such duties as may be assigned by the Committee or the Committee Chairperson.

§ 605.24. Confidentiality

(a) Confidentiality. Disciplinary committee members, committee lawyers, committee employees, and all other individuals officially associated or affiliated with the committee, including pro bono lawyers, bar mediators, law students, stenographers, operators of recording devices and typists who transcribe recorded testimony shall keep committee matters confidential in accordance with applicable law.

(b) Waiver. Upon the written waiver of confidentiality by any Respondent, all participants shall thereafter hold the matter confidential to the extent required by the terms of the waiver.

PART 606. LEGAL AND MEDICAL SERVICES; DUTIES OF COUNSEL RESPECTING APPEALS

§ 606.1. Assignments Pursuant to Section 35 of the Judiciary Law

(a) Counsel.

(1) Whenever in a proceeding described in section 35 of the Judiciary Law the court shall find that counsel should be assigned to represent a person who does not have legal representation and who is financially unable to obtain counsel, the court shall appoint the attorney-in-charge of the criminal courts branch or of the civil branch of the Legal Aid Society as the attorney of record to represent such person. If, however, the court deems the assignment of other counsel to be required because of either a conflict of interest or other good cause, it shall enter an order appointing the attorney designated by the administrator of the Assigned Counsel Plan in the First Judicial Department from the panels of attorneys established under that plan. Designations of counsel by the administrator shall, as nearly as practicable, be by rotation.

(2) The term "legal representation" shall include representation by a member of the bar, representation by the Director of the Mental Hygiene Legal Service, or representation by a corporation approved pursuant to the provisions of Judiciary Law § 495.

(3) A copy of each such order of appointment shall be forwarded by the court to the Administrator of the Assigned Counsel Plan. Claims for compensation by counsel or the Legal Aid Society shall be submitted to the court which made the assignment on prescribed forms, specifying the time expended (in court and out of court), the services rendered and the expenses reasonably incurred, and stating that no payment or promise of payment has been received in respect of such services and expenses.

(b) Psychiatrists and Physicians.

(1) Whenever in a proceeding described in section 35 of the Judiciary Law the court shall find that a psychiatrist or physician should be appointed to examine and report and, if required, to testify at the hearing upon the condition of a person, the court shall request the Mental Health Information Service to designate such psychiatrist or physician for such purposes. If the court deems that because of a conflict of interest or other good cause the Service should not make the designation, it shall request the Impartial Medical Panel Office of the Supreme Court, First Judicial District, to do so. Designations shall, as nearly as possible, be by rotation from panels of psychiatrists and physicians recommended by the New York Academy of Medicine in consultation with the Bronx County and New York County Chapters of the American Psychiatric Association, Bronx County Medical Society, and the Medical Society of the County of New York, including the panel heretofore furnished to the Mental Health Information Service, First Judicial Department.

(2) A copy of each order of appointment entered by the court shall be forwarded to the director of the Mental Health Information Service. Claims for compensation by a psychiatrist or physician shall be submitted to the court which made the assignment on prescribed forms, specifying the time expended (in court and out of court), the services rendered and the expenses reasonably incurred, and stating that no payment or promise of payment has been received in respect of such services and expenses.

Cross References

Judiciary Law, see McKinney's Book 29.

§ 606.2. Compensation for Extraordinary Services

(a) Whenever an attorney, psychiatrist or physician, or a person providing investigative, expert or other services, seeks compensation in excess of the statutory limits prescribed by article 18–B of the County Law or section 35 of the Judiciary Law, because of extraordinary circumstances, he shall submit with his claim a detailed affidavit stating the nature of the proceeding, the manner in which the time was expended, the necessity therefor, and all other facts which tend to demonstrate extraordinary circumstances. In addition, if the claim is by an attorney he shall state the disposition of the matter.

(b) An application seeking compensation in excess of the statutory limits prescribed by Article 18–b of the County Law or section 35 of the Judiciary Law shall be reviewed, *sua sponte* or upon the request of any person or governmental body affected by the order, by the appropriate administrative judge pursuant to section 127.2 of this Part.

Cross References

County Law, see McKinney's Book 11.

Judiciary Law, see McKinney's Book 29.

§ 606.3. Expenses of Assigned Counsel, Psychiatrists or Physicians

The term "expenses reasonably incurred," whenever used in this part, shall not include normal office expenses such as local telephone service, postage, secretarial and other office overhead, or mileage for use of automobile, parking fees, taxi fares, etc., in traveling to a court, hospital or place of detention located within the City of New York and readily accessible by rapid transit.

§ 606.4. Determination of Financial Ability

The appointment of counsel to represent a person who does not have legal representation and who states that he is not financially able to obtain counsel, shall be made upon a finding of inability based either upon such person's affidavit or upon oral testimony in court under oath or by affirmation, or by such other proof as the court may direct.

§ 606.5. Duties of Counsel With Respect to Representation of Defendants in Criminal Actions

(a) Duties of Assigned or Retained Counsel.

(1) It shall be the duty of counsel assigned to or retained for the defense of a defendant in a criminal action or proceeding to represent defendant in the trial court until the action or proceeding has been terminated in that court, and to comply with the provisions of paragraphs (b)(1) or (d)(2) of this section, after which the duties of assigned counsel shall be ended.

(2) It shall be the duty of counsel assigned to prosecute or defend an appeal on behalf of an indigent defendant to accept said assignment and to prosecute the appeal until entry of the order of the appellate court terminating the appeal, and to comply with the provisions of paragraphs (b)(2) or (d)(2) of this section, after which the duties of assigned counsel shall be ended.

(b) Notification of Right to Appeal or to Apply for a Certificate Granting Leave to Appeal; Obligation to File Profile Statement With Notice of Appeal.

(1) *After Conviction and Sentence.* Where there has been a conviction after trial or otherwise, or where there has been an adverse decision upon an application for a writ of habeas corpus, upon a motion to vacate a judgment made pursuant to section 440.10 of the Criminal Procedure Law, upon a motion to set aside a sentence made pursuant to section 440.20 of the Criminal Procedure Law, or where there has been a determination revoking parole, it shall be the duty of counsel, retained or assigned, immediately after the pronouncement of sentence or service of a copy of the order disposing of the application for a writ of habeas corpus, of a motion to vacate a judgment made pursu-

ant to section 440.10 of the Criminal Procedure Law, of a motion to set aside a sentence made pursuant to section 440.20 of the Criminal Procedure Law, or of a notice of the determination revoking parole, to advise the defendant or parolee in writing of his right to appeal or to apply for a certificate granting leave to appeal pursuant to subdivision 4 of section 460.10 of the Criminal Procedure Law, the time limitations involved, in the manner of instituting an appeal and of obtaining a transcript of the testimony, and of the right of a person who has an absolute right to appeal or has received a certificate granting leave to appeal and is unable to pay the cost of an appeal to apply for leave to appeal as a poor person. It shall also be the duty of such counsel to ascertain whether defendant or the parolee wishes to appeal or to apply for a certificate granting leave to appeal, and, if so, to serve and file the necessary notice of appeal from a judgment of conviction or determination revoking parole or to apply for a certificate granting leave to appeal from the denial of a motion made pursuant to section 440.10 or section 440.20 of the Criminal Procedure Law and, if granted, to file the necessary certificate and notice of appeal within the time limitations provided for in subdivision 4 of section 460.10 Criminal Procedure Law. Attached to the notices of appeal, counsel shall file two copies of a profile statement which sets forth:

(i) Title of the action and indictment number;

(ii) County and Court from which the appeal is taken;

(iii) Full names of the defendant and any co-defendants;

(iv) Name(s), address(es) and telephone number(s) of defense counsel;

(v) Charges upon which defendant stands convicted and date judgment was entered;

(vi) Pretrial hearings and dates held;

(vii) Trial dates and/or plea dates; and

(viii) Whether court ordered daily copy of hearing or trial transcripts was received and the date(s) the transcripts were returned.

(2) *After Determination Adverse to Defendant.* Immediately after entry of an order affirming a judgment of conviction or an order modifying or reversing an order or sentence appealed by the People pursuant to section 450.20 of the Criminal Procedure Law or an order denying an application for a writ of habeas corpus, a motion to vacate a judgment made pursuant to section 440.10 of the Criminal Procedure Law, or a motion to set aside a sentence made pursuant to section 440.20 of the Criminal Procedure Law, it shall be the duty of counsel, retained or assigned, to advise defendant of his right to apply for permission to appeal and of the additional right of a person who is unable to pay the cost of a further appeal (in the event permission shall have been granted) to apply for leave to prosecute such appeal as a poor person. It shall

also be the duty of such counsel to ascertain whether defendant wishes to apply for permission to appeal to the Court of Appeals, and, if so, counsel shall make a timely application therefor. If permission to appeal is granted, and poor person's relief and the assignment of counsel are necessary, counsel shall make timely application for such relief. In the case of an order affirming a judgment dismissing a writ of habeas corpus, such counsel shall advise the relator of his or her right to appeal where there is a dissent by at least two justices on a question of law, or of the right to apply for permission to appeal where the determination is unanimous or there is a dissent by fewer than two justices. In the case of a parolee, his counsel shall advise the parolee, after notice of an adverse determination by the Board of Parole of an appeal from a determination revoking parole, of his right to commence a proceeding pursuant to article 78 of the Civil Practice Law and Rules and of the time limitation applicable thereto.

(c) Notification to Defendants Who Appear Without Counsel.

(1) *After conviction or denial of a motion to vacate a judgment made pursuant to section 440.10 of the Criminal Procedure Law, or of a motion to set aside a sentence made pursuant to section 440.20 of the Criminal Procedure Law.* If a defendant has appeared pro se, the trial court shall advise a defendant of his right to appeal from a judgment of conviction, or of his right to apply for a certificate granting leave to appeal from an order denying a motion to vacate a judgment made pursuant to section 440.10 of the Criminal Procedure Law, or of a motion to set aside a sentence made pursuant to section 440.20 of the Criminal Procedure Law. It shall also advise a defendant of the right of a person unable to pay the cost of an appeal to apply for leave to appeal as a poor person. If the defendant so requests, the clerk of the court shall prepare and file and serve forthwith a notice of appeal on behalf of the defendant from a judgment of conviction. If the defendant so requests in writing within 30 days after service upon him of a copy of an order denying a motion to vacate a judgment made pursuant to section 440.10 of the Criminal Procedure Law, or of a motion to set aside a sentence made pursuant to section 440.20 of the Criminal Procedure Law, and no previous application for a certificate granting leave to appeal has been made, the clerk of the court shall serve a copy of such request upon the district attorney and shall transmit the request and the original record of the proceedings sought to be reviewed to the appellate court. Upon determination of the application the original record of proceedings shall be returned to the trial court together with a certified copy of the order entered upon the application; a certified copy of the order shall also be sent to the defendant at his address shown in the application.

(2) *After Determination Adverse to Defendant.*

(i) If on an appeal from a judgment of conviction after trial or otherwise, or on an appeal from an order or sentence appealed by the People pursuant to section 450.20 of the Criminal Procedure Law, or from an order denying a motion to vacate a judgment made pursuant to section 440.10 of the Criminal Procedure Law, or of a motion to set aside a sentence made pursuant to section 440.20 of the Criminal Procedure Law, a defendant has appeared pro se and the judgment, order or sentence is adverse to the defendant the copy of the order of affirmance, with notice of entry, which is served on the defendant shall have annexed or appended thereto the following notice:

NOTICE AS TO FURTHER APPEAL

Pursuant to section 460.20 of the Criminal Procedure Law, defendant has the right to apply for leave to appeal to the Court of Appeals by making application to the chief judge of that court by submitting such application to the clerk of that court, or to a justice of the Appellate Division of the Supreme Court of this department on reasonable notice to the respondent within 30 days after service of a copy of the order or affirmance with notice of entry.

Denial of the application for permission to appeal by the judge or justice first applied to is final and no new application may thereafter be made to any other judge or justice.

(ii) Where an order determining an appeal from a judgment that determines either a writ of habeas corpus or a petition in an article 78 proceeding affecting a criminal case is adverse to a relator or petitioner appearing pro se, the following notice shall be annexed or appended to the copy of the order served, with notice of entry, upon such relator or petitioner:

NOTICE AS TO FURTHER APPEAL

If the determination by the Appellate Division is unanimous or there is a dissent by fewer than two justices, an appeal may be taken to the Court of Appeals only pursuant to CPLR 5602 by permission of the Appellate Division granted before application to the Court of Appeals or by permission of the Court of Appeals upon refusal of the Appellate Division to grant permission, or by direct application to the Court of Appeals.

An application for permission to appeal must be made within 30 days after service of a copy of the order of affirmance with notice of entry.

If the determination by the Appellate Division is not unanimous and at least two justices dissent on a question of law, relator or petitioner may take an appeal to the Court of Appeals as a matter of right pursuant to CPLR 5601(a) by serving on the adverse party a notice of appeal within 30 days after service of a copy of the order appealed from, with notice of entry, and filing the notice of appeal in the office where the judgment or order of the court of original instance is entered.

(d) Notification to Defendants of People's Appeals.

(1) It shall be the duty of trial counsel, upon service of an order appealable by the People pursuant to Criminal Procedure Law Article 450 to forthwith notify defendant in writing that the People have the right to take an appeal, the consequences of the People's appeal and the defendant's rights, including the right to retain appellate counsel or, if indigent, to apply for leave to appear as a poor person.

(2) It shall be the duty of appellate counsel upon service of a notice of appeal or an order of appointment to notify the client in writing that the People have taken an appeal from an order of the trial court and the consequences of the appeal.

(3) In the event no appellate counsel has appeared on behalf of the defendant, assigned trial counsel, upon receipt of the People's brief, shall make diligent efforts to locate the defendant and notify the defendant, in writing, that the People have filed a brief, the consequences of the People's appeal and the defendant's rights, including the right to retain appellate counsel, or if indigent, to apply for leave to appeal as a poor person.

Cross References

CPLR, see McKinney's Book 7B.

Criminal Procedure Law, see McKinney's Book 11A.

§ 606.6. Additional Duties of the Court and of Defendant's Counsel in Connection With Trial Court Transcripts

Where furnishing of a daily copy of a transcript is ordered by the court, the ribbon copy thereof shall be delivered to the court and a carbon copy to counsel for the defendant. Both the court and counsel for the defendant shall be duty-bound to preserve their respective copies. At the conclusion of the trial or hearing, trial counsel for the defendant shall, if an appeal is taken, deliver said carbon copy to appellant's counsel immediately on being advised of the name and address of said appellant's counsel. At the conclusion of the trial or hearing and forthwith after the decision or verdict, as the case may be, the ribbon copy shall be delivered by the court to the county clerk for filing. The ribbon copy and the carbon copy shall constitute the two transcripts of the proceedings required by section 460.70 of the Criminal Procedure Law.

Cross References

Criminal Procedure Law, see McKinney's Book 11A.

§ 606.7. Assignment of Counsel in Family Court

Counsel to be assigned pursuant to Family Court Act, section 262, shall be selected from such panels as have been established in the First Judicial Department in conformity with article 18–B of the County Law, as amended.

§ 606.8. Appointment of Law Guardians in Family Court

Where for sufficient reason law guardians to be appointed pursuant to Family Court Act, section 249, cannot otherwise be designated as provided in section 243(a) of the Family Court Act, appointment of such law guardians shall be made from the panels heretofore established pursuant to section 243(c) of such act, and in such event, the panel of law guardians shall be deemed to be the Family Court panels established pursuant to Family Court Act, section 262.

§ 606.9. Assignment of Counsel in Surrogate's Court

Counsel to be assigned pursuant to SCPA section 407 shall be selected from such panels as have been established in the First Judicial Department for use in the Family Court in conformity with article 18–B of the County Law.

Cross References

County Law, see McKinney's Book 11.

SCPA, see McKinney's Book 58A.

PART 608. PRACTICE OF LAW BY ORGANIZATIONS AND PROFESSIONAL SERVICE CORPORATIONS

§ 608.1. Practice of Law by Organizations Pursuant to Judiciary Law Sections 495 and 496

Any organization which offers prepaid legal services, any nonprofit organization whether incorporated or unincorporated, organized and operating primarily for a purpose other than the provision of legal services and which furnishes legal services as an incidental activity in furtherance of its primary purpose, or any organization which has as its primary purpose the furnishing of legal services to indigent persons, which has its principal office located in the First Judicial Department, shall file with this department a statement describing the nature and purposes of the organization, the composition of its governing body, the type of legal services being made available, and the names and addresses of any attorneys and counselors-at-law employed by the organization or with whom commitments have been made. An updating of this information shall be furnished this department on or before July first of each year and the names and addresses of attorneys and counselors-at-law who rendered legal services during that year shall be included.

§ 608.2. Practice of Law by Professional Service Corporations Pursuant to Business Corporation Law Section 1514

Any professional service corporation organized for the purpose of practicing law pursuant to the Business Corporation Law Article 15 and which has its principal office located in the First Judicial Department shall file with this department on or before July first every three years a statement listing the name and residence address of each shareholder, director and officer of the corporation and certifying that all such individuals are duly authorized to practice law in this state. The statement shall be signed by the president or any vice-president of the corporation and attested to by the secretary or any assistant secretary of the corporation.

PART 610. LICENSING OF LEGAL CONSULTANTS

§ 610.1. Applications for Licenses as Legal Consultants; Referral to Committee on Character and Fitness

(a) The committee on character and fitness appointed by this court to investigate the character and fitness of applicants for admission to practice as attorneys and counselors at law in the courts of this State is hereby also authorized to investigate the qualifications and the character and fitness of applicants for licenses to practice as legal consultants pursuant to the Judiciary Law (§ 53, subd. 6) and the rules of the Court of Appeals (Part 521).

(b) Every applicant for a license to practice as a legal consultant shall complete, verify and file with the clerk of this court the standard form of questionnaire, and shall comply with all the other requirements, prescribed for that purpose by this court.

(c) Every application in this department for such a license shall be referred to the committee on character and fitness for the judicial district in which the applicant actually resides at the time of such application, and, unless otherwise ordered by the court, no such license shall be granted without a certificate from such committee that it has found that the applicant possesses the qualifications and the character and fitness required therefor.

Cross References

Judiciary Law, see McKinney's Book 29.

§ 610.2. Documents, Affidavits and Other Proof Required

Every applicant for a license to practice as a legal consultant shall file the following additional papers with his application:

(a) A certificate from the authority having final jurisdiction over professional discipline in the foreign country in which the applicant was admitted to practice, which shall be signed by a responsible official or one of the members of the executive body of such authority and shall be attested under the hand and seal, if any, of the clerk of such authority, and which shall certify:

(1) As to the authority's jurisdiction in such matters;

(2) As to the applicant's admission to practice in such foreign country and the date thereof and as to his good standing as an attorney or counselor at law or the equivalent therein, and

(3) As to whether any charge or complaint has ever been filed against the applicant with such authority, and, if so, the substance of each such charge or complaint and the disposition thereof.

(b) A letter of recommendation from one of the members of the executive body of such authority or from one of the judges of the highest law court or court of general original jurisdiction of such foreign country, certifying to the applicant's professional qualifications, together with a certificate under the hand and seal, if any, of the clerk of such authority or of such court, as the case may be, attesting to the office held by the person signing the letter and the genuineness of his signature.

(c) Affidavits as to the applicant's good moral character and fitness from three reputable persons residing in this State and not related to the applicant, one of whom shall be a practicing New York attorney.

(d) Affidavits from two attorneys or counselors at law or the equivalent admitted in and practicing in such foreign country, stating the nature and extent of their acquaintance with the applicant and their personal knowledge as to the nature, character and extent of the applicant's practice, and as to the applicant's good standing, as an attorney or counselor at law or the equivalent in such foreign country, and the duration and continuity of such practice.

(e) Such additional evidence as the applicant may see fit to submit with respect to his educational and professional qualifications and his good moral character and fitness.

(f) A duly authenticated English translation of every paper submitted by the applicant which is not in English.

(g) A duly acknowledged instrument designating the clerk of this court the applicant's agent for service of process as provided in section 521.4(a)(2)(iii) of the rules of the Court of Appeals.

§ 610.3. College and Law School Certificates

A certificate shall be submitted from each college and law school attended by the applicant, setting forth the information required by forms which shall be provided to the applicant for that purpose.

§ 610.4. Exceptional Situations

In the event that the applicant is unable to comply strictly with any of the foregoing requirements, the applicant shall set forth the reasons for such inability in an affidavit, together with a statement showing in detail the efforts made to fulfill such requirements.

§ 610.5. Authority of Committee on Character and Fitness to Require Additional Proof

The committee on character and fitness may in any case require the applicant to submit such additional proof or information as it may deem appropriate and may also require the applicant to submit a report of the National Conference of Bar Examiners with respect to his character and qualifications.

§ 610.6. Undertaking

Prior to taking custody of any money, securities (other than unindorsed securities in registered form), negotiable instruments, bullion, precious stones or other valuables, in the course of his practice as a legal consultant, for or on behalf of any client domiciled or residing in the United States, every person licensed to practice as a legal consultant shall obtain, and shall maintain in effect for the duration of such custody, an undertaking issued by a duly authorized surety company, and approved by a justice of this court, to assure the faithful and fair discharge of his duties and obligations arising from such custody. The undertaking shall be in an amount not less than the amount of any such money, or the fair market value of any such property other than money, of which the legal consultant shall have custody, except that this court may in any case in its discretion for good cause direct that such undertaking shall be in a greater or lesser amount. The undertaking or a duplicate original thereof shall be promptly filed by the legal consultant with the clerk of this court.

§ 610.7. Disciplinary Procedure

Disciplinary proceedings and proceedings under section 603.16 of these rules against any legal consultant shall be initiated and conducted in the manner and by the same agencies as prescribed by law for disciplinary proceedings against attorneys.

§ 610.8. Filing

Every application in this department for a license as a legal consultant, together with all the papers submitted thereon, shall upon its final disposition be filed in the office of the clerk of this court.

PART 611. LAW GUARDIAN PLAN

§ 611.1. Introduction

(a)(1) The Family Court panels now established in the First Judicial Department pursuant to article 18–B of the County Law and pertinent provisions of the Family Court Act, shall continue in effect and shall constitute the Family Court Panel Plan in the First Judicial Department.

(2) The law guardian roster of attorneys certified pursuant to the Rules of the Chief Administrator Part 36 and the former Rules of the Court Part 614, to accept appointment as a law guardian for an infant child or children pursuant to Family Court § 249(a), Civil Practice Law and Rules § 1202, or Uniform Rules of the Trial Court § 202.16(f)(3), shall continue in effect in this department as part of the Law Guardian Plan.

(3) The Family Court Panel Plan and the law guardian roster are merged to form the Law Guardian Plan. An attorney certified for appointment in one capacity shall be deemed certified for appointment in the other capacity and by virtue of the certification agrees to accept assignments and appointments in Supreme Court or Family Court.

(b) The Law Guardian Director, appointed by the Presiding Justice of the Appellate Division, First Department, shall administer the Law Guardian Plan.

Cross References

County Law, see McKinney's Book 11.

Family Court Act, see McKinney's Book 29A, Part 1.

§ 611.2. Assignment of Counsel in the Family Court

Counsel to be assigned pursuant to the Family Court Act, section 262, shall be selected from such panels as have been established by the Assigned Counsel Plan in the First Judicial Department.

Cross References

Family Court Act, see McKinney's Book 29A, Part 1.

§ 611.3. Appointment of Law Guardians in Family Court

Where for sufficient reason law guardians to be appointed pursuant to section 249 of the Family Court Act cannot otherwise be designated as provided in section 243(a) of such act, the court may draw upon such panels as have been established by the Assigned Counsel Plan for the First Judicial Department as if such panels had been separately established pursuant to section 243(c) of such act.

Cross References

Family Court Act, see McKinney's Book 29A, Part 1.

§ 611.4. Certification of Attorneys

Certification of an attorney as a member of any panel of the Law Guardian Plan shall be for a one year term subject to: (a) annual redesignation pursuant to Family Court Act, § 244(b); and, (b) recertification as directed by the justices of the Appellate Division, First Department.

§ 611.5. Departmental Advisory Committee

Commencing January 1, 1980 the justices of the Appellate Division, First Department established a Departmental Advisory Committee. This Committee shall remain in operation and have the authority and responsibility to oversee the operation of the Law Guardian Plan and to consider all matters that pertain to the qualifications, performance and professional conduct of individual plan attorneys in their assignments and appointments as plan attorneys, and the representation of indigent parties in Family Court proceedings.

§ 611.6. Composition of the Departmental Advisory Committee

(a) The Committee shall be composed of no fewer than fifteen attorneys who shall be experienced in Family Court and domestic relations proceedings, three Family Court judges, one mental health expert, one representative from each of the three bar associations designated in the Rules of the Court § 612.3, one faculty member of an accredited law school in the First Judicial Department, the Law Guardian Director and the Assigned Counsel Plan Administrator.

(b) The Justices of the Appellate Division, First Department shall nominate all Committee members, except the representatives of the three bar associations, who shall be nominated by the respective presidents of those associations. The Presiding Justice may appoint such additional members to the Committee as will facilitate its operation. The term of appointment for each Committee member, except the Law Guardian Director and Assigned Counsel Plan Administrator, shall be staggered and for a period of three years subject to renomination by the justices of the Appellate Division. The term of appointment for the Law Guardian Director and the Assigned Counsel Plan Administrator shall be co-extensive with the term of their respective positions.

(c) The Presiding Justice shall designate a chair and vice-chair of the Committee.

Cross References

Public Officers Law, see McKinney's Book 46.

§ 611.7. Duties of the Departmental Advisory Committee

The Departmental Advisory Committee shall conduct its activities and carry out the duties enumerated in this Part pursuant to the Bylaws of the Assigned Counsel Plan Central Screening Committee, set forth in Part 612 Appendix A of the Rules of the Court. The Law Guardian Director shall be substituted where reference in the Bylaws is made to the Administrator.

§ 611.8. Screening Process

(a) All applicants for plan membership shall be screened by the Departmental Advisory Committee.

(b) The Committee, in accordance with standards for admission to the panels entitled "General Requirements for All Applicants to the Family Court Panels" and "General Requirements for Law Guardian to Qualify for Appointment in Domestic Relations Matters", shall make a determination as to whether an attorney is qualified for membership on any of the panels.

§ 611.9. Continuing Legal Education

(a) The Departmental Advisory Committee, in co-operation with the Assigned Counsel Plan, the Continuing Legal Education Office and the three bar associations designated in the Rules of the Court § 612.3, shall: (1) on a continuing basis, develop and conduct training and education programs that focus on domestic relations law and practice before the Family Court; (2) annually promulgate a list of recommended training and education programs pertaining to domestic relations and family law sponsored by independent providers of legal education; and, (3) organize and operate a co-counsel program.

(b) Members of the Law Guardian Plan biennially must complete at least eight hours of training and education programs that are either sponsored by the Departmental Advisory Committee or included on the list of recommended programs referred to in subsection (a).

§ 611.10. Annual Report

(a) No later than September 30 of each calendar year the Departmental Advisory Committee shall file with the Appellate Division a written evaluation of the panels and the panel attorneys, setting forth information regarding: the performance of plan attorneys, efficiency of the panels as a means of representing indigent parties, the training and education programs sponsored and recommended by the Committee, and proposals for improving the operation of the Law Guardian Plan. In preparing the written evaluation, the Committee may consult with Family Court judges and bar associations. Plan attorneys shall cooperate with the Committee in preparing the evaluation.

(b) An annual report of the operation of the Family Court panels shall be filed by the Appellate Division with the Chief Administrator of the Unified Court System no later than January 31, of each calendar year.

§ 611.11. Continuity of Powers

Nothing contained in this Part shall be construed to limit the powers of the Appellate Division or the presiding justice thereof or the Administrator of the Assigned Counsel Plan otherwise granted pursuant to laws.

§ 611.12. Members of the Departmental Advisory Committee as Volunteers

The members of the Departmental Advisory Committee, as volunteers, are expressly authorized to participate in a State-sponsored volunteer program within the meaning of Public Officers Law section 17(a).

Cross References

Public Officers Law, see McKinney's Book 46.

§ 611.13. Complaints

The Departmental Advisory Committee may receive and investigate complaints against individual plan members appointed pursuant to this part according to the procedures set forth in Part 612 Appendix A of the Rules of the Court.

§ 611.14. Use of Records

All papers, records and documents involving a complaint relating to the discharge of a panel attorney's duties shall be sealed and deemed private and confidential. However, upon good cause being shown, the justices of the Appellate Division or the presiding justice thereof may, by written order, permit to be divulged all or any part of such papers, records and documents. In the discretion of the presiding justice, such order may be made either with notice to the persons or attorneys to be affected thereby, or upon such notice to them as the presiding justice may direct. Records of the Departmental Advisory Committee shall be made available, upon request, without the necessity for such order, to the Departmental Disciplinary Committee for the Appellate Division, First Judicial Department.

PART 612. RULES TO IMPLEMENT A CRIMINAL COURTS PANEL PLAN

§ 612.0. Introduction

The justices of the Appellate Division of the Supreme Court in and for the First Judicial Department, by virtue of the authority vested in them by law and pursuant to article 18–B of the County Law as implemented by Executive Order No. 178 of the Mayor of the City of New York effective December 1, 1965, and by the Assigned Counsel Plan, approved by the Administrative Board of the Judicial Conference of the State of New York on April 28, 1966, do hereby, effective July 1, 1980, adopt this Part to establish rules governing the Criminal Courts Panel Plan of the Assigned Counsel Plan for the Appellate Division, First Judicial Department, and to set forth rules and standards regulating the selection, designation, performance and professional conduct of individual panel plan attorneys appointed to furnish representation for indigent defendants in criminal proceedings.

Cross References

County Law, see McKinney's Book 11.

§ 612.1. Previous Measures Continued

The Assigned Counsel Plan and the Criminal Courts Panels previously established in the First Judicial Department pursuant to article 18–B of the County Law shall continue in effect in this department.

Cross References

County Law, see McKinney's Book 11.

§ 612.2. Term of Appointments

Appointments of attorneys to any of the Indigent Defendant Legal Panels shall be for an indefinite term subject to recertification as directed by the justices of the Appellate Division First Department.

§ 612.3. Authority of Screening Committee

The Departmental Central Screening Committee heretofore established on January 4, 1979, upon the agreement and recommendation of the participating bar associations to the Assigned Counsel Plan (*i.e.*, Association of the Bar of the City of New York, New York County Lawyers' Association, Bronx County Bar Association), is continued in effect in this department. The Departmental Screening Committee shall have the authority and responsibility to oversee the operation of the panel plan and to consider all matters which pertain to the performance and professional conduct of individual panel plan attorneys in their assignments as panel attorneys and the representation of indigent parties in criminal proceedings.

§ 612.4. Membership of Screening Committee

The membership of the Central Screening Committee shall consist of members from each of the aforesaid bar associations, such members to be nominated by the presidents of the associations or the justices of the Appellate Division First Department. The chair vice-chair and secretary shall be designated by the presiding justice from among the nominees. The term of appointment for each member shall be for a period of three years subject to renomination by the justices of the Appellate Division.

§ 612.5. Duties of Screening Committee

The Central Screening Committee shall promulgate bylaws, subject to the approval of the Appellate Division, First Judicial Department, pursuant to which the committee may conduct its activities and carry out those duties as enumerated in this Part.

§ 612.6. Screening Process

(a) All applications for panel membership shall be screened by the Central Screening Committee.

(b) The committee, in accordance with standards for admission to the panels, entitled "General Requirements For All Applicants To The Indigent Defendants Legal Panel", shall make a determination as to whether an applicant is qualified for membership on any of the panels.

§ 612.7. Written Evaluation

(a) As directed by the Court, an employee of the Assigned Counsel Plan Office shall monitor and report to the Court the status of pending criminal appeals assigned to members of the Appellate Legal Panel.

(b) No later than the last day of each calendar year, the Central Screening Committee shall file with the Appellate Division a written evaluation of the plan and of panel attorneys, including Criminal Court, Supreme Court, homicide and appellate panels, setting forth all appropriate information with respect to the efficiency of the panel plan, problems which may exist in the operation plan, and procedures which have been or will be followed to improve the quality of legal representation in the Criminal Courts. In preparing the written evaluation, the Central Screening Committee may seek evaluations of the plan and Administrator of the Assigned Counsel Plan in the First Judicial Department, the Association of the Bar of the City of New York, the New York County Lawyers' Association, the Bronx County Bar Association and panel attorneys shall cooperate with the Central Screening Committee in this evaluation.

§ 612.8. Training Program

Pursuant to the obligations of the participating bar associations under article 18–B of the County Law and the Assigned Counsel Plan, the bar associations shall, after consultation with the Appellate Division and the administrator of the Assigned Counsel Plan, provide a continuing program of training and education which will allow panel attorneys to improve their profession-

al competence in criminal law. This program should provide for, but not be confined to, the establishment of a continuing cocounsel program and a professional course in criminal advocacy.

Cross References

County Law, see McKinney's Book 11.

§ 612.9. Panel Attorneys

(a) The Appellate Division, pursuant to the provisions of the Assigned Counsel Plan, may at any time make additions to or deletions from the panels.

(b) The Central Screening Committee may continue to process complaints against panel attorneys which relate to the discharge of an attorney's duties under the panel plan, and shall, in consultation with the administrator of the Assigned Counsel Plan, and subject to the approval of the Appellate Division, adopt rules for the processing of such complaints.

§ 612.10. Use of Records

All papers, records and documents involving a complaint relating to the discharge of a panel attorney's duties shall be sealed and be deemed private and confidential. However, upon good cause being shown, the justices of the Appellate Division or the presiding justice thereof may, by written order, permit to be divulged all or any part of such papers, records and documents. In the discretion of the presiding justice or the acting presiding justice, such order may be made either without notice to the persons or attorneys to be affected thereby, or upon such notice to them as he may direct. Records of the Central Screening Committee, however, shall be made available, upon request, without the necessity for such order, to the Departmental Disciplinary Committee for the Appellate Division, First Judicial Department.

§ 612.11. Members of Departmental Screening Committee as Volunteers

The members of the Departmental Central Screening Committee, as volunteers, are expressly authorized to participate in a State-sponsored volunteer program within the meaning of subdivision 1 of section 17 of the Public Officers Law.

Cross References

Public Officers Law, see McKinney's Book 46.

§ 612.12. Present Powers Retained

Nothing contained in this Part shall be construed to limit the power of the Appellate Division, the presiding justice thereof, the participating bar associations to the Assigned Counsel Plan or the administrator of the Assigned Counsel Plan otherwise granted by the Assigned Counsel Plan.

APPENDIX A. CENTRAL SCREENING COMMITTEE INDIGENT DEFENDANTS ASSIGNED COUNSEL PLAN

The Appellate Division, First Judicial Department, in furtherance of its obligation to provide indigent criminal defendants with competent counsel, approves the bylaws contained herein. Membership on all assigned counsel panels is a privilege granted to qualified attorneys by the Appellate Division, First Judicial Department.

BYLAWS

1. Quorum and Voting.

1.1   A quorum of a majority of the Committee is required for the conduct of business.

1.2   Final action on proposed guidelines, applications and complaints requires a majority vote of a quorum.

2. Application for Certification or Recertification.

2.1   All applications for certification or recertification to the panels shall be addressed to the Administrator. The provisions of this section shall apply to applications seeking initial certification or recertification to the panels.

2.2   The Administrator shall examine each application for facial sufficiency. If it is found to be insufficient, the Administrator shall return the application to the applicant.

2.3   The Administrator shall promptly assign every application not returned pursuant to 2.2 to a Committee member for his or her review.

2.4   Within sixty days of receiving the application, the assigned committee member shall contact two-thirds of the required references, at least two in each category (judges, adversaries and colleagues) and shall recommend in writing, to the Chair, the action to be taken on the application. A copy of the recommendation shall be submitted to the Administrator. Requests for extension of the sixty day period shall be made in writing to the Administrator.

2.5   Upon receipt of the assigned committee member's recommendation, the Chair shall accept the recommendation or refer the application to the Committee for review. When the Chair refers an application to the Committee, the Chair shall invite the applicant to appear before the Committee. Upon a review of the assigned committee member's recommendation, the application and any other relevant material, the Committee shall vote on the application pursuant to § 1.2 of these bylaws. The Chair or the Committee shall take the following action on an application:

(1) Certify the applicant to the panel(s) for which he or she is qualified;

(2) Deny certification of the applicant to any of the panels for which he or she is not qualified;

(3) Set conditions that the applicant must meet to establish the necessary qualifications for certification.

2.6   Applicants shall be advised by letter of the determination. In the event the applicant is denied certification, the letter must specify the reasons therefor.

2.7   The Committee's action is appealable to the presiding justice of the Appellate Division, First Judicial Department by the submission of a letter requesting review of the Committee's determination. The presiding justice's review of the Committee's determination is final and non-appealable.

2.8   An applicant denied certification to any panel may reapply for that panel one year after the date of the letter denying certification unless a shorter time or other conditions are set by the Chair or the Committee pursuant to § 2.5.

3. Complaints and Sanctions.

3.1   The Administrator, in consultation with the Chair, shall accept and keep records of written complaints concerning the competence and conduct of panel attorneys. Complaints made to the Administrator shall be forwarded to the Chair.

3.2   The Chair, in consultation with the Administrator, may dismiss complaints. Complaints not dismissed shall be referred to a committee member designated by the Chair for further investigation within thirty days of receipt of the complaint.

3.3   Once a complaint has been referred for further investigation, a subcommittee consisting of the Chair, the Administrator, and two additional committee members shall vote as to whether the attorney should be suspended. Suspension shall be imposed upon a majority vote of the subcommittee. The suspension shall continue pending a resolution of the complaint.

3.4   A panel member who is the subject of a complaint shall receive notice of the substance of the complaint. The notice shall advise the attorney that he or she may respond in writing.

3.5   Investigation by the designated subcommittee member shall be completed within ninety days. Extension of time to investigate a complaint may be granted by the Chair. Upon the completion of an investigation, the designated committee member shall make a report, with findings and recommendations, to the Committee.

3.6 The Committee shall, upon receipt of the report, invite the attorney to appear before the Committee, and upon having duly considered the attorney's statements and other relevant submissions, shall take one or more of the following actions, as shall be appropriate:

(1) Dismiss the complaint;

(2) Adopt the recommendation;

(3) Reject the recommendation;

(4) Suspend the panel attorney from any or all panels to which the attorney is certified and impose conditions upon the attorney's restoration to the panels;

(5) Recommend the substitution of the panel attorney on some or all of the cases to which the attorney is currently assigned by notification to the trial court where the cases are pending;

(6) Remove the attorney from any or all panels to which the attorney is certified.

3.7 At any time the Committee or subcommittee may vote to transmit the information it has developed to the District Attorney or the Departmental Disciplinary Committee.

3.8 The Chair shall promptly notify the attorney in writing of the Committee's action. In the event the determination imposes a restriction on the attorney's panel membership, the letter shall set forth the reasons therefor.

3.9 The determination of the Committee is appealable to the presiding justice of the Appellate Division, First Judicial Department by the submission of a letter requesting review of the Committee's determination. The presiding justice's review of the Committee's determination is final and non-appealable.

3.10 Nothing contained in these bylaws limits the authority of the Appellate Division to suspend or remove an attorney from the panels.

4. Responsibilities of Committee Members.

4.1 Committee members shall act expeditiously on applications and complaints referred to them. Any Committee member who fails to take timely action twice during any twelve month period shall be removed by the Presiding Justice.

5. Responsibilities of Officers.

5.1 An executive committee shall be formed, consisting of the Chair, the Vice-chair, Administrator and three members designated by the Chair. One of the three designees shall serve as Secretary.

5.2 The executive committee may act in place of the Committee in any matter that requires action by the Committee during a period in which the Committee is not scheduled to meet for more than thirty days. Any action taken by the executive committee shall be ratified by the Committee at its next meeting.

5.3 The Chair may designate subcommittees and may designate committee members to serve as chairs therefor.

5.4 All officers and executive committee members shall serve in their respective capacities for three years and may be reappointed by the Appellate Division.

PART 613. RULES TO IMPLEMENT AN INDIGENT DEFENSE ORGANIZATION OVERSIGHT COMMITTEE

§ 613.1. Introduction

The justices of the Appellate Division of the Supreme Court in and for the First Judicial Department, by virtue of the authority vested in them by law and pursuant to article 18–B of the County Law as implemented by Executive Order No. 178 of the Mayor of the City of New York effective December 1, 1965, the Assigned Counsel Plan approved by the Administrative Board of the Judicial Conference of the State of New York on April 28, 1966, and now upon the request of the City of New York and the participating bar associations to the Assigned Counsel Plan (i.e., Association of the Bar of the City of New York, New York County Lawyers' Association and the Bronx County Bar Association) do hereby, effective November 1, 1995, adopt this Part to establish rules governing the Indigent Defense Organization Oversight Committee for the Appellate Division, First Judicial Department, and to set forth rules and standards regulating the performance and professional conduct of indigent defense organizations and the attorneys in the employ of such organization who are appointed to furnish representation for indigent defendants in criminal proceedings.

§ 613.2. Previous Measures Continued

The Assigned Counsel Plan and the Criminal Courts Panels previously established in the First Judicial Department pursuant to Article 18–B of the County Law shall continue in effect in this department.

§ 613.3. Authority of Oversight Committee

The Indigent Defense Organization Oversight Committee hereby established, upon the agreement and recommendation of the City of New York and the participating bar associations to the Assigned Counsel Plan (i.e., Association of the Bar of the City of New York, New York County Lawyers' Association, and the Bronx County Bar Association) shall have the authority and responsibility to monitor the operation of organizations that contract with the City of New

York to represent indigent defendants in criminal proceedings, and to consider all matters that pertain to the performance and professional conduct of such organizations and the individual attorneys in their employ who are assigned to represent indigent parties in criminal proceedings.

§ 613.4. Membership of Oversight Committee

The membership of the Oversight Committee shall consist of lawyers to be nominated by the presidents of the bar associations and by the justices of the Appellate Division, First Department. The chair and vice-chair shall be designated by the presiding justice from among the nominees. The term of appointment for each member shall be for a period of three years subject to renomination by the justices of the Appellate Division, with the exception that four nominees will be appointed for an initial term of four years.

§ 613.5. Duties of Oversight Committee

The Oversight Committee shall promulgate bylaws and standards to be entitled "General Requirements for All Organized Providers of Defense Services to Indigent Defendants", subject to the approval of the Appellate Division, First Judicial Department, pursuant to which the committee may conduct its activities and carry out those duties as enumerated in this Part to ensure that indigent defendants are afforded quality legal representation.

§ 613.6. Monitoring Process

(a) All organizations awarded contracts by the City of New York for the provision of defense services shall be monitored from the time the contract is awarded by the Oversight Committee.

(b) The Committee, in accordance with the "General Requirements For All Organized Providers of Defense Services to Indigent Defendants", shall make a determination as to whether the organizations that contract with the City of New York meet those standards.

§ 613.7. Written Evaluation

The Oversight Committee shall file with the Appellate Division a written evaluation of the organizations providing indigent defense services, setting forth all appropriate information with respect to the organizations' performance, problems which may exist in their operation, and procedures which have been or will be followed to improve the quality of legal representation rendered to indigent defendants. Unless the Court directs otherwise, the Oversight Committee shall file the written evaluations biennially, commencing June 1, 2002. In preparing the written evaluations, the Oversight Committee may seek evaluations of the organizations' performance and the Administrator of the Assigned Counsel Plan in the First Judicial Department, the Association of the Bar of the City of New York, the New York County Lawyers' Association,

and the Bronx County Bar Association shall cooperate with the Oversight Committee in this evaluation.

§ 613.8. Cooperation of Indigent Defense Organizations

All organizations awarded contracts by the City of New York to provide representation to indigent defendants in criminal proceedings shall cooperate with and otherwise assist the Oversight Committee in the discharge of its duties.

§ 613.9. Training Program

Pursuant to the obligations of the participating bar associations under article 18–B of the County Law and the Assigned Counsel Plan, the bar associations shall, after consultation with the Appellate Division and the Oversight Committee, provide a continuing program of training and education which will enable indigent defense organizations and the attorneys in their employ to improve their professional competence in criminal law. This program should provide for, but not be confined to, a professional course in criminal advocacy.

§ 613.10. Complaints

The Oversight Committee may receive and investigate complaints against organizations providing representation to indigent defendants and the attorneys in their employ which relate to the discharge of an organization's or an individual attorney's duties pursuant to an order of appointment, and shall, subject to the approval of the Appellate Division, adopt rules for the processing of such complaints.

§ 613.11. Use of Records

All papers, records and documents involving a complaint against an organization providing representation to indigent defendants or an attorney in its employ shall be sealed and be deemed private and confidential. However, upon good cause being shown, the justices of the Appellate Division or the presiding justice thereof may, by written order, permit to be divulged all or any part of such papers, records and documents. In the discretion of the presiding justice such order may be made either without notice to the organization, persons or attorneys to be affected thereby, or upon such notice to them as he may direct. Records of the Oversight Committee, however, shall be made available, upon request, without the necessity for such order, to the Departmental Disciplinary Committee for the Appellate Division, First Judicial Department.

§ 613.12. Members of First Department Indigent Defense Organization Oversight Committee as Volunteers

The members of the First Department Indigent Defense Organization Oversight Committee, as volunteers, are expressly authorized to participate in a State-sponsored volunteer program within the meaning of subdivision 1 of section 17 of the Public Officers Law.

§ 613.13. Present Powers Retained

Nothing contained in this Part shall be construed to limit the power of the Appellate Division, the presiding justice thereof, or the participating bar associations to the Assigned Counsel Plan otherwise granted by the Assigned Counsel Plan.

PART 614. COMMITTEE TO CERTIFY LAW GUARDIANS FOR APPOINTMENT IN DOMESTIC RELATIONS MATTERS [RESCINDED]

PART 620. RULES OF THE JURY SYSTEM IN THE CITY OF NEW YORK [REPEALED]

PART 622. MENTAL HYGIENE LEGAL SERVICE

(Statutory authority: Mental Hygiene Law § 47.01)

§ 622.1. Definitions

Except as otherwise appears herein, whenever used in this Part any term defined in Mental Hygiene Law [section] 1.03 shall have the meaning set forth therein and, in addition, the following terms shall have the following meanings:

(a) Service means the Mental Hygiene Legal Service.

(b) Director means the head of the Service referred to in Mental Hygiene Law section 47.01 or his or her duly authorized designee.

(c) Court shall mean Supreme Court, County Court or Surrogate's Court.

(d) Patient shall mean a person residing in a facility for the mentally disabled which is licensed or operated by the Department of Mental Hygiene or the Department of Correctional Services, or a person residing in any other place for whom the Service has been appointed counsel or court evaluator pursuant to Article 81 of the Mental Hygiene Law.

(e) Guardian shall mean a person or entity appointed as a guardian, standby guardian or limited guardian as provided in article 17–A of the Surrogate's Court Procedure Act or article 81 of the Mental Hygiene Law.

§ 622.2. Duties of the Director

(a) With regard to patients in facilities governed by the Mental Hygiene Law:

(1) The director shall inform each patient of his or her rights to a judicial hearing, to review pursuant to Mental Hygiene Law sections 9.35 and 15.35, to an appeal and to be represented by the Service or by privately retained counsel.

(2) In every case in which a hearing is requested or ordered or in which an application or petition is made to the court with regard to a patient which may or may not require a hearing, the director shall investigate the patient's case, examine the patient's records, interview the patient and also, in the discretion of the director, interview other persons having information relevant to the patient's case. If the patient has counsel the court may request the director to perform any services on behalf of the patient within the scope of and consistent with the Service's statutory duties.

(3) The director shall examine the patient's facility records as often as the director deems necessary.

(4) The court may request the director to render or undertake any assistance or service on behalf of a patient consistent with the Service's statutory duties.

(5) When a hearing has not been demanded, if the director determines that the case of a patient should be heard by the court, or be reviewed by a court or court and jury, the director may, in his or her discretion, demand a hearing on behalf of such patient or may request that the case of the patient be reviewed by the court, or court and jury, in accordance with the power granted to the Service in the Mental Hygiene Law.

(6)(i) The director shall ascertain that the notices to be given to patients and other persons required under the Mental Hygiene Law have been duly served and posted and that there has been compliance with the procedures required by the Mental Hygiene Law for the hospitalization, transfer, retention and release of patients.

(ii) The director shall ascertain that all requirements of law as to patients' admissions, treatment and discharge affecting patients' rights have been complied with.

(7) The director shall review the status of every person who has been an informal patient or a voluntary patient for a period of 12 consecutive months and shall ascertain that there has been compliance with the Mental Hygiene Law. If the director finds that

the patient is willing and suitable for continued hospitalization in such status he or she shall so certify in the patient's record. If the director finds that the patient is unwilling or unsuitable for continued hospitalization in such status he or she shall take whatever action he or she deems necessary in accordance with the Mental Hygiene Law.

(b) In those guardianship proceedings pursuant to article 81 of the Mental Hygiene Law or article 17–A of the Surrogate's Court Procedure Act in which the Service participates as counsel, court evaluator, guardian-ad-litem or party:

(1) Upon receipt of notice of application in such proceedings, the director shall:

    (i) examine the papers and ascertain that the notices required to be given to parties and patients and, as far as known to the director, to other persons entitled thereto, have been duly served and that there has been due compliance with the prescribed statutory procedure;

    (ii) examine the records relating to the affairs or medical or psychiatric condition of the party or patient;

    (iii) interview every such party or patient, advise him or her of the nature of the proceeding and of his or her legal rights including the right to legal representation and the right to a court hearing, determine whether he or she has any objections to the proceeding or to the proposed guardian or whether he or she has any other objections;

    (iv) interview any psychiatrist, examining physician or psychologist, or such other psychiatrist or physician who has knowledge of the party or patient's mental and physical condition;

    (v) obtain all available information as to the extent and nature of the party or patient's assets;

    (vi) obtain all available information concerning the party or patient's family, background and any other fact that may be necessary or desirable.

(2)(i) The director shall notify the court of any request for hearing.

    (ii) In the director's discretion, and in the interest of the party or patient, the director may demand a hearing.

(3) The director shall inform the party or patient of the progress and status of all proceedings.

(4) In all proceedings for the discharge of a guardian, the enforcement or modification of a guardianship order, or the approval of a guardian's report or accounting, intermediate or final, the director shall inform the party or patient of the nature of the proceeding and his or her rights. The director may perform such additional services on behalf of the party or patient as are within the scope of, and consistent with, the Service's statutory duties.

(5) The director may, in an appropriate case and in his or her discretion, apply to the court for the discharge of the guardian or the enforcement or modification of an order appointing the guardian.

(6) The director is authorized to apprise the examiners charged with the review of accounts or reports with regard to any matter within the jurisdiction of such examiner affecting the welfare and property of a party or patient for whom a guardian has been appointed.

(7) The director shall perform such other duties and responsibilities as may be required by Article 81 of the Mental Hygiene Law.

(c) With regard to inmates, defendants or patients committed to, transferred to or placed in facilities for the mentally disabled pursuant to the Correction Law or to the Criminal Procedure Law:

(1) In all matters or proceedings in which the Service is required to be served with notice, the director shall:

    (i) examine the papers, and shall ascertain that the notices required to be given have been duly served and that there has been due compliance with the prescribed procedure;

    (ii) inform the inmate, defendant or patient of his or her rights including the right to judicial hearing, to review, to appeal and to be represented by the Service or by privately retained counsel;

    (iii) when a hearing has not been demanded, if the director determines that the case should be heard by the court or be reviewed by a court, or court and jury, the director may, in his or her discretion, demand a hearing or may request that the case be reviewed by the court or court and jury;

    (iv) examine the records of the inmate, defendant or patient;

    (v) interview the attending psychiatrist, examining physician or psychologist who has knowledge of the condition of the inmate, defendant or patient;

    (vi) interview all other persons having information relevant to the matter or proceeding;

    (vii) perform such other services on behalf of the inmate, defendant or patient as the director in his or her discretion may determine. The court may request the director to perform additional services within the scope of, and consistent with, the Service's statutory duties.

(d) With regard to applications for authorization to administer psychotropic medication and to perform surgery, electro-convulsive therapy or major medical treatment in the nature of surgery upon parties or patients in facilities:

(1) Copies of notice of such applications shall be served upon the director of the Service of the judicial department in which the proceeding is brought and

the director of the Service of the judicial department in which the facility is located.

(2) In all such proceedings the director shall:

(i) examine the papers, and shall ascertain that the notices required to be given have been duly served;

(ii) interview and inform the party or patient of the nature of the proceeding and of his or her rights, including the right to a judicial hearing, to appeal and to be represented by the Service or by privately retained counsel, and determine whether he or she has any objection to the proceeding;

(iii) when a hearing has not been demanded, if the director determines that the case should be heard by the court, the director may, in his or her discretion, demand a hearing on behalf of the party or patient;

(iv) examine the records of the party or patient;

(v) interview the party or patient's attending and consulting psychiatrist, physician or psychologist who has knowledge of the party or patient's condition;

(vi) interview all other persons having information relevant to the matter or proceeding;

(vii) perform such other services on behalf of the party or patient, as the court may request or the director may determine, consistent with the Service's statutory duties.

(e) In all the foregoing proceedings, the Service shall represent the inmate, defendant, party or patient unless they otherwise have counsel or counsel has been dispensed with pursuant to Article 81 of the Mental Hygiene Law.

(f) In all the foregoing proceedings, the director may, in his or her discretion, submit briefs, affidavits, affirmations or trial memoranda, consistent with the Service's role in the proceeding.

(g) In all of the foregoing proceedings the director shall assist the directors of the Service in the other judicial departments in regard to any proceeding pending in any other judicial department which pertains to a patient residing in the First Judicial Department.

§ 622.3. Guardian Ad Litem and Court Evaluator

In any proceeding before the court involving a patient, the court may appoint the Service as guardian ad litem or court evaluator consistent with, and within the scope of the Service's statutory duties, except when the Service advises the court that such appointment would create a conflict of interest with the Service's duties as counsel pursuant to 623.2 of this Part.

§ 622.4. Additional Psychiatric, Psychological, Medical or Expert Opinion

(a) Pursuant to Judiciary Law section 35 or any other statute, rule or regulation providing for additional opinion the director shall assist in obtaining, through a panel or otherwise, such additional opinion.

(b)(1) A panel of highly qualified psychiatrists shall be constituted and maintained by the presiding justice in cooperation with the New York Academy of Medicine in consultation with the local chapters or branches of the psychiatric or medical profession.

(2) The designation of a psychiatrist shall be made, except when the patient pays for his or her own psychiatrist or when the appointment is made pursuant to Article 81, from the aforesaid panel and shall be as far as possible on rotation basis.

(3) No psychiatrist, psychologist, physician or other expert shall be appointed by the court if he or she is disqualified under provisions of the Mental Hygiene Law or if he or she is employed at the institution in which the patient is hospitalized or residing or to which the patient may be transferred as a result of the proceeding in which the expert is to render his or her opinion.

§ 622.5. Review of Proposed Transfer of Patient or of Changes of Status of Patients

(a) In every case in which it is proposed to transfer a patient from one facility to another facility or to change his or her admission status to another, the director shall review the proposed transfer or change of status.

(b) In any such case, the director, in his or her discretion, may request a hearing on behalf of the patient.

§ 622.6. Fees

(a) When authorized by statute the director may request that the court award the Service a reasonable fee.

(b) The director's requests for fees for the services of attorneys shall not exceed the hourly rates of compensation set forth in Judiciary Law § 35; and the director's requests for fees for the services of non-lawyer professionals shall not exceed the hourly rate of compensation set forth in the Unified Court System's compensation guidelines for court-appointed non-lawyer professionals.

(c) Fees awarded the Service shall be maintained and dispensed in accordance with law.

§ 622.7. Records to Be Confidential

(a) All records and files of the director in any proceedings covered by this Part shall be confidential.

(b) All such records and files of the director may be exhibited only at the discretion of the director or upon order of the court.

PART 630. MISCELLANEOUS RULES [RESCINDED]
PART 635. JOINT ADMINISTRATIVE ORDERS

§§ 635.1 to 635.8. [Rescinded]

§ 635.9. Joint Administrative Order 453: Control and Supervision of City Marshals

The Appellate Division of the Supreme Court, First Judicial Department, and the Appellate Division of the Supreme Court, Second Judicial Department, pursuant to the authority vested in each of them, and for the purpose of providing controls and close supervision of city marshals, do hereby jointly order as follows:

(1) The Commissioner of Investigation of the City of New York or his designee, is empowered to supervise and monitor the official acts of New York City marshals and to take complaints, make inquiries and conduct investigations into all aspects of marshals' activities.

(2) The Commissioner of Investigation or his designee, in order to investigate and monitor the activities of city marshals, may hold hearings, compel the attendance of and examine under oath a marshal and his employees regarding the official acts of any marshal.

(3)(a) Each marshal shall keep detailed books and records and maintain bank accounts as prescribed by the appellate divisions or the Department of Investigation.

(b) A city marshal's official books, records and bank accounts are public records and as such are subject to unannounced inspections by the Department of Investigation or anyone designated for that purpose by the Commissioner of Investigation or the appellate divisions.

(c) Should the Commissioner of Investigation deem it proper, the Department of Investigation may take into its custody any or all of the official records of a city marshal for the purpose of inspecting them.

(d) Each city marshal shall surrender all official books and records including, but not limited to, cash books, docket books, check books, bank statements, and cancelled checks to the Department of Investigation upon termination of office. Should it become necessary, access to such official books and records for the purpose of examination shall be accorded to the city marshal surrendering the same. Upon termination of office, each city marshal shall further prepare a final report of his official acts, as prescribed by the Department of Investigation, which shall include a final statement of monies held in trust, expenses incurred, and fees earned.

(e) A city marshal is entitled to only those fees for those services which are prescribed by law and set forth in an official schedule of fees issued by the Commissioner of Investigation. A city marshal shall perform all other services required of him by law without any other fees or charges, except as otherwise expressly prescribed by law. No fee to which a city marshal is entitled may be waived without specific written authorization of the Commissioner of Investigation.

(f) Each city marshal shall henceforth, in accordance with the procedures prescribed by the Department of Investigation, provide for a fiduciary who shall, upon the death or incapacity of said marshal, assume complete responsibility for the marshal's bank accounts and official records, and shall distribute any monies held in trust or otherwise collected by the marshal to the proper judgment creditors or to any other individual(s) to whom such monies are due and owing. Such a fiduciary shall be compensated at the marshal's own expense.

(4)(a) The Commissioner of Investigation is empowered to continue to issue directives regarding marshals' official day-to-day activities, including, but not limited to, the official records to be kept by city marshals, the procedures for performing their duties, and the conduct of marshals and their employees. Copies of all directives shall be forwarded to the appellate divisions, and each directive shall remain in full force and effect unless and until nullified by joint order of both appellate divisions.

(b) Any handbook of regulations for city marshals which may be promulgated by the Department of Investigation shall become effective upon the approval of both appellate divisions. Any substantial policy changes therein shall require similar approval. However, copies of any other changes therein by directive or otherwise shall be forwarded to the appellate divisions, and such changes shall remain in full force and effect unless and until nullified by joint order of both appellate divisions.

(5) The Director of the Bureau of Marshals at the Department of Investigation or any other person or persons designated by the Commissioner of Investigation may, after an investigation, present evidence of incompetency, misconduct, or other wrongdoing as set forth in subdivision (6) of this section to the Commis-

sioner of Investigation. The commissioner may accordingly designate a deputy commissioner, assistant commissioner or other qualified person to hear charges as provided herein or, in the alternative, at the option of the commissioner, refer these charges and this evidence to the appellate divisions for disciplinary action or removal proceedings.

(6)(a) The Commissioner of Investigation may, after a hearing on charges preferred against a city marshal, impose penalties upon him including, but not limited to, suspension from the performance of his official duties for a period not to exceed six months for violation of the civil laws, the rules of the Appellate Divisions of the First and Second Departments, the rules of the Civil Court of the City of New York, the directives of the Department of Investigation, or for incompetency or misconduct.

(b) A city marshal against whom such disciplinary action is proposed shall have written notice thereof and of the reasons therefor, shall be furnished a copy of the charges preferred against him, and shall be allowed at least eight days for answering the same in writing. The marshal shall be entitled to a full and complete hearing with the assistance and presence of counsel.

(c) The hearing upon which such charges shall be held by such deputy commissioner, assistant commissioner or other person designated by the Commissioner of Investigation for that purpose. Such deputy commissioner or assistant commissioner may, pursuant to chapter 34 of the New York City Charter, issue subpoenas, administer oaths and shall take evidence and make a record of such hearing which shall, with his recommendation, be referred to the Commissioner of Investigation for review and decision.

(d) The deputy commissioner or assistant commissioner holding such hearing shall, upon the request of the city marshal against whom charges are preferred, permit him to be represented by counsel, and shall allow him to summon witnesses in his behalf. The burden of proving incompetency, misconduct or other wrongdoing shall be upon the Director of the Bureau of Marshals or other person designated by the Commissioner of Investigation for the purpose of prefer-

ring charges and shall be by a fair preponderance of evidence. The deputy or assistant commissioner holding such hearing shall receive evidence in the same manner as if this hearing were held pursuant to section 75 of the Civil Service Law, in that compliance with technical rules of evidence shall not be required.

(e) If the city marshal is found guilty, a transcript of the hearing, and a written statement of the determination and the reasons therefor, shall be filed in the office of the Department of Investigation. A copy of the transcript shall, upon request of the city marshal affected, be furnished to him without charge.

(f) If desired, the city marshal may appeal any decision by the Commissioner of Investigation to the appellate divisions. The marshal shall file such appeal in writing within 20 days after service of written notice of the determination to be reviewed, such written notice to be delivered personally or by registered mail to the last known office address of such city marshal. When notice is given by registered mail, such city marshal shall be allowed an additional three days in which to file such an appeal.

(7) A marshal, after being furnished with a copy of the charges preferred against him, may knowingly waive a hearing as provided in subdivision (6) of this section, and agree to a penalty prescribed by the Commissioner of Investigation.

(8) Perjury by a city marshal or his failure to testify concerning his official duties at an investigative or administrative hearing held at the Department of Investigation after being granted immunity from the use of the testimony in a criminal prosecution shall be ground for removal.

(9) Failure to comply with penalties imposed by the Commissioner of Investigation shall be ground for removal.

This Order is effective immediately and shall remain in full force and effect unless and until modified or nullified by joint order of both appellate divisions.

DATED: November 12, 1975

Cross References

Civil Service Law, see McKinney's Book 9.

PART 636. MISCELLANEOUS ORDERS

§§ 636.1 to 636.4. [Rescinded]

§ 636.5. Adoption of Standard Forms for Applications for Admission to Practice as Attorney and Counsellor at Law

The Committee to Regularize Bar Admission Procedures appointed by the Administrative Board of the Judicial Conference of this State having recommended the adoption in all four judicial departments of the

State of certain standard forms of questionnaire, instruction sheet and affidavits for applications for admission to practice as an attorney and counsellor-at-law pursuant to paragraph 1a or 1b of section 90 of the Judiciary Law, and the Appellate Divisions of the Supreme Court in the several departments having all agreed to adopt such forms, it is hereby

ORDERED that such standard forms, copies of which are annexed to this order,[1] shall be the forms used for all such applications for admission to practice made to this Court; and it is further

ORDERED that no changes or amendments shall be made in such forms except after consultation with respect thereto between this Court and the Appellate Divisions of the Supreme Court in the other three departments, acting through their respective Presiding Justices or Associate Justices designated by them.

DATED: January 17, 1973.

[1] The approved standard forms are not published herein. Each applicant for admission will be furnished with a questionnaire, affidavits of character, affidavits of legal employment, and forms for college and law school certificates. All inquiries concerning admission procedures are to be directed to the appropriate office of the Appellate Division to which the applicant has been certified by the State Board of Law Examiners.

Cross References

Judiciary Law, see McKinney's Book 29.

§§ 636.6 to 636.9. [Rescinded]

§ 636.10. Authorization for Committee on Character and Fitness to Continue to Inquire Concerning Any Criminal Actions and Proceedings Involving Applicants for Admission

The Justices of the Appellate Division of the Supreme Court in and for the First Judicial Department, upon reading Chapter 877 of the Laws of 1976, which amended section 160.50 of the Criminal Procedure Law and added a new section 160.60 thereto, and also amended section 296 of the Executive Law of the State of New York, do hereby

ORDER that the Committee on Character and Fitness delegated by this court to investigate applicants for admission to the Bar may continue to inquire concerning any criminal actions or proceedings involving the applicant, including actions or proceedings which were terminated in the applicant's favor, and may continue to require the applicants to answer questions and give information with respect to such matters.

DATED: December 13, 1976.

Cross References

Criminal Procedure Law, see McKinney's Book 11A.

Executive Law, see McKinney's Book 18.

SUPREME COURT, APPELLATE TERM, FIRST DEPARTMENT

Including Amendments Received Through September 15, 2008

Westlaw Electronic Research

These rules may be searched electronically on Westlaw® in the NY–RULES database; updates to these rules may be found on Westlaw in NY–RULESUP-DATES. For search tips and a summary of database content, consult the Westlaw Scope Screens for each database.

Table of Sections

PART 640. RULES OF PRACTICE

§ 640.1. Jurisdiction

The Appellate Term of the Supreme Court for the First Judicial Department shall hear and determine all appeals from the Civil Court of the City of New York and the Criminal Court of the City of New York in the Counties of New York and Bronx at such times and places as may be designated by the Appellate Division of the Supreme Court, First Judicial Department.

§ 640.2. Appeals From Civil Court; Papers Required on Appeals

(a) Appeals from the Civil Court shall be heard upon the return made by the clerk pursuant to the provisions of New York City Civil Court Act, section 1704 and five copies of the record and briefs, or upon the clerk's return and five copies of the briefs and appendices, typewritten or reproduced by any other method authorized by CPLR 5529.

(b) Appeals from the small claims part of the Civil Court shall be heard upon the clerk's return and five copies of the briefs reproduced by any authorized method.

(c) The parties may elect to proceed upon a statement in lieu of a record in accordance with the provisions of CPLR 5527. In the event of such election, the appeal shall be heard upon five copies of the statement and briefs reproduced by any authorized method.

(d) Where copies of the record are filed, the reproduced record shall be of the size specified in CPLR 5529 and on paper of a quality approved by the State Administrator with a substantial cover and fastened at the left hand edge. The pages of the record shall be consecutively numbered at the bottom, and at the top of each page containing testimony there shall be noted the name of the witness, by whom called and whether the examination is on direct, cross or re-direct.

Cross References

CPLR, see McKinney's Book 7B.

New York City Civil Court Act, see McKinney's Book 29A, Part 3.

§ 640.3. Appeals From Criminal Court; Papers Required on Appeal

(a) Appeals from the Criminal Court shall be heard on the original papers, certified by the clerk of the Criminal Court, a stenographic transcript of the minutes of proceedings, certified by the judge before whom the action was tried, or in the case of the death or disability of such judge, in such manner as the court directs, and five copies of the briefs.

(b) For good cause shown, the court may hear the appeal on an abbreviated record containing so much of the evidence or other proceedings as it may deem necessary to a consideration of the questions raised thereby, and five copies of the briefs.

(c) The appellant's brief must contain, at the beginning, the statement required by CPLR 5531 and a statement setting forth whether defendant is presently incarcerated. If the defendant was admitted to bail, the statement should set forth the date of the order and the court which admitted defendant to bail. If a fine was paid, the statement should set forth the amount of the fine, the date of payment, the Criminal Court part or the prison in which payment was made and the receipt number.

Cross References

CPLR, see McKinney's Book 7B.

§ 640.4. Exhibits

Each exhibit or copies thereof shall have affixed thereto a notation as to the page of the transcript where it was admitted in evidence.

§ 640.5. Briefs—What to Contain

(a) Briefs shall be on paper of the same size and quality as is required for the record on appeal by subdivision (a) of section 640.2. The name of counsel who is to argue or submit the appeal shall appear at the upper right hand corner of the first or cover page of the brief and the calendar number of the appeal shall be stated in the upper left hand corner.

(b) In the absence of a specification that the appeal is to be argued, it shall be marked submitted and oral argument shall not be heard.

(c) Testimony referred to in a brief must be accompanied by reference to the page of the record or transcript where such testimony appears.

(d) The main brief of any party shall not exceed 50 pages, and reply briefs shall not exceed 20 pages unless authorized by a justice of the court prior to the filing of any such brief. On appeals from the Criminal Court, appellant's brief shall contain the statement required by subdivision (c) of section 640.3.

(e) Unless authorized by the court, or these rules, briefs to which are added or appended any matter shall not be accepted for filing.

§ 640.6. Time Within Which to Perfect Appeal; Calendar of Pending Appeals; Dismissals

(a) **Appeals From the Civil Court.**

(1) Appellant shall procure the clerk's return pursuant to section 1704 of the New York City Civil Court Act to be filed within 30 days after the filing of the notice of appeal.

(2) Fifteen days before the first day of each term, the clerk of the Appellate Term shall cause a calendar to be published in the New York Law Journal of all appeals in which the clerk's return has been filed since the last publication of such a calendar. The appeals shall be listed in the order that the returns are received and the date each return was filed shall be stated. The publication of the calendar shall serve as notice to the parties of the filing of the return.

(3) Within 60 days after the filing of the return either party may notice the appeal for argument:

(i) If noticed by appellant, the appellant shall file a notice of argument at least fifty-three days before the first day of the term for which the appeal shall have been noticed, together with the following: proof of service thereof; five copies of the record or appendix with proof of service of one copy, if the appeal is to be heard on copies of the record or appendix; five copies of appellant's brief with proof of service of one copy; and such exhibits or copies thereof as are not included in the record or return, unless such exhibits are in the possession of the respondent. At least thirty-one days before the beginning of the term, respondent shall file five copies of the answering brief with proof of service of one copy and such exhibits or copies thereof not required to be filed by appellant. Five copies of a reply brief with proof of service of one copy may be filed at least twenty-four days before the first day of the term for which the appeal shall have been noticed.

(ii) The respondent may notice the appeal for argument by serving and filing a notice of argument at least sixty-eight days before the first day of the term for which respondent shall notice the appeal with proof of service. At least fifty-three days before the first day of the term, unless the court otherwise directs, appellant shall file five copies of appellant's brief with proof of service of one copy of the brief. Where appellant so files, respondent may serve and file an answering brief at least thirty-one days before the first day of the term. If appellant fails to serve and file the brief and fails to appear on the call of the calendar, the court may affirm the judgment or order appealed from or, in its discretion, dismiss the appeal with costs upon the call of the calendar. Five copies of the reply brief with proof of service of one copy may be filed twenty-four days before the first day of such term.

(iii) If neither party notices the appeal for argument within the time prescribed by this section, the appeal shall be dismissed unless for good cause shown an enlargement of time is granted by the court.

(b) Appeals From the Criminal Court.

(1) Appellant shall procure the original papers or abbreviated record to be filed within thirty days after service of the notice of appeal, and appellant shall then notice the appeal for argument or submission, within 120 days from the date of service of the notice of appeal, by filing the notice of argument and briefs, with proof of service of one copy of each paper filed at least fifty-three days before the first day of the appointed term; proof of service of one copy of a transcript of the minutes of the proceedings shall be filed with the notice of argument, such copy to be returned to the appellant upon the argument or submission of the appeal. Unless otherwise ordered, five copies of the respondent's brief with proof of service of one copy shall be filed not later than thirty-one days prior to the first day of the term and five copies of a reply brief with proof of service of one copy may be filed not later than twenty-four days prior to the first day of the appointed term. An appellant who is incarcerated under the judgment appealed from may bring the appeal on for argument or submission on ten days' notice, after the record is filed, by filing a notice of argument and five copies of the appellant's brief, with due proof of service of one copy, in which event five copies of the respondent's brief with proof of service of one copy shall be filed not later than seven days after the service of appellant's brief, and five copies of a reply brief with proof of service of one copy may be filed not later than two days after the service of respondent's brief.

(2) If appellant fails to notice the appeal within the time specified in the foregoing paragraph, the appeal will be dismissed on motion of the respondent unless an enlargement of time is granted by the court for good cause shown.

(3) Fifteen days before the first day of each term, the clerk shall cause a calendar to be published in the *New York Law Journal* of all cases in which a copy of the notice of appeal has been filed with him in accordance with the provisions of section 460.10 of the Criminal Procedure Law. If an appeal is not noticed for argument within 120 days from the date of service of the notice of appeal and no enlargement of time is obtained, such appeal may be dismissed by the court.

(4) The clerk shall prepare a special day calendar for each appointed term of the appeals subject to dismissal for failure on the part of the appellant to comply with this section. Each such special day calendar shall be published in the *New York Law Journal* at least five days prior to, as well as on the day when that calendar is to be called, and the clerk shall cause a postal card notice to be mailed to the appellant at his last known address and to his attorney five days prior to the first day of such publication.

Cross References

Criminal Procedure Law, see McKinney's Book 11A.

New York City Civil Court Act, see McKinney's Book 29A, Part 3.

§ 640.7. Calendar; Argument of Appeals

(a) Unless otherwise ordered, the calendar of appeals shall be called on the first day of the term for which they have been noticed. The calendar call shall commence at such time as the court shall direct.

(b) The clerk shall cause the calendar of appeals and the time the calendar will be called to be published in the *New York Law Journal* six days before the first day of each term.

(c) At any time prior to the call of the calendar the parties may file a stipulation submitting an appeal without oral argument provided, however, that all of the required papers have been served and filed. In the event of the filing of such stipulation, attendance at the calendar call shall not be required.

(d) Not more than 15 minutes shall be allowed to each side for argument except in such cases where additional time is granted by the court. No brief, communication or other paper shall be accepted after submission or argument of an appeal unless authorized by the court.

§ 640.8. Motions Generally

(a) Motions may be noticed for any day of the term and must be submitted without oral argument. The appropriate county clerk's index number must appear on all motion papers.

(b) If an appeal on the calendar is affected by the motion, the calendar number of the appeal must be stated on the moving papers.

(c) All moving and opposing papers, with proof of service, shall be filed with the clerk on or before the return day at 10 a.m. and submitted without oral argument.

§ 640.9. Reargument; Leave to Appeal to Appellate Division; Stay

(a) Reargument.

(1) Motions for reargument shall be made within thirty days after the date of the order determining the appeal.

(2) Papers in support of a motion for reargument shall concisely state the points claimed to have been overlooked or misapprehended by the court, with proper reference to the particular portion of the record, and the authorities relied upon.

(b) Leave to Appeal to the Appellate Division in Civil Matters.

(1) Applications for permission to appeal to the Appellate Division pursuant to CPLR 5703(a) shall be made in the manner and within the time prescribed by CPLR 5513(c) and 5516.

(2) The moving papers shall set forth the questions to be reviewed by the Appellate Division. If the appeal is to review a determination granting or affirming the granting of a new trial or hearing, the moving papers must also contain a stipulation by the appellant consenting to the entry of judgment absolute against the appellant in the event of an affirmance by the Appellate Division.

(c) **Stay.** If a stay is desired pending a determination of a motion for reargument or leave to appeal, application may be made for an order incorporating such stay.

Cross References

CPLR, see McKinney's Book 7B.

Forms

Notice of motion for permission to appeal to appellate division from order of appellate term, determining appeal from lower court, see West's McKinney's Forms, CPLR, § 9:122.

Affidavit in support of motion for permission to appeal to appellate division from order of appellate term determining appeal from lower court, see West's McKinney's Forms, CPLR, § 9:123.

Order of appellate term granting permission to appeal to appellate division, see West's McKinney's Forms, CPLR, § 9:124.

§ 640.10. Leave to Appeal to the Court

(a) Applications to a justice of the Appellate Term for leave to appeal pursuant to the provisions of section 1702(c) of the New York City Civil Court Act shall be made on notice and within the time prescribed by CPLR 5513(c).

(b) The papers in support of such application must contain a copy of the opinion, if any, and a copy of the record in the court below, a concise statement of the grounds of alleged error, and a copy of the order of the lower court denying leave, if any.

(c) Applications for a certificate granting leave to appeal pursuant to the provisions of sections 450.15 and 460.15 of the Criminal Procedure Law must be made in the following manner:

(1) the application must be addressed to the court for assignment to a justice of the Appellate Term;

(2) the application must be in writing and upon reasonable notice to the people;

(3) the application must be made within 30 days after service upon the defendant of a copy of the order from which he seeks to appeal; and

(4) the application must set forth the questions of law or fact to be reviewed, and must contain a statement as to whether or not any such application has previously been made.

Cross References

CPLR, see McKinney's Book 7B.

Criminal Procedure Law, see McKinney's Book 11A.

New York City Civil Court Act, see McKinney's Book 29A, Part 3.

SUPREME COURT,
NEW YORK AND BRONX COUNTIES

Including Amendments Received Through September 15, 2008

See, also, Part 200 (§ 200.1 et seq.), Uniform Rules for Courts Exercising Criminal Jurisdiction, and Part 202 (§ 202.1 et seq.), Uniform Civil Rules for the Supreme Court and County Court

---

Westlaw Electronic Research

These rules may be searched electronically on Westlaw® in the NY–RULES database; updates to these rules may be found on Westlaw in NY–RULESUP-DATES. For search tips and a summary of database content, consult the Westlaw Scope Screens for each database.

PART 660. CIVIL ACTIONS AND PROCEEDINGS [RESCINDED]

PART 661. CRIMINAL ACTIONS AND PROCEEDINGS

§§ 661.1 to 661.6. [Rescinded]

§ 661.7. Additional Duties of the Court and of Defendant's Counsel in Connection With Trial Court Transcripts

Where furnishing of a daily copy of a transcript is ordered by the court, the ribbon copy thereof shall be delivered to the court and a carbon copy to counsel for the defendant. Both the court and counsel for the defendant shall be duly bound to preserve their respective copies. At the conclusion of the trial or hearing, trial counsel for the defendant shall, if an appeal is taken, deliver said carbon copy to appellant's counsel immediately on being advised of the name and address of said appellant's counsel. At the conclusion of the trial or hearing and forthwith after the decision or verdict, as the case may be, the ribbon copy shall be delivered by the court to the county clerk for filing. The ribbon copy and the carbon copy shall constitute the two transcripts of the proceedings required by section 460.70 of the Criminal Procedure Law.

Cross References

Criminal Procedure Law, see McKinney's Book 11A.

§ 661.8. [Rescinded]

SUPREME COURT, APPELLATE DIVISION, SECOND DEPARTMENT

Including Amendments Received Through September 15, 2008

Westlaw Electronic Research

These rules may be searched electronically on Westlaw® *in the NY–RULES database; updates to these rules may be found on* Westlaw *in NY–RULESUP-DATES. For search tips and a summary of database content, consult the* Westlaw *Scope Screens for each database.*

Table of Sections

Parts 1100 to 1510 (§ 1100.1 et seq.) have been promulgated as joint rules of the Appellate Divisions and are set out following Appellate Division, Fourth Department, Part 1040, post.

PART 670. PROCEDURE IN THE APPELLATE DIVISION

§ 670.1. Court Sessions

(a) Unless otherwise ordered, the court will convene at 10 o'clock in the forenoon on Monday, Tuesday, Thursday, and Friday.

(b) Special sessions of the court may be held at such times and for such purposes as the court from time to time may direct.

(c) When a cause is argued or submitted with four Justices present, it shall, whenever necessary, be deemed submitted also to any other duly qualified Justice unless objection is noted at the time of argument or submission.

§ 670.2. General Provisions and Definitions

(a) Unless the context requires otherwise, as used in this part:

(1) The word cause includes an appeal, a special proceeding transferred to this court pursuant to CPLR 7804(g), a special proceeding initiated in this court, and an action submitted to this court pursuant to CPLR 3222 on a case containing the agreed statement of facts upon which the controversy depends.

(2) Any reference to the court means this court; any reference to a Justice means a Justice of this court; any reference to the clerk means the clerk of this court.

(3) Wherever reference is made to a judgment, order, or determination it shall also be deemed to include a sentence.

(4) The word perfection refers to the requirements for placing a cause on the court's calendar, e.g. the filing of a record and brief.

(5) The word consolidation refers to combining two or more causes arising out of the same action or proceeding in one record and one brief.

(6) The word concurrent, when used to describe appeals, is intended to refer to those appeals which have been taken separately from the same order or judgment by parties whose interests are not adverse to one another. The term cross appeal refers to an appeal taken by a party whose interests are adverse to a party who previously appealed from the same order or judgment.

(b) Unless the context requires otherwise, if a period of time prescribed by this Part for the performance of an act ends on a Saturday, Sunday, or holiday, the act will be deemed timely if performed before 5:00 P.M. on the next business day.

(c) If a period of time prescribed by this Part is measured from the service of a record, brief, or other paper and service is by mail, five days shall be added to the prescribed period. If service is by overnight delivery, one day shall be added to the prescribed period.

(d) All records on appeal, briefs, appendices, motions, affirmations, and other papers will be deemed filed in this court only as of the time they are actually received by the clerk and they shall be accompanied by proof of service upon all necessary parties pursuant to CPLR 2103.

(e) An appellate division docket number will be assigned to every cause. All papers and correspondence thereafter filed shall prominently display the docket number or numbers in the upper right hand corner of the first page opposite the title of the action or proceeding. In the event of concurrent and/or cross appeals from a judgment or order, all parties shall use the docket number first assigned to the appeal from that judgment or order.

(f) In any civil cause, and in any criminal cause where the defendant appears by retained counsel, the clerk will send to the party a copy of the decision on an appeal or a motion, if the party provides the clerk with a self-addressed, stamped envelope.

(g) If a cause or the underlying action or proceeding is wholly or partially settled or if any issues are wholly or partially rendered moot, or if any cause should not be calendared because of bankruptcy or death of a party, inability of counsel to appear, an order of rehabilitation, or for some other reason, the parties or their counsel shall immediately notify the court. Any attorney or party who, without good cause shown, fails to comply with the requirements of this subdivision shall be subject to the imposition of such costs and/or sanctions as the court may direct.

(h) Any attorney or party to a civil cause who, in the prosecution or defense thereof, engages in frivolous conduct as that term is defined in section 130–1.1(c) of this Title, shall be subject to the imposition of such costs and/or sanctions authorized by subpart 130–1 of this Title as the court may direct.

(i) The original of every paper submitted for filing in the office of the clerk of this court shall be signed in ink in accordance with the provisions of section 130–1.1–a(a) of this Title. Copies of the signed original shall be served upon all opposing parties and shall be filed in the office of the clerk whenever multiple copies of a paper are required to be served and filed by this Part.

(j) Pursuant to CPLR 5525(a), in all causes the petitioner or appellant may request that the court reporter or stenographer prepare only one copy of the transcript of the stenographic record of the proceedings. When the appendix method or original record method of prosecuting an appeal is being used, the copy prepared by the court reporter, or one of equal quality, shall be filed in the office of the clerk of the court in which the action or proceeding was commenced, prior to the issuance of a subpoena for the original papers as required by section 670.9(b)(1) or (d)(2) of this Part.

Cross References

CPLR, see McKinney's Book 7B.

§ 670.3. Filing of Notice of Appeal, Request for Appellate Division Intervention, Order of Transfer

(a) Where an appeal is taken in a civil action or proceeding, the notice of appeal, or the order of the court of original instance granting permission to appeal, shall be filed by the appellant in the office in which the judgment or order of the court of original instance is filed. Two additional copies of the notice of appeal or order granting permission to appeal shall be filed by the appellant, to each of which shall be affixed a completed Request for Appellate Division Intervention—Civil (Form A), a copy of the order or judgment appealed from, and a copy of the opinion or decision, if any. In the event that the notice of appeal covers two or more judgments or orders, the appellant shall also complete and affix to each Form A an Additional Appeal Information form (Form B) describing the additional judgments or orders appealed from, and affix copies of the judgments or orders and the opinions or decisions upon which they were based, if any. Thereupon, the clerk of the court of original instance shall endorse the filing date upon such instruments and transmit the two additional copies to the clerk of this court.

(b) Where an appeal is taken in a criminal action, the notice of appeal shall be filed by the appellant in duplicate in the office in which the judgment or order of the court of original instance is filed. Thereupon the clerk of the court of original instance shall endorse the filing date upon such instruments, shall execute a Request for Appellate Division Intervention—Criminal (Form D) and shall transmit it together with the duplicate notice of appeal to the clerk of this court.

(c) In any case in which an order is made transferring a proceeding to this court, the petitioner shall file forthwith in the office of the clerk of this court two copies of such order, to each of which shall be affixed a copy of a Request for Appellate Division Intervention—Civil (Form A) and a copy of any opinion or decision by the transferring court.

(d) A Request for Appellate Division Intervention—Attorney Matters (Form E) shall be filed in connection with attorney disciplinary proceedings instituted in this court and applications made to this court pursuant to sections 690.17 and 690.19 of the rules of this court.

(e) In all other actions or proceedings instituted in this court, and applications pursuant to CPLR 5704, a Request for Appellate Division Intervention—Civil (Form A) shall be filed.

§ 670.4. Management of Causes

(a) Active Management.

(1) The court may, in the exercise of discretion, direct that the prosecution of any cause or class of causes be actively managed.

(2) The clerk shall issue a scheduling order or orders directing the parties to a cause assigned to the active management program to take specified action to expedite the prosecution thereof, including but not limited to the ordering of the transcript of the proceedings and the filing of proof of payment therefor, the making of motions, the perfection of the cause, and the filing of briefs. Notwithstanding any of the time limitations set forth in this part, a scheduling order shall set forth the date or dates on or before which such specified action shall be taken.

(3) If any party shall establish good cause why there cannot be compliance with the provisions of a scheduling order, the clerk may amend the same consistent with the objective of insuring expedited prosecution of the cause. An application to amend a scheduling order shall be made by letter, addressed to the clerk, with a copy to the other parties to the cause. The determination of the clerk in amending or declining to amend a scheduling order shall be reviewable by motion to the court on notice pursuant to section 670.5 of this Part.

(4) No filing directed by a scheduling order shall be permitted after the time to do so has expired unless the order is amended in accordance with paragraph (3) of subdivision (a) of this section.

(5) Upon the default of any party in complying with the provisions of a scheduling order, the clerk shall issue an order to show cause, on seven days notice, why the cause should not be dismissed or such other sanction be imposed as the court may deem appropriate.

(b) Civil Appeals Management Program.

(1) The court, in those cases in which it deems it appropriate, will issue a notice directing the attorneys for the parties and/or the parties themselves to attend a pre-argument conference before a designated Justice of this court or such other person as it may designate, to consider the possibility of settlement, the limitation of the issues, and any other matters which the designated Justice or other person determines may aid in the disposition of the appeal or proceeding.

(2) Any attorney or party who, without good cause shown, fails to appear for a regularly scheduled pre-argument conference, or who fails to comply with the terms of a stipulation or order entered following a pre-argument conference, shall be subject to the imposition of such costs and/or sanctions as the court may direct.

§ 670.5. Motions and Proceedings Initiated in this Court—Generally

(a) Unless otherwise required by statute, rule, or order of the court or any Justice, every motion and every proceeding initiated in this court shall be made returnable at 9:30 A.M. on any Friday. Cross motions shall be made returnable on the same day as the original motion and shall be served and filed at least three days before the return date. Motions shall be on notice prescribed by CPLR 2214 and CPLR article 78 proceedings shall be on notice prescribed by CPLR 7804(c).

(b) All motions and proceedings initiated by notice of motion or notice of petition, shall be filed with the clerk at least one week before the return date. All papers in opposition shall be filed with the clerk before 4 P.M. of the business day preceding the return date. All papers in opposition to any motion or proceeding initiated in this court by an order to show cause shall be filed with the clerk on or before 9:30 A.M. of the return date, and shall be served by a method calculated to place the movant and other parties to the motion in receipt thereof on or before that time. The originals of all such papers shall be filed. On the return date the motion or proceeding will be deemed submitted to the court without oral argument. Counsel will not be required to attend and a note of issue need not be filed.

(c) Every notice, petition, or order to show cause instituting a motion or proceeding must state, inter alia:

(1) the nature of the motion or proceeding;

(2) the specific relief sought;

(3) the return date; and

(4) the names, addresses, and telephone numbers of the attorneys and counsel for all parties in support of and in opposition to the motion or proceeding.

(d) The papers in support of every motion or proceeding must contain a copy of:

(1) the order, judgment, or determination sought to be reviewed and the decision, if any; and

(2) the notice of appeal or other paper which first invoked the jurisdiction of this court.

(e) Except as hereinafter provided, when an order to show cause presented for signature makes provision for a temporary stay or other interim relief pending determination of the motion, or when an application is presented pursuant to CPLR 5704, the party seeking such relief must give reasonable notice to his or her adversary of the day and time when, and the location where, the order to show cause or CPLR 5704 application will be presented and the relief being requested. If notice has been given, the order to show cause or the application pursuant to CPLR 5704 must be accompanied by an affidavit or affirmation stating the time, place, by whom given, the manner of such notification, and to the extent known, the position taken by the opposing party. If notice has not been given, the affidavit or affirmation shall state whether the applicant has made an attempt to give notice and the reasons for the lack of success. If the applicant is unwilling to give notice, the affidavit or affirmation shall state the reasons for such unwillingness. An order to show cause providing for a temporary stay or other interim relief or an application pursuant to CPLR 5704 must be personally presented for signature by the party's attorney or by the party if such party is proceeding pro se.

(f) The clerk may reject papers or deem a motion or proceeding to be withdrawn or abandoned for the failure to comply with any of these rules.

Cross References

CPLR, see McKinney's Book 7B.

§ 670.6. Motions—Reargue; Resettle; Amend; Leave to Appeal; Admission Pro Hac Vice.

(a) Motions to Reargue, Resettle, or Amend. Motions to reargue a cause or motion, or to resettle or amend a decision and order, shall be made within 30 days after service of a copy of the decision and order determining the cause or motion, with notice of its entry, except that for good cause shown, the court may consider any such motion when made at a later date. The papers in support of every such motion shall concisely state the points claimed to have been overlooked or misapprehended by the court, with appropriate references to the particular portions of the record or briefs and with citation of the authorities relied upon. A copy of the order shall be attached.

(b) Motions for Leave to Appeal to Appellate Division.

(1) Motions for leave to appeal to the Appellate Division pursuant to CPLR 5701 (c) and Family Court Act § 1112 shall be addressed to the court and shall contain a copy of the order or judgment and the decision of the lower court.

(2) Motions for leave to appeal from an order of the Appellate Term shall contain a copy of the opinions, decisions, judgments, and orders of the lower courts, including: A copy of the Appellate Term order denying leave to appeal; a copy of the record in the Appellate Term if such record shall have been printed or otherwise reproduced; and a concise statement of the grounds of alleged error. If the application is to review an Appellate Term order which either granted a new trial or affirmed the trial court's order granting a new trial, the papers must also contain the applicant's stipulation consenting to the entry of judgment absolute against him in the event that this court should affirm the order appealed from.

(c) Motions for leave to appeal to the Court of Appeals shall set forth the questions of law to be reviewed by the Court of Appeals and, where appropriate, the proposed questions of law decisive of the correctness of this court's determination or of any separable portion within it. A copy of this court's order shall be attached.

(d) Motions for leave to appeal to the Court of Appeals pursuant to CPL 460.20 shall be made to any Justice who was a member of the panel which decided the matter. A copy of this court's order shall be attached.

(e) Motions for Admission Pro Hac Vice. An attorney and counselor-at-law or the equivalent may move for permission to appear pro hac vice with respect to a cause pending before this court pursuant to section 520.11(a)(1) of this Title. An affidavit in support of the motion shall state that the attorney and counselor-at-law is a member in good standing in all the jurisdictions in which he or she is admitted to practice and is associated with a member in good standing of the New York Bar, which member shall appear with him or her on the appeal or proceeding and shall be the person upon whom all papers in connection with the cause shall be served. Attached to the affidavit shall be a certificate of good standing from the bar of the state in which the attorney and counselor-at-law maintains his or her principal office for the practice of law.

Forms

Appeals. See West's McKinney's Forms, CPLR, § 9:1 et seq.

Appeals in criminal cases. See West's McKinney's Forms, Criminal Procedure, Articles 450, 460, and 470.

§ 670.7. Calendar; Preferences; Consolidation

(a) There shall be a general calendar for appeals. Appeals will be placed on the general calendar in the order perfected and, subject to the discretion of the court, will be heard in order.

(b) Preferences.

(1) Any party to an appeal entitled by law to a preference in the hearing of the appeal may serve and file a demand for a preference which shall set forth the provision of law relied upon for such preference and good cause for such preference. If the demand is sustained by the court, the appeal shall be preferred.

(2) A preference under CPLR 5521 may be obtained upon good cause shown by a motion directed to the court on notice to the other parties to the appeal.

(c) Consolidation.

(1) A party may consolidate appeals from civil orders and/or judgments arising out of the same action or proceeding provided that each appeal is perfected timely pursuant to section 670.8(e)(1) of this Part; and

(2) Appeals from orders or judgments in separate actions or proceedings cannot be consolidated but may, upon written request of a party, be scheduled by the court to be heard together on the same day.

Cross References

CPLR, see McKinney's Book 7B.

Forms

Order to show cause why a preference in hearing of appeal should not be granted, see West's McKinney's Forms, CPLR, § 9:244.

Affidavit in support of motion for preference in hearing of appeal, see West's McKinney's Forms, CPLR, § 9:245.

§ 670.8. Placing Civil or Criminal Causes on Calendar; Time Limits for Filing

(a) **Placing Cause on General Calendar.** An appeal may be placed on the general calendar by filing with the clerk the record on appeal pursuant to one of the methods set forth in section 670.9 of this Part and by filing nine copies of a brief, with proof of service of two copies upon each of the other parties. Unless the court shall otherwise direct, when an appeal is prosecuted upon the original record, only one copy of the brief need be served. An extra copy of the statement required by CPLR 5531 shall be filed together with the record or appendix. If an appeal is taken on the original record, the extra copy of the statement shall be filed with the appellant's brief.

(b) **Answering and Reply Briefs.** Not more than 30 days after service of the appellant's brief, each respondent or opposing party shall file nine copies of the answering brief with proof of service of two copies upon each of the other parties. Not more than 10 days after service of respondent's brief, the appellant may file nine copies of a reply brief with proof of service of two copies upon each of the other parties. If one copy of the appellant's brief was served, only one copy of answering and reply briefs need be served.

(c) **Concurrent and Cross Appeals.**

(1) Unless otherwise ordered by the court, all parties appealing from the same order or judgment shall consult and thereafter file a joint record or joint appendix which shall include copies of all notices of appeal. The cost of the joint record or the joint appendix, and the transcript, if any, shall be borne equally by the appealing parties.

(2) The joint record or joint appendix and the briefs of concurrent appellants shall be served and filed together. The time to do so in accordance with subdivision (e) of this rule shall be measured from the latest date on the several concurrent notices of appeal.

(3) The answering brief on a cross appeal shall be served and filed not more than 30 days after service of the appellant's brief or briefs and the joint record or joint appendix, and it shall include the points of argument on the cross appeal. An appellant's reply brief may be served and filed not more than 30 days after service of the answering brief. A cross appellant's reply brief may be served and filed not more than 10 days after service of the appellant's reply brief.

(d) **Enlargements of Time.** Except where a scheduling order has been issued pursuant to section 670.4(a)(2) of this Part or where the court has directed that a cause be perfected or that a brief be served and filed by a date certain, an enlargement of time to perfect or to serve and file a brief may be obtained as follows:

(1) *By Stipulation.* The parties may stipulate to enlarge the time to perfect a cause by up to 60 days, to file an answering brief by up to 30 days, and to file a reply brief by up to 10 days. Not more than one such stipulation per perfection or filing shall be per-

mitted. Such a stipulation shall not be effective unless so ordered by the clerk.

(2) *For Cause.* Where a party shall establish a reasonable ground why there cannot or could not be compliance with the time limits prescribed by this section, or such time limits as extended by stipulation pursuant to paragraph (1) of this subdivision, the clerk or a Justice may grant reasonable enlargements of time to comply. An application pursuant to this paragraph shall be made by letter, addressed to the clerk, with a copy to the other parties to the cause. Orders made pursuant to this paragraph shall be reviewable by motion to the court on notice pursuant to section 670. 5 of this Part.

(e) Notwithstanding any of the provisions of this Part, a civil appeal, action, or proceeding shall be deemed abandoned unless perfected

(1) within six months after the date of the notice of appeal, order granting leave to appeal, or order transferring the proceeding to this court, or,

(2) within six months of the filing of the submission with the county clerk in an action on submitted facts pursuant to CPLR 3222,

unless the time to perfect shall have been extended pursuant to subdivision (d) of this section. The clerk shall not accept any record or brief for filing after the expiration of such six-month period or such period as extended.

(f) Notwithstanding any of the provisions of this Part, an unperfected criminal appeal by a defendant shall be deemed abandoned in all cases where no application has been made by the defendant for the assignment of counsel to prosecute the appeal within nine months of the date of the notice of appeal, unless the time to perfect shall have been extended pursuant to subdivision (d) of this section.

(g) Notwithstanding any of the provisions of this Part, an appeal by the People pursuant to CPL 450.20(1), (1–a) or (8) shall be deemed abandoned unless perfected within three months after the date of the notice of appeal, unless the time to perfect shall have been extended pursuant to subdivision (d) of this section. All other appeals by the People shall be deemed abandoned unless perfected within six months after the date of the notice of appeal, unless the time to perfect shall have been extended pursuant to subdivision (d) of this section.

(h) The clerk shall periodically prepare a calendar of all civil causes which have been ordered to be perfected by a date certain and which have not been perfected and a calendar of all civil causes which have been assigned an appellate division docket number and have not been perfected within the time limitations set forth in subdivision (e) of this section. Such calendars shall be published in the New York Law Journal for five consecutive days. Upon the failure of the appellant to make an application to enlarge time to

perfect within 10 days following the last day of publication, an order shall be entered dismissing the cause.

Cross References

CPLR, see McKinney's Book 7B.

Forms

Statement pursuant to CPLR 5531, see West's McKinney's Forms, CPLR, § 9:226.

§ 670.9. Alternate Methods of Prosecuting Appeals

An appellant may elect to prosecute an appeal upon a reproduced full record (CPLR 5528[a][5]); by the appendix method (CPLR 5528[a][5]); upon an agreed statement in lieu of record (CPLR 5527); or, where authorized by statute or this Part or order of the court, upon a record consisting of the original papers.

(a) **Reproduced Full Record.** If the appellant elects to proceed on a reproduced full record on appeal as authorized by CPLR 5528(a)(5), the record shall be printed or otherwise reproduced as provided in section 670.10.1 and 670.10.2 of this Part. Nine copies of the record, one of which shall be marked "original", duly certified as provided in section 670.10.2(f), shall be filed with proof of service of two copies upon each of the other parties.

(b) **Appendix Method.**

(1) If the appellant elects to proceed by the appendix method, the appellant shall subpoena from the clerk of the court from which the appeal is taken all the papers constituting the record on appeal and cause them to be filed with the clerk of this court prior to the filing of the appendix.

(2) The clerk from whom the papers are subpoenaed shall compile the original papers constituting the record on appeal and transmit them to the clerk of this court, together with a certificate listing the papers constituting the record on appeal and stating whether all such papers are included in the papers transmitted.

(3) If a settled transcript of the stenographic minutes, or an approved statement in lieu of such transcript, or any relevant exhibit is not included in the papers so filed with the clerk of this court, the appellant shall cause such transcript, statement, or exhibit to be filed together with the brief.

(4) The appendix shall be printed or otherwise reproduced as provided in section 670.10.1 and 670.10.2 and may be bound with the brief or separately. Nine copies of the appendix, one of which shall be marked "original", duly certified as provided in section 670.10.2(f) shall be filed with proof of service of two copies upon each of the other parties.

(c) **Agreed Statement in Lieu of Record Method.** If the appellant elects to proceed by the agreed statement method in lieu of record (CPLR 5527), the statement shall be reproduced as provided in section

670.10.1 and 670.10.2 as a joint appendix. The statement required by CPLR 5531 shall be appended. Nine copies of the statement shall be filed with proof of service of two copies upon each of the other parties.

(d) Original Record.

(1) The following appeals may be prosecuted upon the original record, including a properly settled transcript of the trial or hearing, if any:

(i) appeals from the Appellate Term;

(ii) appeals from the Family Court;

(iii) appeals under the Election Law;

(iv) appeals under the Human Rights Law (Executive Law § 298);

(v) appeals where the sole issue is compensation of a judicial appointee;

(vi) other appeals where an original record is authorized by statute;

(vii) appeals where permission to proceed upon the original record has been authorized by order of this court;

(viii) appeals in criminal causes; and

(ix) appeals under Correction Law §§ 168–d(3) and 168–n(3).

(2) When an appeal is prosecuted upon the original record the appellant shall subpoena from the clerk of the court from which the appeal is taken all the papers constituting the record on appeal and cause them to be filed with the clerk of this court prior to the filing of the briefs.

Cross References

CPLR, see McKinney's Book 7B.

Election Law, see McKinney's Book 17.

Executive Law, see McKinney's Book 18.

Family Court Act, see McKinney's Book 29A, Part 1.

Forms

Appeals. See West's McKinney's Forms, CPLR, § 9:1 et seq.

Appeals in criminal cases. See West's McKinney's Forms, Criminal Procedure, Articles 450, 460, and 470.

§ 670.10. [Repealed]

§ 670.10.1. Form and Content of Records, Appendices, and Briefs—Generally

(a) Compliance with Civil Practice Law and Rules. Briefs, appendices and to the extent practicable, reproduced full records, shall comply with the requirements of CPLR 5528 and 5529 and reproduced full records shall, in addition, comply with the requirements of CPLR 5526.

(b) Method of Reproduction. Briefs, records, and appendices shall be reproduced by any method that produces a permanent, legible, black image on white paper. To the extent practicable, reproduction on both sides of the paper is encouraged.

(c) Paper Quality, Size, and Binding. Paper shall be of a quality approved by the chief administrator of the courts and shall be opaque, unglazed, white in color, and measure 11 inches along the bound edge by 8½ inches. Records, appendices, and briefs shall be bound on the left side in a manner that shall keep all the pages securely together; however, binding by use of any metal fastener or similar hard material that protrudes or presents a bulky surface or sharp edge is prohibited. Records and appendices shall be divided into volumes not to exceed two inches in thickness.

(d) Designation of Parties. The parties to all appeals shall be designated in the record and briefs by adding the word "Appellant," "Respondent," etc., as the case may be, following the party's name, e.g., "Plaintiff–Respondent," "Defendant–Appellant," "Petitioner–Appellant," "Respondent–Respondent," etc. Parties who have not appealed and against whom the appeal has not been taken, shall be listed separately and designated as they were in the trial court, e.g., "Plaintiff," "Defendant," "Petitioner," "Respondent." In appeals from the Surrogate's Court or from judgments on trust accountings, the caption shall contain the title used in the trial court including the name of the decedent or grantor, followed by a listing of all parties to the appeal, properly designated. In proceedings and actions originating in this court, the parties shall be designated "Petitioner" and "Respondent" or "Plaintiff" and "Defendant."

(e) Docket Number. The cover of all records, briefs, and appendices shall display the appellate division docket number assigned to the cause in the upper right-hand portion opposite the title.

(f) Rejection of Papers. The clerk may refuse to accept for filing any paper that does not comply with these rules, is not legible, or is otherwise unsuitable.

§ 670.10.2. Form and Content of Records and Appendices

(a) Format. Records and appendices shall contain accurate reproductions of the papers submitted to the court of original instance, formatted in accordance with the practice in that court, except as otherwise provided in subdivision (d) of this section. Reproductions may be slightly reduced in size to fit the page and to accommodate the page headings required by CPLR 5529(c), provided, however, that such reduction does not significantly impair readability.

(b) Reproduced Full Record. The reproduced full record shall be bound separately from the brief, shall contain the items set forth in CPLR 5526, and shall contain in the following order so much of the following items as shall be applicable to the particular cause:

(1) A cover which shall contain the title of the action or proceeding on the upper portion and, on the

lower portion, the names, addresses, and telephone numbers of the attorneys, the county clerk's index or file number, and the indictment number;

(2) The statement required by CPLR 5531;

(3) A table of contents which shall list and briefly describe each paper included in the record. The part of the table relating to the transcript of testimony shall separately list each witness and the page at which direct, cross, redirect and recross examinations begin. The part of the table relating to exhibits shall concisely indicate the nature or contents of each exhibit and the page in the record where it is reproduced and where it is admitted into evidence. The table shall also contain references to pages where a motion to dismiss the complaint or to direct or set aside a verdict or where an oral decision of the court appears;

(4) The notice of appeal or order of transfer, judgment or order appealed from, judgment roll, corrected transcript or statement in lieu thereof, relevant exhibits and any opinion or decision in the cause;

(5) An affirmation, stipulation or order, settling the transcript pursuant to CPLR 5525;

(6) A stipulation or order dispensing with reproducing exhibits.

(i) Exhibits which are relevant to a cause may be omitted upon a stipulation of the parties which shall contain a list of the exhibits omitted and a brief description of each exhibit or, if a party unreasonably refuses to so stipulate, upon motion directed to the court. Exhibits thus omitted, unless of a bulky or dangerous nature, shall be filed with the clerk at the same time that the appellant's brief is filed. Exhibits of a bulky or dangerous nature (cartons, file drawers, ledgers, machinery, narcotics, weapons, etc.) thus omitted need not be filed but shall be kept in readiness and delivered to the court on telephone notice. A letter, indicating that a copy has been sent to the adversary, listing such exhibits and stating that they will be available on telephone notice, shall be filed with the clerk at the same time that the appellant's brief is filed.

(ii) Exhibits which are not relevant to a cause may be omitted upon stipulation of the parties which shall contain a list of the exhibits omitted, a brief description of each exhibit, and a statement that the exhibits will not be relied upon or cited in the briefs of the parties. If a party unreasonably refuses to so stipulate, a motion to omit the exhibits may be directed to the court. Such exhibits need not be filed; and

(7) The appropriate certification or stipulation pursuant to subdivision (f) of this section.

(c) Appendix.

(1) The appendix shall contain those portions of the record necessary to permit the court to fully consider the issues which will be raised by the appellant and the respondent including, where applicable, at least the following:

(i) notice of appeal or order of transfer;

(ii) judgment, decree, or order appealed from;

(iii) decision and opinion of the court or agency, and report of a referee, if any;

(iv) pleadings, if their sufficiency, content or form is in issue or material; in a criminal case, the indictment, or superior court information;

(v) material excerpts from transcripts of testimony or from papers in connection with a motion. Such excerpts must contain all the testimony or averments upon which the appellant relies and upon which it may be reasonably assumed the respondent will rely. Such excerpts must not be misleading or unintelligible by reason of incompleteness or lack of surrounding context;

(vi) copies of critical exhibits, including photographs, to the extent practicable; and

(vii) The appropriate certification or stipulation pursuant to subdivision (f) of this section.

(2) If bound separately from the brief, the appendix shall have a cover complying with subdivision (b)(1) of this section and shall contain the statement required by CPLR 5531 and a table of contents.

(d) Condensed Format of Transcripts Prohibited. No record or appendix may contain a transcript of testimony given at a trial, hearing, or deposition that is reproduced in condensed format such that two or more pages of transcript in standard format appear on one page.

(e) Settlement of Transcript or Statement. Regardless of the method used to prosecute any civil cause, if the record contains a transcript of the stenographic minutes of the proceedings or a statement in lieu of such transcript, such transcript or statement must first be either stipulated as correct by the parties or their attorneys or settled pursuant to CPLR 5525.

(f) Certification of Record. A reproduced full record or appendix shall be certified either by: (1) a certificate of the appellant's attorney pursuant to CPLR 2105; (2) a certificate of the proper clerk; or (3) a stipulation in lieu of certification pursuant to CPLR 5532. The reproduced copy containing the signed certification or stipulation shall be marked "Original."

§ 670.10.3. Form and Content of Briefs

(a) Computer–generated briefs. Briefs prepared on a computer shall be printed in either a serifed, proportionally spaced typeface such as Times Roman, or a serifed, monospaced typeface such as Courier. Narrow or condensed typefaces and/or condensed font spacing may not be used. Except in headings, words may not be in bold type or type consisting of all capital letters.

(1) *Briefs set in a proportionally spaced typeface.* The body of a brief utilizing a proportionally spaced typeface shall be printed in 14–point type, but footnotes may be printed in type of no less than 12 points.

(2) *Briefs set in a monospaced typeface.* The body of a brief utilizing a monospaced typeface shall be printed in 12–point type containing no more than 10½ characters per inch, but footnotes may be printed in type of no less than 10 points.

(3) *Length.* Computer–generated appellants' and respondents' briefs shall not exceed 14,000 words, and reply and amicus curiae briefs shall not exceed 7,000 words, inclusive of point headings and footnotes and exclusive of pages containing the table of contents, table of citations, proof of service, certificate of compliance, or any authorized addendum containing statutes, rules, regulations, etc.

(b) Typewritten briefs. Typewritten briefs shall be neatly prepared in clear type of no less than elite in size and in a pitch of no more than 12 characters per inch. The ribbon typescript of the brief shall be signed and filed as one of the number of copies required by section 670.8 of this Part. Typewritten appellants' and respondents' briefs shall not exceed 70 pages and reply briefs and amicus curiae briefs shall not exceed 35 pages, exclusive of pages containing the table of contents, table of citations, proof of service, certificate of compliance, or any authorized addendum containing statutes, rules, regulations, etc.

(c) Margins, line spacing, and page numbering of computer-generated and typewritten briefs. Computer–generated and typewritten briefs shall have margins of one inch on all sides of the page. Text shall be double-spaced, but quotations more than two lines long may be indented and single-spaced. Headings and footnotes may be single-spaced. Pages shall be numbered consecutively in the center of the bottom margin of each page.

(d) Handwritten briefs. Pro se litigants may serve and file handwritten briefs. Such briefs shall be neatly prepared in cursive script or hand printing in black ink. Pages shall be numbered consecutively in the center of the bottom margin of each page. The submission of handwritten briefs is not encouraged. If illegible or unreasonably long, handwritten briefs may be rejected for filing by the clerk.

(e) Application for permission to file oversized brief. An application for permission to file an oversized brief shall be made to the clerk by letter stating the number of words or pages by which the brief exceeds the limits set forth in this section and the reasons why submission of an oversize brief is necessary. The letter shall be accompanied by a copy of the proposed brief, including a certificate if required by subdivision (f) hereof to the effect that the brief is in all other respects compliant with this section. The determination of the clerk may be reviewed by motion to the court on notice in accordance with section 670.5 of this Part.

(f) Certification of compliance. Every brief, except those that are handwritten, shall have at the end thereof a certificate of compliance with this rule, stating that the brief was prepared either on a typewriter, a computer, or by some other specified means. If the brief was typewritten, the certificate shall further specify the size and pitch of the type and the line spacing used. If the brief was prepared on a computer, the certificate shall further specify the name of the typeface, point size, line spacing, and word count. A party preparing the certificate may rely on the word count of the processing system used to prepare the brief. The signing of the brief in accordance with section 130–1.1–a(a) of this Title shall also be deemed the signer's representation of the accuracy of the certificate of compliance.

(g) Content of Briefs.

(1) *Cover.* The cover shall set forth the title of the action or proceeding. The upper right hand section shall contain a notation stating; whether the cause is to be argued or submitted; if it is to be argued, the time actually required for the argument; and the name of the attorney who will argue (see § 670.20). The lower right hand section shall contain the name, address, and telephone number of the attorney filing the brief and shall indicate whom the attorney represents.

(2) *Appellant's Brief.* The appellant's brief shall contain, in the following order:

(i) the statement required by CPLR 5531;

(ii) a table of contents including the titles of the points urged in the brief;

(iii) a concise statement of the questions involved without names, dates, amounts, or particulars. Each question shall be numbered, set forth separately, and followed immediately by the answer, if any, of the court from which the appeal is taken;

(iv) a concise statement of the nature of the action or proceeding and of the facts which should be known to determine the questions involved, with supporting references to pages in the record or the appendix, including, if such be the case, a statement that proceedings on the judgment or order appealed from have been stayed pending a determination of the appeal;

(v) the appellant's argument, which shall be divided into points by appropriate headings distinctively printed;

(vi) if a civil cause is perfected on the original papers, the brief shall include either a copy of the order or judgment appealed from, the decision, if any, and the notice of appeal, or a copy of any order transferring the proceeding to this court;

(vii) if the appeal is from an order involving
pendente lite relief in a matrimonial action, the brief
shall state whether issue has been joined and, if so,
the date of joinder of issue, and whether the case
has been noticed for trial;

(viii) in criminal causes, the appellant's brief at
the beginning shall also set forth

(A) whether an order issued pursuant to CPL
460.50 is outstanding, the date of such order, the
name of the judge who issued it and whether the
defendant is free on bail or on his or her own
recognizance, and

(B) whether there were co-defendants in the
trial court, the disposition with respect to such co-
defendants, and the status of any appeals by such
co-defendants; and

(ix) a certificate of compliance, if required by
subdivision (f) of this section.

(3) *Respondent's Brief.* The respondent's brief
shall contain, in the following order;

(i) a table of contents including the titles of points
urged in the brief;

(ii) a counterstatement of the questions involved
or of the nature and facts of the action or proceeding, if the respondent disagrees with the statement
of the appellant;

(iii) the argument for the respondent, which shall
be divided into points by appropriate headings distinctively printed; and

(iv) a certificate of compliance, if required by
subdivision (f) of this section.

(4) *Appellant's Reply Brief.* The appellant's reply
brief, unless otherwise ordered by the court, shall not
contain an appendix, but shall contain, in the following
order:

(i) a table of contents;

(ii) the reply for the appellant to the points raised
by the respondent, without repetition of the arguments contained in the main brief, which shall be
divided into points by appropriate headings distinctively printed; and

(iii) a certificate of compliance, if required by
subdivision (f) of this section.

(h) Addenda to Briefs.

(1) Briefs may contain an addendum composed of
decisions, statutes, ordinances, rules, regulations, local
laws, or other similar matter, cited therein that were
not published or that are not otherwise readily available.

(2) Unless otherwise authorized by order of the
court, briefs may not contain maps, photographs, or
other addenda.

(i) Constitutionality of State Statute. Where the
constitutionality of a statute of the State is involved in

an appeal in which the State is not a party, the party
raising the issue shall serve a copy of the brief upon
the Attorney General of the State of New York who
will be permitted to intervene in the appeal.

§ 670.11.　Amicus Curiae Briefs

(a) Permission to file an amicus curiae brief shall
be obtained by persons who are not parties to the
action or proceeding by motion on notice to each of
the parties.

(b) Unless otherwise ordered by the court, oral
argument is not permitted.

§ 670.12.　Appeals in Criminal Actions

(a) Except as otherwise provided herein, an appeal
in a criminal action shall be prosecuted in the same
manner as a civil appeal.

**(b) Application for Certificate Granting Leave to
Appeal.**

(1) An application pursuant to CPL 450.15 and CPL
460.15 for leave to appeal to this court from an order
shall be made in writing within 30 days after service
of the order upon the applicant, on 15 days notice to
the district attorney, or other prosecutor, as the case
may be.

(2) The application shall be addressed to the court
for assignment to a Justice and shall include:

(i) the name and address of the applicant and the
name and address of the district attorney or other
prosecutor, as the case may be;

(ii) the indictment, or superior court information
number;

(iii) the questions of law or fact which it is
claimed ought to be reviewed;

(iv) any other information, data, or matter which
the applicant may deem pertinent in support of the
application;

(v) a statement that no prior application for such
certificate has been made; and

(vi) a copy of the order sought to be reviewed
and a copy of the decision of the court of original
instance or a statement that there was no decision.

(3) Within 15 days after service of a copy of the
application the district attorney or other prosecutor
shall file answering papers or a statement that there
is no opposition to the application. Such answering
papers shall include a discussion of the merits of the
application or shall state, if such be the case, that the
application does not contain any allegations other than
those alleged in the papers submitted by the applicant
in the trial court and that the prosecutor relies on the
record; the answering papers in the trial court; and
the decision of such court, if any.

(4) Unless the Justice designated to determine the
application shall otherwise direct, the matter shall be

submitted and determined upon the foregoing papers and without oral argument.

(c) Appeal From Sentence. Where the only issue to be raised on appeal concerns the legality, propriety, or excessiveness of sentence, the appeal may be prosecuted by submitting a concise statement setting forth the reasons urged in support of the reversal or modification of sentence. Such statement shall contain the information required by CPLR 5531 and by section 670.10.3(g)(2)(viii) of this Part and shall contain a statement by counsel for the appellant that no other issues are asserted.

(1) Such appeals may be brought on as though they were motions made in accordance with the provisions of section 670.5 of this Part and shall be placed upon a special calendar for appeals submitted in accordance with this subdivision. The respondent shall serve and file papers in opposition within 14 days after service of the motion papers.

(2) The appellant shall submit the transcripts of sentence and the transcripts of the underlying plea or trial. The parties shall file an original and four copies of their respective papers, including the necessary transcripts.

(d) When an appeal in a criminal action is prosecuted on the original record or by the appendix method, the appellant shall serve a copy of the transcript of the proceedings upon the respondent together with the brief and appendix.

(e) Appeals by the People pursuant to CPL 450.20(1–a) shall be granted a preference upon the request of either the appellant or the respondent. The appellant's brief shall include an appendix containing a copy of the indictment, the order appealed from and the decision. The respondent's brief may also include an appendix, if necessary. The appellant shall file, separate from the record, one copy of the grand jury minutes (see Rules of the Chief Administrator of the Courts, Part 105).

(f) Appeals to the Court of Appeals. Service of a copy of an order on an appellant as required by CPL 460.10(5)(a) shall be made pursuant to CPLR 2103.

(g) In the event the defendant is represented by counsel the following shall be filed together with the brief filed on behalf of the defendant:

(1) Proof of mailing of a copy of the brief to the defendant at his or her last known address; and

(2) Where a brief pursuant to *Anders v California* (386 US 738) has been filed, a copy of a letter to the defendant advising that he or she may file a pro se supplemental brief and, if he or she wishes to file such a brief, that he or she must notify this court no later than 30 days after the date of mailing of counsel's letter of the intention to do so.

(h) A defendant represented by counsel who has not submitted a brief pursuant to *Anders v California*

(386 US 738) who wishes to file a *pro se* supplemental brief, must make an application for permission to do so not later than 30 days after the date of mailing to the defendant of a copy of the brief prepared by counsel. The affidavit in support of the motion shall briefly set forth the points that the appellant intends to raise in the supplemental brief.

Cross References

CPL, see McKinney's Book 11A.

Forms

Appeals in criminal cases. See West's McKinney's Forms, Criminal Procedure, articles 450, 460, and 470.

§ 670.13. Appeals From the Appellate Term

(a) Appeals from the Appellate Term of the Supreme Court to this court may be prosecuted upon the record as presented to the Appellate Term; its order; its opinion or decision; and the order granting leave to appeal.

(b) When this court has made an order granting leave to appeal, the appellant shall file with the clerk of the Appellate Term a copy of the order. Within 20 days after an order granting leave to appeal shall have been filed with the clerk of the Appellate Term, such clerk or the appellant shall cause the record to be filed with the clerk of this court. Thereafter the appeal may be brought on for argument by the filing of briefs in the same manner as any other cause.

Cross References

CPLR, see McKinney's Book 7B.

§ 670.14. Appeals From Orders Concerning Grand Jury Reports

The mode, time, and manner for perfecting an appeal from an order accepting a report of a grand jury pursuant to CPL 190.85(1)(a) or from an order sealing a report of a grand jury pursuant to CPL 190.85(5) shall be in accordance with the provisions of this Part governing appeals in criminal cases. Appeals from such orders shall be preferred causes and may be added to the calendar by stipulation approved by the court or upon motion directed to the court. The record, briefs, and other papers on such an appeal shall be sealed and not available for public inspection except as permitted by CPL 190.85(3).

Cross References

CPL, see McKinney's Book 11A.

Forms

Appeals in criminal cases. West's McKinney's Forms, Criminal Procedure, Articles 450, 460, and 470.

§ 670.15. Appeals Where the Sole Issue Is Compensation of a Judicial Appointee

If the sole issue sought to be reviewed on appeal is the amount of compensation awarded to a judicial appointee (i.e., referee, arbitrator, guardian, guardian ad litem, conservator, committee of the person or a committee of the property of an incompetent or patient, receiver, person designated to perform services for a receiver, such as but not limited to an agent, accountant, attorney, auctioneer, appraiser, or person designated to accept service), the appeal may be prosecuted in accordance with any of the methods specified in section 670.9 of this Part; or the appeal may be prosecuted by motion in accordance with the procedure applicable to special proceedings as set forth in section 670.5 of this Part. In such event, the review may be had on the original record and briefs may be filed at the option of any party.

§ 670.16. Transferred CPLR Article 78 Proceedings

CPLR article 78 proceedings transferred to this court pursuant to CPLR 7804(g) may be prosecuted in accordance with any of the methods specified in section 670.9 of this Part. Where applicable, every such proceeding shall be governed by this Part as if it were an appeal.

§ 670.17. Transferred Proceedings Under the Human Rights Law (Executive Law § 298)

(a) A proceeding under the Human Rights Law which is transferred to this court for disposition shall be prosecuted upon the original record which shall contain:

(1) copies of all papers filed in the Supreme Court;

(2) the decision of the Supreme Court, or a statement that no decision was rendered;

(3) the order of transfer; and

(4) the original record before the State Division of Human Rights, including a copy of the transcript of the public hearing.

(b) In all other respects every proceeding so transferred shall be governed by this Part as if it were an appeal.

(c) In the event that the original record which was before the State Division of Human Rights was not previously submitted to the Supreme Court, the Division shall file the original record with this court within 45 days after entry of, or service upon it of, a copy of the order of transfer.

Cross References

CPLR, see McKinney's Book 7B.

Executive Law, see McKinney's Book 18.

§ 670.18. Special Proceedings Pursuant to Eminent Domain Procedure Law § 207; Public Service Law §§ 128, 170; Labor Law § 220; Public Officers Law § 36; or Real Property Tax Law § 1218

(a) Special proceedings initiated in this court pursuant to Eminent Domain Procedure Law § 207, Public Service Law §§ 128 or 170, Labor Law § 220, Public Officers Law § 36, or Real Property Tax Law § 1218 shall be commenced by the filing of a petition in the office of the clerk of this court pursuant to CPLR 304. Service of the petition with a notice of petition or order to show cause shall be made in accordance with CPLR 306–b on at least 20 days notice to the respondent. In proceedings pursuant to sections 207, 128, or 170 such notice shall be accompanied by a demand upon the respondent to file a copy of the transcript of the hearing before it and a copy of its determinations and findings.

(b) The respondent shall file an answer to the petition and, in proceedings pursuant to sections 207, 128, or 170, the transcript of the hearing and the determination and findings.

(c) Within three months after service of the answer, the petitioner shall file nine copies of a brief, with proof of service of one copy upon the respondent. Not more than 30 days after service of petitioner's brief, the respondent shall file nine copies of an answering brief, with proof of service of one copy upon the petitioner. Not more than 10 days after service of the respondent's brief the petitioner may file a reply brief.

(d) The proceeding will be heard upon the original record which shall contain:

(1) the notice of petition and petition;

(2) if applicable, the demand for the transcript, determination, and findings;

(3) the original record before the respondent including a copy of the transcript of the hearing, if any; and

(4) the determination and findings of the respondent.

(e) In all other respects such a proceeding shall be governed by this Part as if it were an appeal.

Cross References

CPLR, see McKinney's Book 7B.

Eminent Domain Procedure Law, see McKinney's Book 16A.

Labor Law, see McKinney's Book 30.

Public Service Law, see McKinney's Book 47.

§ 670.19. Action on Submitted Facts

(a) An action submitted to this court pursuant to CPLR 3222 shall be prosecuted on a printed submission which shall be bound separately from the brief and shall contain in the following order:

(1) a cover complying with subdivision (b)(1) of section 670.10.2 of this Part;

(2) the statement required by CPLR 5531;

(3) the case required by CPLR 3222(a), duly executed and acknowledged by all the parties in the form required to entitle a deed to be recorded, containing:

(i) the agreed statement of facts upon which the controversy depends;

(ii) a statement that the controversy is real and is made in good faith for the purpose of determining the rights of the parties;

(iii) a provision designating the particular county clerk of one of the counties within the Second Judicial Department with whom the papers are to be filed; and,

(iv) a provision in conformity with CPLR 3222(b)(3) stipulating that the action be heard and determined by this court; and,

(4) proof of filing of the papers comprising the submission with the designated county clerk.

(b) Where applicable, every such action shall be governed by this Part as if it were an appeal. The submission and the briefs of the respective parties shall be served and filed in accordance with section 670.8 of this Part and the form of the briefs shall be governed by section 670.10.3 of this Part.

§ 670.20. Oral Argument

(a) Not more than 30 minutes shall be allowed for argument to each attorney who has filed a brief on:

(1) appeals from judgments, orders, or decrees made after a trial or hearing;

(2) appeals from orders of the Appellate Term; and

(3) special proceedings transferred to or instituted in this court to review administrative determinations made after a hearing.

(b) Not more than 15 minutes shall be allowed for argument to each attorney who has filed a brief on all other causes except as set forth in subdivision (c).

(c) Argument is not permitted on issues involving maintenance; spousal support; child support; counsel fees; the legality, propriety or excessiveness of sentences; determinations made pursuant to the sex offender registration act; grand jury reports; and calendar and practice matters including but not limited to preferences, bills of particulars, correction of pleadings, examinations before trial, physical examinations, discovery of records, interrogatories, change of venue, and transfers of actions to and from the Supreme Court. Applications for permission to argue such issues shall be made at the call of the calendar on the day the cause appears on the calendar. Notice of intention to make such an application shall be given to the court and the other parties at least seven days before the cause appears on the calendar.

(d) The court, in its discretion, may deny oral argument of any cause.

(e) Where the total time requested for argument by the attorneys on each side exceeds 30 minutes on appeals under subdivision (a) of this section or 15 minutes on appeals under subdivision (b) of this section, the court may, in its discretion, reduce the argument time requested. Not more than one attorney will be heard for each brief unless, upon application made before the beginning of the argument, the court shall have granted permission to allow more than one attorney to argue. A party who has not filed a brief may not argue.

(f) In the event that any party's main brief shall fail to set forth the appropriate notations indicating that the cause is to be argued and the time required for argument (see 670.10.3[g][1]) the cause will be deemed to have been submitted without oral argument by that party.

(g) If any party shall have filed the main brief late and such late brief be accepted, the court or any Justice may deem that the party has waived oral argument and has submitted the cause without argument.

(h) A party who originally elected to argue may notify the clerk of the intention to submit the cause without argument and need not appear on the calendar call.

(i) No briefs, letters, or other communications in connection with a cause will be accepted after the argument or submission of a cause unless permission is granted by the court.

Cross References

CPLR, see McKinney's Book 7B.

Forms

Notice of time requested for argument or intention to submit appeal without argument, see West's McKinney's Forms, CPLR, § 9:246.

§ 670.21. Decisions and Orders; Costs

(a) An order or judgment of this court determining a cause or an order of this court determining a motion shall be drafted by the court and shall be entered in the office of the clerk of this court. Such an order or judgment shall be deemed entered on the date upon which it was issued.

(b) Costs and disbursements upon any cause or motion shall be allowed only as directed by the court. In the absence of a contrary direction, the award by this court of costs upon any cause shall be deemed to include disbursements.

§ 670.22. Fees of the Clerk of the Court

(a) Pursuant to CPLR 8022, the clerk is directed to charge and is entitled to receive on behalf of the State:

(1) A fee of $315, payable upon the filing of a record on a civil appeal or statement in lieu of record on a civil appeal and upon the filing of a notice of petition

or order to show cause commencing a special proceeding.

(2) A fee of $45, payable upon the filing of each motion or cross motion with respect to a civil appeal or special proceeding, except that no fee shall be imposed for a motion or cross motion which seeks leave to appeal as a poor person pursuant to CPLR 1101(a).

(b) Pursuant to Judiciary Law § 265, the clerk is directed to charge and is entitled to receive in advance the following fees on behalf of the State:

(1) For making a photocopy of an order, decision, opinion, or other filed paper or record, $1 for the first page and 50 cents for each additional page.

(2) For comparing the copy of a prepared order, decision, opinion, or other paper or record with the original on file, $1 for the first page and 50 cents for each additional page, with a minimum fee of $2.

(3) For certifying the copy of an order, decision, record, or other paper on file or for affixing the seal of the court, $1; and for authenticating the same, an additional $5.

(4) For certifying in any form that a search of any records in his custody has been made and giving the result of such search, $1.

(5) For an engraved parchment diploma attesting to admission as an attorney and counselor at law, $25.

(6) For a printed certificate attesting to admission or to good standing as an attorney and counselor at law, $5.

(c) The clerk shall not, however, charge or receive any fees set forth in subdivision (b) of this section from the following parties who shall be exempt from the payment of such fees in this court.

(1) The United States or any state, city or county, or any political subdivision or agency or department of any of them;

(2) any judge, court, official character committee or board of examiners, or any recognized agency serving the court or such committee or board;

(3) any duly recognized bar association;

(4) any party specifically exempted by law from the payment of fees; and

(5) any party to the cause for furnishing a copy of an opinion or order.

Cross References

CPLR, see McKinney's Book 7B.

Judiciary Law, see McKinney's Book 29.

§ 670.23. Court's Waiver of Compliance

In any civil or criminal cause, the court, either upon its own or upon any party's motion and either with or without notice to the adverse parties, may waive compliance by any party with any provision of this Part or may vary the application of any such provision.

§ 670.24. Forms

Supreme Court of the State of New York
Appellate Division: Second Judicial Department
Form A—Request for Appellate Division Intervention—Civil

See § 670.3 of the rules of this court for directions on the use of this form
(22 NYCRR 670.3).

Case Title: Set forth the title of the case as it appears on the summons, notice of petition or order to show cause by which the matter was or is to be commenced, or as amended.

For Court of Original Instance

Date Notice of Appeal Filed

For Appellate Division

Case Type		Filing Type	
☐ Civil Action	☐ CPLR article 78 Proceeding		☐ Transferred Proceeding
☐ CPLR article 75 Arbitration	☐ Special Proceeding Other	☐ Appeal	☐ CPLR 5704 Review
	☐ Habeas Corpus Proceeding	☐ Original Proceed-ing	

Nature of Suit: Check up to five of the following categories which best reflect the nature of the case.

A. Administrative Review	D. Domestic Relations	F. Prisoners	I. Torts
☐ 1 Freedom of Information Law	☐ 1 Adoption	☐ 1 Discipline	☐ 1 Assault, Battery, False Imprisonment
☐ 2 Human Rights	☐ 2 Attorney's Fees	☐ 2 Jail Time Calculation	
☐ 3 Licenses	☐ 3 Children— Support	☐ 3 Parole	☐ 2 Conversion
☐ 4 Public Employment	☐ 4 Children— Custody/ Visitation	☐ 4 Other	☐ 3 Defamation
☐ 5 Social Services		**G. Real Property**	☐ 4 Fraud
☐ 6 Other	☐ 5 Children— Terminate Parental Rights	☐ 1 Condemnation	☐ 5 Intentional Infliction of Emo-tional Distress
B. Business & Other Relationships		☐ 2 Determine Title	
	☐ 6 Children— Abuse/Neglect	☐ 3 Easements	☐ 6 Interference with Contract
☐ 1 Partnership/ Joint Venture	☐ 7 Children— JD/PINS	☐ 4 Environmental	
☐ 2 Business	☐ 8 Equitable Distribution	☐ 5 Liens	☐ 7 Malicious Prosecution/ Abuse of Process
☐ 3 Religious		☐ 6 Mortgages	
☐ 4 Not-for-Profit	☐ 9 Exclusive Occupancy of Residence	☐ 7 Partition	☐ 8 Malpractice
☐ 5 Other		☐ 8 Rent	☐ 9 Negligence
C. Contracts		☐ 9 Taxation	☐ 10 Nuisance
☐ 1 Brokerage	☐ 10 Expert's Fees	☐ 10 Zoning	☐ 11 Products Liability
☐ 2 Commercial Paper	☐ 11 Maintenance/ Alimony	☐ 11 Other	☐ 12 Strict Liability
☐ 3 Construction	☐ 12 Marital Status	**H. Statutory**	☐ 13 Trespass and/or Waste
☐ 4 Employment	☐ 13 Paternity	☐ 1 City of Mount Vernon Charter §§ 120, 127–f, or 129	☐ 14 Other
☐ 5 Insurance	☐ 14 Spousal Support		**J. Wills & Estates**
☐ 6 Real Property	☐ 15 Other	☐ 2 Eminent Domain Procedure Law § 207	☐ 1 Accounting
☐ 7 Sales	**E. Miscellaneous**		☐ 2 Discovery
☐ 8 Secured	☐ 1 Constructive Trust	☐ 3 General Municipal Law § 712	☐ 3 Probate/ Administration
☐ 9 Other	☐ 2 Debtor & Creditor	☐ 4 Labor Law § 220	☐ 4 Trusts
	☐ 3 Declaratory Judgment	☐ 5 Public Service Law §§ 128 or 170	☐ 5 Other
	☐ 4 Election Law		
	☐ 5 Notice of Claim	☐ 6 Other	
	☐ 6 Other		

Form A–RADI–Civil

Appeal
Paper Appealed From (check one only): ☐ Amended Decree ☐ Determination ☐ Order ☐ Resettled Order ☐ Amended Judgment ☐ Finding ☐ Order & Judgment ☐ Ruling ☐ Amended Order ☐ Interlocutory Decree ☐ Partial Decree ☐ Other (specify): ☐ Decision ☐ Interlocutory ☐ Resettled Decree ☐ Decree   Judgment ☐ Resettled Judgment   ☐ Judgment

Court:	County:
Dated:	Entered:
Judge (name in full):	Index No.:
Stage: ☐ Interlocutory ☐ Final ☐ Post–Final	Trial: ☐ Yes ☐ No If Yes: ☐ Jury ☐ Non–Jury

Prior Unperfected Appeal Information
Are any unperfected appeals pending in this case? ☐ Yes ☐ No. If yes, do you intend to perfect the appeal or appeals covered by the annexed notice of appeal with the prior appeals? ☐ Yes ☐ No. Set forth the Appellate Division Cause Number(s) of any prior, pending, unperfected appeals:

Original Proceeding
Commenced by: ☐ Order to Show Cause ☐ Notice of Petition ☐ Writ of Habeas Corpus │ Date Filed:
Statute authorizing commencement of proceeding in the Appellate Division:

Proceeding Transferred Pursuant to CPLR 7804(g)	
Court:	County:
Judge (name in full):	Order of Transfer Date:

CPLR 5704 Review of Ex Parte Order	
Court:	County:
Judge (name in full):	Dated:

Description of Appeal, Proceeding or Application and Statement of Issues
Description: If an appeal, briefly describe the paper appealed from. If the appeal is from an order, specify the relief requested and whether the motion was granted or denied. If an original proceeding commenced in this court or transferred pursuant to CPLR 7804(g), briefly describe the object of the proceeding. If an application under CPLR 5704, briefly describe the nature of the ex parte order to be reviewed.   **Amount:** If an appeal is from a money judgment, specify the amount awarded. **Issues:** Specify the issues proposed to be raised on the appeal, proceeding, or application for CPLR 5704 review.

Issues Continued:

Use Form B for Additional Appeal Information

Party Information

Instructions: Fill in the name of each party to the action or proceeding, one name per line. If this form is to be filed for an appeal, indicate the status of the party in the court of original instance and his, her, or its status in this court, if any. If this form is to be filed for a proceeding commenced in this court, fill in only the party's name and his, her, or its status in this court.

Examples of a party's original status include: plaintiff, defendant, petitioner, respondent, claimant, defendant third-party plaintiff, third-party defendant, and intervenor. Examples of a party's Appellate Division status include: appellant, respondent, appellant-respondent, respondent-appellant, petitioner, and intervenor.

No.	Party Name	Original Status	Appellate Division Status
1			
2			
3			
4			
5			
6			
7			
8			
9			
10			
11			
12			
13			
14			
15			
16			
17			
18			
19			
20			

Attorney Information

Instructions: Fill in the names of the attorneys or firms of attorneys for the respective parties. If this form is to be filed with the notice of petition or order to show cause by which a special proceeding is to be commenced in the Appellate Division, only the name of the attorney for the petitioner need be provided.

In the event that a litigant represents herself or himself, the box marked "Pro Se" must be checked and the appropriate information for that litigant must be supplied in the spaces provided.

Attorney/Firm Name:				
Address:				
City:	State:	Zip:	Telephone No.:	
Attorney Type: ☐ Retained ☐ Assigned ☐ Government ☐ Pro Se ☐ Pro Hac Vice				
Party or Parties Represented (set forth party number[s] from table above or from Form C):				

Attorney/Firm Name:				
Address:				
City:	State:	Zip:	Telephone No.:	
Attorney Type: ☐ Retained ☐ Assigned ☐ Government ☐ Pro Se ☐ Pro Hac Vice				
Party or Parties Represented (set forth party number[s] from table above or from Form C):				

Attorney/Firm Name:				
Address:				
City:	State:	Zip:	Telephone No.:	
Attorney Type: ☐ Retained ☐ Assigned ☐ Government ☐ Pro Se ☐ Pro Hac Vice				
Party or Parties Represented (set forth party number[s] from table above or from Form C):				

Attorney/Firm Name:				
Address:				
City:	State:	Zip:	Telephone No.:	
Attorney Type: ☐ Retained ☐ Assigned ☐ Government ☐ Pro Se ☐ Pro Hac Vice				
Party or Parties Represented (set forth party number[s] from table above or from Form C):				

Attorney/Firm Name:				
Address:				
City:	State:	Zip:	Telephone No.:	
Attorney Type: ☐ Retained ☐ Assigned ☐ Government ☐ Pro se ☐ Pro Hac Vice				
Party or Parties Represented (set forth party number[s] from table above or from Form C):				

Attorney/Firm Name:				
Address:				
City:	State:	Zip:	Telephone No.:	
Attorney Type: ☐ Retained ☐ Assigned ☐ Government ☐Pro Se ☐ Pro Hac Vice				
Party or Parties Represented (set forth party number[s] from table above or from Form C):				

Use Form C for Additional Party and/or Attorney Information

The use of this form is explained in § 670.3 of the rules of the Appellate Division, Second Department (22 NYCRR 670.3). If this form is to be filed for an appeal, place the required papers in the following order: (1) the Request for Appellate Division Intervention [Form A, this document], (2) any required Additional Appeal Information Forms [Form B], (3) any required Additional Party and Attorney Information Forms [Form C], (4) the notice of appeal or order granting leave to appeal, (5) a copy of the paper or papers from which the appeal or appeals covered in the notice of appeal or order granting leave to appeal is or are taken, and (6) a copy of the decision or decisions of the court of original instance, if any.

Supreme Court of the State of New York
Appellate Division: Second Judicial Department

Form B—Additional Appeal Information

Use this Form For Each Additional Paper Covered by the Notice of Appeal to be filed with Form A			
Paper Appealed From (check one only):			
☐ Amended De-cree	☐ Determination	☐ Order	☐ Resettled Order
☐ Amended Judg-ment	☐ Finding	☐ Order & Judg-ment	☐ Ruling
☐ Amended Order	☐ Interlocutory Decree	☐ Partial Decree	☐ Other (specify):
☐ Decision	☐ Interlocutory Judgment	☐ Resettled De-cree	
☐ Decree		☐ Resettled Judg-ment	
	☐ Judgment		

Court:	County:
Dated:	Entered:
Judge (name in full):	Index No.:
Stage: ☐ Interlocutory ☐ Final ☐ Post–Final	Trial: ☐ Yes ☐ No If Yes: ☐ Jury ☐ Non–Jury

Description of Appeal

Description: Briefly describe the paper appealed from. If the appeal is from an order, specify the relief requested and whether the motion was granted or denied.

Amount: If the appeal is from a money judgment, specify the amount awarded.
Issues: Specify the issues proposed to be raised on the appeal.

Form B–RADI–Civil

Supreme Court of the State of New York
Appellate Division: Second Judicial Department

Form C—Additional Party and Attorney Information

\multicolumn{4}{c}{**Additional Party Information**}			
No.	Party Name	Original Status	Appellate Division Status
21			
22			
23			
24			
25			
26			
27			
28			
29			
30			
31			
32			

Additional Attorney Information

Attorney/Firm Name:

Address:

City: State: Zip: Telephone No.:

Attorney Type: ☐ Retained   ☐ Assigned   ☐ Government   ☐ Pro Se
☐ Pro Hac Vice

Party or Parties Represented
(set forth party number[s] from table above or from Form A):

Attorney/Firm Name:

Address:

City: State: Zip: Telephone No.:

Attorney Type: ☐ Retained   ☐ Assigned   ☐ Government   ☐ Pro Se
☐ Pro Hac Vice

Party or Parties Represented
(set forth party number[s] from table above or from Form A):

Attorney/Firm Name:

Address:

City: State: Zip: Telephone No.:

Attorney Type: ☐ Retained   ☐ Assigned   ☐ Government   ☐ Pro Se
☐ Pro Hac Vice

Party or Parties Represented
(set forth party number[s] from table above or from Form A):

Attorney/Firm Name:

Address:

City: State: Zip: Telephone No.:

Attorney Type: ☐ Retained   ☐ Assigned   ☐ Government   ☐ Pro Se
☐ Pro Hac Vice

Party or Parties Represented
(set forth party number[s] from table above or from Form A):

Form C–RADI–Civil

Supreme Court of the State of New York
Appellate Division: Second Judicial Department
Form D—Request For Appellate Division Intervention—Criminal

Instructions: Use a separate copy of this form for each judgment, sentence or order appealed from. Multiple convictions under different accusatory instruments, even if the judgments were rendered in the same court on the same day, require the completion of separate copies of this form. Please type or print and answer all questions.

Attach a copy of the notice of appeal. If the appeal is from an order, attach a copy. If the appeal is from a judgment or sentence, attach a copy of the commitment order or an extract of the clerk's minutes.

Case Title:	For Appellate Division Use Only
The People of the State of New York, vs.	Case No.:
	File Opened:

Appellate Division Status: Place a √ in the appropriate box to indicate the Appellate Division status of the parties.

Plaintiff ☐ Appellant ☐ Respondent
Defendant ☐ Appellant ☐ Respondent

Type of Crime: If this is an appeal from a judgment of conviction, a sentence or an order granting or denying post-conviction relief, place a √ mark in up to five of the following boxes to indicate the type of crime or crimes of which the defendant was convicted. If the conviction was for more than five crimes, check the five most serious charges. Check the O to indicate that the conviction was for the substantive crime and check the ☐ to indicate that the conviction was for an attempt to commit that crime. In the event that the precise crime of which the defendant was convicted does not appear on the following list, check the box comparable to the article of the Penal Law in which the substantive crime is set forth. If this is an appeal by the People from an interlocutory order, check up to five boxes to indicate the crimes of which the defendant has been charged.

O =Substantive Crime ☐ =Attempt to Commit Crime

O ☐ 1 Arson	O ☐ 18 False Written Statements—Offenses Involving	O ☐ 35 Marital Relationship, Offenses Affecting
O ☐ 2 Assault & Related Offenses		O ☐ 36 Motor Vehicle, Operating Under Influence
O ☐ 3 Bribery, Not Public Servant & Related Offenses	O ☐ 19 Firearms & Dangerous Weapons, Possession	
O ☐ 4 Bribery, Public Servants & Related Offenses	O ☐ 20 Firearms & Dangerous Weapons, Use	O ☐ 37 Motor Vehicle, Other
O ☐ 5 Burglary & Related Offenses	O ☐ 21 Firearms & Dangerous Weapons, Other	O ☐ 38 Obscenity & Related Offenses
O ☐ 6 Children & Incompetents, Offenses Affecting	O ☐ 22 Forgery & Related Offenses	O ☐ 39 Offenses Relating to Judicial & Other Proceedings
O ☐ 7 Computer Offenses	O ☐ 23 Frauds on Creditors	O ☐ 40 Official Misconduct, Obstruction of Public Servants
O ☐ 8 Conspiracy	O ☐ 24 Frauds, Other	
O ☐ 9 Controlled Substances, Possession	O ☐ 25 Gambling Offenses	O ☐ 41 Perjury & Related Offenses
O ☐ 10 Controlled Substances, Sale	O ☐ 26 Homicide, Abortion	O ☐ 42 Privacy, Offenses Against
O ☐ 11 Controlled Substances, Other	O ☐ 27 Homicide, Criminally Negligent	O ☐ 43 Prostitution Offenses
O ☐ 12 Criminal Facilitation	O ☐ 28 Homicide, Manslaughter	O ☐ 44 Public Order, Offenses Against
O ☐ 13 Criminal Mischief & Related Offenses	O ☐ 29 Homicide, Murder	O ☐ 45 Public Sensibilities, Offenses Against
O ☐ 14 Criminal Possession of Stolen Property	O ☐ 30 Homicide, Vehicular Manslaughter	O ☐ 46 Robbery
	O ☐ 31 Insurance Fraud	O ☐ 47 Sex Offenses, Rape
O ☐ 15 Criminal Solicitation	O ☐ 32 Kidnapping, Coercion & Related Offenses	O ☐ 48 Sex Offenses, Sexual Abuse
O ☐ 16 Enterprise Corruption	O ☐ 33 Larceny	O ☐ 49 Sex Offenses, Sodomy
O ☐ 17 Escape & Offenses Relating to Custody	O ☐ 34 Marihuana Offenses	O ☐ 50 Theft Offenses, Other
		O ☐ 51 Other

Original Court Information (Use another Form D for additional appeals):

Appeal From (Check one only): ☐ Judgment ☐ Order ☐ Sentence ☐ Amended Judgment ☐ Amended Order ☐ Amended Sentence ☐ Resettled Order ☐ Decision ☐ Other (specify):

Dated or Rendered:	Indictment or Superior Court Information No.:
Court:	County:
Stage: ☐ Interlocutory ☐ Final ☐ Post-Final	Judge (name in full):

Conviction: ☐ Plea of Guilty ☐ Jury Verdict ☐ Nonjury Trial ☐ Not Applicable

Codefendants: Were there any codefendants under this accusatory instrument? ☐ Yes ☐ No
Names of codefendants convicted under this accusatory instrument:

Defendant Information (Please supply any available information):	NYSHS No.:
Prisoner Identification No.:	FBI No.:
Address:	

RADI Form D

App.Div.: 2nd Dept.

Supreme Court of the State of New York
Appellate Division: Second Judicial Department

Form E—Request for Appellate Division Intervention—Attorney Matters

See § 670.3 of the rules of this court for directions on the use of this form
(22 NYCRR 670.3).

Case Title: Set forth the title of the case as it appears on the notice of petition or order to show cause by which the matter is to be commenced.	For Appellate Division Use
In the Matter of _____ an Attorney and Counselor at Law.	

Case Type	Special Proceeding Other	Filing Type	Attorney Matter

Agency			
Grievance Committee for:	☐ 2nd & 11th	☐ 9th	☐ 10th Judicial District(s)
Committee on Character and Fitness for:	☐ 2nd, 10, & 11th	☐ 9th	Judicial District(s)

Attorney or Applicant Information

Name Under Which Admitted or to be Admitted to Bar:			
Department of Admission:	Date of Admission:		Date of Birth:
Roll of Attorneys: Volume No.		Page No.	Attorney Registration No.:
Current Address:			
City:	State:	Zip:	Telephone No.:

Counsel for Attorney or Applicant

Counsel/Firm Name:			
Address:			
City:	State:	Zip:	Telephone No.:

Issues Raised

☐ Admission to Practice—Character & Fitness	☐ Conviction of a "Serious Crime" under 22 NYCRR 691.7
☐ Aiding and Abetting a Non–Lawyer in the Practice of Law	☐ Dishonesty, Fraud, Deceit, or Misrepresentation
☐ Commingling Funds	☐ Failure to Cooperate
☐ Conduct Adversely Reflecting on the Fitness to Practice Law	☐ Failure to Keep Records
	☐ Failure to Register or Re–Register
☐ Conduct Involving Moral Turpitude	☐ Mental or Physical Incapacity
☐ Conduct Prejudicial to the Administration of Justice	☐ Neglect
☐ Conflict of Interest—Overreaching	☐ Reciprocal Discipline
☐ Conversion	☐ Reinstatement—Character & Fitness
☐ Conviction of a Felony	☐ Other (specify):
☐ Conviction of Other Crime	

Form E–RADI–Attorney Matters

§§ 670.25 to 670.33.   [Rescinded]

PART 671.   ADDITIONAL DUTIES OF COUNSEL AND THE COURT CLERK IN CRIMINAL ACTIONS, IN HABEAS CORPUS AND CPLR ARTICLE 78 PROCEEDINGS, IN PROCEEDINGS INSTITUTED BY MOTION MADE PURSUANT TO CPL 440.10 OR 440.20 AND FAMILY COURT ACT PROCEEDINGS

§ 671.1.   Application

(a) This Part of the rules is applicable in criminal actions or proceedings and in proceedings involving post-judgment motions made pursuant to CPL 440.10 or 440.20, and in habeas corpus and CPLR Article 78 proceedings arising out of criminal actions or proceedings or accusatory instruments, indictments or informations.

(b) Unless the context requires otherwise, any reference herein to the defendant means either the defendant in a criminal action or proceeding or the defendant, the petitioner or the relator in a proceeding instituted on motion made pursuant to CPL 440.10 or 440.20 or in a proceeding under CPLR Article 78 or in a habeas corpus proceeding.

(c) Unless the context requires otherwise, any reference herein to counsel for the defendant means every attorney who represents the defendant (as herein defined), regardless of whether such attorney shall have been retained or whether he shall have been assigned by the court or whether he be the public defender.

(d) Unless the context requires otherwise, any reference herein to the People's counsel means either the district attorney or other prosecutor as defined in CPL 1.20, or, as the case may be, the Attorney General or the county attorney or any other attorney who may appear for the People or for any public official joined as a party in his official capacity.

Cross References

CPLR, see McKinney's Book 7B.

Criminal Procedure Law, see McKinney's Book 11A.

§ 671.2.   Duration of Representation by Counsel for Defendant

In every criminal action or proceeding specified in section 671.1 hereof the duration of the representation by counsel for the defendant shall be as follows:

(a) in the trial court, until determination of the action or proceeding and until counsel shall have performed the additional duties imposed upon him by these rules; and

(b) in the appellate court, until entry of the order determining the appeal and until counsel shall have performed the additional duties imposed upon him by these rules. Thereupon such counsel's representation shall come to an end.

§ 671.3.   Additional Duties of Defendant's Counsel in the Trial Court

(a) Upon conviction in the trial court or upon denial in that court of a motion made pursuant to CPL 440.10 or 440.20 or the denial or dismissal of an application in a habeas corpus or CPLR article 78 proceeding, it shall be the duty of the counsel for the defendant, immediately after the pronouncement of sentence or after service upon him of a copy of the order denying the motion or of the order or judgment denying or dismissing the application, to give, either by mail or personally, written notice to his client advising him of his right to appeal or to make application for permission to appeal or for a certificate granting leave to appeal pursuant to CPL 460.10 (subdivision 4); and requesting his written instructions as to whether he desires to take an appeal or make such application. Thereafter, if the client gives to counsel timely written notice of his desire to appeal or to make such application, counsel shall promptly serve and file the necessary formal notice of appeal or application to the appropriate appellate court. If the application be granted, then, within the time limitations and in the manner provided in CPL 460.10 (subdivision 4), counsel shall also file the order or certificate granting leave to appeal together with a written notice of appeal. Unless counsel shall have been retained to prosecute the appeal, the notice of appeal in every case shall contain the additional statement that it is being served and filed on appellant's behalf pursuant to this rule and that it shall not be deemed to be counsel's appearance as appellant's attorney upon the appeal.

(b) In counsel's written notice to his client advising him of the right to appeal or to make application for permission to appeal or for a certificate granting leave to appeal, counsel shall also set forth:

(1) the applicable time limitations with respect to the making of the application for permission to appeal or for a certificate granting leave to appeal and the prosecution of the appeal;

(2) the manner of instituting the appeal and, if a trial or hearing was held and stenographic minutes taken, the manner of obtaining a typewritten transcript of such minutes; and

(3) the appellant's right, upon proof of his financial inability to retain counsel and to pay the costs and expenses of the appeal, to make application to the appellate court for the following relief: for the assign-

ment of counsel to prosecute the appeal; for leave to prosecute the appeal as a poor person and to dispense with printing; and if stenographic minutes were taken, for a direction to the clerk and the stenographer of the trial court that a typewritten transcript of such minutes be furnished without charge to the appellant's assigned counsel or, if appellant prosecutes the appeal pro se, to appellant.

(4) In such notice counsel shall also request the written instructions of his client, and if the client thereafter gives counsel timely written notice of his desire to make application for permission to appeal or for a certificate granting leave to appeal or to apply for the relief provided in paragraph (3) hereof, or to make any one or all of these applications, counsel shall proceed promptly to do so.

(c) Counsel shall also advise the client that in those cases where permission to appeal or where certificates granting leave to appeal are required, applications for the foregoing relief will be considered only if, as and when such permission is granted or such certificate is issued.

(d) In the event the People are the appellant and they elect to serve a copy of their notice of appeal upon the defendant, pursuant to their authority to do so under CPL 460.10, subdivision 1(c), they shall also serve a copy thereof upon the attorney who last appeared for the defendant in the court in which the order or sentence being appealed was entered.

(e) If, pursuant to CPL 460.10, subdivision 1(c), the People as appellant elect to serve a copy of their notice of appeal in the first instance upon the attorney who last appeared for the defendant in the court in which the order or sentence being appealed was entered, or if they serve the attorney as required in subdivision (d) hereof, it shall be the duty of the attorney so served to give, either by mail or personally, written notice to his client confirming the fact that such appeal has been taken by the People. Such notice shall also advise his client of his right (1) to retain counsel to represent him as respondent on the appeal, or (2) to respond to the appeal pro se, or (3) upon proof of his financial inability to retain counsel and to pay the cost and expenses of responding to the appeal, to make application to the appellate court for the following relief: for the assignment of counsel to represent him as the respondent on the appeal; for leave to respond to the appeal as a poor person and to dispense with printing; and, if stenographic minutes were taken, for a direction to the clerk and the stenographer of the trial court that a typewritten transcript of such minutes be furnished without charge to the respondent's assigned counsel or, if the defendant appears as respondent pro se, to respondent. In such notice counsel shall also request the written instructions of his client, and, if the client thereafter gives counsel timely written notice of his desire to make such application, counsel shall proceed promptly to do so.

(f) In the event, however, the attorney was the defendant's assigned counsel in the court in which the order or sentence being appealed was entered, such assignment shall remain in effect and counsel shall continue to represent the defendant as the respondent on the appeal until entry of the order determining the appeal and until counsel shall have performed any additional applicable duties imposed upon him by these rules, or until counsel shall have been otherwise relieved of his assignment. In the event the assignment remains in effect as herein provided, the written notice to the client as provided in subdivision (e) hereof may be dispensed with, except to the extent of confirming the fact that such appeal has been taken by the People.

Cross References

CPLR, see McKinney's Book 7B.

Criminal Procedure Law, see McKinney's Book 11A.

§ 671.4. Additional Duties of Defendant's Counsel in the Appellate Division or Other Intermediate Appellate Court

(a) Immediately after entry of the order of the Appellate Division or other intermediate appellate court affirming the judgment of conviction or sentence or the order denying a motion made pursuant to CPL 440.10 or 440.20 or the order or judgment denying or dismissing a habeas corpus or CPLR Article 78 application or proceeding, it shall be the duty of the counsel for the defendant, to give, either by mail or personally, written notice to his client advising him:

(1) of his right to make application for permission to take a further appeal or for a certificate granting leave to appeal to the Court of Appeals; and

(2) in the event such permission is granted or such certificate is issued, of his additional right, upon proof of his financial inability to retain counsel and to pay the costs and expenses of such further appeal, to make a concurrent application to the Court of Appeals for the assignment of counsel and for leave to prosecute such further appeal as a poor person and to dispense with printing. In such notice counsel shall also request the written instructions of his client. If the client thereafter gives to counsel timely written notice of his desire to make either or both of such applications, counsel shall proceed promptly to do so.

(b) In a habeas corpus or CPLR article 78 proceeding, however, if any two judges shall have dissented from the affirmance and if the dissent is on a stated question of law in relator's or petitioner's favor, counsel in his said written notice shall advise his client of his absolute right, without permission, to take a further appeal to the Court of Appeals. Upon receiving from the client written notice of his desire to prosecute such appeal, counsel shall file and serve promptly a formal notice of appeal accordingly. Unless counsel shall have been retained to prosecute the appeal, the notice of appeal shall contain the additional statement that it is being served and filed on appellant's behalf pursuant to this rule and that it shall not be deemed counsel's appearance as appellant's attorney upon the appeal.

(c) In the event the People are the appellant and they elect to serve a copy of their notice of appeal upon the defendant pursuant to their authority to do so under CPL 460.10, subdivision 5(c), they shall also serve a copy thereof upon the attorney who appeared for the defendant in the intermediate court.

(d) If, pursuant to said CPL 460.10, subdivision 5(c), the People as appellant elect in the first instance to serve a copy of their notice of appeal on the attorney who appeared for the defendant in the intermediate appellate court, or, if they serve the attorney as required in subdivision (c) of this section, it shall be the duty of counsel for the defendant to give, either by mail or personally, written notice to his client confirming the fact that such appeal has been taken by the People. Such notice shall also advise him of his right (1) to retain counsel to represent him as respondent on the appeal, or (2) to respond to the appeal, pro se, or (3) upon proof of his financial inability to retain counsel and to pay the costs and expenses of responding to such appeal, to apply to the Court of Appeals for the assignment of counsel, for leave to respond to the appeal as a poor person and to dispense with printing. In such notice counsel shall also request the written instructions of his client. If the client thereafter gives counsel timely written notice of his desire to make such application, counsel shall proceed promptly to do so.

(e) In the event the appeal by the People results in an order of an intermediate appellate court adverse or partially adverse to the defendant-respondent, it shall be the duty of counsel to comply with the written notice provisions of subdivision (a) of this section applicable to an affirmance on an appeal by the defendant except that the term "further appeal" in paragraphs (1) and (2) thereof shall be deemed to read "appeal."

Cross References
CPLR, see McKinney's Book 7B.

Criminal Procedure Law, see McKinney's Book 11A.

§ 671.5. Additional Duties of the Court and the Court Clerk, Where Defendant Appears Pro Se in the Trial Court

If a defendant shall have appeared pro se in the trial court, then, upon imposing sentence or upon the denial of a motion made pursuant to CPL 440.10 or 440.20 or the denial or dismissal of the habeas corpus or CPLR Article 78 application or proceeding, the trial court shall concurrently advise the defendant of his right to appeal or to make application for permission to appeal or for a certificate granting leave to

appeal, as the case may be. The court shall also concurrently advise the defendant of his additional right, upon proof of his financial inability to retain counsel and to pay the cost and expenses of the appeal, to apply to the appellate court for the assignment of counsel and for leave to prosecute the appeal as a poor person and to dispense with printing; and that where permission to appeal or a certificate granting leave to appeal is required, such application for poor person relief will be entertained only if, as and when such permission or certificate is granted. If in open court the defendant orally so requests or if thereafter he so requests in writing and such written request be timely received by the clerk of the trial court, said clerk shall forthwith prepare and serve and file an appropriate notice of appeal on defendant's behalf, or, if a certificate granting leave to appeal is required, serve and file the application therefor in accordance with the rule hereinabove provided with respect to such application. As a part of every such application the clerk shall annex and transmit the original record of the proceedings to the appellate court. Upon the determination of the application, the original record of the proceedings shall be returned to the trial court together with a certified copy of the order entered upon the application. A certified copy of such order shall also be sent to the defendant at his address shown in the application.

Cross References
CPLR, see McKinney's Book 7B.

Criminal Procedure Law, see McKinney's Book 11A.

§ 671.6. Additional Duties of Counsel for the People, Where Defendant Appears Pro Se in Appellate Court on Appeal in Criminal Action or Proceeding Instituted Upon Motion Made Pursuant to CPL 440.10 or 440.20

On an appeal from a judgment of conviction or sentence or on an appeal from an order denying a motion made pursuant to CPL 440.10 or 440.20, if the defendant shall have appeared pro se and if the judgment, sentence or order shall have been affirmed, the copy of the order of affirmance which the People's counsel thereafter serves on the defendant shall have annexed or appended thereto or endorsed thereon the following notice:

NOTICE AS TO FURTHER APPEAL

Pursuant to CPL 460.20, within 30 days after service upon you of a copy of the order of affirmance with notice of its entry, you have the right to apply for a certificate granting leave to take a further appeal to the Court of Appeals. Such application must be made either to the Chief Judge of the Court of Appeals by submitting it to the clerk of that court, as prescribed in CPL 460.20 (subdivisions 3b and 4), or to a justice of the Appellate Division of the Supreme Court in this department, as prescribed in section 670.7 of these rules and in CPL 460.20 (subdivisions 3a and 4).

The denial of such application by the first judge or justice to whom it is presented is final; thereafter a new application may not be made to any other judge or justice.

Cross References

Criminal Procedure Law, see McKinney's Book 11A.

§ 671.7. Additional Duties of Counsel for the People, Where Defendant Appears Pro Se in Appellate Court on Appeal in Habeas Corpus or CPLR Article 78 Proceeding

On an appeal from a judgment or order denying or dismissing a habeas corpus or a CPLR Article 78 application or proceeding, if the defendant shall have appeared pro se and if the judgment or order shall have been affirmed or modified, the copy of the order which the People's counsel thereafter serves on the defendant shall have annexed or appended thereto or endorsed thereon the following notice:

NOTICE AS TO FURTHER APPEAL

If the affirmance by the Appellate Division is unanimous, then, pursuant to statute (CPLR 5602), within 30 days after service upon you a copy of the order of affirmance with notice of its entry, you may make application for permission to take a further appeal to the Court of Appeals. Such application must be made either: to the Appellate Division, or, upon its refusal, to the Court of Appeals; or directly to the Court of Appeals without first applying to the Appellate Division. If such permission be granted by either court, the appeal to the Court of Appeals will be deemed to have been taken without the necessity of serving or filing a formal notice of appeal.

If the affirmance by the Appellate Division is not unanimous and if the dissent is in your favor with respect to a stated question of law; or if the judgment or order appealed from is modified in a substantial respect, and if you are aggrieved by the modification and it is one which is within the power of the Court of Appeals to review, then, pursuant to statute (CPLR 5513, 5515, 5601), within 30 days after service upon you of a copy of the order with notice of its entry, you have the right (without permission) to take a further appeal to the Court of Appeals by serving your notice of appeal on the adverse party or upon his attorney and by filing such notice in the office where the judgment or order of the court of original instance was entered.

Cross References

CPLR, see McKinney's Book 7B.

§ 671.8. [Rescinded]

§ 671.9. Additional Duties of the Court and of Defendant's Counsel in Connection With Trial Court Transcripts

Where furnishing of a daily copy of a transcript is ordered by the court, the ribbon copy thereof shall be delivered to the court and a carbon copy to counsel for the defendant. Both the court and counsel for the defendant shall be duty-bound to preserve their respective copies. At the conclusion of the trial or hearing, trial counsel for the defendant shall, if an appeal is taken, deliver said carbon copy to appellant's counsel immediately on being advised of the name and address of said appellant's counsel. At the conclusion of the trial or hearing and forthwith after the decision or verdict, as the case may be, the ribbon copy shall be delivered by the court to the county clerk for filing. The ribbon copy and the carbon copy shall constitute the two transcripts of the proceedings required by section 460.70 of the Criminal Procedure Law.

Cross References

Criminal Procedure Law, see McKinney's Book 11A.

§ 671.10. Duties of Assigned Counsel in the Surrogate's Court and the Family Court

(a) Upon the entry of an order in the Surrogate's Court and Family Court from which an appeal may be taken, it shall be the duty of assigned counsel for the unsuccessful party, immediately after the entry of the order, to give either by mail or personally, written notice to the client advising of the right to appeal or to make application for permission to appeal, and request written instructions as to whether he or she desires to take an appeal or to make such application. Thereafter, if the client gives to counsel timely written notice of his or her desire to appeal or to make such application, counsel shall promptly serve and file the necessary formal notice of appeal, or make application to this court for permission to appeal. Unless counsel shall have been retained to prosecute the appeal, the notice of appeal may contain the additional statement that it is being served and filed on appellant's behalf pursuant to this rule and that it shall not be deemed to be counsel's appearance as appellant's attorney on the appeal.

(b) In counsel's written notice to the client advising of the right to appeal or to make application for permission to appeal, counsel shall also set forth:

(1) the applicable time limitations with respect to the taking of the appeal or the making of the application for permission to appeal;

(2) the manner of instituting the appeal and, if a trial or hearing was held and stenographic minutes taken, the manner of obtaining a typewritten transcript of such minutes;

(3) the client's right, upon proof of his or her financial inability to retain counsel and to pay the costs and expenses of the appeal, to make application to this court for the assignment of counsel to prosecute the appeal; and, if stenographic minutes were taken, for a direction to the clerk and the stenographer of the trial court that a typewritten transcript of such minutes be furnished without charge to assigned counsel or, if the client prosecutes the appeal pro se, to the client; and

(4) in such notice counsel shall also request the written instructions of his client, and if the client thereafter gives counsel timely written notice of his or her desire to make application for permission to appeal or to apply for the relief provided in paragraph (3), or to make any one or all of these applications, counsel shall proceed promptly to do so.

(c) Counsel shall also advise the client that in those cases where permission to appeal is required, applications for the foregoing relief will be considered only if such permission is granted.

(d) If the assigned counsel represented the successful party in the court in which the order being appealed was entered, such assignment shall remain in effect and counsel shall continue to represent the successful party as the respondent on the appeal until entry of the order determining the appeal and until counsel shall have performed any additional applicable duties imposed upon him or her by these rules, or until counsel shall have been otherwise relieved of his assignment.

Cross References

Family Court Act, see McKinney's Book 29A, Part 1.

PARTS 672 TO 677.   [RESERVED]

PART 678.   ASSIGNED COUNSEL PLAN, SECOND AND ELEVENTH JUDICIAL DISTRICTS

Part 678 heading, Assigned Counsel Plan, Second and Eleventh Judicial Districts, is effective until January 1, 2009.   Part 678 heading was amended by ADM 2008–0918 to read Assigned Counsel Plan, Second, Eleventh, and Thirteenth Judicial Districts, effective January 1, 2009.

§ 678.1.   Introduction

Text effective until January 1, 2009. For text effective January 1, 2009, see § 678.1 post.

This Part is hereby adopted to establish rules governing the Assigned Counsel Plan for the Second and Eleventh Judicial Districts and to establish rules and standards regulating the selection, designation, performance and professional conduct of individual panel plan attorneys appointed to furnish representation for indigent defendants in criminal proceedings.

§ 678.1.   Introduction

Text effective January 1, 2009.   For text effective prior to January 1, 2009, see § 678.1 ante.

This Part is hereby adopted to establish rules governing the assigned counsel plan for the Second, Eleventh, and Thirteenth Judicial Districts and to establish rules and standards regulating the selection, designation, performance and professional conduct of individual panel plan attorneys appointed to furnish representation for indigent defendants in criminal proceedings.

§ 678.2.   Previous Measures Continued

The Assigned Counsel Plan and the Criminal Trials and Appeals Panels, under the Plan previously established for the Second and Eleventh Judicial Districts pursuant to Article 18–B of the County Law, shall continue in effect subject to the provisions of this Part.

§ 678.3.   Administrator

Text effective until January 1, 2009. For text effective January 1, 2009, see § 678.3 post.

The administrative authority over the Assigned Counsel Plan for the Second and Eleventh Judicial Districts shall be delegated to the Administrator of the Assigned Counsel Plan. The Administrator shall administer the plan in accordance with applicable statutes, the Assigned Counsel Plan, this Part, the rules of the Appellate Division, and with the procedures formulated by the Advisory Committee and approved by the Appellate Division.

§ 678.3.   Administrator

Text effective January 1, 2009.   For text effective prior to January 1, 2009, see § 678.3 ante.

The administrative authority over the assigned counsel plan for the Second, Eleventh, and Thirteenth Judicial Districts shall be delegated to the administrator of the assigned counsel plan. The administrator shall administer the plan in accordance with applicable statutes, the assigned counsel plan, this Part, the rules of the Appellate Division, and with the procedures formulated by the advisory committee and approved by the Appellate Division.

§ 678.4.   Advisory Committee

(a) There shall be established an assigned counsel plan advisory committee for the counties of Kings,

Queens and Richmond, which shall be composed of eighteen members, as follows:

(1) six members of the judiciary, who at the time of their initial appointment shall be either Judges of the Criminal Court of the City of New York or Justices of the Supreme Court, and one of whom shall be a Supervising Judge of the Criminal Court or his or her designee and another of whom shall be an Administrative Judge of the Supreme Court or his or her designee;

(2) two representatives of the bar associations in each county;

(3) a member of the faculty of an accredited law school; and

(4) five additional members, at least one of whom shall not be an attorney.

The committee members shall be appointed by the Presiding Justice for a term of three years and may be reappointed for additional three-year terms. The administrator of the assigned counsel plan shall sit as an ex officio member of the advisory committee.

(b) The members of the Advisory Committee as volunteers are expressly authorized to participate in a state-sponsored program within the meaning of section 17 of the Public Officers Law.

§ 678.5. Duties of the Advisory Committee

Subject to the supervision of the Appellate Division, the Advisory Committee shall establish procedures for appointment and reappointment of attorneys to serve on the panels; periodic evaluation of attorneys; training of attorneys; investigating complaints made against members of the panels; suspension and removal of attorneys from the panels; and periodic review of the Plan.

§ 678.6. Eligibility Requirements

(a) General requirements are:

(i) Admission to the New York State Bar for at least two years. The requirement may not be waived except in the following circumstances; where an attorney has been admitted in another state more than two years and has exceptional criminal law experience in that other state.

(ii) Attorneys may only be a member of one trial court panel and one parole panel in one county, except an attorney may be on both the felony panel and the "A" Felony panel in the one county. No attorney may be placed on the appellate panels of more than one department, but an attorney may be on the trial panels of a county and the appellate panel of the same or different department.

(iii) An attorney's primary office must be located in the county of the panel or in an adjoining county within New York City which shall be applied as follows: Kings—adjoining counties: New York and Queens; Richmond—adjoining counties: New York

and Kings; Queens—adjoining counties: Kings and New York.

(iv) Primary office shall be readily available to clients and families.

(v) No matters involving the attorney shall be pending before a Grievance Committee.

(b) The advisory committee shall establish the eligibility requirements for the selection to each panel. Additionally, the advisory committee shall establish procedures and guidelines for review of all applications.

§ 678.7. Bar Association Screening Committee

Each of the county bar associations shall continue to maintain a screening committee which will review the applications of attorneys and recommend qualified attorneys to be added to the panels. The review by the committees shall be in accordance with the eligibility requirement and guidelines established by the advisory committee. The recommendations will be forwarded to the administrator for his or her review and approval to the appropriate panel.

§ 678.8. Designation of Panels

The Appellate Division shall designate the panel for each county from attorneys recommended by the bar association screening committees and approved by the administrator. Appointments to the panels shall be for a term of three years, but successive designations may be made.

§ 678.9. Periodic Evaluation of Panel Members

The advisory committee shall periodically evaluate the qualifications of panel attorneys and shall establish procedures to recertify these attorneys to individual panels. The advisory committee shall not recommend for reappointment any attorney whose past performance the committee determines to be unsatisfactory. Judicial members of the advisory committee may participate in the determination.

§ 678.10. Training and Education

The advisory committee, in cooperation with the administrator, shall establish training and educational programs. It shall determine which programs are mandatory for continued membership on the panels. It shall also, in cooperation with the administrator, establish mentor programs to assist new and current panel members in developing their skills.

§ 678.11. Assignment of Counsel

Assignment of counsel by the Family Court, Supreme Court or Surrogate's Court to represent indigent adults in proceedings pursuant to section 262 of the Family Court Act, shall be made from law guardian panels designated pursuant to Part 679 of this

Title (The rules of the Appellate Division, Second Department). Attorneys so assigned shall be subject to those court rules including the rules relating to evaluation and removal.

§ 678.12. Suspension and Removal

(a) The administrator may suspend any panel attorney for a violation of the assigned counsel plan's rules or procedures, professional misconduct with respect to assigned counsel cases, or other misconduct which would affect the attorney's ability to properly represent assigned counsel clients.

(b) All attorneys who are suspended by the administrator for ineffective representation, professional or other misconduct, or other situations which the administrator deems appropriate, may be referred to the advisory committee for further investigation and recommendations.

(c) The advisory committee will develop procedures for investigation and review with respect to complaints against attorneys.

(d) Based upon its finding, the advisory committee may recommend to the Presiding Justice that an attorney be removed or reinstated to a panel. Judicial members of the committee may participate in the recommendation. Such recommendation shall not be required where an attorney is not reappointed at the expiration of his or her term.

(e) The administrator may, for violations of the plan's rules and procedures, recommend to the Presiding Justice that an attorney be removed from the panel.

§ 678.13. Reappointment of Attorney to Panel

(a) Attorney previously denied certification:

(1) An attorney who has previously served on an assigned counsel plan panel and who was denied recertification, may be granted permission to reapply to the assigned counsel plan under the following conditions:

(i) at least one year has elapsed since denial of recertification;

(ii) the attorney submits at least three letters of reference from lawyers who have served as opposing counsel in litigated matters in the past year;

(iii) the attorney submits at least three letters from judges of courts of record before whom she/he has practiced in the past year;

(iv) the letters referred to in subparagraphs (ii) and (iii) of this paragraph must address at least the following issues: the attorney's trial skills or appellate skills, integrity, knowledge of criminal law, and her/his vigor of advocacy; and

(v) the attorney submits two writing samples, including a brief or motion papers prepared in the past year.

(2) Materials required by paragraph (1) of this subdivision shall be submitted to the advisory committee for the assigned counsel plan.

(3) Upon receipt of the materials required by paragraph (1) of this subdivision, the chairperson shall select a subcommittee of three members to interview the applicant, review the applicant's qualifications and make a recommendation.

(4) The subcommittee shall report to the advisory committee its recommendation and underlying reasons.

(5) Upon review of the subcommittee's report and recommendations, the advisory committee shall decide whether to grant or deny permission to the attorney to reapply to the screening committee of the county bar association.

(b) Attorney previously removed for cause:

(1) An attorney who has previously served on an assigned counsel plan panel and who was removed for cause from the panel must submit a letter to the advisory committee indicating the reason why she/he was removed from the panel and the specific panel to which the attorney seeks appointment.

(2) No letter may be submitted until at least two years have elapsed since the removal of the attorney.

(3) The advisory committee shall consider the request to reapply and, in the event permission is granted, the attorney shall submit materials required in subparagraphs (a)(1)(ii), (iii), (iv) and paragraph (2) of this section to the screening committee of the county bar association.

(c) Attorney who has become inactive:

(1) An attorney who has previously served on the assigned counsel plan panel and who resigned or was removed because of inactivity for a period of three years, may be reinstated by the administrator or at the discretion of the administrator, referred to the advisory committee provided:

(i) at least one year has elapsed since leaving the panel; and

(ii) the attorney submits a letter to the administrator stating the reasons she/he left the panel, details of her/his professional work since leaving the panel, a certificate of good standing and a statement that there are no pending disciplinary matters, and that she/he did not have any disciplinary matters during the time she/he was off the panel.

(2) The administrator at her/his discretion may refer the request to the advisory committee for its review, if the administrator believes a more in-depth review of the attorney should be conducted.

(3) The advisory committee shall consider the request and if it decides more information is required it can request the attorney to submit the information required in subparagraphs (a)(1)(ii), (iii), (iv) and (v) of this section.

(4) The advisory committee can grant or deny the request to be reinstated. If permission to reapply is denied pursuant to subdivision (a), (b) or (c) of this section, a new request may not be submitted for at least one year.

§ 678.14. Annual Evaluations

On June 30th of each year, commencing with June 30, 1991, the advisory committee shall submit to the Appellate Division an evaluation of the operation of the plan and the training programs, and recommendations as to procedures, if any, which should be adopted to improve the performance of the plan and the training programs.

§ 678.15. Annual Reports

An annual report of the operation of the plan shall be filed by the Appellate Division with the Chief Administrator of the Courts.

§ 678.16. Construction

Nothing contained in this Part shall be construed to limit the powers of the Appellate Division, the Presiding Justice, or the administrator [of] the assigned counsel plan, otherwise granted pursuant to law.

PART 679. FAMILY COURT LAW GUARDIAN PLAN

§ 679.1. Family Court Law Guardian Plan Established

There is hereby established in the counties of the Second Judicial Department a plan for the operation of the Family Court law guardian panels designated pursuant to Family Court Act § 243(c).

Cross References

Family Court Act, see McKinney's Book 29A, Part 1.

§ 679.2. Administration of Law Guardian Plan

The law guardian plan for the Second Judicial Department shall be administered by the director of the law guardian program who shall be appointed by the Appellate Division of the Supreme Court, Second Judicial Department, and supervised by the Presiding Justice.

§ 679.3. Law Guardian Director

The director of the law guardian program shall administer the plan in accordance with the law, these rules, and with the procedures promulgated by the law guardian advisory committees.

§ 679.4. Advisory Committees

The following Family Court law guardian advisory committees shall be established:

(a) There shall be a single committee for the counties of Kings, Queens and Richmond, which shall be composed of the Deputy New York City Administrative Judge-Family Division or his or her designee, a representative of each of the county bar associations, a member of the faculty of an accredited law school, and three additional members at least one of whom shall be a non-attorney.

(b) In Nassau County, the committee shall be composed of the Deputy Administrative Judge of the Family Court, a representative of the county bar association, a member of the faculty of an accredited law school, and three additional members at least one of whom shall be a non-attorney.

(c) In Suffolk County, the committee shall be composed of the Deputy Administrative Judge of the Family Court, a representative of the county bar association, a member of the faculty of an accredited law school, and three additional members at least one of whom shall be a non-attorney.

(d) There shall be a single committee for the counties of Dutchess, Orange, Putnam, Rockland and Westchester, which shall be composed of the Deputy Administrative Judge of the Family Court, Ninth Judicial District, a representative from each county bar association, a member of the faculty of an accredited law school, and nine additional members at least three of whom shall be non-attorneys.

(e) On each advisory committee the Family Court Judge member shall serve as chairperson. All the members shall be designated by the Appellate Division, Second Judicial Department, for three-year terms, and may be reappointed for additional terms. The bar association representative members shall be appointed upon recommendation of the respective bar associations. Committee members may not serve on the law guardian panels.

(f) The director of the law guardian program shall sit as an officio member of each advisory committee.

(g) The members of the law guardian advisory committees as volunteers are expressly authorized to participate in a State-sponsored volunteer program within the meaning of the Public Officers Law § 17.

§ 679.5. Duties of the Advisory Committees

Subject to the supervision of the Appellate Division, the advisory committees shall establish procedures for appointment and reappointment of attorneys to serve on the law guardian panels, for periodic evaluation of attorneys who serve on the law guardian panels, for training of attorneys on the law guardian panels, for investigating complaints made against members of the law guardian panels, and for removal of attorneys from the law guardian panels.

§ 679.6.   Eligibility Requirements

(a) To be eligible for recommendation for appointment to a panel designated pursuant to Family Court Act § 243 or to a panel established for attorneys assigned pursuant to Family Court Act § 243, an attorney shall be admitted to the bar of the State of New York, in good standing, and shall have served as counsel or co-counsel in the Family Court in a minimum of three proceedings under Family Court Act article 3, article 6 and article 10.

(b) The advisory committees shall establish co-counsel or mentoring programs to provide experience to admitted attorneys who wish to serve on the panel but lack the qualifications required by paragraph (a).

(c) The minimum requirements may be waived if, in the opinion of the advisory committees, the applicant is otherwise qualified by reason of education, training or substantial trial experience.

(d) The advisory committees may set forth such additional requirements and procedures as they see fit, subject to approval by the Appellate Division.

Cross References
Family Court Act, see McKinney's Book 29A, Part 1.

§ 679.7.   Designation of Panels

The Appellate Division shall designate the law guardian panel for each county from attorneys recommended by the advisory committees. Appointments to the panel shall not exceed one year, but any panel member may be reappointed.

§ 679.8.   Periodic Evaluation of Law Guardians

The advisory committees shall establish procedures to periodically evaluate the representation provided to juveniles by each member of the law guardian panel. In conducting the periodic evaluation the advisory committees shall seek information from Family Court judges and other appropriate and knowledgeable persons. The advisory committees shall not recommend for reappointment any attorney whose representation the committees determine to be unsatisfactory.

Cross References
Family Court Act, see McKinney's Book 29A, Part 1.

§ 679.9.   Training and Education

The advisory committees, in cooperation with the director of the law guardian program shall establish a training and education program for members of the law guardian panels. Such a program may be established in conjunction with bar associations, local law schools or other competent organizations. The advisory committees shall make attendance at training

programs a requirement for continued membership on the law guardian panels.

Cross References
Family Court Act, see McKinney's Book 29A, Part 1.

§ 679.10.   Recommendation for Removal

An advisory committee may, at any time, recommend to the Presiding Justice that an attorney be removed from the panel. Such recommendation shall be submitted in writing, together with a report of the basis for such recommendation. Such recommendation shall not be required where an attorney is not reappointed at the expiration of his or her term. The Presiding Justice shall have the power to remove members of the Family Court law guardian panels and members of panels established for attorneys assigned pursuant to Family Court Act § 262.

§ 679.11.   Assignments of Counsel

Assignments of counsel by the Family Court, Supreme Court or Surrogate's Court to represent children in proceedings wherein compensation is paid privately by one or more of the parties, or is authorized pursuant to Judiciary Law § 35 shall be made from law guardian panels designated pursuant to these rules. This section shall not apply to institutional providers appointed pursuant to Family Court Act § 243(a).

§ 679.12.   Annual Evaluations

On June 30th of each year, commencing with June 30, 1991, each advisory committee shall submit to the Appellate Division an evaluation of the operation of the plan and the training programs, and recommendations as to procedures, if any, which should be adopted to improve the performance of the plan and the training programs.

§ 679.13.   Annual Reports

A report of the operation of the law guardian panels shall be filed by the Appellate Division with the Chief Administrator of the Courts on August 1st of each year, commencing August 1, 1991.

§ 679.14.   Compensation of Law Guardians

(a) Claims by law guardians for services rendered pursuant to Family Court Act § 245 shall be submitted for approval to the Family Court Judge on forms authorized by the Chief Administrator of the Courts. After approval or modification, the Family Court shall forward the claim to the Appellate Division for review by the Presiding Justice or his or her designee. If approved, the Presiding Justice or designee shall certify the claim to the Comptroller for payment.

(b) Claims for compensation by law guardians in excess of the statutory limits set by Family Court Act § 245 and Judiciary Law § 35 shall be accompanied by a sworn statement by the law guardian describing the nature of the proceeding, specifying the time and services rendered and expenses incurred, and detailing the circumstances deemed to be extraordinary that justify a fee in excess of the statutory limits. In the absence of the law guardian's supporting affidavit, excess compensation shall not be allowed. The Family Court, in granting an excess compensation claim, shall make a written finding setting forth the extraor-

dinary circumstances justifying a fee in excess of statutory limits.

§ 679.15. Construction

Nothing contained in this Part shall be construed to limit the powers of the Appellate Division, the Presiding Justice, or the administrator of the assigned counsel plan, otherwise granted pursuant to law.

PART 680. MENTAL HEALTH PROFESSIONALS PANEL

§ 680.1. Access to Mental Health Professionals

In custody and visitation, delinquency, persons in need of supervision, child abuse and neglect, termination of parental rights, family offense, and adoption cases, an evaluation of the parties by a mental health professional is often necessary to assist the court in reaching an appropriate decision. To assure that the court and the parties have access to qualified mental health professionals, a panel of social workers, psychologists and psychiatrists shall be established in the First and Second Judicial Departments in accordance with this part and part 623 of this Title.

§ 680.2. Mental Health Professionals Certification Committee

(a) A mental health professionals certification committee shall be established for the First and Second Judicial Departments.

(b) The committee shall be composed of no fewer than two justices of the Supreme Court, two judges of the Family Court, two lawyers, two social workers, two psychologists, and two psychiatrists. Half of the members in each class shall be appointed by the Presiding Justices of the First and Second Departments of the Appellate Division, respectively, for three year terms. Committee members shall be eligible for reappointment for additional terms. The Law Guardian Directors for the Appellate Division in the First and Second Judicial Departments, respectively, or their designees, shall be ex-officio members.

(c) The members of the committee shall serve as volunteers, authorized to participate in a state-sponsored volunteer program within the meaning of the Public Officers Law § 17.

§ 680.3. Duties of Mental Health Professionals Certification Committee

Subject to the supervision of the Presiding Justices of the Appellate Division of the First and Second Judicial Departments, the mental health professionals certification committee shall establish procedures for (a) the appointment of applicants for membership on the panel of mental health professionals, (b) periodic evaluation of panel members, (c) training of panel members, (d) investigating complaints made against

panel members, and (e) removal of mental health professionals from the panel.

§ 680.4. Establishment of Mental Health Professionals Panel

(a) Eligibility Requirements

A member of the mental health professionals panel shall:

(1) be a social worker, psychologist, or psychiatrist licensed by the State of New York;

(2) complete six hours of introductory training approved by the Presiding Justices of the Appellate Division of the First and Second Judicial Departments;

(3) demonstrate that he or she has forensic experience, including having testified as an expert and/or having submitted a clinical report in connection with one or more of the following types of court proceedings: custody and visitation, delinquency, persons in need of supervision, child abuse and neglect, termination of parental rights, family offense, and adoption;

(4) maintain professional malpractice insurance; and

(5) meet such additional requirements as shall be established by the mental health professionals certification committee with the approval of the Presiding Justices of the Appellate Divisions of the First and Second Judicial Departments.

(b) Application

Licensed social workers, psychologists, and psychiatrists may apply for membership on the mental health professionals panel for the First and Second Judicial Departments by completing a questionnaire in the form prescribed by the mental health professionals certification committee.

(c) Appointments to Panel

(1) The mental health professionals committee shall review applications and identify those mental health professionals who meet the eligibility requirements.

(2) The Presiding Justices of the Appellate Division in the First and Second Judicial Departments shall, by joint order, appoint the members of the mental health professionals panel from among those social workers,

psychologists and psychiatrists recommended by the committee.

(3) Appointments to the panel shall be for a term of three years. Panel members may be reappointed to successive terms. Any panel member may be removed prior to the expiration of his or her term by the joint order of the Presiding Justices of the Appellate Divisions of the First and Second Judicial Departments upon the recommendation of the committee.

§ 680.5. Appointment of Mental Health Professionals From Panel

(a) Appointment

A court may appoint a mental health professional or professionals to evaluate adults and children in any case involving custody and visitation, delinquency, persons in need of supervision, child abuse and neglect, termination of parental rights, family offense, and adoption wherein compensation is paid privately or pursuant to Judiciary Law § 35 or County Law article 18–B. Such appointments shall be from the mental health professionals panel promulgated pursuant to these rules. A court, upon a finding of good cause, may appoint a mental health professional who is not a member of the mental health professionals panel. The court's finding shall be set forth in the order of appointment. This section shall not apply to providers of mental health services pursuant to a governmental contract.

(b) Order of Appointment

The court appointing a mental health professional shall issue a written order setting forth the terms and conditions of the appointment including the method and rate of compensation and by whom such compensation is to be paid. A copy of the order shall be provided to the mental health professional and to every party to the case, including the attorney, if any, for each child.

§ 680.6. Compensation of Mental Health Professionals

(a) The compensation for mental health professionals appointed pursuant to Judiciary Law § 35 or County Law article 18–B shall be at rates prescribed by the Chief Administrator of the Courts. Applications for payment for services rendered pursuant to those sections shall be submitted for approval to the court that appointed the panel member on forms authorized by the Chief Administrator of the Courts or by the appropriate local fiscal authority.

(b) The compensation of mental health professionals appointed in cases in which their fees shall be borne in whole or in part by the parties shall be at rates fixed by the court in accordance with the charge for such services prevailing in the community and the financial circumstances of the parties. Such compensation shall not exceed a sum certain to be set forth in the order of appointment, which sum shall be based on the selected rate and the estimated number of hours required to perform the necessary services. In the event that a greater expenditure of time is required than originally estimated, the mental health professional may apply to the court for additional fees in excess of the sum set forth in the order. The application shall be made by letter, a copy of which shall be forwarded to the party or parties responsible for the payment of the fee.

§ 680.7. Training and Education

The mental health professionals certification committee shall establish a training and education program for members of the mental health professionals panel. The program shall include, but not be limited to, the topics of cultural diversity, learning disabilities, developmental and neuropsychological disorders, substance abuse, sexual abuse, physical and emotional abuse, and neglect. The program may be established in cooperation with relevant professional organizations. The committee may make attendance at training sessions a requirement for continued membership on the panel of mental health professionals.

§ 680.8. Periodic Evaluation of Panel Members

The mental health professionals certification committee shall establish procedures by which it shall periodically evaluate the work performed by each member of the panel of mental health professionals. In conducting its evaluation the committee shall seek information from judges and other appropriate and knowledgeable persons. The committee shall not recommend for reappointment to the panel any member whose performance has been determined to be unsatisfactory.

§ 680.9. Recommendation for Removal

The Presiding Justices of the Appellate Division of the First and Second Judicial Departments may, by joint order, remove members of the mental health professionals panel upon recommendation of the mental health professionals certification committee upon a showing of good cause for such removal. Such a recommendation shall be in writing stating the grounds for removal. A copy of the recommendation shall be provided to the panel member, who shall be afforded a reasonable opportunity to respond thereto in writing.

§ 680.10. Annual Report of the Mental Health Professionals Certification Committee

On June 1st of each year the mental health professionals certification committee shall submit to the Presiding Justices of the Appellate Division in the First and Second Judicial Departments an annual report containing an evaluation of the operation of the mental health professionals panel and the training program and any recommendations concerning measures that should be adopted to improve the performance of the panel and the training program. A copy of that report shall be forwarded to the Chief Administrator of the Courts.

PARTS 681 TO 683. [RESCINDED]

PART 684. MEDICAL MALPRACTICE ACTIONS IN THE SUPREME COURT IN THE SECOND JUDICIAL DEPARTMENT [REPEALED]

PART 685. RULES GOVERNING ELECTRONIC RECORDING OF DEPOSITIONS IN CIVIL CASES [RESCINDED]

PART 690. ADMISSION TO PRACTICE OF ATTORNEYS AND COUNSELORS AT LAW

§ 690.1. Form of Questionnaire and Statement

The prescribing by the Committee on Character and Fitness for each judicial district in the Second Department of a forum of questionnaire and statement, as authorized by CPLR 9404, and the amendment thereof from time to time under the supervision and direction of the Presiding Justice, are hereby approved by this court and the justices thereof.

Cross References

CPLR, see McKinney's Book 7B.

§ 690.2. Clerk of Court May Divulge to Governmental Agencies Papers and Records on Applications for Admission to the Bar

The clerk of the Appellate Division of the Supreme Court, Second Judicial Department, is hereby authorized, without further court order, to divulge and make available to any department, agency, board, bureau, court or judge of the Federal, State or local governments, upon an appropriate written request, the papers and records on any application to said court for admission to the bar and on any motion incident or related to such application.

§ 690.3. Admission Without Examination; Pro Hac Vice

(a) For a Particular Cause. An attorney and counselor-at-law or the equivalent from another state, territory, district or foreign country may be admitted pro hac vice to participate in the trial or argument of a particular cause in which the attorney may be employed, upon application to and in the discretion of the court in which the cause is pending.

(b) Graduate Students, Graduate Assistants and Law School Teachers. An attorney and counselor at law or the equivalent from another state, territory, district or foreign country, who is a graduate student or graduate assistant enrolled in an approved law school in this department, or a teacher employed in such a law school, may apply to this court, by duly verified petition, for admission pro hac vice, to advise and represent clients or participate in the trial or argument of any case during the continuance of such enrollment or employment, if engaged to advise or represent such clients through participation in an organization, described in subdivision 7 of section 495 of the Judiciary Law.

(c) Law School Graduates. An attorney and counselor-at-law or the equivalent from another state, territory, district or foreign country, who is a graduate of an approved law school, may apply to this court, by duly verified petition, for admission pro hac vice, to advise and represent clients and participate in the trial or argument of any case while employed or associated with an organization, described in subdivision 7 of section 495 of the Judiciary Law, whose principal office is located in this department; but such admission pro hac vice shall be for no longer than 18 months.

(d) Term for Rendering Legal Services. Upon granting of the applicant's petition pursuant to either subdivision (b) or (c) of this section, the applicant may render the specified legal services for the organization with which applicant is associated or employed in any court of this State for the period specified in this court's order granting said applicant's petition.

(e) Filing of Annual Report by the Organization. Every organization, described in subdivision 7 of section 495 of the Judiciary Law, employing attorneys admitted pro hac vice pursuant to subdivisions (b) and (c) of this section shall file an annual report with this court on or about January 31st supplying the names and addresses of the attorneys and the type of legal services in which they are engaged in the courts of this State.

Cross References

Judiciary Law, see McKinney's Book 29.

§ 690.4. Volunteer Program

The members of the committees on character and fitness, as volunteers, are expressly authorized to participate in a State-sponsored volunteer program within the meaning of subdivision 1 of section 17 of the Public Officers Law.

Cross References

Public Officers Law, see McKinney's Book 46.

§ 690.5. Filing of Application Papers

Every applicant for admission to practice as an attorney and counselor at law pursuant to subdivision 1(a) or 1(b) of section 90 of the Judiciary Law, may obtain the standard forms and instructions for that purpose from the secretary of the committee on character and fitness. Every applicant for admission to practice pursuant to subdivision 1(a) of section 90 of the Judiciary Law may obtain such forms and instructions immediately after taking the bar examination, and may file a completed application, consisting of the standard form of questionnaire and the other required papers as directed by the instructions, at any time thereafter, regardless of whether the results of the bar examination have yet been issued. As soon as the applicant shall receive a letter from the State Board of Law Examiners stating that the applicant has passed the bar examination, the applicant shall file that letter with the secretary of the committee on character and fitness, and if the applicant's questionnaire was verified more than 45 days prior to such filing, the applicant shall also file a supplemental affidavit stating whether there have been any changes in the facts stated therein and setting forth any such changes.

Cross References

Judiciary Law, see McKinney's Book 29.

§ 690.6. Referral to Committee on Character and Fitness

Every completed application shall be referred for investigation of the applicant's character and fitness to a committee on character and fitness designated by the Appellate Division of the department to which the applicant is eligible for certification by the State Board of Law Examiners after passing the bar examination, or to which the applicant is applying for admission without examination in accordance with the rules of the Court of Appeals for the admission of attorneys and counselors at law.

§ 690.7. Quorum for Committee Action

A majority of the entire committee shall constitute a quorum for the transaction of business by a committee on character and fitness if it consists of less than 10 members, and one fifth of the entire committee, but not less than five members, shall constitute a quorum if it consists of 10 or more members.

§ 690.8. Investigation and Interview

The committee may commence the required investigation at any time after the applicant's completed application has been filed, except that the personal interview of an applicant for admission pursuant to subdivision 1(a) of section 90 of the Judiciary Law shall not be held until after the applicant has been notified by the State Board of Law Examiners that the applicant has passed the bar examination and has been certified to apply for admission. The committee may itself conduct the required investigation, including an interview of the applicant, or it may authorize its chairman or acting chairman to designate one or more of its members to do so and to make a recommendation to the committee.

Cross References

Judiciary Law, see McKinney's Book 29.

§ 690.9. Procedure Upon Recommendation of Approval

If the committee shall approve the application following its own investigation, or if it shall accept a recommendation of approval submitted by the member or members conducting an investigation pursuant to designation, the chairman or acting chairman shall certify to the Appellate Division on behalf of the committee that the applicant possesses the requisite character and fitness.

§ 690.10. Procedure Upon Recommendation of Disapproval, Deferral or Committee Consideration

If the committee shall fail to approve the application following its own investigation, or following a recommendation submitted by the member or members conducting an investigation pursuant to designation that the application be disapproved or that action thereon be deferred, a hearing on the application shall be held expeditiously before the committee or a subcommittee of at least two members designated by the chairman or acting chairman. Such a hearing shall also be held if the member or members conducting an investigation pursuant to designation shall recommend consideration of the application by the committee and the committee shall fail to approve the application following such consideration.

§ 690.11. Notice of Hearing; Waiver

Unless waived in writing by the applicant, a written notice of hearing of not less than twenty days, specifying the time and place of the hearing, shall be served on the applicant. In addition, the notice of hearing shall inform the applicant of the matters to be inquired into and of the applicant's right to be represented by an attorney, and such information shall also be given to the applicant prior to the hearing if the applicant has waived notice of hearing.

§ 690.12. Procedure at Hearing

At the hearing, hearsay evidence may be received and considered and adherence to strict rules of evidence shall not be required. The applicant shall be given an opportunity to call and cross-examine witnesses and to challenge, examine and controvert any adverse evidence. Upon timely request, subpoenas for the attendance of witnesses or the production of papers shall be issued to the applicant by the clerk of the Appellate Division, the subpoena fees and mileage to be paid by the applicant.

§ 690.13. Stenographic Record or Tape Recording

A stenographic record or tape recording shall be made of the hearing, and the applicant may obtain a transcript or copy of the recording at the applicant's expense.

§ 690.14. Decision or Report Following Hearing

Where the hearing has been conducted by the committee, the committee shall render a decision, and where the hearing has been conducted by a subcommittee, the subcommittee shall render a report, within sixty days after the matter is finally submitted, unless the time is extended by consent of the applicant or order of the Appellate Division. The decision of the committee or the report of the subcommittee, as the case may be, may recommend approval or disapproval of the applicant or deferral of action on the application for a period not to exceed six months.

§ 690.15. Transmittal of Decision to Appellate Division Following Hearing Conducted by Committee

Where the hearing has been conducted by the committee, the committee shall transmit its decision to the Appellate Division, together with the appropriate certificate if it recommends approval of the applicant. If the decision recommends disapproval of the applicant or deferral of action on the application, it shall include a statement of the grounds on which it is based, and a copy thereof shall be served on the applicant or the applicant's attorney.

§ 690.16. Review by Committee Following Hearing Conducted by Subcommittee

Where the hearing has been conducted by a subcommittee, the subcommittee's report and the stenographic record or tape recording of the hearing shall be referred for consideration and review to the committee, which shall render a decision thereon expeditiously. The committee's decision may confirm, reverse or modify the subcommittee's report, or direct that a further hearing be held before the same or another subcommittee. If the committee's decision recommends disapproval of the applicant or deferral of action on the application, it shall include a state-

ment of the grounds on which it is based, and a copy thereof shall be served on the applicant or the applicant's attorney. The decision shall be transmitted to the Appellate Division, together with the appropriate certificate, if it recommends approval of the applicant. The deliberations of the committee shall be confidential and the applicant shall not be entitled to compel disclosure thereof.

§ 690.17. Petition to Appellate Division Following Adverse Decision

If the committee's decision is adverse to the applicant, the applicant may, within sixty days after service of a copy thereof, petition the Appellate Division, in accordance with CPLR 9404, on notice of not less than eight days served on the committee together with any supporting papers, for an order granting the application for admission to practice notwithstanding the committee's decision.

Cross References

CPLR, see McKinney's Book 7B.

§ 690.18. Petition to Appellate Division in Case of Unreasonable Delay

In any case in which it is claimed that the committee has unreasonably delayed action on an application for admission to practice, the applicant may petition the Appellate Division, in accordance with CPLR 9404, on notice of not less than eight days served on the committee together with any supporting papers, for an order granting the application notwithstanding the committee's failure to complete action thereon, or for other appropriate relief.

Cross References

CPLR, see McKinney's Book 7B.

§ 690.19. Petition for Advance Ruling With Respect to Past Conduct

(a) Any person who is a matriculated student in an approved law school, as an approved law school is defined in the Rules of the Court of Appeals for the Admission of Attorneys and Counselors at Law, or who has applied for admission to such a law school, and who has previously been (i) convicted of a felony or misdemeanor, or (ii) suspended, removed or dismissed from public office or employment, or (iii) dishonorably discharged from the armed services of the United States, may petition the appellate division of the department in which such person resides or is employed full-time, or, if such person does not reside and is not employed full-time in the State, the Appellate Division of the Third Department, for an advance ruling, in accordance with this section, as to whether such conviction, suspension, removal or dismissal from public office or employment, or dishonorable discharge, as the case may be, would operate to disqualify the petitioner, on character grounds, from being admitted to practice as an attorney and counselor at law in this State.

(b) The petition shall include a detailed statement of the facts with respect to the petitioner's conviction, suspension, dismissal or removal from public office or employment, or dishonorable discharge, as the case may be, and of the petitioner's activities subsequent thereto which the petitioner believes bear on character and fitness to practice law.

(c) The petitioner shall also submit a completed and verified questionnaire, on the standard form furnished by the committee on character and fitness, and affidavits of good moral character from two reputable persons who have known the petitioner for at least one year. In addition, the petitioner shall submit a letter from a person in authority at the approved law school in which the petitioner is a matriculated student, or to which the petitioner has applied for admission, stating that such law school would retain or accept the petitioner as a student therein, as the case may be, if the petitioner's conviction, suspension, dismissal or removal from public office or employment, or dishonorable discharge, as the case may be, would not operate to disqualify the petitioner from being admitted to practice as an attorney and counselor at law in this State.

(d) The petition and other papers submitted by the petitioner shall be referred to the appropriate committee on character and fitness, which shall process and investigate the petition in accordance with the procedures set forth in the preceding sections of this Part. The committee may recommend that a ruling be made either in favor of or against the petitioner, or that no ruling be made, and its recommendation shall be transmitted to the Appellate Division.

(e) A ruling made by the Appellate Division in favor of the petitioner shall determine that the peti-

tioner's prior conviction, suspension, removal or dismissal from public office or employment, or dishonorable discharge, as the case may be, and the acts committed by the petitioner which resulted therein, would not operate to disqualify the petitioner, on character grounds, from being admitted to practice as an attorney and counselor at law in this State. Such a ruling shall have binding force throughout the State with respect to the determination thus made by it. In the event that the Appellate Division should rule against the petitioner or should refuse to make a ruling, its determination shall be without prejudice to the petitioner's right, after passing the bar examination, to apply for a favorable ruling with respect to character and fitness.

§ 690.20.   Manner of Service

Service of any notice or other papers required under any of these rules may be made by mail or in the manner provided for service of a summons.

§ 690.21.   Orientation to the Profession

(a) Orientation Program. This court shall regularly conduct an orientation program on the subject of professional ethics and related topics for applicants seeking admission to practice as attorneys and counselors-at-law.

(b) Required Attendance. Every person admitted to the practice of law after January 1, 2006, shall have attended and successfully completed such an orientation program within one year prior to the date of admission.

(c) Waivers. The Presiding Justice or his or her designee may, in individual cases involving undue hardship or extenuating circumstances, upon written request, grant waivers and modifications of this requirement.

PART 691. CONDUCT OF ATTORNEYS

§ 691.1.   Application

(a) This Part shall apply to all attorneys who are admitted to practice, reside in, commit acts in or who have offices in the Second Judicial Department, or who are admitted to practice by a court of another jurisdiction and who regularly practice within this department as counsel for governmental agencies or as house counsel to corporations or other entities, or otherwise. In addition, any attorney from another state, territory, district or foreign country admitted pro hac vice to participate in the trial or argument of a particular cause in any court in the Second Judicial Department, or who in any way participates in an action or proceeding therein, shall be subject to this Part.

(b) The imposition of discipline pursuant to this Part shall not preclude the imposition of any further or additional sanctions prescribed or authorized by

law, and nothing contained in this Part shall be construed to deny to any other court such powers as are necessary for that court to maintain control over proceedings conducted before it, such as the power of contempt, nor to prohibit bar associations from censuring, suspending or expelling their members from membership in the association or from admonishing attorneys in minor matters; provided, however, that such action by a bar association shall be reported to the appropriate committee appointed pursuant to section 691.4 (a) of this Part, and provided further, that such action by a bar association shall not be a bar to the taking of other and different disciplinary action by this court or by a committee appointed pursuant to section 691.4(a) of this Part.

§ 691.2.   Professional Misconduct Defined

Any attorney who fails to conduct himself, either professionally or personally, in conformity with the standards of conduct imposed upon members of the bar as conditions for the privilege to practice law, and any attorney who violates any provision of the rules of this court governing the conduct of attorneys, or any disciplinary rule of the Code of Professional Responsibility adopted jointly by the Appellate Divisions of the Supreme Court, effective September 1, 1990, or any canon of the Canons of Professional Ethics adopted by the New York State Bar Association, or any other rule or announced standard of this court governing the conduct of attorneys, shall be deemed to be guilty of professional misconduct within the meaning of subdivision (2) of section 90 of the Judiciary Law.

Cross References

Judiciary Law, see McKinney's Book 29.

Code of Professional Responsibility, see Appendix to McKinney's Judiciary Law Book, Book 29.

§ 691.3. Discipline of Attorneys for Professional Misconduct in Foreign Jurisdiction

(a) Any attorney to whom this Part shall apply pursuant to section 691.1 of this Part, who has been disciplined in another State, territory or district, may be disciplined by this court because of the conduct which gave rise to the discipline imposed in such other State, territory or district.

(b) Upon receipt from the foreign jurisdiction of a certified or exemplified copy of the order imposing such discipline and of the record of the proceedings upon which such order was based, this court, directly, or by a committee appointed pursuant to section 691.4(a) of this Part, shall give written notice to such attorney pursuant to subdivision (6) of section 90 of the Judiciary Law, according him the opportunity within twenty days of the giving of such notice, to file a verified statement setting forth any defense to a discipline enumerated under subdivision (c) of this section, and a written demand for a hearing at which consideration shall be given to any and all defenses enumerated in said subdivision (c) of this section. Such notice shall further advise the attorney that, in default of such filing by him, this court will impose such discipline or take such disciplinary action as it deems appropriate.

(c) This court, in default of the attorney's filing a verified statement and demand as provided for in subdivision (b) of this section, may discipline such attorney unless an examination of the entire record before this court, including the record of the foreign jurisdiction and such other evidence as this court in its discretion may receive, discloses (1) that the procedure in the foreign jurisdiction was so lacking in notice or opportunity to be heard as to constitute a deprivation of due process; or (2) that there was such an infirmity of proof establishing the misconduct as to give rise to the clear conviction that this court could not, consistent with its duties, accept as final the finding of the court in the foreign jurisdiction as to the

attorney's misconduct; or (3) that the imposition of discipline by this court would be unjust.

(d) **Opportunity for Hearing.** Where an attorney shall have duly filed both his verified statement setting forth any defense (as enumerated in subdivision (c) of this section) to the imposition of discipline by this court and his written demand for a hearing with respect to such defense, no discipline, by way of suspension or otherwise, shall be imposed without affording the attorney an opportunity to have a hearing.

(e) Any attorney to whom this Part shall apply who has been disciplined in a foreign jurisdiction shall promptly advise this court of such discipline.

Cross References

Judiciary Law, see McKinney's Book 29.

§ 691.4. Appointment of Grievance Committees; Commencement of Investigation of Attorney Misconduct; Complaints; Procedure

*Text of subdivision (a) effective
until January 1, 2009.*

(a) This court shall appoint three grievance committees for the Second Judicial Department. One of these grievance committees shall be charged with the duty and power to investigate and prosecute matters arising in or concerning attorneys practicing, or currently residing or having resided in the second and eleventh judicial districts at the time of their admission to practice by the Appellate Division; another shall have the duty and power to investigate and prosecute matters arising in or concerning attorneys practicing, or currently residing or having resided in the ninth judicial district at the time of their admission to practice by the Appellate Division; and the third shall have the duty and power to investigate and prosecute matters arising in or concerning attorneys practicing, or currently residing or having resided in the tenth judicial district at the time of their admission to practice by the Appellate Division. These committees shall also have the power and duty to investigate and prosecute matters concerning attorneys to whom this Part applies pursuant to section 691.1 of this Part.

Text of subdivision (a) effective January 1, 2009.

(a) This court shall appoint three grievance committees for the Second Judicial Department. One of these grievance committees shall be charged with the duty and power to investigate and prosecute matters arising in or concerning attorneys practicing, or currently residing or having resided in the Second, Eleventh, and Thirteenth Judicial Districts at the time of their admission to practice by the Appellate Division; another shall have the duty and power to investigate and prosecute matters arising in or concerning attorneys practicing, or currently residing or having resided in the Ninth Judicial District at the time of their admission to practice by the Appellate Division; and the third shall have the duty and power to investigate and prosecute matters arising in or concerning attorneys practicing, or currently residing or having resided in the Tenth Judicial District at the time of their admission to practice by the Appellate Division. These committees shall also have the power and duty to investigate and prosecute matters concerning attorneys to whom this Part applies pursuant to section 691.1 of this Part.

(b)(1) Each grievance committee shall consist of 19 members and a chairman, all of whom shall be appointed by this court and 16 of whom shall be attorneys. The chairman shall have the power to appoint an acting chairman from among the members of the grievance committee. Appointments may be made from lists of prospective members submitted by the following county bar associations within the second judicial department: Brooklyn Bar Association, Dutchess County Bar Association, Bar Association of Nassau County, New York, Inc., Orange County Bar Association, Putnam County Bar Association, Queens County Bar Association, Richmond County Bar Association, Rockland County Bar Association, Inc., Suffolk County Bar Association and Westchester County Bar Association. This court shall, in consultation with the committees, appoint a chief counsel to each such grievance committee and such assistant counsel and supporting staff as it deems necessary.

(2) Five persons shall be appointed to each such committee for a term of one year, five persons for a term of two years, five persons for a term of three years and five persons for a term of four years. Thereafter, yearly appointments of five persons shall be made to each such committee for a term of four years. No person who has served two consecutive terms shall be eligible for reappointment until the passage of one year from the expiration of his second such term. The person appointed chairman shall serve as chairman for a term of two years and shall be eligible for reappointment as chairman for not more than one additional term of two years.

(3) The members of the joint bar association grievance committees as volunteers are expressly authorized to participate in a state-sponsored volunteer program within the meaning of subdivision 1 of section 17 of the Public Officers Law.

(c) Investigation of professional misconduct may be commenced upon receipt of a specific complaint by this court or by any such committee, or such investigation may be commenced sua sponte by this court or such a committee. Complaints must be in writing and signed by the complainant but need not be verified. Complainants shall be notified by the committee of actions taken by it with respect thereto.

(d) Each grievance committee shall have the power to appoint its members to subcommittees of not less than three members, two of whom shall constitute a quorum and shall have power to act. At least two members of a subcommittee shall be attorneys. The chairman of the committee shall designate a member of the subcommittee to act as its chairman. Such subcommittees may hold hearings as hereinafter authorized.

(e) Upon receipt or initiation of a specific complaint of professional misconduct, any such committee may, after preliminary investigation and upon a majority vote of the full committee:

(1) dismiss the complaint and so advise the complainant and the attorney;

(2) conclude the matter by issuing a letter of caution to the attorney and by appropriately advising the complainant of such action;

(3) conclude the matter by privately admonishing the attorney, which admonition shall clearly indicate the improper conduct found and the disciplinary rule, canon or special rule which has been violated, and by appropriately advising the complainant of such action;

(4) serve written charges upon the attorney and hold a hearing on the matter as set forth in subdivision (f) of this section;

(5) forthwith recommend to this court the institution of a disciplinary proceeding where the public interest demands prompt action and where the available facts show probable cause for such action.

(f) Except as otherwise provided for in paragraph (5) of subdivision (e) of this section, if, after preliminary investigation, the committee shall deem a matter of sufficient importance, written charges predicated thereon, plainly stating the matter or matters charged, together with a notice of not less than 20 days, shall be served upon the person concerned, either personally, by certified mail, or in such other manner as the committee may direct. The person so served shall file a written answer at the time and place designated in the notice and the committee or a subcommittee shall proceed to hold a hearing of the case. The person concerned (hereinafter referred to as the respondent) may be represented and assisted by counsel. The committee or subcommittee shall decide all questions of evidence. Stenographic minutes of the hearing shall be kept.

(g) Whenever in the course of a hearing evidence is presented upon which another charge or charges against the respondent might be made, it shall not be necessary for the committee to prepare and serve an additional charge or charges on the respondent, but the committee or the subcommittee may, after reasonable notice to the respondent and an opportunity to answer and be heard, proceed to the consideration of such additional charge or charges as if the same had been made and served at the time of the service of the original charge or charges.

(h) If the hearing was held before a subcommittee, it shall make findings of fact and report those findings to the committee. Upon the completion of a hearing, the committee shall promptly meet and either dismiss or sustain the charges and, as to any charges sustained, shall either issue a letter of caution, admonish the respondent, or recommend that probable cause exists for the filing of disciplinary charges against the respondent in this court. A letter of caution may also be issued where the charges have been dismissed. The approval of a recommendation of the filing of disciplinary charges in this court shall be by a majority vote of the full committee.

(i) In the event that a minority of the committee disagrees with a final determination, such minority report shall be filed with this court along with any majority report and the written report of the subcommittee. Upon such filing, the committee shall await the determination of this court before otherwise disposing of the matter.

(j) Unless otherwise provided for by this court, all proceedings conducted by a grievance committee shall be sealed and be deemed private and confidential.

(k) Disciplinary proceedings shall be granted a preference by this court.

(l)(1) An attorney who is the subject of an investigation, or of charges by a grievance committee of professional misconduct, or who is the subject of a disciplinary proceeding pending in this court against whom a petition has been filed pursuant to this section, or upon whom a notice has been served pursuant to section 691.3(b) of this Part, may be suspended from the practice of law, pending consideration of the charges against the attorney, upon a finding that the attorney is guilty of professional misconduct immediately threatening the public interest. Such a finding shall be based upon:

(i) the attorney's default in responding to the petition or notice, or the attorney's failure to submit a written answer to pending charges of professional misconduct or the attorney's failure to submit a written answer to a complaint of professional misconduct within 10 days of receipt of a demand for such an answer by the grievance committee, served either personally or by certified mail upon the attorney or the attorney's failure to comply with any of the lawful demand of this court or the grievance committee made in connection with any investigation, hearing, or disciplinary proceeding; or

(ii) a substantial admission under oath that the attorney has committed an act or acts of professional misconduct; or

(iii) other uncontroverted evidence of professional misconduct.

(2) The suspension shall be made upon the application of the grievance committee to this court, after notice of such application has been given to the attorney pursuant to subdivision 6 of section 90 of the Judiciary Law. The court shall briefly state its reasons for its order of suspension which shall be effective immediately and until such time as the disciplinary matters before the committee have been concluded, and until further order of this court.

(m) Diversion Program.

(1) If during the course of an investigation, the consideration of charges by a grievance committee, or the course of a formal disciplinary proceeding, it appears that the attorney whose conduct is the subject thereof is or may be suffering from alcoholism or other substance abuse or dependency, the court may upon application of the attorney or committee, or on its own motion, stay the investigation, charges, or proceeding and direct the attorney to complete a monitoring program sponsored by a lawyers' assistance program approved by the court. In determining whether to divert an attorney to a monitoring program, the court shall consider (i) whether the alleged misconduct occurred during a time period when the attorney suffered from alcohol or other substance abuse or dependency; (ii) whether the alleged misconduct is related to such alcohol or other substance abuse or dependency; (iii) the seriousness of the alleged misconduct; and (iv) whether diversion is in the best interest of the public, the legal profession, and the attorney.

(2) Upon submission of written proof of successful completion of the monitoring program, the court may direct the discontinuance or resumption of the investigation, charges, or proceeding, or take other appropriate action.

(3) In the event the attorney is not accepted into or fails to successfully complete the monitoring program as ordered by the court, or the attorney commits additional misconduct after diversion is directed pursuant to this subdivision, the court may, upon notice to the attorney affording him or her the opportunity to be heard, rescind the order diverting the attorney to the monitoring program and reinstate the investigation, charges, or proceeding, or take other appropriate action.

(4) Any costs associated with the attorney's participation in a monitoring program pursuant to this subdivision shall be paid by the attorney.

(n) Medical and Psychological Evidence. Whenever an attorney who is the subject of charges of professional misconduct and a hearing before a grievance committee or is the subject of a disciplinary proceeding pending in this court intends to offer medical or psychological evidence at a hearing in mitigation of the charges, he or she shall give written notice to counsel for the committee of the intention to do so not later than 20 days before the scheduled date of the hearing. Said notice shall be accompanied by (1) a duly executed and acknowledged written authorization permitting counsel for the committee to obtain and make copies of the records of the treating physician, psychiatrist, psychologist, or other such health care professionals regarding the attorney's physical or mental condition at issue, and (2) a copy of the written reports, if any, of the health care professionals who the attorney proposes to call as witnesses.

(*o*) **Disqualification from Representation.** No former staff counsel to a grievance committee or former member of such a committee may accept a retainer or otherwise represent an attorney who is the subject of an investigation, or of charges by a grievance committee of professional misconduct, or of a disciplinary proceeding in this court, if such investigation, charges, and/or proceeding were pending before such committee during the term of service of that former staff counsel or committee member.

No former special referee appointed to hear and report on the issues raised in a formal disciplinary proceeding may accept a retainer or otherwise represent an attorney who is the subject of an investigation, or of charges by a grievance committee of professional misconduct, or of a disciplinary proceeding in this judicial department, until the expiration of two years from the date of the submission of his or her final report.

Cross References

Judiciary Law, see McKinney's Book 29.

Public Officers Law, see McKinney's Book 46.

§ 691.5. Investigation of Professional Misconduct on the Part of an Attorney; Subpoenas and Examination of Witnesses Under Oath

(a) Upon application by the chairman or acting chairman of any such committee, or upon application by counsel to such committee, disclosing that such committee is conducting an investigation of professional misconduct on the part of any attorney, or upon application by an attorney under such investigation, the clerk of this court may issue subpoenas, in the name of the presiding justice, for the attendance of witnesses and the production of books and papers before such committee or such counsel or any subcommittee thereof designated in such application, at a time and place therein specified.

(b) Any such committee or a subcommittee thereof is empowered to take and cause to be transcribed the evidence of witnesses who may be sworn by any person authorized by law to administer oaths.

§ 691.5–a. Formal Disciplinary Proceedings; Subpoenas, Depositions, and Motions

In the event that a formal disciplinary proceeding pursuant to section 90 of the Judiciary Law or other provision of this part is commenced in this court against an attorney, the following shall apply:

(a) Subpoenas. Upon application by the petitioner or the respondent, the clerk of this court may issue subpoenas for the attendance of witnesses and the production of books and papers before the referee, justice, or judge designated by the court to conduct a hearing on the issues raised in the proceeding, at a time and place therein specified.

(b) Depositions. When there is good cause to believe that a potential witness will be unavailable at the time of a hearing, the testimony of that witness may be taken by deposition. Such a deposition shall be initiated and conducted in the manner provided by, and the use thereof at a hearing shall be in accordance with, the provisions of article 31 of the Civil Practice Law and Rules.

(c) Motions. Motions made during the course of a formal disciplinary proceeding shall be addressed to the court and shall be made and noticed in the manner provided in section 670.5 of this title. The court may refer the motion to a referee, justice, or judge appointed by it to either hear and determine or hear and report on the same.

§ 691.6. Reprimand; Admonition; Letter of Caution; Confidentiality

(a) The chairman or acting chairman of any such committee may, after investigation and upon a majority vote of the full committee, issue a reprimand or an admonition or a letter of caution in those cases in which professional misconduct, not warranting proceedings before this court, is found. A reprimand is discipline imposed after a hearing. An admonition is discipline imposed without a hearing. A letter of caution may issue when it is believed that the attorney acted in a manner which, while not constituting clear professional misconduct, involved behavior requiring comment. In cases in which an admonition or a letter of caution is issued, the attorney to whom such admonition or letter of caution is directed may, within 30 days after the issuance of the admonition or letter of caution, request a hearing before the committee or a subcommittee thereof, and after such hearing, the committee shall take such steps as it deems advisable. In cases in which a reprimand is issued, the attorney to whom such reprimand is issued, may within 30 days of the issuance of the reprimand, petition this court to vacate the reprimand. Upon such petition, this court may consider the entire record and may vacate the reprimand or impose such other discipline as the record may warrant.

(b) A copy of any reprimand or admonition or letter of caution given pursuant to this section shall be filed with this court.

(c) A confidential record of the proceedings resulting in such reprimand or admonition or letter of caution shall be permanently maintained by such committee (except that the complainant shall be notified of any reprimand or admonition or letter of caution which has become final and is not subject to further review) and may be considered in determining the extent of discipline to be imposed in the event other charges of misconduct are brought against the attorney subsequently.

(d) The provisions for confidentiality contained in this or any other section of this Part are not intended to proscribe the free interchange of information among the committees.

§ 691.7. Attorneys Convicted of Serious Crimes; Record of Conviction Conclusive Evidence

(a) Upon the filing with this court of a certificate that an attorney has been convicted of a serious crime as hereinafter defined in a court of record of any State, territory or district, including this State, this court shall cause formal charges to be made and served upon the respondent and shall enter an order immediately referring the matter to a referee, justice or judge appointed by this court to conduct forthwith disciplinary proceedings, whether the conviction resulted from a plea of guilty or nolo contendere or from a verdict after trial or otherwise, and regardless of the pendency of an appeal.

(b) The term "serious crime" shall include any felony, not resulting in automatic disbarment under the provisions of subdivision (4) of section 90 of the Judiciary Law, and any lesser crime a necessary element of which, as determined by the statutory or common law definition of such crime, involves interference with the administration of justice, criminal contempt of court, false swearing, misrepresentation, fraud, willful failure to file income tax returns, deceit, bribery, extortion, misappropriation, theft, an attempt or a conspiracy or solicitation of another to commit a "serious crime" or a crime involving moral turpitude.

(c) A certificate of the conviction of an attorney for any crime shall be conclusive evidence of his guilt of that crime in any disciplinary proceeding instituted against him based on the conviction, and the attorney may not offer evidence inconsistent with the essential elements of the crime for which he was convicted as determined by the statute defining the crime.

(d) Upon the filing with the court of a certificate that an attorney has been convicted of a crime not constituting a serious crime as hereinbefore defined in a court of record in any State, territory or district, including this State, this court shall either refer the matter to a committee appointed pursuant to section 691.4(a) of this Part for whatever action may be appropriate, or cause formal charges to be made and served upon the respondent and enter an order immediately referring the matter to a referee, justice or judge appointed by this court to conduct forthwith disciplinary proceedings, whether the conviction resulted from a plea of guilty or nolo contendere or from

a verdict after trial or otherwise, and regardless of the pendency of an appeal.

(e) The clerk of any court within the judicial department in which an attorney admitted to practice in this State is convicted of a crime shall within five days of said conviction forward a certificate thereof to the clerk of this court and to the clerk of the Appellate Division of the Supreme Court in the judicial department in which said person was admitted to practice.

(f) Any such committee, upon receiving information that an attorney to whom these rules shall apply pursuant to section 691.1 of this Part, has been convicted of a crime in a court of record of any State, territory or district, shall determine whether the clerk of the court where the conviction occurred has forwarded a certificate of the conviction to this court. If the certificate has not been forwarded by the clerk, such committee shall obtain a certificate of the conviction and forward it to this court.

Cross References

Judiciary Law, see McKinney's Book 29.

§ 691.8. Effect of Restitution on Disciplinary Proceedings

Restitution made by an attorney or on his behalf to a client for funds converted, or to reimburse him for losses suffered as a result of the attorney's wrongdoing, shall not be a bar to the commencement or continuance of disciplinary proceedings.

§ 691.9. Resignation of Attorneys Under Investigation

(a) An attorney who is the subject of an investigation into allegations of misconduct may tender his resignation by submitting to the appropriate committee appointed pursuant to section 691.4(a) of this Part an affidavit stating that he intends to resign and that:

(1) his resignation is freely and voluntarily rendered; he is not being subjected to coercion or duress; and he is fully aware of the implications of submitting his resignation;

(2) he is aware that there is pending an investigation into allegations that he has been guilty of misconduct, the nature of which shall be specifically set forth; and

(3) he acknowledges that if charges were predicated upon the misconduct under investigation, he could not successfully defend himself on the merits against such charges.

(b) Upon receipt of the required affidavit, such committee shall file it with this court, which may enter an order either disbarring him or striking his name from the roll of attorneys.

§ 691.10. Conduct of Disbarred, Suspended or Resigned Attorneys; Abandonment of Practice by Attorney

(a) **Compliance With Judiciary Law.** Disbarred, suspended or resigned attorneys at law shall comply fully and completely with the letter and spirit of sections 478, 479, 484 and 486 of the Judiciary Law relating to practicing as attorneys at law without being admitted and registered, and soliciting of business on behalf of an attorney at law and the practice of law by an attorney who has been disbarred, suspended or convicted of a felony.

(b) **Compensation.** A disbarred, suspended or resigned attorney may not share in any fee for legal services performed by another attorney during the period of his removal from the bar. A disbarred, suspended or resigned attorney may be compensated on a quantum meruit basis for legal services rendered and disbursements incurred by him prior to the effective date of the disbarment or suspension order or of his resignation. The amount and manner of payment of such compensation and recoverable disbursements shall be fixed by the court on the application of either the disbarred, suspended or resigned attorney or the new attorney, on notice to the other as well as on notice to the client. Such applications shall be made at special term in the court wherein the action is pending or at special term in the Supreme Court in the county wherein the moving attorney maintains his office if an action has not been commenced. In no event shall the combined legal fees exceed the amount the client would have been required to pay had no substitution of attorneys been required.

(c) **Notice to Clients Not Involved in Litigation.** A disbarred, suspended or resigned attorney shall promptly notify, by registered or certified mail, return receipt requested, all clients being represented in pending matters, other than litigated or administrative matters or proceedings pending in any court or agency, of his disbarment, suspension or resignation and his consequent inability to act as an attorney after the effective date of his disbarment, suspension or resignation and shall advise said clients to seek legal advice elsewhere.

(d) **Notice to Clients Involved in Litigation.**

(1) A disbarred, suspended or resigned attorney shall promptly notify, by registered or certified mail, return receipt requested, each of his clients who is involved in litigated matters or administrative proceedings, and the attorney or attorneys for each adverse party in such matter or proceeding, of his disbarment, suspension or resignation and consequent inability to act as an attorney after the effective date of his disbarment, suspension or resignation. The notice to be given to the client shall advise of the prompt substitution of another attorney or attorneys in his place.

(2) In the event the client does not obtain substitute counsel before the effective date of the disbarment, suspension or resignation, it shall be the responsibility of the disbarred, suspended or resigned attorney to move pro se in the court in which the action is pending, or before the body in which an administrative proceeding is pending, for leave to withdraw from the action or proceeding.

(3) The notice given to the attorney or attorneys for an adverse party shall state the place of residence of the client of the disbarred, suspended or resigned attorney. In addition, notice shall be given in like manner to the Office of Court Administration of the State of New York in each case in which a retainer statement has been filed.

(e) **Conduct After Entry of Order.** The disbarred, suspended or resigned attorney, after entry of the disbarment or suspension order or after entry of the order accepting the resignation, shall not accept any new retainer or engage in any new case or legal matter of any nature as attorney for another. However, during the period between the entry date of the order and its effective date he may wind up and complete, on behalf of any client, all matters which were pending on the entry date.

(f) **Filing Proof of Compliance and Attorney's Address.** Within 10 days after the effective date of the disbarment or suspension order or the order accepting the resignation, the disbarred, suspended or resigned attorney shall file with the clerk of the Appellate Division for the Second Judicial Department an affidavit showing:

(1) that he has fully complied with the provisions of the order and with these rules; and

(2) that he has served a copy of such affidavit upon the petitioner or moving party.

Such affidavit shall also set forth the residence or other address of the disbarred, suspended or resigned attorney where communications may be directed to him.

(g) **Appointment of Attorney to Protect Clients' Interests and Interests of Disbarred, Suspended or Resigned Attorney.** Whenever it shall be brought to the court's attention that a disbarred, suspended or resigned attorney shall have failed or may fail to comply with the provisions of subdivisions (c), (d) or (f) of this section, this court, upon such notice to such attorney as this court may direct, may appoint an attorney or attorneys to inventory the files of the disbarred, suspended or resigned attorney and to take such action as seems indicated to protect the interests of his clients and for the protection of the interests of the disbarred, suspended or resigned attorney.

(h) **Disclosure of Information.** Any attorney so appointed by this court shall not be permitted to disclose any information contained in any file so inventoried without the consent of the client to whom such file relates except as necessary to carry out the order of this court which appointed the attorney to make such inventory.

(i) Fixation of Compensation. This court may fix the compensation to be paid to any attorney appointed by it under this section. The compensation may be directed by this court to be paid as an incident to the costs of the proceeding in which the charges are incurred and shall be charged in accordance with law.

(j) Required Records. A disbarred, suspended or resigned attorney shall keep and maintain records of the various steps taken by him under this Part so that, upon any subsequent proceeding instituted by or against him, proof of compliance with this Part and with the disbarment or suspension order or with the order accepting the resignation will be available.

(k) Abandonment of Practice by Attorney. When, in the opinion of this court, an attorney has abandoned his practice, this court, upon such notice to such attorney as it may direct, may appoint the chief counsel of the appropriate joint bar association grievance committee, or an individual attorney, to take custody and inventory the files of such attorney and to take such action as seems indicated to protect the interests of his clients.

Cross References
Judiciary Law, see McKinney's Book 29.

§ 691.11. Reinstatement Following Suspension, Disbarment, or Striking of Name from Roll of Attorneys

(a) Timing of Application. No attorney disbarred after a hearing or on consent, or whose name has been stricken from the roll of attorneys pursuant to subdivision 4 of section 90 of the Judiciary Law or section 691.9 of this Part may apply for reinstatement until the expiration of at least seven years from the effective date of the disbarment or removal. An attorney suspended under the provisions of this Part shall be entitled to apply for reinstatement after such an interval as this court may direct in the order of suspension or any modification thereof.

(b) Form and Notice of Application. An application for reinstatement shall be made in the form of a motion in accordance with instructions specified by administrative order of the court. The instructions shall be available in the office of the clerk of the court and on the court's internet site. The motion for reinstatement shall be made upon notice to the appropriate grievance committee and the Lawyers' Fund for Client Protection, which may submit papers in opposition or in relation thereto.

(c) Required Showing. An application for reinstatement may be granted by the court only upon a showing:

(1) by clear and convincing evidence, that the applicant has complied with the provisions of the order disbarring or suspending him or her, or striking his or her name from the roll of attorneys, and that he or she possesses the character and general fitness to practice law; and,

(2) if the applicant was disbarred or suspended from the practice of law for more than one year, that (i) subsequent to the entry of such order, he or she attained a passing score on the Multistate Professional Responsibility Examination described in section 520.9(a) of the rules of the Court of Appeals for the admission of attorneys and counselors-at-law, the passing score thereon being that determined by the New York State Board of Law Examiners pursuant to section 520.9(c) of such rules, and (ii) he or she has successfully completed one credit hour of continuing legal education accredited in accordance with Part 1500 of this Title for each month of disbarment or suspension up to a maximum of twenty-four credits. The continuing legal education required by clause (ii) of this paragraph shall be completed during the period of disbarment or suspension and within the two years preceding reinstatement. Compliance with clause (ii) of this paragraph may, upon request of the applicant, be deferred pending notification that the court has conditionally granted the application for reinstatement subject to the completion of required continuing legal education; or,

(3) if the applicant was suspended from the practice of law for one year, that during the period of suspension (i) he or she and successfully completed eighteen credit hours of continuing legal education accredited in accordance with Part 1500 of this Title, six credit hours of which were in the area of ethics and professionalism as defined in subdivision (c) of section 1500.2 of this Title, or (ii) he or she has successfully completed twelve credit hours of continuing legal education accredited in accordance with Part 1500 of this Title and has attained a passing score on the Multistate Professional Responsibility Examination as set forth in clause (i) of paragraph (2) of this subdivision; or,

(4) if the applicant was suspended from the practice of law for less than one year, that during the period of suspension he or she has successfully completed one credit hour of continuing legal education accredited in accordance with Part 1500 of this Title for each month of suspension.

(d) Character and Fitness Review. The court shall refer an application for reinstatement after a suspension of more than one year or after a disbarment to a Committee on Character and Fitness in this judicial department or to a referee, justice, or judge for a report before granting that application and, in its discretion, may similarly refer an application for reinstatement after a suspension of one year or less.

(e) Renewed Motion for Reinstatement. No renewed motion for reinstatement shall be accepted for filing within one year of the entry of an order of this court denying a prior motion for such relief, unless the order denying the prior motion provides otherwise.

(f) Expenses. The court may direct that the necessary expenses incurred in the investigation and processing of a motion for reinstatement be paid by the applicant.

INSTRUCTIONS

**Application for Reinstatement to the Bar After Disbarment
or Suspension of More than One Year**

An application pursuant to Judiciary Law § 90 and § 691.11 of the rules of this court for reinstatement to the bar after disbarment or a suspension from practice of more than one year shall comply with the following requirements:

§ 1. The application shall be made in the form of a motion.

§ 2. The moving papers shall bear the caption and the Appellate Division docket number of the proceeding that led to the movant's disbarment or suspension.

§ 3. The motion shall be made on notice to the Departmental Grievance Committee that prosecuted the proceeding leading to the movant's disbarment or suspension and to the Lawyers' Fund for Client Protection.

§ 4. The motion shall be made, noticed, and filed in accordance with § 670.5 of the rules of procedure of this court. Payment of the $45 fee required by CPLR 8022(b) shall accompany the filing of the motion papers, unless the movant is exempt from payment thereof pursuant to CPLR 1102. Checks shall be made payable to "Clerk of the Court."

§ 5. The motion shall be supported by the affidavit or affirmation of the movant, subscribed and sworn to or affirmed before a notary public or other person authorized to administer an oath or affirmation.

§ 6. The supporting affidavit or affirmation shall be worded and numbered as follows:

State of New York   )
County of _____) ss.:

_____, being duly sworn, deposes and says (or affirms under the penalty of perjury) that:

1. I hereby apply, pursuant to Judiciary Law § 90 and 22 NYCRR 691.11, for reinstatement as an attorney and counselor-at-law licensed to practice in all of the courts of the State of New York.

2. My full name is _____. The name under which I was admitted to the practice of law is _____. My name was changed on the Roll of Attorneys and Counselors–at–Law to _____ by reason of (marriage, divorce or annulment, or a court order legally changing the movant's name). I have also been known by the following names:

3. I was born on (date) in (city, state, country).

4. I currently reside at (street, town or city, state, and zip code).

5. The telephone numbers at which I can be contacted are:

    Home   _____

    Work   _____

    Mobile   _____

6. The e-mail address at which I can be contacted is _____.

7. I was admitted to the New York State Bar on (date) in the _____ Judicial Department.

8. By opinion and order of this court dated (date), I was (suspended for ___ years/disbarred) from the practice of law. My use of the term "discipline" hereinafter refers to the sanction imposed by this court in the foregoing opinion and order.

    A copy of the opinion and order imposing discipline is attached as exhibit A hereto.

9. Other than the location specified in paragraph 4 hereof, I have resided at the following addresses since the effective date of discipline (in reverse chronological order state the approximate dates of residence, street, town or city, state, and zip code):

10. The discipline imposed upon me was predicated upon, or arose out of, my misappropriation or misuse of the real or personal property of others, or the failure to return legal fees received but unearned by me. I have made full restitution to the owners of the property or the clients in question, and if any part of a loss occasioned by my conduct was the subject of an award by the Lawyers' Fund for Client Protection pursuant to 22 NYCRR Part 7200, I have made full restitution to the Fund, except as follows:

    A statement listing each property, its dollar value, the name of the true owner, and the extent to which I have made or have yet to make restitution is attached as exhibit _____ hereto.

11. I have also been admitted to practice in the following jurisdictions:

    Certificates of Good Standing, issued within the 30 days preceding the execution of this affidavit (or affirmation) by all such jurisdictions, except those in which I have not been reinstated as set forth in paragraph 12 hereof, are attached as exhibit _____ hereto.

12. Since the imposition of discipline, I have also been the subject of professional discipline in the following other jurisdictions (state the jurisdiction, the date, the nature of the discipline imposed, and whether or not you have been reinstated to practice and are now in good standing in such jurisdiction):

    A copy of each order or judgment imposing such discipline is attached as exhibit _____ hereto. A copy of each order or judgment reinstating me to practice is attached as exhibit _____ hereto.

13. On the effective date of discipline, the following matters, which were not the basis of this court's opinion and order, were pending against me before any grievance committee in the State of New York (state the nature of the complaint, the disciplinary authority before which it was pending, and the disposition thereof):

14. From the date of my admission to the New York State Bar until the present, the following other disciplinary sanctions have been imposed upon me due to my misconduct as an attorney, in this or any other jurisdiction (state the jurisdiction, the nature of the misconduct, the date, and the nature of the discipline imposed):

15. Since the imposition of discipline, I have engaged in the practice of law in the following other jurisdictions and in the following manner:

16. Since the imposition of discipline, I have engaged in the following employment or have been engaged in the following businesses (in ascending chronological order, state the dates so engaged, and the name and address of the employer or business):

    A letter from each such employer, attesting to my employment history, is attached as exhibit _____ hereto, except _____, the absence of which is explained as follows:

17. At the time discipline was imposed, I took the following affirmative steps to comply with the order imposing discipline and with 22 NYCRR 691.10:

18. Pursuant to 22 NYCRR 691.10(f), I filed an affidavit of compliance on (date).

A copy of that affidavit of compliance is attached as exhibit _____ *hereto.*

- or -

I failed to file an affidavit of compliance as required by 22 NYCRR 691.10(f) for the following reason(s):

19. Since the imposition of discipline, I or a corporation or an entity of which I am or was a principal, have or has been involved in the following lawsuits, either as a party, witness, or counsel to a party, to the extent indicated (state the title of the suit, the court in which it is or was pending, the index number, the nature of the suit, and the capacity [plaintiff, defendant, counsel, etc.] in which the movant is or was involved):

20. There presently exist(s) the following unsatisfied judgment(s) against me and/or any corporation or entity of which I am or was a principal (state the name and address of the judgment creditor, the court which rendered the judgment, the date and amount of the judgment, the nature of the claim on which it was based, and the amount thereof remaining unpaid):

21. Since the imposition of discipline, I have defaulted in the performance or discharge of an obligation or duty imposed upon me by the following courts, and/or governmental or administrative agencies (state the nature of the obligation or duty, the court or agency by which it was imposed, the date performance was due, and the reason for the default).

22. Other than the judgments set forth in paragraph 20 hereof, I have incurred the following debts with a balance over $500 that are presently overdue by at least 60 days (state the name and address of each creditor, the nature of the debt, the original amount of the indebtedness and date incurred, the due date, and the balance due):

23. I or any firm, corporation, or business entity in which I have or had an ownership interest filed a petition in bankruptcy on (date) to (court).

Copies of any bankruptcy petitions, schedules, and or discharge orders are attached as exhibit _____ *hereto.*

24. Since the imposition of discipline, I have filed all required Federal, state, and local income tax returns when due or have received an extension to file the same, except as follows:

Copies of all such returns are attached as exhibit _____ *hereto.*

25. Since the imposition of discipline, I have applied for the following licenses that required proof of good character (state the nature of the license, the name of the licensing authority, the date of the application, and the result thereof):

26. Since my admission to the New York State Bar, I have had the following licenses suspended or revoked (state the nature of the license, the name of the licensing authority, the date and reason for the action, and whether the license was revoked or suspended):

27. Since the imposition of discipline, I have been arrested, charged with, indicted, convicted, tried, and/or entered a plea of guilty to the following felonies, misdemeanors, violations, and/or traffic infractions (state the court, the offense charged, and date and nature of disposition):

28. Since my admission to the Bar, I have been the subject of the following governmental investigation(s) (state the name of the investigating agency and the nature and date of the investigation):

29. Since the imposition of discipline, I have suffered from or have been treated for a mental or emotional disorder, alcoholism and/or substance abuse or dependency (state the date or dates of each instance, the name of any health professional or institution consulted or affording treatment, and the circumstances):

30. Since the imposition of discipline, I have complied with the requirements of 22 NYCRR 691.11(c)(2) by attaining a passing score on the Multistate Professional Responsibility Examination (MPRE) and, within the two years preceding this application for reinstatement, successfully completing one credit hour of continuing legal education (CLE) accredited in accordance with 22 NYCRR Part 1500 for each month of suspension or disbarment up to a maximum of 24 credits.

Proof of passage of the MPRE and certificates attesting to my completion of the required CLE are attached as exhibit _____ hereto.

- or -

Since the imposition of discipline, I have complied with the requirements of 22 NYCRR 691.11(c)(2) to the extent of attaining a passing score on the Multistate Professional Responsibility Examination (MPRE). However I have not complied with the requirement that, within the two years preceding this application for reinstatement, I successfully complete 24 credit hours of continuing legal education (CLE) accredited in accordance with 22 NYCRR Part 1500. For the following reasons, I hereby request that the court conditionally approve this application subject to the completion of the CLE requirement before reinstatement to the bar:

Proof of passage of the MPRE is attached as exhibit _____ hereto.

31. Within the 30 days preceding the execution of this affidavit (affirmation), I have read the disciplinary rules set forth in 22 NYCRR Part 1200 of the joint rules of the Appellate Divisions and I have read 22 NYCRR Part 691 of the rules of this court. I am familiar with the provisions of the Code of Professional Responsibility. If reinstated to the practice of law, I will conform my conduct to those rules and the ethical considerations set forth in the Code.

32. Other than the passage of time and the absence of additional acts of misconduct, the following facts establish that I possess the requisite character and general fitness to be reinstated as an attorney and counselor–at–law:

33. The following facts, not heretofore disclosed to this court, are relevant to this application and might tend to influence the court to look less favorably upon reinstating me to the practice of law:

34. I understand that the court may take such investigative steps as it deems appropriate to evaluate my character and fitness for reinstatement to the Bar. I will fully cooperate with any request for additional information and make myself available to answer questions under oath or affirmation, as required.

WHEREFORE, I request that the court grant this application for my reinstatement as an attorney and counselor-at-law licensed to practice in all of the courts of the State of New York.

Dated: (city or town, state)

 _____ _____, 200__

 _____

Subscribed to and sworn to before me
this _____ day of _____, 200__

 _____
 Notary Public

§ 7. In completing the supporting affidavit or affirmation, the movant should not omit inapplicable passages. If an entire paragraph is inapplicable, the appropriate answer is "Not Applicable." If portions of the paragraph are inapplicable, the movant may so indicate by the use of strikethrough characters as in the following example:

    2. My full name is _____. The name under which I was admitted to the practice of law is _____. ~~My name was changed on the Roll of Attorneys and Counselors-at-Law to by reason of (marriage, divorce or annulment, or a court order legally changing the movant's name).~~ I have also been known by the following names:

§ 8. The application may be supplemented by the affidavits or affirmations of counsel and character witnesses, and with additional appropriate exhibits.

§ 9. Place the moving papers in the following order:

    a. The notice of motion or order to show cause;

    b. The applicant's form affidavit or affirmation;

    c. The exhibits supporting that form affidavit or affirmation;

    d. Any additional supporting affidavits or affirmations and exhibits thereto; and

    e. An affidavit of service of the moving papers upon the appropriate Departmental Grievance Committee and the Lawyer's Fund for Client Protection.

Application for Reinstatement to the Bar After Suspension of One Year or Less

An application pursuant to Judiciary Law § 90 and § 691.11 of the rules of this court for reinstatement to the bar after a suspension from practice of one year or less shall comply with the following requirements:

§ 1. The application shall be made in the form of a motion.

§ 2. The moving papers shall bear the caption and the Appellate Division docket number of the proceeding that led to the movant's suspension.

§ 3. The motion shall be made on notice to the Departmental Grievance Committee that prosecuted the proceeding leading to the movant's suspension and to the Lawyers' Fund for Client Protection.

§ 4. The motion shall be made, noticed, and filed in accordance with § 670.5 of the rules of procedure of this court. Payment of the $45 fee required by CPLR 8022(b) shall accompany the filing of the motion papers, unless the movant is exempt from payment thereof pursuant to CPLR 1102. Checks shall be made payable to "Clerk of the Court."

§ 5. The motion shall be supported by the affidavit or affirmation of the movant, subscribed and sworn to or affirmed before a notary public or other person authorized to administer an oath or affirmation.

§ 6. The supporting affidavit or affirmation shall be worded and numbered as follows:

    State of New York   )
    County of _____   ) ss.:

_____, being duly sworn, deposes and says (or affirms under the penalty of perjury) that:

    1. I hereby apply, pursuant to Judiciary Law § 90 and 22 NYCRR 691.11, for reinstatement as an attorney and counselor-at-law licensed to practice in all of the courts of the State of New York.

    2. My full name is _____. The name under which I was admitted to the practice of law is _____. My name was changed on the Roll of Attorneys and Counselors-at-Law to _____ by reason of (marriage, divorce or annulment, or a court order legally changing the movant's name). I have also been known by the following names:

3. I was born on (date) in (city, state, country).

4. I currently reside at (street, town or city, state, and zip code).

5. The telephone numbers at which I can be contacted are:

    Home   _____

    Work   _____

    Mobile   _____

6. The e-mail address at which I can be contacted is _____.

7. I was admitted to the New York State Bar on (date) in the _____ Judicial Department.

8. By opinion and order of this court dated (date), I was suspended from the practice of law for a period of (___ months/one year). My use of the term "discipline" hereinafter refers to the sanction imposed by this court in the foregoing opinion and order.

    A copy of the opinion and order imposing discipline is attached as exhibit A hereto.

9. Other than the location specified in paragraph 4 hereof, I have resided at the following addresses since the effective date of discipline (in reverse chronological order state the approximate dates of residence, street, town or city, state, and zip code):

10. I have also been admitted to practice in the following jurisdictions:

    Certificates of Good Standing, issued within the 30 days preceding the execution of this affidavit (or affirmation) by all such jurisdictions, except those in which I have not been reinstated as set forth in paragraph 11 hereof, are attached as exhibit _____ hereto.

11. Since the imposition of discipline, I have also been the subject of professional discipline in the following other jurisdictions (state the jurisdiction, the date, the nature of the discipline imposed, and whether or not you have been reinstated to practice and are now in good standing in such jurisdiction):

    A copy of each order or judgment imposing such discipline is attached as exhibit _____ hereto. A copy of each order or judgment reinstating me to practice is attached as exhibit _____ hereto.

12. On the effective date of discipline, the following matters, which were not the basis of this court's opinion and order, were pending against me before any grievance committee in the State of New York (state the nature of the complaint, the disciplinary authority before which it was pending, and the disposition thereof):

13. From the date of my admission to the New York State Bar until the present, the following other disciplinary sanctions have been imposed upon me due to my misconduct as an attorney, in this or any other jurisdiction (state the jurisdiction, the nature of the misconduct, the date, and the nature of the discipline imposed):

14. Since the imposition of discipline, I have engaged in the practice of law in the following other jurisdictions and in the following manner:

15. Since the imposition of discipline, I have engaged in the following employment or have been engaged in the following businesses (in ascending chronological order, state the dates so engaged, and the name and address of the employer or business):

16. At the time discipline was imposed, I took the following affirmative steps to comply with the order imposing discipline and with 22 NYCRR 691.10:

603

17. Pursuant to 22 NYCRR 691.10(f), I filed an affidavit of compliance on (date).

A copy of that affidavit of compliance is attached as exhibit _____ hereto.

- or -

I failed to file an affidavit of compliance as required by 22 NYCRR 691.10(f) for the following reason(s):

18. There are no unsatisfied judgments against me and/or any corporation or entity of which I am or was a principal, nor have I defaulted in the performance or discharge of an obligation or duty imposed upon me by a court, governmental, or administrative agency, except as follows:

19. Other than the judgments set forth in paragraph 18 hereof, I have incurred the following debts with a balance over $500 that are presently overdue by at least 60 days (state the name and address of each creditor, the nature of the debt, the original amount of the indebtedness and date incurred, the due date, and the balance due):

20. Since the imposition of discipline, I have filed all required Federal, state, and local income tax returns when due or have received an extension to file the same, except as follows:

Copies of all such returns are attached as exhibit _____ hereto.

21. Since the imposition of discipline, I have had the following licenses suspended or revoked (state the nature of the license, the name of the licensing authority, the date and reason for the action, and whether the license was revoked or suspended):

22. Since the imposition of discipline, I have been arrested, charged with, indicted, convicted, tried, and/or entered a plea of guilty to the following felonies, misdemeanors, violations, and/or traffic infractions (state the court, the offense charged, and date and nature of disposition):

23. Since the imposition of discipline, I have suffered from or have been treated for a mental or emotional disorder, alcoholism and/or substance abuse or dependency (state the date or dates of each instance, the name of any health professional or institution consulted or affording treatment, and the circumstances):

24. I was suspended from the practice of law for less than one year, and since the imposition of discipline I have complied with the requirements of 22 NYCRR 691.11(c)(4) by successfully completing one credit hour of continuing legal education (CLE) accredited in accordance with 22 NYCRR Part 1500 for each month of suspension.

Certificates attesting to my completion of the required CLE are attached as exhibit _____ hereto.

25. I was suspended from the practice of law for one year, and since the imposition of discipline I have complied with the requirements of 22 NYCRR 691.11(c)(3) by:

successfully completing 18 credit hours of continuing legal education (CLE) accredited in accordance with 22 NYCRR Part 1500, at least 6 of which were in the field of attorney ethics.

Certificates attesting to my completion of the required CLE are attached as exhibit _____ hereto.

- or -

successfully completing 12 credit hours of continuing legal education (CLE) accredited in accordance with 22 NYCRR Part 1500 and by attaining a passing grade on the Multistate Professional Responsibility Examination.

Certificates attesting to my completion of the required CLE and proof of passage of the MPRE are attached as exhibit _____ hereto.

26. Within the 30 days preceding the execution of this affidavit (affirmation), I have read the disciplinary rules set forth in 22 NYCRR Part 1200 of the joint rules of the Appellate Divisions and I have read 22 NYCRR Part 691 of the rules of this court. I am familiar with the provisions of the Code of Professional Responsibility. If reinstated to the practice of law, I will conform my conduct to those rules and the ethical considerations set forth in the Code.

27. Other than the passage of time and the absence of additional acts of misconduct, the following facts establish that I possess the requisite character and general fitness to be reinstated as an attorney and counselor–at–law:

28. The following facts, not heretofore disclosed to this court, are relevant to this application and might tend to influence the court to look less favorably upon reinstating me to the practice of law:

29. I understand that the court may take such investigative steps as it deems appropriate to evaluate my character and fitness for reinstatement to the Bar. I will fully cooperate with any request for additional information and make myself available to answer questions under oath or affirmation, as required.

WHEREFORE, I request that the court grant this application for my reinstatement as an attorney and counselor-at-law licensed to practice in all of the courts of the State of New York.

Dated: (city or town, state)

_____ _____, 200__

_____

Subscribed to and sworn to before me
this _____ day of _____, 200__

_____
Notary Public

§ 7. In completing the supporting affidavit or affirmation, the movant should not omit inapplicable passages. If an entire paragraph is inapplicable, the appropriate answer is "Not Applicable." If portions of the paragraph are inapplicable, the movant may so indicate by the use of strikethrough characters as in the following example:

2. My full name is _____. The name under which I was admitted to the practice of law is _____. ~~My name was changed on the Roll of Attorneys and Counselors–at–Law to by reason of (marriage, divorce or annulment, or a court order legally changing the movant's name).~~ I have also been known by the following names:

§ 8. The application may be supplemented by the affidavits or affirmations of counsel and character witnesses, and with additional appropriate exhibits.

§ 9. Place the moving papers in the following order:

a. The notice of motion or order to show cause;

b. The applicant's form affidavit or affirmation;

c. The exhibits supporting that form affidavit or affirmation;

d. Any additional supporting affidavits or affirmations and exhibits thereto; and

e. An affidavit of service of the moving papers upon the appropriate Departmental Grievance Committee and the Lawyer's Fund for Client Protection.

Cross References

Judiciary Law, see McKinney's Book 29.

§ 691.11–a. Reinstatement After Voluntary Resignation

(a) Form and Notice of Application. An application for reinstatement by a person who has voluntarily resigned from the bar of this state shall be made in the form of a motion in accordance with instructions specified by administrative order of the court. The instructions shall be available in the office of the clerk of the court and on the court's internet site. The motion for reinstatement shall be made upon notice to the grievance committee in the judicial district in which the applicant last maintained an office for the practice of law, or if none, to the grievance committee in the judicial district in which the applicant resided when admitted to practice, which may submit papers in opposition or in relation thereto.

(c)[1] **Required Showing.** An application for reinstatement may be granted by the court only upon an affidavit or affirmation stating:

(1) the circumstances of the applicant's resignation from the bar and the reason for applying for reinstatement;

(2) whether the applicant has been the subject of a disciplinary complaint or proceeding in any other jurisdiction and the results thereof;

(3) that the applicant is in good standing at the bar of any other jurisdiction in which he or she is admitted to practice; and,

(4) that the applicant has successfully completed one credit hour of continuing legal education accredited in accordance with Part 1500 of this Title for each month since the date of the order of this court accepting the resignation and removing his or her name from the roll of attorneys, up to a maximum of twenty-four credits.

Attached to the moving papers shall be a current certificate of good standing from each jurisdiction in which the applicant is admitted to practice and certificates establishing compliance with the continuing legal education requirement of paragraph (4) of this subdivision.

(d) Character and Fitness Review. The court may refer an application for reinstatement after a voluntary resignation to a Committee on Character and Fitness in this judicial department or to a referee, justice, or judge for a report before granting that application.

[1] So in original. No paragraph (b) has been enacted.

INSTRUCTIONS

Application for Reinstatement to the Bar After Voluntary Resignation

An application pursuant to Judiciary Law § 90 and § 691.11–a of the rules of this court for reinstatement to the bar after a voluntary resignation shall comply with the following requirements:

§ 1. The application shall be made in the form of a motion.

§ 2. The moving papers shall bear the caption and the Appellate Division docket number of the order accepting the movant's voluntary resignation.

§ 3. The motion shall be made on notice to the Departmental Grievance Committee in the judicial district in which the applicant last maintained an office for the practice of law, or if none, to the Departmental Grievance Committee in the judicial district in which the applicant resided when admitted to practice.

§ 4. The motion shall be made, noticed, and filed in accordance with § 670.5 of the rules of procedure of this court. Payment of the $45 fee required by CPLR 8022(b) shall accompany the filing of the motion papers, unless the movant is exempt from payment thereof pursuant to CPLR 1102. Checks shall be made payable to "Clerk of the Court."

§ 5. The motion shall be supported by the affidavit or affirmation of the movant, subscribed and sworn to or affirmed before a notary public or other person authorized to administer an oath or affirmation.

§ 6. The supporting affidavit or affirmation shall be worded and numbered as follows:

State of New York   )
County of _____) ss.:

_____, being duly sworn, deposes and says (or affirms under the penalty of perjury) that:

1. I hereby apply, pursuant to Judiciary Law § 90 and 22 NYCRR 691.11, for reinstatement as an attorney and counselor-at-law licensed to practice in all of the courts of the State of New York.

2. My full name is _____. The name under which I was admitted to the practice of law is _____. My name was changed on the Roll of Attorneys and Counselors-at-Law to _____ by reason of (marriage, divorce or annulment, or a court order legally changing the movant's name). I have also been known by the following names:

3. I was born on (date) in (city, state, country).

4. I currently reside at (street, town or city, state, and zip code).

5. The telephone numbers at which I can be contacted are:

   Home   _____

   Work   _____

   Mobile   _____

6. The e-mail address at which I can be contacted is _____.

7. I was admitted to the New York State Bar on (date) in the _____ Judicial Department.

8. By decision and order of this court dated (date), my voluntary resignation from the Bar of this State was accepted by the court.

   A copy of the decision and order accepting my voluntary resignation is attached as exhibit A hereto.

9. I have also been admitted to practice in the following jurisdictions:

   Certificates of Good Standing, issued within the 30 days preceding the execution of this affidavit (or affirmation) by all jurisdictions in which I am admitted are attached as exhibit _____ hereto.

10. Since the effective date of my resignation, I have been the subject of complaints of professional misconduct or of professional discipline in the following other jurisdictions (state the jurisdiction, the date, the nature of the complaint or the discipline imposed, and whether or not you are now in good standing in such jurisdiction):

11. Since the effective date of my resignation, I have been arrested, charged with, indicted, convicted, tried, and/or entered a plea of guilty to the following felonies, misdemeanors, violations, and/or traffic infractions (state the court, the offense charged, and date and nature of disposition):

12. Since the effective date of my resignation, I have suffered from or have been treated for a mental or emotional disorder, alcoholism and/or substance abuse or dependency (state the date or dates of each instance, the name of any health professional or institution consulted or affording treatment, and the circumstances):

13. Since the effective date of my resignation, I have complied with the requirements of 22 NYCRR 691.11–a(c)(4) by successfully completing one credit hour of continuing legal education (CLE) accredited in accordance with 22 NYCRR Part 1500 for each month since the date of the order of this court accepting the resignation and removing my name from the roll of attorneys, up to a maximum of twenty-four credits.

Certificates attesting to my completion of the required CLE are attached as exhibit _____ hereto.

14.   Within the 30 days preceding the execution of this affidavit (affirmation), I have read the disciplinary rules set forth in 22 NYCRR Part 1200 of the joint rules of the Appellate Divisions and I have read 22 NYCRR Part 691 of the rules of this court. I am familiar with the provisions of the Code of Professional Responsibility. If reinstated to the practice of law, I will conform my conduct to those rules and the ethical considerations set forth in the Code.

15.   I understand that the court may take such investigative steps as it deems appropriate to evaluate my character and fitness for reinstatement to the Bar. I will fully cooperate with any request for additional information and make myself available to answer questions under oath or affirmation, as required.

WHEREFORE, I request that the court grant this application for my reinstatement as an attorney and counselor-at-law licensed to practice in all of the courts of the State of New York.

Dated: (city or town, state)

_____ _____, 200__

Subscribed to and sworn to before me
this _____ day of _____, 200__

_____
Notary Public

§ 7.   In completing the supporting affidavit or affirmation, the movant should not omit inapplicable passages. If an entire paragraph is inapplicable, the appropriate answer is "Not Applicable." If portions of the paragraph are inapplicable, the movant may so indicate by the use of strikethrough characters as in the following example:

2.   My full name is _____. The name under which I was admitted to the practice of law is _____. ~~My name was changed on the Roll of Attorneys and Counselors-at-Law to by reason of (marriage, divorce or annulment, or a court order legally changing the movant's name).~~ I have also been known by the following names:

§ 8.   The application may be supplemented by the affidavits or affirmations of counsel and character witnesses, and with additional appropriate exhibits.

§ 9.   Place the moving papers in the following order:

a.   The notice of motion or order to show cause;

b.   The applicant's form affidavit or affirmation;

c.   The exhibits supporting that form affidavit or affirmation;

d.   Any additional supporting affidavits or affirmations and exhibits thereto; and

e.   An affidavit of service of the moving papers upon the appropriate Departmental Grievance Committee.

Cross References

Judiciary Law, see McKinney's Book 29.

§ 691.12. Regulations and Procedures for Random Review and Audit and Biennial Affirmation of Compliance

(a) Availability of Bookkeeping Records; Random Review and Audit. The financial records required by section 1200.46 of this Title shall be available at the principal New York State office of the attorneys subject hereto, for inspection, copying and determination of compliance with said section 1200.46, to a duly authorized representative of the court pursuant to the issuance, on a randomly selected basis, of a notice or subpoena by this Court or the appropriate Grievance Committee.

(b) Confidentiality. All matters, records and proceedings relating to compliance with section 1200.46 of this Title, including the selection of an attorney for review hereunder, shall be kept confidential in accordance with applicable law, as and to the extent required of matters relating to professional discipline.

(c) Prior to the issuance of any notice or subpoena in connection with the random review and audit program established by this section, the appropriate Grievance Committee shall propose regulations and procedures for the proper administration of the program. The Court shall approve such of the regulations and procedures of the Grievance Committee as it may deem appropriate, and only such regulations and procedures as have been approved by the Court shall become effective.

(d) Any attorney subject to this court's jurisdiction shall execute that portion of the biennial registration statement provided by the Office of Court Administration affirming that the attorney has read and is in compliance with section 1200.46 of this Title. The affirmation shall be available at all times to the Grievance Committees. No affirmation of compliance shall be required from a full-time judge or justice of the unified court system of the State of New York or of a court of any other state, or of a federal court.

§ 691.13. Proceedings Where Attorney Is Declared Incompetent or Alleged to Be Incapacitated

(a) Suspension Upon Judicial Determination of Incompetency or on Involuntary Commitment. Where an attorney subject to the provisions of section 691.1 of this Part has been judicially declared incompetent or involuntarily committed to a mental hospital, this court, upon proper proof of the fact, shall enter an order suspending such attorney from the practice of the law, effective immediately and for an indefinite period and until the further order of this court. A copy of such order shall be served upon such attorney, his committee, and/or the director of the mental hospital in such manner as this court may direct.

(b) Proceeding to Determine Alleged Incapacity and Suspension Upon Such Determination.

(1) Whenever a committee appointed pursuant to section 691.4(a) of this Part shall petition this court to determine whether an attorney is incapacitated from continuing to practice law by reason of mental infirmity or illness or because of addiction to drugs or intoxicants, this court may take or direct such action as it deems necessary or proper to determine whether the attorney is so incapacitated, including examination of the attorney by such qualified medical experts as this court shall designate. If, upon due consideration of the matter, this court is satisfied and concludes that the attorney is incapacitated from continuing to practice law, it shall enter an order suspending him on the ground of such disability for an indefinite period and

until the further order of this court and any pending disciplinary proceedings against the attorney shall be held in abeyance.

(2) This court may provide for such notice to the respondent-attorney of proceedings in such matter as it deems proper and advisable and may appoint an attorney to represent the respondent, if he is without adequate representation.

(3) Any report prepared by a qualified medical expert designated by the court pursuant to paragraph (1) of this subdivision and filed in the office of the clerk of this court shall be made available to counsel for the committee and to counsel for the respondent.

(c) Procedure When Respondent Claims Disability During Course of Proceeding.

(1) If, during the course of a disciplinary proceeding, the respondent contends that he is suffering from a disability by reason of mental infirmity or illness, or because of addiction to drugs or intoxicants, which makes it impossible for the respondent adequately to defend himself, this court thereupon shall enter an order suspending the respondent from continuing to practice law until a determination is made of the respondent's capacity to continue the practice of law in a proceeding instituted in accordance with the provisions of subdivision (b) of this section.

(2) If, in the course of a proceeding under this section or in a disciplinary proceeding, this court shall determine that the respondent is not incapacitated from practicing law, it shall take such action as it deems proper and advisable, including a direction for the resumption of the disciplinary proceeding against the respondent.

(d) Appointment of Attorney to Protect Client's and Suspended Attorney's Interest.

(1) Whenever an attorney is suspended for incapacity or disability, this court, upon such notice to him as it may direct, may appoint an attorney or attorneys to inventory the files of the suspended attorney and to take such action as it deems proper and advisable to protect the interest of his clients and for the protection of the interest of the suspended attorney.

(2) Any attorney so appointed by this court shall not be permitted to disclose any information contained in any file so inventoried without the consent of the client to whom such file relates, except as is necessary to carry out the order of this court which appointed the attorney to make such inventory.

(e) Reinstatement Upon Termination of Disability.

(1) Any attorney suspended under the provisions of this section shall be entitled to apply for reinstatement at such intervals as this court may direct in the order of suspension or any modification thereof. Such application shall be granted by this court upon a showing by clear and convincing evidence that the

attorney's disability has been removed and he is fit to resume the practice of law. Upon such application, this court may take or direct such action as it deems necessary or proper for a determination as to whether the attorney's disability has been removed, including the direction of an examination of the attorney by such qualified medical experts as this court shall designate. In its discretion, this court may direct that the expense of such examination shall be paid by the attorney.

(2) Where an attorney has been suspended by an order in accordance with the provisions of subdivision (a) of this section and thereafter, in proceedings duly taken, has been judicially declared to be competent, this court may dispense with further evidence that his disability has been removed and may direct his reinstatement upon such terms as it deems proper and advisable.

(f) Burden of Proof. In a proceeding seeking an order of suspension under this section, the burden of proof shall rest with the petitioner. In a proceeding seeking an order terminating a suspension under this section, the burden of proof shall rest with the suspended attorney.

(g) Waiver of Doctor-Patient Privilege Upon Application for Reinstatement. The filing of an application for reinstatement by an attorney suspended for disability shall be deemed to constitute a waiver of any doctor-patient privilege existing between the attorney and any psychiatrist, psychologist, physician or hospital who or which has examined or treated the attorney during the period of his disability. The attorney shall be required to disclose the name of every psychiatrist, psychologist, physician and hospital by whom or at which the attorney has been examined or treated since his suspension and he shall furnish to this court written consent to each to divulge such information and records as is requested by court-appointed medical experts or by the clerk of this court.

(h) Payment of Expenses of Proceedings.

(1) The necessary costs and disbursements of an agency, committee or appointed attorney in conducting a proceeding under this section shall be paid in accordance with subdivision (6) of section 90 of the Judiciary Law.

(2) The court may fix the compensation to be paid to any attorney or medical expert appointed by this court under this section. The compensation may be directed by this court to be paid as an incident to the cost of the proceeding in which the charges are incurred and shall be paid in accordance with law.

Cross References

Judiciary Law, see McKinney's Book 29.

§§ 691.14, 691.15. [Repealed]

§ 691.16. Attorneys Assigned by the Court as Counsel for a Defendant in a Criminal Case

(a) No attorney assigned by a court as counsel for a defendant in any criminal case shall in any manner demand, accept, receive or agree to accept or receive any payment, compensation, emolument, gratuity or reward or any promise of payment, compensation, emolument, gratuity or reward or any money, property or thing of value or of personal advantage from such defendant or from any other person, except as expressly authorized by statute.

(b) No attorney assigned by a court as counsel for an indigent defendant in any criminal case shall, during the pendency thereof, accept a private retainer to represent the defendant in that or any other case.

(c) Violation of this section shall result in the removal of the attorney's name from the panel of attorneys eligible to receive assignment pursuant to article 18-B of the County Law and shall constitute a violation of § 1200.3(5) of this Title.

§ 691.17. [Repealed]

§ 691.18. [Rescinded]

§ 691.19. Compromise of Claims or Actions Belonging to Infants

(a) An application for the approval by the court of a settlement of a claim or cause of action belonging to an infant must be made as provided in CPLR 1207 and 1208.

(b) In the case of a claim or demand belonging to an infant, any sum collected by an attorney shall be deposited in a special account apart from his personal account, in accordance with the provisions of section 691.12 of this Part, and a statement of the amount received shall be delivered personally to the duly qualified guardian of the infant or mailed to such guardian by registered or certified mail addressed to said guardian's last known address. But no payment or withdrawal shall be made from such deposit in the said account to the credit of the infant's claim except pursuant to an order of the court after application as provided in section 474 of the Judiciary Law, upon at least two days' notice to the guardian.

Cross References

CPLR, see McKinney's Book 7B.

Judiciary Law, see McKinney's Book 29.

Forms

Settlement of action or claim by infant, incapacitated person, incompetent, or conservatee, see West's McKinney's Forms, CPLR, §§ 3:1321 to 3:1326.

§ 691.20. Claims or Actions for Personal Injury, Property Damage, Wrongful Death, Loss of Services Resulting From Personal Injuries, Due to Negligence or Any Type of Malpractice, and Claims in Connection With Condemnation or Change of Grade Proceedings

(a) Statements as to Retainers; Blank Retainers.

(1) Every attorney who, in connection with any action or claim for damages for personal injury or for property damages, or for death or loss of services resulting from personal injuries, due to negligence or any type of malpractice, or in connection with any claim in condemnation or change of grade proceedings, accepts a retainer or enters into an agreement, express or implied, for compensation for services rendered or to be rendered in such action, claim or proceeding, whereby his compensation is to be dependent or contingent in whole or in part upon the successful prosecution or settlement thereof, shall, within 30 days from the date of any such retainer or agreement of compensation, sign personally and file with the Office of Court Administration of the State of New York a written statement of such retainer or agreement of compensation, containing the information hereinafter set forth. Such statement may be filed personally by the attorney or his representative at the main office of the Office of Court Administration in the City of New York, and upon such filing he shall receive a date-stamped receipt containing the code number assigned to the original so filed. Such statement may also be filed by ordinary mail only addressed to:

Office of Court Administration—Statements
Post Office Box No. 2016
New York, New York 10008

Statements filed by mail must be accompanied by a self-addressed stamped postal card, containing the words "Retainer Statement", the date of the retainer and the name of the client. The Office of Court Administration will date-stamp the postal card, make notation thereon of the code number assigned to the retainer statement and return such card to the attorney as a receipt for the filing of such statement. It shall be the duty of the attorney to make due inquiry if such receipt is not returned to him within 10 days after his mailing of the retainer statement to the Office of Court Administration.

(2) A statement of retainer must be filed in Connection with each action claim or Proceeding for which the attorney has been retained. Such statement shall be on one side of Paper 8½ inches by 11 inches and be in the following form and contain the following information:

Retainer Statement   For office Use:

TO THE OFFICE OF COURT ADMINISTRATION OF THE STATE OF NEW YORK

1. Date of agreement as to retainer ....

2. Terms of compensation ....

3. Name and home address of client ....

4. If engaged by an attorney, name and office address of retaining attorney ....

5. If claim for personal injuries, wrongful death or property damage, date and place of occurrence ....

6. If a Condemnation or change of grade proceeding:

(a) Title and description ....

(b) Date proceeding was commenced ....

(c) Number or other designation of the parcels affected ....

7. Name, address, occupation and relationship of person referring the client ....

Dated: ...., N.Y. .... day of ...., 20...

    Yours, etc.

    ....
    Signature of Attorney

    ....
    Attorney

    ....
    Office and P.O. Address

    ..... Dist. ..... Dept. ..... County

    (Print or Type)

NOTE: CPLR 2104 AND 3217 REQUIRE THAT THE ATTORNEY FOR THE DEFENDANT FILE A STIPULATION OR STATEMENT OF DISCONTINUANCE WITH THE COURT UPON DISCONTINUANCE OF AN ACTION.

(3) An attorney retained by another attorney, on a contingent fee basis, as trial or appeal counsel or to assist in the preparation, investigation, adjustment or settlement of any such action, claim or proceeding shall, within 15 days from the date of such retainer, sign personally and file with the Office of Court Administration a written statement of such retainer in the manner and form as above set forth, which statement shall also contain particulars as to the fee arrangement, the type of services to be rendered in the matter, the code number assigned to the statement of retainer filed by the retaining attorney and the date when said statement of retainer was filed.

(4) No attorney shall accept or act under any written retainer or agreement of compensation in which

the name of the attorney was left blank at the time of its execution by the client.

(b) Closing Statement; Statement Where No Recovery.

(1) A closing statement shall be filed in connection with every claim, action or proceeding in which a retainer statement is required, as follows: Every attorney upon receiving, retaining or sharing any sum in connection with a claim, action or proceeding subject to this section shall, within 15 days after such receipt, retention or sharing, sign personally and file with the Office of Court Administration and serve upon the client a closing statement as hereinafter provided. Where there has been a disposition of any claim, action or proceeding, or a retainer agreement is terminated, without recovery, a closing statement showing such fact shall be signed personally by the attorney and filed with the Office of Court Administration within 30 days after such disposition or termination. Such statement may be filed personally by the attorney or his representative at the main office of the Office of Court Administration in the City of New York and upon such filing he shall receive a date-stamped receipt. Such statement may also be filed by ordinary mail only addressed to:

Office of Court Administration—Statements
Post Office Box No. 2016
New York, N. Y. 10008

Statements filed by mail must be accompanied by a self-addressed stamped postal card containing the words "Closing Statement", the date the matter was completed, and the name of the client. The Office of Court Administration will date-stamp the postal card, make notation thereon of the code number assigned to the closing statement and return such card to the attorney as a receipt for the filing of such statement. It shall be the duty of the attorney to make due inquiry if such receipt is not returned to him within ten days after his mailing of the closing statement to the Office of Court Administration.

(2) Each closing statement shall be on one side of paper 8½ inches by 11 inches and be in the following form and contain the following information:

Closing Statement   For office use:

TO THE OFFICE OF COURT ADMINISTRATION
OF THE STATE OF NEW YORK

1. Code number appearing on Attorney's receipt for filing of retainer statement.

. . . .

2. Name and present address of client

. . . .

3. Plaintiff(s)

. . . .

4. Defendant(s)

. . . .

5. (a) If an action was commenced, state the date: _____, 20_____, _____ Court, _____ County.

(b) Was the action disposed of in open court? _____

If not, and a request for judicial intervention was filed, state the date the stipulation or statement of discontinuance was filed with the clerk of the part to which the action was assigned. _____.

If not, and an index number was assigned but no request for judicial intervention was filed, state the date the stipulation or statement of discontinuance was filed with the County Clerk. _____.

6. Check items applicable: Settled ( ); Claim abandoned by client ( ); Judgment ( )

Date of payment by carrier or defendant . . . . . . day of . . . . . ., 20. . .

Date of payment to client . . . . . . day of . . . . . ., 20. . .

7. Gross amount of recovery (if judgment entered, include any interest, costs and disbursements allowed) $. . . . (of which $. . . . was taxable costs and disbursements).

8. Name and address of insurance carrier or person paying judgment or claim and carrier's file number, if any . . . .

9. Net amounts: to client $. . . .; compensation to undersigned $. . . .; names, addresses and amounts paid to attorneys participating in the contingent compensation . . . .

10. Compensation fixed by: retainer agreement ( ); under schedule ( ); or by court ( ).

11. If compensation fixed by court: Name of Judge. . . . . ., Court . . . . Index No. . . . . . Date of order . . . .

12. Itemized statement of payments made for hospital, medical care or treatment, liens, assignments, claims and expenses on behalf of the client which have been charged against the client's share of the recovery, together with the name, address, amount and reason for each payment . . . .

13. Itemized statement of the amounts of expenses and disbursements paid or agreed to be paid to others for expert testimony, investigative or other Services properly chargeable to the recovery of damages together with the name, address and reason for each payment . . . .

14. Date on which a copy of this closing statement has been forwarded to the client. . . ., 20. . .

NOTE: CPLR 2104 AND 3217 REQUIRE THAT THE ATTORNEY FOR THE DEFENDANT FILE A STIPULATION OR STATEMENT OF DISCONTINUANCE WITH THE COURT UPON DISCONTINUANCE OF AN ACTION.

Dated: ...., N.Y. .... day of ...., 20...

  Yours, etc.

....
Signature of Attorney

....
Attorney

....
Office and P.O. Address

..... Dist. ..... Dept. ..... County

(Print or Type)

(If space provided is insufficient, riders on sheets 8½ inches by 11 inches and signed by the attorney may be attached.)

(3) A joint closing statement may be served and filed in the event that more than one attorney receives, retains or shares in the contingent compensation in any claim, action or proceeding, in which event the statement shall be signed by each such attorney.

(c) Confidential Nature of Statements.

(1) All statements of retainer or closing statements filed shall be deemed to be confidential and the information therein contained shall not be divulged or made available for inspection or examination except upon written order of the presiding justice of the Appellate Division. (See subdivision (g) of this section).

(2) The Office of Court Administration of the State of New York shall microphotograph all statements filed pursuant to this section on film of durable material by use of a device which shall accurately reproduce on such film the original statements in all details thereof, and shall thereafter destroy the originals so reproduced. Such microphotographs shall be deemed to be an original record for all purposes, and an enlargement or facsimile thereof may be introduced in evidence in all courts and administrative agencies and in any action, hearing or proceeding in place and stead of the original statement so reproduced, with the same force and effect as though the original document were presented.

(d) Deposit of Collections; Notice.

(1) Whenever an attorney, who has accepted a retainer or entered into an agreement as above referred to, shall collect any sum of money upon any such action, claim or proceeding, either by way of settlement or after a trial or hearing, he shall forthwith deposit the same in a special account in accordance with the provisions of section 691.12 of this Part. Within 15 days after the receipt of any such sums he shall cause to be delivered personally to such client or sent by registered or certified mail, addressed to such client at the client's last known address, a copy of the closing statement required by this section. At the same time the attorney shall pay or remit to the client the amount shown by such statement to be due the client, and he may then withdraw for himself the amount so claimed to be due him for compensation and disbursements. For the purpose of calculating the 15 day period, the attorney shall be deemed to have collected or received or been paid a sum of money on the date that he receives the draft endorsed by the client, or if the client's endorsement is not required, on the date the attorney receives the sum. The acceptance by a client of such amount shall be without prejudice to the latter's right in an appropriate action or proceeding, to petition the court to have the question of the attorney's compensation or reimbursement for expenses investigated and determined by it.

(2) Whenever any sum of money is payable upon any such claim, action or proceeding, either by way of settlement or after trial or hearing, and the attorney is unable to locate a client, the attorney shall apply pursuant to subdivision f–1 of section 1200.46 of the Disciplinary Rules of the Code of Professional Responsibility to the court in which such action or proceeding was pending, or if no action had been commenced, then to the Supreme Court in the county in which the attorney maintains an office, for an order directing payment to be made to the attorney of the fees and reimbursable disbursements determined by the court to be due said attorney and to the Lawyers' Fund for Client Protection of the balance due to the client, for the account of the client, subject to the charge of any lien found by the court to be payable therefrom.

(e) Contingent Fees in Claims and Actions for Personal Injury and Wrongful Death.

(1) In any claim or action for personal injury or wrongful death, or loss of services resulting from personal injury or for property or money damages, resulting from negligence or any type of malpractice, other than one alleging medical, dental or podiatric malpractice, whether determined by judgment or settlement, in which the compensation of claimant's or plaintiff's attorney is contingent, that is, dependent in whole or in part upon the amount of recovery, the receipt, retention or sharing by such attorney pursuant to agreement or otherwise, of compensation which is equal to or less than that contained in any schedule of fees adopted by this department is deemed to be fair and reasonable. The receipt, retention or sharing of compensation which is in excess of such scheduled fees shall constitute the exaction of unreasonable and unconscionable compensation in violation of any provi-

sions of the Code of Professional Responsibility, as adopted by the New York State Bar Association, or of any Canon of the Canons of Ethics, as adopted by such bar association, unless authorized by a written order of the court as hereinafter provided.

(2) The following is the schedule of reasonable fees referred to in paragraph (1) of this subdivision: either

Schedule A

(i) 50 percent on the first $1000 of the sum recovered;

(ii) 40 percent on the next $2000 of the sum recovered;

(iii) 35 percent on the next $22,000 of the sum recovered; or,

(iv) 25 percent on any amount over $25,000 of the sum recovered; or,

Schedule B

(v) A percentage not exceeding 33⅓ percent of the sum recovered, if the initial contractual arrangement between the client and the attorney so provides, in which event the procedure hereinafter provided for making application for additional compensation because of extraordinary circumstances shall not apply.

(3) Such percentage shall be computed on the net sum recovered after deducting from the amount recovered expenses and disbursements for expert medical testimony and investigative or other services properly chargeable to the enforcement of the claim or prosecution of the action. In computing the fee, the costs as taxed, including interest upon a judgment, shall be deemed part of the amount recovered. For the following or similar items there shall be no deduction in computing such percentages: liens, assignments or claims in favor of hospitals, for medical care and treatment by doctors and nurses, or self-insurers or insurance carriers.

(4) In the event that claimant's or plaintiff's attorney believes in good faith that Schedule A above because of extraordinary circumstances, will not give him adequate compensation, application for greater compensation may be made upon affidavit with written notice and an opportunity to be heard to the client and other persons holding liens or assignments on the recovery. Such application shall be made to the justice of the trial part to which the action had been sent for trial; or, if it had not been sent to a part for trial, then to the justice presiding at the trial term calendar part of the court in which the action had been instituted; or, if no action had been instituted, then to the justice presiding at the trial term calendar part of the Supreme Court for the county in the judicial department in which the attorney who filed the statement of retainer, pursuant to this section, has an office. Upon such application, the justice, in his discretion, if extraordinary circumstances are found to be present,

and without regard to the claimant's or plaintiff's consent, may fix as reasonable compensation for legal services rendered an amount greater than that specified in Schedule A above, provided, however, that such greater amount shall not exceed the fee fixed pursuant to the contractual arrangement, if any, between the client and the attorney. If the application be granted, the justice shall make a written order accordingly, briefly stating the reasons for granting the greater compensation; and a copy of such order shall be served on all persons entitled to receive notice of the application.

(5) The provisions of subdivision (e) of this section shall not apply to an attorney retained as counsel in a claim or action for personal injury or wrongful death by another attorney, if such other attorney is not subject to the provisions of this section in such claim or action, but all other subdivisions of this section shall apply.

(6) Nothing contained in subsection (e) of this section shall be deemed applicable to the fixing of compensation for attorneys representing infants or other persons, where the statutes or rules provide for the fixation of such compensation by the court.

(7) Nothing contained in subsection (e) of this section shall be deemed applicable to the fixing of compensation for attorneys for services rendered in connection with the collection of first party benefits as defined by Article XVIII of the Insurance Law.

(8) The provisions of paragraph (2) of this subdivision shall not apply to claims alleging medical, dental, or podiatric malpractice. Compensation of claimant's or plaintiff's attorney for services rendered in claims or actions for personal injury alleging medical, dental or podiatric malpractice shall be computed pursuant to the fee schedule in section 474–a of the Judiciary Law.

(f) **Preservation of Records of Claims and Actions.** Attorneys for both plaintiff and defendant in the case of any such claim or cause of action shall preserve, for a period of seven years after any settlement or satisfaction of the claim or cause of action or any judgment thereon or after the dismissal or discontinuance of any action, the pleadings and other papers pertaining to such claim or cause of action, including, but not limited to, letters or other data relating to the claim of loss of time from employment or loss of income; medical reports, medical bills, X-ray reports, X-ray bills; repair bills, estimates of repairs; all correspondence concerning the claim or cause of action; and memoranda of the disposition thereof as well as canceled vouchers, receipts and memoranda evidencing the amounts disbursed by the attorney to the client and others in connection with the aforesaid claim or cause of action and such other records as are required to be maintained under section 691.12 of this Part.

(g) **Special Authorization to Divulge Retainer and Closing Statements Filed by Attorneys.** Pursuant to subdivision (c)(1) of this section, the presiding justice of the Appellate Division of the Supreme Court in the second judicial department does hereby order that, without his further specific order, the clerk of the said Appellate Division and the Office of Court Administration of the State of New York, jointly and severally, are authorized to permit any agent or representative of the Treasury Department or of the district director of Internal Revenue of the United States, upon the presentation of written authorization from a supervising official or head in the office of said department or district director, to examine and copy any retainer or closing statement heretofore or hereafter filed by any attorney in the office of the said clerk or the Office of Court Administration of the State of New York, in accordance with said rules regulating the conduct of attorneys and counselors at law.

(h) Omnibus Filings in Property Damage Actions or Claims. Attorneys prosecuting actions or claims for property damage may make semi-annual omnibus filings of retainer statements and closing statements.

Cross References

Insurance Law, see McKinney's Book 27.

Code of Professional Responsibility, see Appendix to McKinney's Book 29.

§ 691.21. Preliminary Investigation of Any Party Unlawfully Practicing Law or Assuming to Practice Law

(a) Upon application by the chairman or acting chairman of the committee or subcommittee on unlawful practice of the law of any recognized bar association in any county in the Second Judicial Department, alleging that such committee or subcommittee has reasonable cause to believe that any party (to wit: any person, firm, corporation or other organization) is unlawfully practicing law or unlawfully assuming to practice law or is engaging in any business or activity which may involve the unlawful practice of law, and further alleging that such committee or subcommittee is conducting or intends to conduct an investigation with respect to such practice, business or activity, the clerk of this court is empowered and authorized to issue, in the name of the presiding justice of the court, subpoenas directing the attendance of witnesses and the production of books, papers and records before such committee or subcommittee at the time when and at the place where it will convene. The clerk of the court is also empowered and authorized to issue such subpoenas upon the application of any such party.

(b) Every committee or subcommittee conducting such preliminary investigation is empowered to take the testimony of witnesses under oath and to transcribe such testimony. Such witnesses may be sworn by any person authorized by law to administer oaths.

§ 691.22. [Repealed]

§ 691.23. Attorney's Affidavit in Agency and Private Placement Adoptions

(a) Every attorney appearing for an adoptive parent, a natural parent, or an adoption agency in an adoption proceeding in the courts within this judicial department, shall, prior to the entry of an adoption decree, file with the Office of Court Administration of the State of New York, and with the court in which the adoption proceeding has been initiated, a signed statement under oath setting forth the following information:

(1) Name of attorney;

(2) Association with firm (if any);

(3) Business address;

(4) Telephone number;

(5) Docket number of adoption proceeding;

(6) Court where adoption has been filed;

(7) The date and terms of every agreement, written or otherwise, between the attorney and the adoptive parents, the natural parents, or anyone else on their behalf, pertaining to any compensation or thing of value paid, or given or to be paid or given by or on behalf of the adoptive parents or the natural parents, including but not limited to retainer fees;

(8) The date and amount of any compensation paid or thing of value given, and the amount of total compensation to be paid or thing of value to be given to the attorney by the adoptive parents, the natural parents, or by anyone else on account of or incidental to any assistance or service in connection with the proposed adoption;

(9) A brief statement of the nature of the services rendered;

(10) The name and address of any other attorney or attorneys who shared in the fees received in connection with the services, or to whom any compensation or thing of value was paid or is to be paid, directly or indirectly, by the attorney; the amount of such compensation or thing of value;

(11) The name and address of any other attorney or attorneys, if known, who received or will receive any compensation or thing of value, directly or indirectly, from the adoptive parents, natural parents, agency, or other source, on account of or incidental to any assistance or service in connection with the proposed adoption; the amount of such compensation or thing of value, if known;

(12) The name and address of any other person, agency, association, corporation, institution, society or organization who received or will receive any compensation or thing of value from the attorney, directly or indirectly, on account of or incidental to any assistance

or service in connection with the proposed adoption; the amount of such compensation or thing of value;

(13) The name and address, if known, of any person, agency, association, corporation, institution, society, or organization to whom compensation or thing of value has been paid or given, or is to be paid or given by any source for the placing out of, or on account of, or incidental to assistance in arrangements for the placement or adoption of the adoptive child; the amount of such compensation or thing of value and the services performed or the purposes for which the payment was made; and

(14) A brief statement as to the date and manner in which the initial contact occurred between the attorney and the adoptive parents or natural parents with respect to the proposed adoption.

(b) Names or other information likely to identify the natural or adoptive parents or the adoptive child are to be omitted from the information to be supplied in the attorney's statement.

(c) Such statement may be filed personally by the attorney, or his representative, at the main office of the Office of Court Administration in the City of New York, and upon such filing he shall receive a date-stamped receipt containing the code number assigned to the original so filed. Such statement may also be filed by ordinary mail, addressed to:

Office of Court Administration—
Adoption Affidavits
Post Office Box No. 2016
New York, New York 10008

(d) All statements filed by attorneys shall be deemed to be confidential, and the information therein contained shall not be divulged or made available for inspection or examination to any person, other than the client of the attorney in the adoption proceeding, except upon written order of the presiding justice of the Appellate Division.

§ 691.24. Compensation of Attorneys Representing Claimants Against Lawyers' Fund for Client Protection

No attorney shall charge a fee for or accept compensation for representation of claimants against the lawyers fund for client protection of the State of New York except as approved by the trustees of the fund.

§ 691.25. Bar Association Screening Committees; Members as Volunteers, Public Officers Law, § 17

The members of the screening committees of the Bar Associations of Kings, Queens and Richmond Counties, which committees are established under the authority of section 722 of the County Law for the purpose of providing counsel to persons charged with a crime, as volunteers, are expressly authorized to participate in a State-sponsored volunteer program within the meaning of subdivision one of section 17 of the Public Officers Law.

Cross References

County Law, see McKinney's Book 11.

Public Officers Law, see McKinney's Book 46.

PART 692.   LICENSING LEGAL CONSULTANTS

§ 692.1. Applications for Licenses as Legal Consultants; Referral to Committee on Character and Fitness

(a) The committees on character and fitness appointed by this court for the respective judicial districts in this department to investigate the character and fitness of applicants for admission to practice as attorneys and counselors at law in the courts of this State are hereby also authorized to investigate the qualifications and the character and fitness of applicants for licenses to practice as legal consultants pursuant to the Judiciary Law (§ 53, subd. 6) and the Rules of the Court of Appeals. (22 NYCRR Part 521)

(b) Every applicant for a license to practice as a legal consultant shall complete, verify and file with the clerk of this court the standard form of questionnaire, and shall comply with all the other requirements prescribed for that purpose by this court.

(c) Every application in this department for such a license shall be referred to the committee on character and fitness for the judicial district in which the appli-

cant actually resides at the time of such application, and, unless otherwise ordered by the court, no such license shall be granted without a certificate from such committee that it has found that the applicant possesses the qualifications and the character and fitness required therefor.

Cross References

Judiciary Law, see McKinney's Book 29.

§ 692.2. Documents, Affidavits and Other Proof Required

Every applicant for a license to practice as a legal consultant shall file the following additional papers with his application:

(a) A certificate from the authority having final jurisdiction over professional discipline in the foreign country in which the applicant was admitted to practice, which shall be signed by a responsible official or one of the members of the executive body of such authority and shall be attested under the hand and seal, if any, of the clerk of such authority, and which shall certify:

(1) As to the authority's jurisdiction in such matters,

(2) As to the applicant's admission to practice in such foreign country and the date thereof, and as to his good standing as an attorney or counselor at law or the equivalent therein, and

(3) As to whether any charge or complaint has ever been filed against the applicant with such authority, and, if so, the substance of each such charge or complaint and the disposition thereof.

(b) A letter of recommendation from one of the members of the executive body of such authority or from one of the judges of the highest law court or court of general original jurisdiction of such foreign country, certifying to the applicant's professional qualifications, together with a certificate under the hand and seal, if any, of the clerk of such authority or of such court, as the case may be, attesting to the office held by the person signing the letter and the genuineness of his signature.

(c) Affidavits as to the applicant's good moral character and fitness from three reputable persons residing in this State and not related to the applicant, one of whom shall be a practicing New York attorney.

(d) Affidavits from two attorneys or counselors at law or the equivalent admitted in and practicing in such foreign country, stating the nature and extent of their acquaintance with the applicant and their personal knowledge as to the nature, character and extent of the applicant's practice, and as to the applicant's good standing, as an attorney or counselor at law or the equivalent in such foreign country, and the duration and continuity of such practice.

(e) Such additional evidence as the applicant may see fit to submit with respect to his educational and professional qualifications and his good moral character and fitness.

(f) A duly authenticated English translation of every paper submitted by the applicant which is not in English.

(g) A duly acknowledged instrument designating the clerk of this court the applicant's agent for service of process as provided in section 521.4(a)(2)(iii) of the rules of the Court of Appeals.

§ 692.3.   College and Law School Certificates

A certificate shall be submitted from each college and law school attended by the applicant, setting forth the information required by forms which shall be provided to the applicant for that purpose.

§ 692.4.   Exceptional Situations

In the event that the applicant is unable to comply strictly with any of the foregoing requirements, the applicant shall set forth the reasons for such inability in an affidavit, together with a statement showing in detail the efforts made to fulfill such requirements.

§ 692.5.   Authority of Committees on Character and Fitness to Require Additional Proof

The committees on character and fitness may in any case require the applicant to submit such additional proof or information as they may deem appropriate and may also require the applicant to submit a report of the National Conference of Bar Examiners with respect to his character and qualifications.

§ 692.6.   Undertaking

Prior to taking custody of any money, securities (other than unendorsed securities in registered form), negotiable instruments, bullion, precious stones or other valuables, in the course of his practice as a legal consultant, for or on behalf of any client domiciled or residing in the United States, every person licensed to practice as a legal consultant shall obtain, and shall maintain in effect for the duration of such custody, an undertaking issued by a duly authorized surety company, and approved by a justice of this court, to assure the faithful and fair discharge of his duties and obligations arising from such custody. The undertaking shall be in an amount not less than the amount of any such money, or the fair market value of any such property other than money, of which the legal consultant shall have custody, except that this court may in any case in its discretion for good cause direct that such undertaking shall be in a greater or lesser amount. The undertaking or a duplicate original thereof shall be promptly filed by the legal consultant with the clerk of this court.

§ 692.7.   Disciplinary Procedure

(a) Disciplinary proceedings against any legal consultant shall be initiated and conducted in the same manner as prescribed by law for disciplinary proceedings against attorneys.

(b) Any committee authorized by this court to conduct preliminary investigations of charges of professional misconduct by attorneys shall have authority to conduct preliminary investigations of charges of professional misconduct or unauthorized activities on the part of any licensed legal consultant in the same manner as in investigations relating to attorneys.

§ 692.8.   Filing

Every application in this department for a license as a legal consultant, together with all the papers submitted thereon, shall upon its final disposition be filed in the office of the clerk of this court.

PART 693. [RESERVED]
PART 694. MENTAL HYGIENE LEGAL SERVICE

(Statutory authority: Mental Hygiene Law § 47.01)

§ 694.1. Definitions

Except as otherwise appears herein, whenever used in this Part any term defined in Mental Hygiene Law section 1.03 shall have the meaning set forth therein and, in addition, the following terms shall have the following meanings:

(a) Service means the Mental Hygiene Legal Service.

(b) Director means the head of the Service referred to in Mental Hygiene Law section 47.01 or his or her duly authorized designee.

(c) Court shall mean Supreme Court, County Court or Surrogate's Court.

(d) Patient shall mean a person residing in a facility for the mentally disabled which is licensed or operated by the Department of Mental Hygiene or the Department of Correctional Services, or a person residing in any other place for whom the Service has been appointed counsel or court evaluator pursuant to Mental Hygiene Law article 81.

(e) Guardian shall mean a person or entity appointed as a guardian, standby guardian or limited guardian as provided in the Surrogate's Court Procedure Act article 17–A or Mental Hygiene Law article 81.

Cross References

Mental Hygiene Law, see McKinney's Book 34A.

SCPA, see McKinney's Book 58A.

§ 694.2. Duties of the Director

(a) With regard to patients in facilities governed by the Mental Hygiene Law:

(1) The director shall inform each patient of his or her rights to a judicial hearing, to review pursuant to Mental Hygiene Law sections 9.35 and 15.35, to an appeal and to be represented by the Service or by privately retained counsel.

(2) In every case in which a hearing is requested or ordered or in which an application or petition is made to the court with regard to a patient which may or may not require a hearing, the director shall investigate the patient's case, examine the patient's records, interview the patient and also, in the discretion of the director, interview other persons having information relevant to the patient's case. If the patient has counsel the court may request the director to perform any services on behalf of the patient within the scope of and consistent with the Service's statutory duties.

(3) The director shall examine the patient's facility records as often as the director deems necessary.

(4) The court may request the director to render or undertake any assistance or service on behalf of a patient consistent with the Service's statutory duties.

(5) When a hearing has not been demanded, if the director determines that the case of a patient should be heard by the court, or be reviewed by a court or court and jury, the director may, in his or her discretion, demand a hearing on behalf of such patient or may request that the case of the patient be reviewed by the court, or court and jury, in accordance with the power granted to the Service in the Mental Hygiene Law.

(6)(i) The director shall ascertain that the notices to be given to patients and other persons required under the Mental Hygiene Law have been duly served and posted and that there has been compliance with the procedures required by the Mental Hygiene Law for the hospitalization, transfer, retention and release of patients.

(ii) The director shall ascertain that all requirements of law as to patients' admissions, treatment and discharge affecting patients' rights have been complied with.

(7) The director shall review the status of every person who has been an informal patient or a voluntary patient for a period of 12 consecutive months and shall ascertain that there has been compliance with the Mental Hygiene Law. If the director finds that the patient is willing and suitable for continued hospitalization in such status he or she shall so certify in the patient's record. If the director finds that the patient is unwilling or unsuitable for continued hospitalization in such status he or she shall take whatever action he or she deems necessary in accordance with the Mental Hygiene Law.

(b) In those guardianship proceedings pursuant to Mental Hygiene Law article 81 or the Surrogate's Court Procedure Act article 17–A in which the Service participates as counsel, court evaluator, guardian-ad-litem or party:

(1) Upon receipt of notice of application in such proceedings, the director shall:

(i) examine the papers and ascertain that the notices required to be given to parties and patients and, as far as known to the director, to other persons entitled thereto, have been duly served and that there has been due compliance with the prescribed statutory procedure;

(ii) examine the records relating to the affairs or medical or psychiatric condition of the party or patient;

(iii) interview every such party or patient, advise him or her of the nature of the proceeding and of his or her legal rights including the right to legal representation and the right to a court hearing, determine whether he or she has any objections to the proceeding or to the proposed guardian or whether he or she has any other objections;

(iv) interview any psychiatrist, examining physician or psychologist, or such other psychiatrist or physician who has knowledge of the party or patient's mental and physical condition;

(v) obtain all available information as to the extent and nature of the party or patient's assets;

(vi) obtain all available information concerning the party or patient's family, background and any other fact that may be necessary or desirable.

(2)(i) The director shall notify the court of any request for hearing.

(ii) In the director's discretion, and in the interest of the party or patient, the director may demand a hearing.

(3) The director shall inform the party or patient of the progress and status of all proceedings.

(4) In all proceedings for the discharge of a guardian, the enforcement or modification of a guardianship order, or the approval of a guardian's report or accounting, intermediate or final, the director shall inform the party or patient of the nature of the proceeding and his or her rights. The director may perform such additional services on behalf of the party or patient as are within the scope of, and consistent with, the Service's statutory duties.

(5) The director may, in an appropriate case and in his or her discretion, apply to the court for the discharge of the guardian or the enforcement or modification of an order appointing the guardian.

(6) The director is authorized to apprise the examiners charged with the review of accounts or reports with regard to any matter within the jurisdiction of such examiner affecting the welfare and property of a party or patient for whom a guardian has been appointed.

(7) The director shall perform such other duties and responsibilities as may be required by Mental Hygiene Law article 81.

(c) With regard to inmates, defendants or patients committed to, transferred to or placed in facilities for the mentally disabled pursuant to the Correction Law or to the Criminal Procedure Law:

(1) In all matters or proceedings in which the Service is required to be served with notice, the director shall:

(i) examine the papers, and shall ascertain that the notices required to be given have been duly served and that there has been due compliance with the prescribed procedure;

(ii) inform the inmate, defendant or patient of his or her rights including the right to judicial hearing, to review, to appeal and to be represented by the Service or by privately retained counsel;

(iii) when a hearing has not been demanded, if the director determines that the case should be heard by the court or be reviewed by a court, or court and jury, the director may, in his or her discretion, demand a hearing or may request that the case be reviewed by the court or court and jury;

(iv) examine the records of the inmate, defendant or patient;

(v) interview the attending psychiatrist, examining physician or psychologist who has knowledge of the condition of the inmate, defendant or patient;

(vi) interview all other persons having information relevant to the matter or proceeding;

(vii) perform such other services on behalf of the inmate, defendant or patient as the director in his or her discretion may determine. The court may request the director to perform additional services within the scope of, and consistent with, the Service's statutory duties.

(d) With regard to applications for authorization to administer psychotropic medication and to perform surgery, electro-convulsive therapy or major medical treatment in the nature of surgery upon parties or patients in facilities:

(1) Copies of notice of such applications shall be served upon the director of the Service of the judicial department in which the proceeding is brought and the director of the Service of the judicial department in which the facility is located.

(2) In all such proceedings the director shall:

(i) examine the papers, and shall ascertain that the notices required to be given have been duly served:

(ii) interview and inform the party or patient of the nature of the proceeding and of his or her rights, including the right to a judicial hearing, to appeal and to be represented by the Service or by privately retained counsel, and determine whether he or she has any objection to the proceeding;

(iii) when a hearing has not been demanded, if the director determines that the case should be heard by the court, the director may, in his or her discretion, demand a hearing on behalf of the party or patient;

(iv) examine the records of the party or patient;

(v) interview the party or patient's attending and consulting psychiatrist, physician or psychologist who has knowledge of the party or patient's condition;

(vi) interview all other persons having information relevant to the matter or proceeding;

(vii) perform such other services on behalf of the party or patient, as the court may request or the director may determine, consistent with the Service's statutory duties.

(e) In all the foregoing proceedings, the Service shall represent the inmate, defendant, party or patient unless they otherwise have counsel or counsel has been dispensed with pursuant to Mental Hygiene Law article 81.

(f) In all the foregoing proceedings, the director may, in his or her discretion, submit briefs, affidavits, affirmations or trial memoranda, consistent with the Service's role in the proceeding.

(g) In all of the foregoing proceedings the director shall assist the directors of the Service in the other judicial departments in regard to any proceeding pending in any other judicial department which pertains to a patient residing in the Second Judicial Department.

Cross References

Correction Law, see McKinney's Book 10B.

Criminal Procedure Law, see McKinney's Book 11A.

Mental Hygiene Law, see McKinney's Book 34A.

SCPA, see McKinney's Book 58A.

§ 694.3. Guardian Ad Litem and Court Evaluator

In any proceeding before the court involving a patient, the court may appoint the Service as guardian ad litem or court evaluator consistent with, and within the scope of the Service's statutory duties, except when the director advises the court that such appointment would create a conflict of interest with the Service's duties as counsel pursuant to 694.2 of this Part.

§ 694.4. Additional Psychiatric, Psychological, Medical or Expert Opinion

(a) Pursuant to Judiciary Law section 35 or any other statute, rule or regulation providing for additional opinion the director shall assist in obtaining, through a panel or otherwise, such additional opinion.

(b) No psychiatrist, psychologist, physician or other expert shall be appointed by the court if he or she is disqualified under provisions of the Mental Hygiene Law or if he or she is employed at the institution in which the patient is hospitalized or residing or to which the patient may be transferred as a result of the proceeding in which the expert is to render his or her opinion.

Cross References

Judiciary Law, see McKinney's Book 29.

Mental Hygiene Law, see McKinney's Book 34A.

§ 694.5. Review of Proposed Transfer of Patient or of Changes of Status of Patients

(a) In every case in which it is proposed to transfer a patient from one facility to another facility or to change his or her admission status to another, the director shall review the proposed transfer or change of status.

(b) In any such case, the director, in his or her discretion, may request a hearing on behalf of the patient.

§ 694.6. Fees

(a) When authorized by statute the director may request that the court award the Service a reasonable fee.

(b) The director's requests for fees for the services of attorneys shall not exceed the hourly rates of compensation set forth in section 35 of the judiciary law; and the director's requests for fees for the services of non-lawyer professionals shall not exceed the hourly rates of compensation set forth in the Unified Court System's compensation rate guidelines for court-appointed non-lawyer professionals.

(c) Fees awarded the Service shall be maintained and dispensed in accordance with law.

Cross References

Mental Hygiene Law, see McKinney's Book 34A.

§ 694.7. Records to Be Confidential

(a) All records and files of the director in any proceedings covered by this Part shall be confidential.

(b) All such records and files of the director may be exhibited only at the discretion of the director or upon order of the court.

PART 695. MENTAL HEALTH INFORMATION SERVICE PROCEDURE [REPEALED]

PARTS 696 TO 699. [RESERVED]

PART 700. COURT DECORUM

§ 700.1. Application of Rules

These rules shall apply in all actions and proceedings, civil and criminal, in courts subject to the jurisdiction of the Appellate Division of the Supreme Court in the Second Judicial Department. They are intended to supplement, but not to supersede, the Code of Professional Responsibility and the Canons of Judicial Ethics, as adopted by the New York State Bar Association. In the event of any conflict between the provisions of these rules and that Code or those Canons, the Code and the Canons shall prevail.

Cross References

Code of Judicial Conduct, see Appendix to McKinney's Judiciary Law, Book 29.

Code of Professional Responsibility, see Appendix to McKinney's Judiciary Law, Book 29.

§ 700.2. Importance of Decorum in Court

The courtroom, as the place where justice is dispensed, must at all times satisfy the appearance as well as the reality of fairness and equal treatment. Dignity, order and decorum are indispensable to the proper administration of justice. Disruptive conduct by any person while the court is in session is forbidden.

§ 700.3. Disruptive Conduct Defined

Disruptive conduct is any intentional conduct by any person in the courtroom that substantially interferes with the dignity, order and decorum of judicial proceedings.

§ 700.4. Obligations of the Attorney

(a) The attorney is both an officer of the court and an advocate. It is his professional obligation to conduct his case courageously, vigorously, and with all the skill and knowledge he possesses. It is also his obligation to uphold the honor and maintain the dignity of the profession. He must avoid disorder or disruption in the courtroom and he must maintain a respectful attitude toward the court. In all respects the attorney is bound, in court and out, by the provisions of the Code of Professional Responsibility.

(b) The attorney shall use his best efforts to dissuade his client and witnesses from causing disorder or disruption in the courtroom.

(c) The attorney shall not engage in any examination which is intended merely to harass, annoy or humiliate the witness.

(d) No attorney shall argue in support of or against an objection without permission from the court; nor shall any attorney argue with respect to a ruling of the court on any objection without such permission. However, an attorney may make a concise statement of the particular grounds for an objection or exception, not otherwise apparent, where it is necessary to do so in order to call the court's attention thereto, or to preserve an issue for appellate review. If an attorney believes in good faith that the court has wrongly made an adverse ruling, he may respectfully request reconsideration thereof.

(e) The attorney has neither the right nor duty to execute any directive of a client which is not consistent with professional standards of conduct. Nor may the attorney advise another to do any act or to engage in any conduct in any manner contrary to these rules.

(f) Once a client has employed an attorney who has entered an appearance, the attorney shall not withdraw or abandon the case without

(1) justifiable cause,

(2) reasonable notice to the client, and

(3) permission of the court.

(g) The attorney is not relieved of these obligations by what he may regard as a deficiency in the conduct or ruling of a judge or in the system of justice; nor is he relieved of these obligations by what he believes to be the moral, political, social, or ideological merits of the cause of any client.

Cross References

Code of Professional Responsibility, see Appendix to McKinney's Judiciary Law, Book 29.

§ 700.5. Obligations of the Judge

(a) In the administration of justice the judge shall safeguard the rights of the parties and the interests of the public. The judge at all times shall be dignified, courteous, and considerate of the parties, attorneys, jurors, and witnesses. In the performance of his duties, and in the maintenance of proper court decorum the judge is in all respects bound by the Canons of Judicial Ethics.

(b) The judge shall use his judicial power to prevent disruptions of the trial.

(c) A judge before whom a case is moved for trial shall preside at such trial unless he is satisfied, upon challenge or sua sponte, that he is unable to serve with complete impartiality, in fact or appearance, with regard to the matter at issue or the parties involved.

(d) Where the judge deems it appropriate in order to preserve or enhance the dignity, order and decorum of the proceedings, he shall prescribe and make known the rules relating to conduct which the parties, attorneys, witnesses and others will be expected to follow in the courtroom.

(e) The judge should be the exemplar of dignity and impartiality. He shall suppress his personal predilections, control his temper and emotions, and otherwise avoid conduct on his part which tends to demean the proceedings or to undermine his authority in the courtroom. When it becomes necessary during trial for him to comment upon the conduct of witnesses, spectators, counsel, or others, or upon the testimony, he shall do so in a firm and polite manner, limiting his comments and rulings to what is reasonably required for the orderly progress of the trial, and refraining from unnecessary disparagement of persons or issues.

(f) The judge is not relieved of these obligations by what he may regard as a deficiency in the conduct of any attorney who appears before him; nor is he relieved of these obligations by what he believes to be the moral, political, social, or ideological deficiencies of the cause of any party.

Cross References

Code of Judicial Conduct, see Appendix to McKinney's Judiciary Law, Book 29.

PART 701. EXERCISE OF THE JUDICIAL CONTEMPT POWER

§ 701.1. Application of Rules

These rules shall apply in all actions and proceedings, civil and criminal, in courts subject to the jurisdiction of the Appellate Division of the Supreme Court in the Second Judicial Department. They are intended to supplement, but not to supersede, the Code of Professional Responsibility and the Canons of Judicial Ethics, as adopted by the New York State Bar Association. In the event of any conflict between the provisions of these rules and that Code or those Canons, the Code and the Canons shall prevail.

Cross References

Code of Judicial Conduct, see Appendix to McKinney's Judiciary Law, Book 29.

Code of Professional Responsibility, see Appendix to McKinney's Judiciary Law, Book 29.

§ 701.2. Exercise of the Summary Contempt Power

(a) The power of the court to punish summarily any contempt committed in its immediate view and presence shall be exercised only in exceptional and necessitous circumstances, as follows: (1) Where the offending conduct disrupts or threatens to disrupt proceedings actually in progress; or (2) where the offending conduct destroys or undermines or tends seriously to destroy or undermine the dignity and authority of the court in a manner and to the extent that it appears unlikely that the court will be able to continue to conduct its normal business in an appropriate way, provided that in either case the court reasonably believes that a prompt summary adjudication of contempt may aid in maintaining or restoring and maintaining proper order and decorum.

(b) Wherever practical, punishment should be determined and imposed at the time of the adjudication of contempt. However, where the court deems it advisable the determination and imposition of punishment may be deferred following a prompt summary adjudication of contempt which satisfies the necessity for immediate judicial corrective or disciplinary action.

(c) Before any summary adjudication of contempt the accused shall be given a reasonable opportunity to make a statement in his defense or in extenuation of his conduct.

§ 701.3. Exercise of the Contempt Power After Hearing

In all other cases, notwithstanding the occurrence of the contumacious conduct in the view and presence of the sitting court, the contempt shall be adjudicated at a plenary hearing with due process of law including notice, written charges, assistance of counsel, compulsory process for production of evidence and an opportunity of the accused to confront witnesses against him.

§ 701.4. Judicial Warning of Possible Contempt

Except in the case of the most flagrant and offensive misbehavior which in the court's discretion requires an immediate adjudication of contempt to preserve order and decorum, the court should warn and admonish the person engaged in alleged contumacious conduct that his conduct is deemed contumacious and give him an opportunity to desist before adjudicating him in contempt. Where a person so warned desists from further offensive conduct, there is ordinarily no occasion for an adjudication of contempt. Where a person is summarily adjudicated in contempt and punishment deferred, if such person desists from further offensive conduct the court should consider carefully whether there is any need for punishment for the adjudicated contempt.

§ 701.5.   Disqualification of Judge

The judge before whom the alleged contumacious conduct occurred is disqualified from presiding at the plenary hearing or trial (as distinguished from summary action) except with the defendant's consent:

(a) If the allegedly contumacious conduct consists primarily of personal disrespect to or vituperative criticism of the judge; or

(b) If the judge's recollection of, or testimony concerning the conduct allegedly constituting contempt, is necessary for an adjudication; or

(c) If the judge concludes that in view of his recollection of the events he would be unable to make his decision solely on the basis of the evidence at the hearing.

PART 702.   CONDUCT OF CRIMINAL TRIAL THREATENED BY DISRUPTIVE CONDUCT

§ 702.1.   Application of Rules

These rules shall apply in all criminal actions and proceedings in courts subject to the jurisdiction of the Appellate Division of the Supreme Court in the Second Judicial Department. They are intended to supplement, but not supersede, the Code of Professional Responsibility and the Canons of Judicial Ethics, as adopted by the New York State Bar Association. In the event of any conflict between the provisions of these rules and that Code or those Canons, the Code and the Canons shall prevail.

Cross References

Code of Professional Responsibility, see Appendix to McKinney's Judiciary Law, Book 29.

§ 702.2.   Removal of Disruptive Defendant

(a) If a defendant engages in disruptive conduct by word or action in the courtroom in the course of his trial, the trial judge may order the defendant to be removed from the courtroom and placed in custody, and the trial judge may proceed with the trial in the absence of the defendant.

(b) The trial judge may not exclude the defendant except after warning that further disruptive conduct will lead to removal of the defendant from the courtroom.

(c) The defendant shall be returned to the courtroom immediately upon a determination by the court that the defendant is not likely to engage in further disruptive conduct.

§ 702.3.   Communication Between Defendant and Courtroom

If the defendant shall have been removed from the courtroom under the provisions of the preceding section, the trial judge shall make reasonable efforts to establish methods of communication linking the defendant with the courtroom while his trial is in progress. For such a defendant the trial judge may provide such methods of communication as may be suitable to the physical facilities of the courthouse and consonant with the goal of providing adequate communication to the courtroom and to defense counsel.

§ 702.4.   Restraint of Defendant

(a) If a defendant engages in disruptive conduct in the course of the trial and the trial judge determines not to take action under the preceding sections, he may order the defendant to be physically restrained in the courtroom while his trial continues.

(b) However, the trial judge shall not direct the restraint authorized in the preceding subdivision unless he shall have first warned the defendant, following his disruptive conduct, that any further misconduct by him will lead to his physical restraint in the courtroom.

(c) The physical restraint of the defendant shall be terminated immediately upon a determination by the court that the defendant is not likely to engage in further disruptive conduct.

PART 704.   JUDICIARY RELATIONS COMMITTEES [RESCINDED]

PART 710.   JOINT ADMINISTRATIVE ORDERS

Joint administrative orders are set forth in Part 635, supra.

PART 711.   MISCELLANEOUS ORDERS

§§ 711.1, 711.2.   [Rescinded]

§ 711.3. ADM 79–0328: Authorization for Committee on Character and Fitness to Continue to Inquire Concerning Any Criminal Actions and Proceedings Involving Applicants for Admission

The justices of the Appellate Division of the Supreme Court in and for the Second Judicial Department upon reading chapter 877 of the Laws of 1976, which amended section 160.50 of the Criminal Procedure Law and added a new section 160.60 thereto, and also amended section 296 of the Executive Law of the State of New York, do hereby:

Order that the committees on character and fitness delegated by this court to investigate applicants for admission to the bar may continue to inquire concerning any criminal actions or proceedings involving the applicant, including actions or proceedings which were terminated in the applicant's favor, and may continue to require the applicants to answer questions and give information with respect to such matters.

DATED: March 28, 1979

Cross References

Criminal Procedure Law, see McKinney's Book 11A.

Executive Law, see McKinney's Book 18.

SUPREME COURT, APPELLATE TERM, SECOND DEPARTMENT

Including Amendments Received Through September 15, 2008

Westlaw Electronic Research

These rules may be searched electronically on Westlaw® *in the NY–RULES database; updates to these rules may be found on* Westlaw *in NY–RULESUP-DATES. For search tips and a summary of database content, consult the* Westlaw *Scope Screens for each database.*

Table of Sections

PART 730. ESTABLISHMENT AND JURISDICTION OF APPELLATE TERMS

§ 730.1. Establishment and Jurisdiction of Appellate Terms

The Appellate Division of the Supreme Court, Second Judicial Department, pursuant to the authority vested in it, does hereby, effective January 2, 1968 and as amended:

Text of subdivision (a) effective until January 1, 2009.

(a)(1) Establish an Appellate Term of the Supreme Court in and for the Second and Eleventh Judicial Districts, which shall be held from time to time at such places in those judicial districts as may be designated by the Chief Administrator of the Courts.

(2) The Chief Administrator of the courts shall, with the approval of the Presiding Justice of the Appellate Division, Second Judicial Department, designate the Supreme Court justices assigned to the Appellate Term of the Supreme Court in and for the second and eleventh judicial districts * * * [such designations shall be set forth in the orders issued from time to time].

Text of subdivision (a) effective January 1, 2009.

(a)(1) Establish an Appellate Term of the Supreme Court in and for the Second, Eleventh, and Thirteenth Judicial Districts, which shall be held from time to time at such places in those judicial districts as may be designated by the Chief Administrator of the Courts.

(2) The Chief Administrator of the Courts shall, with the approval of the Presiding Justice of the Appellate Division, Second Judicial Department, designate the Supreme Court justices assigned to the Appellate Term of the Supreme Court in and for the Second, Eleventh, and Thirteenth Judicial Districts.

Text of subdivision (b) effective until January 1, 2009.

(b) Direct that the Appellate Term of the Supreme Court in and for the second and eleventh judicial districts, hereinabove established, shall have jurisdiction to hear and determine all appeals authorized by law to be taken:

(1) from an order or judgment of the Civil Court of the City of New York entered in the counties of Kings, Queens and Richmond, and

(2) from a judgment, sentence or order of the Criminal Court of the City of New York in any of said counties.

Text of subdivision (b) effective January 1, 2009.

(b) Direct that the Appellate Term of the Supreme Court in and for the Second, Eleventh, and Thirteenth Judicial Districts, hereinabove established, shall have

jurisdiction to hear and determine all appeals authorized by law to be taken:

(1) from an order or judgment of the Civil Court of the City of New York entered in the counties of Kings, Queens and Richmond, and

(2) from a judgment, sentence or order of the Criminal Court of the City of New York in any of said counties.

(c)(1) Establish an Appellate Term of the Supreme Court in and for the ninth and tenth judicial districts which shall be held from time to time at such places in those judicial districts as may be designated by the Chief Administrator of the Courts.

(2) The Chief Administrator of the courts shall, with the approval of the Presiding Justice of the Appellate Division, Second Judicial Department, designate the Supreme Court justices assigned to the Appellate Term of the Supreme Court in and for the ninth and tenth judicial districts * * * [such designations shall be set forth in the orders issued from time to time].

(d) Direct that the Appellate Term of the Supreme Court in and for the ninth and tenth judicial districts, hereinabove established, shall have jurisdiction to hear and determine all appeals now or hereafter authorized by law to be taken to the County Court or to the Appellate Division from any court in any county within the ninth judicial district or the tenth judicial district other than appeals from the Supreme Court, the Surrogate's Court, the Family Court or criminal appeals from the County Court.

(1) Direct that an appeal authorized by CPL 450.10 and 450.20 to be taken to intermediate courts shall be taken to the Appellate Term of the Supreme Court in and for the ninth and tenth judicial districts, hereinabove established, in accordance with its rules applicable thereto but not inconsistent with the applicable provisions of the CPL where such appeal is from a judgment, sentence or order of a local criminal court and all classifications thereof (as defined and set forth in CPL 10.10) located in this department but outside New York City.

(2) In addition to, but not in limitation, of the foregoing, such Appellate Term shall have jurisdiction to hear and determine all appeals:

(i) from the District Court of Nassau County, the District Court of Suffolk County and any other district court hereafter established in any county within the ninth judicial district, and

(ii) from any town, village or city court within either the ninth judicial district or the tenth judicial district, and

(iii) in civil matters, from any county court within either the ninth judicial district or the tenth judicial district.

*Text of subdivision (e) effective
until January 1, 2009.*

(e) The Appellate Term of the Supreme Court in and for the second and eleventh judicial districts and the Appellate Term of the Supreme Court in and for the ninth and tenth judicial districts shall jointly employ the nonjudicial personnel heretofore appointed to and employed in the predecessor Appellate Term previously discontinued, reserving for further order the disposition to be made of the books, records, papers, documents, furniture, equipment and other property of such predecessor Appellate Term, which in the interim shall be held jointly by, and may be used in the conduct severally of the business of, the aforesaid separate Appellate Terms hereby established.

Text of subdivision (e) effective January 1, 2009.

(e) The Appellate Term of the Supreme Court in and for the Second, Eleventh, and Thirteenth Judicial Districts and the Appellate Term of the Supreme Court in and for the Ninth and Tenth Judicial Districts shall jointly employ the nonjudicial personnel heretofore appointed to and employed in the predecessor Appellate Term previously discontinued, reserving no further order the disposition to be made of the books, records, papers, documents, furniture, equipment and other property of such predecessor Appellate Term, which in the interim shall be held jointly by, and may be used in the conduct severally of the business of, the aforesaid separate Appellate Terms hereby established.

(f) Direct that all motions addressed to either of the Appellate Terms shall be made returnable and all briefs, stipulations, and correspondence shall be filed in the Office of the Clerk of the Court, 141 Livingston Street, 15th Floor, Brooklyn, New York 11201.

Cross References

Criminal Procedure Law, see McKinney's Book 11A.

§ 730.2. Civil Appeals Management Program

(a) The chief clerk of the appellate terms, in appropriate cases, may issue a notice directing the attorneys for the parties and/or the parties themselves to attend a pre-argument conference before a designated Justice or other designated person, to consider the possibility of settlement, the limitation of the issues, and any other matters which the designated Justice or other person determines may aid in the disposition of the appeal or proceeding.

(b) Any attorney or party who, without good cause shown, fails to appear for a regularly scheduled pre-argument conference, or who fails to comply with the terms of a stipulation or order entered following a pre-argument conference, shall be subject to the imposition of such costs and/or sanctions as the court may direct.

§ 730.3. General Provisions and Definitions

(a) Unless the context requires otherwise, as used in this part and parts 731 and 732 of this title:

(1) The word perfection refers to the filing of an appellant's brief after an appeal is on the general calendar.

(2) The term cross appeal refers to an appeal taken by a party whose interests are adverse to a party who has appealed from the same order or judgment.

(b) All briefs, motions, affirmations, and any other papers will be deemed filed only as of the time they are actually received by the clerk and they shall be accompanied by proof of service as required by CPLR 2103.

(c) If a period of time prescribed by this part and parts 731 and 732 is measured from the service of a record, brief, or other paper and service is by mail, five days shall be added to the prescribed period. If service is by overnight delivery, one day shall be added to the prescribed period.

(d) Unless the context requires otherwise, if a period of time prescribed by parts 731 and 732 for the performance of an act ends on a Saturday, Sunday, or public holiday, the act will be deemed timely if performed by 5 P.M. of the next business day.

(e) An Appellate Term docket number will be assigned to every appeal. All papers and correspondence thereafter filed shall prominently display the applicable docket number or numbers in the upper left hand corner of the first page above the title of the case.

(f) If an appeal or the underlying action or proceeding is wholly or partially settled or if any issues are wholly or partially rendered moot, or if the calendaring, restoration, or disposition of the appeal is affected by the bankruptcy or death of a party, the inability of counsel to appear, an order of rehabilitation, or some other circumstance, the parties or their counsel shall immediately notify the court. Any attorney or party who, without good cause shown, fails to comply with the requirements of this subdivision shall be subject to such costs and/or sanctions as the court may direct.

(g) Any attorney or party to a civil appeal who, in the prosecution or defense thereof, engages in frivolous conduct as that term is defined in 22 NYCRR subpart 130–1.1(c), shall be subject to the imposition of such costs and/or sanctions as authorized by 22 NYCRR subpart 130–1 as the court may direct.

PART 731. RULES OF PRACTICE FOR THE SECOND AND ELEVENTH JUDICIAL DISTRICTS

Part 731 heading, Rules of Practice for the Second and Eleventh Judicial Districts, is effective until January 1, 2009. Part 731 heading was amended by ADM 2008–0918 to read Rules of Practice for the Second, Eleventh, and Thirteenth Judicial Districts, effective January 1, 2009.

§ 731.1. Records on Appeal

(a) In civil actions or proceedings, the clerk's return, as required to be made and filed pursuant to section 1704 of the Civil Court Act, shall constitute the record on appeal.

(b)(1) In criminal actions or proceedings, the appeal shall be heard on the original papers, certified by the clerk of the court from which the appeal is taken, the court's return when the same is required by statute, a stenographic transcript of the proceedings settled by the judge before whom the action was tried, or in case of the death or disability of such judge, in such manner as this court directs.

(2) For good cause shown, the court may hear the appeal on an abridged record containing so much of the evidence or other proceedings as it may deem necessary to a consideration of the questions raised on the appeal.

(c) Unless otherwise ordered by the court, an appellant may, but need not, print copies of the record on appeal.

Cross References

New York City Civil Court Act, see McKinney's Book 29A, Part 3.

Forms

Matters relating to transcript, record, and briefs. See West's McKinney's Forms, CPLR, §§ 9:216 to 9:241.

§ 731.2. Briefs

(a) The form, style and content of all briefs shall conform to the provisions of CPLR 5528 and 5529. Briefs may, but need not, be printed and may be reproduced by any authorized method or may be typewritten.

(1) The calendar number of the appeal shall be stated at the upper left-hand corner of the cover page of each brief.

(2) In all cases, civil and criminal, each party's main brief, upon the upper right-hand corner of the cover page, shall specify whether the cause is to be argued or submitted, and shall state the name of counsel who is to argue or submit.

(b) In all causes, unless otherwise directed by statute, the court, or these rules, the appellant's main brief shall include at the beginning the statement required by CPLR 5531.

(c) In criminal causes, the appellant's main brief at the beginning shall also set forth:

(1) either the entire judgment or order appealed from, or its material provisions, including its date;

(2) the sentence imposed, if any; and

(3) a statement whether an order issued pursuant to CPL 460.50 is outstanding and, if so, the date of such order, the name of the judge who issued it and whether the appellant is free on bail or on his own recognizance.

Cross References

CPLR, see McKinney's Book 7B.

Criminal Procedure Law, see McKinney's Book 11A.

Forms

Matters relating to transcript, record, and briefs. See West's McKinney's Forms, CPLR §§ 9:216 to 9:241.

§ 731.3. Court Sessions

Unless otherwise ordered, the court will convene at 9:30 o'clock in the forenoon on the first day of each appointed term. The court may be convened on any subsequent day or days during the term by order of the presiding justice or, in his absence, the associate presiding justice, which order shall specify the three justices who shall constitute the court at any such session.

§ 731.4. Calendar of Appeals

(a) The general calendar shall consist of

(1) all appeals in civil cases in which records on appeal have been filed with the clerk of this court, and

(2) all appeals in criminal cases in which a duplicate notice of appeal or an affidavit of errors and the court's return have been transmitted to said clerk as provided in CPL 460.10(1)(e), 460.10(2) and 460.10(3)(d).

(b) An appeal on the general calendar in which a record has been filed may be placed on the appeal calendar to be assigned to an appointed term by filing an original and five copies of the appellant's brief as set forth in subdivision (c) of this section.

(c) The original and five copies of the appellant's brief, with proof of service of one copy, shall be filed with the court within the time prescribed by section 731.8 of this part. In addition to the foregoing, in criminal appeals proof of service upon the respondent of one copy of a transcript of the minutes of all proceedings shall be filed together with the appellant's brief, such copy to be returned by the respondent to the appellant upon the argument or submission of the appeal. The original and five copies of the respondent's brief, with proof of service of one copy, shall be filed not more than 21 days after service of the appellant's brief. The original and five copies of a reply brief, with proof of service of one copy, shall be filed not more than seven days after service of respondent's brief.

(d) A day calendar listing the appeals scheduled for argument or submission on a particular date shall be published in the *New York Law Journal* not less than 12 days prior to such date. Appellants and respondents, or their attorneys, shall be notified of the calendar date by mail not less than five days prior to such date. Notification by either of such means shall be deemed sufficient.

Cross References

Criminal Procedure Law, see McKinney's Book 11A.

§ 731.5. Preferences; Consolidation

(a) Preferences.

(1) Any party to an appeal entitled by law to a preference in the hearing of the appeal may serve and file a demand for preference which shall set forth the provision of law relied upon for such preference and good cause for such preference. If the demand is sustained by the court, the appeal shall be preferred.

(2) A preference under CPLR 5521 may be obtained upon good cause shown by a motion directed to the court on notice to the other parties to the appeal.

(b) Consolidation.

(1) A party may consolidate appeals from civil orders and/or judgments arising out of the same action or proceeding provided that each appeal is perfected timely pursuant to section 731.8 of this part.

(2) Appeals from orders or judgments in separate actions or proceedings cannot be consolidated but may, upon written request of a party, be scheduled by the court to be heard together on the same day.

Forms

Order to show cause why a preference in hearing of appeal should not be granted, see West's McKinney's Forms, CPLR, § 9:244.

Affidavit in support of motion for preference in hearing of appeal, see West's McKinney's Forms, CPLR, § 9:245.

§ 731.6. Oral Argument or Submission

(a) No more than 15 minutes will be allowed for argument on each side, except by express permission of the court.

(b) In the event that any party's main brief shall fail to set forth the appropriate notations with respect to the argument or submission of the cause, as re-

quired by section 731.2(a)(2) of this Part, the cause will be deemed to have been submitted without oral argument by the defaulting party.

(c) When any party shall have noted on his or her filed brief, or, before the appeal appears on the day calendar, shall have filed his or her written consent or stipulation or otherwise notified the clerk that he or she intends to submit the appeal without argument, such party need not appear on the calendar call.

(d) The court, in its discretion, may deny oral argument of any appeal.

§ 731.7. Motions

Motions may be noticed for any day of the term and must be submitted without oral argument. All papers in support of the motion (which must include a copy of the notice of appeal) or in opposition thereto shall be filed before 10 o'clock in the forenoon of the return day of the motion.

§ 731.8. Dismissals on the Court's Own Motion; Enlargements of Time

(a) Unless an enlargement of time is granted in accordance with subdivision (d) of this section, an appeal in a civil case which has not been perfected after having been on the general calendar for more than 90 days shall be subject to dismissal.

(b) Except as otherwise provided in CPL 460.70 and subject to the applicable provisions of CPL 470.60, and unless an enlargement of time is granted in accordance with subdivision (d) of this section, an appeal in a criminal case which has not been perfected within 90 days after the notice of appeal was filed shall be dismissed.

(c) The clerk shall prepare a calendar of the appeals subject to dismissal for failure on the part of the appellant to perfect the same in compliance with this rule. Such dismissal calendar shall be published in the *New York Law Journal* at least five days prior to, as well as on the dismissal day. In criminal cases, the clerk shall cause a notice to be mailed to the appellant and his or her attorney five days prior to the first day of such publication.

(d) Enlargements of Time. Except where the court has directed that an appeal be perfected or that a brief be served and filed by a date certain, an enlargement of time to perfect or to serve and file a brief may be obtained as follows:

(1) *By Stipulation.* The parties may stipulate to enlarge the time to perfect an appeal by up to 60 days, to file an answering brief by up to 30 days, and to file a reply brief by up to 10 days. Not more than one such stipulation per perfection or filing shall be permitted. Such a stipulation shall not be effective unless so ordered by the clerk.

(2) *For Cause.* Where a party shall establish a reasonable ground why there cannot or could not be

compliance with the time limits prescribed by this section, or such time limits as extended by stipulation pursuant to paragraph (1) of this subdivision, the clerk or a Justice may grant reasonable enlargements of time to comply. An application pursuant to this paragraph shall be made by letter, addressed to the clerk, with a copy to the other parties to the appeal. Orders made pursuant to this paragraph shall be reviewable by motion to the court on notice pursuant to section 731.7 of this part.

Cross References

Criminal Procedure Law, see McKinney's Book 11A.

Forms

Extension of time. See West's McKinney's Forms, CPLR, §§ 9:252 to 9:256.

Extension or enlargement of time in criminal appeals. See West's McKinney's Forms, Criminal Procedure, § 460.30, Forms 1 to 3, § 460.70, Forms 2 to 4, 8, 9.

§ 731.9. Appeals in Criminal Cases; Adjournments; Extensions of Time

(a) Every application for an extension or enlargement of time or for an adjournment in an appeal from a judgment of conviction in a criminal case, whether on motion or stipulation, shall include, in addition to a showing of good cause, a statement subscribed by counsel setting forth:

(1) the sentence imposed and whether the defendant is free on bail or on his own recognizance by reason of the issuance of an order pursuant to CPL 460.50 and, if so, the date of such order and the name of the judge who issued the same; and

(2) whether the court has previously granted any enlargement of time.

(b) Where such application pertains to an appeal on the special day calendar referred to in subdivision (c) of section 731.8, such application shall be filed with the clerk of the court at least two days prior to the day on which the appeal is scheduled to appear on such calendar.

Cross References

Criminal Procedure Law, see McKinney's Book 11A.

Forms

Extension or enlargement of time in criminal appeals. See West's McKinney's Forms, Criminal Procedure, § 460.30, Forms 1 to 3, § 460.70, Forms 2 to 4, 8, 9.

§ 731.10. Leave to Appeal to the Appellate Term

(a) Applications to a justice of the Appellate Term for leave to appeal pursuant to the provisions of CPLR 5701(c) and Civil Court Act, section 1702(c) shall be made on notice within the time prescribed by CPLR 5513(b).

(b) The papers in support of such application must contain a copy of the opinion, if any, and a concise statement of the grounds of alleged error, and shall show whether a similar application was made in the court below.

(c) Applications for certificates or orders granting leave to appeal under the Criminal Procedure Law (CPL 450.15, 460.15) shall be governed by the following special rules:

(1) The application shall be in writing and shall be made and filed with the clerk of this court (with proof of service upon the district attorney or any other prosecutor who appeared for the People in the criminal court in which the order sought to be reviewed was rendered) within 30 days after service upon the applicant of a copy of the order.

(2) The application shall be addressed to the court for assignment to a justice and shall include:

(i) the name and address of the applicant and the name and address of the district attorney or other prosecutor, as the case may be;

(ii) the docket or index number;

(iii) the questions of law or fact which it is claimed ought to be reviewed;

(iv) any other information, data, or matter which the applicant may deem pertinent in support of the application; and

(v) a statement that no prior application for such certificate has been made.

(3) In addition, the papers in support of the application shall include a copy of the order sought to be reviewed and a copy of the memorandum or opinion of the court below or a statement that there was none.

(4) Within 15 days after service upon him of a copy of the application and of the papers, if any, in support thereof, the district attorney or other prosecutor (as the case may be) shall file answering papers or a statement that there is no opposition to the application (with proof of service upon the applicant, if appearing pro se, or upon the attorney making the application on behalf of the applicant). Such answering papers shall include a discussion of the merits of the application or shall state, if such be the case, that the application does not contain any allegations other than those alleged in the papers submitted by the applicant in the court below and that the prosecutor relies on the record, his answering papers contained therein and the memorandum or opinion of such court, if there be any.

(5) Unless the justice designated to determine the application shall in his discretion otherwise direct, the matter shall be submitted and determined upon the foregoing papers and without oral argument.

Cross References

CPLR, see McKinney's Book 7B.

Criminal Procedure Law, see McKinney's Book 11A.

New York City Civil Court Act, see McKinney's Book 29A, Part 3.

§ 731.11. Motions to Reargue, Resettle or Amend; Motions for Leave to Appeal to the Appellate Division

(a) Motions to reargue a cause or to resettle an order or to amend a decision shall be made within 30 days after the cause shall have been decided, except that for good cause shown, the court may consider any such motion when made at a later date.

(b) In an appeal in a civil case, a motion for leave to appeal to the Appellate Division from an adverse determination of the Appellate Term shall be made in the manner and within the time prescribed by CPLR 5513(b) and 5516.

(c) The papers in support of such motion shall concisely state the points claimed to have been overlooked or misapprehended by the court, with appropriate references to the particular portions of the record or briefs and with citation of the authorities relied upon.

(d) A motion for leave to appeal to the Appellate Division in a civil case from an order granting or affirming the granting of a new trial or hearing shall contain a stipulation that if the order appealed from be affirmed, judgment absolute may be entered against the moving party.

Cross References

CPLR, see McKinney's Book 7B.

Forms

Notice of motion for permission to appeal to appellate division from order of appellate term determining appeal from lower court, see West's McKinney's Forms, CPLR, § 9:122.

Affidavit in support of motion for permission to appeal to appellate division from order of appellate term determining appeal from lower court, see West's McKinney's Forms, CPLR, § 9:123.

Order of appellate term granting permission to appeal to appellate division, see West's McKinney's Forms, CPLR, § 9:124.

PART 732. RULES OF PRACTICE FOR THE NINTH AND TENTH JUDICIAL DISTRICTS

§ 732.1. Records on Appeal

(a) In civil actions or proceedings, the return required to be filed by the clerk shall constitute the record on appeal, except in civil appeals from the County Court, which shall conform to the requirements of CPLR 5525, et seq.

(b)(1) In criminal actions or proceedings, the appeal shall be heard on the original papers, certified by the clerk of the court from which the appeal is taken, the court's return when the same is required by statute, a stenographic transcript of the proceedings settled by the judge or justice before whom the action was tried, or in case of the death or disability of such judge or justice, in such manner as this court directs.

(2) For good cause shown, the court may hear the appeal on an abridged record containing so much of the evidence or other proceedings as it may deem necessary to a consideration of the questions raised on the appeal.

(c) Unless otherwise ordered by the court, an appellant may, but need not, print copies of the record on appeal.

Cross References

CPLR, see McKinney's Book 7B.

Forms

Matters relating to transcript, record, and briefs. See West's McKinney's Forms, CPLR §§ 9:216 to 9:241.

§ 732.2. Briefs

(a) The form, style and content of all briefs shall conform to the provisions of CPLR 5528 and 5529. Briefs may, but need not, be printed and may be reproduced by any authorized method or may be typewritten.

(1) The calendar number of the appeal shall be stated at the upper left-hand corner of the cover page of each brief.

(2) In all cases, civil and criminal, each party's main brief, upon the upper right-hand corner of the cover page, shall specify whether the cause is to be argued or submitted, and shall state the name of counsel who is to argue or submit.

(b) In all causes, unless otherwise directed by statute, the court, or these rules, the appellant's main brief shall include at the beginning the statement required by CPLR 5531.

(c) In criminal causes, the appellant's main brief at the beginning shall also set forth:

(1) either the entire judgment or order appealed from, or its material provisions, including its date;

(2) the sentence imposed, if any; and

(3) a statement whether an order issued pursuant to CPL 460.50 is outstanding and, if so, the date of such order, the name of the judge who issued it and whether the appellant is free on bail or on his own recognizance.

Cross References

CPLR, see McKinney's Book 7B.

Criminal Procedure Law, see McKinney's Book 11A.

Forms

Matters relating to transcript, record, and briefs. See West's McKinney's Forms, CPLR, §§ 9:216 to 9:241.

§ 732.3. Court Sessions

Unless otherwise ordered, the court will convene at 10 o'clock in the forenoon on the first day of each appointed term. The court may be convened on any subsequent day or days during the term by order of the presiding justice or, in his absence, the associate presiding justice, which order shall specify the three justices who shall constitute the court at any such session.

§ 732.4. Calendar of Appeals

(a) The general calendar shall consist of

(1) all appeals in civil cases in which records on appeal have been filed with the clerk of this court; and

(2) all appeals in criminal cases in which a duplicate notice of appeal or an affidavit of errors and the court's return have been transmitted to said clerk as provided in CPL 460.10(1)(e), 460.10(2) and 460.10(3)(d).

(b) An appeal on the general calendar in which a record has been filed may be placed on the appeal calendar to be assigned to an appointed term by filing an original and five copies of the appellant's brief as set forth in subdivision (c) of this section.

(c) The original and five copies of the appellant's brief, with proof of service of one copy, shall be filed with the court within the time prescribed by section 732.8 of this part. In addition to the foregoing, in criminal appeals proof of service upon the respondent of one copy of a transcript of the minutes of all proceedings shall be filed together with the appellant's brief, such copy to be returned by the respondent to the appellant upon the argument or submission of the appeal. The original and five copies of the respondent's brief, with proof of service of one copy, shall be filed not more than 21 days after service of the appellant's brief. The original and five copies of a reply brief, with proof of service of one copy, shall be filed not more than seven days after service of the respondent's brief.

(d) A day calendar listing the appeals scheduled for argument or submission on a particular date shall be published in the *New York Law Journal* not less than twelve days prior to such date. Appellants and respondents, or their attorneys, shall be notified of the calendar date by mail not less than five days prior to such date. Notification of either of such means shall be deemed sufficient.

Cross References

Criminal Procedure Law, see McKinney's Book 11A.

§ 732.5. Preferences; Consolidation

(a) Preferences.

(1) Any party to an appeal entitled by law to a preference in the hearing of the appeal may serve and file a demand for preference which shall set forth the provision of law relied upon for such preference and good cause for such preference. If the demand is sustained by the court, the appeal shall be preferred.

(2) A preference under CPLR 5521 may be obtained upon good cause shown by a motion directed to the court on notice to the other parties to the appeal.

(b) Consolidation.

(1) A party may consolidate appeals from civil orders and/or judgments arising out of the same action or proceeding provided that each appeal is perfected timely pursuant to section 732.8 of this part.

(2) Appeals from orders or judgments in separate actions or proceedings cannot be consolidated but may, upon written request of a party, be scheduled by the court to be heard together on the same day.

Forms

Order to show cause why a preference in hearing of appeal should not be granted, see West's McKinney's Forms, CPLR, § 9:244.

Affidavit in support of motion for preference in hearing of appeal, see West's McKinney's Forms, CPLR, § 9:245.

§ 732.6. Oral Argument or Submission

(a) No more than 15 minutes will be allowed for argument on each side, except by express permission of the court.

(b) In the event that any party's main brief shall fail to set forth the appropriate notations with respect to the argument or submission of the cause, as required by section 732.2(a)(2) of these rules, the cause will be deemed to have been submitted without oral argument by the defaulting party.

(c) When any party shall have noted on his or her filed brief, or, before the appeal appears on the day calendar, shall have filed his or her written consent or stipulation or otherwise notified the clerk that he or she intends to submit the appeal without argument, such party need not appear on the calendar call.

(d) The court, in its discretion, may deny oral argument of any appeal.

§ 732.7. Motions

Motions may be noticed for any day of the term and must be submitted without oral argument. All papers in support of the motion (which must include a copy of the notice of appeal) or in opposition thereto shall be filed before 10 o'clock in the forenoon of the return day of the motion.

§ 732.8. Dismissals on the Court's Own Motion; Enlargements of Time

(a) Unless an enlargement of time is granted in accordance with subdivision (d) of this section, an appeal in a civil case which has not been perfected after having been on the general calendar for more than 90 days shall be subject to dismissal.

(b) Except as otherwise provided in CPL 460.70 and subject to the applicable provisions of CPL 470.60, and unless an enlargement of time is granted in accordance with subdivision (d) of this section, an appeal in a criminal case which has not been perfected within 90 days after the notice of appeal was filed shall be dismissed.

(c) The clerk shall prepare a calendar of the appeals subject to dismissal for failure on the part of the appellant to perfect the same in compliance with this rule. Such dismissal calendar shall be published in the *New York Law Journal* at least five days prior to, as well as on the dismissal day. In criminal cases, the clerk shall cause a notice to be mailed to the appellant and his or her attorney five days prior to the first day of such publication.

(d) **Enlargements of Time.** Except where the court has directed that an appeal be perfected or that a brief be served and filed by a date certain, an enlargement of time to perfect or to serve and file a brief may be obtained as follows:

(1) *By Stipulation.* The parties may stipulate to enlarge the time to perfect an appeal by up to 60 days, to file an answering brief by up to 30 days, and to file a reply brief by up to 10 days. Not more than one such stipulation per perfection or filing shall be permitted. Such a stipulation shall not be effective unless so ordered by the clerk.

(2) *For Cause.* Where a party shall establish a reasonable ground why there cannot or could not be compliance with the time limits prescribed by this section, or such time limits as extended by stipulation pursuant to paragraph (1) of this subdivision, the clerk or a Justice may grant reasonable enlargements of time to comply. An application pursuant to this paragraph shall be made by letter, addressed to the clerk, with a copy to the other parties to the appeal. Orders made pursuant to this paragraph shall be reviewable by motion to the court on notice pursuant to section 732.7 of this part.

Cross References

Criminal Procedure Law, see McKinney's Book 11A.

Forms

Extension of time. See West's McKinney's Forms, CPLR, §§ 9:252 to 9:256.

Extension or enlargement of time in criminal appeals. See West's McKinney's Forms, Criminal Procedure, § 460.30, Forms 1 to 3, § 460.70, Forms 2 to 4, 8, 9.

§ 732.9. Appeals in Criminal Cases; Adjournments; Extensions of Time

(a) Every application for an extension or enlargement of time or for an adjournment in an appeal from a judgment of conviction in a criminal case, whether on motion or stipulation, shall include, in addition to a showing of good cause, a statement subscribed by counsel setting forth:

(1) the sentence imposed and whether the defendant is free on bail or on his own recognizance by reason of the issuance of an order pursuant to CPL 460.50 and, if so, the date of such order and the name of the judge who issued the same, and

(2) whether the court has previously granted any enlargement of time.

(b) Where such application pertains to an appeal on the special day calendar referred to in subdivision (c) of section 732.8, such application shall be filed with the clerk of the court at least two days prior to the day on which the appeal is scheduled to appear on such calendar.

Cross References

Criminal Procedure Law, see McKinney's Book 11A.

Forms

Extension or enlargement of time in criminal appeals. See West's McKinney's Forms, Criminal Procedure, § 460.30, Forms 1 to 3, § 460.70, Forms 2 to 4, 8, 9.

§ 732.10. Leave to Appeal to the Appellate Term

(a) Applications to a justice of the Appellate Term for leave to appeal pursuant to the provisions of CPLR 5701(c) and 1702(c) of the appropriate court acts, i.e., the UDCA, UCCA and UJCA shall be made on notice within the time prescribed by CPLR 5513(b).

(b) The papers in support of such application must contain a copy of the opinion, if any, and a concise statement of the grounds of alleged error, and shall show whether a similar application was made in the court below.

(c) Applications for certificates or orders granting leave to appeal under the Criminal Procedure Law (CPL 450.15, 460.15) shall be governed by the following special rules:

(1) The application shall be in writing and shall be made and filed with the clerk of this court (with proof of service upon the district attorney or any other prosecutor who appeared for the People in the criminal court in which the order sought to be reviewed was rendered) within 30 days after service upon the applicant of a copy of the order.

(2) The application shall be addressed to the court for assignment to a justice and shall include:

(i) the name and address of the applicant and the name and address of the district attorney or other prosecutor, as the case may be;

(ii) the docket or index number;

(iii) the questions of law or fact which it is claimed ought to be reviewed;

(iv) any other information, data, or matter which the applicant may deem pertinent in support of the application; and

(v) a statement that no prior application for such certificate has been made.

(3) In addition, the papers in support of the application shall include a copy of the order sought to be reviewed and a copy of the memorandum or opinion of the court below or a statement that there was none.

(4) Within 15 days after service upon him of a copy of the application and of the papers, if any, in support thereof, the district attorney or other prosecutor (as the case may be) shall file answering papers or a statement that there is no opposition to the application (with proof of service upon the applicant, if appearing pro se, or upon the attorney making the application on behalf of the applicant). Such answering papers shall include a discussion of the merits of the application or shall state, if such be the case, that the application does not contain any allegations other than those alleged in the papers submitted by the applicant in the court below and that the prosecutor relies on the record, his answering papers contained therein and the memorandum or opinion of such court, if there be any.

(5) Unless the justice designated to determine the application shall in his discretion otherwise direct, the matter shall be submitted and determined upon the foregoing papers and without oral argument.

Cross References

CPLR, see McKinney's Book 7B.

Criminal Procedure Law, see McKinney's Book 11A.

Uniform District, City and Justice Court Acts, see McKinney's Book 29A, Part 3.

§ 732.11. Motions to Reargue, Resettle or Amend; Motions for Leave to Appeal to the Appellate Division

(a) Motions to reargue a cause or to resettle an order or to amend a decision shall be made within 30 days after the cause shall have been decided, except

that for good cause shown, the court may consider any such motion when made at a later date.

(b) In an appeal in a civil case, a motion for leave to appeal to the Appellate Division from an adverse determination of the Appellate Term shall be made in the manner and within the time prescribed by CPLR 5513(b) and 5516.

(c) The papers in support of such motion shall concisely state the points claimed to have been overlooked or misapprehended by the court, with appropriate references to the particular portions of the record or briefs and with citation of the authorities relied upon.

(d) A motion for leave to appeal to the Appellate Division in a civil case from an order granting or affirming the granting of a new trial or hearing shall contain a stipulation that if the order appealed from be affirmed, judgment absolute may be entered against the moving party.

Cross References

CPLR, see McKinney's Book 7B.

Forms

Notice of motion for permission to appeal to appellate division from order of appellate term determining appeal from lower court, see West's McKinney's Forms, CPLR, § 9:122.

Affidavit in support of motion for permission to appeal to appellate division from order of appellate term determining appeal from lower court, see West's McKinney's Forms, CPLR, § 9:123.

Order of appellate term granting permission to appeal to appellate division, see West's McKinney's Forms, CPLR, § 9:124.

§ 732.12. Stay of Judgment Pending Appeal to the Appellate Term

Upon application of a defendant, pursuant to section 460.50 of the Criminal Procedure Law, for an order staying or suspending the execution of the judgment pending the determination of an appeal taken to the Appellate Term, such order may be issued by a justice of the Appellate Term or a justice of the Supreme Court of the judicial district embracing the county in which the judgment was entered.

Cross References

Criminal Procedure Law, see McKinney's Book 11A.

Forms

See West's McKinney's Forms, Criminal Procedure, § 460.50, Form 1 et seq.

PARTS 733 TO 734. [RESERVED]

PART 735. MISCELLANEOUS RULES APPLICABLE TO BOTH APPELLATE TERMS

§ 735.1. [Establishment and Jurisdiction of Appellate Terms]

See Part 730 of these rules.

§ 735.2. [Additional Duties of Counsel, the Court and the Court Clerk in Criminal Actions and in Coram Nobis, Habeas Corpus and CPLR Article 78 Proceedings]

See Part 671 of these rules.

§ 735.3. [Conduct of Attorneys and Counselors-at-Law]

See Part 691 of these rules.

§ 735.4. [Courthouses]

See Part 679 of these rules.

SECOND JUDICIAL DISTRICT, SECOND DEPARTMENT

Westlaw Electronic Research

These rules may be searched electronically on Westlaw® in the NY–RULES database; updates to these rules may be found on Westlaw in NY–RULESUP-DATES. For search tips and a summary of database content, consult the Westlaw Scope Screens for each database.

SUPREME COURT, KINGS COUNTY

Including Amendments Received Through September 15, 2008

See, also, Part 200 (§ 200.1 et seq.), Uniform Rules for Courts Exercising Criminal Jurisdiction, and Part 202 (§ 202.1 et seq.), Uniform Civil Rules for the Supreme Court and County Court

PARTS 750 TO 752. [RESCINDED]
PART 754. MISCELLANEOUS RULES

§ 754.1. [Additional Duties of Counsel, the Court and the Court Clerk in Criminal Actions and in Coram Nobis, Habeas Corpus and CPLR Article 78 Proceedings]

See Part 671 of these rules.

§ 754.2. [Conduct of Attorneys and Counselors-at-Law]

See Part 691 of these rules.

§§ 754.3 to 754.9. [Rescinded]

§§ 754.3 to 754.9 were rescinded effective Jan. 6, 1986, and are now covered under the Uniform Rules for the New York State Trial Courts set out under Part 200 et seq., ante.

§ 754.10. [Courthouses]

See Part 679, supra.

§§ 754.11 to 754.13. [Rescinded]

§§ 754.11 to 754.13 were rescinded effective Jan. 6, 1986, and are now covered under the Uniform Rules for the New York State Trial Courts set out under Part 200 et seq., ante.

SUPREME COURT, RICHMOND COUNTY

Including Amendments Received Through September 15, 2008

See, also, Part 200 (§ 200.1 et seq.), Uniform Rules for Courts Exercising Criminal Jurisdiction, and Part 202 (§ 202.1 et seq.), Uniform Civil Rules for the Supreme Court and County Court

PART 755. RULES OF PRACTICE [RESCINDED]
PART 759. MISCELLANEOUS RULES

§ 759.1. [Additional Duties of Counsel, the Court and the Court Clerk in Criminal Actions and in Coram Nobis, Habeas Corpus and CPLR Article 78 Proceedings]

See Part 671 of these rules.

§ 759.2. [Conduct of Attorneys and Counselors-at-Law]

See Part 691 of these rules.

§§ 759.3 to 759.9. [Rescinded]

§§ 759.3 to 759.9 were rescinded effective Jan. 6, 1986, and are now covered under the Uniform Rules for the New York State Trial Courts set out under Part 200 et seq., ante.

§ 759.10. [Courthouses]

See Part 679, supra.

§§ 759.11 to 759.13. [Rescinded]

§§ 759.11 to 759.13 were rescinded effective Jan. 6, 1986, and are now covered under the Uniform Rules for the New York State Trial Courts set out under Part 200 et seq., ante.

NINTH JUDICIAL DISTRICT, SECOND DEPARTMENT

Westlaw Electronic Research

These rules may be searched electronically on Westlaw® *in the NY–RULES database; updates to these rules may be found on* Westlaw *in NY–RULESUP-DATES. For search tips and a summary of database content, consult the* Westlaw *Scope Screens for each database.*

SUPREME COURT, DUTCHESS COUNTY

Including Amendments Received Through September 15, 2008

See, also, Part 200 (§ 200.1 et seq.), Uniform Rules for Courts Exercising Criminal Jurisdiction, and Part 202 (§ 202.1 et seq.), Uniform Civil Rules for the Supreme Court and County Court

PART 760.   RULES OF PRACTICE [RESCINDED]

PART 764.   MISCELLANEOUS RULES

§ 764.1. [Additional Duties of Counsel, the Court and the Court Clerk in Criminal Actions and in Coram Nobis, Habeas Corpus and CPLR Article 78 Proceedings]

See Part 671 of these rules.

§ 764.2. [Conduct of Attorneys and Counselors-at-Law]

See Part 691 of these rules.

§§ 764.3 to 764.9. [Rescinded]

§§ 764.3 to 764.9 were rescinded effective Jan. 6, 1986, and are now covered under the Uniform Rules for the New York State Trial Courts set out under Part 200 et seq., ante.

§ 764.10. [Courthouses]

See Part 679, supra.

§ 764.11. [Jury System]

See Part 693 of these rules.

§§ 764.12 to 764.15. [Rescinded]

§§ 764.12 to 764.15 were rescinded effective Jan. 6, 1986, and are now covered under the Uniform Rules for the New York State Trial Courts set out under Part 200 et seq., ante.

SUPREME COURT, ORANGE COUNTY

Including Amendments Received Through September 15, 2008

See, also, Part 200 (§ 200.1 et seq.), Uniform Rules for Courts Exercising Criminal Jurisdiction, and Part 202 (§ 202.1 et seq.), Uniform Civil Rules for the Supreme Court and County Court

PART 765. RULES OF PRACTICE [RESCINDED]

PART 769. MISCELLANEOUS RULES

§ 769.1. [Additional Duties of Counsel, the Court and the Court Clerk in Criminal Actions and in Coram Nobis, Habeas Corpus and CPLR Article 78 Proceedings]

See Part 671 of these rules.

§ 769.2. [Conduct of Attorneys and Counselors-at-Law]

See Part 691 of these rules.

§§ 769.3 to 769.9. [Rescinded]

§§ 769.3 to 769.9 were rescinded effective Jan. 6, 1986, and are now covered under the Uniform Rules for the New York State Trial Courts set out under Part 200 et seq., ante.

§ 769.10. [Courthouses]

See Part 679, supra.

§ 769.11. [Jury System]

See Part 693 of these rules.

§§ 769.12 to 769.14. [Rescinded]

§§ 769.12 to 769.14 were rescinded effective Jan. 6, 1986, and are now covered under the Uniform Rules for the New York State Trial Courts set out under Part 200 et seq., ante.

SUPREME COURT, PUTNAM COUNTY

Including Amendments Received Through September 15, 2008

See, also, Part 200 (§ 200.1 et seq.), Uniform Rules for Courts Exercising Criminal Jurisdiction, and Part 202 (§ 202.1 et seq.), Uniform Civil Rules for the Supreme Court and County Court

PART 770.   RULES OF PRACTICE [RESCINDED]

PART 774.   MISCELLANEOUS RULES

§ 774.1.   [Additional Duties of Counsel, the Court and the Court Clerk in Criminal Actions and in Coram Nobis, Habeas Corpus and CPLR Article 78 Proceedings]

See Part 671 of these rules.

§ 774.2.   [Conduct of Attorneys and Counselors-at-Law]

See Part 691 of these rules.

§§ 774.3 to 774.9.   [Rescinded]

§§ 774.3 to 774.9 were rescinded effective Jan. 6, 1986, and are now covered under the Uniform Rules for the New York State Trial Courts set out under Part 200 et seq., ante.

§ 774.10.   [Courthouses]

See Part 679, supra.

§ 774.11.   [Jury System]

See Part 693 of these rules.

§§ 774.12 to 774.15.   [Rescinded]

§§ 774.12 to 774.15 were rescinded effective Jan. 6, 1986, and are now covered under the Uniform Rules for the New York State Trial Courts set out under Part 200 et seq., ante.

SUPREME COURT, ROCKLAND COUNTY

Including Amendments Received Through September 15, 2008

See, also, Part 200 (§ 200.1 et seq.), Uniform Rules for Courts Exercising Criminal Jurisdiction, and Part 202 (§ 202.1 et seq.), Uniform Civil Rules for the Supreme Court and County Court

PART 775. [RULES OF PRACTICE] [RESCINDED]

PART 779. MISCELLANEOUS RULES

§ 779.1. [Additional Duties of Counsel, the Court and the Court Clerk in Criminal Actions and in Coram Nobis, Habeas Corpus and CPLR Article 78 Proceedings]

See Part 671 of these rules.

§ 779.2. [Conduct of Attorneys and Counselors-at-Law]

See Part 691 of these rules.

§§ 779.3 to 779.9. [Rescinded]

§§ 779.3 to 779.9 were rescinded effective Jan. 6, 1986, and are now covered under the Uniform Rules for the New York State Trial Courts set out under Part 200 et seq., ante.

§ 779.10. [Courthouses]

See Part 679, supra.

§ 779.11. [Jury System]

See Part 693 of these rules.

§§ 779.12 to 779.15. [Rescinded]

§§ 779.12 to 779.15 were rescinded effective Jan. 6, 1986, and are now covered under the Uniform Rules for the New York State Trial Courts set out under Part 200 et seq., ante.

SUPREME COURT, WESTCHESTER COUNTY

Including Amendments Received Through September 15, 2008

See, also, Part 200 (§ 200.1 et seq.), Uniform Rules for Courts Exercising Criminal Jurisdiction, and Part 202 (§ 202.1 et seq.), Uniform Civil Rules for the Supreme Court and County Court

PART 780. RULES OF PRACTICE [RESCINDED]

PART 784. MISCELLANEOUS RULES

§ 784.1. [Additional Duties of Counsel, the Court and the Court Clerk in Criminal Actions and in Coram Nobis, Habeas Corpus and CPLR Article 78 Proceedings]

See Part 671 of these rules.

§ 784.2. [Conduct of Attorneys and Counselors-at-Law]

See Part 691 of these rules.

§§ 784.3 to 784.9. [Rescinded]

§§ 784.3 to 784.9 were rescinded effective Jan. 6, 1986, and are now covered under the Uniform Rules for the New York State Trial Courts set out under Part 200 et seq., ante.

§ 784.10. [Courthouses]

See Part 679, supra.

§ 784.11. [Jury System]

See Part 693 of these rules.

§§ 784.12 to 784.14. [Rescinded]

§§ 784.12 to 784.14 were rescinded effective Jan. 6, 1986, and are now covered under the Uniform Rules for the New York State Trial Courts set out under Part 200 et seq., ante.

TENTH JUDICIAL DISTRICT, SECOND DEPARTMENT

Westlaw Electronic Research

These rules may be searched electronically on Westlaw® in the NY–RULES database; updates to these rules may be found on Westlaw in NY–RULESUP-DATES. For search tips and a summary of database content, consult the Westlaw Scope Screens for each database.

SUPREME COURT, NASSAU COUNTY

Including Amendments Received Through September 15, 2008

See, also, Part 200 (§ 200.1 et seq.), Uniform Rules for Courts Exercising Criminal Jurisdiction, and Part 202 (§ 202.1 et seq.), Uniform Civil Rules for the Supreme Court and County Court

PART 785. RULES OF PRACTICE [RESCINDED]

PART 789. MISCELLANEOUS RULES

§ 789.1. [Additional Duties of Counsel, the Court and the Court Clerk in Criminal Actions and in Coram Nobis, Habeas Corpus and CPLR Article 78 Proceedings]

See Part 671 of these rules.

§ 789.2. [Conduct of Attorneys and Counsel-ors-at-Law]

See Part 691 of these rules.

§§ 789.3 to 789.9. [Rescinded]

§§ 789.3 to 789.9 were rescinded effective Jan. 6, 1986, and are now covered under the Uniform Rules for the New York State Trial Courts set out under Part 200 et seq., ante.

§ 789.10. [Courthouses]

See Part 679, supra.

§ 789.11. [Jury System]

See Part 693 of these rules.

§§ 789.12, 789.13. [Rescinded]

§§ 789.12 and 789.13 were rescinded effective Jan. 6, 1986, and are now covered under the Uniform Rules for the New York State Trial Courts set out under Part 200 et seq., ante.

SUPREME COURT, SUFFOLK COUNTY

Including Amendments Received Through September 15, 2008

See, also, Part 200 (§ 200.1 et seq.), Uniform Rules for Courts Exercising Criminal Jurisdiction, and Part 202 (§ 202.1 et seq.), Uniform Civil Rules for the Supreme Court and County Court

PART 790. RULES OF PRACTICE [RESCINDED]
PART 794. MISCELLANEOUS RULES

§ 794.1. [Additional Duties of Counsel, the Court and the Court Clerk in Criminal Actions and in Coram Nobis, Habeas Corpus and CPLR Article 78 Proceedings]

See Part 671 of these rules.

§ 794.2. [Conduct of Attorneys and Counsel-ors-at-Law]

See Part 691 of these rules.

§§ 794.3 to 794.9. [Rescinded]

§§ 794.3 to 794.9 were rescinded effective Jan. 6, 1986, and are now covered under the Uniform Rules for the New York State Trial Courts set out under Part 200 et seq., ante.

§ 794.10. [Courthouses]

See Part 679, supra.

§ 794.11. [Jury System]

See Part 693 of these rules.

§§ 794.12 to 794.14. [Rescinded]

§§ 794.12 to 794.14 were rescinded effective Jan. 6, 1986, and are now covered under the Uniform Rules for the New York State Trial Courts set out under Part 200 et seq., ante.

ELEVENTH JUDICIAL DISTRICT, SECOND DEPARTMENT

Westlaw Electronic Research

These rules may be searched electronically on Westlaw® in the NY–RULES database; updates to these rules may be found on Westlaw in NY–RULESUP-DATES. For search tips and a summary of database content, consult the Westlaw Scope Screens for each database.

SUPREME COURT, QUEENS COUNTY

Including Amendments Received Through September 15, 2008

See, also, Part 200 (§ 200.1 et seq.), Uniform Rules for Courts Exercising Criminal Jurisdiction, and Part 202 (§ 202.1 et seq.), Uniform Civil Rules for the Supreme Court and County Court

PARTS 795 AND 796. [RESCINDED]
PART 799. MISCELLANEOUS RULES

§ 799.1. [Additional Duties of Counsel, the Court and the Court Clerk in Criminal Actions and in Coram Nobis, Habeas Corpus and CPLR Article 78 Proceedings]

See Part 671 of these rules.

§ 799.2. [Conduct of Attorneys and Counselors-at-Law]

See Part 691 of these rules.

§§ 799.3 to 799.9. [Rescinded]

§§ 799.3 to 799.9 were rescinded effective Jan. 6, 1986, and are now covered under the Uniform Rules for the New York State Trial Courts set out under Part 200 et seq., ante.

§ 799.10. [Courthouses]

See Part 679, supra.

§§ 799.11 to 799.13. [Rescinded]

§§ 799.11 to 799.13 were rescinded effective Jan. 6, 1986, and are now covered under the Uniform Rules for the New York State Trial Courts set out under Part 200 et seq., ante.

SUPREME COURT, APPELLATE DIVISION, THIRD DEPARTMENT

Including Amendments Received Through September 15, 2008

Westlaw Electronic Research

These rules may be searched electronically on Westlaw® *in the NY–RULES database; updates to these rules may be found on* Westlaw *in NY–RULESUP-DATES. For search tips and a summary of database content, consult the* Westlaw *Scope Screens for each database.*

Table of Sections

Parts 1100 to 1510 (§ 1100.1 et seq.) have been promulgated as joint rules of the Appellate Divisions and are set out following Appellate Division, Fourth Department, Part 1040, post.

PART 800. RULES OF PRACTICE

§ 800.1. Court Sessions; Four Justices Present

Unless otherwise ordered, court sessions shall commence at 1:00 p.m., except on Friday and the last session day of a term, when they shall commence at 9:30 a.m. A term of court shall be deemed to continue until the day on which the next term convenes, and the court may reconvene at any time during recess. When a cause is argued or submitted to the court with four justices present, it shall, whenever necessary, be deemed submitted also to any other duly qualified justice of the court, unless objection is noted at the time of argument or submission.

§ 800.2. Motions; Special Proceedings; Stays

(a) **Motions.** Unless otherwise directed by order to show cause, motions shall be made returnable on Monday (or if Monday falls on a holiday, on the next business day), whether or not court is actually in session, upon notice prescribed by CPLR 2214. Motions may not be argued except by permission of the court or a justice thereof. Counsel shall promptly notify the court clerk when such permission is granted. A notice of motion shall give notice to adverse parties that the motion will be submitted on the papers and that their personal appearance in opposition to the motion is neither required nor permitted. An order to show cause shall also give notice to adverse parties (1) whether the motion will be argued or submitted and (2) whether their personal appearance in opposition to the motion is permitted. Papers and memoranda shall be typewritten. The original moving papers shall be filed with proof of service as soon as possible. Papers in opposition to a motion made pursuant to notice of motion shall be filed at or before 11 a.m. on the Friday before the return day. Papers in opposition to an order to show cause shall be filed at or before 9 a.m. of the return date of the order. The moving papers on motions for permission to appeal to the Court of Appeals on certified questions shall state the questions proposed. A motion for permission to appeal to the Court of Appeals pursuant to CPLR 5602(a) shall be granted upon the approval of a majority of the justices comprising the panel assigned to consider the motion. On motions for reargument, a copy of the decision and any opinion of the court shall be attached to the moving papers.

(b) **Special Proceedings.** Unless otherwise directed by order to show cause, original special proceedings instituted in this court (e.g., removal proceedings, mandamus and prohibition) shall be made returnable on a motion day, at 1:30 p.m., upon notice prescribed by CPLR 403 or CPLR 7804(c), unless a different time is otherwise fixed by applicable statute. The moving and opposing parties shall submit the original and six copies of their papers with proof of service of a copy on each adversary. Moving papers shall be filed within 24 hours after service upon respondent, and opposing papers shall be filed as prescribed by applicable CPLR section, unless otherwise directed by the court.

(c) Review Proceedings Under Education Law, Labor Law, Public Health Law, and Tax Law. Unless otherwise provided by order to show cause, review proceedings commenced in this court pursuant to section 6510 of the Education Law, sections 220 or 220–b of the Labor Law, section 230–c of the Public Health Law or section 2016 of the Tax Law shall be made returnable on a motion day, on not less then 20 days' notice, as provided in CPLR 7804(c). Within 60 days from service of respondent's answer, petitioner shall file an original and nine copies of a reproduced full record on review and 10 copies of petitioner's brief, or a single copy of the record and 10 copies of petitioner's brief and appendix, with proof of service of one copy of the record and two copies of the brief, or two copies of the brief and appendix, upon respondent. Within 45 days from service of petitioner's brief, respondent shall file 10 copies of a brief or brief and appendix, with proof of service of two copies on petitioner. Petitioner may file a reply brief within 10 days of service of respondent's brief. The record to be filed by petitioner shall be stipulated to by the parties and shall include the petition, answer, reply and affidavits, if any, the administrative determination sought to be reviewed, and the hearing transcript and exhibits. In proceedings pursuant to section 2016 of the Tax Law, the stipulated record shall also include the determination of the administrative law judge, the decision of the tax appeals tribunal, the stenographic transcript of the hearing before the administrative law judge, the transcript of any oral proceedings before the tax appeals tribunal and any exhibit or document submitted into evidence at any proceeding in the division of tax appeals upon which such decision is based.

(d) Stays. When an order to show cause presented for signature makes provision for a temporary stay or other interim relief, except as to the time and manner of service, the party seeking such relief must inform the justice or the clerk at the time of submission of the order that the opposing party has been notified of the application and whether such party opposes or consents to the granting of the interim relief sought.

Cross References

CPLR, see McKinney's Book 7B.

Education Law, see McKinney's Book 16.

Tax Law, see McKinney's Book 59.

Forms

Proceeding against body or officer (article 78 proceeding). See West's McKinney's Forms, CPLR, § 10:601 et seq.

Review proceedings under Education Law. See West's McKinney's Forms, Selected Consolidated Laws, Education Law.

Review proceedings under Tax Law. See West's McKinney's Forms, Tax Practice and Procedure, Tax Law.

Stays. See West's McKinney's Forms, CPLR, §§ 12:732 to 12:736.

§ 800.3. Applications to a Justice for Leave to Appeal to Appellate Division or Court of Appeals

An application to a justice of the Appellate Division for leave to appeal in a civil case (CPLR 5701(c)), or in a criminal action or proceeding (CPL 460.15; 460.20), may, but need not be, addressed to a named justice, and, unless otherwise directed by order to show cause, shall be made returnable at the court's address in Albany, in the manner provided in section 800.2(a) of this Part. Such an application may not be argued unless the justice to whom it is made or referred otherwise directs.

Cross References

CPLR, see McKinney's Book 7B.

Criminal Procedure Law, see McKinney's Book 11A.

Forms

See West's McKinney's Forms, CPLR, §§ 9:122 to 9:134; West's McKinney's Forms, Criminal Procedure, § 460.15, Forms 1 et seq., § 460.20, Forms 1 et seq.

§ 800.4. Alternative Methods of Prosecuting Appeals and Review Proceedings

An appeal or transferred review proceeding may be prosecuted upon a full record reproduced by any method approved for briefs and appendixes by CPLR 5529, by the appendix method, or upon an agreed statement in lieu of record.

(a) Reproduced Full Record. When the full record is reproduced, appellant shall file with the clerk the original and nine copies prepared in accordance with section 800.5 of this Part, with proof of service of one copy upon each adverse party.

(b) Appendix Method. When the appendix method is used, appellant shall file with the clerk a single copy of the papers constituting the record on appeal or record on review prepared in accordance with section 800.5 of this Part, with proof of service of a copy upon each adverse party or, in lieu thereof, appellant may file with the clerk proof of service of a notice upon each adverse party that the single copy of the record has been filed in the office of the clerk of this court. In the alternative, when serving appellant's brief, appellant may serve the single copy of the record upon respondent and shall so state in an affidavit of service. A respondent upon whom the single copy of the record has been served shall file the record with the clerk of this court within 30 days from the date of its service upon him. When there are two or more adverse parties, appellant shall obtain instructions from the clerk for use of a single record by respondents and its filing with the clerk. Appellant's or petitioner's brief shall contain an appendix in compliance with section 800.8(b) of this Part.

(c) Appeals by Indigent Parties. An appeal in a criminal case, or in a civil case by a person who has been granted permission by this court to proceed as a poor person, may be prosecuted by the appendix method authorized by subdivision (b) of this section. Appellant shall file seven copies of a typewritten brief and appendix with proof of service of one copy upon each adversary. Respondent may likewise file seven copies of a brief with proof of service of one copy upon each adversary. The clerk of the court from which the appeal is taken, after service upon him of a copy of the decision of this court, shall furnish without charge to a person granted permission to proceed as a poor person one copy of the stenographic transcript of trial or hearing minutes and one copy of any other paper or document on file in his office which is material and relevant to the appeal. In criminal and family court cases, the court may, where such is necessary for perfection of the appeal, direct the clerk of the court to send a copy of the stenographic transcript of trial or hearing minutes on file in his office to the clerk of this court, who shall attach it to the single copy record upon which the appeal shall be prosecuted.

(d) Agreed Statement in Lieu of Record. If an appeal is prosecuted pursuant to CPLR 5527, appellant shall reproduce the agreed statement as a joint appendix in a manner authorized by CPLR 5529; shall prefix thereto a statement pursuant to CPLR 5531, and shall, within 30 days after approval of the statement by the court from which the appeal is taken, file the required number of copies, with proof of service of one copy upon each adverse party.

Cross References

CPLR, see McKinney's Book 7B.

Forms

Matters relating to transcript, record, and briefs. See West's McKinney's Forms, CPLR, §§ 9:216 to 9:241.

§ 800.5. Record on Appeal or Review

(a) Form and Content. A record on appeal or record on review shall be on good quality, white, unglazed paper and shall comply with CPLR 5526 as to size and form. Carbon copies will not be accepted. Bulky records shall be divided into volumes not to exceed one and one-half inches in thickness and shall be bound on the left margin with a flat clasp or similar type of fastener. The record shall contain, in the following order, so much of the following items as shall be applicable to the particular appeal or proceeding:

(1) a soft cover containing the title and the names, addresses and telephone numbers of attorneys;

(2) a table of contents which shall list and briefly describe each paper included in the record, each witness' testimony and each exhibit. The part relating to a transcript of testimony shall separately state as to each witness the page at which direct, cross, redirect and recross examination begins. The part relating to exhibits shall briefly describe each exhibit and shall indicate the page where offered or admitted in evidence and whether the exhibit has been omitted from the record;

(3) a statement pursuant to CPLR 5531;

(4) the notice of appeal or order of transfer, judgment or order appealed from, judgment roll, corrected transcript or statement in lieu thereof, any affidavits and relevant exhibits or copies of them, and any opinion or decision in the case;

(5) a stipulation or order settling the transcript pursuant to CPLR 5525(c);

(6) a stipulation dispensing with reproducing any exhibits. Exhibits may be omitted from the record pursuant to stipulation of counsel or by permission of the presiding justice. Omitted exhibits which are material to the issues raised on appeal shall be filed when briefs are filed. All exhibits, whether omitted from the record or not, shall be listed and briefly described in the table of contents;

(7) the appropriate certification or stipulation as required by section 800.7 of this Part.

(b) Exhibits. Exhibits which are material to the issues raised by any party shall be made available to the court. Exhibits not relevant, as well as bulky, dangerous or irreplaceable exhibits, need not, however, be filed unless the clerk otherwise directs. Except in appropriation cases, appellant when filing his brief shall also file the original or a certified copy of each exhibit upon which he relies or has reason to believe a respondent will rely. Exhibits under a respondent's control or under the control of a third person shall be filed either pursuant to a five-day written demand served by appellant upon a respondent or pursuant to a subpoena duces tecum issued in accordance with CPLR article 23. Appellant shall also file with his brief proof of service of such a demand or subpoena, together with a list of all relevant exhibits. In appropriation cases, each party shall file with his brief two copies of each appraisal report upon which he relies.

Cross References

CPLR, see McKinney's Book 7B.

Forms

Matters relating to transcript, record, and briefs. See West's McKinney's Forms, CPLR, §§ 9:216 to 9:241.

§ 800.6. Transcript

(a) Number Required. In civil cases, the court reporter or stenographer shall furnish petitioner or appellant with the ribbon copy of the typewritten transcript and, when the appendix method of appeal is used, the ribbon copy, or a copy of equal quality, shall be included in the single-copy record on appeal for use by the parties and the court.

(b) Form. Court reporters and stenographers who report administrative agency hearings shall furnish transcripts on 11 by 8½ inch white, opaque paper of good quality. Pages shall contain page headings as required for appendixes by CPLR 5529(c). The transcript shall be prefaced with a table of contents showing the location of direct, cross and redirect examination of witnesses; motions for dismissal; the jury charge; the verdict and motions addressed to it; and the admission of exhibits in evidence, with a brief description of each.

(c) Settlement of Transcript. A transcript shall be stipulated to by the parties or settled in the manner provided by CPLR 5525(c).

Cross References

CPLR, see McKinney's Book 7B.

Forms

Matter relating to transcript, record, and briefs. See West's McKinney's Forms, CPLR, §§ 9:216 to 9:241.

§ 800.7. Certification of Record

(a) Reproduced Full Record. A reproduced full record shall be certified either by: (1) a certificate of appellant's or petitioner's attorney pursuant to CPLR 2105; (2) a certificate of the proper clerk; or (3) a stipulation in lieu of certification pursuant to CPLR 5532. The reproduced copy containing the signed certification or stipulation shall be marked "Original Record". When a record contains a transcript, it shall be settled in the manner provided in section 800.6(c) of this Part.

(b) Single Copy of Record. When the appendix method is used, the single copy of the record must be stipulated to by the parties or, if the parties are unable to stipulate, settled by the judge before whom the proceedings were held. The procedure for settlement of a single copy record shall be in the manner provided by CPLR 5525(c), except that, if respondent shall fail to make any proposed amendments or objections to the record within twenty days after service of it upon respondent, the record, certified as correct by appellant's or petitioner's attorney, shall be deemed correct and may be filed with an affirmation by counsel certifying to compliance with the requirements of this section and the lack of proposed amendments or objections by respondent.

(c) Law Guardian. Upon any appeal in which a law guardian appears for a non-appellant child, the provisions of this section permitting or requiring respondent to stipulate to the record on appeal shall also apply to and include the law guardian.

Cross References

CPLR, see McKinney's Book 7B.

Forms

Certification pursuant to CPLR 2105, see West's McKinney's Forms, CPLR, § 9:233.

Stipulation in lieu of certification, see West's McKinney's Forms, CPLR, § 9:234.

§ 800.8. Form and Content of Brief and Appendix

(a) Briefs. Briefs shall comply with CPLR 5528 and 5529, shall contain on the cover the name and address of counsel who will argue the appeal and the estimated time of argument, and shall be on good quality, white, unglazed paper. Carbon copies will not be accepted. Except with permission of the court, briefs shall not exceed the following limitations: petitioner's or appellant's brief, 50 printed or 70 typewritten pages; respondent's brief, 25 printed or 35 typewritten pages; reply brief, 10 printed or 15 typewritten pages; amicus curiae brief, 25 printed or 35 typewritten pages.

(b) Appendixes. An appendix shall comply with CPLR 5529 and may be bound in the brief or separately. Appellant's appendix shall contain such parts of the record on appeal as are necessary to consider the questions involved, including at least the following:

(1) notice of appeal;

(2) judgment, decree or order appealed from;

(3) decision and opinion of the court or agency, and report of a referee, if any;

(4) pleadings, if their sufficiency, content or form is in issue or material; in a criminal case, the indictment;

(5) relevant excerpts from transcripts of testimony or of averments in motion papers upon which appellant relies or has reason to believe respondent will rely; in addition, in a criminal case, the sentencing minutes;

(6) charge to the jury; and

(7) copies of critical exhibits, including photographs, to the extent practicable.

(c) Inadequate Appendix. If an appendix fails to comply with this section, the adverse party, within 10 days from its receipt, may move to compel a party to file a further appendix. A respondent may also file an appendix to respondent's brief containing relevant portions of the record omitted from appellant's brief.

Cross References

CPLR, see McKinney's Book 7B.

Forms

Matters relating to transcript, record, and briefs. See West's McKinney's Forms, CPLR, §§ 9:216 to 9:241.

§ 800.9. Filing and Service of Papers

(a) Record and Appellant's Brief. Except where a different time limit or a different number of copies of papers is otherwise permitted herein, appellant shall cause to be filed with the clerk of this court, within 60 days after service of the notice of appeal, either:

(1) the original and nine copies of a reproduced full record and 10 copies of appellant's brief;

(2) the single copy of the record, together with 10 copies of a brief and appendix, or

(3) 10 copies of the agreed statement in lieu of record and 10 copies of a brief; with proof of service of one copy of the record and two copies of the brief, or two copies of a brief and appendix, upon each respondent.

(b) Respondent's Brief. After the record on appeal and appellant's brief, or brief and appendix, have been accepted for filing, the clerk shall mail to each respondent a scheduling memorandum which shall require respondent to serve and file respondent's brief within 45 days from the date of the memorandum or within such shorter time as the memorandum may direct. Each respondent shall file the same number of copies of respondent's brief as appellant shall have filed, with proof of service of two copies upon each appellant. Upon any appeal in which a law guardian appears for a non-appellant child, the provisions of this subdivision regarding mailing of the scheduling memorandum and filing of respondent's brief shall also apply to and include the law guardian.

(c) Reply Brief. Appellant may file a corresponding number of copies of a reply brief within 10 days after service of respondent's brief, with proof of service of two copies upon each respondent.

(d) Effect of Failure to Comply. Upon appellant's or petitioner's failure to comply with any provision of this Part, or for any other unreasonable delay in prosecuting an appeal or proceeding, respondent may move to dismiss for lack of prosecution. Upon respondent's failure to comply with any provision of this Part, in the discretion of the court, costs and disbursements of the appeal may be imposed against respondent or respondent's attorney, irrespective of the outcome of the appeal.

(e) Cross-Appeals. In the case of cross-appeals, unless otherwise directed by order of the court made pursuant to a motion on notice, the plaintiff shall be appellant and shall file and serve the record and brief, or brief and appendix, first. The answering brief and appendix shall be filed and served within 30 days after service of the first brief and shall include the points of argument on the cross-appeal. A reply brief shall be filed and served within 10 days after service of the answering brief. A reply brief to the cross-appeal may be served within 10 days after service of appellant's reply brief.

Forms

Matters relating to transcript, record, and briefs. See West's McKinney's Forms, CPLR, §§ 9:216 to 9:241.

§ 800.10.　Oral Argument

(a) Unless otherwise permitted by the court, oral argument shall not be allowed in the following cases:

(1) appeals from the Workers' Compensation Board;

(2) appeals from the Unemployment Insurance Appeal Board;

(3) appeals from judgments of conviction in criminal cases challenging only the legality, propriety or excessiveness of the sentence imposed;

(4) appeals in or transfers of CPLR article 78 proceedings in which the sole issue raised is whether there is substantial evidence to support the challenged determination; and

(5) any other case in which the court, in its discretion, determines that argument is not warranted.

(b) Any party seeking permission for oral argument in any of the cases specified in subdivision (a)(1) through (4) of this section shall submit a letter application therefor, on notice to all parties, within 10 days after the filing of appellant's or petitioner's brief together with proof of service upon respondent. Any party seeking permission for oral argument in a case specified in subdivision (a)(5) of this section shall submit a letter application therefor, on notice to all parties, within 10 days after being advised by the clerk that there will be no oral argument. The application shall specify the reasons why oral argument is appropriate and the amount of time requested.

(c) In cases not specified in subdivision (a) of this section, each counsel shall notify the clerk whether argument is desired and, if so, shall indicate on the cover of the brief the amount of time requested. Unless otherwise ordered, each side shall be allowed not more than 30 minutes for argument on appeals from judgments, in actions on submitted facts, and in special proceedings transferred to or instituted in this court and 15 minutes on appeals from nonfinal orders.

Forms

Notice of time requested for argument or intention to submit appeal without argument, see West's McKinney's Forms, CPLR, § 9:246.

§ 800.11.　Day Calendar Assignments; Adjournments; Additions

The clerk shall prepare day calendars for each court term by scheduling for argument or submission cases in which the record and appellant's brief have been filed and in which the respondent's brief has been filed or the date for filing and serving respondent's brief has been fixed pursuant to section 800.9(b) of this Part. The clerk shall give counsel notice of the date on which a case will be argued. After notice of day calendar assignment has been given, a case may not be moved to a different day unless request is made at least 14 days prior to commencement of the term for which it has been scheduled. The granting of a request to reschedule a case shall not serve to extend the time to file respondent's brief. A case not argued by a party when reached shall be submitted without oral argument on the papers filed. A case may be added to a term upon written stipulation signed by counsel and approved by the court.

§ 800.12. Appeals and Proceedings Deemed Abandoned

A civil appeal or proceeding shall be deemed to have been abandoned where appellant or petitioner shall fail to serve and file a record and brief within nine months after the date of the notice of appeal or order of transfer, or, in the case of a proceeding instituted in this court, within nine months after the date of the order to show cause or notice of petition commencing the proceeding; and the clerk of this court shall not accept or file any record or brief attempted to be filed beyond the nine-month period unless directed to do so by order of the court. Such an order shall be granted only pursuant to a motion on notice supported by an affidavit setting forth a reasonable excuse for the delay and facts showing merit to the appeal or proceeding.

§ 800.13. Appeals From Family Court

An appeal from Family Court shall be prosecuted by the appendix method authorized by section 800.4(b) of this Part upon a single copy of the record prepared in accordance with section 800.5 of this Part and upon seven copies of a brief and appendix in compliance with section 800.8(b) of this Part. Application for assignment of counsel and for permission to proceed as a poor person shall be made to this court pursuant to section 1120 of the Family Court Act.

Cross References

Family Court Act, see McKinney's Book 29A, Part 1.

§ 800.14. Appeals in Criminal Cases

An appeal authorized by the Criminal Procedure Law shall be prosecuted by the appendix method authorized by section 800.4(b) of this Part. The single copy record in a criminal case shall comply with section 800.5 of this Part, except that, in addition to the relevant items listed in section 800.5(a) of this Part, it shall also contain the indictment, hearing and trial transcripts, motion papers, if any, and sentencing minutes. When the clerk of the trial court has been directed, pursuant to section 800.4(c) of this Part, to furnish a copy of a transcript to this court, the transcript may be omitted from the single copy record.

(a) **Briefs and Appendixes.** Briefs and appendixes shall comply with CPLR 5528 and section 800.8 of this Part.

(b) **When to Be Heard; Service of Briefs.** Unless appellant's time is enlarged by order, appellant's counsel shall file the single copy record and seven copies of a brief and appendix within 60 days after the last day for filing a notice of appeal, with proof of service of one copy upon the appellant and one copy upon respondent. Respondent, within 30 days after service of appellant's brief and appendix, shall file seven copies of a brief and appendix, with proof of service of two copies upon appellant's counsel, who shall forthwith furnish a copy of respondent's brief to appellant. The clerk shall schedule the appeal for argument or submission at the next term of court commencing more than 30 days after the service and filing of the record on appeal and appellant's brief and appendix, unless an extension to file respondent's brief shall have been granted pursuant to section 800.9(b) of this Part.

(c) **Enlargement of Time.** Application by appellant for an enlargement of time in a criminal case shall be by motion on notice and shall be accompanied by an affidavit satisfactorily explaining the delay. The affidavit shall state: (1) the date of conviction; (2) whether by trial or plea; (3) whether appellant is free on bail; (4) the date the notice of appeal was filed; (5) the date the trial transcript was ordered; (6) whether the transcript has been filed; (7) if the complete transcript has not been filed, the date it is expected to be filed; and (8) the date appellant's brief and appendix will be filed.

(d) **Oral Argument.** Unless otherwise ordered by the court, appeals may be submitted without oral argument. The time allowed for oral argument shall be as provided in section 800.10 of this Part.

(e) **Remittitur.** Upon entry of the order on this court's decision, the original record on appeal shall be remitted to the clerk of the criminal court with a copy of the order.

(f) **Reargument of Appeal.** Motions for reargument must be made within 60 days after service upon the moving party of a copy of the court's order, with written notice of its entry, except that when a party has entered the order, the time shall be computed from the date of entry.

(g) **Where Only Sentence in Issue.** When the sole question raised on appeal concerns the legality, propriety or excessiveness of the sentence imposed, the appeal may be heard upon a shortened record on appeal consisting of the notice of appeal, sentencing minutes and minutes of the plea, if appellant pleaded guilty. The record, which shall be clearly labeled "Record on Appeal from Sentence", shall contain a statement pursuant to CPLR 5531 and shall be stipulated to or settled in the manner provided in section 800.7(b) of this Part. The appeal shall be prosecuted, and may be scheduled for oral argument or submission, in the manner provided in subdivision (b) of this section. A copy of the presentence investigation report shall be filed with the clerk.

(h) Expedited Criminal Appeal of Order Reducing Indictment or Dismissing Indictment and Directing Filing of Prosecutor's Information.

(1) This subdivision shall govern the procedure for an expedited appeal, pursuant to CPL 210.20(6)(c), 450.20(1–a) and 450.55, of an order by a superior court reducing a count or counts of an indictment or dismissing an indictment and directing the filing of a prosecutor's information.

(2) After the people file and serve a notice of appeal pursuant to CPL 460.10(1), either party may request that the court expedite the appeal. If a request is made, the court shall hear the appeal on an expedited basis as set forth in this subdivision.

(3)(i) The court shall establish an expedited briefing schedule for the appeal. Briefs may be typewritten or reproduced. The people shall file nine copies of a brief and an appendix, which shall include a copy of the indictment and the trial court's decision and order. The respondent shall file nine copies of a brief and, if necessary, an appendix. One copy of the brief and appendix shall be served on opposing counsel.

(ii) The appeal may be taken on one original record, which shall include copies of the indictment, the motion papers, the trial court's decision and order, and the notice of appeal.

(iii) The People shall file with the Appellate Division, separately from the record, one copy of the grand jury minutes.

(iv) The court shall give preference to the hearing of an appeal perfected pursuant to this subdivision and shall determine the appeal as expeditiously as possible.

(4) Unless otherwise ordered by the Appellate Division, if the defendant is represented in the superior court by court-assigned counsel, such counsel shall continue to represent the defendant in any appeal by the People of an order reducing an indictment or dismissing an indictment and directing the filing of a prosecutor's information.

(i) Service of Order. Service of a copy of the order upon appellant in accordance with CPL 460.10(5)(a) shall be made pursuant to CPLR 2103.

Cross References

CPLR, see McKinney's Book 7B.

Criminal Procedure Law, see McKinney's Book 11A.

Forms

Appeals in criminal cases. See West's McKinney's Forms, Criminal Procedure, articles 450, 460, and 470.

§ 800.15. Appeals From Orders Concerning Grand Jury Reports

The mode, time and manner for perfecting an appeal from an order accepting a report of a grand jury pursuant to paragraph (a) of subdivision 1 of section

190.85 of the Criminal Procedure Law, or from an order sealing a report of a grand jury pursuant to subdivision 5 of section 190.85 of the Criminal Procedure Law, shall be in accordance with section 800.14 of this Part governing appeals in criminal cases. Appeals from such orders shall be preferred causes and may be added to a term calendar either by stipulation or upon motion. The record, briefs and other papers on such an appeal shall be sealed and not be available for public inspection. Unless otherwise directed by the court, oral argument will not be allowed.

Cross References

Criminal Procedure Law, see McKinney's Book 11A.

§ 800.16. Appeals in Election Cases

Appeals in proceedings brought pursuant to any provision of the Election Law shall be prosecuted upon a single-copy record and seven copies of a brief and appendix pursuant to the method specified in section 800.4(b) of this Part. Such appeal shall be given preference and shall be brought on for argument on such terms and conditions as the presiding justice may direct upon application of any party to the proceeding.

Cross References

Election Law, see McKinney's Book 17.

§ 800.17. Unemployment Insurance Appeals

An appeal from a decision of the Unemployment Insurance Appeal Board may be prosecuted in accordance with written instructions which are available from the clerk of the court or the Department of Law, Employment Security Bureau, 120 Broadway, 26th Floor, New York, New York 10271.

§ 800.18. Workers' Compensation Appeals

(a) Papers on Appeal. An appeal from a decision of the Workers' Compensation Board shall be heard upon one copy of the papers constituting the record list as herein prescribed, together with an appendix to appellant's brief, which shall comply with section 800.8 of this Part and contain a copy of each item of the record necessary to consider the questions raised, including those items appellant reasonably assumes will be relied upon by a respondent. Respondent's brief may contain an appendix which, however, shall contain only such additional parts of the record as are necessary to consider the questions involved, or the parties may agree upon a joint appendix. Where all papers in the record on appeal are deemed relevant to the issues, appellant may proceed upon the required number of copies of the record on appeal, and in the event of such an election an appendix shall not be required.

(b) Record List.

(1) Appellant shall prepare a statement of the issues he intends to present for review by the Appellate

Division, together with a list of the papers relevant to those issues. Transcripts of testimony shall be listed according to date, and each paper and exhibit listed shall, where possible, be designated by date and brief description.

(2) Unless, within 45 days after service of a notice of appeal, the Workers' Compensation Board shall vacate, modify or rescind the decision which is the subject of the appeal, within 30 days after expiration of said 45 days or, in the event the Board sooner determines that it will not vacate, modify or rescind the decision, within 30 days after the Board serves a notice of such determination on appellant, appellant shall serve a copy of the proposed record list upon the Attorney General and each party affected by the Board decision, together with a written stipulation reciting that the papers, testimony and exhibits listed therein constitute all of the papers necessary and relevant to the issues. Appellant shall also serve upon the parties affected a written request to stipulate to the contents of the record list within 20 days. Within 20 days after such service, any party so served may make objections, or amendments to the record list and serve them upon appellant.

(3) If a party timely served with a proposed record list shall fail to serve objections or amendments within said 20 days, the record list shall be deemed correct as to that party, and appellant shall affix to the record on appeal an affirmation certifying to the timely service of the proposed record list and request to stipulate and to the failure of one or more parties to comply with the request or to make objections or amendments thereto within the time prescribed.

(4) Within 20 days after service of a proposed record list, a party respondent shall serve upon appellant any proposed objections or amendments thereto. Appellant and the objecting party shall have 20 days thereafter in which to agree upon the objections and amendments to the record list and to stipulate in writing thereto. If they are unable to agree, within 10 days after expiration of said 20 days, appellant shall make application to the Board for settlement of the record list. A copy of the Board's decision shall be attached to the record list.

(5) When filing the original record on appeal, appellant shall file the record list, together with the stipulation, Board decision or affirmation. Hearing transcripts, certified as correct by the hearing reporter, shall, in the absence of objection, also be deemed correct.

(6) A decision of the Board upon an application to settle a record list shall be reviewable by motion pursuant to section 800.2(a) of this Part. The moving papers shall contain a copy of the Board decision and the papers submitted to the Board upon the application. Where necessary, the court will obtain the Board's file for use on the motion.

(c) **Form and Content of Record.** A record on an appeal pursuant to section 23 of the Workers' Compensation Law shall comply as to form with section 800.5(a) of this Part and shall contain:

(1) a soft cover containing the title and names, addresses and telephone numbers of the attorneys;

(2) a table of contents which shall list and briefly describe each paper, including the date thereof, included in the record and each exhibit. The part relating to a transcript of testimony shall separately state as to each witness the page at which direct, cross, redirect and recross examination begins. The part relating to exhibits shall briefly describe each exhibit and shall indicate the page where admitted in evidence and whether the exhibit has been omitted from the record;

(3) a statement pursuant to CPLR 5531;

(4) the notice of appeal and, in chronological order, the papers set forth in the record list;

(5) a stipulation dispensing with reproducing any exhibits in the record. Omitted exhibits which are material to the issues raised shall be filed when briefs are filed; and

(6) a certification or stipulation in lieu thereof.

(d) **Certification of Record.** The record on appeal shall be certified as true and correct by the secretary or other designee of the Workers' Compensation Board by a certificate of appellant's attorney pursuant to CPLR 2105, or by a stipulation in lieu of certification pursuant to CPLR 5532.

(e) **Filing and Service of Papers.** Within 60 days after the last day to agree upon objections or amendments to the record list, or, when the parties are unable to agree, within 60 days from settlement of the record list by the board, or, if no objections or amendments to the record list have been served, within 60 days from the last day to serve them, appellant shall file with the clerk the record on appeal together with 10 copies of appellant's brief and appendix, with proof of service of one copy of the record and two copies of appellant's brief and appendix upon the Attorney General and each respondent affected by the board's decision. Respondent's brief shall be served and filed in accordance with the provisions of section 800.9(b) of this Part, except that a respondent shall file proof of service of two copies of a respondent's brief upon every other interested party to the appeal.

(f) **When to Be Heard; Application of Rules.** Appeals shall be scheduled at terms designated for workers' compensation appeals in accordance with the provisions of section 800.11 of this Part. The attorney general may continue an appeal to a subsequent term by filing, within 14 days from service of appellant's brief, proof of service of a notice of adjournment. Except as otherwise provided in this section, the provisions of this Part governing appeals generally shall apply to workers' compensation appeals.

(g) Remittitur. Upon entry of the order on the court's decision, the record on appeal shall be remitted to the attorney general with a copy of the order for filing with the Workers' Compensation Board.

Cross References

CPLR, see McKinney's Book 7B.

Workers' Compensation Law, see McKinney's Book 64.

§ 800.19. Transferred Proceedings

An article 78 proceeding transferred to this court pursuant to CPLR 7804(g), and an appeal transferred from another department pursuant to CPLR 5711, may be prosecuted in any manner authorized by section 800.4 of this Part. Unless otherwise ordered by the court, the rules governing the content, number and form of records, briefs and appendixes shall apply, except that petitioner or appellant shall serve and file the required papers within 60 days after the entry of the order of transfer.

Cross References

CPLR, see McKinney's Book 7B.

§ 800.20. State Human Rights Matters

(a) Appeals. An appeal from an order or judgment of the Supreme Court determining a proceeding pursuant to section 298 of the Executive Law shall be prosecuted upon a record consisting of the original papers and the record before the State Division of Human Rights together with seven copies of appellant's brief and appendix, with proof of service of one copy upon each respondent. Appellant's appendix shall contain at least the notice of appeal, the order or judgment appealed from, the decision of the court below and the determination and order of the State Division of Human Rights. Each respondent shall file seven copies of a brief with proof of service of one copy upon appellant. Briefs and appendices shall comply with and be filed within the time specified by sections 800.8 and 800.9 of this Part.

(b) Transferred Proceedings. A proceeding transferred to this court for disposition pursuant to section 298 of the Executive Law may be prosecuted upon a single copy of the record on review which shall consist of the notice of petition and petition, answer, reply, if any, the original record and transcript of the public hearing held before the State Division of Human Rights and the division's determination and order. Petitioner shall file seven copies of a brief and appendix, with proof of service of one copy upon each named respondent. Each respondent shall file seven copies of a brief or brief and appendix with proof of service of one copy upon petitioner. Briefs and appendices shall comply with and be filed within the time specified by sections 800.8 and 800.19 of this Part. Unless the court directs otherwise, the division shall file the original record and transcript of public hearing within 45 days of entry of the order of transfer.

Cross References

Executive Law, see McKinney's Book 18.

§ 800.21. Action on Submitted Facts

An original agreed statement of facts in an action submitted to this court pursuant to CPLR 3222 shall be filed in the office of the county clerk, and a copy shall be appended to appellant's brief as a joint appendix. A statement required by CPLR 5531 shall be prefixed thereto. Briefs shall be served and filed in the manner and in accordance with the time requirements prescribed by sections 800.9 and 800.11 of this Part for appeals.

Cross References

CPLR, see McKinney's Book 7B.

Forms

Action on submitted facts, see West's McKinney's Forms, CPLR, §§ 4:409 to 4:417.

Statement pursuant to CPLR 5531, see West's McKinney's Forms, CPLR, § 9:226.

§ 800.22. Orders; Costs

The orders, appointments, assignments and directions of the court shall be signed by the presiding justice or the clerk of the court. Costs in workers' compensation and unemployment insurance appeals shall be taxed by the clerk in accordance with CPLR 8403.

Cross References

CPLR, see McKinney's Book 7B.

§ 800.23. Fees of the Clerk of the Court

(a) Fee on Civil Appeals and Proceedings. In accordance with CPLR 8022, the clerk of the court is directed to charge and is entitled to receive a fee of three hundred fifteen dollars, payable in advance, upon the filing of a record on a civil appeal or statement in lieu of record on a civil appeal, or upon the filing of a notice of petition or order to show cause commencing a special proceeding. The fee shall be paid by check or money order and payment in full shall accompany the record on appeal, statement in lieu of record, notice of petition or order to show cause. A civil appeal or special proceeding shall not be scheduled for argument or submission until the fee is received and the clerk may return a document not accompanied by the fee. The clerk shall not charge or receive a fee from: (1) the State, or any agency or officer thereof, or any party or governmental entity specifically exempted by law from the payment of such fee; (2) any party who by statute, rule or order of the court has been authorized to proceed as a poor person; or (3) a claimant upon an appeal from a decision of the Unemployment Insurance Appeal Board.

(b) Fee on Motions and Cross Motions. In accordance with CPLR 8022, the clerk of the court is also entitled, upon the filing of each motion or cross motion with respect to a civil appeal or special proceeding, to a fee of forty-five dollars, payable in advance. No fee shall be imposed for a motion or cross motion which seeks leave to appeal as a poor person pursuant to CPLR 1101(a).

(c) Other Fees. In accordance with Judiciary Law § 265, the clerk of the court is directed to charge and is entitled to receive in advance the following fees on behalf of the State:

(1) For a large, embossed certificate attesting to admission as an attorney and counsellor at law, twenty dollars.

(2) For a printed certificate attesting to admission, good standing and registration as an attorney and counsellor at law, five dollars.

Cross References

CPLR, see McKinney's Book 7B.

§ 800.24–a. Pre–Calendar Statement for Civil Appeals

(a) In every civil case in which a notice of appeal is filed or an order granting leave to appeal is entered, except in appeals in proceedings pursuant to the Election Law and CPLR articles 70 and 78, appeals in Family Court proceedings involving child abuse or neglect, juvenile delinquency or persons in need of supervision, appeals from decisions of the Unemployment Insurance Appeal Board and Workers' Compensation Board, and appeals pursuant to section 168–n (subd. 3) of the Correction Law, appellant shall also file, together with the notice of appeal or order granting leave to appeal, a pre-calendar statement.

(b) The pre-calendar statement, entitled as same, must set forth:

(1) The title of the underlying action or proceeding and the date of commencement;

(2) The full names of the original parties and any change in the parties;

(3) The name, address, telephone number and facsimile telephone number of counsel for appellant;

(4) The name, address, telephone number and facsimile telephone number of counsel for each respondent and counsel for each other party;

(5) The court, judge or justice, and county from which the appeal is taken, together with the index number and the request for judicial intervention (RJI) number;

(6) The specific nature and object of the underlying action or proceeding (*e.g.*, automobile negligence personal injury action seeking money damages; breach of contract action seeking specific performance; Family Court proceeding seeking modification of child custody and visitation order; divorce action involving equitable distribution; real property action involving a boundary-line dispute and adverse possession);

(7) A clear and concise statement of the issues to be raised on the appeal and the grounds for reversal or modification to be advanced;

(8) Whether there is another pending appeal or pending related action or proceeding, briefly describing same.

(c) Appellant shall attach to the pre-calendar statement a copy of the order or judgment appealed from, the opinion or decision, if any, and a copy of the notice of appeal or order granting leave to appeal.

(d) The clerk of the court from which the appeal is taken shall promptly transmit the pre-calendar statement and its attachments to the Appellate Division, Third Department.

(e) Forms. The pre-calendar statement shall read substantially as follows:

PRE–CALENDAR STATEMENT

State of New York
Supreme Court—Appellate Division
Third Judicial Department

Case Title: Set forth the full case title.

County Index No. _____
RJI No. _____
Date of Commencement ____

Parties Involved: Set forth the full names of the original parties and any change in parties.

Party Name (eg. John E. Doe)	Original Status (eg. Defendant)	Appellate Status (eg. Appellant)

Counsel for Appellant(s):   Set forth the name, address, telephone number and facsimile telephone number of counsel for appellant(s).

Counsel for Respondent(s) and Counsel for Other Parties: Set forth the name, address, telephone number and facsimile telephone number of counsel for respondent(s) and for each other party.

Court, Judge and County: Identify the court, judge or justice, and the county from which the appeal is taken.

Nature and Object of Action or Proceeding: Concisely set forth the nature and object of the underlying action or proceeding.

Appellate Issue(s):   Set forth a clear and concise statement of the issue(s) to be raised on the appeal, the grounds for reversal or modification to be advanced and the specific relief sought on the appeal.

Other Related Matters: Indicate if there is another related action or proceeding, identifying and briefly describing same.

Submitted by:

_____

Signature

Print Name:
Attorney for:
Date:

Attachments: Check

1.   Copy of order or judgment appealed from.   ____ attached

2.   Copy of opinion or decision.   ____ attached
                                                     ____ does not exist

3.   Copy of notice of appeal or order granting leave to appeal.   ____ attached

Attach copies, not originals. File this original form with attachments when original notice of appeal is filed in the office where the judgment or order of court of original instance is entered. A copy of this document must be served upon all counsel and pro se parties.

§ 800.24–b. Civil Appeals Settlement Program

(a) The court, in those cases in which it deems it appropriate, will issue a notice directing the attorneys for the parties and the parties themselves (unless the court excuses a party's personal presence) to attend a pre-calendar conference before such person as it may designate to consider settlement, the limitation of issues and any other matter which such person determines may aid in the disposition of the appeal or resolution of the action or proceeding. Where parties are represented by counsel, only attorneys fully familiar with the action or proceeding, and authorized to make binding stipulations or commitments, or accompanied by a person empowered to act on behalf of the party represented, shall appear at the conference.

(b) Any attorney or party who, without good cause shown, fails to appear for or participate, with the familiarity and authorization described in subdivision (a) of this section, in a regularly scheduled pre-calendar conference, or who fails to comply with the terms of a stipulation or order entered following a pre-calendar conference, may be subject to such sanctions and/or to such costs in the form of reimbursement for actual expenses incurred and reasonable attorneys' fees as the court may direct.

(c) Should a pre-calendar conference not be scheduled within 30 days after the filing of a pre-calendar statement, any party may, upon notice, apply to the court by letter requesting such conference. The application shall include a brief statement indicating why a conference would be appropriate.

PART 805. ADMISSION OF ATTORNEYS

§ 805.1. Admission of Attorneys

(a) Filing of Application Papers. Every applicant for admission to practice as an attorney and counselor at law pursuant to subdivision 1(a) or 1(b) of section 90 of the Judiciary Law, may obtain the standard forms and instructions for that purpose from the clerk of the Appellate Division. Every applicant for admission to practice pursuant to subdivision 1(a) of section 90 of the Judiciary Law may obtain such forms and instructions immediately after taking the bar examination, and may file a completed application, consisting of the standard form of questionnaire and the other required papers as directed by the instructions, at any time thereafter, regardless of whether the results of the bar examination have yet been issued. As soon as the applicant shall receive a letter from the State Board of Law Examiners stating that the applicant has passed the bar examination, the applicant shall file that letter with the clerk of the Appellate Division, and if the applicant's questionnaire was verified more than 45 days prior to such filing, the applicant shall also file a supplemental affidavit stating whether there have been any changes in the facts stated therein and setting forth any such changes.

(b) Referral to Committee on Character and Fitness. Every completed application shall be referred for investigation of the applicant's character and fitness to a committee on character and fitness designated by the Appellate Division of the department to which the applicant is eligible for certification by the State Board of Law Examiners after passing the bar examination, or to which the applicant is applying for admission without examination in accordance with the rules of the Court of Appeals for the admission of attorneys and counselors at law.

(c) Quorum for Committee Action. A majority of the entire committee shall constitute a quorum for the transaction of business by a committee on character

and fitness if it consists of less than ten members, and one-fifth of the entire committee, but not less than five members, shall constitute a quorum if it consists of ten or more members.

(d) Investigation and Interview. The committee may itself conduct the required investigation, including an interview of the applicant, or it may authorize its chairman or acting chairman to designate one or more of its members to do so and to make a recommendation to the committee. The committee or the member or members thereof conducting the investigation may require the applicant to furnish such additional information or proofs of good character as the committee or such member or members may consider pertinent. The committee may commence the required investigation at any time after the applicant's completed application has been filed, except that the personal interview of an applicant for admission pursuant to subdivision 1(a) of section 90 of the Judiciary Law shall not be held until after the applicant has been notified by the State Board of Law Examiners that the applicant has passed the bar examination and has been certified to apply for admission.

(e) Procedure Upon Recommendation of Approval. If the committee shall approve the application following its own investigation, or if it shall accept a recommendation of approval submitted by the member or members conducting an investigation pursuant to designation, the chairman or acting chairman shall certify to the Appellate Division on behalf of the committee that the applicant possesses the requisite character and fitness.

(f) Procedure Upon Recommendation of Disapproval, Deferral or Committee Consideration. If the committee shall fail to approve the application following its own investigation or following a recommendation submitted by the member or members conducting an investigation pursuant to designation that the application be disapproved or that action thereon be deferred, a hearing on the application shall be held expeditiously before the committee or subcommittee of at least two members designated by the chairman or acting chairman. Such a hearing shall also be held if the member or members conducting an investigation pursuant to designation shall recommend consideration of the application by the committee and the committee shall fail to approve the application following such consideration.

(g) Notice of Hearing; Waiver. Unless waived in writing by the applicant, a written notice of hearing of not less than twenty days, specifying the time and place of the hearing, shall be served on the applicant. In addition, the notice of hearing shall inform the applicant of the matters to be inquired into and of the applicant's right to be represented by an attorney, and such information shall also be given to the applicant prior to the hearing if the applicant has waived notice of hearing.

(h) Procedure at Hearing. At the hearing, hearsay evidence may be received and considered and adherence to strict rules of evidence shall not be required. The applicant shall be given an opportunity to call and cross-examine witnesses and to challenge, examine and controvert any adverse evidence. Upon timely request, subpoenas for the attendance of witnesses or the production of papers shall be issued to the applicant by the clerk of the Appellate Division, the subpoena fees and mileage to be paid by the applicant.

(i) Stenographic Record or Tape Recording. A stenographic record or tape recording shall be made of the hearing, and the applicant may obtain a transcript or copy of the recording at the applicant's expense.

(j) Decision or Report Following Hearing. Where the hearing has been conducted by the committee, the committee shall render a decision, and where the hearing has been conducted by a subcommittee, the subcommittee shall render a report, within 60 days after the matter is finally submitted, unless the time is extended by consent of the applicant or order of the Appellate Division. The decision of the committee or the report of the subcommittee, as the case may be, may recommend approval or disapproval of the applicant or deferral of action on the application for a period not to exceed six months.

(k) Transmittal of Decision to Appellate Division Following Hearing Conducted by Committee. Where the hearing has been conducted by the committee, the committee shall transmit its decision to the Appellate Division, together with the appropriate certificate if it recommends approval of the applicant. If the decision recommends disapproval of the applicant or deferral of action on the application, it shall include

a statement of the grounds on which it is based and a copy thereof shall be served on the applicant or the applicant's attorney.

(*l*) Review by Committee Following Hearing Conducted by Subcommittee. Where the hearing has been conducted by a subcommittee, the subcommittee's report and the stenographic record or tape recording of the hearing shall be referred for consideration and review to the committee, which shall render a decision thereon expeditiously. The committee's decision may confirm, reverse or modify the subcommittee's report or direct that a further hearing be held before the same or another subcommittee. If the committee's decision recommends disapproval of the applicant or deferral of action on the application, it shall include a statement of the grounds on which it is based and a copy thereof shall be served on the applicant or the applicant's attorney. The decision shall be transmitted to the Appellate Division, together with the appropriate certificate if it recommends approval of the applicant. The deliberations of the committee shall be confidential and the applicant shall not be entitled to compel disclosure thereof.

(m) Petition to Appellate Division Following Adverse Decision. If the committee's decision is adverse to the applicant, the applicant may, within 60 days after service of a copy thereof, petition the Appellate Division, in accordance with CPLR 9404, on notice of not less than eight days served on the committee together with any supporting papers, for an order granting the application for admission to practice notwithstanding the committee's decision.

(n) Petition to Appellate Division in Case of Unreasonable Delay. In any case in which it is claimed that the committee has unreasonably delayed action on an application for admission to practice, the applicant may petition the Appellate Division, in accordance with CPLR 9404, on notice of not less than eight days served on the committee together with any supporting papers, for an order granting the application notwithstanding the committee's failure to complete action thereon, or for other appropriate relief.

(o) Petition for Advance Ruling With Respect to Past Conduct.

(1) Any person who is a matriculated student in an approved law school, as an approved law school is defined in the rules of the Court of Appeals for the admission of attorneys and counselors at law, or who has applied for admission to such a law school, and who has previously been:

(i) convicted of a felony or misdemeanor;

(ii) suspended, removed or dismissed from public office or employment; or

(iii) dishonorably discharged from the armed services of the United States, may petition the Appellate Division of the department in which such person resides or is employed full-time, or if such person does not reside and is not employed full-time in the State, the Appellate Division of the Third Department, for an advance ruling, in accordance with this section, as to whether such conviction, suspension, removal or dismissal from public office or employment, or dishonorable discharge, as the case may be, would operate to disqualify the petitioner, on character grounds, from being admitted to practice as an attorney and counselor at law in this State.

(2) The petition shall include a detailed statement of the facts with respect to the petitioner's conviction, suspension, dismissal or removal from public office or employment, or dishonorable discharge, as the case may be, and of the petitioner's activities subsequent thereto which the petitioner believes bear on character and fitness to practice law.

(3) The petitioner shall also submit a completed and verified questionnaire on the standard form furnished by the committee on character and fitness and affidavits of good moral character from two reputable persons who have known the petitioner for at least one year. In addition, the petitioner shall submit a letter from a person in authority at the approved law school in which the petitioner is a matriculated student or to which the petitioner has applied for admission, stating that such law school would retain or accept the petitioner as a student therein, as the case may be, if the petitioner's conviction, suspension, dismissal or removal from public office or employment or dishonorable discharge, as the case may be, would not operate to disqualify the petitioner from being admitted to practice as an attorney and counselor at law in this State.

(4) The petition and other papers submitted by the petitioner shall be referred to the appropriate committee on character and fitness, which shall process and investigate the petition in accordance with the procedures set forth in the preceding sections of this Part. The committee may recommend that a ruling be made either in favor of or against the petitioner, or that no ruling be made, and its recommendation shall be transmitted to the Appellate Division.

(5) A ruling made by the Appellate Division in favor of the petitioner shall determine that the petitioner's prior conviction, suspension, removal or dismissal from public office or employment, or dishonorable discharge, as the case may be, and the acts committed by the petitioner which resulted therein, would not operate to disqualify the petitioner, on character grounds, from being admitted to practice as an attorney and counselor at law in this State. Such a ruling shall have binding force throughout the State with respect to the determination thus made by it. In the event that the Appellate Division should rule against the petitioner or should refuse to make a ruling, its determination shall be without prejudice to the petitioner's right, after passing the bar examination, to apply for a favorable ruling with respect to character and fitness.

(p) Manner of Service. Service of any notice or other papers required under any of these rules may be made by mail or in the manner provided for service of a summons.

Cross References

CPLR, see McKinney's Book 7B.

Judiciary Law, see McKinney's Book 29.

§ 805.2. Defense and Indemnification of Members of Committees on Character and Fitness

Members of the committees on character and fitness in the Third Judicial Department, as volunteers, are expressly authorized to participate in a State-sponsored volunteer program within the meaning of subdivision 1 of section 17 of the Public Officers Law.

Cross References

Public Officers Law, see McKinney's Book 46.

§ 805.3. Admission Pro Hac Vice

(a) Application in this department for admission pro hac vice, pursuant to section 520.11(a)(1) of the rules of the Court of Appeals, to participate in the trial or argument of any particular cause, shall be made to the court in which the action or proceeding is pending.

(b) Application for admission pro hac vice, pursuant to section 520.11(a)(2), shall be made only to this court, and shall be made upon a verified petition which shall set forth:

(1) facts showing compliance with the requirements of the section;

(2) the nature of the legal services to be performed;

(3) the courts in which applicant seeks permission to appear; and

(4) the period for which authorization is sought.

(c) Upon approval of an application, the order shall specify the scope and extent of the authorized legal services, the courts in which applicant may appear and the period of authorization.

§ 805.4. Licensing of Legal Consultants

(a) Applications for Licenses as Legal Consultants; Referral to Committee on Character and Fitness.

(1) The committees on character and fitness appointed by this court to investigate the character and fitness of applicants for admission to practice as attorneys and counselors-at-law in the courts of this State are hereby also authorized to investigate the qualifications and the character and fitness of applicants for licenses to practice as legal consultants pursuant to the Judiciary Law (§ 53, subd. 6) and the rules of the Court of Appeals (22 NYCRR Part 521).

(2) Every applicant for a license to practice as a legal consultant shall complete, verify and file with the clerk of this court the standard form of questionnaire, and shall comply with all the other requirements prescribed for that purpose by this court.

(3) Every application in this department for such a license shall be referred to the committee on character and fitness for the judicial district in which the applicant actually resides at the time of such application, and, unless otherwise ordered by the court, no such license shall be granted without a certificate from such committee that it has found that the applicant possesses the qualifications and the character and fitness required therefor.

(b) Documents, Affidavits and Other Proof Required. Every applicant for a license to practice as a legal consultant shall file the following additional papers with his application:

(1) A certificate from the authority having final jurisdiction over professional discipline in the foreign country in which the applicant was admitted to practice, which shall be signed by a responsible official or one of the members of the executive body of such authority and shall be attested under the hand and seal, if any, of the clerk of such authority, and which shall certify:

(i) as to the authority's jurisdiction in such matters;

(ii) as to the applicant's admission to practice in such foreign country and the date thereof, and as to his good standing as an attorney or counselor at law or the equivalent therein; and

(iii) as to whether any charge or complaint has ever been filed against the applicant with such authority, and, if so, the substance of each such charge or complaint and the disposition thereof.

(2) A letter of recommendation from one of the members of the executive body of such authority or from one of the judges of the highest law court or court of general original jurisdiction of such foreign country, certifying to the applicant's professional qualifications, together with a certificate under the hand and seal, if any, of the clerk of such authority or of such court, as the case may be, attesting to the office held by the person signing the letter and the genuineness of his signature.

(3) Affidavits as to the applicant's good moral character and fitness from three reputable persons residing in this State and not related to the applicant, one of whom shall be a practicing New York attorney.

(4) Affidavits from two attorneys or counselors-at-law or the equivalent admitted in and practicing in such foreign country, stating the nature and extent of their acquaintance with the applicant and their personal knowledge as to the nature, character and extent of the applicant's practice, and as to the applicant's good standing, as an attorney or counselor-at-law or the equivalent in such foreign country, and the duration and continuity of such practice.

(5) Such additional evidence as the applicant may see fit to submit with respect to his educational and professional qualifications and his good moral character and fitness.

(6) A duly authenticated English translation of every paper submitted by the applicant which is not in English.

(7) A duly acknowledged instrument designating the clerk of this court the applicant's agent for service of process as provided in section 521.4(a)(2)(iii) of the rules of the Court of Appeals.

(c) College and Law School Certificates. A certificate shall be submitted from each college and law school attended by the applicant, setting forth the information required by forms which shall be provided to the applicant for that purpose.

(d) Exceptional Situations. In the event that the applicant is unable to comply strictly with any of the foregoing requirements, the applicant shall set forth the reasons for such inability in an affidavit, together with a statement showing in detail the efforts made to fulfill such requirements.

(e) Authority of Committee on Character and Fitness to Require Additional Proof. A committee on character and fitness may in any case require the applicant to submit such additional proof or information as it may deem appropriate and may also require the applicant to submit a report of the National Conference of Bar Examiners with respect to his character and qualifications.

(f) Undertaking. Prior to taking custody of any money, securities (other than unendorsed securities in registered form), negotiable instruments, bullion, precious stones or other valuables, in the course of his practice as a legal consultant, for or on behalf of any client domiciled or residing in the United States, every person licensed to practice as a legal consultant shall obtain, and shall maintain in effect for the duration of such custody, an undertaking issued by a duly authorized surety company, and approved by a justice of this court, to assure the faithful and fair discharge of his duties and obligations arising from such custody. The undertaking shall be in an amount not less than the amount of any such money, or the fair market value of any such property other than money, of which the legal consultant shall have custody, except that this court may in any case in its discretion for good cause direct that such undertaking shall be in a greater or lesser amount. The undertaking or a duplicate original thereof shall be promptly filed by the legal consultant with the clerk of this court.

(g) Disciplinary Procedure.

(1) Disciplinary proceedings against any legal consultant shall be initiated and conducted in the same

manner as prescribed by law for disciplinary proceedings against attorneys.

(2) Any committee authorized by this court to conduct preliminary investigations of charges of professional misconduct by attorneys shall have authority to conduct preliminary investigations of charges of professional misconduct or unauthorized activities on the part of any licensed legal consultant in the same manner as in investigations relating to attorneys.

(h) Filing. Every application in this department for a license as a legal consultant, together with all the papers submitted thereon, shall upon its final disposition be filed in the office of the clerk of this court.

Cross References

Judiciary Law, see McKinney's Book 29.

§ 805.5. Activities of Eligible Law Students and Law School Graduates Authorized by Sections 478 and 484 of the Judiciary Law

(a) Any officer or agency of the state, or of a subdivision thereof, or any legal aid organization whose principal office is located in this department, may make application to the presiding justice of this court for an order authorizing the employment or utilization of law students who have completed at least two semesters of law school and eligible law school graduates as law interns to render and perform legal services, to the extent set forth in paragraph (b) hereof, which the officer, agency or organization making the application is authorized to perform. The application shall set forth the names and addresses of the persons to be appointed and facts showing their eligibility for appointment, together with applicant's certification that they are of good character and competent legal ability.

(b) Authorized Activities. Law students who have completed at least two semesters of law school and law school graduates appointed as law interns are authorized to engage in the following activities:

(1) in the Appellate Division, Third Department, to prepare briefs and memoranda of law and, upon prior approval of the court and when under immediate supervision of a supervising attorney, to argue appeals and motions in both civil and criminal actions and proceedings;

(2) in criminal matters, in superior courts, under general supervision of a supervising attorney, to render legal services at arraignments, bail applications, pleas, sentencings, preliminary hearings and post-conviction proceedings, including appeals;

(3) in criminal matters, in inferior courts, under general supervision, to render legal services at arraignments, pleas, sentencings, preliminary hearings, post-conviction proceedings and at nonjury trials in cases involving misdemeanors and lesser offenses; and, when under immediate supervision of a supervising attorney, at jury trials in cases involving misdemeanors;

(4) in family court, under general supervision, to render legal services on motions and in uncontested proceedings, and in contested matters when under immediate supervision of a supervising attorney;

(5) in civil actions and proceedings in or before any court or administrative agency, under general supervision, to render legal services in motions and uncontested matters, and, under immediate supervision, in contested civil matters. Appearances before federal courts and state and federal administrative agencies shall be subject to the rules and regulations of the particular court or agency involved.

(c) Requirements and Limitations. A law intern may appear in the courts and administrative agencies specified in paragraph (b) above if the person on whose behalf the intern is appearing and the supervising attorney have indicated in writing their consent to the appearance. The consents referred to shall be filed with and brought to the attention of the presiding officer of the court or administrative agency. Pleadings, legal documents, briefs and memorandums shall be indorsed by the supervising attorney and may contain the name of the law intern who participated in their preparation.

(d) Limitations on Legal Aid Programs and Organizations. Law students who have completed at least two semesters of law school and law school graduates engaged as law interns in a legal aid organization or legal services program whose principal office is located in this department shall be authorized to render legal services to and represent only persons who are financially unable to pay for legal services and are eligible to qualify for free legal services in accordance with the standards and guidelines of the organization or program in which they are engaged. They may not act in bankruptcy proceedings, libel and slander cases, decedent estate matters or contingent fee matters, except where three private attorneys have rejected the case; but, subject to the scope of the purposes of the organization or program in which they are engaged, they may render assistance to indigent persons in any matter in which a party does not have the right to assignment of counsel and to indigent inmates of correctional institutions or other persons who request assistance in preparing applications for post-conviction relief. A law intern shall neither ask for nor receive any compensation or remuneration for services from the party on whose behalf the services are rendered.

(e) Supervision. A supervising attorney shall be the head of the department, agency or legal aid organization making the application, or his or her designee, and shall have at least two years of actual practice in this state. The supervising attorney shall assume personal professional responsibility for any work undertaken by a law intern and shall supervise the preparation of the intern's work. Immediate supervision of a law intern shall mean that the supervising attorney shall be personally present throughout the proceedings.

(f) Length of Appointment. A law student who has completed at least two semesters of law school or law school graduate may be employed to render legal services, as authorized herein, until he or she shall have been admitted to the bar or notified that he or she failed the New York State bar examination which was given immediately following graduation from law school. A person who shall fail to pass that examination but shall apply to take the next available New York State bar examination may be redesignated upon application to the presiding justice. The length of the period of service shall be specified in the order of appointment.

PART 806. CONDUCT OF ATTORNEYS

§ 806.1. Application

This Part shall apply to all attorneys who are admitted to practice, reside or have an office in, or who are employed or transact business in, the third judicial department.

§ 806.2. Professional Misconduct Defined

Any attorney who fails to conduct himself or herself in conformity with the standards of conduct imposed upon members of the bar as conditions for the privilege to practice law, and any attorney who violates any Disciplinary Rule of the Code of Professional Responsibility adopted jointly by the Appellate Divisions of the Supreme Court, effective September 1, 1990, or any other rule or announced standard of the court governing the conduct of attorneys, shall be deemed to be guilty of professional misconduct within the meaning of subdivision 2 of section 90 of the Judiciary Law.

Cross References

Judiciary Law, see McKinney's Book 29.

Code of Professional Responsibility, see Appendix to McKinney's Judiciary Law, Book 29.

§ 806.3. Third Department Grievance Program

(a) Committee on professional standards. This court shall appoint a committee on professional standards for the Third Judicial Department, which shall consist of a chairperson and 20 members, three of whom shall be nonlawyers. Appointment of lawyers shall, as far as practicable, be made equally from practicing attorneys in each of the judicial districts in the Third Judicial Department. Appointments shall be for a term of three years or for such shorter term as the court deems appropriate. No person who has served two consecutive three-year terms shall be eligible for reappointment until the passage of three years from the expiration of his or her second term. Seven members of the committee shall constitute a quorum and the concurrence of six members shall be necessary for any action taken. The chairperson and vice-chairperson shall be named by the court after considering the recommendations of the committee. The chairperson may appoint an executive committee consisting of at least one member of the committee from each judicial district.

(b) Duties of Committee on Professional Standards. The committee shall (1) consider and cause to be investigated all matters called to its attention, whether by complaint or otherwise, involving alleged misconduct by an attorney in the third judicial department, (2) supervise the professional staff in the performance of its duties to the committee, (3) furnish the court quarterly statistical reports concerning the disposition of all matters before the committee and maintain such records as directed by the court, and (4) submit a proposed annual budget to the court for approval.

(c) Defense and Indemnification of Committee Members. Members of the committee on professional standards, as volunteers, are expressly authorized to participate in a State-sponsored volunteer program within the meaning of subdivision 1 of section 17 of the Public Officers Law.

(d) Professional Staff. The court shall, in consultation with the committee, appoint a professional staff and such supporting staff as shall be necessary. The chief attorney shall be authorized to disburse funds within the amounts appropriated and allocated. The expenses of the staff and committee shall not exceed the amounts segregated and assigned by the Office of Court Administration, and shall be incurred according to rules and regulations promulgated by that office.

(e) Duties of Professional Staff. The chief attorney, under the supervision of the committee, shall (1) answer and take appropriate action respecting all inquiries concerning an attorney's conduct and (2) investigate all matters involving alleged misconduct by an attorney in the Third Judicial Department.

Cross References

Public Officers Law, see McKinney's Book 46.

§ 806.4. Procedure

(a) Investigation Generally. Investigation of professional misconduct may be commenced by the committee, through the chief attorney, upon receipt of a specific complaint, or by the committee on its own motion. Complaints must be in writing and signed by the complainant, but need not be verified. Prior to initiating an investigation on its own motion, the committee shall file as part of its record a written inquiry signed by the chief attorney, which inquiry shall serve as the basis for such investigation.

(b) Investigation by Chief Attorney. Before initiating an investigation of a specific complaint against an attorney, the chief attorney shall determine whether the allegations, if true, are sufficient to establish a charge of professional misconduct. If deemed sufficient, the chief attorney shall forward a copy of the complaint to the attorney, together with a statement of the nature of the alleged professional misconduct and a request that the attorney furnish a written statement concerning the complaint, and shall advise the attorney that a copy of his statement may, in the discretion of the committee, be furnished to the complainant for reply. Attorneys shall be expected to cooperate with all investigations. As part of an investigation, the chief attorney may request an attorney to appear pursuant to written notice to be examined under oath by the chief attorney or a staff attorney, and may, when necessary, apply pursuant to subdivision (e) of this section for a subpoena directing the attorney to appear for such examination. Stenographic minutes of such examination shall be made and a transcript made available to the attorney upon his request and payment of the stenographic fees. If an attorney requests that an examination be conducted before a third person, the chairman of the committee shall designate a member of the committee as the person before whom the examination shall be held. Upon the conclusion of an investigation, the chief attorney shall make a report to the committee. An attorney who fails to comply with a subpoena directing him to appear for examination may, in the court's discretion, be suspended pending his compliance or until further order of the court.

(c) Action by Committee.

(1) If, after an investigation, the committee determines that no action is warranted, the complaint shall be dismissed and the complainant and the attorney shall be so notified in writing; or, if the investigation was undertaken on the committee's own motion, the investigation shall be discontinued. If, after an investigation, the committee determines that a complaint warrants action, it may:

(i) direct that a disciplinary proceeding be commenced against the attorney; or

(ii) admonish the attorney, either orally or in writing, or both, if the acts of misconduct have been established by clear and convincing evidence and the committee determines in light of all of the circumstances that the misconduct is not serious enough to warrant commencement of a disciplinary proceeding; or

(iii) issue a letter of caution, if the acts of misconduct have been so established and the committee determines in light of all the circumstances that the

misconduct is not serious enough to warrant either commencement of a disciplinary proceeding or imposition of an admonition; or

(iv) issue a letter of education, if the committee determines that the actions of the attorney warrant comment.

(2) Prior to imposition of an admonition, the committee shall give the attorney 20 days' notice by mail of the committee's proposed action. The attorney may request reconsideration of the committee's proposed admonition. Such request shall be made by letter, certified mail, return receipt requested, within 14 days from the date of mailing of the committee's notice. The request shall be considered by the executive committee. If it is determined by a majority of the executive committee that reconsideration is warranted, the matter shall be resubmitted to the committee.

(3) No prior notice to the attorney is necessary for the issuance of a letter of caution. The attorney may, however, request reconsideration of the committee's action in issuing a letter of caution. Such request shall be made by letter, certified mail, return receipt requested, within 14 days from the date of mailing of the committee's letter. The request shall be considered by the executive committee. If it is determined by a majority of the executive committee that reconsideration is warranted, the matter shall be resubmitted to the committee.

(4) Following a request for reconsideration of an admonition or letter of caution, where the committee adheres to its action, or where reconsideration is not sought, the attorney may file a motion with the court for review of the admonition or letter of caution, on notice to the chief attorney, within 30 days from the date of mailing or scheduled issuance of the committee's determination. An attorney who receives a letter of education may similarly file a motion with the court for review thereof, upon a showing that the matter giving rise to the letter involves a fundamental constitutional right. Upon such motion, the court may consider the entire record and may confirm or vacate the admonition, or letter of caution or education, or make whatever other disposition it determines to be warranted under all the circumstances.

(5) When an attorney has been admonished or cautioned, the committee shall promptly notify the complainant that appropriate action has been taken. The committee's records relating to its investigation and sanction shall be confidential. An admonition or letter of caution may be considered by the court and the committee in determining whether to impose discipline and the extent of discipline to be imposed in the event other charges of misconduct are subsequently brought against the attorney.

(d) Protective Orders. An attorney aggrieved by any investigation may apply to the court by affidavit, upon notice to the chief attorney in such manner as a justice of the court may direct, for a protective order denying, limiting, conditioning or regulating the use of any information being sought by the chief attorney.

(e) Subpoenas. If it appears that the examination of any person is necessary for a proper determination of the validity of a complaint, the chief attorney or the attorney under investigation may apply to the clerk of this court for issuance of a subpoena for the attendance of the person as a witness and for the production of relevant books and papers. Application for issuance of a subpoena shall be made by setting forth factual allegations showing the relevancy of the testimony, and of any books and papers specified, to the subject matter of the investigation. Subpoenas, which shall be entitled "In the Matter of the Investigation by the Committee on Professional Standards of the Professional Conduct of an Attorney", shall be issued by the clerk in the name of the presiding justice and may be made returnable at a time and place therein specified before the chief attorney or any member of the committee designated to conduct the examination. The committee, or a member thereof designated by the chairman, or the chief attorney or a staff attorney, is empowered to take and cause to be transcribed the testimony of a witness, who may be sworn by any person authorized by law to administer oaths. If the committee is required to obtain a subpoena in order to compel an attorney's appearance for examination, the attorney shall be required to reimburse the committee for the stenographic costs of the examination within ten days of being advised of the amount of such costs.

(f) Suspension of Attorneys Pending Consideration of Disciplinary Charges.

(1) An attorney who is the subject of an investigation into allegations of misconduct and who has been examined by the committee under oath or who is the subject of a disciplinary proceeding commenced in this court pursuant to a petition filed under section 806.5 of this Part, or pursuant to a notice served under section 806.19(b) of this Part, may be suspended from the practice of law pending consideration of the disciplinary charges against the attorney upon a finding that the attorney is guilty of professional misconduct immediately threatening the public interest. Such a finding shall be based upon:

(i) the attorney's default in responding to the petition or notice, or

(ii) a substantial admission under oath to commission of an act or acts of such professional misconduct, or

(iii) other uncontroverted evidence of the misconduct.

(2) The suspension shall be made upon application of the committee to this court, after written notice of such application has been given to the attorney, and shall commence upon service on the attorney of an order of this court granting the application. The court shall briefly state the reasons for the suspension which shall continue until such time as the disciplinary matter has been concluded and until further order of the court.

(3) An order of suspension together with any decision issued pursuant to the provisions of this subdivision shall be deemed a public record. The papers submitted in connection with the application therefor shall be deemed confidential until such time as the disciplinary matter against the attorney has been concluded and the charges are sustained by the court.

(g) Diversion program

(1) During the course of an investigation or disciplinary proceeding, when the attorney raises alcohol or other substance abuse or dependency as a mitigating factor, or upon recommendation of the committee, the Court may, upon application of the attorney or committee, stay the investigation or disciplinary proceeding and direct the attorney to complete a monitoring program sponsored by a lawyers' assistance program approved by the Court. In determining whether to divert an attorney to a monitoring program, the Court shall consider (i) whether the alleged misconduct occurred during a time period when the attorney suffered from alcohol or other substance abuse or dependency; (ii) whether the alleged misconduct is related to such alcohol or other substance abuse or dependency; (iii) the seriousness of the alleged misconduct; and (iv) whether diversion is in the best interests of the public, the legal profession, and the attorney.

(2) Upon submission of written proof of successful completion of the monitoring program, the Court may direct discontinuance or resumption of the investigation or disciplinary proceeding, or take other appropriate action.

(3) In the event the attorney is not accepted into or fails to successfully complete the monitoring program as ordered by the Court, or the attorney commits additional misconduct after diversion is directed pursuant to this subdivision, the Court may, upon notice to the attorney affording him or her an opportunity to be heard, rescind the order diverting the attorney to the monitoring program and reinstate the investigation or disciplinary proceeding, or take other appropriate action.

(4) Any costs associated with the attorney's participation in a monitoring program pursuant to this subdivision shall be the responsibility of the attorney.

§ 806.5. Disciplinary Proceedings

Upon determining that a disciplinary proceeding should be instituted, the committee shall file with the court the original and one copy of the notice of petition and petition of charges with proof of service of a copy upon the attorney. Service of the notice and petition shall be made either personally or by certified mail. If service is made by certified mail and the attorney shall fail to answer or respond within the time specified by the notice, a copy of the notice and petition shall be served upon the attorney personally. The court shall refer issues of fact to a judge or referee to hear and report. If no factual issue is raised, the court may, upon application of either party, fix a time at which the attorney may be heard in mitigation or otherwise, or the court may refer the matter for such purpose.

§ 806.6. County Bar Association Grievance Committees and Mediation Programs

(a) County Bar Association Grievance Committees.

(1) A county bar association which receives a complaint against an attorney shall initially refer the complaint to the committee.

(2) If the chief attorney, or the committee after investigation, determines that the complaint is a matter involving undue delay in rendering legal services not constituting neglect, a fee dispute to which Part 137 of the Rules of the Chief Administrator does not apply, or inadequate representation not constituting professional misconduct, the complaint may be referred back to the county bar association for resolution. A complaint submitted directly to the committee may also be referred by the committee or chief attorney to the county bar association in the first instance.

(3) The county bar association shall complete an investigation and attempt to resolve the complaint within 90 days after receipt of the complaint from the committee or chief attorney. If the county bar association is unable to resolve the complaint within this time period, it shall, upon request of the chief attorney, return its complete file to the committee for further consideration.

(4) The county bar association shall render a quarterly report to the committee within 15 days after the end of each calendar quarter. The report shall contain the names of all attorneys against whom complaints were received or were pending during the preceding quarter. If a county bar association resolves a complaint, it shall forward its complete original file to the committee together with its quarterly report.

(b) County Bar Association Mediation Programs. Upon receipt of a complaint submitted directly to the committee, or following referral of a complaint by a county bar association, the committee or chief attorney, upon determining that the matter is appropriate for mediation, may refer the complaint to a county bar association mediation program pursuant to Part 1220 of the joint rules of the Appellate Divisions.

§ 806.7. Attorneys Convicted of a Crime

Upon the filing with this court of a certificate of a felony conviction of an attorney, the court shall issue an order directing the attorney to show cause why an order should not be entered striking his name from the roll of attorneys pursuant to the provisions of subdivision 4 of section 90 of the Judiciary Law. Upon the filing of the record of conviction of an attorney convicted of a serious crime, as defined in subdivision 4 of section 90 of the Judiciary Law, the court shall issue an order suspending the attorney until a further or final order is made. An attorney who has been suspended may apply for reinstatement upon expiration of the period of suspension.

Cross References

Judiciary Law, see McKinney's Book 29.

§ 806.8. Resignation of Attorneys

(a) An attorney who is the subject of a disciplinary proceeding or of an investigation into allegations of misconduct may resign by tendering his resignation to the court, together with an affidavit stating that he wishes to resign and:

(1) that he is acting freely and voluntarily and is fully aware of the consequences of his resignation;

(2) that he is aware of the pending investigation or disciplinary proceeding concerning allegations of misconduct, the nature of which shall be specifically set forth; and

(3) that he does not contest the allegations of professional misconduct and recognizes that his failure to do so precludes him from asserting his innocence of the professional misconduct alleged.

(b) If the court accepts an attorney's resignation, it shall enter an order of disbarment.

§ 806.9. Conduct of Disbarred, Suspended or Resigned Attorneys

(a) Compliance With Judiciary Law. Disbarred, suspended or resigned attorneys shall comply fully with sections 478, 479, 484 and 486 of the Judiciary Law.

(b) Compensation. A disbarred, suspended or resigned attorney may not share in any fee for legal services performed by another attorney during the period of his removal from the bar, but he or she may be compensated on a quantum meruit basis for legal services rendered and disbursements incurred prior to the effective date of removal. In the absence of agreement, the amount and manner of payment of such compensation and disbursements shall be fixed by the court on application of either the disbarred, suspended or resigned attorney or the new attorney, on notice to the other, as well as on notice to the client. Such applications shall be made at special term of the court in which the action is pending, or at a special term of Supreme Court in the county in which the moving attorney maintains his office if an action has not been commenced. In no event shall the combined legal fees exceed the amount the client would have been required to pay had no substitution of attorneys been required.

(c) Notice to Clients Not Involved in Litigation. A disbarred, suspended or resigned attorney shall promptly notify by registered or certified mail, return receipt requested, all clients being represented in pending matters, other than litigated or administrative matters or proceedings pending in any court or agency, of his disbarment, suspension or resignation and shall advise said clients to seek other legal advice.

(d) Notice to Clients Involved in Litigation.

(1) A disbarred, suspended or resigned attorney shall promptly notify, by registered or certified mail, return receipt requested, each of his clients who is involved in litigated matters or administrative proceedings, and the attorney or attorneys for each adverse party in such matter or proceeding, of his disbarment, suspension or resignation and consequent inability to act as an attorney after the effective date of his disbarment, suspension or resignation. The notice to the client shall request the prompt substitution of another attorney. The notice to the attorney for an adverse party shall state the residence address of the client of the disbarred, suspended or resigned attorney.

(2) In the event a client does not obtain substitute counsel before the effective date of the disbarment, suspension or resignation, it shall be the responsibility of the disbarred, suspended or resigned attorney to move pro se in the court in which the action is pending, or before the body in which an administrative proceeding is pending, for leave to withdraw from the action or proceeding.

(e) Conduct After Entry of Order. A disbarred, suspended or resigned attorney, after entry of the disbarment or suspension order or after entry of the order accepting a resignation, shall not accept any new retainer or engage in any new case or legal matter of any nature as attorney for another. However, during the period between the entry date of the order and its effective date, he may wind up and complete, on behalf of any client, all matters which were pending on the entry date. After the effective date, the use of the name of a disbarred, suspended or resigned attorney, who is a member of a partnership or professional corporation, in the name of said partnership or professional corporation, shall be discontinued. The disbarred, suspended or resigned attorney shall not share in any income generated by the firm or professional corporation with which he was associated after the date of disbarment or resignation or during the period of suspension.

(f) Filing Proof of Compliance and Attorney's Address. Within thirty days after the effective date of the disbarment, suspension order or the order

accepting a resignation, the disbarred, suspended or resigned attorney shall file with the clerk of this court an affidavit reporting that he has fully complied with the provisions of the order and with these rules and that he has served a copy of such affidavit upon the chief attorney. Such affidavit shall also set forth the residence or other address to which communications may be directed to the disbarred, suspended or resigned attorney.

(g) Required Records. A disbarred, suspended or resigned attorney shall keep and maintain records of the steps taken by him to comply with this section so that, on any subsequent proceeding instituted by or against him, proof of compliance with this section and with the disbarment or suspension order, or with the order accepting the resignation, will be available.

Cross References

Judiciary Law, see McKinney's Book 29.

§ 806.10. Mental Incapacity of Attorney; Protection of Clients of Disbarred and Suspended Attorneys

(a) Proceeding to Determine Alleged Incapacity of Attorney. Whenever, during the investigation of a complaint of professional misconduct or the prosecution of a disciplinary proceeding against an attorney, it shall appear that the attorney is incapacitated from continuing to practice law by reason of mental illness, drug addiction or alcoholism, or is otherwise mentally irresponsible, it shall be the duty of the chief attorney to petition the court to take appropriate action for determination of the attorney's mental condition, including examination by such qualified medical experts as the court shall designate. If the court is satisfied from the evidence that the attorney is so incapacitated, it shall suspend him from practice for such mental incapacity indefinitely and until further order, and any pending proceedings against him shall be held in abeyance. The court may appoint counsel to represent the attorney, if he lacks adequate representation.

(b) Procedure When Respondent Claims Disability During Course of Disciplinary Proceeding. If during the course of a disciplinary proceeding respondent contends that he is suffering from a disability by reason of mental infirmity or illness, or because of addiction to drugs or intoxicants which makes it impossible for him adequately to defend himself, the court thereupon shall enter an order suspending respondent from continuing to practice law until a determination is made of the respondent's capacity to do so.

(c) Expenses of Proceedings. The court may fix the compensation of any attorney or medical expert appointed pursuant to this section and direct that payment be made as an incident of the expenses of a disciplinary proceeding.

§ 806.11. Appointment of Attorneys to Protect Clients' Interests

Whenever an attorney is disbarred or suspended for incapacity, disability or other reason, or whenever there are reasonable grounds to believe that an attorney has abandoned or is seriously neglecting his practice to the prejudice of his clients, the court, upon such notice to him as it may direct, may appoint one or more attorneys to inventory his files and take appropriate action to protect the interests of his clients. An attorney so appointed shall not render legal services to clients of the attorney with respect to any file so inventoried, nor disclose any information contained therein without the consent of the client to whom such file relates, except as may be necessary to carry out the provisions of the order which appointed him. Whenever necessary, an attorney so appointed may apply to the court for appropriate instructions for the proper discharge of his duties.

§ 806.12. Reinstatement

(a) An attorney who has been disbarred or whose name has been struck from the roll of attorneys pursuant to subdivision (4) of section 90 of the Judiciary Law may not apply for reinstatement until the expiration of at least seven years from the effective date of the disbarment or removal. An attorney who has been suspended may apply for reinstatement upon expiration of the period of suspension. An attorney suspended pursuant to section 806.10 of this Part who applies for reinstatement shall waive any doctor-patient privilege which would otherwise exist regarding medical or psychiatric care during his or her disability, and shall submit a list of the persons by whom and the facilities at which treatment was received, together with authorizations for the release of records relating thereto. The court may direct the appointment of medical experts to examine the attorney at his or her own expense.

(b) An application for reinstatement may be granted by this court only upon a showing by the applicant (i) by clear and convincing evidence that applicant has fully complied with the provisions of the order disbarring or suspending applicant, or striking applicant's name from the roll of attorneys, and that applicant possesses the character and general fitness to resume the practice of law and (ii) that, subsequent to the entry of such order, applicant has taken and attained a passing score on the Multistate Professional Responsibility Examination described in section 520.9(a) of the Rules of the Court of Appeals for the Admission of Attorneys and Counselors at Law, the passing score thereon being that determined by the New York State Board of Law Examiners pursuant to section 520.9(c) of such rules. A copy of an application for reinstatement shall be served on the committee on professional standards and written notice thereof shall be provided by applicant to the Lawyers' Fund for Client Protection. The committee shall inquire into the merits of,

and may be heard in opposition to, the application. The application may be referred to the appropriate committee on character and fitness or to a judge or referee for a hearing and report to the court.

(c) The court in its discretion may direct that an applicant pay the necessary expenses incurred in connection with an application for reinstatement.

Cross References

Judiciary Law, see McKinney's Book 29.

§ 806.13. Contingent Fees in Claims and Actions for Personal Injury and Wrongful Death

(a) In any claim or action for personal injury or wrongful death, other than one alleging medical, dental or podiatric malpractice, whether determined by judgment or settlement, in which the compensation of claimant's or plaintiff's attorney is contingent, that is, dependent in whole or in part upon the amount of the recovery, the receipt, retention or sharing by such attorney, pursuant to agreement or otherwise, of compensation which is equal to or less than that contained in the schedule of fees in subdivision (b) of this section is deemed to be fair and reasonable. The receipt, retention or sharing of compensation which is in excess of such schedule of fees shall constitute the exaction of unreasonable and unconscionable compensation, unless authorized by a written order of the court as provided in this section. Compensation of claimant's or plaintiff's attorney for services rendered in claims or actions for personal injury alleging medical, dental or podiatric malpractice shall be computed pursuant to the fee schedule in Judiciary Law § 474–a.

(b) The following is the schedule of reasonable fees referred to in subdivision (a) of this section: either,

Schedule A

(1) 50 per cent on the first $1,000 of the sum recovered,

(2) 40 per cent on the next $2,000 of the sum recovered,

(3) 35 per cent on the next $22,000 of the sum recovered,

(4) 25 per cent on any amount over $25,000 of the sum recovered; or,

Schedule B

A percentage not exceeding 33⅓ per cent of the sum recovered, if the initial contractual arrangement between the client and the attorney so provides, in which event the procedure provided in this section for making application for additional compensation because of extraordinary circumstances shall not apply.

(c) Such percentage shall be computed on the net sum recovered after deducting from the amount recovered expenses and disbursements for expert testimony and investigative or other services properly chargeable to the enforcement of the claim or prosecution of the action. In computing the fee, the costs as taxed, including interest upon a judgment, shall be deemed part of the amount recovered. For the following or similar items there shall be no deduction in computing such percentages: liens, assignments or claims in favor of hospitals, for medical care and treatment by doctors and nurses, or self-insurers or insurance carriers.

(d) In the event that claimant's or plaintiff's attorney believes in good faith that Schedule A of paragraph (b) of this section, because of extraordinary circumstances, will not give him adequate compensation, application for greater compensation may be made upon affidavit with written notice and an opportunity to be heard to the client and other persons holding liens or assignments on the recovery. Such application shall be made to the justice of the trial part to which the action had been sent for trial; or, if it had not been sent to a part for trial, then to the justice presiding at the trial term calendar part of the court in which the action had been instituted; or, if no action had been instituted, then to a special term of Supreme Court in the judicial district in which the attorney has an office. Upon such application, the justice, in his discretion, if extraordinary circumstances are found to be present, and without regard to the claimant's or plaintiff's consent, may fix as reasonable compensation for legal services rendered an amount greater than that specified in Schedule A provided, however, that such greater amount shall not exceed the fee fixed pursuant to the contractual arrangement, if any, between the client and the attorney. If the application be granted, the justice shall make a written order accordingly, briefly stating the reasons for granting the greater compensation; and a copy of such order shall be served on all persons entitled to receive notice of the application.

(e) Nothing contained in this section shall be deemed applicable to the fixing of compensation for attorneys representing infants or other persons, where the statutes or rules provide for the fixation of such compensation by the court.

(f) Nothing contained in this section shall be deemed applicable to the fixing of compensation of attorneys for services rendered in connection with collection of first-party benefits as defined in Article XVIII of the Insurance Law.

Cross References

Insurance Law, see McKinney's Book 27.

§ 806.14. Attorney's Affidavit in Agency and Private Placement Adoptions

(a) Every attorney appearing for an adoptive parent, a natural parent or an adoption agency in an adoption proceeding in the courts within this judicial department, shall, prior to the entry of an adoption decree, file with the Office of Court Administration of the State of New York and with the court in which the adoption proceeding has been initiated, a signed statement, under oath, setting forth the following information:

(1) name of attorney;

(2) association with firm (if any);

(3) business address;

(4) telephone number;

(5) docket number of adoption proceeding;

(6) court where adoption has been filed;

(7) the date and terms of every agreement, written or otherwise, between the attorney and the adoptive parents, the natural parents or anyone else on their behalf, pertaining to any compensation or thing of value paid or given or to be paid or given by or on behalf of the adoptive parents or the natural parents, including but not limited to retainer fees;

(8) the date and amount of any compensation paid or thing of value given, and the amount of total compensation to be paid or thing of value to be given to the attorney by the adoptive parents, the natural parents or by anyone else on account of or incidental to any assistance or service in connection with the proposed adoption;

(9) a brief statement of the nature of the services rendered;

(10) the name and address of any other attorney or attorneys who shared in the fees received in connection with the services or to whom any compensation or thing of value was paid or is to be paid, directly or indirectly, by the attorney. The amount of such compensation or thing of value;

(11) the name and address of any other attorney or attorneys, if known, who received or will receive any compensation or thing of value, directly or indirectly, from the adoptive parents, natural parents, agency or other source, on account of or incidental to any assistance or service in connection with the proposed adoption. The amount of such compensation or thing of value, if known;

(12) the name and address of any other person, agency, association, corporation, institution, society or organization who received or will receive any compensation or thing of value from the attorney, directly or indirectly, on account of or incidental to any assistance or service in connection with the proposed adoption. The amount of such compensation or thing of value;

(13) the name and address, if known, of any person, agency, association, corporation, institution, society or organization to whom compensation or thing of value has been paid or given or is to be paid or given by any source for the placing out of, or on account of or incidental to assistance in arrangements for the place-

ment or adoption of the adoptive child. The amount of such compensation or thing of value and the services performed or the purposes for which the payment was made; and

(14) a brief statement as to the date and manner in which the initial contact occurred between the attorney and the adoptive parents or natural parents with respect to the proposed adoption.

(b) Names or other information likely to identify the natural or adoptive parents or the adoptive child are to be omitted from the information to be supplied in the attorney's statement.

(c) Such statement may be filed personally by the attorney or his representative at the main office of the Office of Court Administration in the City of New York, and upon such filing he shall receive a date-stamped receipt containing the code number assigned to the original so filed. Such statement may also be filed by ordinary mail addressed to:

> Office of Court Administration—
> Adoption Affidavits
> Post Office Box No. 2016
> New York, New York 10008

(d) All statements filed by attorneys shall be deemed to be confidential, and the information therein contained shall not be divulged or made available for inspection or examination to any person other than the client of the attorney in the adoption proceeding, except upon written order of the presiding justice of the Appellate Division.

§ 806.15. [Repealed]

§ 806.16. Compensation of Attorneys Representing Claimants Against the Lawyers' Fund for Client Protection

No attorney shall charge a fee for or accept compensation for representation of claimants against the lawyers' fund for client protection of the State of New York except as approved by the trustees of the fund.

§ 806.17. Examiners of Reports of Guardians, Committees and Conservators Pursuant to Article 81 of the Mental Hygiene Law

(a) **Appointment.** Annually in the month of December, the Presiding Justice shall appoint examiners of the reports of guardians, as well as of committees and conservators appointed prior to April 1, 1993, in accordance with section 81.32(b) of the Mental Hygiene Law.

(b) **Duties of Examiners.**

(1) The examiner appointed by the Presiding Justice shall examine initial and annual reports within the times and in the manner required by section 81.32(a) of the Mental Hygiene Law.

(2) The examiner shall file a report, with regard to an initial report of a guardian, within 60 days after the filing of such report. With respect to an annual report filed in the month of May, the examiner's report shall be filed on or before September 15 of the same year. When a court has authorized the filing of an annual report at any other time, the examiner's report shall be filed within 90 days thereafter. Examiner's reports shall be in the form prescribed by the order appointing the examiner.

(3) Examiner's reports shall, on five days notice to the guardian, committee or conservator, be filed in the office of the clerk of the court which appointed the guardian, committee or conservator. A copy of the examiner's report shall, within five days of the date of such filing, also be filed with the office of the Clerk of the Appellate Division, Third Department.

(4) If a guardian, committee or conservator shall fail to file a report within the time specified by law, or shall file an incomplete report, the examiner shall serve a demand and take the other steps necessary to insure compliance as set forth in section 81.32(c) and (d) of the Mental Hygiene Law.

(5) In his or her discretion, the examiner may examine the guardian, committee or conservator and other witnesses under oath and reduce their testimony to writing.

(c) **Compensation.**

(1) For examination of an initial report, an examiner shall be entitled to a fee of $100 and to reimbursement for necessary and reasonable disbursements.

(2) For examination of an annual report, an examiner shall be entitled to reimbursement for necessary and reasonable disbursements and to a fee fixed in accordance with the following schedule:

Closing balance of estate examined:	Fee
Under $5,000	$150
5,001–25,000	200
25,001–50,000	250
50,001–100,000	300
100,001–150,000	400
150,001–225,000	500
225,001–350,000	600
350,001–500,000	700
500,001–750,000	800
750,001–1,000,000	900
Over 1,000,000	1000

The fee shall be computed on the net value of the estate at the end of the calendar year for which the guardian's report has been submitted. A fee in excess of the amount set forth in the above schedule may be awarded upon a showing of extraordinary circumstances.

(3) The fee for examination of annual reports filed for previous years shall be fixed on a quantum meruit basis.

(4) The examiner's claim for a fee and disbursements in estates of less than $5,000 shall be made by standard state voucher and shall be approved by the Presiding Justice or his or her designee. In estates of $5,000 or more, the examiner's claim for a fee and disbursements shall be set forth in the examiner's report and shall be approved by order of the Presiding Justice for payment by the estate.

(5) Within 15 days after receipt of an order directing payment by the estate of the examiner's fee and disbursements, the guardian, committee or conservator may, by written request, upon notice to the examiner, apply to the Presiding Justice for review and reconsideration of any allowance deemed excessive.

Cross References

CPLR, see McKinney's Book 7B.

Mental Hygiene Law, see McKinney's Book 34A.

§ 806.18.   [Repealed]

§ 806.19.   Discipline of Attorneys for Professional Misconduct in Other Jurisdictions

(a) Any attorney to whom this Part shall apply, who has been disciplined in a jurisdiction other than the State of New York, may be disciplined by the court for the conduct which gave rise to the discipline imposed in the other jurisdiction.

(b) It shall be the responsibility of the attorney to file, within 30 days of the date of the disciplinary order in the other jurisdiction, a copy of said order with the court. The failure of the attorney to do so may be deemed professional misconduct.

(c) Upon the filing by the attorney or the committee of a certified or exemplified copy of the disciplinary order, the court, either directly or upon application of the committee, shall give written notice to such attorney pursuant to subdivision 6 of section 90 of the Judiciary Law, according the attorney an opportunity within 20 days of the giving of such notice to file an affidavit or affirmation setting forth any defense to discipline enumerated in subdivision (d) of this section. The notice shall further advise the attorney that in default of such filing, the court may proceed to impose discipline or take other appropriate action. Upon the filing of such affidavit or affirmation, the court may fix a time at which the attorney can be heard in mitigation or otherwise if the attorney requests such appearance in writing.

(d) The court may impose discipline upon the attorney unless an examination of the papers before it and such other evidence as the court in its discretion may receive, discloses 1) that the procedure in the other jurisdiction deprived the attorney of due process; or 2) that there was such an infirmity of proof establishing the misconduct that the court cannot accept as final the finding of misconduct made in the other jurisdiction; or 3) that the imposition of discipline would be unjust. If the attorney raises either or both of the first two defenses enumerated in this subdivision, it shall be the attorney's responsibility to file with the court a copy of the record of the proceedings in the other jurisdiction. The court may require the attorney to file a copy of said record, or portion thereof, in any case in which such evidence is deemed necessary to determine the issues presented.

Cross References

Judiciary Law, see McKinney's Book 29.

PART 820.   [RESERVED]

PART 821.   DUTIES OF COUNSEL IN CRIMINAL ACTIONS AND HABEAS CORPUS PROCEEDINGS

§ 821.1.   Duties of Assigned or Retained Counsel

(a) It shall be the duty of counsel assigned to or retained for the defense of a defendant in a criminal action or proceeding to represent defendant until the action or proceeding has been terminated in the trial court, and to comply with the provisions of subdivision (a) of section 821.2 hereof, after which the duties of assigned counsel shall be ended.

(b) It shall be the duty of counsel assigned to prosecute an appeal on behalf of an indigent defendant to accept said assignment and to prosecute the appeal until entry of the order of the appellate court terminating the appeal, and to comply with the provisions of subdivision (b) of section 821.2 hereof, after which his duties as assigned counsel shall be ended.

§ 821.2.   Notification of Right to Appeal or to Apply for a Certificate Granting Leave to Appeal

(a) **After Conviction or Denial of Post-Conviction or Habeas Corpus Relief.** Where there has been a conviction after trial or otherwise, or where there has been an adverse decision upon an application for a writ of habeas corpus or upon a motion made pursuant to section 440.10 or section 440.20, Criminal Procedure Law, it shall be the duty of counsel, retained or assigned, and of the public defender, immediately after the pronouncement of sentence or the service of a copy of a judgment or order disposing of an application for a writ of habeas corpus or a motion made pursuant to section 440.10 or section 440.20, Criminal Procedure Law, to advise the defendant in writing of his right to appeal or to apply for a certificate granting leave to appeal pursuant to subdivision 4, section 460.10, Criminal Procedure Law, the time limitations involved, the manner of instituting an appeal and of obtaining a transcript of the testimony, and of the right of a person who has an absolute right to appeal or has received a certificate granting leave to appeal and is unable to pay the cost of an appeal to apply for leave to appeal as a poor person. It shall also be the duty of such counsel to ascertain whether defendant wishes to appeal or to apply for a certificate granting leave to appeal and, if so, to serve and file the necessary notice of appeal from a judgment of conviction or to apply for a certificate granting leave to appeal from the denial of a motion made pursuant to section 440.10 or section 440.20, Criminal Procedure Law, and, if granted, to file the necessary certificate and notice of appeal within the time limitations provided for in subdivision 4, section 460.10, Criminal Procedure Law.

(b) After Affirmance of Conviction or of Order or Judgment Denying Post-Conviction or Habeas Corpus Relief. Immediately after entry of an order affirming a judgment of conviction, a judgment denying an application for a writ of habeas corpus, or an order denying a motion made pursuant to section 440.10 or section 440.20, Criminal Procedure Law, it shall be the duty of counsel retained or assigned, and of the public defender, to advise defendant of his right to apply for permission to appeal and of the additional right of a person who is unable to pay the cost of a further appeal (in the event permission shall have been granted) to apply for leave to prosecute such appeal as a poor person. It shall also be the duty of such counsel to ascertain whether defendant wishes to apply for permission to appeal and, if so, to make a timely application therefor. In the case of a nonunanimous affirmance of a judgment dismissing a writ of habeas corpus, such counsel shall also advise the relator of his absolute right to appeal without permission if the dissent is on a stated question of law in his favor.

Cross References

Criminal Procedure Law, see McKinney's Book 11A.

§ 821.3. Notification to Defendants Who Appear Without Counsel

(a) After Conviction or Denial of Post-Conviction Relief. If a defendant has appeared pro se, the trial court shall advise a defendant of his right to appeal from a judgment of conviction, or of his right to apply for a certificate granting leave to appeal from an order denying a motion made pursuant to section 440.10 or section 440.20, Criminal Procedure Law. It shall also advise a defendant of the right of a person unable to pay the cost of an appeal to apply for leave to appeal as a poor person. If the defendant so requests, the clerk of the court shall prepare and file and serve forthwith a notice of appeal on behalf of the defendant from a judgment of conviction. If the defendant so requests in writing, within 30 days after service upon him of a copy of an order denying a motion made pursuant to section 440.10 or section 440.20, Criminal Procedure Law, and no previous application for a certificate granting leave to appeal has been made, the clerk of the court shall serve a copy of such request upon the district attorney and shall transmit the request and the original record of the proceedings sought to be reviewed to the appellate court. Upon determination of the application the original record of proceedings shall be returned to the trial court together with a certified copy of the order entered upon the application; a certified copy of the order shall also be sent to the defendant at his address shown in the application.

(b) After Affirmance on Appeal.

(1) If on an appeal from a judgment of conviction after trial or otherwise, or from an order denying a motion made pursuant to section 440.10 or section 440.20, Criminal Procedure Law, a defendant has appeared pro se and the judgment or order be affirmed, the copy of the order of affirmance, with notice of entry, which is served on the defendant shall have annexed or appended thereto the following notice:

NOTICE AS TO FURTHER APPEAL

Pursuant to section 460.20 of the Criminal Procedure Law, defendant has the right to apply for leave to appeal to the Court of Appeals by making application to the chief judge of that court by submitting such application to the clerk of that court, or to a justice of the Appellate Division of the Supreme Court of this department, as provided in section 800.26, Rules of Practice, Appellate Division, Third Department within 30 days after service of a copy of the order of affirmance with notice of entry.

Denial of the application for permission to appeal by the judge or justice first applied to is final and no new application may thereafter be made to any other judge or justice.

(2) If on an appeal from a judgment dismissing a writ of habeas corpus or from a judgment dismissing a petition in an article 78 proceeding affecting a criminal case, the relator or petitioner has appeared pro se, the copy of the order of affirmance, with notice of entry, which is served on the relator or petitioner shall have annexed or appended thereto the following notice:

NOTICE AS TO FURTHER APPEAL

If the affirmance by the Appellate Division is by a unanimous court, an appeal may be taken to the

Court of Appeals only pursuant to section 5602 of the Civil Practice Law and Rules by permission of the Appellate Division or by permission of the Court of Appeals upon refusal of the Appellate Division to grant permission, or by direct application to the Court of Appeals.

An application for permission to appeal must be made within 30 days after service of a copy of the order of affirmance with notice of entry.

If there is a dissent in the Appellate Division or there is a modification of the judgment appealed from, relator or petitioner may take an appeal to the Court of Appeals as a matter of right pursuant to section 5601(a) of the Civil Practice Law and Rules by serving on the adverse party a notice of appeal within 30 days after service of a copy of the order appealed from, with notice of entry, and filing the notice of appeal in the office where the judgment or order of the original instance is entered.

Cross References

CPLR, see McKinney's Book 7B.

Criminal Procedure Law, see McKinney's Book 11A.

PART 822. ASSIGNMENT OF COUNSEL AND APPOINTMENT OF PHYSICIANS

§ 822.1. Assignment of Counsel

(a) Upon a hearing in a proceeding described in subdivision 1(a) of section 35 of the Judiciary Law, wherein petitioner is financially unable to retain counsel, the court shall assign counsel furnished in accordance with a plan, conforming to the requirements of subdivision 3 of section 722 of the County Law, which is in operation in the county wherein the hearing is held; provided, however, that when such county has not placed in operation a plan conforming to that prescribed in subdivision 3 of section 722 of the County Law, counsel shall be assigned from a list of attorneys maintained by the Appellate Division.

(b) Attorneys holding the following public offices shall not be assigned to act as counsel pursuant to section 35 of the Judiciary Law or section 722 of the County Law: the office of district attorney; assistant district attorney; judge or justice of a city, town or village court; or law clerk to a judge or justice; provided, however, that any such attorney may apply to this court for waiver of this subdivision so as to permit the attorney to be assigned as appellate counsel in cases arising outside of the county where the attorney holds public office. In addition, no attorney shall be assigned to act as counsel if the court determines, in its discretion, that such assignment may involve an ethical or legal conflict of interest.

(c) The court may assign counsel other than in the manner prescribed in subdivision (a) hereof only when it is satisfied that special circumstances require such assignment.

(d) Assignments of counsel by the supreme court or a surrogate's court to represent children in proceedings wherein compensation is authorized pursuant to Judiciary Law § 35(7) shall be made from a law guardian panel designated under section 835.2(a) of Part 835 of these rules.

Cross References

County Law, see McKinney's Book 11.

Judiciary Law, see McKinney's Book 29.

§ 822.2. Maintenance of Lists of Approved Attorneys

The judge of each court having countywide jurisdiction in a county which has not placed in operation a plan conforming to that described in subdivision 3 of section 722 of the County Law, shall submit to the Appellate Division on or before the first day of June each year, a list of attorneys residing within such county for approval by the Appellate Division for the purpose of assignment as counsel pursuant to section 35 of the Judiciary Law. As far as practicable, a judge or justice shall assign attorneys from the approved list in rotation.

Cross References

County Law, see McKinney's Book 11.

Judiciary Law, see McKinney's Book 29.

§ 822.3. Appointment of Psychiatrists or Physicians

Psychiatrists or physicians employed at a state institution shall not be assigned by the court pursuant to section 35, subdivision 3 of the Judiciary Law.

Cross References

Judiciary Law, see McKinney's Book 29.

§ 822.4. Compensation of Counsel and Physicians in Excess of Statutory Limits

(a) This rule shall apply to all claims in this department, pursuant to section 35 of the Judiciary Law, for compensation in excess of the statutory limits for services rendered in a trial court, except for claims in excess of statutory limits by law guardians pursuant to section 245 of the Family Court Act and section 35 of the Judiciary Law.

(b) The claim of an attorney, physician or other person for compensation in excess of the statutory limits, in addition to the information required by statute, shall be supported by a sworn statement describing the circumstances deemed to be extraordinary.

Cross References

County Law, see McKinney's Book 11.

Judiciary Law, see McKinney's Book 29.

PART 823. MENTAL HYGIENE LEGAL SERVICE

§ 823.1. Definitions

Except as otherwise appears herein, whenever used in this Part any term defined in Mental Hygiene Law section 1.03 shall have the meaning set forth therein and, in addition, the following terms shall have the following meanings:

(a) Service means the Mental Hygiene Legal Service.

(b) Director means the head of the Service referred to in Mental Hygiene Law section 47.01 or his or her duly authorized designee.

(c) Court shall mean Supreme Court, County Court or Surrogate's Court.

(d) Patient shall mean a person residing in a facility for the mentally disabled which is licensed or operated by the Department of Mental Hygiene or the Department of Correctional Services, or a person residing in any other place for whom the Service has been appointed counsel or court evaluator pursuant to Article 81 of the Mental Hygiene Law.

(e) Guardian shall mean a person or entity appointed as a guardian, standby guardian or limited guardian as provided in article 17–A of the Surrogate's Court Procedure Act or article 81 of the Mental Hygiene Law.

Cross References

Mental Hygiene Law, see McKinney's Book 34A.

SCPA, see McKinney's Book 58A.

§ 823.2. Duties of the Director

(a) With regard to patients in facilities governed by the Mental Hygiene Law:

(1) The director shall inform each patient of his or her rights to a judicial hearing, to review pursuant to Mental Hygiene Law sections 9.35 and 15.35, to an appeal and to be represented by the Service or by privately retained counsel.

(2) In every case in which a hearing is requested or ordered or in which an application or petition is made to the court with regard to a patient which may or may not require a hearing, the director shall investigate the patient's case, examine the patient's records, interview the patient and also, in the discretion of the director, interview other persons having information relevant to the patient's case. If the patient has counsel the court may request the director to perform any services on behalf of the patient within the scope of and consistent with the Service's statutory duties.

(3) The director shall examine the patient's facility records as often as the director deems necessary.

(4) The court may request the director to render or undertake any assistance or service on behalf of a patient consistent with the Service's statutory duties.

(5) When a hearing has not been demanded, if the director determines that the case of a patient should be heard by the court, or be reviewed by a court or court and jury, the director may, in his or her discretion, demand a hearing on behalf of such patient or may request that the case of the patient be reviewed by the court, or court and jury, in accordance with the power granted to the Service in the Mental Hygiene Law.

(6)(i) The director shall ascertain that the notices to be given to patients and other persons required under the Mental Hygiene Law have been duly served and posted and that there has been compliance with the procedures required by the Mental Hygiene Law for the hospitalization, transfer, retention and release of patients.

(ii) The director shall ascertain that all requirements of law as to patients' admissions, treatment and discharge affecting patients' rights have been complied with.

(7) The director shall review the status of every person who has been an informal patient or a voluntary patient for a period of 12 consecutive months and shall ascertain that there has been compliance with the Mental Hygiene Law. If the director finds that the patient is willing and suitable for continued hospitalization in such status he or she shall so certify in the patient's record. If the director finds that the patient is unwilling or unsuitable for continued hospitalization in such status he or she shall take whatever action he or she deems necessary in accordance with the Mental Hygiene Law.

(b) In those guardianship proceedings pursuant to article 81 of the Mental Hygiene Law or article 17–A of the Surrogate's Court Procedure Act in which the Service participates as counsel, court evaluator, guardian-ad-litem or party:

(1) Upon receipt of notice of application in such proceedings, the director shall:

(i) examine the papers and ascertain that the notices required to be given to parties and patients and, as far as known to the director, to other persons entitled thereto, have been duly served and that there has been due compliance with the prescribed statutory procedure;

(ii) examine the records relating to the affairs or medical or psychiatric condition of the party or patient;

(iii) interview every such party or patient, advise him or her of the nature of the proceeding and of his or her legal rights including the right to legal representation and the right to a court hearing, determine whether he or she has any objections to the proceeding or to the proposed guardian or whether he or she has any other objections;

(iv) interview any psychiatrist, examining physician or psychologist, or such other psychiatrist or physician who has knowledge of the party or patient's mental and physical condition;

(v) obtain all available information as to the extent and nature of the party or patient's assets;

(vi) obtain all available information concerning the party or patient's family, background and any other fact that may be necessary or desirable.

(2)(i) The director shall notify the court of any request for hearing.

(ii) In the director's discretion, and in the interest of the party or patient, the director may demand a hearing.

(3) The director shall inform the party or patient of the progress and status of all proceedings.

(4) In all proceedings for the discharge of a guardian, the enforcement or modification of a guardianship order, or the approval of a guardian's report or accounting, intermediate or final, the director shall inform the party or patient of the nature of the proceeding and his or her rights. The director may perform such additional services on behalf of the party or patient as are within the scope of, and consistent with, the Service's statutory duties.

(5) The director may, in an appropriate case and in his or her discretion, apply to the court for the discharge of the guardian or the enforcement or modification of an order appointing the guardian.

(6) The director is authorized to apprise the examiners charged with the review of accounts with regard to any matter within the jurisdiction of such examiner affecting the welfare and property of a party or patient for whom a guardian has been appointed.

(7) The director shall perform such other duties and responsibilities as may be required by Article 81 of the Mental Hygiene Law.

(c) With regard to inmates, defendants or patients committed to, transferred to or placed in facilities for the mentally disabled pursuant to the Correction Law or to the Criminal Procedure Law:

(1) In all matters or proceedings in which the Service is required to be served with notice, the director shall:

(i) examine the papers, and shall ascertain that the notices required to be given have been duly served and that there has been due compliance with the prescribed procedure;

(ii) inform the inmate, defendant or patient of his or her rights including the right to judicial hearing, to review, to appeal and to be represented by the Service or by privately retained counsel;

(iii) when a hearing has not been demanded, if the director determines that the case should be heard by the court or be reviewed by a court, or court and jury, the director may, in his or her discretion, demand a hearing or may request that the case be reviewed by the court or court and jury;

(iv) examine the records of the inmate, defendant or patient;

(v) interview the attending psychiatrist, examining physician or psychologist who has knowledge of the condition of the inmate, defendant or patient;

(vi) interview all other persons having information relevant to the matter or proceeding;

(vii) perform such other services on behalf of the inmate, defendant or patient as the director in his or her discretion may determine. The court may request the director to perform additional services within the scope of, and consistent with, the Service's statutory duties.

(d) With regard to applications for authorization to administer psychotropic medication and to perform surgery, electro-convulsive therapy or major medical treatment in the nature of surgery upon parties or patients in facilities:

(1) Copies of notice of such applications shall be served upon the director of the Service of the judicial department in which the proceeding is brought and the director of the Service of the judicial department in which the facility is located.

(2) In all such proceedings the director shall:

(i) examine the papers, and shall ascertain that the notices required to be given have been duly served:

(ii) interview and inform the party or patient of the nature of the proceeding and of his or her rights, including the right to a judicial hearing, to appeal and to be represented by the Service or by privately retained counsel, and determine whether he or she has any objection to the proceeding;

(iii) when a hearing has not been demanded, if the director determines that the case should be heard by the court, the director may, in his or her discretion, demand a hearing on behalf of the party or patient;

(iv) examine the records of the party or patient;

(v) interview the party or patient's attending and consulting psychiatrist, physician or psychologist who has knowledge of the party or patient's condition;

(vi) interview all other persons having information relevant to the matter or proceeding;

(vii) perform such other services on behalf of the party or patient, as the court may request or the director may determine, consistent with the Service's statutory duties.

(e) In all the foregoing proceedings, the Service shall represent the inmate, defendant, party or patient unless they otherwise have counsel or counsel has been dispensed with pursuant to Article 81 of the Mental Hygiene Law.

(f) In all the foregoing proceedings, the director may, in his or her discretion, submit briefs, affidavits, affirmations or trial memoranda, consistent with the Service's role in the proceeding.

(g) In all of the foregoing proceedings, the director shall assist the directors of the Service in the other judicial departments in regard to any proceeding pending in any other judicial department which pertains to a patient residing in the Third Judicial Department.

Cross References

Correction Law, see McKinney's Book 10B.

Criminal Procedure Law, see McKinney's Book 11A.

Mental Hygiene Law, see McKinney's Book 34A.

SCPA, see McKinney's Book 58A.

§ 823.3. Guardian Ad Litem and Court Evaluator

In any proceeding before the court involving a patient, the court may appoint the director as guardian ad litem or court evaluator consistent with, and within the scope of the director's statutory duties, except when the director advises the court that such appointment would create a conflict of interest with the director's duties as counsel pursuant to 823.2 of this Part.

§ 823.4. Additional Psychiatric, Psychological, Medical or Expert Opinion

(a) Pursuant to Judiciary Law section 35 or any other statute, rule or regulation providing for addi-

tional opinion the director shall assist in obtaining, through a panel or otherwise, such additional opinion.

(b) No psychiatrist, psychologist, physician or other expert shall be appointed by the court if he or she is disqualified under provisions of the Mental Hygiene Law or if he or she is employed at the institution in which the patient is hospitalized or residing or to which the patient may be transferred as a result of the proceeding in which the expert is to render his or her opinion.

Cross References

Judiciary Law, see McKinney's Book 29.

Mental Hygiene Law, see McKinney's Book 34A.

§ 823.5. Review of Proposed Transfer of Patient or of Changes of Status of Patients

(a) In every case in which it is proposed to transfer a patient from one facility to another facility or to change his or her admission status to another, the director shall review the proposed transfer or change of status.

(b) In any such case, the director, in his or her discretion, may request a hearing on behalf of the patient.

§ 823.6. Fees

(a) When authorized by statute the director may request that the court award the Service a reasonable fee.

(b) The director's requests for fees for the services of attorneys shall not exceed the hourly rates of compensation set forth in section 35 of the judiciary law; and the director's requests for fees for the services of non-lawyer professionals shall not exceed the hourly rate of compensation set forth in the Unified Court System's compensation rate guidelines for court-appointed non-lawyer professionals.

(c) Fees awarded the Service shall be maintained and dispensed in accordance with law.

Cross References

Mental Hygiene Law, see McKinney's Book 34A.

§ 823.7. Records to Be Confidential

(a) All records and files of the director in any proceedings covered by this Part shall be confidential.

(b) All such records and files of the director may be exhibited only at the discretion of the director or upon order of the court.

PART 824. MENTAL HEALTH INFORMATION PROCEDURE [RESCINDED]

PART 830. RULES GOVERNING ELECTRONIC RECORDING OF DEPOSITIONS IN CIVIL CASES [RESCINDED]

PART 835. FAMILY COURT LAW GUARDIAN PANELS

§ 835.1. Departmental Advisory Committee

The presiding justice shall appoint a departmental advisory committee consisting of at least one Supreme Court justice, one Family Court judge, one law guardian panel member, one representative of a family and child welfare agency, one law school professor, one county attorney, and such additional persons as the presiding justice deems necessary to perform the functions of the advisory committee. The clerk of the Appellate Division, third judicial department, shall be a member of the committee ex officio. The term of appointment shall be for two years. The departmental advisory committee shall oversee the operation of the law guardian program in this department and shall annually make recommendations to the presiding justice with respect to promulgation of standards and administrative procedures for improvement of the quality of law guardian representation in the department.

§ 835.2. Law Guardian Panels

(a) Initial Designation to Law Guardian Panel.

(1) *Eligibility.* An attorney is eligible for designation as a member of the law guardian panel of a county of this department when the attorney:

(A) Is a member in good standing of the Bar of the State of New York;

(B) Has attended twelve hours of introductory law guardian training conducted by the Appellate Division; and

(C) Has attained experience in law guardian representation by:

(i) Substantial participation, either as counsel of record or as co-counsel with a law guardian mentor, in:

(1) A juvenile delinquency or person in need of supervision proceeding;

(2) A child abuse, child neglect, or termination of parental rights proceeding; and

(3) A custody or visitation proceeding; and

(ii) Participation as counsel or co-counsel in, or observation of, two hearings in Family Court at which testimony is taken.

(2) *Application.* An attorney may, at any time, apply for membership on a law guardian panel designated for a county in this department. Such an application shall be in the form prescribed by the Appellate Division, and shall be submitted to a Family Court judge of the county.

(3) *Action by the Family Court Judge.* The Family Court judge shall review the application, and take one of the following actions:

(A) When the judge determines that the attorney has met the eligibility requirements of paragraph (1) above, and is otherwise qualified to provide appropriate representation for children, the judge shall approve the application and forward it to the Appellate Division with the recommendation that the attorney be added to the county law guardian panel;

(B) Except as provided in (C) below, when the judge determines that the attorney has not met the eligibility requirements of paragraph (1) above, the judge shall defer action on the application, forward a copy of the application to the Appellate Division, and refer the attorney to a law guardian mentor;

(C) When the judge determines for good cause that an attorney should not be designated as a law guardian panel member, the judge shall deny the application in writing, stating the basis for the denial, regardless of whether or not the attorney has met the eligibility requirements of paragraph (1) above. The attorney may request review of such denial by the Appellate Division.

(4) *Waiver of Eligibility Requirements.* The Appellate Division may waive the eligibility requirements set forth in paragraphs (1)(B) and (C) above when:

(A) An attorney requests such waiver in writing, endorsed by a judge of Family Court; and

(B) The attorney has sufficient relevant experience in the practice of law to demonstrate clearly the ability to represent children effectively; provided, however, that an attorney added to a law guardian panel based on a waiver granted pursuant to this paragraph must attend two days of introductory training conducted by the Appellate Division within one year of designation.

(5) *Law Guardian Mentors.* When a judge of Family Court has deferred action on the application of an attorney for membership on a law guardian panel

pursuant to paragraph (3)(B) above, the judge shall designate an experienced law guardian as a mentor to assist the attorney in meeting the eligibility requirements of paragraph (1)(C) above, and to familiarize the attorney with the representation of children and the operation of the Law Guardian Program. With the agreement of the mentor, the attorney may act as co-counsel in a proceeding specified in paragraph (1)(C)(i) above to which the mentor has been assigned as law guardian, provided, however, that the mentor shall be the attorney of record in the proceeding and shall be responsible for all aspects of the representation provided. When the attorney has met the eligibility requirements, he or she shall so inform the Family Court judge, who shall then take action as provided in paragraph (3) above.

(b) Redesignation of Panels.

(1) The Appellate Division shall, on or before January first of each year, designate an annual law guardian panel for each county in the department from lists of attorneys approved with respect to their competency by the Family Court judges of such counties upon consideration of the following factors:

(A) Rapport with clients;

(B) Case preparation;

(C) Legal knowledge;

(D) Vigor of advocacy; and

(E) Punctuality.

(2) All current members of an annual law guardian panel for a county shall be redesignated to the annual law guardian panel, provided the law guardian has complied with the appropriate training and education requirement set forth in section 835.4(b) of this Part, and provided further that the law guardian has been found qualified for redesignation upon consideration of the factors of law guardian competency in paragraph (b)(1)(A–E) above.

(3) When a Family Court judge determines that a current law guardian should not be redesignated to the annual county law guardian panel, the judge shall submit to the Appellate Division a written recommendation to that effect, setting forth the basis of the recommendation with specific reference to the factors of law guardian competency. The Appellate Division shall provide written notice of the recommendation and a copy of the written recommendation to the law guardian concerned, who may submit to the Appellate Division a written response and such additional documentation as the law guardian believes may assist the Appellate Division in considering the judge's recommendation.

(c) Limitations on Annual Law Guardian Panel Membership. When adequate numbers of attorneys are available in a county:

(1) Only the names of attorneys who reside or maintain an office in the county should appear on the panel list for that county; and

(2) The Family Court judge or judges of the county may decline to designate additional attorneys to the panel.

(d) Removal From Annual Law Guardian Panel. An attorney may, at any time, apply to a Family Court judge of the county in which he or she serves on a law guardian panel to have his or her name removed from the panel list. Upon receipt of such request, the Family Court judge may make a written recommendation to the Appellate Division that the attorney's name be removed; upon receipt of such recommendation, the Appellate Division shall remove the attorney's name from the panel list, if appropriate. If the Family Court judge denies such request, such denial shall be in writing and state the reasons for the denial. The attorney may request review of such denial by the Appellate Division.

Notwithstanding the provisions of subdivision (b) above, a Family Court judge may, at any time, recommend to the Appellate Division the removal of an attorney's name from an annual law guardian panel for good cause, including, but not limited to, misconduct or lack of diligence in performing law guardian assignments.

The Appellate Division may, on its own motion at any time, remove an attorney's name from an annual law guardian panel.

Cross References

Family Court Act, see McKinney's Book 29A, Part 1.

§ 835.3. Assignment of Law Guardians

(a) Any attorney designated to an annual law guardian panel in a county may also be assigned as a law guardian in any other county in the Third Department, provided the assigning Family Court judge has obtained the prior approval of a Family Court judge of the county in which the attorney has been designated to an annual law guardian panel and of the Appellate Division.

(b) The following factors, among others, should be considered when law guardian assignments are made:

(1) the experience and qualifications of the law guardian;

(2) the nature and difficulty of the case;

(3) continuity of representation of the minor in successive proceedings;

(4) that assignments among law guardians on a panel are made in a fair and impartial manner.

(c) No law guardian shall be assigned to represent a minor when such assignment may involve a legal or ethical conflict of interest. Law guardians serving in the following positions or employed by any of the following offices shall not be assigned to serve as a law guardian in those types of proceedings in which, by virtue of such position or employment, they have either similar or equivalent subject matter jurisdiction or responsibilities or, in the county in which they are employed, the office by which they are employed participates as a party: judge or justice of a city, town or village court; law clerk to a judge or justice; district attorney; county attorney, or municipal corporation counsel. Whenever an attorney designated to an annual law guardian panel accepts employment in any of the above positions or offices, the attorney shall inform a Family Court judge of the county in which he or she serves on an annual law guardian panel of such employment; the attorney may complete any matter previously assigned to him, provided the Family Court judge approves of the completion of such assignment and provided completion of such assignment involves no legal or ethical conflict of interest.

§ 835.4. Training and Education

(a) Law guardians shall be expected to be thoroughly familiar with:

(1) provisions of the Family Court Act and relevant provisions of the Domestic Relations Law, Social Services Law, Penal Law and Criminal Procedures Law;

(2) the basic principles of child development and behavior;

(3) the existence and availability of community-based treatment resources and residential facilities; and

(4) recent case law and legislation relating to the foregoing.

(b) To be eligible for redesignation to a law guardian panel in this department pursuant to section 835.2(b) of this Part, a law guardian shall have completed within the preceding two years at least six hours of training and education for law guardians sponsored or co-sponsored by the Appellate Division, Third Department. If prior approval is obtained from the Appellate Division, Third Department, by the law guardian or the sponsoring organization, attendance at an appropriate educational and training program sponsored or co-sponsored by one or more of the following or similar organizations may be substituted: the Appellate Divisions of the First, Second or Fourth Departments; the American Bar Association; the New York State Bar Association; a Family Court; a local or regional bar association or law guardian association; a law school; or a legal aid society. This biennial continuing education and training requirement for law guardians may also be fulfilled by (a) viewing videotapes approved for such purpose by the Appellate Division, Third Department, and filing with the Appellate Division, Third Department an affidavit attesting to such a viewing or (b) attendance at six hours of training and education for newly-designated law guardians as described in section 835.2(a)(1)(B) of this Part.

For good cause shown and upon the written recommendation of a Family Court judge, the Appellate Division, Third Department may waive or defer the training and education requirement set forth herein.

Cross References

Criminal Procedure Law, see McKinney's Book 11A.

Domestic Relations Law, see McKinney's Book 14.

Family Court Act, see McKinney's Book 29A, Part 1.

Penal Law, see McKinney's Book 39.

Social Services Law, see McKinney's Book 52A.

§ 835.5. Compensation

(a) Claims by law guardians for services rendered pursuant to Family Court Act § 245 shall be submitted for approval to the Family Court Judge on forms authorized by the Chief Administrator of the Courts; after approval or modification, the Family Court shall forward the claim to the Appellate Division for approval and certification to the Comptroller for payment. If a claim is received by the Appellate Division more than 90 days after the date of completion of services, the law guardian may be requested to provide an affidavit (i) stating that counsel has not previously applied for payment or been paid for the services in question, and (ii) explaining the reasons for the delay in submitting the claim for payment. The Appellate Division reserves the right to disapprove any claim for compensation by a law guardian received more than 90 days after the date of completion of services.

(b) Claims for compensation by law guardians in excess of the statutory limits set by Family Court Act § 245 and Judiciary Law § 35 shall be accompanied by a sworn statement by the law guardian describing the nature of the proceeding, specifying the time and services rendered and expenses incurred, and detailing the circumstances deemed to be extraordinary justifying a fee in excess of the statutory limits. In the absence of the attorney's affidavit in support of the excess fee, compensation in excess of statutory limits shall not be allowed.

(1) The following are among the factors which may be considered in determining whether extraordinary circumstances exist justifying a fee in excess of statutory limits:

(i) Unusually complex factual or legal issues;

(ii) Novel issues of law requiring extensive legal research;

(iii) Lengthy and necessary trial or other in-court proceedings which alone raise the compensation claim above statutory limits;

(iv) Other unique or unusual circumstances which required the law guardian to spend time on a case raising the compensation claim above statutory limits.

(2) The expenditure of time alone will not ordinarily be considered an extraordinary circumstance warranting additional compensation.

(c) When a law guardian expects the reasonable expenses allowable pursuant to Family Court Act § 245 and Judiciary Law § 35 to exceed the sum of $1,000, for investigative, expert or other services, the law guardian, before incurring such expenses, shall obtain the approval of the judge presiding in the proceeding and of the Appellate Division.

Cross References

Judiciary Law, see McKinney's Book 29.

Family Court Act, see McKinney's Book 29A, Part 1.

PART 839. MISCELLANEOUS RULES [RESCINDED]

PART 840. ORDERS

§ 840.1. [Rescinded]

§ 840.2. Notification of Institution of Disciplinary Proceedings; To Whom Given

WHEREAS, pursuant to the provisions of section 90, subdivision 10, of the Judiciary Law of the State of New York, the institution of disciplinary proceedings against an attorney are to be deemed confidential; and

WHEREAS, a clerk of an Appellate Division of the Supreme Court, or the Clerk of the Court of Appeals, may be called upon to issue a certificate of good standing to an attorney against whom disciplinary proceedings may have been instituted in another Appellate Division; and

WHEREAS, a clerk of an Appellate Division of the Supreme Court, or the Clerk of the Court of Appeals, may desire to affix a legend or notation to such certificate of good standing to be issued to an attorney against whom disciplinary proceedings may have been instituted in another Appellate Division to the effect that such proceedings are pending in such other Appellate Division, it is

ORDERED that, solely for the purpose of enabling a Clerk of an Appellate Division of the Supreme Court or the Clerk of the Court of Appeals to make such notation or affix such legend to a certificate of good standing, the Clerk of this Court is authorized to furnish to the Clerk of the Court of Appeals and the Clerks of the Appellate Divisions of the First, Second and Fourth Departments, a certified copy of each order entered by this Court directing a hearing on, or a reference to hear and report with respect to, charges of unprofessional conduct against an attorney contained in a petition filed with the Clerk of this Court by a Bar Association or other authorized person, body, or agency.

DATED AND ENTERED: October 26, 1966

AMENDMENT

WHEREAS, this court by order entered October 26, 1966, authorized the clerk of this court to transmit to the clerk of the Court of Appeals and to the clerks of the Appellate Divisions of the First, Second and Fourth Departments a certified copy of each order entered by this court directing a hearing on, or a reference to hear and report with respect to, charges of unprofessional conduct against an attorney contained in a petition filed with the clerk of this court by a Bar Association, or other authorized person, body or agency; and

WHEREAS, said order was entered because it had been assumed that a clerk of such other courts might issue a certificate of good standing of a member of the bar who had been admitted in another Department; and

WHEREAS, it appears that only the clerk of the Appellate Division of the Department in which an attorney has been admitted to practice will issue a certificate of his good standing, it is

ORDERED that the order of this court dated October 26, 1966, be amended so as to provide for transmittal solely to the clerk of the Appellate Division in which the attorney was admitted of a certified copy of an order of this court directing such a hearing or reference.

DATED AND ENTERED: October 23, 1973

Cross References

Judiciary Law, see McKinney's Book 29.

§§ 840.3, 840.4. [Rescinded]

§ 840.5. Authorization for Committees on Character and Fitness to Continue to Inquire Concerning Any Criminal Actions or Proceedings Involving Applicants for Admission

Upon reading chapter 877 of the Laws of 1976, which amended section 160.50 of the Criminal Procedure Law and added a new section 160.60 thereto, and also amended section 296 of the Executive Law of the State of New York, it is

ORDERED, that the Committees on Character and Fitness delegated by this court to investigate applicants for admission to the Bar may continue to inquire concerning any criminal actions or proceedings involving the applicant, including actions or proceedings which were terminated in the applicant's favor, and may continue to require the applicants to answer questions and give information with respect to such matters.

DATED AND ENTERED: December 16, 1976

Cross References

Criminal Procedure Law, see McKinney's Book 11A.

Executive Law, see McKinney's Book 18.

§ 840.6.   Disclosure of Jury Lists

Any application made by counsel for a party pursuant to Judiciary Law, § 509(a), for disclosure of the list of potential jurors for use in counsel's trial preparation shall be directed to and determined by the trial judge or justice.

Such applications shall be made upon notice to the Commissioner of Jurors and the other parties to the litigation.

This procedure shall be effective November 10, 1989.

§ 840.7.   Admission to New York Bar Without Examination

WHEREAS, Judiciary Law section 90(1)(b), as amended by chapter 307 of the Laws of 1988, and section 520.9(a)(1) of the Rules of the Court of Appeals, as amended on October 1, 1988, provide, inter alia, that this Court may admit to practice without examination an applicant who has been admitted to practice in another State or territory or the District of Columbia or in a foreign country, provided that at least one such jurisdiction in which the applicant is so admitted would similarly admit an attorney admitted to practice in New York to its Bar without examination; and

WHEREAS, it is the recommendation of the Advisory Committee on Admission of Attorneys that the Appellate Divisions of the Supreme Court maintain a list of reciprocal jurisdiction; it is

ORDERED, that the Clerk of this Court, in consultation with the Clerks of the other Appellate Divisions, shall prepare and maintain a list of reciprocal jurisdictions; and it is further

ORDERED, that jurisdictions shall not be added to or deleted from said list except after consultation by and among the Clerks of the Appellate Divisions.

DATED AND ENTERED: August 28, 1990

RULES FOR TRIAL AND SPECIAL TERMS OF SUPREME COURTS IN THIRD JUDICIAL DEPARTMENT

Including Amendments Received Through September 15, 2008

See, also, Part 200, Uniform Rules for Courts Exercising Criminal Jurisdiction, and Part 202, Uniform Civil Rules for the Supreme Court and County Court

---

Westlaw Electronic Research

These rules may be searched electronically on Westlaw® *in the NY–RULES database; updates to these rules may be found on* Westlaw *in NY–RULESUP-DATES. For search tips and a summary of database content, consult the* Westlaw *Scope Screens for each database.*

PARTS 860 TO 867.   [RESCINDED]

SUPREME COURT, APPELLATE DIVISION, FOURTH DEPARTMENT

Including Amendments Received Through September 15, 2008

Westlaw Electronic Research

These rules may be searched electronically on Westlaw® in the NY–RULES database; updates to these rules may be found on Westlaw in NY–RULESUP-DATES. For search tips and a summary of database content, consult the Westlaw Scope Screens for each database.

Table of Sections

PART 1000.   RULES OF PRACTICE

§ 1000.1.   Terms and Sessions of Court

The presiding justice shall designate by order the terms of court, and the clerk shall provide notice of designated terms to the bar.   Unless otherwise ordered by the presiding justice, the court shall convene at 10 a.m. each day during a designated term.

§ 1000.2.   Appeal Defined; Time Limitations; Perfection of Appeals; Responding and Reply Briefs

(a) Appeal Defined.   For the purposes of these rules the word *appeal* shall mean appeal or cross appeal, unless otherwise indicated by text or context.

(b) Perfecting Appeals Generally.   Unless otherwise provided by statute, rule or order of this court or justice of this court, all appeals shall be perfected pursuant to section 1000.3 of this Part within 60 days of service on the opposing party of the notice of appeal.   An appeal not perfected within the 60–day period is subject to dismissal on motion pursuant to section 1000.12(a) of this Part.   An appeal or cross appeal not perfected within nine months of service of the notice of appeal is subject to dismissal without motion pursuant to section 1000.12(b) of this Part.

(c) Perfecting Appeals in Which Counsel Has Been Assigned.

(1) *Appeals Taken Pursuant to Family Court Act.* An appeal taken pursuant to the Family Court Act in which this court has assigned counsel shall be perfected within 60 days of receipt of the transcript of the proceedings upon which the order or judgment appealed from is based, as provided in Family Court Act, section 1121(7).

(2) *Appeals Taken Pursuant to Criminal Procedure Law.*   An appeal taken pursuant to the Criminal Procedure Law in which this court has assigned coun-

sel shall be perfected within 120 days of receipt of the transcript of the proceedings upon which the judgment appealed from is based, as provided in section 1021.1(a)(3) of this Title.

(d) Respondent's Briefs. Unless otherwise provided by order of this court or justice of this court, a respondent or respondent-appellant shall file and serve briefs within 30 days of service of the brief of the appellant or appellant-respondent. If a respondent or respondent-appellant elects not to submit a brief, that party shall notify the court in writing prior to the expiration of the 30-day period. The failure to timely submit a brief or to timely notify the court that the party does not intend to file a brief may result in the imposition of sanctions pursuant to section 1000.16(a) of this Part.

(e) Reply Briefs. Unless otherwise provided by order of this court or justice of this court, an appellant or appellant-respondent may file and serve reply briefs within 10 days of service of the brief of respondent or respondent-appellant.

(f) Surreply Briefs. Unless otherwise provided by order of this court or justice of this court, a respondent-appellant may file and serve surreply briefs within 10 days of service of the reply brief of appellant-respondent. The contents of a surreply brief are to be limited to issues raised by a cross appeal. In the absence of a cross appeal, surreply briefs shall not be permitted.

(g) Appendices. When the filing of an appendix is authorized, it shall be filed and served by a party at the same time that the party files and serves a brief.

Cross References

Criminal Procedure Law, see McKinney's Book 11A.

Family Court Act, see McKinney's Book 29A, Part 1.

§ 1000.3. Necessary Documents; Perfection of Appeals; Briefs.

(a) Complete and Timely Filing Required. In all appeals, a complete and timely filing is required. The Clerk shall reject a partial or untimely filing.

(b) Perfecting Appeals Generally. Except in appeals in which permission to proceed as a poor person has been granted, or except as otherwise provided by rule or court order, an appellant or appellant-respondent shall make a complete filing that shall consist of: a complete record, along with the original stipulation executed by all the parties or their attorneys or the original order settling the record; 10 additional copies of the record; 10 copies of the brief; proof of service of two copies of the record and brief on each opposing party to the appeal; when necessary, a demand for exhibits (see section 1000.4[g][3] of this Part) with proof of service thereof; the filing fee as required by CPLR 8022; and a copy of any prior order entered by this court or the trial court affecting the appeal including, but not limited to, an order that: expedites the

appeal; grants permission to proceed on appeal as a poor person or on less than the required number of records; assigns counsel; grants an extension of time to perfect the appeal; grants a stay or injunctive relief; grants relief from dismissal of the appeal; or grants permission to exceed page limitations provided for by section 1000.4(f)(3) of this Part.

(c) Appeals in Which Poor Person Relief has Been Granted.

(1) *Criminal Appeal.* Unless otherwise directed by court order, in a criminal appeal in which poor person relief has been granted by this court, the appellant shall file 10 copies of a brief with proof of service of one copy on each opposing party to the appeal; a certified transcript of the trial or hearing, if any; a copy of the pre-sentence investigation report, if relevant to the appeal; when necessary, a demand for exhibits (see section 1000.4[g][3]) with proof of service thereof; and one copy of an appendix with proof of service of one copy on each opposing party. The appendix shall contain the description of the action pursuant to CPLR 5531; a copy of the notice of appeal along with proof of service and filing; a copy of the certificate of conviction and the judgment of the court from which the appeal is taken; a copy of the indictment, superior court information or other accusatory instrument; a copy of any motion papers, affidavits and, to the extent practicable, written and photographic exhibits that are relevant and necessary to the determination of the appeal; and the original stipulation to the record executed by all the parties or their attorneys or the original order settling the record. The appellant shall also file a copy of any prior order entered by this court or the trial court affecting the appeal including, but not limited to, an order that: expedites the appeal; grants permission to proceed on appeal as a poor person or on less than the required number of records; assigns counsel; grants an extension of time to perfect the appeal; grants a stay or injunctive relief; grants relief from dismissal of the appeal; or grants permission to exceed page limitations provided for by section 1000.4(f)(3) of this Part.

(2) *Civil Appeals.* In a civil appeal in which poor person relief has been granted by this court, (including appeals taken pursuant to the Family Court Act, appeals in proceedings taken pursuant to article 78 of the CPLR and appeals in habeas corpus proceedings) and, unless otherwise directed by court order, the appellant or appellant-respondent shall file 10 copies of a brief with proof of service of one copy on each opposing party to the appeal and one copy of the complete record on appeal along with the original stipulation to the record executed by all parties or their attorneys or the original order of settlement, proof of service of one copy of the record on each other party to the appeal and, when necessary, a demand for exhibits (see section 1000.4[g][3]), with proof of service thereof. Appellant shall also file a copy of any prior order entered by this court or the

trial court affecting the appeal including, but not limited to, an order that: expedites the appeal; grants permission to proceed on appeal as a poor person or on less than the required number of records; assigns counsel; grants an extension of time to perfect the appeal; grants a stay or injunctive relief; grants relief from dismissal of the appeal; or grants permission to exceed page limitations provided for by section 1000.4(f)(3) of this Part.

(d) Alternate Methods of Appeal.

(1) *The Appendix Method.* In appeals perfected on the appendix method pursuant to section 1000.4(d) of this Part, the appellant or appellant-respondent shall file one complete record and, in lieu of 10 copies of the record on appeal, 10 copies of the appendix and shall serve one copy of the record on appeal and two copies of the appendix on each party. In all other respects, the appellant or appellant-respondent shall comply with the requirements of section 1000.3(b) of this Part. When a respondent's appendix, reply appendix or joint appendix is submitted, 10 copies shall be filed with proof of service of two copies on each party.

(2) *Statement in Lieu of a Complete Record.* In appeals perfected pursuant to CPLR 5527 and section 1000.4(c) of this Part, the appellant or appellant-respondent shall file and serve, in lieu of the complete record and copies thereof, the joint appendix and 10 copies thereof. In all other respects, the appellant or appellant-respondent shall comply with the requirements of section 1000.3(b) of this Part.

(e) Responding and Reply Briefs. A party submitting a respondent's brief, a respondent-appellant's brief, a reply brief or, when permitted, a surreply brief, shall file 10 copies of the brief with proof of service of two copies of the brief on each party. In an appeal in which permission to proceed as a poor person has been granted, only one copy of a brief need be served on each party. When an extension of time to file and serve a brief has been granted, a copy of the order granting such permission shall be filed with the brief.

(f) Supplemental Briefs in Criminal Appeals. An appellant in a criminal appeal who is represented by assigned counsel may file 10 copies of a *pro se* supplemental brief, with proof of service of one copy on assigned counsel and the People, no later than 45 days after the date on which assigned counsel mails to the appellant the brief prepared, filed and served by assigned counsel. When a *pro se* supplemental brief is filed and served, the People may file and serve 10 copies of a responding brief, with proof of service of one copy on the appellant and assigned counsel, no later than 45 days after the appellant has served the *pro se* supplemental brief.

(g) Service of Papers in Criminal Appeals by the People. In an appeal taken by the people, the people shall serve the defendant in any manner authorized by CPLR 2103.

(h) Companion Filings on Interactive Compact Disk, Read–Only Memory (CD–ROM).

(1) *Companion Filings on CD–ROM.*

(i) The submission of records, appendices and briefs on interactive compact disk, read–only memory (CD–ROM) as companions to the required number of printed records, appendices or briefs in accordance with 22 NYCRR 1000.3 is allowed and encouraged provided that all parties have stipulated to the filing of the companion CD–ROM.

(ii) The Court may, by order on motion by any party or *sua sponte*, require the filing of a companion CD–ROM.

(2) *Technical Specifications.* The companion CD–ROM record, appendix or brief shall comply with the current technical specifications available from the Office of the Clerk.

(3) *Content.* The companion CD–ROM record, appendix or brief shall be identical in content and format (including page numbering) to the printed record, appendix or brief, except that each may also provide electronic links (hyperlinks) to the complete text of any authorities cited therein and to any other document or other material constituting a part of the record.

(4) *Number.* Ten disks or sets of disks shall be filed with proof of service of one disk or set of disks on each party to the appeal, together with a copy of the stipulation of the parties to the filing of the companion CD–ROM or the order of the Court directing the filing of the companion CD–ROM.

(5) *Filing Deadline.* Unless otherwise directed by order of the Court, a companion CD–ROM shall be filed no later than ten (10) days after the printed record, appendix or brief is filed.

Cross References

CPLR, see McKinney's Book 7B.

Family Court Act, see McKinney's Book 29A, Part 1.

Forms

Submission of controversy, see West's McKinney's Forms, CPLR, §§ 4:409 to 4:417.

Matters relating to transcript, record, and briefs, see West's McKinney's Forms, CPLR, §§ 9:216 to 9:241.

Application for leave to prosecute appeal as poor person, see West's McKinney's Forms, CPLR, §§ 9:247 to 9:251.

§ 1000.4. Content and Form of Records, Appendices and Briefs; Exhibits

(a) The Complete Record on Appeal.

(1) *Stipulated or Settled Complete Record.* The complete record on appeal shall be stipulated or settled.

(i) The parties or their attorneys may stipulate to the correctness of the contents of the complete record (see CPLR 5532).

(ii) When the parties or their attorneys are unable to agree and stipulate to the contents of the complete record on appeal, the contents of the record must be settled by the court from which the appeal is taken. It shall be the obligation of the appellant to make the application to settle the record.

(iii) In a criminal matter, the failure of the parties or their attorneys to list in the stipulation to the record on appeal any transcript, exhibit or other document that constituted a part of the underlying prosecution shall not preclude the court from considering such transcript, exhibit or other document in determining the appeal.

(2) *Contents of the Complete Record on Appeal.* The complete record on appeal shall include, in the following order: the notice of appeal with proof of service and filing; the order or judgment from which the appeal is taken; the decision, if any, of the court granting the order or judgment; the judgment roll, if any; the pleadings of the action or proceeding; the corrected transcript of the action or proceeding or statement in lieu of transcript, if any; all necessary and relevant motion papers; and, to the extent practicable, all necessary and relevant exhibits (see CPLR 5526). When the appeal is from a final judgment, the complete record on appeal shall also include any other reviewable order. The complete record on appeal shall also include the description of the action required by CPLR 5531 and the stipulation to the complete record or the order settling the record.

(3) *Form of the Complete Record.*

(i) The complete record on appeal shall be bound on the left side in a manner that properly secures all the pages and keeps them firmly together; however, such binding shall not be done by using metal fastener or similar hard material that protrudes or presents a bulky surface or sharp edge.

(ii) The complete record on appeal shall be reproduced by standard typographic printing or by any other duplicating process that produces a clear black image on white paper. The record shall be reproduced on opaque, unglazed white paper, measuring 8½ by 11 inches. Printing shall be of no less than 11–point size.

(iii) The cover of the complete record on appeal shall be white and shall contain the title of the matter clearly identifying the parties to the appeal and the action or proceeding; the names, addresses and telephone numbers of counsel for the parties or, when appropriate, of the parties; in a civil matter, the index number or, in a court of claims matter, claim number or motion number assigned in the court from which the appeal is taken; in a criminal matter, the indictment or information number; and

the Appellate Division docket number if one has been assigned.

(iv) The complete record on appeal shall be preceded by a table of contents listing and briefly describing the papers included in the record pursuant to paragraph (2) of this subdivision. The table of contents shall list all trial or hearing exhibits, briefly describing the nature of each exhibit, indicating the page of the record where the exhibit is admitted into evidence and indicating where in the record the exhibit is reproduced.

(v) The pages of the complete record on appeal shall be consecutively paginated. The subject matter of each page of the complete record on appeal shall be stated at the top thereof, except, for papers other than testimony, the subject matter may be stated at the top of the first page of the paper, together with the first and last pages thereof. When testimony is reproduced, the name of the witness, by whom the witness was called and whether the testimony is direct, cross, redirect or recross examination shall be stated at the top of each page (see CPLR 5526).

(b) Records in Consolidated Appeals.

(1) *Multiple Appellants.* When two or more parties take an appeal from a single order or judgment, the appeals may be consolidated on motion pursuant to section 1000.13(n) of this Part or on stipulation of the parties or their attorneys. A stipulation consolidating appeals shall be signed by the parties to the appeals or their attorneys, shall designate the party bearing primary responsibility for filing the record and shall be duly filed with this court.

(2) *Multiple Orders or Judgments.* When one party appeals from two or more orders or judgments in the same action, the party may move to consolidate the appeals pursuant to section 1000.13(n) of this Part.

(3) *Form and Content of Records.* When appeals have been consolidated and are perfected on the complete record, the record shall comply with subdivision (a) of this section and the papers related to each appeal shall be clearly identified in the table of contents and shall be physically separated and conspicuously identified within the record (i.e., by insertion of a tab page or colored divider).

(c) Contents of a Statement in Lieu of a Complete Record on Appeal—Joint Appendix.

(1) Pursuant to CPLR 5527, when the questions raised by an appeal can be determined without an examination of all the pleadings and proceedings, the parties or their attorneys may stipulate to a statement showing how the questions arose and were determined by the court from which the appeal is taken and setting forth only those facts alleged and proved or sought to be proved as are necessary to the determination of the appeal. The statement may also include

portions of the transcript of the proceedings and other relevant material. The statement shall include a copy of the order or judgment appealed from, the notice of appeal and a statement of the issues to be determined. The stipulated statement shall be presented for approval to the court from which the appeal is taken within 20 days after the notice of appeal has been filed and served. The court from which the appeal is taken may make corrections or additions as necessary to present fully the questions raised by the appeal. The approved statement shall constitute the record on appeal and shall be bound, along with the description required by CPLR 5531 and the order approving the statement, as a joint appendix.

(2) The joint appendix on appeal shall be bound, printed and reproduced as set forth in subdivision (a)(3) of this section.

(d) Appendices—CPLR Article 55.

(1) *Complete Record on Appeal.* When an appeal is perfected on the appendix method pursuant to CPLR article 55, the complete record on appeal shall comply with CPLR 5525 and subdivision (a) of this section. In the case of consolidated appeals, there shall also be compliance with subdivision (b) of this section.

(2) *Content of Appendix.*

(i) The appellant's appendix shall contain those parts of the record on appeal necessary to consider the questions involved, including those parts of the record that the appellant can reasonably expect to be relied upon by the respondent (see CPLR 5528[a][5]).

(ii) The respondent's appendix shall contain only such additional parts of the record on appeal necessary to consider the questions involved (see CPLR 5528[b]).

(iii) The appellant's reply appendix shall contain only those parts of the record necessary to consider the questions on appeal that have not been included in either the appellant's appendix or the respondent's appendix.

(iv) A joint appendix may be submitted when the parties stipulate to the contents of an appendix.

(3) *Form of Appendix.* An appendix shall be bound, printed and reproduced as set forth in subdivision (a)(3) of this section.

(e) Appendices—Criminal Appeals.

(1) *Content of Appendix.* In a criminal appeal, when permission to proceed as a poor person has been granted (see section 1000.14 of this Part), the appendix to be filed and served by the appellant shall contain, in the following order: the description of the action required by CPLR 5531; a copy of the notice of appeal with proof of service and filing; a copy of the certificate of conviction and the judgment from which the appeal is taken; a copy of the indictment, superior court information or other accusatory instrument; all motion papers, affidavits and, to the extent practicable, written and photographic exhibits relevant and necessary to the determination of the appeal; and the stipulation of the parties or their attorneys to the complete record or the order settling the record. The appellant shall also file a copy of any prior order entered by this court or the trial court affecting the appeal including, but not limited to, an order that: expedites the appeal; grants permission to proceed on appeal as a poor person or on less than the required number of records and briefs; assigns counsel; grants an extension of time to perfect the appeal; grants a stay or injunctive relief; grants relief from dismissal of the appeal; or grants permission to exceed page limitations provided for by subdivision (f)(3) of this section.

(2) *Form of Appendix.* The appendix shall be bound, printed and reproduced as set forth in subdivision (a)(3) of this section.

(f) Briefs.

(1) *Binding.* A brief on appeal or a proceeding shall be bound on the left side in a manner that properly secures all the pages and keeps them firmly together; however, such binding shall not be done by any metal fastener or similar hard material that protrudes or presents a bulky surface or a sharp edge.

(2) *Paper; printing.* The brief shall be reproduced by standard typographical printing or other duplicating process that produces a clear black image on white paper, with one inch margins. The brief shall be reproduced on opaque, unglazed white paper, measuring 8 ½ by 11 inches. Printing shall be of no less than 11–point size, and shall be double-spaced. A brief shall contain no footnotes.

(3) *Page Limits.* The brief of an appellant, petitioner, respondent or respondent-appellant shall not exceed 70 pages. The reply brief of an appellant, petitioner or appellant-respondent or the surreply brief of a respondent-appellant shall not exceed 35 pages. The pages shall be consecutively paginated.

(4) *Cover of Brief; Information.* The cover of a brief shall contain the title to the matter; the name, address and telephone number of the person submitting the brief; in a civil matter, the index number or, in a court of claims matter, claim number or motion number assigned in the court from which the appeal is taken; in a criminal matter, the indictment or information number; the Appellate Division docket number if one has been assigned; and, in the upper right-hand corner, the name of the person requesting oral argument and the time requested for argument, or the name of the person submitting.

(5) *Cover of Brief; Color.* Except in those appeals in which permission to proceed as a poor person has been granted, the cover of a brief of an appellant or petitioner shall be blue; the cover of a brief of a respondent shall be red; the cover of a reply brief

shall be gray; the cover of a surreply brief shall be yellow; and the cover of a brief of an intervenor or an amicus curiae shall be green. The cover of a supplemental brief submitted pro se in a criminal appeal shall be white.

(6) *Contents of Brief.* A brief shall contain, in the following order: a table of contents; a table of citations; a concise statement, not exceeding two pages, of the questions involved in the matter, with each question numbered and followed immediately by the answer, if any, from the court from which the appeal is taken; a concise statement of the nature of the matter and of the facts necessary and relevant to the determination of the questions involved, with supporting references to pages in the record, transcript or appendix, as appropriate; and the argument of the issues, divided into points by appropriate headings, distinctively printed (see CPLR 5528). A brief shall contain no footnotes.

(7) New York decisions shall be cited from the official reports, if any. All other decisions shall be cited from the official reports, if any, and also from the National Reporter System if they are there reported. Decisions not reported officially or in the National Reporter System shall be cited from the most available source (CPLR 5529[e]).

(8) When an extension of time to file and serve a brief has been granted, a copy of the order granting such permission shall be filed with the brief.

(g) Exhibits.

(1) *In General.* Absent a court order or stipulation of the parties, all exhibits shall be submitted to the court. The parties or their attorneys may agree and stipulate that particular exhibits are not relevant or necessary to the determination of an appeal. In such case, the appellant shall file a stipulation of the parties or their attorneys listing the exhibits neither relevant nor necessary to the appeal.

(2) *Printed Exhibits.* To the extent that it is practicable, all relevant and necessary exhibits shall be printed in the record on appeal.

(3) *Original Exhibits.* Absent a stipulation of the parties pursuant to paragraph (1) of this subdivision, all original exhibits shall be submitted to the court. Upon perfecting an appeal, an appellant shall file the original exhibits or, when the exhibits are in the control of a respondent or a third party, a five-day written demand for the exhibits or a subpoena duces tecum for the exhibits issued in accordance with CPLR article 23, with proof of service thereof. The failure of a respondent to comply with a five-day demand may result in sanctions pursuant to section 1000.16(a) of this Part.

(4) *Criminal Appeals; Physical Exhibits.* In a criminal appeal, in lieu of submitting original physical exhibits (weapons, contraband, e.g.) to the Court, the appellant may file a stipulation of the parties identify-

ing the particular exhibits, identifying the party in custody and control of each exhibit and providing that each exhibit shall be made available to the Court upon the request of the Clerk.

(h) Compliance. The clerk shall reject any record, appendix or brief that does not comply with these rules, is not legible or is otherwise unsuitable.

Cross References

CPLR, see McKinney's Book 7B.

Forms

Matters relating to transcript, record, and briefs, see West's McKinney's Forms, CPLR, §§ 9:216 to 9:241.

§ 1000.5. Appeals Taken Pursuant to the Election Law

(a) Original Papers. Appeals in proceedings brought pursuant to the Election Law shall be prosecuted upon one original record that has been stipulated to by all counsel or settled by the court from which the appeal is taken, and the original exhibits.

(b) Briefs and Oral Argument. Appeals taken pursuant to the Election Law shall be accorded a preference pursuant to Election Law, section 16–116. Upon notification by the appellant that an appeal pursuant to the Election Law is to be perfected, the clerk shall expeditiously calendar the appeal and issue a schedule for the filing and service of the record and briefs. Appellant shall file 10 copies of a brief with proof of service of one copy on each opposing party to the appeal. Each respondent shall file and serve a like number of briefs.

Cross References

Election Law, see McKinney's Book 17.

§ 1000.6. Actions on Submitted Facts

In an action submitted to this court pursuant to CPLR 3222 and, unless otherwise ordered by this court, the agreed statement of facts shall be printed or reproduced by any method authorized by court rule. A copy of the statement required by CPLR 5531 shall be prefixed to the papers constituting the submission. Appellant shall file the original submission and 10 copies thereof along with 10 briefs and proof of service of two copies of the submission and the brief on each opposing party, and shall otherwise comply with the requirements of section 1000.3(b) of this Part.

Cross References

CPLR, see McKinney's Book 7B.

§ 1000.7. Expedited People's Appeals Pursuant to CPL 450.20(1–a)

(a) Request to Expedite Appeal. When the people appeal pursuant to CPL 450.20(1–a) from an order reducing a count or counts of an indictment or dismissing an indictment and directing the filing of a prosecutor's information, either party may request that the appeal be conducted on an expedited basis (*see also*, CPL 210.20[6][c]; 450.55; Part 105 of this Title). The request to expedite the appeal may be made after the people file and serve the notice of appeal.

(b) Order Granting Expedited Appeal. When a request has been made pursuant to subdivision (a) of this section, an order shall be issued establishing an expedited briefing schedule and designating a term of court for argument of the appeal, giving a preference to the appeal. The appeal shall be expeditiously determined.

(c) Absent a contrary order of this court, if the defendant was represented in the superior court by court-assigned counsel, such counsel shall continue to represent the defendant in an appeal taken pursuant to CPL 450.20(1–a) and this section (see section 105.4 of this Title).

(d) Brief and Appendix of the People. The people shall file nine copies of a brief and appendix. The appendix shall include a copy of the indictment and the order and decision of the court from which the appeal is taken. Briefs may be typewritten or reproduced. The form of the brief and appendix shall otherwise conform with section 1000.4 of this Part. One copy of the brief and appendix shall be served on counsel for respondent.

(e) Brief and Appendix of Respondent. Respondent shall file nine copies of a brief and shall serve one copy on counsel for the people. The brief may be typewritten or reproduced and shall otherwise conform with section 1000.4 of this Part. Respondent may, if necessary, file nine copies of an appendix and serve one copy of the appendix on counsel for the people. The appendix shall conform with section 1000.4 of this Part, in the same number as respondent's brief.

(f) Record on Appeal. The appeal shall be heard and determined on the original papers, which shall include the notice of appeal with proof of service and filing, the indictment, the motion papers and the order and decision of the court from which the appeal is taken. The people shall file the original papers with their brief and appendix.

(g) Grand Jury Minutes. The people shall file, separately from the record, one copy of the Grand Jury minutes with their brief and appendix.

Cross References

Criminal Procedure Law, see McKinney's Book 11A.

§ 1000.8. Transferred Proceedings

(a) Original Papers. A proceeding transferred to this court shall be prosecuted upon the original papers, which shall include the notice of petition or order to show cause and petition, answer, any other transcript or document submitted to Supreme Court, the

transcript of any proceedings at Supreme Court, the order of transfer and any other order of Supreme Court. When the proceeding has been transferred prior to the filing and service of an answer, a respondent shall file and serve an answer within 25 days of filing and service of the order of transfer. When a proceeding has been transferred to this court pursuant to Executive Law, section 298, the State Division of Human Rights shall file with the clerk the record of the proceedings within 45 days of the date of entry of the order of transfer.

(b) Briefs, Transcripts and Oral Argument. Upon receipt of the order of transfer and other documents from the court from which the transfer has been made, the clerk shall issue a schedule for the filing and service of briefs, if any, the production of necessary transcripts and the calendaring of the proceeding.

(1) A petitioner shall file 10 copies of a brief, with proof of service of one copy on each respondent, as set forth in the scheduling order. If the brief is not timely filed and served, and no motion to extend the time for filing and service is made, the proceeding shall be deemed dismissed, without the necessity of an order.

(2) A respondent shall file 10 copies of a brief, with proof of service of one copy on each other party, as set forth in the scheduling order.

Cross References

Executive Law, see McKinney's Book 18.

§ 1000.9. Original Proceedings

(a) Return Date. Unless otherwise required by statute or by order of this court or justice of this court, original special proceedings commenced in this court shall be made returnable at 10:00 a.m. on any Monday (or, if Monday is a legal holiday, the first business day of the week), regardless of whether the court is in session. The return date shall fall not less than 25 days after service of the notice of petition and petition on each respondent.

(b) Necessary Papers. Unless otherwise directed by statute or by order of this court or justice of this court, a petitioner shall file the original notice of petition and petition and 10 copies thereof and the filing fee as required by CPLR 8022. Each respondent shall file and serve a like number of copies of an answer or other lawful response.

(1) A party commencing an original proceeding by order to show cause (see section 1000.13[b] of this Part) shall, in advance, remit the filing fee as required by CPLR 8022.

(2) Proof of service of two copies of the notice of petition and petition on each respondent shall be filed not later than 15 days after the applicable Statute of Limitations has expired (*see*, CPLR 306–b).

(c) Briefs and Oral Argument. Upon the filing of a notice of petition and petition with proof of service, the clerk shall issue a schedule for the filing and service of briefs, if any, and for the calendaring of the proceeding. A party shall submit 10 copies of a brief.

Cross References

CPLR, see McKinney's Book 7B.

§ 1000.10. Calendaring of Appeals and Proceedings

(a) Scheduling Order. After the appellant has perfected the appeal, the clerk shall issue a scheduling order. The order will specify the term of court for which the matter has been scheduled and set a deadline for the service and filing of respondent's briefs and reply briefs, if any. A proceeding shall be scheduled pursuant to section 1000.8 or 1000.9 of this Part, as appropriate.

(b) Respondent's Brief; Request for Extension of Time. A respondent on an appeal must serve and file 10 copies of a brief on the deadline set by the clerk in the scheduling order, which shall be 30 days from service on respondent of appellant's brief. In a proceeding, a party shall file 10 copies of a brief as set forth by the clerk in the scheduling order. When a respondent to an appeal or a party to a proceeding is unable to comply with a deadline, a motion for an extension of time shall be filed and served prior to the expiration of the deadline (see section 1000.13[h] of this Part). When an extension of time to file and serve a brief has been granted, a copy of the order granting such permission shall be filed with the brief.

(c) Notice of Counsel's Unavailability for Oral Argument. A party or his or her attorney shall notify the clerk in writing within 15 days of the date that the scheduling order was mailed of unavailability for oral argument on a specific date or dates during the term.

(d) Expedited Appeals or Proceedings. A party or his or her attorney may file and serve a motion to expedite an appeal or proceeding. The motion must be made within 15 days of the date that the scheduling order was mailed. The motion must be supported by an affidavit setting forth with particularity the compelling circumstances requiring that the appeal or proceeding be scheduled at the earliest available date (see section 1000.13[m] of this Part).

(e) Day Calendar. The clerk shall prepare calendars for each day of a court term by designating for argument or submission appeals or proceedings that have been perfected and scheduled. A notice to appear for oral argument will be mailed by the clerk to all parties or their attorneys not less than 20 days prior to the term. Counsel must appear as directed or submit on the brief.

§ 1000.11. Oral Argument

(a) Generally. A party or his or her attorney who is scheduled to argue before the court shall sign in with the clerk's office prior to 10:00 a.m. on the day of the scheduled argument. When oral argument is scheduled to commence at a time other than 10:00 A.M., a party or counsel shall sign in with the Clerk's Office prior to the time designated for the commencement of argument. Not more than one person shall be heard on behalf of a party. When a brief has not been filed on behalf of a party, no oral argument shall be permitted except as otherwise ordered by this court.

(b) Requests for Oral Argument. Requests for oral argument shall be made by indicating on the cover of the brief the amount of time requested. The amount of time allowed shall be within the discretion of the court. When no time is indicated on the cover of the brief, the appeal or proceeding shall be deemed submitted.

(c) No Argument Permitted in Particular Cases. Unless otherwise provided by order of this court, oral argument shall not be permitted in the following cases:

(1) an appeal from a judgment of conviction in a criminal case that challenges only the legality or length of the sentence imposed;

(2) a CPLR article 78 proceeding transferred to this court in which the sole issue is whether there is substantial evidence to support the challenged determination; and

(3) any other case in which this court, in its discretion, determines that oral argument is not warranted.

(d) Cases Deemed Submitted. An appeal or proceeding in which no argument time has been requested shall be deemed submitted. When oral argument has been requested and counsel fails to appear when the case is called by the presiding justice or justice presiding, the matter shall be deemed submitted.

(e) Disqualification or Unavailability of Justice. When a justice is absent or unavailable at the time that the appeal or proceeding is argued, the matter will be heard by the four justices present and deemed submitted to any other qualified justice unless counsel objects at the time of oral argument.

(f) No Rebuttal Permitted. Rebuttal argument is not permitted and no time may be reserved by counsel for the purpose of rebuttal.

(g) Post–Argument Submissions. Except as otherwise ordered by this court, no post-argument submissions shall be accepted unless filed, with proof of service of one copy on each other party, within five business days of the argument date.

Cross References

CPLR, see McKinney's Book 7B.

§ 1000.12. Dismissal of Appeals for Failure to Perfect

(a) On Motion. A motion to dismiss for failure to perfect an appeal may be made pursuant to section 1000.13(e) of this Part when an appellant has failed to perfect an appeal within 60 days of service of the notice of appeal.

(b) Without Motion. A civil appeal, except an appeal taken pursuant to the Family Court Act in which this court has assigned counsel, shall be deemed abandoned and dismissed, without the necessity of an order or motion, when an appellant has failed to perfect an appeal within nine months of service of the notice of appeal. A motion to vacate such an abandonment and dismissal may be made pursuant to section 1000.13(g) of this Part.

Cross References

Family Court Act, see McKinney's Book 29A, Part 1.

Forms

Dismissal of appeal for failure to prosecute, see West's McKinney's Forms, CPLR, §§ 9:257 to 9:265.

§ 1000.13. Motions

(a) General Procedures.

(1) *Return Date.* Unless otherwise provided by statute or by order of this court or justice of this court, a motion to this court shall be returnable at 10:00 a.m. on any Monday (or, if Monday is a legal holiday, the first business day of the week), regardless of whether the court is in session. A motion shall not be adjourned except upon the written consent or stipulation of the moving party or by order of this court.

(i)[1] A motion for permission to appeal shall be made returnable on a Monday (or, if Monday is a legal holiday, the first business day of the week) at least eight days but not more than 15 days after the notice of motion is served (see CPLR 5516).

(2) *Notice and Service of Papers.* A notice of motion and supporting papers shall be served with sufficient notice to all parties, as set forth in the CPLR. In computing the notice period, the date upon which service is made shall not be included (see General Construction Law, section 20).

(i) When motion papers are personally served, at least eight-days notice shall be given (CPLR 2214[b]).

(ii) When motion papers are served by regular mail, at least 13–days notice shall be given (CPLR 2103[b][2]).

(iii) When motion papers are served by overnight delivery service, at least nine-days notice shall be given (CPLR 2103[b][6]).

(iv) When motion papers are served by electronic means, there shall be compliance with CPLR 2103(b)(5), and at least eight-days notice shall be given.

(3) *Cross Motions.* Cross motions shall be made returnable on the same date as the original motion. A cross motion shall be served either personally or by overnight delivery service at least four days before the return date.

(4) *Filings of Papers.*

(i) All papers in support of or in opposition to a motion or cross motion shall be filed in the clerk's office no later than 5:00 p.m. on the Friday preceding the return date. When Friday is a legal holiday, papers shall be filed no later than 5:00 p.m. on the Thursday preceding the return date.

(ii) Filing is accomplished by the physical delivery of the necessary papers to the clerk's office.

(iii) A submission to the clerk's office by electronic means will be accepted, provided that it otherwise complies with these rules and the original papers and one copy thereof are sent to the clerk's office on the date of the electronic transmission.

(5) *Necessary Papers.*

(i) Except as otherwise authorized by statute or rule or by order of this court or justice of this court, the papers on a motion or cross motion shall consist of a notice of motion (CPLR 2214), supporting affidavit(s), proof of service on all parties (CPLR 306), a copy of the notice of appeal or order of transfer with proof or admission of service, a copy of the order or judgment being appealed, along with the court's decision, if any, and a copy of any prior order of this court.

(ii) When an appellate docket number has been assigned to a matter by the clerk's office, a notice of motion or cross motion and any supporting affidavits shall conspicuously bear that number.

(iii) An original and one copy of all papers shall be filed.

(iv) Incomplete filings are not acceptable. A failure to comply with the rules for the submission of a motion shall result in the rejection of the motion papers.

(v) In accordance with CPLR 8022, a fee of forty-five dollars must be remitted upon the filing of each motion or cross motion with respect to a civil appeal or special proceeding, except that no fee shall be imposed for a motion or cross motion seeking poor person relief pursuant to CPLR 1101(a) and 22 NYCRR 1000.14.

(6) *Oral Argument.* Oral argument of motions is not permitted.

(b) Orders to Show Cause and Applications Pursuant to CPLR 5704.

(1) *Orders to Show Cause.* When a moving party seeks a temporary stay or other emergency interim

relief pending the return and determination of a motion, the motion may be brought by an order to show cause. The order to show cause shall be directed to a justice of this court with chambers in the judicial district from which the appeal arises. The party bringing the order to show cause must give reasonable notice to all other parties of the date and time when, and the location where, the order to show cause will be presented to a justice of this court, and all counsel may be present upon the presentation of the order to show cause. When the presence of counsel for an adverse party cannot be obtained, the papers in support of the order to show cause shall include an affidavit setting forth the manner in which reasonable notice has been given and an explanation for the failure to obtain the presence of adverse counsel. Unless otherwise ordered by a justice of this court, all papers in opposition to a motion brought by an order to show cause shall be served and filed in the clerk's office no later than noon of the return date set in the order to show cause.

(i)[1] A party commencing an original proceeding (see section 1000.9 of this Part) by an order to show cause shall remit the filing fee in advance, as required by CPLR 8022.

(2) *CPLR 5704(a)*. An application for relief pursuant to CPLR 5704(a) shall be made using the procedures for an order to show cause set forth in paragraph (1) of this subdivision.

(c) Stays of Judgments in Criminal Proceedings (CPL 460.50).

(1) *Initial Application*. Unless otherwise ordered by a justice of this court, an application by a defendant or the attorney for a defendant for a stay of judgment pending appeal may be made by motion on notice, as set forth in subdivision (a) of this section, or by order to show cause, as set forth in subdivision (b)(1) of this section.

(2) *Extensions*. When a defendant or the attorney for a defendant seeks to extend a stay of judgment pending appeal, the application shall be made by motion on notice, as set forth in subdivision (a) of this section. The papers in support of the motion shall include an affidavit stating either that the transcript of the proceeding to be reviewed has been filed pursuant to CPL 460.70 or that the transcript has been ordered, along with an explanation for the delay in completing and filing the transcript.

(d) Stays in Appeals Pursuant to the Family Court Act (Family Court Act, Section 1114).

(1) *Initial Application*. Unless otherwise ordered by a justice of this court, an application for a stay pursuant to Family Court Act, section 1114 shall be made by order to show cause, as set forth in subdivision (b)(1) of this section (see also, Family Court Act, section 1114[d]).

(2) *Extensions*. An application to extend a stay granted pursuant to Family Court Act, section 1114 and paragraph (1) of this subdivision shall be made by motion on notice, as set forth in subdivision (a) of this section. The papers in support of the motion shall include an affidavit demonstrating reasonable efforts to obtain the transcript of the proceeding to be reviewed and otherwise explaining the delay.

(e) Dismissal for Failure to Perfect. A motion to dismiss for failure to perfect the appeal may be made pursuant to section 1000.12(a) of this Part. An order dismissing the appeal shall be entered, unless the appellant timely serves and files an affidavit demonstrating a reasonable excuse for the delay and an intent to perfect the appeal within a reasonable time. When an appellant has made the required showing, an order shall be entered dismissing the appeal unless the appellant perfects the appeal by a date certain and further providing that the appeal shall be dismissed without further order if appellant should fail to perfect on or before the date certain.

(f) Extension of Time to Perfect. In an appeal subject to dismissal pursuant to section 1000.12(b) of this Part or order of this court, a motion for an extension of time to perfect the appeal may be made on or before the date by which the appellant must perfect the appeal. In support of the motion, the appellant shall submit an affidavit demonstrating a reasonable excuse for the delay and an intent to perfect the appeal within a reasonable time.

(g) Vacate Dismissal of Appeal. When an appeal has been dismissed pursuant to section 1000.12(b) of this Part or an order of this court, a motion to vacate the dismissal may be made within one year of the date of the dismissal. In support of the motion, the appellant shall submit an affidavit demonstrating a reasonable excuse for the delay and an intent to perfect the appeal within a reasonable time and setting forth sufficient facts to demonstrate a meritorious appeal.

(h) Extension of Time to File a Brief. A motion for an extension of time to file and serve a petitioner's brief, a respondent's brief, a reply brief or, when permitted, a surreply brief or a pro se supplemental brief shall be supported by an affidavit demonstrating a reasonable excuse for the delay and an intent to file and serve the brief within a reasonable time. When an extension of time to file and serve a brief has been granted, a copy of the order granting such permission shall be filed with the brief.

(i) Extension of Time to Take a Criminal Appeal. A motion pursuant to CPL 460.30 to extend the time to take an appeal shall be made within one year of the date on which the time to take an appeal expired. An affidavit in support of the motion shall set forth facts demonstrating that the appeal was not timely taken because of the improper conduct of a public servant, the improper conduct, death or disability of the defendant's attorney or the inability of the defendant and the defendant's attorney to communicate about whether an appeal should be taken before the time to take the appeal expired.

(1)[2] Filed with the motion papers shall be proof of service of the papers on defendant's trial counsel.

(j) [Repealed].

(k) Briefs Amicus Curiae. A person who is not party to an appeal or proceeding may make a motion to serve and file a brief amicus curiae. An affidavit in support of the motion shall briefly set forth the issues to be briefed and the movant's interest in the issues. The proposed brief may not duplicate arguments made by a party to the appeal or proceeding. When permission to submit a brief amicus curiae is granted, the person to whom it is granted shall file 10 copies of the brief with proof of service of two copies on each party. A person granted permission to appear amicus curiae shall not be entitled to oral argument.

(*l*) Admission Pro Hac Vice on a Particular Matter. An attorney and counselor-at-law or the equivalent may move for permission to appear pro hac vice with respect to a particular matter pending before this court (see section 520.11[a][1] of this Title). An affidavit in support of the motion shall state that the attorney and counselor-at-law is a member in good standing in all the jurisdictions in which the attorney and counselor-at-law is admitted to practice and that the attorney is associated with a member in good standing of the New York Bar, which member shall be the attorney of record in the matter. Attached to the affidavit shall be a certificate of admission in good standing from each Bar to which the attorney and counselor-at-law is admitted.

(m) Expedite Appeal. A motion to expedite an appeal or proceeding shall be supported by an affidavit setting forth with particularity the compelling circumstances justifying an expedited appeal or proceeding.

(n) Consolidation. A motion to consolidate appeals shall be supported by an affidavit setting forth the appeals to be consolidated and the reasons justifying consolidation (see section 1000.4[b][2]).

(o) Applications for Leave to Appeal Pursuant to CPL 460.15. An application pursuant to CPL 460.15 for a certificate granting leave to appeal to this court shall be supported by an affidavit setting forth the questions of law or fact for which review is sought and stating that no prior application has been made. The applicant shall attach to the affidavit a copy of the order and decision, if any, sought to be reviewed and a copy of all papers submitted to the court whose order is sought to be reviewed. The motion shall be submitted to the court for determination by an individual justice thereof.

(p) Reargument and Leave to Appeal to Court of Appeals.

(1) *Time of Motion.* A motion for reargument of or leave to appeal to the Court of Appeals from an order of this court shall be made within 30 days of service of the order of this court with notice of entry. The time to make the motion shall be extended five days if the order is served by mail and by one day if the order is served by overnight delivery service.

(2) *Necessary Papers.* Papers on a motion for reargument or leave to appeal to the Court of Appeals shall include a notice of motion (CPLR 2214), supporting affidavit, proof of service on all parties (CPLR 306) and a copy of the order and memorandum or opinion, if any, of this court.

(3) *Reargument.* An affidavit in support of a motion for reargument shall briefly set forth the points alleged to have been overlooked or misapprehended by this court.

(4) *Leave to Appeal to Court of Appeals.*

(i) An affidavit in support of a motion for leave to appeal to the Court of Appeals shall briefly set forth the questions of law sought to be reviewed by the Court of Appeals and the reasons that the questions should be reviewed by the Court of Appeals.

(ii) In a civil matter, a motion for leave to appeal to the Court of Appeals shall be determined by the panel of justices that determined the appeal.

(iii) In a criminal matter, a motion for leave to appeal to the Court of Appeals may be submitted to and shall be determined by any member of the panel of justices who determined the appeal. The affidavit in support of the motion shall state that no other application for leave to appeal to the Court of Appeals has been made.

(iv) A motion for permission to appeal shall be made returnable on a Monday (or, if Monday is a legal holiday, the first business day of the week) at least eight days but not more than 15 days after the notice of motion is served (see, CPLR 5516).

(q) Withdrawal of Counsel; Assigned Criminal Appeals. An attorney assigned to perfect a criminal appeal on behalf of an indigent defendant pursuant to 22 NYCRR 1022.11 may move, after conferring with the defendant and trial counsel, to be relieved of the assignment (*see People v Crawford*, 71 AD2d 38). In support of the motion, the attorney shall submit an affidavit accompanied by a brief in which the attorney states all points that may arguably provide a basis for appeal, with references to the record and citation to legal authorities. The brief must be served upon the defendant, together with the motion, at least 30 days before the return date of the motion. Together with the motion papers, the brief, and proof of service of the motion papers and the brief upon defendant, counsel shall submit the papers that would constitute the record on appeal pursuant to 22 NYCRR 1000.3(c)(1). Counsel shall also submit a copy of a letter to the defendant advising that he or she may elect to file a pro se response to the motion and/or a pro se supplemental brief.

(r) Other Motions. A motion seeking relief not specifically provided for herein is not precluded. Any such motion shall be submitted to the clerk's office in conformity with subdivision (a) of this section.

¹ So in original. No par. (ii) has been enacted.
² So in original. No par. (2) has been enacted.

Cross References

CPLR, see McKinney's Book 7B.

Criminal Procedure Law, see McKinney's Book 11A.

Family Court Act, see McKinney's Book 29A, Part 1.

General Construction Law, see McKinney's Book 21.

Forms

Permission or leave to appeal, see West's McKinney's Forms, CPLR, § 9:121 et seq.

Leave to appeal in criminal cases, see West's McKinney's Forms, Criminal Procedure, § 460.15, Forms 1 et seq.; § 460.20, Forms 1 et seq.

Extension or enlargement of time in criminal appeals, see West's McKinney's Forms, Criminal Procedure, § 460.30, Forms 1 to 3; § 460.70, Forms 2 to 4, 8, 9.

§ 1000.14. Poor Persons

(a) Motion. A motion for permission to proceed on appeal as a poor person and for assignment of counsel may be made by any party pursuant to section 1000.13 (a) of this Part.

(1) *Supporting Papers; All Appeals.* An affidavit in support of a motion for permission to proceed on appeal as a poor person and for assignment of counsel shall set forth the amount and sources of the movant's income; that the movant is unable to pay the costs, fees and expenses necessary to prosecute or respond to the appeal; and whether any other person is beneficially interested in any recovery sought and, if so, whether every such person is unable to pay such costs, fees and expenses (see, CPLR 1101 [a]; Judiciary Law § 35 (1); County Law § 722).

(2) *Supporting Papers; Civil Appeals.* In a civil appeal, an affidavit in support of a motion for permission to proceed on appeal as a poor person shall also set forth sufficient facts so that the merit of the contentions can be ascertained (CPLR 1101 [a]).

(i) ¹Exceptions. This subdivision has no application to appeals described in Family Court Act § 1120 (a), SCPA 407 (1) and Judiciary Law § 35 (1).

(3) *Service on County Attorney.* A motion for permission to proceed on appeal as a poor person and assignment of counsel shall be served with sufficient notice on the county attorney in the county from which the appeal arises (see, CPLR 1101 [c]).

(4) *Certification in lieu of Motion.* In appeals pursuant to the Family Court Act, in lieu of a motion, an application for either permission to proceed as a poor person or for permission to proceed as a poor person and assignment of counsel may be made by trial counsel or the Law Guardian, as appropriate, by filing with the Clerk a certification of continued indigency and continued eligibility for assignment of counsel pursuant to Family Court Act § 1118. Counsel shall attach to the certification a copy of the order from which the appeal is taken together with the decision, if any, and a copy of the notice of appeal with proof of service and filing.

(b) Stenographic Transcripts. Except as provided by order of this Court, the clerk of the court from which the appeal is taken shall provide a party granted permission to proceed on appeal as a poor person with a stenographic copy of the minutes of the proceeding upon which the appeal is based, along with one copy of any other paper or document on file in the clerk's office that is relevant and necessary to the appeal.

(c) Records and Briefs. A person granted permission to proceed on appeal as a poor person shall perfect the appeal by filing 10 copies of a brief with proof of service of one copy on each respondent.

(1) In a criminal appeal, a person granted permission to proceed on appeal as a poor person shall file a properly certified transcript of the trial or hearing underlying the appeal, if any; a copy of the Pre-Sentence Investigation Report, if relevant and necessary; one copy of an appendix consisting of the documents described in section 1000.4(e) of this Part with proof of service of one copy of the appendix on each respondent; and exhibits as required by section 1000.4 (g) of this Part.

(2) In a civil appeal, a person granted permission to proceed on appeal as a poor person shall file one copy of the stipulated or settled record with proof of service of one copy on each party to the appeal and shall file exhibits as required by section 1000.4 (g) of this Part.

(d) Filing Fee. A person granted permission to proceed on appeal as a poor person shall not be required to pay a filing fee (CPLR 1102 [d]).

(e) Respondent. When an appellant has been granted permission to appeal as a poor person, a respondent shall file 10 briefs with proof of service of one copy on appellant.

¹ So in original. No par. (ii) has been enacted.

Cross References

CPLR, see McKinney's Book 7B.

County Law, see McKinney's Book 11.

Family Court Act, see McKinney's Book 29A, Part 1.

Judiciary Law, see McKinney's Book 29.

§ 1000.15. Lesser Number of Records

(a) Motion. A motion for permission to perfect an appeal on less than the required number of records may be made by any party pursuant to section 1000.13(a) of this Part.

(b) Supporting Papers. An affidavit in support of a motion to perfect an appeal on less than the required number of records shall comply with section 1000.14(a)(1) of this Part.

(c) Relief Under Motion. When a motion to perfect an appeal on less than the required number of records has been granted, an appellant shall perfect the appeal as set forth in section 1000.14(c)(2) of this Part. A respondent shall comply with section 1000.14(e) of this Part.

§ 1000.16.   Sanctions; Signing of Papers

(a) Sanctions. An attorney or party who fails to comply with a rule or order of this court or who engages in frivolous conduct as defined in section 130–1.1(c) of this Title shall be subject to such sanction as the court may, in its discretion, impose. The imposition of sanctions or costs may be made upon motion or upon the court's own initiative, after a reasonable opportunity to be heard. The court may award costs or impose sanctions upon a written decision setting forth the conduct on which the award of costs or imposition of sanctions is made and the reasons for the determination that such an award or sanction is appropriate.

(b) Signing of Papers. In a civil appeal or proceeding, except in an appeal arising from a proceeding commenced pursuant to Family Court Act article three, seven, eight or 10, the original of every paper submitted for filing with the Clerk of Court shall be signed in ink by an attorney or, when a party is not represented by an attorney, a party in accordance with section 130–1.1–a of this Title.

§ 1000.17.   Orders and Decisions

(a) Entry of Orders. An order of this court determining an appeal or motion shall be entered by the clerk in the office of the clerk of this court (see CPLR 5524[a]). Unless otherwise directed by this court or justice of this court, the clerk shall draft the order.

(b) Service of Order. The person prevailing on an appeal or motion shall serve a copy of the order with notice of entry in the office of the clerk of this court on all parties.

(c) Service of Order; Criminal Appeals. Service of a copy of an order on appellant in accordance with CPL 460.10(5)(a) shall be made pursuant to CPLR 2103.

(d) Remittitur. Unless otherwise ordered by this court, an order determining an appeal shall be remitted, together with the record on appeal, to the clerk of the court from which the appeal is taken (see CPLR 5524[b]).

(e) Decisions. Unless otherwise directed by this court, the memorandum decisions and opinions of this court on decided appeals and proceedings shall be published in a list at 3:00 p.m. on the day falling two weeks after the last day of a term of court. A copy of the order determining the appeal or proceeding shall be mailed by the clerk's office to the prevailing party on the appeal or proceeding.

Cross References

CPLR, see McKinney's Book 7B.

§ 1000.18.   Withdrawal of Motion, Appeal or Proceeding; Settlement of Appeal or Proceeding or Issue Therein

(a) Motion. A motion may be withdrawn at any time prior to its return date upon the written request of the moving party.

(b) Appeal or Proceeding. An appeal or proceeding may be withdrawn and discontinued at any time prior to its determination only upon the filing with this court of a written stipulation of discontinuance, which must be signed by the parties or their attorneys and, in criminal appeals and appeals in which counsel has been assigned, by the appellant personally. When an appeal or proceeding is withdrawn or discontinued, the court shall be promptly notified.

(c) Settlement of appeal or proceeding or issue therein. The parties or their attorneys shall immediately notify the Court when there is a settlement of an appeal or proceeding or any issue therein or when an appeal or proceeding or any issue therein has been rendered moot. The parties or their attorneys shall likewise immediately notify the Court if the appeal should not be calendared because of bankruptcy or the death of a party. Any party or attorney who, without good cause shown, fails to comply with the requirements of this subdivision shall be subject to the imposition of such sanction as the Court may, in its discretion, impose pursuant to 22 NYCRR 1000.16(a).

§ 1000.19.   Electronic Recording and Audio–Visual Coverage of Court Proceedings

(a) Generally. Except as authorized by the presiding justice upon written application, audiotaping, photographing, filming or videotaping the proceedings of this court is prohibited.

(b) Application for Permission to Conduct. Written application for permission to photograph or conduct audio or video coverage of court proceedings must be submitted to the presiding justice at least five days prior to the scheduled proceeding. The application must specify, pursuant to section 29.2 of this Title: the type of equipment that will be utilized; the number of personnel that will be employed to conduct the coverage; and the pooling arrangements that have been made with other interested members of the media.

PART 1010. CIVIL APPEALS SETTLEMENT PROGRAM [REPEALED]

§§ 1010.1 to 1010.10. [Repealed]

§§ 1010.1 to 1010.10 were repealed effective February 1, 2007.

PART 1021. INDIGENT CRIMINAL APPEALS MANAGEMENT PROGRAM

§ 1021.1. Establishment of Program; Goals

(a) An Indigent Criminal Appeals Management Program is hereby established to oversee and monitor the assigned counsel program in the Fourth Judicial Department and to improve the delivery of services of assigned appellate counsel to indigent criminal defendants.

(1) It shall be the goal of the program to implement such improvements in the operation and staffs of the legal aid and public defender offices in the Fourth Department so that existing backlogs are eliminated and appeals assigned to such offices are perfected promptly.

(2) It shall be a goal of the program to implement such improvements in the operation of the assigned counsel plans in the Fourth Department so that a disposition is made on all appeals previously assigned to private attorneys participating in such plans and so that future appeals so assigned are perfected promptly.

(3) To assure that these goals are met it shall be the duty of all assigned counsel, including the public defender and legal aid offices, to perfect appeals within a deadline of 120 days after the receipt of the transcripts unless that deadline is extended for good cause shown upon application to the associate justice assigned to chair the council in the appropriate judicial district. Notwithstanding the foregoing, the associate justice assigned to chair such council may set a different deadline for any particular appeal.

(b) In order to achieve the goals specified in subdivision (a) of this section an Indigent Criminal Appeals Council is created in each of the three judicial districts comprising the Fourth Department. The presiding justice shall designate an associate justice to chair each council which shall consist of the permanent members specified by this section, in addition to such other individuals as the presiding justice deems appropriate. The permanent members shall include:

(1) the attorneys in charge of the appeals divisions of the public defender and legal aid offices of those counties in which such offices are assigned to perfect appeals or, if no such division exists, the public defender or attorney in charge of such office;

(2) the assigned counsel administrator of those counties in which criminal appeals are assigned to

private counsel participating in an assigned counsel plan pursuant to County Law, section 722(3);

(3) the assistant district attorneys in charge of the appeals divisions of the district attorney's offices or if no such division exists, the district attorney; and

(4) the administrative court reporter for each judicial district.

(c) The councils shall meet annually during the month of June on a date to be fixed by the chairpersons thereof and at such other times as the Presiding Justice or Chairpersons deem appropriate. The presiding justice shall furnish to each chairperson at least five days prior to each meeting an agenda of matters to be discussed. The chairperson may add such additional matters to the agenda as are deemed appropriate. The duties of the councils shall include, but not be limited to, the following:

(1) the evaluation of the efficiency of the operation of the legal aid societies and public defender offices within the counties situate within the jurisdiction of each council with respect to:

(i) the number of assigned appeals pending, and the length of time the appeals have been pending;

(ii) the number of attorneys available to perfect assigned appeals and whether such attorneys are available on a full-time basis;

(iii) the number of appeals perfected annually;

(iv) availability of alternative representation in those cases involving conflict of interests;

(v) the length of time necessary to obtain transcripts of stenographic minutes necessary to perfect assigned appeals; and

(vi) any matter of concern raised by the presiding justice, chairperson or any member of the council relating to indigent criminal appeals;

(2) the evaluation of the operation of the assigned counsel plans in each county utilizing such a plan for the assignment of appeals with respect to:

(i) the number of attorneys in each county willing to accept assignments of appeals;

(ii) individual caseloads and the length of time such cases have been pending;

(iii) the length of time necessary to obtain transcripts of the stenographic minutes necessary for the perfection of appeals; and

(iv) any matter of concern raised by the presiding justice, chairperson or member of the council relating to indigent criminal appeals;

(3) the submission to the presiding justice of recommendations for the elimination of appeal backlogs in the public defender offices or legal aid societies and the achievement of the time and calendaring goals established by these rules.

(d) Each council shall submit to the presiding justice no later than 30 days after the date of the meeting of the council, a report of the council's deliberations and recommendations.

(e) Public defender and legal aid offices assigned to perfect criminal appeals and assigned council administrators, at least two weeks before each meeting of the council, shall file a report with the council chairperson showing the status of all assigned appeals in their counties and measures they have taken with respect to delinquent appeals.

(f) The presiding justice shall take such steps as are deemed appropriate to implement the recommendations of the councils in conjunction with this court, the Chief Administrator of the Courts, the Chief Administrative Judge of a judicial district or local authorities responsible for funding the public defender offices, legal aid offices or the assigned counsel plan.

§ 1021.2.   Council Members as Volunteers

Members of the Indigent Criminal Appeals Councils, as volunteers, are expressly authorized to participate in a State-sponsored volunteer program within the meaning of subdivision 1 of section 17 of the Public Officers Law.

PART 1022.   ATTORNEYS

§ 1022.1.   Application

(a) This Part shall apply to all attorneys who are admitted to practice, or have offices or practice within the fourth department.

(b) The imposition of discipline pursuant to this Part shall not preclude further or additional sanctions prescribed or authorized by law, or prohibit bar associations from censuring, suspending or expelling their members.

§ 1022.2.   [Repealed]

§ 1022.3.   [Repealed]

§ 1022.4.   Confidential Nature of Statements

(a) All statements filed pursuant to former sections 1022.2 and 1022.3 of this Part and the contents thereof shall be available to only those individuals designated by written order of a justice of the Appellate Division.

(b) The Office of Court Administration shall microfilm all such statements and shall thereafter destroy the originals.

§ 1022.5.   Filing of Statements Pursuant to BCL 1514

A professional service corporation organized for the purpose of practicing law pursuant to the Business Corporation Law, article 15 that has its principal office located in the Fourth Judicial Department shall file with this department on or before July first every three years a statement listing the name and residence address of each shareholder, director and officer of the corporation and certifying that all such individuals are duly authorized to practice law in this State. The statement shall be signed by the president or any vice-president of the corporation and attested to by the secretary or any assistant secretary of the corporation.

§ 1022.6.   Deposit of Infants' Funds; Withdrawals; Accounting

(a) Except as otherwise provided by CPLR 1206 or in proceedings governed by Article 17 of the Surrogate's Court Procedure Act, any sum collected by an attorney as a result of a claim or demand belonging to or on behalf of an infant shall be deposited in the attorney's fiduciary account pursuant to section 1022.5. A statement of the amount received and deposited shall be served personally or by mail upon the infant's guardian.

(b) The attorney shall not retain, withhold or withdraw any portion of the amount collected or recovered as his compensation or reimbursement or disbursements except as authorized by an order of a court, as provided in section 474 of the Judiciary Law.

(c) Infants' funds shall not be withdrawn except by court order. A petition for the withdrawal of such funds shall comply with CPLR 1211 and in addition contain:

(1) an explanation of the purpose of withdrawal;

(2) an estimate of the cost of the proposed expenditure;

(3) the date and amounts of the recovery both by the infant and the parent, if any;

(4) the nature of the infants' injuries and his present state of health; and

(5) any other facts material to the application.

(d) No authorization shall be granted to withdraw such funds where the parents are financially able to support the infant. Except in unusual circumstances, no authorization shall be granted for any purpose other than education or necessaries where the parents are not financially able to support the infant.

(e) No allowance, except for necessary disbursements, shall be made to attorneys upon an application to withdraw infants' funds, unless justified by exceptional circumstances. Such application shall be considered part of the duty of attorneys representing infants in their actions and shall not entitle the attorneys further compensation except as herein provided.

Cross References

CPLR, see McKinney's Book 7B.

Judiciary Law, see McKinney's Book 29.

Surrogate's Court Procedure Act, see McKinney's Book 58A.

§ 1022.7.   [Repealed]

§ 1022.8.   Obligation of Attorneys to Expedite Court Cases

Every attorney representing any party or client in any criminal or civil court proceeding shall arrange his affairs so as to give preference to such court cases, and shall be diligent to assure the earliest disposition consistent with the interest of his client. To this end he shall be punctual at all scheduled appearances or meetings and cooperative with the court and his adversary in efforts to schedule the disposition of his cases in the order of their ages.

§ 1022.9.   Admission Pro Hac Vice

(a) Applications for admission pro hac vice with respect to a pending appeal or proceeding shall be made pursuant to section 1000.13(*l*) of this Title.

(b) Applications for admission pro hac vice pursuant to section 520.11(a)(2) and (3) of this Title shall be made only to the Appellate Division.

§ 1022.10.   [Repealed]

§ 1022.11.   Duties of Criminal Defense Counsel

(a) Counsel assigned to or retained for the defendant in a criminal action or proceeding shall represent the defendant until the matter has been terminated in the trial court. Where there has been a conviction or an adverse decision on an application for a writ of habeas corpus, or on a motion under section 440.10 or 440.20 of the Criminal Procedure Law, immediately after the pronouncement of sentence or the service of a copy of the order disposing of such application or motion, counsel shall advise the defendant in writing of his right to appeal or to apply for permission to appeal, the time limitations involved, the manner of instituting an appeal or applying for permission and of obtaining a transcript of the testimony, and of the right of the person who is unable to pay the cost of an appeal to apply for leave to appeal as a poor person.

Such counsel shall also ascertain whether defendant wishes to appeal or to apply for permission to appeal, and, if so, counsel shall serve the necessary notice of appeal or application for permission and shall file the necessary notice of appeal or application for permission with proof of service on or an admission of service by the opposing party.

(b) Counsel assigned to prosecute an appeal on behalf of an indigent defendant shall prosecute the appeal until entry of the order of the appellate court determining the appeal. Immediately upon entry of an order affirming the judgment of conviction or the order denying an application for a writ of habeas corpus or a motion under section 440.10 or 440.20 of the Criminal Procedure Law, counsel, assigned or retained, shall advise the defendant in writing of his right to apply for permission to appeal and of the right of a person who is unable to pay the cost of a further appeal (in the event that permission is granted) to apply for leave to appeal as a poor person. Counsel shall ascertain whether defendant wishes to apply for permission to appeal, and if so, make timely application therefor. In a habeas corpus proceeding, where the order of the Appellate Division is appealable to the Court of Appeals pursuant to CPLR 5601, counsel shall advise the relator of his absolute right to appeal without permission.

(c) On or before the date of filing appellant's brief, assigned counsel shall mail a copy of the brief to appellant at his last known address and advise the clerk in writing of the date of mailing.

(d) When counsel who has been assigned to perfect an appeal on behalf of an indigent defendant determines, after conferring with the defendant and trial counsel, that the appeal is frivolous, counsel may move to be relieved of the assignment pursuant to section 1000.13(q) of this Title (*see People v Crawford*, 71 AD2d 38). The motion must be accompanied by a brief in which counsel states all points that may arguably provide a basis for appeal, with references to the record and citation to legal authorities. A copy of the brief must be served upon the defendant, together with the motion papers, at least 30 days before the return date of the motion. Together with the motion papers, the brief, and proof of service of the motion papers and the brief upon defendant, counsel shall submit the papers that would constitute the record on appeal pursuant to section 1000.3(c)(1) of this Title. Counsel shall also submit a copy of a letter to the defendant advising that he or she may elect to file a pro se response to the motion and/or a pro se supplemental brief.

Cross References

Criminal Procedure Law, see McKinney's Book 11A.

§ 1022.11a.   Duties of Counsel in Family Court and Surrogate's Court

(a) This rule applies in proceedings commenced pursuant to Family Court Act articles three, seven

701

and 10 and article six, part one, and Social Services Law § 358–a, 384–b and 392 (*see*, Family Court Act § 1121).

(b) Counsel assigned to or retained by a party and the law guardian in an applicable proceeding shall represent the client until the matter is terminated by the entry of an order. Upon the entry of an order, it shall be the duty of counsel promptly to advise the parties of the right to appeal to the Appellate Division or to make a motion for permission to appeal. In the written notice, counsel shall set forth: the time limitations applicable to taking an appeal or moving for permission to appeal; the possible reasons upon which an appeal may be based; the nature and possible consequences of the appellate process; the manner of instituting an appeal or moving for permission to appeal; the procedure for obtaining a transcript of testimony, if any; and the right to apply for permission to proceed as a poor person.

(c) When a party or the law guardian determines to appeal or to move for permission to appeal, counsel or the law guardian shall serve the notice of appeal or motion for permission and shall file the notice of appeal or motion for permission with proof of service on or an admission of service by the opposing parties, including the law guardian when a law guardian has been appointed.

(d) Except when counsel has been retained to prosecute the appeal, the notice of appeal may include the statement that it is being filed and served on behalf of appellant pursuant to 22 NYCRR 1022.11A(c) and that it shall not be deemed an appearance by counsel as counsel for appellant on the appeal.

(e) When a party has indicated a desire to appeal, counsel shall, when appropriate, move for permission to proceed as a poor person and assignment of counsel pursuant to 22 NYCRR 1000.14.

§ 1022.12. Compensation of Attorneys Assigned as Defense Counsel

(a) No attorney assigned as defense counsel in a criminal case shall demand, accept, receive or agree to accept any payment, gratuity or reward, or any promise of payment, gratuity, reward, thing of value or personal advantage from the defendant or other person, except as expressly authorized by statute or by written order of a court.

(b) All vouchers submitted by attorneys, psychiatrists or physicians, pursuant to section 35 of the Judiciary Law and section 722(b) of the County Law in which the compensation sought exceeds the statutory limits shall be submitted to the judge or justice before whom the matter was heard for approval or modification. The attorney, psychiatrist or physician shall attach thereto an affidavit describing the unusual or extraordinary circumstances which warrant the additional fee. Time itself does not necessarily constitute an extraordinary circumstance.

(c) A judge or justice approving such a fee, shall certify that the circumstances are unusual or extraordinary and that therefore a fee in excess of the statutory limit has been earned and the amount thereof. Such certification shall state circumstances, other than additional time, which justify the fee recommended. In the absence of either the attorney's affidavit or the court's certification, additional compensation shall not be allowed.

Cross References

County Law, see McKinney's Book 11.

Judiciary Law, see McKinney's Book 29.

§ 1022.13. Combining or Grouping of Claims

No attorney for a plaintiff or claimant shall for purposes of settlement or payment combine or group two or more unrelated claims or causes of action on behalf of clients and each such claim or cause of action shall be settled or paid independently on its own merit. No attorney for a defendant shall participate in the settlement of claims or causes of action combined or grouped in violation of this section.

§ 1022.14. Gratuities to Public Employees

No attorney shall give any gift or gratuity to any employee of any court or other governmental agency with which such attorney has had or is likely to have any professional or official transaction.

§ 1022.15. Practice of Law by Non-judicial Personnel

(a) Attorneys Employed Full-Time in the Unified Court System. An attorney employed full-time as determined by the time and leave program of the director of administration who is a law secretary to an Appellate Division justice or confidential clerk or deputy confidential clerk to a Supreme Court justice or an employee of the Office of Court Administration or of the Appellate Division shall not participate, directly or indirectly, as attorney or counsel in any action or proceeding pending before any court or any administrative board, agency, committee or commission of any government, or in the preparation or subscription of briefs, papers or documents pertaining thereto. Subject to the approval of a justice of the Appellate Division in each case, such an attorney may participate as attorney or counsel in noncontested matters in the Surrogate's Court, noncontested accountings in the Supreme Court, or other ex parte applications not preliminary or incidental to litigated or contested matters.

(b) Attorneys Employed Part-Time as Confidential Clerks or Deputy Confidential Clerks to Supreme Court Justices or Law Secretaries to Appellate Division Justices. An attorney who is employed part-time as defined by the time and leave program of the director of administration, as a confidential clerk or deputy confidential clerk to a Supreme Court justice or law secretary to an Appellate Division justice shall not appear as attorney or counsel in any action or proceeding pending in the Supreme Court or a County Court, nor shall he subscribe his name to papers or documents pertaining thereto. The attorney may engage in any other practice of law which is compatible with and would not reflect adversely upon the performance of his duties. No partner or associate of the attorney employed as a part-time confidential clerk or deputy confidential clerk or law secretary shall practice law before the justice by whom the attorney is employed.

§ 1022.16. [Repealed]

§ 1022.17. Professional Misconduct Defined

A violation of any rule of the Disciplinary Rules of the Code of Professional Responsibility as set forth in 22 NYCRR part 1200, or any other rule or announced standard of the Appellate Division governing the conduct of attorneys, shall constitute professional misconduct within the meaning of Judiciary Law § 90(2).

Cross References

Judiciary Law, see McKinney's Book 29.

Code of Professional Responsibility, see Appendix to McKinney's Judiciary Law, Book 29.

§ 1022.18. Effect of Restitution on Disciplinary Proceedings

The restitution by an attorney of client funds converted or misapplied by the attorney shall not bar the commencement or continuation of grievance or disciplinary proceedings.

§ 1022.19. Fourth Judicial Department Grievance Plan

(a) Attorney Grievance Committee Structure.

(1) There shall be an attorney grievance committee for each judicial district in the Fourth Judicial Department. There shall be at least one member from each county in each judicial district.

(2) The Appellate Division shall appoint the members of the committees, after consultation with the presidents of the county bar associations. A chairperson of each committee shall be appointed by the Presiding Justice. An appointment shall be for a term of three years. A member who has completed two consecutive three-year terms shall not be eligible for reappointment until three years after the expiration of the second term and vacancies on the committee shall be filled for the remainder of the unexpired term. Each committee shall be composed of 21 members, including three nonlawyers. All members of a committee shall reside in the respective judicial district. Twelve members of a committee constitute a quorum. Members of the committees are volunteers and are expressly authorized to participate in a State-

sponsored volunteer program, pursuant to Public Officers Law, section 17(1).

(3) A member of a current or former committee member's law firm shall not be prohibited from representing a respondent in a disciplinary proceeding, or during an investigation conducted pursuant to these rules, provided that such representation is in accordance with section 1200.45 of this Title.

(b) Duties of Attorney Grievance Committee.

The attorney grievance committee shall:

(1) consider and investigate all matters involving allegations of misconduct by an attorney engaged in the practice of law in the respective judicial district. An investigation may be commenced by the committee upon receipt of a complaint, a referral by this Court or by the committee on its own initiative;

(2) supervise staff attorneys in the performance of their duties before the committee;

(3) appoint sub-committees to assist in investigations when necessary and appropriate;

(4) refer cases directly to the Appellate Division when the public interest requires prompt action or when the matter involves an attorney who has been convicted of a felony or a crime involving conduct that adversely reflects upon the attorney's honesty, trustworthiness or fitness as an attorney; and

(5) maintain and provide to the Appellate Division statistical reports summarizing the processing and disposition of all matters before the committee.

(c) Staff structure.

(1) There shall be a legal staff, which shall include a chief attorney and such staff attorney positions as may be provided for in the State budget. Staff attorneys, including the chief attorney, shall be appointed by the Appellate Division. Staff attorneys shall reside within the Fourth Department. The chief attorney may hire investigative and clerical staff as provided for in the State budget.

(d) Duties and authority of legal staff.

(1) *Investigation of complaints.* Investigation of all complaints shall be initiated by the chief attorney and conducted by the staff attorneys. Staff attorneys are authorized to:

(i) request from the subject of a complaint that a written response be filed within 14 days; a copy of the response may be provided to the complainant;

(ii) interview witnesses and obtain any records and reports necessary to determine the validity of a complaint;

(iii) direct the subject of the complaint to appear before the chief attorney or a staff attorney for a formal interview or examination under oath;

(iv) when it appears that the examination of any person is necessary for a proper determination of the validity of a complaint or that the production of relevant books and papers is necessary, the chief attorney may apply to the clerk of the Appellate Division for a judicial subpoena to compel the attendance of the person as a witness or the production of relevant books and papers; the application for the subpoena shall be supported by sufficient facts to demonstrate the relevancy of the testimony and of any books and papers specified; subpoenas shall be issued by the clerk in the name of the presiding justice and may be made returnable before the chief attorney or staff attorney at a time and place specified therein; and

(v) when it appears that a complaint involves a minor matter, such as a personality conflict between attorney and client, a fee dispute or a delay that resulted in no harm to the client, the staff attorney may refer the complaint, upon notice to the attorney and the complainant, to an appropriate committee of the local bar association.

(2) Authorized dispositions of matters not warranting institution of formal disciplinary proceedings. After investigation of a complaint and consultation with the appropriate committee chairperson, the chief attorney or designated staff attorney may:

(i) dismiss a complaint as unfounded by letter to the complainant and subject attorney; or

(ii) refer a complaint to a mediation or monitoring program, pursuant to section 1220.2 of this Title; or

(iii) when it appears that the factors set forth in 22 NYCRR 1022.20(d)(3)(a) are present, make a written recommendation to the Appellate Division, on notice to the attorney who is the subject of the complaint or investigation, that the matter under investigation be stayed and that the attorney be diverted to a monitoring program approved by the Appellate Division; or

(iv) when it appears that the subject attorney has engaged in inappropriate behavior that does not constitute professional misconduct, issue a letter of caution to the attorney, with written notification to the complainant that such action has been taken; or

(v) recommend to the appropriate committee that a letter of admonition be issued to the subject attorney. A report summarizing the matter along with the recommendation shall be provided to the attorney. The attorney shall be afforded the right to appear before the committee and be heard. A letter of admonition shall be issued upon the approval of a majority of the committee members present. The letter of admonition shall state the nature of the inappropriate conduct and the basis for the determination. The issuance of a letter of admonition shall constitute the imposition of formal discipline. The complainant shall receive written notification that such action has been taken. In the event that a majority of the committee members

decline to approve the issuance of a letter of admonition, the matter may be disposed of in any manner set forth in subparagraph (i), (ii) or (iv) of this paragraph.

(3) *Appeals.*

(i) Appeal from letter of caution. An attorney may appeal to the committee from a letter of caution by filing a letter stating objections to the letter of caution. The letter appeal shall be directed to the chairperson of the appropriate district committee, and shall be served on the chief attorney. The letter appeal shall be filed within 30 days of the date on the letter of caution. The chief attorney may file a reply within 10 days of service of the letter of appeal. Oral argument of the appeal is not permitted.

(ii) Appeal from letter of admonition. An attorney may appeal to the three district committee chairpersons from a letter of admonition by filing a letter stating objections to the letter of admonition. The letter appeal shall be filed within 30 days of the date on the letter of admonition, and shall be served on the chief attorney. The chief attorney may file a reply within 10 days of service of the letter appeal. Appearances on such appeals shall be within the discretion of the committee chairpersons.

(iii) Appeal by chief attorney. The chief attorney may appeal to the three committee chairpersons from a committee determination declining to approve the issuance of a letter of admonition by filing a letter stating objections to the determination. The letter appeal shall be filed within 30 days of the date of the adverse determination, and shall be served on the subject attorney. The attorney may file a reply within 10 days of service of the letter appeal. Appearances on such appeals shall be within the discretion of the committee chairpersons.

On appeals taken pursuant to this paragraph, the chairperson or chairpersons shall review all issues raised by the complaint or complaints and the entire record that was before the chief attorney or the committee.

(e) Duties of county and local bar associations. A county or local bar association may review, investigate and determine complaints against attorneys involving allegations of minor delay that resulted in no harm to the client, fee disputes, personality conflicts between attorney and client, and other minor matters.

(1) The bar association shall provide to the chief attorney, within 20 days of receipt of a complaint, a report, in a form prescribed by the chief attorney, a copy of the complaint and any other relevant correspondence.

(2) When a bar association retains jurisdiction over a complaint after notifying the chief attorney as required by paragraph (1) of this subdivision, the association shall complete its investigation and forward the

file along with a status report in a form prescribed by the chief attorney, to the chief attorney within 60 days of the date of receipt of the complaint. When the bar association has not reached a determination resolving the complaint within the 60–day period, the district committee shall assume jurisdiction of the matter. The association may make a written request to the chief attorney for an extension of the 60–day period.

(3) A complaint received by a bar association that involves a matter other than a minor delay, fee dispute or personality conflict shall be forwarded to the chief attorney as soon as possible and in no event more than 20 days after receipt.

(4) Each bar association shall file quarterly reports on attorney grievance matters in a form prescribed by the chief attorney. The report shall be filed within 15 days of the end of each quarter.

Cross References

Judiciary Law, see McKinney's Book 29.

Public Officers Law, see McKinney's Book 46.

§ 1022.20. Formal Disciplinary Proceedings

(a) Authorization for commencement of proceedings.

The chief attorney may recommend to the committee that disciplinary proceedings be commenced when there is probable cause to believe that an attorney has committed professional misconduct or when an attorney has been convicted of a crime involving conduct that adversely reflects upon the attorney's honesty, trustworthiness or fitness as a lawyer. The chief attorney shall present the matter to the committee along with a written recommendation, which shall be provided to the attorney who is the subject of the proceeding. The attorney shall have the right to appear before the committee and to be heard in response to the charges. When a majority of the committee members present vote to approve the filing of charges upon a determination that there is probable cause to believe that an attorney has committed professional misconduct or has been convicted of a crime involving conduct that adversely reflects upon the attorney's honesty, trustworthiness or fitness as a lawyer, the chief attorney shall institute formal proceedings against the attorney.

(b) Appeal by chief attorney.

The chief attorney may appeal to the three district chairpersons from a committee determination declining to approve the filing of formal charges by filing a letter stating objections to the determination. The letter appeal shall be filed within 30 days of the date of the adverse determination, and shall be served on the subject attorney. The attorney may file a reply within 10 days of service of the letter appeal. On appeals taken pursuant to this subdivision, the chairpersons shall review all issues raised by the complaint or complaints and the entire record that was before the committee.

(c) Procedure for filing charges.

(1) To commence a proceeding in the Appellate Division, the chief attorney shall file the original notice of petition and petition and 5 copies thereof with proof of service of one copy on the respondent attorney. Unless otherwise directed by the Appellate Division, the proceeding shall be made returnable at 2 p.m. on the second Tuesday of the next scheduled court term. The notice of petition and petition shall be served in the manner set forth in Judiciary Law, section 90 (6), and with sufficient notice to all parties, as set forth in the CPLR, and shall be filed at least 20 days prior to the commencement of the court term when it is returnable.

(2) An attorney subject to formal disciplinary charges shall personally appear before the Appellate Division on the return date of the matter and thereafter on any adjourned date, except as provided in paragraph (1) of this subdivision.

(3) *Answer.* An attorney subject to formal disciplinary charges shall file in the Appellate Division the original answer and five copies thereof with proof of service of one copy on the chief attorney or staff counsel within 20 days from the date of service of the petition.

(d) Disposition by Appellate Division.

(1) When a respondent, in the answer, denies a material allegation of the petition, thereby raising an issue of fact, the Appellate Division may dispense with respondent's appearance and refer the matter to a justice of the Supreme Court or a referee designated by the Appellate Division to hear and report without recommendation. Unless otherwise directed by the Appellate Division, the referee shall give the matter a preference, shall schedule the hearing on consecutive dates, to the extent possible, and shall complete the hearing within 60 days following the date of the entry of the order of reference. The parties shall make final submissions, including proposed findings of fact, if any, within 15 days following the date on which the stenographic transcript of the minutes of the hearing is completed, and the referee's report shall be completed within 30 days thereafter.

(2) When no issue of fact is raised, or after completion of the hearing and report on such issue, the Appellate Division shall fix a time at which the respondent may be heard in mitigation or otherwise, unless the respondent waives in writing the privilege to be heard.

(3) (a) When an attorney who is the subject of a disciplinary investigation or proceeding raises in defense of the charges or as a mitigating factor alcohol or substance abuse, or, upon the recommendation of chief counsel or a designated staff attorney pursuant to 22 NYCRR 1022.19(d) (2)(iii), the Appellate Divi-

sion may stay the matter under investigation or the determination of the charges and direct that the attorney complete a monitoring program sponsored by a lawyers' assistance program approved by the Appellate Division upon a finding that:

    (i) the alleged misconduct occurred during a time period when the attorney suffered from alcohol or other substance abuse or dependency;

    (ii) the alleged misconduct is not such that disbarment from the practice of law would be an appropriate sanction; and

    (iii) diverting the attorney to a monitoring program is in the public interest.

(b) Upon submission of written proof of successful completion of the monitoring program, the Appellate Division may dismiss the disciplinary charges. In that event, the chief attorney or a designated staff attorney shall provide written notice to the complainant of the disposition. In the event of an attorney's failure to successfully complete a Court ordered monitoring program, or, the commission of additional misconduct by the attorney during the pendency of the proceeding, the Appellate Division may, upon notice to the attorney and after affording the attorney an opportunity to be heard, rescind the order diverting the attorney to the monitoring program and reinstate the disciplinary charges or investigation.

(c) Any costs associated with the attorney's participation in a monitoring program pursuant to this section shall be the responsibility of the attorney.

(d) Suspension pending disposition.

An attorney who is the subject of an investigation or proceeding may be suspended during the pendency of the investigation or proceeding on motion of the chief attorney, on notice to the attorney, upon a finding by the Appellate Division that the attorney has committed misconduct immediately threatening the public interest. Such a finding may be based upon the attorney's default in responding to a petition, or notice to appear for questioning or subpoena; an admission under oath to the commission of professional misconduct; or other uncontroverted evidence of misconduct.

(e) Investigations of persons or parties unlawfully practicing or assuming to practice law.

(1) A bar association recognized in a county within the Fourth Department or a committee thereof engaged in an investigation into the alleged unlawful practice of law or the subject of such an investigation may apply to this Court for the issuance of a subpoena directing the attendance of witnesses or the production of books, papers and records before the association or committee thereof. Subpoenas shall be issued by the Clerk of this Court in the name of the Presiding Justice upon a determination that there is reasonable cause to believe that a person, firm, corporation or other organization is unlawfully practicing law or assuming to practice law or is engaged in any business or activity that may involve the unlawful practice of law.

(2) Associations or committees referred to in subdivision (1) of this rule are authorized to take and cause to be transcribed testimony under oath.

§ 1022.21.   Attorneys Convicted of a Crime

(a) Attorneys Convicted of a Felony. The Appellate Division shall, upon receipt of proof that an attorney has been convicted of a felony, as that term is defined in Judiciary Law § 90(4)(e), enter an order striking the attorney's name from the roll of attorneys.

(b) Attorneys Convicted of a Serious Crime.

(1) The Appellate Division shall, upon receipt of proof that an attorney has been convicted of a serious crime, as that term is defined in Judiciary Law § 90(4)(d), enter an order suspending the attorney pending the entry of a final order of disposition.

The Appellate Division may, upon the application of the attorney and for good cause shown, as provided in Judiciary Law § 90(4)(f), vacate the suspension.

(2) The Appellate Division shall, upon entry of the judgment of conviction, direct the attorney to show cause why a final order of discipline should not be entered. When an attorney requests a hearing, the Appellate Division shall refer the matter to a referee for a hearing, report and recommendation.

(c) Referral to Grievance Committee. When it is determined by the Appellate Division that the crime of which the attorney has been convicted is not a serious crime, pursuant to Judiciary Law § 90(4)(d), the Appellate Division may refer the matter to a district grievance committee for investigation and appropriate disciplinary action.

(d) Effect of Reversal of Conviction or Pardon. When an attorney has been suspended or disbarred based upon a conviction of a serious crime or felony and the conviction is subsequently reversed on appeal, or, the attorney is pardoned by the President of the United State or a governor of any state, the Appellate Division may vacate or modify the order of suspension or disbarment, as provided in Judiciary Law § 90(5).

Cross References

Judiciary Law, see McKinney's Book 29.

§ 1022.22.   Imposition of Discipline for Misconduct Committed in Other Jurisdiction

When the Appellate Division receives notice that an attorney admitted to practice by the Fourth Department has been disciplined by another state, territory or district, it shall direct the attorney to appear and show cause why similar discipline should not be imposed for the underlying misconduct. The attorney may file, within 20 days of service of the order to show cause, an affidavit stating any defense to the imposition of discipline and raising any mitigating factors. After the attorney has been heard, or, after the appearance has been waived, and upon review of the attorney's affidavit, the order entered by the foreign jurisdiction and the record of the proceeding in that jurisdiction, the Appellate Division may discipline the attorney for the misconduct committed in the foreign jurisdiction unless it finds that the procedure in the foreign jurisdiction deprived the attorney of due process of law, that there was insufficient proof that the attorney committed the misconduct, or, that the imposition of discipline would be unjust.

Cross References

Judiciary Law, see McKinney's Book 29.

§ 1022.23. Incompetency or Incapacity of Attorney

(a) When the Appellate Division is presented with proof of a judicial determination that an attorney is in need of involuntary care or treatment in a facility for the mentally disabled or is the subject of an order of incapacity, retention, commitment or treatment pursuant to the Mental Hygiene Law, it may enter an order immediately suspending the attorney from the practice of law. The chief attorney shall serve a copy of the order upon the attorney, a guardian appointed on behalf of the attorney or upon the director of the appropriate facility, as directed by the Appellate Division.

(b) At any time during the pendency of a disciplinary proceeding or an investigation conducted pursuant to these rules, the chief attorney, or the attorney who is the subject of the proceeding or investigation, may apply to the Appellate Division for a determination that the attorney is incapacitated from practicing law by reason of mental disability or condition, addiction to alcohol or illegal substances or any other condition that renders the attorney incapacitated from practicing law. The application shall be by notice of motion and shall be served with sufficient notice to all parties, as set forth in the CPLR. An affidavit shall be filed in support of the application, setting forth facts demonstrating that the attorney is incapacitated. The Appellate Division may appoint a medical expert to examine the attorney and render a report and may assign counsel to represent the attorney. When the Appellate Division finds that an attorney is incapacitated from practicing law, the Appellate Division shall enter an order immediately suspending the attorney from the practice of law and may stay the pending proceeding or investigation.

§ 1022.24. Appointment of Attorney to Protect Clients of Suspended, Disbarred, Incapacitated, or Deceased Attorney

(a) **Suspension, Disbarment, Incapacitation or Death.** When an attorney is suspended, disbarred, incapacitated from practicing law pursuant to 22 NYCRR 1022.23, has abandoned the practice of law, or is deceased or is otherwise unable to adequately protect the interests of clients, the Appellate Division may appoint one or more attorneys to take possession of the attorney's files, examine the files, advise the clients to secure another attorney or take any other action necessary to protect the clients' interests.

(b) **Report to Court.** An attorney appointed pursuant to 22 NYCRR 1022.24 shall file, within 30 days of the order of appointment or any other time period set by the Appellate Division, a status report, which shall include the name and address of each client and the disposition of each client's file.

(c) **Compensation.** The Appellate Division may fix the compensation of any attorney appointed pursuant to 1022.24 (a), and may direct that compensation shall be a cost of the underlying disciplinary or incapacitation proceeding.

§ 1022.25. Responsibilities of Retired Attorneys

(a) An attorney shall, at least sixty days prior to retirement from the practice of law, notify by certified mail, return receipt requested, each client and the attorney for each adverse party in any pending matter involving the client, that the attorney is retiring and shall advise each client to secure another attorney. The attorney shall also, with respect to each matter in which a retainer statement has been filed pursuant to 22 NYCRR 1022.2 notify the Office of Court Administration that the attorney is retiring.

(b) In the event that a retired attorney fails to comply with subdivision (a), the Appellate Division may appoint an attorney to take possession of the retired attorney's files, examine the files, advise the clients to secure another attorney or take any other action necessary to protect the clients' interest.

§ 1022.26. Resignation From Practice of Law

(a) **Resignation of Attorney During Pendency of Disciplinary Proceeding or Investigation.** The Appellate Division shall enter an order striking from the roll of attorneys the name of an attorney who is the subject of a disciplinary proceeding or an investigation conducted pursuant to these rules upon receipt of an affidavit or affirmation in the form included in Appendix A, with proof of service on the chief attorney, which sets forth the nature of the charges or the allegations under investigation and shows that:

(1) the resignation is voluntarily rendered without duress and with full awareness of the consequences;

(2) the resignor admits the charges or allegations of misconduct;

(3) the resignor has no defense to the charges or allegations of misconduct; and

(4) when the charges or allegations include the wilful misappropriation or misapplication of clients' funds or property, the resignor consents to the entry of an order of restitution.

(b) Resignation of Attorney for Non-Disciplinary Reasons. An attorney may resign from the practice of law for non-disciplinary reasons by submitting to the Appellate Division an affidavit or affirmation in the form included in Appendix A, showing:

(1) the jurisdiction or jurisdictions where the attorney is admitted, along with the respective dates of admission;

(2) the attorney's current address and, when applicable, date that the attorney left the State of New York;

(3) that the attorney is in good standing in each jurisdiction where admitted and that the attorney is not currently the subject of a disciplinary proceeding or complaint;

(4) the specific reason for the resignation; and

(5) when the resignation is submitted by an attorney residing out-of-state who does not want to submit attorney registration fees, that the attorney does not intend to return to the State of New York to resume the practice of law.

When the Appellate Division determines that an attorney is eligible to resign for non-disciplinary reasons, it shall enter an order removing from the roll of attorneys the attorney's name and stating the non-disciplinary nature of the resignation.

Cross References

Judiciary Law, see McKinney's Book 29.

§ 1022.27. Conduct of Disbarred, Suspended or Resigned Attorneys

(a) Prohibition Against Practicing Law. Attorneys disbarred, suspended or resigned from practice shall comply with Judiciary Law §§ 478, 479, 484 and 486.

(b) Notification of Clients. When an attorney is disbarred, suspended from the practice of law or removed from the roll of attorneys after resignation, the attorney shall promptly notify, by registered or certified mail, each client, the attorney for each party in a pending matter and, for each action where a retainer statement has been filed pursuant to former 22 NYCRR 1022.2, the Office of Court Administration. The notice shall state that the attorney is unable to act as counsel due to disbarment, suspension or removal from the roll of attorneys. A notice to a client shall advise the client to obtain new counsel. A notice to counsel for a party in a pending action or to the Office of Court Administration in connection with an action where a retainer statement has been filed pur-

suant to former 22 NYCRR 1022.2 shall include the name and address of the disbarred, suspended or resigned attorney's client.

(c) Duty to Withdraw From Pending Action or Proceeding. When a client in a pending action or proceeding fails to obtain new counsel, the disbarred, suspended or resigned attorney shall move, in the court where the action or proceeding is pending, for permission to withdraw as counsel.

(d) Affidavit of Compliance. A disbarred, suspended or resigned attorney shall file with the Appellate Division, no later than 30 days after the date of the order of disbarment, suspension or removal from the roll of attorneys, an affidavit showing a current mailing address for the attorney and that the attorney has complied with the order and these Rules. The affidavit shall be served on the chief attorney and proof of service shall be filed with the Appellate Division.

(e) Compensation. A disbarred, suspended or resigned attorney may not share in any fee for legal services rendered by another attorney during the period of disbarment, suspension or removal from the roll of attorneys but may be compensated on a quantum meruit basis for services rendered prior to the effective date of the disbarment, suspension or removal from the roll of attorneys. The amount and manner of compensation shall be determined, on motion of the disbarred, suspended or resigned attorney, by the court or agency where the action is pending, or, if the action has not been commenced, at a special term of the Supreme Court in the county where the moving attorney maintained an office. The total amount of the legal fee shall not exceed the amount that the client would have owed if no substitution of counsel had been required.

(f) Required Records. A disbarred, suspended or resigned attorney shall keep and maintain records of the attorney's compliance with 22 NYCRR 1022.27 and with the order of disbarment, suspension or removal from the roll of attorneys.

§ 1022.28. Reinstatement

The Appellate Division may enter an order reinstating an attorney who has been disbarred, suspended or removed from the roll of attorneys for nondisciplinary reasons, when it appears to the satisfaction of the Appellate Division that the attorney has established by clear and convincing evidence that: the attorney has complied with the order of disbarment, suspension or the order removing the attorney from the roll; the attorney has complied with the rules of the court; the attorney has the requisite character and fitness to practice law; and it would be in the public interest to reinstate the attorney to the practice of law.

(a) Disbarred attorneys.

(1) *Time of application.* An attorney disbarred by order of the Appellate Division for misconduct, or stricken from the roll of attorneys pursuant to Judiciary Law, section 90 (4) or section 1022.26 (a) of this Part, may apply for reinstatement to practice after the expiration of seven years from the entry of the order of disbarment or the order striking the attorney from the roll of attorneys. The Appellate Division may deny the application with leave to renew upon submission of proof of successful completion of the New York State Bar Examination described in section 520.8 of this Title.

(2) *Procedure.* An application for reinstatement shall be made by motion, which shall be served with sufficient notice to all parties as set forth in the CPLR. The motion shall be returnable at 2 p.m. on the date scheduled by the Appellate Division for disciplinary matters, or as otherwise directed by the Appellate Division. The disbarred attorney shall personally appear before the Appellate Division on the return date of the application, unless otherwise directed by the Appellate Division. The motion and all supporting papers, as set forth in paragraph (3) of this subdivision, shall be filed in the Appellate Division no later than Friday preceding the return date.

(3) *Necessary papers.* An applicant for reinstatement shall file an original and five copies of the application. Papers on an application for reinstatement following disbarment shall include: a notice of motion; a copy of the order of disbarment or the order striking the attorney from the roll of attorneys; a copy of the Per Curiam Opinion of the Appellate Division, if any; a completed questionnaire in the form included in Appendix A of this section; proof of successful completion of the Multistate Professional Responsibility Examination described in section 520.9 of this Title; proof of service of one copy of the application on the chief attorney; and a copy of a letter to The Lawyers' Fund for Client Protection notifying the Fund that the application has been filed.

(4) *Responding papers.* Papers in response to an application for reinstatement must be in the form of an affidavit or affirmation and shall be filed, along with five copies thereof and proof of service of one copy on the disbarred attorney, no later than the Friday preceding the return date of the application.

(b) Attorneys suspended for misconduct.

(1) *Time of application.* A suspended attorney may apply for reinstatement after the expiration of the period of suspension and as provided in the order of suspension. When an attorney has been suspended for a period of more than one year, the Appellate Division may deny the application with leave to renew upon submission of proof of successful completion of the New York State Bar Examination described in section 520.8 of this Title.

(2) *Procedure.* An attorney suspended for misconduct by order of the Appellate Division may apply for reinstatement by making a motion, as provided in paragraph (a)(2) of this section. When an attorney has been suspended for a period of more than six months, the attorney shall personally appear before the Appellate Division on the return date of the application, unless otherwise directed by the Appellate Division. An attorney suspended for a period of six months or less shall not be required to appear before the Appellate Division, unless otherwise directed by the Appellate Division.

(3) *Necessary papers.* An applicant for reinstatement shall file an original and five copies of the application. When an attorney has been suspended for a period of more than six months, papers on an application for reinstatement following suspension shall include: a notice of motion; a copy of the order of suspension; a copy of the per curiam opinion of the Appellate Division, if any; a completed questionnaire in the form included in Appendix A of this section; proof of successful completion of the Multistate Professional Responsibility Examination described in section 520.9 of this Title; proof of service of one copy of the application on the chief attorney; and a copy of a letter to The Lawyers' Fund for Client Protection notifying the Fund that the application has been filed. When an attorney has been suspended for a period of six months or less, papers on an application for reinstatement following suspension shall include: an affidavit of the suspended attorney demonstrating compliance with the order of suspension and with section 1022.27 of this Part; a copy of the order of suspension; a copy of the per curiam opinion of the Appellate Division, if any; proof of service of one copy of the application on the chief attorney; and a copy of a letter to The Lawyers' Fund for Client Protection notifying the Fund that the application has been filed. The Appellate Division may direct an attorney to file a completed questionnaire in the form included in Appendix A of this section.

(4) *Responding papers.* Papers in response to an application for reinstatement must be in the form of an affidavit or affirmation and shall be filed, along with five copies thereof and proof of service of one copy on the disbarred attorney, no later than the Friday preceding the return date of the application.

(c) Attorneys suspended pursuant to section 1022.23 of this Part.

(1) *Time of application.*

An attorney suspended pursuant to section 1022.23 (a) of this Part may apply for reinstatement at such time as the attorney is declared competent.

An attorney suspended pursuant to section 1022.23 (b) of this Part may apply for reinstatement as provided in the order of suspension or at such time as the attorney is no longer incapacitated from practicing law.

(2) *Procedure.*

An attorney suspended pursuant to section 1022.23 (a) or (b) of this Part may apply for reinstatement by making a motion as provided in paragraph (a)(2) of this section. The attorney shall personally appear before the Appellate Division on the return date of the application, unless otherwise directed by the Appellate Division. The Appellate Division may appoint a medical expert to examine the suspended attorney or may require the suspended attorney to be examined at the attorney's expense. The Appellate Division may require the suspended attorney to submit records of medical or psychiatric care made during the period of disability.

(3) *Necessary papers.* An applicant for reinstatement shall file an original and five copies of the application. Papers on an application for reinstatement following suspension pursuant to section 1022.23 of this Part shall include a notice of motion; a copy of the order of suspension; a copy of the per curiam opinion of the Appellate Division, if any; proof, in evidentiary form, of a declaration of competency or of the attorney's capacity to practice law; proof of service of one copy of the application on the chief attorney; and, when the suspension was for a period of one year or more, a completed questionnaire in the form included in Appendix A of this section; proof of successful completion of the Multistate Professional Responsibility Examination described in section 520.9 of this Title; proof of service of one copy of the application on the chief attorney; and a copy of a letter to The Lawyers' Fund for Client Protection notifying the Fund that the application has been filed.

(4) *Responding papers.* Responding papers may be filed, as provided in paragraph (a) (4) of this section.

(d) Attorneys removed from roll of attorneys after voluntary resignation.

(1) *Time of application.* Attorneys removed from the roll of attorneys after voluntarily resigning from practice pursuant to section 1022.26(b) of this Part may apply for reinstatement to practice at any time upon a showing of changed circumstances. When the attorney has been removed from the roll of attorneys for a period of one year or more, the Appellate Division may require that the attorney submit proof of successful completion of the Multistate Professional Responsibility Examination described in section 520.9 of this Title or may direct that the application be denied with leave to renew upon submission of proof of successful completion of the New York State Bar Examination described in section 520.8 of this Title.

(2) *Procedure.* An attorney removed from the roll of attorneys pursuant to section 1022.26(b) of this Part may apply for reinstatement to practice by submitting to the Appellate Division an affidavit along with supporting documentation showing:

(i) the jurisdiction or jurisdictions where the attorney is admitted and that the attorney is in good standing in each jurisdiction where admitted and is not the subject of a pending disciplinary proceeding or complaint;

(ii) the attorney's current address and, when applicable, date that the attorney left the State of New York;

(iii) facts demonstrating a change of circumstances subsequent to entry of the order accepting the attorney's voluntary resignation; and

(iv) payment of attorney registration fees outstanding at the time of the voluntary resignation and that accrued during the period between the entry of the order removing the attorney from the roll of attorneys and the filing of the application for reinstatement.

When the attorney has been removed from the roll of attorneys for a period of one year or more, the attorney shall personally appear before the Appellate Division at 2 p.m. on the next date scheduled for disciplinary proceedings following the filing of the application, unless otherwise directed by the Appellate Division. Attorneys removed from the roll of attorneys for a period of less than one year prior to the application for reinstatement shall not be required to appear before the Appellate Division, unless otherwise directed by the Appellate Division. Five copies of the application shall be filed in the Appellate Division no later than the Friday preceding the next scheduled disciplinary date, along with proof of service of one copy of the application on the chief attorney; and a copy of a letter to The Lawyers' Fund for Client Protection notifying the Fund that the application has been filed.

(3) *Necessary papers.* Unless otherwise directed by the Appellate Division pursuant to paragraph (2) of this subdivision, papers on an application for reinstatement following the entry of an order of voluntary resignation shall include the affidavit described in paragraph (2) of this subdivision; a copy of the order removing the attorney from the roll of attorneys; the per curiam opinion of the Appellate Division, if any; proof of service of one copy of the application on the chief attorney; and a copy of a letter to The Lawyers' Fund for Client Protection notifying the Fund that the application has been filed. The Appellate Division may direct an attorney to file a completed questionnaire in the form included in Appendix A of this section.

(4) *Responding papers.* Responding papers may be filed as provided in paragraph (a) (4) of this section.

APPENDIX A.
APPELLATE DIVISION, FOURTH DEPARTMENT

Application for Resignation

I, _____, an attorney admitted to practice by the Appellate Division, Fourth Department on _____, hereby apply to resign from the bar of the State of New York. I submit this resignation voluntarily and with full awareness of the consequences. I submit the following information in support of my application:

1. I was admitted to practice in the following jurisdictions on the dates indicated:

_____

_____

_____.

2. I am the subject of the following pending disciplinary charges, as set forth in the petition dated: _____/ I am currently the subject of an investigation into the following allegations of professional misconduct:

_____

_____

_____.

3. I admit that I committed the acts of professional misconduct charged in the petition/ I admit the allegations of misconduct.

4. I have no defense to the charges/allegations of misconduct.

5. I consent to the entry of an order directing that I make restitution to the following clients in the amounts set forth: _____

_____

_____

_____.

6. I understand that acceptance of my resignation by the Court will result in the entry of an order sustaining the charges/allegations against me and striking my name from the roll of attorneys. I understand further that the order and the records and documents in relation thereto, including this affirmation, shall be deemed public records pursuant to Judiciary Law § 90 (10).

I hereby affirm, under penalties of perjury, that the above-stated information is true to the best of my knowledge, except for any information stated to be made on information and belief, and as to that information, I believe it to be true.

Date: _____

_____
Signature of Applicant

APPELLATE DIVISION, FOURTH DEPARTMENT

Application for Voluntary Resignation

I, _____, an attorney admitted to practice by the Appellate Division, Fourth Department on _____, hereby apply to resign from the bar of the State of New York and submit the following information in support of my application:

1. I was admitted to practice in the following jurisdictions on the dates indicated:

_____

_____

_____

_____

2. I ☐ am / ☐ am not in good standing in each of the jurisdictions where I am admitted. If not, please explain: _____

_____

_____

3. I ☐ am / ☐ am not currently the subject of a disciplinary proceeding or complaint in any jurisdiction. If yes, please explain: _____

_____

_____

4. My current address is: _____

_____

5. I left the State of New York on _____ and I have no present intention to return to the State of New York to resume the practice of law.

6. The specific reason for my resignation is: _____

_____

_____

7. I ☐ do / ☐ do not presently have clients in the State of New York.

8. I have stated below any additional facts that are relevant to the Court's determination of my application: _____

_____

_____

I hereby affirm, under penalties of perjury, that the above-stated information is true to the best of my knowledge, except for any information stated to be made on information and belief, and as to that information, I believe it to be true.

Date: _____

_____

Signature of Applicant

APPELLATE DIVISION, FOURTH DEPARTMENT

Petition for Reinstatement

I, _____, hereby petition the Appellate Division for reinstatement to practice pursuant to Judiciary Law § 90 and 22 NYCRR 1022.28. I submit the following information in support of my application:

1. My full name is: _____

2. I have also been known by the following names: _____. (I have attached certified copies of any court orders changing my name)

3. My date and place of birth are: _____

_____.

4. I currently reside at the following address: _____

_____.

    My telephone number is: _____.

5. During the period of my disbarment/suspension, I resided at the following addresses:_____

_____.

6. I am currently employed by: _____.

    My duties are: _____.

7. During the period of my disbarment/suspension, I was employed in the following positions: _____

_____

_____.

8. I was admitted to practice by the Appellate Division, _____ Department on _____, and was disbarred/suspended for a period of ____ years by order entered _____. (I have attached copies of the order and Per Curiam Opinion of the Appellate Division)

9. I am admitted to practice in the following other jurisdictions: _____. I have been disciplined in other jurisdictions in the following ways: _____. (I have attached certified copies of orders imposing discipline)

10. During the period of my suspension, I have engaged in the practice of law in the following jurisdictions, in the manner specified: _____

_____.

11. I have complied with the Appellate Division order imposing discipline upon me in all respects, including payment of all restitution ordered, and I have complied with 22 NYCRR 1022.27. My affidavit of compliance was filed with the Appellate Division on _____.

12. I did not comply with the following provisions of the Appellate Division order or 22 NYCRR 1022.27 for the reasons stated: _____

_____

_____.

13. Since the effective date of the discipline imposed, the following disciplinary complaints have been filed against me in the jurisdictions specified: _____

_____.

14. Prior to the effective date of the discipline imposed, the following disciplinary action was taken against me in the jurisdiction specified: _____

_____

_____.

15. I have listed below any outstanding judgments entered against me or a partnership, corporation or other business entity that I have an ownership interest in: _____

16.   I have listed below any lawsuits pending against me or a partnership, corporation or other business entity that I have an ownership interest in: _____

17.   I have listed below the court, location and date of any petition in bankruptcy filed by me or a partnership, corporation or other business entity that I have an ownership interest in: _____

18.   I have listed below any arrests or convictions of any crimes or violations, including traffic violations, that occurred subsequent to the effective date of my discipline: _____

19.   I have listed below any licenses that I hold, other than a license to practice law, that have been suspended or revoked since the effective date of my discipline, along with the reason for the suspension or revocation: _____

20.   I have listed below any applications that I have submitted since the effective date of my discipline for the issuance of a license that requires proof of good character and I have indicated whether the applications were granted or denied:

21.   I have disclosed below any mental or emotional condition or substance abuse problem that may adversely affect my ability to practice law: _____

22.   I have listed below any educational programs, including continuing legal education programs, that I have attended since the effective date of my discipline and any other steps that I have taken to remain current with developments in the law: _____

23.   I have listed below the amounts of any outstanding attorney registration fees for any jurisdiction in which I am admitted to practice law: _____

24.   I understand that I may be required to furnish to the Appellate Division copies of federal or state tax returns filed by me during the past two years, or, during the period of my discipline, and I agree to furnish the same upon request.

25.   I understand that my application for reinstatement may be referred to the Grievance Committee or the Committee on Character and Fitness for further investigation and I agree to cooperate fully with any committee investigation regarding my application.

26.   I have stated below any additional facts, not disclosed in any other part of my application, that are relevant to the Appellate Division's determination of my present character and fitness to practice law: _____

_____

_____

_____

_____

Petitioner

STATE OF _____)
) ss.:
COUNTY OF _____)

    I, _____, being duly sworn, say that: I have read the foregoing petition and know the contents thereof; the information provided is true of my own knowledge, except if stated to be made upon information and belief, and, as to such information, I believe it to be true.

_____

Petitioner

    Subscribed and sworn to before me this ___ day of _____, 20 ___.

_____
          Notary Public

Cross References

Judiciary Law, see McKinney's Book 29.

§§ 1022.29, 1022.30. [Repealed]

§ 1022.31. Contingent Fees in Claims and Actions for Personal Injury and Wrongful Death

    (a) In any claim or action for personal injury or wrongful death, other than one alleging medical, dental or podiatric malpractice, whether determined by judgment or settlement, in which the compensation of claimant's or plaintiff's attorney is contingent, that is, dependent in whole or in part upon the amount of the recovery, the receipt, retention or sharing by such attorney, pursuant to agreement or otherwise, of compensation which is equal to or less than that contained in any schedule of fees adopted by this department is deemed to be fair and reasonable. The receipt, retention or sharing of compensation which is in excess of such scheduled fees shall constitute the exaction of unreasonable and unconscionable compensation in violation of any provision of the Code of Professional Responsibility, as adopted jointly by the Appellate Divisions of the Supreme Court, effective September 1, 1990, unless authorized by a written order of the court as hereinafter provided.

    (b) The following is the schedule of reasonable fees referred to in subdivision (a) of this section: either

SCHEDULE A

    (1) 50 percent on the first $1,000 of the sum recovered,

    (2) 40 percent on the next $2,000 of the sum recovered,

    (3) 35 percent on the next $22,000 of the sum recovered,

    (4) 25 percent on any amount over $25,000 of the sum recovered; or

SCHEDULE B

    A percentage not exceeding 33⅓ percent of the sum recovered, if the initial contractual arrangement between the client and the attorney so provides, in which event the procedure hereinafter provided for making application for additional compensation because of extraordinary circumstances shall not apply.

Compensation of claimant's or plaintiff's attorney for services rendered in claims or actions for personal injury alleging medical, dental or podiatric malpractice shall be computed pursuant to the fee schedule contained in Judiciary Law, section 474–a.

    (c) Such percentage shall be computed on the net sum recovered after deducting from the amount recovered expenses and disbursements for expert testimony and investigative or other services properly chargeable to the enforcement of the claim or prosecution of the action. In computing the fee, the costs as taxed, including interest upon a judgment, shall be deemed part of the amount recovered. For the following or similar items there shall be no deduction in computing such percentages: liens, assignments or claims in favor of hospitals, for medical care and treatment by doctors and nurses, or of self-insurers or insurance carriers.

(d) In the event that claimant's or plaintiff's attorney believes in good faith that schedule A, above, because of extraordinary circumstances, will not give the attorney adequate compensation, application for greater compensation may be made upon affidavit with written notice and an opportunity to be heard to the client and other persons holding liens or assignments on the recovery. Such application shall be made to the justice of the trial part to which the action had been sent for trial; or, if it had not been sent to a part for trial, then to the justice presiding at the trial term calendar part of the court in which the action had been instituted; or, if no action had been instituted, then to the justice presiding at the trial term calendar part of the Supreme Court for the county in the judicial department in which the attorney making the application has an office. Upon such application, the justice, in his or her discretion, if extraordinary circumstances are found to be present, and without regard to the claimant's or plaintiff's consent, may fix as reasonable compensation for legal services rendered an amount greater than that specified in schedule A, above, provided, however, that such greater amount shall not exceed the fee fixed pursuant to the contractual arrangement, if any, between the client and the attorney. If the application be granted, the justice shall make a written order accordingly, briefly stating the reasons for granting the greater compensation; and a copy of such order shall be served on all persons entitled to receive notice of application.

(e) Nothing contained in this section shall be deemed applicable to the fixing of compensation for attorneys representing infants or other persons, where the statutes or rules provide for the fixation of such compensation by the court.

(f) Nothing contained in this section shall be deemed applicable to the fixing of compensation of attorneys for services rendered in connection with collection of first-party benefits as defined in article XVIII of the Insurance Law.

Cross References

Insurance Law, see McKinney's Book 27.

Code of Professional Responsibility, see Appendix to McKinney's Judiciary Law, Book 29.

§ 1022.32. Examiners of Reports of Guardians, Committees and Conservators Pursuant to Article 81 of the Mental Hygiene Law

(a) Appointment of Court Examiners.

(1) *Appointment.* On or before September 1 of each year, the Presiding Justice shall appoint, for each County within the Appellate Division, Fourth Department, examiners of the reports of guardians, as well as the reports of committees and conservators appointed prior to April 1, 1993.

(2) *Eligibility.*

(i) Only persons who have satisfied training and education requirements approved by the Presiding Justice shall be appointed as court examiners.

(ii) Court examiners shall maintain compliance with 22 NYCRR part 36.

(b) Duties of Court Examiners.

(1) *Generally.* In examining the report of a guardian, committee or conservator, the court examiner shall ascertain whether a guardian, committee or conservator has completed a timely and complete report as required by article 81 of the Mental Hygiene Law; whether a guardian, committee or conservator has complied with the order of appointment; and whether a guardian, committee or conservator has satisfied the duties set forth in Mental Hygiene Law § 81.20.

(2) *Initial Reports.* With respect to an initial report of a guardian, the court examiner shall file a report within 30 days of the filing of the guardian's report.

(3) *Annual Reports.* With respect to an annual report of a guardian, committee or conservator, the court examiner shall file a report within 30 days of the filing of the report of the guardian, committee or conservator.

(4) *Filing Requirements.*

(i) The court examiner shall file the court examiner's report in the office of the clerk of the court that appointed the guardian, committee or conservator, with proof of service of the report on the guardian, committee or conservator.

(ii) Within 10 days of the filing of the court examiner's report, the court examiner shall file a copy of the report with the Clerk of the Appellate Division, Fourth Department, together with proof of the filing and service required by 22 NYCRR 1000.32(b)(4)(i).

(5) *Untimely and Incomplete Reports.* In the event that a guardian, committee or conservator fails to file a timely report or files an incomplete report, the court examiner shall serve the guardian, committee or conservator with a demand for the report and shall take such actions as are necessary to compel compliance, pursuant to Mental Hygiene Law § 81.32 (c) and (d).

(6) *Examination Under Oath.* The court examiner may examine a guardian, committee, conservator or other witness under oath and reduce the testimony to writing.

(7) *Forms.* For court examiner reports, the court examiner shall use forms designated by the Appellate Division, Fourth Department.

(c) Compensation.

(1) *Initial Reports.* For the examination of an initial report, a court examiner is entitled to a fee of $100, together with reimbursement for reasonable and necessary disbursements.

(2) *Annual Reports.* For the examination of an annual report, a court examiner is entitled to reimbursement for reasonable and necessary disbursements and a fee fixed pursuant to the following fee schedule:

Closing balance of Estate examined	Fee
$5,000 and under	$150
$5001—$25,000	$200
$25,001—$50,000	$250
$50,001—$100,000	$300
$100,001—$150,000	$400
$150,001—$225,000	$500
$225,001—$350,000	$600
$350,001—$500,000	$700
$500,001—$750,000	$800
$750,001—$1,000,000	$900
Over $1,000,000	$1000

(3) The fee shall be calculated on the net value of the estate at the close of the calendar year for which the annual report has been filed. Upon a showing of extraordinary circumstances, a fee in excess of the fee fixed by the schedule may be awarded.

(4) An application for a fee for an estate with a value of $5000 or less shall be made by standard voucher and shall be approved by the Presiding Justice or the designee of the Presiding Justice.

(5) An application for a fee for an estate with a value of more than $5000 shall be set forth in the report of the court examiner and shall be approved by order of the Presiding Justice for payment by the estate. The court examiner shall serve a copy of the order approving payment on the guardian, committee or conservator, and shall file a copy of the order with the clerk of the court that appointed the guardian.

(6) A guardian, committee or conservator may apply to the Presiding Justice for review and reconsideration of any fee on the ground of excessiveness. Such application shall be in writing and shall be made within 20 days of service by the court examiner of the order directing payment of the fee from the estate.

(d) Transition.

(1) The appointment of any court examiner, appointed pursuant to former 22 NYCRR 1022.32, due to expire on March 31, 2008, shall be continued to August 31, 2008.

§ 1022.33. Attorney's Affidavit in Agency and Private Placement Adoptions

(a) Every attorney appearing for an adoptive parent, a natural parent or an adoption agency, in an adoption proceeding in the courts within this judicial department, shall, prior to the entry of an adoption decree, file with the Office of Court Administration of the State of New York and with the court in which the adoption proceeding has been initiated, a signed statement, under oath, setting forth the following information:

(1) name of attorney;

(2) association with firm (if any);

(3) business address;

(4) telephone number;

(5) docket number of adoption proceeding;

(6) court where adoption has been filed;

(7) the date and terms of every agreement, written or otherwise, between the attorney and the adoptive parents, the natural parents or anyone else on their behalf, pertaining to any compensation or thing of value paid or given or to be paid or given by or on behalf of the adoptive parents or the natural parents, including but not limited to retainer fees;

(8) the date and amount of any compensation paid or thing of value given, and the amount of total compensation to be paid or thing of value to be given to the attorney by the adoptive parents, the natural parents or by anyone else on account of or incidental to any assistance or service in connection with the proposed adoption;

(9) a brief statement of the nature of the services rendered;

(10) the name and address of any other attorney or attorneys who shared in the fees received in connection with the services, or to whom any compensation or thing of value was paid or is to be paid, directly or indirectly, by the attorney; the amount of such compensation or thing of value;

(11) the name and address of any other attorney or attorneys, if known, who received or will receive any compensation or thing of value, directly or indirectly, from the adoptive parents, natural parents, agency or other source, on account of or incidental to any assistance or service in connection with the proposed adoption; the amount of such compensation or thing of value, if known;

(12) the name and address of any other person, agency, association, corporation, institution, society or organization who received or will receive any compensation or thing of value from the attorney, directly or indirectly, on account of or incidental to any assistance or service in connection with the proposed adoption; the amount of such compensation or thing of value;

(13) the name and address, if known, of any person, agency, association, corporation, institution, society or organization to whom compensation or thing of value has been paid or given or is to be paid or given by any source for the placing out of, or on account of or incidental to assistance in arrangements for the placement or adoption of the adoptive child; the amount of such compensation or thing of value and the services performed or the purposes for which the payment was made; and

(14) a brief statement as to the date and manner in which the initial contact occurred between the attorney and the adoptive parents or natural parents with respect to the proposed adoption.

(b) Names or other information likely to identify the natural or adoptive parents or the adoptive child are to be omitted from the information to be supplied in the attorney's statement.

(c) Such statement may be filed personally by the attorney or his representative at the main office of the Office of Court Administration in the City of New York, and upon such filing he shall receive a date-stamped receipt containing the code number assigned to the original so filed. Such statement may also be filed by ordinary mail addressed to:

Office of Court Administration—
Adoption Affidavits
Post Office Box 2016
New York, New York 10008

(d) All statements filed by attorneys shall be deemed to be confidential, and the information therein contained shall not be divulged or made available for inspection or examination to any person other than the client of the attorney in the adoption proceeding, except upon written order of the presiding justice of the Appellate Division.

§ 1022.34. Admission of Attorneys

(a) **Filing of Application Papers.** Every applicant for admission to practice as an attorney and counselor at law pursuant to subdivision 1(a) or 1(b) of section 90 of the Judiciary Law may obtain the standard forms and instructions for that purpose from the clerk of the Appellate Division. Every applicant for admission to practice pursuant to subdivision 1(a) of section 90 of the Judiciary Law may obtain such forms and instructions immediately after taking the bar examination, and may file a completed application, consisting of the standard form of questionnaire and the other required papers as directed by the instructions, at any time thereafter, regardless of whether the results of the bar examination have yet been issued. As soon as the applicant shall receive a letter from the State Board of Law Examiners stating that the applicant has passed the bar examination, the applicant shall file that letter with the clerk of the Appellate Division, and if the applicant's questionnaire was verified more than 45 days prior to such filing, the

applicant shall also file a supplemental affidavit stating whether there have been any changes in the facts stated therein and setting forth any such changes.

(b) **Referral to Committee on Character and Fitness.** Every completed application shall be referred for investigation of the applicant's character and fitness to a committee on character and fitness designated by the Appellate Division of the department to which the applicant is eligible for certification by the State Board of Law Examiners after passing the bar examination, or to which the applicant is applying for admission without examination in accordance with the rules of the Court of Appeals for the admission of attorneys and counselors at law.

(c) **Quorum for Committee Action.** A majority of the entire committee shall constitute a quorum for the transaction of business by a committee on character and fitness if it consists of less than 10 members, and one-fifth of the entire committee, but not less than five members, shall constitute a quorum if it consists of 10 or more members.

(d) **Investigation and Interview.** The committee may itself conduct the required investigation, including an interview of the applicant, or it may authorize its chairman or acting chairman to designate one or more of its members to do so and to make a recommendation to the committee. The committee or the member or members thereof conducting the investigation may require the applicant to furnish such additional information or proofs of good character as the committee or such member or members may consider pertinent. The committee may commence the required investigation at any time after the applicant's completed application has been filed, except that the personal interview of an applicant for admission pursuant to subdivision 1(a) of section 90 of the Judiciary Law shall not be held until after the applicant has been notified by the State Board of Law Examiners that the applicant has passed the bar examination and has been certified to apply for admission.

(e) **Procedure Upon Recommendation of Approval.** If the committee shall approve the application following its own investigation, or if it shall accept a recommendation of approval submitted by the member or members conducting an investigation pursuant to designation, the chairman or acting chairman shall certify to the Appellate Division on behalf of the committee that the applicant possesses the requisite character and fitness.

(f) **Procedure Upon Recommendation of Disapproval, Deferral or Committee Consideration.** If the committee shall fail to approve the application following its own investigation, or following a recommendation submitted by the member or members conducting an investigation pursuant to designation that the application be disapproved or that action thereon be deferred, a hearing on the application shall be held expeditiously before the committee or a subcommittee of at least two members designated by the chairman or acting chairman. Such a hearing shall also be held if the member or members conducting an investigation pursuant to designation shall recommend consideration of the application by the committee and the committee shall fail to approve the application following such consideration.

(g) Notice of Hearing; Waiver. Unless waived in writing by the applicant, a written notice of hearing of not less than 20 days, specifying the time and place of the hearing, shall be served on the applicant. In addition, the notice of hearing shall inform the applicant of the matters to be inquired into and of the applicant's right to be represented by an attorney, and such information shall also be given to the applicant prior to the hearing if the applicant has waived notice of hearing.

(h) Procedure at Hearing. At the hearing, hearsay evidence may be received and considered and adherence to strict rules of evidence shall not be required. The applicant shall be given an opportunity to call and cross-examine witnesses and to challenge, examine and controvert any adverse evidence. Upon timely request, subpoenas for the attendance of witnesses or the production of papers shall be issued to the applicant by the clerk of the Appellate Division, the subpoena fees and mileage to be paid by the applicant.

(i) Stenographic Record or Tape Recording. A stenographic record or tape recording shall be made of the hearing, and the applicant may obtain a transcript or copy of the recording at the applicant's expense.

(j) Decision or Report Following Hearing. Where the hearing has been conducted by the committee, the committee shall render a decision, and where the hearing has been conducted by a subcommittee, the subcommittee shall render a report, within 60 days after the matter is finally submitted, unless the time is extended by consent of the applicant or order of the Appellate Division. The decision of the committee or the report of the subcommittee, as the case may be, may recommend approval or disapproval of the applicant or deferral of action on the application for a period not to exceed six months.

(k) Transmittal of Decision to Appellate Division Following Hearing Conducted by Committee. Where the hearing has been conducted by the committee, the committee shall transmit its decision to the Appellate Division, together with the appropriate certificate if it recommends approval of the applicant. If the decision recommends disapproval of the applicant or deferral of action on the application, it shall include a statement of the grounds on which it is based and a copy thereof shall be served on the applicant or the applicant's attorney.

(l) Review by Committee Following Hearing Conducted by Subcommittee. Where the hearing has been conducted by a subcommittee, the subcommittee's report and the stenographic record or tape recording of the hearing shall be referred for consideration and review to the committee, which shall render a decision thereon expeditiously. The committee's decision may confirm, reverse or modify the subcommittee's report or direct that a further hearing be held before the same or another subcommittee. If the committee's decision recommends disapproval of the applicant or deferral of action on the application, it shall include a statement of the grounds on which it is based and a copy thereof shall be served on the applicant or the applicant's attorney. The decision shall be transmitted to the Appellate Division, together with the appropriate certificate if it recommends approval of the applicant. The deliberations of the committee shall be confidential and the applicant shall not be entitled to compel disclosure thereof.

(m) Petition to Appellate Division Following Adverse Decision. If the committee's decision is adverse to the applicant, the applicant may, within 60 days after service of a copy thereof, petition the Appellate Division, in accordance with rule 9404 of the Civil Practice Law and Rules, on notice of not less than eight days served on the committee together with any supporting papers, for an order granting the application for admission to practice notwithstanding the committee's decision.

(n) Petition to Appellate Division in Case of Unreasonable Delay. In any case in which it is claimed that the committee has unreasonably delayed action on an application for admission to practice, the applicant may petition the Appellate Division, in accordance with rule 9404 of the Civil Practice Law and Rules, on notice of not less than eight days served on the committee together with any supporting papers, for an order granting the application notwithstanding the committee's failure to complete action thereon, or for other appropriate relief.

(o) Petition for Advance Ruling With Respect to Past Conduct.

(1) Any person who is a matriculated student in an approved law school, as an approved law school is defined in the rules of the Court of Appeals for the admission of attorneys and counselors at law, or who has applied for admission to such a law school, and who has previously been:

(i) convicted of a felony or misdemeanor;

(ii) suspended, removed or dismissed from public office or employment; or

(iii) dishonorably discharged from the armed services of the United States,

may petition the Appellate Division of the department in which such person resides or is employed full-time, or if such person does not reside and is not employed full-time in the State, the Appellate Division of the

Third Department, for an advance ruling, in accordance with this section, as to whether such conviction, suspension, removal or dismissal from public office or employment, or dishonorable discharge, as the case may be, would operate to disqualify the petitioner, on character grounds, from being admitted to practice as an attorney and counselor at law in this State.

(2) The petition shall include a detailed statement of the facts with respect to the petitioner's conviction, suspension, dismissal or removal from public office or employment, or dishonorable discharge, as the case may be, and of the petitioner's activities subsequent thereto which the petitioner believes bear on character and fitness to practice law.

(3) The petitioner shall also submit a completed and verified questionnaire on the standard form furnished by the committee on character and fitness, and affidavits of good moral character from two reputable persons who have known the petitioner for at least one year. In addition, the petitioner shall submit a letter from a person in authority at the approved law school in which the petitioner is a matriculated student or to which the petitioner has applied for admission, stating that such law school would retain or accept the petitioner as a student therein, as the case may be, if the petitioner's conviction, suspension, dismissal or removal from public office or employment or dishonorable discharge, as the case may be, would not operate to disqualify the petitioner from being admitted to practice as an attorney and counselor at law in this State.

(4) The petition and other papers submitted by the petitioner shall be referred to the appropriate committee on character and fitness, which shall process and investigate the petition in accordance with the procedures set forth in the preceding sections of this Part. The committee may recommend that a ruling be made either in favor of or against the petitioner, or that no ruling be made, and its recommendation shall be transmitted to the Appellate Division.

(5) A ruling made by the Appellate Division in favor of the petitioner shall determine that the petitioner's prior conviction, suspension, removal or dismissal from public office or employment, or dishonorable discharge, as the case may be, and the acts committed by the petitioner which resulted therein, would not operate to disqualify the petitioner, on character grounds, from being admitted to practice as an attorney and counselor at law in this State. Such a ruling shall have binding force throughout the State with respect to the determination thus made by it. In the event that the Appellate Division should rule against the petitioner or should refuse to make a ruling, its determination shall be without prejudice to the petitioner's right, after passing the bar examination, to apply for a favorable ruling with respect to character and fitness.

(p) Manner of Service. Service of any notice or other papers required under any of these rules may be made by mail or in the manner provided for service of a summons.

Cross References

CPLR, see McKinney's Book 7B.

Judiciary Law, see McKinney's Book 29.

§ 1022.35. Compensation of Attorneys Representing Claimants Against Lawyers' Fund for Client Protection

No attorney shall charge a fee for or accept compensation for representation of claimants against the Lawyers' Fund for Client Protection, except as approved by the trustees of the fund.

§ 1022.36. Application for Disclosure of Records Pursuant to Judiciary Law, § 90(10)

(a) An application made pursuant to Judiciary Law, section 90(10), shall consist of a notice of petition and petition returnable on the opening day of a term of this court or on the first business day of any week during the term. If the requested disclosure relates to a complaint, inquiry, investigation or proceeding involving the Office of Grievance Committees for the Fourth Judicial Department, the application shall be on notice to such office as provided by CPLR 2214(b). It shall also be served upon the subject attorney, unless the application requests, and the Presiding Justice approves, dispensing with such service.

(b) The petition shall specify:

(1) the nature and scope of the inquiry or investigation for which disclosure is sought;

(2) the papers, records or documents sought to be disclosed; and

(3) other methods, if any, of obtaining the information sought, and the reasons such methods are unavailable or impractical.

(c) Upon written request of a representative of the Lawyers' Fund for Clients' Protection certifying that a person or persons has filed a claim or claims seeking reimbursement from the Lawyers' Fund for Clients' Protection for the wrongful taking of client money or property by an attorney who has been disciplined by this Court, the offices of the Grievance Committees for the Fourth Judicial Department are authorized to disclose to the Lawyers' Fund for Clients' Protection such information as they may have on file relating thereto.

Cross References

CPLR, see McKinney's Book 7B.

Judiciary Law, see McKinney's Book 29.

PART 1023. MENTAL HYGIENE LEGAL SERVICE

§ 1023.1. Definitions

Except as otherwise appears herein, whenever used in this Part any term defined in Mental Hygiene Law § 1.03 shall have the meanings set forth therein and, in addition, the following terms shall have the following meanings:

(a) Service means the Mental Hygiene Legal Service.

(b) Director means the head of the Service referred to in Mental Hygiene Law § 47.01 or his/her duly authorized designee.

(c) Court shall mean Supreme Court, County Court or Surrogate's Court.

(d) Patient shall mean a person residing in a facility for the mentally disabled which is licensed or operated by the Department of Mental Hygiene or the Department of Correctional Services, or a person residing in any other place for whom the Service has been appointed counsel or court evaluator pursuant to Mental Hygiene Law article 81.

(e) Guardian shall mean a person or entity appointed as a guardian, standby guardian or limited guardian as provided in Surrogate's Court Procedure Act article 17–A or Mental Hygiene Law article 81.

Cross References

Mental Hygiene Law, see McKinney's Book 34A.

SCPA, see McKinney's Book 58A.

§ 1023.2. Duties of the Director

(a) With regard to patients in facilities governed by the Mental Hygiene Law:

(1) The director shall inform each patient of his or her rights to a judicial hearing, to a review pursuant to Mental Hygiene Law §§ 9.35 and 15.35, to an appeal and to be represented by the Service or by privately retained counsel.

(2) In every case in which a hearing is requested or ordered or in which an application or petition is made to the court with regard to a patient which may or may not require a hearing, the director shall investigate the patient's case, examine the patient's records, interview the patient and also, in the discretion of the director, interview other persons having information relevant to the patient's case. If the patient has counsel the court may request the director to perform any services on behalf of the patient within the scope of and consistent with the Service's statutory duties.

(3) The director shall examine the patient's facility records as often as the director deems necessary.

(4) The court may request the director to render or undertake any assistance or service on behalf of a patient consistent with the Service's statutory duties.

(5) When a hearing has not been demanded, if the director determines that the case of a patient should be heard by the court or be reviewed by a court, or court and jury, the director may, in his or her discretion, demand a hearing on behalf of such patient or may request that the case of the patient be reviewed by the court, or court and jury, in accordance with the power granted to the Service in the Mental Hygiene Law.

(6)(i) The director shall ascertain that the notices to be given to patients and other persons required under the Mental Hygiene Law have been duly served and posted and that there has been compliance with the procedures required by the Mental Hygiene Law for the hospitalization, transfer, retention and release of patients.

(ii) The director shall ascertain that all requirements of law as to patients' admissions, treatment and discharge affecting patients' rights have been complied with.

(7) The director shall review the status of every person who has been an informal patient or a voluntary patient for a period of 12 consecutive months and shall ascertain that there has been compliance with the Mental Hygiene Law. If the director finds that the patient is willing and suitable for continued hospitalization in such status he or she shall so certify in the patient's record. If the director finds that the patient is unwilling or unsuitable for continued hospitalization in such status he or she shall take whatever action he or she deems necessary in accordance with the Mental Hygiene Law.

(b) In those guardianship proceedings pursuant to Mental Hygiene Law article 81 or Surrogate's Court Procedure Act article 17–A in which the Service participates as counsel, court evaluator, guardian ad litem or party:

(1) Upon receipt of notice of application in such proceedings, the director shall:

(i) examine the papers and ascertain that the notices required to be given to parties and patients and, as far as known to the director, to other persons entitled thereto, have been duly served and that there has been due compliance with the prescribed statutory procedure;

(ii) examine the records relating to the affairs or medical or psychiatric condition of the party or patient;

(iii) interview every such party or patient, advise him or her of the nature of the proceedings and of his or her legal rights including the right to legal representation and the right to a court hearing, determine whether he or she has any objections to the proceeding or to the proposed guardian or whether he or she has any other objections;

(iv) interview any psychiatrist, examining physician or psychologist, or such other psychiatrist or physician who has knowledge of the party or patient's mental and physical condition;

(v) obtain all available information as to the extent and nature of the party or patient's assets;

(vi) obtain all available information concerning the party or patient's family, background and any other fact that may be necessary or desirable.

(2)(i) The director shall notify the court of any request for a hearing.

(ii) In the director's discretion, and in the interest of the party or patient, the director may demand a hearing.

(3) The director shall inform the party or patient of the progress and status of all proceedings.

(4) In all proceedings for the discharge of a guardian, the enforcement or modification of a guardianship order, or the approval of a guardian's report or accounting, intermediate or final, the director shall inform the party or patient of the nature of the proceeding and his or her rights. The director may perform such additional services on behalf of the party or patient as are within the scope of, and consistent with, the Service's statutory duties.

(5) The director may, in an appropriate case and in his or her discretion, apply to the court for the discharge of the guardian or the enforcement or modification of an order appointing the guardian.

(6) The director is authorized to apprise the examiners charged with the review of accounts with regard to any matter within the jurisdiction of such examiner affecting the welfare and property of a party or patient for whom a guardian has been appointed.

(7) The director shall perform such other duties and responsibilities as may be required by Mental Hygiene Law article 81.

(c) With regard to inmates, defendants or patients committed to, transferred to or placed in facilities for the mentally disabled pursuant to the Correction Law or to the Criminal Procedure Law:

(1) In all matters or proceedings in which the Service is required to be served with notice, the director shall:

(i) examine the papers, and shall ascertain that the notices required to be given have been duly served and that there has been due compliance with the prescribed procedure;

(ii) inform the inmate, defendant or patient of his or her rights including the right to a judicial hearing, to review, to appeal and to be represented by the Service or by privately retained counsel;

(iii) when a hearing has not been demanded, if the director determines that the case should be heard by the court or be reviewed by a court, or court and jury, the director may, in his or her discretion, demand a hearing or may request that the case be reviewed by the court, or court and jury;

(iv) examine the records of the inmate, defendant or patient;

(v) interview the attending psychiatrist, examining physician or psychologist who has knowledge of the condition of the inmate, defendant or patient;

(vi) interview all other persons having information relevant to the matter or proceeding; and

(vii) perform such other services on behalf of the inmate, defendant or patient as the director in his or her discretion may determine. The court may request the director to perform additional services within the scope of, and consistent with, the Service's statutory duties.

(d) With regard to applications for authorization to administer psychotropic medication and to perform surgery, electro-convulsive therapy or major medical treatment in the nature of surgery upon parties or patients in facilities:

(1) Copies of notice of such applications shall be served upon the director(s) of the Service of the judicial department in which the proceeding is brought and the director of the Service of the judicial department in which the facility is located.

(2) In all such proceedings the director shall:

(i) examine the papers, and shall ascertain that the notices required to be given have been duly served;

(ii) interview and inform the party or patient of the nature of the proceeding and of his or her rights, including the right to a judicial hearing, to appeal and to be represented by the Service or by privately retained counsel, and determine whether he or she has any objection to the proceeding;

(iii) when a hearing has not been demanded, if the director determines that the case should be heard by the court, the director may, in his or her discretion, demand a hearing on behalf of the party or patient;

(iv) examine the records of the party or patient;

(v) interview the party or patient's attending and consulting psychiatrist, physician or psychologist who has knowledge of the party or patient's condition;

(vi) interview all other persons having information relevant to the matter or proceeding; and

(vii) perform such other services on behalf of the party or patient, as the court may request or the director may determine, consistent with the Service's statutory duties.

(e) In all the foregoing proceedings, the Service shall represent the inmate, defendant, party or patient unless they otherwise have counsel or counsel has been dispensed with pursuant to Mental Hygiene Law article 81.

(f) In all the foregoing proceedings, the director may, in his or her discretion, submit briefs, affidavits, affirmations or trial memoranda, consistent with the Service's role in the proceeding.

(g) In all of the foregoing proceedings the director shall assist the directors of the Service in the other judicial departments in regard to any proceeding pending in any other judicial department which pertains to a patient residing in the Fourth Judicial Department.

Cross References

Correction Law, see McKinney's Book 10B.

Criminal Procedure Law, see McKinney's Book 11A.

Mental Hygiene Law, see McKinney's Book 34A.

SCPA, see McKinney's Book 58A.

§ 1023.3. Guardian Ad Litem and Court Evaluator

In any proceeding before the court involving a patient, the court may appoint the director as guardian ad litem or court evaluator consistent with, and within the scope of the director's statutory duties, except when the director advises the court that such appointment would create a conflict of interest with the director's duties as counsel pursuant to § 1023.2 of this Part.

§ 1023.4. Additional Psychiatric, Psychological, Medical or Expert Opinion

(a) Pursuant to Judiciary Law § 35 or any other statute, rule or regulation providing for additional opinion the director shall assist in obtaining, through a panel or otherwise, such additional opinion.

(b) No psychiatrist, psychologist, physician or other expert shall be appointed by the court if he or she is disqualified under provisions of the Mental Hygiene Law or if he or she is employed at the institution in which the patient is hospitalized or residing or to which the patient may be transferred as a result of the proceeding in which the expert is to render his or her opinion.

Cross References

Judiciary Law, see McKinney's Book 29.

Mental Hygiene Law, see McKinney's Book 34A.

§ 1023.5. Review of Proposed Transfer of Patient or of Changes of Status of Patients

(a) In every case in which it is proposed to transfer a patient from one facility to another facility or to change his or her admission status to another, the director shall review the proposed transfer or change in status.

(b) In any such case, the director, in his or her discretion, may request a hearing on behalf of the patient.

§ 1023.6. Fees

(a) When authorized by statute the director may request that the court award the Service a reasonable fee.

(b) The director's requests for fees for the services of attorneys shall not exceed the hourly rates of compensation set forth in section 35 of the Judiciary Law; and the director's requests for fees for the services of non-lawyer professionals shall not exceed the hourly rate of compensation set forth in the Unified Court System's compensation rate guidelines for court-appointed non-lawyer professionals.

(c) Fees awarded the Service shall be maintained and dispensed in accordance with law.

§ 1023.7. Records to Be Confidential.

(a) All records and files of the director in any proceedings covered by this Part shall be confidential.

(b) All such records and files of the director may be exhibited only at the discretion of the director or upon order of the court.

PART 1024.   UNIFORM CALENDAR AND PRACTICE RULES [RESCINDED]

PART 1025.   ORGANIZATION AND PROCEDURE OF COUNTY JURY BOARDS [RESCINDED]

PARTS 1026 AND 1027.   [RESCINDED]

PART 1028.   MEDICAL MALPRACTICE PANELS

§ 1028.1.   Medical Malpractice Panel Established

(a) There is hereby established in the Seventh and Eighth Judicial Districts of the Fourth Department a medical malpractice panel to facilitate the disposition of medical malpractice actions in the Supreme Court, and a separate malpractice panel in each of said judicial districts for actions against podiatrists in the Supreme Court.

(b) The presiding justice of the Appellate Division, or a designee of the presiding justice, with the assistance of the Medical Society of the State of New York, county medical societies, or the New York Academy of Medicine, shall prepare a list or lists of physicians regularly admitted to practice medicine in the State of New York, divided into lists of physicians according to the particular specialty of each, and a separate list or lists of licensed podiatrists.

(c) The presiding justice or designee shall prepare a list or lists of attorneys with trial experience, not confined, however, to the field of medical malpractice.

(d) The presiding justice or designee may add to a list or delete from a list at any time the name of a physician, podiatrist or attorney in the discretion of the presiding justice or designee.

(e) The names of physicians, podiatrists and attorneys appearing on lists compiled for a judicial district in the Fourth Judicial Department may be utilized, where practicable, in another judicial district in that department where a medical malpractice panel has been established. The names of physicians, podiatrists and attorneys from another judicial department may be utilized in the Fourth Judicial Department upon agreement of the respective presiding justices.

§§ 1028.2 to 1028.7.   [Rescinded]

PART 1029.   LICENSING OF LEGAL CONSULTANTS

§ 1029.1.   Applications for Licenses as Legal Consultants; Referral to Committee on Character and Fitness

(a) The committee on character and fitness appointed by this court for each judicial district in this department to investigate the character and fitness of applicants for admission to practice as attorneys and counselors at law in the courts of this State is hereby also authorized to investigate the qualifications and the character and fitness of applicants for licenses to practice as legal consultants pursuant to the Judiciary Law (§ 53, subd. 6) and the Rules of the Court of Appeals (22 NYCRR Part 521).

(b) Every applicant for a license to practice as a legal consultant shall complete, verify and file with the clerk of this court the standard form of questionnaire, and shall comply with all the other requirements, prescribed for that purpose by this court.

(c) Every application in this department for such a license shall be referred to the committee on character and fitness for the judicial district in which the applicant actually resides at the time of such application, and, unless otherwise ordered by the court, no such license shall be granted without a certificate from such committee that it has found that the applicant possesses the qualifications and the character and fitness required therefor.

Cross References

Judiciary Law, see McKinney's Book 29.

§ 1029.2.   Documents, Affidavits and Other Proof Required

Every applicant for a license to practice as a legal consultant shall file the following additional papers with his application:

(a) A certificate from the authority having final jurisdiction over professional discipline in the foreign country in which the applicant was admitted to practice, which shall be signed by a responsible official or one of the members of the executive body of such authority and shall be attested under the hand and seal, if any, of the clerk of such authority, and which shall certify:

(1) as to the authority's jurisdiction in such matters,

(2) as to the applicant's admission to practice in such foreign country and the date thereof and as to his good standing as an attorney or counselor at law or the equivalent therein, and

(3) as to whether any charge or complaint has ever been filed against the applicant with such authority, and, if so, the substance of each such charge or complaint and the disposition thereof.

(b) A letter of recommendation from one of the members of the executive body of such authority or from one of the judges of the highest law court or court of general original jurisdiction of such foreign country, certifying to the applicant's professional qualifications, together with a certificate under the hand and seal, if any, of the clerk of such authority or of such court, as the case may be, attesting to the office held by the person signing the letter and the genuineness of his signature.

(c) Affidavits as to the applicant's good moral character and fitness from three reputable persons residing in this State and not related to the applicant, one of whom shall be a practicing New York attorney.

(d) Affidavits from two attorneys or counselors at law or the equivalent admitted in and practicing in such foreign country, stating the nature and extent of their acquaintance with the applicant and their personal knowledge as to the nature, character and extent of the applicant's practice, and as to the applicant's good standing as an attorney or counselor at law or the equivalent in such foreign country, and the duration and continuity of such practice.

(e) Such additional evidence as the applicant may see fit to submit with respect to his educational and professional qualifications and his good moral character and fitness.

(f) A duly authenticated English translation of every paper submitted by the applicant which is not in English.

(g) A duly acknowledged instrument designating the clerk of this court the applicant's agent for service of process as provided in section 521.4(a)(2)(iii) of the Rules of the Court of Appeals.

§ 1029.3. College and Law School Certificates

A certificate shall be submitted from each college and law school attended by the applicant, setting forth the information required by forms which shall be provided to the applicant for that purpose.

§ 1029.4. Exceptional Situations

In the event that the applicant is unable to comply strictly with any of the foregoing requirements, the applicant shall set forth the reasons for such inability in an affidavit, together with a statement showing in detail the efforts made to fulfill such requirements.

§ 1029.5. Authority of Committee on Character and Fitness to Require Additional Proof

The committee on character and fitness may in any case require the applicant to submit such additional proof or information as it may deem appropriate and may also require the applicant to submit a report of the National Conference of Bar Examiners with respect to his character and qualifications.

§ 1029.6. Undertaking

Prior to taking custody of any money, securities (other than unendorsed securities in registered form), negotiable instruments, bullion, precious stones or other valuables, in the course of his practice as a legal consultant, for or on behalf of any client domiciled or residing in the United States, every person licensed to practice as a legal consultant shall obtain, and shall maintain in effect for the duration of such custody, an undertaking issued by a duly authorized surety company, and approved by a justice of this court, to assure the faithful and fair discharge of his duties and obligations arising from such custody. The undertaking shall be in an amount not less than the amount of any such money, or the fair market value of any such property other than money, of which the legal consultant shall have custody, except that this court may in any case in its discretion for good cause direct that such undertaking shall be in a greater or lesser amount. The undertaking or a duplicate original thereof shall be promptly filed by the legal consultant with the clerk of this court.

§ 1029.7. Disciplinary Procedure

(a) Disciplinary proceedings against any legal consultant shall be initiated and conducted in the same manner as prescribed by law for disciplinary proceedings against attorneys.

(b) Any committee authorized by this court to conduct preliminary investigations of charges of professional misconduct by attorneys shall have authority to conduct preliminary investigations of charges of professional misconduct or unauthorized activities on the part of any licensed legal consultant in the same manner as in investigations relating to attorneys.

§ 1029.8. Filing

Every application in this department for a license as a legal consultant, together with all the papers submitted thereon, shall upon its final disposition be filed in the office of the clerk of this court.

PART 1030.   RULES GOVERNING ELECTRONIC RECORDING OF DEPOSITIONS IN CIVIL CASES [RESCINDED]

PART 1032.   OPERATION OF LAW GUARDIAN PROGRAM

§ 1032.1.   Law Guardian Office; Law Guardian Director

(a) A law guardian office for the Fourth Judicial Department is established to ensure the provision of the highest quality of representation for children and to administer the law guardian program in a manner sensitive to local needs.

(b) The function of the law guardian office shall be to provide continuing administrative direction to the law guardian program in the Fourth Judicial Department and to secure the cooperation of local bar associations, law schools and governmental agencies in order to achieve the goal specified in subdivision (a) of this section.

(c) The law guardian office shall be administered by a law guardian director who shall be appointed by the Appellate Division and supervised by the presiding justice. The duties of the law guardian director shall include but not be limited to the following:

(1) to administer the law guardian program office in accordance with the law and these rules;

(2) with the approval of the presiding justice and in consultation with the departmental advisory committee, to implement standards, guidelines and procedures for the improvement of the law guardian program in the Fourth Judicial Department;

(3) in conjunction with local family courts, local bar associations, law schools or any other competent organization and in consultation with the departmental advisory committee, to provide a continuing program of law guardian training and education that will allow applicant attorneys to satisfy requirements for designation to the panel, and to improve and maintain the professional competence of attorneys serving as law guardians;

(4) to consult with the law guardian directors in the First, Second and Third Judicial Departments and with the Office of Court Administration to coordinate the operation of the programs in each department; and

(5) to prepare the annual report on the operation of the law guardian program in the Fourth Department.

§ 1032.2.   Departmental Advisory Committee

(a) The presiding justice shall appoint a chairperson and the members of the departmental advisory committee, which shall consist of at least one Supreme Court judge, one Family Court judge, one law guardian engaged in private practice, one representative of a family and child care agency, one law school professor, one county attorney, one person who is not an attorney and who is not an employee of any branch of government, a member of the staff of the Appellate Division who shall be a nonvoting member and such other members as the presiding justice deems necessary to enable the committee to perform the functions specified in this section. The term of appointment shall be staggered and for a period of two years subject to reappointment by the presiding justice.

(b) The departmental advisory committee may make recommendations to the presiding justice and the law guardian director with respect to:

(1) training of law guardians;

(2) the promulgation of rules, standards and administrative procedures for effective law guardian representation in the department;

(3) procedures necessary to insure that panel members are designated and assigned in a fair and impartial manner, having regard to the nature and difficulty of each case and the special qualifications of panel members; and

(4) procedures necessary to improve the operation thereof throughout the department.

§ 1032.3.   Members of Departmental Advisory Committee Are Volunteers.

Each member of the departmental advisory committee is a volunteer expressly authorized to participate in a State-sponsored volunteer program as provided in section 17(1) of the Public Officers Law.

§ 1032.4.   Law Guardian Panel

(a) Initial designation to law guardian panel.

(1) *Eligibility*. An attorney is eligible for designation as a member of the law guardian panel of a county of this department when the attorney:

(i) is a member in good standing of the Bar of the State of New York and in any other jurisdiction in which the attorney is admitted to the practice of law;

(ii) has attended 12 hours of law guardian introductory training conducted by the law guardian program; and

(iii) has obtained experience in law guardian representation by appearing either as attorney of record, associate counsel or co-counsel for a party in a minimum of three proceedings under article 3, article 6, article 7, or article 10 of the Family Court Act; or has been found by a Family Court judge to be well qualified by reason of education, training or substantial trial experience.

(2) *Application.* An attorney may, at any time, apply for membership on a county law guardian panel in this department. Such application shall be in the form prescribed by the Appellate Division and shall be submitted for consideration to the supervising judge of Family Court in those counties where the supervising judge sits and in other counties to the senior Family Court judge.

(3) *Action by the Family Court judge.* The supervising or senior Family Court judge shall review the application and take one of the following actions:

(i) When the judge determines that the attorney has met the eligibility requirements of paragraph (1) of this subdivision and is otherwise qualified to provide appropriate representation for children, the judge shall approve the application and forward it for consideration by the Appellate Division. If the judge finds the attorney to be well qualified under subparagraph (1) (iii) of this subdivision, the judge shall submit the basis of the finding in writing to the Appellate Division.

(ii) When the judge determines for good cause that an attorney should not be designated as a law guardian panel member, the judge shall deny the application and state the reason for the denial in writing. The attorney may request reconsideration of such denial by the Appellate Division.

(4) *Waiver of eligibility requirements.* The Appellate Division may waive the eligibility requirements set forth in subparagraphs (1)(ii) and (iii) of this subdivision when an attorney requests such waiver in writing, endorsed by the supervising or senior Family Court judge; and

(i)[1] the attorney has sufficient relevant experience in the practice of law to demonstrate clearly the ability to represent children effectively; provided, however, that an attorney added to a law guardian panel based upon a waiver granted pursuant to this paragraph must attend 12 hours of introductory training conducted by the law guardian program within one year of designation.

(5) *Action by the Appellate Division.* Upon receipt of the application and the recommendation of the supervising or senior Family Court judge that an attorney be placed on the law guardian panel, the Appellate Division shall:

(i) designate the attorney to a county panel; or

(ii) request further information from the applicant, which may include an interview; or

(iii) decline to designate the attorney to a county panel. If not designated to a county panel, the

attorney shall be informed of the basis of the decision and may request reconsideration.

(b) Redesignation of panels.

(1) The Appellate Division shall, on or before April 1 of each year, designate an annual law guardian panel for each county in the department from lists of attorneys who have been found competent by the supervising judge of Family Court in those counties where the supervising Family Court judge sits and in other counties by the senior Family Court judge upon consideration of the following factors:

(i) legal knowledge;

(ii) rapport with clients;

(iii) vigorous advocacy;

(iv) case preparation; and

(v) courtroom demeanor.

(2) To be eligible for redesignation to a panel a law guardian shall:

(i) have completed within the preceding two years at least one training program conducted by the law guardian program. If prior approval is obtained from the Appellate Division, attendance at an appropriate educational and training program sponsored or cosponsored by another New York State Judicial Department, bar association, law school or legal aid society, may be substituted for training conducted by the law guardian program; and

(ii) have been found competent by the supervising or senior Family Court judge of the county upon consideration of the factors of law guardian competency set forth in subparagraph (1)(i)—(v) of this subdivision.

1 So in original. No par. (ii) has been enacted.

§ 1032.5. Assignment of Law Guardians

(a) Any attorney designated to a law guardian panel in the Fourth Department may be assigned as a law guardian in any adjoining county in the Fourth Department and in any other county not adjoining may be assigned upon prior approval of the Appellate Division.

(b) No law guardian shall be assigned to represent a minor when such assignment involves an ethical conflict of interest. Attorneys serving in the following positions or employed by the following offices, if otherwise eligible for designation, shall disclose such employment to the court: judge or justice of a city, town or village court; law clerk to a judge or justice; district attorney; county attorney; and municipal corporation counsel. Attorneys serving in any of the above positions or employed by any of the above offices, shall not be appointed as a law guardian in proceedings in which, by virtue of such position or employment, they have similar or equal subject matter jurisdiction or, in the county in which they are employed, the office in which they are employed participates as a party.

(c) Removal from law guardian panel. An attorney may request that his or her name be removed from a law guardian panel. Upon receipt of such request, the Appellate Division shall remove the attorney's name from the panel. A Family Court judge, Supreme Court justice or surrogate may, at any time, recommend to the Appellate Division the removal of an attorney's name from a law guardian panel for good cause, including, but not limited to, misconduct, lack of diligence in performing law guardian assignments, or unwillingness to serve. An attorney whose name appears on a law guardian panel for two consecutive years and who has not served as a law guardian shall be removed from the list by the Appellate Division. The Appellate Division may, on its own motion at any time, remove an attorney's name from an annual law guardian panel. Regardless of the basis for removal from the law guardian panel, an attorney may request reconsideration of such removal.

(d) Assignment of counsel by the Supreme or a Surrogate's Court to represent children in proceedings wherein compensation is authorized pursuant to Judiciary Law § 35 (7) shall be made from the panel designated pursuant to subdivision 1032.4.

§ 1032.6. Compensation

(a) A law guardian seeking compensation for services rendered pursuant to Family Court Act § 245 shall submit a claim for approval to the Family Court on forms authorized by the Chief Administrator of the Courts. The Family Court shall certify the claim, subject to appropriate modifications, and shall forward the claim to the Appellate Division for approval and certification to the Comptroller for payment. When a claim is received by the Appellate Division more than 90 days after the law guardian has completed the assignment, the law guardian shall provide an affidavit

stating that the law guardian has not been paid for the services rendered, that a claim has not been submitted previously, and the reasons why the claim was not received within the 90-day period. The Appellate Division may, in the exercise of its discretion, disapprove any claim not received with the 90-day period.

(b) Compensation in excess of the limits established by Family Court Act § 245 and Judiciary Law § 35 shall not be approved absent a showing of extraordinary circumstances. A law guardian submitting a claim for compensation in excess of the statutory limits shall submit, with the claim, an affidavit detailing the nature of the proceeding in which the services were rendered, the services rendered, the time expended, the expenses incurred and the facts that would support a finding of extraordinary circumstances. Absent such an affidavit, a fee in excess of the statutory limits shall not be approved.

(c) In determining whether there are extraordinary circumstances warranting compensation in excess of the statutory limits, the Family Court and the Appellate Division shall consider:

(1) Whether the matter involved unusually complex factual or legal issues;

(2) Whether a novel issue of law, which required extensive legal research was involved;

(3) Whether a lengthy trial or other in-court proceedings were necessary; and

(4) Any other unique or unusual circumstances.

The expenditure of time alone, however, shall not constitute an extraordinary circumstance.

(d) When a law guardian anticipates that expenses, as authorized pursuant to Family Court Act § 245 and Judiciary Law § 35, will exceed $300, the law guardian shall, before incurring such expenses, obtain approval of the Family Court and the Appellate Division.

PART 1039. MISCELLANEOUS RULES

§ 1039. Notification of Right to Appeal to Defendants Appearing Pro Se

(a) Upon a judgment of conviction or an order denying a motion pursuant to Criminal Procedure Law section 440.10 or 440.20, if a defendant has appeared pro se, the trial court shall advise the defendant of the right to appeal or to move for permission to appeal, as the case may be, and of the right of a defendant to move for permission to proceed on appeal as a poor person. If the defendant so requests, the clerk shall promptly prepare, file and serve a notice of appeal on behalf of the defendant.

(b) Upon an order affirming or modifying a judgment of conviction or an order affirming an appeal from an order denying a motion for permission to

appeal pursuant to Criminal Procedure Law section 460.15, a defendant appearing pro se shall be served with a copy of the order, with notice of entry, together with the following notice:

NOTICE AS TO FURTHER APPEAL

Pursuant to Criminal Procedure Law section 460.20, a defendant has the right to apply for leave to appeal to the Court of Appeals. A defendant may apply for leave to appeal from an order of the Appellate Division by making an application to the Chief Judge of the Court of Appeals, by submitting the application to the Clerk of the Court of Appeals, or by making application to a Justice of the Appellate Division of this Department. A defendant may apply for leave to appeal from an order of any other intermediate appellate court by making an application to the Chief Judge of the Court of Appeals. Such application shall be submitted to the Clerk of the Court of Appeals within 30 days after service of a copy of the order of the intermediate appellate court. Denial of the initial application for leave to appeal is final, and no further application may be made to any other Judge or Justice (see, 22 NYCRR 500.10; 1000.13 [p]).

(c) Upon an order affirming or modifying a judgment denying or dismissing a petition for a writ of habeas corpus, a petitioner proceeding pro se shall be served with a copy of the order, with notice of entry, together with the following notice:

NOTICE AS TO FURTHER APPEAL

A petitioner may appeal to the Court of Appeals as a right, pursuant to CPLR 5601 (a) if two justices dissent, or pursuant to CPLR 5601 (b) if the provisions of this subdivision are met. The appeal shall be taken within 30 days of service of the order of the Appellate Division, with notice of entry, by serving all adverse parties with a notice of appeal and filing the notice of appeal in the Office of Clerk of the court where the judgment or order appealed to the Appellate Division was entered.

An appeal from any other order of the Appellate Division determining the appeal may be taken to the Court of Appeals only by permission pursuant to CPLR 5602. An application for permission to appeal may be made to the Appellate Division or to the Court of Appeals. The application to the Court of Appeals may be made either directly or following refusal by the appellate division. The application shall be made within 30 days of the service of a copy of the order of the Appellate Division, with notice of entry (see, 22 NYCRR 500.11 [d]; 1000.13 [p]).

§§ 1039.1, 1039.2. [Rescinded]

§ 1039.3. [Repealed]

§§ 1039.4 to 1039.16. [Rescinded]

PART 1040. ORDERS

§ 1040.1. Committee Inquiries

Upon reading chapter 877 of the Laws of 1976, which amended section 160.50 of the Criminal Procedure law and added a new section 160.60 thereto, and also amended section 296 of the Executive Law of the State of New York.

It is hereby ORDERED, That the Committees on Character and Fitness appointed by this court pursuant to CPLR 9401 to investigate applicants for admission to the bar may continue to inquire concerning any criminal actions or proceedings involving the applicant, including actions or proceedings which were terminated in the applicant's favor, and may continue to require the applicants to answer questions and give information with respect to such matters.

DATED AND ENTERED: December 21, 1976

Cross References

CPLR, see McKinney's Book 7B.

Criminal Procedure Law, see McKinney's Book 11A.

Executive Law, see McKinney's Book 18.

§ 1040.2. Committee Participation

Members of the Committees on Character and Fitness, as volunteers, are expressly authorized to participate in a State-sponsored volunteer program within the meaning of subdivision 1 of section 17 of the Public Officers Law.

Cross References

Public Officers Law, see McKinney's Book 46.

SUPREME COURT, APPELLATE DIVISION, ALL DEPARTMENTS

Including Amendments Received Through September 15, 2008

Westlaw Electronic Research

These rules may be searched electronically on Westlaw® *in the NY–RULES database; updates to these rules may be found on* Westlaw *in NY–RULESUP-DATES. For search tips and a summary of database content, consult the* Westlaw *Scope Screens for each database.*

Table of Features

PART 1100. UNIFORM PROCEDURES FOR APPEALS FROM PRETRIAL FINDINGS OF MENTAL RETARDATION IN CAPITAL CASES

Table of Sections

§ 1100.1. General

This Part shall govern the procedure for an expedited appeal by the People to the Appellate Division, pursuant to Criminal Procedure Law 400.27(12)(f) and 450.20(10), of an order by a superior court finding a defendant charged with Murder in the First Degree to be mentally retarded.

§ 1100.2. Procedure

(a) Upon filing the notice of appeal, the People shall give notice to the Appellate Division that an appeal is pending pursuant to Criminal Procedure Law 400.27(12)(f) and request that an expedited briefing schedule be set.

(b) The Appellate Division shall establish an expedited briefing schedule for the appeal. Briefs may be typewritten or reproduced. Both the People and the defendant shall file nine copies of a brief, and one copy of the brief shall be served on opposing counsel.

(c) The appeal may be taken on one original record, which shall include copies of the indictment, the motion papers, the minutes of, and all exhibits in, the hearing on mental retardation held in the superior court, the court's decision and order, and the notice of appeal.

(d) The Appellate Division shall give preference to the hearing of an appeal perfected pursuant to this Part and shall determine the appeal as expeditiously as possible.

§ 1100.3. Representation by Court–Assigned Counsel in the Appellate Division

In any appeal by the People from an order pursuant to this Part, the Appellate Division shall assign counsel to represent a defendant who is represented in the superior court by court-assigned counsel, and may direct that the court-assigned counsel in the superior court represent the defendant on appeal.

PART 1200.   DISCIPLINARY RULES OF THE CODE OF PROFESSIONAL RESPONSIBILITY

The Disciplinary Rules of the Code of Professional Responsibility, promulgated as joint rules of the Appellate Divisions of the Supreme Court effective September 1, 1990, are now Part 1200 of Title 22 of New York Codes, Rules and Regulations (NYCRR).

Table of Sections

§ 1200.1. Definitions*

(a) Differing interests include every interest that will adversely affect either the judgment or the loyalty of a lawyer to a client, whether it be a conflicting, inconsistent, diverse, or other interest.

(b) Law firm includes, but is not limited to, a professional legal corporation, a limited liability company or partnership engaged in the practice of law, the legal department of a corporation or other organization and a qualified legal assistance organization.

(c) Person includes a corporation, an association, a trust, a partnership, and any other organization or legal entity.

(d) Professional legal corporation means a corporation, or an association treated as a corporation, authorized by law to practice law for profit.

(e) State includes the District of Columbia, Puerto Rico, and other Federal territories and possessions.

(f) Tribunal includes all courts, arbitrators and other adjudicatory bodies.

(g) [Reserved]

(h) Qualified legal assistance organization means an office or organization of one of the four types listed in section 1200.8(d)(1) through (4), inclusive, that meets all the requirements thereof.

(i) Fraud does not include conduct, although characterized as fraudulent by statute or administrative rule, which lacks an element of scienter, deceit, intent to mislead, or knowing failure to correct misrepresentations which can be reasonably expected to induce detrimental reliance by another.

(j) Domestic relations matters means representation of a client in a claim, action or proceeding, or preliminary to the filing of a claim, action or proceeding, in either Supreme Court or Family Court, or in any court of appellate jurisdiction, for divorce, separation, annulment, custody, visitation, maintenance, child support, or alimony, or to enforce or modify a judgment or order in connection with any such claims, actions or proceedings.

(k) "Advertisement" means any public or private communication made by or on behalf of a lawyer or law firm about that lawyer or law firm's services, the primary purpose of which is for the retention of the lawyer or law firm. It does not include communications to existing clients or other lawyers.

(l) "Computer-accessed communication" means any communication made by or on behalf of a lawyer or law firm that is disseminated through the use of a computer or related electronic device, including, but not limited to, web sites, weblogs, search engines, electronic mail, banner advertisements, pop-up and pop-under advertisements, chat rooms, list servers, instant messaging, or other internet presences, and any attachments or links related thereto.

* "Confidence" and "Secret" are defined in section 1200.19(a) of this Part. "Sexual relations" is defined in section 1200.29–(a) of this Part. "Copy" is defined in section 1200.41(d)(10) of this Part.

§ 1200.2. [DR 1–101] Maintaining Integrity and Competence of the Legal Profession

(a) A lawyer is subject to discipline if the lawyer has made a materially false statement in, or has deliberately failed to disclose a material fact requested in connection with, the lawyer's application for admission to the bar.

(b) A lawyer shall not further the application for admission to the bar of another person that the lawyer knows to be unqualified in respect to character, education, or other relevant attribute.

§ 1200.3. [DR 1–102] Misconduct

(a)[1] A lawyer or law firm shall not:

(1) Violate a disciplinary rule.

(2) Circumvent a disciplinary rule through actions of another.

(3) Engage in illegal conduct that adversely reflects on the lawyer's honesty, trustworthiness or fitness as a lawyer.

(4) Engage in conduct involving dishonesty, fraud, deceit, or misrepresentation.

(5) Engage in conduct that is prejudicial to the administration of justice.

(6) Unlawfully discriminate in the practice of law, including in hiring, promoting or otherwise determining conditions of employment, on the basis of age, race, creed, color, national origin, sex, disability, marital status, or sexual orientation. Where there is a tribunal with jurisdiction to hear a complaint, if timely brought, other than a Departmental Disciplinary Committee, a complaint based on unlawful discrimination shall be brought before such tribunal in the first instance. A certified copy of a determination by such a tribunal, which has become final and enforceable, and as to which the right to judicial or appellate review has been exhausted, finding that the lawyer has engaged in an unlawful discriminatory practice shall constitute *prima facie* evidence of professional misconduct in a disciplinary proceeding.

(7) Engage in any other conduct that adversely reflects on the lawyer's fitness as a lawyer.

[1] So in original. No par. (b) has been enacted.

§ 1200.4. [DR 1–103] Disclosure of Information to Authorities

(a) A lawyer possessing knowledge, (1) not protected as a confidence or secret, or (2), not gained in the lawyer's capacity as a member of a bona fide lawyer assistance or similar program or committee, of a violation of section 1200.3 of this Part that raises a substantial question as to another lawyer's honesty, trustworthiness or fitness as a lawyer shall report such knowledge to a tribunal or other authority empowered to investigate or act upon such violation.

(b) A lawyer possessing knowledge or evidence, not protected as a confidence or secret, concerning another lawyer or a judge shall reveal fully such knowledge or evidence upon proper request of a tribunal or other authority empowered to investigate or act upon the conduct of lawyers or judges.

§ 1200.5. [DR 1–104] Responsibilities of a Partner or Supervisory Lawyer and Subordinate Lawyers

(a) A law firm shall make reasonable efforts to ensure that all lawyers in the firm conform to the disciplinary rules.

(b) A lawyer with management responsibility in the law firm or direct supervisory authority over another lawyer shall make reasonable efforts to ensure that the other lawyer conforms to the disciplinary rules.

(c) A law firm shall adequately supervise, as appropriate, the work of partners, associates and nonlawyers who work at the firm. The degree of supervision required is that which is reasonable under the circumstances, taking into account factors such as the experience of the person whose work is being supervised, the amount of work involved in a particular matter, and the likelihood that ethical problems might arise in the course of working on the matter.

(d) A lawyer shall be responsible for a violation of the disciplinary rules by another lawyer or for the conduct of a nonlawyer employed or retained by or associated with the lawyer that would be a violation of the disciplinary rules if engaged in by a lawyer if:

(1) The lawyer orders, or directs the specific conduct, or, with knowledge of the specific conduct, ratifies it; or

(2) The lawyer is a partner in the law firm in which the other lawyer practices or the nonlawyer is employed, or has supervisory authority over the other lawyer or the nonlawyer, and knows of such conduct, or in the exercise or reasonable management or supervisory authority should have known of the conduct so that reasonable remedial action could be or could have been taken at a time when its consequences could be or could have been avoided or mitigated.

(e) A lawyer shall comply with these Disciplinary Rules notwithstanding that the lawyer acted at the direction of another person.

(f) A subordinate lawyer does not violate these Disciplinary Rules if that lawyer acts in accordance with a supervisory lawyer's reasonable resolution of an arguable question of professional duty.

§ 1200.5–a. [DR 1–105] Disciplinary Authority and Choice of Law

(a) A lawyer admitted to practice in this state is subject to the disciplinary authority of this state, regardless of where the lawyer's conduct occurs. A lawyer may be subject to the disciplinary authority of both this state and another jurisdiction where the lawyer is admitted for the same conduct.

(b) In any exercise of the disciplinary authority of this state, the rules of professional conduct to be applied shall be as follows:

(1) For conduct in connection with a proceeding in a court before which a lawyer has been admitted to practice (either generally or for purposes of that proceeding), the rules to be applied shall be the rules of the jurisdiction in which the court sits, unless the rules of the court provide otherwise; and

(2) For any other conduct:

(i) If the lawyer is licensed to practice only in this state, the rules to be applied shall be the rules of this state, and

(ii) If the lawyer is licensed to practice in this state and another jurisdiction, the rules to be applied shall be the rules of the admitting jurisdiction in which the lawyer principally practices; provided, however, that if particular conduct clearly has its predominant effect in another jurisdiction in which the lawyer is licensed to practice, the rules of that jurisdiction shall be applied to that conduct.

§ 1200.5–b. [DR 1–106] Responsibilities Regarding Nonlegal Services

(a) With respect to lawyers or law firms providing nonlegal services to clients or other persons:

(1) A lawyer or law firm that provides nonlegal services to a person that are not distinct from legal services being provided to that person by the lawyer or law firm is subject to these Disciplinary Rules with respect to the provision of both legal and nonlegal services.

(2) A lawyer or law firm that provides nonlegal services to a person that are distinct from legal services being provided to that person by the lawyer or law firm is subject to these Disciplinary Rules with respect to the nonlegal services if the person receiving the services could reasonably believe that the nonlegal services are the subject of an attorney-client relationship.

(3) A lawyer or law firm that is an owner, controlling party or agent of, or that is otherwise affiliated with, an entity that the lawyer or law firm knows to be providing nonlegal services to a person is subject to these Disciplinary Rules with respect to the nonlegal services if the person receiving the services could

reasonably believe that the nonlegal services are the subject of an attorney-client relationship.

(4) For purposes of sections 1200.5–b(a)(2) and (a)(3), it will be presumed that the person receiving nonlegal services believes the services to be the subject of an attorney-client relationship unless the lawyer or law firm has advised the person receiving the services in writing that the services are not legal services and that the protection of an attorney-client relationship does not exist with respect to the nonlegal services, or if the interest of the lawyer or law firm in the entity providing nonlegal services is de minimis.

(b) Notwithstanding the provisions of section 1200.5–b(a), a lawyer or law firm that is an owner, controlling party, agent, or is otherwise affiliated with an entity that the lawyer or law firm knows is providing nonlegal services to a person shall not permit any nonlawyer providing such services or affiliated with that entity to direct or regulate the professional judgment of the lawyer or law firm in rendering legal services to any person, or to cause the lawyer or law firm to compromise its duty under sections 1200.19(b) and (d) with respect to the confidences and secrets of a client receiving legal services.

(c) For purposes of this section, "nonlegal services" shall mean those services that lawyers may lawfully provide and that are not prohibited as an unauthorized practice of law when provided by a nonlawyer.

§ 1200.5–c. [DR 1–107] Contractual Relationship Between Lawyers and Nonlegal Professionals

(a) The practice of law has an essential tradition of complete independence and uncompromised loyalty to those it serves. Recognizing this tradition, clients of lawyers practicing in New York State are guaranteed "independent professional judgment and undivided loyalty uncompromised by conflicts of interest".[1] Indeed, these guarantees represent the very foundation of the profession and allow and foster its continued role as a protector of the system of law. Therefore, a lawyer must remain completely responsible for his or her own independent professional judgment, maintain the confidences and secrets of clients, preserve funds of clients and third parties in his or her control, and otherwise comply with the legal and ethical principles governing lawyers in New York State.

Multi–disciplinary practice between lawyers and nonlawyers is incompatible with the core values of the legal profession and therefore, a strict division between services provided by lawyers and those provided by nonlawyers is essential to protect those values. However, a lawyer or law firm may enter into and maintain a contractual relationship with a nonlegal professional or nonlegal professional service firm for the purpose of offering to the public, on a systematic and continuing basis, legal services performed by the lawyer or law firm, as well as other nonlegal profes-

sional services, notwithstanding the provisions of section 1200.20(a), provided that:

1. The profession of the nonlegal professional or nonlegal professional service firm is included in a list jointly established and maintained by the Appellate Divisions pursuant to Section 1205.3 of the Joint Appellate Division rules.

2. The lawyer or law firm neither grants to the nonlegal professional or nonlegal professional service firm, nor permits such person or firm to obtain, hold or exercise, directly or indirectly, any ownership or investment interest in, or managerial or supervisory right, power or position in connection with the practice of law by the lawyer or law firm, nor, as provided in section 1200.8(b)(1), shares legal fees with a nonlawyer or receives or gives any monetary or other tangible benefit for giving or receiving a referral; and

3. The fact that the contractual relationship exists is disclosed by the lawyer or law firm to any client of the lawyer or law firm before the client is referred to the nonlegal professional service firm, or to any client of the nonlegal professional service firm before that client receives legal services from the lawyer or law firm; and the client has given informed written consent and has been provided with a copy of the "Statement of Client's Rights in Cooperative Business Arrangements" pursuant to section 1205.4 of the Joint Appellate Divisions rules.

(b) For purposes of section 1205–c(a):

(1) Each profession on the list maintained pursuant to a joint rule of the Appellate Divisions shall have been designated sua sponte, or approved by the Appellate Divisions upon application of a member of a nonlegal profession or nonlegal professional service firm, upon a determination that the profession is composed of individuals who, with respect to their profession:

(a) have been awarded a Bachelor's Degree or its equivalent from an accredited college or university, or have attained an equivalent combination of educational credit from such a college or university and work experience;

(b) are licensed to practice the profession by an agency of the State of New York or the United States Government; and

(c) are required under penalty of suspension or revocation of license to adhere to a code of ethical conduct that is reasonably comparable to that of the legal profession.

(2) The term "ownership or investment interest" shall mean any such interest in any form of debt or equity, and shall include any interest commonly considered to be an interest accruing to or enjoyed by an owner or investor.

(c) Section 1200.5–c(a) shall not apply to relationships consisting solely of nonexclusive reciprocal referral agreements or understandings between a law-yer or law firm and a nonlegal professional or nonlegal professional service firm.

(d) Notwithstanding section 1200.17(a), a lawyer or law firm may allocate costs and expenses with a nonlegal professional or nonlegal professional service firm pursuant to a contractual relationship permitted by section 1200.5–c(a), provided the allocation reason-ably reflects only the costs and expenses incurred or expected to be incurred by each.

1 "Statement of Client's Rights" 22 NYCRR Part 1210.

§ 1200.6. [DR 2–101] Advertising

(a) A lawyer or law firm shall not use or dissemi-nate or participate in the use or dissemination of any advertisement that:

(1) contains statements or claims that are false, deceptive or misleading; or

(2) violates a disciplinary rule.

(b) Subject to the provisions of subdivision (a) of this section, an advertisement may include information as to:

(1) legal and nonlegal education, degrees and other scholastic distinctions, dates of admission to any bar; areas of the law in which the lawyer or law firm practices, as authorized by this Part; public offices and teaching positions held; publications of law relat-ed matters authored by the lawyer; memberships in bar associations or other professional societies or or-ganizations, including offices and committee assign-ments therein; foreign language fluency; and bona fide professional ratings;

(2) names of clients regularly represented, provided that the client has given prior written consent;

(3) bank references; credit arrangements accepted; prepaid or group legal services programs in which the lawyer or law firm participates; nonlegal services provided by the lawyer or law firm or by an entity owned and controlled by the lawyer or law firm; the existence of contractual relationships between the law-yer or law firm and a nonlegal professional or nonlegal professional service firm, to the extent permitted by section 1200.5–c of this Part and the nature and extent of services available through those contractual rela-tionships; and

(4) legal fees for initial consultation; contingent fee rates in civil matters when accompanied by a state-ment disclosing the information required by subdivi-sion (p) of this section; range of fees for legal and nonlegal services, provided that there be available to the public free of charge a written statement clearly describing the scope of each advertised service; hour-ly rates; and fixed fees for specified legal and nonle-gal services.

(c) An advertisement shall not:

(1) include an endorsement of, or testimonial about, a lawyer or law firm from a client with respect to a matter that is still pending;

(2) include a paid endorsement of, or testimonial about, a lawyer or law firm without disclosing that the person is being compensated therefor;

(3) include the portrayal of a judge, the portrayal of a fictitious law firm, the use of a fictitious name to refer to lawyers not associated together in a law firm, or otherwise imply that lawyers are associated in a law firm if that is not the case;

(4) use actors to portray the lawyer, members of the law firm, or clients, or utilize depictions of fiction-alized events or scenes, without disclosure of same;

(5) rely on techniques to obtain attention that dem-onstrate a clear and intentional lack of relevance to the selection of counsel, including the portrayal of lawyers exhibiting characteristics clearly unrelated to legal competence;

(6) be made to resemble legal documents; or

(7) utilize a nickname, moniker, motto or trade name that implies an ability to obtain results in a matter.

(d) An advertisement that complies with subdivi-sion (e) of this section may contain the following:

(1) statements that are reasonably likely to create an expectation about results the lawyer can achieve;

(2) statements that compare the lawyer's services with the services of other lawyers;

(3) testimonials or endorsements of clients, where not prohibited by subdivision (c)(1) of this section, and of former clients; or

(4) statements describing or characterizing the quality of the lawyer's or law firm's services.

(e) It is permissible to provide the information set forth in subdivision (d) of this section provided:

(1) its dissemination does not violate subdivision (a) of this section;

(2) it can be factually supported by the lawyer or law firm as of the date on which the advertisement is published or disseminated; and

(3) it is accompanied by the following disclaimer: "Prior results do not guarantee a similar outcome."

(f) Every advertisement other than those appear-ing in a radio or television advertisement or in a directory, newspaper, magazine or other periodical (and any websites related thereto), or made in person pursuant to section 1200.8(a)(1) of this Part, shall be labeled "Attorney Advertising" on the first page, or on the home page in the case of a web site. If the communication is in the form of a self-mailing bro-chure or postcard, the words "Attorney Advertising" shall appear therein. In the case of electronic mail, the subject line shall contain the notation "ATTORNEY ADVERTISING."

(**g**) A lawyer or law firm shall not utilize:

(1) a pop-up or pop-under advertisement in connection with computer- accessed communications, other than on the lawyer or law firm's own web site or other internet presence; or

(2) meta tags or other hidden computer codes that, if displayed, would violate a disciplinary rule.

(**h**) All advertisements shall include the name, principal law office address and telephone number of the lawyer or law firm whose services are being offered.

(**i**) Any words or statements required by this rule to appear in an advertisement must be clearly legible and capable of being read by the average person, if written, and intelligible if spoken aloud.

(**j**) A lawyer or law firm advertising any fixed fee for specified legal services shall, at the time of fee publication, have available to the public a written statement clearly describing the scope of each advertised service, which statement shall be available to the client at the time of retainer for any such service. Such legal services shall include all those services which are recognized as reasonable and necessary under local custom in the area of practice in the community where the services are performed.

(**k**) All advertisements shall be pre-approved by the lawyer or law firm and a copy shall be retained for a period of not less than three years following its initial dissemination. Any advertisement contained in a computer-accessed communication shall be retained for a period of not less than one year. A copy of the contents of any website covered by this section shall be preserved upon the initial publication of the web site, any major web site redesign, or a meaningful and extensive content change, but in no event less frequently than once every 90 days.

(*l*) If a lawyer or law firm advertises a range of fees or an hourly rate for services, the lawyer or law firm shall not charge more than the fee advertised for such services. If a lawyer or law firm advertises a fixed fee for specified legal services, or performs services described in a fee schedule, the lawyer or law firm shall not charge more than the fixed fee for such stated legal service as set forth in the advertisement or fee schedule, unless the client agrees in writing that the services performed or to be performed were not legal services referred to or implied in the advertisement or in the fee schedule and, further, that a different fee arrangement shall apply to the transaction.

(**m**) Unless otherwise specified in the advertisement, if a lawyer publishes any fee information authorized under this disciplinary rule in a publication which is published more frequently than once per month, the lawyer shall be bound by any representation made therein for a period of not less than 30 days

after such publication. If a lawyer publishes any fee information authorized under this rule in a publication which is published once per month or less frequently, the lawyer shall be bound by any representation made therein until the publication of the succeeding issue. If a lawyer publishes any fee information authorized under this rule in a publication which has no fixed date for publication of a succeeding issue, the lawyer shall be bound by any representation made therein for a reasonable period of time after publication, but in no event less than 90 days.

(**n**) Unless otherwise specified, if a lawyer broadcasts any fee information authorized under this rule, the lawyer shall be bound by any representation made therein for a period of not less than 30 days after such broadcast.

(**o**) A lawyer shall not compensate or give any thing of value to representatives of the press, radio, television or other communication medium in anticipation of or in return for professional publicity in a news item.

(**p**) All advertisements that contain information about the fees charged by the lawyer or law firm, including those indicating that in the absence of a recovery no fee will be charged, shall comply with the provisions of Judiciary Law § 488(3).

§ 1200.7. [DR 2–102] Professional Notices, Letterheads, and Signs

(**a**) A lawyer or law firm may use internet web sites, professional cards, professional announcement cards, office signs, letterheads or similar professional notices or devices, provided the same do not violate any statute or court rule, and are in accordance with section 1200.6 of this Part, including the following:

(1) A professional card of a lawyer identifying the lawyer by name and as a lawyer, and giving addresses, telephone numbers, the name of the law firm, and any information permitted under sections 1200.6(b) or 1200.10 of this Part. A professional card of a law firm may also give the names of members and associates.

(2) A professional announcement card stating new or changed associations or addresses, change of firm name, or similar matters pertaining to the professional offices of a lawyer or law firm or any nonlegal business conducted by the lawyer or law firm pursuant to section 1200.5-b. It may state biographical data, the names of members of the firm and associates and the names and dates of predecessor firms in a continuing line of succession. It may state the nature of the legal practice if permitted under section 1200.10 of this Part.

(3) A sign in or near the office and in the building directory identifying the law office and any nonlegal business conducted by the lawyer or law firm pursuant to section 1200.5-b. The sign may state the nature of the legal practice if permitted under section 1200.10 of this Part.

(4) A letterhead identifying the lawyer by name and as a lawyer, and giving addresses, telephone numbers, the name of the law firm, associates and any information permitted under sections 1200.6(b) or 1200.10 of this Part. A letterhead of a law firm may also give the names of members and associates, and names and dates relating to deceased and retired members. A lawyer or law firm may be designated "Of Counsel" on a letterhead if there is a continuing relationship with a lawyer or law firm, other than as a partner or associate. A lawyer or law firm may be designated as "General Counsel" or by similar professional reference on stationery of a client if the lawyer or the firm devotes a substantial amount of professional time in the representation of that client. The letterhead of a law firm may give the names and dates of predecessor firms in a continuing line of succession.

(b) A lawyer in private practice shall not practice under a trade name, a name that is misleading as to the identity of the lawyer or lawyers practicing under such name, or a firm name containing names other than those of one or more of the lawyers in the firm, except that the name of a professional corporation shall contain "P.C." or such symbols permitted by law, the name of a limited liability company or partnership shall contain "L.L.C.," "L.L.P." or such symbols permitted by law, and, if otherwise lawful, a firm may use as, or continue to include in its name the name or names of one or more deceased or retired members of the firm or of a predecessor firm in a continuing line of succession. Such terms as "legal clinic", "legal aid", "legal service office", "legal assistance office", "defender office" and the like, may be used only by qualified legal assistance organizations, except that the term "legal clinic" may be used by any lawyer or law firm provided the name of a participating lawyer or firm is incorporated therein. A lawyer or law firm may not include the name of a nonlawyer in its firm name, nor may a lawyer or law firm that has a contractual relationship with a nonlegal professional or nonlegal professional service firm pursuant to section 1200.5–c to provide legal and other professional services on a systematic and continuing basis include in its firm name the name of the nonlegal professional service firm or any individual nonlegal professional affiliated therewith. A lawyer who assumes a judicial, legislative or public executive or administrative post or office shall not permit his or her name to remain in the name of a law firm or be used in professional notices of the firm during any significant period in which the lawyer is not actively and regularly practicing law as a member of the firm and, during such period, other members of the firm shall not use the lawyer's name in the firm name or in professional notices of the firm.

(c) A lawyer shall not hold himself or herself out as having a partnership with one or more other lawyers unless they are in fact partners.

(d) A partnership shall not be formed or continued between or among lawyers licensed in different jurisdictions unless all enumerations of the members and associates of the firm on its letterhead and in other permissible listings make clear the jurisdictional limitations on those members and associates of the firm not licensed to practice in all listed jurisdictions; however, the same firm name may be used in each jurisdiction.

(e) A lawyer or law firm may utilize a domain name for an internet web site that does not include the name of the lawyer or law firm provided:

(1) all pages of the web site clearly and conspicuously include the actual name of the lawyer or law firm;

(2) the lawyer or law firm in no way attempts to engage in the practice of law using the domain name;

(3) the domain name does not imply an ability to obtain results in a matter; and

(4) the domain name does not otherwise violate a disciplinary rule.

(f) A lawyer or law firm may utilize a telephone number which contains a domain name, nickname, moniker or motto that does not otherwise violate a disciplinary rule.

§ 1200.8. [DR 2–103] Solicitation and Recommendation of Professional Employment

(a) A lawyer shall not engage in solicitation:

(1) by in-person or telephone contact, or by real-time or interactive computer-accessed communication unless the recipient is a close friend, relative, former client or existing client; or

(2) by any form of communication if:

(i) the communication or contact violates sections 1200.6(a), 1200.8(g) or 1200.41–a of this Part;

(ii) the recipient has made known to the lawyer a desire not to be solicited by the lawyer;

(iii) the solicitation involves coercion, duress or harassment;

(iv) the lawyer knows or reasonably should know that the age or the physical,emotional or mental state of the recipient makes it unlikely that the recipient will be able to exercise reasonable judgment in retaining a lawyer; or

(v) The lawyer intends or expects, but does not disclose, that the legal services necessary to handle the matter competently will be performed primarily by another lawyer who is not affiliated with the soliciting lawyer as a partner, associate or of counsel.

(b) For purposes of this section "solicitation" means any advertisement initiated by or on behalf of a lawyer or law firm that is directed to, or targeted at, a specific recipient or group of recipients, or their family members or legal representatives, the primary purpose of which is the retention of the lawyer or law firm, and a significant motive for which is pecuniary gain. It does not include a proposal or other writing prepared and delivered in response to a specific request of a prospective client.

(c) A solicitation directed to a recipient in this State, shall be subject to the following provisions:

(1) a copy of the solicitation shall at the time of its dissemination be filed with the attorney disciplinary committee of the judicial district or judicial department wherein the lawyer or law firm maintains its principal office. Where no such office is maintained, the filing shall be made in the judicial department where the solicitation is targeted. A filing shall consist of:

(i) a copy of the solicitation;

(ii) a transcript of the audio portion of any radio or television solicitation; and

(iii) if the solicitation is in a language other than English, an accurate English language translation.

(2) such solicitation shall contain no reference to the fact of filing.

(3) if a solicitation is directed to a predetermined recipient, a list containing the names and addresses of all recipients shall be retained by the lawyer or law firm for a period of not less than three years following the last date of its dissemination.

(4) solicitations filed pursuant to this subdivision shall be open to public inspection.

(5) the provisions of this subdivision shall not apply to:

(i) a solicitation directed or disseminated to a close friend, relative, or former or existing client;

(ii) a web site maintained by the lawyer or law firm, unless the web site is designed for and directed to or targeted at a prospective client affected by an identifiable actual event or occurrence or by an identifiable prospective defendant; or

(iii) professional cards or other announcements the distribution of which is authorized by section 1200.7(a) of this Part.

(d) A lawyer shall not compensate or give anything of value to a person or organization to recommend or obtain employment by a client, or as a reward for having made a recommendation resulting in employment by a client, except that:

(1) A lawyer or law firm may refer clients to a nonlegal professional or nonlegal professional service firm pursuant to a contractual relationship with such nonlegal professional or nonlegal professional service firm to provide legal and other professional services on a systematic and continuing basis as permitted by section 1200.5–c, provided however that such referral

shall not otherwise include any monetary or other tangible consideration or reward for such, or the sharing of legal fees; or

(2) A lawyer may pay the usual and reasonable fees or dues charged by a qualified legal assistance organization or referral fees to another lawyer as permitted by section 1200.12 of this Part.

(e) A written solicitation shall not be sent by a method that requires the recipient to travel to a location other than that at which the recipient ordinarily receives business or personal mail or that requires a signature on the part of the recipient.

(f) A lawyer or the lawyer's partner or associate or any other affiliated lawyer maybe recommended, employed or paid by, or may cooperate with one of the following offices or organizations which promote the use of the lawyer's services or those of a partner or associate or any other affiliated lawyer, or request one of the following offices or organizations to recommend or promote the use of the lawyer's services or those of the lawyer's partner or associate, or any other affiliated lawyer as a private practitioner, if there is no interference with the exercise of independent professional judgment on behalf of the client:

(1) a legal aid office or public defender office:

(i) operated or sponsored by a duly accredited law school;

(ii) operated or sponsored by a bona fide, nonprofit community organization;

(iii) operated or sponsored by a governmental agency; or

(iv) operated, sponsored, or approved by a bar association;

(2) a military legal assistance office;

(3) a lawyer referral service operated, sponsored or approved by a bar association or authorized by law or court rule;

(4) any bona fide organization which recommends, furnishes or pays for legal services to its members or beneficiaries provided the following conditions are satisfied:

(i) Neither the lawyer, nor the lawyer's partner, nor associate, nor any other affiliated lawyer nor any nonlawyer, shall have initiated or promoted such organization for the primary purpose of providing financial or other benefit to such lawyer, partner, associate or affiliated lawyer.

(ii) Such organization is not operated for the purpose of procuring legal work or financial benefit for any lawyer as a private practitioner outside of the legal services program of the organization.

(iii) The member or beneficiary to whom the legal services are furnished, and not such organization, is recognized as the client of the lawyer in the matter.

(iv) The legal service plan of such organization provides appropriate relief for any member or beneficiary who asserts a claim that representation by counsel furnished, selected or approved by the organization for the particular matter involved would be unethical, improper or inadequate under the circumstances of the matter involved; and the plan provides an appropriate procedure for seeking such relief.

(v) The lawyer does not know or have cause to know that such organization is in violation of applicable laws, rules of court or other legal requirements that govern its legal service operations.

(vi) Such organization has filed with the appropriate disciplinary authority, to the extent required by such authority, at least annually a report with respect to its legal service plan, if any, showing its terms, its schedule of benefits, its subscription charges, agreements with counsel and financial results of its legal service activities or, if it has failed to do so, the lawyer does not know or have cause to know of such failure.

(g) No solicitation relating to a specific incident involving potential claims for personal injury or wrongful death shall be disseminated before the 30th day after the date of the incident, unless a filing must be made within 30 days of the incident as a legal prerequisite to the particular claim, in which case no unsolicited communication shall be made before the 15th day after the date of the incident.

(h) Any solicitation made in writing or by computer-accessed communication and directed to a predetermined recipient, if prompted by a specific occurrence involving or affecting a recipient, shall disclose how the lawyer obtained the identity of the recipient and learned of the recipient's potential legal need.

(i) If a retainer agreement is provided with any solicitation, the top of each page shall be marked "SAMPLE" in red ink in a type size equal to the largest type size used in the agreement and the words "DO NOT SIGN" shall appear on the client signature line.

(j) Any solicitation covered by this section shall include the name, principal law office address and telephone number of the lawyer or law firm whose services are being offered.

(k) The provisions of this section shall apply to a lawyer or members of a law firm not admitted to practice in this State who solicit retention by residents of this State.

§ 1200.9. [DR 2–104] Suggestion of Need of Legal Services

(a) (Repealed)

(b) (Repealed)

(c) A lawyer may accept employment which results from participation in activities designed to educate the public to recognize legal problems, to make intelligent selection of counsel or to utilize available legal services.

(d) A lawyer who is recommended, furnished or paid by a qualified legal assistance organization may represent a member or beneficiary thereof, to the extent and under the conditions prescribed therein.

(e) Without affecting the right to accept employment, a lawyer may speak publicly or write for publication on legal topics so long as the lawyer does not undertake to give individual advice.

(f) If success in asserting rights or defenses of a client in litigation in the nature of a class action is dependent upon the joinder of others, a lawyer may accept employment from those contacted for the purpose of obtaining their joinder, provided such acceptance does not violate any statute or court rule in the judicial department in which the lawyer practices.

§ 1200.10. [DR 2–105] Identification of Practice and Specialty

(a) A lawyer or law firm may publicly identify one or more areas of law in which the lawyer or the law firm practices, or may state that the practice of the lawyer or law firm is limited to one or more areas of law, provided that the lawyer or law firm shall not state that the lawyer or law firm is a specialist or specializes in a particular field of law, except as provided in section 1200.10(b), (c) or (d) of this Part.

(b) A lawyer admitted to engage in patent practice before the United States Patent and Trademark Office may use the designation "Patent Attorney" or a substantially similar designation.

(c) A lawyer may state that the lawyer has been recognized or certified as a specialist only as follows:

(1) A lawyer who is certified as a specialist in a particular area of law or law practice by a private organization approved for that purpose by the American Bar Association may state the fact of certification if, in conjunction therewith, the certifying organization is identified and the following statement is prominently made: "The [name of the private certifying organization] is not affiliated with any governmental authority. Certification is not a requirement for the practice of law in the State of New York and does not necessarily indicate greater competence than other attorneys experienced in this field of law."

(2) A lawyer who is certified as a specialist in a particular area of law or law practice by the authority having jurisdiction over specialization under the laws of another state or territory may state the fact of certification if, in conjunction therewith, the certifying state or territory is identified and the following statement is prominently made: "Certification granted by the [identify state or territory] is not recognized by any governmental authority within the State of New

York. Certification is not a requirement for the practice of law in the State of New York and does not necessarily indicate greater competence than other attorneys experienced in this field of law."

§ 1200.11. [DR 2–106] Fee for Legal Services

(a) A lawyer shall not enter into an agreement for, charge or collect an illegal or excessive fee.

(b) A fee is excessive when, after a review of the facts, a lawyer of ordinary prudence would be left with a definite and firm conviction that the fee is in excess of a reasonable fee. Factors to be considered as guides in determining the reasonableness of a fee may include the following:

(1) The time and labor required, the novelty and difficulty of the questions involved and the skill requisite to perform the legal service properly.

(2) The likelihood, if apparent or made known to the client, that the acceptance of the particular employment will preclude other employment by the lawyer.

(3) The fee customarily charged in the locality for similar legal services.

(4) The amount involved and the results obtained.

(5) The time limitations imposed by the client or by circumstances.

(6) The nature and length of the professional relationship with the client.

(7) The experience, reputation and ability of the lawyer or lawyers performing the services.

(8) Whether the fee is fixed or contingent.

(c) A lawyer shall not enter into an arrangement for, charge, or collect:

(1) A contingent fee for representing a defendant in a criminal case.

(2) Any fee in a domestic relations matter:

(i) The payment or amount of which is contingent upon the securing of a divorce or in any way determined by reference to the amount of maintenance, support, equitable distribution, or property settlement;

(ii) Unless a written retainer agreement is signed by the lawyer and client setting forth in plain language the nature of the relationship and the details of the fee arrangement. A lawyer shall not include in the written retainer agreement a nonrefundable fee clause; or

(iii) Based upon a security interest, confession of judgment or other lien, without prior notice to the client in a signed retainer agreement and approval from a tribunal after notice to the adversary. A lawyer shall not foreclose on a mortgage placed on the marital residence while the spouse who consents to the mortgage remains the titleholder and the residence remains the spouse's primary residence.

(3) A fee proscribed by law or rule of court.

(d) Promptly after a lawyer has been employed in a contingent fee matter, the lawyer shall provide the client with a writing stating the method by which the fee is to be determined, including the percentage or percentages that shall accrue to the lawyer in the event of settlement, trial or appeal, litigation and other expenses to be deducted from the recovery and whether such expenses are to be deducted before or, if not prohibited by statute or court rule, after the contingent fee is calculated. Upon conclusion of a contingent fee matter, the lawyer shall provide the client with a written statement stating the outcome of the matter, and if there is a recovery, showing the remittance to the client and the method of its determination.

(e) Where representation is in a civil matter, a lawyer shall resolve fee disputes by arbitration at the election of the client pursuant to a fee arbitration program established by the Chief Administrator of the Courts and approved by the justices of the Appellate Divisions.

(f) In domestic relations matters, a lawyer shall provide a prospective client with a statement of client's rights and responsibilities at the initial conference and prior to the signing of a written retainer agreement.

§ 1200.12. [DR 2–107] Division of Fees Among Lawyers

(a) A lawyer shall not divide a fee for legal services with another lawyer who is not a partner in or associate of the lawyer's law firm, unless:

(1) The client consents to employment of the other lawyer after a full disclosure that a division of fees will be made.

(2) The division is in proportion to the services performed by each lawyer or, by a writing given to the client, each lawyer assumes joint responsibility for the representation.

(3) The total fee of the lawyers does not exceed reasonable compensation for all legal services they rendered the client.

(b) This Disciplinary Rule does not prohibit payment to a former partner or associate pursuant to a separation or retirement agreement.

§ 1200.13. [DR 2–108] Agreements Restricting the Practice of a Lawyer

(a) A lawyer shall not be a party to or participate in a partnership or employment agreement with another lawyer that restricts the right of a lawyer to practice law after the termination of a relationship created by the agreement, except as a condition to payment of retirement benefits.

(b) In connection with the settlement of a controversy or suit, a lawyer shall not enter into an agreement that restricts the right of a lawyer to practice law.

§ 1200.14. [DR 2–109] Obligation to Decline Employment

(a)[1] A lawyer shall not accept employment on behalf of a person if the lawyer knows or it is obvious that such person wishes to:

(1) Bring a legal action, conduct a defense, or assert a position in litigation, or otherwise have steps taken for such person merely for the purpose of harassing or maliciously injuring any person.

(2) Present a claim or defense in litigation that is not warranted under existing law, unless it can be supported by good faith argument for an extension, modification, or reversal of existing law.

[1] So in original. No par. (b) has been enacted.

§ 1200.15. [DR 2–110] Withdrawal From Employment

(a) In General.

(1) If permission for withdrawal from employment is required by the rules of a tribunal, a lawyer shall not withdraw from employment in a proceeding before that tribunal without its permission.

(2) Even when withdrawal is otherwise permitted or required under section 1200.15(a)(1), (b) or (c) of this Part, a lawyer shall not withdraw from employment until the lawyer has taken steps to the extent reasonably practicable to avoid foreseeable prejudice to the rights of the client, including giving due notice to the client, allowing time for employment of other counsel, delivering to the client all papers and property to which the client is entitled and complying with applicable laws and rules.

(3) A lawyer who withdraws from employment shall refund promptly any part of a fee paid in advance that has not been earned.

(b) Mandatory Withdrawal. A lawyer representing a client before a tribunal, with its permission if required by its rules, shall withdraw from employment, and a lawyer representing a client in other matters shall withdraw from employment, if:

(1) The lawyer knows or it is obvious that the client is bringing the legal action, conducting the defense, or asserting a position in the litigation, or is otherwise having steps taken, merely for the purpose of harassing or maliciously injuring any person.

(2) The lawyer knows or it is obvious that continued employment will result in violation of a disciplinary rule.

(3) The lawyer's mental or physical condition renders it unreasonably difficult to carry out the employment effectively.

(4) The lawyer is discharged by his or her client.

(c) Permissive Withdrawal. Except as stated in DR 2–110(A), a lawyer may withdraw from representing a client if withdrawal can be accomplished without material adverse effect on the interests of the client, or if:

(1) The client:

(i) Insists upon presenting a claim or defense that is not warranted under existing law and cannot be supported by good faith argument for an extension, modification, or reversal of existing law.

(ii) Persists in a course of action involving the lawyer's services that the lawyer reasonably believes is criminal or fraudulent.

(iii) Insists that the lawyer pursue a course of conduct which is illegal or prohibited under the disciplinary rules.

(iv) By other conduct renders it unreasonably difficult for the lawyer to carry out employment effectively.

(v) Insists, in a matter not pending before a tribunal, that the lawyer engage in conduct which is contrary to the judgment and advice of the lawyer but not prohibited under the disciplinary rules.

(vi) Deliberately disregards an agreement or obligation to the lawyer as to expenses or fees.

(vii) Has used the lawyer's services to perpetrate a crime or fraud.

(2) The lawyer's continued employment is likely to result in a violation of a disciplinary rule.

(3) The lawyer's inability to work with co-counsel indicates that the best interests of the client likely will be served by withdrawal.

(4) The lawyer's mental or physical condition renders it difficult for the lawyer to carry out the employment effectively.

(5) The lawyer's client knowingly and freely assents to termination of the employment.

(6) The lawyer believes in good faith, in a proceeding pending before a tribunal, that the tribunal will find the existence of other good cause for withdrawal.

§ 1200.15–a. [DR 2–111] Sale of Law Practice

(a) A lawyer retiring from a private practice of law, a law firm one or more members of which are retiring from the private practice of law with the firm, or the personal representative of a deceased, disabled or missing lawyer, may sell a law practice, including good will, to one or more lawyers or law firms, who may purchase the practice. The seller and the buyer may agree on reasonable restrictions on the seller's private practice of law, notwithstanding any other provision of this Code. Retirement shall include the cessation of the private practice of law in the geographic area, that is, the county and city and any county or city contiguous thereto, in which the practice to be sold has been conducted.

(b) Confidences and Secrets.

(1) With respect to each matter subject to the contemplated sale, the seller may provide prospective buyers with any information not protected as a confidence or secret under section 1200.19 of this Part.

(2) Notwithstanding section 1200.19, the seller may provide the prospective buyer with information as to individual clients:

    (i) concerning the identity of the client, except as provided in section 1200.15–a(b)(6) of this Part;

    (ii) concerning the status and general nature of the matter;

    (iii) available in public court files; and

    (iv) concerning the financial terms of the attorney-client relationship and the payment status of the client's account.

(3) Prior to making any disclosure of confidences or secrets that may be permitted under section 1200.15–a(b)(2) of this Part, the seller shall provide the prospective buyer with information regarding the matters involved in the proposed sale sufficient to enable the prospective buyer to determine whether any conflicts of interest exist. Where sufficient information cannot be disclosed without revealing client confidences or secrets, the seller may make the disclosures necessary for the prospective buyer to determine whether any conflict of interest exists, subject to section 1200.15–a(b)(6) of this Part. If the prospective buyer determines that conflicts of interest exist prior to reviewing the information, or determines during the course of review that a conflict of interest exists, the prospective buyer shall not review or continue to review the information unless seller shall have obtained the consent of the client in accordance with section 1200.19(c)(1) of this Part.

(4) Prospective buyers shall maintain the confidentiality of and shall not use any client information received in connection with the proposed sale in the same manner and to the same extent as if the prospective buyers represented the client.

(5) Absent the consent of the client after full disclosure, a seller shall not provide a prospective buyer with information if doing so would cause a violation of the attorney-client privilege.

(6) If the seller has reason to believe that the identity of the client or the fact of the representation itself constitutes a confidence or secret in the circumstances, the seller may not provide such information to a prospective buyer without first advising the client of the identity of the prospective buyer and obtaining the client's consent to the proposed disclosure.

(c) Written notice of the sale shall be given jointly by the seller and the buyer to each of the seller's clients and shall include information regarding:

(1) The client's right to retain other counsel or to take possession of the file;

(2) The fact that the client's consent to the transfer of the client's file or matter to the buyer will be presumed if the client does not take any action or otherwise object within 90 days of the sending of the notice, subject to any court rule or statute requiring express approval by the client or a court;

(3) The fact that agreements between the seller and the seller's clients as to fees will be honored by the buyer;

(4) Proposed fee increases, if any, permitted under section 1200.15–a(e) of this Part; and

(5) The identity and background of the buyer or buyers, including principal office address, bar admissions, number of years in practice in the state, whether the buyer has ever been disciplined for professional misconduct or convicted of a crime, and whether the buyer currently intends to re-sell the practice.

(d) When the buyer's representation of a client of the seller would give rise to a waivable conflict of interest, the buyer shall not undertake such representation unless the necessary waiver or waivers have been obtained in writing.

(e) The fee charged a client by the buyer shall not be increased by reason of the sale, unless permitted by a retainer agreement with the client or otherwise specifically agreed to by the client.

§ 1200.16. [DR 3–101] Aiding Unauthorized Practice of Law

(a) A lawyer shall not aid a non-lawyer in the unauthorized practice of law.

(b) A lawyer shall not practice law in a jurisdiction where to do so would be in violation of regulations of the profession in that jurisdiction.

§ 1200.17. [DR 3–102] Dividing Legal Fees With a Non-lawyer

(a)[1] A lawyer or law firm shall not share legal fees with a non-lawyer, except that:

(1) An agreement by a lawyer with his or her firm, partner, or associate may provide for the payment of money, over a reasonable period of time after the lawyer's death, to the lawyer's estate or to one or more specified persons.

(2) A lawyer who undertakes to complete unfinished legal business of a deceased lawyer may pay to the estate of the deceased lawyer that proportion of the total compensation which fairly represents the services rendered by the deceased lawyer.

(3) A lawyer or law firm may compensate a non-lawyer employee, or include a non-lawyer employee in a retirement plan, based in whole or in part on a profit-sharing arrangement.

[1] So in original. No par. (b) has been enacted.

§ 1200.18. [DR 3–103] Forming a Partnership With a Non-lawyer

(a)[1] A lawyer shall not form a partnership with a non-lawyer if any of the activities of the partnership consist of the practice law.

[1] So in original. No par. (b) has been enacted.

§ 1200.19. [DR 4–101] Preservation of Confidences and Secrets of a Client

(a) *Confidence* refers to information protected by the attorney-client privilege under applicable law, and *secret* refers to other information gained in the professional relationship that the client has requested be held inviolate or the disclosure of which would be embarrassing or would be likely to be detrimental to the client.

(b) Except when permitted under DR 4–101(C), a lawyer shall not knowingly:

(1) reveal a confidence or secret of a client;

(2) use a confidence or secret of a client to the disadvantage of the client; and

(3) use a confidence or secret of a client for the advantage of the lawyer or of a third person, unless the client consents after full disclosure.

(c) A lawyer may reveal:

(1) Confidences or secrets with the consent of the client or clients affected, but only after a full disclosure to them.

(2) Confidences or secrets when permitted under disciplinary rules or required by law or court order.

(3) The intention of a client to commit a crime and the information necessary to prevent the crime.

(4) Confidences or secrets necessary to establish or collect the lawyer's fee or to defend the lawyer or his or her employees or associates against an accusation of wrongful conduct.

(5) Confidences or secrets to the extent implicit in withdrawing a written or oral opinion or representation previously given by the lawyer and believed by the lawyer still to be relied upon by a third person where the lawyer has discovered that the opinion or representation was based on materially inaccurate information or is being used to further a crime or fraud.

(d) A lawyer shall exercise reasonable care to prevent his or her employees, associates, and others whose services are utilized by the lawyer from disclosing or using confidences or secrets of a client, except that a lawyer may reveal the information allowed by subdivision (c) of this section through an employee.

§ 1200.20. [DR 5–101] Conflicts of Interest; Lawyers Own Interests

(a)[1] A lawyer shall not accept or continue employment if the exercise of professional judgment on behalf of the client will be or reasonably may be affected by the lawyer's own financial, business, property, or personal interests, unless a disinterested lawyer would believe that the representation of the client will not be adversely affected thereby and the client consents to the representation after full disclosure of the implications of the lawyer's interest.

[1] So in original. No par. (b) has been enacted.

§ 1200.20–a. Participation in Limited Pro Bono Legal Service Programs

(a) A lawyer who, under the auspices of a program sponsored by a court, government agency, bar association or not-for-profit legal services organization, provides short-term limited legal services to a client without expectation by either the lawyer or the client that the lawyer will provide continuing representation in the matter:

(1) shall comply with sections 1200.20, 1200.24, and 1200.27 of these rules, concerning restrictions on representations where there are or may be conflicts of interest as that term is defined in this part, only if the lawyer has actual knowledge at the time of commencement of representation that the representation of the client involves a conflict of interest;

(2) shall comply with sections 1200.20, 1200.24 and 1200.27 only if the lawyer has actual knowledge at the time of commencement of representation that another lawyer associated with the lawyer in a law firm is affected by those sections;

(b) Except as provided in paragraph (a)(2), sections 1200.24 and 1200.27 are inapplicable to a representation governed by this section.

(c) Short-term limited legal services are services providing legal advice or representation free of charge as part of a program described in subdivision (a) with no expectation that the assistance will continue beyond what is necessary to complete an initial consultation, representation or court appearance.

(d) The lawyer providing short-term limited legal services must secure the client's informed consent to the limited scope of the representation, and such representation shall be subject to the provisions of section 1200.19.

(e) The provisions of this section shall not apply where the court before which the representation is pending determines that a conflict of interest exists or, if during the course of the representation, the attorney providing the services become aware of the existence of a conflict of interest precluding continued representation.

§ 1200.21.   [DR 5–102] Lawyers as Witnesses

(a) A lawyer shall not act, or accept employment that contemplates the lawyer's acting, as an advocate on issues of fact before any tribunal if the lawyer knows or it is obvious that the lawyer ought to be called as a witness on a significant issue on behalf of the client, except that the lawyer may act as an advocate and also testify:

(1) If the testimony will relate solely to an uncontested issue.

(2) If the testimony will relate solely to a matter of formality and there is no reason to believe that substantial evidence will be offered in opposition to the testimony.

(3) If the testimony will relate solely to the nature and value of legal services rendered in the case by the lawyer or the lawyer's firm to the client.

(4) As to any matter, if disqualification as an advocate would work a substantial hardship on the client because of the distinctive value of the lawyer as counsel in the particular case.

(b) Neither a lawyer nor the lawyer's firm shall accept employment in contemplated or pending litigation if the lawyer knows or it is obvious that the lawyer or another lawyer in the lawyer's firm may be called as a witness on a significant issue other than on behalf of the client, and it is apparent that the testimony would or might be prejudicial to the client.

(c) If, after undertaking employment in contemplated or pending litigation, a lawyer learns or it is obvious that the lawyer ought to be called as a witness on a significant issue on behalf of the client, the lawyer shall not serve as an advocate on issues of fact before the tribunal, except that the lawyer may continue as an advocate on issues of fact and may testify in the circumstances enumerated in paragraphs (a)(1) through (4) of this section.

(d) If, after undertaking employment in contemplated or pending litigation, a lawyer learns or it is obvious that the lawyer or a lawyer in his or her firm may be called as a witness on a significant issue other than on behalf of the client, the lawyer may continue the representation until it is apparent that the testimony is or may be prejudicial to the client at which point the lawyer and the firm must withdraw from acting as an advocate before the tribunal.

§ 1200.22.   [DR 5–103] Avoiding Acquisition of Interest in Litigation

(a) A lawyer shall not acquire a proprietary interest in the cause of action or subject matter of litigation he or she is conducting for a client, except that the lawyer may:

(1) Acquire a lien granted by law to secure the lawyer's fee or expenses.

(2) Except as provided in section 1200.11(c)(2) or (3) of this Part, contract with a client for a reasonable contingent fee in a civil case.

(b) While representing a client in connection with contemplated or pending litigation, a lawyer shall not advance or guarantee financial assistance to the client, except that:

(1) A lawyer representing an indigent or pro bono client may pay court costs and expenses of litigation on behalf of the client;

(2) A lawyer may advance court costs and expenses of litigation, the repayment of which may be contingent on the outcome of the matter; and

(3) A lawyer, in an action in which an attorney's fee is payable in whole or in part as a percentage of the recovery in the action, may pay on the lawyer's own account court costs and expenses of litigation. In such case, the fee paid to the attorney from the proceeds of the action may include an amount equal to such costs and expenses incurred.

§ 1200.23.   [DR 5–104] Transactions Between Lawyer and Client

(a) A lawyer shall not enter into a business transaction with a client if they have differing interests therein and if the client expects the lawyer to exercise professional judgment therein for the protection of the client, unless:

(1) The transaction and terms on which the lawyer acquires the interest are fair and reasonable to the client and are fully disclosed and transmitted in writing to the client in a manner that can be reasonably understood by the client;

(2) The lawyer advises the client to seek the advice of independent counsel in the transaction; and

(3) The client consents in writing, after full disclosure, to the terms of the transaction and to the lawyer's inherent conflict of interest in the transaction.

(b) Prior to conclusion of all aspects of the matter giving rise to employment, a lawyer shall not negotiate or enter into any arrangement or understanding:

(1) With a client or a prospective client by which the lawyer acquires an interest in literary or media rights with respect to the subject matter of the employment or proposed employment.

(2) With any person by which the lawyer transfers or assigns any interest in literary or media rights with respect to the subject matter of employment by a client or prospective client.

§ 1200.24. [DR 5–105] Conflict of Interest: Simultaneous Representation

(a) A lawyer shall decline proffered employment if the exercise of independent professional judgment in behalf of a client will be or is likely to be adversely affected by the acceptance of the proffered employment, or if it would be likely to involve the lawyer in representing differing interests, except to the extent permitted under subdivision (c) of this section.

(b) A lawyer shall not continue multiple employment if the exercise of independent professional judgment in behalf of a client will be or is likely to be adversely affected by the lawyer's representation of another client, or if it would be likely to involve the lawyer in representing differing interests, except to the extent permitted under subdivision (c) of this section.

(c) In the situations covered by subdivisions (a) and (b) of this section, a lawyer may represent multiple clients if a disinterested lawyer would believe that the lawyer can competently represent the interest of each and if each consents to the representation after full disclosure of the implications of the simultaneous representation and the advantages and risks involved.

(d) While lawyers are associated in a law firm, none of them shall knowingly accept or continue employment when any one of them practicing alone would be prohibited from doing so under section 1200.20(a), 1200.24(a) or (b),1200.27(a) or (b), or 1200.45(b) of this Part except as otherwise provided therein.

(e) A law firm shall keep records of prior engagements, which records shall be made at or near the time of such engagements and shall have a policy implementing a system by which proposed engagements are checked against current and previous engagements, so as to render effective assistance to lawyers within the firm in complying with section 1200.24(d) of this Part. Failure to keep records or to have a policy which complies with this subdivision, whether or not a violation of section 1200.24(d) of this Part occurs, shall be a violation by the firm. In cases in which a violation of this subdivision by the firm is a substantial factor in causing a violation of section 1200.24(d) of this Part by a lawyer, the firm, as well as the individual lawyer, shall also be responsible for the violation of section 1200.24(d) of this Part.

§ 1200.25. [DR 5–106] Settling Similar Claims of Clients

A lawyer who represents two or more clients shall not make or participate in the making of an aggregate settlement of the claims of or against the clients, unless each client has consented after full disclosure of the implications of the aggregate settlement and the advantages and risks involved, including the existence and nature of all the claims involved and the participation of each person in the settlement.

§ 1200.26. [DR 5–107] Avoiding Influence by Others Than the Client

(a) Except with the consent of the client after full disclosure a lawyer shall not:

(1) Accept compensation for legal services from one other than the client.

(2) Accept from one other than the client any thing of value related to his or her representation of or employment by the client.

(b) Unless authorized by law, a lawyer shall not permit a person who recommends, employs, or pays the lawyer to render legal service for another to direct or regulate his or her professional judgment in rendering such legal services, or to cause the lawyer to compromise the lawyer's duty to maintain the confidences and secrets of the client under section 1200.19(b) of this Part.

(c) A lawyer shall not practice with or in the form of a limited liability company, limited liability partnership or professional corporation authorized to practice law for a profit, if:

(1) A non-lawyer owns any interest therein, except that a fiduciary representative of the estate of a lawyer may hold the stock or interest of the lawyer for a reasonable time during administration;

(2) A non-lawyer is a member, corporate director or officer thereof; or

(3) A nonlawyer has the right to direct or control the professional judgment of a lawyer.

§ 1200.27. [DR 5–108] Conflict of Interest— Former Client

(a) Except as provided in section 1200.45(b) with respect to current or former government lawyers, a lawyer who has represented a client in a matter shall not, without the consent of the former client after full disclosure:

(1) Thereafter represent another person in the same or a substantially related matter in which that person's interests are materially adverse to the interests of the former client.

(2) Use any confidences or secrets of the former client except as permitted by section 1200.19(c) of this Part or when the confidence or secret has become generally known.

(b) Except with the consent of the affected client after full disclosure, a lawyer shall not knowingly represent a person in the same or a substantially related matter in which a firm with which the lawyer formerly was associated had previously represented a client:

(1) Whose interests are materially adverse to that person; and

(2) About whom the lawyer had acquired information protected by section 1200.19(b) of this Part that is material to the matter.

(c) Notwithstanding the provisions of section 1200.24(d) of this Part, when a lawyer has terminated an association with a firm, the firm is prohibited from thereafter representing a person with interests that are materially adverse to those of a client represented by the formerly associated lawyer and not currently represented by the firm only if the law firm or any lawyer remaining in the firm has information protected by section 1200.19(b) of this Part that is material to the matter, unless the affected client consents after full disclosure.

§ 1200.28. [DR 5–109] Organization as Client

(a) When a lawyer employed or retained by an organization is dealing with the organization's directors, officers, employees, members, shareholders or other constituents, and it appears that the organization's interests may differ from those of the constituents with whom the lawyer is dealing, the lawyer shall explain that the lawyer is the lawyer for the organization and not for any of the constituents.

(b) If a lawyer for an organization knows that an officer, employee or other person associated with the organization is engaged in action, intends to act or refuses to act in a matter related to the representation that is a violation of a legal obligation to the organization, or a violation of law that reasonably might be imputed to the organization, and is likely to result in substantial injury to the organization, the lawyer shall proceed as is reasonably necessary in the best interest of the organization. In determining how to proceed, the lawyer shall give due consideration to the seriousness of the violation and its consequences, the scope and nature of the lawyer's representation, the responsibility in the organization and the apparent motivation of the person involved, the policies of the organization concerning such matters and any other relevant considerations. Any measures taken shall be designed to minimize disruption of the organization and the risk of revealing information relating to the representation to persons outside the organization. Such measures may include, among others:

(1) Asking reconsideration of the matter;

(2) Advising that a separate legal opinion on the matter be sought for presentation to appropriate authority in the organization; and

(3) Referring the matter to higher authority in the organization, including, if warranted by the seriousness of the matter, referral to the highest authority that can act in behalf of the organization as determined by applicable law.

(c) If, despite the lawyer's efforts in accordance with section 1200.28(b) of this Part, the highest authority that can act on behalf of the organization insists upon action, or a refusal to act, that is clearly a violation of law and is likely to result in a substantial injury to the organization, the lawyer may resign in accordance with section 1200.15 of this Part.

§ 1200.29. [DR 5–110] Membership in Legal Services Organization

(a)[1] A lawyer may serve as a director, officer or member of a not-for-profit legal services organization, apart from the law firm in which the lawyer practices, notwithstanding that the organization serves persons having interests that differ from those of a client of the lawyer or the lawyer's firm, provided that the lawyer shall not knowingly participate in a decision or action of the organization.

(1) If participating in the decision or action would be incompatible with the lawyer's duty of loyalty to a client under section 1200.20 through 1200.29 of this Part; or

(2) where the decision or action could have a material adverse effect on the representation of a client of the organization whose interests differ from those of a client of the lawyer or the lawyer's firm.

[1] So in original. No par. (b) has been enacted.

§ 1200.29–a. Sexual Relations With Clients

(a) "Sexual relations" means sexual intercourse or the touching of an intimate part of another person for the purpose of sexual arousal, sexual gratification, or sexual abuse.

(b) A lawyer shall not:

(1) Require or demand sexual relations with a client or third party incident to or as a condition of any professional representation.

(2) Employ coercion, intimidation, or undue influence in entering into sexual relations with a client.

(3) In domestic relations matters, enter into sexual relations with a client during the course of the lawyer's representation of the client.

(c) Section 1200.29–a(b) shall not apply to sexual relations between lawyers and their spouses or to ongoing consensual sexual relationships that predate the initiation of the lawyer-client relationship.

(d) Where a lawyer in a firm has sexual relations with a client but does not participate in the representation of that client, the lawyers in the firm shall not be subject to discipline under this rule solely because of the occurrence of such sexual relations.

§ 1200.30. [DR 6–101] Failing to Act Competently

(a)[1] A lawyer shall not:

(1) Handle a legal matter which the lawyer knows or should know that he or she is not competent to

handle, without associating with a lawyer who is competent to handle it.

(2) Handle a legal matter without preparation adequate in the circumstances.

(3) Neglect a legal matter entrusted to the lawyer.

[1] So in original. No par. (b) has been enacted.

§ 1200.31. [DR 6–102] Limiting Liability to Client

(a) [1] A lawyer shall not seek, by contract or other means, to limit prospectively the lawyer's individual liability to a client for malpractice, or, without first advising that person that independent representation is appropriate in connection therewith, to settle a claim for such liability with an unrepresented client or former client.

[1] So in original. No par. (b) has been enacted.

§ 1200.32. [DR 7–101] Representing a Client Zealously

(a) A lawyer shall not intentionally:

(1) Fail to seek the lawful objectives of the client through reasonably available means permitted by law and the disciplinary rules, except as provided by subdivision (b) of this section. A lawyer does not violate this disciplinary rule, however, by acceding to reasonable requests of opposing counsel which do not prejudice the rights of the client, by being punctual in fulfilling all professional commitments, by avoiding offensive tactics, or by treating with courtesy and consideration all persons involved in the legal process.

(2) Fail to carry out a contract of employment entered into with a client for professional services, but the lawyer may withdraw as permitted under sections 1200.15, 1200.21 and 1200.24 of this Part.

(3) Prejudice or damage the client during the course of the professional relationship, except as required under section 1200.33(b) or as authorized by section 1200.15 of this Part.

(b) In the representation of a client, a lawyer may:

(1) Where permissible, exercise professional judgment to waive or fail to assert a right or position of the client.

(2) Refuse to aid or participate in conduct that the lawyer believes to be unlawful, even though there is some support for an argument that the conduct is legal.

§ 1200.33. [DR 7–102] Representing a Client Within the Bounds of the Law

(a) In the representation of a client, a lawyer shall not:

(1) File a suit, assert a position, conduct a defense, delay a trial, or take other action on behalf of the client when the lawyer knows or when it is obvious that such action would serve merely to harass or maliciously injure another.

(2) Knowingly advance a claim or defense that is unwarranted under existing law, except that the lawyer may advance such claim or defense if it can be supported by good faith argument for an extension, modification, or reversal of existing law.

(3) Conceal or knowingly fail to disclose that which the lawyer is required by law to reveal.

(4) Knowingly use perjured testimony or false evidence.

(5) Knowingly make a false statement of law or fact.

(6) Participate in the creation or preservation of evidence when the lawyer knows or it is obvious that the evidence is false.

(7) Counsel or assist the client in conduct that the lawyer knows to be illegal or fraudulent.

(8) Knowingly engage in other illegal conduct or conduct contrary to a disciplinary rule.

(b) A lawyer who receives information clearly establishing that:

(1) The client has, in the course of the representation, perpetrated a fraud upon a person or tribunal shall promptly call upon the client to rectify the same, and if the client refuses or is unable to do so, the lawyer shall reveal the fraud to the affected person or tribunal, except when the information is protected as a confidence or secret.

(2) A person other than the client has perpetrated a fraud upon a tribunal shall promptly reveal the fraud to the tribunal.

§ 1200.34. [DR 7–103] Performing the Duty of Public Prosecutor or Other Government Lawyer

(a) A public prosecutor or other government lawyer shall not institute or cause to be instituted criminal charges when he or she knows or it is obvious that the charges are not supported by probable cause.

(b) A public prosecutor or other government lawyer in criminal litigation shall make timely disclosure to counsel for the defendant, or to a defendant who has no counsel, of the existence of evidence, known to the prosecutor or other government lawyer, that tends to negate the guilt of the accused, mitigate the degree of the offense or reduce the punishment.

§ 1200.35. [DR 7–104] Communicating With Represented and Unrepresented Parties

(a) During the course of the representation of a client a lawyer shall not:

(1) Communicate or cause another to communicate on the subject of the representation with a party the lawyer knows to be represented by a lawyer in that

matter unless the lawyer has the prior consent of the lawyer representing such other party or is authorized by law to do so.

(2) Give advice to a party who is not represented by a lawyer, other than the advice to secure counsel, if the interests of such party are or have a reasonable possibility of being in conflict with the interests of the lawyer's client.

(b) Notwithstanding the prohibitions of section 1200.35(a) of this Part, and unless prohibited by law, a lawyer may cause a client to communicate with a represented party, if that party is legally competent, and counsel the client with respect to those communications, provided the lawyer gives reasonable advance notice to the represented party's counsel that such communications will be taking place.

§ 1200.36. [DR 7–105] Threatening Criminal Prosecution

(a)[1] A lawyer shall not present, participate in presenting, or threaten to present criminal charges solely to obtain an advantage in a civil matter.

1 So in original. No par. (b) has been enacted.

§ 1200.37. [DR 7–106] Trial Conduct

(a) A lawyer shall not disregard or advise the client to disregard a standing rule of a tribunal or a ruling of a tribunal made in the course of a proceeding, but the lawyer may take appropriate steps in good faith to test the validity of such rule or ruling.

(b) In presenting a matter to a tribunal, a lawyer shall disclose:

(1) Controlling legal authority known to the lawyer to be directly adverse to the position of the client and which is not disclosed by opposing counsel.

(2) Unless privileged or irrelevant, the identities of the clients the lawyer represents and of the persons who employed the lawyer.

(c) In appearing as a lawyer before a tribunal, a lawyer shall not:

(1) State or allude to any matter that he or she has no reasonable basis to believe is relevant to the case or that will not be supported by admissible evidence.

(2) Ask any question that he or she has no reasonable basis to believe is relevant to the case and that is intended to degrade a witness or other person.

(3) Assert personal knowledge of the facts in issue, except when testifying as a witness.

(4) Assert a personal opinion as to the justness of a cause, as to the credibility of a witness, as to the culpability of a civil litigant, or as to the guilt or innocence of an accused; but the lawyer may argue, upon analysis of the evidence, for any position or conclusion with respect to the matters stated herein.

(5) Fail to comply with known local customs of courtesy or practice of the bar or a particular tribunal without giving to opposing counsel timely notice of the intent not to comply.

(6) Engage in undignified or discourteous conduct which is degrading to a tribunal.

(7) Intentionally or habitually violate any established rule of procedure or of evidence.

§ 1200.38. [DR 7–107] Trial Publicity

(a) A lawyer participating in or associated with a criminal or civil matter, or associated in a law firm or government agency with a lawyer participating in or associated with a criminal or civil matter, shall not make an extrajudicial statement that a reasonable person would expect to be disseminated by means of public communication if the lawyer knows or reasonably should know that it will have a substantial likelihood of materially prejudicing an adjudicative proceeding in that matter. Notwithstanding the foregoing, a lawyer may make a statement that a reasonable lawyer would believe is required to protect a client from the substantial prejudicial effect of recent publicity not initiated by the lawyer or the lawyer's client. A statement so made shall be limited to such information as is necessary to mitigate the recent adverse publicity.

(b) A statement ordinarily is likely to prejudice materially an adjudicative proceeding when it refers to a civil matter triable to a jury, a criminal matter, or any other proceeding that could result in incarceration, and the statement relates to:

(1) The character, credibility, reputation or criminal record of a party, suspect in a criminal investigation or witness, or the identity of a witness, or the expected testimony of a party or witness.

(2) In a criminal case or proceeding that could result in incarceration, the possibility of a plea of guilty to the offense or the existence or contents of any confession, admission, or statement given by a defendant or suspect or that person's refusal or failure to make a statement.

(3) The performance or results of any examination or test or the refusal or failure of a person to submit to an examination or test, or the identity or nature of physical evidence expected to be presented.

(4) Any opinion as to the guilt or innocence of a defendant or suspect in a criminal case or proceeding that could result in incarceration.

(5) Information the lawyer knows or reasonably should know is likely to be inadmissible as evidence in a trial and would if disclosed create a substantial risk of prejudicing an impartial trial.

(6) The fact that a defendant has been charged with a crime, unless there is included therein a statement explaining that the charge is merely an accusation and

that the defendant is presumed innocent until and unless proven guilty.

(c) Provided that the statement complies with section 1200.39(a) of this Part, a lawyer involved with the investigation or litigation of a matter may state the following without elaboration:

(1) The general nature of the claim or defense.

(2) The information contained in a public record.

(3) That an investigation of the matter is in progress.

(4) The scheduling or result of any step in litigation.

(5) A request for assistance in obtaining evidence and information necessary thereto.

(6) A warning of danger concerning the behavior of a person involved, when there is reason to believe that there exists the likelihood of substantial harm to an individual or to the public interest.

(7) In a criminal case:

(i) The identity, age, residence, occupation and family status of the accused.

(ii) If the accused has not been apprehended, information necessary to aid in apprehension of that person.

(iii) The fact, time and place of arrest, resistance, pursuit, use of weapons, and a description of physical evidence seized, other than as contained only in a confession, admission, or statement.

(iv) The identity of investigating and arresting officers or agencies and the length of the investigation.

§ 1200.39. [DR 7–108] Communication With or Investigation of Jurors

(a) Before the trial of a case a lawyer connected therewith shall not communicate with or cause another to communicate with anyone the lawyer knows to be a member of the venire from which the jury will be selected for the trial of the case.

(b) During the trial of a case:

(1) A lawyer connected therewith shall not communicate with or cause another to communicate with any member of the jury.

(2) A lawyer who is not connected therewith shall not communicate with or cause another to communicate with a juror concerning the case.

(c) DR 7–108(A) and (B) do not prohibit a lawyer from communicating with members of the venire or jurors in the course of official proceedings.

(d) After discharge of the jury from further consideration of a case with which the lawyer was connected, the lawyer shall not ask questions of or make comments to a member of that jury that are calculated

merely to harass or embarrass the juror or to influence the juror's actions in future jury service.

(e) A lawyer shall not conduct or cause, by financial support or otherwise, another to conduct a vexatious or harassing investigation of either a member of the venire or a juror.

(f) All restrictions imposed by DR 7–108 upon a lawyer also apply to communications with or investigations of members of a family of a member of the venire or a juror.

(g) A lawyer shall reveal promptly to the court improper conduct by a member of the venire or a juror, or by another toward a member of the venire or a juror or a member of his or her family of which the lawyer has knowledge.

§ 1200.40. [DR 7–109] Contact With Witnesses

(a) A lawyer shall not suppress any evidence that the lawyer or the client has a legal obligation to reveal or produce.

(b) A lawyer shall not advise or cause a person to hide or to leave the jurisdiction of a tribunal for the purpose of making the person unavailable as a witness therein.

(c) A lawyer shall not pay, offer to pay, or acquiesce in the payment of compensation to a witness contingent upon the content of his or her testimony or the outcome of the case. But a lawyer may advance, guarantee, or acquiesce in the payment of:

(1) Expenses reasonably incurred by a witness in attending or testifying.

(2) Reasonable compensation to a witness for the loss of time in attending, testifying, preparing to testify or otherwise assisting counsel.

(3) A reasonable fee for the professional services of an expert witness.

§ 1200.41. [DR 7–110] Contact With Officials

(a) A lawyer shall not give or lend anything of value to a judge, official, or employee of a tribunal except as permitted by the Code of Judicial Conduct, but a lawyer may make a contribution to the campaign fund of a candidate for judicial office in conformity with the Code of Judicial Conduct.

(b) In an adversary proceeding, a lawyer shall not communicate, or cause another to communicate, as to the merits of the cause with a judge or an official before whom the proceeding is pending, except:

(1) in the course of official proceedings in the cause;

(2) in writing if the lawyer promptly delivers a copy of the writing to opposing counsel or to an adverse party who is not represented by a lawyer;

(3) orally upon adequate notice to opposing counsel or to an adverse party who is not represented by a lawyer; or

(4) as otherwise authorized by law, or by the Code of Judicial Conduct.

§ 1200.41–a. [DR 7–111] Communication After Incidents Involving Personal Injury or Wrongful Death

(a) In the event of an incident involving potential claims for personal injury or wrongful death, no unsolicited communication shall be made to an individual injured in the incident or to a family member or legal representative of such an individual, by a lawyer or law firm, or by any associate, agent, employee or other representative of a lawyer or law firm, seeking to represent the injured individual or legal representative thereof in potential litigation or in a proceeding arising out of the incident before the 30th day after the date of the incident, unless a filing must be made within 30 days of the incident as a legal prerequisite to the particular claim, in which case no unsolicited communication shall be made before the 15th day after the date of the incident.

(b) This provision limiting contact with an injured individual or the legal representative thereof applies as well to lawyers or law firms or any associate, agent, employee or other representative of a lawyer or law firm who represent actual or potential defendants or entities that may defend and/or indemnify said defendants.

§ 1200.42. [DR 8–101] Action as a Public Official

(a) [1] A lawyer who holds public office shall not:

(1) use the public position to obtain, or attempt to obtain, a special advantage in legislative matters for the lawyer or for a client under circumstances where the lawyer knows or it is obvious that such action is not in the public interest;

(2) use the public position to influence, or attempt to influence, a tribunal to act in favor of the lawyer or of a client; or

(3) accept anything of value from any person when the lawyer knows or it is obvious that the offer is for the purpose of influencing the lawyer's action as a public official.

[1] So in original. No par. (b) has been enacted.

§ 1200.43. [DR 8–102] Statements Concerning Judges and Other Adjudicatory Officers

(a) A lawyer shall not knowingly make false statements of fact concerning the qualifications of a candidate for election or appointment to a judicial office.

(b) A lawyer shall not knowingly make false accusations against a judge or other adjudicatory officer.

§ 1200.44. [DR 8–103] Lawyer Candidate for Judicial Office

A lawyer who is a candidate for judicial office shall comply with section 100.5 of the Chief Administrator's Rules Governing Judicial Conduct (22 NYCRR) and Canon 5 of the Code of Judicial Conduct.

§ 1200.45. [DR 9–101] Avoiding Even the Appearance of Impropriety

(a) A lawyer shall not accept private employment in a matter upon the merits of which the lawyer has acted in a judicial capacity.

(b) Except as law may otherwise expressly permit:

(1) A lawyer shall not represent a private client in connection with a matter in which the lawyer participated personally and substantially as a public officer or employee, and no lawyer in a firm with which that lawyer is associated may knowingly undertake or continue representation in such a matter unless:

(i) the disqualified lawyer is effectively screened from any participation, direct or indirect, including discussion, in the matter and is apportioned no part of the fee therefrom; and

(ii) there are no other circumstances in the particular representation that create an appearance of impropriety.

(2) A lawyer having information that the lawyer knows is confidential government information about a person, acquired when the lawyer was a public officer or employee, may not represent a private client whose interests are adverse to that person in a matter in which the information could be used to the material disadvantage of that person. A firm with which that lawyer is associated may knowingly undertake or continue representation in the matter only if the disqualified lawyer is effectively screened from any participation, direct or indirect, including discussion, in the matter and is apportioned no part of the fee therefrom.

(3) A lawyer serving as a public officer or employee shall not:

(i) participate in a matter in which the lawyer participated personally and substantially while in private practice or nongovernmental employment, unless under applicable law no one is, or by lawful delegation may be, authorized to act in the lawyer's stead in the matter; or

(ii) negotiate for private employment with any person who is involved as a party or as attorney for a party in a matter in which the lawyer is participating personally and substantially.

(c) A lawyer shall not state or imply that the lawyer is able to influence improperly or upon irrelevant grounds any tribunal, legislative body, or public official.

(d) A lawyer related to another lawyer as parent, child, sibling or spouse shall not represent in any matter a client whose interests differ from those of another party to the matter who the lawyer knows is represented by the other lawyer unless the client consents to the representation after full disclosure and the lawyer concludes that the lawyer can adequately represent the interests of the client.

§ 1200.46. [DR 9–102] Preserving Identity of Funds and Property of Others; Fiduciary Responsibility; Commingling and Misappropriation of Client Funds or Property; Maintenance of Bank Accounts; Recordkeeping; Examination of Records

(a) Prohibition Against Commingling and Misappropriation of Client Funds or Property. A lawyer in possession of any funds or other property belonging to another person, where such possession is incident to his or her practice of law, is a fiduciary, and must not misappropriate such funds or property or commingle such funds or property with his or her own.

(b) Separate Accounts.

(1) A lawyer who is in possession of funds belonging to another person incident to the lawyer's practice of law, shall maintain such funds in a banking institution within the State of New York which agrees to provide dishonored check reports in accordance with the provisions of Part 1300 of the joint rules of the Appellate Divisions. *Banking institution* means a state or national bank, trust company, savings bank, savings and loan association or credit union. Such funds shall be maintained, in the lawyer's own name, or in the name of a firm of lawyers of which he or she is a member, or in the name of the lawyer or firm of lawyers by whom he or she is employed, in a special account or accounts, separate from any business or personal accounts of the lawyer or lawyer's firm, and separate from any accounts which the lawyer may maintain as executor, guardian, trustee or receiver, or in any other fiduciary capacity, into which special account or accounts all funds held in escrow or otherwise entrusted to the lawyer or firm shall be deposited; provided, however, that such funds may be maintained in a banking institution located outside the State of New York if such banking institution complies with such Part 1300, and the lawyer has obtained the prior written approval of the person to whom such funds belong which specifies the name and address of the office or branch of the banking institution where such funds are to be maintained.

(2) A lawyer or the lawyer's firm shall identify the special bank account or accounts required by section 1200.46(b)(1) of this Part as an "Attorney Special Account," or "Attorney Trust Account," or "Attorney Escrow Account," and shall obtain checks and deposit slips that bear such title. Such title may be accompanied by such other descriptive language as the lawyer may deem appropriate, provided that such additional language distinguishes such special account or accounts from other bank accounts that are maintained by the lawyer or the lawyer's firm.

(3) Funds reasonably sufficient to maintain the account or to pay account charges may be deposited therein.

(4) Funds belonging in part to a client or third person and in part presently or potentially to the lawyer or law firm shall be kept in such special account or accounts, but the portion belonging to the lawyer or law firm may be withdrawn when due unless the right of the lawyer or law firm to receive it is disputed by the client or third person, in which event the disputed portion shall not be withdrawn until the dispute is finally resolved.

(c) Notification of Receipt of Property; Safekeeping; Rendering Accounts; Payment or Delivery of Property. A lawyer shall:

(1) promptly notify a client or third person of the receipt of funds, securities, or other properties in which the client or third person has an interest;

(2) identify and label securities and properties of a client or third person promptly upon receipt and place them in a safe deposit box or other place of safekeeping as soon as practicable;

(3) maintain complete records of all funds, securities, and other properties of a client or third person coming into the possession of the lawyer and render appropriate accounts to the client or third person regarding them; and

(4) promptly pay or deliver to the client or third person as requested by the client or third person the funds, securities, or other properties in the possession of the lawyer which the client or third person is entitled to receive.

(d) Required Bookkeeping Records. A lawyer shall maintain for seven years after the events which they record:

(1) The records of all deposits in and withdrawals from the special accounts specified in section 1200.46(b) of this Part and of any other bank account which records the operations of the lawyer's practice of law. These records shall specifically identify the date, source and description of each item deposited, as well as the date, payee and purpose of each withdrawal or disbursement.

(2) A record for special accounts, showing the source of all funds deposited in such accounts, the names of all persons for whom the funds are or were held, the amount of such funds, the description and

amounts, and the names of all persons to whom such funds were disbursed;

(3) copies of all retainer and compensation agreements with clients;

(4) copies of all statements to clients or other persons showing the disbursement of funds to them or on their behalf;

(5) copies of all bills rendered to clients;

(6) copies of all records showing payments to lawyers, investigators or other persons, not in the lawyer's regular employ, for services rendered or performed;

(7) copies of all retainer and closing statements filed with the Office of Court Administration; and

(8) All checkbooks and check stubs, bank statements, prenumbered cancelled checks and duplicate deposit slips with respect to the special accounts specified in DR 9–102(B) (subdivision (b) of this section) and any other bank account which records the operations of the lawyer's practice of law.

(9) Lawyers shall make accurate entries of all financial transactions in their records of receipts and disbursements, in their special accounts, in their ledger books or similar records, and in any other books of account kept by them in the regular course of their practice, which entries shall be made at or near the time of the act, condition or event recorded.

(10) For Purposes of section 1200.46(d) of this Part, a lawyer may satisfy the requirements of maintaining copies by maintaining any of the following items; original records, photocopies, microfilm, optical imaging, and any other medium that preserves an image of the document that cannot be altered without detection.

(e) **Authorized Signatories.** All special account withdrawals shall be made only to a named payee and not to cash. Such withdrawals shall be made by check or, with the prior written approval of the party entitled to the proceeds, by bank transfer. Only an attorney admitted to practice law in New York State shall be an authorized signatory of a special account.

(f) **Missing Clients.** Whenever any sum of money is payable to a client and the lawyer is unable to locate the client, the lawyer shall apply to the court in which the action was brought if in the unified court system, or, if no action was commenced in the unified court system, to the Supreme Court in the county in which the lawyer maintains an office for the practice of law, for an order directing payment to the lawyer of any fees and disbursements that are owed by the client and the balance, if any, to the Lawyers' Fund for Client Protection for safeguarding and disbursement to persons who are entitled thereto.

(g) **Designation of Successor Signatories.**

(1) Upon the death of a lawyer who was the sole signatory on an attorney trust, escrow or special account, an application may be made to the Supreme Court for an order designating a successor signatory for such trust, escrow or special account who shall be a member of the bar in good standing and admitted to the practice of law in New York State.

(2) An application to designate a successor signatory shall be made to the Supreme Court in the judicial district in which the deceased lawyer maintained an office for the practice of law. The application may be made by the legal representative of the deceased lawyer's estate; a lawyer who was affiliated with the deceased lawyer in the practice of law; any person who has a beneficial interest in such trust, escrow or special account; an officer of a city or county bar association; or counsel for an attorney disciplinary committee. No lawyer may charge a legal fee for assisting with an application to designate a successor signatory pursuant to this rule.

(3) The Supreme Court may designate a successor signatory and may direct the safeguarding of funds from such trust, escrow or special account, and the disbursement of such funds to persons who are entitled thereto, and may order that funds in such account be deposited with the Lawyers' Fund for Client Protection for safeguarding and disbursement to persons who are entitled thereto.

(h) **Dissolution of a Firm.** Upon the dissolution of any firm of lawyers, the former partners or members shall make appropriate arrangements for the maintenance by one of them or by a successor firm of the records specified in section 1200.46(d) of this part. In the absence of agreement on such arrangements, any partner or former partner or member of a firm in dissolution may apply to the Appellate Division in which the principal office of the law firm is located or its designee for direction and such direction shall be binding upon all partners, former partners or members.

(i) **Availability of Bookkeeping Records; Records Subject to Production in Disciplinary Investigations and Proceedings.** The financial records required by this Disciplinary Rule shall be located, or made available, at the principal New York State office of the lawyers subject hereto and any such records shall be produced in response to a notice or subpoena duces tecum issued in connection with a complaint before or any investigation by the appropriate grievance or departmental disciplinary committee, or shall be produced at the direction of the appropriate Appellate Division before any person designated by it. All books and records produced pursuant to this subdivision shall be kept confidential, except for the purpose of the particular proceeding, and their contents shall not be disclosed by anyone in violation of the lawyer-client privilege.

(j) Disciplinary Action. A lawyer who does not maintain and keep the accounts and records as specified and required by this Disciplinary Rule, or who does not produce any such records pursuant to this Rule, shall be deemed in violation of these Rules and shall be subject to disciplinary proceedings.

APPENDIX A.   STANDARDS OF CIVILITY

Preamble

The New York State Standards of Civility for the legal profession set forth principles of behavior to which the bar, the bench and court employees should aspire.   They are not intended as rules to be enforced by sanction or disciplinary action, nor are they intended to supplement or modify the Rules Governing Judicial Conduct, the Code of Professional Responsibility and its Disciplinary Rules, or any other applicable rule or requirement governing conduct.   Instead they are a set of guidelines intended to encourage lawyers, judges and court personnel to observe principles of civility and decorum, and to confirm the legal profession's rightful status as an honorable and respected profession where courtesy and civility are observed as a matter of course.   The Standards are divided into four parts: lawyers' duties to other other lawyers, litigants and witnesses; lawyers' duties to the court and court personnel; judges' duties to lawyers, parties and witnesses; and court personnel's duties to lawyers and litigants.

As lawyers, judges and court employees, we are all essential participants in the judicial process.   That process cannot work effectively to serve the public unless we first treat each other with courtesy, respect and civility.

Lawyers' Duties to Other Lawyers, Litigants and Witnesses

I.   Lawyers should be courteous and civil in all professional dealings with other persons.

A.   Lawyers should act in a civil manner regardless of the ill feelings that their clients may have toward others.

B.   Lawyers can disagree without being disagreeable.   Effective representation does not require antagonistic or acrimonious behavior.   Whether orally or in writing, lawyers should avoid vulgar language, disparaging personal remarks or acrimony toward other counsel, parties or witnesses.

C.   Lawyers should require that persons under their supervision conduct themselves with courtesy and civility.

II.   When consistent with their clients' interests, lawyers should cooperate with opposing counsel in an effort to avoid litigation and to resolve litigation that has already commenced.

A.   Lawyers should avoid unnecessary motion practice or other judicial intervention by negotiating and agreeing with other counsel whenever it is practicable to do so.

B.   Lawyers should allow themselves sufficient time to resolve any dispute or disagreement by communicating with one another and imposing reasonable and meaningful deadlines in light of the nature and status of the case.

III.   A lawyer should respect the schedule and commitments of opposing counsel, consistent with protection of their clients' interests.

A.   In the absence of a court order, a lawyer should agree to reasonable requests for extensions of time or for waiver of procedural formalities when the legitimate interests of the client will not be adversely affected.

B.   Upon request coupled with the simple representation by counsel that more time is required, the first request for an extension to respond to pleadings ordinarily should be granted as a matter of courtesy.

C.   A lawyer should not attach unfair or extraneous conditions to extensions of time.   A lawyer is entitled to impose conditions appropriate to preserve rights that an extension might otherwise jeopardize, and may request, but should not unreasonably insist on, reciprocal scheduling concessions.

D.   A lawyer should endeavor to consult with other counsel regarding scheduling matters in a good faith effort to avoid scheduling conflicts.   A lawyer should likewise cooperate with opposing counsel when scheduling changes are requested, provided the interests of his or her client will not be jeopardized.

E.   A lawyer should notify other counsel and, if appropriate, the court or other persons at the earliest possible time when hearings, depositions, meetings or conferences are to be canceled or postponed.

IV.   A lawyer should promptly return telephone calls and answer correspondence reasonably requiring a response.

V.   The timing and manner of service of papers should not be designed to cause disadvantage to the party receiving the papers.

A.   Papers should not be served in a manner designed to take advantage of an opponent's known absence from the office.

B.   Papers should not be served at a time or in a manner designed to inconvenience an adversary.

C.   Unless specifically authorized by law or rule, a lawyer should not submit papers to the court without serving copies of all such papers upon opposing counsel in such a manner that opposing counsel will receive them before or contemporaneously with the submission to the court.

VI.   A lawyer should not use any aspect of the litigation process, including discovery and motion practice, as a means of harassment or for the purpose of unnecessarily prolonging litigation or increasing litigation expenses.

A. A lawyer should avoid discovery that is not necessary to obtain facts or perpetuate testimony or that is designed to place an undue burden or expense on a party.

B. A lawyer should respond to discovery requests reasonably and not strain to interpret the request so as to avoid disclosure of relevant and non-privileged information.

VII. In depositions and other proceedings, and in negotiations, lawyers should conduct themselves with dignity and refrain from engaging in acts of rudeness and disrespect.

A. Lawyers should not engage in any conduct during a deposition that would not be appropriate in the presence of a judge.

B. Lawyers should advise their clients and witnesses of the proper conduct expected of them in court, at depositions and at conferences, and, to the best of their ability, prevent clients and witnesses from causing disorder or disruption.

C. A lawyer should not obstruct questioning during a deposition or object to deposition questions unless necessary.

D. Lawyers should ask only those questions they reasonably believe are necessary for the prosecution or defense of an action. Lawyers should refrain from asking repetitive or argumentative questions and from making self-serving statements.

VIII. A lawyer should adhere to all express promises and agreements with other counsel, whether oral or in writing, and to agreements implied by the circumstances or by local customs.

IX. Lawyers should not mislead other persons involved in the litigation process.

A. A lawyer should not falsely hold out the possibility of settlement as a means for adjourning discovery or delaying trial.

B. A lawyer should not ascribe a position to another counsel that counsel has not taken or otherwise seek to create an unjustified inference based on counsel's statements or conduct.

C. In preparing written versions of agreements and court orders, a lawyer should attempt to correctly reflect the agreement of the parties or the direction of the court.

X. Lawyers should be mindful of the need to protect the standing of the legal profession in the eyes of the public. Accordingly, lawyers should bring the New York State Standards of Civility to the attention of other lawyers when appropriate.

Lawyers' Duties to the Court and Court Personnel

I. A lawyer is both an officer of the court and an advocate. As such, the lawyer should always strive to uphold the honor and dignity of the profession, avoid disorder and disruption in the courtroom, and maintain a respectful attitude toward the court.

A. Lawyers should speak and write civilly and respectfully in all communications with the court and court personnel.

B. Lawyers should use their best efforts to dissuade clients and witnesses from causing disorder or disruption in the courtroom.

C. Lawyers should not engage in conduct intended primarily to harass or humiliate witnesses.

D. Lawyers should be punctual and prepared for all court appearances; if delayed, the lawyer should notify the court and counsel whenever possible.

II. Court personnel are an integral part of the justice system and should be treated with courtesy and respect at all times.

Judges' Duties to Lawyers, Parties and Witnesses

A judge should be patient, courteous and civil to lawyers, parties and witnesses.

A. A judge should maintain control over the proceedings and insure that they are conducted in a civil manner.

B. Judges should not employ hostile, demeaning or humiliating words in opinions or in written or oral communications with lawyers, parties or witnesses.

C. Judges should, to the extent consistent with the efficient conduct of litigation and other demands on the court, be considerate of the schedules of lawyers, parties and witnesses when scheduling hearings, meetings or conferences.

D. Judges should be punctual in convening all trials, hearings, meetings and conferences; if delayed, they should notify counsel when possible.

E. Judges should make all reasonable efforts to decide promptly all matters presented to them for decision.

F. Judges should use their best efforts to insure that court personnel under their direction act civilly toward lawyers, parties and witnesses.

Duties of Court Personnel to the Court, Lawyers and Litigants

Court personnel should be courteous, patient and respectful while providing prompt, efficient and helpful service to all persons having business with the courts.

A. Court employees should respond promptly and helpfully to requests for assistance or information.

B. Court employees should respect the judge's directions concerning the procedures and atmosphere that the judge wishes to maintain in his or her courtroom.

PART 1205. COOPERATIVE BUSINESS ARRANGEMENTS BETWEEN LAWYERS AND NON–LEGAL PROFESSIONALS

§ 1205.1. Application

This Part shall apply to all lawyers who, pursuant to a cooperative business arrangement, (1) undertake to provide legal services to a client referred by a nonlegal service provider or (2) refer an existing client to a nonlegal service provider.

§ 1205.2. Definition

A "cooperative business arrangement" is a contractual relationship between a lawyer or law firm and a nonlegal professional or nonlegal professional service firm for the purpose of offering to the public, on a systematic and continuing basis, legal services performed by the lawyer or law firm, as well as other nonlegal professional services, as authorized by section 1200.5–c of the Disciplinary Rules of the Code of Professional Responsibility.

§ 1205.3. List of Professions

(a) The Appellate Divisions jointly shall establish and maintain a list of professions, set forth in section 1205.5 of this Part designated by the Appellate Divisions sua sponte or approved by them upon application of a member of a nonlegal profession or nonlegal professional service firm, with whose members a lawyer may enter into a cooperative business arrangement to perform legal and nonlegal services as authorized by section 1200.5–c of the Disciplinary Rules.

(b) A member of a nonlegal profession may apply to the Appellate Division to have that profession included in the list by submitting to the Appellate Division Clerk's Office in any Judicial Department a petition to establish that the profession is composed of individuals who, with respect to their profession, meet the requirements set forth in section 1200.5–c(b)(1) of the Disciplinary Rules.

§ 1205.4. Statement of Client's Rights in Cooperative Business Arrangements

In the furtherance of a cooperative business arrangement, (a) prior to the commencement of legal representation of a client referred by a nonlegal service provider or (b) prior to the referral of an existing client to a nonlegal service provider, a lawyer shall provide the client with a statement of client's rights. That statement shall include a consent to the referral to be signed by the client and shall contain the following:

STATEMENT OF CLIENT'S RIGHTS IN COOPERATIVE BUSINESS ARRANGEMENTS

Your lawyer is providing you with this document to explain how your rights may be affected by the referral of your particular matter by your lawyer to a nonlegal service provider, or by the referral of your particular matter by a nonlegal service provider to your lawyer.

To help avoid any misunderstanding between you and your lawyer please read this document carefully. If you have any questions about these rights, do not hesitate to ask your lawyer.

Your lawyer has entered into a contractual relationship with a nonlegal professional or professional service firm, in the form of a cooperative business arrangement which may include sharing of costs and expenses, to provide legal and nonlegal services. Such an arrangement may substantially affect your rights in a number of respects. Specifically, you are advised:

1. A lawyer's clients are guaranteed the independent professional judgment and undivided loyalty of the lawyer, uncompromised by conflicts of interest. The lawyer's business arrangement with a provider of nonlegal services may not diminish these rights.

2. Confidences and secrets imparted by a client to a lawyer are protected by the attorney/client privilege and may not be disclosed by the lawyer as part of a referral to a nonlegal service provider without the separate written consent of the client.

3. The protections afforded to a client by the attorney/client privilege may not carry over to dealings between the client and a nonlegal service provider.

Information that would be protected as a confidence or secret, if imparted by the client to a lawyer, may not be so protected when disclosed by the client to a nonlegal service provider. Under some circumstances, the nonlegal service provider may be required by statute or a code of ethics to make disclosure to a government agency.

4. Even where a lawyer refers a client to a nonlegal service provider for assistance in financial matters, the lawyer's obligation to preserve and safeguard client funds in his or her possession continues.

You have the right to consult with an independent lawyer or other third party before signing this agreement.

Client's Consent:

I have read the above Statement of Client's Rights in Cooperative Business Arrangements and I consent to the referral of my particular matter in accordance with that Statement.

_____

Client's signature

_____

Date

§ 1205.5. Nonlegal Professions Eligible to Form Cooperative Business Arrangements with Lawyers

Members of the following nonlegal professions are eligible to form contractual business relationships with lawyers:

Architecture

Certified Public Accountancy

Professional Engineering

Land Surveying

Certified Social Work

PART 1210. STATEMENT OF CLIENT'S RIGHTS

Table of Sections

§ 1210.1. Posting

Every attorney with an office located in the State of New York shall insure that there is posted in that office, in a manner visible to clients of the attorney, a statement of client's rights in the form set forth below. Attorneys in offices that provide legal services without fee may delete from the statement those provisions dealing with fees. The statement shall contain the following:

STATEMENT OF CLIENTS RIGHTS

1. You are entitled to be treated with courtesy and consideration at all times by your lawyer and the other lawyers and personnel in your lawyer's office.

2. You are entitled to an attorney capable of handling your legal matter competently and diligently, in accordance with the highest standards of the profession. If you are not satisfied with how your matter is being handled, you have the right to withdraw from the attorney-client relationship at any time (court approval may be required in some matters and your attorney may have a claim against you for the value of services rendered to you up to the point of discharge).

3. You are entitled to your lawyer's independent professional judgment and undivided loyalty uncompromised by conflicts of interest.

4. You are entitled to be charged a reasonable fee and to have your lawyer explain at the outset how the fee will be computed and the manner and frequency of billing. You are entitled to request and receive a written itemized bill from your attorney at reasonable intervals. You may refuse to enter into any fee arrangement that you find unsatisfactory. In the event of a fee dispute, you may have the right to seek arbitration; your attorney will provide you with the necessary information regarding arbitration in the event of a fee dispute, or upon your request.

5. You are entitled to have your questions and concerns addressed in a prompt manner and to have your telephone calls returned promptly.

6. You are entitled to be kept informed as to the status of your matter and to request and receive copies of papers. You are entitled to sufficient information to allow you to participate meaningfully in the development of your matter.

7. You are entitled to have your legitimate objectives respected by your attorney, including whether or not to settle your matter (court approval of a settlement is required in some matters).

8. You have the right to privacy in your dealings with your lawyer and to have your secrets and confidences preserved to the extent permitted by law.

9. You are entitled to have your attorney conduct himself or herself ethically in accordance with the Code of Professional Responsibility.

10. You may not be refused representation on the basis of race, creed, color, religion, sex, sexual orientation, age, national origin or disability.

PART 1215. WRITTEN LETTER OF ENGAGEMENT

Table of Sections

§ 1215.1.   Requirements

(a) Effective March 4, 2002, an attorney who undertakes to represent a client and enters into an arrangement for, charges or collects any fee from a client shall provide to the client a written letter of engagement before commencing the representation, or within a reasonable time thereafter (i) if otherwise impracticable or (ii) if the scope of services to be provided cannot be determined at the time of the commencement of representation. For purposes of this rule, where an entity (such as an insurance carrier) engages an attorney to represent a third party, the term "client" shall mean the entity that engages the attorney. Where there is a significant change in the scope of services or the fee to be charged, an updated letter of engagement shall be provided to the client.

(b) The letter of engagement shall address the following matters:

(1) Explanation of the scope of the legal services to be provided;

(2) Explanation of attorney's fees to be charged, expenses and billing practices; and, where applicable, shall provide that the client may have a right to arbitrate fee disputes under Part 137 of the Rules of the Chief Administrator.

(c) Instead of providing the client with a written letter of engagement, an attorney may comply with the provisions of subdivision (a) by entering into a signed written retainer agreement with the client, before or within a reasonable time after commencing the representation, provided that the agreement addresses the matters set forth in subdivision (b).

§ 1215.2.   Exceptions

This section shall not apply to (1) representation of a client where the fee to be charged is expected to be less than $3000, (2) representation where the attorney's services are of the same general kind as previously rendered to and paid for by the client, or (3) representation in domestic relations matters subject to Part 1400 of the Joint Rules of the Appellate Division (22 NYCRR) or (4) representation where the attorney is admitted to practice in another jurisdiction and maintains no office in the State of New York, or where no material portion of the services are to be rendered in New York.

PART 1220. MEDIATION OF ATTORNEY–CLIENT DISPUTES

Table of Sections

§ 1220.1.   Referral to Mediation

The Grievance Committee or the Office of Chief Counsel ("disciplinary office") may refer attorney-client disputes to mediation pursuant to this Part when it determines, upon receipt of a complaint relating to an attorneys conduct, that mediation may be an appropriate alternative method of resolving the dispute. Disputes involving the following matters shall not be eligible for mediation:

(1) Escrow violations.

(2) Allegations of criminal conduct.

(3) A pattern of similar misconduct or behavior (existing over a reasonable period of time).

(4) Allegations of abuse of alcohol or drugs or of physical or mental impairment.

§ 1220.2.   Mediation Program

(a) **Mediators.** Mediators shall consist of attorneys appointed by the Court or by the bar associations who have agreed to serve as volunteer mediators and who meet the experience and training requirements deemed appropriate by the Court.

(b) **Bar association mediation coordinator.** Bar associations may designate a member of their association to serve as a mediation coordinator ("coordinator"), who shall assist in the administration of the mediation program. In counties within a judicial department where there are fewer than 200 registered attorneys, bar associations may designate a regional mediation coordinator to represent the interests of the respective bar associations.

(c) **Public Officers Law § 17(1).** Mediators, as volunteers, are expressly authorized to participate in a state-sponsored volunteer program within the meaning of subdivision 1 of section 17 of the Public Officers Law.

§ 1220.3.   Procedure

(a) When the disciplinary office determines that a complaint is appropriate for mediation, it shall forward copies of the complaint and any other correspondence related to the complaint, to the appropriate mediator or coordinator, with notification to the attorney and the complainant of the referral. The mediator or coordinator then shall notify the attorney by first class mail, to submit within 20 days a response to the complaint, if a response was not previously submitted. This notice also shall state that, if no response is received within 20 days, the complaint will be automatically returned to the disciplinary office for investigation under the appropriate Appellate Division rules.

(b) Upon receipt of the attorney's response, the matter shall be assigned to or retained by an impartial mediator. The mediator shall schedule a mediation conference within 14–21 days after assignment of the matter, or if the matter has been directly handled by the mediator, within 14–21 days after receipt of the response. Any additional correspondence from the attorney or the complainant concerning the dispute must be submitted to the mediator no later than 10 days prior to the mediation conference. The mediator may grant an adjournment of the conference for good cause, but in no event may the conference be held more than 45 days after the response has been received or after referral to the coordinator, whichever is later. The mediator may conduct the mediation by teleconference. If the parties have resolved their dispute by mediation, a written agreement shall be produced and signed by both parties.

(c) If the coordinator or the mediator determines at any time during the mediation process that the matter is unsuitable for mediation, or that the matter involves the type of ineligible conduct described in section 1220.1, or that the mediation should not proceed because the attorney or complainant is uncooperative, then the complaint shall be returned to the disciplinary office for appropriate action.

§ 1220.4.   Mediation Report

Within 10 days following the conclusion of the mediation, the mediator shall send a report to the disciplinary office advising of any disposition.

(a) If the parties have resolved their dispute by mediation, the report shall be accompanied by the original written agreement signed by both parties, together with all other correspondence related to the dispute. Copies of the agreement shall be provided to the parties.

(b) If the parties are unable to resolve their dispute, the complaint shall be returned to the disciplinary office for appropriate action.

§ 1220.5. Compliance with Mediation Agreement

Compliance with the terms of the mediation agreement shall result in dismissal of the complaint by the disciplinary office. Failure to comply with the terms of the mediated agreement shall constitute "conduct prejudicial to the administration of justice" and shall result in the complaint being investigated as a disciplinary matter under the appropriate Appellate Division rules. A complainant's failure to comply with the terms of the mediated agreement shall result in dismissal of the complaint.

§ 1220.6. Confidentiality

All mediated proceedings are confidential pursuant to Judiciary Law, § 90(10).

APPENDIX A.   GUIDELINES FOR ATTORNEYS, CLIENTS AND MEDIATORS

1. Introduction to Program

It is the responsibility of the Appellate Divisions of the Supreme Court to ensure that attorneys are fit to practice law and adhere to proper ethical standards through the disciplinary programs administered by the Grievance Committee or the Office of Chief Counsel ("disciplinary office") in each judicial department. When clients assert that an attorney's conduct jeopardizes the public interest or severely prejudices a client's rights, such misconduct is subject to formal disciplinary procedures. These procedures can result in private sanctions, public censure, suspension or disbarment. When clients assert grievances that may not warrant formal disciplinary procedures, such grievances may be appropriate for referral by the disciplinary office to the Program for Mediation of Attorney–Client Disputes that has been established by the Appellate Divisions at 22 NYCRR Part 1220 (April 1998).

2. The Mediation Process

Mediation is a proven means of dispute resolution which enables parties to meet together in an informal atmosphere with the assistance of a neutral mediator in order to find solutions that address their interests and needs. Mediation can provide attorneys, clients and the disciplinary office with an effective means of resolving minor disputes in a non-adversarial manner. Mediation provides an opportunity to address a client's underlying interests and needs, while minimizing costs for attorneys in defending minor complaints and encouraging a positive relationship between attorneys and their clients and the disciplinary office.

3. Complaints Subject to Mediation

The disciplinary office will evaluate a client's complaint about an attorney's conduct to determine whether it is appropriate for mediation. Referral to mediation is entirely within the discretion of the disciplinary office and neither the complainant nor the attorney has any presumptive right to have a complaint referred to mediation. However, once the disciplinary office deems a complaint appropriate for mediation, and the parties agree to mediate, each party shall cooperate in the mediation process. The types of cases that will be referred to mediation generally are those in which there has been a breakdown in the attorney-client relationship and where the complaint could be resolved best through conciliation and not formal disciplinary proceedings.

4. Complaints Excluded from Mediation

(a) *Misconduct in the Complaint.* Since avoidance of ethical misconduct by attorneys is a matter of public interest to the State and the courts, a complaint will not be considered appropriate for referral to mediation when it asserts ethical misconduct that could be subject to private sanctions, public censure, suspension or disbarment, including, but not limited to:

(i) escrow violations;

(ii) allegations of criminal conduct;

(iii) a pattern of similar misconduct or behavior (existing over a reasonable period of time);

(iv) allegations of abuse of alcohol or drugs or of physical or mental impairment.

(b) *Misconduct Revealed During Mediation.* When an attorney engages in material ethical misconduct at the mediation session or a party to the mediation reveals that the attorney has engaged in material ethical misconduct that was not previously known by the disciplinary office, whether that conduct is related to or unrelated to the complaint being mediated, the mediator shall terminate the mediation process and report the misconduct to the disciplinary office in the mediation summary report. Such report shall be accompanied by the complaint and response originally submitted to the mediator. A copy of the mediation summary report will also be provided to the mediation coordinator for inclusion in the mediation file. The mediation report constitutes an exception to the confidentiality of all phases of the mediation process.

5.   Mediator Panels

(a) *Mediators.* Mediators shall consist of attorneys appointed by the court or by the bar associations who have agreed to serve as volunteer mediators and who meet the experience and training requirements deemed appropriate by the Court.

(b) *Mediation Coordinators.* Bar associations may appoint one of their members to serve as a mediation coordinator ("coordinator") to assist the disciplinary office in administering the program, including maintaining files, scheduling mediation, assessing conflicts of interest between a potential mediator and the parties to the mediation before appointing the mediators, and appointing mediators on a rotating basis from the lists of available mediators. In counties within a judicial department where there are fewer than 200 registered attorneys, local bar associations may designate a regional coordinator to represent the interests of the respective bar associations in administering the program.

(c) *Mediator Training.* Mediator Training Programs may include the following:

(1) conflict resolution, negotiation, and mediation theory;

(2) standard mediation process and techniques, including mediation skills that relate to active listening, eliciting interests that may not seem legally relevant, probing, reframing of concerns, and introducing ordinary standards of professional practice to those unfamiliar with them;

(3) standards for conduct of mediators concerning impartiality, ethics and confidentiality;

(4) statutes, rules and practices governing mediated settlement conferences; and

(5) identification of cases that are not appropriate for mediation.

(d) *Mediator Immunity.* The mediator will not be liable for any act or omission while serving as an approved volunteer mediator except for wilful misconduct. Attorneys serving as volunteer mediators in this program are entitled to the protections afforded to State-sponsored volunteers within the meaning of subdivision (1) of section 17 of the Public Officers Law.

(e) *Conflicts of Interest and Impartiality.* Upon receipt of the file, mediators, prior to the start of mediation or as part of the assignment process by the coordinator, shall determine whether there exists any conflict of interest between the mediator and the parties to the mediation. Conflicts include, but are not limited to, a personal or business relationship by the mediator with one of the parties during the last five years; an adversarial relationship between the mediator or an attorney in his or her firm and either party within the last five years; or legal representation of one of the parties by the mediator or by an attorney in his or her firm that concluded within the last five years. Where such a conflict of interest exists and is not waived by the parties, the matter shall be assigned to another mediator. In addition, if at the start of the mediation process either party objects for cause to the assigned mediator, or the mediator does not believe that he or she can serve as an impartial mediator, a new mediator should be appointed.

The mediator will conduct the conference informally. At the outset of the process, the mediator should describe the rules by which the mediation will proceed and make clear to the parties that he or she is serving as a mediator and not a judge.

The mediator's role is to facilitate communication and suggest ways of resolving the dispute, and not to impose a settlement on the parties. The mediator shall make every effort to hear all the relevant facts, review all the relevant documents, become familiar with any controlling legal principles and seek to bring about an acceptable compromise between the parties. The mediator should refrain from using legal jargon and assure that any proposal discussed as a means of resolving the matter is clearly understood by the parties.

6.   Mediation Process

The disciplinary office, upon determining that a complaint is appropriate for mediation, will send copies of the complaint and any other correspondence related to the complaint, to the appropriate mediator or coordinator, and notify the attorney and the complainant of the referral. The mediator or coordinator then will notify the attorney by first class mail to submit within 20 days a response to the complaint, if a response was not previously submitted. If no response is received within 20 days, the complaint will be returned to the disciplinary office for investigation.

Upon receipt of the attorney's response, the matter will be assigned to or retained by an impartial mediator. The mediator will schedule a mediation conference within 14- 21 days after assignment of the matter, or if the matter has been directly handled by the mediator, within 14–21 days after receipt of the response. Any additional correspondence from the attorney or the complainant concerning the dispute must be submitted to the mediator no later than 10 days prior to the mediation conference. The mediator may grant an adjournment of the conference for good cause, but in no event may the conference be held more than 45 days after the response has been received or after referral to the coordinator, whichever is later.

Within 10 days following the conclusion of the mediation, the mediator shall send a mediation summary report to the disciplinary office.

7. Limited Confidentiality for Attorney–Client Mediation Processes

The significant public interest involved in regulating an attorney's fitness to practice law requires that mediation shall be confidential except as stated below and except as required by section 90(10) of the Judiciary Law. Mediators shall inform the parties to the mediation about these exceptions in the mediator's opening statement in the mediation session.

(a) *Mediators Shall Report Misconduct.* Mediators shall report to the disciplinary office whenever an attorney engages in material ethical misconduct during a mediation session or when a party to the mediation reveals that the attorney engaged in material ethical misconduct that was not previously known by the disciplinary office, whether such conduct is related to or unrelated to the complaint being mediated. Mediators shall terminate the mediation process and report the misconduct to the disciplinary office in the mediation summary report. Such report shall be accompanied by the complaint and response originally submitted to the mediator. A copy of the report shall be provided to the coordinator for inclusion in the mediation file. The conduct reported by the mediator under this section along with the allegations of the original complaint are subject to investigation by the disciplinary office.

(b) *Mediated Agreements Shall be Forwarded to Disciplinary Offices.* Upon the termination of mediation, the mediator shall include a duplicate original of any full or partial signed agreement reached by the parties at the mediation session with the mediation summary report that must be filed with the coordinator or the disciplinary office. Coordinators will forward the agreement and report to the disciplinary office.

(c) *Report Shall be Filed upon Unsuccessful Mediation.* The coordinator or mediator shall report a termination of the mediation process to the disciplinary office on a mediation summary report when a complainant fails to respond to a notice or to appear, when the complainant withdraws the complaint, or when the mediator terminates the mediation on his or her own accord if agreement cannot be reached.

(d) *Correspondence Shall be Labeled "Confidential."* All correspondence by disciplinary offices, coordinators or mediators to the parties shall bear the legend, "PERSONAL AND CONFIDENTIAL."

(e) *Files Shall be Confidential with Exceptions.* Except as provided in (f) below, documents submitted to the mediator shall be used only for the mediation process and shall be returned to the party who provided them at the close of the mediation process, including brief statements that the mediator requests from the parties before the start of mediation process after the response to the complaint is filed. The complaint and response to the complaint along with any mediated agreement will remain part of the mediation file.

The files created for the mediation program, including administrative documents created by the coordinator, shall be marked as "CONFIDENTIAL" and all reasonable steps shall be taken by the disciplinary office, coordinator and staff, and mediators to assure such confidentiality, except as specifically provided in these rules. Absent an order from the Appellate Divisions to the contrary pursuant to section 90(10) of the Judiciary Law, the only persons who shall have access to the confidential files are coordinators and their administrative staffs, members of the disciplinary offices, appropriate Appellate Division staff, and the complainant and attorney, or their respective legal representatives. Mediators shall only have access to the files for cases on which they serve as mediators.

(f) *Mediation Sessions Shall be Confidential with Exceptions.* Mediation sessions shall be held in circumstances assuring confidentiality of the process. Mediators should assure the availability of confidential individual caucus sessions with each party to encourage parties to discuss their genuine interests and needs that may assist the mediator in helping the parties reach acceptable mutual resolutions. Mediators have an obligation to report to the disciplinary offices any evidence not previously known by the disciplinary office that raises a substantial question as to the attorney's honesty, trustworthiness or fitness as a lawyer in other respects. Mediators shall not reveal information to another party to the mediation when it is identified as confidential by the revealing party. Mediators and parties agree they shall not reveal any statements, conduct or documents used during mediation to third parties, except as specifically required by these rules.

8. Outcome of the Mediation Process

(a) *Failure to Cooperate.* If an attorney fails to respond to a complaint or to appear at a mediation session, the mediator shall terminate the mediation and file a mediation summary report. If a complainant fails to cooperate in the mediation process, the mediator shall terminate the mediation process and file with the disciplinary office a recommendation that the complaint be dismissed.

(b) *Dismissal of complaint upon an attorney's compliance with Mediated Agreement.* When a mediation results in a mediated agreement, an attorney's compliance with the terms of a mediated agreement in a timely and good faith manner will result in dismissal of the complaint by the disciplinary office. Mediated agreements should set forth a reasonable time frame for compliance whenever feasible.

(c) *Failure to Comply with a Mediated Agreement.* Before the close of the mediation session, the mediator will inform the client that an attorney's failure to comply with the mediated agreement in the time period specified in the agreement will result in the matter being referred to the disciplinary office. If an attorney fails to comply with the terms of a mediated agreement on file with the disciplinary office, the disciplinary office may initiate a disciplinary investigation on the original charges and on "conduct prejudicial to the administration of justice" arising from noncompliance with the mediated agreement. If such investigation is commenced, the mediated agreement, complaint and response to the complaint can be used by the disciplinary office in its investigation.

(d) *Failure to Reach Agreement.* When parties do not reach agreement in the mediation, the mediator shall report termination of the process without agreement on the mediation summary report sent to the disciplinary office which may continue its investigation of the original complaint.

PART 1230. FEE ARBITRATION

Table of Sections

§ 1230.1. Establishment of Fee Arbitration Program

(a) The Chief Administrator of the Courts shall establish a fee arbitration program, which shall be approved by the justices of the Appellate Divisions and which shall provide for the resolution by arbitrators of fee disputes between an attorney and client based upon representation in civil matters.

(b) The fee arbitration program established by the Chief Administrator pursuant to this Part shall provide for arbitration that shall be binding upon both attorney and client unless de novo review is sought in the courts.

PART 1300.   DISHONORED CHECK REPORTING RULES FOR ATTORNEY SPECIAL, TRUST AND ESCROW ACCOUNTS

Table of Sections

§ 1300.1.   Dishonored Check Reports

(a) Special bank accounts required by Disciplinary Rule 9–102 (22 NYCRR 1200.46) shall be maintained only in banking institutions which have agreed to provide dishonored check reports in accordance with the provisions of this section.

(b) An agreement to provide dishonored check reports shall be filed with the Lawyers' Fund for Client Protection, which shall maintain a central registry of all banking institutions which have been approved in accordance with this section, and the current status of each such agreement.   The agreement shall apply to all branches of each banking institution that provides special bank accounts for attorneys engaged in the practice of law in this state, and shall not be cancelled by a banking institution except on thirty days prior written notice to the Lawyers' Fund for Client Protection.

(c) A dishonored check report by a banking institution shall be required whenever a properly payable instrument is presented against an attorney special, trust or escrow account which contains insufficient available funds, and the banking institution dishonors the instrument for that reason.   A "properly payable instrument" means an instrument which, if presented in the normal course of business, is in a form requiring payment under the laws of the State of New York.

(d) A dishonored check report shall be substantially in the form of the notice of dishonor which the banking institution customarily forwards to its customer, and may include a photocopy or a computer-generated duplicate of such notice.

(e) Dishonored check reports shall be mailed to the Lawyers' Fund for Client Protection, 119 Washington Avenue, Albany, NY 12210, within five banking days after the date of presentment against insufficient available funds.

(f) The Lawyers' Fund for Client Protection shall hold each dishonored check report for ten business days to enable the banking institution to withdraw a report provided by inadvertence or mistake; except that the curing of an insufficiency of available funds by a lawyer or law firm by the deposit of additional funds shall not constitute reason for withdrawing a dishonored check report.

(g) After holding the dishonored check report for ten business days, the Lawyers' Fund for Client Protection shall forward it to the attorney disciplinary committee for the judicial department or district having jurisdiction over the account holder, as indicated by the law office or other address on the report, for such inquiry and action that attorney disciplinary committee deems appropriate.

(h) Every lawyer admitted to the Bar of the State of New York shall be deemed to have consented to the dishonored check reporting requirements of this section.   Lawyers and law firms shall promptly notify their banking institutions of existing or new attorney special, trust, or escrow accounts for the purpose of facilitating the implementation and administration of the provisions of this section.

PART 1400. PROCEDURE FOR ATTORNEYS IN DOMESTIC RELATIONS MATTERS

Table of Sections

---

§ 1400.1. Application

This Part shall apply to all attorneys who, on or after November 30, 1993, undertake to represent a client in a claim, action or proceeding, or preliminary to the filing of a claim, action or proceeding, in either Supreme Court or Family Court, or in any court of appellate jurisdiction, for divorce, separation, annulment, custody, visitation, maintenance, child support, or alimony, or to enforce or modify a judgment or order in connection with any such claims, actions or proceedings. This Part shall not apply to attorneys representing clients without compensation paid by the client, except that where the client is other than a minor, the provisions of section 1400.2 shall apply to the extent they are not applicable to compensation.

§ 1400.2. Statement of Client's Rights and Responsibilities

An attorney shall provide a prospective client with a statement of client's rights and responsibilities, in a form prescribed by the Appellate Divisions, at the initial conference and prior to the signing of a written retainer agreement. If the attorney is not being paid a fee from the client for the work to be performed on the particular case, the attorney may delete from the statement those provisions dealing with fees. The attorney shall obtain a signed acknowledgement of receipt from the client. The statement shall contain the following:

STATEMENT OF CLIENT'S RIGHTS AND RESPONSIBILITIES

Your attorney is providing you with this document to inform you of what you, as a client, are entitled to by law or by custom. To help prevent any misunderstanding between you and your attorney please read this document carefully.

If you ever have any questions about these rights, or about the way your case is being handled, do not hesitate to ask your attorney. He or she should be readily available to represent your best interests and keep you informed about your case.

An attorney may not refuse to represent you on the basis of race, creed, color, sex, sexual orientation, age, national origin or disability.

You are entitled to an attorney who will be capable of handling your case; show you courtesy and consideration at all times; represent you zealously; and preserve your confidences and secrets that are revealed in the course of the relationship.

You are entitled to a written retainer agreement which must set forth, in plain language, the nature of the relationship and the details of the fee arrangement. At your request, and before you sign the agreement, you are entitled to have your attorney clarify in writing any of its terms, or include additional provisions.

You are entitled to fully understand the proposed rates and retainer fee before you sign a retainer agreement, as in any other contract.

You may refuse to enter into any fee arrangement that you find unsatisfactory.

Your attorney may not request a fee that is contingent on the securing of a divorce or on the amount of money or property that may be obtained.

Your attorney may not request a retainer fee that is nonrefundable. That is, should you discharge your attorney, or should your attorney withdraw from the case, before the retainer is used up, he or she is entitled to be paid commensurate with the work performed on your case and any expenses, but must return the balance of the retainer to you. However, your attorney may enter into a minimum fee arrangement with you that provides for the payment of a specific amount below which the fee will not fall based upon the handling of the case to its conclusion.

You are entitled to know the approximate number of attorneys and other legal staff members who will be working on your case at any given time and what you will be charged for the services of each.

You are entitled to know in advance how you will be asked to pay legal fees and expenses, and how the retainer, if any, will be spent.

At your request, and after your attorney has had a reasonable opportunity to investigate your case, you are entitled to be given an estimate of approximate future costs of your case, which estimate shall be made in good faith but may be subject to change due to facts and circumstances affecting the case.

You are entitled to receive a written, itemized bill on a regular basis, at least every 60 days.

You are expected to review the itemized bills sent by counsel, and to raise any objections or errors in a timely manner. Time spent in discussion or explanation of bills will not be charged to you.

You are expected to be truthful in all discussions with your attorney, and to provide all relevant information and documentation to enable him or her to competently prepare your case.

You are entitled to be kept informed of the status of your case, and to be provided with copies of correspondence and documents prepared on your behalf or received from the court or your adversary.

You have the right to be present in court at the time that conferences are held.

You are entitled to make the ultimate decision on the objectives to be pursued in your case, and to make the final decision regarding the settlement of your case.

Your attorney's written retainer agreement must specify under what circumstances he or she might seek to withdraw as your attorney for nonpayment of legal fees. If an action or proceeding is pending, the court may give your attorney a "charging lien," which entitles your attorney to payment for services already rendered at the end of the case out of the proceeds of the final order or judgment.

You are under no legal obligation to sign a confession of judgment or promissory note, or to agree to a lien or mortgage on your home to cover legal fees. Your attorney's written retainer agreement must specify whether, and under what circumstances, such security may be requested. In no event may such security interest be obtained by your attorney without prior court approval and notice to your adversary. An attorney's security interest in the marital residence cannot be foreclosed against you.

You are entitled to have your attorney's best efforts exerted on your behalf, but no particular results can be guaranteed.

If you entrust money with an attorney for an escrow deposit in your case, the attorney must safeguard the escrow in a special bank account. You are entitled to a written escrow agreement, a written receipt, and a complete record concerning the escrow. When the terms of the escrow agreement have been performed, the attorney must promptly make payment of the escrow to all persons who are entitled to it.

In the event of a fee dispute, you may have the right to seek arbitration. Your attorney will provide you with the necessary information regarding arbitration in the event of a fee dispute, or upon your request.

Receipt Acknowledged:

_____

Attorney's signature

_____

Client's signature

_____

Date

§ 1400.3.   Written Retainer Agreement

An attorney who undertakes to represent a party and enters into an arrangement for, charges or collects any fee from a client shall execute a written agreement with the client setting forth in plain language the terms of compensation and the nature of services to be rendered. The agreement, and any amendment thereto, shall be signed by both client and attorney, and, in actions in Supreme Court, a copy of the signed agreement shall be filed with the court with the statement of net worth. Where substitution of counsel occurs after the filing of the net worth statement, a signed copy of the attorney's retainer agreement shall be filed with the court within 10 days of its execution. A copy of a signed amendment shall be filed within 15 days of signing. A duplicate copy of the filed agreement and any amendment shall be provided to the client. The agreement shall be subject to the provisions governing confidentiality contained in Domestic Relations Law, section 235(1). The agreement shall contain the following information:

RETAINER AGREEMENT

1. Names and addresses of the parties entering into the agreement;

2. Nature of the services to be rendered;

3. Amount of the advance retainer, if any, and what it is intended to cover;

4. Circumstances under which any portion of the advance retainer may be refunded. Should the attorney withdraw from the case or be discharged prior to

the depletion of the advance retainer, the written retainer agreement shall provide how the attorney's fees and expenses are to be determined, and the remainder of the advance retainer shall be refunded to the client;

5. Client's right to cancel the agreement at any time; how the attorney's fee will be determined and paid should the client discharge the attorney at any time during the course of the representation;

6. How the attorney will be paid through the conclusion of the case after the retainer is depleted; whether the client may be asked to pay another lump sum;

7. Hourly rate of each person whose time may be charged to the client; any out-of-pocket disbursements for which the client will be required to reimburse the attorney. Any changes in such rates or fees shall be incorporated into a written agreement constituting an amendment to the original agreement, which must be signed by the client before it may take effect;

8. Any clause providing for a fee in addition to the agreed-upon rate, such as a reasonable minimum fee clause, must be defined in plain language and set forth the circumstances under which such fee may be incurred and how it will be calculated.

9. Frequency of itemized billing, which shall be at least every 60 days; the client may not be charged for time spent in discussion of the bills received;

10. Client's right to be provided with copies of correspondence and documents relating to the case, and to be kept apprised of the status of the case;

11. Whether and under what circumstances the attorney might seek a security interest from the client, which can be obtained only upon court approval and on notice to the adversary;

12. Under what circumstances the attorney might seek to withdraw from the case for nonpayment of fees, and the attorney's right to seek a charging lien from the court.

13. Should a dispute arise concerning the attorney's fee, the client may seek arbitration; the attorney shall provide information concerning fee arbitration in the event of such dispute or upon the client's request.

§ 1400.4. Nonrefundable Retainer Fee

An attorney shall not enter into an arrangement for, charge or collect a nonrefundable retainer fee from a client. An attorney may enter into a "minimum fee" arrangement with a client that provides for the payment of a specific amount below which the fee will not fall based upon the handling of the case to its conclusion.

§ 1400.5. Security Interests

(a) An attorney may obtain a confession of judgment or promissory note, take a lien on real property, or otherwise obtain a security interest to secure his or her fee only where:

(1) the retainer agreement provides that a security interest may be sought;

(2) notice of an application for a security interest has been given to the other spouse; and,

(3) the court grants approval for the security interest after submission of an application for counsel fees.

(b) Notwithstanding the provisions of subdivision (a) of this section, an attorney shall not foreclose on a mortgage placed on the marital residence while the spouse who consents to the mortgage remains the titleholder and the residence remains the spouse's primary residence.

§ 1400.6. [Deleted]

§ 1400.7. Fee Arbitration

In the event of a fee dispute between attorney and client, the client may seek to resolve the dispute by arbitration pursuant to a fee arbitration program established by the Chief Administrator of the Courts and subject to the approval of the justices of the Appellate Divisions.

APPENDIX A. STATEMENT OF CLIENT'S RIGHTS AND RESPONSIBILITIES

Your attorney is providing you with this document to inform you of what you, as a client, are entitled to by law or by custom. To help prevent any misunderstanding between you and your attorney please read this document carefully.

If you ever have any questions about these rights, or about the way your case is being handled, do not hesitate to ask your attorney. He or she should be readily available to represent your best interests and keep you informed about your case.

An attorney may not refuse to represent you on the basis of race, creed, color, sex, sexual orientation, age, national origin or disability.

You are entitled to an attorney who will be capable of handling your case; show you courtesy and consideration at all times; represent you zealously; and preserve your confidences and secrets that are revealed in the course of the relationship.

You are entitled to a written retainer agreement which must set forth, in plain language, the nature of the relationship and the details of the fee arrangement. At your request, and before you sign the agreement, you are entitled to have your attorney clarify in writing any of its terms, or include additional provisions.

You are entitled to fully understand the proposed rates and retainer fee before you sign a retainer agreement, as in any other contract.

You may refuse to enter into any fee arrangement that you find unsatisfactory.

Your attorney may not request a fee that is contingent on the securing of a divorce or on the amount of money or property that may be obtained.

Your attorney may not request a retainer fee that is nonrefundable. That is, should you discharge your attorney, or should your attorney withdraw from the case, before the retainer is used up, he or she is entitled to be paid commensurate with the work performed on your case and any expenses, but must return the balance of the retainer to you. However, your attorney may enter into a minimum fee arrangement with you that provides for the payment of a specific amount below which the fee will not fall based upon the handling of the case to its conclusion.

You are entitled to know the approximate number of attorneys and other legal staff members who will be working on your case at any given time and what you will be charged for the services of each.

You are entitled to know in advance how you will be asked to pay legal fees and expenses, and how the retainer, if any, will be spent.

At your request, and after your attorney has had a reasonable opportunity to investigate your case, you are entitled to be given an estimate of approximate future costs of your case, which estimate shall be made in good faith but may be subject to change due to facts and circumstances affecting the case.

You are entitled to receive a written, itemized bill on a regular basis, at least every 60 days.

You are expected to review the itemized bills sent by counsel, and to raise any objections or errors in a timely manner. Time spent in discussion or explanation of bills will not be charged to you.

You are expected to be truthful in all discussions with your attorney, and to provide all relevant information and documentation to enable him or her to competently prepare your case.

You are entitled to be kept informed of the status of your case, and to be provided with copies of corre-

spondence and documents prepared on your behalf or received from the court or your adversary.

You have the right to be present in court at the time that conferences are held.

You are entitled to make the ultimate decision on the objectives to be pursued in your case, and to make the final decision regarding the settlement of your case.

Your attorney's written retainer agreement must specify under what circumstances he or she might seek to withdraw as your attorney for nonpayment of legal fees. If an action or proceeding is pending, the court may give your attorney a "charging lien," which entitles your attorney to payment for services already rendered at the end of the case out of the proceeds of the final order or judgment.

You are under no legal obligation to sign a confession of judgment or promissory note, or to agree to a lien or mortgage on your home to cover legal fees. Your attorney's written retainer agreement must specify whether, and under what circumstances, such security may be requested. In no event may such security interest be obtained by your attorney without prior court approval and notice to your adversary. An attorney's security interest in the marital residence cannot be foreclosed against you.

You are entitled to have your attorney's best efforts exerted on your behalf, but no particular results can be guaranteed.

If you entrust money with an attorney for an escrow deposit in your case, the attorney must safeguard the escrow in a special bank account. You are entitled to a written escrow agreement, a written receipt, and a complete record concerning the escrow. When the terms of the escrow agreement have been performed, the attorney must promptly make payment of the escrow to all persons who are entitled to it.

In the event of a fee dispute, you may have the right to seek arbitration. Your attorney will provide you with the necessary information regarding arbitration in the event of a fee dispute, or upon your request.

Receipt Acknowledged:

_____   _____
Attorney's signature   Client's signature

_____
Date

APPENDIX B.   STATEMENT OF CLIENT'S RIGHTS AND RESPONSIBILITIES
[To Be Used Only When Representation Is Without Fee]

Your attorney is providing you with this document to inform you of what you, as a client, are entitled to by law or by custom. To help prevent any misunderstanding between you and your attorney please read this document carefully.

If you ever have any questions about these rights, or about the way your case is being handled, do not hesitate to ask your attorney. He or she should be readily available to represent your best interests and keep you informed about your case.

An attorney may not refuse to represent you on the basis of race, creed, color, sex, sexual orientation, age, national origin or disability.

You are entitled to an attorney who will be capable of handling your case; show you courtesy and consideration at all times; represent you zealously; and preserve your confidences and secrets that are revealed in the course of the relationship.

You are expected to be truthful in all discussions with your attorney, and to provide all relevant information and documentation to enable him or her to competently prepare your case.

You are entitled to be kept informed of the status of your case, and to be provided with copies of correspondence and documents prepared on your behalf or received from the court or your adversary.

You have the right to be present in court at the time that conferences are held.

You are entitled to make the ultimate decision on the objectives to be pursued in your case, and to make the final decision regarding the settlement of your case.

You are entitled to have your attorney's best efforts exerted on your behalf, but no particular results can be guaranteed.

If you entrust money with an attorney for an escrow deposit in your case, the attorney must safeguard the escrow in a special bank account. You are entitled to a written escrow agreement, a written receipt, and a complete record concerning the escrow. When the terms of the escrow agreement have been performed, the attorney must promptly make payment of the escrow to all persons who are entitled to it.

Receipt Acknowledged:

_____   _____
Attorney's signature   Client's signature

_____
Date

773

PART 1500.   MANDATORY CONTINUING LEGAL EDUCATION PROGRAM FOR ATTORNEYS IN THE STATE OF NEW YORK

Table of Sections

SUBPART A.   STRUCTURE OF PROGRAM

§ 1500.1.   Scope

There shall be a mandatory continuing legal education program in the State of New York (hereinafter Program) which shall include a transitional legal education program for newly admitted attorneys, as set forth in Subpart B, and a legal education program for all other admitted attorneys, as set forth in Subpart C. A Continuing Legal Education Board shall accredit and oversee, as set forth in this Subpart, the courses, programs and other educational activities that will satisfy the requirements of the Program.

§ 1500.2.   Definitions

(a) Accredited Course or Program is a continuing legal education course or program that has met the standards set forth in § 1500.4(b) and has received advance accreditation approval by the Continuing Legal Education Board.

(b) Accredited Provider is a person or entity whose continuing legal education program has been accredited by the Continuing Legal Education Board, and who has been certified by the Continuing Legal Education Board as an accredited provider of continuing legal education courses and programs in accordance with § 1500.4(c).

(c) Ethics and Professionalism may include, among other things, the following: the norms relating to lawyers' professional obligations to clients (including the obligation to provide legal assistance to those in need, confidentiality, competence, conflicts of interest, the allocation of decision making, and zealous advocacy and its limits); the norms relating to lawyers' professional relations with prospective clients, courts and other legal institutions, and third parties (including the lawyers' fiduciary, accounting and record-keeping obligations when entrusted with law client and escrow monies, as well as the norms relating to civility); the sources of lawyers' professional obligations (including disciplinary rules, judicial decisions, and relevant constitutional and statutory provisions); recognition and resolution of ethical dilemmas; the mechanisms for enforcing professional norms; substance abuse control; and professional values (including professional development, improving the profession, and the promotion of fairness, justice and morality).

(d) Skills must relate to the practice of law and may include, among other things, problem solving, legal analysis and reasoning, legal research and writing, drafting documents, factual investigation (as taught in courses on areas of professional practice), communication, counseling, negotiation, mediation, arbitration, organization and trial advocacy.

(e) Law Practice Management must relate to the practice of law and may encompass, among other

774

things, office management, applications of technology, state and federal court procedures, stress management, management of legal work and avoiding malpractice and litigation.

(f) Areas of Professional Practice may include, among other things, corporations, wills/trusts, elder law, estate planning/administration, real estate, commercial law, civil litigation, criminal litigation, family law, labor and employment law, administrative law, securities, tort/insurance practice, bankruptcy, taxation, compensation, intellectual property, municipal law, landlord/tenant, environmental law, entertainment law, international law, social security and other government benefits, and alternative dispute resolution procedures.

(g) Regulations and Guidelines refers to the Regulations and Guidelines of the Continuing Legal Education Board set forth in Part 7500 of Volume 22 of the New York Codes, Rules, and Regulations.

§ 1500.3. The Continuing Legal Education Board

(a) The Continuing Legal Education Board. The Continuing Legal Education Board (CLE Board) is hereby established.

(b) Board Composition. The CLE Board shall consist of 16 resident members of the bench and bar. Three (3) members shall be chosen by each of the Presiding Justices of the Appellate Divisions, and four (4) members shall be chosen by the Chief Judge of the State of New York. The Chief Judge shall designate the Chair. Board members shall serve at the pleasure of the Administrative Board of the Courts.

(c) Quorum. Nine (9) members shall constitute a quorum of the entire CLE Board.

(d) Term of Service. The term of Board members shall be three years. Board members shall be appointed for no more than one three-year term.

(e) Duties and Responsibilities. The CLE Board is authorized to: accredit providers of courses, programs, and other educational activities that will satisfy the requirements of the Program; determine the number of credit hours for which continuing legal education credit will be given for particular courses or programs; adopt or repeal regulations and forms consistent with these rules; examine course materials and the qualifications of continuing legal education instructors; consult and appoint committees in furtherance of its official duties as necessary; foster and encourage the offering of accredited courses and programs, particularly in geographically isolated regions; and report annually on its activities to the Chief Judge, the Presiding Justices of the Appellate Divisions and the Chief Administrator of the Courts.

(f) Expenses. Members of the CLE Board shall serve without compensation but shall be reimbursed for their reasonable, actual and direct expenses incurred in furtherance of their official duties.

(g) Confidentiality. The files, records and proceedings of the CLE Board, as they relate to an attorney's satisfying the requirements of this Part, shall be confidential and shall not be disclosed except in furtherance of the duties of the Board or upon the request of the attorney affected, or as they may be introduced in evidence or otherwise produced in proceedings implementing this Part.

(h) Appeal of Determinations. Any person or organization aggrieved by a determination pursuant to this Part may seek administrative review of that determination pursuant to the Regulations and Guidelines adopted by the CLE Board.

§ 1500.4. Accreditation

(a) Procedure. Unless a provider has been granted Accredited Provider status pursuant to subdivision (c), accreditation of continuing legal education courses or programs must be sought at least 60 days prior to the occurrence of the course or program, except in extenuating circumstances and with prior permission of the CLE Board.

(b) Standards. Continuing legal education courses or programs to be accredited shall comply with the following guidelines:

(1) One (1) hour of continuing legal education credit shall consist of at least 50 minutes of instruction, exclusive of introductory remarks, meals, breaks, or other noneducational activities.

(2) The course or program must have significant intellectual or practical content and its primary objective must be to increase the professional legal competency of the attorney in ethics and professionalism, skills, practice management and/or areas of professional practice.

(3) The course or program shall be taught by instructors with expertise in the subject matter being taught and shall be specifically tailored to attorneys.

(4) (*Effective January 1, 2008*) The faculty of the course or program shall include at least one attorney in good standing, who shall actively participate in the course or program.

(5) The course or program shall not be taught by a disbarred attorney, whether the disbarred attorney is the sole presenter or one of several instructors.

(6) The continuing legal education course or program must be offered by a provider that has substantial, recent experience in offering continuing legal education to attorneys, or that has demonstrated an ability to effectively organize and present continuing legal education to attorneys.

(7) Thorough, high quality, readable and carefully prewritten materials must be made available to all participants at or before the time the course or pro-

gram is presented, unless the absence of materials, or the provision of such materials shortly after the course or program, is pre-approved by the CLE Board. Written materials shall satisfy the criteria set forth in the Regulations and Guidelines.

(8) The cost of continuing legal education courses or programs to the participating attorney shall be reasonable.

(9) Providers must have a financial hardship policy as provided in the Regulations and Guidelines.

(10) The course or program must be conducted in a physical setting that is comfortable and conducive to learning.

(11) At the conclusion of the course or program, each participant must be given the opportunity to complete an evaluation questionnaire addressing the quality, effectiveness and usefulness of the particular course or program. A summary of the results of the survey(s) must be submitted to the CLE Board at the end of the calendar year in which the course or program was given. Providers must maintain the questionnaires for a period of four (4) years following the course or program.

(12) Providers of continuing legal education courses or programs shall provide a Certificate of Attendance to all persons completing the continuing legal education course or program.

(13) Providers of continuing legal education courses or programs must maintain an official attendance list of participants in the program, and the time, date, location, title, speaker(s) and amount of approved CLE credit for each course or program, for at least four (4) years after the completion date.

(14) Programs that satisfy these standards and that cross academic lines, such as accounting-tax seminars, may be considered for approval by the CLE Board.

(c) Accredited Provider Status.

(1) *Procedure.* Application may be made for Accredited Provider status by submitting the appropriate forms and materials to the CLE Board pursuant to CLE Board Regulations and Guidelines.

(2) *Requirements.* Accredited Provider status may be granted at the discretion of the CLE Board to applicants satisfying the requirements of this section and, as well, the following requirements:

(i) The provider has presented, within the prior three (3) years, separate programs of continuing legal education that meet the standards set forth in subdivision (b) and the Regulations and Guidelines of the CLE Board, or

(ii) The provider has demonstrated to the Board that its CLE activities have consistently met the standards set forth in subdivision (b) and the Regulations and Guidelines of the CLE Board.

Providers that meet the foregoing requirements may include bar associations, law schools, law firms and legal departments (including corporate, nonprofit and municipal and state law departments).

(3) *Duration of Accredited Provider Status.* Once a provider has been granted Accredited Provider status, the continuing legal education courses or programs sponsored by that provider are presumptively approved for credit for a period of three (3) years from the date of the grant of such status.

(4) *Accredited Provider Reports.* Providers granted Accredited Provider status shall file a written report with the CLE Board each year at a time fixed by the Board. The report shall describe the continuing legal education activities conducted during the prior 12 months and shall be in such detail and form as required by the Board and by the Regulations and Guidelines. The accredited status of a provider may be continued by filing an application for renewal with the Board before the end of the provider's accreditation period.

(5) *Renewal of Accredited Provider Status.* Renewal of Accredited Provider status shall be for periods of three (3) years. The CLE Board shall determine if there are pending or past breaches of these Rules or Regulations and Guidelines, and the Board, in its discretion, may condition renewal upon the provider meeting additional requirements specified by the Board.

(i) If an application for renewal is timely filed, the accredited status shall continue until the Board acts on the application.

(ii) If an application for renewal is not filed before the end of the provider's accreditation period, the provider's accredited status will terminate at the end of the period. Any application received thereafter shall be considered by the Board as an initial application for Accredited Provider status.

(6) *Revocation.* Accredited Provider status may be revoked by the Board if the reporting requirements of these Rules and Regulations and Guidelines are not met or, if upon review of the provider's performance, the CLE Board determines that the content of the course or program materials, the quality of the CLE activities, or the provider's performance does not meet the standards set forth in these Rules and Regulations and Guidelines. In such event, the CLE Board shall send the provider a 30–day notice of revocation by first class mail. The provider may request a review of such revocation, and the CLE Board shall determine the request within 90 days of receipt of such request. The decision of the CLE Board shall be final after such review.

(d) Provider List. A list of accredited providers whose continuing legal education courses or activities have been presumptively approved for credit shall be compiled and published periodically by the CLE

Board. Lists shall be made available at each of the Appellate Divisions and at such other offices and electronic sites as the Chief Administrator of the Courts shall determine.

(e) Announcement. Providers who have received approval for continuing legal education courses and programs may indicate that their course or program has received CLE Board approval as follows:

"This (transitional) continuing legal education course (or program) has been approved in accordance with the requirements of the Continuing Legal Education Board for a maximum of _____ credit hours, of which _____ credit hours can be applied toward the _____ requirement, and _____ credit hours can be applied toward the _____ requirement."

Where a program or segment of a program might reasonably be used to satisfy more than one category of instruction, e.g., either ethics or areas of professional practice, the approved provider may so indicate, but must state that duplicate credit for the same hour of instruction is not permitted; an election must be made by the attendee, and each hour may be counted as satisfying only one category of instruction. The following language may be used:

and an aggregate of _____ credit hours can be applied toward the _____ requirement or the _____ requirement.

§ 1500.5. Waivers, Modifications and Exemptions

(a) Waivers and Modifications. The Continuing Legal Education Board may, in individual cases involving undue hardship or extenuating circumstances, grant waivers and modifications of Program requirements to attorneys, upon written request, in accordance with the Regulations and Guidelines established by the CLE Board and this Part.

(b) Exemptions. The following persons shall be exempt from the requirements of New York's continuing legal education program:

(1) Subject to the requirements in §§ 1500.12(f) and 1500.22(n), attorneys who do not practice law in New York. Attorneys practice law pursuant to this section if, during the reporting period, they give legal advice or counsel to, or provide legal representation for, a particular body or individual in a particular situation in either the public or private sector. The practice of law does not include the performance of judicial or quasi-judicial (e.g., administrative law judge, hearing officer) functions;

(2) Full-time active members of the United States Armed Forces and members of the military service of the state serving on active duty;

(3) Attorneys with offices outside of New York who are temporarily admitted to practice in a court within New York for a case or proceeding;

(4) Attorneys who certify that they are retired from the practice of law pursuant to § 468–a of the Judiciary Law.

SUBPART B. MANDATORY CONTINUING LEGAL EDUCATION FOR NEWLY ADMITTED ATTORNEYS

§ 1500.10. Application

(a) The requirements of this Subpart shall apply to all newly admitted attorneys, who are not exempt from these requirements pursuant to § 1500.5(b), during the first two years after their admission to the Bar of the State of New York.

(b) A newly admitted attorney is an attorney who has successfully passed the New York State Bar examination administered by the State Board of Law Examiners and who becomes duly admitted to the practice of law in New York after October 1, 1997.

(c) Attorneys who have been engaged in the practice of law in another state, the District of Columbia, any territory of the United States or any foreign jurisdiction, for at least five (5) of the seven (7) years immediately preceding admission to the New York Bar, shall not be deemed newly admitted attorneys for the purposes of this Subpart, and shall be required to comply with the requirements of Subpart C to the extent they are applicable.

§ 1500.11. Statement of Purpose

Mandatory Continuing Legal Education for Newly Admitted Attorneys in the State of New York is a transitional continuing legal education program designed to help recent graduates and newly admitted attorneys become competent to deliver legal services at an acceptable level of quality as they enter practice and assume primary client service responsibilities. The Program seeks to help the newly admitted attorney establish a foundation in certain practical skills, techniques and procedures, which are and can be essential to the practice of law, but may not have been adequately addressed in law school. It includes courses targeting ethics and professionalism, skills, practice management and areas of professional practice.

§ 1500.12. Minimum Requirements

(a) Credit Hours. Each newly admitted attorney shall complete a minimum of 32 credit hours of accredited transitional education within the first two (2) years of the date of admission to the Bar. Sixteen (16) accredited hours shall be completed in each of the first two (2) years of admission to the Bar as follows:

-Three (3) hours of ethics and professionalism;

-Six (6) hours of skills; and

-Seven (7) hours of practice management and areas of professional practice.

Ethics and professionalism, skills, law practice management and areas of professional practice are defined in § 1500.2. The ethics and professionalism and skills components may be intertwined with other courses.

(b) Carry–Over Credit. Except as provided in section 1500.13(b)(2), a newly admitted attorney who accumulates more than the 16 hours of credit required in the first year of admission to the Bar may carry over to the second year of admission to the Bar a maximum of eight (8) credits. Six (6) credits in excess of the 16–hour requirement in the second year of admission to the Bar may be carried over to the following biennial reporting cycle to fulfill the requirements of Subpart C. Ethics and professionalism credit may not be carried over.

(c) Accredited Courses or Programs Only. Transitional continuing legal education credit will be granted only for courses and programs approved as such by the CLE Board, except as provided in subdivision (d). No transitional continuing legal education course or program consisting of nontraditional formats, such as self-study, correspondence work, videotapes, audiotapes, motion picture presentations or on-line programs may be accepted for credit without prior permission from the CLE Board, except as provided in the Regulations and Guidelines.

(d) Other Jurisdictions. Transitional continuing legal education courses approved by another state, the District of Columbia, any territory of the United States or any foreign jurisdiction with requirements meeting the standards adopted by the CLE Board shall count toward the newly admitted attorney's compliance with New York's transitional CLE Program requirements in accordance with the Regulations and Guidelines established by the CLE Board and this Part.

(e) Post–Graduation/Pre–Admission. A maximum of 16 credit hours of approved transitional CLE courses taken from the date of graduation from law school up through the date of admission to the New York Bar may be applied toward a newly admitted attorney's first-year CLE Program requirements. Credit hours in excess of 16 may not be carried over and applied toward the second-year CLE requirement.

(f) Obligations of Attorneys exempt from the Program Requirements.

(1) An attorney who is exempt from the requirements of this Program and who is required to comply with the continuing legal education requirements of another jurisdiction shall comply with those requirements and shall certify to this compliance on the attorney's biennial attorney registration statement.

(2) An attorney who is exempt from the requirements of this Program and who is not required to comply with the continuing legal education requirements of another jurisdiction shall so certify on the attorney's biennial attorney registration statement.

(3) An attorney who is exempt from the requirements of this Program and who thereafter ceases to be exempt and commences the practice of law in New York during the first two years after admission to the Bar shall be required to complete by the end of those two years 1.5 credit hours of accredited legal education as set forth in section 1500.12(a), in any combination of categories set forth in said section, for each full month of the two-year period during which the attorney practices law in New York.

(4) An Attorney who permanently ceases to practice law in New York while commencing or continuing the practice of law in another jurisdiction shall be exempt from the requirements of this Program for the year in which the permanent cessation from New York practice occurred, and shall comply with the requirements of any jurisdiction in which the attorney practices law during that year.

§ 1500.13. Reporting Requirements

(a) Attorney Obligations. Each newly admitted attorney subject to New York's transitional continuing legal education requirements shall retain the Certificate of Attendance for each approved transitional education course or program for at least four (4) years from the date of the course or program.

(b) Certification. (1) Except as otherwise authorized by this Part, each newly admitted attorney subject to New York's transitional continuing legal education requirements is required to certify along with the submission of his or her biennial attorney registration statement that the attorney has satisfactorily completed 32 credit hours of transitional continuing legal education (16 credit hours in the first year of admission to the Bar, 16 credit hours in the second year of admission to the Bar) and that the attorney has retained the Certificates of Attendance or other documentation required by the CLE Board for the accredited courses or programs.

(2) A newly admitted attorney who is required to file his or her biennial attorney registration statement prior to completing the second year of admission to the Bar shall certify the actual number of credit hours of transitional continuing legal education completed at the time the statement is filed. The attorney shall remain responsible for completing the 16 second-year credit hours of transitional continuing legal education by the end of that second year after admission, but may apply 12 of the 16 credit hours to fulfilling the

requirements of Subpart C as set forth in § 1500.22(b)(3).

§ 1500.14. Waivers or Modifications

(a) A newly admitted attorney may apply in writing to the CLE Board for a waiver or modification of Program requirements based upon extenuating circumstances preventing the newly admitted attorney from complying with the requirements, in accordance with the Regulations and Guidelines established by the CLE Board and this Part.

(b) Requests for extensions of time in which to complete Program requirements based upon extenuating circumstances shall be made pursuant to the procedures contained in the Regulations and Guidelines and shall not be granted for a period of greater than 90 days absent special circumstances. If an extension is granted, the period of time by which a newly admitted attorney must complete the mandatory continuing legal education requirements applicable to all attorneys as set forth in Subpart C remains the same.

§ 1500.15. Noncompliance

The names of newly admitted attorneys who fail to comply with transitional continuing legal education requirements will be submitted to the Appellate Division for appropriate action.

§ 1500.16. Effective Date

Mandatory Continuing Legal Education for Newly Admitted Attorneys in the State of New York shall become effective on October 1, 1997.

SUBPART C. MANDATORY CONTINUING LEGAL EDUCATION FOR ATTORNEYS OTHER THAN NEWLY ADMITTED ATTORNEYS

§ 1500.20. Application

The requirements of this Subpart shall apply to all attorneys who have been duly admitted to the practice of law in New York, are not exempt from these requirements pursuant to § 1500.5(b), and are not newly admitted attorneys subject to the requirements of Subpart B of this Part.

§ 1500.21. Statement of Purpose

It is of utmost importance to members of the Bar and to the public that attorneys maintain their professional competence by continuing their legal education throughout the period of their active practice of law. This Program establishes the minimum requirements for continuing legal education for attorneys other than newly admitted attorneys in New York State.

§ 1500.22. Minimum Requirements

(a) Credit Hours. Each attorney shall complete a minimum of 24 credit hours of accredited continuing legal education each biennial reporting cycle in ethics and professionalism, skills, law practice management or areas of professional practice, at least four (4) credit hours of which shall be in ethics and professionalism. Ethics and professionalism, skills, law practice management and areas of professional practice are defined in § 1500.2. The ethics and professionalism components may be intertwined with other courses.

(b) Biennial Reporting Cycle.

(1) The biennial reporting cycle shall be the two-year period between the dates of submission of the attorney's biennial registration statement.

(2) An attorney shall comply with the requirements of this Subpart commencing from the time of the filing of the attorney's biennial attorney registration statement in the second calendar year following admission to the Bar.

(3) A newly admitted attorney whose transitional two year post-Bar admission period has not been completed as of the last day the attorney registration statement in paragraph (2) is required to be filed may apply 12 credit hours of the second-year accredited transitional education credits required in section 1500.12(a) to fulfilling the requirements of this Subpart.

(c) Carry–Over Credit. An attorney who accumulates more than the 24 hours of credit in any one biennial reporting cycle may carry over a maximum of six (6) credits to the next biennial reporting cycle.

(d) Course or Program Formats. Continuing legal education courses or programs may include traditional live classroom or audience settings; teleconferences; video conferences; satellite transmissions; videotapes; audiotapes; motion picture presentations; interactive video instruction; activities electronically transmitted from another location; self-study; correspondence work; and on-line computer courses.

(e) Credit for Speaking and Teaching Activities. Credit may be earned through speaking, teaching or participating in a panel in an accredited CLE program. Where teaching is done in tandem or by panel, teaching credit shall be given to all participants.

(f) Credit for Teaching Law School Classes. Credit may be earned through teaching in an ABA-accredited law school as may be permitted pursuant to the Regulations and Guidelines of the CLE Board.

(g) Credit for Attending Law School Courses. Credit may be earned for attending courses at an ABA-accredited law school after admission to practice in New York provided (i) the attorney is officially registered for the course, and (ii) the attorney completed the course as required by the terms of registration.

(h) Credit for Judging Law Competitions. Credit may be earned for preparing students for and judging law competitions, mock trials and moot court arguments, including those in high school, pursuant to the Regulations and Guidelines of the CLE Board.

(i) Credit for Publications. Credit may be earned, as may be permitted pursuant to the Regulations and Guidelines of the CLE Board, for legal research-based writing upon application to the CLE Board, provided the activity (i) produced material published or to be published, in print or electronically, in the form of an article, chapter or book written, in whole or in substantial part, by the applicant, and (ii) contributed substantially to the continuing legal education of the applicant and other attorneys.

(j) Credit for Performing Pro Bono Legal Services. Credit may be earned for performing uncompensated legal services for clients unable to afford counsel pursuant to (a) assignment by a court; or (b) a program, accredited by the CLE Board, of a bar association, legal services provider or other entity. Credit shall be awarded pursuant to the Regulations and Guidelines of the CLE Board, provided that no more than six hours of CLE credit may be awarded in a two-year reporting period for performing pro bono legal services, and no more than one credit hour of CLE credit may be awarded for every six hours of legal work performed.

(k) Accredited Courses, Programs and Activities Only. Continuing legal education credit will be granted only for courses, programs and activities approved by the CLE Board, except where credit is extended as provided in subdivision (m).

(*l*) Individual Course Approval. An attorney seeking approval of a course or program that has not otherwise been approved shall apply to the CLE Board for approval in accordance with Board procedures. Such approval must be sought at least 60 days prior to the occurrence of the course or program, except in extenuating circumstances and only with prior permission of the Board.

(m) Other Jurisdictions. Continuing legal education courses approved by another state, the District of Columbia, any territory of the United States or any foreign jurisdiction with requirements meeting the standards adopted by the CLE Board shall count toward the attorney's compliance with New York's CLE Program requirements in accordance with the Regulations and Guidelines established by the CLE Board and this Part.

(n) Obligations of Attorneys exempt from the Program Requirements.

(1) An attorney who is exempt from the requirements of this Program and who is required to comply with the continuing legal education requirements of another jurisdiction shall comply with those requirements and shall certify this compliance on the attorney's biennial attorney registration statement.

(2) An attorney who is exempt from the requirements of this Program and who is not required to comply with the continuing legal education requirements of another jurisdiction shall so certify on the attorney's biennial attorney registration statement.

(3) An attorney who is exempt from the requirements of this Program and who thereafter ceases to be exempt and commences the practice of law in New York during a biennial reporting cycle shall be required to complete by the end of the reporting cycle one credit hour of accredited continuing legal education as set forth in section 1500.22(a), in any combination of categories set forth in said section, for each full calendar month of the biennial reporting cycle during which the attorney practices law in New York.

(4) An attorney who permanently ceases to practice law in New York while commencing or continuing the practice of law in another jurisdiction shall be exempt from the requirements of this Program for the reporting cycle in which the permanent cessation from New York practice occurred, and shall comply with the requirements of the jurisdiction in which the attorney practices law during that cycle.

§ 1500.23.   Reporting Requirements

(a) Attorney Obligations. Each attorney subject to New York's continuing legal education requirements shall retain the Certificate of Attendance or other documentation required by the Board for each approved education course, program or activity for at least four (4) years from the date of the course, program or activity.

(b) Certification. Except as otherwise authorized by this Part, each attorney subject to New York's continuing legal education requirements is required to certify along with the submission of his or her biennial attorney registration statement that the attorney has satisfactorily completed 24 credit hours of continuing legal education for the current biennial reporting cycle and that the attorney has retained the Certificates of Attendance or other documentation required by the CLE Board for the accredited courses, programs or activities.

§ 1500.24.   Waivers or Modifications

(a) An attorney may apply in writing to the CLE Board for a waiver or modification of Program requirements based upon extenuating circumstances preventing the attorney from complying with the requirements, in accordance with the Regulations and Guidelines established by the CLE Board and this Part.

(b) Requests for extensions of time in which to complete Program requirements based upon extenuating circumstances shall be made pursuant to the procedures contained in the Regulations and Guidelines and shall not be granted for a period of greater than 90 days absent special circumstances. If an extension is granted, the period of time by which the attorney must complete the mandatory continuing legal education requirements of the next biennial reporting cycle remains the same.

§ 1500.25. Noncompliance

The names of attorneys who fail to comply with continuing legal education requirements will be submitted to the Appellate Division for appropriate action.

§ 1500.26. Effective Date and Transition

The requirements of this Subpart shall become effective on December 31, 1998. Compliance with the certification requirement shall commence with biennial attorney registration statements filed on or after January 1, 2000, as follows:

(1) Attorneys who file their biennial registration statement in calendar year 2000 shall complete 12 credit hours of accredited continuing legal education as of the date of the filing in any combination of the categories set forth in § 1500.22(a). Attorneys who accumulate more than 12 credit hours at the time of this filing may carry over a maximum of six (6) credit hours to the next biennial cycle;

(2) Attorneys who file their biennial registration statement in calendar year 2001 must complete the full 24 credit hours of accredited continuing legal education as set forth in § 1500.22(a).

Approved CLE credits earned from January 1, 1998, may be applied toward fulfilling the requirements for the initial biennial reporting cycle.

APPENDIX A.   REGULATIONS AND GUIDELINES

Section 1. Publication of New York State CLE Board Regulations and Guidelines for the Mandatory Continuing Legal Education Program for Attorneys in the State of New York

Pursuant to Part 1500, Title 22 of the Official Compilations of Codes, Rules and Regulations of the State of New York, the following Regulations and Guidelines have been promulgated by the New York State Continuing Legal Education Board ("CLE Board") to clarify the "Mandatory Continuing Legal Education Program for Attorneys in the State of New York." These Regulations and Guidelines shall be read with the Program Rules for a full understanding of New York State's continuing legal education requirement. All written requests to the New York State CLE Board may be sent to:

The New York State Continuing
Legal Education Board

25 Beaver Street, Room 888

New York, New York 10004

Section 2. Mandatory Continuing Legal Education Program for Newly Admitted Attorneys

A. Requirement — Newly admitted attorneys shall fulfill their continuing legal education requirement by taking accredited transitional continuing legal education courses or programs in traditional live classroom settings or through attendance at fully interactive videoconferences if the videoconference technology has been separately approved by the CLE Board for use by newly admitted attorneys.

1. Newly admitted attorneys who are exempt from the CLE requirement and who thereafter cease to be exempt and commence the practice of law in New York during the first two years of admission to the Bar, shall be required to complete by the end of those two years 1.5 credit hours of accredited continuing legal education as set forth in § 1500.12(a) of the Program Rules in any combination of categories set forth in that section, for each month of the two-year period during any part of which the attorney practices law in New York.

2. Subject to the requirements of § 1500.12(f)(4) of the Program Rules, newly admitted attorneys who are practicing law in New York at the commencement of the reporting cycle and who thereafter cease to practice law in New York and become exempt from the CLE requirement during the first two years of admission to the Bar, and remain exempt through the end of the first two years of admission to the Bar, shall be required to complete by the end of those two years 1.5 credit hours of accredited continuing legal education as set forth in § 1500.12(a) of the Program Rules in any combination of categories set forth in that section, for each month of the two-year period during any part of which the attorney practices law in New York.

B. Transitional Courses — Transitional continuing legal education courses are courses designed to help recent graduates and newly admitted attorneys establish a foundation in the practical skills, techniques and procedures essential to the practice of law. The specific requirements and breakdown of categories of credit are described in Subpart B of the Program Rules.

C. Transitional CLE Course Formats — Transitional CLE credit hours may be earned by (1) attendance at accredited continuing legal education courses or programs presented in traditional live classroom settings or (2) attendance at fully interactive videoconferences if the videoconference technology has been separately approved by the CLE Board for use by newly admitted attorneys. Videoconferences using videoconference technology that has not received separate approval by the CLE Board for use by newly admitted attorneys may not be used by newly admitted attorneys except as set forth in section 2(F) of these Regulations and Guidelines. Any provider seeking approval of videoconferences for newly admitted attorneys must make a separate application for approval of the videoconference technology to the CLE Board pursuant to sections 8(A)(5), 8(B)(5) and 8(C)(7) of these Regulations and Guidelines.

D. Limitations on CLE Credit Awards

1. *Partial Credit* — Credit shall be awarded only for attendance at an entire course or program, or for attendance at an entire session of a course or program. No credit shall be awarded for attending a portion of a course or a portion of a session.

2. *Repeat Attendance* — No CLE credit hours may be earned for repeating the same course or program, in any format, even if the course or program is repeated in a subsequent reporting cycle.

E. CLE Activities — Newly admitted attorneys may not earn transitional CLE credit hours for the CLE activities set forth in section 3(D) of these Regulations and Guidelines.

F. Nontraditional CLE Course Formats — Except as set forth in sections 2(C) and 2(F)(1) of these Regulations and Guidelines, no newly admitted attorney shall earn transitional CLE credit hours through nontraditional CLE course formats except in extenuating circumstances and only with prior permission from the CLE Board. Nontraditional formats are any formats other than the traditional live classroom format. Nontraditional formats include, but are not limited to, audio recordings, video recordings (for individual viewing), video replays (group showings of video recordings), live satellite broadcasts, teleconferences, videoconferences, webcasts, webconferences and online courses.

1. *Exception for Newly Admitted Attorneys in Foreign Offices* — Newly admitted attorneys based in law offices outside of the United States may fulfill up to 12 credit hours of accredited transitional continuing legal education through nontraditional course formats

without prior permission from the CLE Board. Videoconferences as provided in section 2(C) of these Regulations and Guidelines do not fall within this limitation.

2. *Procedure* — Requests to fulfill the transitional CLE requirement through nontraditional CLE course formats as set forth in this section shall be made in writing and submitted to the CLE Board at least 60 days prior to the date of the course or program. The request shall set forth the specific extenuating circumstances warranting this exception and include supporting documentation. The CLE Board shall notify the attorney of its decision by first class mail.

3. *Nontraditional Format Credit Hour Limit* — No newly admitted attorney may earn more than 12 CLE credit hours through nontraditional format CLE courses. CLE credit hours earned through nontraditional format courses pursuant to sections 2(C) and 2(F)(1) of these Regulations and Guidelines do not fall within this limitation.

G. Postgraduate/Preadmission Credit — Subject to the requirements of § 1500.12(e) of the Program Rules, transitional CLE credit hours may be earned for attending approved transitional CLE courses from the date of graduation from law school through the date of admission to the New York Bar, except that no credit will be awarded for attendance at such courses occurring more than two years before the date of admission to the New York Bar.

H. Postgraduate Enrollment — Transitional CLE credit hours may be earned for attending courses for credit or by audit at an ABA–accredited law school after admission to the New York Bar provided that (1) the attorney is officially registered for the course and (2) the attorney completed the course as required by the terms of the registration. Credit for approved attendance at law school courses shall be for the number of 50–minute classes attended. Attorneys shall obtain from the school an official transcript or other appropriate documentation indicating the name of attorney, name, date and location of course, New York credit hours earned, a breakdown of categories of credit and the attorney's successful completion of the course. Attorneys shall retain proof of completion of such postgraduate work for a period of four (4) years after completion of such course work.

I. Ethics and Professionalism Credit — Ethics and professionalism credit may not be carried over from the first year of admission to the Bar to fulfill the requirement for the second year of admission. Ethics and professionalism credit may not be carried over from the second year of admission to the Bar to fulfill the requirement for the following biennial reporting cycle. Notwithstanding § 1500.13(b)(2) of the Program Rules, a newly admitted attorney who is required to file a biennial registration statement prior to completing the second year of admission to the Bar may not apply ethics and professionalism credit hours to the requirement for the following biennial reporting cycle.

Section 3. Mandatory Continuing Legal Education Program for Attorneys Other Than Newly Admitted Attorneys

A. Requirement — Experienced attorneys may take accredited transitional and nontransitional continuing legal education courses or programs towards their Program requirements. The specific requirements are described in Subpart C of the Program Rules.

1. Experienced attorneys who are exempt from the CLE requirement and who thereafter cease to be exempt and commence the practice of law in New York during the two-year reporting cycle shall be required to complete by the end of the reporting cycle one (1) credit hour of accredited continuing legal education as set forth in § 1500.22(a) of the Program Rules, in any category, for each month of the reporting cycle during any part of which the attorney practices law in New York.

2. Subject to the requirements of § 1500.22(n), experienced attorneys who are practicing law in New York at the commencement of the reporting cycle and who thereafter cease to practice law in New York and become exempt from the CLE requirement during the two-year reporting cycle, and remain exempt through the end of the two-year reporting cycle, shall be required to complete by the end of the reporting cycle one (1) credit hour of accredited continuing legal education as set forth in § 1500.22(a) of the Program Rules, in any category, for each month of the reporting cycle during any part of which the attorney practices law in New York.

3. A newly admitted attorney who is exempt from New York's transitional CLE requirements under § 1500.10(c) of the Program Rules and is subject to the CLE requirements for experienced attorneys, may apply to the initial biennial reporting cycle a maximum of 16 CLE credit hours for attending approved transitional or nontransitional CLE courses taking place before the date of admission to the New York Bar, except that no credit may be applied for attendance at such courses

occurring more than two years before the date of admission to the New York Bar.

B. Course or Program Formats — Experienced attorneys may earn CLE credit hours in a number of formats including, for example, the traditional live classroom setting, audio recordings, video recordings (for individual viewing), video replays (group showings of video recordings), live satellite broadcasts, teleconferences, videoconferences, webcasts, webconferences and online courses, if the CLE Board has accredited the provider to offer the particular format. Credit may not be earned for reading legal materials unless specifically preapproved by the CLE Board.

C. Limitations on CLE Credit Awards

1. *Partial Credit* — Credit shall be awarded only for attendance at an entire course or program, or for attendance at an entire session of a course or program. No credit shall be awarded for attending a portion of a course or a portion of a session.

2. *Repeat Attendance* — No CLE credit hours may be earned for repeating the same course or program, in any format, even if the course or program is repeated in a subsequent reporting cycle.

D. CLE Activities

1. *Speaking and Teaching* — Credit may be earned for speaking and teaching at an accredited CLE program, including accredited programs presented to summer associates or to nonattorney judges or justices. Three (3) CLE credit hours are awarded for each 50 minutes of presentation. No additional credit may be earned for preparation time. The sponsor of the CLE activity is responsible for issuing appropriate certification to the speaker documenting the name of attorney, name, date and location of course or program, breakdown of categories of credit and the number of New York CLE credit hours earned.

2. *Panel Presentations* — Credit may be earned for participating in panel presentations accredited by the CLE Board. The panel member earns three (3) CLE credit hours for each 50 minutes of participation on the panel. No additional credit may be earned for preparation time. The sponsor of the CLE activity is responsible for issuing appropriate certification to panel members documenting the name of attorney, name, date and location of activity, breakdown of categories of credit and the number of New York CLE credit hours earned.

3. *Moderators* — Credit may be earned for moderating CLE activities accredited by the CLE Board. The moderator earns one (1) CLE credit hour for each 50 minutes of participation. No additional credit may be earned for preparation time. The sponsor of the CLE activity is responsible for issuing appropriate certification to the moderator documenting the name of attorney, name, date and location of activity, breakdown of categories of credit and the number of New York CLE credit hours earned.

4. *In–House CLE* — Credit may be earned for speaking, teaching or participating in an accredited in-house program as set forth in subsections 3(D)(1)–(3) above. No CLE credit may be earned for activity in connection with a pending case. The sponsor of the CLE activity is responsible for issuing appropriate certification documenting the name of attorney, name, date and location of course or program and the number of New York CLE credit hours earned.

5. *Law Competitions* — Credit may be earned for preparing students for and judging law competitions, mock trials and moot court arguments, including those at the high school or college level. Ethics and professionalism credit hours are not available for participation in this type of CLE activity. CLE credit hours are not available for grading written briefs or other written papers in connection with this type of CLE activity. No additional credit may be earned for preparation time. The sponsor of the CLE activity is responsible for issuing appropriate certification documenting the name of attorney, name, date and location of course or program and the number of New York CLE credit hours earned.

a. **Law School Competitions** — One (1) credit hour may be earned for each 50 minutes of participation in an ABA-accredited law school competition. A maximum of six (6) CLE credit hours may be earned for participation in this type of CLE activity during any one reporting cycle.

b. **High School and College Competitions**

i. **Application** — The sponsor, or an attorney participant, shall submit an application for accreditation of the law competition to the CLE Board for review with a cover letter and any supporting documentation, including: (1) a description of the competition, (2) the date(s) and time(s) of the competition, (3) a copy or description of the written materials to be distributed to the participants, (4) the name(s) and credentials of the faculty participant(s) in the competition and (5) the name of the contact person at the sponsoring school.

ii. **Application Deadline** — Accreditation of high school and college law competitions shall be sought no later than 15 days after the occurrence of the law competition.

iii. **Calculation of Credit** — One (1) CLE credit hour may be earned for each 50 minutes of participation in a high school or college law competition. A maximum of three (3) CLE credit hours may be earned for this type of CLE activity during any one reporting cycle.

c. **In–House** — Credit may be earned for preparing participants for, demonstrating for and judging accredited in-house mock trial, moot court and other trial advocacy exercises. Credit shall be awarded as set forth in sections 3(D)(5) and 3(D)(5)(a) above. No CLE credit may be earned for activity in connection with a pending case.

d. **Credit Hour Limit** — Subject to the requirements of section 3(D)(5)(b)(iii) above, a combined maximum of six (6) CLE credit hours may be earned for the activities set forth in subsections 3(D)(5)(a)–(c) during any one reporting cycle.

6. *Teaching Law Courses* — Credit may be earned for teaching law courses at an ABA-accredited law school. One (1) CLE credit hour is awarded for each 50 minutes of instruction. No additional credit may be earned for preparation time. The ABA-accredited law school is responsible for issuing appropriate certification to the instructor documenting the name of attorney, name, date and location of course, breakdown of categories of credit and the number of New York CLE credit hours earned.

7. *Repeat Presentations* — CLE credit hours may be earned for repeat presentations of any of the foregoing CLE activities set forth in 3(D) of this section except as indicated below:

a. One (1) CLE credit hour may be earned for each 50 minutes of repeat presentation as a speaker, teacher or panel member at an accredited CLE activity within any one reporting cycle.

b. No additional credit may be earned for moderating repeat presentations of the same CLE program within any one reporting cycle.

8. *Written Materials* — Credit may be obtained for either speaking at an accredited CLE

activity or for the preparation of written materials for that same CLE activity, but not for both. Written materials distributed in conjunction with an accredited CLE activity are eligible for CLE credit only if (i) such written material is sufficient in substance and citation to stand by itself as an instructional tool (in contrast to an outline that is merely an adjunct or aid to the speaker's presentation), and (ii) such written material meets the criteria for CLE publications set forth in section 3(D)(10) of these Regulations and Guidelines.

9. *Postgraduate Enrollment* — CLE credit hours may be earned for attending courses for credit or by audit at an ABA–accredited law school after admission to practice in New York provided that (i) the attorney is officially registered for the course and (ii) the attorney completed the course as required by the terms of the registration. Credit for approved attendance at law school courses shall be for the number of 50–minute classes attended. Attorneys shall obtain from the school an official transcript or other appropriate documentation indicating the name of attorney, name, date and location of course, breakdown of categories of credit, the number of New York credit hours earned and the attorney's successful completion of the course. Attorneys shall retain proof of completion of such postgraduate work for a period of four (4) years after completion of such course work.

10. *Publications* — Credit may be earned for legal research-based writing that (i) is published or accepted for publication, in print or electronically, in the form of an article, chapter, book, revision or update, (ii) is written in whole or in substantial part by the applicant and (iii) contributed substantially to the continuing legal education of the applicant and other attorneys. "Legal research-based writing," under this subsection, is defined as writing that has as its primary purpose to increase the professional legal competency of attorneys in ethics and professionalism, skills, law practice management and/or areas of professional practice.

   a. **Limitations** — The following shall not qualify for CLE publication credit:

   i. Editing legal research-based writing;

   ii. Authorship of published decisions;

   iii. Writing appearing in a publication for general circulation or in a publication directed to a nonlawyer audience; and

   iv. Legal research-based writing appearing in any publication, whether print or electronic, that is controlled by the applicant or by the applicant's firm or employer.

   b. **Application** — The applicant shall submit the legal research-based writing to the CLE Board for review with a New York State Continuing Legal Education Board "Application for Publication Credit" and supporting documentation including, but not limited to: (i) proof that the legal research-based writing has been published or has been accepted for publication, (ii) the date of publication or acceptance for publication, (iii) the time the applicant spent on research or writing, (iv) the total number of CLE credit hours requested, (v) a breakdown of the categories of credit, (vi) the date of the applicant's admission to the New York Bar, and (vii) an English translation of legal research-based writing not written in English. Each joint author seeking credit shall submit a separate application. Applicants not listed as authors shall submit with their application a letter from a listed author attesting to the applicant's contribution to the legal research-based writing and describing the nature and extent of the contribution.

   c. **Calculation of Credit**

   i. one (1) CLE credit hour may be awarded for each 50 minutes of research and writing.

   ii. A maximum of 12 CLE publication credit hours may be earned during any one reporting cycle.

   iii. Credit, if awarded, shall be awarded as of the date of publication or the date of acceptance for publication.

   d. **Notification** — The Board shall notify the applicant by first class mail of its decision to grant, deny or grant with modifications the request for CLE publication credit.

11. *Pro Bono Legal Services* — Credit may be earned for performing eligible pro bono legal services for clients unable to afford counsel pursuant to (i) assignment by a court or (ii) participation in a pro bono CLE program sponsored by an Approved Pro Bono CLE Provider. CLE credit shall not be awarded for pro bono legal services performed outside of New York State.

   a. **Definitions**

   i. **Eligible pro bono legal services** are (1) legal services for which there is no compensation to the attorney performing the legal services or (2) legal services for which the compensation to the attorney performing the legal services is provided by someone other than the recipient of those services, and such compensation would be provided regardless of whether the attorney performed those services. Legal services provided by assigned counsel who receive compensation for those services from any source and/or legal services provided by legal services organization attorneys within the scope of their employment, are not eligible pro bono legal services.

ii. **A pro bono CLE program** is a program, activity or case that is sponsored by, and to which attorneys are assigned by an Approved Pro Bono CLE Provider, and in which all recipients of the legal services provided by the program have been screened for financial eligibility.

b. **Court Assignment** — Pro Bono CLE credit may be earned for the provision of eligible pro bono legal services to clients unable to afford counsel, pursuant to assignment by a court.

c. **Approved Pro Bono CLE Providers**

i. **Eligibility** — Eligibility for designation by the CLE Board as an Approved Pro Bono CLE Provider is limited to the following organizations:

(1) Legal services organizations, or subsidiaries or subdivisions thereof, that have as their primary purpose the furnishing of legal services to indigent persons and that have filed a statement with the Appellate Division in the Judicial Department in which their principal office is located, pursuant to New York Judiciary Law § 496; or

(2) Subsidiaries or programs of bar associations that have as their primary purpose the furnishing of legal services to indigent persons.

ii. **Approval** — An eligible organization seeking to become an Approved Pro Bono CLE Provider must submit to the CLE Board a letter requesting approval. The letter shall include a description of the organization's pro bono CLE programs and the name of a pro bono CLE contact person at the organization. The organization requesting approval as an Approved Pro Bono CLE Provider shall be furnished with written notice of the CLE Board's determination to approve, conditionally approve or deny the request by first class mail at the address reflected on the letter requesting approval. Pro bono CLE programs sponsored by Approved Pro Bono CLE Providers are deemed approved for pro bono CLE credit for a period of three (3) years from the date of the CLE Board's approval of the Pro Bono CLE Provider.

d. **Calculation of Credit** — Credit for eligible pro bono legal services shall be awarded in the following ratio: one (1) CLE credit hour for every six (6) 50–minute hours (300 minutes) of eligible pro bono legal service. Credit shall be awarded in increments of no less than .5 CLE credit hour. Ethics and professionalism credit is not available for participation in pro bono CLE activities. A maximum of six (6) pro bono CLE credit hours may be earned during any one reporting cycle.

e. **Attorney Obligations** — In order to receive pro bono CLE credit, attorneys shall maintain records of their participation in pro bono CLE activities as follows:

i. **Court Assignment** — An attorney who performs eligible pro bono legal services pursuant to assignment by a court shall calculate the CLE credit hours earned pursuant to section 3(D)(11)(d), above. The attorney shall retain for a period of four (4) years the CLE credit hour calculation and a copy of the court order assigning the attorney to the pro bono activity.

ii. **Pro Bono CLE Program Assignment** — An attorney who performs eligible pro bono legal services for a pro bono CLE program pursuant to assignment by an Approved Pro Bono CLE Provider shall complete an affirmation describing the services provided, and stating the number of hours of eligible pro bono legal service that the attorney performed. The attorney shall submit the affirmation to the sponsoring Approved Pro Bono CLE Provider. The attorney shall retain for a period of four (4) years the time records of the attorney's participation in eligible pro bono legal services, a copy of the attorney's affirmation and the Letter of Participation issued to the attorney by the Approved Pro Bono CLE Provider as set forth in section 3(D)(11)(f)(i), below.

f. **Obligations of Approved Pro Bono CLE Providers**

i. **Letters of Participation** — Approved Pro Bono CLE Providers shall furnish participating attorneys with a Letter of Participation indicating: (1) the name of the

Approved Pro Bono CLE Provider, (2) the date(s) of assignment, and the location and name, if applicable, of the pro bono CLE program, (3) the name of the attorney participant, (4) the number of hours of eligible pro bono service provided by the attorney pursuant to section 3(D)(11)(e)(ii) above and (5) the number of pro bono CLE credit hours earned, calculated pursuant to section 3(D)(11)(d), above.

ii. **Participation List** — Approved Pro Bono CLE Providers shall retain for a period of four (4) years a list of participants in each pro bono CLE program along with the number of hours of eligible pro bono service claimed and the number of pro bono CLE credit hours earned by each participant.

iii. **Year–End Reports** — Approved Pro Bono CLE Providers shall complete and submit to the CLE Board a year-end report at the end of each calendar year during which the organization has been an Approved Pro Bono CLE Provider. The report shall contain information for pro bono CLE programs sponsored during the calendar year, including: (1) the total number of pro bono CLE programs sponsored, (2) the total number of attorneys participating in the pro bono CLE programs, (3) the total number of attorneys to whom Letters of Participation were issued, (4) the total number of pro bono CLE credits issued and (5) the total pro bono CLE hours reported on attorney affirmations.

g. **Carry–Over Credit for Newly Admitted Attorneys** — Newly admitted attorneys may earn pro bono CLE credit as set forth in this section 3(D)(11), solely for the purpose of carrying over pro bono CLE credit to the following biennial reporting cycle in partial fulfillment of the requirements for experienced attorneys. A maximum of six (6) CLE credit hours, including pro bono CLE credit, may be carried over to the following biennial reporting cycle. Newly admitted attorneys may not apply pro bono CLE credit to their minimum requirements as set forth in § 1500.12(a) of the Program Rules and section 2(A) of these Regulations and Guidelines. Newly admitted attorneys shall maintain records of their participation in pro bono CLE activities as set forth in section 3(D)(11)(e), above, and shall retain those records for a period of six (6) years.

h. **Effective Date** — Pro bono CLE credit pursuant to this section D(11) may be earned only for eligible pro bono legal services performed after January 1, 2000.

Section 4. Guidelines for Waivers, Modifications, Extensions of Time and Exemptions

A. Waivers and Modifications

1. *Rule* — The CLE Board may grant a waiver or modification of Program requirements based on undue hardship or extenuating circumstances that prevent the attorney from complying with Program requirements.

2. *Application* — An attorney seeking a waiver or modification of Program requirements shall submit a New York State Continuing Legal Education Board "Application for Waiver or Modification of the CLE Requirement" to the CLE Board as soon as possible. The request shall include:

a. a full description of the undue hardship or extenuating circumstances necessitating the request;

b. a statement as to whether the applicant practices law in New York; and

c. a list of the CLE courses completed for the relevant reporting cycle.

3. *Review* — The CLE Board shall review the request and any supporting documentation, and notify the attorney by first class mail of its decision to grant, deny or grant with modifications the relief requested.

4. *Effective Date* — The effective date for any waiver or modification granted under the Program Rules and these Regulations and Guidelines shall be the date the attorney filed the request for a waiver or modification. The attorney must notify the CLE Board immediately of any material change in the circumstances that led to the grant of a waiver or modification of the attorney's CLE requirements.

5. *Reporting Requirement* — An attorney who has been granted a waiver or modification of Program requirements shall certify to that fact on the biennial attorney registration statement, and shall retain supporting documentation demonstrating the attorney's eligibility for a waiver or modification of New York's Program requirements.

B. Extensions of Time

1. *Rule* — The CLE Board may grant requests for extensions of time in which to complete Program requirements based on undue hardship or extenuating circumstances for a period of 90 days or less, absent compelling circumstances.

2. *Application* — An attorney seeking an extension of time in which to complete Program requirements shall submit a New York State Continuing Legal Education Board "Application for an Extension of Time" to the CLE Board as soon as possible. The request shall include:

a. a description of the undue hardship or extenuating circumstances necessitating the request;

b. a list of accredited courses and the number of CLE credits completed for the relevant reporting cycle; and

c. a plan of action outlining how the attorney intends to complete the requirement if an extension is granted.

3. *Review* — The CLE Board shall review the request and any supporting documentation, and notify the attorney by first class mail of its determination.

4. The grant of an extension of time in which to complete Program requirements shall not affect the date by which the attorney shall complete the continuing legal education requirements for the following reporting cycle.

C. Exemptions

1. *Rule* — Section 1500.5(b) of the Program Rules sets forth the categories of exemptions from New York's CLE requirements. If the period during which an attorney qualifies for exemption is less than the entire biennial reporting cycle, the attorney may be eligible for a prorated CLE requirement as set forth in sections 2(A)(1), (2) and 3(A)(1), (2) of these Regulations and Guidelines.

2. *Not Practicing Law in New York Exemption* — The issue of whether an attorney is practicing law in New York is a question of law that must be determined by the individual attorney. All members of the New York Bar are presumed to be practicing law in New York unless otherwise shown; the burden of proof is on the individual attorney. In determining whether an attorney is practicing law in New York, the attorney should be guided by case law and the Restatement of Law, Third, the Law Governing Lawyers, Chapter 1, § 3. Attorneys who determine that they are not practicing law in New York must retain supporting documentation for audit purposes and comply with the requirements of §§ 1500.12(f) and 1500.22(n) of New York's CLE Program Rules.

Neither the CLE Board nor its staff shall advise attorneys on the issue of whether their specific activities constitute the practice of law in New York.

3. *Reporting Requirement* — An attorney who is exempt from New York's CLE requirements shall retain supporting documentation demonstrating the attorney's eligibility for an exemption from New York's Program requirements, and shall certify to the exemption on the biennial attorney registration statement.

4. *Exemption from Newly Admitted Attorney CLE Requirement* — An attorney who has been engaged in the practice of law in another state, the District of Columbia, any territory of the United States or any foreign jurisdiction, for five (5) of the seven (7) years immediately preceding admission to the New York Bar, shall not be deemed a newly admitted attorney for purposes of the CLE requirement, but shall be required to comply with the requirements of Subpart C of the Program Rules and section 3 of these Regulations and Guidelines, to the extent they are applicable.

Section 5. Reporting Procedures

Attorneys shall retain proof of compliance with Program requirements (*e. g.*, certificates of attendance) and supporting documentation (*e.g.*, for waivers, modifications, extensions of time or exemptions from New York's requirement) for a period of four (4) years. Attorneys shall certify on the biennial registration statement that they have completed the appropriate number of credit hours and are in full compliance with the Program Rules and these Regulations and Guidelines.

Section 6. New York's Approved Jurisdiction Policy

A. **Rule** — A New York attorney who completes an eligible Approved Jurisdiction course or program may claim New York CLE credit for the course or program in accordance with the requirements of the Program Rules and these Regulations and Guidelines.

B. **Definitions.**

1. An *eligible Approved Jurisdiction course or program* is an out-of-state course or program that is accredited by a New York Approved Jurisdiction and that is (a) presented in the live classroom format or (b) if the course or program is presented in a nontraditional format (i.e., a format other than the traditional live classroom format), the provider of the program has independently verified the attorney's participation in accordance with New York's standards.

2. *Out-of-state course or program.* A live classroom-format program is an "out-of-state" course or program if it takes place outside of New York State. A nontraditional format

program is an "out-of-state" course or program if the headquarters of the provider organization is located outside of New York State.

3. A *New York Approved Jurisdiction* is any state, the District of Columbia, territory of the United States or foreign jurisdiction whose CLE accreditation standards for live classroom-format courses or programs have been approved by the CLE Board as meeting New York's accreditation standards for live classroom-format courses or programs. A list of New York Approved Jurisdictions is available on the CLE website, www.nycourts.gov/attorneys/cle, or may be obtained by contacting the CLE Board.

C. **Procedures for Claiming Credit and Attorney Obligations** — An attorney completing an eligible Approved Jurisdiction course or program may claim New York CLE credit in accordance with the requirements of the Program Rules and these Regulations and Guidelines. The attorney must obtain from the provider, and retain for a period of four (4) years, the following:

1. documentation that the course or program was approved by the CLE agency of a New York Approved Jurisdiction;

2. a certificate of attendance indicating (a) the attorney's name, (b) the name, date and location of the course or program, (c) whether the course is (i) transitional and appropriate for newly admitted attorneys, (ii) nontransitional and not acceptable for newly admitted attorneys or (iii) appropriate for both newly admitted and experienced attorneys, (d) a breakdown of categories of credit as defined in § 1500.2(c)-(f) of the Program Rules, and (e) the number of CLE credit hours earned based on a 50-minute hour; and

3. for nontraditional format courses, proof that the provider of the course independently verified the attorney's participation in accordance with New York's standards (e.g., a copy of the attorney affirmation used to report an embedded alphanumeric code to the provider, or a copy and results of a test used by the provider to verify participation, or a written statement from the provider describing the verification method used by the provider).

D. **Limitations** — Credit may be claimed only in a manner consistent with the Program Rules and these Regulations and Guidelines.

1. *Newly Admitted Attorneys* — Newly admitted attorneys who complete eligible Approved Jurisdiction courses or programs may earn CLE credit only in accordance with the requirements of section 2 of these Regulations and Guidelines. (E.g., newly admitted attorneys may not earn New York CLE credit for participation in programs offered in a nontraditional format, even if this activity has been approved for credit by an Approved Jurisdiction, as CLE credit is not available to newly admitted attorneys for this activity under these Regulations and Guidelines except as provided in sections 2(C) and 2(F).)

2. *Attorneys other than Newly Admitted Attorneys* — Attorneys other than newly admitted attorneys may earn credit for completion of eligible Approved Jurisdiction courses or programs only in accordance with the requirements of section 3 of these Regulations and Guidelines. (E.g., New York attorneys may not earn New York CLE credit for reading legal materials, even if this activity has been approved for credit by a New York Approved Jurisdiction, as CLE credit is not available for this activity under these Regulations and guidelines except as provided in section 3(B).) Credit may be earned for any of the activities set forth in section 3(D)(1)–(4) and (7), for an eligible Approved Jurisdiction course or program, to the extent that credit is available under these Regulations and Guidelines.

E. **Procedure for Nonapproved Out-of-State Courses or Programs** — An attorney or sponsoring organization seeking New York CLE credit for an out-of-state course or program that is not an eligible Approved Jurisdiction course or program shall comply with the accreditation application procedures for individual courses and programs. (See section 8 of these Regulations and Guidelines.)

Section 7. Confidentiality

The files, records and proceedings of the CLE Board, as they relate to an attorney's satisfying the requirements of the Program Rules and these Regulations and Guidelines, shall be confidential and shall not be disclosed except in furtherance of the duties of the CLE Board or upon the request of the attorney affected, or as they may be introduced in evidence or otherwise produced in proceedings implementing the Rules and Regulations and Guidelines.

Section 8. The Accreditation Process

A. **Individual Courses or Programs**

1. *Application for Individual Courses or Programs* — Sponsoring organizations (or individuals on their own behalf) may seek accreditation of individual courses or programs offered in New York, or offered out of state and not accredited by a New York approved jurisdiction, by completing the New York State Continuing Legal Education Board

"Application for Accreditation of an Individual Course Activity." An original and one (1) copy of the application form and supporting information shall accompany all requests for accreditation of CLE courses and programs. Continuing legal education courses that are granted accreditation by the CLE Board are deemed approved for credit as of the date of the course or program, in traditional live classroom settings only, unless otherwise indicated in the CLE Board approval letter.

2. *Supporting Information* — Applications shall be submitted with all required attachments. Failure to do so will delay consideration of the application. Required attachments include but are not limited to:

a. timed course or program outline;

b. faculty biographies, including educational background and degrees;

c. complete set of written materials for the course or program;

d. computation of New York credit hours;

e. breakdown of categories of credit;

f. financial aid policy as required under section 8(A)(4)(i) of these Regulations and guidelines;

g. attendance verification procedures; and

h. sample or description of any nontraditional course format(s) as required under section 8(A)(5) of these Regulations and Guidelines.

3. *Application Deadline* — Applications for accreditation of CLE courses or programs shall be submitted by sponsoring organizations or individuals on their own behalf, in accordance with the following application deadlines:

a. **Sponsoring Organizations** — Applications submitted by sponsoring organizations shall be postmarked at least 60 days prior to the occurrence of the course or program. All applications should be submitted as far in advance of the date of the course or program as possible to ensure a timely response by the CLE Board.

i. Applications postmarked less than 60 days prior to the occurrence of the course or program will not be accepted for review except in extenuating circumstances and with prior permission from the CLE Board. A cover letter detailing the extenuating circumstances shall be included with the late application.

ii. No application for accreditation will be accepted for review after a course or program has occurred except under extraor-

dinary circumstances. A cover letter detailing the extraordinary circumstances shall be included with the late application.

b. **Individual Attorneys** — Applications submitted by individual attorneys seeking CLE credit on their own behalf, as participants in a CLE course or program, shall be submitted as follows:

i. Applications shall be postmarked at least 60 days prior to the occurrence of the course or program. All applications should be submitted as far in advance of the date of the course or program as possible to ensure a timely response by the CLE Board.

ii. Applications postmarked up to 30 days after the conclusion of the course or program will be accepted for review where the individual attorney is unable to obtain the supporting information required under section 8(A)(2) of these Regulations and Guidelines at least 60 days prior to the occurrence of the course or program.

iii. Applications postmarked more than 30 days after the conclusion of the course or program will not be accepted for review, except for good cause shown.

4. *Standards for Approval* — Accredited continuing legal education courses or programs shall comply with the following guidelines:

a. One (1) hour of continuing legal education credit shall consist of at least 50 minutes of instruction or other accredited activity, exclusive of introductory remarks, meals, breaks or other noneducational activities. Credit hours shall be calculated in no less than 25–minute (.5–hour) increments.

i. Each 0–24 minute session of instruction or other accredited activity shall equal zero (0) CLE credit hours.

ii. Each 25–49 minute session of instruction or other accredited activity shall equal one-half (.5) credit hour.

iii. Each 50–74 minute session of instruction or other accredited activity shall equal one (1) credit hour.

iv. Each 75–99 minute session of instruction or other accredited activity shall equal one and one-half (1.5) credit hours.

b. The program shall have significant intellectual or practical content and its primary objective shall be to increase the professional legal competency of attorneys in ethics and professionalism, skills, law practice management and/or areas of professional practice.

c. The continuing legal education course or program shall be offered in New York State, offered out of state and not accredited by a New York Approved Jurisdiction, or offered in any nontraditional format, by a provider that has substantial, recent experience in offering continuing legal education, or that has demonstrated an ability to effectively organize and present continuing legal education to attorneys.

d. The continuing legal education course or program shall be taught by instructors with expertise in the subject matter being taught and shall be specifically tailored to a legal audience.

   i. The faculty of the course or program shall include at least one attorney in good standing who shall actively participate in the course or program.

   ii. The faculty of the course or program shall not include any disbarred attorney.

e. Thorough, high quality, readable and carefully prewritten materials shall be made available to all participants at or before the time the course or program is presented, unless the absence of materials, or the provision of such materials shortly after the course or program, is approved in advance by the CLE Board.

f. Written materials for approved courses and programs shall satisfy the following additional criteria:

   i. Materials shall be prepared or compiled specifically for the accredited course or program, and shall specifically address each topic presented in the course or program;

   ii. Materials shall be prepared or adopted and approved by the speaker and shall be distributed to the attendees at or before the time the course or program is to be held, unless the absence of materials, or the provision of such material shortly after the program, is approved in advance by the CLE Board;

   iii. Materials shall reflect that they are timely or that they have been updated with specific reference to the course or program;

   iv. Materials shall cover those matters that one would expect for a comprehensive and professional treatment of the subject matter of the course or program; and

   v. Brief outlines without citations or explanatory notations shall not constitute compliance with Program accreditation criteria.

g. The course or program shall be conducted in a physical setting that is comfortable and conducive to learning.

h. The cost of continuing legal education courses or programs to the participating attorney, apart from optional meals, lodging and travel, shall be reasonable.

i. Except in situations where courses are offered free of charge or where the CLE Board has determined that a financial aid policy is not appropriate, a financial aid policy shall be submitted with all applications.

   i. The CLE Board will review a provider's financial aid policy and procedures for New York attorneys who wish to participate in its courses or programs but who are unable to participate due to cost considerations.

   ii. Financial aid policies shall be described in detail in the application. The description shall include the specific procedures to be followed by applicants seeking financial aid as well as the specific criteria for the receipt of such aid. The types of financial aid available may include, but are not limited to, discounts, reduced fees, scholarship awards or waivers of course fees.

   iii. Upon grant of accreditation, providers shall include a statement that they have a financial aid policy and shall identify the procedure for applying for consideration in all their continuing legal education advertisements and brochures for courses and programs offered to New York attorneys, whether those advertisements and brochures are printed or distributed electronically.

   iv. Provider applications that do not include a financial aid policy for courses or programs offered for a fee are ineligible for CLE Board review.

j. The continuing legal education course or program, whether presented in traditional live classroom format or in nontraditional format, shall include a procedure to be used by the provider to verify that the attorney completed the entire course or completed an entire session of the course. A provider's attendance verification procedure may not rely solely on statements made by a participating attorney. Applications that do not include appropriate procedures to verify that an attorney completed the entire course or an entire session of the course shall not be approved.

k. Programs that cross academic lines, such as accounting-tax seminars, that are designed in part for a legal audience and otherwise meet the standards of quality and accreditation criteria set forth in the Program Rules and these Regulations and Guidelines may be considered for approval by the CLE Board.

5. *Nontraditional Format Courses* — A nontraditional format is any format other than the traditional live classroom format. Nontraditional formats include, but are not limited to, the various forms of audio recordings and video recordings, live broadcasts, teleconferences, videoconferences, webcasts, webconferences and online courses. In addition to the requirements set forth in the Program Rules and these Regulations and Guidelines, sponsoring organizations that wish to have a course approved in one or more nontraditional formats (or individual attorneys applying on their own behalf for credit for completion of a nontraditional format course) shall submit the following for each format:

a. a description of the method of participation (group activity and/or self-study);

b. a description of the procedures used by the provider to verify that an attorney completed an entire course or an entire session of a course, noting that a provider's attendance verification procedures may not rely solely on statements made by participating attorneys, and must be appropriate for both the method of presentation and the format; and

c. A sample of each type of nontraditional format course (compact disc, audiotape, etc.), or for an online program, a password and instructions for online access. Where submission of a sample may not be possible (e.g., for a webconference or teleconference), the provider shall submit a description of the technology used (including whether the program is live or archived and the level of interactivity). Individual attorneys applying on their own behalf need only submit a description of the technology used, and not a sample.

6. *Announcement Pending Approval* — Providers of courses or programs for which accreditation has been sought but not yet approved may announce:

"Application for accreditation of this course or program in New York is currently pending."

7. *Announcement* — Providers of approved courses and programs may announce in information brochures or registration materials the following:

"This course or program has been approved in accordance with the requirements of the New York State Continuing Legal Education Board for a maximum of ___ credit hours, of which ___ credit hours can be applied toward the _____ requirement, and ___ credit hours can be applied toward the _____ requirement."

B. Accredited Provider Status

1. *Accreditation* — Continuing legal education courses or programs sponsored by Accredited Providers that meet the standards for accreditation of individual courses as set forth in section 8(A)(4) of these Regulations and Guidelines are deemed approved for credit for a period of three (3) years from the date of the grant of such status, for traditional live classroom settings only, unless otherwise indicated in the CLE Board approval letter.

a. **Eligibility** — Providers that are legal organizations and that have sponsored, organized and administered, over the prior three (3) years, with at least one (1) in each year, eight (8) or more separate and distinct continuing legal education courses or programs offered in New York, offered outside of New York and not approved by an Approved Jurisdiction or offered in any nontraditional format, and meeting the standards set forth in section 8(A)(4)(a)-(j) of these Regulations and Guidelines, may seek Accredited Provider status. A "legal organization" under this subsection is defined as a provider whose courses are (1) taught primarily by attorneys and (2) designed primarily for attorney audiences. Committees, departments or divisions of New York Accredited Providers are not eligible for Accredited Provider status unless otherwise approved by the New York State CLE Board.

b. **Application** — An organization seeking Accredited Provider status shall complete the New York State Continuing Legal Education Board "Application for Accredited Provider Status." A completed application form and supporting information must accompany all requests for Accredited Provider status. A maximum of one application for Accredited Provider status will be approved per continuing legal education provider.

c. **Application Deadline** — Application for Accredited Provider status may be submitted as soon as the requirements for Accredited Provider status have been satisfied.

2. *Course or Program Sampling* — All applications for Accredited Provider status shall include a list of CLE courses sponsored, organized and administered by the applicant over the prior three (3) years. The list shall include the title, date, location and faculty names for each course or program, and shall indicate which faculty members, if any, are attorneys. The application shall also be accompanied by supporting information for three (3) of those courses or programs, one from each of the prior three (3) years (*e.g.*, a provider applying for Accredited Provider status in 2008 must submit one (1) course each from 2005, 2006, and 2007).

3. *Supporting Information* — Applications for Accredited Provider status shall be accompanied by all required attachments for each course or program submitted for the CLE Board's review. Failure to do so will delay consideration of the application. Required attachments for each submitted course or program include but are not limited to:

a. timed course or program outline;

b. faculty biographies, including educational background and degrees;

c. complete set of written materials distributed for each course or program;

d. computation of New York credit hours;

e. breakdown of categories of credit;

f. financial aid policy as required under section 8(A)(4)(i) of these Regulations and Guidelines;

g. attendance verification procedures; and

h. sample or description of any nontraditional course format(s) as required under section 8(A)(5) of these Regulations and Guidelines.

4. *Standards for Approval* — Accredited Provider status may be granted at the discretion of the CLE Board to eligible applicants satisfying the following criteria:

a. The provider has sponsored, organized and administered, within the prior three (3) years, with at least one (1) in each year, eight (8) or more separate and distinct programs of continuing legal education that satisfy the requirements of the Program Rules and section 8(A)(4)(a)-(j) of these Regulations and Guidelines.

b. The provider has established CLE Board-approved financial aid policies and procedures in accordance with section 8(A)(4)(i) of these Regulations and Guidelines. Upon grant of Accredited Provider status, providers shall include a statement that they have a financial aid policy and shall identify the procedure for applying for consideration in all their continuing legal education advertisements and brochures in accordance with section 8(A)(4)(i) of these Regulations and Guidelines.

c. The provider has established CLE Board-approved procedures for verifying that an attorney completed a course, or completed a session of a course, for each format and method of presentation (group participation and/or self-study) for which approval is sought, in accordance with sections 8(A)(4)(j) and 8(B)(5) of these Regulations and Guidelines.

5. *Nontraditional Formats* — A nontraditional format is any format other than the traditional live classroom format. Nontraditional formats include, but are not limited to, various forms of audio recordings and video recordings, live broadcasts, teleconferences, videoconferences, webcasts, webconferences and online courses. In addition to the requirements set forth in the Program Rules and these Regulations and Guidelines, providers that wish to have one or more nontraditional formats approved shall submit the following for each format:

a. a description of the method of participation (group activity and/or self-study);

b. a description of the procedures used by the provider to verify that an attorney completed an entire course or an entire session of a course, noting that a provider's attendance verification procedures may not rely solely on statements made by participating attorneys, and must be appropriate for both the method of presentation and the format; and

c. A sample of each type of nontraditional format course (compact disc, audiotape, etc.), or for an online program, a password and instructions for online access. Where submission of a sample may not be possible (e.g., for a webconference or teleconference), the provider shall submit a description of the technology used (including whether the program is live or archived and the level of interactivity).

6. *Announcement Pending Approval* — Providers of courses or programs for which Accredited

Provider status has been sought but not yet approved may announce:

"Application for Accredited Provider status in New York is currently pending."

7. *Announcement* — Where a provider has applied for and has been approved as an Accredited Provider, the provider may announce in information brochures or registration materials the following:

"[Provider] has been certified by the New York State Continuing Legal Education Board as an Accredited Provider of continuing legal education in the State of New York [_____ 200x— _____ 200x]."

8. *Renewal of Accredited Provider Status*

a. An Accredited Provider may request renewal of its Accredited Provider status for an additional three-year period. The request shall be made in writing to the CLE Board at least 45 days before the end of the accreditation period.

b. The CLE Board shall determine if there are pending or past breaches of the Program Rules or of these Regulations and Guidelines, and the Board, at its discretion, may condition renewal of the Accredited Provider status upon the provider meeting additional requirements specified by the CLE Board. The provider shall be furnished with written notice by first class mail of the CLE Board's determination to approve, conditionally approve or deny, or deny the request for renewal of Accredited Provider status.

c. If a request for renewal is timely, the Accredited Provider status shall continue until the CLE Board acts on the application.

d. If an application for renewal is not received by the CLE Board at least 45 days before the end of the accreditation period, the provider's Accredited Provider status will terminate at the end of the period. Any application received thereafter shall be considered by the CLE Board as an initial request for Accredited Provider status.

e. Eligibility for renewal of Accredited Provider status is limited to organizations meeting the eligibility requirements for Accredited Provider status set forth in section 8(B)(1)(a) of these Regulations and Guidelines.

C. **Hybrid Accreditation of Individual Courses or Programs**

1. *Application* — Sponsoring organizations (or individuals on their own behalf) that do not meet the criteria for Accredited Provider status may seek hybrid accreditation for repeat presentations of individual courses or programs offered in New York, offered out of state and not accredited by a New York approved jurisdiction or offered in any non-traditional format, by completing the New York State Continuing Legal Education Board "Application for Accreditation of an Individual Course Activity." Applicant shall indicate that it is seeking hybrid accreditation of its course or program. An original and one (1) copy of the application form and supporting information shall accompany all requests for accreditation of CLE courses and programs.

2. *Accreditation Period* — Continuing legal education courses that are granted hybrid accreditation by the CLE Board may be approved for credit for a period of one (1) to three (3) years from the date of the grant of such status, in traditional live classroom settings only, unless otherwise indicated in the CLE Board approval letter.

Examples

a. Multiple presentations of continuing legal education courses given over the course of a year (*e.g.*, single course or program presented five (5) times a year) meeting the Board's accreditation criteria may be approved for credit for one (1) year without separate application to the Board for each presentation within the year.

b. Repeat presentations of a continuing legal education course given over the course of several years (*e.g.*, single course or program presented twice a year over the last four (4) years) meeting the Board's accreditation criteria may be approved for a period of up to three (3) years.

3. *Modifications or Updates* — Modifications or updates that substantially change the course during the accreditation period, including, but not limited to, substantial changes to the course material or to the faculty presenting the program, must be submitted to the CLE Board for approval, prior to the date of the program.

4. *Supporting Information* — Applications for hybrid accreditation of individual courses or programs shall be accompanied by all required attachments. Required attachments for each submitted course or program include but are not limited to:

a. timed course or program outline;

b. faculty biographies, including educational background and degrees;

c. complete set of written materials for the course or program;

d. computation of New York credit hours;

e. breakdown of categories of credit;

f. financial aid policy as required under section 8(A)(4)(i) of these Regulations and Guidelines;

g. attendance verification procedures; and

h. sample or description of any nontraditional course format(s) as required under section 8(A)(5) of these Regulations and Guidelines.

5. *Application Deadline* — Applications for hybrid accreditation of individual courses or programs shall be postmarked at least 60 days prior to the occurrence of the course or program. All applications should be submitted as far in advance of the date of the course or program as possible to assure a timely response by the CLE Board.

6. *Standards for Approval* — Hybrid accreditation of individual courses or programs may be granted at the discretion of the CLE Board to applicants satisfying the requirements of the Program Rules and section 8(A)(4) of these Regulations and Guidelines.

7. *Nontraditional Format Courses* — A nontraditional format is any format other than the traditional live classroom format. Nontraditional formats include, but are not limited to, the various forms of audio recordings and video recordings, live broadcasts, teleconferences, videoconferences, webcasts, webconferences and online courses. In addition to the requirements set forth in the Program Rules and these Regulations and Guidelines, sponsoring organizations that wish to have a course approved in one or more nontraditional formats shall submit the following for each format:

a. a description of the method of participation (group activity and/or self-study);

b. a description of the procedures used by the provider to verify that an attorney completed an entire course or an entire session of a course, noting that a provider's attendance verification procedures may not rely solely on statements made by participating attorneys, and must be appropriate for both the method of presentation and the format; and

c. A sample of each type of nontraditional format course (compact disc, audiotape, etc.), or for an online program, a password and instructions for online access. Where submission of a sample may not be possible

(e.g., for a webconference or teleconference), the provider shall submit a description of the technology used (including whether the program is live or archived and the level of interactivity).

8. *Announcement Pending Approval* — Providers of courses or programs for which hybrid accreditation has been sought but not yet approved may announce:

"Application for accreditation of this course or program in New York is currently pending."

9. *Announcement* — Providers of courses or programs that have been approved for hybrid accreditation may announce in information brochures or registration materials the following:

"This course or program has been approved in accordance with the requirements of the New York State Continuing Legal Education Board for a maximum of ___ credit hours, of which ___ credit hours can be applied toward the _____ requirement and ___ credit hours can be applied toward the _____ requirement."

10. *Extension of Hybrid Accreditation*

a. A provider may request extension of its hybrid accreditation for an additional period of up to three (3) years. The request shall be made in writing to the CLE Board at least 45 days before the end of the accreditation period.

b. The CLE Board shall determine if there are pending or past breaches of the Program Rules or of these Regulations and Guidelines, and the Board, at its discretion, may condition extension of the hybrid accreditation period upon the provider meeting additional requirements specified by the CLE Board. The provider shall be furnished with written notice by first class mail of the CLE Board's determination to approve, conditionally approve or deny, or deny the request for extension of its hybrid accreditation.

c. If a request for extension is timely, the hybrid accreditation shall continue until the CLE Board acts on the request.

d. If a request for extension of the hybrid accreditation is not received by the CLE Board at least 45 days before the end of the accreditation period, the provider's hybrid accreditation will terminate at the end of the period. Any request received thereafter shall be considered by the CLE Board as an initial application for hybrid accreditation.

Section 9. Revocation

Accredited Provider status or hybrid accreditation of courses may be revoked by the CLE Board if the requirements of the Program Rules and these Regulations and Guidelines are not met or, if upon review of the provider's performance, the CLE Board determines that the content of the course, the program materials, the quality of the CLE activities or the provider's performance does not meet the standards set forth in the Program Rules and these Regulations and Guidelines. In such event, the Board shall send the provider a 30–day notice of revocation by first class mail containing a written statement of the reasons for the revocation and affording an opportunity for the provider to request a review of the revocation by making an explanation and submitting facts in opposition. The CLE Board shall provide such additional hearing as thereafter may be required. Unless there are special circumstances, the CLE Board shall determine the request within 180 days of receipt of such request. The decision of the CLE Board shall be final after such review.

Section 10. Obligations of Accreditation

A. **Attendance List** — Providers of continuing legal education courses or programs shall retain an official attendance list of participants in the program, including the name, time, date and location of the course or program, for at least four (4) years.

B. **Certificates of Attendance** — Providers of continuing legal education courses or programs shall, within 60 days after the occurrence of the course or program, or within 30 days after the CLE Board's written notice of accreditation of the course or program, whichever is later, provide a "New York CLE Certificate of Attendance" to all persons completing the course or program. The certificate of attendance shall contain the following information, all of which shall be completed by the provider: name of attorney, course or program title, date, location (city and state) and format; breakdown of categories of credit and the number of New York CLE credit hours earned; whether the course is (i) transitional and appropriate for newly admitted attorneys, (ii) nontransitional and not acceptable for newly admitted attorneys or (iii) appropriate for both newly admitted and experienced attorneys; and provider information. All certificates of attendance must be signed by the provider or an agent thereof. Providers may not issue blank certificates of attendance. A sample certificate of attendance shall be retained by the provider for at least four (4) years.

1. Credit shall be awarded only for attendance at an entire course or program, or for attendance at an entire session of a course or program. No credit shall be awarded for attend-ing a portion of a course or a portion of a session.

2. Attorneys who attend multiple breakout sessions must be issued a certificate of attendance completed by the provider indicating the specific sessions attended by the attorney.

3. Certificates of attendance shall not be sent to the CLE Board unless specifically requested by the CLE Board.

C. **Evaluation Surveys** — At the conclusion of the course or program, each participant shall be given a written evaluation questionnaire to complete addressing the content, instruction and written materials of the particular course or program, and, where applicable, the physical setting and/or technology. Providers shall retain the completed questionnaires for at least four (4) years.

D. **Individual Courses or Programs** — Providers of individual courses or programs shall complete and submit to the CLE Board a "New York State Continuing Legal Education Board Course Summary" form for each course or program accredited by the CLE Board for which New York CLE credit was awarded to at least one attorney during the calendar year.

E. **Accredited Providers** — New York Accredited Providers shall complete and submit to the CLE Board a "New York State Continuing Legal Education Board Accredited Provider Year–End Report" at the end of each calendar year for which Accredited Provider status has been granted. The report shall describe the accredited continuing legal education activities conducted in New York State, conducted out of state and not accredited by a New York Approved Jurisdiction or conducted in a nontraditional format for which New York credit was issued, during the calendar year. The "Accredited Provider Year–End Report" shall be submitted to the CLE Board between January 1 and January 31 of the following year.

F. **Retention of Documents** — In addition to the requirements of sections 10(A), 10(B) and 10(C) of these Regulations and Guidelines, Accredited Providers shall retain for a period of at least four (4) years, for each program conducted in New York, or conducted out of state and not accredited by a New York Approved Jurisdiction, or presented in a nontraditional format for which New York CLE credit was issued, (i) a copy of the timed agenda, (ii) a course brochure or a copy of the advertisement, where applicable and (iii) a copy of the course materials.

G. **Publication of Financial Aid Policy** — Providers approved by the New York State CLE Board shall publish the existence of a financial aid policy for courses or programs offered to New York attorneys in all advertisements and brochures as required by section 8(A)(4)(i) of these Regulations and Guidelines.

H. Publication of Transitional and/or Nontransitional Courses or Programs — Providers shall indicate in their brochures and advertisements whether a course or program is (i) transitional and appropriate for newly admitted attorneys, (ii) nontransitional and not acceptable for newly admitted attorneys or (iii) appropriate for both newly admitted and experienced attorneys.

I. Notification of Changes in Provider Information — Providers of accredited continuing legal education programs shall notify the New York State Continuing Legal Board of any change in address and/or contact person within 30 days of the effective date of the change.

Section 11. CLE Board Review of Applications, Notification of Decision and Appeals

A. Review — Upon receipt of the written and completed application, the CLE Board with the assistance of the staff shall:

1. examine and evaluate the application pursuant to the accreditation standards established by § 1500.4 of the Program Rules and these Regulations and Guidelines;

2. approve, conditionally approve, or deny all or any portion of the application; and

3. determine the number of credit hours and the breakdown of categories of credit for individual courses or programs.

B. Decision

1. *Written Notice* — The individual or organization requesting accreditation shall be provided with written notice of the CLE Board's determination to approve, conditionally approve, or deny the application for accreditation by first class mail at the address reflected on the application for accreditation.

2. *Contents of Notice* — The written notice shall include, but is not limited to, the following:

   a. If the application for accreditation of an individual course or program is approved, the notice shall state the number of approved credit hours allocated to the course or program and the breakdown of categories of credit (*i.e.*, for transitional courses, ethics and professionalism, skills, law practice management and/or areas of professional practice, and for nontransitional courses, general and/or ethics and professionalism).

   b. If the application is denied, the notice shall state the reasons for the determination and

advise the applicant of the right to seek a review of the determination. Applicants whose applications have been denied must immediately notify all attorney registrants by first class mail that the course or program has been denied CLE accreditation. If an appeal of the denial is pending, the provider may notify the registrants of this fact.

C. Appeal

1. *Review* — Any person or organization whose application for Accredited Provider status or for accreditation of a continuing legal education course or program, or publication, has been denied may seek review of the CLE Board's decision by filing a written request with the CLE Board's Application Review Committee stating the reasons for the request.

2. *Time for Filing* — Any request for review of the CLE Board's decision shall be sent by first class mail to the Application Review Committee within 14 days following the date of the notice of denial.

3. *Additional Information* — The applicant may present additional written information to the Application Review Committee.

4. *Decision of Application Review Committee* — Following its review, the Application Review Committee may take such action as it deems appropriate. The Committee will notify the applicant by first class mail of its finding and the action. Unless the applicant files a petition for review, the CLE Board's decision shall be final.

Section 12. CLE Board Audit

Providers shall permit the CLE Board and its staff to attend, free of charge, any continuing legal education course or program. Such attendance shall not qualify for continuing legal education credit.

Section 13. Nonaccredited Activities

The following categories of courses or programs shall not qualify for continuing legal education credit:

A. Courses or programs designed primarily for nonattorneys that do not advance the legal knowledge, legal education and legal skills of attorneys;

B. Bar review courses or programs taken in preparation for bar examinations;

C. Law courses not taught at the law school level (*e.g.*, law courses at colleges, universities, graduate schools, paralegal schools);

D. Courses or programs taken in preparation for licensure exams for nonlawyer professionals; and

E. Business meetings or committee meetings of legal   and law-related associations.

PART 1510. MANDATORY CONTINUING LEGAL EDUCATION FOR NEWLY ADMITTED ATTORNEYS IN THE STATE OF NEW YORK [REPEALED]

Pub. Note: See, now, Subpart B of Part 1500 of these rules.

COUNTY COURT RULES, FOURTH DEPARTMENT

Including Amendments Received Through September 15, 2008

Westlaw Electronic Research

These rules may be searched electronically on Westlaw® *in the NY–RULES database; updates to these rules may be found on* Westlaw *in NY–RULESUP-DATES. For search tips and a summary of database content, consult the* Westlaw *Scope Screens for each database.*

Table of Sections

PART 1590. UNIFORM CALENDAR AND PRACTICE RULES FOR COUNTY COURTS

§§ 1590.1 to 1590.10. [Rescinded]

§ 1590.11. Length of Juror Service

In all counties except Erie, Monroe, Onondaga, Niagara, and Oneida, in the Fourth Judicial Department, the county court judge assigned to a jury term may extend juror service any period of time up to the start of the next jury term in that county.

PARTS 1600 TO 1720. [REPEALED]

Pub. Note: Parts 1600 to 1720, formerly prescribing rules for County Courts in the Fourth Department, were rescinded eff. January 6, 1986, upon the promulgation of the Uniform Rules for the New York State Trial Courts. See now, Parts 200 and 202.

PART 1722. COMMITTEES OF ESTATES OF INCOMPETENT PERSONS (ONEIDA COUNTY)

§ 1722.1. Commissions

Committees will not be allowed to take out in advance one-half commissions on receiving the corpus of the estate.

§ 1722.2. Attorney's Fees on Annual Account

A committee will not usually, and if the committee is an attorney will not in any ordinary case, be allowed attorney's fees for making up his annual account.

§ 1722.3. Fees Paid to Personal Sureties

No allowance will be made for fees paid to personal sureties on committees' bonds.

§ 1722.4. Traveling Expenses

Committees will not be allowed for traveling beyond actual disbursements, necessarily incurred.

§ 1722.5. Charges for Legal Services Rendered to Committee

Charges for legal services rendered to the committee of the estate will not be allowed unless the nature thereof and the occasion for the expenditure are shown.

§ 1722.6. Name of Depository to Be Given

Where funds are deposited in a bank, the name of the depository must be given and where mortgage is taken, the county clerk's office in which it is recorded, with the book and page of record, should be stated.

§ 1722.7. Original Vouchers to Be Submitted With Annual Account

All annual accounts must be accompanied by original vouchers except for trivial expenditures.

SURROGATE'S COURT—LOCAL RULES, SECOND, THIRD AND FOURTH JUDICIAL DEPARTMENTS

Including Amendments Received Through September 15, 2008

Westlaw Electronic Research

These rules may be searched electronically on Westlaw® *in the NY–RULES database; updates to these rules may be found on* Westlaw *in NY–RULESUP-DATES. For search tips and a summary of database content, consult the* Westlaw *Scope Screens for each database.*

Table of Sections

PART 1850. SUFFOLK COUNTY

§ 1850.1. Proceedings to Compel Production of Wills

In all proceedings pursuant to SCPA § 1401, costs and sanctions will be imposed against any attorney who wilfully withholds production of a will.

§ 1850.2. Service of the Account

In all proceedings for the judicial settlement of an account filed in the Surrogate's Court, Suffolk County, counsel are advised that all waivers of citation and citation must be accompanied by a full copy of the schedules constituting the account for review by the respective person or persons interested. Disbursements for photocopying and postage in this regard may be presented to the court for approval as a proper administration expense of the estate.

§ 1850.3. Service of Wills With Citation and Waivers of Citation in Probate Proceedings

In all probate proceedings, waivers of citation and citation, except those to be served by publication, must have a copy of the will attached thereto, and the affidavits of service of citation shall recite the service of same.

§ 1850.4. Advance Payment of Legal Fees

In all proceedings for the advance payment of legal fees to an attorney-fiduciary, instituted pursuant to the provisions of SCPA § 2111, the petitioner shall file with his (her) application, acknowledged consents to the relief requested signed by all those persons whose interests in the estate would be affected by the proceeding, or, alternatively, shall cause citation to issue to such persons.

§ 1850.5. Legal Fees and Commissions of Attorney–Fiduciaries

Whenever there is an attorney acting as a fiduciary of an estate, he (she) will be required to file an informal account with the Surrogate's Court no later than twelve (12) months from the issuance of Letters (or twenty-four [24] months if the estate must file a Federal estate tax return), and shall not be entitled to payment of fiduciary commissions and, except where SCPA § 2111(2) applies, to payment of legal fees, without further court order. In the event legal fees are paid pursuant to SCPA § 2111(2), the reasonableness of said legal fees are subject to review by this court upon the filing of an informal account by the personal representative of the estate.

Accordingly, all decrees issued in Probate and Administration proceedings involving an attorney-fiduciary shall contain the following additional language:

ORDERED, ADJUDGED AND DECREED, that the personal representative of the estate shall file an informal account with this court no later than twelve (twenty-four months if the estate must file a Federal estate tax return) months from the date of this decree and his (her) failure to do so will result in the revocation of letters; and it is further

ORDERED, ADJUDGED AND DECREED, that there shall be no payment of fiduciary commissions without further order of this court; and it is further

ORDERED, ADJUDGED AND DECREED, that, except where SCPA § 2111(2) is applicable, there shall be no payment of legal fees without further order of this court. In the event legal fees are paid pursuant to SCPA § 2111(2), the reasonableness of said legal fees are subject to review by this court upon the filing of an informal account by the personal representative of the estate.

§ 1850.6. Attorney–Fiduciaries

(a) In all probate proceedings, with respect to a will and/or codicil executed prior to February 1, 1991, but after September 1, 1988, where the will and/or codicil of the deceased nominates an attorney as a fiduciary, there shall be annexed to the probate petition an affidavit of the testator/testatrix setting forth the following:

(1) that the testator/testatrix was advised at or about the time of the execution of the will and/or codicil, that the nominated attorney may be entitled to a legal fee, in addition to the fiduciary commissions authorized by statute;

(2) where there are co-fiduciaries, that the testator/testatrix was advised of the fact that multiple commissions may be due and payable out of the funds of the estate; and

(3) the testator's/testatrix's reasons for nominating the attorney to serve as fiduciary; and it is

FURTHER ORDERED that

(b) In all probate proceedings, with respect to a will and/or codicil executed on or before September 1, 1988, where the will and/or codicil of the deceased nominates an attorney as a fiduciary, there shall be annexed to the probate petition an affidavit of the attorney setting forth the following:

(1) whether the testator/testatrix was advised, at or about the time of the execution of the will and/or codicil, that the attorney may be entitled to a legal fee, in addition to the fiduciary commissions authorized by statute;

(2) where there are co-fiduciaries, whether the testator/testatrix was advised of the fact that multiple

commissions may be due and payable out of the funds of the estate; and

(3) the circumstances surrounding the attorney's appointment as fiduciary; and it is

FURTHER ORDERED that

(c) With respect to a will and/or codicil executed on or before September 1, 1988, and providing that the testator/testatrix is not then deceased, and is competent, the attorney shall exercise all reasonable efforts to procure an affidavit from the testator/testatrix, which shall be annexed to the probate petition, and shall be in the form as set forth in ordered subdivision (d) of this section; and it is

FURTHER ORDERED that

(d) In all probate proceedings, with respect to a will and/or codicil executed after February 1, 1991, where the will and/or codicil of the deceased nominates an attorney as a fiduciary, there shall be annexed to the probate petition an affidavit of the testator/testatrix setting forth the following:

(1) that the testator/testatrix, was advised at or about the time of the execution of the will and/or codicil, that the nominated attorney-fiduciary is entitled to commissions, payable out of the funds of the estate and/or trust, pursuant to either New York SCPA section 2307 or section 2309, which are estimated to be in the sum of $_____, predicated upon an estate and/or trust valued at $_____;

(2) where there are co-fiduciaries, that the testator/testatrix was further advised of the fact that each co-fiduciary is entitled to receive a commission payable out of the funds of the estate and/or trust, pursuant to either New York SCPA section 2307 or section 2309, and that such commission is estimated to be in the sum of $_____ for each fiduciary, predicated upon an estate and/or trust valued at $_____; and

(3) that the testator/testatrix was further advised that the nominated attorney-fiduciary may be entitled to a legal fee, in addition to the statutory fiduciary commissions pursuant to either New York SCPA section 2307 or section 2309 and the manner in which said fee shall be determined; and

(4) the testator's/testatrix's reason for nominating the attorney to serve as fiduciary.

Failure to submit any one of the foregoing affidavits may warrant the scheduling of a hearing in order to determine whether the appointment of the attorney as fiduciary was procured by the exercise of fraud and/or undue influence upon the decedent.

§ 1850.7. [Reserved]

§ 1850.8. Legal Fees and Commissions of Attorney–Fiduciaries

Pursuant to the provisions of Part 207 of the Uniform Rules for the Surrogate's Court, § 207.1(c), and Part 9 of the Rules of the Chief Judge (22 NYCRR Part 9), the court, on March 31, 1988 having issued an order with regard to its local rule requiring an attorney-fiduciary to file an informal account, and to request an order of the court in advance of making payment of fiduciary commissions and legal fees, and said order having failed to set forth the effective date of said local rule as October 1, 1986, it is

ORDERED that the order of the court, dated March 31, 1988, is hereby amended to set forth the effective date of the aforesaid local rule of the court as October 1, 1986, and it is further

ORDERED that, in all other respects, the order of the court, dated March 31, 1988 is, hereby ratified and confirmed.

§ 1850.9. Retainer Agreements of Counsel

Pursuant to the authority contained in Uniform Court Rule § 207.1(c), the Surrogate's Court of Suffolk County does hereby adopt the following court rule, effective January 1, 1989:

(a) Whenever an attorney is retained, after the effective date of this rule, by a client, to render services in connection with any action, claim or proceeding in the Surrogate's Court, the attorney shall be required to enter into a written retainer with the client stating, inter alia, the services to be performed, the compensation to be paid for such services, and the mode of payment therefor.

(b) The said written retainer agreement shall be annexed to any petitions filed by a fiduciary for the judicial settlement of his/her account, as well as any and all applications submitted to the court for the fixation of legal fees.

§ 1850.10. Attorney–Fiduciary–Trustees

In all instances where an attorney is appointed as trustee, he/she shall not be entitled to receiving or paying commissions without prior court approval, except as provided in SCPA, sections 2308 and 2309, and he/she shall not be authorized to pay any legal fees, except as provided in SCPA, section 2111. In the event legal fees are paid pursuant to SCPA § 2111(2), the reasonableness of said legal fees are subject to review by this court.

§ 1850.11. Procedure at Pre-trial Conferences in Contested Matters

ORDERED that all contested matters shall be placed on this court's reserve trial and hearing calendar and a pre-trial conference shall be scheduled, and it is further

ORDERED that pursuant to Uniform Rule 207.29, a detailed schedule for an exchange of bills of particulars, of all pre-trial discovery procedures, and a firm trial date shall be set forth in a pre-trial stipulation to be executed by the attorneys in attendance and "So Ordered" by the court, and it is further

ORDERED that any modification of same can only be made upon leave of the court, and in the event that there has been noncompliance with the order, a conference shall be scheduled to determine the reason for said noncompliance, and it is further

ORDERED that the foregoing rule shall be effective immediately.

§ 1850.12. Telephone Conferences

All counsel who have duly appeared in a proceeding in compliance with Surrogate's Court Procedure Act article 4, will be permitted, in the discretion of the court, to participate in pre-trial conferences and to argue pre-trial motions telephonically, where extended distance to the courthouse or other compelling circumstances render a personal appearance impractical upon the following procedure:

(a) **Pre-trial Conferences.** At least five court days prior to the scheduled conference date, counsel requesting a telephone appearance must notice the court in writing of:

(1) the reason counsel wishes to appear telephonically;

(2) the names of all other counsel who will attend such conference;

(3) that counsel has secured the consent of all other counsel that he be permitted to appear telephonically;

(4) that the official court reporter will or will not be required; and

(5) that on the date and hour of the scheduled conference, said counsel will institute a telephone call to the court and remain available for the conference to commence.

(6) Where two or more counsel wish to appear telephonically at the same conference, in lieu of a separate request from each party, all counsel should designate one party to make the foregoing written request and, in addition to the required information, such request must inform the court that on the date and hour of scheduled conference, a designated party will institute a telephone conference call between the court and all counsel appearing telephonically.

(b) **Pre-trial Motions.** Simultaneous with the filing of any pre-trial motion, answering or reply papers, but at least five court days prior to the return date, counsel requesting leave of court to argue for or against said motion telephonically must include among the pleadings, his separate affirmation setting forth:

(1) the reason counsel wishes to appear telephonically;

(2) that he has obtained the consent of all other counsel that he be permitted to appear telephonically; and

(3) that on the hour of the return date of said motion said counsel will institute a telephone call to the court and remain available for the argument of the motion.

(4) Where two or more counsel wish to argue for and against the same motion telephonically, it shall be the duty of that counsel first requesting leave to argue telephonically on the date and hour of the return date of such motion to institute a telephone conference call between the court and all counsel appearing telephonically.

(c) **Notification.** After the court has reviewed the request of counsel to appear telephonically, written notification will be sent to counsel approving or denying such application, and it is further

ORDERED, that the foregoing rule shall be effective immediately.

§ 1850.13. Filing of Documents That Are Not the Official Surrogate's Court Forms

(a) Any document submitted for filing in this court that is not an Official Surrogate's Court Form, for which the Chief Administrative Judge has prescribed a form, shall be on standard eight and one-half inch by eleven inch paper, the text must be legible and, other than instructions, it must be a standard typeline of 10 to 12 point characters, the margins shall be no less than one-half inch, and the form shall have attached thereto the following certification from either the attorney or the party who prepared the said document:

"The undersigned hereby certifies that the attached document submitted for filing is the same as the prescribed form and that the substantive text has not been altered."

(b) The instructional portion of the Official Surrogate's Court Form that is being copied need not appear on the document submitted for filing.

PART 1851. RICHMOND COUNTY

§ 1851.1. Retainer Agreements

(A) Whenever an attorney is retained by a client to render services in connection with any action, claim or proceeding in the Surrogate's Court, the attorney shall be required to enter into a written retainer with the client stating, inter alia, the services to be performed, the compensation to be paid for such services and the mode of payment therefor. Attorneys shall include a copy of a retainer agreement with the initial filing of any court papers.

(B) Failure to enter into and file such retainer agreement will be considered by the court on any application for legal fees and may constitute a ground for disallowance of fees.

§ 1851.2. Appearances

(A) All attorneys, other than those whose representation has been noted by a pleading, must file a notice of appearance and authorization to appear.

(B) Substitutions of attorney. No subsequent attorney representing a party will be permitted to appear unless there is filed with the clerk a consent to the change signed by the retiring attorney and signed and acknowledged by the party.

§ 1851.3. Pleadings and Papers Filed With Court

(A) The Court will not accept submissions via facsimile transmission.

(B) Any pleading or paper supplemental thereto, e.g. waiver and consent, renunciation, affidavit etc., that is dated more than six months prior to the date of filing, is considered stale and shall not be accepted for filing by the Court.

(C) No party in interest in a proceeding may act as notary for any papers filed in the proceeding.

(D) Any document submitted for filing in this court that is not an Official Surrogate's Court Form, but for which the Chief Administrative Judge has prescribed a form, shall be on standard eight and one-half-inch by eleven-inch paper, the text must be legible, the standard typeline shall be of 10 to 12–point characters (other than instructions), the margins shall be no less than one-half-inch, and the form shall have attached thereto the following certification from either the attorney or the party who prepared the document:

> "The undersigned hereby certifies that the attached document submitted for filing is the same as the prescribed form, and the substantive text of that prescribed form has not been altered."

§ 1851.4. Motions

(A) All return dates for motions will be fixed by the clerk. Any motion submitted to the Court with a return date not selected by the clerk shall be rejected.

(B) Appearance is required by counsel for all parties on the return date of the motion, and all motions are to be orally argued.

§ 1851.5. Calendar

(A) The calendar will be called promptly at 9:30 A.M. All attorneys must appear in person.

(B) No adjournment shall be granted without prior approval of the Court. Prior approval of the Court must be sought, in writing, no later than two full business days prior to the scheduled court date. A request for an adjournment must be made directly to the Law Department and not the Clerk's Office. A party seeking an adjournment must attempt to obtain the consent of all parties prior to seeking approval of the Court, and must indicate to the Court at the time approval is sought whether consent has or has not been obtained.

(C) At every pre–trial conference, all parties must appear.

§ 1851.6. Pre-trial Discovery

(A) Upon completion of the SCPA 1404 examination of attesting witnesses, counsel shall notify the Law Department before leaving the Court, and the matter will be restored to the Court's calendar for the fourth Wednesday after said examination. Any post-SCPA 1404 objections to probate of the instrument being offered must be filed with the Court no later than the close of business on the Friday immediately preceding the adjourned date. If no objections are filed by that time, the matter will proceed as an uncontested probate and be marked "for decree" at the call of the calendar.

(B) Upon the filing of objections or an answer, and after SCPA 1411 jurisdiction has been obtained, if required, a discovery conference will be scheduled with the Court. At such conference, a detailed schedule for an exchange of bills of particulars and of all pre-trial discovery procedures, and a firm trial date shall be set forth in a pre-trial stipulation to be executed by the attorneys in attendance and "So Ordered" by the Court. Immediately upon completion of discovery, a note of issue with a certificate of readiness and an affidavit of service shall be filed with the Court. Thereafter the Court will schedule a pre-trial conference that counsel and all parties shall attend.

§ 1851.7. Preliminary/Temporary Letters

Any order granting preliminary or temporary letters will provide that such letters will expire six months after the date of issuance. The order will further provide for the petitioner to post a bond for the full amount of the estate assets alleged in the petition. Preliminary or temporary letters may be of limited authority as determined by the Court.

§ 1851.8. Accounting Rules

(A) The accounting party must sign each page in the Account of Proceedings.

(B) A copy of the Account of Proceedings must be served with each Citation, and the Affidavit of Service of Citation must recite that a copy of the Account of Proceedings was also served.

(C) A copy of the Account of Proceedings must be served on each party signing a Waiver and Consent and the Waiver and Consent must acknowledge the receipt of the Account.

(D) If attorney's fees, commissions, disallowances of claims or like matters must be approved, these items with the monetary values thereof must specifically be set forth on all Petitions, Citations and Waivers and Consents.

(E) If any attorney other than the accounting party's attorney appears, or if a Guardian Ad Litem is appointed, all accounting decrees must contain a Notice of Settlement unless the decree is approved by said persons as to form and content.

(F) In order for an accounting to be accepted for filing by the Court, the petition must state whether or not an inventory of assets pursuant to Uniform Rule of the Surrogate's Court 207.20 has been filed with the Court.

(G) In all accounting proceedings, the petitioner may either cite the State Tax Commission as a party in interest, or submit proof of fixation and payment of tax or a no-tax letter, prior to the entry of a final decree.

(H) In all judicial accounting proceedings, an affidavit of legal services pursuant to Uniform Rule of the Surrogate's Court 207.45 must be filed with the account of proceeding.

§ 1851.9. Distribution of Estates

(A) In all estates, proof of full distribution in the form of receipts and releases must be filed with the court.

(B) Whenever the estate of a decedent has not been fully distributed within two years from the date when the first permanent letters of administration or letters testamentary were issued, where the gross taxable estate of such decedent does not require the filing of a federal estate tax return, and within three years if a federal estate tax return is required, the executor or administrator shall, file with the clerk of the court a statement substantially in the form prescribed in section 207.42 of the Uniform Rules for Surrogate's Court.

§ 1851.10. Safe Deposit Box Openings

A representative of the Surrogate's Court shall be present at all safe deposit box openings ordered pursuant to SCPA 2003(1).

§ 1851.11. Guardianship Rules

In addition to the requirements contained in the maintenance petition, all applicants requesting withdrawal in guardianship accounts must submit the federal and state income tax returns of the guardian and/or the guardian's spouse for the last three years.

§ 1851.12. Variance

Any of the rules set forth herein may be varied in the discretion of the Court for good cause shown.

PARTS 1852 TO 1857. [RESERVED]
PART 1858. QUEENS COUNTY

PROCESS CALENDAR

The Process Calendar is called every Thursday. When a holiday falls on a Thursday, the calendar is called on Wednesday of the same week.

SERVICE OF PROCESS AND PROOF OF SERVICE

1. Motions must be made returnable every week on the day on which the process calendar is called. Counsel must check with the Clerk of the Court as to the appropriate date to be entered for return of notice of motion prior to serving and filing. Any motion noticed with an incorrect date will be returned to counsel and not placed on the calendar until the correct date is inserted on the notice of motion and served on all respondents. Oral argument is required on all motions.

2. Where service of process is permitted by certified or registered mail, there is no need to file a signed return receipt unless directed by the Court. The affidavit of service, however, must include a statement that the mailing was not returned to the sender as undeliverable.

PLEADINGS AND PAPERS FILED WITH COURT

1. Any pleading, or paper supplemental thereto (e.g. waiver and consent, renunciation, affidavit, etc.) that is dated more than six months prior to date of filing is considered stale and will not be accepted for filing by the Court.

2. No party in interest in a proceeding can act as a notary for any papers filed in the proceeding.

TRIALS

The calendar for the trial of contested proceedings is called every Monday. When a holiday falls on a Monday, the calendar is called on Tuesday of the same week.

SELF-REPRESENTED PETITIONERS

All self-represented petitioners for letters testamentary must be personally interviewed by the Chief Clerk, Deputy Chief Clerk, or one of their designees, prior to filing their petition with the Court.

PROBATE DEPARTMENT

1. Personal appearance and examination under oath by the Clerk must be had of any witness to a will offered for probate that was executed within 90 days of the date of the decedent's death. Where all the parties in interest in the proceeding are adult and competent and sign an acknowledged waiver and consent to entry of the will to probate, the Court will dispense with this requirement.

2. When a probate proceeding is marked for decree subject to examination of subscribing witnesses, such examination shall be conducted on the date set on the return date of process or, if no date has been set, then within 90 days of the return date, or else objections will be deemed waived. The time provided for by statute for filing objections after completion of the examination of subscribing witnesses may be extended by stipulation of counsel filed with the Court and so ordered.

3. A petition requesting leave to extend preliminary letters beyond 180 days must be accompanied by a cash flow statement detailing the assets marshaled and claims paid by the petitioner. Any discrepancy between the value of estate assets set forth in the cash flow statement and the original petition for probate requires the filing of an affidavit explaining the discrepancy. If leave for extension is granted, preliminary letters will be extended for an additional 180 days.

ADMINISTRATION DEPARTMENT

1. In order to dispense with the necessity of a bond pursuant to SCPA 805, the petitioner for letters of administration must not only submit the unanimous, acknowledged consent of all distributees, but also a copy of a paid funeral bill.

2. In a proceeding under SCPA Article 13, the Court may require submission of a third party affidavit of kinship if it is alleged that the petitioner is the sole distributes of the decedent.

3. The certificate of letters of voluntary administration issued pursuant to SCPA Article 13 will specifically identify the alleged assets of an estate on its face, e.g. bank name and account number, and will limit the right of the voluntary administrator to marshal only such identified assets.

EXEMPT PROPERTY FOR BENEFIT OF FAMILY—EPTL 5–3.1

Certificates may be issued to a spouse, or children under the age of 21 years of the decedent, identifying exempt property set forth in EPTL 5–3.1, when necessary.

ACCOUNTING DEPARTMENT

1. A copy of the account must be served with the citation on all parties interested in the account. Proof of service must reflect service of both citation and account, as must any waiver and consent signed by a party. Expenses for photocopies and mailings of the account and citation shall be allowed as a legal disbursement.

2. General language approving the account, or compromise and account, shall not be permitted in a waiver and consent signed by a party. A waiver and consent by a residuary legatee or distributes is not acceptable unless it specifically consents to every prayer for relief set forth in the petition and citation. All other interested parties need only specifically consent to relief which affects their interest.

3. Where real property is sold by a fiduciary, only the sum equal to the net proceeds of sale is to be included in Schedule A of the Account, and a copy of the closing statement is to be submitted with the Account. All expenses incurred in connection with the sale (e.g. RPT tax, broker's commissions, attorney's fees, etc.) and the satisfaction of outstanding liens (e.g. mortgage, Parking Violation Bureau judgments, etc.), must be deducted from the gross sale price prior to entry in Schedule A.

4. A petition for permission to sell real property, pursuant to SCPA Article 19, must be accompanied by a copy of the contract of sale and a current appraisal of the subject property.

5. A petition to fix and determine attorney's fees, pursuant to SCPA 2110, must allege the specific dollar amount of the fee requested and must be accompanied by an affidavit of legal services.

COMPROMISE AND ACCOUNT

1. Jurisdiction over either the defendant or the defendant's insurance carrier must be obtained in any proceeding to compromise a cause of action for personal injury or wrongful death. This requirement is satisfied by either:

(a) a letter on insurance company letterhead advising of the settlement of a cause of action for a specific dollar sum on behalf of their insured defendant;

(b) an original signed stipulation of settlement or court certified copy of stipulation placed on the record;

(c) a waiver and consent signed and acknowledged by an insurance company officer who has the authority to execute; or

(d) service of citation on the insurance carrier and the named defendant in the underlying action.

2. A copy of the attorney's retainer agreement must be filed with the petition regardless whether the parties are competent adults and have consented to the fee requested.

3. A formal judicial account must be filed along with the petition to compromise where either:

(a) any party is under a disability (e.g. infancy, incompetency);

(b) there are disputed creditor's claims;

(c) there are estate assets other than settlement proceeds; or

(d) the petition seeks to compromise both a cause of action for personal injury and for wrongful death.

VARIANCE

ANY OF THE RULES SET FORTH HEREIN MAY BE VARIED IN THE DISCRETION OF THE COURT FOR GOOD CAUSE SHOWN.

PART 1900. SARATOGA COUNTY

§ 1900.1. Fingerprinting

Commencing on January 1, 1990, applications in adoption proceedings in this Court shall be accompanied by the fingerprints of the adoptive parent or

parents. The cost of said fingerprinting and processing shall be borne by the adoptive parent or parents. The Court will furnish the necessary cards for such fingerprinting.

PART 1901. ULSTER COUNTY

§ 1901.1. Requirements for Submission of Orders

In cases where the Court has required that counsel submit and order in conformance with a decision of the Court and/or a stipulation entered into by and between the parties, the following rules will apply in connection with submission of such orders in the Ulster County Family Court:

(a) Proposed orders, with proof of service on all parties, must be submitted for signature unless otherwise directed by the Court within 30 days after the signing and filing of the decision directing that the order be settled or submitted, or within 30 days of receiving this notice, whichever comes first.

(b) The proposed order should be noticed for settlement at 8:30 a.m. 15 days after the date it is mailed to the Court, all counsel and/or pro se litigants.

(c) Proposed counter-orders shall be made returnable on the same date and at the same place, and shall be served on all parties by personal service, not less

than two days or by mail, not less than seven days before the date of settlement.

(d) When submitting proposed orders or counter-orders, in addition to submitting the original proposed order or counter-order, counsel must submit sufficient copies of same for mailing to all counsel involved in the proceeding as well as litigants if they appear pro se. Furthermore, counsel must also submit an addressed stamped envelope containing sufficient postage to mail the final order to each and every individual who should receive a copy of same.

(e) If proposed orders are not submitted in a timely manner, the Court will dismiss the action on its own motion. If counsel are unable to comply with any of the requirements herein, counsel must advise the Court in writing before the expiration of such time period as to any reasons for such inability and provide an explanation justifying the request for a new date at which time the proposed order or counter-order will be submitted. Copies of such letter must be sent to all parties involved in the proceedings.

PART 1913. SCHENECTADY COUNTY

§ 1913.1. Filing of Estate Tax Returns

Pursuant to section 972(c) of the Tax Law of the State of New York, the Schenectady County Surrogate's Court hereby adopts, effective immediately, a local rule requiring the filing of a duplicate copy of estate tax returns, statements or other documents, or copies thereof, with the Schenectady County Surro-

gate's Court, when such documents are required to be filed pursuant to section 971 of the Tax Law.

This local rule shall apply to all cases in which a petition for probate or administration is filed with the Schenectady County Surrogate's Court. In implementing this local rule, the Schenectady County Surrogate's Court shall apply the provisions of section 207.43 of the Uniform Rules of the Surrogate's Court.

PART 1921. CHENANGO COUNTY

§ 1921.1. Estate Tax Return

WHEREAS, chapter 389 of the Laws of 1997 permits individual Surrogate's Courts, at their discretion

and by local rule, to require the filing of an estate tax return with the Surrogate's Court; and

WHEREAS, the filing requirements of section 9.1 of the Rules of the Chief Judge require the filing of a local rule with the Chief Administrator of the Courts.

Effective immediately, and applicable to the estates of persons dying on or after February 1, 2000, it is the rule of the Surrogate's Court of Chenango County that a person filing a petition for probate or administration in the Surrogate's Court of Chenango County and obligated to file an estate tax return with the Commissioner of Taxation and Finance, also file a copy of the estate tax return, without fee, with the Surrogate's Court of Chenango County.

PART 1950. OSWEGO COUNTY

§ 1950.1. Retainer Statements

Attorneys shall include a copy of a retainer agreement with the initial filing of any court papers. Said agreement should state, inter alia, when and by whom the attorney was retained, the terms of the retainer and a brief statement as to the services to be performed.

§ 1950.2. Filing of an Affidavit Regarding Wills and/or Codicils

In all probate proceedings where the purported will and/or codicil of the deceased nominates an attorney as a fiduciary or co-fiduciary, there shall be annexed to the probate petition an affidavit of the testator setting forth the following:

(1) that the testator was advised that the nominated attorney may be entitled to a legal fee as well as to the commissions authorized by statute for the fiduciary;

(2) that where an attorney is nominated to serve as co-fiduciary, that the testator was told of the fact that multiple commissions may be due and payable out of estate funds; and

(3) what the testator's reasons for nominating an attorney to serve as fiduciary or co-fiduciary were. Failure to submit an affidavit of this nature may result in the denial of letters to an attorney. This rule shall be effective for all wills and codicils executed on or after June 1, 1990.

[§ 1950.3. Filing of an Affidavit of Assets With the Petition for Probate or Administration]*

Attorneys shall file an affidavit of property with the initial filing of a petition for probate or a petition for administration. Said affidavit should state the personal, real and jointly owned property of the decedent insofar as the attorney and/or the proposed fiduciary may be able to provide. Thereafter, a full disclosure of assets shall be furnished in accordance with the provisions of section 207.20 of the Uniform Rules for Surrogate's Court.

* Section designation editorially provided.

PARTS 1951 TO 1962. [RESERVED]

PART 1963. WAYNE COUNTY

§ 1963.1. General

Service of Process and Proof of Service

1. Pursuant to Rule 207.7(c) all proofs of service of process, notices of motion, and orders to show cause, must be filed two days prior to the return date.

2. Counsel shall check with the clerk of the court as to the appropriate date to be entered for return of notice of motion prior to serving and filing.

3. Where, by court order, service of process is permitted by certified or registered mail it is not necessary to file a signed return receipt unless directed by the court. The affidavit of service, however, must include a statement that the mailing was not returned to the sender as undeliverable.

Pleadings and Papers Filed With Court

4. Any pleading or paper supplemental thereto (waiver and consent, renunciation, affidavit, etc.) which is dated more than six months prior to date of filing is considered stale and not accepted for filing by the court.

5. Where it appears that a pleading must be amended, amendment may be accomplished by the affidavit of the petitioner or petitioner's attorney unless directed otherwise by the clerk of the court.

6. No party in interest in a proceeding can act as a notary public for any papers filed in the proceeding.

Status of the Parties; Proof of Kinship

7. Pursuant to Rule 207.17(d) the court will not accept an affidavit of kinship signed by the spouse or issue of a petitioner claiming to be the sole statutory distributee.

8. Pursuant to Rule 207.50 the court will require service of process on an alleged divorced spouse unless either a certified copy of the divorce decree or

other acceptable proof of divorce is filed with the petition.

9. The court may also require that where the sole statutory distributee is an alleged surviving spouse, a copy of the marriage certificate be filed with the petition.

§ 1963.2. Probate

Witnesses

1. The court requires the personal appearance and examination under oath by the clerk of any witness to a will offered for probate which was executed within 90 days of the date of the decedent's death. Where all the parties in interest in the proceeding are adult and competent and sign an acknowledged waiver, the court will dispense with this requirement.

Objections to Probate

2. The time for filing objections after completion of the examination of subscribing witnesses, if requested pursuant to SCPA section 1404, shall be filed within 30 days, which may be extended by stipulation of counsel.

Attorney–Fiduciary

3. (a) Where the petition for probate requests that letters testamentary issue to a person who is also an attorney, not related by blood or affinity with the decedent, the court requires that the attorney-fiduciary submit an affidavit explaining his relationship with the decedent and the circumstances surrounding his nomination as executor. After the required affidavit is filed, the court shall determine whether a hearing is necessary on the issue of the attorney-fiduciary's qualifications and the facts surrounding his or her appointment.

(b) If the attorney-fiduciary is found to be qualified to act as executor, he or she must comply with Rule 207.60.

Preliminary Letters

4. Any order granting preliminary letters will provide that such letters will expire six months after the date of issuance. The order will further provide for the petitioner to post a bond for the full amount of the estate assets alleged in the petition for probate.

5. A petition requesting leave to extend preliminary letters beyond six months must be accompanied by a cash flow statement detailing the assets marshalled and claims paid by the petitioner. Any discrepancy between the value of estate assets set forth in the cash flow statement and the original petition for probate requires the filing of an affidavit explaining the discrepancy. If leave for extension is granted, preliminary letters will be extended only for an additional six months.

Bequest to Confidant

6. In addition to the common practice of requiring an affidavit and hearing regarding any bequest in the decedent's will to an attorney (*Matter of Putnam*, 257 NY 140), the court requires the submission of an affidavit detailing the relationship of the legatee to the testator and the facts surrounding a bequest to any person having a confidential relationship with the decedent (clergyman, accountant, doctor, nurse, home care attendant, etc.). The required affidavit, together with the petition, is submitted to the court to determine whether a hearing on the bequest is necessary.

Wrongful Death

7. Where a cause of action for personal injury or wrongful death is listed as an asset of the estate and any of the parties in interest in the estate, either as legatees or distributees, are under a disability (infancy, incompetency, unknown, etc.), letters testamentary issued by the court will be restricted to provide that the cause of action cannot be settled or compromised without further order of the court.

Trials

8. A note of issue and statement of readiness in compliance with Rule 207.29 and statement of issues in compliance with Rule 207.30 must be timely served and filed 10 days prior to the trial date set. Once a day certain and time for trial is fixed by the court, no adjournments will be granted barring extraordinary circumstances.

§ 1963.3. Administration

1. If the petition for letters of administration sets forth a cause of action for personal injury or wrongful death as an asset of the estate, the court follows the common practice of restricting letters to provide that the administrator be prohibited from compromising or collecting the proceeds from such cause of action without further order of the court. In addition, the court requires that the petitioner and the petitioner's attorney both file separate affidavits stating that they will not compromise, or collect proceeds of the cause of action without further order of the court.

2. In order to dispense with the necessity of a bond pursuant to SCPA section 805, the petitioner for letters of administration must not only submit the unanimous acknowledged consent of all distributees but also a copy of a paid funeral bill.

3. Absent a showing of special circumstances, the court will not entertain a petition for letters of administration where the sole asset of the estate is title to real property which in theory passes by operation of law without the necessity of letters of administration.

§ 1963.4. Small Estate Administration

1. In a proceeding under article 13 of the SCPA, the court may require submission of a third party

affidavit of kinship if it is alleged that the petitioner is the sole distributee of the decedent.

2. The certificate of letters of voluntary administrator, issued pursuant to article 13 of the SCPA, will specifically identify the alleged assets of an estate on its face (bank name, account number, etc.) and limit the right of the voluntary administrator to marshall only such identified assets.

§ 1963.5. Accounting

1. The court requires that a copy of the account be served with the citation on all parties in interest in the account. Proof of service must reflect such receipt, as must any waiver and consent signed by a party in interest. Expenses for photocopies and mailings of the account and citation shall be allowed as a legal disbursement.

2. In order for an accounting to be accepted for filing by the court, the petition must state whether or not an inventory of assets pursuant to Rule 207.20 has been filed with the court.

3. In any estate with gross taxable assets in excess of $108,000, the petitioner may either cite the State Tax Commission as a party in interest or submit proof of fixation and payment of tax prior to the entry of a final decree.

4. Where it appears from the papers on file that either attorney fees or fiduciary commissions have been improperly taken in advance of an accounting (restricted or limited letters), the petition must request that such advance payment be approved by the court nunc pro tunc.

5. The court will not permit general language approving the account in a waiver and consent signed by a party in interest. A waiver and consent by a residuary legatee or distributee is not acceptable unless it specifically consents to every prayer for relief set forth in the petition and citation. All other interested parties need only specifically consent to relief which affects their interest.

6. Where real property is sold by a fiduciary, only the sum equal to the net proceeds of sale is to be included in Schedule A of the account and a copy of the closing statement is to be submitted with the account. All expenses incurred in connection with the sale and the satisfaction of outstanding liens must be deducted from gross sale price prior to entry in Schedule A.

§ 1963.6. Miscellaneous

Sale of Real Property

1. A petition for permission to sell real property pursuant to article 19 of SCPA must be accompanied by a copy of the contract of sale and a current appraisal of the subject property.

Inventory of Assets

2. (a) A notice of the requirements of Rule 207.20 shall be sent by the clerk with original certificates of letters testamentary or administration. In general this rule requires the filing of an inventory of the assets which constitute the gross taxable estate within six months after the issuance of letters.

(b) If the required inventory is not filed 90 days after the date due, letters may be suspended and will not be reinstated until the requirements of Rule 207.20 are complied with.

Attorney Fees

3. A petition to fix and determine attorney fees pursuant to SCPA section 2110, must allege the specific dollar amount of the fee requested and must be accompanied by an affidavit of legal services.

Compromise and Account

4. The court requires that jurisdiction over either the defendant or the defendant's insurance carrier be obtained in any proceeding to compromise a cause of action for personal injury or wrongful death. This requirement is satisfied by either:

(a) a letter on insurance company letterhead advising of the settlement of a cause of action for a specific dollar sum in behalf of their insured defendant; or

(b) an original signed stipulation of settlement or court certified copy of stipulation placed on the record; or

(c) a waiver and consent signed and acknowledged by an insurance company officer who has the authority to execute; or

(d) service of citation on either the insurance carrier or the named defendant in the negligence action.

5. A statement of whether or not all funeral and medical expenses have been paid must be set forth in the petition.

6. A copy of the attorney's retainer agreement must be filed with the petition, regardless of whether the parties in interest are competent adults and have consented to the fee requested.

7. Regardless of whether the petition requests that settlement proceeds be allocated to wrongful death (which are nontaxable) or personal injury (which are taxable as estate assets), the court may require that the State Tax Department be cited for any settlement in excess of $108,000 and the Internal Revenue Service be served for any settlement in excess of $600,000.

8. A formal judicial account must be filed along with the petition for leave to compromise where:

(a) either any party in interest is under a disability; or

(b) there are disputed creditor's claims; or

(c) there are estate assets other than settlement proceeds; or

(d) the petitioner seeks to compromise both a cause of action for personal injury and wrongful death.

§ 1963.7. Variance

Any of the rules set forth herein may be varied in the discretion of the court for good cause shown.

STATE BOARD OF LAW EXAMINERS

Including Amendments Received Through September 15, 2008

Westlaw Electronic Research

These rules may be searched electronically on Westlaw® *in the NY–RULES database; updates to these rules may be found on* Westlaw *in NY–RULESUP-DATES. For search tips and a summary of database content, consult the* Westlaw *Scope Screens for each database.*

Table of Sections

PART 6000. RULES

§ 6000.1. Board Office

(a) All correspondence or other written communications to the members of the Board or the administrative officers of the Board, with the exceptions designated in sub-division (b) of this Part, shall be addressed to the Board's office at New York State Board of Law Examiners, Bldg. 3 Corporate Plaza, 254 Washington Ave. Extension, Albany, NY 12203-5195.

(b) The Board may, in its discretion, designate a different address solely for receipt of the materials described in Sections 6000.2(a) and (d) and 6000.3(a) of this part. Such address shall be displayed prominently in the application materials furnished to the applicants, and on the Board's Web site (www.nybarexam.org).

§ 6000.2. Proof Required of Applicants for Examination

(a) Each first time applicant shall file in the office of the Board, at least 90 days but no more than 120 days before the date of the examination for which such applicant intends to apply, an affidavit on a form furnished or approved by the Board, stating compliance with the requirements of Section 520.3, 520.4, 520.5, or 520.6 of the Rules of the Court of Appeals. That affidavit shall specify the address in or outside the State where the applicant resides and the place in the State, if any, where the applicant is employed full time. If the applicant changes either address before the examination for which application has been made, the applicant shall notify the Board in writing of such change of address. Written notification of such change of address must be received no later than the first day of the month in which the examination for which application has been made will be given to ensure that the change is made for mailing of the seating assignment.

(b) Each first time applicant shall cause to be filed in the office of the Board, on a form furnished or approved by the Board, proof of compliance with the requirements of section 520.3, 520.4, 520.5, or 520.6 of the rules of the Court of Appeals. Such proof of compliance must be received by the Board no later than the first day of the month in which the examination for which application has been made will be given.

(c) Handwriting specimen. Each first time applicant shall file or cause to be filed a handwriting specimen on a form furnished by the Board, in the usual handwriting of the applicant and bearing the applicant's signature at the end thereof, containing a certification by an authorized official of the law school from which the applicant has or will be graduated; or by an attorney with whom the applicant has studied; or by a notary public, depending upon whether the applicant qualified under section 520.3, 520.4, 520.5, or 520.6 of the Rules of the Court of Appeals no later than the first day of the month in which the examination for which application has been made will be given. If a law school is not able to certify an applicant's handwriting, such applicant shall file a written confirmation of that fact from the school and a handwriting specimen certified by a notary public.

(d) Re-examination. Except as provided in the following sentence, an applicant for re-examination shall, at least 90 but not more than 120 days before the examination for which such applicant intends to apply, file an affidavit, on a form furnished or approved by the Board. An applicant who failed the immediately preceding administration of the examination shall file the prescribed affidavit and pay the required fee by the later of:

(1) the 90th day preceding the examination; or

(2) the 21st day following the date of the Board's notification of failure to such applicant.

(e) Additional Proofs. The Board in its discretion may order additional proofs to be filed, and may require an applicant to appear in person before it, or a member thereof, and be examined concerning the applicant's qualifications to be admitted to the examination.

§ 6000.3. Fees

(a) Payment of the fee for examination or re-examination, in the amount prescribed by section 465 of the Judiciary Law, shall be made by certified check, cashier's check, or money order, payable to "State Board of Law Examiners," at the time of application for examination or re-examination. An application shall not be considered to be filed unless the affidavit required by section 6000.2(a) or (d) of this Part and the payment required herein are postmarked no later than 90 days before the date of the examination for which such applicant intends to apply.

(b) If, after applying for examination or re-examination and paying the prescribed fee therefor, an applicant desires to withdraw such application, the applicant may do so upon notice to the Board in writing. If such notice is received in the office of the Board no later than the first day of the month in which the examination for which application has been made will be given the Board will credit the fee paid by such applicant for a period not to exceed three years. If written notification of withdrawal is not received by the foregoing date, the Board will consider the reason for withdrawal and lateness of notification and may, in its discretion, credit the fee paid by the applicant for good cause shown.

(c) No applicant will receive a credit on more than one occasion, and any applicant who withdraws from more than one examination will be required to pay a new fee, in the full amount, with each subsequent application.

(d) Payment of the fee for a certificate of educational compliance required of applicants for admission to the Bar on motion, in the amount prescribed by section 465 of the Judiciary Law, shall be made by certified check, cashier's check, or money order, payable to "State Board of Law Examiners," at the time application for such certificate is made.

(e) Applicants requesting the certification to any jurisdiction of an MBE score obtained prior to February 1996 shall pay a fee of $25 for each such transfer. Such fee shall be paid at the time of request by a certified check, cashier's check or money order, payable to "State Board of Law Examiners." If a request for transfer of a prior score is not made at least 60 days prior to the date of the examination for which the requestor is applying in the other jurisdiction, the Board cannot guarantee that the score will be transferred prior to the date of the other jurisdiction's examination.

(f) Any request for a duplicate original of the Board's letter notifying the applicant of successful completion of the bar examination and of certification to the Supreme Court, Appellate Division must be in the form of a letter containing the applicant's name, social security number, examination passed (month and year), and address to which the duplicate is to be sent, accompanied by a certified check, cashier's check, or money order in the amount of $10, payable to "State Board of Law Examiners."

Cross References

Judiciary Law, see McKinney's Book 29.

§ 6000.4. Examination Accommodations for Applicants With Disabilities

(a) The bar examination is intended to test all qualified applicants for knowledge and skills relevant to the practice of law. Accordingly, it is the policy of the New York State Board of Law Examiners to provide accommodations in testing conditions during the administration of the examination to applicants with disabilities, to the extent such accommodations are timely requested, reasonable, consistent with the nature and purpose of the examination, and necessitated by the applicant's disability.

(b) The Board shall make available to applicants a Request for Test Accommodations Form and Guidelines for Documentation of a Disability to be utilized by candidates with disabilities in making requests for accommodation. If an applicant is requesting test accommodations, the completed form, together with all supporting documentation specified by such form and the Board's guidelines, shall be sent to the Board's Albany office located at New York State Board of Law Examiners, Bldg. 3 Corporate Plaza, 254 Washington Ave. Extension, Albany, NY 12203-5195. Requests for test accommodations should be filed as early in the application period as possible and shall, in any event, be postmarked no later than the general application deadline which is 90 days prior to the first day of the examination. Any requests for test accommodations which are not timely filed and/or are not complete at the time of filing may be denied.

(c) If an applicant wishes to obtain a determination of eligibility for test accommodations prior to the application filing period, the Request for Test Accommodations Form is available upon request from the Board's Albany office. A completed Request for Test Accommodations Form together with all supporting documentation which complies with the Board's guidelines may be submitted up to six months prior to the examination for which the applicant seeks accommodation.

(d) The Request for Test Accommodations Form referred to in subsection (b) hereof shall require the applicant to describe with specificity the requested accommodation(s) and submit documentation prepared by a qualified professional which complies with the Board's guidelines for documentation of a disability and which states the nature of the applicant's disability, the causal relationship between such disability and the applicant's ability to take the bar examination without the requested accommodation(s) and the reasons the specific accommodations requested are required. The form shall also require documentation of prior test accommodations, if any, granted to the applicant by academic institutions, licensure authorities, or other test administrators.

(e) If the request for test accommodations is based upon a learning disability, Attention Deficit/Hyperactivity Disorder (ADHD), or other cognitive disability, the documentation may not be more than four years old. If the request for test accommodations is based upon any other type of disability, the documentation from the qualified professional may not be more than one year old. The documentation must be comprehensive and shall include all test protocols, the qualified professional's evaluation and observations, and shall otherwise comply with the Board's General Guidelines for Documentation of a Disability, Guidelines for Documentation of Learning Disabilities, and Guidelines for Documentation of Attention Deficit/Hyperactivity Disorder which are contained in the request for test accommodations packet.

(f) The Board reserves the right to have any request for accommodations, together with all documentation, evaluated by an expert in the field retained by the Board. The Board may, in its discretion, require the applicant to provide additional information relating to the disability and/or prior accommodations, and may also require that the applicant submit to examination by an expert designated by the Board in connection with the candidate's request for testing accommodations.

(g) The Board shall act upon any request for accommodations submitted in full compliance with the foregoing provisions of this section 6000.4, and shall notify the applicant of its determination no later than twenty (20) days prior to the date of the examination for which such accommodations are requested. If the requested test accommodations are denied in whole or in part, the Board's notification shall state the reason(s) for such denial.

(h) The applicant may forthwith appeal the notification of denial of the applicant's request for accommodations to the full Board pursuant to the provisions of Judiciary Law section 460–b. Such an appeal shall be in the form of a verified petition setting forth the applicant's name, age and residence address, the facts relied upon and a prayer for relief. The appeal shall be accompanied by any further supporting documentation the applicant elects to provide in response to the Board's stated reason(s) for denial of the applicant's request, but may not set forth for consideration any new diagnosis or disability which was not discussed in the applicant's initial request for accommodations. Such appeal must be received at the Board's Albany office, New York State Board of Law Examiners, Bldg. 3 Corporate Plaza, 254 Washington Ave. Extension, Albany, NY 12203-5195, no later than 14 days from the date of the letter denying the applicant's request. The Board shall make a determination upon such appeal and shall notify the applicant of such determination.

(i) For purposes of this section, the term *disability* shall mean a disability under the Americans with Disabilities Act of 1990 (ADA) and accompanying regulations which define a person with a disability as someone with a physical or mental impairment that substantially limits one or more major life activities. The term *applicants with disabilities* shall mean otherwise qualified candidates having such disabilities. The term *qualified professional* shall mean a licensed physician, psychiatrist or other health care provider who has comprehensive training in the field related to the applicant's disability. (Where the applicant is claiming a learning disability, ADHD, or other cognitive disorder, the following professionals would generally be considered qualified to provide an evaluation provided that they have additional training in the specific field and direct experience in working with an adult population: clinical or educational psychologists, school psychologists, neuropsychologists, psychiatrists, learning disabilities specialists, and medical doctors.)

(j) The Board may, in its discretion, delegate to any of its members, or to its Executive Director or Deputy

Executive Director, all or any part of its duties and responsibilities under the foregoing provisions of this section 6000.4, other than its responsibilities under subsection (h) of this section in connection with appeals pursuant to section 460–b of the New York State Judiciary Law.

§ 6000.5. Assignment and Certification of Applicants

(a) Each applicant admitted to the examination shall be assigned to a test center designated for the judicial department in which, as shown by the papers filed by the applicant with the Board, the applicant resides or, if not a resident of the State, in which such papers show that the applicant is employed full-time, or if such papers do not show that the applicant resides or is employed full-time in the State, to a test center in the Third Department.

(b) Every applicant who, after completing the examination, becomes a resident of the State or a full-time employee therein or who changes the place of residence or full-time employment in the State, shall immediately file written notice thereof with the Board.

(c) Every applicant who passes the examination will be certified to the Appellate Division of the department in which, as shown by the papers filed by the applicant with the Board, the applicant resides, or, if not a resident of the State, the applicant is employed full-time in the State. If such papers do not show that the applicant resides or is employed full-time in the State, the applicant shall be certified to the Appellate Division of the Third Department. Any written notification of a change of address as described in paragraph (b) of this section which would result in a change of department to which the applicant will be certified must be received at least two weeks prior to the release of the results of the examination to ensure that such change is made.

§ 6000.6. Examination

(a) The board shall hold examinations twice each year, on two consecutive days, being the last Tuesday and Wednesday, of February and July. The final total weighted scale score required to pass the bar examination is as follows:

DATE OF ADMINISTRATION	REQUIRED SCORE
February 2005 and before	660
July 2005 and February 2006	665
July 2006 and February 2007	670
July 2007 and thereafter	675

(b) The first day of each examination (the New York section) will consist of 50 multiple choice questions and five essay questions in substantive and procedural law, on the subjects listed in subsection (c) below, and the Multistate Performance Test (MPT). One 90-minute test item of the MPT, developed by the National Conference of Bar Examiners, will be given on each administration of the examination.

(c) The multiple choice and essay questions presented on the first day of the examination may test the following subjects:

(1) business relationships;

(2) conflict of laws;

(3) constitutional law (N.Y. and Federal);

(4) contracts;

(5) criminal law and procedure;

(6) evidence;

(7) family law;

(8) New York and federal civil jurisdiction and procedure;

(9) professional responsibility;

(10) real property;

(11) remedies;

(12) torts (including statutory no-fault provisions);

(13) trusts, wills and estates;

(14) UCC articles 2, 3 and 9.

(d) The Multistate Bar Examination (MBE) will be administered on the second day of the examination. The MBE consists of 200 multiple choice questions developed by the National Conference of Bar Examiners dealing with the following subjects:

(1) contracts;

(2) torts;

(3) constitutional law;

(4) criminal law;

(5) real property; and

(6) evidence.

(e) An applicant shall have the option to take the Multistate Bar Examination in another jurisdiction on the same day that such examination is given in New York, and the MBE scale score attained in such other jurisdiction will be combined with the applicant's scores on the New York section of the examination, in the same manner as if the applicant had taken the Multistate Bar Examination in New York. An applicant exercising this option shall notify the Board in writing of such exercise, at the same time that the application to take the New York State bar examination is filed.

(f) Every applicant must take both the New York section of the examination at the designated location in New York State and the MBE section, either in New York State or concurrently in another jurisdiction. No applicant will be admitted to the examination more than one half hour after the examination begins. Any applicant who is not present for the New York section will not be permitted to take the MBE in New York on the following day. Any examination papers submitted by an applicant who does not take the entire examination will not be graded.

§ 6000.7. Automatic Regrading of Certain Examination Answers

(a) The essay answers for each applicant who receives a total weighted scale score within the regrading range set forth below following the initial grading of his or her bar examination shall be regraded by graders other than the initial graders. For each essay the initial scale score and the scale score resulting from regrading shall be averaged to determine the applicant's final scale score for that essay. The applicant's scores shall then be recomputed to arrive at a final total weighted scale score. The range of scores obtained on the initial grading which are subject to this rule are as follows:

DATE OF ADMINISTRATION	REGRADING RANGE
February 2005 and before	650–669
July 2005 and February 2006	655–674
July 2006 and February 2007	660–679
July 2007 and thereafter	665–684

(b) Each applicant who has received a final examination score below the required passing score may obtain one set of copies of his or her own answers to the essay questions by written request accompanied by a certified check, cashier's check, or money order, payable to the order of "State Board of Law Examiners", in the amount of $40, to the Board's office at Bldg. 3 Corporate Plaza, 254 Washington Ave. Extension, Albany, NY 12203–5195. Such request shall be made no later than 30 days after the Board's failure notice to the applicant.

(c) Failed applicants may also, in the same written request, order copies of the essay questions and the selected applicants' answers referred to in section 6000.8(a) of this Part for an additional $30, or $15 each for the questions only or the answers only. The fee for a total packet containing the failed applicant's essay answers, the essay questions, and selected applicants' answers is $70. All of the fees described in this subsection must be in the form of a certified check or money order, payable to "State Board of Law Examiners."

§ 6000.8. Publication of Essay Questions and Selected Applicant's Answers

(a) No later than 60 days after the promulgation of the results of each bar examination, the Board shall release, to one or more newspapers of general circulation, copies of the essay questions that appeared on such examination and copies of selected applicants' answers to those essay questions. The answers shall be ones which received scores superior to the average scale score awarded for the relevant essay. Such answers, which shall be selected by the Board, shall be released in a format designed to protect the anonymity of the authors and shall not be released without the authors' consent.

(b) Sets of the essay questions and selected applicants' answers from the three most recent bar examinations will be available, upon written request accompanied by a certified check, cashier's check, or money order, payable to "State Board of Law Examiners", in the amount of $50, to the Board's office at Bldg. 3 Corporate Plaza, 254 Washington Ave. Extension, Albany, NY 12203–5195. These questions and answers shall also be published on the Board's website (www. nybarexam.org).

Cross References

Judiciary Law, see McKinney's Book 29.

§ 6000.9. Fraud, Dishonesty and Other Misconduct

(a) If it shall appear to the Board that there is credible evidence which would establish that an applicant has:

(1) either by omission or commission falsified the application or proofs required for admission to the bar examination or misrepresented the applicant's eligibility to sit for the New York State bar examination;

(2) either by omission or commission falsified the proofs required for admission to practice with or without examination;

(3) either by omission or commission falsified documentation submitted in support of a request for test accommodations under Rule 6000.4 or secured such documentation under false pretenses;

(4) brought unauthorized items or materials into the examination room or otherwise violated the Board's examination security policy;

(5) broken the seal on the question book, opened the question booklet, or reviewed the questions in the question book prior to the announcement that the examination has begun, or otherwise violated any of the oral or written instructions given in connection with the administration of the New York State bar examination;

(6) possessed in any manner, reviewed and/or utilized any unauthorized notes, books, recordings, electronically retrievable data or other unauthorized materials during the bar examination, or secreted such materials for such use;

(7) written or designated any answers to questions on the bar examination prior to the announcement of the beginning of the examination session or written or designated any answers or other information (unless specifically instructed by a proctor to insert non-answer information) on an answer sheet or booklet after the announcement of the conclusion of the session;

(8) sought, obtained or used answers or information from or given answers or information to another

applicant or any other person during the bar examination;

(9) removed any examination materials or notes made during the examination from the examination room;

(10) memorized questions for the purpose of reporting and/or reported the substance of questions to any person or entity engaged in, or affiliated with any person or entity engaged in, the preparation of applicants to take the bar examination or otherwise violated the copyright protection afforded to bar examination materials;

(11) engaged in fraud, dishonesty or other misconduct in connection with the applicant's application to or the administration of the Multistate Professional Responsibility Examination (MPRE) or to a bar examination of any other jurisdiction;

(12) sat for the bar examination without having a *bona fide* intention to seek admission to practice law in the State of New York; or

(13) compromised or disrupted the process for admission to or administration of the bar examination,

applicant's examination papers and grades shall be impounded by the Board pending a full investigation by the Board and the Board shall serve written charges on such applicant by mail at the last address provided to the Board by the applicant, stating with particularity the facts upon which such charges are based. The applicant's examination results shall be withheld pending the determination of the charges by the Board.

(b) The applicant, no later than 30 days after the service of charges shall cause to be delivered to the office of the Board a verified answer to such charges. Such answer shall identify with specificity the charges disputed by the applicant, who shall set forth any evidence which can be adduced by the applicant in contradiction of such charges. The applicant may include in such written answer a request that the Board hold a hearing.

(c) In the event such applicant does not submit a written and verified answer as provided in Subsection (b) the Board shall deem the facts set forth in the written charges to be true.

(d) In the event such applicant does not request a hearing, and the Board does not on its own motion determine to conduct a hearing, the Board shall make a determination based on the evidence submitted.

(e) If the applicant shall request a hearing, or if the Board, on its own motion, determines to conduct a hearing, the Board shall set a date for a hearing by the Board or by one or more members of the Board who shall make a report and recommendation to the full Board which shall render a written decision. Rea-

sonable notice of the hearing shall be provided to the applicant.

(f) If the applicant shall be found guilty by reason of:

(1) applicant's admission that such charges are true, in whole or in part; or

(2) applicant's default in answering the written charges, in whole or in part; or

(3) determination of the Board, after a hearing, or where no hearing was conducted, after the Board's review of the evidence submitted,

such determination shall be set forth in the Board's written decision and one or more of the following penalties, and any other penalty which the Board may deem appropriate, may be imposed:

(i) forfeiture of all fees paid by such applicant;

(ii) nullification of the examination taken or the application made by such applicant;

(iii) disqualification of the applicant from taking the New York State Bar Examination or applying for admission on motion for a period not to exceed six years from the date of such admission or determination;

(iv) invalidation or striking of one or more answers of the examination taken by such applicant, or the reduction of applicant's final score by one or more points;

(v) transmission of a written report of the matter to the Committee on Character and Fitness in New York State having jurisdiction of the applicant;

(vi) transmission of a written report of the matter to the bar admission authority and/or disciplinary authority in every jurisdiction of the United States and, where applicable, to any foreign jurisdiction deemed appropriate by the Board.

(g) The Board shall notify the applicant of its decision in writing as soon as practicable.

(h) The applicant shall be entitled to be represented and advised by counsel, at his or her own expense, at every stage of the proceeding. Any person who voluntarily appears or who is compelled to attend, and submit proof or testimony, at any hearing held pursuant to Subsection (e) of this Part shall be entitled to be represented and advised by counsel, at his or her own expense.

§ 6000.10.   Application for Waiver of Rules

The Board, upon application and for good cause shown, may in its discretion vary the application of or waive any provision of these rules where strict compliance will cause unwarranted hardship to the applicant. Such application shall be in the form of a verified petition which shall set forth the applicant's name, age and residence address, the facts relied upon, and a prayer for relief.

COMMITTEES ON CHARACTER AND FITNESS OF APPLICANTS FOR ADMISSION TO THE BAR

Including Amendments Received Through September 15, 2008

Westlaw Electronic Research

These rules may be searched electronically on Westlaw® *in the NY–RULES database; updates to these rules may be found on* Westlaw *in NY–RULESUP- DATES. For search tips and a summary of database content, consult the* Westlaw *Scope Screens for each database.*

PART 6020. INSTRUCTIONS TO APPLICANTS FOR ADMISSION TO THE BAR IN THE SECOND, NINTH, TENTH AND ELEVENTH JUDICIAL DISTRICTS [REPEALED]

STATE COMMISSION ON JUDICIAL CONDUCT

Including Amendments Received Through September 15, 2008

Westlaw Electronic Research

These rules may be searched electronically on Westlaw® *in the NY–RULES database; updates to these rules may be found on* Westlaw *in NY–RULESUP-DATES. For search tips and a summary of database content, consult the* Westlaw *Scope Screens for each database.*

Table of Sections

PART 7000. OPERATING PROCEDURES AND RULES

§ 7000.1. Definitions

For the purpose of this Part, the following terms have the meanings indicated below:

(a) "Administrator" means the person appointed by the commission as administrator.

(b) "Administrator's complaint" means a complaint signed by the administrator at the direction of the commission, which is filed as part of the commission's records.

(c) "Answer" means a verified response, in writing, to a formal written complaint.

(d) "Complaint" means a written communication to the commission signed by the complainant, making allegations against a judge as to his qualifications, conduct, fitness to perform, or the performance of his official duties, or an administrator's complaint.

(e) "Commission" means the State Commission on Judicial Conduct.

(f) "Dismissal" means a decision at any stage not to proceed further.

(g) "Formal written complaint" means a writing, signed and verified by the administrator of the commission, containing allegations of judicial misconduct against a judge for determination at a hearing.

(h) "Hearing" means an adversary proceeding at which testimony of witnesses may be taken and evidentiary data and material relevant to the formal

823

written complaint may be received, and at which the respondent judge is entitled to call and cross-examine witnesses and present evidentiary data and material relevant to the formal written complaint.

(i) "Initial review and inquiry" means the preliminary analysis and clarification of the matters set forth in a complaint, and the preliminary fact-finding activities of commission staff intended to aid the commission in determining whether or not to authorize an investigation with respect to such complaint.

(j) "Investigation", which may be undertaken only at the direction of the commission, means the activities of the commission or its staff intended to ascertain facts relating to the accuracy, truthfulness or reliability of the matters alleged in a complaint. An investigation includes the examination of witnesses under oath or affirmation, requiring the production of books, records, documents or other evidence that the commission or its staff may deem relevant or material to an investigation, and the examination under oath or affirmation of the judge involved before the commission or any of its members.

(k) "Judge" means a judge or justice of any court in the unified court system of the State of New York.

(*l*) "Letter of dismissal and caution" means the written confidential comments, suggestions and recommendations referred to in sections 7000.3(c) and 7000.4 of this Part and issued by the Commission to a judge in lieu of a formal written complaint.

(m) "Letter of Caution" means the written confidential comments, suggestions and recommendations referred to in section 7000.7 of this part and issued by the commission to a judge at the conclusion of proceedings pursuant to a formal written complaint, upon a finding that the judge's misconduct is established.

(n) "Retirement" means a retirement for physical or mental disability preventing the proper performance of judicial duties.

(*o*) "Referee" means any person designated by the commission pursuant to section 43, subdivision 2, of the Judiciary Law to hear and report on any matter in accordance with the provisions of section 44, subdivision 4, of the Judiciary Law.

Cross References

Judiciary Law, see McKinney's Book 29.

§ 7000.2. Complaints

The commission shall receive, initiate, investigate and hear complaints against any judge with respect to his qualifications, conduct, fitness to perform, or the performance of his official duties. Prior to commencing an investigation of a complaint initiated by the commission, the commission shall file as part of its records an administrator's complaint.

§ 7000.3. Investigations and Dispositions

(a) When a complaint is received or when the administrator's complaint is filed, an initial review and inquiry may be undertaken.

(b) Upon receipt of a complaint, or after an initial review and inquiry, the complaint may be dismissed by the Commission or, when authorized by the commission, an investigation may be undertaken.

(c) During the course of, or after, an investigation, the commission may dismiss the complaint, direct further investigation, request a written response from the judge who is the subject of the complaint, direct the filing of a formal written complaint or take any other action authorized by section 22 of Article 6 of the Constitution or Article 2–A of the Judiciary Law. Notwithstanding the dismissal of a complaint, the commission, in connection with such dismissal, may issue to the judge a letter of dismissal and caution containing confidential comments, suggestions and recommendations with respect to the complaint, the commission's initial review and inquiry, or the commission's investigation as they pertain to the judge.

(d) Any member of the commission, or the administrator, may administer oaths or affirmations, subpoena witnesses, compel their attendance, examine them under oath or affirmation, and require the production of any books, records, documents or other evidence that may be deemed relevant or material to an investigation. The commission may, by resolution, delegate to staff attorneys and other employees designated by the commission the power to administer oaths and take testimony during investigations authorized by the commission. If testimony is taken of a judge under investigation, during the course of an investigation authorized by the commission, at least one member of the commission, or a referee designated by the commission, shall be present.

(e) In the course of the investigation, the commission may require the appearance of the judge involved before the commission, or any of its members, or a referee designated by the commission, in which event the judge shall be notified in writing of his required appearance either personally, at least three days prior to such appearance, or by certified mail, return receipt requested, at least five days prior to such appearance. A copy of the complaint shall be served upon the judge at the time of such notification.

(f) The judge shall have the right to be represented by counsel during any and all stages of the investigation at which his appearance is required, and to present evidentiary data and material relevant to the complaint by submitting such data and material, including a written statement, or by making an oral statement which shall be transcribed. Counsel for the judge shall be permitted to advise him of his rights and otherwise confer with him, subject to reasonable limitations to prevent obstruction of or interference with the orderly conduct of the investigatory proceeding. A transcript of the judge's testimony shall be made available to the judge without cost.

(g) A nonjudicial witness required to appear before the commission shall have the right to be represented by his or her counsel who may be present with the witness and may advise the witness, but may not otherwise take any part in the proceeding.

Cross References

Constitution, see McKinney's Book 2.

Judiciary Law, see McKinney's Book 29.

§ 7000.4. Use in Subsequent Proceedings of Letter of Dismissal and Caution or Letter of Caution

(a) A letter of dismissal and caution issued in lieu of a formal written complaint may be used in subsequent proceedings only as follows:

(1) The fact that a judge had received a letter of dismissal and caution may not be used to establish the misconduct alleged in a subsequent proceeding. However, the underlying conduct described in the letter of dismissal and caution may be charged in a subsequent formal written complaint, and evidence in support thereof may be presented at the hearing.

(2) Where the underlying conduct described in the letter of dismissal and caution is charged in a subsequent formal written complaint, a judge may be questioned with respect to receipt of the prior letter of dismissal and caution, and upon a finding by the commission of a judge's misconduct with respect to the facts underlying the letter of dismissal and caution, such letter of dismissal and caution may be considered by the commission in determining the sanction to be imposed.

(b) As to any prior letter of dismissal and caution or letter of caution to the respondent judge that is not already in the record of a proceeding commenced by the filing of a formal written complaint, the administrator and respondent may address such letter in their briefs to the commission and at oral argument before the commission, for purposes of sanction only. Any prior letter used in such a manner would become part of the record of the present proceeding.

§ 7000.5. Use of Letter of Suggestions and Recommendations of Former State Commission on Judicial Conduct and Temporary State Commission on Judicial Conduct

A letter of suggestions and recommendations sent to a judge by the former State Commission on Judicial Conduct or the Temporary State Commission on Judicial Conduct may be used in the same manner and for the same purposes in subsequent proceedings as a letter of dismissal and caution may be used as indicated in section 7000.4 of this Part.

§ 7000.6. Procedure Upon a Formal Written Complaint

(a) Applicable Law. If the commission determines that a hearing is warranted, the procedures to be followed are those set forth in section 44, subdivision 4, of the Judiciary Law.

(b) Answer. A judge who is served with a formal written complaint shall serve his answer, verified by him, within 20 days of service of the formal written complaint. The answer shall contain denials of those factual allegations known or believed to be untrue. The answer shall also specify those factual allegations as to the truth of which the judge lacks knowledge or information sufficient to form a belief, and this shall have the effect of a denial. All other factual allegations in the charges are deemed admitted. The answer may also contain affirmative and other defenses, and may assert that the specified conduct alleged in the formal written complaint is not improper or unethical. Failure to answer the formal written complaint shall be deemed an admission of its allegations.

(c) Summary Determination. Either party may move before the commission for a summary determination upon all or any part of the issues being adjudicated, if the pleadings, and any supplementary materials, show that there is no genuine issue as to any material fact and that the moving party is entitled to such decision as a matter of law. If a summary determination is granted, the commission shall provide reasonable opportunity for the submission of briefs and oral argument with respect to possible sanctions.

(d) Agreed Statement of Facts. Subject to the approval of the commission, the administrator and the respondent may agree on a statement of facts and may stipulate in writing that the hearing shall be waived. In such a case, the commission shall make its determination upon the pleadings and the agreed statement of facts.

(e) Subpoenas. The judge who is the subject of a formal written complaint may request the referee designated by the commission to issue subpoenas on the judge's behalf. The referee shall grant reasonable requests for subpoenas.

(f) Motions.

(1) The commission shall decide the following motions:

(i) a motion for summary determination;

(ii) a motion to dismiss;

(iii) a motion to confirm or disaffirm the findings of the referee; and

(iv) a motion made prior to the appointment of the referee, except that the commission may refer such motion to the referee when such referral is not inconsistent with the other provisions of this section.

(2) The referee designated by the commission shall decide all other motions.

(3) In deciding a motion, the commission members shall not have the aid or advice of the administrator or commission staff who has been or is engaged in the investigative or prosecutive functions in connection with the case under consideration or a factually related case.

(4) Motions to dismiss a formal written complaint must be made within 30 days of service.

(5) Motions for the disqualification of a referee are to be made to that referee within 10 days of the parties being notified of the designation of the referee. The commission will hear appeals from determinations made within 10 days thereof. All proceedings will be stayed until the commission has rendered its decision.

(6) Motions for reconsideration of a commission determination must be made within 30 days of service of the determination upon respondent. In a motion to reconsider on grounds of newly discovered evidence, the moving party must demonstrate that the proffered evidence, if introduced at the hearing before the referee or otherwise properly before the commission, (1) would probably have resulted a different determination and (2) could not have been discovered in time to introduce at the hearing or otherwise be properly before the commission prior to the rendering of the determination. The commission reserves the authority to direct a hearing before a referee for the purpose of evaluating the newly discovered evidence.

(7) Moving parties shall obtain a return date from the Clerk of the Commission for all motions to be decided by the Commission.

(g) Hearings. The referee shall set a prompt hearing date, regulate the course of the hearing, make appropriate rulings, set the time and place for adjourned or continued hearings and, consistent with paragraphs (k) and (l) of this section, fix the time for filing briefs and other documents, and shall have such other authority as specified by the commission, not inconsistent with the provisions of article 2–A of the Judiciary Law.

(h) Discovery. (1) Upon the written request of the respondent, the administrator shall, at least ten days prior to the hearing or any adjourned date thereof, make available to the respondent without cost copies of all documents which the administrator intends to present at such hearing, a list of the witnesses the administrator intends to call to give testimony, and any written statements made by witnesses who will be called to give testimony by the administrator. The administrator shall, in any case, make available to the respondent at least ten days prior to the hearing or any adjourned date thereof, any exculpatory evidentiary data, and material relevant to the formal written complaint. The failure of the commission to furnish timely any documents, statements and/or exculpatory evidentiary data, and material provided for herein shall not affect the validity of any proceedings before the commission, provided that such failure is not substantially prejudicial to the judge.

(2) Upon the written request of the administrator, respondent shall, at least five days prior to the hearing or any adjourned date thereof, make available to the administrator without cost copies of all documents that respondent intends to present at such hearing, a list of the witnesses respondent intends to call to give testimony and any written statements made by witnesses who will be called to give testimony by respondent.

(i) Burden of Proof and Rules of Evidence at Hearing.

(1) The attorney for the commission has the burden of proving, by a preponderance of the evidence, the facts justifying a finding of misconduct.

(2) At the hearing, the testimony of witnesses may be taken and evidentiary data and material relevant to the formal written complaint may be received. The rules of evidence applicable to nonjury trials shall be followed.

(j) Post–Hearing Procedures. Within a reasonable time following a hearing, the commission shall furnish to the respondent, without cost, a copy of the transcript of the hearing.

(k) The respondent who is the subject of the hearing, and the administrator, shall be afforded a reasonable opportunity to present to the referee written argument on issues of law and fact. The respondent and the administrator may file briefs and proposed findings with the referee no later than four weeks after their receipt of the transcript of the hearing. For good cause, the referee may grant a reasonable extension or may shorten the period.

(l) The referee shall submit a report to the commission with proposed findings of fact and conclusions of law. No recommendation shall be made with respect to a sanction to be imposed by the commission. The referee shall endeavor to submit such report: (i) no later than 30 days after receipt of the briefs referred to in subdivision (k) of this section, or (ii) no later than 30 days after failure to the respondent or the administrator to file such brief within the time prescribed in subdivision (k) of this section. A copy of the referee's report shall be sent to the respondent.

(m) Following service of a formal written complaint upon the respondent, the respondent may request and authorize in writing that a copy of any determination filed by the commission with the Chief Judge of the Court of Appeals and served by the Chief Judge upon the respondent pursuant to section 44, subdivision 7, of the Judiciary Law, and a copy of any correspondence sent by the Chief Judge to the respondent, be forwarded by the Chief Judge to the respondent's counsel. The commission shall make available to the respondent a form for such request and authorization.

(n) Following the appearance of counsel representing a judge in any matter before the commission, at any stage of the proceeding, such counsel may not withdraw as counsel in the matter without the permission of the commission.

Cross References

Judiciary Law, see McKinney's Book 29.

§ 7000.7. Procedure for Consideration of Referee's Report or Agreed Statement of Facts

(a) The commission shall consider the referee's report or agreed statement of facts and shall provide reasonable opportunity for the submission of briefs and oral argument with respect to such report or agreed statement of facts and with respect to possible sanctions. The respondent judge shall file an original and 10 copies of any brief submitted to the commission.

(b) In making a determination following receipt of a referee's report or agreed statement of facts, the commission members shall not have the aid or advice of the administrator or commission staff who has been or is engaged in the investigative or prosecutive functions in connection with the case under consideration or a factually related case.

(c) If the commission determines that a judge who is the subject of a hearing shall be admonished, censured, removed or retired, the commission shall transmit its written determination, together with its findings of fact and conclusions of law and the record of the proceedings upon which the determination is based, to the Chief Judge of the Court of Appeals.

(d) If the commission determines that the respondent judge's misconduct is established but that a determination other than admonition, censure, removal or retirement from office is appropriate, the commission may issue to the judge a letter of caution containing confidential comments, suggestions and recommendations with respect to the formal written complaint.

(e) If the commission determines that the formal written complaint is not sustained, that the judge's misconduct is not established and that no further action is necessary, the formal written complaint shall be dismissed.

(f) The commission shall notify the complainant of its disposition of the complaint.

§ 7000.8. Confidentiality of Records

The confidentiality of the commission's records shall be governed by section 45 of the Judiciary Law. Disciplining staff for breaches of confidentiality shall be governed by procedures set forth in section 46 of the Judiciary Law.

Cross References

Judiciary Law, see McKinney's Book 29.

§ 7000.9. Standards of Conduct

(a) A judge may be admonished, censured or removed for cause, including but not limited to misconduct in office, persistent failure to perform his duties, habitual intemperance, and conduct on or off the bench, prejudicial to the administration of justice, or retired for mental or physical disability preventing the proper performance of his judicial duties.

(b) In evaluating the conduct of judges, the commission shall be guided by:

(1) the requirement that judges uphold and abide by the Constitution and laws of the United States and the State of New York; and

(2) the requirement that judges abide by the Code of Judicial Conduct, the rules of the Chief Administrator and the rules of the respective Appellate Divisions governing judicial conduct.

Cross References

Code of Judicial Conduct, see Appendix to McKinney's Judiciary Law, Book 29.

§ 7000.10. Amending Rules

The rules of the commission may be amended with the concurrence of at least six members.

§ 7000.11. Quorum, Voting

(a) Six members of the commission shall constitute a quorum of the commission except for any action taken pursuant to section 43, subdivision 2, and section 44, subdivisions 4 through 8, of the Judiciary Law, in which case eight members shall constitute a quorum. A member who abstains from, or does not participate in, voting shall be considered to be present for purposes of quorum.

(b) For any action taken by the commission pursuant to its statutory functions, powers or duties, the concurrence of six members shall be necessary, except any action taken pursuant to section 44, subdivision 1, 2 or 3 of the Judiciary Law, and any designation of a panel provided for in section 43, subdivision 1 of the Judiciary Law shall require the concurrence of a majority of those members present.

Cross References

Judiciary Law, see McKinney's Book 29.

§ 7000.12. Commission's Principal Office

The commission's principal office shall be its New York City office.

§ 7000.13. Designation of Clerk of the Commission

The commission shall designate a clerk of the commission who shall be a member of the bar of the State of New York. The clerk shall not participate in the investigation or in an adversarial capacity in any matter before the commission. The clerk shall assist the commission in all matters concerning its consideration of formal charges. The clerk shall serve as the commission's liaison to referees appointed pursuant to section 43 of the Judiciary Law; shall correspond on behalf of the commission with attorneys with matters before the commission, including the administrator; shall schedule oral arguments and other matters before the commission; shall assist the commission in the preparation of determinations and orders and shall transmit the record of matters to the Court of Appeals, pursuant to section 44, subdivision 7, of the Judiciary Law. The clerk shall advise complainants of the commission's disposition of complaints, pursuant to section 44, subdivisions 1 and 6, of the Judiciary Law. The clerk shall perform such additional duties as may be assigned by the commission. The clerk shall serve at the pleasure of the commission and the terms and conditions of employment shall be established by the commission.

§ 7000.14. Special Rules For Commission Members

(a) **Campaigns for judicial office.** No commission member shall participate in or contribute to any campaign for judicial office, except where the member is a candidate for judicial office. When a commission member is associated with a bar association committee or other organization that endorses or rates candidates for judicial office, the member shall not participate in that process.

(b) **Campaigns for non-judicial office.** A commission member who is involved in any political campaign for non-judicial office shall not make reference to the member's affiliation with the commission or act in any way that indicates support for the candidate by the commission.

(c) **Disqualification based on fiduciary appointment.** A commission member who has accepted a discretionary fiduciary appointment from a judge shall be disqualified from participating in any complaint involving that judge or the judge who approves the commission member's fee for such appointment, for the period beginning on the date of the appointment and ending two years after the appointment is formally terminated or the member's final fee for the appointment is awarded, whichever comes later.

PART 7001. PUBLIC ACCESS TO RECORDS OF THE STATE COMMISSION ON JUDICIAL CONDUCT

§ 7001.1. Definitions

(a) "Records" shall mean a written determination filed in the Court of Appeals and served upon a judge in accordance with applicable provisions of law, and related findings of fact, conclusions of law and the record of proceedings upon which such a determination is based, and other documents which may, by law, be made public.

(b) "Information" shall mean information which may, by law, be provided.

§ 7001.2. Purpose and Scope

(a) This Part provides procedures by which records may be obtained.

(b) Personnel shall furnish to the public information and records as defined in section 7001.1 of this Part.

§ 7001.3. Designation of Records Access Officer

(a) The State Commission on Judicial Conduct is responsible for insuring compliance with the regulations herein and designates its administrator as records access officer. The administrator will delegate to a staff employee in each office the functions of receiving requests for records and providing assistance to the public.

(b) The records access officer is responsible for insuring appropriate agency response to public requests for access to records.

(c) The records access officer shall insure that personnel:

(1) maintain an up-to-date subject matter list;

(2) assist the requester in identifying requested records, if necessary;

(3) upon locating the records, take one of the following actions:

(i) make records available for inspection; or

(ii) deny access to the records in whole or in part and explain in writing the reasons therefor;

(4) upon request for copies of records, make a copy available upon payment or offer to pay established fees, if any, in accordance with section 7001.9 of this Part;

(5) upon request, certify that a record is a true copy; and

(6) upon failure to locate records, certify that:

(i) the State Commission on Judicial Conduct is not the custodian for such records; or

(ii) the records of which the State Commission on Judicial Conduct is a custodian cannot be found after diligent search.

§ 7001.4. Location

Records shall be available for public inspection at:

(a) 61 Broadway, New York, N.Y. 10006;

(b) 400 Andrews Street, Rochester, N.Y. 14604; and

(c) 38–40 State Street, Albany, N.Y. 12207.

§ 7001.5. Hours for Public Inspection

Requests for public access to records shall be accepted and records produced upon reasonable notice during all hours regularly open for business. These hours are 9 a.m. to 5 p.m., Monday through Friday.

§ 7001.6. Requests for Public Access to Records

(a) A written request may be required, but oral requests may be accepted when records are readily available.

(b) A response shall be given regarding any request reasonably describing the record or records sought within five business days of receipt of the request.

(c) A request shall reasonably describe the record or records sought. Whenever possible, a person requesting records should supply information regarding dates, file designations or other information that may help to describe the records sought.

(d) If the records access officer does not provide or deny access to the record sought within five business days of receipt of a request, he or she shall furnish a written acknowledgment of receipt of the request and a statement of the approximate date when the request will be granted or denied. If access to records is neither granted nor denied within 10 business days after the date of acknowledgment of receipt of a request, the request may be construed as a denial of access that may be appealed.

§ 7001.7. Subject Matter List

(a) The records access officer shall maintain a reasonably detailed current list by subject matter of all records in its possession as defined in section 7001.1 of this Part.

(b) The subject matter list shall be sufficiently detailed to permit identification of the category of the record sought.

(c) The subject matter list shall be updated not less than twice per year. The most recent update shall appear on the first page of the subject matter list.

§ 7001.8. Denial of Access to Records

(a) Denial of access to records shall be in writing, stating the reason therefor and advising the requester of the right to appeal to the State Commission on Judicial Conduct.

(b) If requested records are not provided promptly, as required in subdivision (d) of section 7001.6 of this Part, such failure shall also be deemed a denial of access.

(c) The State Commission on Judicial Conduct shall hear appeals for denial of access to records under the Freedom of Information Law.

(d) The time for deciding an appeal by the State Commission on Judicial Conduct shall commence upon receipt of a written appeal identifying:

(1) the date of the appeal;

(2) the date and location of the requests for records;

(3) the records to which the requester was denied access;

(4) whether the denial of access was in writing or due to failure to provide records promptly, as required by subdivision (d) of section 7001.6 of this Part; and

(5) the name and return address of the requester.

(e) The State Commission on Judicial Conduct shall inform the requester of its decision in writing promptly following its first meeting after receipt of the appeal.

(f) The State Commission on Judicial Conduct shall transmit to the Committee on Public Access to Records copies of all appeals upon receipt of appeals. Such copies shall be addressed to:

Committee on Public Access to Records
Department of State
162 Washington Avenue
Albany, N.Y. 12231

(g) The State Commission on Judicial Conduct shall inform the appellant and the Committee on Public Access to Records of its determination in writing promptly, following its first meeting after receipt of an appeal. The determination shall be transmitted to the Committee on Public Access to Records in the same manner as set forth in subdivision (f) of this section.

Cross References

Freedom of Information Law, see McKinney's Book 46.

§ 7001.9. Fees

(a) There shall be no fee charged for:

(1) inspection of records;

(2) search for records; or

(3) any certification pursuant to this Part.

(b) Copies of records shall be provided at a cost of 25 cents per photocopy page.

§ 7001.10. Public Notice

A notice containing the title or name and business address of the records access officer and appeals body and the location where records can be seen or copied shall be posted in a conspicuous location wherever records are kept.

§ 7001.11. Severability

If any provision of this Part or the application thereof to any person or circumstance is adjudged invalid by a court of competent jurisdiction, such judgment shall not affect or impair the validity of the other provisions of this Part or the application thereof to other persons and circumstances.

JUDICIAL NOMINATION COMMISSION

Including Amendments Received Through September 15, 2008

Westlaw Electronic Research

These rules may be searched electronically on Westlaw® *in the NY–RULES database; updates to these rules may be found on* Westlaw *in NY–RULESUP-DATES. For search tips and a summary of database content, consult the* Westlaw *Scope Screens for each database.*

Table of Sections

PART 7100. RULES OF PROCEDURE

§ 7100.1. Chairperson [1]

The chairperson of the commission shall preside at any meeting of the commission at which the chairperson is present, and, if absent, shall designate another member to preside. The chairperson shall be the sole spokesperson for the commission unless unable to so act, in which case the chairperson shall designate another member of the commission or counsel as spokesperson in a specific regard. In any event, the confidentiality mandated by Judiciary Law, article 3–A, section 66(1) [2] shall be maintained by all members and staff. The chairperson shall have such other functions and duties as may be assigned by the commission, or are customary for the office.

[1] The term "chairperson" as used in this part refers to the "chairman" authorized by Judiciary Law § 62(4).

[2] Judiciary Law, article 3–A sections will be referred to hereinafter by section number only.

Cross References

Judiciary Law, see McKinney's Book 29.

§ 7100.2. Counsel

The counsel of the commission shall assist the chairperson, supervise the implementation of the rules and resolutions of the commission, organize and implement the investigation of candidates, report upon investigations to the commission, supervise other commission staff, if any, serve, when present, as secretary of commission meetings and fulfill such other duties as may be delegated by the commission or chairperson.

§ 7100.3. Meetings

(a) Meetings of the commission may be called by the chairperson, or a majority of the members of the commission, by written notice to the other members specifying the time and place of meeting. Such notice shall be mailed or sent at least seven days before the time specified, except that a meeting may be held on shorter notice, and by telephonic notice, if it is impractical to do otherwise. Notice of meeting may be waived by any member before or after the meeting, and attendance at a meeting by a member shall constitute a waiver of notice. At least one meeting of the commission shall be held in every calendar year.

(b) Meetings of the commission may be held without notice whenever the commission, at a previous meeting, shall have designated the time and place for the meeting.

§ 7100.4. Quorum for Meetings

(a) Section 62(6) of the Judiciary Law states that a quorum shall consist of 10 members of the commission. Ten members of the commission must, therefore, be present at the time any vote of the full commission is taken. In the event that it is impractical for a quorum to be physically present for such a vote, except as to the selection or elimination of nominees, the chairperson may direct that the members be polled by telephone and a vote so taken shall have the same force and effect as a vote taken when a quorum is physically present.

(b) In the event that seven or more members are present in person at a duly called meeting at which a quorum fails to appear, those members who are present at such meeting are constituted a committee of the commission, and are authorized to conduct all business of the commission and enact resolutions on behalf of the commission, except as to the selection or elimination of nominees; provided that the absent members of the commission are given prompt telephonic or written notice of any action taken by the committee; and provided that any action taken by that committee is ratified at the next commission meeting at which 10 members are present in person, or is ratified by a writing, or writings, signed by all the absent members of the commission.

Cross References

Judiciary Law, see McKinney's Book 29.

§ 7100.5.   Solicitation of Candidates

(a) When the commission has been duly notified that a vacancy on the Court of Appeals has occurred, or is about to occur, the chairperson and counsel shall arrange for broadly disseminated public notice of the existence of the vacancy, of the procedure to be followed by prospective candidates in order to be considered by the commission, and of any date that has been set after which questionnaires may no longer be accepted.

(b) Each member of the commission, and counsel, shall encourage persons who may be well qualified to become candidates for nomination to the Court of Appeals vacancy by filing an executed questionnaire with the commission. In seeking recommendations or encouraging prospective candidates, members of the commission, and counsel, should make clear that no commitment or support for nomination is implied.

§ 7100.6.   Investigation of Candidates

(a) In order to receive consideration by the commission, candidates must set forth and verify all the information called for by the questionnaire furnished by the commission, and execute the accompanying forms by which the commission is given access to information or records that may be otherwise confidential.

(b) Counsel shall cause such inquiry to be made as to the background and qualifications of a candidate as is necessary to determine that all statutory or constitutional criteria for appointment to the Court of Ap

peals are met, and to ensure that the commission shall have the fullest possible information available for its deliberations with respect to the candidate.

(c) Counsel is authorized to utilize, on the commission's behalf, the power granted to the commission by section 64(3) of the Judiciary Law, to request from any agency of the State assistance, information and data and, specifically, shall procure the assistance of the State Police in acquiring background information with respect to candidates.

(d) In the event that the chairperson, counsel or any member believes that the power granted by section 64(2) of the Judiciary Law to administer oaths or affirmations, or to subpoena witnesses or documents, should be utilized, they shall request the authority to do so from the commission at a duly constituted meeting; except that, in the event the chairperson believes that any such power should be utilized on an emergency basis, the chairperson may do so pursuant to the agreement of a majority of the commission given by telephone or in writing. Subpoenas, or other process, issued on behalf of the commission shall be signed by the chairperson or, if unavailable, by counsel; and the chairperson (or a member of the commission designated by the chairperson) and counsel are hereby empowered to administer oaths or affirmations on behalf of the commission.

Cross References

Judiciary Law, see McKinney's Book 29.

§ 7100.7.   Consideration of Candidates

(a) Initial Screening Procedures.

(1) The commission will establish a date by which questionnaires must be filed for a particular vacancy, and after that date the procedures for initial screening of candidates shall commence.

(2) Each member of the commission shall be furnished with a copy of each application received, together with any further necessary background information, and the chairperson shall request each member to provide prompt written advice as to the names of those candidates that the member believes merit further consideration as part of the final nomination process. The chairperson's request shall indicate the date by which the members should submit such names, and should remind each member of the desirability of restricting the number of candidates receiving further consideration. Candidates whose names have not been submitted to the chairperson by at least one member, within the specified time, or who are not proposed for further consideration by the chairperson, shall not be given further consideration for the particular vacancy.

(3) The chairperson shall call a meeting of the commission for a date following the date by which the members are to have proposed candidates who merit further consideration, the purpose of which will be to

assess the relative merit of the remaining candidates and to determine the procedures to be followed for their further consideration. Such procedures may include the use of panels of commission members to conduct an initial interview. Following the utilization of the procedures then adopted, the commission shall meet again to determine the number of candidates that may be feasibly interviewed by the full commission, and to determine which candidates will be so interviewed, as part of the nomination procedures described in subdivision (b) of this section.

(b) Nomination Procedures.

(1) If the nominations are for the office of Chief Judge, the number to be nominated shall be seven pursuant to section 63(2)(a) of the Judiciary Law. If the nominations are for the office of Associate Judge, the number to be nominated shall be the maximum number specified by section 63(2)(b) or (c) of the Judiciary Law, unless fewer candidates receive the affirmative vote of at least eight members of the commission.

(2) When the number of candidates has been reduced by the commission to a number feasible for interview by the full commission, as part of the final nomination procedures, the chairperson shall call a meeting, or series of meetings, for the purpose of considering candidates and determining those to be nominated by the commission to the Governor, and each remaining candidate shall be invited to be interviewed by the commission. Each remaining candidate will be requested to file with the commission, prior to the candidate's interview, a sworn financial statement in a form supplied by the commission. Thereafter, the commission will discuss the relative merits of the remaining candidates and attempt to reach a consensus as to which candidates should be nominated (bearing in mind that each nomination must have the affirmative vote of eight members). In the event a consensus is not reached as to all nominations, the balloting procedure described below shall commence. The balloting procedure will be utilized only as to those nominations which have not been made by consensus.

(3) Each member of the commission present, including the chairperson, will be given a ballot which will contain the names of each remaining candidate in alphabetical order. Each member voting shall place a number next to the name of each candidate, which number indicates the member's order of preference; that is, next to the member's first choice the member will place the number "1."

(4) The numbers each candidate receives shall be added, and the aggregate is referred to, hereinafter, as the candidate's "points." In order for a candidate to be nominated, he must be among those receiving the lowest number of points, and he must have the affirmative votes of eight members of the commission—pursuant to section 63(3) of the Judiciary Law.

For example, in the case of a nomination for the office of Chief Judge, and assuming that no nominations have been made by consensus, a nominee must be among the seven receiving the lowest number of points (in the aggregate) and must be among the seven receiving the least points on each of eight members' ballots.

(5) If this first balloting yields an indecisive result as to one or more nominations because of a tie, or because a candidate who has received among the lowest number of points has not received eight affirmative votes, additional balloting shall be conducted. On ballots subsequent to the first one, there shall be listed only those candidates not receiving nomination on a prior ballot or by consensus. No candidate shall be considered nominated if he or she has received a higher number of points than a candidate as to whom the result is indecisive. The members will vote again by listing their order of preference. This balloting procedure will be continued until all nominees are selected for the particular vacancy.

(6) Following the completion of a ballot, the chairperson may call for further discussion on the relative merits of all candidates not previously nominated. At any time following the completion of the first ballot, in the case of a vacancy in the office of Associate Judge, a member may offer a resolution reducing the number of candidates to be nominated, within the range stated in section 63(2)(b) or (c) of the Judiciary Law.

(7) All votes taken with respect to nominations will be by secret ballot.

(8) Pursuant to section 65(4) of the Judiciary Law, upon the completion by the commission of its consideration and evaluation of the qualifications of a candidate, there shall be no reconsideration of that candidate for the vacancy for which the candidate was considered, except with the concurrence of nine members of the commission. For this purpose, the commission will not be considered to have completed its consideration and evaluation of the qualifications of a candidate until the conclusion of the meeting at which the candidate was nominated or eliminated for the particular vacancy.

Cross References

Judiciary Law, see McKinney's Book 29.

§ 7100.8. Report to the Governor

Following the conclusion of the meeting of the commission at which nomination procedure has been concluded, and the appropriate number of candidates nominated by the commission, the chairperson and counsel shall prepare, and the chairperson sign, a single written report to the Governor or Governor-elect, as the case may be, which shall contain the commission's nominations, and which report shall be in conformance with section 63(3) of the Judiciary Law.

§ 7100.9. Amendment or Waiver of Rules

Any rule adopted by the commission may be amended or revoked by the commission, by the vote of a majority of a quorum present at a duly constituted meeting. Any rule of the commission may be waived by the commission, in a specific instance, by the affirmative vote of eight members of the commission present at a duly constituted meeting.

LAWYERS' FUND FOR CLIENT PROTECTION

Including Amendments Received Through September 15, 2008

Westlaw Electronic Research

These rules may be searched electronically on Westlaw® *in the NY–RULES database; updates to these rules may be found on* Westlaw *in NY–RULESUP-DATES. For search tips and a summary of database content, consult the* Westlaw *Scope Screens for each database.*

PART 7200.   TRUSTEES' REGULATIONS AND PROCEDURES

§ 7200.1.   Purpose of Fund

The purpose of the Lawyers' Fund for Client Protection is to promote public confidence in the administration of justice and the integrity of the legal profession by reimbursing losses caused by the dishonest conduct of attorneys admitted and licensed to practice law in the courts of New York State.

§ 7200.2.   Organization

(a) The fund shall be administered by a board of trustees appointed by the Court of Appeals of the State of New York.

(b) The board of trustees shall consist of seven members. Of the trustees first appointed, three shall be appointed for terms of three years, two for a term of two years, and two for a term of one year. As each term expires, each new appointment shall be for a term of three years.

(c) The trustees shall serve without compensation, but shall be entitled to receive their actual and necessary expenses incurred in the discharge of their duties.

(d) The trustees shall from time to time elect from their membership a chairman, vice-chairman, treasurer and such additional officers as they deem necessary or appropriate.

(e) The trustees shall retain an executive director to serve as the chief administrative officer of the fund.

§ 7200.3.   Meetings

(a) The trustees shall meet at least quarterly each year at such locations, or in such manner, as the chairman shall designate. Special meetings may be called by the chairman, and shall be called by the chairman upon the request of at least two trustees. Special meetings may be conducted by telephone conference. The chairman shall provide reasonable notice of all meetings.

(b) Four trustees shall constitute a quorum. A majority of the trustees present at any meeting of the board may exercise any power held by the trustees, except as otherwise provided in this Part.

§ 7200.4.   Powers of Trustees

In the exercise of the authority granted the trustees, the trustees have the power to:

(a) receive, hold, manage and distribute 50 per centum of the monies collected pursuant to the provisions of section 468–a of the Judiciary Law and such other monies as may be credited or otherwise transferred from any other fund or source, pursuant to law, including voluntary contributions, together with any interest accrued thereon. All deposits of such revenues not otherwise required for the payment of claims shall be secured and invested as required by the provisions of section 97–t of the State Finance Law;

(b) adopt regulations for the administration of the fund and procedures for the presentation, determination and payment of claims, including the establishment of a maximum limitation for awards to claimants;

(c) investigate claims for reimbursement of losses as the trustees deem appropriate using staff and other available resources;

(d) coordinate and cooperate with the Appellate Divisions of the Supreme Court in the investigation of claims;

(e) examine witnesses and, in accordance with the provisions of the Civil Practice Law and Rules and the regulations of the trustees, administer oaths or affirmations and issue subpoenas;

(f) hold such hearings as the trustees deem appropriate;

(g) determine, in the trustees' sole discretion, the merits of claims presented for reimbursement, the amount of reimbursement to be awarded, the terms under which reimbursement shall be made and the order of payment;

(h) prosecute claims for restitution to which the fund may be entitled;

(i) engage in studies and programs for client protection and prevention of dishonest conduct in the practice of law;

(j) employ and at pleasure remove employees, legal counsel, agents and consultants, and fix their compensation within the amounts made available therefor;

(k) furnish the Court of Appeals with such reports and audits as the court may require; and

(l) perform all other acts necessary or proper for the fulfillment of the purposes of the fund and its effective administration.

Cross References

CPLR, see McKinney's Book 7B.

Judiciary Law, see McKinney's Book 29.

State Finance Law, see McKinney's Book 55.

§ 7200.5.   Duties of Officers

(a) The chairman shall preside at all meetings of the trustees, generally supervise the administration of the fund, and exercise such other functions and duties that the trustees may assign or delegate, or that are customary to the office of chairman.

(b) The vice-chairman shall assume the duties of chairman in the absence or disability of the chairman.

(c) The treasurer shall maintain the financial records of the fund and, jointly with the chairman, certify vouchers of the fund that authorize the State Comptroller to make payments to claimants.

(d) The executive director shall assist the trustees, supervise the implementation of regulations and policies of the trustees, coordinate the investigation of claims and prepare reports thereon, supervise staff, serve as secretary at meetings, and fulfill such other duties as may be assigned or delegated by the chairman or the trustees.

§ 7200.6.   Conflict of Interest

A trustee with a past or present relationship with a claimant or the attorney whose alleged conduct is the subject of the claim shall disclose such relationship to the trustees and, if the trustees deem appropriate, that trustee shall not participate in any proceeding relating to such claim.

§ 7200.7.   Reports

(a) On or before the first day of April each year, the trustees shall prepare an annual report of the activities and operations of the fund during the preceding year. The report shall be transmitted to the Court of Appeals, the Governor, the Legislature and the State Comptroller.

(b) The trustees may also issue periodic reports to the public concerning the activities and procedures of the fund.

§ 7200.8.   Eligible Claims

(a) The trustees shall consider claims for the reimbursement of losses caused by the dishonest conduct of attorneys admitted to practice in New York State, provided that:

(1) the dishonest conduct alleged constituted the wrongful taking of money, securities or other property belonging to a law client or other person who entrusted it with an attorney admitted to the practice of law in New York State;

(2) the dishonest conduct occurred in the practice of law by an attorney admitted to practice law in New York State;

(3) there is, in the trustees' discretion, a sufficient nexus between the dishonest conduct alleged in the claim and the practice of law in New York State;

(4) the claim is made directly by the client or other person, or their representative;

(5) the loss occurred or was discovered on or after June 1, 1981; and

(6) unless the trustees decide otherwise, the attorney has been suspended or removed from practice, is

dead, or the attorney's whereabouts cannot be determined.

(b) The claimant shall have the responsibility to provide satisfactory evidence of an eligible loss.

(c) For the purposes of this section, "dishonest conduct" shall include the misappropriation or willful misapplication of money, securities or property in the practice of law; and unlawful acts in the nature of theft, larceny, embezzlement, fraud or conversion.

(d) Losses not eligible for reimbursement include damages resulting from an attorney's negligence, malpractice or neglect; losses incurred by government agencies; losses incurred by financial institutions; losses incurred by business organizations having twenty or more employees; and losses arising from financial transactions with attorneys that do not occur within an attorney-client relationship and the practice of law.

(e)(1) In a loss resulting from an attorney's refusal or failure to refund an unearned legal fee as required by the Lawyer's Code of Professional Responsibility, "dishonest conduct" shall include an attorney's misrepresentation, or false promise, to provide legal services to a law client in exchange for the advance payment of a legal fee.

(2) An attorney's failure to perform or complete a legal engagement shall not constitute, in itself, evidence of misrepresentation, false promise or dishonest conduct.

(3) Reimbursement of a legal fee may be allowed only if: (i) the attorney provided no legal services to the client in the engagement; or (ii) the legal services that the attorney actually provided were, in the trustees' judgment, minimal or insignificant; or (iii) the claim is supported by a determination of a court, a fee conciliation bureau, or an accounting acceptable to the trustees that establishes that the client is owed a refund of a legal fee. No award reimbursing a legal fee shall exceed the actual fee that the client paid the attorney.

(4) In the event that a client is provided equivalent legal services by another attorney without cost to the client, the legal fee paid to the predecessor attorney will not be eligible for reimbursement, except in extraordinary circumstances.

§ 7200.9. Filing Claims

(a) Claims for reimbursement from the fund shall be written and verified. The fund shall provide an official claim form which shall require the following information: the name and address of the claimant; the name and last-known address of the attorney who is alleged to have committed a dishonest act; the terms of the attorney's professional engagement for the claimant; the amount of loss incurred; the date of the loss or the period of time when the loss occurred; the place and manner in which the loss occurred; the

date and manner in which the claimant discovered the loss; a description of what steps the claimant has taken to recover the loss from the attorney or any other source; and whether there are other sources, such as insurance, fidelity bonds or surety agreements, to reimburse the claimant's loss. The trustees may require a claimant to submit additional information that may be necessary to determine a claim.

(b) The fund shall promptly acknowledge receipt of the claim, which shall be assigned a claim number.

(c) A claim shall be filed with the fund within two years after the following dates, whichever is later:

(1) the date when the alleged dishonest conduct occurred; or

(2) the date when such dishonest conduct was first discovered.

(d) The trustees, in their discretion, may permit the late filing of claims upon a showing that compliance with the time limitations of this section may cause undue hardship or result in an injustice.

(e) In the discretion of the trustees, a claim shall be deemed filed when any writing specifying the claim is received by the fund, a bar association, an attorney grievance committee, or a police or other government agency.

§ 7200.10. Processing Claims

(a) Whenever it appears that a claim is not eligible for reimbursement pursuant to section 7200.8 of this Part, the claimant shall be advised of the reasons why the claim is not eligible for reimbursement, and that unless additional facts to support eligibility are submitted to the fund within 30 days the claim shall be dismissed.

(b) All claims that are eligible for reimbursement from the fund shall be investigated in such manner as the trustees deem appropriate. The trustees shall be furnished a written report of each investigation.

(c) The appropriate Appellate Division of the Supreme Court shall be requested to assist the trustees, to the extent the court deems appropriate, in the investigation of claims for reimbursement from the fund.

(d) A certified copy of an order disciplining an attorney for the same act of conduct alleged in a claim, or a final judgment imposing civil or criminal liability therefor, shall, for the purpose of this Part, be evidence that the attorney committed such act.

(e) Upon receipt of the investigation report, the trustees shall determine whether to conduct additional investigation. If the attorney whose alleged conduct gave rise to the claim has not been previously notified of the claim, a copy shall be provided the attorney. The attorney shall be invited to respond to the claim within 20 days.

(f) The trustees may request that testimony be presented to complete the record. Upon request, the claimant and the attorneys, or their respective representatives, shall be given an opportunity to be heard.

(g) The trustees shall determine, in their sole discretion, whether a claim merits reimbursement from the fund and the amount, time, manner of its payment and the conditions upon which payment shall be made. The award of a claim shall require the affirmative vote of at least four trustees.

(h) Unless the trustees direct otherwise, no claim shall be awarded during the pendency of a disciplinary proceeding involving the same act of conduct that is alleged in the claim.

(i) In the exercise of their discretion in determining claims, the trustees shall consider, together with such other factors as they deem appropriate:

(1) the amount of money available and likely to become available to the fund for the payment of claims, and the size and number of claims that have been or are likely to be presented;

(2) the amount of the claimant's loss as compared with the amount of losses sustained by other claimants who may merit reimbursement from the fund;

(3) the degree of hardship suffered by the claimant as a result of the loss;

(4) any conduct of the claimant that contributed to the loss; and

(5) the existence of other sources to reimburse the claimant's loss, such as insurance, fidelity bonds or surety agreements.

(j) Written notice of the trustees' determination shall be provided the claimant and the attorney whose alleged conduct gave rise to the claim, or their representatives.

§ 7200.11.　Reconsideration of Claims

A claimant who is denied reimbursement in whole or in part may request that the trustees reconsider the claim by filing an application with the fund no later than 30 days following receipt of the trustees' determination. If a claimant fails to request reconsideration, or the original determination of the trustees is confirmed, the trustees' determination shall be final.

§ 7200.12.　Legal Right to Payment From Fund

No person or organization shall have any legal right to payment from the fund as a claimant, third-party beneficiary or otherwise.

§ 7200.13.　Payment of Awards

(a) Claimants shall be reimbursed for losses in amounts to be determined by the trustees. No award shall exceed $300,000.

(b) Awards Shall Not Include Interest. Attorneys' fees and other incidental out-of-pocket expenses shall not be reimbursed by the fund. Additional taxes, interest, late charges and similar penalties finally incurred by a claimant as the direct result of an attorney's misappropriation may be eligible for reimbursement in the discretion of the trustees. The investigation report in a claim which involves such an element of loss shall contain an estimate of the amount of such loss and a recommendation whether the loss merits reimbursement from the fund. Unless the trustees determine otherwise, payment thereof may be processed as a supplemental award of reimbursement without further action by the trustees, provided the claimant provides proof of loss within six months following the trustees' approval of the underlying claim. The executive director shall report quarterly to the trustees on the payment of all supplemental awards during the preceding quarter.

(c) No claim for reimbursement shall be paid until the claimant transfers to the fund, in such form as the trustees shall authorize, the claimant's rights against the attorney whose dishonest conduct caused the claimant's loss and any other person or entity who may be liable for the claimant's loss.

(d) Payment of claims shall be made in such amounts and at such times as the trustees deem appropriate and may be paid in lump-sum or installment amounts.

(e) If a claimant is a minor or an incompetent, the award may be paid to a parent, guardian, committee or the attorney of the claimant, on the behalf of and for the benefit of the claimant.

(f) All payments of awards of reimbursement from the fund shall be made by the State Comptroller on vouchers certified by the chairman and the treasurer.

§ 7200.14.　Representation by Counsel

(a) A claimant and the attorney whose alleged conduct resulted in the claim shall have the right to be represented by an attorney.

(b) In accordance with rules of the Appellate Divisions of the Supreme Court, no attorney who assists a claimant process a claim with the fund shall charge or accept compensation for those services, without the prior written approval of the trustees. No fee applications by attorneys, including public officers and court-appointed fiduciaries, shall be approved by the trustees absent a showing of extraordinary circumstances.

§ 7200.15.　Confidentiality

(a) Except as otherwise provided, all claims and proceedings and the records relating thereto shall be sealed and confidential.

(b) All information provided by an Appellate Division of the Supreme Court shall remain sealed and confidential to the extent required by section 90 of the Judiciary Law.

(c) The trustees' final determination awarding reimbursement of a claim, and the facts relating to the claimant's loss, shall be a public record.

(d) An attorney whose alleged conduct gave rise to the claim may waive confidentiality.

(e) This section shall not be construed to deny access to information by the Court of Appeals, and Appellate Division of the Supreme Court, or to any court of competent jurisdiction in a judicial review proceeding.

Cross References

Judiciary Law, see McKinney's Book 29.

§ 7200.16. Amendment of Regulations

New regulations may be adopted, and any regulation may be amended or repealed, by the trustees at any regular or special meeting, provided that notice of the proposed adoption, amendment or repeal have been given all trustees at least seven days before the meeting. New regulations, amendments and repeals shall be published in the *State Register*. Copies of all regulations shall be made available to the public at all offices of the fund.

§ 7200.17. Construction of Regulations

These regulations shall be liberally construed to accomplish the objectives of the fund and the policies of the trustees.

STATE REPORTER

Including Amendments Received Through September 15, 2008

Westlaw Electronic Research

These rules may be searched electronically on Westlaw® *in the NY–RULES database; updates to these rules may be found on* Westlaw *in NY–RULESUP-DATES. For search tips and a summary of database content, consult the* Westlaw *Scope Screens for each database.*

PART 7300. RULES CONCERNING PUBLICATION OF OPINIONS IN THE MISCELLANEOUS REPORTS

§ 7300.1. Approval

No opinion shall be made available for publication in any official or unofficial reports, except the *New York Law Journal*, without the approval of the State Reporter or the Committee on Opinions.

§ 7300.2. Copies of Opinion

Before an opinion is made available for publication other than in the *New York Law Journal*, two copies thereof shall be sent to the State Reporter at One Commerce Plaza, 17th Floor, Albany, NY 12210.

§ 7300.3. Notification

If the State Reporter determines that the opinion is acceptable for publication, he will so notify the judge who wrote the opinion and, within 48 hours after such determination, mail a copy thereof to the West Publishing Company.

§ 7300.4. Appeal

If the State Reporter determines that the opinion is not acceptable for publication, he will so notify the judge who wrote the opinion.

(a) If the judge agrees with the State Reporter's determination, the opinion will, without more, be withheld from publication.

(b) If the judge disagrees with the State Reporter's determination, the opinion will be submitted, upon the judge's written request, to a member of the Committee on Opinions. If the member of the committee determines that the opinion should not be published, that determination shall be final and the opinion will be withheld from publication.

§ 7300.5. Conditional Approval

In some cases, an opinion may be approved for publication on condition: for example, that excessively long quotations from opinions, texts or other writings be eliminated or summarized; or that an exceedingly long statement of the facts be eliminated or condensed.

§ 7300.6. Policies

Opinions to be published should be written as concisely as possible, without repetition or lengthy dissertations on well-known legal principles; opinions dealing with matters which are essentially of interest only to the attorneys and parties involved should not be presented for publication; and opinions covering legal matters which are of relatively incidental interest or which involve primarily factual or discretionary matters or dicta should not be submitted for publication.

§ 7300.7.   Committee on Opinions

The Committee on Opinions consists of one justice from each of the departments of the Appellate Division.

RULES OF THE ETHICS COMMISSION FOR THE UNIFIED COURT SYSTEM

[See Part 40. Rules of the Chief Judge]

Adopted and effective January 1, 1991

Including Amendments Received Through September 15, 2008

Westlaw Electronic Research

These rules may be searched electronically on Westlaw® *in the NY–RULES database; updates to these rules may be found on* Westlaw *in NY–RULESUP-DATES. For search tips and a summary of database content, consult the* Westlaw *Scope Screens for each database.*

Table of Sections

PART 7400. PROCEDURES

§ 7400.1. Requesting Exemptions From Filing Financial Disclosure Statements

(a) Definitions.

(1) "Annual compensation" shall mean the basic annual salary which an individual receives to perform the duties of the position in which he or she serves. Annual salary shall not include location pay, payment of overtime, retroactive salary benefits, uniform or clothing allowance, reimbursements, or any one time payment, bonus or award.

(2) "Commission" shall mean the Ethics Commission for the Unified Court System.

(3) "Employee" shall mean a state-paid judge, justice, officer or employee of the Unified Court System.

(4) "Employee organization" shall mean an employee organization that is recognized or certified pursuant to section 204 of the Civil Service Law to represent public employees of a public employer.

(5) "File" shall mean to make delivery to the offices of the Commission personally or by mail. The filing date shall be the date the document filed is received in the offices of the Commission.

(6) "Financial disclosure statement" shall mean the annual statement approved by the Chief Judge pursuant to subdivision 4 of section 211 of the Judiciary Law.

(7) "Job title" shall mean the title of the position to which an employee has been elected or appointed.

(8) "Rule" shall mean Part 40 of the Rules of the Chief Judge of the State of New York (22 NYCRR).

(b) Scope. Pursuant to section 40.1(i)(8) of the Rule, the Commission shall permit an employee who is not a policy maker pursuant to section 40.2 of the Rule, and who is required to file a financial disclosure statement, to request an exemption from filing. This request will be granted if, in the discretion of the Commission, the public interest does not require disclosure and the employee's duties do not involve any of the duties set forth in section 40.1(i)(8) of the Rule.

(c) Procedure.

(1) An employee individually, or an employee organization on behalf of persons who share the same job title, may request an exemption from filing a financial disclosure statement by filing a written request with the Commission on or before March 1st of the year in which the exemption is requested.

(2) The request for the exemption shall include:

(i) the name, work address, home address, work telephone number and job title of the employee if the request is on an individual basis, or the name of the employee organization, and name, address and telephone number of its authorized representative filing on behalf of persons who share the same job title;

(ii) the job title for which an exemption is requested where the request is by an employee organization;

(iii) a copy of the title specifications of the job title for which an exemption is requested;

(iv) a statement in support of the claim of the filing employee or employee organization that the public interest does not require disclosure and that the job title for which the exemption is requested does not involve any of the duties set forth in section 40.1(i)(8) of the Rule, giving specific reasons and justifications therefor. Documentation supporting this statement may be annexed to the request.

(3) The request for an exemption must be signed by the employee, if requesting an individual exemption, or by the authorized representative of the employee organization requesting an exemption on behalf of persons who share the same job title.

(d) Commission Action.

(1) Upon receipt of a request for an exemption from filing a financial disclosure statement, the Commission shall review the material filed to determine whether the public interest requires disclosure and whether the duties of the job title include any of the duties set forth in section 40.1(i)(8) of the Rule.

(2) If the Commission determines that additional information would be useful, it may obtain such information from the Office of Court Administration, from the individual employee requesting an exemption, from the employee organization requesting an exemption on behalf of persons who share the same job title, or from any source deemed appropriate by the Com-

mission. The Commission, in its discretion, may request a meeting with the individual employee or the representative of an employee organization to discuss the exemption request.

(3) If the Commission requests additional information from an individual employee or an employee organization, such additional information must be filed with the Commission within twenty-one [21] business days of the date the request is mailed from the Commission offices. If the Commission does not receive such information within the said twenty-one [21] days, it may render a decision on the information available.

(4) Unless the Commission decides that the public interest does not require disclosure and that a job title does not involve the duties set forth in section 40.1(i)(8) of the rule, the Commission shall deny the request for an exemption from filing a financial disclosure statement.

In applying the public interest standard, the Commission considers the duties the employee may be called upon to perform. The Commission weighs the strong public interest in disclosure against the employee's privacy rights. In this weighing process, the Commission considers the employee's role in the judicial, administrative or managerial process of the Unified Court System. The Commission also considers the potential for conflict of interest and use of public office for personal gain in the performance of the employee's actual or potential job duties.

Judiciary Law, section 211(4) and 22 NYCRR Part 40 establish a strong public policy favoring disclosure. Thus employees otherwise required to file, who have requested an exemption from filing, must demonstrate that an individual exception to this policy is warranted.

(5) The Commission shall give written notification of its decision to the employee and/or the employee organization, as appropriate, and to the Chief Administrator of the Courts.

(6) Once an exemption has been granted for a job title, an employee, as long as he or she holds that job title, will not be required to file a financial disclosure statement in any subsequent year for which one would otherwise be required unless:

(i) the duties of the job title change; or

(ii) it is determined that the employee holds a policymaking position by: the Chief Judge of the Court of Appeals, as to personnel of that Court; the Presiding Justice of each Appellate Division, as to personnel of that Court; or the Chief Administrator of the Courts, as to all other state-paid personnel of the Unified Court System; or

(iii) the Commission, upon review of its decision to grant such exemption, determines the exemption is no longer appropriate.

§ 7400.2. Requesting an Extension of Time to File a Financial Disclosure Statement, and Automatic Extensions of Time to File Supplementary Financial Disclosure Statements

(a) Definitions.

(1) "Commission" shall mean the Ethics Commission for the Unified Court System.

(2) "Employee" shall mean a state-paid judge, justice, officer or employee of the Unified Court System.

(3) "File" shall mean to make delivery to the offices of the Commission personally or by mail. The filing date shall be the date the document filed is received in the offices of the Commission.

(4) "Financial disclosure statement" shall mean the annual statement approved by the Chief Judge pursuant to subdivision 4 of section 211 of the Judiciary Law.

(5) "Job title" shall mean the title of the position to which an employee has been elected or appointed.

(6) "Rule" shall mean Part 40 of the Rules of the Chief Judge of the State of New York (22 NYCRR).

(b) Scope.

(1) Pursuant to section 40.1(i)(3) of the Rule, the Commission shall permit an employee who is required to file a financial disclosure statement to request an additional period of time within which to file such statement. This request will be granted if the Commission finds that there is justifiable cause for the extension or that the timely filing of the statement would cause undue hardship.

(2) Pursuant to section 40.2(a)(2)(i) of the Rule, the Commission shall allow an employee who has timely filed an application for automatic extension with the Internal Revenue Service to file a supplementary statement of financial disclosure.

(c) Procedure for Requesting an Extension of Time to File a Financial Disclosure Statement.

(1) An employee may request an extension of time to file a financial disclosure statement after May 15th of the year in which filing is required by filing a written request with the Commission on or before May 15th of the year in which such extension is requested.

(2) The request for the extension shall include:

(i) the name, home address, work address, work telephone number, and job title of the employee requesting the extension;

(ii) a statement in support of the employee's claim that an extension of time to file a financial disclosure statement is necessary due to justifiable cause or undue hardship, giving specific reasons and justifications therefor. Documentation supporting this statement may be annexed to the request;

(iii) the date certain by which the employee will file his or her financial disclosure statement.

(3) The request for an extension must be signed by the employee requesting the extension.

(d) Commission Action.

(1) Upon receipt of a request for extension of time to file a financial disclosure statement, the Commission shall review the material filed to determine if there has been a showing of justifiable cause or undue hardship.

(2) If the Commission determines that additional information would be useful, it may request such information from the employee requesting the extension. The Commission, in its discretion, may request a meeting with the employee to discuss the extension request.

(3) Unless the Commission decides that there is justifiable cause for an extension of time to file a financial disclosure statement, or that timely filing of such statement would cause undue hardship, the Commission shall deny the request for an extension of time to file a financial disclosure statement.

(4) The Commission shall give written notice of its decision to the employee requesting an extension of time to file. If the extension is granted, the decision shall include the date certain on or before which the employee's financial disclosure statement must be filed. In the event the Commission determines that such written notice of its decision would not reach the employee requesting the extension before May 15th of the year for which the extension is requested, the Commission shall notify the employee of its decision by telephone, to be followed by written notice of decision.

(5) Vacation periods, and the ordinary and necessary tasks, routines, and obligations of an employee's personal and work life shall not constitute undue hardship or justifiable cause for an extension of time to file a financial disclosure statement.

(6) No extension of time to file a financial disclosure statement shall be granted beyond September 30th of the year in which such extension is requested.

(e) Supplementary Financial Disclosure Statements.

(1) An employee who timely filed with the Internal Revenue Service an application for automatic extension of time in which to file his or her individual income tax return for the immediately preceding calendar or fiscal year is required to file a financial disclosure statement on or before May 15th of the year that filing is required. The employee, however, may indicate on the timely filed financial disclosure statement that information regarding a particular item of disclosure is lacking and will be supplied in a

supplementary statement of financial disclosure to be filed on or before the seventh day after the expiration of the period of such automatic extension of time within which to file such individual tax return.

(2) The employee must submit a written statement with the timely filed financial disclosure statement. This written statement shall include:

(i) the name, home address, work address, work telephone number and job title of the employee;

(ii) a copy of the application filed with the Internal Revenue Service for automatic extension of time in which to file the employee's individual income tax return for the immediately preceding calendar or fiscal year;

(iii) a description of the nature of the information which cannot be timely provided on the financial disclosure statement, including the question number(s) where the information would otherwise be reported; and

(iv) the date that the employee's automatic extension expires.

(3) Failure to file a supplementary financial disclosure statement, or the filing of an incomplete or deficient supplementary financial disclosure statement, shall be subject to the notice and penalty provisions of the Rule as if the supplementary statement were an annual statement of financial disclosure.

§ 7400.3. Requesting an Exemption From Reporting One or More Items of Information Which Pertain to an Employee's Spouse or Unemancipated Children; Statement of Separation From Spouse

(a) **Definitions.**

(1) "Commission" shall mean the Ethics Commission for the Unified Court System.

(2) "Employee" shall mean a state-paid judge, justice, officer or employee of the Unified Court System.

(3) "File" shall mean to make delivery to the offices of the Commission personally or by mail. The filing date shall be the date the document filed is received in the offices of the Commission.

(4) "Financial disclosure statement" shall mean the annual statement approved by the Chief Judge pursuant to subdivision 4 of section 211 of the Judiciary Law.

(5) "Job title" shall mean the title of the position to which an employee has been elected or appointed.

(6) "Rule" shall mean Part 40 of the Rules of the Chief Judge of the State of New York (22 NYCRR).

(7) "Spouse" shall mean husband or wife of the employee filing a financial disclosure statement unless the husband or wife has been living separate and

apart from such employee during the entire reporting year:

(i) pursuant to a judicial order, decree or judgment or a legally binding separation agreement; or

(ii) with the intention of terminating the marriage or remaining permanently separated.

(8) "Unemancipated child" shall mean any son, daughter, stepson or stepdaughter of the employee filing a financial disclosure statement who is under the age of eighteen [18] and unmarried.

(b) **Scope.** Pursuant to section 40.1(i)(7) of the Rule, the Commission shall permit an employee who is required to file a financial disclosure statement to request an exemption from the requirement to report one or more items of information which pertain to the employee's spouse or unemancipated children. This request will be granted by the Commission upon a finding by a majority of the total number of its members without vacancy that the employee's spouse, on his or her own behalf or on behalf of an unemancipated child, or the employee on behalf of an unemancipated child, objects to providing the information necessary to make such disclosure, and that the information that would otherwise be required to be reported will have no material bearing on the discharge of the employee's official duties.

(c) **Procedure.**

(1) An employee may request an exemption from any requirement to report one or more items of information that pertain to his or her spouse or unemancipated children by filing a written request with the Commission on or before April 1st of the year in which such exemption is requested.

(2) The request for the exemption shall include:

(i) the name, home address, work address, work telephone number, and job title of the employee requesting the exemption;

(ii) the specific information the spouse or employee objects to reporting on the employee's financial disclosure statement;

(iii) a statement that the employee or his or her spouse objects to reporting the information on the financial disclosure statement, giving specific reasons and justifications therefor;

(iv) a statement in support of the employee's claim that the information that would otherwise be required to be reported on the financial disclosure statement will have no material bearing on the discharge of the employee's official duties, giving specific reasons and justifications therefor;

(v) documentation supporting the aforesaid statements may be annexed to the request.

(3) The request for exemption must be signed by the employee requesting the exemption.

(d) **Commission Action.**

(1) Upon receipt of a request for an exemption from the requirement to report one or more items of information which pertain to an employee's spouse or unemancipated children, the Commission shall review the material filed to determine whether an objection has been made by the appropriate person to the reporting of the information, and whether the information for which an exemption is requested will have a material bearing on the discharge of the employee's official duties.

(2) If the Commission determines that additional information would be useful, it may request such information from the employee requesting the exemption. Such additional information must be filed with the Commission within twenty-one [21] business days of the date the request is mailed from the Commission offices. If the Commission has not received such information within the said twenty-one [21] days, it may render its decision on the information available. The Commission, in its discretion, may request a meeting with the employee, or his or her spouse, to discuss the exemption request.

(3) Unless the Commission decides by a majority of the total members of the Commission without vacancy that the employee or his or her spouse objects to providing the information necessary to make disclosure, and that the information that would otherwise be required to be reported will have no material bearing on the discharge of the employee's official duties, the Commission shall deny the request for exemption.

In applying the material bearing standard to decide exemption requests, the Commission weighs competing public and private interests including the following:

(i) Whether the information is of a personal or particularly intimate nature;

(ii) Whether the disclosure of the information could pose a safety threat to the employee or his or her family, and the nature of that threat, including its seriousness and imminence;

(iii) Whether the information may relate in a substantial and important way to the employee's official duties;

(iv) Whether the information could reveal or relate to an actual or potential conflict of interest;

(v) The employee's role in the judicial, administrative or managerial process of the Unified Court System;

(vi) Whether the standard is being applied in the case of a spousal/child exemption request or a deletion request. The employee's burden is far greater when seeking an exemption request. The granting of an exemption request means that the relevant information will not be reported at all on the financial disclosure statement, while the granting of a deletion request means that the information will be reported on the financial disclosure statement, but deleted from the copy made available to the public;

(vii) Such other factors as may be relevant.

If an employee requests a spousal exemption on the grounds that he or she has no knowledge of his or her spouse's assets or income, and that his or her spouse refuses to supply this information to him or her, the employee must so state specifically in the form of an affidavit. The employee must, at a minimum, convince the Commission that his or her spouse refuses to provide the information, that he or she has no other source regarding this information, and that he or she has made a bona fide attempt to obtain, and cannot obtain, the information. Other potentially relevant, but not necessarily controlling, matters include the circumstances of, and reasons for, a spouse's refusal to provide the employee with the relevant information, the duration and consistency over time of his or her spouse's refusal to disclose such information to the employee, and whether the employee and his or her spouse file or have filed joint federal, state or local tax returns. If the employee and his or her spouse have filed a joint tax return, the employee must at a minimum report such information as is available from that return.

Judiciary Law § 211(4) and 22 NYCRR Part 40 establish a strong public policy favoring disclosure. Thus employees otherwise required to file, who have requested exemptions, must demonstrate that an individual exception to this policy is warranted.

(4) The Commission shall give written notice of its decision to the employee requesting the exemption.

(e) **Statement of Separation.** If the husband or wife of the employee filing a financial disclosure statement is not a spouse as hereinbefore defined, the employee shall file with his or her financial disclosure statement a statement signed by the employee indicating that he or she has been living separate and apart from his or her husband or wife for the entire reporting year pursuant to a judicial order, decree, judgment or legally binding separation agreement, or with the intention of terminating the marriage or remaining permanently separated. This statement shall set forth the date of the separation and the current address of the employee's husband or wife.

§ 7400.4. Deletion of One or More Items of Information From the Copy of the Financial Disclosure Statement Made Available to the Public

(a) **Definitions.**

(1) "Commission" shall mean the Ethics Commission for the Unified Court System.

(2) "Employee" shall mean a state-paid judge, justice, officer or employee of the Unified Court System.

(3) "File" shall mean to make delivery to the offices of the Commission personally or by mail. The filing date shall be the date the document filed is received in the offices of the Commission.

(4) "Financial disclosure statement" shall mean the annual statement approved by the Chief Judge pursuant to subdivision 4 of section 211 of the Judiciary Law.

(5) "Job title" shall mean the title of the position to which an employee has been elected or appointed.

(6) "Rule" shall mean Part 40 of the Rules of the Chief Judge of the State of New York (22 NYCRR).

(b) Scope. Pursuant to section 40.1(i)(6) of the Rule, the Commission shall permit an employee who is required to file a financial disclosure statement to request that the Commission delete from the copy of the financial disclosure statement made available for public inspection one or more items of information. This request will be granted by the Commission upon a finding by a majority of the total number of its members without vacancy that the information that would otherwise be required to be made available for public inspection will have no material bearing on the discharge of the employee's official duties.

(c) Procedure.

(1) An employee may request deletion of one or more items of information from the copy of the financial disclosure statement made available to the public by filing a written request with the Commission on or before May 15th of the year in which the deletion is requested.

(2) The request for the deletion shall include:

(i) the name, home address, work address, work telephone number, and job title of the employee requesting the deletion;

(ii) the information which the employee seeks to have deleted;

(iii) a statement in support of the employee's claim that the information that would otherwise be made available for public inspection will have no material bearing on the discharge of the employee's official duties, giving specific reasons and justifications therefor. Documentation supporting this statement may be annexed to the request.

(3) The request for deletion must be signed by the employee requesting the deletion, and must be filed with a complete financial disclosure statement containing the information sought to be deleted.

(d) Commission Action.

(1) Upon receipt of a request for deletion of one or more items of information from the copy of the financial disclosure statement made available to the public, the Commission shall review the material filed to determine if the information will have a material

bearing on the discharge of the employee's official duties.

(2) If the Commission determines that additional information would be useful, it may request such information from the employee requesting the deletion. The Commission, in its discretion, may request a meeting with the employee to discuss the deletion request.

(3) Unless the Commission decides by a majority of the total members of the Commission without vacancy that the information that would otherwise be required to be made available for public inspection will have no material bearing on the discharge of the employee's official duties, the Commission shall deny the request for deletion.

In applying the material bearing standard to decide deletion requests, the Commission weighs competing public and private interests including the following:

(i) Whether the information is of a personal or particularly intimate nature;

(ii) Whether the disclosure of the information could pose a safety threat to the employee or his or her family, and the nature of that threat, including its seriousness and imminence;

(iii) Whether the information may relate in a substantial and important way to the employee's official duties;

(iv) Whether the information could reveal or relate to an actual or potential conflict of interest;

(v) The employee's role in the judicial, administrative or managerial process of the Unified Court System;

(vi) Whether the standard is being applied in the case of a spousal/child exemption request or a deletion request. The employee's burden is far greater when seeking an exemption request. The granting of an exemption request means that the relevant information will not be reported at all on the financial disclosure statement, while the granting of a deletion request means that the information will be reported on the financial disclosure statement, but deleted from the copy made available to the public;

(vii) Such other factors as may be relevant.

Judiciary Law § 211(4) and 22 NYCRR Part 40 establish a strong public policy favoring disclosure. Thus employees otherwise required to file, who have requested deletions, must demonstrate that an individual exception to this policy is warranted.

(4) The Commission shall give written notice of its decision to the employee requesting the deletion.

§ 7400.5. Public Inspection of Financial Disclosure Statements

(a) Definitions.

(1) "Commission" shall mean the Ethics Commission for the Unified Court System.

(2) "Employee" shall mean a state-paid judge, justice, officer or employee of the Unified Court System.

(3) "File" shall mean to make delivery to the offices of the Commission personally or by mail. The filing date shall be the date the document filed is received in the offices of the Commission.

(4) "Financial disclosure statement" shall mean the annual statement approved by the Chief Judge pursuant to subdivision 4 of section 211 of the Judiciary Law.

(5) "Rule" shall mean Part 40 of the Rules of the Chief Judge of the State of New York (22 NYCRR).

(b) Scope. Pursuant to section 40.1(p) of the Rule, the Commission shall make available for public inspection the information set forth in annual statements of financial disclosure required to be filed for the seven reporting years prior to and including the current year, except that categories of value or amount and the names of unemancipated children, and any other item of information deleted from public inspection by the Commission pursuant to section 40.1(i)(6) of the Rule, shall remain confidential and not available for public inspection. The Commission shall also make Notices of Delinquency available for public inspection.

(c) Statement Inspection Officer.

(1) The Executive Director of the Commission is designated as the Statement Inspection Officer.

(2) The Statement Inspection Officer shall:

(i) maintain a current list of financial disclosure statements available for public inspection;

(ii) respond to all inquiries regarding public inspection of financial disclosure statements;

(iii) receive and process requests for public inspection of financial disclosure statements;

(iv) insure that information deleted from public inspection pursuant to law and regulation is not made available for public inspection;

(v) maintain a schedule of copying fees;

(vi) designate one or more members of the staff of the Commission to serve as Assistant Statement Inspection Officer; such Assistant(s) shall have the same function and responsibilities as the Statement Inspection Officer except as to the designation of other Assistants.

(d) Public Inspection of Statements.

(1) Financial disclosure statements shall be available for public inspection, by appointment, at the Commission office at 25 Beaver Street, New York, New York, every day the office is open for business, during the hours 10:00 A.M. through 12:00 P.M. and 2:00 P.M. through 4:00 P.M. Statements may be made available for public inspection at other times at the discretion of the Statement Inspection Officer.

(2) A person may obtain a copy of a financial disclosure statement in person, or by mail, upon the payment of copying fees. The copying fee is $7.00 for each statement copy obtained in person from the Commission office and $7.50 for each statement copy mailed from the office. The copying fee will be waived for all federal, state or local government agencies and departments.

(3) The financial disclosure statement of an employee who has filed an exemption or deletion request, or whose statement has been returned for revision, shall not be available for public inspection pending a decision on the request, or the receipt of the revised statement. The fact that an exemption or deletion request has been made will be kept confidential; the record and substance of the request will also be confidential and not available for public inspection.

(4) If the Commission has denied an exemption or deletion request, the financial disclosure statement of the employee who made the request shall not be available for public inspection for twenty-one (21) days from the date on which notice of the denial is mailed to the employee by the Commission.

(5) No documents pertaining to a request for public inspection shall be available for public inspection. The identities of public inspectors, and the fact that a statement has been inspected, are confidential and will not be made available to the public or to filers.

§ 7400.6. Investigation by Commission

(a) Definitions.

(1) "Commission" shall mean the Ethics Commission for the Unified Court System.

(2) "Executive Director" shall mean the executive director of the Ethics Commission for the Unified Court System as appointed pursuant to section 40.1(i)(1) of the Chief Judge's Rule.

(3) "Employee" shall mean a state-paid judge, justice, officer or employee of the Unified Court System.

(4) "File" shall mean to make delivery to the office of the Commission personally or by mail. The filing date shall be the date the document filed is received in the office of the Commission.

(5) "Financial disclosure statement" shall mean the annual statement approved by the Chief Judge pursuant to subdivision 4 of Section 211 of the Judiciary Law.

(6) "Rule" shall mean Part 40 of the Rules of the Chief Judge of the State of New York (22 NYCRR).

(b) Scope. Pursuant to section 40.1(o)(2) of the Rule, the Commission is authorized to conduct any investigation necessary to carry out its responsibilities under the provisions of section 40.1. In the course of an investigation, the Commission is authorized to administer oaths or affirmations, subpoena witnesses, compel their attendance and require the production of any books or records or other materials which it may deem relevant or material.

(c) Procedure.

(1) The subjects of a Commission investigation may include but are not limited to the timeliness or accuracy of an employee's filing of a financial disclosure statement, an employee's request for an extension of time to file, an employee's request for an exemption from the requirement to file, an employee's request for an exemption from reporting information pertaining to his or her spouse or child, or an employee's request for deletion of certain information from the copy of his or her statement made available to the public, or such other matters as may arise in connection with the discharge of the Commission's duties.

(2) The Commission may contact the employee who did file, or should have filed, the financial disclosure statement that is the subject of the investigation, another employee, or any other person, to obtain information relevant to the investigation. This contact may be by telephone or by letter.

(3) If the employee or other person fails or refuses to respond to the telephone call or letter, or if the Commission has reasonable cause to believe that it is necessary or appropriate, the Commission may require the appearance of the employee or other person before the Commission, or, if so authorized by the Commission, one or more of its members, in which event the employee or other person shall be notified in writing of his or her required appearance either personally, at least ten days prior to such appearance, or by certified mail, to be deposited in the U.S. mail at least ten days prior to such appearance. Such written notice shall set forth the time and place of the appearance, the nature of the information the Commission is seeking, and the books, records or other materials that the employee or other person must present to the Commission.

(4) If the employee or other person fails to appear or secure an adjournment in response to such written notice, or fails to produce the sought after books, records or other materials, the Commission may compel his or her appearance and/or the production of the required books, records or other materials with a subpoena and/or subpoena duces tecum issued pursuant to CPLR § 2303.

(5) The employee or other person may request, in writing, an adjournment of his or her appearance. An adjournment will be granted for good cause only. If the request is granted, the Commission will notify the employee or other person in writing of the new date.

(d) Appearance Before the Commission.

(1) An employee or other person appearing before the Commission shall answer questions and produce the books, records or other materials sought by the Commission. He or she shall have the right to be represented by an attorney and make an oral statement and to present relevant data and material, including a written statement. The attorney shall be permitted to advise the employee or other person and otherwise confer with her or him.

(2) At the commencement of the appearance, the Chair of the Commission, or his or her designee, may swear in the employee or other person by administering an oath or affirmation.

(3) The appearance may be recorded in any way permitted by the CPLR. If the appearance is recorded, a transcript shall be provided to the employee or other person without fee upon his or her written request.

(e) Commission Action. If the Commission finds that further action is necessary or appropriate, it may give written notification to the Chief Administrator of the Courts, the Commission on Judicial Conduct, or any other appropriate agency or authority of the results of its investigation and request that further action be taken. The Commission shall give written notification to the employee who was the subject of the investigation that it has determined that further action is necessary and that the matter has been referred to the Chief Administrator of the Courts, the Commission on Judicial Conduct, or other appropriate agency or authority.

§ 7400.7. Filing Requirements for Certain Judicial Candidates

(a) Definitions

(1) "Candidate" shall mean a candidate for public election to judicial office, who is required to file an annual statement of financial disclosure pursuant to 22 NYCRR Part 100. "Candidate" shall not mean a candidate for judicial office in the town and village courts.

(2) "Commission" shall mean the Ethics Commission for the Unified Court System.

(3) "File" shall mean to make delivery to the offices of the Commission personally or by mail. The filing date shall be the date the document filed is received in the offices of the Commission.

(4) "Financial disclosure statement" shall mean the annual statement of financial disclosure approved by the Chief Judge pursuant to subdivision 4 of section 211 of the Judiciary Law.

(b) Scope

(1) Pursuant to 22 NYCRR Section 100.5(A)(4)(g), a judge or a non-judge who is a candidate for public election to judicial office shall file a financial disclosure statement with the Commission within twenty days following the date on which he or she becomes a candidate. However, a judge or non-judge who is an officer or employee of the Unified Court System re-

quired to file an annual statement of financial disclosure pursuant to 22 NYCRR Part 40 is not required to file pursuant to 22 NYCRR Part 100.

(2) The Commission shall permit a candidate to request an additional period of time within which to file. This request will be granted if the Commission finds that there is justifiable cause for the extension or that the timely filing of the statement would cause undue hardship.

(3) The Commission shall permit a candidate to request that the Commission delete one or more items of information from the copy of his or her financial disclosure statement made available for public inspection. This request will be granted by the Commission upon a finding by a majority of the total number of its members without vacancy that the information that would otherwise be required to be made available for public inspection will have no material bearing on the discharge of the candidate's official duties should he or she be elected.

(4) The Commission shall make available for public inspection the information set forth in financial disclosure statements required to be filed for the seven reporting years prior to and including the current year, except that categories of value or amount and the names of unemancipated children, and any other item of information deleted from public inspection by the Commission pursuant to 22 NYCRR Section 40.1(1)(6) shall remain confidential and not available for public inspection.

(c) **Procedure Regarding Filing Extension**

(1) A candidate may request an extension of time to file a financial disclosure statement more than twenty days after he or she becomes a candidate by filing a written request with the Commission on or before the 20th day after he or she becomes a candidate.

(2) The request for the extension shall include:

(i) the name, home address, work address, work telephone number, and job title of the candidate requesting the extension;

(ii) a statement in support of the candidate's claim that an extension of time to file a financial disclosure statement is necessary due to justifiable cause or undue hardship, giving specific reasons and justifications therefor. Documentation supporting this statement may be annexed to the request;

(iii) the date certain by which the candidate will file his or her financial disclosure statement.

(3) The request for an extension must by signed by the candidate requesting the extension.

(d) **Commission Action Regarding Extension Requests**

(1) Upon receipt of a request for extension of time to file a financial disclosure statement, the Commission shall review the material filed to determine if there has been a showing of justifiable cause or undue hardship.

(2) If the Commission determines that additional information would be useful, it may request such information from the candidate requesting the extension. The Commission, in its discretion, may request a meeting with the candidate to discuss the extension request.

(3) Unless the Commission decides that there is justifiable cause for an extension of time to file a financial disclosure statement, or that timely filing of such statement would cause undue hardship, the Commission shall deny the request for an extension of time to file a financial disclosure statement.

(4) The Commission shall give written notice of its decision to the candidate requesting an extension of time to file. If the extension is granted, the decision shall include the date certain on or before which the candidate's financial disclosure statement must be filed. In the event the Commission determines that such written notice of its decision would not reach the candidate requesting the extension before the 20th day after he or she becomes a candidate, the Commission shall notify the candidate of its decision by telephone, to be followed by written notice of decision.

(5) Vacation periods, and the ordinary and necessary tasks, routines, and obligations of a candidate's personal and work life shall not constitute undue hardship or justifiable cause for an extension of time to file a financial disclosure statement.

(6) No extension of time to file a financial disclosure statement shall be granted to a candidate beyond thirty-five days after he or she becomes a candidate.

(e) **Procedure Regarding Deletion Requests**

(1) A candidate may request deletion of one or more items of information from the copy of the financial disclosure statement made available to the public by filing a written request with the Commission together with his or her financial disclosure statement.

(2) The request for the deletion shall include:

(i) the name, home address, work address, and work telephone number of the candidate requesting the deletion;

(ii) the information which the candidate seeks to have deleted;

(iii) a statement in support of the candidate's claim that the information that would otherwise be made available for public inspection will have no material bearing on the discharge of the candidate's official duties, if he or she is elected, giving specific reasons and justifications therefor. Documentation supporting this statement may be annexed to the request.

(3) The request for deletion must be signed by the candidate requesting the deletion, and must be filed

with a complete financial disclosure statement containing the information sought to be deleted.

(f) Commission Action Regarding Deletion Requests

(1) Upon receipt of a request for deletion of one or more items of information from the copy of the financial disclosure statement made available to the public, the Commission shall review the material filed to determine if the information will have a material bearing on the discharge of the candidate's official duties, if he or she is elected.

(2) If the Commission determines that additional information would be useful, it may request such information from the candidate requesting the deletion. The Commission, in its discretion, may request a meeting with the candidate to discuss the deletion request.

(3) Unless the Commission decides by a majority of the total members of the Commission without vacancy that the information that would otherwise be required to be made available for public inspection will have no material bearing on the discharge of the candidate's official duties, if he or she is elected, the Commission shall deny the request for deletion.

In applying the material bearing standard to decide deletion requests, the Commission weighs competing public and private interests including the following:

(i) Whether the information is of a personal of particularly intimate nature;

(ii) Whether the disclosure of the information could pose a safety threat to the candidate or his or her family, and the nature of that threat, including its seriousness and imminence;

(iii) Whether the information may relate in a substantial and important way to the candidate's official duties, if he or she is elected;

(iv) Whether the information could reveal or relate to an actual or potential conflict of interest;

(v) Such other factors as may be relevant.

Judiciary Law § 211(4) and 22 NYCRR Part 40 establish a strong public policy favoring disclosure.

Thus candidate otherwise required to file, who have requested deletions, must demonstrate that an individual exception to this policy is warranted.

(4) The Commission shall give written notice of its decision to the candidate requesting the deletion, by overnight mail. The Commission shall also advise the candidate of its decision by telephone.

(g) Public Inspection of Statements

(1) Financial disclosure statements shall be available for public inspection, by appointment, at the Commission office at 25 Beaver Street, New York, New York, every day the office is open for business during the hours 10:00 A.M. through 12:00 P.M. and 2:00 P.M. through 4:00 P.M. Statements may be made available for public inspection at other times at the discretion of the Statement Inspection Officer.

(2) A person may obtain a copy of a financial disclosure statement in person, or by mail, upon the payment of copying fees. The copying fee is $7.00 for each statement copy obtained in person from the Commission office and $7.50 for each statement copy mailed from the office. The copying fee will be waived for all federal, state or local government agencies and departments.

(3) The financial disclosure statement of a candidate who has filed a deletion request shall not be available for public inspection pending a decision on the request. The fact that a deletion request has been made will be kept confidential; the record and substance of the request will also be confidential and not available for public inspection.

(4) If the Commission has denied a deletion request, the financial disclosure statement of the candidate who made the request shall not be available for public inspection for three days from the date on which notice of the denial is mailed to the candidate by the Commission.

(5) No documents pertaining to a request for public inspection shall be available for public inspection. The identities of public inspectors, and the fact that a statement has been inspected, are confidential and will not be made available to the public or to filers.

COURT DIRECTORY

GENERAL INFORMATION
1–800–COURTNY or 1–800–268–7869
www.courts.state.ny.us
www.nycourts.gov
TDD: (212) 428–2511

STATE-WIDE ADMINISTRATIVE OFFICES AND ASSOCIATIONS

Office of Court Administration
4 Empire State Plaza, Suite 2001
Albany, NY 12223–1450
Tel. (518) 474–7469
Fax. (518) 473–5514
      or
25 Beaver Street
New York, NY 10004
Tel. (212) 428–2700

New York State CLE Board
25 Beaver Street, Room 888
New York, NY 10004
Tel. (212) 428–2105
Tel. 1–877–NYS–4CLE
www.nycourts.gov/attorneys/cle

Community Dispute Resolution Centers Program
New York State Unified Court System
98 Niver Street
Cohoes, NY 12047–4712
Tel. (518) 238–2888
Fax. (518) 238–2951
www.nycourts.gov/ip/adr/cdrc.shtml

Commission on Judicial Conduct
61 Broadway
New York, NY 10006
Tel. (212) 809–0566
Fax. (212) 809–3664
      or
38–40 State Street
Albany, NY 12207
Tel. (518) 474–5617
Fax. (518) 486–1850
      or
400 Andrews Street
Rochester, NY 14604
Tel. (585) 232–5756
Fax. (585) 232–7834
www.scjc.state.ny.us/

New York State Board of Law Examiners
Corporate Plaza – Building 3
254 Washington Avenue Extension
Albany, NY 12203–5195
Tel. (518) 452–8700 or (800) 342–3335
Fax. (518) 452–5729
www.nybarexam.org

OCA – Attorney Registration Unit
P.O. Box 2806
Church Street Station
New York, NY 10008
Tel. (212) 428–2800
Fax. (212) 428–2804
Email: attyreg@courts.state.ny.us
www.nycourts.gov/attorneys/registration/

Lawyers' Fund for Client Protection
119 Washington Avenue
Albany, NY 12210
Tel. (518) 434–1935 or (800) 442–FUND
Email: info@nylawfund.org
www.nylawfund.org

New York State Bar Association
1 Elk Street
Albany, NY 12207–1096
Tel. (518) 463–3200
Fax. (518) 487-5517
www.nysba.org

Department of State
One Commerce Plaza
99 Washington Avenue
Albany, NY 12231–0001
Tel. (518) 474–4752
Fax. (518) 474–4597
Email: info@dos.state.ny.us
www.dos.state.ny.us
      or
123 William Street
New York, NY 10038–3804
Tel. (212) 417–5800
Fax. (212) 417–2383

COURT DIRECTORY

New York State Department of State
Division of Corporations, State Records, and Uniform
  Commercial Code
One Commerce Plaza
99 Washington Avenue
Suite 600
Albany, NY 12231–0001
Email: corporations@dos.state.ny.us
Corporations—General Information:
Tel. (518) 473–2492
Fax. (518) 474–1418
State Records:
Tel. (518) 474–4770
Uniform Commercial Code:
Tel. (518) 474–4763
Fax. (518) 474–4478

Department of Family Assistance

www.dfa.state.ny.us

Office of Children and Family Services
General information Tel. (518) 473–7793
Abandoned Infant Protection Act Tel. (866) 505-SAFE
  (7233)
Adoption and other children's programs Tel. (800) 345–
  KIDS (5437)
Adult Protective Services Tel. (800) 342-3009 (dial 6)
Child abuse hotline Tel. (800) 342–3720
Child care complaint line Tel. (800) 732–5207
Domestic Violence Hotline (English) Tel. (800) 942–
  6906
Domestic Violence Hotline (Spanish) Tel. (800) 942–
  6908
www.ocfs.state.ny.us/main/

Office of Temporary and Disability Assistance
40 North Pearl Street
Albany, NY 12243
Tel. (518) 474–9516

COURT OF APPEALS
Court of Appeals Hall
20 Eagle Street
Albany, NY 12207–1095
Tel. (518) 455–7700
www.courts.state.ny.us/ctapps/

APPELLATE DIVISIONS
First Department
27 Madison Avenue
New York, NY 10010
Tel. (212) 340–0400
www.courts.state.ny.us/courts/ad1

Second Department
45 Monroe Place
Brooklyn, NY 11201
Tel. (718) 875–1300
www.courts.state.ny.us/courts/ad2

Third Department
Empire State Plaza
Justice Building, Room 511
Albany, NY 12223
Mailing Address:
P.O. Box 7288, Capitol Station
Albany, NY 12224–0288
Tel. (518) 471–4777
Fax. (518) 471–4750
www.nycourts.gov/ad3

Fourth Department
M. Dolores Denman Courthouse
50 East Avenue
Rochester, NY 14604
Tel. (585) 530–3100
www.nycourts.gov/ad4

COURT OF CLAIMS

www.nyscourtofclaims.state.ny.us

Clerk of the Court of Claims
P.O. Box 7344
Capitol Station
Albany, NY 12224
Tel. (518) 432–3411
Fax. (866) 413–1069
Email: rdecatal@courts.state.ny.us

26 Broadway
New York, NY 10004
Tel. (212) 361-8100

State Office Building
44 Hawley Street
Binghamton, NY 13901–4418
Tel. (607) 721–8623
Fax. (607) 721–8621

State Office Building
130 South Elmwood Avenue
Suite 300
Buffalo, NY 14202
Tel. (716) 515–4810

State Office Building, 3rd Floor
Veterans Memorial Highway
Hauppauge, NY 11787
Tel. (631) 952–6542
Fax. (631) 952–6727

Supreme Court Building
100 Supreme Court Drive
Mineola, NY 11501
Tel. (516) 571–2873

500 Court Exchange Building
144 Exchange Boulevard
Rochester, NY 14614–2108
Tel. (585) 325–4500
Fax. (585) 262–5715

65 South Broadway
Saratoga Springs, NY 12866
Tel. (518) 583–5330

205 South Salina Street
Syracuse, NY 13202
Tel. (315) 466–7151
Fax. (315) 466–7154

State Office Building
207 E. Genessee Street
Utica, NY 13501
Tel. (315) 793–2601
Fax. (315) 793–2606

140 Grand Street
White Plains, NY 10601
Tel. (914) 289–2310
Fax. (914) 289–2313

ALBANY COUNTY
[3rd Judicial District, 3rd Judicial Department]
www.nycourts.gov/courts/3jd

Supreme Court
Albany County Courthouse
16 Eagle Street, Room 102
Albany, NY 12207
Tel. (518) 285–8989
Fax. (518) 487–5020

County Court
Albany County Courthouse
6 Lodge Street
Albany, NY 12207
Tel. (518) 285–8989
Fax. (518) 487–5020

Family Court
30 Clinton Avenue
Albany, NY 12207
Tel. (518) 285–8600
Fax. (518) 462–4248

Surrogate's Court
Albany County Family Court Building
30 Clinton Avenue
Albany, NY 12207
Tel. (518) 487–5393
Fax. (518) 487–5087

Albany City Court–Civil Part
Albany City Hall, Room 209
24 Eagle Street
Albany, NY 12207
(518) 434–5115
Fax. (518) 434–5034

Albany City Court–Traffic Part
Albany City Hall, Basement
24 Eagle Street
Albany, NY 12207
(518) 434–5095
Fax. (518) 434–5084

Albany City Court–Criminal Part
Public Safety Building
1 Morton Avenue
Albany, NY 12202
Tel. (518) 462–6714
Fax. (518) 462–8778

Cohoes City Court
City Hall, Room 219
97 Mohawk Street
P.O. Box 678
Cohoes, NY 12047
Tel. (518) 233–2133
Fax. (518) 233–8202

Watervliet City Court
City Hall
2 Fifteenth Street
Watervliet, NY 12189
Tel. (518) 270–3803
Fax. (518) 270–3812

Frances Bergan Law Library
Albany County Courthouse, Room 316
16 Eagle Street
Albany, NY 12207
Tel. (518) 270–3717

COURT DIRECTORY

Sheriff
Albany County Court House
16 Eagle Street
Albany, NY 12207
Tel. (518) 487–5440
Fax. (518) 487–5037

ALLEGANY COUNTY

[8th Judicial District, 4th Judicial Department]

Supreme Court
Allegany County Courthouse
7 Court Street
Belmont, NY 14813–1084
Tel. (585) 268–5800
Fax. (585) 268–7090

County Court
Allegany County Courthouse
7 Court Street
Belmont, NY 14813–1084
Tel. (585) 268–5800
Fax. (585) 268–7090

Family Court
Allegany County Courthouse
7 Court Street
Belmont, NY 14813–1084
Tel. (585) 268–5816
Fax. (585) 268–7090

Surrogate's Court
Allegany County Courthouse
7 Court Street
Belmont, NY 14813–1084
Tel. (585) 268–5815
Fax. (585) 268–7090

Allegany County Law Library
Allegany County Courthouse
7 Court Street
Belmont, NY 14813–1084
Tel. (716) 268–5813

Sheriff
4884 State Route 19
Belmont, NY 14813
Tel. (585) 268–9200
Fax. (585) 268-9475
Email: Tompkiw@alleganyco.com

BRONX COUNTY

[12th Judicial District, 1st Judicial Department]

Supreme Court
851 Grand Concourse
Bronx, NY 10451
Tel. (718) 618–1400

Family Court
900 Sheridan Avenue
Bronx, NY 10451
Tel. (212) 374–3700
Fax. (718) 590–2681
www.courts.state.ny.us/famhome.htm

Surrogate's Court
851 Grand Concourse
Bronx, NY 10451
Tel. (718) 590–3618

Civil Court of the City of New York
Bronx County Branch
851 Grand Concourse
Bronx, NY 10451–2988
Tel. (646) 386–5700

Criminal Court of the City of New York
Bronx County Branch
215 East 161st Street
Bronx, NY 10451
Tel. (718) 590–2858
Fax. (718) 590–2857

Bronx County Housing Court
1118 Grand Concourse
Bronx, NY 10456
Tel. (718) 466–3005
Fax. (718) 466–3006

Bronx County Law Library
851 Grand Concourse, Room 817
Bronx, NY 10451
Tel. (718) 590–3678

Sheriff
332 E. 149th Street
Bronx, NY 10451–5606
Tel. (718) 585–1230

BROOME COUNTY

[6th Judicial District, 3rd Judicial Department]

COURT DIRECTORY

Supreme Court
Broome County Courthouse
92 Court St., P.O. Box 1766
Binghamton, NY 13902–1766
Tel. (607) 778–2448
Fax. (607) 778–6426

County Court
Family and County Court Building
65 Hawley St., P.O. Box 1766
Binghamton, NY 13902–1766
Tel. (607) 778–2448
Fax. (607) 778–6426

Family Court
Family and County Court Building
65 Hawley Street
Binghamton, NY 13902–1766
Tel. (607) 778–2156
Fax. (607) 778–2439

Surrogate's Court
Broome County Courthouse
92 Court St.
Binghamton, NY 13902
Tel. (607) 778–2111
Fax. (607) 778–2308

Binghamton City Court
City Hall, Governmental Plaza
38 Hawley Street, 5th Floor
Binghamton, NY 13901
Tel. (607) 772–7006
Fax. (607) 772–7041

Binghamton County Law Library
Broome County Courthouse
92 Court Street, Room 107
Binghamton, NY 13901
Tel. (607) 778–2119
Fax. (607) 772–8331

Sheriff
155 Lt. Van Winkle Drive
Binghamton, NY 13905
Tel. (607) 778–1911
Fax. (607) 778-2100
Email: bcsheriff@co.broome.ny.us

CATTARAUGUS COUNTY

[8th Judicial District, 4th Judicial Department]

Supreme Court
303 Court Street
Little Valley, NY 14755
Tel. (716) 938–9111
Fax. (716) 938–9328
   or
Supreme Court
One Leo Moss Drive
Olean, NY 14760
Tel. (716) 373–8035
Fax. (716) 373–0449

County Court
303 Court Street
Little Valley, NY 14755
Tel. (716) 938–9111
Fax. (716) 938–6413

Family Court
One Leo Moss Drive
Suite 1140
Olean, NY 14760–1152
Tel. (716) 373–8035
Fax. (716) 373–0449

Surrogate's Court
303 Court Street
Little Valley, NY 14755
Tel. (716) 938–9111
Fax. (716) 938–6983
   or
Surrogate's Court
One Leo Moss Drive
Olean, NY 14760
Tel. (716) 373–8043
Fax. (716) 373–0449

Olean City Court
Municipal Building
101 East State Street
P.O. Box 631
Olean, NY 14760–0631
Tel. (716) 376–5620
Fax. (716) 376–5623

Salamanca City Court
225 Wildwood Avenue
Salamanca, NY 14779
Tel. (716) 945–4153
Fax. (716) 945–2362

Cattaraugus County Law Library
303 Court Street
Little Valley, NY 14755–1028
Tel. (716) 938–9111 ext. 326

COURT DIRECTORY

Sheriff
301 Court Street
Little Valley, NY 14755–1090
Tel. (716) 938–9191 or (800) 443–3403
Fax. (716) 938–6552
Email: dbjohn@cattco.org
www.sheriff.cattco.org

CAYUGA COUNTY
[7th Judicial District, 4th Judicial Department]

Supreme Court
Cayuga County Courthouse
152 Genesee Street
Auburn, NY 13021
Tel. (315) 255–4320
Fax. (315) 255–4322

County Court
Cayuga County Courthouse
152 Genesee Street
Auburn, NY 13021
Tel. (315) 255–4320
Fax. (315) 255–4322

Family Court
Cayuga County Courthouse
157 Genesee Street
Auburn, NY 13021–3476
Tel. (315) 255–4306
Fax. (315) 255–4312

Surrogate's Court
Cayuga County Courthouse
152 Genesee Street
Auburn, NY 13021
Tel. (315) 255–4316
Fax. (315) 255–4324

Auburn City Court
157 Genesee Street
Auburn, NY 13021
Tel. (315) 253–1570
Fax. (315) 253–1085

New York Cayuga County Law Library
Court House Building
154 Genesee Street
Auburn, NY 13021
Tel. (315) 255–4310
Fax. (315) 255–4322

Sheriff
7445 County House Road
P.O. Box 518
Auburn, NY 13021
Tel. (315) 253–1222
Fax. (315) 253–4575
Email: sheriff@cayugacounty.us

CHAUTAUQUA COUNTY
[8th Judicial District, 4th Judicial Department]

Supreme Court
Chautauqua County Courthouse
1 North Erie Street
P.O. Box 292
Mayville, NY 14757–0292
Tel. (716) 753–4266
Fax. (716) 753–4993

County Court
Chautauqua County Courthouse
1 North Erie Street
P.O. Box 292
Mayville, NY 14757–0292
Tel. (716) 753–4000

Family Court
Gerace Office Building
3 North Erie Street
P.O. Box 149
Mayville, NY 14757–0149
Tel. (716) 753–4351
Fax. (716) 753–4350

Surrogate's Court
Gerace Office Building
3 North Erie Street
P.O. Box C
Mayville, NY 14757
Tel. (716) 753–4337
Fax. (716) 753–4600

Dunkirk City Court
City Hall
342 Central Avenue
Dunkirk, NY 14048–2122
Tel. (716) 366–2055
Fax. (716) 366–3622

Jamestown City Court
Municipal Building
200 East Third Street
Jamestown, NY 14701–5494
Tel. (716) 483–7561
Fax. (716) 483–7519

Chautauqua County Law Library
Chautauqua County Courthouse
1 North Erie Street
Mayville, NY 14757–0292
Tel. (716) 753–7111

Sheriff
15 East Chautauqua Street
P.O. Box 128
Mayville, NY 14757–0128
Tel. (716) 753–4900
Fax. (716) 753–4969
Email: jg@sheriff.us
www.sheriff.us/

CHEMUNG COUNTY
[6th Judicial District, 3rd Judicial Department]

Supreme Court
Hazlett Building
203–205 Lake Street
P.O. Box 588
Elmira, NY 14902–0588
Tel. (607) 737–3560
Fax. (607) 737–3562

County Court
Chemung County Courthouse
224 Lake Street
P.O. Box 588
Elmira, NY 14902–0588
Tel. (607) 737–2940
Fax. (607) 732–3343

Family Court
Justice Building
203–209 William Street
P.O. Box 588
Elmira, NY 14902–0588
Tel. (607) 737–2902 or 737–2903
Fax. (607) 737–2898

Surrogate's Court
224 Lake Street
P.O. Box 588
Elmira, NY 14902–0588
Tel. (607) 737–2946 or (607) 737–2819
Fax. (607) 737–2874

Elmira City Court
317 East Church Street, Suite 3
Elmira, NY 14901
Tel. (607) 737–5681
Fax. (607) 737–5820

Chemung County Law Library
Hazlett Building
203–205 Lake Street
P.O. Box 588
Elmira, NY 14901
Tel. (607) 737–2983
Fax. (607) 733–9863

Sheriff
203 William Street
P.O. Box 588
Elmira, NY 14902–0588
Tel. (607) 737–2987
Fax. (607) 737–2931
Email: cmoss@co.chemung.ny.us

CHENANGO COUNTY
[6th Judicial District, 3rd Judicial Department]

Supreme Court
County Office Building
5 Court Street
Norwich, NY 13815
Tel. (607) 337–1457
Fax. (607) 337–1835

County Court
County Office Building
5 Court Street
Norwich, NY 13815–1676
Tel. (607) 337–1457
Fax. (607) 337–1835

Family Court
County Office Building
5 Court Street
Norwich, NY 13815
Tel. (607) 337–1824
Fax. (607) 337–1835

Surrogate's Court
County Office Building
5 Court Street
Norwich, NY 13815
Tel. (607) 337–1827
Fax. (607) 337–1834

Norwich City Court
One Court Plaza
Norwich, NY 13815
Tel. (607) 334–1224
Fax. (607) 334–8494

COURT DIRECTORY

Chenango County Law Library
David L. Follett Library
5–9 West Main Street, 2nd Floor
Norwich, NY 13815
Tel. (607) 334–9463
Fax. (607) 334–9236

Sheriff
279 County Route 46
Norwich, NY 13815–1698
Tel. (607) 337–1857
Fax. (607) 336–1568
www.chenangosheriff.us

CLINTON COUNTY
[4th Judicial District, 3rd Judicial Department]

Supreme Court
137 Margaret Street, Third Floor
Plattsburgh, NY 12901–2990
Tel. (518) 565–4715
Fax. (518) 565–4708

County Court
137 Margaret Street, Third Floor
Plattsburgh, NY 12901–2990
Tel. (518) 565–4715
Fax. (518) 565–4708

Family Court
137 Margaret Street , Third Floor
Suite 311
Plattsburgh, NY 12901–2964
Tel. (518) 565–4658
Fax. (518) 565–4688

Surrogate's Court
137 Margaret Street , Third Floor
Plattsburgh, NY 12901
Tel. (518) 565–4630
Fax. (518) 565–4769

Plattsburgh City Court
24 U.S. Oval
Plattsburgh, NY 12903
Tel. (518) 563–7870
Fax. (518) 563–3124

Clinton County Law Library
72 Clinton Street
Plattsburgh, NY 12901
Tel. (518) 565–4808
Fax. (518) 562–1193

Sheriff
25 McCarthy Drive
Plattsburgh, NY 12901–6203
Tel. (518) 565–4330
Fax. (518) 565–4333

COLUMBIA COUNTY
[3rd Judicial District, 3rd Judicial Department]

Supreme Court
Columbia County Courthouse
401 Union Street
Hudson, NY 12534
Tel. (518) 828–7858
Fax. (518) 828–1603

County Court
Columbia County Courthouse
401 Union Street
Hudson, NY 12534
Tel. (518) 828–7858
Fax. (518) 828–1603

Family Court
Columbia County Courthouse
401 Union Street
Hudson, NY 12534
Tel. (518) 828–0315
Fax. (518) 828–1603

Surrogate's Court
Columbia County Courthouse
401 Union Street
Hudson, NY 12534
Tel. (518) 828–0414
Fax. (518) 828–1603

Hudson City Court
425 Warren Street
Hudson, NY 12534
Tel. (518) 828–5763
Fax. (518) 828–7692

Columbia County Law Library
Supreme Court Courthouse
401 Union Street
Hudson, NY 12534
Tel. (518) 828–3206
Fax. (518) 828–2101

Sheriff
85 Industrial Tract
Hudson, NY 12534
Tel. (518) 828–0601
Fax. (518) 828–9088

COURT DIRECTORY

CORTLAND COUNTY

[6th Judicial District, 3rd Judicial Department]

Supreme Court
Cortland County Courthouse
46 Greenbush Street, Suite 301
Cortland, NY 13045
Tel. (607) 753–5013
Fax. (607) 756–3409

County Court
Cortland County Courthouse
46 Greenbush Street, Suite 301
Cortland, NY 13045
Tel. (607) 753–5013
Fax. (607) 756–3409

Family Court
Cortland County Courthouse
46 Greenbush Street, Suite 301
Cortland, NY 13045
Tel. (607) 753–5353
Fax. (607) 756–3409

Surrogate's Court
Cortland County Courthouse
46 Greenbush Street, Suite 301
Cortland, NY 13045
Tel. (607) 753–5355
Fax. (607) 756–3409

Cortland City Court
25 Court Street
Cortland, NY 13045
Tel. (607) 753–1811
Fax. (607) 753–9932

Cortland County Law Library
Cortland County Courthouse
46 Greenbush Street
Cortland, NY 13045
Tel. (607) 753–5011
Fax. (607) 756–3409

Sheriff
54 Greenbush Street
Cortland, NY 13045
Tel. (607) 758–5599
Fax. (607) 753–6649

DELAWARE COUNTY

[6th Judicial District, 3rd Judicial Department]

Supreme Court
Delaware County Courthouse
3 Court Street
Delhi, NY 13753
Tel. (607) 746–2131
Fax. (607) 746–3253

County Court
Delaware County Courthouse
3 Court Street
Delhi, NY 13753
Tel. (607) 746–2131
Fax. (607) 746–3253

Family Court
Delaware County Courthouse
3 Court Street
Delhi, NY 13753
Tel. (607) 746–2298
Fax. (607) 746–2288

Surrogate's Court
Delaware County Courthouse
3 Court Street
Delhi, NY 13753
Tel. (607) 746–2126
Fax. (607) 746–3253

Delaware County Law Library
Delaware County Courthouse
3 Court Street
Delhi, NY 13753
Tel. (607) 746–3959
Fax. (607) 746–8198

Sheriff
280 Phoebe Lane, Suite 1
Delhi, NY 13753
Tel. (607) 746–2336
Fax. (607) 746–2632

DUTCHESS COUNTY

[9th Judicial District, 2nd Judicial Department]

Supreme Court
Dutchess County Courthouse
10 Market Street
Poughkeepsie, NY 12601
Tel. (845) 486–2260
Fax. (845) 473–5403

COURT DIRECTORY

County Court
Dutchess County Courthouse
10 Market Street
Poughkeepsie, NY 12601
Tel. (845) 486–2260
Fax. (845) 473–5403

Family Court
50 Market Street
Poughkeepsie, NY 12601–3204
Tel. (845) 486–2500
Fax. (845) 486–2510

Surrogate's Court
Dutchess County Courthouse
10 Market Street
Poughkeepsie, NY 12601
Tel. (845) 486–2235
Fax. (845) 486–2234

Beacon City Court
1 Municipal Plaza, Suite 2
Beacon, NY 12508
Tel. (845) 838–5030
Fax. (845) 838–5041

Poughkeepsie City Court
62 Civic Center Plaza
P.O. Box 300
Poughkeepsie, NY 12601
Tel. (845) 451–4091
Fax. (845) 451–4094

Dutchess County Law Library
50 Market Street
Poughkeepsie, NY 12601
Tel. (845) 486–2215

Sheriff
150 North Hamilton Street
Poughkeepsie, NY 12601
Tel. (845) 486–3800
Fax. (845) 486–3927

ERIE COUNTY
[8th Judicial District, 4th Judicial Department]

Supreme Court
Erie County Court Building
25 Delaware Avenue
Buffalo, NY 14202
Tel. (716) 845–9301
Fax. (716) 851–3293

Supreme Court
Erie County Hall
92 Franklin Street
Buffalo, NY 14202
Tel. (716) 845–9300
Fax. (716) 851–3293

Supreme Court
Buffalo City Court Building
50 Delaware Avenue
Buffalo, NY 14202

Supreme Court
Eagle Street Office Building
77 West Eagle Street
Buffalo, NY 14202

County Court
Erie County Court Building
25 Delaware Avenue
Buffalo, NY 14202
Tel. (716) 845–9301
Fax. (716) 851–3293

Family Court
One Niagara Plaza
Buffalo, NY 14202
Tel. (716) 845–7400
Fax. (716) 858–8432

Surrogate's Court
Erie County Hall
92 Franklin Street
Buffalo, NY 14202
Tel. (716) 845–2560
Fax. (716) 853–3741

Buffalo City Court
50 Delaware Avenue
Buffalo, NY 14202
Tel. (716) 845–2600
Fax. (716) 847–8257

Lackawanna City Court
714 Ridge Road
Lackawanna, NY 14218
Tel. (716) 827–6486
Fax. (716) 825–1874

Tonawanda City Court
200 Niagara Street
Tonawanda, NY 14150
Tel. (716) 845–2160
Fax. (716) 693–1612

COURT DIRECTORY

Erie County Law Library
77 West Eagle Street
Buffalo, NY 14202
Tel. (716) 845–9400
Fax. (716) 852–3454

Sheriff
10 Delaware Avenue
Buffalo, NY 14202
Tel. (716) 858–7608
Fax. (716) 858–7680
www.erie.gov/sheriff

ESSEX COUNTY
[4th Judicial District, 3rd Judicial Department]

Supreme Court
Essex County Courthouse
7559 Court Street
P.O. Box 217
Elizabethtown, NY 12932
Tel. (518) 873–3375
Fax. (518) 873–3376

County Court
Essex County Courthouse
7559 Court Street
P.O. Box 217
Elizabethtown, NY 12932
Tel. (518) 873–3375
Fax. (518) 873–3376

Family Court
Essex County Courthouse
7559 Court Street
Elizabethtown, NY 12932
Tel. (518) 873–3324
Fax. (518) 873–3626

Surrogate's Court
Essex County Courthouse
7559 Court Street
P.O. Box 505
Elizabethtown, NY 12932
Tel. (518) 873–3384
Fax. (518) 873–3731

Essex County Court Law Library
Essex County Courthouse
7559 Court Street
P.O. Box 217
Elizabethtown, NY 12932
Tel. (518) 873–3377
Fax. (518) 873–3376

Sheriff
702 Stowersville Road
P.O. Box 68
Lewis, NY 12950
Tel. (518) 873–6321
Fax. (518) 873–3340

FRANKLIN COUNTY
[4th Judicial District, 3rd Judicial Department]

Supreme Court
Franklin County Courthouse
355 West Main Street
Malone, NY 12953–1817
Tel. (518) 481–1681
Fax. (518) 481–5456

County Court
Franklin County Courthouse
355 West Main Street
Malone, NY 12953–1817
Tel. (518) 481–1681
Fax. (518) 481–5456

Family Court
Franklin County Courthouse
355 West Main Street
Malone, NY 12953–1817
Tel. (518) 481–1742
Fax. (518) 481–5453

Surrogate's Court
Franklin County Courthouse
355 West Main Street
Malone, NY 12953–1817
Tel. (518) 481–1737
Fax. (518) 483–7583

Franklin County Court Law Library
Franklin County Courthouse
63 West Main Street
Malone, NY 12953–1817
Tel. (518) 481–1732

Sheriff
45 Bare Hill Road
Malone, NY 12953
Tel. (518) 483–6795
Fax. (518) 483-3205

FULTON COUNTY
[4th Judicial District, 3rd Judicial Department]

COURT DIRECTORY

Supreme Court
Fulton County Office Building
223 West Main Street
Johnstown, NY 12095
Tel. (518) 736–5539
Fax. (518) 762–5078

County Court
Fulton County Office Building
223 West Main Street
Johnstown, NY 12095
Tel. (518) 762–5078

Family Court
11 North William Street
Johnstown, NY 12095–2116
Tel. (518) 762–3840
Fax. (518) 762–9540

Surrogate's Court
Fulton County Office Building
223 West Main Street
Johnstown, NY 12095
Tel. (518) 736–5685
Fax. (518) 762–6372

Gloversville City Court
City Hall
3 Frontage Road
Gloversville, NY 12078
Tel. (518) 773–4527
Fax. (518) 773–4599

Johnstown City Court
33–41 East Main Street, Suite 105
Johnstown, NY 12095
Tel. (518) 762–0007
Fax. (518) 762–2720

Fulton County Court Law Library
Fulton County Office Building
223 West Main Street
Johnstown, NY 12095
Tel. (518) 762–5685
Fax. (518) 762–6372

Sheriff
2712 State Highway 29
Johnstown, NY 12095
Tel. (518) 736–2100
Fax. (518) 736–2126

GENESEE COUNTY

[8th Judicial District, 4th Judicial Department]

Supreme Court
Genesee County Courts Facility
1 West Main Street
Batavia, NY 14020–2019
Tel. (585) 344–2550 ext. 2239
Fax. (585) 344–8517

County Court
Genesee County Courts Facility
1 West Main Street
Batavia, NY 14020–2019
Tel. (585) 344–2550 ext. 2239
Fax. (585) 344–8517

Family Court
Genesee County Courts Facility
1 West Main Street
Batavia, NY 14020–2019
Tel. (585) 344–2550 ext. 2231
Fax. (585) 344–8520

Surrogate's Court
Genesee County Courts Facility
1 West Main Street
Batavia, NY 14020–2019
Tel. (585) 344–2550 ext. 2240
Fax. (585) 344–8517

Batavia City Court
Genesee County Courts Facility
1 West Main Street
Batavia, NY 14020–2019
Tel. (585) 344–2550 ext. 2417
Fax. (585) 344–8556
Email: lgiambro@courts.state.ny.us

Genesee County Law Library
Genesee County Courts Facility
1 West Main Street
Batavia, NY 14020–2019
Tel. (585) 344–2550 ext. 2224
Fax. (585) 344–8517

Sheriff
165 Park Road
Batavia, NY 14020
Tel. (585) 345–3000
Fax. (585) 344–3102
Email: sheriff@co.genesee.ny.us

COURT DIRECTORY

GREENE COUNTY
[3rd Judicial District, 3rd Judicial Department]

Supreme Court
Greene County Courthouse
320 Main Street
Catskill, NY 12414–1825
Tel. (518) 943–2230
Fax. (518) 943–7763

County Court
Greene County Courthouse
320 Main Street
Catskill, NY 12414–1816
Tel. (518) 943–2230
Fax. (518) 943–7763

Family Court
Greene County Courthouse
320 Main Street
Catskill, NY 12414–1816
Tel. (518) 943–5711
Fax. (518) 943–1864
Email: bvanderm@courts.state.ny.us

Surrogate's Court
Greene County Courthouse
320 Main Street
Catskill, NY 12414–1825
Tel. (518) 943–2484
Fax. (518) 943–1864

Greene County Law Library
Greene County Courthouse
320 Main Street
Catskill, NY 12414
Tel. (518) 943–3130

Sheriff
80 Bridge Street
P.O. Box 231
Catskill, NY 12414
Tel. (518) 943–3300
Fax. (518) 943–6832
Email: sheriff@discovergreene.com

HAMILTON COUNTY
[4th Judicial District, 3rd Judicial Department]

Supreme Court
[Sessions held in Fulton County]
County Clerk's Office
P.O. Box 204
Lake Pleasant, NY 12108

Chief Clerk's Office
White Birch Lane
P.O. Box 780
Indian Lake, NY 12842–0780

County Court
Hamilton County Courthouse
Route 8
Lake Pleasant, NY 12108
Tel. (518) 648–5411
Fax. (518) 648–6286
Mailing address:
Court Chambers
P.O. Box 780
Indian Lake, NY 12842

Family Court
Hamilton County Courthouse
Route 8
Lake Pleasant, NY 12108
Tel. (518) 648–5411
Fax. (518) 648–6286
Mailing address:
Court Chambers
P.O. Box 780
Indian Lake, NY 12842

Surrogate's Court
Hamilton County Courthouse
Route 8
Lake Pleasant, NY 12108
Tel. (518) 648–5411
Fax. (518) 648–6286
Mailing address:
Court Chambers
P.O. Box 780
Indian Lake, NY 12842

Hamilton County Court Law Library
Hamilton County Courthouse
Route 8
P.O. Box 780
Lake Pleasant, NY 12108
Tel. (518) 648–5411
Fax. (518) 648–6286
Mailing address:
Court Chambers
P.O. Box 780
Indian Lake, NY 12842

Sheriff
South Shore Road
P.O. Box 210
Lake Pleasant, NY 12108
Tel. (518) 548–3113
Fax. (518) 548–5704

COURT DIRECTORY

HERKIMER COUNTY
[5th Judicial District, 4th Judicial Department]

Supreme Court
Herkimer County Office & Court Facility
301 North Washington Street
Herkimer, NY 13350
Civil Tel. (315) 867–1209
Crim. Tel. (315) 867–1282
Fax. (315) 866–1802

County Court
Herkimer County Office & Court Facility
301 North Washington Street
Suite 5550
Herkimer, NY 13350
Civil Tel. (315) 867–1209
Crim. Tel. (315) 867–1282
Fax. (315) 866–1802

Family Court
Herkimer County Office & Court Facility
301 North Washington Street
P.O. Box 749
Herkimer, NY 13350
Tel. (315) 867–1139
Fax. (315) 867–1369

Surrogate's Court
Herkimer County Office & Court Facility
301 North Washington Street
Herkimer, NY 13350
Tel. (315) 867–1170
Fax. (315) 866–1802

Little Falls City Court
Little Falls City Hall
659 East Main Street
Little Falls, NY 13365
Tel. (315) 823–1690
Fax. (315) 823–1623

Herkimer County Law Library
Herkimer County Office & Court Facility
301 North Washington Street
Suite 5511
Herkimer, NY 13350
Tel. (315) 867–1172
Fax. (315) 866–7991

Sheriff
320 North Main Street
Herkimer, NY 13350–2922
Tel. (315) 867–1167
Fax. (315) 867–1354

JEFFERSON COUNTY
[5th Judicial District, 4th Judicial Department]

Supreme Court
State Office Building
317 Washington Street
Watertown, NY 13601
Tel. (315) 785–7906
Fax. (315) 785–7909

County Court
Jefferson County Court Complex
163 Arsenal Street
2nd Floor
Watertown, NY 13601
Tel. (315) 785–3010
Fax. (315) 785–3330

Family Court
Jefferson County Court Complex
163 Arsenal Street
2nd Floor
Watertown, NY 13601
Tel. (315) 785–3001
Fax. (315) 785–3198

Surrogate's Court
Jefferson County Court Complex
163 Arsenal Street
3rd Floor
Watertown, NY 13601
Tel. (315) 785–3019
Fax. (315) 785–5194

Watertown City Court
Municipal Building
245 Washington Street
1st Floor
Watertown, NY 13601
Tel. (315) 785–7785
Fax. (315) 785–7856

Jefferson County Law Library
Jefferson County Courthouse
163 Arsenal Street
2nd Floor
Watertown, NY 13601
Tel. (315) 785–3064
Fax. (315) 785–3330

Sheriff
753 Waterman Drive
Watertown, NY 13601
Tel. (315) 786–2660
Fax. (315) 786–2684

COURT DIRECTORY

KINGS COUNTY

[2nd Judicial District, 2nd Judicial Department]

Supreme Court (Criminal)
320 Jay Street
Brooklyn, NY 11201
Tel. (347) 296–1076
   or
Supreme Court (Civil)
360 Adams Street
Brooklyn, NY 11201
Tel. (347) 296–1183

Family Court
330 Jay Street
Brooklyn, NY 11201
Tel. (347) 401–9600
Fax. (347) 401–9609
www.courts.state.ny.us/famhome.htm

Surrogate's Court
2 Johnson Street
Brooklyn, NY 11201
Tel. (347) 404–9700
Fax. (718) 643–6237

Civil Court of the City of New York
Kings County Branch
141 Livingston Street
Brooklyn, NY 11201
General (212) 791–6000
Civil (347) 404–9123
Housing: (347) 404–9201
Small claims: (347) 404–9021

Criminal Court of the City of New York
Kings County Branch
120 Schermerhorn Street
Brooklyn, NY 11201
Tel: (212) 374–5880
Fax. (718) 643–7733

Kings County Housing Court
141 Livingston Street
Brooklyn, NY 11201
Tel. (347) 404–9201

Kings County Law Library
360 Adams Street, Room 349
Brooklyn, NY 11201
Tel. (347) 296–1144
Fax. (718) 643–2412

Sheriff
210 Joralemon Street, Room 911
Brooklyn, NY 11201–3745
Tel. (718) 802-3543

LEWIS COUNTY

[5th Judicial District, 4th Judicial Department]

Supreme Court
Lewis County Courthouse
7660 State Street
Lowville, NY 13367
Tel. (315) 376–5347
Fax. (315) 376–5398

County Court
Lewis County Courthouse
7660 N. State Street
2nd Floor
Lowville, NY 13367–1396
Tel. (315) 376–5366
Fax. (315) 376–4145

Family Court
Lewis County Courthouse
7660 State Street
Lowville, NY 13367
Tel. (315) 376–5345
Fax. (315) 376–5189

Surrogate's Court
Lewis County Courthouse
7660 State Street
Lowville, NY 13367
Tel. (315) 376–5344
Fax. (315) 376–4145

Lewis County Law Library
Lewis County Courthouse
7660 State Street
Lowville, NY 13367–1396
Tel. (315) 376–5383
Fax. (315) 376–4145

Sheriff
Outer Stowe Street
P.O. Box 233
Lowville, NY 13367
Tel. (315) 376–3511
Fax. (315) 376–5232

COURT DIRECTORY

LIVINGSTON COUNTY
[7th Judicial District, 4th Judicial Department]
www.courts.state.ny.us/courts/7jd/

Supreme Court
Livingston County Courthouse
2 Court Street
Geneseo, NY 14454–1030
Tel. (585) 243–7060
Fax. (585) 243–7067

County Court
Livingston County Courthouse
2 Court Street
Geneseo, NY 14454–1030
Tel. (585) 243–7060
Fax. (585) 243–7067

Family Court
Livingston County Courthouse
2 Court Street
Geneseo, NY 14454–1030
Tel. (585) 243–7070
Fax. (585) 243–7076

Surrogate's Court
Livingston County Courthouse
2 Court Street
Geneseo, NY 14454–1030
Tel. (585) 243–7095
Fax. (585) 243–7583

Livingston County Law Library
24 Center Street
Geneseo, NY 14454
Tel. (585) 243–0440

Sheriff
4 Court Street
Geneseo, NY 14454
Tel. (585) 243–7100
Fax. (585) 243–7926

MADISON COUNTY
[6th Judicial District, 3rd Judicial Department]

Supreme Court
Madison County Courthouse
North Court Street
P.O. Box 545
Wampsville, NY 13163
Tel. (315) 366–2266
Fax. (315) 366–2539

County Court
Madison County Courthouse
North Court Street
P.O. Box 545
Wampsville, NY 13163
Tel. (315) 366–2266
Fax. (315) 366–2539

Family Court
Madison County Courthouse
North Court Street
P.O. Box 607
Wampsville, NY 13163
Tel. (315) 366–2291
Fax. (315) 366–2828

Surrogate's Court
Madison County Courthouse
138 North Court Street
P.O. Box 607
Wampsville, NY 13163
Tel. (315) 366–2392
Fax. (315) 366–2539

Oneida City Court
109 North Main Street
Oneida, NY 13421
Tel. (315) 363–1310
Fax. (315) 363–3230

Oneida Public Library
220 Broad Street
Oneida, NY 13421
Tel. (315) 363–3050
Fax. (315) 363–4217

Sheriff
North Court Street
P.O. Box 16
Wampsville, NY 13163
Tel. (315) 366–2318
Fax. (315) 366–2286
Email: sheriff@co.madison.ny.us

MONROE COUNTY
[7th Judicial District, 4th Judicial Department]
www.courts.state.ny.us/courts/7jd/

Supreme Court
Hall of Justice, Room 545
99 Exchange Blvd.
Rochester, NY 14614–2185
Chief Clerk Tel. (585) 428–5001
Civil Tel. (585) 428–2020
Crim. Tel. (585) 428–2331
Fax. (585) 428–2190

COURT DIRECTORY

County Court
Hall of Justice, Room 545
99 Exchange Blvd.
Rochester, NY 14614–2185
Chief Clerk Tel. (585) 428–5001
Civil Tel. (585) 428–2020
Crim. Tel. (585) 428–2331
Fax. (585) 428–2190

Family Court
Hall of Justice, Room 361
99 Exchange Blvd.
Rochester, NY 14614–2187
Tel. (585) 428–5429
Fax. (585) 428–2597

Surrogate's Court
Hall of Justice, Room 541
99 Exchange Blvd.
Rochester, NY 14614–2186
Tel. (585) 428–5200
Fax. (585) 428–2650

Rochester City Court
Civil Branch
Hall of Justice, Room 6
99 Exchange Blvd.
Rochester, NY 14614–2199
Civil Tel. (585) 428–2444
Civil Fax. (585) 428–2588
Crim. Tel. (585) 428–2447
Crim. Fax. (585) 428–2732

Monroe County Law Library
Hall of Justice, Room 525
99 Exchange Blvd.
Rochester, NY 14614
Tel. (585) 428–1854
Fax. (585) 428–3182

Sheriff
130 South Plymouth Avenue
Rochester, NY 14614
Tel. (585) 753–4178
Fax. (585) 753–4524

MONTGOMERY COUNTY
[4th Judicial District, 3rd Judicial Department]

Supreme Court
Montgomery County Courthouse
58 Broadway
P.O. Box 1500
Fonda, NY 12068–1500
Tel. (518) 853–4516
Fax. (518) 853–3596

County Court
Montgomery County Courthouse
58 Broadway
P.O. Box 1500
Fonda, NY 12068–1500
Tel. (518) 853–4516
Fax. (518) 853–3596

Family Court
Montgomery County Courthouse
58 Broadway
P.O. Box 1500
Fonda, NY 12068–1500
Tel. (518) 853–8134
Fax. (518) 853–8148

Surrogate's Court
Montgomery County Courthouse
58 Broadway
P.O. Box 1500
Fonda, NY 12068–1500
Tel. (518) 853–8108
Fax. (518) 853–8230

Amsterdam City Court
One Guy Park Avenue Extension
Public Safety Building, Room 208
Amsterdam, NY 12010
Tel. (518) 842–9510
Fax. (518) 843–8474

Montgomery County Court Law Library
Montgomery County Courthouse
58 Broadway
P.O. Box 1500
Fonda, NY 12068–1500

Sheriff
200 Clark Drive
P.O. Box 432
Fultonville, NY 12072–0432
Tel. (518) 853–5500
Fax. (518) 853–4096

NASSAU COUNTY
[10th Judicial District, 2nd Judicial Department]

Supreme Court
100 Supreme Court Drive
Mineola, NY 11501
Tel. (516) 571–2904
Fax. (516) 571–1575

COURT DIRECTORY

County Court
262 Old Country Road
Mineola, NY 11501
Tel. (516) 571–2800
Fax. (516) 571–2160

Family Court
1200 Old Country Road
Westbury, NY 11590
Tel. (516) 571–9033
Fax. (516) 571–9335

Surrogate's Court
262 Old Country Road
Mineola, NY 11501
Tel. (516) 571–2847
Fax. (516) 571–3803

1st District Court
99 Main Street
Hempstead, NY 11550
Tel. (516) 572-2355
Fax. (516) 572–2507

2nd District Court
99 Main Street
Hempstead, NY 11550
Tel. (516) 572–2264

3rd District Court
435 Middle Neck Road
Great Neck, NY 11023
Tel. (516) 571–8400

4th District Court
99 Main Street
Hempstead, NY 11550
Tel. (516) 571–7090

Glen Cove City Court
13 Glen Street
Glen Cove, NY 11542
Tel. (516) 676–0109
Fax. (516) 676–1570

Long Beach City Court
1 West Chester Street
Long Beach, NY 11561
Tel. (516) 431–1000
Fax. (516) 889–3511

Nassau County Law Library
100 Supreme Court Drive
Mineola, NY 11501
Tel. (516) 571–3883
Fax. (516) 571–0752

Sheriff, Correctional Center
100 Carmen Avenue
East Meadow, NY 11554
Tel. (516) 572–4200
Fax. (516) 572–4300

Sheriff, Family Court Unit
1200 Old Country Road
Westbury, NY 11590
Tel. (516) 571–9050

Sheriff, Mineola Office
240 Old Country Road
Mineola, NY 11501
Tel. (516) 571–2113

NEW YORK COUNTY
[1st Judicial District, 1st Judicial Department]

Supreme Court
Civil Branch
60 Centre Street
New York, NY 10007
Tel. (646) 386–3600
Fax. (212) 374–3326
www.nycourts.gov/courts/nyc/supreme/
    or
Satellite Courthouses
80, 100, and 111 Centre Street
71 Thomas Street
New York, NY 10013

Criminal Term
100 Centre Street
New York, NY 10013
Tel. (646) 386–4000
Fax. (212) 374–0667
    or
Criminal Term
111 Centre Street
New York, NY 10013
Tel. (646) 386–4301
Fax. (212) 374–2637

Appellate Term
60 Centre Street
New York, NY 10007
Tel. (646) 386-3040

COURT DIRECTORY

Family Court
60 Lafayette Street
New York, NY 10013
Tel. (646) 386–5206
Fax. (212) 374–4567
www.nycourts.gov/courts/nyc/family/

Surrogate's Court
31 Chambers Street
New York, NY 10007
Tel. (646) 386–5000
Fax. (212) 374–3250

Civil Court of the City of New York
New York County Branch
111 Centre Street
New York, NY 10013–4390
Tel. (646) 386–5700
Tel. (646) 386–5600
Fax. (212) 374–8053

Criminal Court of the City of New York
100 Centre Street
New York, NY 10013
Tel. (646) 386–4500
Fax. (212) 374–5293

New York County Housing Court
111 Centre Street
New York, NY 10013
Tel. (646) 386–5750
Small Claims (646) 386–5480

NY County Supreme Civil Law Library
60 Centre Street, Room 500
New York, NY 10007–1474
Tel. (646) 386–3670
Fax. (212) 374–8159

Sheriff
31 Chambers Street, 6th Floor
New York, NY 10017
Tel. (212) 788–8731
Fax. (212) 766–9666

Niagara County
[8th Judicial District, 4th Judicial Department]

Supreme Court
Civic Building
775 3rd Street
Niagara Falls, NY 14302–1710
Tel. (716) 278–1800
Fax. (716) 278–1809
Email: mflorian@courts.state.ny.us

County Court
Niagara County Courthouse
175 Hawley Street
Lockport, NY 14094
Tel. (716) 439–7148
Fax. (716) 439–7157
Email: afarnold@courts.state.ny.us

Family Court
Niagara County Courthouse
175 Hawley Street
Lockport, NY 14094
Tel. (716) 439–7172
Fax. (716) 439–7170

Surrogate's Court
Niagara County Courthouse
175 Hawley Street
Lockport, NY 14094
Tel. (716) 439–7130
Fax. (716) 439–7319

Lockport City Court
1 Locks Plaza
Lockport, NY 14094–3694
Civil Tel. (716) 439–6660
Crim. Tel. (716) 439–6671
Traffic Tel. (716) 439–6680
Fax. (716) 439–6684

Niagara Falls City Court
Public Safety Building
520 Hyde Park Boulevard
Niagara Falls, NY 14302
Civil Tel. (716) 278–9860
Crimiinal Tel. (716) 278–9800
Traffic Tel. (716) 278–9840
Fax. (716) 278–9809
Email: mfarbo@courts.state.ny.us

North Tonawanda City Court
City Hall
216 Payne Avenue
North Tonawanda, NY 14120
Tel. (716) 693–1010
Fax. (716) 743–1754

Niagara County Library
Niagara County Courthouse
175 Hawley Street
Lockport, NY 14090
Tel. (716) 439–7145

COURT DIRECTORY

Sheriff
5526 Niagara Street Extension
P.O. Box 496
Lockport, NY 14095–0496
Tel. (716) 438–3393
Fax. (716) 438–3302

ONEIDA COUNTY
[5th Judicial District, 4th Judicial Department]

Supreme Court
Oneida County Courthouse, 4th Floor
200 Elizabeth Street
Utica, NY 13501
Tel. (315) 798–5890
Fax. (315) 798–6436
    or
Supreme Court
NYS Office Building
207 Genesee Street
Utica, NY 13501
Tel. (315) 793–2184
Fax. (315) 793–2217
    or
Supreme Court
Oneida County Courthouse
302 North James St.
Rome, NY 13440

Oneida County Court
Oneida County Courthouse, 4th Floor
200 Elizabeth Street
Utica, NY 13501
Tel. (315) 798–5889
Fax. (315) 798–6047

Oneida County Family Court
Oneida County Courthouse
200 Elizabeth Street, 1st Floor
Utica, NY 13501
Tel. (315) 798–5925
Fax. (315) 798–6404
    or
301 West Dominick Street
Rome, NY 13440
Tel. (315) 337–7492
Fax. (315) 336–3828

Surrogate's Court
Oneida County Office Building
800 Park Avenue, 8th Floor
Utica, NY 13501
Tel. (315) 797–9230
Rome Off. Tel. (315) 336–6860
Fax. (315) 797–9237

Rome City Court
100 West Court Street
Rome, NY 13440
Tel. (315) 337–6440
Fax. (315) 338–0343

Sherrill City Court
373 Sherrill Road
Sherrill, NY 13461
Tel. (315) 363–0996
Fax. (315) 363–1176

Utica City Court
411 Oriskany Street West
Utica, NY 13502
Civil Tel. (315) 724–8157
Fax. (315) 792–8038
Crim. Tel. (315) 724–8227
Fax. (315) 724–0762
Traffic Tel. (315) 724–8158
Fax. (315) 792–0762

Oneida County Law Library
Oneida County Courthouse
235 Elizabeth Street
Utica, NY 13501
Tel. (315) 798–5703
Fax. (315) 798–6470

Sheriff
6065 Judd Road
Oriskany, NY 13424–4218
Tel. (315) 765–2222
Fax. (315) 765–2205

ONONDAGA COUNTY
[5th Judicial District, 4th Judicial Department]

Supreme Court
Onondaga County Courthouse
401 Montgomery Street
Syracuse, NY 13202
Civil Division
Tel. (315) 671–1030
Fax. (315) 671-1176
Criminal Division
Tel. (315) 671–1020
Fax. (315) 671-1191

County Court
Onondaga County Courthouse
505 South State Street
Syracuse, NY 13202–2104
Tel. (315) 671–1020
Fax. (315) 671-1191

Family Court
Onondaga County Courthouse
401 Montgomery Street
Syracuse, NY 13202
Tel. (315) 671–2000
Fax. (315) 671-1163

Surrogate's Court
Onondaga County Courthouse
401 Montgomery Street
Syracuse, NY 13202
Tel. (315) 671–2100
Fax. (315) 671-1162

Syracuse City Court
505 South State Street
Syracuse, NY 13202–2104
Crim. Tel. (315) 671–2760
Crim. Fax. (315) 671–2744
Civil Tel. (315) 671–2782
Civil Fax. (315) 671–2741
Traffic Tel. (315) 671–2770
Traffic Fax. (315) 671–2743

Onondaga County Law Library
Onondaga County Courthouse
401 Montgomery Street
Syracuse, NY 13202
Tel. (315) 671–1150
Fax. (315) 671–1160

Sheriff
407 South State Street
Syracuse, NY 13202
Tel. (315) 435–3044
Fax. (315) 435–2942

ONTARIO COUNTY
[7th Judicial District, 4th Judicial Department]
www.courts.state.ny.us/courts/7jd/

Supreme Court
Ontario County Courthouse
27 North Main Street
Canandaigua, NY 14424
Tel. (585) 396–4239
Fax. (585) 396–4576

County Court
Ontario County Courthouse
27 North Main Street
Canandaigua, NY 14424
Tel. (585) 396–4239
Fax. (585) 396–4576

Family Court
Ontario County Courthouse
27 North Main Street
Canandaigua, NY 14424
Tel. (585) 396–4272
Fax. (585) 396–4576
Email: ontariofamilycourt@courts.state.ny.us

Surrogate's Court
Ontario County Courthouse
27 North Main Street
Canandaigua, NY 14424
Tel. (585) 396–4055
Fax. (585) 396–4576
Email: dcrudele@courts.state.ny.us

Canandaigua City Court
2 North Main Street
Canandaigua, NY 14424
Tel. (585) 396–5011
Fax. (585) 396–5012
Email: lschutz@courts.state.ny.us

Geneva City Court
255 Exchange Street
Geneva, NY 14456
Tel. (315) 789–6560
Fax. (315) 781–2802
Email: jguard@courts.state.ny.us

Ontario County Law Library
Finger Lakes Community College
4355 Lakeshore Drive
Canandaigua, NY 14424
Tel. (585) 394–3500, ext. 7371

Sheriff
74 Ontario Street
Canandaigua, NY 14424
Tel. (585) 394–4560
Fax. (585) 396–4844

ORANGE COUNTY
[9th Judicial District, 2nd Judicial Department]

Supreme Court
285 Main Street
Goshen, NY 10924
Tel. (845) 291–3111
Fax. (845) 291–2595

COURT DIRECTORY

County Court
285 Main Street
Goshen, NY 10924
Tel. (845) 291–3111
Fax. (845) 291–2595

Family Court
285 Main Street
Goshen, NY 10924
Tel. (845) 291–3030
Fax. (845) 291–3054

Surrogate's Court
30 Park Place
Goshen, NY 10924
Tel. (845) 291–2193
Fax. (845) 291–2196

Middletown City Court
2 James Street
Middletown, NY 10940
Tel. (845) 346–4050
Fax. (845) 343–5737

Newburgh City Court
57 Broadway
Newburgh, NY 12550
Tel. (845) 565–3208
Fax. (845) 565–1244

Port Jervis City Court
20 Hammond Street
Port Jervis, NY 12771
Tel. (845) 858–4034
Fax. (845) 858–9883

Orange County Law Library
Orange County Government Center
255–275 Main Street
Goshen, NY 10924
Tel. (845) 297–3138
Fax. (212) 401–9144

Sheriff
110 Wells Farm Road
Goshen, NY 10924–6740
Tel. (845) 291–4033
Fax. (845) 294–1590

ORLEANS COUNTY
[8th Judicial District, 4th Judicial Department]

Supreme Court
3 South Main Street
Courthouse
Albion, NY 14411–1497
Tel. (585) 589–5458
Fax. (585) 589–0632

County Court
3 South Main Street
Courthouse
Albion, NY 14411–1497
Tel. (585) 589–5458
Fax. (585) 589–0632

Family Court
3 South Main Street
Courthouse
Albion, NY 14411–1497
Tel. (585) 589–4457
Fax. (585) 589–0632
Email: mwashak@courts.state.ny.us

Surrogate's Court
3 South Main Street
Courthouse
Albion, NY 14411–1497
Tel. (585) 589–4457
Fax. (585) 589–0632
Email: dberry@courts.state.ny.us

Orleans County Law Library
3 South Main Street
Courthouse
Albion, NY 14411–1497
Tel. (716) 589–4457

Sheriff
13925 State Route 31, Suite 400
Albion, NY 14411–9386
Tel. (585) 590–4142
Fax. (585) 590–4178
Email: ocsher@orleansny.com

OSWEGO COUNTY
[5th Judicial District, 4th Judicial Department]

Supreme Court
Oswego County Courthouse
25 East Oneida Street
Oswego, NY 13126
Tel. (315) 349–3280
Fax. (315) 349–8513

COURT DIRECTORY

County Court
25 East Oneida Street
Oswego, NY 13126
Tel. (315) 349–3277
Fax. (315) 349–8513

Family Court
Oswego County Public Safety Center
39 Churchill Road
Oswego, NY 13126
Tel. (315) 349–3350
Fax. (315) 349–3457

Surrogate's Court
Oswego County Courthouse
25 East Oneida Street
Oswego, NY 13126
Tel. (315) 349–3295
Fax. (315) 349–8514

Fulton City Court
Municipal Building
141 South First Street
2nd Floor
Fulton, NY 13069
Tel. (315) 593–8400
Fax. (315) 592–3415

Oswego City Court
Conway Municipal Building
20 West Oneida Street
Oswego, NY 13126
Tel. (315) 343–0415
Fax. (315) 343–0531

Oswego County Law Library
Oswego County Courthouse
25 East Oneida Street
Oswego, NY 13126
Tel. (315) 349–3297
Fax. (315) 349–3273

Sheriff
Oswego County Public Safety Center
39 Churchill Road
Oswego, NY 13126
Tel. (315) 349–3307
Fax. (315) 349–3483
Email: sheriff@oswegocounty.com

Supreme Court
Otsego County Office Building
197 Main Street
Cooperstown, NY 13326
Tel. (607) 547–4364
Fax. (607) 547–7567

County Court
Otsego County Office Building
197 Main Street
Cooperstown, NY 13326
Tel. (607) 547–4364
Fax. (607) 547–7567

Family Court
Otsego County Office Building
197 Main Street
Cooperstown, NY 13326
Tel. (607) 547–4264
Fax. (607) 547–6412

Surrogate's Court
Otsego County Office Building
197 Main Street
Cooperstown, NY 13326
Tel. (607) 547–4213
Fax. (607) 547–7566

Oneonta City Court
Public Safety Building
81 Main Street
Oneonta, NY 13820
Tel. (607) 432–4480
Fax. (607) 432–2328

Otsego County Law Library
Otsego County Office Building
197 Main Street
Cooperstown, NY 13326–1129
Tel. (607) 547–5425
Fax. (607) 547–6109

Sheriff
172 County Highway 33 West
Cooperstown, NY 13326
Tel. (607) 547–4271
Fax. (607) 547–6413

OTSEGO COUNTY

[6th Judicial District, 3rd Judicial Department]

PUTNAM COUNTY

[9th Judicial District, 2nd Judicial Department]

COURT DIRECTORY

Supreme Court
20 County Center
Carmel, NY 10512
Tel. (845) 208–7830
Fax. (845) 228–9611

County Court
20 County Center
Carmel, NY 10512
Tel. (845) 208–7830
Fax. (845) 228–9611

Family Court
20 County Center
Carmel, NY 10512
Tel. (845) 208–7805
Fax. (845) 228–9614

Surrogate's Court
44 Gleneida Avenue
Carmel, NY 10512
Tel. (845) 208–7860
Fax. (845) 228–5761

Putnam County Law Library
Putnam County Office Building
40 Gleneida Avenue
Carmel, NY 10512
Tel. (845) 225–3641 ext. 297
Fax. (845) 225–4395

Sheriff
3 County Center
Carmel, NY 10512
Tel. (845) 225–4300
Fax. (845) 225–4399

QUEENS COUNTY
[11th Judicial District, 2nd Judicial Department]
www.courts.state.ny.us/courts/11jd/

Supreme Court (Civil Term)
88–11 Sutphin Boulevard, Suite 2
Jamaica, NY 11435
Tel. (718) 298–1000
Fax. (718) 520–2204
    or

(Criminal Term)
125–01 Queens Boulevard
Kew Gardens, NY 11415
Tel. (718) 298–1000
Fax. (718) 520–2494
    or
(Civil and Criminal Terms)
25–10 Court Square
Long Island City, NY 11101
Tel. (718) 298–1000
Fax. (718) 520–2539

Family Court
151–20 Jamaica Avenue
Jamaica, NY 11432
Tel. (718) 298–0197
Fax. (718) 297–2826
www.nycourts.gov/courts/nyc/family

Surrogate's Court
88–11 Sutphin Boulevard, 7th Floor
Jamaica, NY 11435
Tel. (718) 298–0500

Civil Court of the City of New York
Queens County Branch
89–17 Sutphin Boulevard
Jamaica, NY 11435
Tel. (718) 262–7100
Tel. (212) 791–6000
Fax. (718) 262–7107

Criminal Court of the City of New York
Queens County Branch
125-01 Queens Boulevard
Kew Gardens, NY 11415
Tel. (212) 374–5880
Fax. (718) 520–4712

Queens County Housing Court
89–17 Sutphin Boulevard
Jamaica, NY 11435
Tel. (646) 386–5750
www.courts.state.ny.us/courts/nyc/housing

COURT DIRECTORY

Queens County Law Library
Queens County General Courthouse
88–11 Sutphin Boulevard, Room 65
Jamaica, NY 11435
Tel. (718) 298–1206
Fax. (718) 520–3589
Email: law_library_queens@courts.state.ny.us
www.nycourts.gov/library/queens/

Queens County Law Library
125–01 Queens Blvd.
Room 722
Kew Gardens, NY 11415

Sheriff
144–06 94th Avenue
Jamaica, NY 11435
Tel. (718) 298–7550
Fax. (718) 298–7470

RENSSELAER COUNTY
[3rd Judicial District, 3rd Judicial Department]

Supreme Court
80 Second Street
Troy, NY 12180–4098
Tel. (518) 285–5025
Fax. (518) 270–3714

County Court
80 Second Street
Troy, NY 12180–4098
Tel. (518) 285–5025
Fax. (518) 270–3714

Family Court
1504 Fifth Avenue
Troy, NY 12180–4107
Tel. (518) 270–3761
Fax. (518) 272–6573
Email: pbeeler@courts.state.ny.us

Surrogate's Court
80 Second Street
Troy, NY 12180–4098
Tel. (518) 270–3724
Fax. (518) 272–5452

Rensselaer City Court
505 Broadway
Rensselaer, NY 12144
Tel. (518) 462–6751
Fax. (518) 462–3307

Troy City Court – Civil
51 State Street, 3rd Floor
Troy, NY 12180
Tel. (518) 273–2434

Troy City Court – Criminal and Traffic
51 State Street, 2nd Floor
Troy, NY 12180
Tel. (518) 271–1602
Tel. (518) 274–2816

Rensselaer County Law Library
Courthouse
80 Second Street
Troy, NY 12180
Tel. (518) 270–3717
Fax. (518) 274–0590

Sheriff
4000 Main Street
Troy, NY 12180
Tel. (518) 270–5448
Fax. (518) 270–5447

RICHMOND COUNTY
[2nd Judicial District, 2nd Judicial Department]
www.nycourts.gov/courts/2jd/richmond.shtml

Supreme Court (Civil)
18 Richmond Terrace
Staten Island, NY 10301
Tel. (718) 390–5201
Fax. (718) 390–5435
      or
355 Front Street
Staten Island, NY 10304
Tel. (718) 876–6411

Supreme Court (Criminal)
18 Richmond Terrace
Staten Island, NY 10301
Tel. (718) 390–5280
Fax. (718) 390–5435

Family Court
100 Richmond Terrace
Staten Island, NY 10301
Tel. (718) 390–5460/5461
Fax. (718) 390–5247
www.courts.state.ny.us/famhome.htm

COURT DIRECTORY

Surrogate's Court
18 Richmond Terrace
Staten Island, NY 10301
Tel. (718) 390–5400
Fax. (718) 390–8741

Civil Court of the City of New York
Richmond County Branch
927 Castleton Avenue
Staten Island, NY 10310
General Info: (212) 791–6000
Civil Tel. (718) 390–5417
Small claims: (718) 390–5421
Fax. (718) 390–8108

Criminal Court of the City of New York
Richmond County Branch
67 Targee Street
Staten Island, NY 10304
Tel. (212) 374–5880
Fax. (718) 390–8405

Richmond County Housing Court
927 Castleton Avenue
Staten Island, NY 10310
Tel. (718) 390–5420

Richmond County Law Library
Supreme Court Building
18 Richmond Terrace
Staten Island, NY 10301
Tel. (718) 390–5291
Fax. (718) 390–5230
Email: bagnese@courts.state.ny.us

Sheriff
350 Saint Marks Avenue
Staten Island, NY 10301
Tel. (718) 815–8407
Fax. (718) 815–8412

ROCKLAND COUNTY
[9th Judicial District, 2nd Judicial Department]

Supreme Court
Rockland County Courthouse
1 South Main Street
New City, NY 10956
Tel. (845) 638–5393
Fax. (845) 638–5312

County Court
Rockland County Courthouse
1 South Main Street
New City, NY 10956
Tel. (845) 638–5393
Fax. (845) 638–5312

Family Court
Rockland County Courthouse
1 South Main Street
New City, NY 10956
Tel. (845) 638–5300
Fax. (845) 638–5319

Surrogate's Court
Rockland County Courthouse
1 South Main Street
New City, NY 10956
Tel. (845) 638–5330
Fax. (845) 638–5632

Rockland County Law Library
Rockland County Courthouse
1 South Main Street
Suite 235
New City, NY 10956–3551
Tel. (845) 638–5396
Fax. (212) 401–9143

Sheriff
55 New Hempstead Road
New City, NY 10956
Tel. (845) 638–5400
Fax. (845) 638–5035

St. Lawrence County
[4th Judicial District, 3rd Judicial Department]
www.nycourts.gov/courts/4jd/stlawrence/

Supreme Court
St. Lawrence County Courthouse
48 Court Street
Canton, NY 13617–1194
Tel. (315) 379–0326
Fax. (315) 379–2311

County Court
48 Court Street
Canton, NY 13617–1194
Tel. (315) 379–2214
Fax. (315) 379–9934

Family Court
48 Court Street
Canton, NY 13617–1194
Tel. (315) 379–2410
Fax. (315) 386–3197

Surrogate's Court
48 Court Street
Canton, NY 13617–1194
Tel. (315) 379–2217
Fax. (315) 379–2372

Ogdensburg City Court
330 Ford Street
Ogdensburg, NY 13669
Tel. (315) 393–3941
Fax. (315) 393–6839

St. Lawrence County Supreme Court Law Library
St. Lawrence County Courthouse
48 Court Street
Canton, NY 13617–1194
Tel. (315) 379–2279
Fax. (315) 379–2424
Email: tlomaki@courts.state.ny.us

Sheriff
48 Court Street
Canton, NY 13617
Tel. (315) 379–2430
Fax. (315) 379–0335

SARATOGA COUNTY
[4th Judicial District, 3rd Judicial Department]

Supreme Court
Municipal Center
Building 3
30 McMaster Street
Ballston Spa, NY 12020
Tel. (518) 885–2224
Fax. (518) 884–4758

County Court
Municipal Center
Building 3
30 McMaster Street
Ballston Spa, NY 12020
Tel. (518) 885–2224
Fax. (518) 884–4758

Family Court
Saratoga County Municipal Center
Building 2
35 West High Street
Ballston Spa, NY 12020
Tel. (518) 884–9207
Fax. (518) 884–8735

Surrogate's Court
Municipal Center
Building 3
30 McMaster Street
Ballston Spa, NY 12020
Tel. (518) 884–4722
Fax. (518) 884–4774

Saratoga Springs City Court
474 Broadway, Suite 3
Saratoga Springs, NY 12866
Tel. (518) 581–1797
Fax. (518) 584–3097

Mechanicville City Court
36 North Main Street
Mechanicville, NY 12118
Tel. (518) 664–9876
Fax. (518) 664–8606

Saratoga County Supreme Court Law Library
City Hall, 3rd Floor
Suite 10
474 Broadway
Saratoga Springs, NY 12866
Tel. (518) 584–4862
Fax. (518) 581–0966

Sheriff
6010 County Farm Road
Ballston Spa, NY 12020–2207
Tel. (518) 885–6761
Fax. (518) 885–2253

SCHENECTADY COUNTY
[4th Judicial District, 3rd Judicial Department]

Supreme Court
Schenectady County Courthouse
612 State Street
Schenectady, NY 12305
Tel. (518) 388–4389
Fax. (518) 388–4520

COURT DIRECTORY

County Court
Schenectady County Courthouse
612 State Street
Schenectady, NY 12305
Tel. (518) 388–4389
Fax. (518) 388–4520

Family Court
Schenectady County Office Building
620 State Street
Schenectady, NY 12305
Tel. (518) 388–4305
Fax. (518) 388–4496

Surrogate's Court
Schenectady County Courthouse
612 State Street
Schenectady, NY 12305
Tel. (518) 388–4293
Fax. (518) 377–6378

Schenectady City Court (Civil Division)
City Hall
105 Jay Street, Room 214-215
Schenectady, NY 12305
Tel. (518) 382–5077
Fax. (518) 382–5080

Schenectady City Court (Criminal Division)
531 Liberty Street
Schenectady, NY 12305
Tel. (518) 382–5239
Fax. (518) 382–5241

Schenectady County Supreme Court Law Library
612 State Street
Schenectady, NY 12305–2114
Tel. (518) 285–8518
Fax. (518) 377–5909

Sheriff
320 Veeder Avenue
Schenectady, NY 12307
Tel. (518) 388–4300
Fax. (518) 388–4593

SCHOHARIE COUNTY
[3rd Judicial District, 3rd Judicial Department]

Supreme Court
Schoharie County Courthouse
290 Main Street
P.O. Box 669
Schoharie, NY 12157
Tel. (518) 295–8342
Fax. (518) 295–7226

County Court
Schoharie County Courthouse
290 Main Street
P.O. Box 669
Schoharie, NY 12157
Tel. (518) 295–8342
Fax. (518) 295–7226

Family Court
Schoharie County Courthouse
290 Main Street
P.O. Box 669
Schoharie, NY 12157–0669
Tel. (518) 295–8383
Fax. (518) 295–8451

Surrogate's Court
Schoharie County Courthouse
290 Main Street
P.O. Box 669
Schoharie, NY 12157–0669
Tel. (518) 295–8387
Fax. (518) 295–8451

Schoharie County Law Library
Schoharie County Courthouse
290 Main Street
Schoharie, NY 12157–0447
Tel. (518) 295–7900
Fax. (518) 295–8451

Sheriff
157 Depot Lane
P.O. Box 689
Schoharie, NY 12157
Tel. (518) 295–7066
Fax. (518) 295–7094

SCHUYLER COUNTY
[6th Judicial District, 3rd Judicial Department]

Supreme Court
Schuyler County Courthouse
105 Ninth Street, Unit 35
Watkins Glen, NY 14891
Tel. (607) 535–7760
Fax. (607) 535–4918

County Court
Schuyler County Courthouse
105 Ninth Street, Unit 35
Watkins Glen, NY 14891
Tel. (607) 535–7760
Fax. (607) 535–4918

COURT DIRECTORY

Family Court
Schuyler County Courthouse
105 Ninth Street, Unit 35
Watkins Glen, NY 14891
Tel. (607) 535–7143
Fax. (607) 535–4918

Surrogate's Court
Schuyler County Courthouse
105 Ninth Street, Unit 35
Watkins Glen, NY 14891
Tel. (607) 535–7144
Fax. (607) 535–4918

Watkins Glen Public Library
610 South Decatur Street
Watkins Glen, NY 14891
Tel. (607) 535–2346
Fax. (607) 535–7338

Sheriff
106 Tenth Street
Watkins Glen, NY 14891
Tel. (607) 535–8222
Fax. (607) 535–8216

SENECA COUNTY
[7th Judicial District, 4th Judicial Department]
www.courts.state.ny.us/courts/7jd

Supreme Court
48 West Williams Street
Waterloo, NY 13165
Tel. (315) 539–7021
Fax. (315) 539–7929
Email: eyoung@courts.state.ny.us

County Court
48 West Williams Street
Waterloo, NY 13165
Tel. (315) 539–7021
Fax. (315) 539–7929

Family Court
48 West Williams Street
Waterloo, NY 13165
Tel. (315) 539–6291
Fax. (315) 539–4225
Email: cbrown@courts.state.ny.us

Surrogate's Court
48 West Williams Street
Waterloo, NY 13165
Tel. (315) 539–7531
Fax. (315) 539–3267

Seneca County Law Library
47 Cayuga Street
Seneca Falls, NY 13148
Tel. (315) 568–8265

Sheriff
6150 State Route 96
Romulus, NY 14541
Tel. (315) 220–3200
Fax. (315) 220–3478

STEUBEN COUNTY
[7th Judicial District, 4th Judicial Department]
www.courts.state.ny.us/courts/7jd/steuben/

Supreme Court
Steuben County Courthouse
3 East Pulteney Square
Bath, NY 14810–1575
Tel. (607) 776–7879
Fax. (607) 776–5226

County Court
Steuben County Courthouse
3 East Pulteney Square
Bath, NY 14810–1575
Tel. (607) 776–7879
Fax. (607) 776–5226

Family Court
Steuben County Courthouse
3 East Pulteney Square
Bath, NY 14810–1575
Tel. (607) 776–9631
Fax. (607) 776–7857

Surrogate's Court
Steuben County Courthouse
3 East Pulteney Square
Bath, NY 14810
Tel. (607) 776–7126
Fax. (607) 776–4987

Corning City Court
12 Civic Center Plaza
Corning, NY 14830–2884
Tel. (607) 936–4111
Fax. (607) 936–0519

Hornell City Court
82 Main St.
P.O. Box 627
Hornell, NY 14843–0627
Tel. (607) 324–7531
Fax. (607) 324–6325
Email: lbeltz@courts.state.ny.us

COURT DIRECTORY

Steuben County Supreme Court Law Library
3 East Pulteney Square
Bath, NY 14810–1557
Tel. (607) 664–2099
Fax. (607) 776–7715

Sheriff
7007 Rumsey Street Extension
Bath, NY 14810–7827
Tel. (607) 776–7009
Fax. (607) 776–4271

SUFFOLK COUNTY

[10th Judicial District, 2nd Judicial Department]

Supreme Court
400 Carleton Avenue
Central Islip, NY 11722
Tel. (631) 853–5462
Fax. (631) 853–5835
    or
235 Griffing Avenue
Riverhead, NY 11901
Tel. (631) 852–2333
Fax. (631) 852–2340
    or
One Court Street
Riverhead, NY 11901
    or
210 Center Drive
Riverhead, NY 11901

County Court
Arthur M. Cromarty Court Complex
210 Center Drive
Riverhead, NY 11901
Tel. (631) 852–2121
Fax. (631) 852–2568

Family Court
John P. Cohalan, Jr., Courthouse
400 Carleton Avenue
Central Islip, NY 11722–9076
Tel. (631) 853–4648
Fax. (631) 853–4283
    or
Family Court
Millbrook Office Campus
889 East Main Street
Suite 308
Riverhead, NY 11901
Tel. (631) 852–3905
Fax. (631) 852–2851

Surrogate's Court
County Center Building
320 Center Drive
Riverhead, NY 11901
Tel. (631) 852–1745
Fax. (631) 852–1777

District Court—Chief Clerk's Office
John P. Cohalan, Jr. Courthouse
400 Carleton Avenue
Room D255
Central Islip, NY 11722
Tel. (631) 853–4530
Fax. (631) 853–4505

District Court—Criminal Division: Main Office
Cohalan Court Complex
400 Carleton Avenue
Room D220
Central Islip, NY 11722
Tel. (631) 853–7500

1st District Court—Civil
3105 Veterans Memorial Highway
Ronkonkoma, NY 11779
Tel. (631) 854–9676
Fax. (631) 854–9681

2nd District Court
30 East Hoffman Ave
Lindenhurst, NY 11757
Tel. (631) 854–1121
Fax. (631) 854–1127

3rd District Court
1850 New York Avenue
Huntington Station, NY 11746
Tel. (631) 854–4545
Fax. (631) 854–4549

4th District Court
North County Complex, Bldg. #C158
Veterans Memorial Highway
Hauppauge, NY 11787
Tel. (631) 853–5408
Fax. (631) 853–5951

5th District Court
3105 Veterans Memorial Highway
Ronkonkoma, NY 11779
Tel. (631) 854–9676
Fax. (631) 854–9681

6th District Court
150 West Main Street
Patchogue, NY 11772
Tel. (631) 854–1440
Fax. (631) 854–1444

Suffolk County Supreme Court Law Library
Cohalan Court Complex
400 Carleton Avenue
Central Islip, NY 11702
Tel. (516) 853–7530
Fax. (516) 853–7533
    or
Suffolk County Law Library
Arthur M. Cromarty Court Complex
1st Floor
220 Center Drive
Riverhead, NY 11901–3312
Tel. (631) 852–2419

Sheriff
100 Center Drive
Riverhead, NY 11901–3307
Tel. (631) 852–2200
Fax. (631) 852–1898

SULLIVAN COUNTY

[3rd Judicial District, 3rd Judicial Department]

Supreme Court
Sullivan County Courthouse
414 Broadway
Monticello, NY 12701
Tel. (845) 794–4066
Fax. (845) 791–6170

County Court
Sullivan County Courthouse
414 Broadway
Monticello, NY 12701
Tel. (845) 794–4066
Fax. (845) 791–6170
Email: elilley@courts.state.ny.us

Family Court
Sullivan County Government Center
100 North Street
Monticello, NY 12701
Tel. (845) 794–3000, ext. 3460
Fax. (845) 794–0199

Surrogate's Court
County Government Center
100 North Street, Room 250
P.O. Box 5012
Monticello, NY 12701
Tel. (845) 794–3000 ext. 3450
Fax. (845) 794–0310

Sullivan County Law Library
Sullivan County Courthouse
441 Broadway
Monticello, NY 12701
Tel. (845) 794–1547
Fax. (845) 794–6170

Sheriff
4 Bushnell Avenue
Monticello, NY 12701–1304
Tel. (845) 794–7100
Fax. (845) 794–0810

TIOGA COUNTY
[6th Judicial District, 3rd Judicial Department]

Supreme Court
16 Court Street
Courthouse Square
Owego, NY 13827
Tel. (607) 687–0544
Fax. (607) 687–5680

County Court
16 Court Street
Courthouse Square
Owego, NY 13827
Tel. (607) 687–0338
Fax. (607) 687–3240

Family Court
Court Annex Building
20 Court Street
P.O. Box 10
Owego, NY 13827
Tel. (607) 687–1730
Fax. (607) 687–3240

Surrogate's Court
Court Annex Building
20 Court Street
Owego, NY 13827
Tel. (607) 687–1303
Fax. (607) 687–3240

Tioga County Law Library
18 East Street
Waverly, NY 14892
Tel. (607) 565–9341

Sheriff
Tioga County Public Safety Building
103 Corporate Drive
Owego, NY 13827–3249
Tel. (607) 687–1010
Fax. (607) 687–6755

TOMPKINS COUNTY
[6th Judicial District, 3rd Judicial Department]
www.courts.state.ny.us/courts/6jd/tompkins/

Supreme Court
Tompkins County Courthouse
320 North Tioga Street
P.O. Box 70
Ithaca, NY 14851–0070
Tel. (607) 272–0466
Fax. (607) 256–0301

County Court
Tompkins County Courthouse
320 North Tioga Street
P.O. Box 70
Ithaca, NY 14851–0070
Tel. (607) 272–0466
Fax. (607) 256–0301

Family Court
Tompkins County Courthouse
320 North Tioga Street
P.O. Box 70
Ithaca, NY 14851–0070
Tel. (607) 277–1517
Fax. (607) 277–5027

Surrogate's Court
Tompkins County Courthouse
320 North Tioga Street
Ithaca, NY 14851–0070
Tel. (607) 277–0622
Fax. (607) 256–2572

Ithaca City Court
118 East Clinton Street
Ithaca, NY 14850–5689
Tel. (607) 273–2263
Fax. (607) 277–3702

Tompkins County Law Library
Tompkins County Courthouse
P.O. Box 70
320 North Tioga Street
Ithaca, NY 14850
Tel. (607) 272–0045
Fax. (607) 272–3276

Sheriff
779 Warren Road
Ithaca, NY 14850–1255
Tel. (607) 257–1345
Fax. (607) 266–5436

ULSTER COUNTY
[3rd Judicial District, 3rd Judicial Department]

Supreme Court
Ulster County Courthouse
285 Wall Street
Kingston, NY 12401–3817
Tel. (845) 340–3377
Fax. (845) 340–3387

County Court
Ulster County Courthouse
285 Wall Street
Kingston, NY 12401-3817
Tel. (845) 340–3377
Fax. (845) 340–3387

Family Court
16 Lucas Avenue
Kingston, NY 12401–3708
Tel. (845) 340–3600
Fax. (845) 340–3626

Surrogate's Court
240 Fair Street
Kingston, NY 12401–3806
Tel. (845) 340–3348
Fax. (845) 340–3352

Kingston City Court
1 Garraghan Drive
Kingston, NY 12401–6065
Tel. (845) 338–2974
Fax. (845) 338–1443

Ulster County Supreme Court Law Library
285 Wall Street
Kingston, NY 12401
Tel. (845) 340–3053
Fax. (845) 340–3773

COURT DIRECTORY

Sheriff
380 Boulevard
Kingston, NY 12401
Tel. (845) 340–3590
Fax. (845) 331–2810

WARREN COUNTY

[4th Judicial District, 3rd Judicial Department]

Supreme Court
Warren County Municipal Center
1340 State Route 9
Lake George, NY 12845
Tel. (518) 761–6431
Fax. (518) 761–6253

County Court
Warren County Municipal Center
1340 State Route 9
Lake George, NY 12845
Tel. (518) 761–6431
Fax. (518) 791–6253

Family Court
Warren County Municipal Center
1340 State Route 9
Lake George, NY 12845
Tel. (518) 761–6500
Fax. (518) 761–6230

Surrogate's Court
Warren County Municipal Center
1340 State Route 9
Lake George, NY 12845
Tel. (518) 761–6514
Fax. (518) 761–6511

Glens Falls City Court
City Hall
42 Ridge Street, 3rd Floor
Glens Falls, NY 12801
Tel. (518) 798–4714
Fax. (518) 798–0137

Warren County Supreme Court Law Library
Warren County Municipal Center
1340 State Route 9
Lake George, NY 12845
Tel. (518) 761–6442
Fax. (518) 761–6586

Sheriff
1400 State Route 9
Lake George, NY 12845–3434
Tel. (518) 743–2500
Fax. (518) 743–2519

WASHINGTON COUNTY

[4th Judicial District, 3rd Judicial Department]

Supreme Court
383 Broadway
Fort Edward, NY 12828–1015
Tel. (518) 746–2521
Fax. (518) 746–2519

County Court
383 Broadway
Fort Edward, NY 12828–1015
Tel. (518) 746–2521
Fax. (518) 746–2519

Family Court
383 Broadway
Fort Edward, NY 12828–1015
Tel. (518) 746–2501
Fax. (518) 746–2503

Surrogate's Court
383 Broadway
Fort Edward, NY 12828–1015
Tel. (518) 746–2546
Fax. (518) 746–2547

Washington County Law Library
383 Broadway
Fort Edward, NY 12828–1015
Tel. (518) 746–2521

Sheriff
399 Broadway
Fort Edward, NY 12828–1021
Tel. (518) 746–2475
Fax. (518) 746–2398

WAYNE COUNTY

[7th Judicial District, 4th Judicial Department]

Supreme Court
Wayne County Hall of Justice
54 Broad Street, Suite 106
Lyons, NY 14489
Tel. (315) 946–5459
Fax. (315) 946–5456

COURT DIRECTORY

County Court
Wayne County Hall of Justice
54 Broad Street, Suite 106
Lyons, NY 14489
Tel. (315) 946–5459
Fax. (315) 946–5456

Family Court
Wayne County Hall of Justice
54 Broad Street, Suite 106
Lyons, NY 14489
Tel. (315) 946–5420
Fax. (315) 946–5456

Surrogate's Court
Wayne County Hall of Justice
54 Broad Street, Suite 106
Lyons, NY 14489
Tel. (315) 946–5430
Fax. (315) 946–5433

Wayne County Law Library
67 Canal Street
Lyons, NY 14489
Tel. (315) 946–9262

Sheriff
7368 Route 31
Lyons, NY 14489
Tel. (315) 946–9711
Fax. (315) 946–5811

WESTCHESTER COUNTY
[9th Judicial District, 2nd Judicial Department]
www.courts.state.ny.us/courts/9jd/westchester/

Supreme Court
111 Dr. Martin Luther King, Jr. Boulevard
White Plains, NY 10601
Tel. (914) 824–5300/5400
Fax. (914) 995–3427

County Court
111 Dr. Martin Luther King, Jr. Boulevard
White Plains, NY 10601
Tel. (914) 824–5300/5400
Fax. (914) 995–3427

Family Court (New Rochelle)
420 North Avenue
New Rochelle, NY 10801
Tel. (914) 813–5650
Fax. (914) 813–5580

Family Court (White Plains)
Westchester County Courthouse
111 Dr. Martin Luther King, Jr. Boulevard
White Plains, NY 10601
Tel. (914) 824–5500
Fax. (914) 995–4468

Family Court (Yonkers)
53 South Broadway
Yonkers, NY 10701
Tel. (914) 231–2950
Fax. (914) 231–2814

Surrogate's Court
111 Dr. Martin Luther King Jr. Blvd.
White Plains, NY 10601
Tel. (914) 824–5656
Fax. (914) 995–3728

Mount Vernon City Court
2 Roosevelt Square North
Mount Vernon, NY 10550–2060
Tel. (914) 665–2400
Fax. (914) 699–1230

New Rochelle City Court
475 North Avenue
New Rochelle, NY 10801
Tel. (914) 654–2207
Fax. (914) 654–0344

Peekskill City Court
2 Nelson Avenue
Peekskill, NY 10566
Tel. (914) 737–3405
Fax. (914) 736–1889

Rye City Court
21 McCullough Place
Rye, NY 10580
Tel. (914) 967–1599
Fax. (914) 967–3308

White Plains City Court
77 South Lexington Avenue
White Plains, NY 10601
Tel. (914) 824–5675
Fax. (914) 422–6058

Yonkers City Court
100 South Broadway
Yonkers, NY 10701
Tel. (914) 377–6326
Fax. (914) 377–6395

COURT DIRECTORY

Westchester County Law Library
111 Dr. Martin Luther King, Jr. Boulevard
White Plains, NY 10601
Tel. (914) 824–5660

Sheriff
Department of Public Safety
Saw Mill River Parkway
Hawthorne, NY 10532–1027
Tel. (914) 741–4400

WYOMING COUNTY
[8th Judicial District, 4th Judicial Department]

Supreme Court
147 North Main Street
Warsaw, NY 14569
Tel. (585) 786–2253
Fax. (585) 786–2818

County Court
147 North Main Street
Warsaw, NY 14569
Tel. (585) 786–2253
Fax. (585) 786–2818

Family Court
147 North Main Street
Warsaw, NY 14569
Tel. (585) 786–3148
Fax. (585) 786–3800

Surrogate's Court
147 North Main Street
Warsaw, NY 14569
Tel. (585) 786–3148
Fax. (585) 786–3800

Wyoming County Law Library
Wyoming County Courthouse
143 North Main Street
Warsaw, NY 14569–1199
Tel. (585) 786–3148
Fax. (585) 786–3800

Sheriff
151 North Main Street
Warsaw, NY 14569–1123
Tel. (585) 786–8989
Fax: (585) 786–8961
Email: fheimann@wyomingco.net

YATES COUNTY
[7th Judicial District, 4th Judicial Department]
www.courts.state.ny.us/courts/7jd/

Supreme Court
Yates County Courthouse
415 Liberty Street
Penn Yan, NY 14527
Tel. (315) 536–5126
Fax. (315) 536–5190

County Court
Yates County Courthouse
415 Liberty Street
Penn Yan, NY 14527
Tel. (315) 536–5126
Fax. (315) 536–5190

Family Court
415 Liberty Street
Penn Yan, NY 14527
Tel. (315) 536–5127
Fax. (315) 536–5190

Surrogate's Court
415 Liberty Street
Penn Yan, NY 14527
Tel. (315) 536–5130
Fax. (315) 536–5190

Yates County Law Library
214 Main Street
Penn Yan, NY 14527
Tel. (315) 536–6114

Sheriff
227 Main Street
Penn Yan, NY 14527–1720
Tel. (315) 536–4438
Fax. (315) 536–5191

COMBINED INDEX
TO RULES OF STATE COURTS

I–1

CORRECTIONAL INSTITUTIONS—Cont'd
Definitions, actions and proceedings, inmates, § 140.1
Fees, actions and proceedings, § 140.1 et seq.
    Source other than trust fund account, § 140.4
Judges visits, §§ 17.1, 17.2
Mental illness defense commitment, § 110.5 et seq.
Motions, inmates, poor persons, § 140.2
Orders,
    Fees, inmates, poor persons, § 140.3
    Inmates, poor persons, § 140.3
Petitions, inmates, filing, § 140.2
Poor persons, actions and proceedings, inmates, § 140.1 et seq.
Trust fund accounts, actions and proceedings, inmates, § 140.1 et seq.

COSTS AND EXPENSES
Appellate division, first department, §§ 600.13, 600.15
Court of appeals, § 500.3
Freedom of information access, § 124.8
Frivolous conduct in civil actions, § 130–1.1 et seq.
Judicial administration, costs and sanctions, § 37.1
Surrogates Court, this index
Transcripts, § 108.2

COUNSEL
Attorneys, generally, this index

COUNTIES
Courts. County Courts, generally, this index

COUNTY COURTS
Generally, § 202.1 et seq.
Accountings for trusts, § 202.53
Alimony motions, § 202.16
Appeal and review,
    Human rights division orders, § 202.47
    Perfecting civil appeals to county court, § 202.55
    Sidewalk assessment review, § 202.58
    Tax assessment review, post
Applicability of rules, § 202.1
Assessment review proceedings. Tax assessment review, post
Assignment of cases,
    Judicial intervention, request for, § 202.6
    Matrimonial actions, § 202.16
Assignments for benefit of creditors, § 202.63
Attorneys,
    County courts First Department, § 661.7
    Criminal appeals, county appeals, § 200.40
    Engagement of counsel, § 202.32
    Fees pendente lite, motion for, § 202.16
    Trial counsel identification, § 202.31
Bifurcated trials, § 202.42
Bills of particulars,
    Malpractice actions, notice of bills of particulars in, § 202.56
    Submission, § 202.32
Calendar practice, §§ 202.3, 202.22
    Matrimonial actions, § 202.16
    Mistrial, rescheduling after, § 202.45
    Motions, §§ 202.7, 202.8
    Special preferences, §§ 202.24, 202.25
Certificate of readiness, form, § 202.21
Chenango County, estate taxes, returns, § 1921.1
Children and minors,
    Claims and proceedings by, § 202.67
    Indian child custody proceeding, § 202.68

COUNTY COURTS—Cont'd
Children and minors—Cont'd
    Support motions, § 202.16
Conferences, differentiated case management, § 202.19
Coordination, related actions, multiple districts, § 202.69
County appeals, criminal appeals, attorneys, § 200.40
CPLR, applicability of, § 202.1
Creditors, assignments for benefit of, § 202.63
Criminal appeals, § 200.30 et seq.
    Applicability of regulations, § 200.30
    County appeals, attorneys, § 200.40
    Perfecting appeals, § 200.33
Custody of Indian child, § 202.68
Damages,
    Bifurcated trials, § 202.42
    Proof on affidavit, § 202.46
Death action medical report exchange, § 202.17
Default, § 202.27
    Damages, proof, § 202.46
Dental malpractice actions, special rules for, § 202.56
Deposition videotaping, § 202.15
Deposits in court by receivers and assignees, § 202.52
Differentiated case management, § 202.19
Discontinuance, actions and proceedings, § 202.28
Discovery and disclosure,
    Bills of particulars,
        Malpractice action notice, § 202.56
        Submission, § 202.32
    Eminent domain appraisal reports exchange, § 202.61
    Matrimonial financial disclosure, § 202.15
    Medical reports exchange, § 202.17
    Pretrial conference, § 202.26
    Videotaping deposition, § 202.15
Dissolution of business entity, proof, § 202.51
Drug treatment, superior courts, §§ 43.1, 143.1 et seq.
Election proceedings, § 202.64
Eminent domain appraisal reports exchange, § 202.61
Engagement of counsel, § 202.32
Equitable distribution in matrimonial actions, § 202.16
Evidence,
    Damages, proof on affidavit, § 202.46
    Discovery and disclosure, generally, ante
    Dissolution of business entity, § 202.51
Ex parte application, county court judges empowered to hear, § 202.5
Filing of papers, § 202.5 et seq.
Financial disclosure in matrimonial actions, § 202.15
Forms,
    Certificate of readiness, § 202.21
    Malpractice actions, notice of bills of particulars in, § 202.56
    Note of issue, § 202.21
    Notice of motion, § 202.7
Guardians for incompetents, appointment, § 202.54
Human rights division orders review, § 202.47
Hung jury, rescheduling after, § 202.45
Incompetent persons,
    Claims and proceedings by, § 202.67
    Guardians for, § 202.54
Indexing of papers, § 202.5
Indian child custody proceeding, § 202.68
Inquest after default, proof of damages at, § 202.45
Integrated youth court, Westchester County, §§ 45.1, 145.1 et seq.
Judges,
    Assignment of cases to, § 202.3

COURTS—Cont'd
Officers and employees—Cont'd
Fiduciaries, appointments, § 50.2
Financial statements and reports, § 50.2
Improper influence, § 50.5
Obstruction, employee rights, § 50.4
Political activities, §§ 50.2, 50.5
Retirement and pensions, sick leave, banks and banking, § 135.4
Sick leave, banks and banking, § 135.1 et seq.
Parent education and awareness program, § 144.1 et seq.
Political activities, officers and employees, §§ 50.2, 50.5
Practice of law, officers and employees, § 50.6
Preamble, appointments, § 36.0
Preliminary conferences and hearings,
City courts, § 210.10
County courts, § 202.12
Court of claims, § 206.10
Superior Court criminal cases, § 200.12
Procedures, appointments, §§ 36.3, 36.4
Publication, appointments, § 36.5
Records and reports. Chief Administrator of Courts, this index
Retirement and pensions, sick leave, banks and banking, § 135.4
Sick leave, officers and employees, banks and banking, § 135.1 et seq.
Smoking, § 39.1
Supplemental needs trustees, appointments, § 36.0 et seq.
Supreme Court, generally, this index
Surrogates Court, generally, this index
Unified court system, Ethics Commission, §§ 40.1, 7400.1 et seq.

CRIME VICTIMS
Generally, § 129.1 et seq.
Assistance education, § 129.1 et seq.
Definitions, § 129.2
Immunity from suit, § 129.5
Purpose of regulations, § 129.1
Sexual abuse victims, video recording, § 205.86
Standards of fair treatment, checklist of, § 129.3

CRIMES
Criminal Law and Procedure, generally, this index

CRIMINAL LAW AND PROCEDURE
Appearance tickets, local criminal courts, mail and mailing, § 200.25
Appearances of counsel, § 200.5
Applicability of uniform trial court rules, § 200.1
Assignment of cases,
Local criminal courts, § 200.22
Superior courts, § 200.11
Attorney threatening criminal prosecution, § 1200.36
Attorneys, assignment, local criminal courts, § 200.26
Capital punishment. Death Penalty, generally, this index
City courts. Local criminal courts, post
County Courts, this index
Court of appeals, § 500.20
Crime Victims, generally, this index
Death Penalty, generally, this index
Disabilities, certificate of relief from, § 200.9
Disruptive behavior in First Department, § 604.3
Electronic appearances in downstate venues, § 106.1
Family offenses. Family Court, this index
Filing of papers, §§ 200.3, 200.4

CRIMINAL LAW AND PROCEDURE—Cont'd
Forms, §§ 200.3, 200.8
Insanity defense, §§ 110.14, 111.8
Grand Juries, generally, this index
Guilty pleas, mail and mailing, local criminal courts, § 200.25
Indictment and Information, generally, this index
Insanity Defense Procedure, generally, this index
Integrated domestic violence parts, Supreme Court, §§ 41.1, 141.1 et seq.
Interpreters, § 217.1, 217.2
Jury, generally, this index
Juvenile delinquency. Family Court, this index
Local criminal courts, § 200.20 et seq.
Appearance tickets, mail and mailing, § 200.25
Applicability of rules, §§ 200.20, 200.21
Attorneys, assignment, § 200.26
Bail, § 200.26
Bronx County, §§ 42.1, 142.1 et seq.
Court of appeals, § 500.20
Docket, § 200.22
Guilty pleas, mail and mailing, § 200.25
Procedure, rules governing, §§ 200.20, 200.21
Recordkeeping requirements for town and village courts, § 200.23
Securing orders, § 200.26
Transfer of cases, drug treatment, superior courts, § 143.2
Oaths, authorization to administer, § 200.7
Perfecting appeals to county court, § 200.33
Preliminary conference in superior court, § 200.12
Records and reports, §§ 200.23, 200.24
Reporting disposition of cases, § 115.4
Signature of judge, § 200.4
Special district attorneys in superior courts, § 200.15
Stay pending appeal to county court,
Duration of stay, § 200.32
Power to issue, § 200.31
Superior Court Criminal Cases, generally, this index
Terms of court, § 200.2
Town courts. Local criminal courts, post
Transfer of indictments between superior courts, § 200.14
Uniform rules for trial courts, § 200.1 et seq.
Victims. Crime Victims, generally, this index
Village courts. Local criminal courts, post

CUSTODY
Family Court, this index
Indian child custody proceeding,
Family court, § 205.51
Supreme Court, § 202.68
Surrogates court, § 207.59
Parent education and awareness program, § 144.1 et seq.

DAMAGES
Affidavit, proof on, § 202.46
Bifurcated trials,
District court, § 208.35
New York City civil court, § 208.35
City courts, § 210.32
Court of appeals, remittitur by, § 500.19
District court,
Bifurcated trials, § 208.35
Default inquest, § 208.32
New York City civil court,
Bifurcated trials, § 208.35
Default inquest, § 208.32

LANDLORD AND TENANT
Eviction,
    City courts, notice in, § 210.42
    District court, notice in, § 208.42
    New York City civil court, form, § 208.42

LAW GUARDIANS
Family Court, this index

LAW SCHOOL
Admission to bar, §§ 520.3, 520.5, 520.6

LAWYERS
Attorneys, generally, this index

LAWYERS FUND FOR CLIENT PROTECTION
Attorneys, this index

LEAVE OF ABSENCE
Career service for unified court system employees, annual
    leave, § 24.3
Sick leave, court officers and employees, banks and bank-
    ing, § 135.1 et seq.
Unpaid leaves, § 24.7

LEAVE TO APPEAL
Appeal and Review, this index

LIBRARIES
Law libraries,
    Designation, § 123.1
    Materials submission requirements, § 123.2

LISTS AND LISTINGS
Parent education and awareness program, providers,
    § 144.4

LOCAL CRIMINAL COURTS
Criminal Law and Procedure, this index

MARRIAGE
Matrimonial Actions, generally, this index

MATRIMONIAL ACTIONS
Attorney fees, § 1400.1 et seq.
    Arbitration and award, § 1400.7
    Nonrefundable retainer, § 1400.4
    Retainer, §§ 1400.3, 1400.4
    Security interests, § 1400.5
    Statement of client rights, § 1400.2
Attorneys,
    Application, § 1400.1
    Arbitration of fee, § 1400.7
    Clients rights, § 1400.2
    Nonrefundable retainer fee, § 1400.4
    Security interests, § 1400.5
    Written retainer agreement, § 1400.3
County Courts, this index
Expert witness appointment, § 202.18
Judgment proposed, § 202.50
Parent education and awareness program, § 144.1 et seq.
Supreme Court, § 202.16
    Expert witness appointment, § 202.18
    Proposed judgment, § 202.50

MEDIATION
Arbitration and Award, generally, this index

MEDICAL CARE AND TREATMENT
Report exchange in personal injury actions. Medical
    Report Exchange In Personal Injury Actions, general-
    ly, this index

MEDICAL RECORDS
Exchange in personal injury actions. Medical Report
    Exchange In Personal Injury Actions, generally, this
    index

**MEDICAL REPORT EXCHANGE IN PERSONAL INJURY
ACTIONS**
City courts, § 210.13
Court of claims, § 206.14
District court, § 208.13
New York City civil court, § 208.13
Supreme Court uniform rules, § 202.17

MENTAL HEALTH, OFFICE OF
Mentally Ill Persons, generally, this index

MENTAL HEALTH PROFESSIONALS
Supreme court appellate division, departments, § 680.1
    et seq.

MENTALLY ILL PERSONS
Appearance at hearings, § 109.1
Attorneys, first department, § 622.1 et seq.
City courts, settlements in, § 210.36
Claims and proceedings by, § 202.67
Death Penalty, generally, this index
Guardians, § 202.54
Insanity defense, §§ 110.1 et seq., 111.1 et seq.
Judicial departments,
    First department mental hygiene legal service,
        § 622.1 et seq.
    Fourth department, attorneys, mental incapacity,
        § 1022.23
Oneida County, committees for incompetents in, § 1722.1
    et seq.

**MENTALLY RETARDED AND DEVELOPMENTALLY DIS-
ABLED PERSONS**
Appearance at hearings, § 109.1
Attorneys, first department, § 622.1 et seq.
City courts, settlements in, § 210.36
Claims and proceedings by, § 202.67
Guardians, § 202.54
Insanity defense, §§ 110.1 et seq., 111.1 et seq.
Judicial departments,
    First department mental hygiene legal service,
        § 622.1 et seq.
    Fourth department, attorneys, mental incapacity,
        § 1022.23
Oneida County, committees for incompetents in, § 1722.1
    et seq.

MICROFILMING
Library submission requirements, § 123.2

MINORS
Children and Minors, generally, this index

MISTRIAL
Jury, this index

MOTIONS
Alimony, § 202.16
Appellate division, first department, §§ 600.2, 640.8

PRIVILEGED OR CONFIDENTIAL MATTERS
Confidential or Privileged Information, generally, this index

PRIVILEGES AND IMMUNITIES
Family court, CASA programs, § 117.2

PRO BONO SERVICES
Attorneys, conflicts of interest, code of professional responsibility, § 1200.20–a

PRO HAC VICE ADMISSION TO BAR
Foreign attorneys, § 520.11

PROBATE OF WILL
Generally, § 207.19

PROCESS
Attorney admission, agent for service as condition of, § 520.13
City Courts, this index
Commercial claims notice,
    City courts, § 210.41–a
    District court, § 208.41–a
    New York City civil court, § 208.41–a
Court of Appeals, this index
District Courts, this index
Family court,
    Findings of fact, § 205.36
    Motion papers, § 205.11
Justice courts,
    Small claims proceedings, § 214.10
    Summons, § 214.3
New York City Civil Court, this index
Penalties for disobeying summons, § 128.12
Summons,
    City courts, forms in, § 210.6
    District court, § 208.6
    Justice courts, § 214.3
    New York City civil court, § 208.6
    Penalties for disobeying, § 128.12
Surrogates court, § 207.7

PROFESSIONAL SERVICE CORPORATIONS
Attorneys,
    First department, § 608.2
    Fourth department, § 1022.5

PROOF
Evidence, generally, this index

PROPERTY
Eminent Domain, generally, this index

PROSECUTION
Criminal Law and Procedure, generally, this index

PROTECTION ORDERS
Electronic transmission, pilot programs and projects, § 205.7a

PSYCHOLOGISTS AND PSYCHOLOGY
Appointment, § 127.1 et seq.
    First department, § 606.1 et seq.
Capital cases, assignment and compensation, § 127.3
Insanity Defense Procedure, generally, this index

PUBLIC AREAS
Judges, transaction of official business in nonpublic facilities, § 20.1

PUBLIC ASSISTANCE
Social Services Department, generally, this index

PUBLIC HEARINGS
Hearings, generally, this index

PUBLIC OFFICERS AND EMPLOYEES
Unified court system employees. Career Service for Unified Court System Employees, generally, this index

PUBLIC RECORDS
Records and Reports, generally, this index

PUBLIC WELFARE
Social Services Department, generally, this index

PUBLIC WORKS AND CONTRACTS
Court of claims special rules, § 206.23

PUBLICATION
Courts, appointments, § 36.5
Rules and regulations, courts, § 9.1

QUALIFICATION OR DISQUALIFICATION
Neutrals, alternative dispute resolution, §§ 146.4, 146.6

RACIAL DISCRIMINATION
Bias or Prejudice, generally, this index

READINESS CERTIFICATE OR STATEMENT
Forms, this index

REAL PROPERTY
Eminent Domain, generally, this index

REARGUMENT OR RECONSIDERATION
Appellate division, first department, § 600.14
Appellate term, § 640.9
Court of appeals,
    Criminal cases, § 500.20
    Motions, § 500.24

RECEIVERS AND RECEIVERSHIP
Appointment, § 36.0 et seq.
Deposits in court by, § 202.52

RECERTIFICATION
Certificates and Certification, generally, this index

RECORDS AND REPORTS
Attorney client disputes, mediation report, § 1220.4
Board of governors, attorney fees, dispute resolution, § 137.3
Caseload Activity Reporting, generally, this index
Court records. Chief Administrator of Courts, this index
Criminal Law and Procedure, this index
Family Court, this index
Freedom of Information, generally, this index
Judicial nomination commission, disclosure, § 7101.1 et seq.
Jury, this index
Mental health professionals, supreme court appellate division, departments, § 680.10
Publication, First Department notice publication, § 601.1
Surrogates Court, this index
Transcripts, generally, this index

RECYCLING AND RECYCLABLES
Courts, paper, filing of papers, § 215.1 et seq.
Paper, courts, filing of papers, § 215.1 et seq.

SOCIAL SERVICES DEPARTMENT—Cont'd
Foster care—Cont'd
Termination of parental rights, judgments and decrees, suspension, § 205.50
Paternity. Child support, ante
Termination of parental rights, judgments and decrees, suspension, § 205.50

SOLICITATION
Code of professional responsibility, solicitation by attorney, § 1200.8

SOLID WASTE
Disposal, court records, retention and disposition, § 104.1

SPECIAL DISTRICT ATTORNEYS
Superior courts, § 200.15

SPECIAL MASTERS
Supreme Court uniform rules, § 202.14

SPECIAL PROCEEDINGS
First department, appellate division, § 600.2

SPOUSES
Matrimonial Actions, generally, this index

STAFFING
Labor and Employment, generally, this index

STATE BOARD OF LAW EXAMINERS
Generally, § 6000.1 et seq.
Attorneys, generally, this index

STATE RECORDS
Records and Reports, generally, this index

STATE REPORTER
Generally, § 7300.1 et seq.
Reporter of Decisions, generally, this index

STATEMENTS
Disclosure statements,
Judges, elections, § 100.5
Matrimonial actions, § 202.15

STAYS
Appellate term, § 640.9
County court,
Duration of stay, § 200.32
Power to issue, § 200.31

SUBMISSION ON AGREED FACTS
Court of claims, § 206.24
Judicial departments, first department appeals, § 600.7

SUBPOENAS
Conduct and discipline of attorneys,
First department, § 605.17
Fourth department, § 691.5–a
Leaves for employees, § 24.6

SUMMONING JURORS
Generally, § 128.6
Failure to respond, procedure, § 128.12

SUMMONS
Process, this index

SUPERIOR COURT CRIMINAL CASES
Generally, § 200.10 et seq.
Applicability of rules, § 200.10
Docket, § 200.11
Grand jury impanelment, § 200.13
Preliminary conference, § 200.12
Special district attorney, appointment of, § 200.15
Transfer of indictments between superior courts, § 200.14

SUPPLEMENTAL NEEDS TRUSTEES
Appointments, § 36.0 et seq.

SUPPORT OF CHILD OR SPOUSE
Family Court, this index
Supreme Court,
Motions, § 202.16
Referrals to family court, § 205.40
Uniform rules, alimony, § 202.16
Surrogates court allowances, § 207.14

SUPPORTIVE SERVICES
Social Services Department, generally, this index

SUPREME COURT
Generally, § 202.1 et seq.
Accountings for trusts, § 202.53
Alimony motions, § 202.16
Appellate division. Supreme Court Appellate Division, generally, this index
Applicability of rules, § 202.1
Assignments,
Commercial division, § 202.70
Creditors, assignments for benefit of, § 202.63
Deposits in court, § 202.52
Judicial intervention, request for, § 202.6
Matrimonial actions, § 202.16
Bifurcated trials, § 202.42
Bills of particulars,
Malpractice actions, notice of bills of particulars in, § 202.56
Submission, § 202.32
Bronx County, criminal division, §§ 42.1, 142.1 et seq.
Calendar practice, § 202.3
Calendars, § 202.22
Matrimonial actions, § 202.16
Mistrial, rescheduling after, § 202.45
Motions, §§ 202.7, 202.8
Special preferences, §§ 202.24, 202.25
Certificate of readiness, form, § 202.21
Children and minors,
Claims and proceedings by, § 202.67
Indian child custody proceeding, § 202.68
Support motions, § 202.16
Clients rights, posting of statement, § 1210.1
Commercial division, § 202.70
Conferences, differentiated case management, § 202.19
Coordination, related actions, multiple districts, § 202.69
County court, perfecting civil appeals to, § 202.55
CPLR, applicability of, § 202.1
Creditors, assignments for benefit of, § 202.63
Criminal division, Bronx County, §§ 42.1, 142.1 et seq.
Custody of Indian child, § 202.68
Damages,
Bifurcated trials, § 202.42
Proof on affidavit, § 202.46
Death action medical report exchange, § 202.17

†